ECOLOGY AND
CONSERVATION
OF NEOTROPICAL
MIGRANT LANDBIRDS

Based on a symposium hosted by
Manomet Bird Observatory, 6–9 December 1989

ECOLOGY AND CONSERVATION OF NEOTROPICAL MIGRANT LANDBIRDS

Edited by
John M. Hagan III and
David W. Johnston

Preface by Gerry E. Studds

Foreword by Thomas E. Lovejoy

`Patrick`
`Ross`
`Presented`
`with him in 2019`
`in Sara Sota`

Smithsonian Institution Press
Washington and London

Production Editor: Nancy P. Dutro.
Typesetting: Blue Heron, Inc.

Library of Congress Cataloging-in-Publication Data

Ecology and conservation of neotropical migrant landbirds /
    edited by John M. Hagan and David W. Johnston.
        p.   cm.
    Includes Spanish abstracts for each chapter.
    Papers from the Symposium on Ecology and Conserva-
tion of Neotropical Migrant Landbirds, held Dec. 6–9, 1989,
Woods Hole, Mass., and hosted by the Manomet Bird
Observatory.
    Includes bibliographical references and index.
    ISBN 1-56098-113-X   1-56098-140-7 (pbk.)
    1. Birds—Latin America—Ecology—Congresses. 2.
Birds—Latin America—Migration—Congresses. 3. Birds,
Protection of—Latin America—Congresses. I. Hagan, John
M. II. Johnston, David W. III. Manomet Bird Observatory
(Mass.) IV. Symposium on Ecology and Conservation of
Neotropical Migrant Landbirds (1989 : Woods Hole, Mass.)
QL685.7.E36   1991
598.25'098—dc20   91-15396

British Library Cataloguing-in-Publication Data is available.
Manufactured in the United States of America.
97 96 95 94 93 92   5 4 3 2 1

∞ The paper used in this publication meets the minimum
requirements of the American National Standard for Perma-
nence of Paper for Printed Library Materials
Z39.48—1984.

FRONT COVER: The habitat photograph on the cover, by
Jan Erik Pierson, is of Henri Pittier National Park in northern
Venezuela, where numbers of migrants overwinter, including
Olive-sided Flycatchers, Golden-winged Warblers, Blackburnian Warblers, Cerulean Warblers, American Redstarts, Northern Waterthrushes, and Ovenbirds. The Common Yellowthroat, photographed by Barth Schorre, is a bird of marsh
borders and shrublands that winters throughout Central
America.

Symposium sponsors

We are grateful to the following organizations and individuals for sponsoring the symposium in Woods Hole, and for supporting the publication of these proceedings.

National Fish and Wildlife Foundation
Conservation International
International Council for Bird Preservation, U.S.
National Science Foundation
National Wildlife Federation
Nuttall Ornithological Club
Swift Instruments, Inc.
The Nature Conservancy
U.S. Fish and Wildlife Service, International Division
USDA Forest Service
William H. and Helen C. Vanderbilt Foundation
Wharton Trust
Wild Bird Feeding Institute
World Wildlife Fund

Mrs. William P. Ellison
Mrs. Bradley Fisk
Mrs. John Fiske
Mrs. August Meyer
Dr. Josephine Murray
Mr. and Mrs. Peter M. Richards
Mr. and Mrs. Charles L. Smith, Jr.
Anonymous (5)

Reviewers

The editors are especially grateful to the following individuals who reviewed one or more of the manuscripts submitted for publication in this volume: K. Able, W. Arendt, R. Askins, J. Atwood, F. Bairlein, J. Blake, E. Bollinger, W. Buskirk, G. Butcher, A. Cruz, D. Dawson, J. Dinsmore, S. Droege, W. Drury, T. Engstrom, J. Faaborg, M. Ficken, R. Forman, C. Francis, S. Gauthreaux, R. Greenberg, P. Hamel, B. Harrington, L. Harris, D. Heinemann, M. Hunter, D. Hussell, F. James, J. Karr, P. Kerlinger, E. Ketterson, J. Kricher, D. Kroodsma, D. Levey, T. Lloyd-Evans, J. Lynch, S. Mabey, T. Martin, F. Moore, I. Nisbet, V. Nolan, R. O'Connor, D. Pashley, D. Petit, G. Powell, C. Ralph, J. Rappole, J. Reed, R. Repasky, R. Ricklefs, C. Robbins, S. Robinson, N. Rodenhouse, T. Root, S. Sader, J. Sauer, T. Sherry, K. Smith, C. Staicer, G. Stiles, S. Temple, M. Villard, R. Waide, D. Warner, A. Weisbrod, D. Wiedenfeld, D. Wilcove, K. Winker, J. Witham, D. Wood, and J. Wunderle.

Preface

I am not an ornithologist, or even a scientist, but as one charged with making prudent decisions for this country, I depend heavily on the facts provided by the scientific method. I depend on information such as that contained in this book, offered by individuals committed to the conservation of natural systems through scientific inquiry.

Never before has this dependence been so crucial. We humans are witnessing—more important, we are *causing*—the extinction of species at a frightening rate. We are sacrificing the richest and most productive habitats on earth for short-term profit. We are poisoning our air, polluting our water, and tampering with the composition of our atmosphere. It is time that priorities of the nation change. We are one nation, but we have global responsibilities. It is incumbent upon us to be an international leader on environmental isssues, as we are living in a time when some of the most important decisions in human history will be made.

The plight of Neotropical migratory birds is but one of many symptoms of a deteriorating planet. However, these species have an almost mystical power to captivate the human imagination. These small brightly colored creatures full of song, and only a few grams in weight, are able to make annual trips of unimaginable complexity and rigor, only to return each year, often to the same tree or bush. How do they do it? It is a sad fact that we are systematically destroying these homes to which they return. We are slow to realize that it is our home as well.

What should we do? What are we going to do? Our first job is to get federal agencies to consider the environmental impacts of their actions, not only within our borders, but around the world. We have to manage temperate forests with care and intelligence, just as we have suggested that our Latin American neighbors do with tropical forests. We have to build partnerships between conservation organizations and government agencies so that we can channel our expertise and energy efficiently. Finally, we need strong leadership from the Fish and Wildlife Service, and we need to provide them with the means of carrying out their mandate.

While these discrete tasks are necessary, they are not sufficient to meet our global responsibilities. We need a *global alliance for conservation* that will harness the resources of the world, while protecting life, not taking it. This alliance must exclude no country and draw no distinctions between culture or religion or race. The alliance must embrace life *in all its forms*. It must help economies grow without destroying natural resources—an alliance for sustainable development.

Preserving biological diversity, conserving our wildlife, preventing global warming, keeping the Nearctic-Neotropical migratory bird system intact—however you describe it, conservation is a common-sense goal. It is also our responsibility, both individually and collectively, for there is no greater right than that of a child to grow up in a world that is healthy enough to sustain human life, and rich enough in its variety and abundance of plants and animals to make life worth living.

Gerry E. Studds
United States Congress

Foreword

Having reached the quincentennial of Columbus's arrival in the New World, we need only look at the state of those far greater, and in a sense far more daring, voyagers, our Neotropical migrants, to sense the ecological havoc of the last five hundred years. The declines in populations of many of these are as undeniable as the increases of greenhouse gases in the atmosphere. The origins of the problems are multiple and only fuzzily understood, as are the consequences of unnaturally high levels of greenhouse gases for climate change. These are signals of serious environmental trouble, the avian one for the Western Hemisphere, and the atmospheric one for both hemispheres.

In 1970, the Smithsonian convened a conference on the problem of Neotropical migrants, itself an echo of William Vogt's earlier effort in a 1966 Smithsonian symposium on avifauna in a changing ecosystem. In the intervening years, the amount of information on the problem has grown impressively, as has the number of scholars working on the topic. The Manomet conference, which the Smithsonian Institution Press is honored to publish, reflects the progress and a deepening understanding.

The vectors behind the declines are multiple and a result of problems in the Americas, north and south. Almost thirty years after publication of *Silent Spring*, toxic substances, including DDT, still play a role south of the Rio Grande, and one cannot ignore the additional effects global climate change may bring. Yet still and all, the migrant landbird decline seems largely generated by land-use change: habitat destruction and habitat fragmentation. A first reaction has to be that those changes, however ill defined, when taken together, must represent major ecological change. What portents to society do these feathered sentinels represent?

What this means is that slowing and halting the decline is a lot tougher than many endangered species problems, and the solution lies in land-use policies and implementation within both Americas. These problems cannot be solved by a few parks or reserves. If migrant landbirds are to continue to be a significant part of North American summer ecology, as well as of Middle and South American winter ecology, we need to seek ways in which we and these feathered fellow denizens of the New World can coexist. A lot of the solution involves trees and forest lands—also of major importance to stablilizing atmospheric carbon.

As one who enjoys the annual arrival of these travelers of beauty, physical prowess, and almost unfathomable navigational skill (it is one thing to be able to migrate, yet another to do so over thousands of miles), I am deeply puzzled why so few bird watchers share my distress and anger over their decline. Even if blind to the greater environmental signal, one would think more bird watchers would be upset over the decline of the basis of their hobby. Have they not yet noticed it? Or do they feel helpless in the face of the scale of the problem?

The scientific community involved with this work has a heavy responsibility here to wake up the bird-watching community to what is happening. With tens of millions of bird watchers, plus democracy prevalent throughout the hemisphere, there is potentially an interest group with political muscle. Certainly, if those scientists who are knowledgeable do not speak out, we cannot expect the nature-loving segment of society, and certainly not the rest of the population, to bestir themselves.

This volume, while technical, is a step in speaking out. I would urge all who examine it, even in the most casual perusal, to enlist in the effort to stem the decline in the melodious miracle which is the migratory landbird phenomenon. If we can't save this wonder of nature, it augurs grimly for anything else, including ourselves.

Thomas E. Lovejoy
Secretary for External Affairs
Smithsonian Institution

Contents

Introduction

The face of the land changes with time. It always has. With European settlement of the Western Hemisphere, however, the rate of change has accelerated to a point that exceeds the adaptive abilities of many animal species. This is especially true for members of the Nearctic-Neotropical migratory bird system. Whether on their breeding or wintering grounds, suitable habitat for many of these species is eroding away. The consequences for migratory landbirds, and other flora and fauna, are depressing.

To forestall or possibly reverse these patterns of landscape change, we need hard evidence that the changes are having the presumed detrimental effects on animal populations. Only with this information can we expect to convince political leaders to alter the priorities of human affairs. This book represents an effort toward that goal.

Are Neotropical migrant birds declining in number? Are effects of forest fragmentation on their reproductive success diminishing populations rangewide? Can forest fragmentation be stopped or controlled? Is the rapid loss of tropical wintering habitat leading to the demise of these species? What is the prospect for sustainable development of tropical forests, and the survival of organisms that depend on them? These questions, and others, prompted more than 300 scientists to converge on Woods Hole, Massachusetts, for a symposium hosted by Manomet Bird Observatory in December 1989. A major symposium devoted to Neotropical migrant landbirds had not taken place since 1977, when at Front Royal, Virginia, about 40 scientists gathered to discuss migrant bird ecology in the Neotropics.[1] In the 12 intervening years, the leading questions to be answered about these species changed dramatically, a fact that can be verified by comparing the Tables of Contents for the two proceedings volumes. The 1970s had been an exciting time of pioneering the still largely unexplored discipline of nonbreeding season ecology.

That excitement, however, gave way to concern. What changed in such a short time? The primary cause for redirection came from a plethora of sobering publica-

1. Keast, A., and E.S. Morton, eds. 1980. *Migrant Birds in the Neotropics: Ecology, Behavior, Distribution, and Conservation.* Washington: Smithsonian Institution Press.

tions, each indicating that some populations of Neotropical migrant landbirds were declining. At first, it was not obvious whether declines were geographically isolated or widespread. Until further evidence emerged, we hoped for the best. But further evidence did emerge. Between 1977 and 1989, several monitoring programs designed to track bird population changes were reaching fruition. The painstakingly slow process of building our simple graphs of long-term trends in populations, point by point, began to pay off. No fewer than two dozen publications between 1977 and 1989 documented population declines in migratory landbirds in North America, whereas reports of population increases were hard to find.

In the 1980s, it became clear that purely academic research questions would have to yield to more pressing ones regarding causal mechanisms of population change. Two explanations received most of the attention: (1) the effects of wintering habitat loss in the Neotropics, especially in Central America, and (2) forest fragmentation effects on breeding populations in North America. Negative effects on reproductive success from forest fragmentation and the concomitant proliferation of forest edge habitat were empirically documented. But could such effects cause long-term and widespread declines in populations? Rapid loss of tropical habitats, the other causative explanation, was at best correlative. Until wintering-season studies became more sophisticated, and it was established more precisely which tropical habitats are used by which species, this explanation would have to remain largely speculative.

The relative importance of these two mechanisms to population changes caused a polarization within the research community. One goal of the MBO symposium was to dissolve this dichotomous approach. For this particular problem, that of declines of migratory birds, we cannot afford a protracted debate. Time is of the essence. Whether one believes tropical deforestation has played a role in reported declines, or even if one questions whether reported declines are any more than normal population fluctuations, the rate of conversion of both dry and wet tropical forests to agriculture and rangeland will make the most rigorous of scientists succumb to pessimism. Moreover, whether tropical deforestation, temperate forest fragmentation, or neither has been the *primary* cause for reported population changes is moot; there is ample evidence to warrant serious concern about both. Our research agenda should reflect this fact, and proceed in a balanced, complementary, and coordinated manner.

The principal reason for the symposium, however, was to gather, in a single room, as many people as possible who could offer empirical clarification for the problems at hand, to dispense with speculation and offer some

facts, to identify gaps in knowledge of the ecology and conservation of Neotropical migrant landbirds, and to energize one another in pursuit of answers. The purpose was not to solve the problems immediately, but to place us on a proper and focused course for effective research and conservation. Many papers presented in this book may seem to present contradictory information. Some report population declines whereas others do not. Some authors label species as habitat generalists on the wintering grounds, and others label them as specialists. Rather than viewing results as *contradictory*, we prefer to consider them *complementary*. We now have a clearer definition of the questions that need to be answered. Explaining these apparent discrepancies through new lines of research should substantially advance our knowledge of migrant bird ecology.

The 1989 symposium attracted about six times the number present at the 1977 meeting. Moreover, scientists who had previously focused their study on basic questions of behavior and ecology found themselves facing profound conservation issues. Consciences have sharpened the senses of a growing number of us. Is it because a generation could envision the demise of their source of motivation, possibly within their lifetime? We have come face to face with the discipline of conservation biology. We are obliged to respond.

In this book we have attempted to include sound, empirical studies with relevance to the ecology and conservation of Neotropical migratory landbirds. Some papers are clearly more *applied* than others, but conservation merit can be found in them all. We have allowed slightly more speculation than might be found in standard scientific journals in light of the urgency of our questions. We did not want to restrain potentially important conjecture. If you find yourself in disagreement with authors, consider the merits of initiating new lines of investigation to support your case. There is much work to be done.

This book begins with two plenary papers presented at the symposium. The first, by John Terborgh, who has borne careful witness to this ever-depressing saga of population declines, provides a commentary on our current state of affairs. Gary Hartshorn follows with some welcomed news about prospects for sustainable development of tropical forests, and, consequently, offers some hope for long-term survival of species that depend on them. The second section contains a variety of papers that report population trends, the status of populations, or of efforts to further international cooperative studies of these species. Section three is devoted to ecology, conservation, and behavior during the nonbreeding season, including migration. Interestingly, this section contains the largest number of papers, and perhaps reflects the burgeoning interest and recognition of the importance of a poorly understood nonbreeding season ecology. Section four focuses on the breeding grounds, where authors continue to untangle the roles of fragmented habitats, climatic events, and population parameters such as reproductive success and philopatry in observed changes in populations. In the fifth section are papers with especially broad, hemispheric perspectives. They attempt to link breeding season and nonbreeding season ecology and conservation into more holistic views. Eugene S. Morton, a long-time student of migratory birds, opens section six with his views on the road ahead. Finally, a statement from the Latin American participants, which was presented at the symposium, concludes the text. Both North and Latin Americans would be well served by reading what they have to say. An end section includes the resolutions adopted by the participants of this symposium, which reflect the nature and seriousness of this conservation issue and the commitment of the participants to solving it. Not all presentations, either oral or poster, were submitted as manuscripts for publication here, so we reproduce a copy of the 1989 symposium program, including poster presentations.

In an attempt to deflect some criticism of our use of the term *Neotropical* migrants, here we operationally define the term as pertaining to those species that breed in the Nearctic biogeographic realm, but that winter in the Neotropical realm. This definition describes those landbird species that were the subject of this symposium. We are selectively removing from the definition austral Neotropical migrants, and altitudinal migrants whose entire ranges are restricted to the Neotropics. Having defined the term for our purposes, let us consider the alternatives. *Nearctic* migrant is not a sufficient term because it includes many species that winter no farther south than the southern United States. These species were not the focus of the symposium, except in cases where comparison with Neotropical-wintering species was instructive. The most accurate term describing our subjects might be *Nearctic-Neotropical* migrants, which we viewed as excessively cumbersome. Nevertheless, we have let authors use the terms they prefer. Because everyone seems to have a preference, and no single term could please all, we hope readers will concentrate on the issues at hand.

The difficult challenges posed by long-term conservation of the Neotropical migrant bird system might ordi-

narily cause many to abandon ship. Interestingly, the opposite has occurred. More and more conservation scientists and policy makers are joining ranks. As this book goes to press, an international, cooperative, migrant landbird conservation initiative is underway, which was partly precipitated by the 1989 symposium. A plan has recently been adopted that empowers federal agencies, nongovernment organizations, and policy makers to come together as a coordinated problem-solving force. Desire alone is insufficient, however, which is why this effort is all the more exciting. Along with the political mandate for action, substantial funding for this program is possible—a necessary and long-awaited element.

Will this new migratory bird program, or this book, achieve our goals? Both might spark new research to fill persisting gaps in our knowledge. But if a century from now the Wood Thrush is still enjoyed by those who seek its liquid melody, the answer will be *yes*.

The idea for this symposium came in 1987. Two years of preparation for the meeting, and the subsequent review and assembly of these proceedings, required an army of support. Several individuals, however, performed duties that only the most dedicated would undertake. Nancy Richards, who chaired the local committee on arrangements for the symposium, choreographed a flawless performance by a team of wonderful volunteers. The Woods Hole Marine Biological Laboratory and its conference facility staff provided a comfortable and attractive, albeit wintertime, setting. Our steering committee, Jonathan Atwood, Russell Greenberg, Richard Holmes, Trevor Lloyd-Evans, Frank Moore, Eugene Morton, Raymond O'Connor, and Chandler Robbins, provided essential advice and direction. A large number of financial sponsors of both the symposium and this volume, duly noted in the front of this book, supported our endeavor in the most crucial way. Luis Naranjo kindly translated abstracts into Spanish, thereby increasing the book's usefulness. Josette Carter helped with many details of the symposium, and performed the laborious task of checking final manuscripts for consistency and technical accuracy. However, any errors in this book remain our responsibility. Finally, we thank the director, Linda Leddy, and the trustees of Manomet Bird Observatory, for their resolute commitment to the symposium and these proceedings.

John M. Hagan III
David W. Johnston

Plenary addresses

JOHN TERBORGH
Center for Tropical Conservation
Duke University
3705 Erwin Road
Durham, North Carolina 27705

Perspectives on the conservation of Neotropical migrant landbirds

This is the second special symposium on migratory birds I have had the pleasure to attend. The first was at Front Royal, Virginia, 12 years ago, and many of the people who were there are here with us today.

I sense that this time we are participating in a different kind of event. The meeting at Front Royal took place in an atmosphere of excitement and discovery. Twelve years ago we knew surprisingly little about the winter habits and whereabouts of many migratory birds. The presentations emphasized basic information on what species wintered where, in what habitats and in what numbers. Conservation was a recurrent theme, but not an overriding preoccupation of the participants. There was a strong sense of enthusiasm for all the new-found facts and a feeling that we were all participating in a collaborative venture of major scientific importance.

Now, as many of us gather again to consider the same general topic, the mood has changed. The excitement of adventure and discovery has given way to a feeling of grave concern. Our attention is focused on a new set of issues, issues that relate to the conservation of declining and possibly threatened populations. There is a real sense that we are at risk of losing some of our most beloved birds. Few were expressing such concerns at Front Royal. In a mere 12 years our mood and orientation has changed dramatically. What has happened?

The global environmental crisis has caught up with migratory birds. There are simply too many people making ever increasing demands on a fixed supply of resources. It is inconceivable that we can continue on the same reckless path for very long. Eventually we shall arrive at an equilibrium quite different from today's growth oriented world, but in the meantime we are going to pass through a very difficult transition period that will tax our collective wisdom to the utmost. Whether tigers, elephants and many migratory birds will successfully pass through this time of transition is not a call I wish to make. I just do not have a crystal ball. But if we are armed with good scientific information, we may be able to engage in an enlightened form of crisis management that will carry us through to a time of greater stability and restraint.

By clearing forests, draining wetlands, and contaminating the land, sea and air, we are altering the balance of nature. Migratory birds are particularly vulnerable to these alterations because they must pass through a series of environments on their annual peregrinations. If one of these environments is seriously degraded, it becomes the weakest link in a chain. Since North American migratory birds fill every nook and corner of our continent, and reach as far as Tierra del Fuego in their seasonal journeys, there is hardly an environment in the hemisphere that can escape our concern. We must become global in our thinking. What happens somewhere else can and does affect us. And the threat is all the more serious because our ability to do something about it is severely limited. It would be nice if we could pass laws protecting the forests of Central America, but we cannot. I fear that in some cases we shall be as helpless to control events as a sidewalk bystander watching two cars bear down on each other in a collision course. It thus behooves us to do as much as we can as soon as we can to ward off a crisis that is plainly coming in the near future.

Historical perspective

To place the current situation in perspective, it will help to go back to 1492 when Columbus's discovery set off the greatest human migration in history. At that time the population of the Western Hemisphere was about 1/20th of its current size. Pristine nature reigned over most of North and South America. More than half of the population of the entire hemisphere was concentrated in the Mexican plateau and central Andes. The great forests of both continents were essentially intact.

It is hard to say how many migratory birds nested in North America then, but the number was surely far greater than it is today. Some appreciation of this can be gained by examining results published in *American Birds* in the Breeding Bird Census (Table 1). These results clearly indicate that eastern forests hold the largest breeding concentrations of migratory birds, followed by eastern coniferous forests and western deciduous forests.

We have to realize that these forests are not so extensive today as they were when Europeans began to populate the continent. The total area in forest in the 48 states reached a low of 480 million acres in the decade 1910–1920. Since then there has been a significant recovery to around 610 million acres, or approximately 60% of the original area. But not all the 60% that remains is in its original condition; in fact, virtually none of it is. The entire forest estate east of the Great Plains is passing through various stages of succession; most of it is less than 60 years old. Moreover, in the South and parts of the West, mixed forests have been extensively replaced by plantation monocultures which are notoriously poor breeding bird habitats. If we take into account how birds react to a successional gradient (Table 2), it is clear that a considerable portion of today's deciduous forest harbors breeding bird densities appreciably lower than the virgin forests which once carpeted the continent.

Putting all this together—the conversion of forests to cropland, pasture and urban sprawl, the downgrading of virgin stands to second growth, and the conversion of mixed forests to pine monocultures—one comes to the conclusion that the populations of species that breed in the deciduous forest cannot be much more than a quarter of their historical levels. For non-forest birds, the stories undoubtedly vary. Certain ones, such as the Indigo Bunting and Northern Oriole, have undoubtedly

TABLE 1. Densities of Neotropical migrants in some North American habitats

Vegetation	No. censuses	Pairs/km^2	% Migrants	Pairs migrants/km^2
Eastern deciduous forest	10	863	68	587
Eastern coniferous forest	6	644	64	412
Central oak hickory forest	7	417	45	188
Prairie grassland, tall	10	214	47	101
Prairie grassland, short	3	174	3	5
Cultivated field, Iowa	2	24	0	0
Rocky Mt. deciduous forest	6	449	70	315
Rocky Mt. coniferous forest	7	382	18	69
Riparian, California	7	1596	25	399
Chapparal, California	6	608	10	61
Tundra, Alaska	7	79	36	28

SOURCE: *American Birds,* Jan.–Feb. issues of 1983 and 1984

TABLE 2. Diversity and density of breeding birds with plant succession in the Georgia piedmont

Age of plant community (yrs.)	No. of breeding bird spp.	No. of breeding pairs
1–2	2	15
3	2	40
15	8	105
20	13	127
25	10	83
35	12	95
60	24	163
100	23	233
150	22	224

SOURCE: Johnston and Odum 1956

prospered; others such as the Upland Sandpiper have gone the way of the Prairie Chicken and are reduced more drastically than the birds of the deciduous forest.

To appreciate what is happening in the tropics, we have to interpret current trends in the context of what has happened in North America over the last 200 years. If we take the historical condition as our frame of reference, the first major perturbation came with the clearing and plowing of habitats in North America, with a concomitant reduction in the area of available breeding habitat. This disrupted the longstanding balance between breeding and wintering grounds, so that over the last 150 years populations presumably have been limited by the area of available breeding habitat, and more recently by further insults, such as the explosive increase in cowbirds. In the 1980s and 1990s, however, we are seeing another disruption of the balance, this one caused by uncontrolled destruction of winter habitat. The danger in this is that the populations of many species have already been reduced by 75%, so that further downward pressure could quickly bring them to dangerously low levels.

The loss of wintering habitat in some areas is already very advanced. The once extensive forests of the Antilles, for example, are a thing of the past. When Smith wrote his treatise on the forests of Cuba in 1954, he estimated that only 5% of the forest estate of that country remained intact. The situation today can hardly be any better. Alexander Wetmore wrote of traveling for days through unbroken forest between Cotui and La Vega when he explored the Dominican Republic in the early 1900s. I traveled the same route in 1970, and hardly a tree was to be seen. The entire landscape, as far as the eye could see, had been converted to sugarcane. Every one of us knows that Black-throated Blue Warblers, American Redstarts, and Ovenbirds do not winter in sugarcane fields.

In Central America, forests are being felled to expand banana plantations, to create cattle pasture and to provide land to a growing population of desperately poor peasant farmers. Mid-elevation forests in the northern Andes are being replaced by coffee plantations, dairy farms and cornfields. Anyone who reads the conservation literature, or even the newspapers, is familiar with these facts, so I will not belabor them. The main point is that as human populations continue to expand at rates of over 2% per year in the countries to the south, the pressure on the land becomes unsupportable.

The inescapable implication of this for conservation is that there is only a limited amount of time left in which to slow human population growth and to institute other fundamental changes in the countries of this hemisphere or many of our migratory birds will be little more than memories. To appreciate the reality and the inevitability of this prospect, one need only to visit one of the more crowded countries of this hemisphere, let us say, Haiti, El Salvador or Jamaica. Each of these countries has a human population density in excess of 100 per square kilometer, and in each of them there remains almost nothing that can be described as natural habitat. Yellowthroats and Yellow Warblers may be able to winter in such places, but Worm-eating Warblers and Hooded Warblers cannot.

To me, the most frightening aspect of this situation is that one country after another will pass the 100 per square kilometer population threshold in the coming two or three decades. After this has happened, there is really not much that can be done to salvage winter habitat for migratory birds. By then the forest will be gone and the pressure on the land too great to resist. If anything is to be done, it has to be done before this point is reached. I am not suggesting that wholesale extinctions are in the offing, but rather that many formerly common species will become rare and local in their breeding distributions. You can imagine having to travel hundreds of miles to see a Hooded Warbler or Canada Warbler, just as we have always had to do to see a Kirtland's Warbler.

All is not well on the homefront

Loss of tropical wintering habitat is not the only stress being felt by migratory birds. They are clearly suffering the consequences of various sorts of environmental deterioration here in North America as well. These include the continuing loss of wetlands and prairie grassland, further intensification of agricultural practices with the associated application of ever increasing amounts of chemicals, accelerated urban expansion, and a drastic loss of water quality due to agricultural runoff and acid rain. As if these pressures were not enough, we have all become aware since Front Royal of what is commonly called "the forest fragmentation effect," the disappearance of migratory songbirds from suburban and even rural woodlots across much of the East and Midwest.

Research carried out in the last 12 years has done much to clarify the causes of the so-called fragmentation effect. The environment of small and even not-so-small forests in the east is demonstrably not the same as it was in precolonial times. Experiments with artificial nests performed by David Wilcove, John Faaborg and others have shown that there are abnormal numbers of mammalian and avian nest predators near edges and in the vicinity of human habitations. Predation rates are so high, especially near the ground, that virtually all ground-nesting species have declined or disappeared from large areas (Fig. 1).

A second major cause of nesting failure is cowbird parasitism. Brown-headed Cowbirds have increased dramatically since the early decades of this century, expanding their geographical distribution by hundreds of miles while increasing their host range at the same time (Fig. 2). Cowbird parasitism has reached such levels that certain species seem to be unable to raise any young of their own, and one seriously wonders why their populations have not already collapsed. My colleague, Scott Robinson, who has been studying cowbird parasitism in Illinois, found 19 Wood Thrush nests, all parasitized, in the fragmented watershed of a reservoir in the central part of the state. The average nest con-

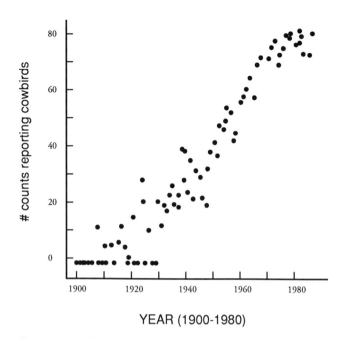

FIGURE 2. Index of abundance of Brown-headed Cowbirds from 1900 to 1980, from Christmas Bird Count records (from Brittingham and Temple 1983).

tained 4.6 cowbird eggs and only 1.2 Wood Thrush eggs. Even in the Shawnee National Forest, the largest contiguous forest tract in the state, he found that all but 7 of 90 Wood Thrush nests were parasitized. The Wood Thrushes of Illinois constitute nothing less than a cowbird factory. A similarly grim story can be told for other species, as Scott will relate in one of the paper sessions to follow.

In another disturbing development, John Faaborg is finding that up to three-quarters of the territorial male Ovenbirds in central Missouri woodlots are unpaired. Such strongly biased sex ratios suggest that the actual breeding populations of these species may be much smaller than would be indicated by normal census methods—the Breeding Bird Survey, for example. Presumably, historical sex ratios were approximately equal. How might one account for such male-biased populations?

Although this is still an unanswered question, a likely possibility is sex-biased overwinter survival. Jim Lynch, Eugene Morton and their associates have recently discovered that male and female Hooded Warblers segregate into different habitats on the Yucatan wintering ground. Males occupy territories in mature forest whereas females are found along edges and in early second growth. After an experimental removal of males along one edge, females in the adjacent habitat did not expand into the vacant male territories, suggesting that

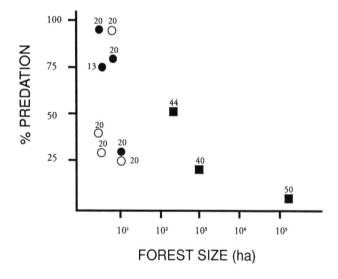

FIGURE 1. Percentage of nests preyed upon as a function of forest size. *Closed squares*—large figure tracts, *open circles*—rural fragments, *closed circles*—suburban fragments. Number above each point is number of nests placed in that forest (from Wilcove 1985).

the observed habitat differences represented sex limited preferences and not exclusion. Sexual segregation into different winter habitats is known for some other species, but had not previously been documented for a Neotropical migrant. Any sort of sex limited habitat use, whether brought about by preference or exclusion, can lead to sex ratio distortions because it is inherently unlikely that survival will be equal in different habitats, or that the available areas of different habitats will be equivalent.

Land-use patterns are changing rapidly in Central America. The changes are likely to induce differential effects within populations that use more than one habitat. If the preferred habitat is, let us say, primary forest, and the area of primary forest is diminished, there will be increasing competition within the population for this habitat. If males are generally able to dominate females in the contest for territories, females will be forced into poor quality habitat where they might experience reduced survival.

A similar argument applies to age classes. A scarcity of prime habitat will favor adults over juveniles, since adults are normally dominant. A probable example of this was discovered by John Rappole and Mario Ramos who found that Wood Thrushes unable to secure winter territories in primary forest in Veracruz, Mexico experienced poor survival in early successional vegetation. Reduced juvenile survivorship can reduce recruitment into the breeding population. Russ Greenberg is currently investigating these issues in Yucatan and will report later on his results.

Finally, in an article that arrived in the latest issue of *American Birds*, John Faaborg documented a steep 15-year decline in the numbers of North American migrants wintering in the Guánica State Forest in Puerto Rico. Precisely what this implies is not yet clear, although it would be difficult to arrive at a positive interpretation of his results.

None of the subjects I have just discussed—forest fragmentation, nest predation, cowbird parasitism, age and sex biased overwinter survival, long-term population declines on the wintering grounds—was the subject of a presentation at Front Royal. The topics are not all new ones, but ones that have come to the forefront of our attention in the years since Front Royal. Collectively, they underscore the seriousness and diversity of the issues we face in conserving migratory birds. In most cases, it is not clear what remedial action can be taken, or even what is within the realm of the possible. Can we dictate land-use practices in Central America? No. Can we persuade people across the country to buy raccoon-proof garbage cans? Doubtfully. Can we cut the cowbird population by 90%? It is not easy to see how. Can we convince farmers not to use so many chemicals on their

fields? That would be difficult, to say the least. In each case we seem to be up against a stone wall.

Where do we go from here?

What then can be done? The best we can hope for is to prevent the situation from slipping much further; going back to where we were 20 to 40 years ago, I am afraid, is impossible. I have painted a gloomy picture, because I believe the prospects for the future are truly gloomy. Nevertheless, there are steps that can be taken to ameliorate the unfolding of a worst case scenario.

Our cause is a subtle one, best noticed by people like me who have a long memory for such things as birds. The man in the street is not so easily convinced that things are amiss in the environment and that strong measures are in order. The absence of a few birds in the park where he walks his dog is something he will never notice. Some individual Congressmen may be concerned, but Congress is a political body that seldom moves against the tide. If legislative action is required, especially if the action is at all expensive or controversial, the Congress is likely to balk unless the case in favor is unarguable. This is why promoting the cause of migratory birds will require strong information of the most unassailable quality.

Take, for example, the recent administration's response to acid rain. There was no consensus among the experts, it was claimed, as to whether acid rain was producing detrimental effects. When Congress held hearings, the administration could produce "expert" witnesses to support its agnostic views. Other explanations were possible, it was argued. The offending sources could not be identified. More research was needed. All of you are familiar with this history, and the fact that we still lack a vigorous program to curtail acid emissions. If anything is to be done about the plight of migratory birds, conservationists are going to have to pull themselves together and design a public relations campaign that will avoid the pitfalls that have hampered progress on acid rain. It will not be easy, but good information will help.

On the scientific front, I can make two recommendations. The first is that the ornithological community institute a nationwide monitoring program for breeding birds that will provide accurate, up-to-the-year information on population trends. The second is that a systematic program be organized to monitor tropical deforestation and land-use trends via remote sensing.

A retort to the first of these recommendations might be that we already have a bird population monitoring system: there is the Blue List, the Breeding Bird Census, the Breeding Bird Atlas, the Breeding Bird Survey, and the Christmas Counts. What more could one want?

More is not the answer. The problem is credibility. For reasons I will not belabor in detail, for the time simply is not sufficient, each of these impressive efforts lacks credibility, because they are all designed in ways that make a scientist want to cry. A witness who was trying to convince a Congressional committee to appropriate more money for migratory birds on the strength of these programs could be cut to ribbons by a sharp-witted opponent. Improving the information base will require making adjustments in the way we are doing things.

A program to monitor deforestation and land use in the tropics is well within our technical capacity. But it would be expensive. As remote sensing capabilities become more refined and accurate, the cost of processing the data rises exponentially. An effort to monitor changes in vegetation cover in just the Western Hemisphere would cost millions of dollars a year. That is why no conservation organization has yet undertaken the task, nor is this a likely prospect. This is a job for Congress to allocate to NASA or some other competent organization.

On the political front, I can offer a number of suggestions that pertain to the dilemma of tropical deforestation, as well as the situation on the homefront.

Even as we are gathered here in Massachusetts to express our mutual concern for migratory birds, legislatures in many of the tropical countries of this hemisphere are debating and approving bills designed to promote colonization and large-scale development in the remaining areas of tropical forest in their countries. These steps are directed toward the stated goal of nearly every tropical nation—to complete the occupation of its entire national territory, so that hitherto inaccessible natural resources can be made available for exploitation. Indeed, throughout the 19th century, the policies of our own government were hardly distinguishable from this. How then can we admonish people who do not have enough to eat for not following in our footsteps in seeking to wring the maximum benefit from their natural resources?

Having no stick, we must do it with the carrot, if we are to do it at all. International financial and assistance organizations such as the World Bank and USAID have enormous leverage in the less developed countries. Few major development projects are initiated without the express approval and financial backing of these organizations. The policies of both the World Bank and USAID toward conservation have changed markedly for the better within the last few years, and will continue to improve. By voicing our concerns to our representatives, we can hope that they in turn will use their influence to press further reforms on the international agencies.

It would help if international organizations ceased to sponsor projects that resulted in the destruction of primary habitat in the tropics. This would include large-scale colonization schemes, such as the transmigration program in Indonesia, road building for the purpose of opening up virgin lands, and dam construction in low-lying river basins. It would help to withdraw financial support from countries that continued to offer subsidies for clearing tropical forest, whether for cattle ranching, plantation agriculture or unsustainable colonization. It would help to promote land-for-debt swaps and to reduce required debt payments in return for agreements to protect the environment. It would help to make assistance available to develop sustainable forestry on lands inherently unsuited to agriculture. And it would help to provide assistance for the reforestation and restoration of abandoned land. These are just a few suggestions. A thoughtful person could easily add to the list.

The problems of migratory birds are not all to be found in the tropics, as I hope I have made clear. In the U.S. the main threats are the loss of certain habitats, particularly prairies and wetlands, the continued deterioration of water quality in many of the nation's lakes and rivers, and the plague of unintentionally subsidized nest predators and cowbirds. As to habitat loss, it would help to consider how a wide range of government subsidies and tax incentives affect land-use patterns across the country. As for water quality, we are gradually coming to grips with the problems caused by human and industrial wastes, and we seem to be inching toward a consensus on acid rain, but agricultural runoff remains a serious and nearly intractable problem. I expect it will be a long time before we find ways of reducing this. Finally, I see little that can be done to abate the plague of nest predators and cowbirds in suburban America. The best hope for forest-dwelling songbirds is to push ahead with expanding and consolidating our National Forests, as these offer the largest contiguous blocks of relatively cowbird-free habitat in the land.

That leaves me wondering, as a last note, about the Least Bell's Vireo, the Black-capped Vireo, the Henslow's Sparrow, the Kirtland's Warbler, and others of their ilk that have no refuge from the curse of the cowbird. What is to become of them? Perhaps some of you have the answers, for I do not.

Literature cited

Brittingham, M.C., and S.A. Temple. 1983. Have cowbirds caused forest songbirds to decline? *BioScience* 33:31–35.

Johnston, D.W., and E.P. Odum. 1956. Breeding bird populations in relation to plant succession on the Piedmont of Georgia. *Ecology* 37:50–61.

Wilcove, D.S. 1985. Nest predation in forest tracts and the decline of migratory songbirds. *Ecology* 66:1211–1214.

GARY S. HARTSHORN
World Wildlife Fund
1250 24th Street NW
Washington D.C. 20037

Forest loss and future options in Central America

This paper is an overview of deforestation patterns and the dwindling options remaining for the tropical forests of Central America. Although we can make inferences about deforestation over the past few centuries (e.g., in prime coffee-growing regions), most deforestation in Central America has occurred since 1950. Rampant deforestation not only destroys forest resources, it also reduces environmental services and eliminates natural habitats for millions of species, including many Neotropical migrant and resident birds (cf. Terborgh 1989). For nonvertebrates, we know very little about patterns of species diversity in the region; as recently as 1980 the flora of Nicaragua was one of the least known national floras of any country in Latin America.

In the second half of the 20th century we have witnessed the pervasive use of modern technology to exploit the region's natural resources: chainsaws and skidders to log and clear forests, bulldozed roads to advance the agricultural frontier deeper into the forested hinterland, heavy dependence on fertilizers and pesticides to produce crops for export, construction of dams for generating hydroelectric power, and depletion of near-shore coastal and marine resources, inter alia (Leonard 1987). Burgeoning human populations, inequitable distribution of agricultural land, insecure land tenure and the emphasis on export commodities combine to exacerbate further the abuse of renewable natural resources in Central America.

The seven countries (Belize, Costa Rica, El Salvador, Guatemala, Honduras, Nicaragua and Panama) comprising Central America differ greatly in size, population, per capita income, etc. (Table 1). As a region, Central America is quite small—roughly equivalent in size to Thailand, the combined states of Utah and Nevada, or the Brazilian state of Minas Gerais.

Not all ecological changes in the region are due simply to deforestation. Particularly in coastal regions, such as the Gulf of Nicoya or the Gulf of Fonseca whose catchments have long been used for growing cotton, there are tremendous problems with pesticide and fer-

TABLE 1. Population and economic features of Central American countries

Country	Area (km^2)	Population (thousands)	GNP ($ million)	Per capita ($)	Foreign debt ($ million)
Belize	22,975	160	130	1,190	139
Costa Rica	51,000	2,700	4,563	1,690	4,437
El Salvador	21,156	5,000	4,700	940	1,692
Guatemala	108,889	8,700	7,830	1,250	2,709
Honduras	112,088	4,800	4,128	860	3,188
Nicaragua	148,000	3,600	2,903	829	7,291
Panama	77,082	2,300	4,876	2,120	5,323
TOTAL	541,190	27,260	29,130		24,779

SOURCES: World Bank 1990, World Resources Institute 1990–1991.

tilizer abuse, as well as run-off into coastal waters. These pollutants have caused a very serious depletion of the coastal fisheries. On the Caribbean coast, sedimentation caused primarily by deforestation has decimated coral reefs (e.g., Cahuita). These are just a few illustrations of coastal and near-shore degradation of valuable and highly productive natural resources.

Deforestation

If we look at the long-term trends of deforestation in Latin America, we see that the region as a whole lost only about 20% of the forest area from 1850 to 1980, which is far less than other regions such as south Asia and China (Table 2). Looking more closely at tropical American deforestation (Table 3), Brazil is by far the leader with almost 1.5 million hectares of tropical forests converted each year. Using total forest loss per year, few other tropical American countries make the top ten list.

However, rates of loss (i.e., the percent of remaining forests lost each year) give a different set of top ten countries (Table 4). During the early 1980s, Costa Rica

had the highest relative rate of deforestation in Central America (3.9%); El Salvador (2.9%), Nicaragua (2.7%), and Honduras (2.4%) also make this top ten list. The total forest loss in the Central American region is about 400,000 hectares per year, which would rank the region fifth when compared with the top ten tropical countries in total area deforested each year (Table 3). This is equivalent to an average 2% rate of deforestation for the Central American region.

To illustrate patterns of deforestation in Central America, I focus on Costa Rica, a tiny country that has lost more than 50% of its tropical forests since 1950. Costa Rica is an ecologically complex country, with 12 ecological life zones (Holdridge et al. 1971) in an area about the size of West Virginia. For comparison, the eastern and central United States has only 11 ecological life zones (Sawyer and Lindsay 1964). Costa Rica's eco-

TABLE 2. Forest depletion by regions, 1850 to 1980

Region	Area (million hectares)				Percent loss
	1850	1900	1950	1980	
Tropical Africa	1,336	1,306	1,188	1,074	20
Latin America	1,420	1,394	1,273	1,151	19
South Asia	317	299	251	180	43
Southeast Asia	252	249	242	235	7
China	96	84	69	58	39
North America	971	954	939	942	3
World	5,919	5,749	5,345	5,007	15

SOURCE: World Resources Institute 1987, Table 18.3, p. 272.

TABLE 3. Top ten tropical countries ranked by annual forest loss in hectares during the period 1981–1985

Rank	Country	Forests, 1980	Annual rate	Deforested per yr
1.	Brazil	396,030,000	0.4%	1,480,000
2.	Colombia	47,351,000	1.7%	820,000
3.	Indonesia	123,235,000	0.5%	600,000
4.	Mexico	47,840,000	1.2%	595,000
5.	Ecuador	14,679,000	2.3%	340,000
6.	Nigeria	7,583,000	4.0%	300,000
7.	Ivory Coast	4,907,000	5.9%	290,000
8.	Peru	70,520,000	0.4%	270,000
9.	Malaysia	21,256,000	1.2%	255,000
10.	Thailand	10,375,000	2.4%	252,000

SOURCE: World Resources Institute 1986, Table 6.1, p. 274.

TABLE 4. Top ten tropical countries ranked by percentage loss of forests (ha) during the period 1981–85

Rank	Country	Forests, 1980	Annual loss	Deforested per yr
1.	Ivory Coast	4,907,000	5.9%	290,000
2.	Paraguay	4,100,000	4.6%	190,000
3.	Nigeria	7,583,000	4.0%	300,000
4.	Costa Rica	1,664,000	3.9%	65,000
5.	Nepal	2,128,000	3.9%	84,000
6.	Haiti	58,000	3.1%	2,000
7.	El Salvador	155,000	2.9%	5,000
8.	Nicaragua	4,508,000	2.7%	121,000
9.	Guinea-Bissau	664,000	2.6%	17,000
10.	Honduras	3,797,000	2.4%	90,000

SOURCE: World Resources Institute 1986, Table 6.1, p. 274.

logical complexity is due primarily to latitude (8–11°N) and a series of NW-SE mountain ranges (peaking at 3,818 m on Chirripó) that cause orographic rainfall and cloud forests on the front ranges, whereas the Pacific versant has a pronounced monsoonal climate.

In such a wet country as Costa Rica, deforestation patterns are strongly correlated to ecologically related features, such as life zones, slope gradient, and transportation network (Sader and Joyce 1988). These authors analyzed changes in primary forest cover over 43 years, based on aerial photos (1940, 1950 and 1961) and LandSat Multispectral Scanner images (1977 and 1983). Their data show the appreciable decline in primary forests remaining in the years 1940 (67%), 1950 (56%), 1961 (45%), 1977 (32%) and 1983 (17%). An independent study put Costa Rica's remaining forest cover at 19.5% (Flores 1984). The main discrepancy was due to misclassification of swamp forests in northeastern Costa Rica by Sader and Joyce (1988).

Of the 33% of Costa Rica deforested prior to 1940, two life zones—tropical dry and tropical premontane moist—had been most affected. The former (all in northwestern Costa Rica) was deforested for large cattle ranches and the latter (mostly in the Central and San Ramón Valleys), for intensive coffee (*Coffea arabica*) plantations. Despite the preeminent socio-economic role of bananas early in the 20th century (Casey 1979), only 16% of the tropical wet life zone was deforested prior to 1940.

Between 1940 and 1950, average annual deforestation rates were highest in the tropical dry (9.9%) and tropical premontane moist (7.9%) life zones; however, the tropical moist life zone (especially in the El General Valley) lost the largest area (1,643 km^2) of primary tropical forests. From 1950 to 1961, an additional 1,867 km^2 of tropical moist life zone was deforested. Between 1961

and 1977, tropical wet (2,251 km^2) and tropical premontane wet (2,655 km^2) life zones lost the most primary forests.

From 1940 to 1977, the average annual rate of deforestation in Costa Rica rose slightly from 1.6% to 1.9%. Between 1977 and 1983, the annual rate of forest loss skyrocketed to 7.7% per year. Such a striking increase in annual deforestation was due largely to the economic boom in beef exports from the mid-1970s to the early 1980s and the massive conversion of forest to cattle ranches (Hartshorn et al. 1982). Over 56% of the deforestation in the 1977–1983 period occurred in the tropical wet (2,515 km^2), tropical premontane wet (801 km^2) and tropical premontane rain (884 km^2) life zones. Even though these wetter life zones are generally unsuitable for productive pastures on a sustainable basis, strong government incentives promoted deforestation (Hartshorn et al. 1982).

The detailed analyses of Costa Rican deforestation over the 1940–1983 period (Sader and Joyce 1988) clearly indicate how the agricultural frontier (including cattle ranching) advanced sequentially through dry, moist, wet and rain life zones. Advancement of the agricultural frontier was abetted by major development of the transportation network (primarily all-weather roads). Between 1967 and 1977, for example, the cumulative total distance of roads nearly tripled (Sader and Joyce 1988). By 1977, the mean distance of forest from a road was only 14.2 km. The national transportation network has reached all but the most remote and therefore inaccessible parts of the country, such as the high Talamancas and Corcovado National Park in southern Costa Rica.

The deforestation patterns in Costa Rica are fairly representative for Central America. Virtually all the dry forests in the Pacific lowlands are gone, making these forests an endangered ecosystem (Janzen 1988). Even though a few sizeable conservation units (Costa Rica's lower Tempisque complex and Guanacaste National Park) have been established, they are still threatened by fires and poaching. The Caribbean lowlands of Central America have several large conservation units (e.g., Belize's Bladen Reserve and the much-expanded Cockscomb Basin Jaguar Reserve, Guatemala's Tikal World Heritage Site, Honduras's Río Plátano Biosphere Reserve and Costa Rica's Barra del Colorado-Tortuguero complex), but consolidation of these "protected" areas has been generally incomplete. Many of the region's conservation units occur at higher elevations, where they perform critical environmental services such as watershed protection and cloud interception.

The sharp rise in the annual rate of deforestation in Costa Rica during the 1980s is indicative of increasing pressure on the rapidly declining forests of Central America. Most deforestation in the region occurs through the slash-and-burn process to convert forests to non-forest uses. In contrast to shifting cultivation as practiced by many indigenous peoples, the slash-and-burn technique is a key element of agricultural colonization that does not rotate small clearings in a forest matrix. Rather, cutting and burning the forest advances the agricultural frontier farther into the forests. It is easy to see why penetration roads play such an important role in tropical deforestation.

Little timber is harvested during the conversion of forest to other land uses, primarily because of lack of immediate access to sawmills. In the smaller countries of Central America, roads are somewhat less important as vehicles of access than they are in the Amazon Basin. When there is anticipation of development activities like a road, colonists will arrive perhaps years before access gets there in order to stake claims. Usually "improving" the land by cutting down forest strengthens the claim of ownership. In some cases, the colonist will fell all but the large timber trees, which can be harvested when road access reaches the property some years hence; this is called "logging a pasture."

In Central America, cattle ranching is the primary cause of deforestation. There was tremendous pressure, particularly in the 1960s and 1970s, to convert tropical forest to extensive pastures for beef cattle (Shane 1980). Especially in the late 1970s, Central America witnessed rampant and indiscriminant deforestation to produce beef for export. By 1980 the region was producing over 350,000 metric tons annually, of which about 40% was exported (Leonard 1987). Beef exports lessened appreciably during the 1980s, primarily because of a precipitous decline in the U.S. beef market. Central American governments also tightened credit for beef cattle operations. Nevertheless, total beef production declined only modestly, as increased domestic consumption of beef more than compensated for sharply declining exports of beef (Leonard 1987).

The rampant deforestation of Central America in the 1970s and 1980s occurred with no concerns or restrictions about suitability or sustainability. Forests were cut and burned regardless of rainfall regime, site quality, steepness of slope, or protection of water courses. All too often the extensive pastures extended from stream bank to ridge top. The cavalier ignorance of site quality and land-use capability in the rush to advance the agricultural frontier for cattle ranching invited disasters. Deforested slopes suffered erosion two orders of magnitudes greater than background erosion under primary forests. The frequency of landslides on deforested slopes increased greatly. Much of the eroded soil was washed into streams, greatly increasing the sediment load. Where a river was dammed (usually for generating hydroelectric power) the enormous sediment loads entering the reservoir quickly reduced the active storage capacity. The rapid filling of reservoirs (e.g., El Sal-

vador's Río Lempa) reduces the utility of hydroelectric and/or irrigation projects to one or two decades. Rivers still without dams carry their greatly increased sediment loads to the sea, literally drowning the productive capacity of near-shore ecosystems, such as mangroves, estuaries, and coral reefs. Deforested watersheds are unable to buffer storms and modulate stream flows, often resulting in more frequent major floods of lowlands and reductions in potable water services to human communities.

Logging, per se, is not a primary cause of deforestation in Central America. Rather, it is the access roads for logging that facilitate colonists advancing the agriculture frontier. In a few cases, such as petroleum exploration in Costa Rica and Guatemala, improved access to remote hinterlands fuels a rapid advance of the deforestation front, often with complete disregard of existing conservation units or the traditional land use and claims of indigenous cultures. Where logging is not the primary cause of deforestation, the frontier is well defined and easily recognizable from aerial photos or satellite imagery. However, the gradient from stable agriculture to primary forest is often longer, more complex, and not so visually abrupt. Colonists may stake out claims in anticipation of improved access several years later. Small clearings or homesteads are established in the forest matrix; often they are abandoned after a few years. If not reclaimed, the abandoned patches are dominated by vigorous growth of secondary forests. Knowledgeable colonists often leave several large timber trees when clearing the primary forest; a few large emergent trees per hectare over 10–20 year-old secondary forest (or even cacao plantations) could be easily misinterpreted on aerial photos or satellite images as primary forest. Such complex gradients from established agriculture (or pasture) to primary forest complicate the quantitative analyses of deforestation.

Because some countries such as Costa Rica are trying to prohibit the clearing of primary forest, entrepreneurs undercut the forest (i.e., cut small trees up to about 20 cm dbh) and plant grass for pasture. They then solicit permits to log the "remnant" timber trees in their pastures. The consequence is that primary forests continue to be cut, even in designated protected areas (e.g., Barra del Colorado Wildlife Sanctuary, Costa Rica).

In contrast to the broad-leaved forests discussed so far, the area of pine forests in northern Central America (Bethel et al. 1976; Hartshorn 1988a) has not declined appreciably in the last 30 to 40 years. The total area in coniferous forests has been stable in Belize, Guatemala, Honduras, and Nicaragua. What is happening though, is a rather considerable degradation of the forest resource. Even though the total area is essentially the same as it was in 1950, the standing volume of coniferous timber is now less than half of what it was in 1950

(Leonard 1987). The principal cause is intensive logging of commercial timber, coupled with inadequate silvicultural management for sustained yield of timber, excessive and repeated burning, and in some cases strong local demand for fuelwood, posts, and stakes.

Sustainable use options

With such a rapidly dwindling resource base of primary forests, there is precious little time remaining to save those forests outside the national system of protected areas. In fact, many conservationists state that just protecting the national parks and equivalent reserves in the region is a major challenge that will become increasingly more difficult in the 1990s. The primary forests in less-stringent "protection" categories (e.g., forest reserves, Indian reserves), as well as privately held forests, have little chance of surviving unless ways are found to use these renewable forest resources (timber and non-timber forest products) without destroying the forests. There is an urgent need to find, to test, and to implement sustainable uses of tropical forests that generate direct economic benefits to the forest owners, neighbors, and their beneficiaries. These options range from nonextractive uses such as ecotourism, to sustained-yield of timber based on natural forest management. A few of these initiatives are highlighted in this section.

Natural history tourism (or ecotourism) is generating considerable economic benefits in many developing countries. In fact, it is ranked third in foreign exchange earnings in Costa Rica. In other tropical countries (e.g., Kenya, Thailand) tourism ranks number one. Because natural history tourism is perceived to be a passive, nondestructive use of tropical forests, it has stimulated much enthusiasm among conservationists (Boo 1990). Increasing interest by visitors to a protected area stimulates local appreciation for conservation and, even more importantly, generates local income. In a few exceptional cases (e.g., the private Monteverde Cloud Forest Reserve) visitors' fees are sufficient to cover maintenance costs. More typically, visitor fees (especially for foreigners) to national parks and reserves are so low that they generate only a small fraction of the operating costs.

In many tropical American countries, ecotourism is booming and the unprepared visitor is usually offered a shoppers' market of nature-tour operators. Some operators have developed their own lodges in or bordering particularly attractive protected areas. Local entrepreneurs often capitalize on ecotourism by offering a range of lodging options. Clearly, the service opportunities for lodging, food, transport, and guides can generate significant improvements in local employment. However, there is considerable leakage of profits away

from the local community. Most profits from ecotourism accrue in the capital city, or are repatriated abroad. Strengthening local capture of ecotourism profits in addition to an expanding service sector are essential if ecotourism is to fulfill expectations for building local support for conservation.

One of the more exciting initiatives for saving tropical forests is the renewed interest and evidence for natural forest management (cf. Gradwohl and Greenberg 1988). Over the past few decades there was a growing consensus that it was ecologically impossible and economically unviable to manage complex tropical forests for sustained yield of timber (Baur 1968; Leslie 1977; Mergen and Vincent 1987). The late 1980s saw a surprising shift in professional opinion to a positive open-mindedness about tropical forest management (Hartshorn et al. 1987, Leslie 1987, Schmidt 1987).

This remarkable change in perspective about tropical forest managment came about through the concordance of several different concerns: (1) traditional approaches to tropical forest management (e.g., enrichment planting) simply were not economically viable; (2) growing alarm over the loss of tropical forests; (3) better understanding of tropical forest dynamics; (4) rapidly improving markets for a wider array of tropical timber species; and (5) a growing realization that tropical forestry must involve local people. Naturally, these, and other factors, have not advanced equally fast or in an integrated manner.

An excellent example of this new approach to sound use of tropical forests is the innovative project being implemented by the Yánesha Forestry Cooperative (COFYAL) in the Peruvian Amazon (Hartshorn 1990; Landis 1990). The Costa Rican Tropical Science Center (TSC) designed a vertically integrated model that involves full control of forest resources, harvesting all trees in narrow strip clear-cuts, local processing of timber, and marketing of forest products (Tosi 1982). In 1986, TSC helped the Amuesha Indians of Peru's Palcazú valley form COFYAL, whose statutory objectives are to: (1) provide a source of employment for members of the native communities; (2) manage the communities' natural forests for sustained yield of forest products; and (3) protect the cultural integrity of the Amuesha people.

A key component of COFYAL's forest management system is the harvesting of all timber in long, narrow (30–40 m wide) strips in primary forests. In effect, each clear-cut strip is an elongated gap in the forest canopy that permits sunlight to reach the forest floor. These forest gaps occur frequently in primary tropical forests and are important sites for natural regeneration of many native tree species (Hartshorn 1978, 1980, 1989a). Gap-phase dynamics of tropical American forests is the ecological cornerstone of the COFYAL forest management system that rotates a series of strip clear-cuts through a production forest for sustained yield of timber. The clear-cutting of narrow strips in primary forests promotes excellent natural regeneration of hundreds of native tree species (Hartshorn 1988b, 1989a,b). Furthermore, the widely spaced strips not only maintain the primary forest structure, but this natural forest management system maintains considerable undisturbed habitat for wildlife and birds. The natural forest management system being implemented by COFYAL is an ecologically sound, economically viable, socially responsible, and politically acceptable initiative that promotes sound forestry by local people to generate attractive economic benefits.

Another innovative approach to tropical forest management is the PORTICO operation in Costa Rica. PORTICO exports hardwood doors made of "royal mahogany" (*Carapa nicaraguensis*, Meliaceae). To ensure adequate supplies of timber, PORTICO has purchased about 8,500 hectares of swamp forest in northeast Costa Rica and is managing their forests for sustained yield of *Carapa*. Because PORTICO's forests are dominated by *Carapa* (McHargue and Hartshorn 1983), the company uses a highly selective harvesting system to remove only a few trees per hectare on a 15-year cutting cycle. After experimenting with logging by contractors, PORTICO switched to using their own employees, which helped the company drastically reduce damage caused by tree felling and log extraction. The company also selects two large, excellent *Carapa* trees on each hectare that are left as seed trees. The careful removal of a few large trees per hectare minimizes damage to smaller trees, while maintaining the primary forest structure.

PORTICO has an active forest guard program to protect their production forests from squatters and hunters. There are very serious threats to unprotected forests in northeastern Costa Rica, as well as considerable deforestation in the Barra del Colorado Wildlife Sanctuary. An independent evaluation (by INBio—Costa Rica's National Biodiversity Institute) of wildlife and plants in the company's managed forests indicates more wildlife in PORTICO's forests than in nearby primary forests that are unprotected. For example, the field team observed green macaws (*Ara ambigua*) feeding on *Dipteryx panamensis* fruits in PORTICO forests. As a consequence of this information the company made an immediate decision to cut no *Dipteryx* trees in their managed forests, so as to help maintain the dwindling population of this wide-ranging frugivore.

Through a MacArthur Foundation funded project at La Selva, we have screened dozens of potentially valuable and usable native tree species to look at the possibilities of incorporating them in reforestation schemes. There is considerable interest on the part of developing agencies, as well as local farmers, to use native (and better known) tree species for reforestation. Some of the La Selva project's promising tree species are *Calophyllum brasiliense*, *Pithecellobium macradenium*, *Vochysia guatemalensis*, and *V. ferruginea*. It takes a tremendous effort to move promising native species through the domestication process; you have to know the phenology of the species, when it is appropriate to collect the seeds, how to handle the seeds, how they can be stored, how to germinate them, and what is the most efficient and economical way of moving them through a nursery situation. This process may take many years to bring fast-growing native tree species to the potential reforestation market.

Summary

Unless we address the growing and legitimate needs of rural people, there is little chance of turning around the rampant deforestation in Central America. We have to find ways to enfranchise and facilitate rural people in their local efforts to use tropical forests sustainably and obtain direct economic returns from the forest resources. There is a growing emphasis in so-called secondary or minor forest products (e.g., Peters et al. 1989) as attractive sources of income for rural people. In many tropical forests, timber is still the primary forest product, thus the sustainable production of timber often is a necessary precursor to managing complex tropical forests for non-timber products.

This decade is a particularly critical time for reversing the exponential loss of tropical forests. Multidisciplinary efforts throughout the tropics are urgently needed to find ways to use forests sustainably without destroying habitats. Many tropical regions such as Central America are in danger of losing virtually all unprotected forests by the year 2000. And if local people are not soon incorporated in the efforts to consolidate established conservation units, few of these national parks and equivalent reserves will survive well into the next century. The deteriorating interaction of tropical forests and migrant birds is a harbinger of the difficult tasks to save tropical forest habitats and the myriad species that they harbor, whether as full-time residents or migratory visitors.

Literature cited

Baur, G.N. 1968. *The Ecological Basis of Rainforest Management.* Sydney, Australia: Forestry Commission of New South Wales.

Bethel, J.S., D.G. Briggs and J.G. Flores. 1976. Forests in Central America: Which kind, how large and where? *Revista Biología Tropical* 24(suppl.):143–175.

Boo, E. 1990. *Ecotourism: The Potentials and Pitfalls.* Washington: World Wildlife Fund, 2 vols.

Casey G., J. 1979. *Limón 1880–1940: Un Estudio de la Industria Bananera en Costa Rica.* San José: Editorial Costa Rica.

Flores R., J.G. 1984. *Diagnóstico del Sector Industrial Forestal y Alternativas de Solución.* San José, Costa Rica: Dirección General Forestal.

Gradwohl, J., and R. Greenberg. 1988. *Saving the Tropical Forests.* London: Earthscan Publ. Ltd.

Hartshorn, G.S. 1978. Tree falls and tropical forest dynamics. Pages 617–638 in *Tropical Trees as Living Systems,* P.B. Tomlinson and M.H. Zimmermann, eds. Cambridge: Cambridge University Press.

———. 1980. Neotropical forest dynamics. *Biotropica* 12(suppl.):23–30.

———. 1988a. Tropical and subtropical vegetation of Meso-America. Pages 365–390 in *North American Terrestrial Vegetation,* M.G. Barbour and W.D. Billings, eds. New York: Cambridge University Press.

———. 1988b. *Natural regeneration of trees on the Palcazú demonstration strips.* San José, Costa Rica: Tropical Science Center.

———. 1989a. Application of gap theory to tropical forest management: Natural regeneration on strip clear-cuts in the Peruvian Amazon. *Ecology* 70(3):567–569.

———. 1989b. Gap-phase dynamics and tropical tree species richness. Pages 65–73 in *Tropical Forests: Botanical Dynamics, Speciation and Diversity,* L. Holm-Nielsen, I. Nielsen, and H. Balslev, eds. London: Academic Press.

———. 1990. Natural forest management by the Yánesha Forestry Cooperative in Peruvian Amazonia. Pages 128–138 in *Alternatives to Deforestation: Steps Toward Sustainable Use of the Amazon Rain Forest,* A.B. Anderson, ed. New York: Columbia University Press.

Hartshorn, G.S., L. Hartshorn, A. Atmella, L. Gomez, A. Mata, L. Mata, R. Morales, R. Ocampo, D. Pool, C. Quesada, C. Solera, R. Solórzano, G. Stiles, J. Tosi, A. Umaña, C. Villalobos, and R. Wells. 1982. *Costa Rica Country Environmental Profile: A Field Study.* San José: Tropical Science Center, 123 p.

Hartshorn, G.S., R. Simeone, and J. Tosi, Jr. 1987. Manejo para rendimiento sostenido de bosques naturales: Un sinopsis del proyecto de desarrollo del Palcazú en la Selva Central de la Amazonía Peruana. Pages 235–243 in *Management of the Forests of Tropical America: Prospects and Technologies,* J.C. Figueroa Colón, F. Wadsworth, and S. Branham, eds. Rio Piedras, Puerto Rico: Institute of Tropical Forestry.

Holdridge, L., W. Grenke, W. Hatheway, T. Liang, and J. Tosi, Jr. 1971. *Forest Environments in Tropical Life Zones: A Pilot Study.* Elmsford, N.Y.: Pergamon Press.

Janzen, D.H. 1988. Tropical dry forests: The most endangered major tropical ecosystem. Pages 130–137 in *Biodiversity,* E.O. Wilson, ed. Washington: National Academy Press.

Landis, S. 1990. Managing a rain forest: A Peruvian experiment in sustained yield. *Fine Woodworking* 82:75–79.

Leonard, H.J. 1987. *Natural Resources and Economic Development in Central America: A Regional Environmental Profile.* New Brunswick, N.J.: Transaction Books.

Leslie, A.J. 1977. When theory and practice contradict. *Unasylva* 29(115):2–17.

———. 1987. A second look at the economics of natural management systems in tropical mixed forests. *Unasylva* 39(155):46–58.

McHargue, L.A., and G.S. Hartshorn. 1983. Seed and seedling ecology of *Carapa guianensis. Turrialba* 33(4):399–404.

Mergen, F., and J.R. Vincent, eds. 1987. *Natural Management of Tropical Moist Forests: Silvicultural and Management Prospects of Sustained Utilization.* New Haven: Yale University Press.

Peters, C., A. Gentry, and R. Mendelsohn. 1989. Valuation of an Amazonian rainforest. *Nature* 339:655–656.

Sader, S.A., and A.T. Joyce. 1988. Deforestation rates and trends in Costa Rica, 1940–1983. *Biotropica* 20:11–19.

Sawyer, J.O., and A.A. Lindsey. 1964. The Holdridge bioclimatic formations of the eastern and central United States. *Proc. Indiana Acad. Sci.* 73:105–112.

Schmidt, R. 1987. Tropical rain forest management. *Unasylva* 39(156):2–17.

Shane, D.R. 1980. *Hoofprints on the Forest: An Inquiry into the Beef Cattle Industry in the Tropical Forest Areas of Latin America.* Washington: U.S. State Department Office of Environmental Affairs.

Terborgh, J. 1989. *Where Have All the Birds Gone?* Princeton: Princeton University Press.

Tosi, J.A., Jr. 1982. *Sustained Yield Management of Natural Forests: Forestry Subproject.* Lima, Peru: USAID Central Selva Resources Management Project.

World Bank. 1990. *World Development Report 1990.* New York: Oxford University Press.

World Resources Institute. 1986. *An Assessment of the Resource Base that Supports the Global Economy.* Washington: World Resources Institute.

———. 1987. *An Assessment of the Resource Base that Supports the Global Economy.* Washington: World Resources Institute.

———. 1990–1991. *An Assessment of the Resource Base that Supports the Global Economy.* Washington: World Resources Institute

Trends
in
populations

RAYMOND J. O'CONNOR
Department of Wildlife
College of Forest Resources
University of Maine
Orono, Maine 04469

Trends in populations: Introduction

For conservation purposes the crucial information as to any species' status is to be found in its population dynamics. No matter how interesting the habitat use patterns of a bird, no matter how readily it forages or breeds in one rather than another habitat, the litmus test is whether its numbers are stable or increasing or unstable and declining. Despite the early work of Lack (1954, 1966), ornithologists have probably not adequately emphasized the need for long-term studies of bird populations, though two recent books (Newton 1989, Stacey and Koenig 1990) have very recently shifted the balance of work in this respect. Conservation biologists have indeed targeted the critically small populations of several threatened or endangered species for emergency attention, but for species that are currently relatively abundant, research into long-term dynamics is poor. For Neotropical migrants in North America the Breeding Bird Survey organized annually since 1966 by the U.S. Fish and Wildlife Service and Canadian Wildlife Service provides invaluable information on trends. Yet, as I have pointed out elsewhere (O'Connor in press a,b), the opportunities that these data provide for study of the long-term dynamics of birds are only now beginning to be appreciated among professional ornithologists and ecologists in the U.S. (Sauer and Droege 1990). Until we develop a significant research effort in this area, with a focus on answering the "Why" rather than the "What" questions, we will continue to be limited to what is called in Britain "fire brigade" research. Such research attacks questions that need urgent answers but with each taken in isolation, so the work never yields any deeper understanding of the broader scientific issues that underlie the problems. Given the horrific estimates of the costs in time and money needed to develop recovery plans for even just those North American species already classified as endangered, it is clear that far-sighted research into the problems raised in the present volume will be necessary if we are not to rush our limited research resources from one crisis to another.

The papers presented in the section introduced here

generally share this concern for the long term. The papers by Sauer and Droege and by Johnston and Hagan re-emphasize the strength of the data that show Neotropical migrants to be in trouble. But at the same time the papers by Witham and Hunter and by Hagan et al. both emphasize that patterns of decline are detectable in small landbirds that winter in the southeastern U.S. James et al., working in that region, present results showing some forest-dwelling species to have increased whilst some open-habitat species have decreased. They point out that such results are not consistent with the view that Neotropical migrant warblers occupying forest habitats are declining. Their conclusion actually holds only for the Southeast: their conclusion can be extended to eastern North America (origin of the strongest evidence of Neotropical migrant declines) only if there is little geographical variation in the population dynamics of these species. However, different processes may operate in different regions, a point I have noticed is generally not adequately considered by ornithologists. Hagan et al.'s findings here are especially relevant to this point, for they show that migration volume at Manomet is more poorly correlated with regional BBS trends the further the region is from Manomet. That is, the BBS trends must change over space. James et al. similarly demonstrate substantial geographic variation in the population trends of individual species, and in my own paper I also report variation between states as to population trends in each. There are sound theoretical reasons for anticipating such variation (Wilcove and Terborgh 1984) and for incorporating it into more general thinking about the processes that occur in bird populations.

One expectation developed by Wilcove and Terborgh (1984) is that we can anticipate low density populations, particularly those at the edge of a species' range, to be the first to decrease when overall numbers fall, with core populations remaining fairly high. One of my concerns about the use of the route-regression procedure (Geissler and Noon 1981) in analyses of BBS data, therefore, is that the weighting factors used weight changes in areas of high density and give low weight to changes in areas of low densities. In this respect the emphasis by James et al. on the significance of the choice of test statistic in evaluating population trends is especially welcome. Their paper also offers an alternative method of treating the BBS data that deserves consideration as a practical alternative to present statistical models (For technical reviews of these models, and a current review of thinking in this area see Sauer and Droege 1990). The paper by Hussell et al. also offers an alternative approach to tracking population changes among Neotropical migrants, by detailed analysis of migration counts at an inland bird observatory, though it is an approach perhaps less likely to become an opera-

tional conservation tool because of the sheer volume of confounding variables present.

Studies of Neotropical migrants on their wintering grounds dominated the reports in Keast and Morton (1980) but figure less prominently in the contributions to this volume, particularly those in the present section. Nevertheless, substantial long-term data are accumulating in wintering ground studies, enabling Faaborg and Arendt to offer intriguing information on trends in the nonbreeding populations and as to factors affecting them. In a further contribution Arendt reports information collected through collaborative work of the type long known on the North American continent but relatively new to the tropics. His initial success both in obtaining information and in obtaining a consensus as to priority topics for further collaboration augurs well for the future. One finding—that habitat generalists appear to have declined less severely than habitat specialists—is especially noteworthy. This result is perhaps not unexpected when viewed against habitat destruction in the tropics—it implies simply that generalists can stay in an area following loss of preferred habitat because they can make use of alternative habitats—but it reflects an avian phenomenon not well appreciated by ornithologists. First suggested by Fretwell and Lucas (1969), the ability to make use of multiple habitats of different intrinsic value can both buffer a species against environmental change and make it harder for conservationists to detect any underlying population decrease. The theory has extensive implications for the long term viability of populations in substitute habitats (O'Connor 1985). González-Alonso also reports on a project in its early stages, to monitor the Neotropical populations of Cuba, the largest land mass in the Caribbean, and to develop improved understanding of the dynamics of wintering migrants and their interactions with the local residents there. One of the earliest findings, of approximately equal survivorship in migrants and residents alike, is relevant to survivorship issues raised elsewhere (Ricklefs, this volume).

Finally, despite their overlap in coverage, the papers in this Section also reflect some of the problems that currently plague research on Neotropical migrant birds. First, each individual paper has its own spatial and temporal domain, making it impossible to resolve differences unequivocally as to time or space or methods used. Second, the papers in general advocate single factor explanations, with inadequate attention to the possibility that different factors may be at work in different parts of North America or of the tropics. Finally, one realizes in reading these papers just how little we do know of the environmental factors impacting the population dynamics of birds: all too often my feeling whilst reading individual papers was that "if only they had information on . . . ," we would be further on in our understanding of the problem. Despite these failings, one must also acknowledge how far we have come since the landmark symposium of Keast and Morton (1980). Then just three papers—Morse (1980), Greenberg (1980) and Fretwell (1980)—addressed the issues examined here but could only sketch out possibilities for future study. Here we present quantitative data building on those ideas whilst at the same time offering fresh ideas and new evidence to promote future research.

Literature cited

Fretwell, S. 1980. Evolution of migration in relation to factors regulating bird numbers. Pages 517–528 in *Migrant Birds in the Neotropics: Ecology, Behavior, Distribution and Conservation*, A. Keast and E.S. Morton, eds. Washington: Smithsonian Institution Press.

Fretwell, S.D., and H.L. Lucas, Jr. 1969. On territorial behavior and other factors influencing habitat distribution in birds. I. Theoretical development. *Acta Biotheor.* 19:16–36.

Geissler, P.H., and B.R. Noon. 1981. Estimates of avian population trends from the North American Breeding Bird Survey. Pages 42–51 in *Estimating Numbers of Terrestrial Birds*, C.J. Ralph and M.J. Scott, eds. Studies in Avian Biology No. 6.

Greenberg, R. 1980. Demographic aspects of long-distance migrations. Pages 493–504 in *Migrant Birds in the Neotropics: Ecology, Behavior, Distribution and Conservation*, A. Keast and E.S. Morton, eds. Washington: Smithsonian Institution Press.

Keast, A., and E.S. Morton, eds. 1980. *Migrant Birds in the Neotropics: Ecology, Behavior, Distribution, and Conservation.* Washington: Smithsonian Institution Press.

Lack, D. 1954. *The Natural Regulation of Animal Numbers.* Oxford: Oxford University Press.

———. 1966. *Population Studies of Birds.* Oxford: Clarendon Press.

Morse, D.H. 1980. Population limitation: Breeding or wintering grounds? Pages 505–516 in *Migrant Birds in the Neotropics: Ecology, Behavior, Distribution and Conservation*, A. Keast and E.S. Morton, eds. Washington: Smithsonian Institution Press.

Newton, I., ed. 1989. *Lifetime reproduction in birds.* London: Academic Press.

O'Connor, R.J. 1985. Behavioural regulation of bird populations: A review of habitat use in relation to migration and residency. Pages 105–142 in *Behavioural Ecology: Ecological Consequences of Adaptive Behavior*, R.M. Sibly and R.H. Smith, eds. Oxford: Blackwell Scientific Publications.

———. In press a. Long-term population studies in the United States. *Ibis.*

———. In press b. Population patterns and process parameters—issues in integrating monitoring and modeling. In *Population Ecology and Wildlife Toxicology of Agricultural Pesticide Use: A Modelling Initiative for Avian Species.* Washington: SETAC.

Sauer, J.R., and S. Droege, eds. 1990. *Survey Designs and Statistical Methods for the Estimation of Avian Population Trends.* U.S. Fish and Wildlife Service Biol. Rept. 90(1).

Stacey, P.B., and W.D. Koenig, eds. 1990. *Cooperative Breeding in Birds: Long-term Studies of Ecology and Behavior.* Cambridge: Cambridge University Press.

Wilcove, D.S., and Terborgh, J.W. 1984. Patterns of population decline in birds. *Am. Birds* 38:10–13.

JOHN R. SAUER
U.S. Fish and Wildlife Service
Patuxent Wildlife Research Center
Laurel, Maryland 20708

SAM DROEGE
U.S. Fish and Wildlife Service
Office of Migratory Bird Management
Laurel, Maryland 20708

Geographic patterns in population trends of Neotropical migrants in North America

Abstract. We use the route-regression method to estimate the population trends of 100 species of Neotropical migrants using data from the North American Breeding Bird Survey (BBS). We examine long-term (1966–1988) and recent (1978–1988) trends. In the long-term, more species of Neotropical migrants were increasing than were decreasing in the eastern and western parts of the continent, but recent trends indicate that more species decreased than increased in their population index in the east. Recent population declines in the eastern part of the continent were primarily associated with bird species that breed in forested habitat. No association was detected between changes in forest acreages by state and population trends of Neotropical migrants in the United States and Canada.

Sinopsis. Utilizando datos del Censo Norteamericano de Aves Anidantes (BBS), nosotros empleamos el método de regresión de ruta para estimar las tendencias poblacionales de 100 especies de aves migratorias neotropicales. Examinamos tendencias a largo plazo (1966–1988) y tendencias recientes (1978–1988). A largo plazo, hubo mas especies de migratorias neotropicales que incrementaron en las partes oriental y occidental del continente de las que disminuyeron, pero las tendencias recientes indican que fueron mas las especies que decrecieron que aquellas que aumentaron su índice poblacional en el este. Las declinaciones poblacionales recientes en el este del continente se asociaron primariamente con especies de aves que anidan en habitat forestal. No se detectó ninguna asociación entre los cambios en la extensión de los bosques por Estado y las tendencias poblacionales de migratorias neotropicales en los Estados Unidos y Canada.

Environmental changes in both the Neotropics and North America might be affecting populations of Neotropical migrant birds. However, it is difficult to document large-scale changes in populations because of the extensive breeding ranges of most Neotropical migrants and the lack of rangewide, systematic surveys. The North American Breeding Bird Survey (Robbins et al. 1986) is the only systematic survey that has gathered data throughout the breeding ranges of most Neotropical migrant birds. Robbins et al. (1989b) used BBS data to document extensive population declines in Neotropical migrant populations in the eastern United States and Canada between 1978 and 1987, and suggested that habitat changes in the Neotropics might be relatively more important than habitat changes in North America in affecting recent population declines of some forest species. However, local changes in presence, size, and distribution of forested habitats in the temperate regions have been shown to affect populations of breeding birds (e.g., Askins and Philbrick 1987, Butcher et al. 1981, Holmes and Sherry 1988). Large-scale changes in the availability of major habitat types should cause some change in the abundance and distribution of Neotropical migrant bird species, many of which exhibit strong habitat preferences (e.g., Ehrlich et al. 1988).

In this paper, we search for regional patterns in population trends of 100 species of Neotropical migrant birds, as determined from analysis of BBS data. We first present continental population trends for the Neotropical migrant species for two time periods, then we examine regional population trends among breeding populations of Neotropical migrants in the United States and Canada to determine whether patterns exist in population changes among states/provinces or physiographic strata (e.g., Droege and Sauer 1989). Finally, we discuss these changes with regard to breeding habitats and changes in forest area within the regions.

Methods

THE NORTH AMERICAN BREEDING BIRD SURVEY

The BBS was initiated in the eastern United States and Canada in 1966 by Chandler S. Robbins, and by 1968 the survey had been expanded to cover the conterminous United States and southern Canada. It is a roadside survey, in which permanent sampling routes are randomly located in physiographic strata within states/provinces (state-stratum units). Each route is 39.4 km (24.5 mi) long, and is surveyed each year in late May or June by an observer who records all birds seen or heard within 0.4 km in a three-minute period at stops located 0.8 km (0.5 mi) apart. Attempts are made to have the same observer run a route for a series of years to maintain the continuity of the data. Data exist for over 3,000 established BBS routes, about 2,000 of which are surveyed in any year. The total count of individuals of each species recorded at the 50 stops is used as an index to the abundance of the species.

STATISTICAL ANALYSIS

ANALYSIS OF POPULATION TRENDS. We use the route-regression method (Geissler and Noon 1981, Geissler 1984, Geissler and Sauer 1990) to estimate population trends for each species. In this method, a population trend is estimated for each route on which at least one individual of the species was observed during the period of interest. Regional trends for the species are then estimated as weighted averages of the route trends.

Route trends are estimated by linear regression of the counts on year. The dependent variable in the regression is the natural logarithm of the count plus 0.5 to prevent the occurrence of zero counts. We include observers as covariables in this regression, thus allowing for their different abilities to perceive and identify birds. The slope coefficient of the year variable, when back-transformed (Bradu and Mundlac 1970, Geissler 1984), is the estimate of annual population change on the route over the interval.

To calculate regional trends for a species, we first estimate trends for each physiographic stratum within all states and provinces in the region. Individual route trends are weighted by mean counts of the species on the route and by the inverse of an estimate of the variance of the slope estimate from the regression of each route (Geissler 1984). To estimate trends for states, provinces, physiographic strata, or other regions, we further weight the state-stratum trends by the state-stratum areas and the number of routes sampled within the state-stratum. In this analysis, a regional estimate of trend incorporates data from each state-stratum in which the species was present on at least one route. We then estimate variances of trend estimates by bootstrapping (Efron 1982), a bias-reduction technique in which 400 subsamples are randomly drawn with replacement from the original sample of routes, and trends are estimated for each subsample. The median value of the bootstrapped estimates is used as our estimate of population trend, and the variance calculated from the subsamples is used as our estimate of variance for the regional trend. Because it is unlikely that this procedure will provide valid variance estimates for small samples, we prefer to use Z-based confidence intervals and not assess significance for small samples (i.e., $n < 10$ routes for state/provinces or physiographic strata, $n < 25$ routes for BBS regions).

TIME PERIODS. We present population trend results for two time periods: the entire survey period (long-term trends: 1966–1988) and a late period (recent trends: 1978–1988). The long-term trends encompass 23 years (21 years for the western United States and western Canada), and represent the longest existing continental data set of trends for breeding populations of nongame birds. The late period trends correspond to the interval for which Robbins et al. (1989b) reported population declines, but the present analysis differs from Robbins et al. (1989b) in that we present (1) both continental and regional trends, (2) more species, and (3) we compare long-term and recent trends, thus providing a longer-term context for the recent results. Because the same data are used to estimate trends for each interval we do not directly compare results by species for the two intervals or adjust significance levels for multiple comparisons.

SPECIES USED IN THE ANALYSIS. We attempted to estimate population trends for all Neotropical migrant birds surveyed by the BBS. To be classified as a Neotropical migrant, a species must winter (for the most part) south of the conterminous United States. Several species were eliminated from the analysis because of taxonomic changes during the survey (e.g., Alder Flycatcher, *Empidonax alnorum*) or small sample sizes. The 100 species for which we could estimate trends (see Table 1) are a diverse group, representing eastern and western species that breed in a variety of habitats.

HABITAT CLASSIFICATION. We placed species into three breeding season habitat use categories: Forest, Scrub, and Unclassified (Table 1). We used Ehrlich et al. (1988) as our primary reference to categorize the breeding habitat of a species. Forest species are considered to be dependent upon forest for breeding, whereas scrub species are largely restricted to successional or scrub habitats. Unclassified species are those that could not be placed into either category.

REGIONS OF ANALYSIS. We examined population trends on several geographic scales. Trends by states, provinces, and physiographic strata were estimated for all species that occurred on at least 10 routes in the state/province or stratum. The physiographic strata used in the analysis are slightly modified versions of those presented in Robbins et al. (1986). A map and list of physiographic strata are given in Droege and Sauer (1989). We also estimated trends for each species of interest at the continental (or surveywide) level and for Eastern, Central, and Western BBS regions (Robbins et al. 1986). A species must have been observed on at least 25 routes to be included in the regional analysis.

SUMMARIZING TREND RESULTS. For the continent and for each of the three BBS regions, we present trend results for each species and the proportion of increasing species within each region for both time periods. Proportions of increasing species are also presented by region for each breeding habitat category. The proportions are used to

determine if region- or habitat-specific differences exist in population trends.

Because of space limitations, we do not present individual state, province, or stratum trends for each Neotropical migrant species. Instead, we present the proportion of species with increasing populations (as shown by a positive estimate of median trend) for each stratum and time period. We present these results on maps, to allow for the examination of patterns of decline. State data are used only to correlate population trends with changes in forest area.

CORRELATING TREND WITH CHANGES IN FOREST AREA. Much research has emphasized the consequences of forest loss or fragmentation in temperate areas for forest-dwelling Neotropical migrants (e.g. Robbins et al. 1989a). Little documentation is available, however, of the effects of regional changes in forest area on regional bird populations. Comparable data on acreages of woodland and forest, excluding preserves, were available by state in *Agricultural Statistics* (USDA 1978, 1980, 1984) for three years (1974, 1978, and 1982) during the interval of the BBS. Using these data, we estimated percent changes in forest areas by state (comparable data for provinces were not available) using linear regression of log-transformed forest acreages on year. The percent changes in forest areas were then correlated with estimates of bird population trends by state for each species. The sample size for each correlation corresponded to the number of states in which the species occurred on at least 10 routes. We also correlated the percent changes in forest area with the proportions of increasing species by state to determine whether regional changes in forest acreages were associated with declines among species.

Results

POPULATION TRENDS

RANGEWIDE TRENDS: 1966–1988. One hundred species of Neotropical migrants had sufficient samples ($n \geq 25$ routes over the species range) for estimation of rangewide trends. Examination of the statistical significance of individual species trends indicated that 23 species had point estimates of trend that were significantly increasing ($P < 0.05$), whereas 18 species had trend estimates that were significantly decreasing in trend (Table 1). The overall proportion of species with positive point estimates of trend was 0.56, which is not statistically different from 0.5 ($P > 0.2$, see Table 5).

RANGEWIDE TRENDS: 1978–1988. During the late period, only 11 species had significant population increases, whereas 23 species had significant declines (Table 1).

TABLE 1. Population trends (in % change/year) of Neotropical migrant species for 1966–1988 (long-term) and 1978–1988 (short-term), sample sizes (number of routes [n]), and statistical significances of the test that the trend is significantly different from 0.0 (*: $P < 0.1$; **: $P < 0.05$; ***: $P < 0.01$)

Species	Long-term			Short-term		
	% change	P	n	% change	P	n
Unclassified Habitat						
Laughing Gull	8.01	***	92	4.47		79
Franklin's Gull	-6.46	*	185	-8.34	*	113
Least Tern	5.07		59	-13.86	***	33
Black Tern	-6.81	***	304	-1.79		220
Wilson's Phalarope	1.64		270	0.77		206
Upland Sandpiper	3.83	***	588	2.91	***	458
Mississippi Kite	0.95		127	0.23		108
Swainson's Hawk	0.75		498	2.91	**	382
Osprey	2.60	**	347	0.71		275
Black-billed Cuckoo	2.37		1152	-2.99	***	944
Common Nighthawk	0.44		1347	-0.86		1014
Lesser Nighthawk	6.48	**	103	9.46	***	67
Chimney Swift	-0.27		1635	0.01		1458
Vaux's Swift	-0.45		126	-1.11		102
Scissor-tailed Flycatcher	-0.47		230	3.17	***	197
Eastern Kingbird	-0.18		2013	-0.03		1794
Western Kingbird	2.00	***	793	2.47	***	646
Ash-throated Flycatcher	2.82	***	319	0.13		256
Olive-sided Flycatcher	-2.94	***	652	-2.52	**	499
Western Wood-Pewee	-0.78		534	-0.76		418
Yellow-bellied Flycatcher	5.15	***	235	3.56		171
Gray Flycatcher	0.64		70	2.25		50
Bobolink	-0.99	***	1016	-3.96	***	874
Scott's Oriole	4.59	**	87	4.76	***	66
Hooded Oriole	-0.06		58	1.32		40
Baltimore Oriole	0.71	**	1450	-2.20	***	1258
Bullock's Oriole	-1.62	*	516	-1.46		420
Black-headed Grosbeak	-0.30		422	1.57	***	345
Dickcissel	-1.40	**	721	1.15		612
Purple Martin	1.74	***	1449	-0.48		1198
Cliff Swallow	2.68	***	1444	2.02	*	1176
Barn Swallow	1.58	***	2384	-0.87	**	2108
Violet-green Swallow	-1.05		415	-0.41		327
Bank Swallow	0.98		1129	-0.86		830
N. Rough-winged Swallow	1.28	*	1842	-2.24		1487
Warbling Vireo	1.57	***	1547	0.88		1298
Cape May Warbler	2.39		205	-5.09	*	154
Northern Waterthrush	2.73	**	534	2.31		398
Blue-gray Gnatcatcher	0.45		1067	0.98		912
Gray-cheeked Thrush	5.63		39	-4.34		29
Forest Habitat						
Am. Swallow-tailed Kite	1.79		32	-4.86		26
Broad-winged Hawk	0.83	*	821	-0.57		618
Yellow-billed Cuckoo	-0.71	***	1499	-6.25	***	1293
Chuck-will's-widow	-0.30		458	-0.36		400
Whip-poor-will	-0.50		542	-1.62	*	382
Great Crested Flycatcher	-0.03		1633	-0.58		1466
Eastern Wood-Pewee	-1.29	***	1570	-1.12	***	1386
Western Flycatcher	205	*	289			0.55
Acadian Flycatcher	-0.14		748			-0.61
Least Flycatcher	-0.19		1006			-0.10

TABLE 1—Continued next page

TABLE 1—*Continued*

Species	Long-term			Short-term		
	% change	P	n	% change	P	n
Rose-breasted Grosbeak	0.99	**	1028	-3.16	***	892
Western Tanager	-0.54		405	0.66		314
Scarlet Tanager	1.25	***	1122	-0.98	**	964
Summer Tanager	0.16		677	-0.59		596
Red-eyed Vireo	1.37	***	1819	0.38		1559
Philadelphia Vireo	1.49		153	2.10		116
Yellow-throated Vireo	0.37		1063	0.08		874
Solitary Vireo	2.25	***	796	2.29	***	624
Black-and-white Warbler	0.62		998	0.44		801
Prothonotary Warbler	0.95		398	-0.01		325
Swainson's Warbler	2.39	***	91	0.85		72
Worm-eating Warbler	-0.57		321	-2.23	*	246
Northern Parula	0.20		840	-1.91	***	688
Black-thr. Blue Warbler	0.14		380	1.78		284
Magnolia Warbler	2.29	**	464	-0.40		368
Cerulean Warbler	-4.08	***	254	-0.39		167
Bay-breasted Warbler	0.86		193	-12.13	***	142
Blackpoll Warbler	4.23		164	-5.66	*	77
Blackburnian Warbler	1.11		453	-1.02		355
Yellow-throated Warbler	0.46		415	0.54		322
Black-thr. Green Warbler	-0.62		555	-3.23	***	443
Ovenbird	0.58	**	1128	-1.07	***	952
Louisiana Waterthrush	-0.24		535	0.40		415
Kentucky Warbler	-1.26	***	599	-1.95	**	495
Hooded Warbler	0.36		511	0.18		413
Canada Warbler	-0.17		446	-2.26	*	340
American Redstart	-0.30		1161	-1.54	*	887
Wood Thrush	-1.91	***	1361	-4.01	***	1204
Veery	-0.87	***	846	-2.29	***	710
Swainson's Thrush	1.07		619	-0.05		471
Scrub Habitat						
Ruby-thr. Hummingbird	1.63		1269	3.79	*	995
Orchard Oriole	-1.61	***	1149	-0.20		1002
Blue Grosbeak	2.17	***	892	2.69	***	775
Indigo Bunting	-0.54	***	1572	-0.69	***	1376
Lazuli Bunting	-0.71		354	1.69	*	293
Painted Bunting	-3.43	***	236	-1.68	**	195
White-eyed Vireo	-0.72	**	826	-2.99	***	717
Bell's Vireo	-2.34	**	272	-0.55		181
Blue-winged Warbler	-0.02		429	-1.36		320
Golden-winged Warbler	-2.28	***	288	-0.83		204
Nashville Warbler	4.10		596	2.63		493
Tennessee Warbler	3.78		294	-11.12	**	216
Yellow Warbler	0.58	**	1901	1.11	***	1577
Chestnut-sided Warbler	-0.78		703	-2.93	***	584
Prairie Warbler	-2.39	***	681	-0.61		565
Connecticut Warbler	3.48		92	6.03		71
Mourning Warbler	1.02		475	-0.82		388
Common Yellowthroat	-0.24		2113	-1.55	***	1865
Yellow-breasted Chat	-1.33	***	1123	1.51	***	934
Wilson's Warbler	1.65	*	457	0.39		343

The proportion of species with positive point estimates of trend for the late period was 0.41, which is less than 0.5 at a significance level of $P < 0.07$ (see Table 5).

EASTERN REGION TRENDS: 1966–1988. In the Eastern BBS Region, trends could be estimated for 79 species (Table 2). Of these, 15 species were increasing significantly and 14 were decreasing significantly. The proportion of species with positive point estimates of trend was 0.62, which is significantly greater than 0.5 (see Table 5, $P < 0.05$).

EASTERN REGION TRENDS: 1978–1988. In the late time period, a much different pattern of increases and declines emerged. Only six species had statistically significant increases, while 21 species showed significant declines. The proportion of species with positive point estimates of trend was 0.32, which is significantly less than 0.5 (see Table 5, $P < 0.001$).

CENTRAL REGION TRENDS: 1966–1988. In the central BBS region trends were estimated for 63 species of Neotropical migrants; nine species showed significant increases and 13 species showed significant declines (Table 3). Overall the proportion of species with increasing point estimates of trends was 0.49, which is close to that expected by chance (see Table 5).

CENTRAL REGION TRENDS: 1978–1988. Trends were estimated for 61 species during the late period (Table 3), and of these, four species showed significant population increases and 11 showed population declines. The proportion of species showing positive point estimates of trend in this interval was 0.41, and was not significantly different from 0.5 (see Table 5).

WESTERN REGION TRENDS: 1966–1988. Twelve of the 48 species showed significantly increasing trends and two showed significant declines in the Western BBS Region (Table 4). Overall, 0.65 had positive point estimates of trend ($P < 0.05$, Table 5).

WESTERN REGION TRENDS: 1978–1988. Fourteen of the 47 species (Table 4) showed significantly increasing trends, and only two species showed significant declines. The proportion of increasing species was 0.68 ($P < 0.05$), which is similar to that of the longer time interval (Table 5).

REGIONAL VARIATION IN POPULATION TRENDS

We calculated the proportion of species with positive point estimates of trend for each breeding habitat type (Forest, Scrub, and Unclassified) for the two time periods, and used the proportions to address several ques-

tions about geographic variation in population changes. In the following sections, we present the questions we examined as section headings.

1. DOES REGIONAL VARIATION EXIST IN THE PROPORTION OF INCREASING SPECIES?

To address this question, we used chi-square tests to determine whether the proportion of increasing species differed among the three regions. We tested the hypothesis for all habitat groups combined and within each of the three habitat groups.

PROPORTION FOR ALL SPECIES COMBINED. For the long-term trends, the proportion of species with increasing trends did not differ among the regions ($\chi^2 = 0.91$, $P > 0.5$). However, differences in proportions do exist in the later period ($\chi^2 = 5.86$, $P < 0.06$), primarily because of a higher proportion of increasing species in the West (Table 5).

PROPORTIONS WITHIN HABITAT GROUPS. Within a habitat group, no significant differences were found among regions using the long-term trends. A pattern of higher proportions of increasing species in the West occurred in each breeding habitat category in the late period (Table 5), but it was not statistically significant.

2. DO TRENDS DIFFER AMONG HABITAT GROUPS WITHIN EACH REGION?

No statistically significant differences existed among the proportion of species with positive trend estimates among habitat groups within BBS regions or thoughout the survey region for either time period (Table 5).

3. DO DIFFERENCES EXIST BETWEEN THE LONG-TERM AND LATE PERIOD TRENDS?

In most instances, proportionally fewer species increased during the late period than during the entire time period (Table 5). Exceptions to this pattern include Unclassified and Scrub habitat groups (and all species together) in the Western BBS Region, and the Scrub habitat group and all species combined in the Central BBS Region. Forest species decreased dramatically in the proportion of positive trends in the late period relative to the entire time period.

4. DO TRENDS DIFFER AMONG PHYSIOGRAPHIC STRATA?

The analyses presented above are based on trends estimated across large geographic areas. However, geographic patterns in population trends might occur at a smaller scale. We expected patterns to be particularly

TABLE 2. Population trends of Neotropical migrants from the Eastern Region of the BBS for 1966–1988 (long-term) and 1978–1988 (short-term), sample sizes (number of routes [n]), and statistical significances of the test that the trend is significantly different from 0.0 (*: P < 0.1; **: P < 0.05; ***: P < 0.01)

Species	Long-term			Short-term		
	% change	P	n	% change	P	n
Unclassified Habitat						
Upland Sandpiper	0.90		262	0.56		176
Mississippi Kite	0.26		45	-0.32		35
Osprey	3.85	***	231	1.22		188
Black-billed Cuckoo	3.46		848	-1.07		698
Common Nighthawk	-2.02	**	512	-3.19	**	354
Chimney Swift	-0.58	**	1269	-0.08		1126
Eastern Kingbird	-0.46		1312	0.18		1175
Olive-sided Flycatcher	-1.23		332	-3.24		243
Yellow-bell. Flycatcher	5.15	***	229	3.61		166
Bobolink	-0.70	*	717	-3.89	***	618
Baltimore Oriole	0.51	*	1000	-2.91	***	878
Dickcissel	-3.10	**	288	3.31	**	234
Purple Martin	0.23		986	-1.65	*	833
Cliff Swallow	2.33	**	595	2.30		472
Barn Swallow	0.73	***	1317	-0.77	***	1179
Bank Swallow	2.23	*	696	-3.40		519
N. Rough-winged Swallow	1.59	***	970	-0.11		787
Warbling Vireo	0.92	**	827	-0.17		703
Cape May Warbler	2.37		203	-5.14	*	152
Northern Waterthrush	1.86		458	1.52		338
Blue-gray Gnatcatcher	0.73		740	1.10		649
Gray-cheeked Thrush	5.63		39	-4.34		29
Forest Habitat						
Am. Swallow-tailed Kite	1.79		32	-4.86		26
Broad-winged Hawk	0.85	*	738	-0.64		558
Yellow-billed Cuckoo	-1.03	***	1069	-6.12	***	921
Chuck-will's-widow	-1.13	*	312	-1.87	*	280
Whip-poor-will	-0.70		477	-1.36		325
Great Crested Flycatcher	0.01		1256	-0.31		1132
Eastern Wood-pewee	-0.90	***	1268	-0.74	**	1124
Acadian Flycatcher	0.18		626	-0.75		525
Least Flycatcher	-1.41	***	762	-0.31		615
Rose-breasted Grosbeak	0.90	*	823	-3.86	***	710
Scarlet Tanager	1.30	***	1036	-0.86	*	900
Summer Tanager	-0.95		470	-0.99	**	425
Red-eyed Vireo	1.45	***	1325	0.66		1178
Philadelphia Vireo	1.64		134	2.06		101
Yellow-throated Vireo	0.46		927	-0.02		761
Solitary Vireo	4.44	***	491	2.19		387
Black-and-white Warbler	0.79		886	0.45		706
Prothonotary Warbler	1.75	*	305	1.06		251
Swainson's Warbler	2.08	**	72	0.14		61
Worm-eating Warbler	-0.18		283	-2.73	**	218
Northern Parula	0.72		727	-1.91	***	59
Black-thr. Blue Warbler	0.14		380	1.79		284
Magnolia Warbler	2.30	**	445	-0.42		357
Cerulian Warbler	-4.11	***	232	-0.35		161
Bay-breasted Warbler	0.86		193	-12.13	***	142
Blackpoll Warbler	4.37		143	-5.43	*	68

TABLE 2—*Continued*

Species	Long-term			Short-term		
	% change	P	n	% change	P	n
Blackburnian Warbler	1.11		448	-1.06		350
Yellow-throated Warbler	0.41		348	0.10		268
Black-thr. Green Warbler	-0.62		555	-3.23	***	443
Ovenbird	0.73	***	1017	-0.89	**	856
Louisiana Waterthrush	-0.43		467	-0.06		362
Kentucky Warbler	-0.58		490	-1.48	*	402
Hooded Warbler	1.58	**	456	0.77		372
Canada Warbler	-0.17		444	-2.26	*	340
American Redstart	-0.41		970	-1.80	*	751
Wood Thrush	-1.93	***	1209	-4.10	***	1082
Veery	-0.80	**	691	-2.51	***	584
Swainson's Thrush	2.34	*	319	0.10		247
Scrub Habitat						
Ruby-thr. Hummingbird	0.45		1059	1.27	**	839
Orchard Oriole	0.18		708	1.41	**	622
Blue Grosbeak	2.81	***	463	3.02	***	424
Indigo Bunting	-0.60	***	1207	-0.64	***	1075
Painted Bunting	-4.38	***	37	-2.32	**	34
White-eyed Vireo	0.10		649	-1.45	***	577
Bell's Vireo	-0.23		46	-1.48		30
Blue-winged Warbler	-0.11		401	-1.68		301
Golden-winged Warbler	-2.28	***	286	-0.81		202
Nashville Warbler	4.17		454	2.30		368
Tennessee Warbler	3.76		234	-11.26	**	175
Yellow Warbler	1.40	***	1126	1.17	**	965
Chestnut-sided Warbler	-0.84		684	-2.95	***	568
Prairie Warbler	-2.16	***	604	-0.33		505
Connecticut Warbler	0.96		64	4.89	***	48
Mourning Warbler	1.01		437	-0.72		353
Common Yellowthroat	-0.35	*	1370	-1.76	***	1232
Yellow-breasted Chat	-2.06	***	701	0.86	*	603
Wilson's Warbler	2.55		161	-5.80	*	122

associated with physiographic strata, which often differ in land use and other features relevant to bird habitat. We present the proportion of increasing species by physiographic stratum for each breeding habitat classification, restricting the analysis to strata with trend estimates for $n > 4$ species, and present the results in terms of ranges in the proportion of increasing species (< 0.40, ≥ 0.40 and < 0.50, ≥ 0.50 and < 0.60, ≥ 0.60). We use figures to present the results for 1966–1988 and 1978–1988 trends.

FOREST-BREEDING SPECIES. Generally, forest-breeding Neotropical migrants increased in most strata over the 1966–1988 period (Fig. 1). Strata showing declines occurred in three groups centering on the Appalachian Mountains, the southcentral United States, and the Rocky Mountains–Coastal ranges.

In the 1978–1988 period, more species declined than

increased in most physiographic strata (Fig. 1). Only a few strata showed more increasing than decreasing species, and many of the northern and eastern strata showed high proportions of declining species. Examination of change in proportions of increasing species from the long-term to the later-period analysis indicates that, with a few exceptions associated with strata that had high proportions of decreasing species in the longer period, most strata had a higher proportion of declining species in the late period than in the long-term.

SCRUB-BREEDING SPECIES. Scrub-breeding species did not show as consistent a pattern of decline as the forest-breeding species (Fig. 2). Generally, strata in the southeast interior tended to have lower proportions of increasing species in the 1966–1988 data (Fig. 2), and a similar but less consistent pattern existed in the late period (Fig. 2). Strata in the north and northeast tend-

TABLE 3. Population trends of Neotropical migrants from the Central Region of the BBS for 1966–1988 (long-term) and 1978–1988 (short-term) periods, sample sizes (number of routes [n]), and statistical significances of the test that the trend is significantly different from 0.0 (*: $P < 0.1$; **: $P < 0.05$; ***: $P < 0.01$)

Species	Long-term			Short-term		
	% change	P	n	% change	P	n
Unclassified Habitat						
Wilson's Phalarope	-1.59		114	-1.96		93
Upland Sandpiper	4.19	***	281	3.06	***	250
Mississippi Kite	0.95		82	0.23		73
Swainson's Hawk	0.50		276	1.29		213
Black-billed Cuckoo	0.29		253	-6.83	***	209
Common Nighthawk	0.94		426	-0.20		338
Lesser Nighthawk	4.24	***	29	.		.
Chimney Swift	0.56		366	0.33		332
Scissor-tailed Flycatcher	-0.43		220	3.17	***	190
Eastern Kingbird	0.65		487	-0.25		445
Western Kingbird	2.12	***	351	2.85	***	304
Ash-throated Flycatcher	1.39	*	56	-1.13		46
Western Wood-Pewee	0.58	***	58	6.76	**	37
Bobolink	-2.43	***	215	-5.03	***	188
Baltimore Oriole	0.13		376	-2.55	***	321
Bullock's Oriole	-1.83		145	-0.13		119
Black-headed Grosbeak	1.67		62	2.48		45
Dickcissel	-1.20	**	429	1.01		375
Purple Martin	3.47	***	361	0.06		305
Cliff Swallow	2.36	**	342	0.72		290
Barn Swallow	3.10	***	525	-0.41		483
Bank Swallow	0.71		232	-0.83		161
N. Rough-winged Swallow	3.32	***	432	2.33		363
Warbling Vireo	1.32	**	311	-1.42		256
Blue-gray Gnatcatcher	-0.25		199	1.09		171
Forest Habitat						
Broad-winged Hawk	0.65		75	-0.50		55
Yellow-billed Cuckoo	-0.53		410	-6.31	***	357
Chuck-will's-widow	0.74		146	1.75	*	120
Whip-poor-will	-0.01		65	-2.26		57
Great Crested Flycatcher	-0.20		360	-1.30		321
Eastern Wood-Pewee	-2.62	***	299	-2.51	***	259
Acadian Flycatcher	-2.11	*	122	-0.09		89
Least Flycatcher	-0.90		122	-3.25		99
Rose-breasted Grosbeak	1.12	*	170	-0.40		152
Scarlet Tanager	0.86		86	-2.76	**	64
Summer Tanager	0.54		192	-0.21		158
Red-eyed Vireo	0.41		319	0.28		248
Yellow-throated Vireo	-0.17		136	0.91		113
Black-and-white Warbler	-0.48		98	1.30		82
Prothonotary Warbler	-1.30		93	-4.01		74
Worm-eating Warbler	-2.20		38	0.35		28
Northern Parula	-2.51	*	113	-1.87		92
Yellow-throated Warbler	1.14		67	3.43		54
Ovenbird	-3.30	**	74	-4.43		64
Louisiana Waterthrush	0.76		68	2.67		53
Kentucky Warbler	-2.34	***	109	-2.70	*	93
Hooded Warbler	-5.43		55	-2.38		41
American Redstart	4.53		100	3.42		66

Table 3—*Continued*

Species	Long-term			Short-term		
	% change	P	n	% change	P	n
Wood Thrush	-1.82	**	152	-2.80		122
Veery	-1.90	***	35	-4.87	***	30
Scrub Habitat						
Ruby-thr. Hummingbird	3.68		195	7.69		145
Orchard Oriole	-3.82	***	432	-2.10	**	372
Blue Grosbeak	0.95		325	0.91		266
Indigo Bunting	-0.32		343	-0.88		285
Lazuli Bunting	-1.53		42	6.55		33
Painted Bunting	-3.67	***	189	-1.75	**	155
White-eyed Vireo	-2.49	***	177	-3.05	***	140
Bell's Vireo	-4.46	***	197	-1.90	*	134
Blue-winged Warbler	2.66		28	.		.
Yellow Warbler	-1.42	**	292	-0.21		223
Prairie Warbler	-4.71	***	77	-3.12		60
Common Yellowthroat	-0.33		418	-2.07	***	374
Yellow-breasted Chat	-0.16		240	1.47	*	189

ed to have increases in the proportions of declining species in the late period.

ALL SPECIES. In the long-term trends for all species combined, most strata showed a preponderance of increasing species, except for a cluster of strata showing declines in the central parts of the eastern and central United States (Fig. 3). In the 1978–1988 period, however, declines in the northeastern, northern, and west-central strata suggested an overall decline (Fig. 3).

5. ARE POPULATION CHANGES CORRELATED WITH CHANGES IN FOREST AREA?

ANALYSIS OF INDIVIDUAL SPECIES. Sufficient data existed to correlate long-term state bird population trends with state forest acreage trends for 91 species. Of these, the correlations were statistically significant ($P < 0.05$) in only five species, three of which were positively correlated (Western Wood-Peewee, *Contopus sordidulus*, Orchard Oriole, *Icterus spurius*, and Prairie Warbler, *Dendroica discolor*), and two of which were negatively correlated (Wilson's Phalarope, *Phalaropus tricolor*, and Ruby-throated Hummingbird *Archilochus colubris*). This number of significant correlations would be expected by chance.

For each breeding habitat group we calculated the proportion of species with positive correlation coefficients without regard to the statistical significance of the correlation. If this proportion is significantly ($P \leq 0.05$) greater or less than 0.5, we can conclude that an association existed between changes in forest acreage and population trends of birds in the species group. Fif-

teen of 37 forest-breeding species (40.5%) showed a positive correlation with forest area trends ($P > 0.3$), as did nine of 18 scrub-breeding species (50.0%), and 22 of 36 unclassified habitat species (61.1%, $P > 0.1$). Overall, population trends of 46 of 91 species had positive correlations with forest changes (50.5%), suggesting no association between forest area trends and bird population trends at the state level.

ANALYSIS OF PROPORTIONS. For each breeding habitat classification, we also calculated the proportion of bird species with positive point estimates of trend (again, without regard to statistical significance of the estimate) for each state, and correlated these proportions with the changes in forest acreage by state. The analysis was conducted for the three breeding habitats using long-term data and late period data. Although all six correlations were negative, none was statistically significant ($P > 0.05$) and only for the unclassified breeding habitat species was the correlation significant at the 0.1 level. Over all species, the correlations were not significant for either period ($P > 0.15$).

Discussion

TRENDS IN NEOTROPICAL MIGRANT BIRD SPECIES

Although our analysis indicates that populations of Neotropical migrant bird species generally have been increasing between 1966 and 1988, recent trends suggest that eastern and some central regional populations have been declining in the years after 1978. We have

TABLE 4. Population trends of Neotropical migrants from the Western Region of the BBS for 1966–1988 (long-term) and 1978–1988 (short-term) periods, sample sizes (number of routes [n]),) and statistical significances of the test of the null hypothesis that the trend is equal to 0.0 (*: $P < 0.1$; **: $P < 0.05$; ***: $P < 0.01$)

Species	Long-term			Short-term		
	% change	P	n	% change	P	n
Unclassified Habitat						
Wilson's Phalarope	3.07	**	152	2.62		110
Upland Sandpiper	3.04	*	45	3.04		32
Swainson's Hawk	1.32	*	220	5.83	**	167
Osprey	0.94		107	0.36		86
Black-billed Cuckoo	1.23		51	-3.07		37
Common Nighthawk	-0.32		409	-2.28	*	322
Lesser Nighthawk	8.49		74	9.20	***	47
Vaux's Swift	-0.45		126	-1.11		102
Eastern Kingbird	-5.80		214	0.44		174
Western Kingbird	1.60	*	435	1.79	*	338
Ash-throated Flycatcher	3.04	***	263	0.35		210
Olive-sided Flycatcher	-3.50	***	311	-2.33	**	252
Western Wood-Pewee	-0.91		476	-1.06	*	381
Gray Flycatcher	0.64		70	2.26		50
Bobolink	5.59		84	4.38		68
Scott's Oriole	4.55	**	82	4.45	***	61
Hooded Oriole	-0.07		48	1.44		31
Baltimore Oriole	4.36	***	74	2.88	**	59
Bullock's Oriole	-1.52	**	371	-2.11		301
Black-headed Grosbeak	-0.34		360	1.56	***	300
Purple Martin	4.86		102	10.18	**	60
Cliff Swallow	3.23	**	507	3.27	*	414
Barn Swallow	-0.13		542	-2.13	**	446
Violet-green Swallow	-1.20		402	-0.53		316
Bank Swallow	-2.66		201	3.57		150
No. Rough-winged Swallow	-0.98		440	-5.80		337
Warbling Vireo	2.02	***	409	1.90	**	339
Northern Waterthrush	6.45	***	75	4.79	**	59
Blue-gray Gnatcatcher	1.58		128	-1.22		92
Forest Habitat						
Western Flycatcher	1.95		280	0.54		211
Least Flycatcher	3.31	***	122	1.54	**	93
Rose-breasted Grosbeak	4.56	***	35	5.79	**	30
Western Tanager	-0.46		395	0.78		305
Red-eyed Vireo	1.66		175	-1.01		133
Solitary Vireo	0.49		298	2.58	***	231
Ovenbird	0.38		37	-4.75		32
American Redstart	1.21		91	1.77		70
Veery	-1.19	*	120	-0.68		96
Swainson's Thrush	-0.21		286	-0.08		213
Scrub Habitat						
Blue Grosbeak	2.89	***	104	5.92		85
Lazuli Bunting	-0.67		312	1.52		260
Bell's Vireo	0.94		29	.		.
Nashville Warbler	2.84	**	138	5.20	**	121
Tennessee Warbler	3.44		54	-4.65		37
Yellow Warbler	0.00		483	1.30	**	389
Common Yellowthroat	2.41	**	325	1.97		259
Yellow-breasted Chat	0.80		182	5.46	***	142
Wilson's Warbler	1.43		294	2.66	**	219

Table 5. Proportions of increasing species, with associated Z-values and sample sizes (n) for the three habitat categories and overall for each BBS region and the entire survey range

Category	1966–1988			1978–1988		
	n	Proportion	Z	n	Proportion	Z
Eastern						
Unclassified	21	0.714	2.17	21	0.380	-1.12
Forest	40	0.625	1.63	40	0.275	-3.19
Scrub	18	0.500	0.00	18	0.333	-1.50
All	79	0.620	2.20	79	0.316	-3.50
Central						
Unclassified	25	0.760	3.04	24	0.541	0.40
Forest	25	0.360	-1.46	25	0.320	-1.93
Scrub	13	0.231	-2.30	12	0.333	-1.22
All	63	0.492	-0.13	61	0.410	-1.43
Western						
Unclassified	29	0.586	0.94	29	0.655	1.76
Forest	10	0.700	1.38	10	0.600	0.65
Scrub	9	0.778	2.00	8	0.875	3.21
All	48	0.646	2.11	47	0.681	2.66
Surveywide						
Unclassified	40	0.625	1.63	40	0.525	0.32
Forest	40	0.575	0.96	40	0.300	-2.76
Scrub	20	0.400	-0.91	20	0.400	-0.91
All	100	0.560	1.28	100	0.410	-1.82

demonstrated geographic and habitat-specific patterns associated with these population changes. Declines were primarily in forest-breeding species in the Eastern BBS Region and scrub species in the Central BBS Region. Hutto (1988) described regional variation in population declines in migrant species, and discussed some of the complexities involved with regional analyses of BBS data. Our analysis demonstrates that large variations in population trends exist among geographic regions and species in the United States and Canada. Thus, geographic scale will likely be an important component of any analysis of population trends.

ARE POPULATION CHANGES ASSOCIATED WITH TROPICAL OR TEMPERATE PHENOMENA? Robbins et al. (1989b) reported that habitat use tended to be similar between breeding and wintering grounds for most Neotropical migrant species, and the six species that differed in seasonal habitat use formed the basis for their argument regarding the relatively greater importance of tropical deforestation in causing declines in bird populations. Although recent research is contributing to our knowledge of habitat use patterns of wintering migrants in the tropics (e.g., Hutto 1989, Lynch 1989, papers in this volume), we do not yet have sufficient information to assess definitively the relative importance of changes in breeding or wintering habitats.

Any assessment is further complicated because regional variation exists in rates and extents of habitat change in both tropical wintering areas and temperate breeding areas, creating mosaics of habitat quality that affect each species differently. Ramos and Warner (1980) demonstrated that mixing of subspecies occurs on the wintering ground. However, in some species a partitioning of the wintering grounds exists along subspecific lines (Am. Ornithol. Union 1957). Unless specific breeding populations can be associated with specific wintering localities, there will always be uncertainty about the relative importance of breeding or wintering habitat changes in affecting declines in breeding populations of Neotropical migrant birds.

CORRELATING HABITAT CHANGES WITH BIRD POPULATION CHANGES. Although it is widely accepted and well documented that forest area and configuration influence bird distribution, we found little evidence to indicate that state population trends of Neotropical migrant bird species correlate with statewide changes in forest acreage on the breeding grounds. In general, habitat changes that affect bird populations are unlikely to be documented adequately by the regional summary data provided in publications such as *Agricultural Statistics*. Vandell and Linder (1981) suggested that Ring-necked Pheasant (*Phasianus colchicus*) populations declined in re-

Proportion Increasing
1966 – 1988 Data: Forest Breeding Species

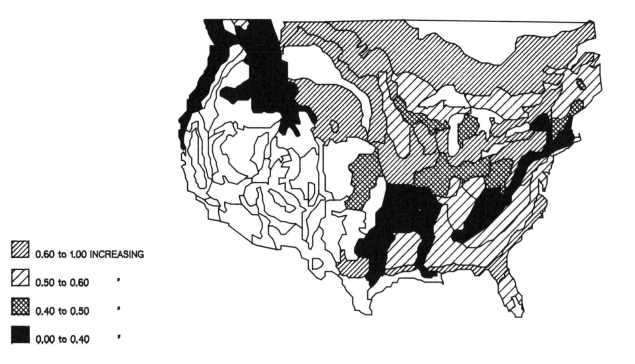

0.60 to 1.00 INCREASING

0.50 to 0.60   "

0.40 to 0.50   "

0.00 to 0.40   "

Proportion Increasing
1978 – 1988 Data: Forest Breeding Species

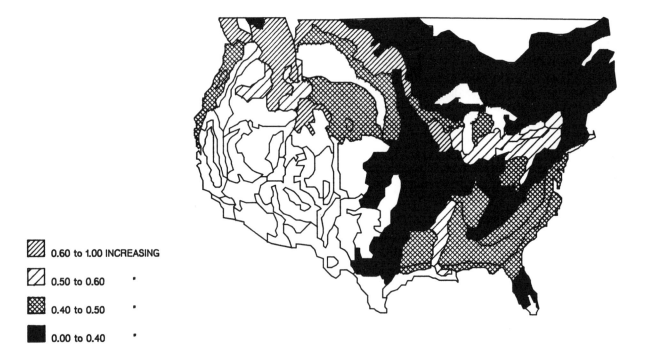

0.60 to 1.00 INCREASING

0.50 to 0.60   "

0.40 to 0.50   "

0.00 to 0.40   "

FIGURE 1. Summary of the proportion of increasing species by physiographic stratum for forest-breeding Neotropical migrant species for long-term (1966–1988) (*top*) and late (1978–1988) (*bottom*) intervals.

Proportion Increasing
1966 – 1988 Data: Scrub Breeding Species

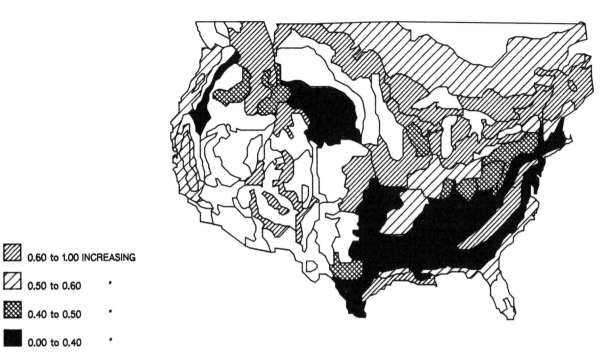

☑ 0.60 to 1.00 INCREASING

☑ 0.50 to 0.60   "

▨ 0.40 to 0.50   "

■ 0.00 to 0.40   "

Proportion Increasing
1978 – 1988 Data: Scrub Breeding Species

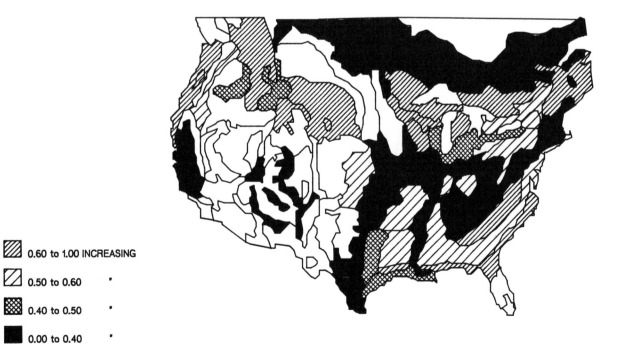

☑ 0.60 to 1.00 INCREASING

☑ 0.50 to 0.60   "

▨ 0.40 to 0.50   "

■ 0.00 to 0.40   "

FIGURE 2. Summary of the proportion of increasing species by physiographic stratum for scrub-breeding Neotropical migrant species for long-term (1966–1988) (*top*) and late (1978–1988) (*bottom*) intervals.

Proportion Increasing
1966 – 1988 Data: All Species

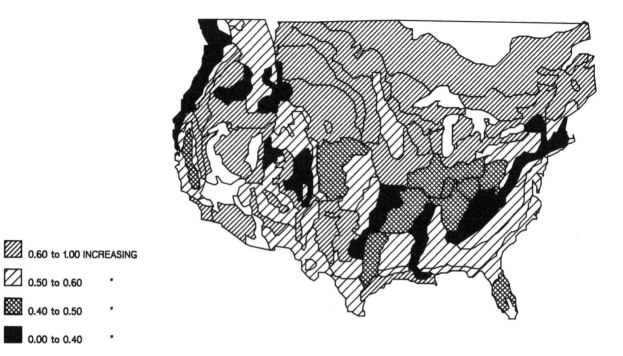

□ 0.60 to 1.00 INCREASING
□ 0.50 to 0.60 "
▨ 0.40 to 0.50 "
■ 0.00 to 0.40 "

Proportion Increasing
1978 – 1988 Data: All Species

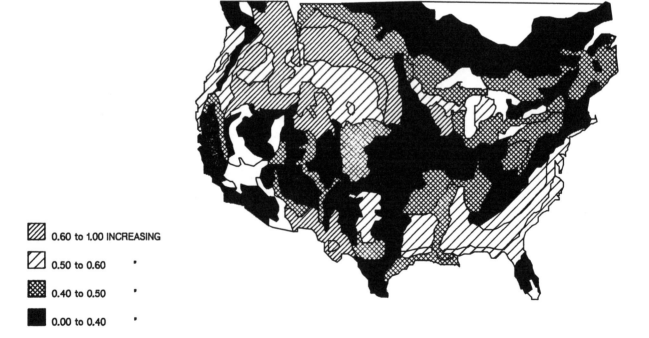

□ 0.60 to 1.00 INCREASING
□ 0.50 to 0.60 "
▨ 0.40 to 0.50 "
■ 0.00 to 0.40 "

FIGURE 3. Summary of the proportion of increasing species by physiographic stratum for all Neotropical migrant species for long-term (1966–1988) (*top*) and late (1978–1988) (*bottom*) intervals.

sponse to changes in the quality of the habitat, although analysis of aerial photography suggested little change in the proportions of cover types. The distribution of forested acreage is also an important determinant of suitability of bird habitat, and species differ in their tolerance to fragmentation of forests (Robbins et al. 1989a). Changes in forest acreage could result from changes in forest management practices, changes in agriculture, or from increased urbanization. Different causes of forest acreage changes might have different effects on bird populations.

WEATHER EFFECTS. Severe weather conditions at any point in the year could lead to widespread mortality or reproductive failure, and have been shown to modify population densities in many species. The effects of severe weather both in winter (for Field Sparrows [*Spizella pusilla*], Eastern Bluebirds [*Sialia sialis*, Sauer and Droege 1990] and other species [Robbins et al. 1986]) and in spring (for Purple Martins [*Progne subis*, Sauer et al. 1987] and Eastern Bluebirds) are clearly visible in BBS results, and provide examples of associations of survey results with an environmental factor. If inhospitable weather occurs over a wide region during the breeding season, then geographic clusters of population declines can occur as a consequence of either decreased productivity or increased mortality.

RESEARCH NEEDS

The suite of factors involved in creating the widescale patterns we observed in population trends of Neotropical migrant species are not readily apparent. The complexities associated with each species' life history and the many geographic differences in wintering and breeding ranges preclude a clear understanding of geographic patterns of change in Neotropical migrants. Perhaps we can come closer to understanding larger scale patterns by focusing our attention at the species level. Designed experiments using mark-recapture methods can be used to assess the effects of changes in habitats on the population dynamics of migrant birds in temperate and tropical regions (e.g., Holmes et al. 1989). Extending our limited knowledge of where breeding populations winter and their relative abundance in different habitats and regions will increase our ability to correlate changes in weather and habitat on the wintering grounds with changes in populations of Neotropical migrants. Given the declines of forest land that are occurring in some sections of the Neotropics, such studies must come quickly, if they are to be of use in the development of conservation strategies for migratory birds.

Acknowledgments

We thank D.K. Dawson, F.C. James, J.D. Nichols, and C.S. Robbins for careful reviews of the manuscript. We thank H. Bourne for assistance with computing and figure preparation. M.E. Keller commented on the forest area–trend correlations.

Literature cited

American Ornithologists' Union. 1957. *Check-list of North American Birds.* American Ornithologists' Union, Washington, D.C.

Askins, R.A., and M.J. Philbrick. 1987. Effect of changes in regional forest abundance on the decline and recovery of a forest bird community. *Wilson Bull.* 99:7–21.

Bradu, D., and Y. Mundlac. 1970. Estimation in lognormal linear models. *J. Am. Stat. Assoc.* 65:198–211.

Butcher, G.S., W.A. Niering, W.J. Barry, and R.H. Goodwin. 1981. Equilibrium biogeography and the size of nature preserves: An avian case study. *Oecologia* 49:29–37.

Droege, S., and J.R. Sauer. 1989. *North American Breeding Bird Survey: Annual Summary 1988.* U.S. Fish and Wildlife Service Biol. Rept. 89(13).

Efron, B. 1982. *The Jackknife, the Bootstrap and Other Resampling Plans.* Philadelphia: Soc. for Industrial Appl. Math.

Ehrlich, P.R., D.S. Dobkin, and D. Wheye. 1988. *The Birder's Handbook: A Field Guide to the Natural History of North American Birds.* New York: Simon and Schuster.

Geissler, P.H. 1984. Estimation of animal population trends and annual indices from a survey of call-counts or other indications. *Proc. Am. Stat. Assoc., Section on Surv. Res. Methods* 1984:472–477.

Geissler, P.H., and B.R. Noon. 1981. Estimates of avian population trends from the North American Breeding Bird Survey. Pages 42–51 in *Estimating Numbers of Terrestrial Birds,* C.J. Ralph and M.J. Scott, eds. Studies in Avian Biology No. 6.

Geissler, P.H., and J.R. Sauer. 1990. Topics in route-regression analyses. Pages 54–57 in *Survey Designs and Statistical Methods for the Estimation of Avian Population Trends,* J.R. Sauer and S. Droege, eds. U.S. Fish and Wildlife Service Biol. Rept. 90(1).

Holmes, R.T., and T.W. Sherry. 1988. Assessing population trends of New Hampshire forest birds: Local vs. regional patterns. *Auk* 105:756–768.

Holmes, R.T., T.W. Sherry, and L. Reitsma. 1989. Population structure, territoriality and overwinter survival of two migrant warbler species in Jamaica. *Condor* 91:545–561.

Hutto, R.L. 1988. Is tropical deforestation responsible for the reported declines in neotropical migrant populations? *Am. Birds* 42:375–379.

———. 1989. The effect of habitat alteration on migratory land birds in a west Mexican tropical deciduous forest: A conservation perspective. *Conserv. Biol.* 3:138–148.

Lynch, J.F. 1989. Distribution of overwintering Nearctic migrants in the Yucatan Peninsula, I: General patterns of occurrence. *Condor* 91:515–544.

Ramos, M.A., and D.W. Warner. 1980. Analysis of North American subspecies of migrant birds wintering in Los Tuxtlas, southern Veracruz, Mexico. Pages 174–180 in *Migrant Birds in the Neotropics: Ecology, Behavior, Distribution and Conservation*, A. Keast and E.S. Morton, eds. Washington: Smithsonian Institution Press.

Robbins, C.S., D. Bystrak, and P.H. Geissler. 1986. *The Breeding Bird Survey: Its First Fifteen Years, 1965–1979*. U.S. Fish and Wildlife Serv. Resource Pub. 157.

Robbins, C.S., D.K. Dawson, and B.A. Dowell. 1989a. *Habitat Area Requirements of Breeding Forest Birds of the Middle Atlantic States*. Wildl. Monogr. 103.

Robbins, C.S., J.R. Sauer, R.S. Greenberg, and S. Droege. 1989b. Population declines in North American birds that migrate to the neotropics. *Proc. Natl. Acad. Sci.* 86:7658–7662.

Sauer, J.R., and S. Droege. 1990. Recent population trends of the Eastern Bluebird. *Wilson Bull.* 102:239–252.

Sauer, J.R., M.K. Klimkiewicz, and S. Droege. 1987. Population trends of the Purple Martin in North America, 1966–1986. *Nature Society News* 22:1–2.

United States Department of Agriculture. 1978, 1980, 1984. *Agricultural Statistics*. Washington: U.S. Government Printing Office.

Vandell, G.M., and R.L. Linder. 1981. Pheasants decline but cover-type acreages remain unchanged on South Dakota study site. *Wildl. Soc. Bull.* 9:299–301.

FRANCES C. JAMES
DAVID A. WIEDENFELD*
Department of Biological Science
Florida State University
Tallahassee, Florida 32306

CHARLES E. MCCULLOCH
Biometrics Unit
Department of Plant Breeding and Biometry
Cornell University
Ithaca, New York 14853

Trends in breeding populations of warblers: Declines in the southern highlands and increases in the lowlands

Abstract. Breeding Bird Survey (BBS) data for the 22-year period 1966–1987 for the southeastern and south central United States show trends in populations of the eight most common species of Neotropical migrant wood-warblers. The populations of two species have declined, two are stable, and four have increased. The four species that increased, the Prothonotary Warbler, Hooded Warbler, Northern Parula, and Yellow-throated Warbler, are all forest-dwelling species. Of the three species that live in open habitats, the number of Yellow-breasted Chats has been stable, but the Common Yellowthroat and Prairie Warbler populations have declined.

These results are not consistent with the view that Neotropical migrant warblers occupying forest habitats are declining. Instead, they suggest that trends in the resource base for insectivorous birds might differ between open and forest habitats. Further study would be required to investigate this possibility and to estimate the extent to which the changes reported here might be due to increases or decreases in the rate of mortality during migration or on the wintering grounds.

When these data were examined separately for upland and lowland areas within the southeastern continental region and by 12 physiographic strata, we found substantial geographic variation in the population trends of each species. The declines in the Common Yellowthroat and the Prairie Warbler were entirely in the uplands, where numbers of the Yellow-breasted Chat and Kentucky Warbler were also declining. All five of the forest-dwelling species were increasing in the lowlands. The number of Prothonotary Warblers increased in the Mississippi Alluvial Plain and the Lower Coastal Plain in the first half of the period and declined in the second half, a pattern not seen elsewhere in the region for this species.

We call our method of analysis nonparametric nonlinear route regression (NNRR). It is an exploratory technique developed especially for BBS data. NNRR was applied to 198 routes taken in nine states. With both NNRR and linear route regression, as applied by Robbins et al. (1986), data for routes are aggregated into physiographic strata within states and then into larger areas. NNRR uses

*Current address: Museum of Natural Science, Room 119 Foster Hall, Louisiana State University, Baton Rouge, LA 70803

LOESS, a locally weighted scatterplot smoother, which can detect nonlinear trends and which allows flexibility in the degree of smoothing of the data. Although NNRR is not designed to test a specific hypothesis, confidence limits can be calculated for population estimates based on NNRR, and various tests of the statistical significance of trends may be applied. We advocate a combination of exploratory analysis to reveal structure in data and more classical statistical methods to test hypotheses. We show that choice of a test criterion and its interpretation require special attention, and we use the example of the Prothonotary Warbler to illustrate the advantages of NNRR over the use of linear regression.

Sinopsis. Datos del Censo Norteamericano de Aves Anidantes (BBS) correspondientes al período de 22 años comprendido entre 1966 y 1987 para el sureste y la parte centro-sur de los Estados Unidos muestran tendencias en poblaciones de las ocho especies mas comunes de Parulinae migratorias neotropicales. Las poblaciones de dos especies han declinado, dos han permanecido estables y cuatro han incrementado. Las cuatro especies que incrementaron, *Protonotaria citrea, Wilsonia citrina, Parula americana* y *Dendroica dominica,* son todas especies habitantes de bosque. De las tres especies que viven en habitats abiertos, los números de *Icteria virens* han sido estables y los de *Geothlypis trichas* y *Dendroica discolor* han declinado.

Estos resultados no son consistentes con el punto de vista de que las Parulinae migratorias neotropicales que ocupan habitats forestales están declinando. Por el contrario, sugieren que las tendencias en la base de recursos para aves insectívoras podría diferir entre habitats abiertos y forestales. Se requerirían estudios adicionales para investigar esta posibilidad y estimar hasta donde los cambios aquí reportados podrían deberse a incrementos o decrecimientos en la tasa de mortalidad durante la migración o en las áreas de invernada.

Cuando examinamos estos datos separadamente para áreas de zonas altas y de zonas bajas dentro de las regiones sureste y centro-sur y para 12 estratos fisiográficos, encontramos variación geográfica en las tendencias poblacionales de cada especie. Las declinaciones de *Geothlypis trichas* y de *Dendroica discolor* ocurrieron enteramente en las zonas altas, en donde los números de *Icteria virens* y *Oporornis formosus* también declinaron. Todas las cinco especies habitantes de bosque incrementaron en las zonas bajas. El número de *Protonotaria citrea* incrementó en la planicie aluvial del Mississippi y en la planicie costera inferior en la primera mitad del período considerado y declinó en la segunda mitad, un patrón no visto en ningún otro sitio de la región para esta especie.

Nosotros llamamos nuestro método de análisis regresión de ruta no lineal y no paramétrica (NNRR). Es una técnica exploratoria desarrollada especialmente para datos del BBS. Se aplicó NNRR a 198 rutas tomadas en nueve estados. Tanto con este método como con el de regresión lineal de ruta, como ha sido aplicado por Robbins et al. (1986), se agregan los datos para las rutas en estratos fisiográficos para cada estado y posteriormente para áreas mayores. La

NNRR utiliza LOESS, un suavizador de gráficos de puntos localmente pesado, el cual puede detectar tendencias no lineares y permite flexibilidad en el grado de normalización de los datos. Aunque la NNRR no está diseñada para examinar una hipótesis específica, pueden calcularse intervalos de confianza para estimativos de población basados en NNRR y aplicarse varias pruebas para la significancia estadística de las tendencias. Nosotros recomendamos una combinación de análisis exploratorios para revelar estructura en los datos y métodos estadísticos mas clásicos para examinar hipótesis. Demostramos que la escogencia de los criterios de examen y su interpretación requieren atención especial y usamos el ejemplo de *Protonotaria citrea* para ilustrar las ventajas de NNRR sobre el uso de la regresión lineal.

Conservationists want to know whether there are long-term declines in populations of migrant landbirds, but it is surprisingly difficult to determine such trends (Myers 1989). The results of several long-term breeding bird censuses (BBCs), taken mostly in the central and northern United States, have documented local declines in several species of migrant forest-dwelling warblers, and local causes have sometimes been invoked to explain these declines (Whitcomb et al. 1981). Also, because we know that major land-use changes are taking place in Middle America and the West Indies, it is tempting to propose that tropical deforestation is causing heavy mortality in migrants in winter and that breeding populations are affected (Keast and Morton 1980, Johnston and Winings 1987). However, Hutto (1989) found higher densities of migrants in mid-successional habitats than in undisturbed forest in western Mexico. He also pointed out that extrapolations of trends in local plots to trends in broad geographic areas are probably not justified (Hutto 1988).

Rather surprisingly, a summary of data taken in the Breeding Bird Survey (BBS), the most comprehensive survey of populations of breeding birds in North America, for the 15-year period 1965–1979 (Robbins et al. 1986) showed stable or increasing populations of almost all species of Neotropical migrant wood-warblers (Parulinae). This finding remains in conflict with the results of BBCs as evidence of the direction of population trends in forest-dwelling migrant land birds in the eastern United States. A more recent paper by Robbins and co-workers (Robbins et al. 1989) reports that, on the basis of additional BBS data, forest-dwelling Neotropical migrants have been declining in the eastern United States and Canada since 1978. Robbins et al. (1989) did not look for evidence of geographic variation in these trends within species.

Here, we take a closer look at trends in breeding pop-

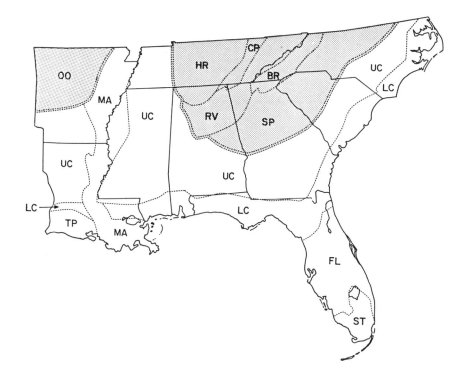

FIGURE 1. Southeastern and south central United States showing physiographic strata. Lowland strata are below the double dotted line. Codes from lower right to left in lowland strata: *ST,* Subtropical; *FL,* Floridian; *LC,* Lower Coastal Plain; *UC,* Upper Coastal Plain; *MA,* Mississippi Alluvial Plain; and *TP,* East Texas Prairies. Codes in upland strata: *SP* Southern Piedmont; *RV,* Ridge and Valley; *CP,* Cumberland Plateau; *BR,* Blue Ridge Mountains; *HR,* Highland Rim; and *OO,* Ozark Ouachita Plateau.

ulations of the eight most common species of migrant wood-warblers (Parulinae) in the southeastern and south central United States (see Table 1), considered in the order of their preferred breeding habitat, from marshes and grassy swales to mature forest. All of the species are widespread in the region, and their breeding ranges extend beyond the region. For each species we organize the results into upland and lowland areas (Fig. 1), and we describe population trends in each of 12 physiographic strata. The objective is to describe the complexities of trends in the data. We show that confidence limits can be calculated for population estimates based on nonparametric nonlinear route regression (NNRR) and that the statistical significance of trends can be calculated.

Methods

The Breeding Bird Survey, a cooperative program sponsored by the U.S. Fish and Wildlife Service (FWS) and the Canadian Wildlife Service, is designed to sample bird populations uniformly across all of North America. Volunteer observers record the birds seen and heard in one morning in June at each of 50 stops along a prescribed route along 25 miles of rural roadway. There is a route in each one-degree latitude-longitude block, but not all routes are run in all years. Because Breeding Bird Surveys are taken along roadsides, the results probably overestimate the numbers of birds that occupy open habitats in relation to the numbers in forest habitats. If roadsides incur increasing development with

time, the results of the BBSs would probably indicate an increase in open-habitat species and a decrease in forest species over and above the true trends in the general area. Also, if a forest-dwelling species increases on a BBS route, it is unlikely that it is declining in nearby continuous forest.

Analysis of BBS data, which are available on request from the FWS, requires decisions about screening for quality, how to treat missing data, how to aggregate data by routes into larger areas, and what model to fit to obtain estimates of trends (James et al. 1990). Aggregation involves decisions about whether to weight the data by area, abundance, and statistical precision. James et al. (1990) show that the number of stops out of 50 on which a species is recorded is a reliable statistic on which to base estimates of the abundance of a species. Here we have retained that statistic. Our criteria for inclusion of a route with missing data were that at least 10 years be represented in the 22-year period and that there be at least one year of data in each of four periods: the first six years, each of the next five-year periods, and the last six years. Of the 399 routes with some data judged to be reliable by the FWS (their Type 1, S. Droege, pers. comm.), we used 198 routes. In this data set of 198 routes, each with 50 stops for up to 22 years, each species was recorded more than 1,200 times (Table 2). The selection of a route did not depend on the presence of the species of interest but only on the reliability of the data, as described above, and the coverage of the period of interest. The data for the number of stops per route on which a species was recorded were averaged

TABLE 1. Estimates of abundances of eight species of wood-warblers in southeastern and south central United States based on averages of number of stops per route on which each species was recorded on Breeding Bird Surveys, 1966–1987

Code	Physiographic stratum	No. routes per stratum	Common Yellowthroat	Prairie Warbler	Yellow-breasted Chat	Kentucky Warbler	Prothonotary Warbler	Hooded Warbler	Northern Parula	Yellow-throated Warbler
	LOWLANDS (L)									
ST	Subtropical	1	0	2.8	0	0	0	0	0	0
FL	Floridian	11	6.6	0	0	0	0	0	0.9	0.1
LC	Lower Coastal Plain	33	9.1	0.5	2.4	0.1	2.2	1.9	5.2	0.9
UC	Upper Coastal Plain	63	7.4	1.3	10.4	1.9	1.2	1.5	1.5	0.3
MA	Mississippi Alluvial Plain	16	9.1	0.1	9.3	0.4	2.9	0.5	1.3	0.1
TP	East Texas Prairies	3	2.7	0	0.3	0	0.4	0	0.1	0
	UPLANDS (U)									
SP	Southern Piedmont	13	5.9	5.0	10.9	0.5	0.1	1.1	0.4	0.4
RV	Ridge and Valley	19	7.5	2.2	9.1	1.4	0.1	0.7	0	0.4
HR	Highland Rim	19	12.6	2.9	14.0	2.1	0.5	0.1	0.3	0.5
OO	Ozark Ouachita Plateau	13	4.1	1.5	9.0	2.9	0.2	0.8	1.1	0.2
CP	Cumberland Plateau	4	14.6	3.6	18.3	6.9	0	4.1	0.6	8.0
BR	Blue Ridge Mountains	3	5.3	1.2	5.7	1.8	0	6.6	2.5	4.1
	AVERAGE[a]		7.4	1.6	8.4	1.3	1.0	1.3	1.5	0.5

a. Weighted by the proportional area of each stratum.

TABLE 2. Summary of trends in Figures 4–11 in eight species of migrant warblers, ordered by habitat from open to forest, 1966-1987. The strata are identified as upland (U) or lowland (L)

Species	No. of times present	Positive (+), negative (–), or no (0) trend in:			Increases[a]	Decreases[a]	Peaks and dips
		U	L	Overall			
SPECIES IN OPEN HABITAT							
Common Yellowthroat	4299	–	0	–	LC(L)	CP(U), RV(U)	
Prairie Warbler	2158	–	0	–	LC(L)	CP(U), SP(U), RV(U)	ST(dip)
Yellow-breasted Chat	3852	–	0	0	LC(L)	CP(U), HR(U), RV(U)	
SPECIES IN FOREST							
Kentucky Warbler	1880	0	+	+	MA(L), UC(L)	RV(U), OO(U), HR(U), BR(U)	CP(peak)
Prothonotary Warbler	1954	0	+	+	LC(L)	OO(U)	MA(peak), UC(peak)
Hooded Warbler	1875	0	+	+	MA(L), LC(L), UC(L)	OO(U)	
Northern Parula	2015	0	+	+	MA(L), LC(L)		CP(peak), RV(peak), OO(dip)
Yellow-throated Warbler	1295	+	+	+	LC(L), UC(L), MA(L), HR(U)		

NOTE: For explanation of strata codes, see Figure 1 and Table 1.

a. Fourteen of 15 increases were in the lowlands; 14 of 14 decreases were in the uplands.

for stratum-within-state units. These averages were weighted by the proportion of the area covered by stratum-within-state units into either state or stratum units. We obtained estimates for the region as a whole by weighting the values by stratum by their areal proportions of the larger region.

Nonlinear nonparametric route regression (NNRR) allows flexible modeling of the routes. It is explained in detail and compared with linear route regression (Geissler and Noon 1981, Geissler 1984, Robbins et al. 1986) and with the Mountford method (Mountford 1982, 1985) by James et al. (1990). NNRR does not force the data into linear trends on a log scale over the time period considered, as does linear route regression. Major differences also exist between NNRR and the other two methods in how the data are weighted and what model is used for the estimation of trends. Unlike linear route regression, with NNRR, routes are weighted only by the sizes of the areas truly represented, without regard for the precision of the estimates. Also, with NNRR, the original unit of abundance (mean stops on which a species was recorded) is retained.

NNRR uses LOESS, a locally weighted scatterplot smoother. Cleveland and co-workers (Cleveland 1979, 1981, Chambers et al. 1983) originally called this technique LOWESS, but Cleveland and Devlin (1988) now use the name LOESS. With NNRR, data can be fit directly on a route-by-route basis, or the smoothing can be performed at higher levels of aggregation. We set the optional smoothing parameter to 0.5, at which value one half of the data are scanned to calculate each fitted value. The procedure for our analysis is given in Appendix 1.

First, we present trends in the eight species in terms of the percentage of the highest abundance of each in the 22-year period. Then, we illustrate the advantages and disadvantages of different degrees of smoothing of the data, and we compare the results of agglomerating routes by states with results of agglomerating them by physiographic strata. Because agglomeration by strata is preferable, we use NNRR to construct graphs (see Figs. 4–11) that allow comparisons of geographic variation in trends within species among strata. Although NNRR is an exploratory technique, we explain how to place confidence limits on estimated values, and we compare two tests to estimate the statistical significance of differences between estimated values for the average number of stops per route for the first five years and last five years of the 22-year period for each species.

Results

GEOGRAPHIC VARIATION IN SIZES OF POPULATIONS

Although some biases might arise from differences in the detectability of species on a BBS route, average

abundances of the eight species can be indicated by the average number of stops per route on which each was recorded (Table 1). Six of the eight species were most numerous in upland strata. Within the uplands, four species, the Common Yellowthroat (*Geothlypis trichas*), Yellow-breasted Chat (*Icteria virens*), Kentucky Warbler (*Oporornis formosus*), and Yellow-throated Warbler (*Dendroica dominica*), were most numerous in the Cumberland Plateau. The Hooded Warbler (*Wilsonia citrina*) was most numerous in the Blue Ridge Mountains, and the Prairie Warbler (*Dendroica discolor*) in the Southern Piedmont (Fig. 1, Table 1). Of the two species that were more numerous in lowland than in upland areas, the Prothonotary Warbler (*Protonotaria citrea*) is most numerous in the Mississippi Alluvial Plain and the Northern Parula (*Parula americana*) in the Lower Coastal Plain (Fig. 1, Table 1).

OVERALL TRENDS

A comparison of trends in the eight species in terms of percentage of the highest abundance that each has achieved in the 22-year period gives their rates of change independently of the differences in abundances among species. In Figure 2 the highest population estimate, which is the maximum number of the 22 averages of stops per route by year for each species, is assigned 100%, and the other averages are scaled accordingly. Of the three species in open habitats (Fig. 2a), the numbers of Common Yellowthroats and Prairie Warblers have been declining, and the numbers of Yellow-breasted Chats have been stable. Of the five species in forest habitats, the Hooded Warbler, Yellow-throated Warbler, and Northern Parula were at their highest level at the end of the 22-year period. The population of the Kentucky Warbler is apparently stable. The numbers of Prothonotary Warblers, although higher at the end of the period than at the beginning, have been declining since the late 1970s.

THE SMOOTHING OPTION

Raw BBS data for the number of stops on which a species was recorded on a particular route each year contain variation other than the best estimate of the population in the one-degree latitude-longitude block it is intended to sample. Some of this variation is attributable to differences in the abilities of observers, the weather, the time of day, and simply chance. The option of variable levels of smoothing of the data in LOESS permits some of this "noise" to be controlled to varying degrees. The level of smoothing must be chosen with care, however, because excessive smoothing can obscure nonlinear trends. The degree of smoothing should depend on the objective of the analysis. For example, if

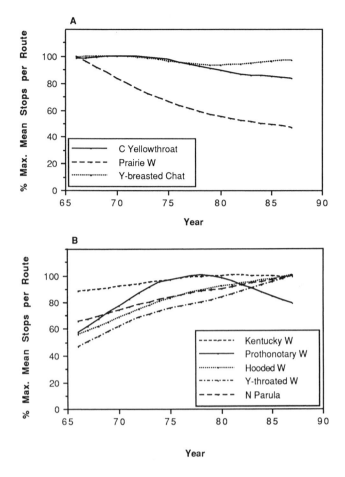

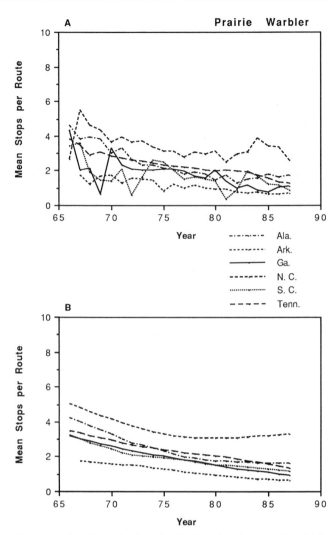

FIGURE 2. Overall trends in breeding populations for eight species of wood-warblers expressed as percentages of their abundance in the peak year. A—open-habitat species; B—forest-dwelling species.

FIGURE 3. Trends in the Prairie Warbler for six states in which there are some upland areas. Figure 3A gives data smoothed only at route level; 3B gives data smoothed at each step of aggregation: route, stratum within state, and state.

the objective were to detect the effect of a particularly hot year, less smoothing would be advisable than if the objective were to detect a general trend for a 22-year period. To demonstrate the usefulness of the smoothing option, we compare a graph of the results of data for the Prairie Warbler for the entire region smoothed only at the route level (Fig. 3a) with a graph of the same data smoothed at each of three levels of aggregation: route, stratum within state, and state (Fig. 3b). Because of the smoothing effect, Figure 3b indicates long-term trends more clearly than does Figure 3a.

GENERAL TRENDS

Differences in trends among strata as presented by species in Figures 4–11 are summarized in Table 2. We give general trends for uplands, lowlands, and the entire region. Then, we identify particular strata where trends are most apparent. The three species that occupy

open habitats, Common Yellowthroat, Prairie Warbler, and Yellow-breasted Chat, have had stable populations in the lowlands and increasing populations in the Lower Coastal Plain. However, all three have been decreasing in the uplands, particularly in the Cumberland Plateau and Ridge and Valley strata. The dramatic decline of the Prairie Warbler in the uplands has been most severe in the Cumberland Plateau (see Fig. 5a). Note, however, that the Prairie Warbler has been stable in the lowlands (see Fig. 5b).

The five forest-dwelling species, Kentucky Warbler, Prothonotary Warbler, Hooded Warbler, Northern Parula, and Yellow-throated Warbler, all have had stable or increasing populations for the region (Table 2, see Overall). As a group, they were recorded at more stops per route in the southeastern and south central states

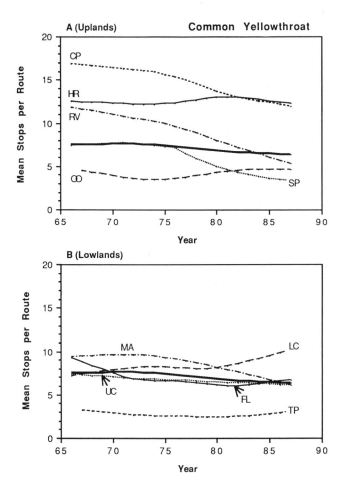

FIGURE 4. Trends in the Common Yellowthroat by upland (A) and lowland (B) strata. Strata are identified in Table 1 and illustrated in Figure 1. Heavy line in both graphs gives the trend for the entire region.

in the mid-1980s than they were in the late 1960s. Except for the Yellow-throated Warbler, which has been increasing throughout the region, the major increases in these species have occurred in the lowlands, and their populations in the uplands have been stable.

SPECIES ACCOUNTS

We present trends in each species by physiographic stratum in Figures 4–11. The upper graph for each species gives results for the upland strata and the lower graph for the lowland strata. For the Yellow-throated Warbler the differences in abundance among strata in the uplands required the addition of a third graph. The single overall trend for each species for the region (the dark line) is repeated in upland and lowland graphs in Figures 4–11. This presentation allows visual comparisons

within species of where each is most common and to what extent the trends by stratum are contributing to the overall trend. Because the overall trend is smoothed again by LOESS and weighted by the proportional size of each stratum, it is not a simple average of the values by year for the strata.

COMMON YELLOWTHROAT. The exceptionally large population of the Common Yellowthroat in the Cumberland Plateau has been declining (Fig. 4a). Similar declines in the Ridge and Valley (RV) and Southern Piedmont (SP) strata also contribute to a general decline in the uplands, although no decline is apparent in the Highland Rim or the Ozark Ouachita Plateau strata. The population in the lowlands has been stable (Fig. 4b). The declines in the uplands have been partially offset by increases in the Lower Coastal Plain (LC) since 1980. The overall trend for the species (heavy line in Fig. 4a, b) shows a decline.

PRAIRIE WARBLER. In the mid-1960s Prairie Warblers were far more numerous in the uplands of the southeastern states than they were in the lowlands (Fig. 5). The formerly high populations in the Cumberland Plateau (CP), Southern Piedmont (SP), and Ridge and Valley (RV) strata have suffered especially sharp declines. In contrast, the less numerous lowland populations have been stable or increasing (Fig. 5b). Note the increase in the isolated nonmigratory population in the Subtropical stratum (ST) in southern Florida since about 1980, after an earlier decline.

YELLOW-BREASTED CHAT. Like the Prairie Warbler, the Yellow-breasted Chat was much more numerous in the uplands than it was in the lowlands in the mid-1960s (cf. Figs. 5 and 6). Sharp declines in the uplands in the Cumberland Plateau (CP), Highland Rim (HR), and Ridge and Valley (RV) strata since that time have reduced this difference. Lowland populations of the Yellow-breasted Chat have either remained stable or shown slight increases (Fig. 6b).

KENTUCKY WARBLER. The Kentucky Warbler, which was especially numerous in the Cumberland Plateau (CU, Fig. 7a), shows a peak and then a decline. Elsewhere in the uplands it has been in a general decline. The decline has been most apparent in the Ridge and Valley stratum. Increases in the lowlands (Fig. 7b) are offset by decreases in the highlands. As a result the overall population in the region has been stable.

PROTHONOTARY WARBLER. A major peak in Prothonotary Warblers in the late 1970s in the Mississippi Alluvial Plain and the Upper Coastal Plain dominates the overall trend for the region (Fig. 8). The smaller popula-

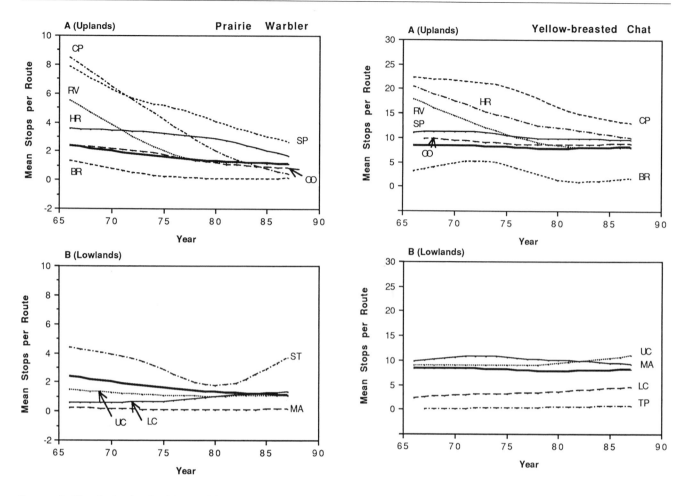

FIGURE 5. Trends in the Prairie Warbler by upland (A) and lowland (B) strata.

FIGURE 6. Trends in the Yellow-breasted Chat by upland (A) and lowland (B) strata.

tions in the uplands have been stable (Fig. 8a), except for a decline in the Ozark Ouachita Plateau (OO).

HOODED WARBLER. A dramatic increase has occurred in the abundance of the Hooded Warbler in the Cumberland Plateau (CP in Fig. 9a), and the species has been increasing in all lowland strata (Fig. 9b). The only decline has been in the Ozark Ouachita Plateau.

NORTHERN PARULA. Numbers of the Northern Parula in the uplands appeared to be stable (Fig. 10a). The species has been especially common in the Lower Coastal Plain (LC in Fig. 10b), where it has been increasing. Further increases have been apparent in two adjacent strata, the Floridian (FL) and the Mississippi Alluvial Plain (MA).

YELLOW-THROATED WARBLER. The number of Yellow-throated Warblers, although small, has been increasing in several strata in both the lowlands and the uplands

(Fig. 11a-c). The dramatic increase in the Cumberland Plateau (Fig. 11c) has been followed by decreasing numbers since about 1980. However, increases in the lowlands persisted throughout the period.

IMPORTANCE OF ANALYSIS BY STRATA

As noise is removed by smoothing and the data are aggregated into trends for larger areas, information about differences among the smaller areal units is lost. The extent of this loss is apparent in Figures 4–11, which give trends in physiographic strata within the region as well as the single line for the overall trend by species. Some of the trends for individual strata are based on more routes than others (Table 1), and the reliability of estimates by stratum increases with sample size. If overall trends are an important function of factors related to resource variation within a region, then the display of geographic variation should be greatest when it is orga-

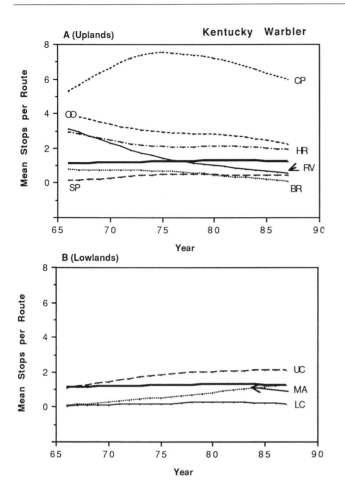

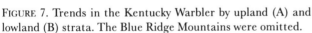

FIGURE 7. Trends in the Kentucky Warbler by upland (A) and lowland (B) strata. The Blue Ridge Mountains were omitted.

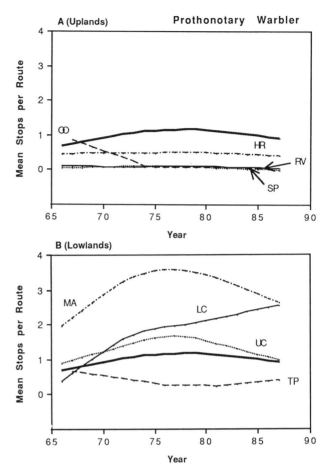

FIGURE 8. Trends in the Prothonotary Warbler by upland (A) and lowland (B) strata.

nized by areal units that are sensitive to this resource variation. For example, one would predict that, if the populations are responding to resources that vary by physiographic strata, then presentation of the results by political units such as states would partly obscure these responses, and variation in trends by state would be expected to be lower than variation by strata. A comparison between Figures 3b and 5a illustrates that for the Prairie Warbler this prediction is correct. For Figure 5 (and also for Figures 4 and 6–11), the data were smoothed at the route, stratum-within-state, and *stratum* levels. For Figure 3b, data were smoothed at the route, stratum-within-state, and *state* levels. Figure 5a presents the results for upland strata for the Prairie Warbler; Figure 3b represents results by state, each of which includes parts of strata in both the uplands and the lowlands. Apparently trends in the Prairie Warbler are sensitive to factors that are associated with the different strata, and presentation of the data by strata, as in Figure 5a, allows this regional variation to be expressed.

CONFIDENCE LIMITS AND STATISTICAL SIGNIFICANCE OF CHANGES IN BIRD POPULATIONS

A linear regression through unsmoothed data for the mean number of stops per route on which the Prothonotary Warbler was recorded, weighted by the proportional area of each stratum and averaged for the region as a whole, gives a statistically significant increase ($Y = -0.16 + 0.012X$, $R^2 = 0.42$, $P = 0.0011$). Inspection of Figure 12a, however, suggests that linear regression is not an appropriate technique for these data. Six of the first seven points fall below the regression line, the next seven are above the line, and the last four are below it. Although the regression is statistically significant, the nonrandom pattern of the residuals suggests that the linear regression might be misleading. This concern is supported by the fact that NNRR showed a linear increase in only one of eight physiographic strata (LC) and an overall trend dominated by data from two strata in which populations declined in the 1980s (Fig. 8).

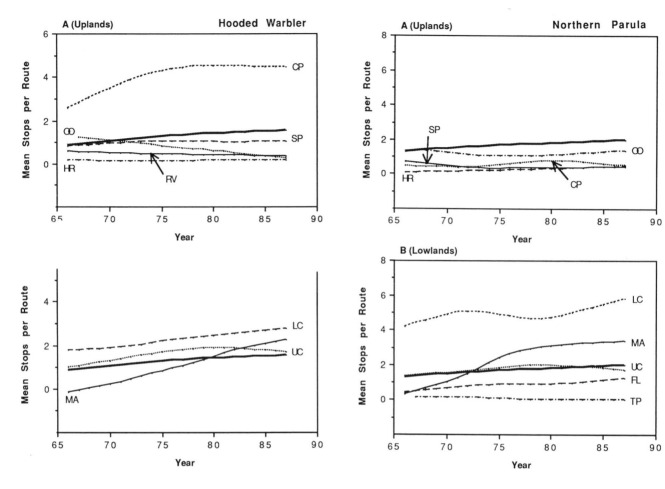

FIGURE 9. Trends in the Hooded Warbler by upland (A) and lowland (B) strata. Blue Ridge Mountains were omitted.

FIGURE 10. Trends in the Northern Parula in the upland (A) and lowland (B) strata. Blue Ridge Mountains were omitted.

A more sensitive way to judge the validity of the trends shown in Figures 4–11 would be to calculate confidence intervals around estimated values. These will become smaller as the degree of smoothing increases. However, oversmoothing can make any trend linear, so biological judgment must enter into the analysis when the degree of smoothing is chosen. Again, using the same data for the Prothonotary Warbler, we give confidence intervals for estimates by year with data smoothed at f =0.5 at the route level (Fig. 12b). The method for calculating the confidence limits (plus and minus two times the standard error of the estimates) is discussed by James et al. (1990). Calculation of confidence limits around LOESS estimates allows assessment of the validity of trends determined by NNRR and can be more sensitive to trends in the data than can linear regression. However, the method of calculation of confidence limits recommended by Cleveland and De-

vlin (1988) would not be appropriate, because it would not use route-to-route variability as the basis for standard error.

To determine whether more birds of a particular species were present at the end of the 22-year period than at the beginning, we performed two types of statistical tests. The dependent variable was the difference between the first five and the last five years in the average estimates of the number of mean stops per route on which a species was recorded. For each species, differences for each stratum were averaged and weighted by the proportional areal differences among strata. The variances (s^2/n) of the differences among strata were also weighted by the proportional differences among strata (Table 3). We give the statistical significance of t-tests for the average difference for each species (see Appendix 2). Because this test is based on the ratio of the average difference to its standard deviation, its P-value

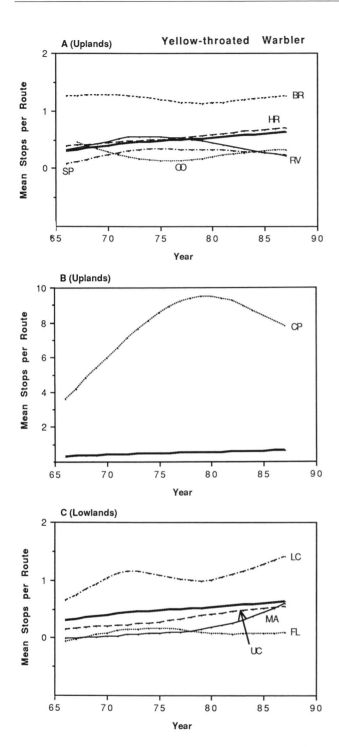

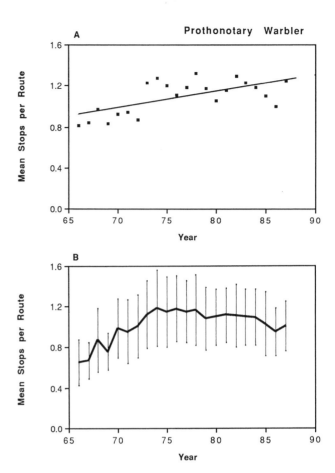

FIGURE 12. Two methods of estimating statistical significance of changes in numbers of Prothonotary Warblers. 12A shows a linear regression through unsmoothed estimates, $Y = -0.16 + 0.012X$, $R^2 = 0.42$, $P = 0.001$; 12B gives confidence limits calculated as by James et al. (1990) for estimates smoothed at route level.

FIGURE 11. Trends in the Yellow-throated Warbler by upland (A,B) and lowland (C) strata. Note different scale in Figure 11B.

is a function of the magnitude of the difference in relation to the variation in differences among routes. This focus on the consistency of the differences is probably not the question of interest. As we have seen, geographic variation in trends is substantial. If we are most interested in whether there are more birds at time 2 than at time 1, geographic variation in that parameter is an independent question.

Also, all P values are an inverse function of sample size. The same difference with the same variance would have a lower P value if the sample size were increased. The t-test is primarily answering the question, "Given a specific sample size, are the set of differences consistent?" This t-test did not identify the biologically significant 20% increase in the Yellow-throated Warbler because it addressed this previous question.

TABLE 3. Two statistical tests of trends as defined by the differences in population estimates between average values for the first and last five years

Species	Percent change[a]	Mean differences[b]	Differences test			Binomial test		
			s^{2c}	z	P	No. of routes	No. > 0	P
Common Yellowthroat	−22	−0.94	0.11	−2.90	0.004	177	65	0.000
Prairie Warbler	−64	−0.90	0.02	−5.70	0.000	133	38	0.000
Yellow-breasted Chat	−16	−0.44	0.13	−1.20	0.211	154	61	0.010
Kentucky Warbler	−2	−0.02	0.02	−0.15	0.881	116	55	0.575
Prothonotary Warbler	+23	0.21	0.01	2.33	0.020	120	70	0.067
Hooded Warbler	+57	0.52	0.03	2.91	0.004	107	55	0.764
Northern Parula	+38	0.57	0.02	3.59	0.000	119	77	0.001
Yellow-throated Warbler	+20	0.11	0.01	1.20	0.230	90	57	0.011

a. Percent change of average estimates for last five years from those of first five years.

b. Mean difference between the mean of the number of stops per route on which the species was recorded between the first and last five-year periods (1966–1987), weighted by the proportional area of each stratum in the region.

c. Variance of differences calculated as $\sum w_i^2 s_i^2$ where w is the proportional area of each stratum in the region. See James et al. (1990) for a similar example in which the variance of the estimate, rather than the difference between two estimates, is calculated.

In a second test, we asked whether there were more increases or decreases in the mean number of stops per route between the beginning and the end of the period than would be expected by chance. The results of binomial tests (Table 3) differ from those of the *t*-tests mainly in that the 57% increase in the Hooded Warbler is not deemed statistically significant by the binomial test. This result means that most of the increases in the Hooded Warbler must have occurred on a small percentage of the routes or on routes in which Hooded Warblers were also recorded in the first five years of the period. In this case, the *P* values measure whether an improbable number of routes changed from recording the species at all, to not recording it, or the reverse. In neither the *t*-test nor the binomial test do the *P* values answer the question of whether there are biologically significant changes in the sizes of the populations. Although interpretation of our graphs is somewhat subjective, we believe it is more informative than the statistical significance of the test results. We want to describe, within known confidence limits, the magnitude and the shape of trends across the period of interest and how they vary geographically. That information will help us design further studies to analyze the multiple causes that probably underlie the behavior of the populations.

Discussion

The common idea that migrant warbler populations are declining in the eastern United States, and that these declines are most extreme in forest-dwelling species, is not supported by BBS data for the eight most common species of warblers in the southeastern and south central states. In particular, declines since 1978 in Kentucky and Yellow-throated Warblers reported by Robbins et al. (1989) for the entire eastern United States are apparent for the region studied here only in the Cumberland Plateau. This area must be the southernmost extension of general declines that are occurring in the Appalachians and in the northeastern part of the continent (Sauer and Droege, this volume). Differences between the linear route regression method used by Robbins and co-workers (Robbins et al. 1986, 1989) and NNRR need to be compared by application of both methods to the same data set to assure that methodological differences are not affecting the detection of trends.

The major findings of our analyses are that there is substantial geographic variation in trends in bird populations and that this variation seems to show interesting patterns. For example, in the region considered here, populations in the lowlands are stable or increasing, whereas those in the uplands are stable or decreasing. The three species that live in open habitats are stable in the lowlands but declining in the uplands; the five species that live in forest habitats are increasing in the lowlands. Declines in some forest species in certain physiographic strata in the uplands could be partly due to forest fragmentation or its correlates, but larger declines in the same strata of open-habitat species weaken this argument. During this 22-year period, although the total area of timberland in the region has been decreasing, the average stand age and the biomass of forest have been increasing (Knight 1987).

The one species that is in a very severe decline is the species that is most characteristically found in early successional habitats, the Prairie Warbler. This decline might be influenced by resources in its wintering areas in the West Indies and in Middle America. Unfortunately no banding returns are available for warblers breeding in the southern states and recovered in the Neotropics or for birds banded in winter and recovered in the southeastern United States in a subsequent breeding season (D. Bystrak, pers. comm.). The decline might also be the result of a decreasing number of oldfields in the region. Analysis of land use patterns in relation to the differing trends in bird populations by physiographic areas is the next logical step for this species, and indeed for all eight species.

The fact that geographic variation in trends in the Prairie Warbler is more obvious when the data are organized by physiographic strata than when organized by states suggests that bird populations are in fact sensitive to resources that covary with the physiographic strata. The covariation of trends among species in the uplands and in the lowlands is further evidence of this phenomenon.

METHODS OF ANALYSIS OF BBS DATA AND THE DEFINITION OF A TREND

With NNRR, standard errors for the fitted lines can be given (Fig. 12b and James et al. 1990), allowing judgments about questions like "Is this peak real?" Confidence limits can also be calculated according to Cleveland's LOWESS procedure, but when data are averaged over routes, the confidence limits are overly narrow. We think that the confidence limits in Fig. 12b allow proper inferences about trends and their variation and that they are more informative than are the statistical tests described next.

For questions like "Is the population really decreasing?" one has to specify what is meant by a trend. With linear route regression (e.g., Robbins et al. 1986) the answer is the slope of the linear regression of the abundance statistic on a log scale against time. It is easy to calculate the statistical significance of this quantity. When the definition of a trend is similarly specified in NNRR, we can also calculate its statistical significance (Fig. 12a and text). We conducted two other tests in Table 3 for average differences between estimates of the abundance statistic for the beginning and the end of the period, another definition of a trend. For the Prothonotary Warbler, all three tests showed significant increases. Because in each case a trend was defined too narrowly, it was not able to detect the fact that the species has been declining since the late 1970s.

NNRR offers the same ability as ordinary regression techniques for testing trends or other quantities of in-

terest defined in prespecified ways. However, because of its flexibility in fitted models, it goes further in that it can suggest many other quantities of interest. As with other types of analysis, the specification of significance levels of data-suggested hypotheses is generally problematic.

Acknowledgments

We thank Sam Droege and John Sauer for supplying BBS data for this study and for their helpful discussions of the problems involved in the analysis. We thank Loretta Wolfe, Ole Martin, and David Eslinger for assistance with data analysis and Lincoln Moses for comments on the manuscript.

Literature cited

Chambers, J.M., W.S. Cleveland, W.S. Kleiner, and P.A. Tukey. 1983. *Graphical Methods for Data Analysis.* Boston: Duxbury Press.

Cleveland, W.S. 1979. Robust locally weighted regression and smoothing scatterplots. *J. Am. Stat. Assoc.* 74:829–836.

———. 1981. LOWESS: A program for smoothing scatterplots by robust locally weighted regression. *Am. Stat.* 35:54.

Cleveland, W.S., and S.J. Devlin. 1988. Locally weighted regression: An approach to regression analysis by local fitting. *J. Am. Stat. Assoc.* 83:596–610.

Geissler, P.H. 1984. Estimation of animal population trends and annual indices from a survey of call-counts or other indications. *Proc. Am. Stat. Assoc., Section on Surv. Res. Methods* 1984:472–477.

Geissler, P.H., and B.R. Noon. 1981. Estimates of avian population trends from the North American Breeding Bird Survey. Pages 42–51 in *Estimating Numbers of Terrestrial Birds,* C.J. Ralph and M.J. Scott, eds. Studies in Avian Biology No. 6.

Hutto, R.L. 1988. Is tropical deforestation responsible for the reported declines in neotropical migrant populations? *Am. Birds* 42:375–379.

———. 1989. The effect of habitat alteration on migratory land birds in a west Mexican tropical deciduous forest: A conservation perspective. *Conserv. Biol.* 3:138–148.

James, F.C., C.E. McCulloch, and L. Wolfe. 1990. Methodological issues in the estimation of trends in bird populations with an example: The Pine Warbler. Pages 84–97 in *Survey Designs and Statistical Methods for the Estimation of Avian Population Trends,* J.R. Sauer and S. Droege, eds. U.S. Fish and Wildlife Service Biol. Rept. 90(1).

Johnston, D.W., and D.I. Winings. 1987. Natural history of Plummers Island, Maryland. XXVII. The decline of forest breeding birds on Plummers Island, Maryland, and vicinity. *Proc. Biol. Soc. Wash.* 100:762–768.

Keast, A., and E.S. Morton, eds. 1980. *Migrant Birds in the Neotropics: Ecology, Behavior, Distribution, and Conservation.* Washington: Smithsonian Institution Press.

Knight, H.A. 1987. The pine decline. *J. Forestry* 85:25–28.

Mountford, M.D. 1982. Estimation of population fluctuations with application to the Common Bird Census. *Appl. Stat.* 31:135–143.

———. 1985. An index of population change with application to the Common Bird Census. Pages 121–132 in *Statistics in Ornithology*, D. Brillinger, S. Fienberg, J. Gani, J. Hartian, and K. Krickenberg, eds. Springer-Verlag, New York.

Myers, J.P. 1989. Nintendo and other birds. *Am. Birds* 43:7–9.

Robbins, C.S., D. Bystrak, and P.H. Geissler. 1986. *The Breeding Bird Survey: Its First Fifteen Years, 1965–1979.* U.S. Fish and Wildlife Serv. Resource Pub. 157.

Robbins, C.S., J.R. Sauer, R.S. Greenberg, and S. Droege. 1989. Population declines in North American birds that migrate to the neotropics. *Proc. Natl. Acad. Sci.* 86:7658–7662.

Whitcomb, R.F., C.S. Robbins, J.F. Lynch, B.L. Whitcomb, M.K. Klimkiewicz, and D. Bystrak. 1981. Effects of forest fragmentation on the avifauna of the eastern deciduous forest. Pages 125–205 in *Forest Island Dynamics in Man-dominated Landscapes*, R.L. Burgess and D.M. Sharpe, eds. New York: Springer-Verlag.

APPENDIX 1. Procedure for nonlinear nonparametric route regression

Analyses of Breeding Bird Survey data were performed on the Florida State University's mainframe CYBER computer with FORTRAN V programs. Plots were produced on an Apple Macintosh SE with Cricket Graph (Cricket Software, Malvern, PA).The data were processed in the following steps:

1. The program LOWFTN selected routes eligible for inclusion as in James et al. (1990). The criteria for inclusion were that each route have: (a) Type 1 (U.S. Fish and Wildlife Service category) data for at least 10 years of the 22-year period from 1966 through 1987; (b) Type 1 data for at least one year in each of the four periods: 1966–1971, 1972–1976, 1977–1981, 1982–1987.

2. The program STRTFIX added a code number for the stratum to which each route belonged.

3. A FORTRAN V program read in the data and called the LOESS smoothing subroutine (obtained from W.S. Cleveland). The parameter F (fraction of the data considered at each point in the smoothing procedure) was set to 0.5; the parameter DELTA to 0; and the number of steps (iterations) to 2. Data for each route were smoothed separately.

4. The smoothed route values were averaged by stratum-within-state units with AVERAG.

5. For analyses not involving further smoothing, AVERAG was used again on stratum-within-state values produced in Step 4 to average the data by successively larger areas. These were weighted by the proportion of the area of each unit. For analyses involving additional smoothing, LOESS was applied at stratum-within-state level, stratum (or state) level, and regional level. Note that lines for strata or states smoothed at each step were smoothed three times and that lines for the region smoothed at each step were smoothed four times.

APPENDIX 2. Calculation of *t*-test for differences between average in first and last five years of 22-year period.

1. Begin with values for smoothed routes.

2. Obtain averages of the mean number of stops on which a species was recorded for the first five years and the last five years of the period for each route.

3. Subtract the beginning average from the ending average. The difference will be called Δ_i.

4. Average the Δ_i by strata and calculate the variance of each as s^2/n.

5. Weight each Δ_i by the proportional area of its stratum; sum the weighted differences. (This calculation gives the average differences in Table 3.)

6. Weight the variances (s^2/n) by the square of the proportional area of their strata and sum the weighted variances. (This calculation gives the value s^2 in Table 3.)

7. Calculate $\Delta/\sqrt{s^2}$ and find its P value in a table for the z distribution.

JOHN FAABORG
Division of Biological Sciences and
School of Natural Resources
University of Missouri-Columbia
Columbia, Missouri 65211

WAYNE J. ARENDT
USDA Forest Service
Southern Forest Experiment Station
Institute of Tropical Forestry, Call Box 25000
Rio Piedras, Puerto Rico 00928-2500

Long-term declines of winter resident warblers in a Puerto Rican dry forest: Which species are in trouble?

Abstract. We studied the ecology of winter resident warblers in tropical deciduous forest in southwestern Puerto Rico from 1972 through 1990. Birds were sampled each year during January or early February with 16 mist-net lines. Winter resident numbers from a single line operated from 1973 through 1990 showed a decline. Some of this decline is a result of the near absence, in recent years, of the formerly common Prairie Warbler (*Dendroica discolor*) and Northern Parula (*Parula americana*). Expanded sampling in 1989 and 1990 showed the continued rarity of these two species, but apparent recovery of other winter resident warbler populations. Factors that may be limiting winter resident populations are discussed, with emphasis on the role of rainfall variation on both wintering and breeding grounds. In particular, the period with lowest populations corresponded to severe drought conditions over much of these species' breeding grounds.

Sinopsis. Desde 1972 hasta 1990, nosotros estudiamos la ecología de los Parulinae residentes de invierno en un bosque deciduo tropical en el suroeste de Puerto Rico. Cada año se muestrearon las aves durante el mes de enero o inicios de febrero utilizando 16 líneas de redes de niebla. Los números de residentes de invierno de una línea particular operada desde 1973 hasta 1990 mostraron una declinación. Parte de este decrecimiento es un resultado de la casi total ausencia, en años recientes, de *Dendroica discolor* y *Parula americana* ambas comunes anteriormente. Muestreos mas extensos en 1989 y 1990 mostraron la continuación en la rareza de estas dos especies, pero la aparente recuperación de otras poblaciones de Parulinae residentes de invierno. Se discuten los factores que pueden estar limitando las poblaciones de residentes de invierno, conénfasis en el papel de la variación en la precipitación tanto en las zonas de cría como en las de invernada. En particular, el período con las menores poblaciones correspondió a condiciones de sequía severa a través de gran parte de las áreas reproductivas de esas especies.

Knowledge of the occurrence and causes of population fluctuations in migrant birds is critical to their conservation. Yet, much of the recent discussion concerning the status of migratory species has relied on data of limited intensity or duration. Long-term studies of tropical birds that include population measures of winter residents are particularly rare.

We have monitored migrant and resident bird populations at a single site in Puerto Rico since 1973. Although of limited coverage, originally consisting of a single line of 16 nets, our long-term sampling effort provides insights into population changes unavailable from more intensive studies of shorter duration. For example, we have seen how variations in amounts and timing of rainfall differentially affected resident birds in different foraging guilds (Faaborg et al. 1984, Faaborg and Arendt in press).

Most importantly, this monitoring showed a distinct decline in the density of winter resident warblers over the first 15 years of study (Faaborg and Arendt 1989). Initial analyses indicated that declines occurred in both "regular" winter resident species (those captured nearly every year and with frequent recaptures between years) and the species that, although fairly common, only rarely showed site fidelity.

In this paper we analyze further these winter resident warbler population variations, benefiting from two additional annual samples of the original net line, plus 15 other samples taken nearby in 1989 and 1990. Although the declines found earlier in some species have continued, other species that declined in the mid-1980s seem to have recovered. Although no proven explanations for the declines are available, we discuss some possible hypotheses. We believe that identification of species that seem to be threatened will help focus conservation efforts more than sweeping generalizations about the decline of all migratory birds.

Study areas and methods

We conducted our studies within the Guánica Forest along the coast of southwest Puerto Rico. This 4,000-ha tract of tropical deciduous forest has been protected by the Commonwealth of Puerto Rico for 60 years and is designated a World Biosphere Reserve. The original 2,079-ha tract, protected in 1919, is considered the best example of natural vegetation remaining in the Subtropical Dry Forest life zone in the world (F. Wadsworth, pers. comm.). The remainder of the forest is in various stages of regeneration. This area receives seasonal rainfall which, when combined with the coralline substrate, results in the sclerophyllous vegetation typical of such habitats throughout the West Indies (see Terborgh and Faaborg 1973 for a more detailed description with pho-

tographs). Habitats outside the forest have been completely altered, such that the Guánica Forest is an island of mature, forested habitat isolated from the forested mountains of the interior of Puerto Rico.

Bird populations were sampled using 36-mm-mesh mist nets placed end-to-end in a straight line through typical forest vegetation. For the line first operated in 1973, a trail was cleared through the forest and the same location for nets was used each year. Other lines operated in 1989 (7 lines) and/or 1990 (8 lines) were placed along trails or narrow roadways where the habitat and topography were minimally disturbed. Net lines were operated from dawn to dark for three consecutive days, with three-day totals compared between net lines or years. All samples discussed here were taken between 4 January and 15 February. We generally captured over 90% of the three-day total of winter residents in the first two days of netting; this suggests that no migratory movement was occurring at this time.

We tested associations between avian population variation and a variety of rainfall measures. Because rainfall measures were unavailable for the forest itself, we used weather data from three stations around the Guánica Forest (see Faaborg et al. 1984 for details). An annual average of these three sites was used as an index of total annual rainfall and rainfall during the first six months of the year. The latter is effectively a measure of the amount of rain that falls to end the December-April dry season, which might be critical to nesting success of resident birds during the May-July breeding season. Because we assumed that winter bird populations reflect the effects of rainfall patterns prior to the sampling, associations were tested between each year's avian population variation and rainfall measures for the previous year, rainfall two years previous, and the sum of the two previous years. The relationship between bird numbers and rainfall in the same calendar year (and subsequent to the sampling) was tested to search for spurious relationships. We also correlated bird numbers with rainfall expressed as the departure from mean rainfall (DFM); DFM is the absolute value of the actual amount of rain minus the long-term average. Thus, 16 different combinations of rainfall measures were compared to bird populations: two rainfall categories (actual rainfall or DFM) times two rainfall totals (annual or six-month) times four time periods (calendar year, previous year, two years previous, sum of two previous years). Because sample sizes for a species or guild in a year were often small, we used Spearman rank correlations for all tests of significance.

Results

Despite a recent increase in the number of winter resident warblers captured in the original net line, a

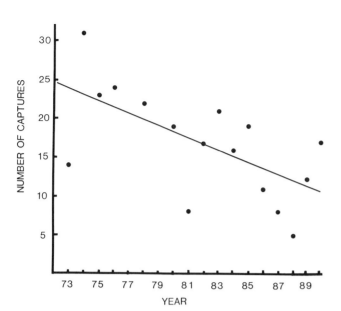

FIGURE 1. Number of winter resident warblers captured in 16 nets during 16 three-day samples between 1973 and 1990 at Guánica Forest, Puerto Rico. The least-squares regression line is drawn for reference only; a Spearman rank correlation showed $P = 0.01$.

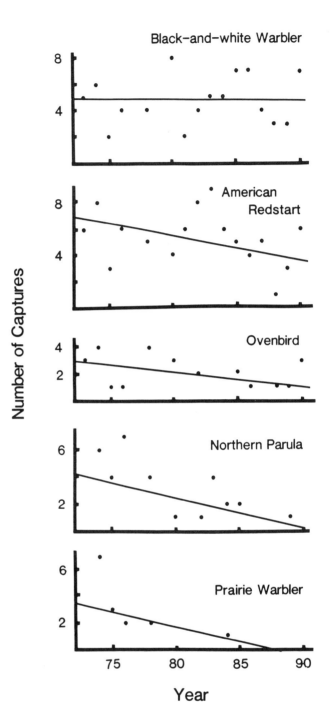

FIGURE 2. Numbers of the five most abundant winter resident warbler species captured at Guánica Forest, 1973–1990. The least-squares regression lines are drawn for reference only; Spearman rank correlations showed $P = 0.01$ for the Prairie Warbler, $P = 0.04$ for the Northern Parula, and $P > 0.05$ for the other species.

significant decline in winter resident warblers for the 18-year period of study has occurred (Fig. 1). That the original line is representative of the forest is suggested by the similarity of average captures with the other net lines (original line 1989 = 12, 1990 = 17; means of other lines, 1989 = 12.6, $n = 7$; 1990 = 16.8, $n = 8$).

Examination of the variation of individual species over 18 years provides insight into the species-specific patterns contributing to this overall decline (Table 1). Four of the five most frequently captured species declined over this period; wintering populations of two species (Northern Parula and Prairie Warbler) have nearly disappeared at this site (Fig. 2). Although the Cape May Warbler showed a pattern of decline, this species occurred irregularly within the Guánica Forest, and sometimes was captured in relatively large numbers. In contrast, the Northern Parula and Prairie Warbler were once common at the study site and their declines appear to be forestwide; only eight Northern Parula and four Prairie Warblers were captured in 17 lines operated in 1989 and 1990, compared to as many as seven captures per species in a single year on the original line.

Most of the decline of the Northern Parula and Prairie Warbler occurred in the 1970s. Excluding their numbers from total captures for the period 1973–1985 results in stable winter resident warbler numbers for this period (Fig. 3). Thus, it appears that the reduction in numbers of two species largely explains the decline in

TABLE 1. Number of winter residents captured in the original Guánica Forest net line, 1973–1990. Number in parentheses is number of birds banded in previous years and recaptured within that year's sample.

Species	1973	1974	1975	1976	1978	1980	1981	1982	1983	1984	1985	1986	1987	1988	1989	1990
Black-and-white Warbler (*Mniotilla varia*)	5	6(1)	2(2)	4	4	8(2)	2	4(2)	5(2)	5(2)	7(3)	7(1)	4(3)	3(1)	3	6(1)
American Redstart (*Setophaga ruticilla*)	6	8	3(1)	6	5(1)	4	5(1)	8(1)	9(4)	5(2)	4(2)	3(1)	4	1	3(2)	6(1)
Ovenbird (*Seiurus aurocapillus*)	3	4	1(1)	1	4	3(2)	1	2			2(1)			1	3	3(1)
Northern Parula (*Parula americana*)		6	4	7	4	1		1	4(1)	2	2(1)	1			1	
Prairie Warbler (*Dendroica discolor*)		7	3	2	2	2				2						
Cape May Warbler (*Dendroica tigrina*)			9	3					3	1	1					
Hooded Warbler (*Wilsonia citrina*)			1					2		1	1					2
Prothonotary Warbler (*Protonotaria citrea*)				1	2(1)	1(1)					1				2	
Wilson's Warbler (*Wilsonia pusilla*)					1											
Northern Waterthrush (*Seiurus noveboracensis*)										1						
TOTAL SPECIES	3	5	7	7	7	6	3	5	4	7	7	3	2	3	5	4
TOTAL INDIVIDUALS	14	31	23	24	22	19	8	17	21	17	18	11	8	5	12	17
RECAPTURES		1	4	2	2	5	1	3	7	4	7	2	3	1	2	3

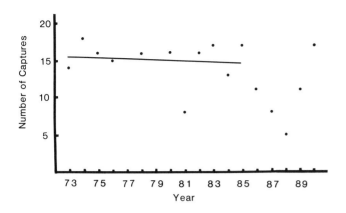

FIGURE 3. Total number of winter resident warblers captured at Guánica Forest, 1973–1990, but excluding the Northern Parula and Prairie Warbler. The least-squares regression line is drawn for reference only using data from 1973 through 1985 (see text).

overall captures for the period 1973–1985.

The sharp decline in winter resident numbers during the period 1986–1988 reflects both sharp declines in the "regular" winter residents (those captured nearly every year and that showed frequent recaptures between years) and a total absence of other species. These "other" species, such as the Hooded or Prothonotary warbler, generally occurred at a rate of one or two per line and could have been missed by chance. For the regular species (Black-and-white Warbler, American Redstart, and Ovenbird) the sharp 1986–1988 decline might reflect the cumulative effects of gradual declines in the American Redstart and Ovenbird (Fig. 2) plus below-average captures in a species that shows no long-term decline in the forest (Black-and-white Warbler). Two of these species are generally widespread through the Guánica Forest and apparently recovered in 1989 and 1990 (4.6 and 3.8 captures per line in 1989 and 6.1 and 5.8 captures in 1990 for the Black-and-white Warbler and Ovenbird, respectively). The American Redstart was captured on only five lines in both 1989 and 1990, with an average of 2.4 birds on those lines where it occurred.

Several correlations occurred between bird populations and rainfall, but few involved winter resident birds (Faaborg and Arendt in press). Spearman rank correlations between total winter resident numbers and rainfall for the first six months of the year were significant for six-month totals from the previous year ($r = -0.70705$, $P = 0.0047$), for six-month totals summed for the two previous years ($r = -0.77940$, $P = 0.0010$), and for the DFM for six-month rainfall from the previous year ($r = 0.56670$, $P = 0.0346$). A series of Spearman rank correlations between the numbers of each of the three regular species captured over 15 years and rainfall

data produced only one significant correlation. Because 36 tests were run, one might expect a significant correlation purely by chance, and little can be said about interactions between single-species populations and rainfall.

Discussion

Explaining population fluctuations in migratory birds is a difficult task. Ecological limitations might occur on the breeding grounds, during migration, and/or on the wintering grounds (Askins et al. 1990). Unfortunately, we have few clues as to where wintering birds in Puerto Rico breed. Yet, some understanding of how populations are regulated is needed to design appropriate conservation strategies. Caution also must be taken in making any generalizations about migrants as a group, because even closely related species can have different strategies of migratory behavior, foraging, and site fidelity (Rappole et al. 1983).

We have documented long-term population fluctuations in local densities of winter resident warblers at a site in which habitat and its juxtaposition relative to other habitats have not changed during the course of study. If available wintering habitat is limiting migratory birds because of tropical deforestation, as suggested by Morton and Greenberg (1989) and Robbins et al. (1989), we would not expect constant decreases within a study site. Rather, we might expect winter resident densities in an unchanging refuge either to increase, as winter residents are forced to pack at higher densities in the remaining space, or to remain the same, if territorial behavior limits winter densities. A decline within the Guánica Forest suggests that other limiting factors may be at work.

Our search for explanations for the long-term decline in winter resident numbers also must consider that the decline seems to have two components, the loss of the Northern Parula and Prairie Warbler in the 1970s, and a general decline in all other species from 1986 through 1988. It seems unlikely that the declines in the once common Northern Parula and Prairie Warbler are related to successional changes or rainfall variation within the Guánica Forest; the losses were too rapid for the former and independent of the latter (Faaborg et al. 1984). A more likely explanation is that factors elsewhere are affecting the populations of these species. Whether this reflects overall population declines, local declines where the "Guánica" birds breed, or shifts in wintering range is unknown.

The second component of the overall decline in winter resident numbers might reflect shorter-term limiting factors. Populations that were stable from 1973–1985 declined during 1986–1988 but then recovered by 1990 (Fig. 3). Arguments can be made for the effects of rainfall limitations on populations on both the breeding and wintering grounds at this time.

Rainfall variation in the Guánica Forest could affect winter resident populations both directly, by affecting food supply (insects), and indirectly, by affecting the number of resident competitors through interactions between rainfall patterns and resident nesting success. We have shown three significant correlations between winter resident numbers and rainfall patterns, all for rainfall measures from the first six months of the year, most of which falls after the winter residents have left Puerto Rico. The eight significant correlations between resident populations and rainfall also involved six-month rainfall measures, as this factor seems to affect nesting success because sufficient rain is necessary to end the December-April dry season (see Faaborg and Arendt in press). Interestingly, winter resident numbers were inversely correlated with rainfall amounts and positively correlated with DFM values, whereas insectivorous permanent residents were positively correlated with six-month rainfall amounts but negatively correlated with DFM values. In contrast, the often heavy but highly variable rains of September-November occur after most breeding by the residents and are not correlated with resident or winter resident populations.

These data suggest that residents and winter residents have opposing responses to rainfall amounts occurring during the first six months of the year in the Guánica Forest. It is doubtful that this reflects a direct response to changes in food supply associated with these rains, as they occur primarily after the winter residents have left for the breeding grounds. Rather, it suggests a response by winter residents to resident numbers, which are a function of breeding success during the period that winter residents are absent. Resident breeding success is greatly affected by April-June rainfall (Faaborg et al. 1984).

The above pattern suggests a scenario where more than a half-dozen winter resident species return to Puerto Rico in the autumn, assess the densities of the four or five resident species that could be considered strong competitors for food, then space themselves in an appropriate fashion. This seems to be an exceptionally fine-tuned social system for a large set of species, most of which are only loosely territorial and rarely vocalize (Faaborg and Arendt 1984, 1989). It also ignores the fact that winter resident populations have varied over sixfold during this period, compared to only a twofold variation among insectivorous residents or rainfall. Despite the lack of correlations with annual rainfall amounts, a more realistic model also would have to add the effects of August-October rainfall upon food supply to the factors evaluated by a prospective winter resident. This would not negate possible effects of competitive interactions with residents, but it would recognize

that food limitation for a winter resident is a function of both resident numbers (which are affected by six-month rainfall) and food supply (which might be affected both by six-month and August-October rains). Obviously, much more information is needed to understand possible interactions between residents and winter residents.

Winter resident densities also could decrease locally if some climatic factor limited nesting success on the breeding grounds. As noted earlier, we do not know the breeding grounds of the winter residents of Guánica Forest, and it is unlikely that all the different species breed in the same general location. Thus, a general population decline in a wintering site would require large-scale climatic limitation. This may have occurred in the mid-1980s. Blake et al. (this volume) show how densities of long-distance migrants in Wisconsin and Michigan declined during a period of moderate to severe drought in 1986–1988. This drought period corresponds with the sharp declines recorded at Guánica Forest, and the drought was widespread through the eastern United States and Canada. Amelioration of this drought also corresponded with the increases in winter resident numbers at Guánica in 1989 and 1990. Given that birds fledged in the previous summer compose 50% or more of many wintering bird populations (Holmes et al. 1989; Sherry and Holmes, this volume), a widespread drought on the breeding grounds could have rapid implications for wintering populations.

CONSERVATION IMPLICATIONS. This study presents distressing information on the status of the Prairie Warbler and Northern Parula in the Guánica Forest, and we encourage a close scrutiny of their populations elsewhere on the wintering grounds and on the breeding grounds. Observed declines in other species might be related to short-term limitations on either wintering or breeding grounds. At Guánica, Black-and-white Warbler populations seem to be stable, whereas those of the Ovenbird and American Redstart still show a general decline, although recent data suggest they might be recovering. Despite correlations between bird numbers and rainfall patterns on both breeding and wintering grounds, we can only speculate about where ecological limitations are occurring until we know the breeding ranges of Guánica Forest winter residents.

Acknowledgments

We thank the many students, spouses, and colleagues who have helped with netting over the years. Financial assistance for early work has come from the Chapman Fund of the American Museum of Natural History, the National Science Foundation, the Research Council of the Graduate School, University of Missouri-Columbia, the U.S. Agency for International Development, and the

USDA Forest Service, Institute of Tropical Forestry, Southern Forest Experiment Station. Expanded work is being done with the support of the National Ecology Research Center, U.S. Fish and Wildlife Service, and is a contribution from the Missouri Cooperative Fish and Wildlife Research Unit (U.S. Fish and Wildlife Service, University of Missouri-Columbia, Missouri Department of Conservation, and Wildlife Management Institute, cooperating). The Puerto Rican Department of Natural Resources has allowed us permission to continue this work within the Guánica Forest. In recent years, forest biologist Miguel Canals and his staff have been very helpful during our field work. Mark Kaiser and James Gibbs provided statistical help. Mercedes Foster, Mark Ryan, Tom Sherry, Therese Donovan, Linda S. Delay, the editors, and an anonymous reviewer provided helpful comments on the manuscript.

Literature cited

Askins, R.A., J.F. Lynch, and R. Greenberg. 1990. Population declines in migratory birds in eastern North America. *Current Ornithol.* 7:1–57.

Faaborg, J., and W.J. Arendt. 1984. Population sizes and philopatry of winter resident warblers in Puerto Rico. *J. Field Ornithol.* 55:376–378.

———. 1989. Long-term declines in winter resident warblers in a Puerto Rican dry forest. *Am. Birds* 43:1226–1230.

———. In press. Rainfall correlates of bird population fluctuations in a Puerto Rican dry forest: A 15-year study. *Ornitologia Caribena.*

Faaborg, J., W.J. Arendt, and M.S. Kaiser. 1984. Rainfall correlates of bird population fluctuations in a Puerto Rican dry forest: A nine year study. *Wilson Bull.* 96:557–595.

Holmes, R.T., T.W. Sherry, and L. Reitsma. 1989. Population structure, territoriality and overwinter survival of two migrant warbler species in Jamaica. *Condor* 91:545–561.

Morton, E.S., and R. Greenberg. 1989. The outlook for migratory songbirds: "Future shock" for birders. *Am. Birds* 43:178–183.

Rappole, J.H., E.S. Morton, T.E. Lovejoy, III, and J.L. Ruos. 1983. *Nearctic Avian Migrants in the Neotropics.* Washington: U.S. Fish and Wildlife Service.

Robbins, C.S., J.R. Sauer, R.S. Greenberg, and S. Droege. 1989. Population declines in North American birds that migrate to the neotropics. *Proc. Natl. Acad. Sci.* 86:7658–7662.

Terborgh, J., and J. Faaborg. 1973. Turnover and ecological release in the avifauna of Mona Island, Puerto Rico. *Auk* 90:759–779.

RAYMOND J. O'CONNOR
Department of Wildlife
College of Forest Resources
University of Maine
Orono, Maine 04469

Population variation in relation to migrancy status in some North American birds

Abstract. Breeding Birds Survey data for Neotropical migrants and permanent residents in the contiguous United States show major differences between the two groups in their population patterns. Over the period 1966–1988, increases in population level between successive years were, on average, larger in both groups than were needed to compensate for years of decreases. Increases were also slightly more frequent than were decreases. Migrants and residents alike should therefore have increased in average numbers through the period, in the absence of compensating dynamics. These tendencies toward net increase were not distributed randomly across species within groups but were offset by density-dependent regulation in just over half of the species tested. Resident species were relatively more tightly coupled with density in this way than were Neotropical migrant species (8 out of 9 residents tested, against 9 of 25 Neotropical migrants tested). Resident species were density-compensated to a greater extent than were migrants. This might be because Neotropical migrants are markedly less abundant than the permanently resident species.

Sinopsis. Datos del Censo Norteamericano de Aves Anidantes para aves migratorias neotropicales y residentes permanentes en los Estados Unidos muestran grandes diferencias entre los dos grupos en sus patrones poblacionales. Durante el período 1966–1988, los incrementos en niveles de población entre años sucesivos fueron en promedio mas grandes de lo necesario en ambos grupos como para compensar los años de decrecimiento. Los incrementos fueron también ligeramente mas frecuentes que los decrecimientos. Migratorias y residentes deben por lo tanto, en promedio, haber incrementado numéricamente durante este período, en la ausencia de una dinámica compensatoria. Estas tendencias hacia el incremento neto no estuvieron distribuidas aleatoriamente para las especies dentro de cada grupo, sino que fueron superadas por la regulación dependiente de la densidad en algo mas de la mitad de las especies examinadas. Las especies residentes estuvieron relativamente mas acopladas con la densidad en esta forma, con respecto a las especies migratorias neotropicales (8 de 9 residentes examinadas contra 9 de 25 migratorias neotropicales examinadas). Las especies residentes fueron compensadas por la densidad en mayor grado que las migratorias. Esto podría deberse a que las migratorias neotropicales son marcadamente menos abundantes que las especies permanentemente residentes.

Population trends of Neotropical migrant landbirds in North America have received considerable attention in recent years as evidence has mounted to show that these populations are being differentially affected by environmental changes on the breeding grounds, in the wintering quarters, or both (e.g., Hall 1984, Johnston and Winings 1987, Wilcove 1985, Wilcove et al. 1986, Robbins et al. 1989). In North America fragmentation of remaining larger expanses of eastern deciduous forests has been held responsible for declines in Neotropical migrant numbers (Robbins 1980, Whitcomb et al. 1981, Wilcove 1985), while on the wintering grounds the absolute loss of forest habitat has been thought to be the major contributor to these declines (Robbins et al. 1989). Implicit in the former explanation is the idea that Neotropical migrants suffer differentially from the effects of fragmentation. Indeed, several authors have described long-distance migration in forest interior species as being associated with a syndrome of biological characteristics that predispose them to suffer in this way (Whitcomb et al. 1981, Lynch and Whigham 1984). One might expect, on these same grounds, that the population dynamics of such species might differ from those of residents (and also of short-distance migrants). Of especial interest is the possibility that Neotropical migrants might be less competitive (and, therefore, more vulnerable to decline) than residents. Long-distance migrants in Britain, for example, have been shown to be more r-selected than resident species and thus to be differentially susceptible to environmental impacts (O'Connor 1981, 1985, in press).

The present paper examines this question through analyses of long-term data for regional populations of various Neotropical migrant and permanent resident species in the United States. Classification of species to these groups followed Droege and Sauer (1989), so short-distance migrants, although technically resident year-round within North America, were not considered to be permanent residents.

Materials and methods

The population data analyzed here were obtained from the North American Breeding Bird Survey (BBS), conducted annually since 1966 by the U.S. Fish and Wildlife Service (Robbins et al. 1986). A BBS route consists of a 24.5-mile (39.4 km) stretch of secondary roads, with 50

three-minute census stops spaced 0.5 mile (0.8 km) apart along its length. The route is run one morning each year at the peak of the breeding season, starting 30 minutes before sunrise. Most routes in the United States are run in June, except in the southern states, where the peak breeding season is in late May. At each stop the observer records the total number of each bird species heard and those seen within 0.25 mile (0.4 km) of the stop point. Each route is restricted to a single latilong degree block and to a single state. The data are subsequently reviewed by BBS staff and a quality code added to reflect adverse weather conditions and other factors that might affect the reliability or comparability of the counts. The data from the individual stops are summed to provide a single route total for each species.

In the present study, analysis was restricted to passerine species. For each species, each state was regarded as a separate geographic sampling unit and, subject to some restrictions detailed below, the BBS data for that state and species were used to calculate a population index. This index was computed as follows. For each pair of years n and $n+1$, the BBS routes within the state that were surveyed in both years were identified. Subsequent analysis was restricted to sets that could be paired in this way. By pairing data across years much route-specific variation is controlled. Next, only year-on-year pairings that involved at least eight routes within the state were considered further, the others being discarded as an inadequate sample. Counts for these matched-year pairs were then summed to yield S_n and S_{n+1} for the two years. This process was repeated for the full period 1966–1988 (i.e., n = 1966 through 1987). If at least 10 pairings of adequate size were available for the period, the data were processed further, otherwise being discarded as an inadequate sample. The number of year-pairs available, therefore, differed between states and between species. (Somewhat different criteria were applied to analyses of national population data below.)

For species and state combinations meeting the above criteria, an index of population change was computed as
$$C_n = \log(S_{n+1}) - \log(S_n)$$
where C_n is the population change between year n and year $n+1$ and where the data were logarithmically ($\log_e$) transformed to reflect the multiplicative nature of population increases or decreases. The computed values (C_n, S_n) were used to derive a series of variables to characterize each state-species population. The mean positive excursion of the population was computed as
$$I = (\Sigma C_n)/n_I, C_n > 0$$
where n_I is the frequency of positive C_n, i.e., the number of year-on-year increases in population size that were recorded over the 22-year period. Similarly, the mean negative excursion of the population was computed as
$$D = (\Sigma C_n)/n_D, C_n < 0$$
where n_D is the frequency of negative C_n, i.e., the num-

ber of year-on-year decreases in population size. The relative frequency of increases was computed as

$$F_I = n_I/(n_I + n_D)$$

where n_I and n_D are as above.

The frequency with which runs of population increases (and separately of decreases) occurred was estimated by tallying the runs of positive (negative) values of C_n. In practice, however, these estimates proved of limited value because of the frequency with which the runs were terminated by missing values of C_n.

"Counts" of each species recorded in the Breeding Bird Survey are not strictly absolute counts but rather the product eP, where e is the census efficiency of the observer in respect of the species censused and P is the true population size. However, in the analyses conducted here, the relative change in population size is independent of observer census efficiency provided the observer is the same in the two years being compared. Only data paired by the same observer across years were used here. A further source of error could arise through the observer changing in efficiency between years. Here, only data from observers rated excellent by the BBS Office were used, ensuring that such drift was, at worst, a second-order effect.

The possibility of density-dependence with each species was tested for by using Morris's (1963) test on the national population data for each species. Population changes at the national level were computed as Bailey's (1967) index, which uses only data from sites paired across years. The resulting estimates of relative change are chained together across years to provide an index of population level. Bailey's method is potentially open to random walk through accumulation of error over time, but this problem is negligible given adequate sample sizes (Moss 1985). Here data were analysed only for species present on at least 20 BBS routes in each year.

Morris's (1963) method is a biased indicator of density dependence, especially when measurement errors are large. In the case of national BBS data, such errors are likely to be fairly small, given the sample sizes involved. Perhaps more significantly, the question of interest here was whether the incidence of density-dependent regulation differed between residents and migrants (see below), that is, a comparison within which absolute bias is of reduced importance. A more complete analysis of the issues involved here is in preparation (R.J. O'Connor and R.P. Boone unpubl. data).

All logarithmically transformed data were back-transformed after averaging, and ratios were converted to the corresponding percentages. In the case of decreases, the sign of the logarithm was reversed to express the decrease as the equivalent compensating increase, that is, a decrease from 100 to 80 is a 20% decrease but needs a 25% increase during population recovery; without this transformation the amplitudes of decreases and increases in a population at equilibrium would not average zero. Before conducting further statistical analysis, the data were checked for normality. As a result of these checks, logarithmic transformations were used with all population and population change data. These results were then aggregated by species to provide a single estimate of each population measure for each species. The number of state-level estimates entering such aggregations varied markedly between species. Finally, these species-specific estimates were compared across groups differing in migratory status.

Data for 88 species were considered. These species comprised those passerines designated by Droege and Sauer (1989) as either Neotropical migrants or as permanent residents. Appendix 1 identifies these species and additionally indicates the number of states from which population data were obtained. In the case of the Tufted Titmouse (*Parus bicolor*) in Texas, only the data for the nominate race were considered; information on the Black-crested Titmouse, initially recorded as a separate species (*P. atricristatus*) within the BBS data set, were not included.

Results

Figure 1 summarizes the mean densities (strictly, indices of density, as noted above) of migrant and resident

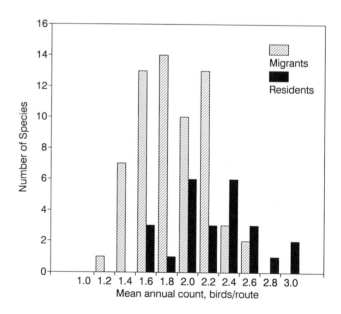

FIGURE 1. Frequency distribution of mean abundance for Neotropical migrant and permanent resident species surveyed in the Breeding Bird Survey in the contiguous United States, 1966–1988. Each species was characterized by its mean count over time within each state before being averaged by state and the species averages were then tallied in 0.2 birds/route intervals.

species, based on those routes involved in the samples described above. Most of the migrant species had low annual mean counts, while most of the resident species had high mean counts. On average, a migrant species reached only 42% of the count achieved by a typical permanent resident, thus paralleling the situation with migrants in Britain (O'Connor 1981). This difference in mean abundance also implies that the resident species are potentially open to greater density dependence than are the migrant species, unless density dependence is itself relatively more intense at a given population level among migrants (see below).

A significant difference was found in the mean amplitude of species-specific population changes between permanent residents and Neotropical migrants (34.9% vs. 30.4%) (Table 1). This implies that the permanent residents were more variable in abundance than were the migrants, a pattern the reverse of that prevailing among migrants and residents in Britain (O'Connor 1981). The major part of this difference came from the average amplitude of population increases (41.0% for permanent residents vs. 34.7% for Neotropical migrants), with a smaller but statistically nonsignificant difference in decrease amplitudes (28.3% vs. 25.1% respectively). (Recall that these decrease amplitudes have been adjusted to a common base with increases.) A possibility here is that increases among permanent residents occurred principally following decreases brought about by adverse winter conditions, as the populations recovered toward their original levels. However, the increases needed to compensate the observed decrease were much smaller in each case than is actually ob-

served in each increase. In both groups, therefore, the average increase was larger than the average decrease (corrected for having to start from the smaller population size after a decrease), so both groups should tend to increase on average unless decreases were more frequent than increases. Table 1 shows, however, that while the frequency of increases and of decreases was fairly similar across groups, increases were actually slightly more frequent in each case than were decreases. Thus increases were both larger and more frequent than decreases within both groups.

The relative frequency of increases and decreases could be confounded by the distribution of increases and decreases across species. However, the relative incidence of increases calculated on a within-species basis was substantially above 50% in both groups (Table 1). By computing the long-term change appropriate to the mean values indicated in Table 1, increase factors of 7.9 for permanent residents and 6.4 for Neotropical migrants are obtained. That is, a migrant or resident characterized by the respective group average dynamical parameters would have increased greatly in abundance over the 22 years of the BBS.

Given that the overall trends actually observed in both groups (Robbins et al. 1986) have been far less than would be expected with this propensity for increase, some additional factor must be operating to minimize the upward trend. An obvious possibility is that of density dependence in population dynamics, such that changes, particularly increases relative to decreases, should be smaller in larger populations and in species with high numbers, and conversely at low num-

TABLE 1. Comparison of population dynamics measures between Neotropical migrants and permanent residents

Variable	Permanent residents (n = 25)		Neotropical migrants (n = 63)		Probability[a]
	Mean	S.D.	Mean	S.D.	
Modulus change[b]	34.9	8.7	30.4	6.0	0.04
Increase size (%)	41.0	10.2	34.7	7.6	0.005
Decrease size (%)	28.3	10.5	25.1	6.0	n.s.
Frequency of increases	10.2	1.5	10.0	1.6	n.s.
Frequency of decreases	8.2	1.7	7.6	1.4	n.s.
Relative incidence of increases (%)[c]	56.0	6.8	57.2	5.2	n.s.
Run length: increases	1.9	0.4	1.8	0.4	n.s.
" : decreases	1.6	0.4	1.53	0.4	n.s.
Frequency of runs : increases	4.9	1.1	4.9	1.2	n.s.
" : decreases	4.8	1.2	4.7	1.2	n.s.

a. Mann-Whitney U test.

b. Amplitude of change, irrespective of sign.

c. Proportion of year-on-year changes that were positive.

TABLE 2. Frequency of intraspecific density dependencies in population change in Neotropical migrants and permanent residents

	Density-dependent species[a]	
	Number	Percent
Permanent residents ($n = 9$)	8	88.9
Neotropical migrants ($n = 25$)	9	36.0

NOTE: Density dependencies were measured across states but within species and only for those species with data available from five or more states. Fisher exact probability = 0.017

a. Species with significant linear regression of log mean population change within state on log mean population size prior to the change.

bers. According to Morris's (1963) procedure for detecting density dependence, some 38 species of the 70 with adequate national data for population levels were significantly density-dependent, that is, their changes in population from year to year were negatively correlated with the prevailing population levels. Statistical evidence of density-dependence in relation to migrancy status showed that permanent residents were slightly more prone to regulation (13 of 20 species, i.e., 65%) than were Neotropical migrants (25 of 50 species or 50%). This difference did not reach statistical significance ($\chi^2 = 0.76$, n.s.). The two groups did, however, differ markedly in the slope of the regression axis computed in the Morris test: the permanent residents averaged 0.680 ± 0.216 against 0.538 ± 0.265 for the Neotropical migrants ($t = 2.32$, d.f. = 68, $P = 0.023$). The two groups, therefore, differed, on average, in the strength of density dependence prevailing.

These ideas were tested further by computing for each species a regression of mean population excursion on mean population size prior to the excursion. Popula-

tion levels and changes were here computed from state averages and only for those species with data from at least five states. This analysis is, as with the Morris (1963) method used on the national data, slightly biased because errors in the estimation of population level for each year tend to generate a negative correlation between population change and previous population level even in the absence of any ecological effect. However, such biases are likely to have a different distribution from those affecting Morris's (1963) test, so that congruence of results provides some confirmation of both approaches. Of the 34 species (9 permanent residents, 25 Neotropical migrants) thus examined, negative slopes were obtained in all but two cases: Nashville Warbler (slope = 0.023) and Northern Parula (slope = 0.255). Although the mean slope differed little between the two groups (residents -0.342 ± 0.115, migrants -0.326 ± 0.184, $t = 1.68$, $P = 0.10$), the distribution of statistically significant slopes differed markedly between the two groups (Table 2). Almost all (89%) of the permanent residents showed statistically significant density dependence, while only 36% of the Neotropical migrants showed this pattern. The one exception among the permanent residents was the Black-billed Magpie. Density dependence thus appeared to be stronger among the resident species.

Table 3 summarizes the relationship across species between the amplitude of population excursions within a species and the preceding population size. Here, these data are averaged across all states for a given species. As before, the analysis contains a potential bias because errors in prior population appear on both axes. However, simulations of the effects of census errors in the initial population showed that this error would account for only a small part of the effects actually found in Table 3. All the regressions were significantly negative, implying greater regulation of population level at higher population densities, both in migrants and in residents. Nevertheless, the regressions for the permanent residents

TABLE 3. Interspecific density-dependencies among permanent residents and among Neotropical migrants

Population change	Group	Slope		Constant		R^2
		Value	S.E.	Value	S.E.	
Increase size	Permanent residents	-0.167	0.044	1.998	0.106	35.9
	Neotropical migrants	-0.117	0.031	1.766	0.064	17.0
Decrease size	Permanent residents	-0.250	0.077	2.058	0.197	28.6
	Neotropical migrants	-0.134	0.034	1.676	0.074	18.9
Modulus change	Permanent residents	-0.194	0.044	2.006	0.109	43.6
	Neotropical migrants	-0.131	0.028	1.747	0.059	25.4

NOTE: All regressions are of the population change indicated regressed on population count before change, both variables logarithmically transformed. All regressions were significant at 0.005 or better

were always markedly steeper than for Neotropical migrants, and they additionally accounted for a greater proportion of the variance (rightmost column of Table 3). In both groups the slope for decrease size regressed on population size was steeper than was the case for increases, but the constants in the corresponding regressions were quite similar. These results suggest that the less abundant species in both groups have less capacity to recover from a population decrease than more abundant species and that the residents (generally the more abundant species) are more tightly coupled in this respect than are Neotropical migrant species.

Discussion

Neotropical migrants in North America were shown in the present study to occur in lower numbers than permanent residents (Fig. 1). This is a trait they share with long-distance migrants in Britain (O'Connor 1981). In Britain many of the more numerous resident species are habitat generalists that occupy a broad range of widely available man-modified habitats but migrant species are more specialized in habitat use (O'Connor 1985, in press). Many habitat generalists in North America are similarly permanent residents or short-distance migrants and typically use small parks, suburbs, and other disturbed areas with some tree cover (Whitcomb et al. 1981). In contrast, Neotropical migrants comprised fewer than half the individuals in such small fragmented tracts, although they often accounted for 80–90% of breeding individuals in extensive tracts of eastern deciduous forest. The lower numbers of Neotropical migrants in the present study may, therefore, be due to widespread forest fragmentation (Robbins 1980, Whitcomb et al. 1981, Wilcove 1985). Alternatively, the relatively low abundance of migrants may reflect a potential bias in the Breeding Bird Survey itself: the roadside counts of the BBS may sample forest edge habitat rather more frequently than is typical for the landscape at large, thus under-sampling Neotropical migrants relative to resident species. The possibility of such a bias has frequently been raised in discussion of BBS results but arguably remains unresolved (Terborgh 1989).

The density indices used in the present analyses are not identical to those used in other analyses of BBS data, for example, by Robbins et al. (1986). Their approach used the method of Geissler and Noon (1981) to generate a statistical model of the continental (or regional) population of each species. The results of each BBS count for the species were weighted by a factor reflecting the relative area attributable to that route within an overall stratified sampling scheme. In addition, each count received weighting reflecting the local abundance of the species, so that, for example, decreases in a high density area received greater emphasis than

did decreases in low density areas. Although at first sight offering a more appropriate model of population change than the approach adopted here, the Geissler-Noon method has limitations. First, the population trends computed are based on just a subset of the North American data in the case of species with significant range in the boreal forests of northern Canada, because these areas lack BBS routes. Secondly, the assumption that changes in high density areas deserve greater weight results in concealing significant information on population change in those species that vary in range in response to population changes (Wilcove and Terborgh 1984, O'Connor and Fuller 1985). In the present analysis, in contrast, greater weight is placed on changes within states, thus emphasizing pattern, rather than amplitude, of change. Because most of the findings of interest here relate to differences between permanent residents and Neotropical migrants, the differences between the two approaches are probably not critically important.

Both permanent residents and Neotropical migrants shared a tendency toward consistent increase in their species-specific long-term dynamics (Table 1). Because the BBS trends between 1966 and 1988 have not in practice been characterized by six- to sevenfold increases in mean numbers, some process countering such consistent increase is clearly at work. Density-dependent population regulation is the most likely process to bring this about, effectively introducing nonlinearity into the relationship of population change to size (Lack 1954, 1966). Such regulation can occur on a variety of scales, typically through habitat-specific reductions in breeding success at high densities (Lack 1966), but regional variation in densities can generate spatial gradients in the intensity of density-dependent processes that lead to overall population regulation (Wilcove and Terborgh 1984, O'Connor and Fuller 1985).

Intraspecific competition can manifest itself as density-dependent reduction in reproductive success, survivorship, or emigration (Lack 1954, 1966). In practice, evidence on density dependence in avian survival is scarcer than is the case for reproduction and emigration, probably mostly because of the problems of demonstrating survivorship differences in the field. Irrespective of the proximate mechanism, however, intraspecific effects are most likely to be apparent in situations of high density, and one would, therefore, expect their manifestation in the form of density-dependent changes in population size in those species that breed at higher densities. This was indeed the case here across all species, and several analyses suggested that the more abundant resident species demonstrated tighter links between population changes (particularly decreases) than did Neotropical migrants. Across states, for example, decreases were well correlated with preceding population counts in residents but were much less so in migrants. Although the analysis for density dependence conducted here was not statistically rigorous, because plotting the differences between each pair of successive counts against the first of those pairs potentially introduces spurious correlation if the counts are not exact (Varley and Gradwell 1968), simulation analyses indicate that such errors are negligible within the present data. An extended analysis to confirm the results presented here is in preparation.

Whitcomb et al. (1981) developed a model of habitat island use that offers a possible explanation for the inverse relationships between population change and population abundance reported here in Tables 2 and 3. Neotropical migrants recolonize the individual breeding territories they vacated the previous fall, but since typically only 40–60% of the adult breeders actually survive the double migratory journey and period of wintering in the tropics, many vacancies are filled by young birds breeding for the first time (O'Connor 1985). However, young birds rarely return to breed at their natal sites, so vacancies are filled largely by individuals fledged elsewhere. At equilibrium, therefore, the size of the breeding population in any given area is a function both of the survival of the adult breeders there and of the rate of colonization of that plot by first-year birds, an idea confirmed by simulation modeling (May 1981). If a plot is of better quality for breeding than is surrounding habitat, its colonization rate will be high; conversely, a patch of poor quality in the midst of better habitat will have low colonization rates. These ideas are essentially those of Fretwell and Lucas (1970), modified to take adult site fidelity into account (Fretwell 1980, 1985, O'Connor 1985). Applying them to the present results, if first-year birds selectively colonize the best available habitats and if these are characterized by higher densities than are poorer habitats, changes in population density will be relatively low in areas of high density and will be disproportionately large in areas of low density, as noted here for many species (Table 2).

One might reasonably anticipate that between two species of different densities the effect just described might operate more at the higher density than in the lower. In the present study this would lead to steeper across-state relationships in residents than in Neotropical migrants, as observed (Table 2). The validity of this extension of the argument of Whitcomb et al. (1981) does, however, depend on a differential in the survival rates for residents and migrants: mortality creates the vacancies to be filled by first-time breeders, so steeper density-dependence implies more mortality among residents. This is consistent with the widely held idea of greater survival of Neotropical migrants (e.g., references in Ricklefs 1990). (This need not be the case, for

colonizing tendencies on the part of the first-year birds of each species might be scaled to their relative densities rather than to their absolute densities. I have no evidence on this point, except that decreases in the BBS counts were typically associated with relatively large counts in migrants, rather than with small counts as expected on a scaling argument.) In addition, where species are loosely colonial, as appears to be the case for many Neotropical migrants (Whitcomb et al. 1981), the social organization might significantly shape the patterns of colonization of new habitat. If newcomers to an area settle preferentially around existing colonies, core densities in a regionally declining population might maintain the appearance of normality, although surrounded by large expanses of suitable but unoccupied habitat in which population changes are amplified (Wilcove and Terborgh 1984).

In the present analyses, population amplitude changes across states within species were correlated negatively with preceding counts both in migrants and in residents, although more so for residents. Greenberg (1980), Morse (1980), and Cox (1985) have pointed out that ultimate limitations for migrants must be a dynamic outcome of processes on both the breeding and the wintering grounds (unless, one might add, conditions during migration are limiting). If long-term conditions on the breeding grounds permit increased reproductive success, either this can be translated into increased fitness or poorer quality wintering areas can be exploited at the original level of fitness. Conversely, without detriment to fitness, any improvements in survival on the wintering ground allow use of additional breeding range formerly too low in reproductive success to be usable. Ricklefs (this volume) derives a model that formally demonstrates an expectation of demographic coupling between migrants and residents. Hence species should, in the long term and at equilibrium, be limited equally in both ranges, with density-dependent factors reducing the quality of each region from its intrinsic value to some lower level common across regions (Cox 1985). This argument implies, however, that resident species that overlap with migrants in resource use will also be limited, either in breeding on the migrant breeding grounds or in wintering on the migrant wintering grounds. Hence, one would expect strong negative relationships between numbers and population decreases in residents, as observed here. In Britain resident and migrant numbers were inversely related except immediately after crashes in resident populations brought about by unusually severe winters, and associated niche expansion and contraction have also been demonstrated (O'Connor 1985).

Similar thinking can be applied to the situation with

Neotropical migrants. The loss of these species from forest islands in the eastern United States has been found to be accompanied by increases in the populations of permanent resident species (Lynch and Whitcomb 1978), suggesting that interspecific competition between the two groups might be superimposed on whatever intraspecific competition might be present. Where this happens, the increased numbers of resident species may have the potential to impede recolonization by, and population growth of, Neotropical migrants with similar nesting or feeding requirements. Neotropical migrants have relatively low reproductive output but rather high survivorship (Whitcomb et al. 1981, Greenberg 1986), and this latter should, according to MacArthur and Wilson (1967), be equivalent to high reproduction in building a stable population in newly colonized (here habitat) islands. But the MacArthur-Wilson argument is true only in a constant environment: in the face of environmental stochasticity, small but long-lived populations, Neotropical migrants, for example, are more likely to be eliminated by chance events than are more fecund populations that more quickly increase to sizes less vulnerable to chance (O'Connor 1986). For example, in Britain many resident species were severely reduced in numbers by the extreme winter of 1962–63, but the speed with which they subsequently recovered their original numbers was directly correlated with seasonal egg production and not at all with survivorship (O'Connor 1981). Because Neotropical migrants have relatively low egg production each season, they are thus less likely to recolonize habitat patches from which they were initially lost by chance. The proximate causes of change in relative numbers of Neotropical migrants and permanent residents need further study.

One bias that must be acknowledged in the present study is that the constraints imposed as to the number of routes and of year-pairs for inclusion of the data in the study constitute an implicit bias in favor of the more abundant species. Lynch and Whigham (1984) note that some species of high conservation interest combine area-sensitivity with rarity, to the extent that statistically significant findings are not possible. Given the conservation interest on such species, this is undesirable but inevitably limits the scope of geographically and temporally extensive studies such as the present one.

Acknowledgments

I am grateful to Sam Droege of the USFWS Patuxent Wildlife Research Center for providing the Breeding Bird Survey data analysed here. I thank Randy Boone for programming help and thank Bruce Lauber, and Tim Jones for assistance in developing database facilities. I also thank Shirley Moulton for secretarial support. Professor Lincoln E. Moses and an anonymous referee provided critical review of an earlier draft of this paper.

Literature cited

Bailey, R.S. 1967. An index of bird population changes on farmland. *Bird Study* 14:195–209.

Cox, G.W. 1985. The evolution of avian migration systems between temperate and tropical regions of the New World. *Am. Nat.* 126:451–474.

Droege, S., and J.R. Sauer. 1989. *North American Breeding Bird Survey: Annual Summary 1988*. U.S. Fish and Wildlife Service Biol. Rept. 89(13).

Fretwell, S. 1980. Evolution of migration in relation to factors regulating bird numbers. Pages 517–527 in *Migrant Birds in the Neotropics: Ecology, Behavior, Distribution and Conservation*, A. Keast and E.S. Morton, eds. Washington: Smithsonian Institution Press.

———. 1985. Why do birds migrate? Inter and intraspecific competition in the evolution of bird migration contributions from population ecology. *Acta 18th Internat. Ornithol. Cong.* (Moscow): 630–637.

Fretwell, S.D., and H.L. Lucas, Jr. 1969. On territorial behavior and other factors influencing habitat distribution in birds. I. Theoretical development. *Acta Biotheor.* 19:16–36.

Geissler, P.H., and B.R. Noon. 1981. Estimates of avian population trends from the North American Breeding Bird Survey. Pages 42–51 in *Estimating Numbers of Terrestrial Birds*, C.J. Ralph and M.J. Scott, eds. Studies in Avian Biology No. 6.

Greenberg, R. 1980. Demographic aspects of long-distance migrations. Pages 493–504 in *Migrant Birds in the Neotropics: Ecology, Behavior, Distribution and Conservation*, A. Keast and E.S. Morton, eds. Washington: Smithsonian Institution Press.

———. 1986. Competition in migrant birds in the nonbreeding season. *Current Ornithol.* 3:281–307.

Hall, G.A. 1984. Population decline of Neotropical migrants in an Appalachian forest. *Am. Birds* 38:14–18.

Johnston, D.W., and D.I. Winings. 1987. Natural history of Plummers Island, Maryland. XXVII. The decline of forest breeding birds on Plummers Island, Maryland, and vicinity. *Proc. Biol. Soc. Wash.* 100:762–768.

Lack, D. 1954. *The Natural Regulation of Animal Numbers*. Oxford: Oxford University Press.

———. 1966. *Population Studies of Birds*. Oxford: Clarendon Press.

Lynch, J.F., and D.F. Whigham. 1984. Effects of forest fragmentation on breeding bird communities in Maryland, U.S.A. *Biol. Conserv.* 28:287–324.

Lynch, J.F., and R.F. Whitcomb. 1978. Effects of the insularization of the eastern deciduous forest on avifaunal diversity and turnover. Pages 461–489 in *Classification, Inventory, and Evaluation of Fish and Wildlife Habitat*, A. Marmelstein, ed. U.S. Fish and Wildlife Serv. Pub. OBS-78176.

MacArthur, R.H., and E.O. Wilson. 1967. *The Theory of Island*

Biogeography. Princeton: Princeton University Press.

May, R.M. 1981. Modeling recolonization by Neotropical migrants in habitats with changing patch structure, with notes on the age structure of populations. Pages 207–213 in *Forest Island Dynamics in Man-dominated Landscapes,* R.L. Burgess and D.M. Sharpe, eds. New York: Springer-Verlag.

Morris, R.F. 1963. Predictive equations based on key-factors. *Mem. Entomol. Soc. Can.* 32:16–21.

Morse, D.H. 1980. Population limitation: Breeding or wintering grounds? Pages 505–516 in *Migrant Birds in the Neotropics: Ecology, Behavior, Distribution and Conservation,* A. Keast and E.S. Morton, eds. Washington: Smithsonian Institution Press.

Moss, D. 1985. Some statistical checks on the Common Birds Census index—20 years on. Pages 175–179 in *Bird Census and Atlas Studies.* K. Taylor, R.J. Fuller, and P.C. Lack, eds. Tring, England: British Trust for Ornithology.

O'Connor, R.J. 1981. Comparisons between migrant and non-migrant birds in Britain. Pages 167–195 in *Animal Migration,* D.J. Aidley, ed. Soc. Exp. Biol. Seminar Series 13, Cambridge: Cambridge University Press.

———. 1985. Behavioural regulation of bird populations: A review of habitat use in relation to migration and residency. Pages 105–142 in *Behavioural Ecology: Ecological Consequences of Adaptive Behavior,* R.M. Sibly and R.H. Smith, eds. Oxford: Blackwell Scientific Publications.

———. 1986. Biological characteristics of invaders among bird species in Britain. *Phil. Trans. R. Soc. Lond.* B 314:583–598.

———. 1990. Some ecological aspects of migrants and residents. Pages 175–182 in *Bird Migration: Physiology and Ecology,* E. Gwinner, ed. Berlin: Springer-Verlag.

O'Connor, R.J., and R.J. Fuller. 1985. Bird population responses to habitat. Pages 197–212 in *Bird Census and Atlas Studies.* K. Taylor, R.J. Fuller, and P.C. Lack, eds. Tring, England: British Trust for Ornithology.

Robbins, C.S. 1980. Effect of forest fragmentation on breeding bird populations in the piedmont of the mid-Atlantic region. *Atlantic Nat.* 33:31–36.

Robbins, C.S., D. Bystrak, and P.H. Geissler. 1986. *The Breeding Bird Survey: Its First Fifteen Years, 1965–1979.* U.S. Fish and Wildlife Serv. Resource Pub. 157.

Robbins, C.S., J.R. Sauer, R.S. Greenberg, and S. Droege. 1989. Population declines in North American birds that migrate to the neotropics. *Proc. Natl. Acad. Sci.* 86:7658–7662.

Terborgh, J. 1989. *Where Have All the Birds Gone?* Princeton: Princeton University Press.

Varley, G.C., and G.R. Gradwell. 1968. Population models for the winter moth. *Symp. Royal Entomol. Soc. Lond.* 9:132–142.

Whitcomb, R.F., C.S. Robbins, J.F. Lynch, B.L. Whitcomb, M.K. Klimkiewicz, and D. Bystrak. 1981. Effects of forest fragmentation on the avifauna of the eastern deciduous forest. Pages 125–205 in *Forest Island Dynamics in Man-dominated Landscapes,* R.L. Burgess and D.M. Sharpe, eds. New York: Springer-Verlag.

Wilcove, D.S. 1985. Nest predation in forest tracts and the decline of migratory songbirds. *Ecology* 66:1211–1214.

Wilcove, D.S., and Terborgh, J.W. 1984. Patterns of population decline in birds. *Am. Birds* 38:10–13.

Wilcove, D.S., C.H. McLellan, and A.P. Dobson. 1986. Habitat fragmentation in the temperate zone. Pages 237–256 in *Conservation Biology: The Science of Scarcity and Diversity,* M.E. Soulé, ed. Sunderland, Mass.: Sinauer Associates Inc.

APPENDIX 1. Migratory status and sample size for species analyzed in this study

Species	Migratory status[a]	States[b]
Eastern Kingbird (*Tyrannus tyrannus*)	N	35
Western Kingbird (*Tyrannus verticalis*)	N	39
Scissor-tailed Flycatcher (*Tyrannus forficatus*)	N	3
Great Crested Flycatcher (*Myiarchus crinitus*)	N	30
Ash-throated Flycatcher (*Myiarchus cinerascens*)	N	3
Acadian Flycatcher (*Empidonax virescens*)	N	11
Willow Flycatcher (*Empidonax traillii*)	N	9
Alder Flycatcher (*Empidonax alnorum*)	N	4
Least Flycatcher (*Empidonax minimus*)	N	10
Hammond's Flycatcher (*Empidonax hammondii*)	N	1
Dusky Flycatcher (*Empidonax oberholseri*)	N	1
Western Flycatcher (*Empidonax difficilis*)	N	2
Eastern Wood-Pewee (*Contopus virens*)	N	29
Western Wood-Pewee (*Contopus sordidulus*)	N	4
Olive-sided Flycatcher (*Contopus borealis*)	N	2
Steller's Jay (*Cyanocitta stelleri*)	P	3
Scrub Jay (*Aphelocoma coerulescens*)	P	1
Black-billed Magpie (*Pica pica*)	P	5
Yellow-billed Magpie (*Pica nuttalli*)	P	1
Common Raven (*Corvus corax*)	P	4
Black-capped Chickadee (*Parus atricapillus*)	P	16
Carolina Chickadee (*Parus carolinensis*)	P	16
Mountain Chickadee (*Parus gambeli*)	P	1
Chestnut-backed Chickadee (*Parus rufescens*)	P	1
Tufted Titmouse (*Parus bicolor*)	P	24
Plain Titmouse (*Parus inornatus*)	P	1
Verdin (*Auriparus flaviceps*)	P	1
Bushtit (*Psaltriparus minimus*)	P	1
Brown-headed Nuthatch (*Sitta pusilla*)	P	2
Wrentit (*Chamaea fasciata*)	P	1
Carolina Wren (*Thryothorus ludovicianus*)	P	17
Cactus Wren (*Campylorhynchus brunneicapillus*)	P	2
(Northern) Mockingbird (*Mimus polyglottos*)	P	28
Curve-billed Thrasher (*Toxostoma curvirostre*)	P	1
California Thrasher (*Toxostoma redivivum*)	P	1
Wood Thrush (*Hylocichla mustelina*)	N	25
Swainson's Thrush (*Catharus ustulatus*)	N	4
Veery (*Catharus fuscescens*)	N	4
Blue-gray Gnatcatcher (*Polioptila caerulea*)	N	15
White-eyed Vireo (*Vireo griseus*)	N	16
Bell's Vireo (*Vireo bellii*)	N	2
Yellow-throated Vireo (*Vireo flavifrons*)	N	10
Solitary Vireo (*Vireo solitarius*)	N	4
Red-eyed Vireo (*Vireo olivaceus*)	N	27
Warbling Vireo (*Vireo gilvus*)	N	17
Black-and-white Warbler (*Mniotilta varia*)	N	9
Prothonotary Warbler (*Protonotaria citrea*)	N	3
Golden-winged Warbler (*Vermivora chrysoptera*)	N	1
Blue-winged Warbler (*Vermivora pinus*)	N	3

APPENDIX 1.—*Continued next page*

APPENDIX 1—*Continued*

Species	Migratory status	States
Nashville Warbler (*Vermivora ruficapilla*)	N	6
Northern Parula (*Parula americana*)	N	7
Yellow Warbler (*Dendroica petechia*)	N	26
Magnolia Warbler (*Dendroica magnolia*)	N	2
Black-throated Blue Warbler (*Dendroica caerulescens*)	N	1
Black-throated Green Warbler (*Dendroica virens*)	N	5
Blackburnian Warbler (*Dendroica fusca*)	N	1
Yellow-throated Warbler (*Dendroica dominica*)	N	1
Chestnut-sided Warbler (*Dendroica pensylvanica*)	N	10
Prairie Warbler (*Dendroica discolor*)	N	9
Ovenbird (*Seiurus aurocapillus*)	N	16
Louisiana Waterthrush (*Seiurus motacilla*)	N	1
Kentucky Warbler (*Oporornis formosus*)	N	5
Mourning Warbler (*Oporornis philadelphia*)	N	3
Common Yellowthroat (*Geothlypis trichas*)	N	35
Yellow-breasted Chat (*Icteria virens*)	N	19
Hooded Warbler (*Wilsonia citrina*)	N	7
Wilson's Warbler (*Wilsonia pusilla*)	N	1
Canada Warbler (*Wilsonia canadensis*)	N	3
American Redstart (*Setophaga ruticilla*)	N	12
House Sparrow (*Passer domesticus*)	P	40
Bobolink (*Dolichonyx oryzivorus*)	N	14
Orchard Oriole (*Icterus spurius*)	N	19
Baltimore (Northern) Oriole (*Icterus galbula*)	N	24
Bullock's (Northern) Oriole (*Icterus galbula*)	N	3
Common Grackle (*Quiscalus quiscula*)	P	35
Scarlet Tanager (*Piranga olivacea*)	N	14
Summer Tanager (*Piranga rubra*)	N	13
(Northern) Cardinal (*Cardinalis cardinalis*)	P	28
Pyrrhuloxia (*Cardinalis sinuatus*)	P	1
Rose-breasted Grosbeak (*Pheucticus ludovicianus*)	N	12
Black-headed Grosbeak (*Pheucticus melanocephalus*)	N	2
Blue Grosbeak (*Guiraca caerulea*)	N	15
Indigo Bunting (*Passerina cyanea*)	N	28
Lazuli Bunting (*Passerina amoena*)	N	2
Painted Bunting (*Passerina ciris*)	N	3
Dickcissel (*Spiza americana*)	N	13
Brown Towhee (*Pipilo fuscus*)	P	2

a. N = Neotropical migrant; P = permanent resident, as defined by Droege and Sauer (1989).

b. Number of states meeting the criterion of at least 10 estimates of year-on-year population change between 1966 and 1988, with each estimate based on at least eight paired routes.

DAVID W. JOHNSTON
5219 Concordia Street
Fairfax, Virginia 22032

JOHN M. HAGAN III
Manomet Bird Observatory
P.O. Box 1770
Manomet, Massachusetts 02345

An analysis of long-term breeding bird censuses from eastern deciduous forests

Abstract. Thirteen data sets of breeding bird censuses in eastern North American deciduous forests were examined for population trends in Neotropical migrant and resident birds. Using linear and quadratic regression models, we found that Neotropical migrant populations at most sites experienced significant declines in the 1960s and 1970s; during the 1980s, the numbers of breeding Neotropical birds were increasing or decreasing at equal numbers of sites. Resident species, however, showed either nonsignificant changes or increased or decreased at equal numbers of sites during the same decades. At five of 13 of the sites we found significant positive correlations in trends between the Neotropical and resident groups, suggesting that some factor(s) might have been affecting both groups. Because breeding bird censuses potentially offer valuable information on population trends, we recommend that efforts be initiated to establish a well-coordinated network of long-term breeding bird censuses over widely spaced geographic areas of eastern deciduous forests. Results from such long-term studies could then be used to develop suitable conservation measures for Neotropical migrant birds.

Sinopsis. Trece conjuntos de datos de censos de aves anidantes en los bosques deciduos del oriente de Norteamérica fueron examinados en busca de tendencias poblacionales de aves residentes y migratorias neotropicales. Usando modelos de regresión lineal y cuadrática, encontramos que las poblaciones de migratorias neotropicales en la mayoría de los sitios experimentaron declinaciones significativas en las décadas de 1960 y 1970; durante los años 1980, las poblaciones de aves neotropicales anidantes incrementaron o decrecieron en igual número de sitios. Sin embargo, las especies residentes o no presentaron cambios significativos o incrementaron o decrecieron en igual número de sitios durante las mismas décadas. En cinco de 13 de los sitios encontramos correlaciones positivas significativas en las tendencias entre los grupos neotropical y residente, lo cual sugiere que algún factor (o factores) podrían haber estado afectando a ambos grupos. Puesto que los censos de aves anidantes potencialmente ofrecen información valiosa sobre tendencias poblacionales, recomendamos que se inicien esfuerzos para establecer una red bien coordinada de censos a largo plazo de aves anidantes a través de áreas de bosque oriental deciduo ampliamente separadas geográficamente. Los resultados de tales estudios a largo plazo pueden entonces usarse para desarrollar medidas de conservación apropiadas para aves migratorias neotropicales.

Long-term records of distribution and abundance patterns have recently been recommended as a powerful and invaluable tool to document population trends (NRC 1986). In 1914, the U.S. Bureau of Biological Survey initiated widespread annual breeding bird censuses to determine abundances and distributions of bird species in the United States. The first years of those censuses in the eastern United States revealed interyear population fluctuations and marked decreases in both migratory and resident species (Cooke 1923). Thus, even 70 years ago geographically widely spaced censuses indicated short-term declines in breeding bird populations. Data sets spanning a decade or more from deciduous forest sites in Ohio (Williams 1936), Michigan (Walkinshaw 1947), and Illinois (Kendeigh 1982) in the 1920s to the 1940s also showed fluctuations in bird populations. Those three census sets were too few to suggest meaningful widespread trends in that time period.

By 1969, Aldrich and Robbins (1970) noted that populations of many species of migratory birds had increased or decreased in recent years in North America, especially in eastern deciduous forests. Since then, declines in breeding landbirds have been reported from scattered sites in the United States by investigators using different sampling techniques, including (1) long-term breeding bird counts or censuses in deciduous forests (Wisconsin, Ambuel and Temple 1982; New Jersey, Serrao 1985; New Hampshire, Holmes et al. 1986; the Washington, D.C. area, Briggs and Criswell 1978, Johnston and Winings 1987); (2) breeding bird censuses in coniferous or mixed deciduous-coniferous forests (Michigan, Walkinshaw 1979; Connecticut, Butcher et al. 1981; West Virginia, Hall 1984a,b; California, Marshall 1988); (3) banding station records (Stewart 1987); and (4) band returns (Leck et al. 1981). However, Breeding Bird Surveys (BBS) from 1965 to 1979 indicated stable or increasing populations of some eastern forest species (Robbins et al. 1986), but in a subsequent analysis of BBS data, Robbins et al. (1989) concluded that most Neotropical migrant bird species breeding in forests of eastern North America declined between 1978 and 1987. A comparative study of breeding bird censuses between 1947 and 1983 in the Great Smoky Mountains revealed no statistically significant decline in Neotropical

migrants (Wilcove 1988). Large fluctuations in numbers of Neotropical migrants over time were reported in a 50-year study in Illinois (Kendeigh 1982) and in 20 years of transect observations in Pennsylvania (Overlease and Overlease 1987). Thus, questions persist as to the direction, magnitude, geographical extent, and time of population changes in birds breeding in deciduous forests of eastern North America.

Our objective in this paper is to examine long-term breeding bird census data sets from eastern deciduous forest sites to determine whether any significant recent changes have occurred in the number of breeding pairs and when such changes might have occurred. Documenting long-term population changes over several decades at several localities will help in our understanding real trends and their causes in Neotropical migrant and resident land birds.

The data sets and methods of analysis

From the published literature we found 13 breeding bird census data sets spanning a decade or more, the sites located in mature deciduous forests in the eastern United States (Table 1). Some of these sites contained "some pine" (e.g., WMS, RCP; abbreviations from Table 1) and probably would not fit the ecological definition of a climax deciduous forest. The authors' site descriptions did not identify the extent of any community successional changes. All sites were dominated by mature hardwoods, chiefly combinations of oak (*Quercus*), hickory (*Carya*), beech (*Fagus*), and maple (*Acer*) species; Table 1. Some census-takers changed at a site over the duration of the censuses, but they consistently used the spot-mapping or territory-mapping technique (Kendeigh 1982, Verner 1985). Potential limitations to this method or the resulting data sets have been identified by Johnston (1990), and include variation in census efforts among years and sites and the absence of censuses at some sites in some years (aperiodic data sets). Despite these possible limitations, we feel that all the data sets identified in Table 1 were probably similarly affected by such limitations and are, therefore, suitably comparable for the present analysis.

The numbers of breeding pairs reported for each year in each of the censuses were standardized to the number of pairs (at HBB Holmes et al. [1986] counted adult individuals) per 40.5 ha (100 acres) to permit comparisons among the different-sized sites. For each year in each data set, we derived two separate series of standardized counts of breeding pairs: (1) "Neotropical" (Neotropical migrants) and (2) "resident" (short-distance or intracontinental migrants and residents or nonmigrants). Within each site, we determined whether the standard counts of the two groups changed in similar ways using Pearson product-moment correlation.

Because simple plots of the raw data showed marked changes in the direction of population trends at some sites, we performed both linear and quadratic (second-order) regressions on the data for each group (Neotropical and resident) for each site. If the second-order regression term was significant, we used the quadratic model to describe the population trend, and defined the inflection point as the year in which the trend changed from increasing to decreasing, or vice versa. Otherwise, we applied a linear regression model to the data. If the linear term was significant, we used the simple linear model to describe the trend. If the linear model was not significant ($P > 0.05$), we concluded that the data set showed no significant trend.

We examined whether similar patterns of population change were evident among sites at the same time by arbitrarily dividing the data sets into 10-year segments. If at least six data points fell within the defined decade segments (e.g., 1970s, 1980s), a linear trend was computed for that site, decade, and each group of birds. We used the slope of the regression line, whether statistically significant or not, to represent the direction of change for the group in that decade.

Results

Only six sites provided data that we considered long-term, that is, more than 20 years (Table 1). However, we also examined trends in shorter-term data sets because population changes, even for short periods, could be instructive when compared with trends at other sites.

Six sites showed significant linear declines in the numbers of Neotropical migrants (Table 2, Fig. 1). Six other sites showed significant quadratic regressions, and for three of those, the trend was negative after the inflection point. For one site (DRV), no significant population trend was found. Thus, for the Neotropical group, an equal number of linear and quadratic patterns in trends was found.

By contrast, for the resident group only two linear trends were found (Table 2). At five sites a quadratic

TABLE 1. Deciduous forest sites used for breeding bird census data in this study

Site	First year	Last year	Number of years censused	Size (ha)	Description[a]
Trelease Woods, IL (TRW)	1927	1976	42	24.0	Mature mixed hardwoods, extant field edge
Cleveland, OH (CLE)	1932	1947	15	26.3	Climax beech-maple, undocumented changes outside
Calhoun Co., MI (CLH)	1938	1947	10	5.0	Oak-hickory forest, part of 40-ha tract
Cabin John, MD (CBJ)	1947	1988	36	7.6	100-year riverine forest, road constructed nearby in 1958
Rock Creek Park, DC (RCP)	1948	1988	31	32.4[b]	80-year hardwood forest with scattered pine, road construction on one side
Greenbrook, NJ (GRB)	1949	1985	11	66.8	Mixed northern hardwoods, "most neighboring woodlands have remained intact."
Wilkesboro, NC (WKB)	1954	1973	20	16.2	Hardwoods, some pine, no major habitat changes inside/outside
Glover-Archbold Pk., DC (GLA)	1959	1988	27	14.2	Mixed upland hardwoods, undocumented changes outside
Calvert Co., MD (CLV)	1960	1986	26	11.3	Mixed upland hardwoods, some logging inside and outside in 1976
Wormsloe Pl., GA (WMS)	1963	1973	11	10.0	Oak with some pine, part of 130-ha tract
Hubbard Brook, NH (HBB)	1969	1988	20	10.0	Part of unfragmented, extensive forest
Clayton, GA (CLA)	1969	1978	10	6.1	Mountain hardwoods, in extensive National Forest
Dranesville, VA (DRV)	1973	1986	14	11.0	Uniform hardwoods, part of 140-ha tract

SOURCES: *Audubon Field Notes, Am. Birds, The Atlantic Nat., J. Field Ornithol.*, and HBB (Holmes et al. 1986), CLH (Walkinshaw 1947), TRW (Kendeigh 1982), CLE (Williams 1936), GRB (Serrao 1985, pers. comm.)

a. Taken from authors' site descriptions.

b. Reduced to 26.3 ha in 1963.

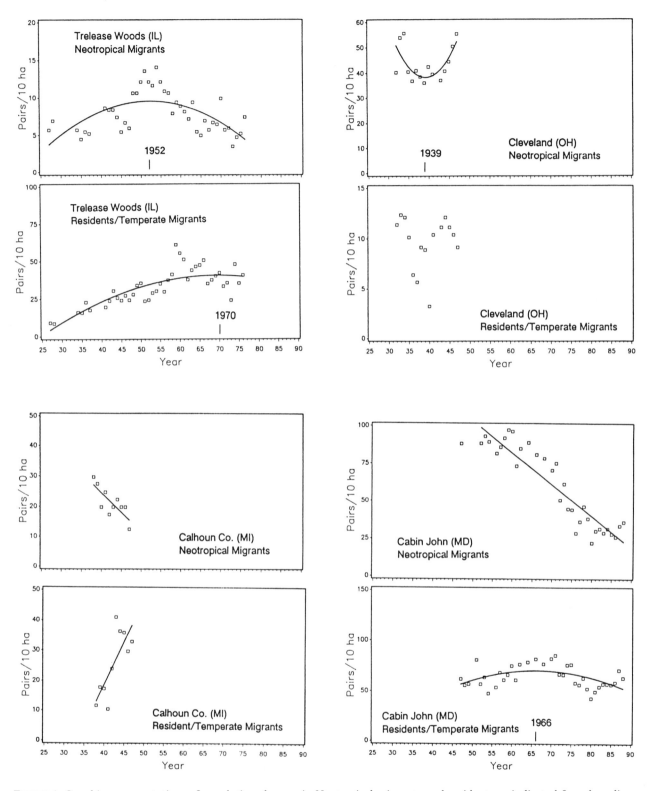

FIGURE 1. Graphic representations of population changes in Neotropical migrants and residents as indicated from breeding bird censuses in eastern deciduous forests. Linear and quadratic regression lines are drawn if statistically significant. See text for explanation of procedures.

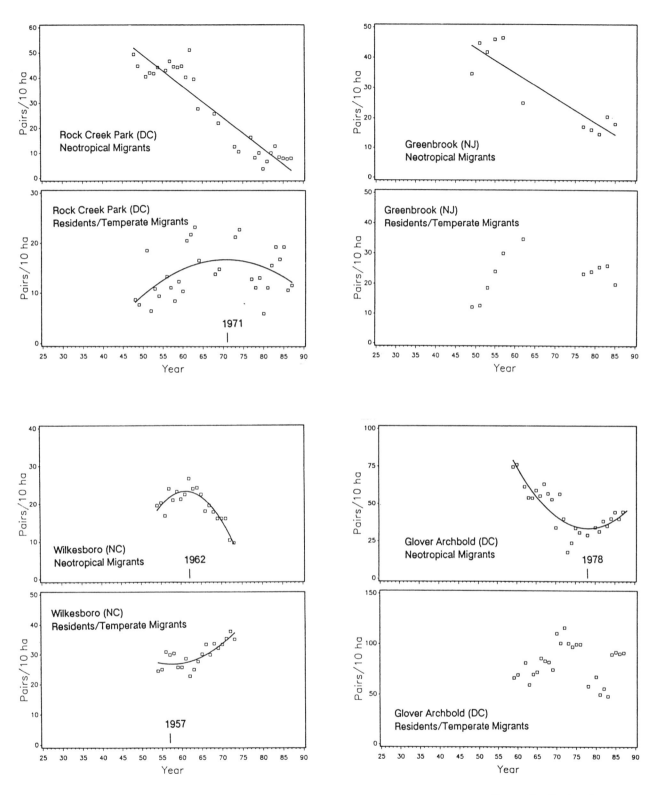

FIGURE 1—*Continued next page*

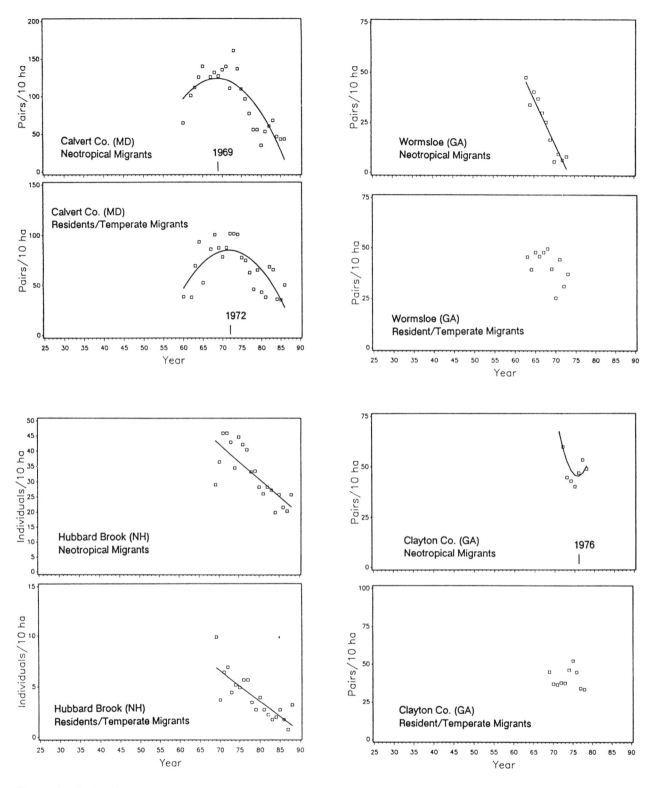

FIGURE 1—*Continued*

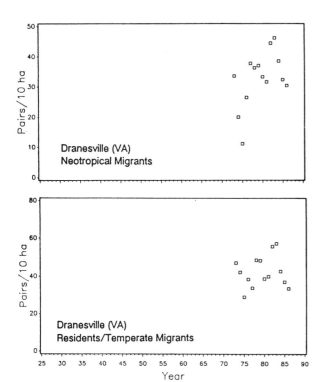

FIGURE 1—*Continued*

TABLE 2. Regression models used to describe patterns of change of migrant and resident groups

Neotropical site	Regression	
	Migrants	Residents
Trelease Woods (IL)	Q(−)	Q(−)
Cleveland (OH)	Q(+)	ns
Calhoun Co. (MI)	L(−)	L(+)
Cabin John (MD)	L(−)	Q(−)
Rock Creek (DC)	L(−)	Q(−)
Greenbrook (NJ)	L(−)	ns
Wilkesboro (NC)	Q(−)	Q(+)
Glover Archbold (DC)	Q(+)	ns
Calvert Co. (MD)	Q(−)	Q(−)
Wormsloe (GA)	L(−)	ns
Hubbard Brook (NH)	L(−)	L(−)
Clayton (GA)	Q(+)	ns
Dranesville (VA)	ns	ns

NOTE: An "L" indicates a significant linear regression ($P < 0.05$) and "Q" indicates significant quadratic regression. Signs in parentheses indicate either the slope of the linear regression line or the trend after the inflection point of a quadratic regression.

model better described the data, and at six other sites we found no significant trend. Four of the five quadratic regressions showed a negative change after the inflection point.

The fact that so many of the regression models were significant, whether linear or quadratic in pattern, suggested that directional changes in populations were taking place at most sites. However, the Neotropical group was more likely to show a significant trend (12 of 13 sites) than the resident group (7 of 13 sites). Also, the Neotropical group tended to show more linear declines than the resident group, and the resident group was more likely to show a quadratic, curvilinear pattern of change.

Although a general difference in patterns of trends between the two groups was revealed by regression analyses, simple correlations performed between the number of Neotropical and resident birds showed a significant positive correlation for five of the 13 sites (Table 3). That is, at these specific sites, populations of each group changed in a similar manner during the time of the censuses, despite differences in site locations and time periods. Even at a site, such as Cabin John, where the Neotropical group showed a steady linear decline and the resident group showed a quadratic pattern that peaked in 1966, a significant positive corre-

lation was found between the numbers of each group (Table 3, Fig. 1). The post-1966 downturn in the resident group was sufficiently similar to the long-term linear decline in the Neotropical group to result in a positive correlation (Fig. 1). The Wilkesboro site showed the only negative correlation between the number of Neotropical and resident pairs. There, the Neotropical group decreased after the quadratic inflection, while the resident group increased.

An analysis of directions of population trends during the 10-year intervals revealed an important difference in the trends of these two groups across the sites. Few data sets provided data from the 1930s through the 1950s, but both the Neotropical and resident groups showed similar numbers of positive or negative trends at that time (Table 4). However, in the 1960s and 1970s, Neotropical migrant populations at most sites were decreasing, while during the same time period the number of sites that showed increasing or decreasing residents was about equal. By the 1980s, the numbers of Neotropical pairs were increasing at as many sites as they were decreasing, indicating a possible change in the patterns of declines seen in the 1960s and 1970s at some sites. During the 1980s, the pattern for resident birds did not appear to change from the pattern during the two previous decades.

TABLE 3. Pearson product-moment correlations between the numbers of Neotropical migrants and residents for each breeding bird census site

Site	r	P	n
Trelease Woods (IL)	+0.09	ns	42
Cleveland (OH)	+0.31	ns	15
Calhoun Co. (MI)	−0.60	ns	10
Cabin John (MD)	+0.34	0.04	36
Rock Creek (DC)	−0.14	ns	30
Greenbrook (NJ)	−0.26	ns	11
Wilkesboro (NC)	−0.81	< 0.0001	20
Glover Archbold (DC)	−0.21	ns	26
Calvert Co. (MD)	+0.78	< 0.0001	25
Wormsloe (GA)	+0.69	0.02	11
Hubbard Brook (NH)	+0.50	0.05	16
Clayton (GA)	−0.30	ns	10
Dranesville (VA)	+0.72	0.004	14

NOTE: Sample size (n) represents the number of years censused.

Discussion

We examined population trends in 13 breeding bird census data sets derived from wide spatial and temporal scales. Both Neotropical and resident groups showed a variety of trends, often different at a given site. Although it is difficult to draw general conclusions about rangewide population changes from these data sets, a few patterns are noteworthy. For example, the Neotropical group showed statistically significant population decreases more often than the residents, whether quadratic or linear in nature. The resident group was more likely to show no significant change or a quadratic pattern.

Inflection points of quadratic regressions might be indicative of time periods when some causal mechanism(s) of population change became influential. However, all the data sets were not collected during the same time periods. The inflection in 1939 (CLV) is probably meaningless to current concerns for migrant land bird populations, but for some of the longer sets spanning the 1960s and 1970s, a preponderance of trend changes (from positive to negative) occurred in the late 1960s and early 1970s (Fig. 1).

Although patterns of population change between the two groups are notable, we can only speculate on the causes of these differences. The Neotropical group showed more significant declines than did the residents, and one might be inclined to implicate events away from the breeding grounds for this result. However, reproductive success of Neotropical migrant species has

TABLE 4. Number of sites showing positive (+) or negative (−) trends in Neotropical migrant and resident species groups by decade

Group		1930s	1940s	1950s	1960s	1970s	1980s
Neotropical	(+)	0	2	2	1	1	3
	(−)	1	1	2	6	6	3
Resident	(+)	0	3	2	4	3	3
	(−)	1	0	2	3	4	3

NOTE: Sites were not included if fewer than six data points were available per decade. A trend does not indicate statistical significance within a decade.

been shown to be more affected by size or spatial extent of the forests in which they breed than temperate resident species (e.g., Robbins 1980). Unless censuses are conducted within large forested areas, interpretation of these results is confounded by the possible differential influence of forest-edge effects on the two groups. One census site, located within a large contiguous forest tract (HBB), showed clear declines in the Neotropical migrant group in the 1970s and 1980s. However, that site also showed a strong linear decline in the resident group, further obfuscating causal mechanisms. Data for two other sites that were also not forest fragments (CLA, WMS) had too few data to draw any strong conclusion about recent trends in the Neotropical migrant group at those sites. Overall, it is not clear from our analysis that resident-group species are increasing or remaining stable, as several authors have suggested (Briggs and Criswell 1978, Askins et al. 1990). Rather, at several sites (HBB, TRW, CBJ, CLV, RCP) the numbers of residents showed clear declines. Parallel declines in both groups in recent decades might indicate an increasingly important role of breeding-ground effects on all bird species.

Many of the longer-term data sets, or early data sets, showed that statistically significant changes are not necessarily recent events. For example, the Neotropical migrant data set from Cleveland (1932–1947) showed a clear quadratic pattern of change well before recent times of concerns about forest fragmentation, brood parasitism, or tropical deforestation. At Trelease Woods, Neotropical species steadily increased until 1952 (inflection point), and the resident group increased until 1970, but causes of these earlier increases remain unknown. Results from these older data sets indicate that causal mechanisms of broad-scale population changes will be difficult to identify because populations might have been changing or fluctuating for many decades. It is, therefore, reasonable to ask whether many recent declines were human-induced or of natural origin, or whether population changes were parts of natural cycles.

At only four of the 13 sites are annual censuses continuing. This is unfortunate because breeding bird censuses provide some advantages over other methods of monitoring bird populations. For a given area, breeding bird censuses are likely to yield a more accurate estimate of bird populations because the site is visited repeatedly during the breeding season, and because territories are mapped. By contrast, the Breeding Bird Survey protocol samples along roadside transects on only one day during the breeding season. Therefore, sampling error is a more significant component of annual counts derived from the BBS versus breeding bird censuses. This means that breeding bird censuses should be more sensitive to changes in populations. Also, census sites can be strategically located in large tracts of contiguous forest, thereby controlling for local effects of forest fragmentation and associated phenomena. BBS, conducted along roadsides, will always be subject to the effects of human encroachment and habitat modification.

However, if the goal is only to document broad-scale changes in populations, the BBS methodology is superior to censuses because of the large number of surveys. Scale is an important consideration in any population monitoring program if the goal is a large scope of inference. At the large scale needed, the BBS is a practical and efficient approach. However, breeding bird censuses can offer valuable, additional information. For example, on a census site it is possible to monitor annual variations in vegetation and food abundance, and to examine interspecific dynamics of the birds. Therefore, the censuses have a greater probability of revealing causal mechanisms of population changes, and understanding these mechanisms is vital to developing conservation strategies. Census sites might also attract more detailed ecological studies by researchers because they are often (or could be) established in stable areas within large parks or protected lands. We recommend that efforts be initiated to reinstitute long-term breeding bird censuses, with a well-structured spatial arrangement of sites. With such a system, we believe that understanding the causal mechanisms of population changes will be realized quicker.

Acknowledgments

Two anonymous reviewers provided useful changes to the manuscript, and Jon Atwood handled the entire editorial process.

Literature cited

Aldrich, J.W., and C.S. Robbins. 1970. Changing abundance of migratory birds in North America. Pages 17–26 in *The Avifauna of Northern Latin America*, H.K. Buechner and J.H. Buechner, eds. Smithsonian Contrib. Zool. 26.

Ambuel, B., and S.A. Temple. 1982. Songbird populations in southern Wisconsin forests: 1954 and 1979. *J. Field Ornithol.* 53:149–158.

Askins, R.A., J.F. Lynch, and R. Greenberg. 1990. Population declines in migratory birds in eastern North America. *Current Ornithol.* 7:1–57.

Briggs, S.A., and J.H. Criswell. 1978. Gradual silencing of spring in Washington. *Atlantic Nat.* 32:19–26.

Butcher, G.S., W.A. Niering, W.J. Barry, and R.H. Goodwin. 1981. Equilibrium biogeography and the size of nature preserves: An avian case study. *Oecologia* 49:29–37.

Cooke, M.T. 1923. *Reports of Bird Censuses in the United States, 1916 to 1920.* U.S. Dept. Agriculture Bull. 1165.

Hall, G.A. 1984a. A long-term bird population study in an Appalachian spruce forest. *Wilson Bull.* 96:228–240.

———. 1984b. Population decline of neotropical migrants in an Appalachian forest. *Am. Birds* 37:14–18.

Holmes, R.T., T.W. Sherry, and F.W. Sturges. 1986. Bird community dynamics in a temperate deciduous forest: Long-term trends at Hubbard Brook. *Ecol. Monogr.* 50:201–220.

Johnston, D.W. 1990. Description of surveys: Breeding bird censuses. Pages 30–34 in *Survey Designs and Statistical Methods for the Estimation of Avian Population Trends*, J.R. Sauer and S. Droege, eds. U.S. Fish and Wildlife Service Biol. Rept. 90(1).

Johnston, D.W., and D.I. Winings. 1987. Natural history of Plummers Island, Maryland. XXVII. The decline of forest breeding birds on Plummers Island, Maryland, and vicinity. *Proc. Biol. Soc. Wash.* 100:762–768.

Kendeigh, S.C. 1982. *Bird Populations in East Central Illinois: Fluctuations, Variations, and Development over a Half-century.* Ill. Biol. Monogr. 52.

Leck, C.F., B.G. Murray, Jr., and J. Swinebroad. 1981. Changes in breeding bird population at Hutcheson Memorial Forest since 1958. *W.L. Hutcheson Mem. For. Bull.* 6:8–15.

Marshall, J.T. 1988. Birds lost from a Giant Sequoia forest during fifty years. *Condor* 90:359–372.

National Research Council. 1986. *Ecological Knowledge and Environmental Problem-solving.* Washington: National Academy Press.

Overlease, W.R., and E.D. Overlease. 1987. A summary of 20 years of observation of bird populations along a portion of Brandywine Creek near Chadds Ford, Pennsylvania 1965–1984. *Proc. Penn. Acad. Sci.* 61:153–169.

Robbins, C.S. 1980. Effect of forest fragmentation on breeding bird populations in the Piedmont of the mid-Atlantic region. *Atlantic Nat.* 33:31–36.

Robbins, C.S., D. Bystrak, and P.H. Geissler. 1986. *The Breeding Bird Survey: Its First Fifteen Years, 1965–1979.* U.S. Fish and Wildlife Serv. Resource Pub. 157.

Robbins, C.S., J.R. Sauer, R.S. Greenberg, and S. Droege. 1989. Population declines in North American birds that migrate to the neotropics. *Proc. Natl. Acad. Sci.* 86:7658–7662.

Serrao, J. 1985. Decline of forest songbirds. *Records of New Jersey Birds* 11:5–9.

Stewart, P.A. 1987. Decline in numbers of wood warblers in spring and autumn migrations through Ohio. *N. Am. Bird Bander* 12:58–60.

Verner, J. 1985. Assessment of counting techniques. *Current Ornithol.* 2:247–302.

Walkinshaw, L.H. 1947. Brushy field, woodlots, and pond. *Aud. Field Notes* 1:214–215.

———. 1979. Forests and wildlife in southern Michigan in the past as compared to 1970–1978. Pages 263–268 in *Proc. Workshop on Management of North Central and Northeastern Forests for Nongame Birds*, R.M. DeGraaf and K.E. Evans, compilers. USDA Forest Service, Gen. Tech. Rept. NC-51.

Wilcove, D.S. 1988. Changes in the avifauna of the Great Smoky Mountains: 1947–1983. *Wilson Bull.* 100:256–271.

Williams, A.B. 1936. The composition and dynamics of a beech-maple climax community. *Ecol. Monogr.* 6:319–408.

JACK W. WITHAM
MALCOLM L. HUNTER, JR.
Department of Wildlife
University of Maine
Orono, Maine 04469

Population trends of Neotropical migrant landbirds in northern coastal New England

Abstract. We examined bird population trends in a coastal strip (ca. 50 km wide) in New Hampshire and Maine. Data from 11 Breeding Bird Survey routes were used to calculate trends (percent annual change) of 59 species for the years 1966–1988 and 1983–1988. Population trends on a 40-ha study area of mature pine/oak forest (Holt Forest, Arrowsic, ME) were calculated from six years (1983–1988) of territory-mapping data. Habitat change was analyzed on BBS routes using aerial photographs from 1962 to 1966 and 1985 to 1987. During the period 1966–1988, 10 of 16 forest-breeding Neotropical migrants had negative trends (two were significant [$P < 0.05$]), while in the later period 1983–1988, 13 of 16 had negative trends, of which seven were significant. Nine of 15 edge/open breeders had negative trends, eight of which were significant. Among the 23 short-distance migrant species, 16 winter primarily in the southeastern United States. Thirteen (81%) of these 16 had negative trends in northern coastal New England (1966–1988), 10 of which were significant. Habitat analysis indicated decreases in the amount of forest (–7%), agricultural (–9%), and non-forest upland (–12%), while rural residential (+23%) and urban/industrial (+4%) increased along BBS routes. These habitat changes might explain the declines in edge/open species but probably do not explain declines in forest-breeding Neotropical migrants. Our findings suggest that conservationists should be concerned about birds that breed in early successional habitats and winter in the southeastern United States, in addition to forest-breeding Neotropical migrants.

Sinopsis. Nosotros examinamos tendencias poblacionales de aves en una franja costera (ca. 50 km de ancho) en New Hampshire y Maine. Datos de 11 rutas del Censo Norteamericano de Aves Anidantes (BBS) fueron empleados para calcular tendencias (porcentaje de cambio anual) de 59 especies para los años 1966–1988 y 1983–1988. Calculamos tendencias poblacionales para un área de estudio de bosque maduro de pino y roble de 40 ha (Bosque Holt, Arrowsic, ME) a partir de seis años (1983–1988) de datos de mapeos de territorios. El cambio de habitat fué analizado sobre rutas del BBS usando fotografías aéreas de 1962–1966 y 1985–1987. Durante el período 1966–1968, 10 de 16 aves migratorias neotropicales anidantes de bosque tuvieron tendencias negativas (dos fueron significativas [$P<0.05$]), mientras que en el período posterior de 1983-1988, 13 de 16 tuvieron tendencias negativas, de las cuales siete fueron significativas. Nueve de 15 anidantes de bordes de bosque y espacios abiertos tuvieron tendencias negativas, ocho de las cuales fueron significativas. De las 23 especies migratorias de distancia corta, 16 invernan primariamente en el sureste de los Estados Unidos. Trece de estas 16 (81%) tuvieron tendencias negativas en el norte de la zona costera de Nueva Inglaterra (1966–1988), 10 de las cuales fueron significativas. Los análisis de habitat indicaron decrecimiento en la extensión de bosque (-7%), terrenos agrícolas (-9%) y tierras altas no boscosas (-12%), mientras que las zonas rurales residenciales (+23%) y urbanas/industriales (+4%) incrementaron a lo largo de las rutas del BBS. Estos cambios de habitat podrían explicar las declinaciones de las migratorias neotropicales anidantes de bosque. Nuestros hallazgos sugieren que los conservacionistas deben estar preocupados por las aves que anidan en habitats sucesionales tempranos e invernan en el sureste de los Estados Unidos, además de las migratorias Neotropicales anidantes de bosque.

Studies have shown that bird populations are quite dynamic, and have identified a number of potential regulating forces, including changes in climate (Kalela 1949), landscapes (Lynch and Whigham 1984, Helle and Jarvinen 1986, Askins and Philbrick 1987), food (Morse 1978, Crawford and Jennings 1989), competitors (Sherry and Holmes 1988), and predators (Wilcove 1985). As with most ecological phenomena, the causal relationships are undoubtedly complex and also vary widely among different species (Holmes and Sherry 1988). Despite these caveats, a well-known generalization has emerged from recent studies of eastern North American passerines: populations of species that winter in the Neotropics are declining (Ambuel and Temple 1982, Holmes et al. 1986, Robbins et al. 1989).

Many writers have ascribed these trends to the degradation of tropical forests (Keast and Morton 1980, Wilcove and Whitcomb 1983, Steinhart 1984, Wallace 1986, Hutto 1988), although forest fragmentation on the breeding grounds might also be a likely cause of population declines (Lynch and Whigham 1984, Wilcove 1988, Morton and Greenberg 1989). Specifically, it is thought that breeding Neotropical migrants might be particularly vulnerable to nest predation and brood parasitism in small forest patches with high edge-to-area ratios (Gates and Gysel 1978, Brittingham and Temple 1983, Temple 1986).

Most of these studies have been conducted in the mid-Atlantic and midwestern United States where extensive areas of forest have been converted to agricul-

ture and residential use (Whitney and Somerlot 1985). In this paper we examine bird population changes, as estimated by Breeding Bird Surveys, and habitat changes in an area of northern coastal New England where the pattern of land use conversion has been rather different from that in other regions. We have also undertaken detailed monitoring of bird populations on one site for six years, thus allowing us to examine changes in some species at a smaller spatial scale.

Study areas and methods

LOCAL POPULATION TRENDS

Local bird densities were estimated at the Holt Research Forest, Arrowsic, Maine (Fig. 1). The 40-ha gridded study area was a mature white pine/red oak forest within a larger 100-ha unfragmented parcel on a 2,170-ha, 95% forested, island in the Kennebec River. Small openings existed within the canopy where juniper (*Juniperus communis*)-covered ledges occurred. The dominant tree species included white pine (*Pinus strobus*), red maple (*Acer rubrum*), and northern red oak (*Quercus rubra*). During the winter of 1987–88 a light harvest was

FIGURE 1. The counties of northern coastal New England with the location of 11 U.S. Fish and Wildlife Service Breeding Bird Survey Routes and the Holt Research Forest.

conducted on 10 ha of the study area when approximately 2,700 trees (12% of total) were removed. To test the possibility that this harvest contributed significantly to changes in number of territories of a species, estimates for 1988 were tested against the mean for 1983–1987 estimates (Sokal and Rolf 1969).

Numbers of territories were estimated using the territory mapping method (IBCC 1969). Sixteen visits were made during each breeding season from late May through early July, 1983–1988, between 0430 and 1030 hr on 50-m interval north/south lines. Population trends at Holt Forest were calculated using the method described by Holmes and Sherry (1988); where changes in abundance for each species over time were used for a simple linear regression model:

$$ln(c_i + 0.5) = year_i(ln[B]) + ln(A),$$

where c_i is the number of territories/40 ha in year i; $ln(A)$ and $ln(B)$ are the fitted constants for the y-intercept and slope, respectively. The trend (non-log-transformed) is then calculated by taking the antilog of the slope of the above regression:

$$trend(t) = e^{(ln[B]-0.5[variance])},$$

where variance is the square of the standard error (SE) of the estimate in the above regression. The average percent annual change is calculated from: $(t–1)(100)$. Trends were considered significant when the slopes from the linear regression were statistically different from zero ($P < 0.05$), based on standard t-tests.

REGIONAL POPULATION TRENDS

To examine regional bird populations all 11 Breeding Bird Survey (BBS) routes between the southern border of New Hampshire and Penobscot Bay, Maine, within 50 km of the coast, were used (Fig. 1). These routes are within the Central New England (Stratum 12) and Northern New England (Stratum 27) physiographic regions of the BBS; we call this area northern coastal New England. In Maine, these routes were Cape Neddick, Westbrook, Biddeford, Kittery Point, Newcastle, Bowdoin Center, and Warren; in New Hampshire, they were Brentwood, Dover, Epsom, and Strafford. This area is reasonably uniform climatically and physiographically and also in terms of recent changes in land use. Most of the routes traverse localities that are, to varying degrees, undergoing significant human population growth (Table 1) and hence, development. Standard breeding bird surveys were conducted on each route for an average of 17 years, ranging from 10 to 23 years per route. (See Robbins et al. 1986 for a complete description of the methodology.)

Population trends (average percent annual change) were provided for two periods (1966–1988 and 1983–1988) by John Sauer, U.S. Fish Wildlife Service, Patuxent Wildlife Research Center. Calculations were made, using data from all 11 routes, by the route regression method as described by Robbins et al. (1989). Population trends within the Central New England and Northern New England BBS regions for the period 1966–1987 were also provided for comparative purposes. Fifty-nine species were selected for analysis of trends; these included all upland species from the orders Columbiformes, Cuculiformes, Piciformes, and Passeriformes with mean counts greater than 0.7 individuals per route per year. Species were categorized (Table 2) as to a preferred breeding habitat type: mature forest (forest with closed canopy over 10 m tall), edge/open (early successional terrestrial ecosystems and edges of forests), and generalists (edges, suburban, openings, forest, and other habitats); and a wintering strategy:

TABLE 1. Human population growth in counties of northern coastal New England with BBS routes (see Figure 1)

| State | County | Census Year | | | | Percent increase |
| | | 1960 | | 1986 | | |
		Total number	Density (no./km²)	Total number	Density (no./km²)	
ME	York	99,402	38.1	158,800	60.8	59.8
	Cumberland	182,751	80.5	228,100	100.5	24.8
	Kennebec	89,150	39.3	112,000	49.3	25.6
	Sagadahoc	22,793	34.2	31,700	47.6	39.1
	Lincoln	18,497	15.6	28,300	23.8	53.0
	Knox	28,575	29.8	35,100	36.6	22.8
NH	Rockingham	99,029	122.1	221,800	273.5	124.0
	Strafford	59,799	62.3	94,000	98.0	57.2

SOURCE: U.S. Bureau of Census (1981, 1988)

TABLE 2. Distribution of species by breeding habitat and wintering strategy

Breeding habitat	Wintering strategy			Total
	Permanent resident	Short-distance migrant	Neotropical migrant	
Mature forest	6	4	16	26
Edge/Open	0	8	7	15
Generalist	5	11	2	18
TOTAL	11	23	25	59

NOTE: See Table 4 for species list and assignments

TABLE 3. Habitat classifications used to describe BBS routes

Habitat	Description
Agricultural	Pasture, field, cropland, orchards.
Forest	All cover types, with closed canopy.
Upland non-forest	Open areas including powerlines, old fields, shrublands, clearcuts.
Rural residential	1–5 buildings within 200 m of point.
Suburban with canopy	Greater than 5 buildings within 200 m radius, canopy estimated >30%.
Suburban without canopy	Greater than 5 buildings within 200 m radius, canopy estimated <30%.
Urban/Industrial	Human structures dominating, includes roads, factories, dense housings.
Open water	Open water includes lakes, rivers, and ocean.
Wetlands	Marshes, shrub swamps, and peatlands.

residents (remaining in the breeding area year-round), short-distant migrants (migrate to other parts of the United States), Neotropical migrants (migrate to the Neotropics). Species classifications were based on the following sources: Rappole et al. 1983, DeGraaf and Rudis 1986, Ehrlich et al. 1988, Robbins et al. 1989, and Root 1988.

The null hypothesis of equal number of decreasing and increasing trends was tested with chi-square for both breeding habitats and wintering strategies. Year to year changes in bird abundance were compared between Holt Forest and northern coastal New England BBS routes. Spearman rank correlation coefficients were calculated from the annual changes rather than numbers of individuals, thereby minimizing problems of autocorrelation.

REGIONAL HABITAT ANALYSIS

Habitat changes along BBS routes were determined by examining aerial photographs. A total of 100 random points were assessed for each route for each of two time periods: 1962–1966 and 1985–1987. Complete sets of early photos were not available for two New Hampshire routes and smaller samples were used (Strafford, $n = 80$; Dover, $n = 51$). All photos were black and white prints at scales of 1:20,000 and 1:80,000 for early and recent photos, respectively.

All points were located within 400 m of the road and evenly distributed along the entire route. The point location was determined by a 0.05-mm dot centered in 3 × 3-mm cells on a 204 × 204-cell gridded transparency. Every 4th and 16th cell (early and recent photos, respectively), through which the route passed, were selected as an assessment point. A 10× loupe was used to facilitate habitat assessments. Each point was assigned to

one of nine habitat classifications (Table 3). The number of points in each habitat category was summed by time period and converted to percent of total.

Results

REGIONAL POPULATION TRENDS

The population trends of the 59 species are listed in Table 4 for northern coastal New England (1966–1988 and 1983–1988) and the Central and Northern New England BBS regions. Following Robbins et al. (1989) we report all increasing and decreasing trends, whether statistically significant or not, plus trends that are significant ($P < 0.05$). Within the northern coastal New England area (1966–1988), 29 species had decreasing trends, of which 15 were significant ($P < 0.05$), and 30 species had increasing trends, of which 11 were significant.

When analyzed by breeding habitat (Tables 5,6), one half of the 26 mature forest species had decreasing trends and one half increasing; only two of the decreasing trends were significant, whereas five increasing trends were significant. Of 15 edge/open breeding

TABLE 4. Species list with breeding habitat, wintering strategy, and trends for northern coastal New England, 1966–88 and 1983–1988, and central and northern New England BBS regions

Species	Wintering strategy	Breeding habitat	Percent annual change			
			Northern coastal NE		BBS regions 1966–87	
			1966–88	1983–88	Central NE	Northern NE
Rock Dove (*Columba livia*)	R	G	2.8	7.8	3.2*	-1.9
Mourning Dove (*Zenaida macroura*)	SD	G	6.7**	3.3	4.3**	8.9**
Black-billed Cuckoo (*Coccyzus erythropthalmus*)	NM	F	-4.1	20.4	-4.7**	0.9
Downy Woodpecker (*Picoides pubescens*)	R	F	1.3	25.3	-1.4	0.3
Hairy Woodpecker (*Picoides villosus*)	R	F	-0.4	3.1	-1.5*	1.9
Northern Flicker (*Colaptes auratus*)	SD	G	-2.1*	-9.2	-2.9**	-4.0**
Eastern Wood-Pewee (*Contopus virens*)	NM	F	0.2	-4.6	0.6	-0.1
Least Flycatcher (*Empidonax minimus*)	NM	F	-4.7**	-3.7	-3.8**	-1.9
Eastern Phoebe (*Sayornis phoebe*)	SD	E/O	-0.01	14.8**	-2.0**	-2.8
Great Crested Flycatcher (*Myiarchus crinitus*)	NM	G	2.3	3.5	-1.3	3.0**
Eastern Kingbird (*Tyrannus tyrannus*)	NM	E/O	2.0	-3.5	-0.7	0.6
Blue Jay (*Cyanocitta cristata*)	SD	F	-1.2	-3.8	-1.9**	1.1
American Crow (*Corvus brachyrhynchos*)	SD	G	4.8**	5.2**	3.4**	2.6**
Black-capped Chickadee (*Parus atricapillus*)	R	F	2.7**	3.1	2.1**	2.5**
Tufted Titmouse (*Parus bicolor*)	R	F	21.6*	4.3	6.6**	6.1*
Red-breasted Nuthatch (*Sitta canadensis*)	R	F	1.0	4.7	0.8	3.1*
White-breasted Nuthatch (*Sitta carolinensis*)	R	F	3.7**	12.2	-0.1	2.9**
House Wren (*Troglodytes aedon*)	SD	G	-1.8	-1.1	-0.6	2.1**
Veery (*Catharus fuscescens*)	NM	F	-2.0	2.7	-1.1	-0.4
Hermit Thrush (*Catharus guttatus*)	SD	F	-11.6	8.1	-1.2	-7.0
Wood Thrush (*Hylocichla mustelina*)	NM	F	-1.8	-7.3**	-2.0**	-1.1
American Robin (*Turdus migratorius*)	SD	G	-1.8**	-0.3	-1.0*	-0.7
Gray Catbird (*Dumetella carolinensis*)[a]	NM	E/O	-1.2	-5.7*	0.7	0.6
Northern Mockingbird (*Mimus polyglottos*)	R	G	9.1**	2.7	12.8**	10.5**
Brown Thrasher (*Toxostoma rufum*)	SD	E/O	-8.3**	-10.0**	-9.6**	-4.9**
Cedar Waxwing (*Bombycilla cedrorum*)	SD	G	3.9*	-9.7*	3.2**	5.0**
European Starling (*Syturnus vulgaris*)	SD	G	-2.3*	-4.8**	-2.1**	-1.7*
Solitary Vireo (*Vireo solitarius*)[a]	NM	F	-2.8*	1.3	0.5	1.5
Warbling Vireo (*Vireo gilvus*)	NM	F	2.4	-11.6*	4.1*	2.4
Red-eyed Vireo (*Vireo olivaceus*)	NM	F	-2.0	-1.9	0.1	1.0
Nashville Warbler (*Vermivora ruficapilla*)	NM	F	-1.4	-7.8	-3.8	3.3*
Yellow Warbler (*Dendroica petechia*)	NM	G	1.2	-3.8	2.9**	0.1
Chestnut-sided Warbler (*Dendroica pensylvanica*)	NM	E/O	-4.3**	-2.0	-2.8*	-0.4
Yellow-rumped Warbler (*Dendroica coronata*)	SD	F	5.1**	-6.1	4.4**	3.4**
Black-thr. Green Warbler (*Dendroica virens*)	NM	F	-0.6	-0.9	-0.3	-2.0
Pine Warbler (*Dendroica pinus*)	SD	F	9.6**	6.4*	5.1*	8.6**
Black-and-white Warbler (*Mniotilta varia*)[a]	NM	F	2.4	-2.8	0.2	0.9
American Redstart (*Setophaga ruticilla*)	NM	F	-3.6	-6.4**	3.0**	-1.6

NOTE: * = $P < 0.05$; ** = $P < 0.01$; E/O = edge/open; F = mature forest; G = generalist; NM = Neotropical migrant; R = Resident; SD = short distance migrant (see text for description).

a. Indicates species that are designated as Neotropical migrants by most authors and therefore here, although a significant portion of the population from this region might winter in the southern U.S. (Rappole et al. 1983, Robbins et al. 1989, Root 1989).

TABLE 4—*Continued next page*

TABLE 4—*Continued*

Species	Wintering strategy	Breeding habitat	Percent annual change			
			Northern coastal NE		BBS regions 1966–87	
			1966–88	1983–88	Central NE	Northern NE
Ovenbird (*Seiurus aurocapillus*)	NM	F	0.7	-1.8	1.2	0.8
Common Yellowthroat (*Geothlypis trichas*)[a]	NM	E/O	-2.0*	-6.6**	-0.5	-0.9
Canada Warbler (*Wilsonia canadensis*)	NM	F	0.2	-6.5	-5.3*	-0.5
Scarlet Tanager (*Piranga olivacea*)	NM	F	-0.1	-6.4**	-0.7	0.2
Northern Cardinal (*Cardinalis cardinalis*)	R	G	13.1**	-2.6	5.6**	6.6**
Rose-breasted Grosbeak (*Pheucticus ludovicianus*)	NM	F	4.1	-2.6	-0.2	4.9**
Indigo Bunting (*Passerina cyanea*)	NM	E/O	2.3	-17.8**	-2.5*	2.1
Rufous-sided Towhee (*Pipilo erythrophthalmus*)	SD	E/O	-10.7**	-9.3**	-9.1**	-10.2**
Chipping Sparrow (*Spizella passerina*)	SD	E/O	0.7	1.8	0.9	-0.3
Field Sparrow (*Spizella pusilla*)	SD	E/O	-8.2**	-13.4*	-8.3**	-6.8**
Song Sparrow (*Melospiza melodia*)	SD	E/O	-2.1*	-0.1	-1.3**	-3.2**
White-throated Sparrow (*Zonotrichia albicollis*)	SD	E/O	-8.6**	-9.0**	-8.0**	-3.8**
Bobolink (*Dolichonyx oryzivorus*)	NM	E/O	0.6	-0.6	1.8	1.2
Eastern Meadowlark (*Sturnella magna*)	SD	E/O	-5.7**	-7.4	-8.1**	-5.1**
Common Grackle (*Quiscalus quiscula*)	SD	G	-2.3**	2.9	-2.5**	1.2
Brown-headed Cowbird (*Molothrus ater*)	SD	G	-2.3*	1.3	-2.4**	-1.2
Northern Oriole (*Icterus galbula*)	NM	G	3.7**	-6.4	0.4	3.8**
Purple Finch (*Carpodacus purpureus*)	SD	G	-3.7	3.5	-2.0*	-1.7
House Finch (*Carpodacus mexicanus*)	R	G	34.2**	26.8**	20.5**	24.7**
American Goldfinch (*Carduelis tristis*)	SD	E/O	1.9	0.2	0.2	-2.0
House Sparrow (*Passer domesticus*)	R	G	1.7	-6.1	-1.3	2.8

NOTE: * = $P < 0.05$; ** = $P < 0.01$; E/O = edge/open; F = mature forest; G = generalist; NM = Neotropical migrant; R = Resident; SD = short distance migrant (see text for description).

a. Indicates species that are designated as Neotropical migrants by most authors and therefore here, although a significant portion of the population from this region might winter in the southern U.S. (Rappole et al. 1983, Robbins et al. 1989, Root 1989).

species, nine had decreasing trends with eight significant, whereas only one of six species with increasing trends was significant. The significantly decreasing edge/open species were Eastern Meadowlark, Chestnut-sided Warbler, Common Yellowthroat, White-throated Sparrow, Field Sparrow, Song Sparrow, Rufous-sided Towhee, and Brown Thrasher.

When analyzed by wintering strategies (Tables 7,8), roughly equal numbers of Neotropical migrant species had decreasing or increasing trends (13 vs. 12, respectively). Four decreasing trends were significant; only one species increased significantly. Among 23 short-distance migrants, 15 had decreasing trends, 73% of which were significant. Of the eight increasing trends, 62% were significant. Only one of 11 resident species had a decreasing trend, whereas 10 species were increasing, six significantly.

Analyses by both breeding habitat and wintering strategy indicate that 10 of 16 forest-breeding Neotropical migrants and three of seven edge/open Neotropical migrants had decreasing trends. Of the nine decreasing edge/open species, six were short-distance migrants.

In general, trends in the northern coastal New England area (1966–1988), as defined for this study, were similar to those in the Central and Northern New England regions (1966–1987) recognized by the BBS (Table 9). Of the 29 decreasing species in the northern coastal New England area, 18 of them were decreasing in both BBS regions and an additional seven species were decreasing in one region or the other. Overall, the shared decreasing species were dominated by short-distance migrant and edge/open species, such as Eastern Meadowlark, White-throated Sparrow, Field Sparrow, Song Sparrow, Rufous-sided Towhee, and Brown Thrasher. Of

TABLE 5. Number of species with increasing and decreasing trends and number of significant trends ($P < 0.05$) for northern coastal New England (1966–88) by breeding habitat with χ^2 results (χ^2 to test null hypothesis of equal number of increasing and decreasing trends)

Breeding habitat	Number of species				
	Increasing trends		Decreasing trends		Total no.
	No. trends	No. significant	No. trends	No. significant	
Mature forest	13	5	13	2	26
Edge/Open	6	1	9	8	15
Generalist	11	6	7	5	18
TOTAL	30	11	29	15	59

$\chi^2 = 1.47$, 2 d.f., $P = 0.48$, NS

TABLE 6. Number of species with increasing and decreasing trends and number of significant trends ($P < 0.05$) for northern coastal New England (1983–88) by breeding habitat with χ^2 results

Breeding habitat	Number of species				
	Increasing trends		Decreasing trends		Total no.
	No. trends	No. significant	No. trends	No. significant	
Mature forest	11	1	15	4	26
Edge/open	2	0	13	7	15
Generalist	10	3	8	2	18
TOTAL	23	4	36	13	59

$\chi^2 = 6.35$, 2 d.f., $P < 0.05$

the 30 species increasing in the northern coastal New England area, 17 of them increased in both BBS regions and 10 more increased in one region or the other.

When the trend analysis was restricted to only the later years (1983–1988) of the study period, the balance between species with decreasing and increasing trends disappeared. The overall number of decreasing and increasing trends was 36 (13 significant) and 23 (4 significant), respectively. Of 15 edge/open breeders, 13 had decreasing trends; seven were significant. Twenty-one of 25 Neotropical migrants had decreasing trends and seven of these were significant.

REGIONAL VERSUS LOCAL POPULATION TRENDS

A total of 23 species occurred regularly ($\bar{X} \geq 1.0$ territory per 40 ha) at the Holt Forest (Table 10). The Veery, with

a decrease in the number of territories in 1988, was the only species with a significant change in postharvest numbers ($t_{.05[4]} = 3.47$, $P < 0.05$), and therefore, it was not included in the analysis because the results suggest that their decline might have been caused by the harvest.

Only two species (Yellow-rumped and Blackburnian warblers) showed significant trends, both increasing. Forest-breeding species had equal numbers of increasing (9) and decreasing (9) trends, two edge/open species decreased and two generalists increased. More Neotropical migrant species were decreasing (8) than increasing (3), while six species of short-distance migrants were increasing and three were decreasing. If we compare Holt Forest trends to the northern coastal New England area (1983–1988) by species, 12 species had similar trends (7 negative and 5 positive) and nine species had opposite

TABLE 7. Number of species with increasing and decreasing trends and number of significant trends (*P* < 0.05) for northern coastal New England (1966–88) by wintering strategy with χ^2 results

| Wintering strategy | Number of species | | | | Total no. |
| | Increasing trends | | Decreasing trends | | |
	No. trends	No. significant	No. trends	No. significant	
Neotropical	12	1	13	4	25
Short-distance	8	5	15	11	23
Resident	10	6	1	0	11
TOTAL	30	11	29	15	59

$\chi^2 = 9.52$, 2 d.f., *P* < 0.01

TABLE 8. Number of species with increasing and decreasing trends and number of significant trends (*P* < 0.05) for northern coastal New England (1983–88) by wintering strategy with χ^2 results

| Wintering strategy | Number of species | | | | Total no. |
| | Increasing trends | | Decreasing trends | | |
	No. trends	No. significant	No. trends	No. significant	
Neotropical	4	0	21	7	25
Short-distance	10	3	13	6	23
Resident	9	1	2	0	11
TOTAL	23	4	36	13	59

$\chi^2 = 14.2$, 2 d.f., *P* < 0.01

trends. Correlations between Holt Forest and regional annual population change were significant for only one species: Hermit Thrush ($r_s = 0.97$, *P* = 0.005).

No overall relationship was found between population trends at Holt Forest and northern coastal New England region. Only one species showed a significant correlation, and this is less than would be expected by chance. Apparently six years of data were not sufficient to show significant relationships or those relationships do not exist; in contrast, 18 years of data in a New Hampshire study were sufficient to show some relationships (Holmes and Sherry 1988).

REGIONAL HABITAT ANALYSES

Most of the nine habitat types changed considerably over the 25-year period (Table 11). Most notable were decreases in agricultural (–9%), forest (–7%), and non-forest upland areas (–12%), and increases in rural residential (+23%) areas. These changes were undoubtedly

related to human population increases in the region (Table 1).

Discussion

Many writers have expressed concern about the impact of tropical deforestation on migrant birds (Keast and Morton 1980, Wilcove and Whitcomb 1983, Steinhart 1984, Wallace 1986, Hutto 1988). In northern coastal New England, for the period 1966–1988, we found no substantial overall decline for Neotropical migrants, because only 13 of 25 species had negative trends. Although our analysis of northern coastal New England for the later period (1983–1988) was undertaken for comparison to Holt Forest data, some changes emerge when 1966–1988 vs. 1983–1988 trends are compared for Neotropical migrants and edge/open breeders. The percentage of edge/open breeders with declining trends changed from 60% in the entire period to 87% in the later period. Neotropical migrants with declining trends

TABLE 9. Comparison of the number of positive and negative trends from northern coastal New England (NCNE) with central New England (CNE) and northern New England (NNE) by wintering and breeding strategy

BBS Region	Number of trends by sign					
	NCNE		CNE		NNE	
	+	−	+	−	+	−
Neotropical; forest	6	10	7	9	9	7
Neotropical; edge/open	4	3	3	4	5	2
Neotropical; generalist	2	0	1	1	2	0
Short-distance; forest	2	2	2	2	3	1
Short-distance; edge/open	2	6	2	6	0	8
Short-distance; generalist	4	7	3	8	5	6
Resident; forest	5	1	3	3	6	0
Resident; generalist	5	0	4	1	4	1
TOTAL	30	29	25	34	34	25

changed from 52% to 84%. These latter results parallel the findings of Robbins et al. (1989) that North American populations of most Neotropical migrants were stable from 1966–1978, but began to decline during 1978–1987. Additionally, when results of our later period were compared with the later period, 1978–1987, of Robbins et al. (1989), among 23 species of Neotropical migrants common to both studies, 14 had the same trend direction and all of these were negative. It is not clear to what extent loss of forest in the breeding range (−7% documented here) vs. winter habitat loss or other factors could explain these declines.

Possibly habitat changes in northern coastal New England have been partially responsible for the changes in abundance of edge/open breeders. Edge/open species would be particularly affected by the large decline in the abundance of upland nonforest (−12%) and agricultural areas (−9%). Much of this loss can be ascribed to an increase in the rural residential habitat types (+23%), a change caused by the proliferation of roadside single-family homes. Some of the decrease in upland nonforest can also be attributed to forest succession. Another study of habitat change (1950s–1984) conducted in two towns in our study region also documented a loss of agricultural lands (−10 and −21%) and an increase in developed area (6 and 11%), whereas forested area (1 and 3%) actually increased slightly (Arbuckle and Lee 1987).

Habitat loss in the southeastern United States might also be responsible for some of the decreasing trends. Sixteen of the 23 species considered to be short-distance migrants winter primarily in the southeastern United States; 13 (81%) of these 16 had negative trends in northern coastal New England (1966–1988) and 10 of the trends were significant. This group includes six of the eight significantly declining edge/open species and four of the five significantly declining habitat generalists. Hagan et al. (this volume), reporting on migration count data at Manomet Bird Observatory, provided data on 11 of the same short-distance migrant species for the period 1970–1988. Eight of the 11 species had concordant trend directions and all of these were negative.

To summarize, although these regional data add support to the widespread concern for population changes in North American landbirds, especially forest-breeders wintering in the Neotropics, they also point to another problem that, at least in this region, is even more conspicuous. This is loss of habitat and population declines for species that inhabit open, early-successional ecosystems and edges, most of which migrate to the southeastern United States. Which of the two groups of birds merits more attention from conservationists?

Clearly, any species threatened with global extinction must have the highest priority. No one should compromise efforts to save the Kirtland's Warbler (*Dendroica kirtlandii*) with an attempt to bolster a locally declining population of American Robins. However, in evaluating priorities for species that are not in such dire straits, the choices are less clear. Given a choice of protecting a tract of mature forest vs. a parcel of abandoned pasture (all other things being equal), what should conservationists in northern coastal New England do?

Our first answer would be: all other things are never equal; inevitably, only addressing a complex array of other considerations (e.g., cost of maintaining the pasture as an early successional ecosystem, anticipated patterns for future landscape change, global population trends of species of concern) will provide an answer. An alternative answer would be to buy neither parcel and use the time and money saved to lobby for new zoning laws that would facilitate cluster development and other techniques designed to stop the inexorable degradation of the entire landscape.

Acknowledgments

We wish to thank John Sauer and Sam Droege of the U.S. Fish and Wildlife Service for providing trends analysis of BBS data sets and the many observers who col-

TABLE 10.   Number of territories at the Holt Forest and average annual percent change from 1983–1988 for Holt Forest (HRF) and northern coastal New England BBS routes

Species	Number of territories	Average annual percent change	
	$\bar{x}(\pm SD^a)$	HRF	BBS
Hairy Woodpecker	1.3 (0.52)	2.7	3.1
Eastern Wood-Pewee	4.5 (2.51)	1.8	-4.6
Blue Jay	2.2 (1.47)	27.9	-3.8
Black-capped Chickadee	9.0 (2.83)	12.9	3.1
Red-breasted Nuthatch	4.2 (1.33)	-3.5	4.7
Brown Creeper	6.3 (1.51)	2.8	26.5
Golden-crowned Kinglet	3.5 (1.87)	25.5	–
Veery	3.8 (1.60)	–	2.7
Hermit Thrush	7.2 (0.75)	2.7	8.1
Solitary Vireo	2.3 (2.58)	-3.5	1.3
Nashville Warbler	4.2 (3.19)	-25.0	-7.8
Yellow-rumped Warbler	9.3 (2.34)	12.3*	-6.1
Black-th. Green Warbler	28.2 (4.17)	-5.6	-0.9
Blackburnian Warbler	11.3 (2.42)	10.4*	-7.8
Pine Warbler	1.2 (0.41)	-7.1	6.4*
Black-and-white Warbler	5.7 (1.75)	-11.8	-2.8
Ovenbird	30.5 (4.37)	-2.3	-1.8
Common Yellowthroat	7.2 (1.47)	-0.9	-6.6**
Canada Warbler	1.0 (0.63)	-16.3	-6.5
Scarlet Tanager	3.0 (0.89)	9.9	-6.4*
White-throated Sparrow	6.3 (2.50)	-7.0	-9.0**
Brown-headed Cowbird	2.0 (0.63)	3.1	1.3
Purple Finch	1.8 (0.41)	-1.6	3.5

NOTE: * = P < 0.05; ** = P < 0.01.

a. Based on 6 years of territory mapping.

TABLE 11. Habitat changes on northern coastal New England BBS routes

Habitat	Percent of total points		Percent change
	1962–1966	1985–1987	
Agriculture	14.6	5.8	-8.8
Forest	37.4	30.1	-7.3
Upland non-forest	18.5	6.3	-12.2
Rural residential	8.8	31.8	23.0
Suburban w/ canopy	2.3	4.1	1.8
Suburban w/o canopy	4.8	5.4	0.6
Urban/Industrial	5.0	9.4	4.4
Open water	2.7	2.7	0.0
Wetlands	5.6	4.5	-1.1
Number of points	1031	1100	

lected the BBS data sets. In addition, we wish to thank Bob Johnston, Maine Geological Survey, Steve Cashman and Mike Lynch, USDA Soil Conservation Service for providing aerial photographs. Steve Sader advised us on aerial photograph interpretation and Bill Halteman advised us on statistics. Bill Drury, Raymond O'Connor, and Tom Sherry reviewed early drafts of the manuscript. Support was provided by the Holt Woodland Research Foundation and MacIntyre Stennis Funds. This is Maine Agricultural Experiment Station Publ. No. 1505.

Literature cited

Ambuel, B., and S.A. Temple. 1982. Songbird populations in southern Wisconsin forests: 1954 and 1979. *J. Field Ornithol.* 53:149–158.

Arbuckle, J., and M. Lee. 1987. *The Cumulative Impacts of Development in Maine: A Study of Habitat Changes in Five Coastal Towns.* Augusta, Maine: Maine State Planning Office.

Askins, R.A., and M.J. Philbrick. 1987. Effect of changes in regional forest abundance on the decline and recovery of a forest bird community. *Wilson Bull.* 99:7–21.

Brittingham, M.C., and S.A. Temple. 1983. Have cowbirds caused forest songbirds to decline? *BioScience* 33:31–35.

Crawford, H.S., and D.T. Jennings. 1989. Predation by birds on spruce budworm *Choristoneura fumiferana*: functional, numerical, and total responses. *Ecology* 70:152–163.

DeGraaf, R.M., and D.D. Rudis. 1986. *New England Wildlife: Habitat, Natural History, and Distribution.* Broomall, Pa.: USDA Forest Serv., N.E. Forest Exp. Sta., Gen. Tech. Rep. NE-108.

Ehrlich, P.R., D.S. Dobkin, and D. Wheye. 1988. *The Birder's Handbook: A Field Guide to the Natural History of North American Birds.* New York: Simon and Schuster.

Gates, J.E., and L.W. Gysel. 1978. Avian nest dispersion and fledgling success in field forest ecotones. *Ecology* 59:871–883.

Helle, P., and O. Jarvinen. 1986. Population trends of North Finnish land birds in relation to their habitat selection and changes in forest structure. *Oikos* 46:107–115.

Holmes, R.T., and T.W. Sherry. 1988. Assessing population trends of New Hampshire forest birds: Local vs. regional patterns. *Auk* 105:756–768.

Holmes, R.T., T.W. Sherry, and F.W. Sturges. 1986. Bird community dynamics in a temperate deciduous forest: Long-term trends at Hubbard Brook. *Ecol. Monogr.* 50:201–220.

Hutto, R.L. 1988. Is tropical deforestation responsible for the reported declines in neotropical migrant populations? *Am. Birds* 42:375–379.

International Bird Census Committee [IBBC]. 1969. Recommendations for an international standard for a mapping method in bird census work. *Bird Study* 16:248–255.

Kalela, O. 1949. Changes in geographic ranges in the avifauna of northern and central Europe in relation to recent changes in climate. *Bird-Banding* 2:77–103.

Keast, A., and E.S. Morton, eds. 1980. *Migrant Birds in the Neotropics: Ecology, Behavior, Distribution, and Conservation.* Washington: Smithsonian Institution Press.

Lynch, J.F., and D.F. Whigham. 1984. Effects of forest fragmentation on breeding bird communities in Maryland, U.S.A. *Biol. Conserv.* 28:287–324.

Morse, D.H. 1978. Populations of Bay-breasted and Cape May warblers during an outbreak of the spruce budworm. *Wilson Bull.* 90:404–413.

Morton, E.S., and R. Greenberg. 1989. The outlook for migratory songbirds: "Future shock" for birders. *Am. Birds* 43:178–183.

Rappole, J.H., E.S. Morton, T.E. Lovejoy, III, and J.L. Ruos. 1983. *Nearctic Avian Migrants in the Neotropics.* Washington: U.S. Fish and Wildlife Service.

Robbins, C.S., D. Bystrak, and P.H. Geissler. 1986. *The Breeding Bird Survey: Its First Fifteen Years, 1965–1979.* U.S. Fish and Wildlife Serv. Resource Pub. 157.

Robbins, C.S., J.R. Sauer, R.S. Greenberg, and S. Droege. 1989. Population declines in North American birds that migrate to the neotropics. *Proc. Natl. Acad. Sci.* 86:7658–7662.

Root, T. 1988. *Atlas of Wintering North American Birds.* Chicago: University of Chicago Press.

Sherry, T.W., and R.T. Holmes. 1988. Habitat selection by breeding American Redstarts in response to a dominant competitor, the Least Flycatcher. *Auk* 105:350–364.

Sokal R.R., and F.J. Rohlf. 1969. *Biometry.* San Francisco: W.H. Freeman and Co.

Steinhart, P. 1984. Trouble in the tropics. *National Wildlife* Dec.-Jan. 1984:16–20.

Temple, S.A. 1986. Predicting impacts of habitat fragmentation on forest birds: A comparison of two models. Pages 301–304 in *Wildlife 2000: Modeling Habitat Relationships of Terrestrial Vertebrates,* J. Verner, M.L. Morrison, and C.J. Ralph, eds. Madison: University of Wisconsin Press.

U.S. Bureau of Census. 1981. *Characteristics of the Population.* Vol. 1. U.S. Summary. PC80-1-A1. Washington: Dept. of Commerce.

———. 1988. *City and County Data Book 1988.* Washington: U.S. Government Printing Office.

Wallace, J. 1986. Where have all the songbirds gone? *Sierra* Mar./Apr. 1986:44–47.

Whitney, G.G., and W.J. Somerlot. 1985. A case study of woodland continuity and change in the American Midwest. *Biol. Conserv.* 31:265–287.

Wilcove, D.S. 1985. Nest predation in forest tracts and the decline of migratory songbirds. *Ecology* 66:1211–1214.

———. 1988. Changes in the avifauna of the Great Smoky Mountains: 1947–1983. *Wilson Bull.* 100:256–271.

Wilcove, D.S., and R.F. Whitcomb. 1983. Gone with the trees. *Nat. History* 92:82–91.

SIDNEY A. GAUTHREAUX, JR.
Department of Biological Sciences
Clemson University
Clemson, South Carolina 29634-1903

The use of weather radar to monitor long-term patterns of trans-Gulf migration in spring

Abstract. WSR-57 radars are operated at eight weather stations around the northern and eastern coasts of the Gulf of Mexico. These radars are capable of detecting the migration of birds across the Gulf and through the coastal areas from Brownsville, Texas around the northern Gulf to Key West, Florida. Film records from the radar stations exist for 33 years (1957–1990) and can be used to quantify the day-to-day and year-to-year patterns of spring migration across the Gulf. The methods of analysis are discussed and preliminary findings suggest a decline in the amount of trans-Gulf migration and changes in the seasonal timing of the flights since the mid-1960s.

Sinopsis. Radares WSR-57 son operados en ocho estaciones meteorológicas alrededor de las costas norte y este del Golfo de México. Estos radares son capaces de detectar la migración de aves a través del Golfo y de las áreas costeras desde Brownsville, Texas, alrededor del extremo norte del Golfo, hasta Key West, Florida.

Existen registros fílmicos de 33 años (1957–1990) de las estaciones de radar y pueden ser usados para cuantificar los patrones de migración primaveral a través del Golfo, día a día y año a año. Se discuten los métodos de análisis y los hallazgos preliminares sugieren una declinación en la magnitud de la migración a través del Golfo y cambios en la cronología estacional de los vuelos desde mediados de la década de 1960.

Since 1957 the U.S. Weather Bureau (National Weather Service) has operated weather surveillance (WSR-57) radars at eight weather stations around the northern coast of the Gulf of Mexico from Brownsville, Texas, to Key West, Florida, and Miami, Florida (Fig. 1). During normal operations a 35-mm or 16-mm film record of the remote radar display is made, and these record films are stored permanently at the National Climatic Data Center in Asheville, North Carolina.

From 1963 to 1967, I evaluated the use of the WSR-57 radars at Lake Charles and New Orleans, Louisiana, to study birds arriving from across the Gulf of Mexico in

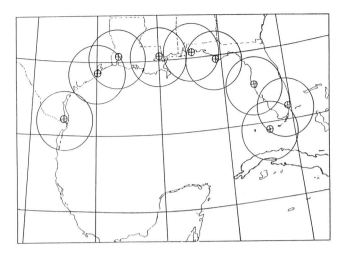

FIGURE 1. Locations of the WSR-57 radar stations around the Gulf of Mexico. Each circle delimits 125 nautical mile range (the standard range for radar film records). From left to right the stations are: Brownsville, TX; Galveston, TX; Lake Charles, LA; New Orleans (Slidell), LA; Pensacola, FL; Apalachicola, FL; Tampa, FL; Key West, FL; and Miami, FL;

spring migration. I quantified the radar displays of bird migration using other quantitative techniques (Gauthreaux 1970), and studied the trans-Gulf migration of songbirds from the Neotropics in spring (Gauthreaux 1971). I determined that the number of migrating birds arriving from over the Gulf of Mexico was related to the spatial extent of the echo pattern of the migration in the film records of the remote radar displays. In this paper I discuss a research project that would involve the quantification and analysis of all of the film records (1957–1990) from the eight radar stations on the Gulf coast in an effort to characterize long-term changes in the trans-Gulf spring migrations. Because most of the migrant songbirds breeding in eastern North America either cross the Gulf of Mexico or move up the Texas coast and the Florida peninsula in spring (Cooke 1904, Lowery 1945, 1951, Stevenson 1957), virtually all of their movements can be monitored by the coastal network of WSR-57 radars. Analysis of the film records should produce a data set that documents the numbers of birds moving into eastern North America each spring over the last 33 years. The data set can then be used as a dependent variable in analyses of the possible influences of several long-term environmental factors (e.g., tropical deforestation, climate change) on the temporal and spatial patterns of spring trans- and circum-Gulf migration over the last three decades.

Equipment and methods

The WSR-57 is a 10-cm wavelength (S-band) surveillance radar operated on two pulse lengths—0.5 sec and

4.0 sec. The longer pulse length is used because of increased sensitivity. The radar has a transmitter power of 500 kw, and the circular antenna 3.7 m in diameter projects a pencil beam of 2° beam width and completes 3 rpm. Although the range can be adjusted from 10 to 250 nautical miles, most of the film records have been made with the radar display on 125 nautical mile range. Although the radar antenna can be elevated from the horizontal, most of the film records have been made with the antenna at 0° elevation. Additional details of the WSR-57 radar can be found in Gauthreaux (1970, 1980).

Two distinct kinds of movement of passerine migrants can be recognized near the northern Gulf coast in spring (Gauthreaux 1971). The first is the arrival of trans-Gulf migrants (often flocks) usually during the daylight hours. The movements are easily recognized because of the characteristic pattern of echoes offshore on the radar screen (Fig. 2a). The second movement is the nocturnal exodus of migrants from the northern Gulf coast (Fig. 2b). These flights include trans-Gulf birds that have landed earlier in the day and migrants that have wintered in the area and are beginning their northward migration. The pattern of echoes on the radar screen is quite different from that produced by arriving trans-Gulf flights during the day. The echo pattern of the exodus is produced by birds flying individually in the night sky.

The range on the radar screen to which an echo pattern produced by migrating birds extends is in part a function of the number of birds migrating in the atmosphere, the altitudinal distribution of the birds, and the elevation of the radar antenna (Nisbet 1963, Gauthreaux 1970). The antenna of the WSR-57 is not elevated during routine surveillance so this variable can be eliminated as an influence. Only when flights are at very low altitudes are they below radar coverage, and these occur when birds encounter strong headwinds when crossing the Gulf. Because weather data are also collected for each day at each station, such occasions are easily noted. When flights are at unusually high altitudes they can be easily detected because of the characteristic "doughnut" display on the radar screen (Gauthreaux 1991). Consequently, the qualitative relationship between the dimensions of the radar display of a migratory flight and the number of birds in the flight is being used to determine the relative amounts of migration from the Gulf on a day-to-day and a year-to-year basis. Although this relationship is qualitative, the relationship is currently being quantified using direct visual means so that the range to which the echo pattern extends can be related quantitatively to the number of birds producing the pattern.

The film record for a given radar station from 1 March through 31 May is on approximately 13–15 100-ft

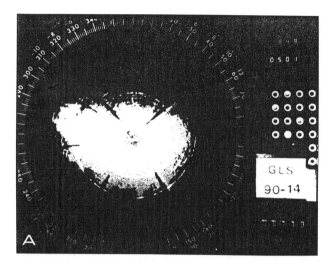

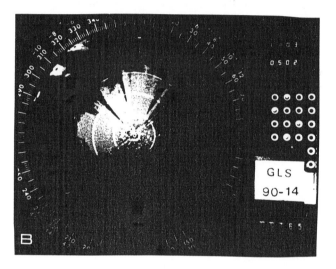

FIGURE 2. Photographs showing the echo pattern on the radar screen characteristic of (A) trans-Gulf migration and (B) the subsequent nocturnal exodus. Galveston, TX, 125 nautical mile range. (A) 1 May 1990, 18:49 GMT, (B) 2 May 1990, 02:03 GMT.

(30.4-m) rolls of film. When no weather echoes are within 125 nautical mile range of the radar, the remote radar display is photographed for one revolution of the antenna every 20 minutes. When weather echoes move into range, the interval between photographic exposures is shortened, and when severe weather is in the vicinity, the radar display might be photographed for every other revolution of the antenna.

During analysis, the radar films are viewed on a large screen editor, and each frame (exposure) has data on radar settings (range and attenuation settings) and the time (GMT) and date of the exposure. For each day the following information is recorded on a data sheet: month and date, time and range of echo pattern at the beginning, peak, and end of the exodus; time and range

of echo pattern at the beginning, peak, and end of a trans-Gulf flight; precipitation during exodus and trans-Gulf flights and amount (isolated, scattered, broken, solid); winds and precipitation over the Gulf of Mexico (poor, marginal, good, excellent conditions for a trans-Gulf flight—see Gauthreaux 1971).

When the spatial extent (range) of a trans-Gulf flight is compared to the spatial extent (range) of the subsequent exodus, the two are highly correlated (e.g., Fig. 3, Pearson product-moment correlation, 50 cases, $r = 0.7$, $P < 0.001$). Consequently, the information on spatial extent and duration of an exodus is useful in attempting to quantify a trans-Gulf flight when it is obscured by precipitation. Likewise, the delayed arrival of a trans-Gulf flight is clearly recognized when the arrival occurs during the evening. On such occasions the display of echoes on the radar screen is quite extensive, and the movement continues for a longer period of time (6–8 hr) than is usual for a regular exodus (2–3 hr). The analyses of the radar film records have only recently begun, so the following discussion is limited to some of the potential results of the analyses.

Results and discussion

Some of the preliminary results of the analyses are presented in Table 1, in which three years (1987–1989) of radar films have been analyzed for two radar stations (Lake Charles, LA, and Galveston, TX). In this analysis the presence or absence of a trans-Gulf flight on a date when conditions for a flight across the Gulf were good to excellent has been coded. The data are grouped into three periods: the last half of March, April and most of

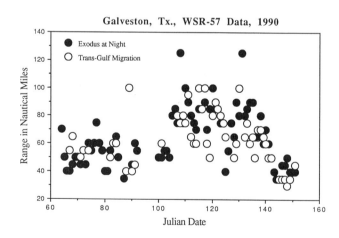

FIGURE 3. Scatter plot of trans-Gulf migrations and subsequent nocturnal exoduses at Galveston, TX, for the spring of 1990. The spatial extent of each movement displayed on the radar screen is coded as the maximum range that the echo pattern extended from the radar station.

TABLE 1.   Sample size (days sampled, *n*), and frequency of trans-Gulf flights (TGF) and exoduses (E) of migrants

Location and year	15 Mar–31 Mar			1 Apr–30 Apr			1 May–27 May		
	n	TGF	E	*n*	TGF	E	*n*	TGF	E
Lake Charles, LA									
1987	17	0	14	30	6	25	27	15	26
1988	17	0	2	30	13	20	27	6	23
1989	11	4	11	22	13	20	27	6	27
Galveston, TX									
1987	14	4	2	19	5	8	26	24	26
1988	14	3	8	30	19	22	27	17	23
1989	13	4	6	30	18	23	21	18	21

the month of May. Within a period the number of dates examined is given first, followed by the number of dates with trans-Gulf flights, and then the number of dates with exoduses. Trans-Gulf flights and exoduses did not occur on every date examined. Although the data do not provide quantitative information on the number of birds in the flight, they do indicate the seasonal temporal pattern of flights for these three years at these two radar stations. In Figure 4 the data are plotted in half-month periods for the Lake Charles, LA station, and in Figure 5 the data are plotted the same way for the Galveston, TX station. Although the data are very limited at this stage of analysis, the pattern of fewer trans-Gulf flights from the middle of March through the middle of April represents a change in the seasonal timing of trans-Gulf migration from that recorded from the late 1950s and early 1960s. Whether the same number of birds are crossing the Gulf in spring in fewer flights, or the number of birds crossing the Gulf has declined

over the last twenty years, cannot be answered with such data. Once the spatial extent of the displays of migration on the radar screen has been quantified, the answer will be forthcoming.

If one compares the percentage of days with trans-Gulf flights in the spring seasons of 1965–1967 with the percentage of days with trans-Gulf flights in the spring seasons of 1987–1989, at Lake Charles, LA, the decline over 20 years is almost 50%. If one examines the number of trans-Gulf flights that occurred in relation to the number of days when flights were possible (because of favorable weather) for the period 8 April–15 May for each year from 1965 to 1967 and from 1987 to 1989, the percentages are as follows: 1965—90%, 1966—95%, 1967—100%, 1987—36%, 1988—43%, and 1989—53%. Although these data are from only one radar station, they are suggestive, and analysis of the radar films for the other seven WSR-57 stations should clarify the picture considerably. It must also be remembered that

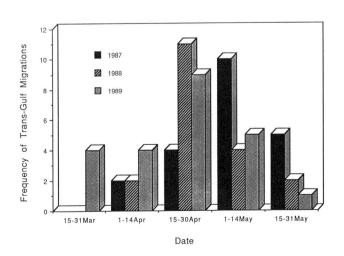

FIGURE 4. Seasonal timing of trans-Gulf flights for Lake Charles, LA.

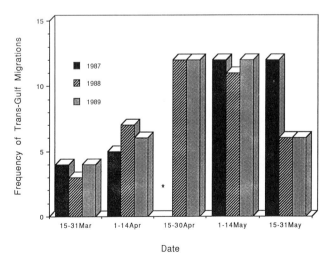

FIGURE 5. Seasonal timing of trans-Gulf flights for Galveston, TX

weather conditions over the Gulf of Mexico can cause considerable year-to-year variation in the amount of trans-Gulf migration. In 1987, virtually all the trans-Gulf migration that spring occurred in May, so it is not surprising that the lowest percentage of days with trans-Gulf migrations for the years 1987–1989 occurred in 1987. With a considerably larger data set (more years and stations), the influence of weather conditions over the Gulf can be measured and its contribution to the year-to-year variation in the patterns of trans-Gulf migration can be accurately assessed.

The analysis of the radar film record for all eight stations around the northern coast of the Gulf of Mexico can also provide additional information on the species composition of flight groups and their geographic origin. Because different species migrate at different times during the spring season, declines in the number of migrants crossing the Gulf during a particular period could be related to a particular group of species. Although very preliminary, the reduction in the number of trans-Gulf flights in early spring would suggest that those species that migrate in late March and early April are perhaps being impacted more than those species that migrate later in the spring. In addition to temporal information, the radar network can also provide data on flights from different geographic areas. The radar stations in Florida are more likely to detect migrations from the West Indies, whereas the Brownsville and Galveston stations would be biased toward detecting migrations from Central America. The analyses of the radar film records will be very time consuming, but the films offer a means of monitoring absolute and relative numbers of spring migrants returning to eastern North America. In addition, the analyses might offer the best means of assessing populations of trans-Gulf migrants over a broad geographic area over a period of 30 years. I know of no other data base that can accomplish this objective.

Acknowledgments

I would like to thank the numerous individuals at the National Climatic Data Center who have assisted me in the analysis of the radar films, particularly Ken Rudine, Sam McCown, and Bob Nagan. I also thank Carroll Belser for her long hours of assistance in reading the radar films and helping with the analysis. Katherine Luhring assisted in the preparation of the illustrations.

Literature cited

Cooke, W.W. 1904. Distribution and migration of North American warblers. U.S. Dept. Agric., Biol. Surv. Bull. No. 18.

Gauthreaux, S.A., Jr. 1970. Weather radar quantification of bird migration. *BioScience* 20:17–20.

———. 1971. A radar and direct visual study of passerine spring migration in southern Louisiana. *Auk* 88:343–365.

———. 1980. Direct visual and radar methods for the detection, quantification, and prediction of bird migration. Special Publ. Dept. Zoology, Clemson University, Clemson, S.C. (Available from the author.)

———. 1991. The flight behavior of migrating birds in changing wind fields: Radar and visual analyses. *Am. Zool.* 31:187–204.

Lowery, G.H., Jr. 1945. Trans-Gulf migration of birds and the coastal hiatus. *Wilson Bull.* 57:92–121.

———. 1951. A quantitative study of the nocturnal migration of birds. *Univ. Kansas Pub. Mus. Nat. Hist.* 3:361–472.

Nisbet, I.C.T. 1963. Quantitative study of migration with 23-centimeter radar. *Ibis* 105:435–460.

Stevenson, H.M. 1957. The relative magnitude of the trans-Gulf and circum-Gulf spring migrations. *Wilson Bull.* 69:39–77.

DAVID J.T. HUSSELL
MONICA H. MATHER
PAMELA H. SINCLAIR
Ontario Ministry of Natural Resources
Wildlife Research Section
P.O. Box 5000
Maple, Ontario, Canada L6A

Trends in numbers of tropical- and temperate-wintering migrant landbirds in migration at Long Point, Ontario, 1961–1988

Abstract. A multiple regression model with variables accounting for the effects of weather, lunar cycle, date, and multiple sites was used to produce annual population indices for 61 species of landbirds counted during migration at Long Point, Ontario in 1961–1988. Rates of change in these migration indices were positively correlated with Breeding Bird Survey (BBS) trends in Ontario for 45 species in 1967–1987, indicating that both sources of data reflect real population changes.

Our migration indices did not follow the pattern found by Robbins et al. (1989), who used BBS data from eastern North America to show that populations of migrants that winter in the Neotropics ("tropical migrants") increased in 1966–1978 and declined in 1978–1987, while migrants that winter in North America ("temperate migrants") did not change in the same periods. We found that nonsignificantly more species of tropical migrants decreased than increased in both periods, while temperate migrants decreased significantly in the first period and increased in the second.

Among 33 species of tropical migrants, migration indices of 29 decreased and only four increased from 1961 to 1988, a significantly greater proportion of decreases than in 23 temperate migrants, in which 12 decreased and 11 increased. Examination of trends within three decades (1961–1970, 1970–1979 and 1979–1988), however, indicated that many species fluctuated in numbers between 1961 and 1988: tropical migrants tended to decrease in the 1960s, increase in the 1970s and decrease in the 1980s, while many temperate migrants followed the opposite pattern. Fluctuations in numbers of many species appeared to be associated with periodic events, such as spruce budworm outbreaks on the breeding grounds and cold winters in the southern U.S. These fluctuations may explain some of the net changes that occurred from 1961 to 1988, but make it difficult to identify long-term trends. Nine of the 33 tropical migrants and three of the 23 temperate migrants had consistent downward trends over the 28 years, but the proportion of declining species did not differ significantly between the two groups. In our view, these declines are unexplained and require continued monitoring and study to identify whether habitat losses or other factors are responsible.

Sinopsis. Un modelo de regresión múltiple incluyendo variables con información sobre efectos climáticos, ciclo lunar, fecha y sitios múltiples, fue utilizado para producir índices poblacionales anuales para 61 especies de aves terrestres contadas durante su migración en Long Point, Ontario, entre 1961 y 1988. Las tasas de cambio en estos índices de migración estuvieron correlacionadas con las tendencias del Censo Norteamericano de Aves Anidantes (BBS) en Ontario para 43 especies entre 1967 y 1987, indicando que ambas fuentes de datos reflejan cambios poblacionales reales.

Nuestros índices de migración no siguieron el patrón encontrado por Robbins et al. (1989), quienes usaron datos del BBS del este de Norteamérica para mostrar que las poblaciones de migratorias que invernan en el neotrópico ("migratorias tropicales") incrementaron entre 1966 y 1978 y declinaron entre 1978 y 1987, mientras que las migratorias que invernan en Norteamérica ("migratorias boreales") no cambiaron en los mismos períodos. Nosotros encontramos que no hubo un número significativamente mayor de especies migratorias tropicales que declinaron en comparación con las que incrementaron en ambos períodos, mientras que las migratorias boreales declinaron significativamente en el primer período e incrementaron en el segundo.

Entre 33 especies de migratorias tropicales, los índices de migración de 28 decrecieron y solamente 5 incrementaron entre 1961 y 1988, lo cual es una proporción significativamente mayor de decrecimientos en comparación con las 23 especies migratorias boreales, de las cuales 11 decrecieron y 12 incrementaron. Sin embargo, el examen de tendencias dentro de las tres décadas (1961–1970, 1970–1979 y 1979–1988) indicó que muchas especies fluctuaron numéricamente entre 1961 y 1988: las migratorias tropicales tendieron a decrecer en los años sesenta, incrementar en los setenta y decrecer en los ochenta, mientras que muchas migratorias boreales siguieron el patrón opuesto. Las fluctuaciones numéricas de muchas especies parecieron estar asociadas con eventos periódicos, tales como sobreabundancia del gusano cogollero del abeto en las regiones de cría e inviernos fríos en el sur de los Estados Unidos. Estas fluctuaciones pueden explicar algunos de los cambios netos que ocurrieron entre 1961 y 1988, pero hacen difícil la identificación de tendencias a largo plazo. Nueve de 33 migratorias tropicales y 3 de las 23 migratorias boreales tuvieron tendencias decrecientes consistentes a través de los 28 años, pero la proporción de especies declinantes no difirió significativamente entre los dos grupos. A nuestro juicio, estas declinaciones siguen sin explicar y requieren la continuación de un seguimiento y estudio para identificar si la pérdida de habitat u otros factores son los responsables de las mismas.

Most of the continental and regional information on population trends of North American migrant birds has come from the Breeding Bird Survey (BBS; Erskine 1978, Robbins et al. 1986, Robbins et al. 1989). The first 15 years of the BBS (1965–1979) provided no evidence for declines in forest migrants, and species belonging to most taxonomic groups containing predominantly forest migrants (other than sparrows) increased (Hutto 1988). A recent analysis showed that among 62 species of migrants that breed in eastern North America and winter in the Neotropics ("tropical" or "Neotropical migrants"), a significantly greater proportion declined than increased in the period 1978–1987, while the reverse was true in the preceding period, 1966–1978 (Robbins et al. 1989). During the same periods, 14 temperate residents and 19 temperate-wintering migrants did not show a general pattern of increase or decrease. This was the first evidence of widespread regional declines in Neotropical migrants.

Counts of birds during migration provide an independent source of information on bird populations (Hussell 1981a, Bednarz et al. 1990). Counts taken at one or a few concentration points on the migration path often involve large numbers of individuals that may come from widespread source populations, although the precise locations of wintering or summering areas may not be known. Migration is strongly influenced by meteorological conditions (Richardson 1978), often resulting in high variances and skewed distributions in counts of migrants. Nevertheless, useful indices of population size can be extracted from migration counts, by using multiple regression to assign variation to seasonal, site, and environmental variables (Hussell 1981a, 1985).

Long Point Bird Observatory has conducted counts of migrant landbirds at Long Point, on the north shore of Lake Erie, since 1961. An earlier analysis of spring migration counts of six species at Long Point showed that migration indices for 1962–1979 were positively related to BBS indices from southern and central Ontario and Quebec (Hussell 1981a). The breeding grounds of nearly all the populations of birds migrating through Long Point are probably north of the Great Lakes, mainly in Ontario and western Quebec. Migration indices for species whose ranges are limited to the areas covered by the BBS should follow the same trends as those derived from the BBS, if both methods track population changes. In Ontario, BBS coverage extends only from

42° N to 50° N, but forested habitat occurs to 56° N. For species whose ranges extend north of the area covered by the BBS, the correlation between BBS and migration indices is likely to be weaker because the two methods do not sample the same populations. For some northern species, such as Gray-cheeked Thrush, Blackpoll Warbler and White-crowned Sparrow, comparisons between the BBS and migration indices are not possible because BBS coverage of the breeding ranges of these species is lacking or inadequate.

In this paper we present information on changes in abundance of tropical- and temperate-wintering migrants at Long Point for the years 1961–1988. Our information is both new and independent of BBS results, because it is derived from a different method of sampling populations and because it samples populations that are not represented in the BBS. Moreover, because our data collection started five years before the BBS, it has the potential to add a longer perspective to observed population changes. First, we relate trends in Long Point migration indices to rates of change in BBS population indices in Ontario in the period 1967–1987. Then, we examine our data to determine whether the trends in tropical and temperate migrants in eastern North America reported from the BBS for the years 1966–1978 and 1978–1987 (Robbins et al. 1989) are evident in the Long Point migration counts. Finally, we look for changes in populations of both groups of migrants over the whole period of our study (1961–1988) and attempt to interpret the observed patterns.

Materials and methods

BIRD MIGRATION COUNTS

The migration counts were "daily counts" (see below) of bird numbers recorded at the Long Point Bird Observatory for 1961–1988. Long Point is a 32-km sandy peninsula on the north shore of Lake Erie in Ontario, Canada (42°33' N, 80°10' W). Data were recorded from three sites on a total of 7,115 site-days between 15 March and 30 November, including 4,238 daily counts from site 1 on the tip of the point, 1,783 counts from site 2, 19 km west of site 1, and 1,094 counts from site 3, which is near the base of the point and 9 km west of site 2. Coverage was most complete in the main migration periods in April–May and August–October. No counts were available from any site in the spring of 1965, and there were very few counts from site 1 in spring 1973 and fall 1974. Coverage of site 2 was intermittent prior to 1975 and was entirely lacking in 1963 and the fall of 1973. Site 3 was in use only from 1980 to 1988, and the size of the area covered was reduced after 1983. In the final

five years, therefore, we treated this as a separate site, but assumed the same environmental and date effects as the original site 3 in the multiple regression analyses (see below).

For each species, a daily count consisted of an estimate of the number of birds occurring at a site on a particular day. This estimate was based on a morning count along a standard survey route, the day's banding totals, and other observations during the day. Observers (normally 1–5) were usually present at a site throughout the day, and in the evening they collaborated in making the day's count estimates. The procedure is explained in more detail elsewhere (Hussell 1981a). Daily counts sometimes included unidentified flycatchers of the genus *Empidonax*. To estimate numbers of Least and Yellow-bellied flycatchers, we prorated unidentified *Empidonax* in the daily counts in proportion to numbers of each species of *Empidonax* in the banded sample (provided that at least five were banded or not more than 10 were unidentified in the daily count). Also, any remaining unidentifed *Empidonax* recorded before 15 May and from 1–14 July were assumed to be Least Flycatchers (Hussell 1981b, 1982, unpubl. data).

The daily counts for each of 61 species at each site, after log transformation, were the dependent variables in the multiple regression analyses used to calculate abundance indices (see below). The species used in the analyses are mainly or exclusively nocturnal migrants, and we believe that daily counts largely represent birds that arrived at Long Point following a nocturnal flight, usually on the previous night.

Daily counts could be affected by bias or error in counting or estimation. Methods of estimating and recording counts remained essentially the same throughout the study period, with somewhat more rigorous standards being followed (through use of a field manual and improved data forms) from the mid-1970s. Many different people were involved in making estimates of bird numbers both within and across years. Bias attributable to individuals would occur mainly in years with relatively poor coverage (which were given low weights in the analyses). Such bias might contribute to variability in the indices, but is unlikely to influence long-term trends.

Long-term changes in bird numbers could be influenced by changes in habitat at the count sites. The water level of Lake Erie has changed markedly over the 28 years and influenced the habitat, particularly at sites 1 and 2, in two ways: by changing the size of ponds in the count areas and by erosion of the shoreline and vegetation. Lake levels were generally low in the 1960s, high in the 1970s and early 1980s, and low in the last two years. After erosion of a substantial section of the southern edge of site 2 in the early 1970s, that count area and its survey route was extended in a northeasterly direction to compensate for the lost area. Site 1 (eastern tip of point) suffered gradual erosion in the 1970s and early 1980s including loss of substantial numbers of small cottonwood trees. After major erosion in a storm in December 1985, this count area was extended in a westerly direction, and its survey route was modified to compensate for the losses.

WEATHER AND LUNAR CYCLE

Weather data used in the analyses were from the NOAA weather station at Erie, Pennsylvania, located at 42°05' N 80°11' W, about 50 km south of Long Point near the south shore of Lake Erie. For each day, six variables (capitalized codes are given below) were constructed from the hourly (Eastern Standard Time) weather records as follows: (1) temperature TP, difference from normal of the mean of dry bulb temperatures (°C) measured at 1900 (preceding day), 0100 and 0700; (normal temperature was calculated from a sixth power polynomial regression of mean temperature on day for all dates from 2 March to 30 November, 1961–1988); (2) precipitation PR, amount (mm of water) accumulated from 0600 to 1200; (3) visibility VS, mean of measurements (in km) at 0100, 0400, and 0700; (4) cloud CL, mean of opaque cloud cover in tenths at 0100, 0400, and 0700, (5) wind speed WS (km/hr), mean of measurements at 0100, 0400 and 0700, and (6) wind direction WD, measured on an 8-point scale (N, NE, E, etc.), derived from vector addition of wind speeds and directions (measured to the nearest 10°) at 0100, 0400, and 0700. An additional variable, days from full moon MN, was calculated from dates of full moon extracted from Meeus (1983).

CALCULATION OF ANNUAL INDICES OF ABUNDANCE

Annual indices of abundance for each of 61 species were calculated separately for each season (spring and fall) using multiple regression, in which the dependent variable was the log-transformed daily count, $\text{Ln}(N_{ijk}+1)$ where N_{ijk} is the daily count of the species present at site i, in year j, on day k. Except for differences in the sets of independent variables, the criteria for excluding data, and omission of the stepwise procedure for selecting variables (see below), the model and regression analysis methods were identical to those described in Hussell (1981a), which should be consulted for a more detailed description.

The model was a 2-way ANCOVA with year and site as factors and date, weather, and lunar variables as co-

variates, whose effects were specific to site. The annual index of abundance was derived from the adjusted mean for year, $\hat{\bar{Y}}_{.j}$, which represented the mean of the transformed daily count under standardized conditions of site, date, weather, and moon (represented by mean values of all independent variables except dummy variables for year). Annual indices in the original (untransformed) scale were calculated by back-transformation, as described in Hussell (1981a), except that the log-transformed adjusted means for year were first corrected upward by one-half the estimated variance about the regression, so that the corrected estimates in the original scale represent the mean instead of the median (Finney 1941, Baskerville 1972, Sprugel 1983, Hussell 1985).

For each species, spring and fall migration periods were chosen. For exclusively migratory species, each period was determined by first excluding records on late or early dates separated by more than four days from any other record in any year, and then selecting start and end dates representing the middle 98% of days on which the species was recorded. For species with locally resident populations at any site, inspection of a plot of counts vs. date enabled us to select arbitrary cut-off dates representing the start or end of migration. Few daily counts were from site 2 after 25 September. To avoid overfitting of sparse data, site 2 data were excluded from fall analyses for those species whose migration period started after 11 September (this provided at least 242 daily counts in fall at site 2 for each remaining species).

In the first run of the regression, the 66 independent variables consisted of three dummy variables for site (representing sites 2 and 3, plus site 3 in 1980–1983; site 1 was the reference site), 15 site-date interaction variables (five for each site), 39 site-weather interaction variables (13 for each site), six site-moon interaction variables (two for each site), and three terms for year (year, year², year³). Site-date, site-weather, and site-moon interaction variables represented effects of date, weather, and moon at sites 1, 2, and 3. First- to fifth-order date terms were used to provide a description of the change in number of migrants through the season. The 13 weather variables were TP, TP^2, CL, $\sqrt{VS}$, PR, and eight wind variables consisting of first- and second-order wind speed terms for four wind directions as described in Hussell (1981a). The two moon variables were MN and MN^2. All independent variables were retained in the regression (rather than using stepwise removal of nonsignificant variables as in Hussell 1981a), so that the final model was consistent among species. In this regression run, year was treated as a continuous variable rather than as a factor, to avoid excessive year-to-year differences in selection of data for the second run (see below), which could have biased subsequent weighted analyses of changes in the annual indices.

The primary purpose of the first regression run was to identify cases (i.e. transformed daily counts and the independent variables for the same site, year and day) that contributed to poor distribution of residuals, so that they could be dropped from the second run (Hussell 1981a). These were mainly cases at the start or end of the migration seasons, when few birds occurred. A second purpose was to provide an objective method for eliminating data for years or sites or species for which the data were inadequate to give an acceptable analysis, as judged by the distribution of residuals (poor fit) and/or number of cases relative to number of variables (overfit). In the second (final) run of the regression, therefore, cases that had predicted values of less than 0.2 birds in the first run were excluded. This criterion (0.2 birds) was more restrictive than that used in Hussell (1981a): it improved the distribution of residuals in the second run and provided an objective method for selecting suitable data. If a site had fewer than 100 cases remaining (with predicted values 0.2 birds in the first run), data from that site (and the dummy and interaction variables representing the site) were excluded, and the first run was repeated before proceeding. This eliminated data for one or more sites that recorded so few birds of a particular species as to be unsuitable for analysis and sometimes excluded data for an entire season (spring or fall) or a species.

The second regression run (with the reduced data set) was similar to the first, except that up to 27 dummy variables for year (representing 1962–1988, with 1961 as the reference) replaced the three year terms. All other variables were the same as in the first run. The total number of independent variables varied with species and season and ranged from 43 to 90 (median = 89), depending on the number of years and sites from which data were used. Fifty-five of 61 spring regressions and 40 of 60 fall regressions used data from all three sites. The median number of daily counts in the final regression runs was 1,265 in spring (minimum = 317, maximum = 2,276, n = 61) and 1,593 in fall (minimum = 331, maximum = 2,457, n = 60). The ratio of cases (daily counts) to independent variables in the spring regressions ranged from 4.9 to 25.6 (median = 14.2, 74% > 10.0), and in the fall regressions from 5.5 to 27.3 (median = 18.7, 87% > 10.0).

Coefficients of the dummy variables for year, estimated in the second regression, were used to calculate annual indices, as described previously. The "indices" referred to in the following sections were all derived from this regression procedure and are always *annual* indices for a *single species*, in *one season* (spring of fall). (See Figs. 1 and 2 for examples.)

RATES OF CHANGE IN ABUNDANCE INDICES

To determine the rate of change in abundance of a species over time we performed a weighted analysis of covariance on annual indices for selected periods of years, with season as a factor and year as a covariate. The natural logarithm of the back-transformed annual index was used as the dependent variable because it is expected that between-season differences among years in numbers of migrants are multiplicative rather than additive, if the same populations were sampled spring and fall. The regression coefficients of year then indicate the average proportionate (exponential) rate of change, spring and fall, which, multiplied by 100, becomes the percent rate of change per year. A weighted analysis, with weights proportional to the number of cases (i.e., number of site-days of counts) on which each annual index was based, was used because variances are likely to be inversely proportional to the number of cases. Annual indices based on fewer than 20 site-days of counts were excluded. Weights of the remaining indices were $n_j N / \Sigma n_j$, where n_j was the number of cases for index j, N was the number of indices, and the sum was taken over all indices (spring and fall) used in the regression. For some species or time periods, no acceptable data were available for one season, and the analysis became a weighted simple linear regression. Because a large number of species and variables were tested, the few significant nonlinear effects and interactions between year and season were considered spurious, and they were omitted from calculation of rates of change.

Rates of change were calculated over several periods that were of interest: (a) 1967–1987 for comparison with breeding bird survey results, (b) 1967–1978 and 1978–1987 for comparison with Robbins et al. (1989) and (c) 1961–1970, 1970–1979 and 1979–1988 to characterize changes within three 10-year periods. In addition, we calculated separate spring and fall rates of change for 1967–1987, for comparison with each other. The estimates of rates of change for 1967–1987 were considered to be acceptable if they were based on at least 12 indices (each with $n_j \geq 20$) in either season, including at least one each before 1970 and after 1984. Estimates for the other time periods were accepted if they were based on at least five indices, either spring or fall.

NET CHANGES IN ABUNDANCE, 1961–1988

A different approach was used to estimate changes between the start and end of the study period, because nonlinear effects became important over the longer time periods. We used indices for 1961–1970 and 1979–1988 to test the significance of the difference between estimates of the 1961 and 1988 indices derived from linear regression of index on year within each of the two ten-year periods. The model was: $I_{js} = a_1 + a_2Z_2 + a_3S + b_1Z_1X_{1j} + b_2Z_2X_{2j} + e_{js}$, where I_{js} is the natural logarithm of the back-transformed index for year j (61, 62, etc.) in season s, S is a dummy variable for season ($S = 0$ for spring, $S = 1$ for fall), Z_1 and Z_2 are dummy variables for period ($Z_1 = 1$ and $Z_2 = 0$ for 1961–1970; $Z_1 = 0$ and $Z_2 = 1$ for 1979–1988), $X_{1j} = j - 61$ and $X_{2j} = j - 88$; a_1, a_2, a_3, b_1 and b_2 are constants estimated by regression analysis and e_{js} is an error term representing unexplained variation. The coefficient a_2 is an estimate of the difference between the regression estimate of I_{js} in 1961 and that in 1988, and $a_2 \times 100/27$ is the estimated exponential percent rate of change per year.

We used a weighted analysis to estimate the regression coefficients, with weights calculated in the same way as for estimating rates of change. We checked whether there were significant interactions between season and time period. In only one species (Red-eyed Vireo) was a significant ($P < 0.05$) interaction found, indicating that the proportional difference between spring and fall indices differed between 1961–1970 and 1979–1988, so we estimated a_2 with the interaction included in the analysis. For all other species, interactions were nonsignificant and were omitted.

BREEDING BIRD SURVEY TRENDS IN ONTARIO

The Breeding Bird Survey measures breeding populations of many species from an annual roadside count along numerous routes throughout North America (Robbins et al. 1986). In Ontario, the BBS started in 1967 (Erskine 1978). For comparison with our migration indices, we used median annual rates of change for the years 1967–1987 for all routes in Ontario, calculated by the U.S. Fish and Wildlife Service using standard route regression methods (Sauer and Droege, this volume; Robbins et al. 1989; Geissler and Noon 1981; S. Droege, pers. comm.). Only species whose rates of change were based on at least 35 routes were included in our comparison.

CLASSIFICATION OF TROPICAL AND TEMPERATE MIGRANTS

We followed Robbins et al. (1989) in classifying 35 species as tropical and seven species as temperate migrants, for species that were common to both studies. We classified an additional three species as tropical migrants and 16 as temperate migrants in accordance with winter distributions (A.O.U. 1983, Root 1988). Species

wintering mainly north of 25° N were classified as temperate and all others were tropical migrants.

STATISTICAL ANALYSES AND TESTS

Multiple regressions and related analyses of the daily estimated totals were performed on a microcomputer using SAS (SAS Institute Inc. 1988). Most other analyses and tests were done in SPSS (Norusis/SPSS Inc. 1988).

Results

MIGRATION INDICES

Examples of spring and fall annual indices of abundance ("migration indices") for eight species of migrants at Long Point are shown in Figures 1 and 2. Each index represents the estimated mean number of birds per day per site that would have occurred if the site coverage, weather, and moon conditions had been identical in all years (i.e., the indices are corrected for the confounding effects of uneven site coverage and differing weather and moon conditions among years). For each season, differences in index values among years represent presumed population changes. Differences between spring and fall indices, however, do not indicate differences between spring and fall population sizes: they merely reflect different patterns of occurrence at Long Point and differences in site coverage between spring and fall. Results presented in the following sections refer to rates of change in these migration indices within specified time periods and to net changes from 1961 to 1988.

CORRELATION BETWEEN RATES OF CHANGE IN LONG POINT MIGRATION INDICES AND THE BBS IN ONTARIO

Rates of change in spring and fall migration indices were positively correlated in 42 species for which acceptable estimates were available for both seasons in 1967–1987 (Spearman rank correlation $r_s = 0.462$, $n = 42$, $P = 0.0021$), so we used combined rates of change for spring and fall indices in all subsequent analyses. To determine if the BBS and migration indices estimated similar population changes, we calculated rates of change in migration indices for 1967–1987 for 45 species for which BBS rates of change for Ontario were also available. Rates of change in combined spring and fall indices were positively correlated with those for the BBS over this time period (Fig. 3, $r_s = 0.599$, $n = 45$, $P = 0.0001$).

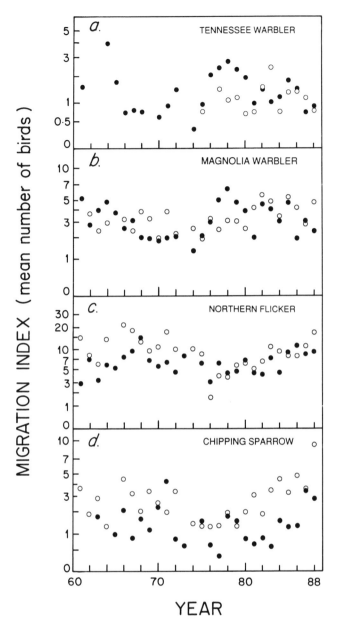

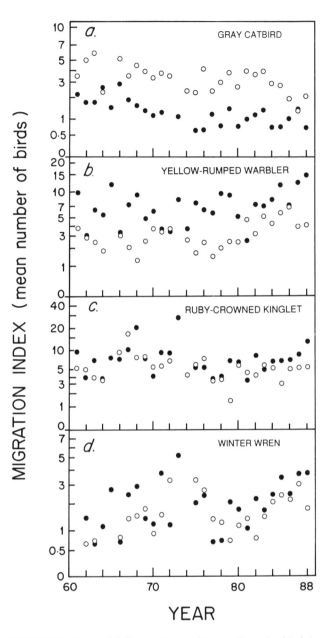

FIGURE 1. Spring and fall migration indices: *a*, Tennessee Warbler; *b*, Magnolia Warbler; *c*, Northern Flicker; *d*, Chipping Sparrow. *Open circles* = spring; *solid circles* = fall. Indices based on fewer than 20 site-days of counts were excluded. The migration index represents the estimated mean number of birds per site-day for standard conditions (i.e., identical coverage by site and date with identical moon and weather).

FIGURE 2. Spring and fall migration indices: *a*, Gray Catbird; *b*, Yellow-rumped Warbler; *c*, Ruby-crowned Kinglet; *d*, Winter Wren. See Figure 1 for further explanation.

RATES OF CHANGE IN THE BBS AND MIGRATION INDICES, 1966–1978 AND 1978–1987

Using BBS data from eastern North America, Robbins et al. (1989) showed that most Neotropical migrants increased in the period 1966–1978 and most decreased in 1978–1987, but no significant changes were found in

temperate-wintering migrants. Their results are summarized in Figure 4 (upper).

We examined changes in Long Point migration indices for 34 tropical migrants and 23 temperate migrants for which adequate data were available for both of the same two time periods. Our results, summarized in Figure 4 (lower), showed that nonsignificantly more

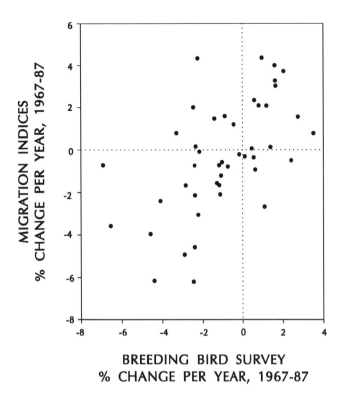

FIGURE 3. Rates of change in combined spring and fall migration indices at Long Point versus trends in the Breeding Bird Survey in Ontario, 1967–1987. Each point represents one species. (Spearman rank correlation, $r_s = 0.599$, $n = 45$, $P = 0.0001$).

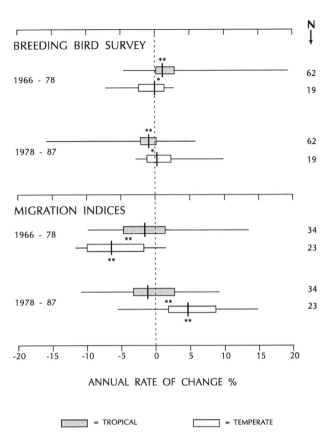

FIGURE 4. Annual rates of change for species of tropical and temperate migrants in the Breeding Bird Survey and Long Point migration indices in 1966–1978 and 1978–1987. Vertical lines, horizontal bars and horizontal lines indicate median, middle 50% and range of values, respectively; N = number of species. Asterisks above or below medians indicate significance (* = $P < 0.05$, ** = $P < 0.01$) of difference of the median from zero (binomial test); asterisks between medians indicate significance of difference between tropical and temperate migrants (Mann-Whitney U-test). BBS results are from Robbins et al. (1989).

tropical migrants decreased than increased in both 1966–1978 and 1978–1987 (in both periods, 21 decreased and 13 increased, binomial test $P = 0.230$). By contrast, significantly more temperate migrants decreased in 1966–1978 (19 decreases vs. 4 increases, $P = 0.003$) and significantly more increased in 1978–1987 (4 decreases vs. 19 increases, $P = 0.003$). The same patterns were apparent when we considered only the 31 tropical and eight temperate migrants that were common to both the BBS (Robbins et al. 1989) and the Long Point data sets, but none was significant. Among the 31 tropical migrants in 1978–1987, however, the proportion of declines (68%) was similar to that reported by Robbins et al. (1989) from the BBS (71%) and approached significance (10 increases, 21 decreases, binomial test $P = 0.073$).

RATES OF CHANGE IN MIGRATION INDICES, 1961–1970, 1970–1979, AND 1979–1988

In 1961–1970, eight tropical migrants had significant decreases while only one had a significant increase (Table 1). Moreover, the proportion of decreases (re-

gardless of individual significance) was significantly greater than that of the increases in 1961–1970 (Fig. 5, 31 decreased, 2 increased, binomial test, $P < 0.0001$). In 1970–1979, most tropical migrants increased, and 10 showed significant increases while only two declined (Table 1). The proportion of increases was significantly greater than decreases in this decade (Fig. 5, 9 decreased, 24 increased, $P = 0.015$). In 1979–1988, another reversal was detected in the direction of population change in tropical migrants with seven significant decreases and four increases (Table 1). Although the proportions of decreases and increases did not differ significantly (Fig. 5, 22 decreases, 16 increases, $P = 0.417$), the median rate of change did differ significantly from

TABLE 1. Rates of change within three decades and overall change 1961–1988 in migration indices of 38 tropical and 23 temperate migrants

Species	Rate of change[a] %/yr			Net change[b] %/yr
	1961–70	1970–79	1979–88	1961–88
TROPICAL MIGRANTS				
Black-billed Cuckoo *Coccyzus erythropthalmus*	-9.1		10.2	-3.9
Eastern Wood-Pewee *Contopus virens*	-6.6	3.3	7.5**	0.8
Yellow-bellied Flycatcher *Empidonax flaviventris*	-15.1*	13.2**	-6.4	-5.4**
Least Flycatcher *Empidonax minimus*	-6.7	8.4**	-0.9	-2.3*
Great Crested Flycatcher *Myiarchus crinitus*		7.4	2.0	
Veery *Catharus fuscescens*	-6.3	1.4	-4.2	-3.3**
Gray-cheeked Thrush *Catharus minimus*	-7.0	-10.8*	3.9	-3.4**
Swainson's Thrush *Catharus ustulatus*	-7.8*	1.2	-3.3	-2.9**
Wood Thrush *Hylocichla mustelina*	-9.4	-0.6	-15.0**	-6.0**
Gray Catbird *Dumetella carolinensis*	-3.7	-1.0	-5.6*	-3.5**
Solitary Vireo *Vireo solitarius*			1.0	
Warbling Vireo *Vireo gilvus*			10.2**	
Philadelphia Vireo *Vireo philadelphicus*			7.8	
Red-eyed Vireo *Vireo olivaceus*	-2.0	0.3	1.6	-0.6
Tennessee Warbler *Vermivora peregrina*	-13.3	16.5**	-4.5	-2.3
Nashville Warbler *Vermivora ruficapilla*	-5.0*	2.0	-6.3	-2.9**
Yellow Warbler *Dendroica petechia*	-3.6	9.1*	4.2	1.2
Chestnut-sided Warbler *Dendroica pensylvanica*	-6.3	5.1	3.0	-0.8
Magnolia Warbler *Dendroica magnolia*	-8.9**	9.8**	-2.0	-1.4
Cape May Warbler *Dendroica tigrina*	-10.3	13.3**	4.6	0.8
Black-thr. Blue Warbler *Dendroica caerulescens*	-1.6	4.3	-1.1	-0.2
Black-throated Green Warbler *Dendroica virens*	-1.3	4.2	-8.2*	-1.5
Blackburnian Warbler *Dendroica fusca*	-8.1*	14.7*	-0.8	-0.6
Palm Warbler *Dendroica palmarum*	-6.6*	-1.0	8.4*	-1.5
Bay-breasted Warbler *Dendroica castanea*	-12.2**	19.8**	-5.1	-0.8
Blackpoll Warbler *Dendroica striata*	-1.7	4.8	6.0	0.7
Black-and-white Warbler *Mniotilta varia*	-6.2	0.4	1.3	-0.9
American Redstart *Setophaga ruticilla*	-6.7*	4.8	-3.3	-2.2**
Ovenbird *Seiurus aurocapillus*	-5.7	0.2	-6.4*	-2.9**
Northern Waterthrush *Seiurus noveboracensis*	-6.1	-1.7	-10.0*	-4.0*
Mourning Warbler *Oporornis philadelphia*			6.8	
Common Yellowthroat *Geothlypis trichas*	-1.8	-1.9	-1.1	-1.6
Wilson's Warbler *Wilsonia pusilla*	-5.9	9.1*	-5.3	-3.2**
Canada Warbler *Wilsonia canadensis*	-7.3	5.6*	-8.3*	-3.7**
Scarlet Tanager *Piranga olivacea*	15.3*	-10.2	-11.5*	-1.4
Rose-breasted Grosbeak *Pheucticus ludovicianus*	-2.0	-4.9	-4.6	-2.4*

NOTE: * = P < 0.05; ** = P < 0.01. Blanks indicate data were inadequate to measure rate of change.

a. Estimated as described in "Rates of change in abundance indices" (Materials and Methods).

b. Estimated as described in "Net changes in abundance, 1961–1988" (Materials and Methods).

TABLE 1—*Continued next page*

TABLE 1—*Continued*

Species	Rate of change[a] %/yr			Net change[b] %/yr
	1961–70	1970–79	1979–88	1961–88
Lincoln's Sparrow *Melospiza lincolnii*	-2.6	0.3	-0.2	-0.6
Northern Oriole *Icterus galbula*	1.0	-8.2**	7.9**	-0.3
TEMPERATE MIGRANTS				
Yellow-bellied Sapsucker *Sphyrapicus varius*	1.6	0.7	0.7	-1.8*
Northern Flicker *Colaptes auratus*	5.3	-9.8*	9.5**	1.9*
Eastern Phoebe *Sayornis phoebe*	4.2	-5.9	7.7*	3.2
Brown Creeper *Certhia americana*	5.2	-2.0	3.7	2.2
House Wren *Troglodytes aedon*	1.8	-7.5*	4.2	0.3
Winter Wren *Troglodytes troglodytes*	6.5	-4.5	10.7**	4.7**
Golden-crowned Kinglet *Regulus satrapa*	7.1	-13.6*	11.1*	5.6*
Ruby-crowned Kinglet *Regulus calendula*	4.4	-8.5*	5.4*	0.8
Hermit Thrush *Catharus guttatus*	-4.7	0.5	3.2	-0.0
American Robin *Turdus migratorius*	6.7	-5.8*	13.9**	4.8**
Brown Thrasher *Toxostoma rufum*	2.8	-12.0**	-3.1	-3.3**
Yellow-rumped Warbler *Dendroica coronata*	-0.2	0.7	8.7**	2.6*
Rufous-sided Towhee *Pipilo erythrophthalmus*	0.4	-14.8**	-3.4	-4.1**
Chipping Sparrow *Spizella passerina*	2.2	-8.4	15.3**	3.3**
Field Sparrow *Spizella pusilla*	1.2	-7.5	8.5**	0.9
Vesper Sparrow *Pooecetes gramineus*	-8.2		21.9*	-1.9
Savannah Sparrow *Passerculus sandwichensis*	-3.0	-3.2	4.4	-1.1
Fox Sparrow *Passerella iliaca*	-6.7	3.2	9.5	-3.0
Song Sparrow *Melospiza melodia*	0.3	-8.2*	5.7	-0.9
Swamp Sparrow *Melospiza georgiana*	0.9	-4.2	3.2	-1.7
White-throated Sparrow *Zonotrichia albicollis*	-4.0	-2.7	-2.7	-2.6*
White-crowned Sparrow *Zonotrichia leucophrys*	3.8	-4.5	1.1	-1.0
Dark-eyed Junco *Junco hyemalis*	-1.6	-4.0	4.5	-0.1

NOTE: * = P < 0.05; ** = P < 0.01. Blanks indicate data were inadequate to measure rate of change.

a. Estimated as described in "Rates of change in abundance indices" (Materials and Methods).

b. Estimated as described in "Net changes in abundance, 1961–1988" (Materials and Methods).

that in the preceding period for 33 species with data in both periods (median rate of change = 3.27 in 1970–1979, –1.99 in 1979–1988, $P = 0.002$, Wilcoxon matched-pairs signed-ranks test).

Among 23 temperate migrants, none increased or decreased significantly in 1961–1970 (Table 1). Increases outnumbered decreases by 16 to 7 in this period, but the proportions of decreases and increases did not differ significantly (Fig. 5, binomial test, $P = 0.093$). In 1970–1979, there were eight significant decreases in temperate migrants and no significant increases (Table 1). Likewise, significantly more overall decreases than increases were found in the 1970s (Fig. 5, 18 decreases, 4 increases, $P = 0.004$). By contrast, in 1979–1988, 10 temperate migrants increased significantly, but none

decreased significantly (Table 1). Of the 23 species of temperate migrants, 20 increased in this period (Fig. 5, $P = 0.0005$).

Eight sequences of positive or negative change are possible within the three decades (Table 2, column 1). If changes occurred randomly and independently within time periods and among species, we would expect equal numbers of species in each of the eight categories. Species were not equally distributed among the change categories (Table 2, $\chi^2 = 37.0$, $P < 0.005$). Moreover, the tropical and temperate migrants considered separately were more strongly nonrandomly distributed than both groups together (Table 2). Tropical migrants were heavily represented (30 of 32 species) among the four categories involving declines in the 1960s, and 16 of

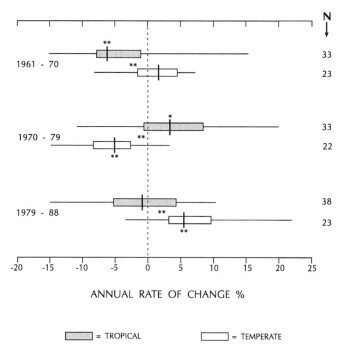

ANNUAL RATE OF CHANGE %

▨ = TROPICAL   ▢ = TEMPERATE

FIGURE 5. Annual rates of change in Long Point migration indices for tropical and temperate migrants in 1961–1970, 1970–1979, and 1979–1988. See Figure 4 for key to format.

TABLE 2. Patterns of change in migration indices during three periods: 1961–1970, 1970–1979, 1979–1988

Change pattern	No. of species		
	Tropical	Temperate	Total
− − −	5	1	6
− − +	2	2	4
− + −	16	0	16
+ − −	1	2	3
+ + −	0	0	0
+ − +	1	13	14
− + +	7	3	10
+ + +	0	1	1
TOTAL	32	22	54
χ^2	52.0	46.4	37.0
P	< 0.005	< 0.005	< 0.005

NOTE: Change pattern indicates direction of change (+ or −) in 61–70, 70–79, and 79–88, respectively. No. of species from Table 1, for species with estimates for all 3 time periods. χ^2 for equal expected frequencies among change pattern categories.

32 species (50%) decreased in the 1960s, increased in the 1970s, and decreased again in the 1980s. Temperate migrants tended to show the opposite pattern: 13 of 22 species (59%) increased in the 1960s, decreased in the 1970s, and increased again in the 1980s.

NET CHANGE IN MIGRATION INDICES, 1961–1988

Among 33 species of tropical migrants, 29 (88%) decreased and only four (12%) increased from 1961 to 1988. Moreover, 14 of the decreases, but none of the increases, were significant ($P < 0.05$, Table 1). Twelve (52%) of the 23 temperate migrants declined while 11 (48%) increased. Four of the declines and six of the increases in temperate migrants were significant. Tropical migrants had a significantly greater proportion of decreases than did temperate migrants ($\chi^2 = 8.81$, d.f.= 1, $P < 0.005$).

Discussion

MIGRATION INDICES AS INDICATORS OF POPULATION CHANGE

The positive correlation between BBS and migration estimates of rates of population change provides further evidence that the Long Point migration indices reflected population levels of migrants, as reported previously (Hussell 1981a). Moreover, the strong positive associa-

tion between spring and fall estimates of rates of change of migration indices provides additional support for this assumption.

If migration indices and BBS indices from the presumed breeding area were perfectly correlated, we would conclude that both methods are excellent indicators of population levels and that migration indices provide no information additional to the BBS. We suggest that an imperfect correlation is expected, because of sampling errors in determining both sets of indices and because migration indices and the BBS sample different populations. Therefore, we believe that Long Point migration indices provide additional information to that from the BBS on population changes of birds that occur in migration at Long Point.

Although changes in habitat at the count sites on Long Point could affect bird numbers, it is difficult to argue that these can account for long-term changes in migration indices reported in this paper, because some species such as Yellow-bellied Sapsucker, Veery, and Nashville Warbler declined, while related species with similar habitat requirements such as Northern Flicker, Hermit Thrush and Yellow Warbler increased or remained unchanged. Use of data from three sites to produce a composite index will have reduced the influence of habitat changes at any one site. Moreover, positive correlations between BBS and migration indices show that effects of habitat change at the count sites, if any, were not large enough to mask population changes.

RATES OF CHANGE IN BBS AND MIGRATION INDICES, 1966–1978 AND 1978–1987

Our analysis of Long Point migration data for Neotropical migrants provided only partial and weak support for the pattern of increases in 1966–1978 and subsequent declines in 1978–1987 reported by Robbins et al. (1989) from BBS results for all of eastern North America. We showed that temperate migrants decreased significantly in 1966–1978 and increased significantly in 1978–1987, in contrast to the lack of change in both periods from BBS results. These discrepancies could be attributed to one or more factors. The two studies sampled different (but overlapping) source populations and species. We recorded a similar, but marginally nonsignificant, proportion of declines in the second period in the 31 tropical migrants that were among the 62 considered in the BBS study, indicating some consistency between the two sets of results. Also, Robbins et al. (1989) chose 1978 to separate the two periods after noting that many Neotropical species in their data peaked in that year. This choice predisposed their analysis to find the increases and declines that they reported for tropical migrants, but did not dictate any pattern for the temperate migrants. If populations in the Great Lakes region peaked at a different time than the subcontinental populations considered in the BBS study, then trends before and after 1978 might be obscured or enhanced depending on when the peaks and troughs occurred.

PATTERNS OF CHANGE IN MIGRATION INDICES 1961–1988

Over the 28-year period, net declines were associated with wintering area, with 88% of tropical migrants but only 52% of temperate migrants decreasing. Examination of changes within the three decades, however, indicates that many species fluctuated in abundance (Table 2). Tropical migrants tended to decrease in the 1960s, increase in the 1970s, and decrease again in the 1980s. This pattern is evident, for example, in the Tennessee and Magnolia warblers (Fig. 1a,b). The opposite pattern occurred in several temperate migrants, including the Northern Flicker and Chipping Sparrow (Fig. 1c,d), which increased in the 1960s, decreased in the 1970s and increased in the 1980s. Based on this pattern, net changes in tropical migrants from 1961–1988 would tend to be negative, as both the first and last decades had declining trends. Likewise, the temperate migrants would tend to show increases, as trends in the first and last decades were both increasing. We conclude that overall declines or increases from 1961 to 1988 in species showing such fluctuations do not necessarily indicate persistent changes in population levels, but are more likely to represent the normal population dynamics of the species.

Among 62 Neotropical migrants whose BBS trends were reported by Robbins et al. (1989), 34 that increased in 1966–1978 subsequently decreased in 1978–1987. These populations might also be undergoing fluctuations similar to those found in the migration indices, but the BBS data probably did not start early enough to document adequately any changes in the 1960s. Among the 19 of those 34 fluctuating species included in our analyses, 17 decreased at Long Point in the 1960s. Robbins et al. (1989) reported only 10 Neotropical migrants that declined in both of their study periods. Seven of those 10 species were not among the ones we studied because their breeding ranges are primarily south of Ontario.

Consistent declines in migration indices throughout all three decades and a significant decrease from 1961–1988, might indicate noncyclic or persistent declines in populations. The five species showing such continuous negative trends consisted of four Neotropical migrants: Gray Catbird (Fig. 2a), Wood Thrush, Northern Waterthrush, and Rose-breasted Grosbeak; plus one temperate migrant: the White-throated Sparrow (Table 1). In addition, seven other migrants had a weak (< 4.0% per year) and nonsignificant increase in one decade combined with a large (> 2.5% per year), highly significant negative change between 1961 and 1988. These species did not show the strongly fluctuating patterns typical of many other migrants. They consisted of five Neotropical migrants: Veery, Gray-cheeked Thrush, Swainson's Thrush, Nashville Warbler, and Ovenbird; and two temperate migrants: Rufous-sided Towhee and Brown Thrasher (Table 1). Using the same criteria, in reverse, to identify long-term increases, only the Yellow-rumped Warbler showed signs of a persistent substantial increase, but most of its increase occurred after 1980 (Fig. 2b, Table 1).

In summary, we conclude that nine of 33 tropical (27%) and three of 23 temperate (13%) species showed persistent population declines, but tropical migrants were not undergoing such changes significantly more than temperate migrants ($\chi = 1.63$, d.f. = 1, $P > 0.10$). Nevertheless, these long-term changes are unexplained and require continued monitoring and study to identify causes. Notably, all four of the Neotropical-migrant thrushes showed long-term declines, but the Hermit Thrush and American Robin, both temperate migrants, did not.

CAUSES OF POPULATION CHANGES

Populations of migrants might be affected by conditions on the breeding grounds, on the wintering range or along the migration routes. They might be influenced by temporary or periodic events, such as variation in food abundance or weather, or by more permanent, nonperiodic changes. Nonperiodic influences could include changes in habitat availability resulting from natural or human-induced causes, including habitat destruction and climate change. Nevertheless, habitat loss will be reflected in decreased populations only if populations are limited by habitat availability in the season in which that habitat is occupied.

We have very limited understanding of the population dynamics of small landbird migrants on either a regional or continental scale. The BBS has provided some of the first wide-scale information on populations of North American birds and has demonstrated patterns that demand explanation. Likewise our migration indices demonstrated population changes that remain to be explained. An appreciation both of the potential complexity of influences on populations of migrant birds and of our ignorance of the subject, indicates that we should be cautious in interpreting the observed patterns and should not expect to find single causes to explain them.

Our data indicated that tropical and temperate migrant populations tended to fluctuate in opposite directions (Fig. 5, Table 2). What could cause these fluctuations? Four tropical migrants showing large fluctuations, including significant double-digit percentage rates of increase in the 1970s, were the Tennessee, Cape May, Blackburnian and Bay-breasted warblers. Three of these four showed similar changes in the BBS (Robbins et al. 1989). All are known to respond strongly to outbreaks of spruce budworm (*Choristoneura fumiferana*) (Kendeigh 1947, Morris et al. 1958, Welsh and Fillman 1980, Welsh 1987), and their recent population changes correspond to widespread outbreaks that peaked in Ontario in 1980 and in the remainder of eastern Canada in 1975 (data from annual forest insect and disease surveys, Canadian Forestry Service). The similar pattern of change recorded in the Blackpoll Warbler by the BBS suggests that its populations might also respond to an abundance of spruce budworm in those parts of its range monitored by the BBS. Other warblers showing similar but less marked changes in migration indices include the Nashville, Magnolia, Black-throated Blue, Black-throated Green, Wilson's, and Canada warblers, American Redstart, and Ovenbird. These results support the suggestion that populations of nearly all warblers might be affected to some degree by spruce budworm outbreaks (D.A. Welsh, pers. comm.). The Least and Yellow-bellied flycatchers fluctuated in the same way as the "budworm warblers" and we suspect that they might also benefit from outbreaks, perhaps by feeding on the adult insects.

Some temperate migrants also feed on the spruce budworm (Crawford et al. 1983, Crawford and Jennings 1989) but their populations did not vary in the same way as those of tropical migrants. Several of the smaller temperate migrants, including the two kinglets and the

Winter Wren, were adversely affected by cold winters in the southern United States in 1976–1977 and 1977–1978 (Robbins et al. 1986), contributing to overall declines in that decade. The effects of those two winters and the wide fluctuations of populations of these species are also apparent in our results (Fig. 2c,d). Declines in other temperate migrants are less easy to attribute to winter weather, although there might have been some impact of severe winters.

The tendency for tropical and temperate migrants to fluctuate in opposite directions suggests the possibility of competitive interactions between these two groups. Direct evidence is lacking for this, however, and there are theoretical reasons for thinking that populations of tropical and temperate migrants are not closely linked to each other (Ricklefs, this volume). It is more likely that long-distance and short-distance migrants are simply subject to differing factors that affect survival and reproductive rates, similar to those conferring advantages and disadvantages to migration and residency (O'Connor 1985). The two groups are clearly not ecologically homogeneous, with more ground-feeding birds (mainly sparrows) among the temperate migrants and many more foliage gleaners (mainly warblers and vireos) and flycatchers among the tropical migrants. Temperate migrants face the possibility of adverse conditions on the wintering range in some years. Tropical migrants escape this by travelling longer distances to what are presumably more predictable winter habitats, but even tropical habitats can be subject to variable conditions. The Sahel drought in Africa and El Niño events in the Pacific have both had extreme effects on mortality or reproductive success of some tropical landbird populations (Lövei 1989, Grant 1986).

In summary, several different factors could have effects that produce large short-term fluctuations in populations of landbird migrants. Variations in some of these factors are consistent with observed patterns of abundance in migrant birds. Because most small landbirds have short longevities and moderate-to-high reproductive rates, we expect to find large year-to-year changes in populations, and the effects of periodic perturbations in the environment are likely to be short-lived, unless the perturbations themselves extend over several years. Major habitat changes caused by humans, although they might be more rapid today than formerly, are nevertheless relatively slow. Given the large fluctuations in populations that can be attributed to short-term or periodic events, it is difficult both to identify longer-term trends and to associate them with habitat changes. Many tropical migrants had relatively low populations in the late 1960s and early 1970s (this study, Robbins et al. 1989), and subsequent large increases clearly indicate that those populations were not limited by habitat availability at that time, but we cannot infer that habitat limited populations at their peak levels in the late 1970s and early 1980s. The most likely candidates for showing longer-term effects of habitat loss or degradation are the nine Neotropical and three temperate migrants that had consistent declines in migration indices from 1961 to 1988. Whether these changes reflect the effects of habitat loss on the summer or winter ranges, along the migration routes, or at all, remains an open question, which warrants further study.

Acknowledgments

Thanks to Long Point Bird Observatory (LPBO), including many staff and numerous volunteers, for collecting and providing the counts of migrant birds. Data were entered into computer files at Queen's University, Kingston, by Patricia Slavin. R.D. Montgomerie provided facilities at Queen's University and Charles Francis gave freely of his expertise in responding to many requests for data. Jon McCracken and Beverly Collier assisted with checking original records at LPBO. Sam Droege provided BBS trend results for Ontario. Bruce Pond compiled the weather data and helped in many other ways. Erica Dunn and Bette Wilkinson assisted with preparation of the manuscript. Audrey Chui drew the figures. Our thanks to Erica Dunn, Brian Collins, John Hagan, Paul Kerlinger, John Richardson and an anonymous reviewer for constructive comments on drafts of the manuscript. Data entry was funded by an Environmental Youth Corps grant from the Ontario Ministry of Natural Resources to LPBO, and analysis was funded by the Ontario Ministry of Natural Resources. This paper is a publication of the Long Point Bird Observatory and is Ontario Ministry of Natural Resources Wildlife Research Section Contribution No. 89-06.

Literature cited

American Ornithologists' Union. 1983. *Check-list of North American Birds.* 6th ed. Washington: American Ornithologists' Union.

Bednarz, J.C., D. Klem, Jr., L.J. Goodrich, and S.E. Senner. 1990. Migration counts of raptors at Hawk Mountain, Pennsylvania as indicators of population trends, 1934–1986. *Auk* 107:96–109.

Baskerville, G.L. 1972. Use of logarithmic regression in estimation of plant biomass. *Can. J. Forestry* 2:49–53.

Crawford, H.S., and D.T. Jennings. 1989. Predation by birds on spruce budworm *Choristoneura fumiferana:* Functional, numerical and total responses. *Ecology* 70:152–163.

Crawford, H.S., R.W. Titterington, and D.T. Jennings. 1983. Bird predation and spruce budworm populations. *J. Forestry* 81:433–435.

Erskine, A.J. 1978. *The First Ten Years of the Co-operative Breeding Bird Survey in Canada.* Can. Wildl. Serv. Rep. Series 42.

Finney, D.J. 1941. On the distribution of a variate whose logarithm is normally distributed. *J. Royal Stat. Soc.* Supplement 7: 155–161.

Geissler, P.H., and B.R. Noon. 1981. Estimates of avian population trends from the North American Breeding Bird Survey. Pages 42–51 in *Estimating Numbers of Terrestrial Birds,* C.J. Ralph and M.J. Scott, eds. Studies in Avian Biology No. 6.

Grant, P.R. 1986. *Ecology and Evolution of Darwin's Finches.* Princeton: Princeton University Press.

Hussell, D.J.T. 1981a. The use of migration counts for detecting population levels. Pages 92–102 in *Estimating Numbers of Terrestrial Birds,* C.J. Ralph and M.J. Scott, eds. Studies in Avian Biology No. 6.

———. 1981b. Migrations of the Least Flycatcher in southern Ontario. *J. Field Ornithol.* 52:97–111.

———. 1982. Migrations of the Yellow-bellied Flycatcher in southern Ontario. *J. Field Ornithol.* 53:223–234.

———. 1985. Analysis of hawk migration counts for monitoring population levels. *Proc. Hawk Migration Conf.* 4:243–254.

Hutto, R.L. 1988. Is tropical deforestation responsible for the reported declines in neotropical migrant populations? *Am. Birds* 42:375–379.

Kendeigh, S.C. 1947. *Bird Population Studies in the Coniferous Forest Biome during a Spruce Budworm Outbreak.* Ontario Department of Lands and Forests, Research Division, Biol. Bull. 1.

Lövei, G. 1989. Passerine migration between the Palearctic and Africa. *Current Ornithol.* 6:143–174.

Meeus, J. 1983. *Astronomical Tables for the Sun, Moon and Planets.* Richmond, Va.: Willman-Bell Inc.

Morris, R.F., W.F. Cheshire, C.A. Miller, and D.G. Mott, 1958. The numerical response of avian and mammalian predators during a gradation of spruce budworm. *Ecology* 39:487–494.

Norusis, M.J./SPSS Inc. 1988. *SPSS/PC+ V2.0 Base Manual for the IBM PC/XT/AT and PS/2.* Chicago: SPSS Inc.

O'Connor, R.J. 1985. Behavioural regulation of bird populations: A review of habitat use in relation to migration and residency. Pages 105–142 in *Behavioural Ecology: Ecological Consequences of Adaptive Behavior,* R.M. Sibly and R.H. Smith, eds. Oxford: Blackwell Scientific Publications.

Richardson, W.J. 1978. Timing and amount of bird migration in relation to weather: A review. *Oikos* 30:224–272.

Root, T. 1988. *Atlas of Wintering North American Birds.* Chicago: University of Chicago Press.

Robbins, C.S., D. Bystrak, and P.H. Geissler. 1986. *The Breeding Bird Survey: Its First Fifteen Years, 1965–1979.* U.S. Fish and Wildlife Serv. Resource Pub. 157.

Robbins, C.S., J.R. Sauer, R.S. Greenberg, and S. Droege. 1989. Population declines in North American birds that migrate to the neotropics. *Proc. Natl. Acad. Sci.* 86:7658–7662.

SAS Institute Inc. 1988. *SAS/STAT User's Guide,* Release 6.03 ed. Cary, N.C.: SAS Institute Inc.

Sprugel, D.G. 1983. Correcting for bias in log-transformed allometric equations. *Ecology* 64:209–210.

Welsh, D.A. 1987. Birds as indicators of forest stand condition in boreal forests of eastern Canada. *ICBP Technical Publ.* 6:259–267.

Welsh, D.A., and D.R. Fillman. 1980. The impact of forest cutting on boreal bird populations. *Am. Birds* 34:84–94

JOHN M. HAGAN III
TREVOR L. LLOYD-EVANS
JONATHAN L. ATWOOD
Manomet Bird Observatory
P.O. Box 1770
Manomet, Massachusetts 02345

D. SCOTT WOOD
Section of Birds
Carnegie Museum of Natural History
Pittsburgh, Pennsylvania 15213

Long-term changes in migratory landbirds in the northeastern United States: Evidence from migration capture data

Abstract. We examined 19 years of fall migration data from two banding stations in the eastern United States for landbird population trends. To verify the usefulness of these data for this purpose, we first present several species case studies relating population indices derived from migration captures with independent sources of data. Migration capture data collected at Manomet Bird Observatory (MBO) in eastern Massachusetts accurately tracked the northward range expansion of the Northern Cardinal and Tufted Titmouse over the last 19 years. Marked declines in Ruby-crowned and Golden-crowned kinglets were evident after an unusually severe winter, and populations indices of three boreal forest warbler species increased after an outbreak of a major food item, the spruce budworm. These results indicate that migration captures can be used as population indices for at least some species. Of 52 species examined, 11 showed significant declines and two showed significant increases between the 1970s and 1980s. Most of the species that declined winter in the southeastern United States, not in the Neotropics. Of 38 species in common with the Breeding Bird Survey (BBS), 24 (63%) showed a positive correlation (P < 0.1) with data from at least one northeastern BBS physiographic stratum. However, significant correlations were more common for physiographic strata near MBO. BBS data from New England also indicated that a greater proportion of temperate-wintering species are declining than tropical-wintering species. Data from the Powdermill Nature Reserve (PNR) from 1970 to 1988, a banding station in western Pennsylvania, showed significant increases for nine species (mostly Neotropical migrants) and no significant decreases. However, correlations between PNR and BBS were few, even for data from proximate physiographic strata. These results, taken together, indicate that regional trends in Neotropical migrants might not mirror overall population declines. It appears that migration capture data can track changes in populations and will be useful as a corroborative data source, but their sensitivity is limited to the general region of sampling.

Sinopsis. Nosotros examinamos 19 años de migración otoñal de dos estaciones de anillamiento en el este de los Estados Unidos para buscar tendencias poblacionales. Para verificar la utilidad de estos datos para este propósito, primero presentamos casos de estudio específicos relacionando índices poblacionales derivados de capturas de migración a partir de fuentes de datos independientes. Los datos de captura de migración colectados en el Observatorio de Aves de Manomet (MBO) en el este de Massachusetts detectaron con exactitud la expansión hacia el norte de *Cardinalis cardinalis* y *Parus bicolor* durante los últimos 19 años. Las declinaciones marcadas de *Regulus calendula* y *Regulus satrapa* fueron evidentes después de un invierno inusualmente severo y los índices poblacionales de tres especies de Parulinae boreales de bosque incrementaron después de la explosión de un item alimenticio principal, el gusano cogollero del abeto. Estos resultados indican que las capturas de migración pueden ser usadas como índices poblacionales para por lo menos algunas especies. De las 52 especies examinadas, 11 mostraron declinaciones significativas y dos presentaron incrementos significativos entre las décadas de 1970 y 1980. La mayoría de las especies que declinaron invernan en el sur de los Estados Unidos y no en el Neotrópico. De 38 especies en común con el Censo Norteamericano de Aves Anidantes (BBS), 24 (63%) mostraron una correlación positiva (P<0.1) con datos de por lo menos un estrato fisiográfico del BBS del noroeste. Sin embargo, las correlaciones significativas fueron mas comunes para los estratos fisiográficos cercanos al MBO. Los datos del BBS de Nueva Inglaterra también indicaron que está declinando una mayor proporción de especies invernantes en la zona templada en comparación con las invernantes del Neotrópico. Los datos de 1970–1988 de la Reserva Natural de Powdermill (PNR), una estación de anillamiento en el oeste de Pennsylvania, mostraron incrementos significativos para nueve especies (en su mayoría migratorias neotropicales) y ningún decrecimiento significativo. Sin embargo, las correlaciones entre los datos de PNR y el BBS fueron muy pocas, incluso para datos de estratos fisiográficos cercanos. Estos resultados, tomados en conjunto, indican que las tendencias regionales de las migratorias neotropicales podrían no revelar declinaciones poblacionales generales. Parece ser que los datos de captura de migración pueden detectar cambios en las poblaciones y serán útiles como una fuente de datos para corroboraciones, pero su sensibilidad está limitada a la región general de muestreo.

Evidence from many recent studies indicates that populations of some Neotropical migrant landbird species are decreasing (Aldrich and Robbins 1970, Temple and Temple 1976, Robbins 1979, Ambuel and Temple 1982, Hall 1984a,b, Holmes et al. 1986, Askins and Philbrick 1987, Johnston and Winings 1987, Holmes and Sherry 1988, Robbins et al. 1989, Askins et al. 1990). This evidence is based on local or regional studies, with the exception of the continental Breeding Bird Survey (Robbins et al. 1989). Although each study has followed largely independent sampling protocols, the basic information from which conclusions have been drawn is the same: the number of territorial males in an area.

Counting breeding birds is an intuitively appealing approach to estimating population sizes, but this technique presents some problems. Logistically, it is difficult to census the entire breeding range of many species, particularly those Neotropical migrants that breed in sparsely populated areas where human access to the breeding grounds is difficult (Hussell 1981). Counts of breeding birds also tend to sample only singing, territorial males, representing a potentially biased index to population size. Variation in skill of human observers to identify correctly birds by song (Cyr 1981, Faanes and Bystrak 1981) adds variation to population estimates. More importantly, the BBS samples breeding birds along roadsides, which might be biased in favor of edge habitats. The reproductive success of many Neotropical species is well known to be negatively affected by factors associated with forest edge (see review in Askins et al. 1990).

A technique that uses completely different methodology for sampling bird populations would substantially strengthen our assessment of population changes. Counts (or captures) of birds passing fixed points along migration routes might provide such a technique. It seems reasonable that the number of birds migrating should be correlated with the number of birds in the population. If so, this technique has several advantages over the BBS: (1) from a single point one can sample birds representing a region, albeit specifically unknown, (2) nonbreeders, floaters, and females are also sampled, (3) there is no observer bias in detectability because birds are trapped and identified in-hand, and (4) the samples are not restricted to birds breeding along roadsides.

Despite a long history of trapping and banding passerines during migration at widespread sites in the United States (Low 1957, Robbins 1968) and Europe, migration capture data have received little attention for monitoring population changes (Langslow 1978, Svensson 1978, Hussell 1981, Riddiford 1983, Jones 1986, Stewart 1987), and the results have been equivocal. Establishing the usefulness of this technique requires comparison of results with a different, well-established technique, such as the Breeding Bird Survey, and then assuming that this reference database is accurate. Svensson (1978) found that migration captures were more variable than breeding bird censuses in southern Sweden. Furthermore, migration captures of temperate zone wintering migrant species were more strongly correlated with breeding bird censuses than were migration captures of tropical migrant species. He concluded that migration captures were a less efficient method of monitoring population trends, or might be preferred only for species breeding in inaccessible areas. However, this argument might be untenable in that not enough is known about true population changes, rendering an assessment of variance for any technique useless (Hussell 1981).

In this study we draw on data from two migration banding stations, Manomet Bird Observatory (MBO) on Cape Cod Bay in Massachusetts, and the Carnegie Museum's Powdermill Nature Reserve (PNR) in western Pennsylvania. Both of these stations have been in operation for more than 20 years, have used standardized sampling techniques, and catch a similar set of migrant species. To establish whether captures of birds during migration might be useful in tracking changes in bird populations, we compare migration indices to well-known population changes, or to environmental factors that should have affected population levels. We concentrate our analyses on MBO data because of a greater familiarity with that data set and bird populations in the New England region. We compare data from both sites with Breeding Bird Survey indices for the northeastern United States.

Methods

STUDY AREAS

Manomet Bird Observatory (MBO), located on the western side of Cape Cod Bay, Plymouth Co., Massachusetts, U.S.A. (41°50' N, 70°30' W), is generally characterized by second-growth deciduous woodland, bordered on the east and south by a steep, eroding coastal bluff and on the west and north by brushy wetlands. Dominant tree species on the 7-ha study plot included black cherry (*Prunus serotina*), shadbush (*Amelanchier* spp.), red maple (*Acer rubrum*), white oak (*Quercus alba*) and pitch pine (*Pinus rigida*); dominant understory shrubs include common catbrier (*Smilax rotundifolia*), bayberry (*Myrica pensylvanica*), staghorn sumac (*Rhus typhina*), honeysuckle (*Lonicera morrowi*), arrowwood (*Vibernum recognitum*), Virginia creeper (*Parthenocissus quinquefolia*), and poison ivy (*Rhus radicans*). The vegetation was not managed to maintain a constant successional stage during the study. Vegetation data were not collected, so successional changes were not quantified. However, because the site is exposed to a coastal environment, the rate of vegetation change is less than at more sheltered, inland localities.

Between 45 and 50 nylon mist nets (12 m length, 2.6 m high, 4-panels, 36 mm extended mesh) were operated

annually from 1970 to 1988, inclusive. Throughout the study period, net sites were maintained at fixed locations to reduce variability in capture effort. From 15 August through 15 November, nets remained open at least five days a week from 0.5 hr prior to sunrise to 0.5 hr after sunset. We closed nets under adverse weather conditions, and kept records of opening and closing times of each net.

Powdermill Nature Reserve (PNR), a banding station operated by the Carnegie Museum of Natural History, is located in the Ligonier Valley, five km south of Rector, Westmoreland Co., Pennsylvania (40°10' N, 79°16' W). Dominant tree species on the 2.4-ha study plot used for the banding operation were red maple and black cherry; dominant understory shrubs included hawthorne (*Crataegus* spp.), wild crabapple (*Pyrus* spp.), speckled alder (*Alnus rugosa*), smooth blackhaw (*Viburnum prunifolium*), and black willow (*Salix nigra*). In comparison with MBO, PNR had somewhat greater habitat changes from 1970 to 1988, the period of study. In addition to relatively more rapid plant succession, wetland areas were modestly increased between 1972 and 1978. However, the qualitative appearance of the vegetation in the vicinity of the net lanes has undergone minor change; these areas were managed to keep vegetation at a constant successional stage.

From 1970 to 1988, inclusive, between 35 and 45 nylon mist nets (12 m length, 2.6 m high, 4-panels, 30 and 36 mm extended mesh) were operated annually by R.C. Leberman. Nets were opened daily throughout fall migration (1 August to 30 November), except under adverse weather conditions. Records were kept of opening and closing times of nets so that capture effort could be calculated (Leberman and Wood 1983). Nets at PNR were usually closed in early afternoon.

COMPUTATION OF POPULATION INDICES

Although we captured birds during migration in both spring and fall, only fall data (15 August to 15 November) are analyzed because banding totals are much greater in fall than in spring for the MBO site. Because we wanted only migrant birds in our calculations of population indices, we applied several restrictions to the data. First we eliminated from analyses all captures or recaptures of locally breeding individuals. From the remaining sample we calculated annual population indices for each species. Because netting effort could change at each site from day-to-day, and year-to-year, it was necessary to adjust population indices accordingly. The temporal window of migration for most species was a subset of each banding station's effort for the season, and varied among the species. Therefore, the temporal adjustment for each species was different, according to site, and its species-specific window of migration. Each species' migration window was defined as those dates after the 1st percentile of captures and before the 99th percentile capture date (all years combined). All population estimates were calculated using these species-specific windows of time.

For each day of banding station operation, we calculated a daily index for each species, providing the date fell within its migration window. This daily index was derived by dividing the number of caught individuals of a species by the total number of net hours of operation for that date. The resulting number was multiplied by 1,000 to produce a daily estimate in birds per 1,000 net hours of operation. We added a constant (one) to this number before taking the natural log; this provided our daily population index for further analysis.

For each site and species we derived an annual population index by calculating the mean of the logged daily indices. We then used these annual estimates in all analyses of trends of populations based on data from the two sites. This procedure prevented a day with an unusually large capture number from unduly influencing the annual population index for a species. Distributions of daily migration captures tend to be skewed due to weather effects (Blokpoel and Richardson 1978, Svensson 1978, Hussell 1981). Thus, the mean of the transformed daily capture number gives a better estimate of the distribution of captures than does the mean or sum of counts in the original scale.

To examine population trends of the MBO and PNR data, we divided the 19 annual indices into two sets: pre-1980 data ($n = 10$), and post-1980 (inclusive, $n = 9$). We then performed a nonparametric Wilcoxon 2-sample test to compare population indices of the 1970s to those of the 1980s. Thus, the hypothesis being tested is whether population indices have changed between these two periods. This approach addressed the problem at hand, that of documenting population changes, while avoiding the limitations imposed by using linear regression.

We also examined population trends of different species groups according to wintering range, wintering habitat, and whether the species was a winter habitat generalist or specialist. We categorized species by wintering range as either northeastern U.S. (resident), southeastern U.S. (short-distance migrants), or Neotropical migrants (long-distance, Central American/Caribbean, or South American wintering species). We classified Central America wintering species as forest or non-forest dwelling species, and as habitat specialists or generalists, using data from Rappole et al. (1983). In cases where species were grouped, we used linear regression to examine population changes. In such cases, superimposing the population indices of many species has a smoothing effect on the resultant annual estimates, making linear regression a more in-

structive method of analysis. Before grouping species, we first standardized all annual species indices so that an abundant species was not given more weight in the derived annual index than less common species.

Annual population indices from BBS data for the species of interest were obtained from S. Droege and J. Sauer at the Patuxent Research Center. We used data from BBS physiographic strata (defined in Robbins et al. 1986) that represented the northeastern United States and the eastern half of Canada (Fig. 1). We did not use BBS indices for any stratum and year when fewer than 10 routes were censused. We compared population estimates from MBO, PNR, and BBS sources using the Pearson product-moment correlation (SAS 1985).

Results

MBO DATA

The MBO migration capture data set consisted of 52 species (Table 1). Twenty-six (50%) of the species were Neotropical migrants, 18 (35%) were short-distance migrants (wintering mainly in the southern United States), and six (12%) were resident species that show little or no seasonal movement. Two species, the Gray Catbird and the Common Yellowthroat, winter in both the southeastern United States and Central America, and, therefore, could not be placed in one of these categories. The 19 years of fall banding data used in this study involved 90,553 individual bird captures and approximately 409,900 net hours of effort.

To establish whether our migration indices are sensi-

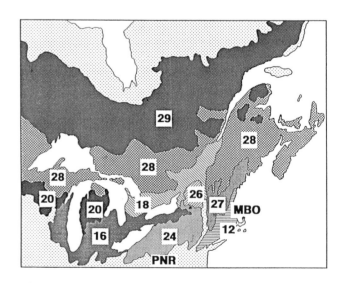

FIGURE 1. Breeding Bird Survey physiographic strata in the northeastern U.S. and southern Canada. Stratum numbers are from Robbins et al. (1986).

TABLE 1. Range, habitat classifications, and population trends of species used in this study

Species	MBO captures	PNR captures	Winter range	Winter habitat	Gen./Spec.	MBO trend	PNR trend
Downy Woodpecker *Picoides pubescens*	483	215	NE			−	+
Northern Flicker *Colaptes auratus*	351	105	NE			−	+
Eastern Phoebe *Sayornis phoebe*	271	nd	SE			− *	
Blue Jay *Cyanocitta cristata*	1439	156	NE			−	+ *
Black-capped Chickadee *Parus atricapillus*	18734	1686	NE			+	+
Tufted Titmouse *Parus bicolor*	2118	328	NE			+ *	−
Brown Creeper *Certhia americana*	988	116	SE			−	−
Golden-crowned Kinglet *Regulus satrapa*	1664	386	SE				+ *
Ruby-crowned Kinglet *Regulus calendula*	1003	3460	SE			−	−
Veery *Catharus fuscescens*	375	172	CA	F	S	+	+
Gray-cheeked Thrush *Catharus minimus*	126	nd	SA			+	+
Swainson's Thrush *Catharus ustulatus*	852	5292	SA			−	+
Hermit Thrush *Catharus guttatus*	855	944	SE			−	−
Wood Thrush *Hylocichla mustelina*	164	551	CA	F	S	−	+ *
American Robin *Turdus migratorius*	4788	269	SE			−	−
Gray Catbird *Dumetella carolinensis*	11851	3938	SE,CA	N	G	+	+
Brown Thrasher *Toxostoma rufum*	231	134	SE			−	−
Philadelphia Vireo *Vireo philadelphicus*	152	nd	CA	F	S	+	+
Red-eyed Vireo *Vireo olivaceus*	1906	2255	SA			+	−
Tennessee Warbler *Vermivora peregrina*	173	nd	CA	F	S	−	
Nashville Warbler *Vermivora ruficapilla*	348	1036	CA	N	G	−	−
Northern Parula *Parula americana*	54	nd	CA	N	G	− *	
Yellow Warbler *Dendroica petechia*	297	90	CA	N	G	−	−
Cape May Warbler *Dendroica tigrina*	382	nd	CA	N	G	− *	
Chestnut-sided Warbler *Dendroica pensylvanica*	83	nd	CA	N	G	−	
Magnolia Warbler *Dendroica magnolia*	432	4278	CA	F	G	+	
Black-thr. Blue Warbler *Dendroica caerulescens*	250	331	CA	N	G	+	+ *
Yellow-rumped Warbler *Dendroica coronata*	14412	5295	SE	N	S	− *	+ *
Black-throated Green Warbler *Dendroica virens*	176	nd	CA	F	G	−	
Bay-breasted Warbler *Dendroica castanea*	646	961	CA	F	S	−	+
Blackpoll Warbler *Dendroica striata*	5480	603	SA			− *	−
Black-and-white Warbler *Mniotilta varia*	875	261	CA	N	G	−	−
American Redstart *Setophaga ruticilla*	2671	2025	CA	F	G	−	+
Ovenbird *Seiurus aurocapillus*	420	1102	CA	N	G	+	+ *
Northern Waterthrush *Seiurus noveboracensis*	626	608	CA	N	S	+	−
Mourning Warbler *Oporornis philadelphia*	194	280	CA,SA			+	+
Common Yellowthroat *Geothlypis trichas*	1384	4656	SE,CA	N	S	− *	+
Wilson's Warbler *Wilsonia pusilla*	519	617	CA	N	G	−	−
Canada Warbler *Wilsonia canadensis*	318	658	CA			−	+
Yellow-breasted Chat *Icteria virens*	694	75	CA	N	S	−	−
Northern Cardinal *Cardinalis cardinalis*	449	541	NE			+ *	−
Rufous-sided Towhee *Pipilo erythrophthalmus*	690	591	SE			− *	+
American Tree Sparrow *Spizella arborea*	116	nd	SE			− *	
Field Sparrow *Spizella pusilla*	237	nd	SE			− *	
Fox Sparrow *Passerella iliaca*	45	nd	SE			−	
Lincoln's Sparrow *Melospiza lincolnii*	130	nd	SE			−	
Swamp Sparrow *Melospiza georgiana*	527	2600	SE			−	+
White-throated Sparrow *Zonotrichia albicollis*	5035	6120	SE			− *	−
Song Sparrow *Melospiza melodia*	1819	5208	SE			−	+ *
Dark-eyed Junco *Junco hyemalis*	1564	2929	SE			− *	
Northern Oriole *Icterus galbula*	630	43	CA	N	G	+	
Purple Finch *Carpodacus purpureus*	591	2599	SE			+	+ *

NOTE: * = $P < 0.05$; CA = Central America; F = mainly forest species; Gen. = generalist; N = nonforest species; NE = northeastern United States; nd = no data; SA = South America; SE = southeastern U.S.; Spec. = specialist.

SOURCES: Rappole et al. 1983 (winter range, winter habitat, G/S); A.O.U. 1983 (winter range).

tive to changes in avian populations, we present several species case studies in an effort to validate our data. We selected species for which good evidence exists for population fluctuation or for environmental features known to affect populations. We first examine whether population indices derived from MBO migration captures are correlated with these independent data, and then compare both to BBS results.

CASE STUDIES

Beddall (1963) described dramatic northward range expansions by Northern Cardinal and Tufted Titmouse during the late 1940s and early 1950s. These species have continued to spread northward, with the first Vermont breeding records occurring in 1962 (Northern Cardinal) and 1975 (Tufted Titmouse) (Laughlin and Kibbe 1985). Spearman rank correlations of National Audubon Society Christmas Bird Count (CBC) data from coastal Massachusetts (Buzzard's Bay, Marshfield, Boston and Concord) with year (1973–1987) indicated highly significant ($P < 0.001$) increases for both species in eastern Massachusetts (Northern Cardinal, $r = 0.81$; Tufted Titmouse, $r = 0.82$).

MBO migration indices for the Northern Cardinal showed a positive, significant correlation with CBC data ($r = 0.60$, $P = 0.015$) but the titmouse indices showed a nonsignificant positive correlation ($r = 0.39$, $P = 0.14$). Migration indices for both species were significantly positively correlated with BBS indices for Stratum 12, the stratum within which MBO lies (see Fig. 2 for Northern Cardinal).

Thus, three independent sources of data (CBC, BBS, and MBO) generally agree on population trends in these two species during the last two decades. This indicates that banding data can reflect changes in species distribution and abundance.

In the eastern U.S., Golden-crowned and Ruby-crowned kinglets winter primarily from the mid-Atlantic states south to the Gulf of Mexico (Lepthien and Bock 1976, Root 1988). Because their small body size (5–6 g) results in a high rate of heat loss (Thaler-Kottek 1986), both species are subject to mortality in severely cold weather. In both Europe (Hilden and Koskimies 1969, Sharrock 1976, Cawthorne and Marchant 1980, Hilden 1982) and North America (Allen 1919, Wilson 1922, Griscom 1923, Laurenzi et al. 1982, Laughlin and Kibbe 1985, Ehrlich et al. 1988), kinglet populations have been shown to decline as a result of severe winter weather.

The winter of 1976–77 was exceptionally cold throughout the wintering ranges of Ruby-crowned and Golden-crowned kinglets, and caused rangewide declines in eastern North American kinglet populations

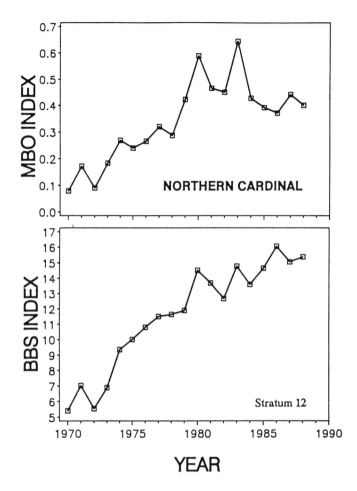

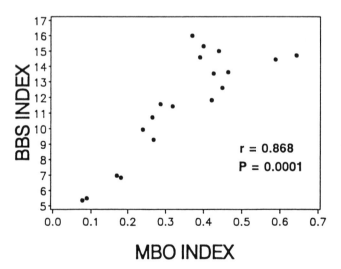

FIGURE 2. Population indices of the Northern Cardinal since 1970 for MBO migration data and BBS data. Correlation between these two data sources shown in lower plot.

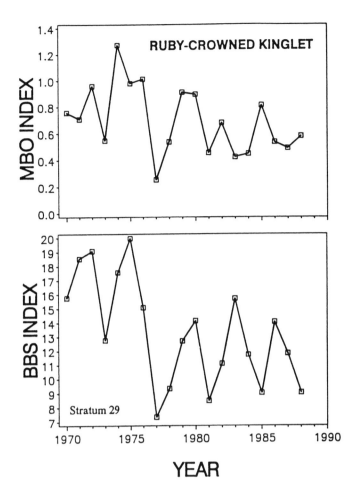

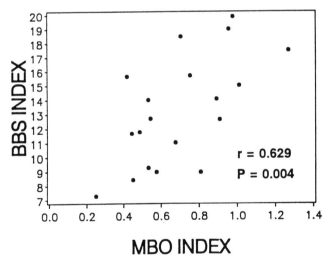

FIGURE 3. Population indices of the Ruby-crowned Kinglet since 1970 for MBO migration data and BBS data. Correlation between these two data sources shown in lower plot.

(Buckley et al. 1977, Hall 1977, Hamilton 1977, LeGrand 1977, Robertson 1977, Scott 1977, Smith 1977, Stevenson 1977, Sabo 1980, Webster 1977, Van Velzen 1978, Robbins et al. 1986). Breeding bird censuses conducted in Allegheny Co., New York showed a 33% decline in the number of breeding pairs of Golden-crowned Kinglets from 1976 to 1977 (Brooks 1977, 1978), and Vickery (1977) reported a 77% decline of Ruby-crowned Kinglets in New Hampshire in the 1977 breeding season. MBO migration capture data for the period 1970–1988 indicate that populations of both Golden-crowned and Ruby-crowned (Fig. 3) kinglets were at their lowest point in 1977, the year following the harsh winter of 1976–77. BBS indices for Stratum 29 for these two species were also at their lowest point during 1977.

For Golden-crowned Kinglets, the BBS indices from Stratum 27 were significantly and positively correlated ($r = 0.56$, $P = 0.028$) with annual MBO migration captures (but not from Strata 24, 26, 28 or 29). For Ruby-crowned Kinglets (Fig. 3), significant correlations with MBO data were obtained for BBS Strata 26 ($r = 0.66$, $P = 0.013$), 27 ($r = 0.47$, $P = 0.059$), 28 ($r = 0.70$, $P = 0.001$) and 29 ($r = 0.63$, $P = 0.004$), but not for Stratum 18. It appears that both migration capture data and BBS indices served as useful indicators of a major decline in North American kinglet populations between the 1976 and 1977 breeding seasons.

Of the North American wood-warblers, the reproductive success of Bay-breasted, Cape May, and Tennessee warblers is closely associated with densities of the spruce budworm (*Choristoneura fumerifana* Clem.), a major defoliator of northern coniferous forests (Kendeigh 1947, MacArthur 1958, Morse 1978, Harrison 1984). In years when this important food item was abundant, increases in reproductive output via larger clutch sizes, greater frequency of second clutches, and enhanced fledging success, often resulted in dramatic increases in the local population levels of these species (Kendeigh 1947, Hensley and Cope 1951, Zach and Falls 1975, Harrison 1984).

We compared yearly migration counts of Bay-breasted, Cape May, and Tennessee warblers at MBO with data on spruce budworm densities obtained within the breeding ranges of each species. We used two indices of spruce budworm abundance in these comparisons: (1) number of hectares defoliated annually by spruce budworms during the period 1970–1980 throughout eastern North America (Hardy et al. 1981), and (2) average counts of moths collected at light traps in Maine from 1970 to 1988 (Trial 1988). We found significant, positive correlations between both of these indices and migration captures of Bay-breasted, Cape May, and Tennessee warblers (Table 2).

Bay-breasted Warbler population indices from MBO

TABLE 2. Correlations between two types of annual spruce budworm indices (defoliation and moth counts), MBO migration count indices, and Breeding Bird Survey indices, for three warbler species known to respond to budworm outbreaks

Data Source	Species	Defoliation[a]			Moth Count[b]		
		n	r	P	n	r	P
MBO	CMWA	11	0.61	0.047	19	0.61	0.005
MBO	TEWA	11	0.79	0.004	19	0.53	0.020
MBO	BBWA	11	0.85	0.001	19	0.58	0.009
BBS (Stratum 28)	BBWA	11	-0.72	0.013	19	-0.06	0.800
BBS (Stratum 29)	BBWA	11	0.46	0.151	18	0.20	0.438

NOTE: n = number of years; P = probability of correlation due to chance; r = Spearman rank correlation; BBWA = Bay-breasted Warbler; CMWA = Cape May Warbler; TEWA = Tennessee Warbler.

a. Index based on number of hectares defoliated annually by spruce budworm throughout eastern North America. For BBWA and CMWA, values used were the totals of Zones A, B, C, and D as provided in Hardy et al. (1981). For the more northerly-distributed Tennessee Warbler (A.O.U. 1983), number of hectares defoliated in Zones C and D (Hardy et al. 1981) were used.

b. Index based on mean number of moths captured annually in light traps in Maine (Trial 1988).

were not significantly correlated with BBS data Stratum 28 or 29 (Fig. 4). However, the MBO sample might have been much more geographically restricted than the area represented by these two large BBS strata. Robbins et al. (1989) reported a nonsignificant increase in this species until 1978; it experienced a strongly significant decline in 1980s, a pattern that fits the budworm explanation for population change. Because of this lack of relationship between BBS data from Stratum 28 or 29, we obtained BBS data for the Bay-breasted Warbler for New Bruswick and Nova Scotia, the most likely areas from where MBO samples come. Plots of BBS data for these two areas are more similar to the MBO pattern (Fig. 5), with elevated populations about the time of the budworm outbreak. Still, neither New Brunswick nor Nova Scotia data were significantly correlated with MBO indices ($P > 0.2$). We did not have BBS data for Cape May or Tennessee warblers.

POPULATION TRENDS IN THE MBO DATA

For all 52 species, the number of birds caught per effort significantly declined over the 19-year span of the data set ($P << 0.01$, $R^2 = 0.54$, Fig. 6). Separating the species into wintering latitude groups indicated that northeastern U.S. wintering species ($n = 6$ species) tended to increase during this time, although not significantly ($P = 0.21$, $R^2 = 0.09$). Neotropical migrants (Central and South American wintering species togeth-

er, $n = 26$ species) tended to decrease, but not significantly ($P = 0.20$, $R^2 = 0.09$, Fig. 7). Southeastern U.S. wintering species ($n = 17$ species), however, showed a strong decline ($P < 0.01$, $R^2 = 0.69$, Fig. 7). (We removed the Yellow-rumped Warbler from the southeastern U.S. analysis because some individuals winter in the tropics.)

We subdivided the Neotropical migrant group into several logical categories for further analysis. Neither the species group that winters primarily in South America ($n = 5$ species, $P = 0.17$, $R^2 = 0.11$, Fig. 8) nor the species group wintering mainly in Central America ($n = 20$ species, $P = 0.28$, $R^2 = 0.07$, Fig. 8), showed significant changes since 1970.

We subdivided the species that winter mainly in Central America as either habitat specialists or generalists (Table 1). In this analysis we only used species for which winter habitat selection data exist in Rappole et al. (1983). A specialist species could be one that is found only in scrub habitat, or one found only in medium-aged or mature forests. Generalists were often found in both habitats. Neither the generalist species group ($n = 14$ species, $P = 0.26$, $R^2 = 0.07$) nor the specialist group showed any significant population changes during this study ($n = 9$ species, $P = 0.16$, $R^2 = 0.11$).

The same Central American wintering species used in the above analysis were reclassified into those that use primarily forest habitats and those that use mainly scrub habitats. A species using either of these habitat

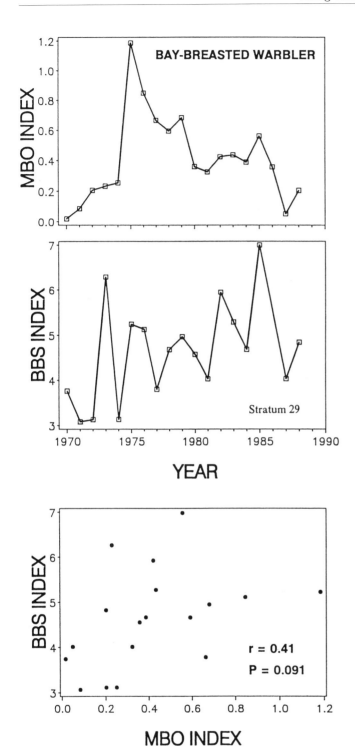

FIGURE 4. Population indices of the Bay-breasted Warbler since 1970 for MBO migration data and BBS data. Correlation between these two data sources shown in lower plot.

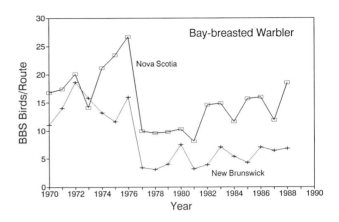

FIGURE 5. Birds/route for the Bay-breasted Warbler in Nova Scotia and New Brunswick using BBS data from 1970 to 1988.

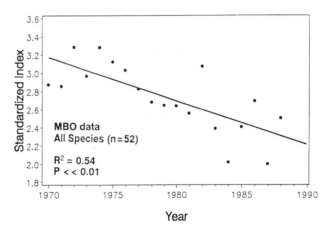

FIGURE 6. MBO standardized population indices since 1970 for all 52 species combined.

types could either be a generalist or a specialist, but displayed some preference for either forest or scrub (see Rappole et al. 1983). The species group comprised mainly of forest-dwelling species showed no significant change ($n = 8$ species, $P > 0.50$), whereas the group using primarily scrub habitats showed a weakly significant decrease in numbers ($n = 15$ species, $P = 0.08$, $R^2 = 0.17$).

An analysis of population trends by species, comparing annual population indices of pre-1980 data ($n = 10$ years) to post-1980 data ($n = 9$ years, inclusive), showed declines in 36 species (69%) and increases in 16 (31%) (Table 1). Of those that decreased, 11 represented significant declines (21% of 52 species, Wilcoxon 2-sample test, $P < 0.05$; see Table 1) and only two species in-

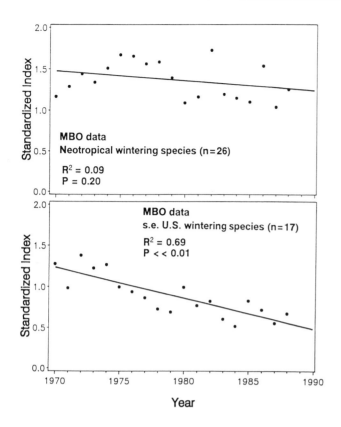

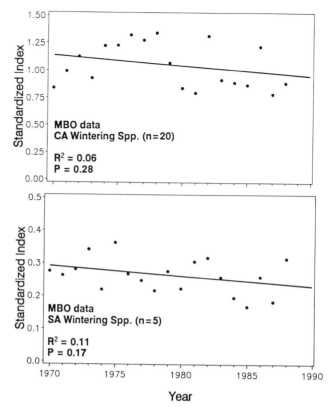

FIGURE 7. MBO standardized population indices since 1970 for the species group that migrates to the Neotropics, and the group that winters in the southeastern United States.

FIGURE 8. MBO standardized population indices since 1970 for the species group that winters in Central America, and the group that winters in South America.

creased significantly (Northern Cardinal and Tufted Titmouse, 4% of 52 species). Of the 11 species showing significant declines, only three were Neotropical migrants (Blackpoll Warbler, Cape May Warbler, and Northern Parula). The Common Yellowthroat also showed a significant decline, but we do not know whether our sample was composed of those wintering in the United States or Central America or both. The remaining seven species that showed significant declines were all short-distance migrants that spend their winters in the southeastern United States (Eastern Phoebe, Yellow-rumped Warbler, Rufous-sided Towhee, Dark-eyed Junco, White-throated Sparrow, American Tree Sparrow, and Field Sparrow).

CORRELATIONS BETWEEN MBO DATA AND THE BBS

Because we obtained annual population estimates for different BBS physiographic strata, we were able to compare annual population indices derived from MBO migration captures to different geographic regions. We

relaxed the significance level for these analyses to $P = 0.10$ because we did not want to omit weakly significant relationships from consideration. Of the 38 species for which we had data from both sources (BBS and MBO), 24 (63%) showed a significant positive correlation ($P < 0.10$) with at least one of the nine BBS strata examined in this study. Twelve of 38 species (32%) showed a significant negative correlation with at least one of the BBS strata. Four species showed a significant positive correlation with at least one stratum while also showing a significant negative correlation with another stratum.

Positive correlations between the MBO data and BBS data were more numerous for strata geographically near MBO, indicating that there is a spatial limit to the usefulness of data from a single banding station (Fig. 9). This is expected because the farther the BBS stratum from MBO, the greater the chance that sampled populations are different.

Because fall migration capture data were composed mostly of hatch-year birds, we were monitoring primarily annual reproductive output for a species, not adult

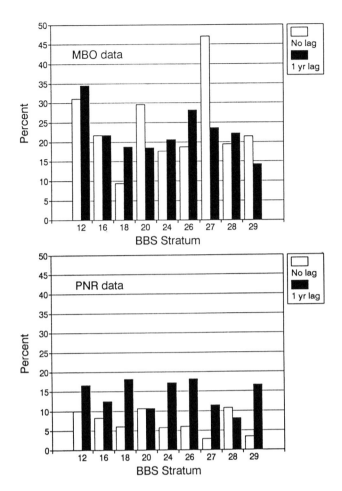

FIGURE 9. Percent of species in MBO and PNR data sets that showed significant ($P < 0.1$) positive correlation with BBS data from each physiographic stratum.

breeding population levels, as does the BBS. Monitoring reproductive output should be compatible with measuring overall population change because an increase in hatch-year birds can be correlated with high survivorship and high returns in subsequent years (Holmes et al. 1986, Holmes and Sherry, this volume). This suggests, however, that the proper comparison between indices from migration data and BBS data might involve a lag of one year. That is, reproductive output in year x (fall migration data) might correlate better with the number of breeding birds in the following year ($x + 1$) (spring BBS data). Correlation between MBO data and BBS data using such a lag function, however, did not substantially improve the number of significant positive correlations (Fig. 9). Some strata showed more correlations and others showed fewer using the lagged relationship.

TRENDS IN REGIONAL BBS DATA

Although Robbins et al. (1989) showed a general pattern of decline for many Neotropical migrants on a continental scale, those patterns do not necessarily represent changes in the New England region alone. For this reason, we assessed population trends in the BBS data using the same decade analysis as performed for the MBO data above. We limited this analysis to Strata 12 and 27, which cover most of New England. Of 30 species analyzed in Stratum 12, seven showed a significant increase ($P < 0.05$, Wilcoxon 2-sample test), and 12 showed a significant decrease. Of 13 Neotropical migrant species, four (31%) showed significantly lower population levels in the later period (1980–1988). Eight of 17 (47%) short-distance migrants and residents showed lower indices in the later decade. In Stratum 27, eight species increased significantly and 15 species declined. Of 15 Neotropical migrant species, six (40%) declined significantly, and of 20 short-distance and resident species, nine (45%) declined significantly. Thus, for the New England region, BBS data also showed more significant declines in short-distance migrant and resident species (eight of 17 species) than in Neotropical migrant species (four of 13 species).

CORRELATIONS BETWEEN MBO AND PNR DATA

Of the 52 species analyzed using the MBO data, 40 of these were also caught in sufficient numbers at PNR to allow correlation analysis of population trends between the sites. Of these 40 species, only one showed a significant positive correlation with the MBO data (Yellow-breasted Chat, $r = 0.72$, $P = 0.021$, $n = 19$). One species showed a significant negative correlation (Tufted Titmouse, $r = -0.68$, $P = 0.041$). Two other species showed weakly significant positive correlations (Magnolia Warbler, $r = 0.67$, $P = 0.053$, and Black-capped Chickadee, $r = 0.66$, $P = 0.065$). This number of correlations could have occurred simply due to chance, as 41 tests were performed. Thus, the two sites showed apparently independent changes in populations for most species.

POPULATION TRENDS IN PNR DATA

Data for 40 species were available for analysis from the PNR site. All species combined, after standardization, showed a positive, significant trend using linear regression ($P = 0.04$, $R^2 = 0.25$, Fig. 10). The subset of Neotropical migrant species ($n = 12$ species) also showed a significant positive increase over time ($P < 0.01$, $R^2 = 0.39$), whereas species wintering in the south-

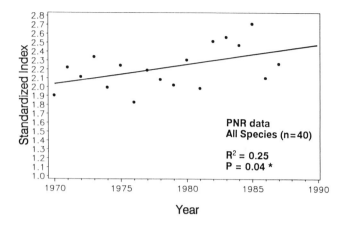

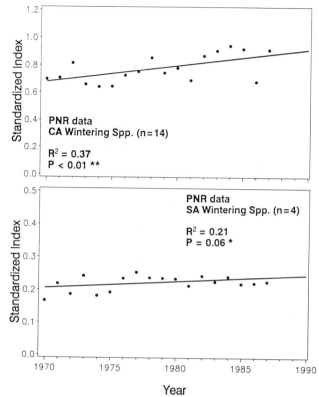

FIGURE 12. PNR standardized population indices since 1970 for the species group that winters in Central America, and the group that winters in South America.

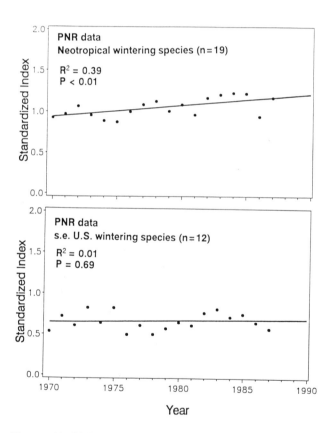

FIGURE 11. PNR standardized population indices since 1970 for the species group that migrates to the Neotropics, and the group that winters in the southeastern United States.

eastern United States showed no significant trend ($P = 0.69$, Fig. 11).

For only the Neotropical migrants, the species group ($n = 4$ species) that migrates to South America showed a weakly significant increase ($P = 0.06$, $R^2 = 0.21$), whereas the group wintering in Central America ($n = 14$ species) showed a strong increase over the last 19 years ($P < 0.01$, $R^2 = 0.37$, Fig. 12).

For only Central American wintering species, habitat specialists ($n = 7$ species) showed no significant change over time ($P > 0.3$), but habitat generalists showed a significant increase over the same time span ($P < 0.01$, $R^2 = 0.45$). Using the same species set, forest-dwelling species in winter ($n = 5$ species) showed a significant increase ($P < 0.01$, $R^2 = 0.48$), but non-forest species ($n = 15$ species) did not ($P = 0.11$, $R^2 = 0.15$).

Of the 40 PNR species analyzed by comparing population indices by decades, 24 (60%) increased in numbers and 16 (40%) decreased. These frequencies are no different from an expected frequency of 20 for each trend type if populations were changing randomly ($\chi^2 =$

1.6, $P >> 0.1$). Of these 40, none showed a significant decrease, while nine showed a significant increase (see Table 1).

CORRELATIONS BETWEEN PNR AND THE BBS

Of 39 species for which we had both PNR and BBS data, 10 (26%) species showed significant positive correlations ($P < 0.05$) with at least one of the nine northeastern BBS strata. Four species (10%) showed significant negative correlations with at least one stratum. Unlike MBO data, PNR data showed poor correlation with BBS data and did not correlate any better with BBS indices from geographically proximate strata (Fig. 9). By using a lag function of one year to relate PNR data to BBS data for the following year, the number of significant correlations increased, but still remained well below that of MBO and BBS correlations (Fig. 9).

Discussion

We have examined long-term migration capture data and shown that they are useful in describing at least regional population changes in some species. Thus, migration capture data appear to be a valid source of information on bird population trends. MBO data for selected species correlated well with documented or expected population changes. Although these observations were only correlative, they are consistent with what we would expect given known information about the species' biology.

MBO annual population indices from capture data correlated reasonably well with the BBS data, with 63% of 38 species showing a significant ($P < 0.1$) positive correlation with at least one BBS stratum. That correlations between the BBS data set and MBO data were more common for nearby BBS strata indicates that the usefulness of migration capture data has geographic limitations. This is further exemplified by the poor correlation of MBO and PNR data. The poor correlation could be explained in several ways. First, the two sites are 800 km apart, and different source populations are likely sampled at each site. Thus, there might be little reason to expect agreement between the two unless population changes are occurring on a rangewide basis. Second, either site might not be accurately tracking population changes because of biases. The most likely source of bias is habitat change at the study sites, which would have affected the numbers and species of birds caught through time. PNR has undergone greater habitat change than MBO. Several ponds were created at PNR in the early 1970s, but the degree of habitat change has not been commensurate with the apparent

increase in the numbers of Neotropical migrants. The MBO site has remained unaltered except for normal vegetational succession, which is slowed because of the coastal climate. Third, it is possible that neither site measures population levels accurately, and that migration captures are of little value in tracking population changes. However, we believe that our case studies using the MBO data convincingly demonstrate that migration captures can monitor real population phenomena, and we are inclined to discount this last explanation.

Lack of agreement between PNR and BBS data is difficult to reconcile. Possible explanations include either biased samples as a result of habitat change at PNR, or inappropriate comparison of the data. Perhaps BBS indices for the physiographic strata north of PNR, which generally have a wide longitudinal extent, do not represent the populations sampled by PNR. A more careful comparison with BBS data using more specific geographic regions is warranted for the PNR data.

Although Robbins et al. (1989) reported continental-scale declines in many species of Neotropical migrant landbirds using BBS data, our data do not support that observation for the northeastern United States. Nor do BBS data from Strata 12 and 27, two New England regions, support that contention. Several studies have shown that regional patterns of change can be different from continental changes (James et al., this volume; Sauer and Droege, this volume). For example, Robbins et al. (1989) described the Ovenbird as increasing from 1966 to 1977, and significantly decreasing thereafter. MBO, PNR, and New England BBS data all showed increases in Ovenbird populations in the 1980s, which might be related to gradual maturation of forests in the region. Moreover, in the Northeast, both the MBO and BBS data set showed a greater percentage of significant declines for short-distance migrants that winter in the southeastern U.S. than for Neotropical migrants. A pattern of increases in some regions and decreases in others suggests that tropical deforestation might not have driven recent declines, unless breeding populations tend to occupy the same wintering areas. Whether this is true is not known.

BBS data from Strata 12 and 27 showed more significant declines and increases between the 1970s and 1980s than MBO data. MBO data showed significant declines in 11 (21%) of 52 species, whereas BBS data showed declines in 12 (40%) of 30 species in Stratum 12, and 15 (43%) of 35 species in Stratum 27. This higher occurrence of significant declines in the BBS data might be explained in several ways. First, BBS data might be more sensitive to population change than migration capture data. Variation in migration captures from year-to-year because of weather differences might render it a less powerful technique for detecting population change (Svennson 1978). Alternatively, the source populations sampled by migration captures are probably very different from BBS source populations. The BBS samples breeding birds along roadsides. Migration indices should have no bias for sampling individuals from any particular area (roadsides or interior forests). That is, they should sample individuals in proportion to the types of areas they inhabit. Thus, migration samples probably consist of a larger proportion of individuals from areas of contiguous forest. This subset of the population might not be declining at the rate of roadside subsets. However, by the time migration capture data show widespread changes in birds that breed in contiguous forest, declines might be so pervasive that conservation action will be ineffective.

Of the 11 species showing significant declines in the MBO data, three were Neotropical migrants (Northern Parula, Cape May Warbler, and Blackpoll Warbler). The Northern Parula and the Cape May Warbler are non-forest dwelling habitat generalists in Central America in winter, whereas the Blackpoll Warbler is a South American forest species. Thus, apparent declines in these species are difficult to reconcile with only a tropical deforestation explanation. Nor does their ecology or range in the breeding season indicate any obvious explanation for declines. Until more is known about their basic ecology, and the source of the migrant sample of these species, it will remain difficult to assess the causes of these apparent population changes.

That many short-distance species showed significant declines in both the MBO and BBS data sets deserves further attention. The Rufous-sided Towhee showed a significant decline in the MBO data, and for Strata 12 and 27. Correlations between MBO and BBS indices were significant and positive for all eight strata in which the species occurs. Thus, population declines in this species appear extensive. Many of the short-distance migrant species that showed declines, such as the towhee, tend to use second-growth habitats. The gradual maturing of forests and loss of former agricultural areas and associated seral stages of habitat might partially explain this pattern. At the same time, this might explain the lower rates of decline, or even stability of Neotropical migrant species in the Northeast, which generally use more mature forests. Witham and Hunter (this volume) reported similar declines for short-distance migrants in coastal Maine and, using old aerial photos, documented a decline in second-growth habitats along BBS routes. Also, loss of second-growth wintering habitat in the southeastern U.S. to large corporate agriculture and monocultures of economically valuable timber might also be responsible for the declines. In our effort to understand factors that affect long-distance

Neotropical migrants, we should not overlook conservation problems facing short-distance migrants with both winter and summer ranges restricted to North America. These species should be monitored as closely as Neotropical-wintering species.

Acknowledgments

We are grateful to the hundreds of volunteers who have helped collect migration capture data at both the PNR and MBO sites over the past two decades. We are especially grateful for the indispensable role of R. Leberman at PNR. J. Sauer and S. Droege kindly provided us with the annual population estimates derived from the BBS data set. D. Hussell and S. Droege provided excellent comments on an earlier draft of this manuscript. Financial support for collecting the migration capture data over the past 20 years has come from many generous sources. Two sources that deserve special note, however, include the Manomet Bird Observatory trustees and Carnegie Foundation.

Literature cited

Allen, F.H. 1919. The scarcity of Golden-crowned Kinglets. *BirdLore* 21:361–362.

Aldrich, J.W., and C.S. Robbins. 1970. Changing abundance of migratory birds in North America. Pages 17–26 in *The Avifauna of Northern Latin America*, H.K. Buechner and J.H. Buechner, eds. Smithsonian Contrib. Zool. 26.

Ambuel, B., and S.A. Temple. 1982. Songbird populations in southern Wisconsin forests: 1954 and 1979. *J. Field Ornithol.* 53:149–158.

American Ornithologists' Union. 1983. *Check-list of North American Birds*. 6th ed. Washington: American Ornithologists' Union.

Askins, R.A., and M.J. Philbrick. 1987. Effect of changes in regional forest abundance on the decline and recovery of a forest bird community. *Wilson Bull* 99:7–21.

Askins, R.A., J.F. Lynch, and R. Greenberg. 1990. Population declines in migratory birds in eastern North America. *Current Ornithol.* 7:1–57.

Beddall, B.G. 1963. Range expansion of the Cardinal and other birds in the northeastern states. *Wilson Bull.* 75:140–158.

Blokpoel, H., and W.J. Richardson. 1978. Weather and spring migration of Snow Geese across southern Manitoba. *Oikos* 30:350–363.

Brooks, E.W. 1977. Breeding Bird Census: Upland mixed pine-spruce-hardwood plantation. *Am. Birds* 31:51–52.

———. 1978. Breeding Bird Census: Upland mixed pine-spruce-hardwood plantation. *Am. Birds* 32:24.

Buckley, P.A., R.O. Paxron, and D.A. Cutler. 1977. Hudson-Delaware Region. *Am. Birds* 31:311–316.

Cawthorne, R.A., and J.H. Marchant. 1980. The effects of the

1978/79 winter on British bird populations. *Bird Study* 27:163-172.

Cyr, A. 1981. Limitation and variability in hearing ability in censusing birds. Pages 327–333 in *Estimating Numbers of Terrestrial Birds,* C.J. Ralph and M.J. Scott, eds. Studies in Avian Biology No. 6.

Ehrlich, P.R., D.S. Dobkin, and D. Wheye. 1988. *The Birder's Handbook: A Field Guide to the Natural History of North American Birds.* New York: Simon and Schuster.

Faanes, C.A., and D. Bystrak. 1981. The role of observer bias in the North American Breeding Bird Survey. Pages 353–359 in *Estimating Numbers of Terrestrial Birds,* C.J. Ralph and M.J. Scott, eds. Studies in Avian Biology No. 6.

Griscom, L. 1923. *Birds of the New York City Region.* Am. Mus. Nat. Hist. Handbook Series No. 9. New York: American Museum of Natural History.

Hall, G.A. 1977. Appalachian Region. *Am. Birds* 31:331–333.

———. 1984a. Population decline of Neotropical migrants in an Appalachian forest. *Am. Birds* 38:14–18.

———. 1984b. A long-term bird population study in an Appalachian spruce forest. *Wilson Bull.* 96:228–240.

Hamilton, R.B. 1977. Central Southern Region. *Am. Birds* 31:339–343.

Hardy, Y., M. Mainville, and D.M. Schmitt. 1981. *An Atlas of Spruce Budworm Defoliation in Eastern North America, 1938–80.* U.S. Dept. Agriculture, Forest Service, Cooperative State Research Service, Misc. Pub. 1449.

Harrison, H.H. 1984. *Wood Warbler's World.* New York: Simon and Schuster.

Hensley, M.M., and J.B. Cope. 1951. Further data on removal and repopulation of breeding birds in a spruce-fir forest community. *Auk* 68:483–493.

Hilden, O. 1982. Winter ecology and partial migration of the Goldcrest *Regulus regulus* in Finland. *Ornis Fenn.* 59:99–122.

Hilden, O., and J. Koskimies. 1969. Effects of the severe winter of 1965/66 upon winter bird fauna in Finland. *Ornis Fenn.* 46:22–31.

Holmes, R.T., and T.W. Sherry. 1988. Assessing population trends of New Hampshire forest birds: Local vs. regional patterns. *Auk* 105:756–768.

Holmes, R.T., T.W. Sherry, and F.W. Sturges. 1986. Bird community dynamics in a temperate deciduous forest: Long-term trends at Hubbard Brook. *Ecol. Monogr.* 50:201–220.

Hussell, D.J.T. 1981. The use of migration counts for detecting population levels. Pages 92–102 in *Estimating Numbers of Terrestrial Birds,* C.J. Ralph and M.J. Scott, eds. Studies in Avian Biology No. 6.

Johnston, D.W., and D.I. Winings. 1987. Natural history of Plummers Island, Maryland. XXVII. The decline of forest breeding birds on Plummers Island, Maryland, and vicinity. *Proc. Biol. Soc. Wash.* 100:762–768.

Jones, E.T. 1986. The passerine decline. *N. Am. Bird Bander* 11:74–75.

Kendeigh, S.C. 1947. *Bird Population Studies in the Coniferous Forest Biome during a Spruce Budworm Outbreak.* Ontario Dept. Lands Forests, Biol. Bull. 1.

Langslow, D.R. 1978. Recent increases of Blackcaps at bird observatories. *Brit. Birds* 71:345–354.

Laughlin, S.B., and D.P. Kibbe. 1985. *The Atlas of Breeding Birds of Vermont.* Hanover, N.H.: University Press of New England.

Laurenzi, A.W., B.W. Anderson, and R.D. Ohmart. 1982. Wintering biology of Ruby-crowned Kinglets in the lower Colorado River Valley. *Condor* 84:385–398.

Leberman, R.C., and D.S. Wood. 1983. *Bird-banding at Powdermill: Twenty Years Reviewed.* P.N.R. Research Rep. 42. Pittsburgh: Carnegie Museum of Natural History.

LeGrand, H.E., Jr. 1977. Southern Atlantic Coast Region. *Am. Birds* 31:319–322.

Lepthien, L.W., and C.E. Bock. 1976. Winter abundance patterns of North American kinglets. *Wilson Bull.* 88:483–485.

Low, S.H. 1957. Banding with mist nets. *Bird-Banding* 28:115–128.

MacArthur, R.H. 1958. Population ecology of some warblers of northeastern coniferous forests. *Ecology* 39:599–619.

Morse, D.H. 1978. Populations of Bay-breasted and Cape May Warblers during an outbreak of the spruce budworm. *Wilson Bull.* 90:404–413.

Rappole, J.H., E.S. Morton, T.E. Lovejoy, III, and J.L. Ruos. 1983. *Nearctic Avian Migrants in the Neotropics.* Washington: U.S. Fish and Wildlife Service.

Riddiford, N. 1983. Recent declines of Grasshopper Warblers (*Locustella naevia*) at British bird observatories. *Bird Study* 30:143–148.

Robbins, C.S. 1968. Net hours: A common denominator for the study of bird populations by banders. *EBBA News* 31:31–35.

———. 1979. Effect of forest fragmentation on bird populations. Pages 198–212 in *Management of North-Central and Northeastern Forests for Nongame Birds; Workshop Proceedings.* R.M. DeGraaf and K.E. Evans, eds. North Central Forest Exp. Stat. Pub. USFS Gen. Tech. Report NC-15.

Robbins, C.S., D. Bystrak, and P.H. Geissler. 1986. *The Breeding Bird Survey: Its First Fifteen Years, 1965–1979.* U.S. Fish and Wildlife Serv. Resource Pub. 157.

Robbins, C.S., J.R. Sauer, R.S. Greenberg, and S. Droege. 1989. Population declines in North American birds that migrate to the neotropics. *Proc. Natl. Acad. Sci.* 86:7658–7662.

Robertson, W.B., Jr. 1977. The changing seasons. *Am. Birds* 31:1103–1109.

Root, T. 1988. *Atlas of Wintering North American Birds.* Chicago: University of Chicago Press.

Sabo, S.R. 1980. Niche and habitat relations in subalpine bird communities of the White Mountains of New Hampshire. *Ecol. Monogr.* 50:241–259.

SAS Institute Inc. 1985. *SAS User's Guide: Statistics,* Version 5 ed. Cary, N.C.: SAS Institute Inc.

Scott, F.R. 1977. Middle Atlantic Coast Region. *Am. Birds* 31:316–319.

Sharrock, J.T.R. 1976. *The Atlas of Breeding Birds in Britain and Ireland.* Calton, England: Poyser.

Smith, K. 1977. The changing seasons. *Am. Birds* 31:292–303.

Stevenson, H.M. 1977. Florida Region. *Am. Birds* 31:322–325.

Stewart, P.A. 1987. Decline in numbers of wood warblers in spring and autumn migration through Ohio. *N. Am. Bird Bander* 12:58–60.

Svensson, S.E. 1978. Efficiency of two methods for monitoring bird population levels: Breeding bird censuses contra counts of migrating birds. *Oikos* 30:373–386.

Temple, S.A., and B.L. Temple. 1976. Avian population trends in central New York State, 1935–1972. *Bird-Banding* 47:238–257.

Thaler-Kottek, E. 1986. Zum Verhalten von Winter und Sommergoldhahnchen (*Regulus regulus, Regulus ignicapillus*)–ethookologische Differenzierung und Anpassung an den Lebensraum. *Ornithol. Beob.* 83:281–289.

Trial, H., Jr. 1988. *Spruce Budworm in Maine: The End of the Outbreak: Biological Conditions in 1986, 1987, and 1988, and a Look at the Future.* Department of Conservation, Maine Forest Service, Insect and Disease Management Div., Tech. Rep. No. 28.

Van Velzen, W.T. 1978. Forty-first Breeding Bird Census. *Am. Birds* 32:49.

Vickery, P.D. 1977. Northeastern Maritime Region. *Am. Birds* 77:1110–1114.

Webster, F.S., Jr. 1977. South Texas Region. *Am. Birds* 31:349–351.

Wilson, G. 1922. Bird changes caused by the winter of 1917–1918. *Auk* 39:270.

Zach, R., and J.B. Falls. 1975. Responses of the Ovenbird (Aves: Parulidae) to an outbreak of the spruce budworm. *Can. J. Zool.* 53:1669–1672.

HIRAM GONZÁLEZ-ALONSO
Instituto de Ecologia y Sistematica
Academia de Ciencias de Cuba
Carretera de Varona km 3.5
Ciudad Habana, Cuba

MARTIN K. MCNICHOLL
218 First Avenue
Toronto, Ontario, Canada M4M 1X4

PAUL B. HAMEL*
Tennessee Department of Conservation
Ecological Services Division
701 Broadway
Nashville, Tennessee 37219-5237

MARTÍN ACOSTA
Facultad de Biologia
Universidad de la Habana
25 e/ J e I, Vedado
Ciudad Habana, Cuba

ESTEBAN GODINEZ
JORGE HERNÁNDEZ
DAYSI RODRÍGUEZ
Instituto de Ecologia y Sistematica
Academia de Ciencias de Cuba
Carretera de Varona km 3.5
Ciudad Habana, Cuba

JEROME A. JACKSON
Department of Biological Sciences
Mississippi State University
Mississippi State, Mississippi 39762

CARMEN MARCOS GREGO
Direccion de Proteccion al Bosque y la Fauna
Ministerio de Agricultura
Virtudes No. 680 Esq. Belascoain
Centro Habana, Cuba

R. DOUGLAS MCRAE
Long Point Bird Observatory
Port Rowan, Ontario, Canada N0E 1M0

JACQUES SIROIS
Canadian Wildlife Service
Box 637
Yellowknife, NWT, Canada X1A 2N5

A cooperative bird-banding project in Peninsula de Zapata, Cuba, 1988–1989

Abstract. Ecological relationships among and between migrant and resident species of the Cuban winter avifauna have been little studied. The purpose of this ongoing collaboration among Canadian, Cuban, and U.S. ornithologists has been to institute a program of bird banding and study that will stimulate investigation of the winter ecology of resident and migratory species in Cuba. We captured 423 birds of 43 species, including 236 of 20 Neotropical migrant species, of which 14 were Parulinae. Forest habitats contained a disproportionately high percentage of captured and censused individuals belonging to species commonly considered forest interior migrants on the breeding grounds. Thirteen percent of the migrants and 12% of the resident individuals captured in 1989 were returns of birds banded in 1988. We believe this project will lead to improved efforts for the conservation of Neotropical migrants on both winter grounds and breeding grounds.

Sinopsis. Las relaciones ecológicas entre especies migrantes y residentes de la avifauna Cubana no han sido estudiadas en detalle. El propósito de esta colaboración entre instituciones Canadienses, Estadounidenses y Cubanas ha sido el instituir un programa de anillado de aves y estudio que estimulará la investigación de la ecología no reproductiva de especies residentes y migratorias en Cuba. Hemos capturado 423 individuos de 43 especies, incluyendo 236 de especies migrantes neotropicales, de las cuales 14 fueron Parulinae. Los habitats de bosque tuvieron un porcentaje desproporcionadamente alto de individuos censados y capturados de especies que normalmente se consideran especies del interior del bosque en las zonas reproductivas. Trece porciento de los individuos migrantes y 12% de los residentes capturados en 1989 fueron aves anilladas en 1988. Creemos que este proyecto producirá mejores esfuerzos para la conservación de los migrantes neotropicales tanto en sus zonas reproductivas como no reproductivas.

Cuba occupies half of the land area of the West Indies (Lucas et al. 1983) at the interface of the Nearctic and Neotropical realms (Udvardy 1975). Because of its size and its geographic location, the Cuban archipelago pro-

*Address correspondence to Paul B. Hamel.

vides wintering and staging habitats important to many North American migrants. Shugart (1984) found that, among Caribbean islands, only Cuba was sufficiently large that old growth habitats can exist, given the frequency of hurricanes and the concomitant habitat destruction they cause. One migrant, Bachman's Warbler (*Vermivora bachmanii*), winters only in Cuba (Hamel 1986). Cuban avifauna contains 21 endemic species, with only one known extinction in historic times, Cuban Macaw (*Ara tricolor*), and the only currently known population of Ivory-billed Woodpecker (*Campephilus principalis*).

Despite a growing network of protected areas and the development of conservation policies (S. Oharriz LLorente, pers. comm.), and although one-fourth of the main island is mountainous (Garrido 1986), difficult to access, and has poor agricultural value (Herrero et al. 1983), activities such as ranching, logging, and agriculture (particularly the cultivation of sugarcane) have contributed greatly to deforestation and forest fragmentation in the last century (Silva Taboada 1983, Herrero et al. 1983). We suspect that this degradation has affected migratory and resident birds in ways similar to those impacts recorded elsewhere in the hemisphere (Keast and Morton 1980, Robbins et al. 1986, Lynch 1989). In 1959, forests occupied about 12% of the Cuban landmass (Herrero et al. 1983). In 1980, Rappole et al. (1983) estimated that 14% of the island was forested as isolated fragments. Few studies of residents and wintering migrants in Cuba have been published; none has addressed the issue of bird distribution in a landscape fragmented by agriculture, forestry, and human settlements. Studies of banded birds have included White-crowned Pigeon (*Columba leucocephala*, Godinez, unpubl. data) and some migrants (Garrido 1986).

This paper is an analysis of data from the first collaborative study by Canadian, Cuban, and U.S. biologists of Neotropical migrants in Cuba. General objectives of the study include: (1) establish a training program in mist-netting and banding techniques, (2) search for good sites for permanent banding stations, (3) initiate examination of Cuban resident and winter bird populations in relation to habitat, (4) search for *Vermivora bachmanii*, and (5) enhance communication among Canadian, Cuban, and U.S. ornithologists. This paper presents the results of the first two years of this effort. Additional information is available in González-Alonso et al. (1990), Sirois et al. (1990), and Hamel (unpubl. data).

Materials and methods

STUDY AREA

We established a banding station and three study areas at Los Sabalos (22°15' N, 81°05' W), in the Cienaga de Zapata, on the Zapata Peninsula, Matanzas Province,

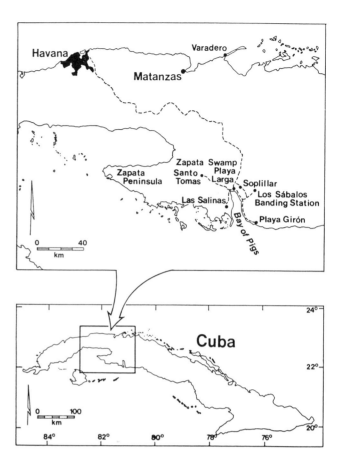

FIGURE 1. Location of the Los Sabalos banding station, Matanzas Province, Cuba.

Cuba (Fig. 1). The peninsula encompassed over 3,400 km² of freshwater, brackish water, and marine wetlands (Scott and Carbonell 1986). Mangrove forest dominated vast areas at sea level, whereas freshwater marshes, shrub swamps, and forested wetlands prevailed inland. The area was flooded in the rainy season (May–October). During the dry season, the forest floor remained damp where canopy was present. The elevation never exceeded 20 meters. Few people now live on the peninsula because of the wet terrain. The climate is tropical with mean daily temperatures from 20°C in January to 27°C in July (Alfonso et al. 1985).

Vegetation at Los Sabalos was upland semideciduous forest, growing on shallow soil over limestone substrates. The dominant tree species throughout the Los Sabalos study area was Jucaro (*Bucida palustris* Borhidi), and was recorded at all three stations. Descriptions presented here result from a small sample of vegetation measurements made at Los Sabalos. The banding stations differed in three ways that may affect bird distribution. The stations exhibited a gradient of soil moisture from more mesic at Stations A and C to drier at Station B; a gradient of forest structure from short and open at Station C, through taller and denser at Stations A, to tallest and densest at Station B; and a gradient from simple composition with few species of canopy trees at Stations A and C to a more complex forest association with many tree species at Station B.

Structure and composition of the vegetation at Los Sabalos reflected the effects of flooding and of human land use practices. Persistent grazing and harvesting of trees for tobacco poles and other wood products have produced a young forest dominated by small trees, with a browse line often apparent. Areas not subjected to wet season flooding had a more diverse suite of woody species. All stations reflected past forest harvest, with obvious extensive coppice growth of many species. Downed logs and leaf litter were present at both stations A and B, but a far greater amount of each was present at Station B. More limestone was exposed at Station B than at the other stations. Herbaceous cover was present at both stations A and C, and much less developed at Station B. In addition to grazing by native fauna, including jutias (*Capromys* sp.), that by white-tailed deer (*Odocoileus virginianus*) and pigs (*Sus scrofa*) occurred throughout the area during the study; horses (*Equus caballus*), goats (*Capra hircus*), and guineafowl (*Numida meleagris*) were also present at Station C.

Differences among the stations permitted comparison of bird communities in the following ways: (1) among two forested sites, one drier with a more diverse composition (Station B) and one wetter with fewer tree species (Station A); and (2) between the forested stations and a seasonally flooded pasture with numerous tall shrubs and small trees (Station C).

FIELD TECHNIQUES

The field methods employed in this study involved capturing and banding birds, censusing birds in the vicinity of the nets, measuring the structure and composition of the vegetation near the nets, and observing the behavior of birds in the field. The techniques are presented here briefly. Birds were caught in 30 standard mist nets 9 x 2 m with 30-mm mesh. Three groups of ten nets were set in subjectively chosen locations along and near forest trails in three different habitats. Two nets at Station B and one at Station C were located near standing water. For each captured bird, we recorded the species, age and sex when known, capture location in detail, standard morphological measurements, and other data. All birds were banded on one leg with US FWS bands and some migrants with an additional band containing an address on the other leg. Birds were released at the banding site.

Estimates of the composition of bird communities in the habitats encompassing the nets were made at six counting points in each habitat using the fixed-radius circular plot technique of Hutto et al. (1986). At each point, 20-min counts were made by one or two observers between 0715 and 0935 on rainless mornings with low wind velocities. Detections of each species were summarized into mean number of encounters/count and frequency within each habitat. Additionally, notation was made for each species in each habitat to indicate whether at least one detection was within 25 m of at least one counting point.

Cursory vegetation measurements were taken in two ways, and the resulting small samples merely indicated vegetation composition and structure at the three banding stations. Trees at least 25 cm in diameter at 1.5 m above ground were identified to species, tallied, and their diameters recorded in two 2-m wide transects at each station. From these data, estimates were derived of the diameter class distribution and basal area by species along each transect. Vegetation in the vicinity of the nets was sampled and resulting data summarized using a protocol based on that of James and Shugart (1970).

Observations of the behavior and habitat use of birds at Los Sabalos and other locations in Matanzas Province were made by following trails through the forest, or by searching for particular species, and then recording specific behaviors of the birds when found. All observers searched for *Vermivora bachmanii*. Indeed, each technique employed in this study involved a means of detecting this species.

Results and discussion

We caught 423 birds of 43 species at Los Sabalos in 1988 and 1989; 20 species were Neotropical migrants and 24 were residents. Each year, approximately 55% of all captured birds were Neotropical migrants. Twenty-nine species of Passeriformes, four Columbiformes, three Piciformes, two Cuculiformes were captured as well as single species each of Apodiformes, Coraciiformes, Strigiformes, and Ciconiiformes. In 1988, 49 of the 238 birds captured were recaptured one to four times, for a total of 74 repeats. In 1989, 64 birds were recaptured a total of 89 times. Twenty-seven of these birds were returns from 1988, 37 were repeats from 1989. The mist nets were open for 17 days (nine in 1988, eight in 1989) between sunrise and sunset, up to 10 hours per day, for a total of 3,865 net hours. Capture rates varied during the day in an expected fashion. Capture rates for the morning hours only (0700–1200 EST) were 0.188 birds/net hr in 1988 and 0.123 birds/net hr in 1989.

In each year the peak capture rate was achieved in the second day in the field. Subsequently, the rate declined. This indicates that efforts to capture a maximum number of birds might be achieved by operating a larger number of individual substations in mornings only, for periods of 4–5 days, rather than keeping a

TABLE 1.   Numbers of captures and recaptures of Neotropical migrants by species in 1988 and 1989 at Los Sabalos, Cuba

Species	Year and station[a]								Total
	1988				1989				
	A	B	C	Total	A	B	C	Total	
Green-backed Heron *Butorides striatus*				0			1	1	1
Yellow-bellied Sapsucker *Sphyrapicus varius*	1		2	3	1		2	3	6
Blue-gray Gnatcatcher *Polioptila caerulea*	1	1		2			2	2	4
Gray Catbird *Dumetella carolinensis*	4	5:1	5:2	14:3	2	4:1		6.1	20.4
Blue-winged Warbler *Vermivora pinus*				0		1		1	1
Northern Parula *Parula americana*	1	4	2	7	4:1	1	4	9:1	16:1
Magnolia Warbler *Dendroica magnolia*	2:1	1:1	3:2	1:1	2		3:1	6:3	
Black-thr. Blue Warbler *Dendroica caerulescens*	4:3	5	2	11:3	4:3	7:2	1	12:5	23:8
Prairie Warbler *Dendroica discolor*				0			2	2	2
Palm Warbler *Dendroica palmarum*	1		22:9	23:9	1		17:8	18:8	41:17
Black-and-white Warbler *Mniotilta varia*	1	3:2	1	5:2	6:1	1	1	8:1	13:3
American Redstart *Setophaga ruticilla*	2:1	8:4	2	12:5	3:1	1:1	4:2	16:7	
Worm-eating Warbler *Helmitheros vermivorus*	1	6	1	8	2	1	3	11	
Ovenbird *Seiurus aurocapillus*	3:1	10:2	5:1	18:4	2	4	2:1	8:1	26:5
Northern Waterthrush *Seiurus noveboracensis*	1	1:1	4:2	6:3	3	7	10:4	16:7	
Louisiana Waterthrush *Seiurus motacilla*	1	1	1	3	1	3	4:1	7:1	
Kentucky Warbler *Oporornis formosus*		1		1			0	1	
Common Yellowthroat *Geothlypis trichas*	2	4:1	11:3	17:4	1	3	4	21:4	
Hooded Warbler *Wilsonia citrina*		1:1		1:1		1		1	2:1
Indigo Bunting *Passerina cyanea*				0		3	3	3	3
TOTAL INDIVIDUALS	25	51	58	134:36	26	27	49	102:25	236:61
PERCENT OF TOTAL	19	38	43	57	26	26	48	43	
TOTAL SPECIES	14	14	12	16	10	12	14	19	20
PERCENT OF TOTAL	88	88	75	80	53	63	72	95	

a. Figures are expressed as number of birds captured:number of birds recaptured.

smaller number of stations open for a longer period. Despite the diminution of capture rate over the sampling period and during afternoon hours, our overall capture rate (0.11 birds/net hr and 0.15 captures/net hr) was higher than that reported in similar studies, by Bosque and Lentino (1987) in Venezuela (0.045 birds/net hr), for example.

CAPTURES AND RECAPTURES OF
NEOTROPICAL MIGRANTS

We caught 134 birds of 16 Neotropical migrant species in 1988, and 102 birds of 19 Neotropical species in 1989 (Table 1). Hotter weather during most of the 1989 banding period probably caused the reduced catch in spite of the greater number of nets used in 1989.

Most of the species caught were expected to be in Cuba during January and February (Garrido and Garcia Montaña 1975, Garrido 1988). However, four species were noteworthy: Blue-winged (*Vermivora pinus*), Worm-eating (*Helmitheros vermivorus*), Kentucky (*Oporornis formosus*), and Hooded warblers (*Wilsonia citrina*); (see Appendix 1).

All but five of the Neotropical migrant species banded were wood-warblers (Parulinae). Gray Catbirds (*Dumetella carolinensis*) were the only non-Paruline migrants caught often. The high proportion of wood-warblers caught is of special interest because some recent banding data of migrants have suggested that several of these species may be declining (Jones 1986; Robbins et al. 1986; Stewart 1987, 1988; Gilbert 1988). Continued work in Cuba will be valuable for clarifying this issue and for interpreting results from other Caribbean islands farther from the North American mainland. Distinguishing long- from short-term fluctuations in numbers, and local or regional trends from continental trends will not be easy.

Banders frequently first detect a species in a given area when it appears in a mist net, but the capture of three Indigo Buntings (*Passerina cyanea*) on different days at Station C in 1989 was enlightening because the species was not observed nearby.

The small numbers of most species caught make detailed comparisons between years or among areas premature. However, certain results were clear. A higher proportion of woodland species, especially Ovenbirds (*Seiurus aurocapillus*), were captured at the more heavily forested Station B. The more open nature of Station C accounted for the high numbers of Palm Warblers (*Dendroica palmarum*), a species often found in open areas in the tropics (Leck 1985). We considered the forest-interior breeding migrants as a group (Hamel et al. 1982, Robbins et al. 1989), and compared the proportion of forest-interior migrants across forested stations (A and B) versus open station (C). The proportions of forest-in-

terior migrants were higher than expected in forested stations and lower in the open station (χ^2, 2 d.f.= 1988: 24.14, $P < 0.01$; 1989: 25.15, $P < 0.01$; years combined: 46.26, $P < 0.01$). These results were consistent with those from the bird counts that indicate a greater similarity between the forested stations than between the forested and open habitats.

In both years, a large proportion of the migrants caught were recaptured at least once, with 36 birds of 10 species recaptured a total of 56 times in 1988 and 25 birds of 10 species recaptured a total of 37 times in 1989 (Table 1). Although the study period each year was just over a week, these data indicated that once on wintering grounds, at least some individuals of these species remained within a prescribed area, rather than wandering widely. This impression was further strengthened by the small number of between-station captures. We detected no movement of birds in either year between Station C and any other station. In 1988, only three birds moved the 250 m between Stations A and B, and two of these were subsequently recaptured at the original banding site. In 1989, all movements were between extreme parts of Station A, 70 m apart. Sightings of banded birds indicated that even more birds remained in the vicinity than were recaptured.

Winter residency and even territoriality has been demonstrated for several Parulines elsewhere in their wintering ranges (Stewart and Connor 1980, Lynch et al. 1985, Greenberg 1986, Morton et al. 1987, Rappole 1988, Holmes et al. 1989). Because some of these warbler species appear to move more widely elsewhere in the Caribbean region (Faaborg and Arendt 1989), much more research is required to clarify the extent and nature of movements and residency of these species on their Cuban wintering grounds.

Among-year site fidelity by Neotropical migrants has been demonstrated through banding returns on the wintering grounds (Nickel 1968; Loftin 1977; Kricher and Davis 1986; and references cited therein). Less is known of such among-year winter site tenacity of Neotropical migrants wintering on Caribbean islands. Banding returns have provided evidence for site fidelity among Neotropical migrants wintering in the Bahamas (Anonymous 1985, Dewey 1989), Haiti (Woods 1975), Jamaica (Diamond and Smith 1973), Puerto Rico (Faaborg and Winters 1979; Faaborg and Arendt 1989), and Trinidad (Snow and Snow 1960).

Similar site fidelity has been suspected in Cuba (O.H. Garrido, pers. comm.; LLanes Sosa et al. 1987; González-Alonso, pers. obs.). The capture by Sanchez et al. (unpubl. data) at Los Sabalos in October 1988 of five birds banded there in the previous winter provided the first substantiation of winter site tenacity in Cuba. Our 1989 recaptures of 16 birds of seven species banded in 1988 (Table 2) provided additional evidence. The

TABLE 2. Neotropical migrant birds captured at Los Sabalos, Cuba, in 1988 and recaptured there in 1989

Species	Station[a]				% of total captured in 1989	Other Caribbean localities[b]
	A	B	C	Total		
Black-throated Blue Warbler *Dendroica caerulescens*		1:1		1:1	8	Haiti, Jamaica
Palm Warbler *Dendroica palmarum*			4:6	4:6	18	Haiti, Bahamas
Black-and-white Warbler *Mniotilta varia*	2:2	1:1[c]		2:3	20	Jamaica, Puerto Rico
American Redstart *Setophaga ruticilla*	1:2	3:4		4:6	50	Jamaica, Puerto Rico
Worm-eating Warbler *Helmitheros vermivorus*			1:1	1:1	25	Jamaica
Ovenbird *Seiurus aurocapillus*		2:4		2:4	20	Jamaica, Puerto Rico, Bahamas
Common Yellowthroat *Geothlypis trichas*		1:1	1:2	2:3	33	Haiti, Jamaica
TOTAL	2:4	8:11	6:9	16:24		

a. Expressed as number of birds:number of captures (e.g. six Palm Warbler recaptures were recorded, but only four birds were involved). All birds were recaptured at the station where they were originally banded, unless otherwise indicated.

b. Other Caribbean islands or localities on which the species has been recaptured in a year subsequent to the original banding on the same island. SOURCES: Haiti (Woods 1975), Jamaica (Diamond and Smith 1973), Puerto Rico (Faaborg and Winters 1979, Faaborg and Arendt 1989), Bahamas (Anonymous 1985, Dewey 1989).

c. Banded at Station B, caught once at Stations A and B

Ovenbird, Black-throated Blue Warbler (*Dendroica caerulescens*), and one of the American Redstarts (*Setophaga ruticilla*) caught by Sanchez et al. (unpubl. data) were also caught by us, whereas the other two redstarts were not. Thus, at least six American Redstarts and 18 Neotropical migrants returned from one winter to another to Los Sabalos (50% of the redstarts banded there in 1988 and 13% of the migrant birds). Each species we recaptured is also known to display site fidelity on at least one other Caribbean island (Table 2).

Because of the perceived threat to migrant birds posed by deforestation in the tropics (Lovejoy 1983), these limited data have important implications for conservation of these species, especially because all of our recaptures between years were of Parulines, as were most of our intra-year recaptures. When individuals of a species display site fidelity on both the breeding and winter grounds, destruction of habitats in either breeding or winter grounds may result in population losses proportionally greater than habitat losses. That is, loss of either winter or breeding habitat may eliminate a segment of the population. Disappearance of a part of the population from an unmodified breeding area may be the result of destruction of the winter habitat, and disappearance of a part of the population from an unmodified wintering area may be the result of destruc-

tion of the breeding habitat. In the extreme, destruction of half of the winter habitat and half of the breeding habitat might be sufficient to eliminate far more than half the population, under conditions that the winter habitat destroyed represents the winter home of that part of the population whose breeding habitat is intact and the breeding habitat destroyed represents the breeding grounds for that segment of the population whose winter habitat is intact.

Some species might be more variable in their winter site tenacity, however. For example, we captured a relatively large number of Gray Catbirds, but had relatively few recaptures and no returns. This result is similar to that of Fisk (1976) in Florida.

CAPTURES AND RECAPTURES OF RESIDENT BIRDS

We caught 186 birds of 24 resident species during the work, including 104 birds of 22 species in 1988 and 82 birds of 21 species in 1989. Those most frequently captured were species that forage on the ground, for example Red-legged Thrush (*Turdus plumbeus*), Gray-headed Quail-Dove (*Geotrygon caniceps*), Ruddy Quail-Dove (*G. montana*), and Common Ground-Dove (*Columbina passerina*); or birds that forage by sallying, for example Loggerhead Kingbird (*Tyrannus caudifasciatus*), La Sagra's

Flycatcher (*Myiarchus sagrae*), Greater Antillean Pewee (*Contopus caribaeus*), and Cuban Tody (*Todus multicolor*). The proportion of recaptures among resident birds in each year was markedly lower than that of the migrants (1988: 12%, 1989: 15%, combined years 13%). Similarly, the numbers of species represented in the sample of recaptures was lower both absolutely and relatively among resident species than among migrants. The proportion of species represented in the sample of returns from 1988 to 1989, as well as the number of birds returning from 1988 to 1989 (11 birds of five species), was lower for the resident species than for the migrants.

More than 75% of the resident birds captured in each year were Passeriformes or Columbiformes. High similarity in species composition of the samples from the two years existed because 19 species were captured each year, corresponding to the capture of most species susceptible to capture by nets deployed in the forest understory. Low similarity of relative abundance of the samples of the several stations indicated that differences existed between the stations, differences that were probably due to the differences in habitat discussed earlier (e.g. in 1988, $S_{AB} = 0.38$, $S_{AC} = 0.40$, and $S_{BC} = 0.48$; while in 1989, $S_{AB} = 0.33$, $S_{AC} = 0.50$, and $S_{BC} = 0.58$; index of similarity is that of Acosta Cruz 1987). Comparisons made between years for each station revealed quantitative similarities below 0.5 for each station indicating considerable annual variation as well.

CIRCULAR PLOTS

We made 48 counts on 23 fixed-radius (25-m) circular plots in this study, 24 by pairs of observers and 24 by single observers (Table 3). A total of 1500 birds of 59 species was recorded (Table 4). Sixteen (27%) of these species were North American migrants, including 13 migratory Parulinae.

Because the number of counts in each habitat was small, detailed analyses and density conversions of these data were not warranted. However, several points did seem justified and relevant. The technique of Hutto et al. (1986) was useful for winter in semideciduous forests such as those of Los Sabalos. At that season birds were not singing and most calls were not audible for the distances required for other circular plot techniques such as that described by Hamel (1984). Only Cuban Vireo (*Vireo gundlachii*), Cuban Tody (*Todus multicolor*), and Cuban Trogon (*Priotelus temnurus*) were detected by song each day. The combination of lack of singing and presence of dense vegetation made the use of fixed-width transects such as that of Järvinen and Väisänen (1977) problematical as well, because silent birds were difficult to detect when screened by vegetation. Because the technique has been used by other workers on winter avifauna of Caribbean and Gulf Coast habitats (Waide and Wunderle, pers. comm.), its use in Cuba will be of considerable comparative value. It was obvious that the

TABLE 3. Summary of bird counts at Los Sabalos, Cuba, 1988–1989 (both resident and migrant species are included)

	Station			
	A	B	C	Total
Sample size, as points (no. of counts, mean no. of observers)	7(15, 1.6)	6(16, 1.4)	6(17, 1.5)	19(48, 1.5)
Starting time, mean value:				
1988	0813	0810	0824	
1989	0852	0906	0847	
TOTAL	0836	0845	0840	
Birds, mean no./count, (range) exclusive of large flocks of *Cathartes aura*	29.5(14–47)	29.9(23–49)	27.3(16–62)	28.8(14–62)
Species richness, mean (range)	16.2(9–22)	17.0(10–27)	16.8(11–24)	16.7(9–27)
Total species	46	41	52	59
Species recorded at one station only	5	2	9	16
Birds recorded within 25 m, mean/count	6.2	9.8	4.8	6.9
Total species recorded within 25 m	29	29	25	43
Species recorded within 25 m at one station only	3	4	8	15
Percent of migrants within 25 m	22	28	28	
Percent of forest interior migrants within 25 m	7	15	2	

TABLE 4. Birds counted at Los Sabalos, Cuba, 1988–1989. Data expressed as mean number/count (frequency, range)

Species	Status[a]	Station A	B	C
Sample Size, Points (Counts)		7(15)	6(16)	6(17)
Olivaceous Cormorant *Phalacrocorax olivaceus*		–	–	0.06(1,–)
Great Blue Heron *Ardea herodias*		0.2	(2,1–1)	0.1(1,–)
Great Egret *Casmerodius albus*		0.2(2,1–1)	–	–
Little Blue Heron *Egretta caerulea*		–	–	0.06(1,–)
Cattle Egret *Bubulcus ibis*		–	–	0.4(4,1–2)
Green-backed Heron *Butorides striatus*		0.1(2,1–1)	–	0.06(1,–)
Wood Stork *Mycteria americana*		0.06(1,–)	–	–
Turkey Vulture *Cathartes aura*		0.5(3,1–3)	0.6(3,1–7)	4.4(8,1–42)
Broad-winged Hawk *Buteo platypterus*		0.06(1,–)	0.1(2,1–1)	0.2(2,1–3)
Red-tailed Hawk *Buteo jamaicensis*		–	–	0.06(1,–)
American Kestrel *Falco sparverius*		–	–	0.06(1,–)
Peregrine Falcon *Falco peregrinus*		–	–	0.06(1,–)
Common Moorhen *Gallinula chloropus*		0.2(4,1–1)	–	–
American Coot *Fulica americana*		0.3(3,1–1)	–	–
Killdeer *Charadrius vociferus*		0.06(1,–)	–	0.4(6,1–3)
White-crowned Pigeon *Columba leucocephala*		0.2(2,1–1)	0.2(2,1–1)[b]	0.4(3,1–3)
Zenaida Dove *Zenaida aurita*		0.9(6,1–4)	0.6(4,1–3)	0.5(7,1–2)[c]
Mourning Dove *Zenaida macroura*		0.5(5,1–3)	0.5(3,2–3)	2.4(14,1–5)[c]
Common Ground-Dove *Columbina passerina*		0.1(3,1–1)	0.6(7,1–2)	0.4(7,1–2)[c]
Gray-headed Quail-Dove *Geotrygon caniceps*		–	0.2(2,1–1)[b]	–
Ruddy Quail-Dove *Geotrygon montana*		0.06(1,–)[c]		0.06(1,–)
Cuban Parrot *Amazona leucocephala*		3.1(13,2–6)	1.4(10,1–5)	1.5(9,1–4)
Great Lizard-Cuckoo *Saurothera merlini*		1.5(9,1–4)[b]	2.1(13,1–4)[b,c]	1.7(12,1–3)[b,c]
Smooth-billed Ani *Crotophaga ani*		0.06(1,–)	0.06(1,–)	0.9(5,1–2)[b]
Cuban Pygmy-Owl *Glaucidium siju*		1.9(13,1–7)[b]	1.2(9,1–3)	1.4(12,1–3)
Cuban Emerald *Chlorostilbon ricordii*		0.9(11,1–2)[b,c]	1.2(12,1–4)[b,c]	0.1(2,1–1)[c]
Cuban Trogon *Priotelus temnurus*		2.1(9,1–9)[c]	2.1(8,1–7)[c]	0.8(8,1–4)[c]
Cuban Tody *Todus multicolor*		1.6(14,1–3)[b,c]	1.1(12,1–2)[b,c]	0.3(3,1–2)[b]
West Indian Woodpecker *Melanerpes superciliaris*		1.9(13,1–4)[b]	0.9(9,1–3)[b]	1.4(9,1–4)
Yellow-bellied Sapsucker *Sphyrapicus varius*	Migrant	0.2(4,1–1)[c]	0.06(1,–)	0.2(2,1–1)[b]
Cuban Green Woodpecker *Xiphidiopicus percussus*		0.1(1,–)[b]	0.3(5,1–1)[b]	0.1(1,–)
Northern Flicker *Colaptes auratus*		0.7(8,1–2)	0.4(3,1–3)	0.8(9,1–4)[c]
Greater Antillean Pewee *Contopus caribaeus*		1.9(14,1–4)[b,c]	2.0(13,1–4)[b,c]	1.8(15,1–4)[b,c]
La Sagra Flycatcher *Myiarchus sagrae*		1.2(11,1–3)[c]	1.3(10,1–4)[b,c]	1.2(12,1–3)[b,c]
Loggerhead Kingbird *Tyrannus caudifasciatus*		0.2(4,1–1)[b]	0.6(5,1–3)[b,c]	0.9(11,1–3)[c]
Blue-gray Gnatcatcher *Polioptila caerulea*	Interior?	1.0(12,1–2)[b,c]	0.7(5,1–4)[b,c]	0.9(9,1–4)[c]
Red-legged Thrush *Turdus plumbeus*		1.8(11,1–4)[b,c]	1.2(9,1–3)[b]	1.8(13,1–8)[b,c]
Gray Catbird *Dumetella carolinensis*	Migrant	0.1(1,–)	0.8(6,1–2)[b]	0.4(3,1–3)[b]
Cuban Vireo *Vireo gundlachii*		0.5(6,1–1)[c]	0.6(6,1–2)[c]	1.4(13,1–4)
Northern Parula *Parula americana*	Interior	0.5(4,1–5)[c]	0.7(5,1–3)[b,c]	0.2(4,1–1)[b]
Magnolia Warbler *Dendroica magnolia*	Interior	0.2(2,1–1)[c]	0.7(8,1–2)[b,c]	0.1(2,1–1)
Black-thr. Blue Warbler *Dendroica caerulescens*	Interior	0.06(1,–)[c]	0.4(6,1–1)[b,c]	0.1(2,1–1)
Black-thr. Green Warbler *Dendroica virens*	Interior	–	0.1(1,–)[c]	0.06(1,–)[c]
Yellow-throated Warbler *Dendroica dominica*	Interior	0.06(1,–)[c]	–	–

a. Resident species are not marked. Migrant species are indicated either as Migrant–migratory species, or as Interior–migratory species that are believed to require large contiguous tracts of forest in the breeding season.

b. Recorded within 25 m on at least one count in this habitat in 1988.

c. Recorded within 25 m on at least one count in this habitat in 1989.

TABLE 4—*Continued*

Species	Status[a]	Station		
		A	B	C
Prairie Warbler *Dendroica discolor*	Migrant	–	–	0.1(2,1–1)[c]
Palm Warbler *Dendroica palmarum*	Migrant	–	–	2.8(14,1–18)[c]
Black-and-white Warbler *Mniotilta varia*	Interior	0.06(1,–)[c]	0.2(2, 1–1)[b]	0.1(2,1–1)
American Redstart *Setophaga ruticilla*	Interior	2.1(14,1–7)[b,c]	1.4(11,1–4)[b,c]	0.4(7,1–1)[c]
Ovenbird *Seiurus aurocapillus*	Interior	0.06(1,–)[c]	0.2(4,1–1)[b,c]	0.06(1,–)
Northern Waterthrush *Seiurus noveboracensis*	Migrant	0.06(1,–)[b]	0.06(1,–)	0.5(9,1–3)[b,c]
Louisiana Waterthrush *Seiurus motacilla*	Interior?	–	0.06(1,–)[b]	–
Common Yellowthroat *Geothlypis trichas*	Migrant	0.06(1,–)[b]	0.2(2,1–1)[b]	0.9(8,1–3)[b,c]
Yellow-headed Warbler *Teretistris fernandinae*		1.4(10,1–4)[c]	2.8(12,1–5)[b,c]	0.4(4,1–3)
Stripe-headed Tanager *Spindalis zena*		0.1(3,1–1)[c]	0.2(3,1–1)[c]	0.06(1,–)
Cuban Bullfinch *Melopyrrha nigra*		–	0.1(1,–)[c]	0.2(2,1–1)
Cuban Grassquit *Tiaris canora*		–	–	0.3(3,1–1)[b]
Yellow-faced Grassquit *Tiaris olivacea*		0.06(1,–)[c]	–	0.4(5,1–4)[b,c]
Cuban Blackbird *Dives atroviolacea*		0.8(5,1–3)[c]	0.5(5,1–3)[b]	0.4(5,1–3)
Black-cowled Oriole *Icterus dominicensis*		0.8(5,1–4)[c]	2.1(12,1–5)[b,c]	0.2(5,1–1)
Unidentified columbid		–	0.1(1,–)	–
Unidentified *Geotrygon*		0.06(1,–)	–	0.2(1,–)
Unidentified picid		0.2(2,1–1)	0.2(2,1–1)	–
Unidentified tyrannid		–	0.1(1,–)	0.06(1,–)
Unidentified parulid		0.2(3,1–1)	0.1(1,–)	0.6(1,–)
Unidentified icterid		0.1(1,–)	–	0.1(1,–)
Unidentified species		–	0.4(2,1–3)	0.1(1,–)

a. Resident species are not marked. Migrant species are indicated either as Migrant–migratory species, or as Interior–migratory species that are believed to require large contiguous tracts of forest in the breeding season.

b. Recorded within 25 m on at least one count in this habitat in 1988.

c. Recorded within 25 m on at least one count in this habitat in 1989.

pairs of observers identified more birds than the single observers during the counts.

Point counts at the several stations indicated differences in detectabilities and occurrence of species among habitats. The stations differed in the total number of species observed and the proportion of species and individuals encountered within 25 m of the counting point. More species were detected in the open habitat of Station C than in either of the more forested stations. However, at the forested Station B a much higher proportion of the birds observed were within 25 m of the counting points, suggesting that actual densities at Station B were higher than those at the other stations.

The proportion of individuals belonging to migratory species was highest at the forested Station B, where the proportion of individuals belonging to the group of forest-interior migrants was almost 10%. *Teretistris fernandinae*, the species on which migrant forest-dwelling birds cue for forming flocks (cf. Quesada and de las Pozas 1984), contributed 13% of the birds in the forested Station B.

Comparison of the lists of species for the several stations provided several additional insights into the winter bird communities of Los Sabalos. Approximately 75% of the combined lists of each pair of stations was made up of species that occurred in each station, for example, 74% of 50 between Stations A and B, 72% of 57 between Stations A and C, and 72% of 52 between Stations B and C. These results indicate that the avian composition of the three habitats was similar. These results were misleading to the extent that large, wide ranging species such as Cuban Parrot (*Amazona leucocephala*) appeared on each list. When the comparison of stations was confined to species observed within 25 m of the counting points, the two forested stations, A and B, were more similar to each other than either was to Station C, whether the comparison concerned migrants, resident species, or all species. Thus, forest habitats at Los Sabalos differed from open habitats in species composition in winter.

We examined the counts of forest-interior species separately. We tested the null hypothesis that the proportion of these species observed within 25 m was the same regardless of station. The proportion of forest-interior migrants at the forested Station A was not different than expected (χ^2, 1 d.f. = 0.201, n.s.). At the forested Station B the proportion of forest interior migrants was significantly higher than expected (χ^2, 1 d.f. = 4.70, $P < 0.05$). At the open Station C the proportion of interior migrants was significantly lower than expected (χ^2, 1 d.f. = 12.2, $P < 0.01$). Because of the differences in habitat between stations B and C, and the concomitant differences in species composition, we suggest that forested habitats in Cuba are important habitats, particularly for wintering migrant birds.

Conclusions

Brief evaluations of each of the objectives of this project can be presented. The number of captures, recaptures, and net hours of effort are indicative of the success of this program as a training effort. Four Cuban ornithologists have visited Long Point Bird Observatory in the past two years for additional training. The work of Sanchez et al. (unpubl. data) indicates that this work stimulated additional effort in Cuba. Our efforts have concentrated upon the single, Los Sabalos site; additional sites have been suggested for further evaluation, and one was employed in 1989 (LLanes Sosa and Melian, unpubl. report, Sirois et al. 1990). The relatively high rate of returns of migrants from one winter to another found in this study, as well as additional findings (Kirkconnell and Hamel, unpubl. data) on flocks of *Teretistris fernandinae* and migrants, indicate the rich potential for further research in Cuba. We found no Bachman's Warblers (Hamel 1988), but have identified likely localities and shown how searches for this species can be conducted in concert with other work. The existence of this project and the combined work of scientists from the three countries demonstrates that this kind of cooperative effort is possible. Our results indicate some winter site fidelity of certain migrants and the importance of forest habitats as wintering grounds for forest interior breeding species, and suggest that particular, identifiable habitats are important for individual migratory and resident species.

Acknowledgments

Orlando Garrido and Gilberto Silva were important to the initial formulation of the project. Graeme Gibson was important as initiator, fundraiser, facilitator, and friend of the project. Robert Waide and Joseph Wunderle provided information concerning their own ongoing projects on migrant birds in the Caribbean region. Iola M. Price, formerly of the Canadian Wildlife Service, helped to bring together the necessary resources outside Cuba. Ileana Yarza of the Academia de Ciencias de Cuba was equally helpful in bringing together the necessary resources inside Cuba. The Canadian Wildlife Service Latin American Programme provided equipment in both years and honoraria for McNicholl and McRae in 1989. World Wildlife Fund (Canada) provided funding for air fares from Canada for McNicholl and McRae. Long Point Bird Observatory provided some equipment to the project. The Pan American Section of the International Council for Bird Preservation supported Hamel's participation in 1988, and the Tennessee Department of Conservation provided assistance to him in 1989. Jackson was supported in part by Mississippi State University. The final manuscript benefited from the comments of Lisa, Dan, and Ken Petit, as well as two anonymous reviewers.

Literature cited

Acosta Cruz, M. 1987. Una expresión de similaridad cuantitativa. Utilización espacial y temporal en aves. *Revista Cubana de Biología* 1(3):67–72.

Alfonso, A.P., H. Elizalde, and O. Solano. 1985. *El mesoclima de la Península de Zapata*. Rep. de Invest. No. 12, Academia de Ciencias de Cuba.

Anonymous. 1985. Banding returns to Andros Island, Bahamas. *Ottawa Banding Group Newsletter* 2(1):1–3.

Bond, J. 1980. *Birds of the West Indies*, 4th ed. Houghton Mifflin, Boston, Massachusetts.

Bosque, C., and M. Lentino. 1987. The passage of North American migratory land birds through xerophytic habitats on the western coast of Venezuela. *Biotropica* 19(3):267–273.

Dewey, J. 1989. Andros Island, Bahamas. *Ottawa Banding Group Newsletter* 6(2):4–8.

Diamond, A.W., and R.W. Smith. 1973. Returns and survival of banded warblers wintering in Jamaica. *Bird-Banding* 44:221–224.

Faaborg, J., and W.J. Arendt. 1989. Longevity estimates of Puerto Rican birds. *N. Am. Bird Bander* 14:11–13.

Faaborg, J., and J.E. Winters. 1979. Winter resident returns and longevity and weights of Puerto Rican birds. *Bird-Banding* 50:216–223.

Fisk, E.J. 1976. Notes on a winter bird-population study: Observations versus netting. *Aud. Field Notes* 30:1075.

Garrido, O.H. 1986. Introduction, Cuba. Pages 483–484 in *A Directory of Neotropical Wetlands*, D.A. Scott and M. Carbonell, compilers. Slimbridge, U.K.: IUCN, Cambridge and IWRB.

———. 1988. *La migracion de las aves en Cuba*. Sevilla, España: Graficas Mirte.

Garrido, O.H., and F. Garcia Montaña. 1975. *Catalogo de las aves de Cuba*. Havana: Academia de Ciencias de Cuba.

Gilbert, W.M. 1988. Warbler population declines. *N. Am. Bird Bander* 13:11.

González-Alonso, H., J. Sirois, M.K. McNicholl, P.B. Hamel, E. Godinez, R.D. McRae, M. Acosta, D. Rodríguez, C. Marcos, y J. Hernández. 1990. *Resultados preliminares de un proyecto cooperativo de anillamiento de aves en la Ciénaga de Zapata, Cuba, enero de 1988*. Canadian Wildlife Service, Progress Notes No. 187.

Greenberg, R. 1986. Competition in migrant birds in the non-breeding season. *Current Ornithol.* 3:281–307.

Hamel, P.B. 1984. Comparison of variable circular-plot and spot-mapping methods in a temperate deciduous forest. *Ornis Scand.* 15:266–274.

———. 1986. *Bachman's Warbler, a Species in Peril.* Washington: Smithsonian Institution Press.

———. 1988. Bachman's Warbler. Pages 624–635 in *Audubon Wildlife Report 1988.* New York: National Audubon Society.

Hamel, P.B., H.E. LeGrand, Jr., M.R. Lennartz, and S.A. Gauthreaux, Jr. 1982. *Bird-habitat Relationships on Southeastern Forest Lands.* Asheville, N.C.: U.S. Forest Service General Technical Report SE-22.

Herrero, J.A., R. Molina, and Y.V. Melchanov. 1983. Los bosques en Cuba, su funcion y significado antierosivo. *Revista forestal Baracao* 13(1):83–93.

Holmes, R.T., T.W. Sherry, and L. Reitsma. 1989. Population structure, territoriality and overwinter survival of two migrant warbler species in Jamaica. *Condor* 91:545–561.

Hutto, R.L., S.M. Pletschet, and P. Hendricks. 1986. A fixed-radius point count method for nonbreeding and breeding season use. *Auk* 103:593–602.

James, F.C., and H.H. Shugart. 1970. A quantitative method of habitat description. *Aud. Field Notes* 24:727–736.

Järvinen, O., and R.A. Väisänen. 1977. Line transect method: A standard for field-work. *Polish Ecol. Studies* 3(4):11–15.

Jones, E.T. 1986. The passerine decline. *N. Am. Bird Bander* 11:74–75.

Keast, A., and E.S. Morton, eds. 1980. *Migrant Birds in the Neotropics: Ecology, Behavior, Distribution, and Conservation.* Washington: Smithsonian Institution Press.

Kricher, J.C., and W.E. Davis, Jr. 1986. Returns and winter-site fidelity of North American migrants banded in Belize, Central America. *J. Field Ornithol.* 57:48–52.

Leck, C.F. 1985. The use of disturbed habitats by North American birds wintering in Mexico. *Biotropica* 17:263–264.

LLanes Sosa, A., A. Kirkconnel Paez, R.M. Posada Rodriguez, and S. Cubillas Hernandez. 1987. Nuevos reportes de fechas de aves migratorias para Cuba. *Miscelanea Zoologica, Academia de Ciencias de Cuba* 36:1–2.

Loftin, H. 1977. Returns and recoveries of banded North American birds in Panama and the tropics. *Bird-Banding* 48:253–258.

Lopez Ornat, A., J.F. Lynch, and B. MacKinnon de Montes. 1989. New and noteworthy records of birds from the eastern Yucatan Peninsula. *Wilson Bull.* 101:390–409.

Lovejoy, T.E. 1983. Tropical deforestation and North American migrant birds. *Bird Conserv.* 1:126–128.

Lucas, G., G. Moreau, and C. Labouret, eds. 1983. *Petit Larousse illustre.* Paris: Larousse.

Lynch, J.F. 1989. Distribution of overwintering Nearctic migrants in the Yucatan Peninsula, I: General patterns of occurrence. *Condor* 91:515–544.

Lynch, J.F., E.S. Morton, and M.E. Van der Voort. 1985. Habitat segregation between the sexes of wintering Hooded Warblers (*Wilsonia citrina*). *Auk* 102:714–721.

Morton, E.S., J.F. Lynch, K. Young, and P. Mehlhop. 1987. Do male Hooded Warblers exclude females from nonbreeding territories in tropical forest? *Auk* 104:133–135.

Nickel, W.P. 1968. Returns of northern migrants to tropical winter quarters and banded birds recovered in the United States. *Bird-Banding* 39:107–116.

Quesada, M., and G. de las Pozas. 1984. Actividad de forrajeo de la Chillina, Teretistris fernandinae (Aves: Parulidae), en un bosque de San Diego de los Baños, Cuba. *Miscelanea Zoologica, Academia de Ciencias de Cuba* 19:1–2.

Rappole, J.H. 1988. Intra- and intersexual competition in migratory passerine birds during the nonbreeding season. *Acta 19th Internat. Ornithol. Cong.* (Ottawa): 2308–2317.

Rappole, J.H., E.S. Morton, T.E. Lovejoy, III, and J.L. Ruos. 1983. *Nearctic Avian Migrants in the Neotropics.* Washington: U.S. Fish and Wildlife Service.

Robbins, C.S., D. Bystrak, and P.H. Geissler. 1986. *The Breeding Bird Survey: Its First Fifteen Years, 1965–1979.* U.S. Fish and Wildlife Serv. Resource Pub. 157.

Robbins, C.S., D.K. Dawson, and B.A. Dowell. 1989. *Habitat Area Requirements of Breeding Forest Birds of the Middle Atlantic States.* Wildl. Monogr. 103.

Scott, D.A., and M. Carbonell, compilers. 1986. *A Directory of Neotropical Wetlands.* Slimbridge, U.K.: IUCN, Cambridge and IWRB.

Shugart, H.H. 1984. *A Theory of Forest Dynamics.* New York: Springer-Verlag.

Silva Taboada, G. 1983. *Los Murcielagos de Cuba.* Havana: Editorial Cientifico-Tecnica.

Sirois, J., M.K. McNicholl, R.D. McRae, and P.B. Hamel. 1990. *A Pilot Study of Wintering Forest Birds in the Zapata Swamp, Cuba, Phase Two: January-February 1989.* Report to Latin American Program, Canadian Wildlife Service.

Snow, D.W., and B.K. Snow. 1960. Northern Waterthrush returning to same winter quarters in successive winters. *Auk* 77:351–352.

Stewart, P.A. 1987. Decline in numbers of wood warblers in spring and autumn migrations through Ohio. *N. Am. Bird Bander* 12:58–60.

———. 1988. Warbler population declines: A reply. *N. Am. Bird Bander* 13:12.

Stewart, P.A., and H.A. Connor. 1980. Fixation of wintering Palm Warblers to a specific site. *J. Field Ornithol.* 51:365–367.

Udvardy, M.D.F. 1975. *A Classification of the Biogeographical Provinces of the World.* IUCN Occasional Paper No. 18. Morges, Switzerland.

Woods, C.A. 1975. Banding and recapture of wintering warblers in Haiti. *Bird-Banding* 46:344–346.

Worth, C.B. 1969. Hooded Warbler in Trinidad, West Indies. *Wilson Bull.* 81:215.

APPENDIX 1. Notes on individual migrant species

BLUE-WINGED WARBLER (*Vermivora pinus*). The Blue-winged Warbler, a male with slight Golden-winged Warbler characteristics, was captured on 28 January 1989 at Station B, where McRae had observed one earlier the same day, and close to where Sanchez et al. (unpubl. data) reported one in October 1988. Bond (1980) considered this species a rare winter resident or transient throughout the West Indies, and Garrido and Garcia Montaña (1975) considered it rare in Cuba, with records only in April, August, September and December. LLanes Sosa et al. (1987) recently provided February and March records, and Garrido (1988) reported fall records from August to November. Thus, because this species has now been reported in Cuba in each month from August through April, it should be considered as a very rare winter resident (Orlando Garrido, pers. comm.).

WORM-EATING WARBLER (*Helmitheros vermivorus*). Although Worm-eating Warblers winter regularly throughout much of the West Indies (Bond 1980), they are fairly rare in winter in Cuba (Garrido and Garcia Montaña 1975). Thus, the 11 caught by us at Los Sabalos in two years provide a higher total than might be expected.

KENTUCKY WARBLER (*Oporornis formosus*). The Kentucky Warbler caught on 15 January 1988 was unusual. This species is rare anywhere in the West Indies (Bond 1980; Lopez Ornat et al. 1989). Previous records for Cuba are from mid-February to mid-April, August, October, and more recently December (Garrido and Garcia Montaña 1975; LLanes Sosa et al. 1987).

HOODED WARBLER (*Wilsonia citrina*). Hooded Warblers are rare in Cuba, although observed annually (Garrido and Garcia Montaña 1975; Garrido 1988); we were surprised to capture this species each year. Previously published records for Cuba are from March to April and August to October (Garrido and Garcia Montaña 1975), and more recently December (Llanes Sosa et al. 1987) and January (Garrido 1988). There are also several unpublished winter records from birdwatching groups visiting Cuba. This species is considered rare anywhere in the West Indies (Bond 1980), but has been observed as far south as Trinidad (Worth 1969).

WAYNE J. ARENDT
USDA Forest Service
Southern Forest Experiment Station
Institute of Tropical Forestry
Call Box 25000
Rio Piedras, Puerto Rico 00928-2500

WITH COLLABORATORS

Status of North American migrant landbirds in the Caribbean region: A summary

Abstract. To summarize the current status of North American landbird migrants in the Caribbean, 24 regional and local collaborators have joined together in a coordinated effort to document: (a) species diversity, (b) distribution (geographically, and among habitats), (c) general abundance on each island, (d) present-day factors affecting migrant populations, both negative and positive, (e) measures that must be taken to mitigate negative impacts on migrant numbers, and (f) professional views on the probable future of Caribbean migrant landbirds in light of the accelerated development currently taking place throughout most of the region. From this consortium has come the following information: (1) More long-term population dynamics studies are needed to monitor temporal (e.g., population fluctuations over time) and spatial (e.g., differential use of habitat) characteristics of both migrant and resident species, especially on the larger islands of the Greater Antilles, where most of the migrant individuals winter. (2) More long-term population monitoring studies are needed on the smaller islands of the Lesser Antillean Archipelago because as habitat continues to be lost in the larger islands, there is evidence that at least some migrant species are extending their nonbreeding season range east and southward in the region as documented by long-time inhabitants. (3) Existing long-term population studies show tendencies for continued population declines in some paruline warbler species on their Puerto Rican dry-forest wintering grounds (e.g., Northern Parula, Ovenbird, Cape May Warbler, and particularly the Prairie Warbler, which is showing commensurate population declines in North America). (4) In contrast to habitat specialists, which are already showing signs of population crashes, migrant species that are habitat generalists may not be threatened with immediate extinction, or even drastic population declines in the near future, because of their ability to adapt to a mosaic of habitat types, including those altered through human activity. (5) There is hope for the future of migrant landbirds in the Caribbean, owing largely to the rough topography and resilient vegetation inherent to several Caribbean islands. Through international cooperation among conservationists, resource managers, governmental policy-makers, and the general public, enough suitable habitat could remain to support viable migrant landbird populations indefinitely in the Caribbean region.

Sinopsis. Para resumir el estado actual de las aves migratorias terrestres Norteamericanas en el Caribe, se han unido 24 colaboradores locales y regionales en un esfuerzo coordinado para documentar: (a) diversidad de especies, (b) distribución (geográfica y habitacional), (c) abundancia general en cada isla, (d) factores que actualmente afectan las poblaciones migratorias tanto negativa como positivamente, (e) medidas que deben tomarse para mitigar impactos negativos sobre los números de migratorias y (f) puntos de vista profesionales sobre el futuro probable de las aves migratorias terrestres en el Caribe a la luz del desarrollo acelerado que actualmente tiene lugar a través de la mayor parte de la región. A partir de este consorcio ha resultado la siguiente información: (1) Se necesitan mas estudios a largo plazo de las dinámicas poblacionales para monitorear características temporales (e.g. fluctuaciones poblacionales a través del tiempo) y espaciales (e.g. uso diferencial del habitat) tanto de especies migratorias como de especies residentes, especialmente en las islas mayores del archipiélago de las Antillas Menores, puesto que a medida que continúa la pérdida de habitat en dichas islas, existe evidencia de que por lo menos algunas especies están extendiendo su areal no reproductivo hacia el este y hacia el sur en la región, como ya ha sido documentado para residentes antiguas. (3) Estudios poblacionales a largo plazo ya existentes muestran tendencias de declinación poblacional continuada en algunas especies de Parulinae en sus zonas de invernada en los bosques secos de Puerto Rico (e.g. *Parula americana*, *Seiurus aurocapillus*, *Dendroica tigrina* y particularmente *D. discolor*, la cual está presentando enormes declinaciones poblacionales en Norteamérica). (4) En contraste con las especialistas de habitat que ya están presentando síntomas de depresión poblacional, especies migratorias que son generalistas de habitat pueden no estar amenazadas de extinción inmediata o inclusive de declinaciones poblacionales drásticas en el futuro cercano, gracias a su habilidad para adaptarse a a un mosaico de tipos de habitat, muchos de los cuales han sido alterados mediante actividad humana. (5) Existe la esperanza por el futuro de las aves terrestres migratorias en el Caribe, basada en la abrupta topografía y la capacidad de recuperación de la vegetación inherente a varias islas caribeñas. A través de la cooperación internacional entre conservacionistas, administradores de recursos, legisladores gubernamentales y el público en general, podría mantenerse suficiente habitat apropiado para mantener poblaciones viables de aves terrestres migratorias indefinidamente en la región del Caribe.

About one half of all landbirds breeding in North America migrate to Mexico and the western Caribbean (the Bahamas, Cuba, and Hispaniola), with many additional individuals reaching even the small islands in the eastern Caribbean (Terborgh and Faaborg 1980). Most landbird migrants are small insectivorous species of flycatchers, vireos, and paruline warblers, of which the latter group makes up the bulk of Nearctic breeders wintering in the Neotropics (Rappole et al. 1983). Many landbird migrants spend up to 75% of each year in the Caribbean region, often in very high concentrations and in an area with a combined landmass only one-eighth the size of the breeding grounds occupied on the North American continent (Terborgh and Faaborg 1980). Thus, it is of paramount importance that the distribution, population dynamics, and ecology of Caribbean migrants be studied to complement research and conservation efforts currently being undertaken on the North American continent in an attempt to reduce population declines in as many species as possible.

Methods

CURRENT STATUS OF CARIBBEAN LANDBIRD MIGRANTS

To summarize the current status of landbird migrants on the major Caribbean islands, a large and diverse group of collaborators has been organized (their names and respective islands are listed in the Appendix). Collaborators have given freely of their time, and in many instances their unpublished data, and have incorporated a wealth of experience, knowledge, and expertise in this paper.

Migrant landbirds in the Caribbean fall into six general categories: (1) transients from North America, (2) mostly transient, with a few individuals remaining as seasonal residents, (3) seasonal residents, that is, substantial numbers remain throughout the Temperate Zone winter months, (4) interisland or "Caribbean-based" migrants, (5) irruptive migrants, and (6) casual (vagrant) visitors.

TRANSIENTS. A good example of a transient migrant is the Blackpoll Warbler (*Dendroica striata*), a species that moves en masse through the Caribbean Archipelago en route to its wintering grounds in South America (Nisbet 1970).

MOSTLY TRANSIENT. Many examples are known for species of migrant landbirds in which the bulk of the population spends the Temperate Zone winter months in the continental tropics, with most individuals migrating through Mexico and Central America. However, individuals from subpopulations of these species either migrate through the Caribbean region or remain as seasonal residents, for example, a few raptorial species and many passerines including flycatchers, swallows, thrushes, vireos, warblers, grosbeaks and allies, emberizines, and icterines (Table 1). On islands in which permanent, year-round populations are found, as in the case of the Turkey Vulture (*Cathartes aura*), Northern Harrier (*Circus cyaneus*), Sharp-shinned Hawk (*Accipiter striatus*), and Yellow Warbler (*Dendroica petechia*), it is impossible in most instances to discern migratory from permanent-resident individuals. It is apparent that additional individuals are present on an island simply because the density of a given species is greater during the Temperate Zone winter months.

SEASONAL RESIDENTS. Caribbean islands host an array of seasonal or "winter" resident landbird migrants that pass the Temperate Zone winter in suitable habitat. Seasonal residents include examples from many taxa, ranging from raptors, cuckoos, caprimulgids, and woodpeckers, to the more numerous passerine species (Table 1). An example of a wide-ranging landbird in which the bulk of the population winters and migrates within continental North America, but which also maintains small populations that migrate into the Greater Antilles, is the Mourning Dove (*Zenaida macroura*) (Aldrich and Duvall 1958).

INTERISLAND MIGRANTS. Although most migrant landbirds breed on the North American continent, some visitors to Caribbean islands are species native to the region and move from island to island or migrate from the Caribbean to Central and South America at different times of the year. Examples of interisland migrants include the Gray Kingbird (*Tyrannus dominicensis*) and the Black-whiskered Vireo (*Vireo altiloquus*). Populations of the Gray Kingbird are partially migratory, moving east and southward in the Greater Antilles after the breeding season (Brodkorb 1950). Although populations of the Black-whiskered Vireo are permanent residents in the Lesser Antilles, most Greater Antillean populations migrate to northern South America after the breeding season. However, a few individuals can be found throughout the year on most islands within the species' normal range in the Greater Antilles (Arendt and others, unpubl. data). Although the White-crowned Pigeon (*Columba leucocephala*) is a wide-ranging interisland migrant throughout the Greater Antilles and the northern Lesser Antilles (Arendt et al. 1979, Norton and Seaman 1985), it also can be considered a North American migrant because of its breeding colonies in south Florida and the Florida Keys (A.O.U. 1983).

IRRUPTIVE MIGRANTS. Some species of migrant landbirds reach Puerto Rico, its satellites, and other Caribbean islands in disproportionate numbers each year. A species might be observed in the tens or even hundreds one year, but might be casually observed or even absent the next. Examples of irruptive migrants include at least

three species of paruline warblers, Magnolia Warbler (*Dendroica magnolia*), Yellow-rumped Warbler (*D. coronata*), and Palm Warbler (*D. palmarum*).

CASUAL MIGRANTS (VAGRANTS). Some species of North American landbird migrants have been recorded only once or very few times in the Caribbean. These species are termed casual migrants or vagrants. Examples of casual migrants include Black-billed Cuckoo (*Coccyzus erythropthalmus*), Ruby-throated Hummingbird (*Archilochus colubris*), and many passerines.

DEFINITIONS OF ABUNDANCE AND HABITAT ASSOCIATIONS

To evaluate current abundances of Caribbean landbird migrants, I compiled an overview of the species and relative numbers of migrants reaching major islands. Because of the heterogeneous group of collaborators, "abundance" definitions were kept simple to minimize ambiguity. The following "abundance" terms (numerically coded in Table 1) were adopted: ABUNDANT: Observed in very large numbers, often in many habitat types. COMMON: Present in moderate numbers, often in many habitat types. UNCOMMON: Present, but in small numbers, often found in a single or very few habitat types. CASUAL: An inclusive category including single records (i.e., VAGRANTS) and those species with just a few reported sightings (RARE species). IRRUPTIVE: Migrants whose numbers fluctuate dramatically (usually on a yearly basis) because of factors such as climate and food. TRANSIENT: A migrant that passes through an area during its annual migration. WINTER RESIDENT: A migrant that resides in an area during the Temperate Zone winter months.

To assess the habitat distribution of landbird migrants on Caribbean islands (Table 2) and also to minimize ambiguity, the following habitat terms (alpha coded in Table 2) were adopted: COAST: Includes offshore cays, shoreline, beaches, bluffs, cliffs, strand vegetation, littoral woodland, brushland, scrub vegetation, and ruinate thickets. DRY FOREST: Includes primary and secondary (disturbed) xerophytic (sclerophyllous) deciduous forest from sea level to 200 m with 50–100 cm of rainfall annually. WET FOREST: Includes primary and secondary (disturbed) mesophytic (above 200 m with 100–200 cm of rainfall annually), wet (above 400 m with up to 400 cm of rainfall annually), and hygrophytic (above 600 m with 400–800 cm of rainfall annually) forest. ELFIN WOODLAND: Includes primary and secondary (disturbed) stunted herbaceous vegetation confined to mountain tops and ridges, often above 750 m; rainfall often exceeds 500 cm annually. WETLANDS: All low-lying land, submerged or inundated periodically by fresh or saline water. Includes primary and secondary (dis-

TABLE 1. Distribution and abundance of 151 species of Caribbean landbird migrants

Species	BH	TC	CU	SI	CI	JM	HT	DR	MO	PR	CL	VQ	ST	SJ	SC	TO	VG	AG	AL	SM	SB	SE	KN	AB	MT	GP	DO	MQ	SL	SV	BB	GN	TT	AR	CO	BN	AP
Cathartes aura	5	6			5	5	6	6		6				5	5																				9	9	9
Pandion haliaetus	10,11	12	9		9	9	9	9	9	9	9	9	9	9	12	9	12	12	9	9	9	9	8		12	12	9	12	8	5	9	8	12	9	9	9	6
Elanoides forficatus		5			5	5																															
Ictinia mississippiensis																																					
Circus cyaneus	9	12			9		6	6	7,8	6				6	6				6	6					6					17	17				9		
Accipiter striatus	6					4		9	5	6				5																							
Buteo lineatus		12			5	5																												5	9	9	
B. platypterus						4																										5	9	9		6	
B. swainsoni	5					5																															
B. regalis						5																															
Falco sparverius	12	12		*	12		6	6																					6	6	5			9	9	12	6
F. columbarius	10,11	8,10	9	*	9	12	9	9	9	9	9	9	9	9	9	9	9	9	9	9	9	9	12		9	9	9	9	5	9	8	9	9	12	9	9	
F. peregrinus	9	9	9	*	9	9	9	9	9	9	9	9	9	9	9	9	9	9	6	6	6	9	6		9	9	9	5	5	5	5	5	9	9	9	9	
Columba leucocephala	9	*	10	*	10	9	9	9	6	9	9	6	9	6,5,7	6	6	6	6	9		6	6	9		5	5	5										6
Zenaida asiatica	6				5	8	8	5		5	6			5																							
Z. macroura	8	8			8	8	8	5	6	6	6																										
Coccyzus	5	5			4	4	5	5	5	5				5												5			17	5			5				
erythropthalmus																																					
C. americanus	10,11	9 7,11	6	*	8	11	8	9	9 7,8	7,8	7,8		6	8	6	6	6	6	5	5	5	6	6		12	12	12	6	11	11	5	5	11	12	12	12	
Athene cunicularia	6	6																															5				
Asio otus	5	5																																			
A. flammeus	8	11	*			12	12	5	8	8			7,8	7,8	8	8	8	8	6	6			9		9	9	9	5	8	5		5	5	9	9	9	
Chordeiles minor	6	12	5		5	910,11	10,11	6	6	6	9	6 7,8	6 7,8	6	9	9	9		6	6			6						5	5				5	5		
Caprimulgus carolinensis																																					
C. vociferus		5		5	5		5	5	5	5				5								5	5	12	5	5	5	8		8	5	5	5	9	5	5	
Cypseloides niger	5	5		5	6		5	5					5	6									5		9	5				5	5		5		5		
Chaetura pelagica	8	5		8	4		5	5						6		5															5	5	5				
Aeronautes saxatalis																																					
Archilochus colubris	5	9		5	12	5	12	5		5				9	9	9	7	*	12			5	9	12	9	9	9	9	6	6	9	9	9	9	9	9	*
Ceryle alcyon	12	11	*	*	12	12	12	12	9	12		9	9	9	9	6	6	6	6	6			9		9	6		9		9	9	9	9	9	9	5	
Sphyrapicus varius	12	12	*		9	12	6	9	9	9		9	6	6	6	6																					
Contopus borealis																																	9				
C. sordidulus		5			4	4																															
C. virens	6	5		*	5									5					5														5	5	5	5	*
Empidonax flaviventris																																					
E. virescens	5	11																																			
E. alnorum		5																																			
E. trailli		8			5	5																															
E. minimus																																					
Sayornis phoebe	5	6																																			
Myiarchus crinitus	5	5																																			
Tyrannus melancholicus		6								5																											
T. verticalis	8	5		5	5		9	9		6	9	9	9	9	9	9	9	9	5	5	5	5	5	5	5	5	5	5	5	5	5	5	9	5	5	5	*
T. tyrannus	8	5	8	*	5	5		9	6	9	9			9			6	6		6													12	9	12	5	*
T. dominicensis	7	7	7	*	7	7	9	9	5	5	9			9			9	6																		12	*
T. forficatus	5	5						5																													

Manomet Symposium 1989

TABLE 1—Continued

Species	BH	TC	CU	SI	CI	JM	HT	DR	MO	PR	CL	VQ	ST	SJ	SC	TO	VG	AG	AL	SM	SB	SE	KN	AB	MT	GP	DO	MQ	SL	SV	BB	GN	TT	AR	CO	BN	AP
T. savana	8																																	8	8	8	
Progne subis	5	11	5		8	5		6	5	5	5	5	5	6	6																			8	8	8	
P. dominicensis	8		5		5	5		5	5,7,8	5	5	5	5	5	6																			8	8	8	
Tachycineta bicolor	6	6	12	5	8	12		5	5	7,8	8	5	5	5	5											5	6	5	5	5	5		5	5	5	5	
T. cyaneoviridis	5		5	5			7,8							5	5																						5
Stelgidopteryx serripennis	5	5	8	5	11	5		7,8			5		5	5	5	5																					*
Riparia riparia	8		8	*	8	8		8	8	7,8		8	8	8	7,8								7			9	9	9	5	9	7	8	12	12	12	12	*
Hirundo rustica	5		8	*	8	5		8	5					6	6								5			5	5	5	6	5		8	5	8	8	8	
H. pyrrhonota					5			5																													
H. fulva	7,11		11	*	7,11	5	12	12	12	12	8		9	10,11	7,11	12	9		7,117,117,11			12	12	9	12	7,8	8	12	7,8	11		9	10,11	10,11	10,11	*
Troglodytes aedon	6		5																																		
Regulus calendula	6		5		5		5																														
Polioptila caerulea	12	9	13		9			5		5																		5						5	5	5	5
Oenanthe oenanthe	5		5							5																					5						
Sialia sialis	5		17																																		
Catharus fuscescens	5		8		5	5		6	5	6		5	6	5	5												5						5	5	5	5	5
C. minimus	11	5	8	*	5	6	7,8	9	6	6		6	6	5	5																		5	5	5	5	5
C. ustulatus	8		11	*	5	5		5	5																										5	5	5
C. guttatus	6																																				
Hylocichla mustelina	5	6	8			4		6	5	5																											
Turdus migratorius	6	5	17		13	9		6	6	6										5										5							*
Dumetella carolinensis	12	8	12	*																																	5
Toxostoma rufum	6		6											6																					5		
Anthus spinoletta	6			5		6																															5
A. spragueii	5																																				
Bombycilla cedrorum	17	7,16			5	17	17	17	6	6				6											5	5	5						6				
Lanius ludovicianus	5																																				
Vireo griseus	9	6	12	*	13	5		6	6	6		5	6	6	6																						
V. solitarius	5		6			4			5					6																							
V. flavifrons	9	5	9	*		4		6		6		5	5	10	5									6					5		5		5		5		
V. gilvus	8		8			5																			5												
V. philadelphicus	5		8			5			5	5			6																								
V. olivaceus	8	5	11	*	5	11		5		5		6	6	5	6	6	6	6	6	6	6	6	6	6	6	5	5	5	5	5	5	5	5	5	5	5	5
V. altiloquus	5	6	6		5	6				7		6		6																			5	5	5	5	*
Vermivora bachmanii	6																																				
V. pinus	6	5	9		6	4		5					6	6							6					5							5				
V. chrysoptera	8		8			4		5		9		6		6																							
V. peregrina	9	5	11		8	6		5		6		6		5												5											
V. celata	6									6			6	6																							
V. ruficapilla	5	5	5		4	6	5	5		12	12		12	14	12	12	12	9	9	12	12	12	12	9	9	9	9		6	9	8	5	5	5	5	5	*
Parula americana	12	12	12	*	12	12		12	9	9	6	9	9	9	9	9	9	6	9	9	6	6	6	5	6	6	6	6	9	5	5	5	6	5	5	5	*
Dendroica petechia	12	*	11	*	11	9		12	6	6	6	6	9	6	6										5	5	5		5	5	5		5	5	5	5	*
D. pensylvanica	8		8		5	6			6	6			6	6	5	5									5	5	5		8		8		5				
D. magnolia	11	5	7,8		7,8	9		7,8	9	17		6	6	6	5						6				8	5	5		8		8		5		5		*

TABLE 1—Continued next page

TABLE 1—Continued

Species																	Island																				
	BH	TC	CU	SI	CI	JM	HT	DR	MO	PR	CL	VQ	ST	SJ	SC	TO	VG	AG	AL	SM	SB	SE	KN	AB	MT	GP	DO	MQ	SL	SV	BB	GN	TT	AR	CO	BN	AP
D. tigrina	12	8	12	*	12	12	12,13,14	15	9	12	9	9	9	12	9	9	9	9	9	12	9	12	9	8	9	9	9	9	9	6	5	6	9	6	6	6	*
D. caerulescens	12	5	12	*	12	12	12	12	7,8	12	6	6	6	9	6	9	12	6						6	6	6	6			6		5	5	5	5	5	*
D. coronata	13,17	6	17	*	17	17	17	17	12	17	6		9	9	6	9								6	6	6	6			6	8	5	5	6	6	6	*
D. townsendi	5																																				
D. virens	9	5	10,11			9	9	9		6			6	6	4					6				6		6							5	5	5	5	5
D. fusca	5	5	8	*	8	5	5	5		6			6	6	6											5							5	5	5	5	
D. dominica	12	5	12	*	13	9	9	9	9	9	9	9	6	6,5,10	6									6		5											
D. pinus	5		6		5	5		11	5	5				5												5											
D. kirtlandii	9							6																													
D. discolor	12	5	12	*	12	12	12	12	12	12	9	9	9	9	9	9		9		9	9	9	9	9		9	5	5		5	5	5	5	5	5	5	*
D. palmarum	14	6	12	*	15	12	12	12	9	17	9		5	9	6	5														5	5			6	6		
D. castanea	5	5	8		8	11	11	6	5	6			5		5					5	5	5		5		5	5		5	5	5		5	5	5	5	
D. striata	11	11	11	*	8	4	11	11	5,7,11	7,11			8	8	8					5					5	8	5	8	5	5	16		8	7,11	7,11	7,11	*
D. cerulea	5	5	5		6	4		5																											5		
Mniotilta varia	12	5	12	*	12	12	12	12	12	12	9	9	12	12	9	12				9	9	9		12	12	9	9	12	6	6	8	6	5	6	6	6	*
Setophaga ruticilla	12	9	12	*	12	12	12	12	12	12	12	12	12	12	12	12				12	12	12		12	12	12	12	12	12	12	9	8	12	10,11	10,11	10,11	*
Protonotaria citrea	8	5	5	*	5	11	9	9	9	9	9	9	9	6	6	6		6	6	6	6	6		6	6	9	9	6	6	6	6	6	9	6	6	6	*
Helmitheros vermivorus	12	5	7	*	9	9	7,8	9	5	9	6			9	7,8	6			6	5				8		9	9										
Limnothlypis swainsonii	5		9	*	6	9			6					6																							
Seiurus aurocapillus	12	9	12	*	9	12	12	12	7,8	12	9	9	9	12	6	9	9	9		8	9	9		12	6	9	9	9	6	6	5	5	5	9	9	9	*
S. noveboracensis	12	6	12	*	12	12	12	12	7,8	12	12	12	12	14	9	12	12	9		9	9	9	9	12	6	12	9	12	12	9	9	8	12	12	12	12	*
S. motacilla	12	12	12	*	7	9	12	7,8	7,8	12	9	9	6	9	6	12				6			9	12	6	6	9	9	6	6	5	5	5	5	5	5	*
Oporornis formosus	5	5	5		6	4	12	6	6	6	5		5	9	5	9				5	5			6	6	6											
O. agilis	5							6	6	6				6	5																			8	8		
O. philadelphia	5				4	4	6	6	5	5	5			6	6						5													5	5		
Geothlypis trichas	6	5	6	*	12	12	6	6	6	12	7,8	7,8	6	6	6	6		5		5	6			6	6	6	6	6			5	5	5	5		5	
Wilsonia citrina	7,8	6	9	*	4	4		5	6	9	7,8	7,8	9	17	5	5				6	6			6	6	9	9	9		6	8	5	5	9		9	*
W. pusilla	5		5		4	4		5	5	5			6	6	6	6										5											
W. canadensis	6		6		4	4		5	6	6			6	6	5	5									5	5	5		5								
Icteria virens	6		6		5				6					6																							
Piranga rubra	6	7,11			8	5	6	5	5	5			6	6	6	5			5		8			8		5			5	5	5	5	9	8		5	
P. olivacea	5	5	5	5	8	5		5	5	5			6	6	5	5			5		8			8	5	5			5	5	8	5	5	8	5	5	*
P. ludoviciana	5	5	11	5	5	5																															
Pheucticus ludovicianus	7,8	7,8		5	9	9	6	6	5	6			5	5	5	5						8		8		5	5		5	5	5		5	8	8	8	*
P. melanocephalus																																					
Guiraca caerulea	11	5								5				5																					5		
Passerina cyanea	13,14	13	12	5	9	9	8	8	5	9	6		6	12	12	9					9												5	9	9	9	*
P. ciris	11	7,8	11	*	4	4																															
Spiza americana	6	5								5																							18	18			
Pipilo chlorurus			4																															16	16		
Spizella passerina	6		6																																		
S. pallida	6		7,8																																		
Pooecetes gramineus	6		5	*																																	
Chondestes grammacus	6		6																																		

TABLE 1—*Continued*

Species		BH	TC	CU	SI	CI	JM	HT	DR	MO	PR	CL	VQ	ST	SJ	SC	TO	VG	AG	AL	SM	SB	SE	KN	AB	MT	GP	DO	MQ	SL	SV	BB	GN	TT	AR	CO	BN	AP
																																						Island
Passerculus sandwichensis		9																																				
Ammodramus savannarum		6		9	5	9			6	5			5																									
Melospiza melodia		6																																				
M. lincolnii		6	7,8	6		6		17		6	6																											
M. georgiana		5								6																												
Zonotrichia albicollis																																			5			
Z. leucophrys		5		5			4			5	5																											
Junco hyemalis		5		5	5	5	5	5		8	8	5	5	8																								
Dolichonyx oryzivorus		11	11	11	11	8		5	6	8	8	5	5	8	8	5									5	5	5	5	5	5	5	5	5	5	11	11	11	
Agelaius phoeniceus		5																																				6
Sturnella magna		5		5	5	5			5	5	5											5											5	5		6	
Xanthocephalus xanthocephalus		5																																				
Euphagus carolinus		5																																				
E. cyanocephalus		5																																				
Molothrus ater		6		4			6																															
Icterus spurius		8	5	5		9		6	6	6	6	6	6	17	6	5							5					5		5	5	5	5	5				11
I. galbula		5		5	*																																	
Carduelis tristis		6																																				

SOURCES for Tables 1 & 2: Aldridge 1987; American Ornithologists' Union 1983; Barlow 1978; Benito-Espinal 1990; Blake 1973–1981; Bond 1956–1982, 1957, 1970; Bradley 1985; Brewer 1977; Buden 1987; Clark 1905; Cory 1909; A. Cruz 1977; Danforth 1930, 1936, 1939, 1983 unpubl. data; Dathe & Fisher 1979; Devas 1970; Diamond 1972; Diamond & Smith 1973; Diamond et al. 1977; Dod 1978, 1981; Downer 1972; Downer & Sutton 1990; Eaton 1953; Evans (unpubl. data); ffrench 1966, 1980; Fisher & Wetmore 1931; Fletcher 1983; Garrido & Montana 1975; Gochfeld 1974, 1979; Gosse Bird Club 1986; Guth 1971; Holland & Williams 1978; Johnston 1975; Keith unpubl. data; La Bastille 1973; Lack & Lack 1972, 1973; Lack et al. 1972; Mayfield 1972; McCandless 1961; Molinares 1980; A.G. Moore 1985; Nicoll 1904; R.L. Norton 1979, 1981, 1982-1988; Pashley 1988a b; Paynter 1956; Perez-Rivera & Bonilla 1983; Perez-Rivera 1980; Raffael 1973, 1981, 1983; Riley 1905; Robertson 1962; Russel et al. 1965; Schwartz & Klinikowski 1963, 1965; Siegel 1983; Snow & Snow 1960; Sorrie 1975; Spendelow 1985; R. Sutton unpubl. data; Terborgh & Faaborg 1980; Van der Werff et al. 1958; Vaurie 1961; Voous 1983; Wells 1902; Williams & Williams 1985; Wiley & Bauer 1985; Woods 1985; Woods & Ottenwalder 1986.

ISLAND CODES: Bahamas (BH); Turks & Caicos (TC); Cuba (CU); Swan Islands (SI); Cayman Islands (CI); Jamaica (JM); Haiti (HT); Dominican Republic (DR); Mona Island (MO); Puerto Rico (PR); Culebra Island (CL); Vieques Islands (VQ); St. Thomas (ST); St. John (SJ); St. Croix (SC); Tortola (TD); Virgin Gorda (VG); Anegada (AG); Anguilla (AL); St. Martin (SM); Saba (SB); St. Eustatius (SE); St. Kitts-Nevis (KN); Antigua & Barbuda (AB); Montserrat (MT); Guadeloupe (GP); Dominica (DO); Martinique (MQ); St. Lucia (SL); St. Vincent (SV); Barbados (BB); Grenada (GN); Trinidad & Tobago (TT); Aruba (AR); Curaçao (CO); Bonaire (BN); San Andres & Providencia (AP).

STATUS CODES: 1 (abundant); 2 (common); 3 (uncommon); 4 (casual); 5 (casual transient); 6 (casual transient & winter resident); 7 (casual winter resident); 8 (uncommon transient); 9 (uncommon transient & winter resident); 10 (uncommon winter resident); 11 (common transient); 12 (common transient & winter resident); 13 (common winter resident); 14 (abundant transient); 15 (abundant transient & winter resident); 16 (irruptive transient); 17 (irruptive transient & winter resident); * indicates that the species has been recorded, but no additional information was given.

TABLE 2—Habitat use by 151 species of Caribbean landbird migrants

Island	*Cathartes aura*	*Pandion haliaetus*	*Elanoides forficatus*	*Ictinia mississippiensis*	*Circus cyaneus*	*Accipiter striatus*	*Buteo lineatus*	*B. platypterus*	*B. swainsoni*	*B. regalis*	*Falco sparverius*	*F. columbarius*	*F. peregrinus*	*Columba leucocephala*	*Zenaida asiatica*	*Z. macroura*	*Coccyzus erythropthalmus*	*C. americanus*	*Athene cunicularia*	*Asio otus*	*A. flammeus*	*Chordeiles minor*	*Caprimulgus carolinensis*
BH	CO	CTLU			CT	CW					CO	CT	CT	CTD	CO	COU	CD	CD	CO		C	CO	CTD
TC	CO	CTLU											CT	*	CO	COU		CDU	CO		C	CO	CTD
CU	CO	CTLU	CTL		TO			CODWU			FOU	CTFU	CTL	CTDWSU		COU	CU	DF	CO	O	CO	OU	DWSF
SI		*									*		*	*				*				OU	
CI	CD	CTLSU	CT	c	CTO	CDW	c	CODU	c	c	CTSOU	CTLOU	CTOU	CTDSU	CO	COU		CDS				*	LS
JM	CO	CTLU	C	c			c		c	c		CWU	CTU	CTDWSU		COU	C	CD				O	CDW
HT	CO	CTLU			CT	WS	c		c			CW	CTU	CTDWSU		COU	DW	DW				OFU	TDW
DR	CO	CTLU			TO	CW					OS	CTSO	TCLU	CTDWSU		COU	DW	DW				C	TDW
MO	CT	CT				W							CT	CTD				CTD				CO	CD
PR	CDO	CTLU			CT							CTWEDU	CTWU	CTDU	CO	COU	CD	TDW				CO	TW
CL		CTL										CTOU	CTOU	CTD	CO	COU		CTD					CTD
VQ		CTLU										CTOU	CTOU	CTD		COU		CD					CTD
ST		CTLU			CT							CTOU	CTOU	CTDW				CD				CO	CD
SJ	C	CTLU			CT	C						CTOU	CTOU	CTW								CO	TD
SC	C	CTLU			CTOU							CTOU	CTOU	CTD	CO			CTDWOU				CU	CDW
TO		CTLU										CTFO	CTOU	CTD	CO			CD				CO	CTD
VG		CTLU										CTFO	CTOU	CTD	CO							CO	CTD
AG		CTLU										CTFO	CTOU	CTD				CD				CO	
AL					CO																		
SM		CTLU			CO							CTOS	CT	CTDW				CTDW				CO	CTDW
SB		CTLU										CTOS	CT	CTDW									CTDW
SE		CTLU										CTOS	CT	CTDW				CTDW					
KN												CTDW	CT	CTDW				CDW					CTDW
AB		CTLU										CWOS	CT	CTDWU				D					CTDW
MT													CT										
GP		CTLU										CW	CT	CT				CDWU				CO	
DO		CTLU			CTDWO							CTLOU	CTLU	CTD			CU	CDWU				CO	
MQ		CTLU										CW	CT	CTO				CTD				CO	
SL		CTLU										CTWDO	CT					DW					
SV		CTLU			T						CO	CW	CT				CU	CDOU				CO	
BB		CTU									CO	CTO	C				CS	OS				SFOU	
GN		CTLU										CT						CD					
TT		CTLU					W	F				CTOU	CTOU				CU	CTWOU					
AR		CTLU										CTOU	CTOU					CTOU		CO		COU	COU
CO		CTLU										CTOU	CTOU					CTOU				COU	COU
BN		CTLU										CTOU	CTOU					CTOU				COU	COU
AP		CTLU										*		CTD				CTOU				COU	COU

HABITAT CODES: C (coast); D (dry forest); E (elfin woodland); F (forest edge); L (littoral); O (open areas); P (pines); R (riparian); S (woodland); T (wetland); U (urban areas); W (wet forest); * indicates that the species has been recorded, but no additional information was given.

ISLAND CODES: See Table 1.

TABLE 2—Continued

Island	C. vociferus	Cypseloides niger	Chaetura pelagica	Aeronautes saxatalis	Archilochus colubris	Ceryle alcyon	Sphyrapicus varius	Contopus borealis	C. sordidulus	C. virens	Empidonax flaviventris	E. virescens	E. alnorum	E. traillii	E. minimus	Sayornis phoebe	Myiarchus crinitus	Tyrannus melancholicus	T. verticalis	T. tyrannus	T. dominicensis	T. forficatus	T. savana	Progne subis	P. dominicensis
BH		CO	C		CU	CL	CDW			CF		CO				C	C		CO	CO	CTDSFOU	C		CO	CTOU
TC			CU				*			CU										C	CTDSFU				CTOU
CU	DW	CO	C		CTU	CTL	TDWSU		DSFU	CDWFU	CFU	CDFU	CD	CFU		COFFU		CT	F	CU	CTLDRSFOU	U		CO	CTOU
SI						*	*			*									CO	*	*		FU		
CI		CO	CTO		COU	CTLS	CTDSU			DLSF				CFU	C					CSU	CTLDSFOU			COU	CTOU
JM		CO	CO	CO	CU	CTL	DWSFU		DSF	CFU				CFU	C					CU	CTLDSFOU				CTOU
HT		CO	CO	CO		CTL	DW														CTLDSFOU			CO	CTOU
DR		CO	CO			CTL	DW														CTLDSFOU			COU	CTOU
MO		C				CT	CD														CD			C	CD
PR		COW			CU	CTL	DWES										C			CO	CTLDSFOU	C		C	CTOU
CL						CTL	CD														CTLDSFOU				CTOU
VQ						CTL	CD														CTLDSFOU				CDOU
ST						CTL	CDW														CTLDSFOU			CO	CDOU
SJ						CT	CDW														CTLDSFOU				CDOU
SC		CO	C			CT	CTLDWOU			C											CTLDWSFOU			CO	CDOU
TO			COU			CTL	CD														CTLDSFOU				
VG			COU			CTL	CD														CTLDSFOU				
AG						CTL	CD														CTLDSFOU				
AL						*	*														*				
SM						CTL	C														CTLDWSFOU				CTO
SB						CTL															CTLDWSFOU				CTO
SE						CTL															CTLDOU				CTO
KN		COU				CTL															CTLDWSFOU				CTDO
AB		COU				CTL															CTLDSFOU				CDO
MT		CO				CTL															CTLDWESFOU				CDO
GP		CO				CTL															CTLDWSFOU				CTOU
DO		COWU				CTL	CM														CTLDWSFOU				CTOU
MQ		COWU				CTL															CTLDWSFOU				CTOU
SL		CWOU				CTL															CTLDWSFOU				CDOU
SV		CWOU				CTL															CTLDWSFOU				COU
BB		CTOU				CTL									U						CTLDSFOU				COU
GN	W	W	C			CTL															CTLDWSFOU				
TT		CO	TW			CTL		WFU													CTDWSFOU				
AR	CO					CTL	CU			CU										CD	CTDSFOU			CTLO	COU
CO		CO				CTL	CU	CU													CTDWSFOU			CTLO	
BN		CO				CTL	CU	CU		CU										CU	CTDWSFOU			CTLO	CTLO
AP						*	*			*										*	*				CTLO

HABITAT CODES: C (coast); D (dry forest); L (littoral); O (open areas); P (pines); R (riparian); S (woodland); T (wetland); U (urban areas); W (wet forest); * indicates that the species has been recorded, but no additional information was given.

ISLAND CODES: See Table 1.

TABLE 2—Continued next page

TABLE 2—Continued

Island	*Tachycineta bicolor*	*T. cyaneoviridis*	*Stelgidopteryx serripennis*	*Riparia riparia*	*Hirundo pyrrhonota*	*H. fulva*	*H. rustica*	*Troglodytes aedon*	*Regulus calendula*	*Polioptila caerulea*	*Oenanthe oenanthe*	*Sialia sialis*	*Catharus fuscescens*	*C. minimus*	*C. ustulatus*	*C. guttatus*	*Hylocichla mustelina*	*Turdus migratorius*	*Dumetella carolinensis*	*Toxostoma rufum*	*Anthus spinoletta*	*A. spraguei*
BH	CO	CO	CO	CO	CO		CO	CU	CU	CD	CO		C	CD	CD	CSU	CSU	CSU	CDW	CD	CLWO	C
TC	CO		CO						CU	CD				C			CDU	C	C			
CU	OT	CO	TO	CO	CO	CO	CTLOU	CD	U	CTLDSFU	COU		CDWSFU	CDWSFU	CDWSFU		CDWSU	CSOU	CDWSFU	CDU		
SI	CO	*	*	*	*	CO	*						*	*	*				*		CO	
CI	COU		CTLO	CTLO	CLO		CTLOU			CTDS			CL	CL					CDSU			
JM	CWOU		CTOU	CTLO	COU		CTOU		CU				DW	CDW	CDW			COU	CDWU		CO	
HT				CTO	COU		CTLO							W				DW	DW			
DR	CTO		CTO	CTO	COU	CD	CO		CU				DW	TDW	CDW			CD	DW			
MO					C		CTO							CD								
PR	CTOU			CTLU		CO	CTOU				C			CTDW			C		D			
CL	CTOU						CTO															
VQ	CO						CTO															
ST	COU		COU	COU	COU		CTO						C	C								
SJ	COU		COU	COU	COU		CTO						C	C								
SC	COU		COU	COU	COU		OU															
TO			COU				CTO															
VG							CTO															
AG							CTO															
AL							CTO												C			
SM							CTO															
SB							CTO															
SE							CTO															
KN							CTO															
AB				CO	C		CO															
MT					C		CTO															
GP				CO	CTOU		CTOU															
DO				CTOU	CTOU		COU															
MQ				CTOU			COU							C								
SL				CO	CO		COU															
SV				C	CO		CTOU				CU											
BB				CTO	CO		O												CU			
GN				CTO			CO															
TT				CO	T		CTOU						W	CU								
AR		C	c	CTO	CO		CTOU				CD		CU	CU	CU							
CO				CTO	CO		CTOU				CD		CU	CU	CU		C			U		
BN				CTO	CO		CTOU						CDU									
AP				*		*	*												*		*	

HABITAT CODES: C (coast); D (dry forest); E (elfin woodland); F (forest edge); L (littoral); O (open areas); P (pines); R (riparian); S (woodland); T (wetland); U (urban areas); W (wet forest); * indicates that the species has been recorded, but no additional information was given.
ISLAND CODES: See Table 1.

Manomet Symposium 1989

TABLE 2—Continued

Island	*Bombycilla cedrorum*	*Lanius ludovicianus*	*Vireo griseus*	*V. solitarius*	*V. flavifrons*	*V. gilvus*	*V. philadelphicus*	*V. olivaceus*	*V. altiloquus*	*Vermivora bachmanii*	*V. pinus*	*V. chrysoptera*	*V. peregrina*	*V. celata*	*V. ruficapilla*	*Parula americana*	*Dendroica petechia*	*D. pensylvanica*	*D. magnolia*
BH	C		CD	CD	DW		C	CTDW	CDWRSFU	CD	W	CDW	CD	C	CU	CDW	CT	C	CD
TC			CS		DU			CSU	CDRSFU		CR		C		D				CD
CU	COS		CDWSU	DS	DSU	CFU	CSFU	CDSFU	CTLDWRSFU	CTOU	CDRSOU	DSU	CDSFU		CU	CTWRSFOU	CTDFU	CTDU	CRU
SI			*		*				*							*	*		
CI	CD		CLD					CDSU	TRSFU		C		CTDS		CU	CTDS	CTDU	CDOU	CTDSU
JM	CDWOU		C	SU	SU		CTDW	CDWU	CTDWSU		CR	WU	DWRSU		CU	TDWSFU	CTDR		DRSU
HT	W								CTDWSU		P				W	DW	CTD		
DR	CDWSU		CDW		CDW				CTDWSU		CDWRSU	CDW				CTDWRSPU	CTDW		CTDWRU
MO	CD		CD						CD						C	CD	CTD		C
PR	CDWU		DWU		CWS			CS	CTDWERSU			CW				CTDWERSU	CTD	WU	D
CL									CDSFU							CTDS	CTD		CD
VQ			C		CDS			CDSU	CDSFU							CTDS	CTD		CTS
ST			CS		CS			SU	CDSFU		CRS					CTDSU	CTDF	DWS	CTSF
SJ	C		CS		CS			SU	CTWFU		CRS	CW				CTDWSU	CTDF	DWS	DTSF
SC			CS		CS				CTDFU		CRS	CW				CTLDWFOU	CTDU		
TO									CDSFU							CDSU	CTD		
VG									CDSFU							CDSU	CTD		
AG									CDSFU							CDSU	CTD		
AL									CDSFU							CDSU	CTD		
SM									CDWRSFU		CDS					CDWRSU	CTD		CSU
SB									CDWRSFU							CDWRSU	CTD		
SE									CDWOFU							CDWRSU	CTD		
KN									CTDWRSFU							DWRSU	CTD		
AB					W		DW	CD	CTDWRSFU		CTDW					DWRSU	CTD		
MT								CD	CTDWRSFU		CTDW					CWRSU	CTD	W	W
GP	CDU								CTDWRSFU							CTDWSU	CTD	D	D
DO	CU								CTDWESU							CTDWRSU	CTD	CDU	DU
MQ	CDU								CTDWSU							CTDWSU	CTD		
SL								CD	CTDWSU							DW	CTD		
SV					C	C			CTDWSU				C			CDWS	CTD		
BB								DS	CDSU			W	T			TSU	CTD	TO	TS
GN					C			CDWSF	CTDWSU							DW	CTD		
TT					CWU			CDWSF	CTDWRSFU							D	CTFOU	CDWFO	TD
AR	U								CTDLU							CD	CTD	C	
CO					C			CU	CTDLU				C			CTWRU	CTD		
BN								CU	CTDLU				C			CTU	CTD	C	

HABITAT CODES: C (coast); D (dry forest); E (elfin woodland); F (forest edge); L (littoral); O (open areas); P (pines); R (riparian); S (woodland); T (wetland); U (urban areas); W (wet forest); * indicates that the species has been recorded, but no additional information was given.

ISLAND CODES: See Table 1.

TABLE 2—*Continued next page*

TABLE 2—Continued

Island	D. tigrina	D. caerulescens	D. coronata	D. townsendi	D. virens	D. fusca	D. dominica	D. pinus	D. kirtlandii	D. discolor	D. palmarum	D. castanea	D. striata	D. cerulea	Mniotilta varia	Setophaga ruticilla
BH	CDW	CDWU	CDO	C	CDW	C	CP	C	CDPU	CTD	CDWO	CD	CDPU	C	CTDW	CDWSU
TC	CDSU	CDSU	CDOU		CDSU	C	CDU		CD	CD	CDOU	CD	CDOU		CTDU	CDSFOU
CU	CDWRU	WRSU	CDU		CDWR	CS	C	CWRP		CTD	CTSU	C	CU	CR	CTDWU	CTDWU
SI	*	*	*				*			*	*		CDWOU		*	*
CI	CTDSFOU	TDSU	CTDSOU		CTDPS	CTDSP	CTDSP			CTDSP	CTDOU	CTO	CTDU	CL	CTDSU	CTLDSFOU
JM	DWFSOU	TDWSOU	CTDWSU		DWU	CWSU	CTDWU	CU		CTDWSFOU	CTDWOU	CDWSU	CU	CU	CTDWSFU	CTDWSFU
HT	WPO	DWSU	CDO		WP		P	WPO		CTDWSFOU	DWO		CDWOU		CTDWPSFOU	DWU
DR	CTDWRU	TDWRSU	CTDRSP		WRS	CW	CTRPU	CWRP	CD	CTDWFRSU	CTDWSOU	DW	CTDWRU		CTDWRSFU	CTDWRSU
MO	CD	C	CDP		DW		C	CD		CTDP	CP	C	C	C	CTDP	CTDP
PR	CTDWEU	TDWESU	CTDWOU				CTD			CTD	CTD	CDW	CDU		CTDWERU	CTDRSU
CL	CTDS	CDU	CDO							CTD	CTDO				CDS	CTDS
VQ	CTDSU	CDSU	CTDOU							CTD	CTDO				CDS	CTDSU
ST	CDS	CDWSU	CDOS		CDW	CW	CT			CTD	CTDO		CDS		CDW	CTDWFU
SJ	CTDWFU	DWSU	CTD		CDW	CW	CD			CTDWF	CTFU		CDS		CDTWFU	CTDWFU
SC	CTDWFOU	WRSU	CTDWOU		CD		U			CTDWFOU	CTFU	CS	CTDWFOU		CDTWSOU	CTDWU
TO	CTDSU		CDO				CDU			CTDU	CTD				CDU	CTDWSU
VG	CTDS		CDO							CTDU					CTDWSU	CTDSU
AG	CDSFOU	C														
AL	CDSFOU															
SM	CDWU				CS					CTD			C		CDTWRS	CDWSRU
SB	CDU		CDWOU							CTD					CDTWRS	CDWSRU
SE	CDWU		CDWOU							CTD					CDTWRS	CDWSRU
KN	CTDWSFU									CTD					DWS	CDWSRU
AB	CTDWSU	W	CD		W		CD			DTW		C	W		DW	CDWSRU
MT	CTDU						CD	T		CTD						
GP	WSU	WS	CTO		W								CDWSU		CDWS	CTDWSU
DO	CTDWRSOU	TDWS	CTDSOU		W							CU	CTDRSFOU		CDTWSU	CTDWSU
MQ	DWU							D		CTD			CDWS		CTDWSU	CTDWSFU
SL	CDWU		DW								DW		DW		CTDWSU	CTDWSU
SV	CDWU	CDWU	CDO									CDU	CDWSU		CTDWSU	DWU
BB	TSU		TS		TS	C				T	CTD	TO	TOS		STU	CTDWSU
GN	CTDWSFU									CTDWSFOU					CTDWSU	TDWSU
TT	CTLDSU	CW	WU		WS	W				T		W	CTWFU		W	CDWU
AR	CDU	CU			CU	C				CU	CU		CDSOU		CTD	CTDWROU
CO	CDU		CDOU		CU	CW				CU	CU	C	CDSWOU		CTD	CTDOU
BN	CDU	CU	CDOU		CU	C				CDU		C	CDSOU	CU	CTDR	CTDWROU
AP	*	*			D					CDU	*	C	*	CU	*	CTDOU *

HABITAT CODES: C (coast); D (dry forest); E (elfin woodland); F (forest edge); L (littoral); O (open areas); P (pines); R (riparian); S (woodland); T (wetlands); U (urban areas); W (wet forest); * indicates that the species has been recorded, but no additional information was given.
ISLAND CODES: See Table 1.

TABLE 2—Continued

Island	Protonotaria citrea	Helmitheros vermivorus	Limnothlypis swainsonii	Seiurus aurocapillus	S. noveboracensis	S. motacilla	Oporornis formosus	O. agilis	O. philadelphia	Geothlypis trichas	Wilsonia citrina	W. pusilla	W. canadensis	Icteria virens	Piranga rubra	P. olivacea	P. ludoviciana	Pheucticus ludovicianus	P. melanocephalus	Guiraca caerulea
BH	CT	DW	CDW	CDS	CT	TL	C	C	C	CDOU	CD	C	C	CD	CS	CS	CS	CDW		CDO
TC	CT	CTD		*	CT		CU		C	CDU	CD					C	CS	CS		CO
CU	CT	CDS	CDS	CTDWRS	CTR	CTLR	CD	CD		CDOU	CD	CDR	C	CRDW	CDWS	C	CR	CDWR		CDS
SI		*		*	*	*				*	*			O	*	*		CS		CTOU
CI	CT	CTLD	CT	CTDP	CTLD	CTL	CLS		CU	CTDS			RU		CLDSU	CL	COU	COU		CDO
JM	CT	CTOW	CTDW	CTDWSOU	DWSU	LWRU	CU	CD		CTLDWSU DWPSO	DRU	RU	RU		CDWSU	CDSU		CDWU		
HT	CT	DW		CDW	CT	TLW												CDW		TDO
DR	CTDP	TDW	CDW	TLDWRS	CTLRU	CTLWRU	CWSU	CD	CTDU	CTDORU	CDWRU	CTRSU	CD		DW	C		CDW		C
MO	CT	CD		CP	CP	CTL			CD	CD	CD	CD	DW			C		CD		C
PR	CT	CTW		TDWE	CTLW	CTLW	CDW	CW		CTDO	CTD	C						CTDWS		
CL	CT			CTD	CT	CTL														
VQ	CT	CD		CDW	CTL	CTL			CD	CTDO	CD	CD	CW	CD		CD		CD		CDO
ST	CT	CTWF	CD	TDWF	CTL	CTLW	W	W		CTDO	CDW		CW	W		W		OU		CO
SJ	CT	CTDW	CD	CTDWU	CTLDF	CTW	WF	W		TDO	CTDWFU		CW			DU				CO
SC	CT			CD	TWR	CTRW	W			T	T		C			DU				
TO	CT			CD	CTWFU					CTO	CDFU					CD				
VG	CT			C	CTL											CDU				
AG	CT				CL					CTO										
AL	CT					CTL										CDU		CD		
SM	CT	CS		C	CT			C	CD		CDW		CW			CDWU		CDWU		CDO
SB					CT						CDW		CW			CDWU		CDWU		CO
SE					CT								C			CDWU				CO
KN						CTLW														
AB	CT	W		W	CTL	LW	W			CD	W			CD		W	CD	CD		
MT				C	CT	C							C			C				
GP	CTD			DTWU	CTWU	CTDWU	TD			CTO	TDU		C			C				
DO	CTD				CTLW	CTLDW				CTDO	CTDW							OU		
MQ	CTD			CDWSU	CTU	CTLU					CTDU					C		CDWU		
SL	CT			DW	CTWU	CTWU				CDU			DW			DW				
SV	CTD			*	*	*					CDU				SU	SU		CU		
BB		U		U	TW	TR									CDWSU	CDWU	U	U		
GN	CT				CT										DWSU	CDWU	CDWU	CDWU		
TT	CTDSU			CDWS	CTLWRU	CTU	CU			CT						CF	WU	WU		
AR	CTLDU			CD	CTL	CTU				CL	S				CW	CU	CU	CU		
CO	CTLDU			CD	CTL	CTU	CU	CU	CU		CU					CU	CU	CU		CU
BN	CTLDU			CD	CTL		CU	CU								CU	CU	CU	CU	CU
AP	*	*		*	*	*	*			DS	CLU *				*	*	*	*		

HABITAT CODES: C (coast); D (dry forest); E (elfin woodland); F (forest edge); L (littoral); O (open areas); P (pines); R (riparian); S (woodland); T (wetlands); U (urban areas); W (wet forest); * indicates that the species has been recorded, but no additional information was given.
ISLAND CODES: See Table 1.

TABLE 2—Continued next page

TABLE 2—Continued

Island	Passerina cyanea	P. ciris	Spiza americana	Pipilo chlorurus	Spizella passerina	S. pallida	Pooecetes gramineus	Chondestes grammacus	Passerculus sandwichensis	Ammodramus savannarum	Melospiza melodia	M. lincolnii	M. georgiana	Zonotrichia albicollis	Z. leucophrys	Junco hyemalis	Dolichonyx oryzivorus	Agelaius phoeniceus	Sturnella magna	Xanthocephalus xanthocephalus	Euphagus carolinus	E. cyanocephalus	Molothrus ater	Icterus spurius	I. galbula	Carduelis tristis
BH	CDPO	CO	CO		CO		CO	CO	CO	CO	CO	CO	CO		C	COU	COU	CO	CO	CO	CO	CO	CO	C	C	
TC	CDSO	CO	CO			CU	CO	CO	CO	CO	CO	CO				COU	COU		CO	CO					CU	
CU	CO	CO	CO	C	CO		CO	CO	CO	CO	CO	CO	CO		COU		C									COU
SI	CO *	*	*		CO	CO	CO	CO	CTO								*		CO	CO			CO	*	CR	
CI	CTSOU	C							COU	CTO		CO		COU	COU	COU	CTSOU			CTL					CTLDS	
JM	CO	CU	CO						CO	CO		W			COU	COU	CTOU							C	CTDSU	
HT	CDO																								CDSU	
DR	CDO																CO								CDSU	
MO	CO									CO		C		COU		COU	CO		C						CDOU	
PR	CO		COU							C		CD					CO		CO	C					CDU	
CL																	CO			CO					CTDU	
VQ										C							CO								CTDSU	
ST	CO															COU	CO								CTDSU	
SJ	CO																CO								CTDFU	
SC	TU																OU								TDSU	
TO	CO																								CU	
VG	CO																									
AG																										
AL																										
SM	COU																COU								CU	
SB																	COU									
SE																	COU									
KN																										
AB																	COU									
MT																										
GP																	COU									
DO																	CO									
MQ																	CO									
SL																	CO								COU	
SV																	C								S	
BB																	TO								COU	
GN																	COU		C						CDWRU	
TT	F		CTO														CU	OU							CU	
AR	COU		CO										C				CTOU								CU	
CO	COU		CO														CTOU									
BN																	CTOU	C							CU	
AP	*																C									

HABITAT CODES: C (coast); D (dry forest); E (elfin woodland); F (forest edge); L (littoral); O (open areas); P (pines); R (riparian); S (woodland); T (wetlands); U (urban areas); W (wet forest); * indicates that the species has been recorded, but no additional information was given.
ISLAND CODES: See Table 1.

turbed) tidal mangrove forest and associated wetlands habitats. LITTORAL: Pertaining to lake-shore habitat and associated vegetation. FOREST EDGE: "Edge" vegetation usually including colonizing species of herbaceous and woody vegetation (i.e., small bushes) in the interphase between grassland-savannah vegetation and forests. OPEN AREAS: Include grasslands (dominated by herbaceous grasses, sometimes used for any herb dominated vegetation) and savannah vegetation (tropical and subtropical grassland, transitional in character between grassland or desert and rain forest; typically having drought resistant vegetation dominated by grasses with scattered tall trees). PINES: Native or introduced coniferous species, including monocultures and mixed-species plantations and natural stands. URBAN: Any human-altered habitat including settings in cities and small towns such as city parks, gardens, golf courses, lawns, vacant lots, airports, hotel and resort grounds, over open sewers, settling tanks, water supplies (reservoirs); it also includes agricultural lands, fields, orchards, irrigation ditches. RIPARIAN: Riverine vegetation growing along the banks of rivers and streams. WOODLANDS: A circumscribed area of vegetation (relict patches of forest) dominated by a more or less closed stand of short trees. Also includes small fragmented woodlots of predominantly secondary forest vegetation characterized by widely scattered trees showing signs of regeneration, but continuing to suffer from periodic cutting and other disturbances such as grazing.

HOW TO USE TABLES 1 AND 2. Caribbean islands are arranged in geographic order from west to east and north to south; migrants (genera and specific names) are listed in phylogenetic order to show each species' distribution and status throughout the region.

Results

Information was gathered from collaborators and the literature for Neotropical landbird migrants in 10 Orders: Falconiformes, and Columbiformes through Passeriformes, with the exception of the Psittaciformes (A.O.U. 1983), for more than 50 major Caribbean Islands. Distribution and abundance information for 151 species of Neotropical landbird migrants using the greater Caribbean region as part of their migration routes or as wintering grounds is summarized in Table 1.

Paruline warblers tend to reach more Caribbean islands than any other major group of Neotropical landbird migrants (Table 1). Of these, most individuals of three species (Cape May, Black-throated Blue, and Prairie warblers) spend the nonbreeding season almost exclusively in the Caribbean (Rappole et al. 1983). In addition, substantial numbers of another 10 species of

paruline warblers spend most of their nonbreeding season in, or passing through, the Caribbean islands. These species must be monitored closely in an effort to detect possible population declines that could be deleterious at the species rather than population level.

Information on habitat use by 151 species of Neotropical landbird migrants is summarized in Table 2. Most migrants, including the paruline warblers, use many habitats in addition to tropical rain forest (e.g., dry forest, wetlands, woodland, and even altered and degraded habitats, plus a variety of urban environments).

FACTORS AFFECTING MIGRANT DISTRIBUTION AND ABUNDANCE IN THE CARIBBEAN REGION

Many geographical, ecological, and human-induced factors affect migrants and their habitats in the greater Caribbean basin. Included are (1) seasonal fluctuations in precipitation and food resulting from prolonged droughts (Faaborg 1982, Faaborg and Arendt 1984, Spendlow 1985), (2) hurricanes (Wadsworth and Englerth 1959, Lindo 1968, Neumann et al. 1978, Lugo et al. 1983, Thompson 1983, Wunderle et al. 1989, Wunderle 1990, Arendt 1990), (3) distance from mainland and landmass of wintering grounds (Terborgh and Faaborg 1980), (4) habitat loss and alteration through deforestation, burning regimes, draining, and spraying of chemicals in wetlands and other ecosystems to induce agricultural and urban development (Westermann 1953, Vogt 1970, Lovejoy 1983, Wilcove and Terborgh 1984, Faaborg and Arendt 1985, ffrench 1985, Rappole and Morton 1985, Serrao 1985), (5) competition and habitat quality (Terborgh and Faaborg 1980), (6) over-hunting (Arendt et al. 1979, Garrido 1985, Wiley 1985), and (7) importation of exotic species (Westermann 1953).

Twenty-four regional and local experts reported that, at present, 11 major factors (with another 9 of less importance) are adversely or favorably affecting the distribution and abundance of Caribbean landbird migrants:

HABITAT LOSS. Habitat loss is, and probably will continue to be, the primary factor adversely impacting migrant populations throughout the Caribbean region. For example, in the Cayman Islands (Greater Antilles), the biggest threat to migrant birds is the drainage of mangrove forest, other wetlands areas, and woodland for urban, recreational, and agricultural use (P. Bradley, in lett.). A strong antienvironmental lobby exists within the Cayman Islands, and it appears that minimal environmental restraints will be built into the new planning laws. Most unfortunately, premium land for developers is also prime migrant bird habitat. A similar situation exists in the U.S. Virgin Islands. On St. John, Norton (in lett.) reports that whereas most habitat loss in the Caribbean is piecemeal, the accumulated loss throughout the Virgin Islands (presently under heavy development to accommodate the tourist industry) is having a negative effect on both migratory and resident bird populations. Likewise, on St. Croix, the continuing emphasis by the government on commercial, tourist, and industrial growth is definitely having a negative impact on the almost 30 species of migrant landbirds dependent upon forest and wetlands habitats (F. Sladen, in lett.). In Jamaica, although the rate of deforestation has been estimated as 3% per annum (FAO 1981), because "forest" was defined as "any habitat with more than 10% canopy cover" (Eyre 1986), the actual rate is undoubtedly much higher (R. Sutton and others, in lett.). At the present rate, most of Jamaica's forested areas will be converted to plantations, hillside agriculture (including marijuana plots), human settlement, and charcoal burning within the next 5–10 years. Since Lack's study (1976), riverine forests and sea level forests have been virtually extirpated. The large tracts of wet montane forest in the Blue Mountains and the wet limestone forest of the Cockpit country and John Crow Mountains depicted by Lack (1976, Fig. 3) no longer exist (M. Gochfeld, in lett.). Such deforestation is a result of much slash-and-burn clearing and extensive cultivation of marijuana at middle and high elevations (Gruber 1984). In Haiti, the dominant factor affecting migrants is habitat loss (Woods 1975). Each year landbird migrants are being restricted to ever-shrinking areas of suitable habitat. Lowland forests have been lost to expanding human activities, especially agriculture. Scrub forest in low to middle elevations has been lost as a result of an increased demand for charcoal. Exploitation of mangrove forests for building supplies and charcoal is increasing. Destruction of mesic forests in middle and upper elevations continues to accelerate, with the land being converted to garden plots and fallen trees being used for building materials and charcoal. Within the Massif de le Selle, a major center of concentration for migrant birds in Haiti, the World Bank is considering an extensive economic development plan for the remaining pine forests at the upper elevations. An accelerating decline of economic conditions within Haiti is responsible for increasing the rate of habitat loss (Woods and Ottenwalder 1983, 1986). In neighboring Dominican Republic, the state of the natural environment is not any better. Habitat loss is by far the most significant factor affecting both resident and migrant bird populations (A. Dod, in lett.). She states that "today, virtually no prime rain forest habitat remains in the Dominican Republic, and the situation is similar for all other forest habitats throughout the country. Massive fires have destroyed large tracts of native pine (*Pinus occidentalis*) in the Cordillera Central, while agriculturists and developers are destroying dry forest and tidal mangrove forest at lower elevations. The once ex-

tensive forests of the limestone karst hills along the southern shores of the Samaná Bay have all but disappeared as a result of cutting and burning by squatters clearing land for their garden plots." Similarly, coastal wetlands habitats are also under the ever-growing threat of destruction by foreign merchants and developers. Arendt documents two examples of long-term aquacultural and agricultural projects undertaken by foreign entrepreneurs that are destroying much of the country's prime wetlands areas. First, not many years ago, a South American-based shrimp company built shrimp farms at three different sites along the country's northern shore from the Samaná Bay to Monte Cristi. To date, construction of the shrimp farms has resulted in extensive destruction of tidal mangrove forest and other wetland habitats, but little production of shrimp. It now appears that the company will go bankrupt and operations will cease. Nevertheless, much wetlands habitat has been irreversibly altered. As a second example, a Japanese firm, with the intent of raising potatoes and onions, has begun a multimillion dollar agricultural venture in the Samaná Bay area. The firm has already begun to drain many wetlands areas from the coastal town of Nagua to the shores of the Samaná Bay. Not only are the acidic soils causing poor crop yields, but drainage of the wetlands is affecting the fisheries industry, the industry upon which most inhabitants of the bay area rely heavily.

On Vieques Island (one of Puerto Rico's satellites), habitat destruction is the major threat facing migrants. "Wetlands are threatened by the alteration of the natural drainage through blockage of tidal channels by improperly maintained road culverts and excess sedimentation caused by overgrazing and erosion of adjacent uplands. Mesic forests on slopes are threatened by loss of undergrowth and replacement seedlings due to overgrazing by cattle." (B. Sorrie, in lett.). Loss of vegetational diversity is not normally conducive to migrant populations.

In the Lesser Antilles, habitat loss was reported by most collaborators as the prime negative factor affecting migrant populations. However, because fewer landbird migrants reach most of these islands, collaborators did not consider that habitat loss would cause the extirpation of their small migrant bird populations. Such is the case on St. Lucia, where migrant landbirds occur on the island as vagrants or as rare "winter" visitors (A. Keith, in lett.). But, on a precautionary note, if the alteration of natural habitat on St. Lucia continues at its present rate, the destruction of natural watersheds, increased soil erosion, heavy siltation of rivers and wetlands, and the fouling of freshwater supplies, now on the increase, will undoubtedly adversely impact migrant as well as resident bird life (C. Cox, in lett.). A similar situation exists in Trinidad and Tobago. R. ffrench (in lett.) writes "I see no immediate threat to migrant landbirds, provided that the present rate of deforestation does not increase . . . although species diversity in migrant landbirds on Trinidad and Tobago is quite high, the number of individuals within most species is quite low. The most numerous species such as the Barn Swallow, Yellow Warbler, and the irruptive Dickcissel, should find a secure future on these islands for many years to come."

On Antigua, heavy development presently taking place, especially construction of condominiums in the vicinity of McKinnon's Pond, is definitely having an adverse affect on migrant landbirds (Spencer in lett.). McKinnon's Pond is a major natural wetlands area and center for migrants (Faaborg and Arendt 1985). Both Antigua and Barbuda suffer from the increasing practice of converting scrub and dry forest to cattle range, thus destroying potential forest habitat for migrants. Barbuda currently has a large sand-mining and exporting venture underway. Extensive areas of beach, strand vegetation, and mangrove forest are being destroyed for the extraction and exportation of sand and other materials used in building, paving, and other types of construction. In the French West Indies, development, deforestation, and the conversion of native habitat to monocultures continues throughout the territory and is greatly affecting the status of migratory warblers, both transients and "winter" residents (E. Benito-Espinal, in lett.).

On St. Vincent, Kirby (in lett.) writes that "one of the main threats to the environment and migratory bird populations is the drying up of the littoral swamps inland of the sand dunes." These swamps began drying up in the 1930s, desiccation being accelerated via road construction and rechanneling of natural drainage systems. Currently, along the south coast, limited wetlands habitat remains at Prospect and none at Righton or Diamond. In St. Vincent, the rate of deforestation differs in different parts of the island, with the windward slopes showing more extensive cultivation, either as established plots and plantations, or shifting agriculture (M. Kelsey, in lett.). However, some extensive and relatively undisturbed forest can be found on the leeward side of St. Vincent, particularly in the upper Buccament, Wallibou and Cumberland valleys.

On Barbados, a low-relief island, extirpation of the natural vegetation has been virtually complete to accommodate agriculture, urban development, and the tourist industry. Only one small area of the island's original forest cover remains. Turner's Hall Wood, a 20-ha patch of secondary mesophytic, semideciduous forest, is located at St. Andrew in the rugged Scotland District. Some small fringes of woodland survive below the steep rocky escarpment bordering the Scotland District. The prime woodlot, located at Joe's River, has been claimed

by government for forestry purposes and a variety of potential timber species has been planted during the past 15 years. Coastal woodland has been either eliminated or greatly altered along the west and south coasts. In addition to a handful of small areas of white mangrove (*Laguncularia racemosa*) surviving among numerous houses and hotels along the west and south coasts, one small 32-ha tract of mangrove and sedge swamp remains, the Graeme Hill Swamp in Christ Church. In 1972, the western portion (12 ha) of the swamp was drained by land developers. Some 5 ha of prime development land bordering the 1.6-ha natural estuarine pool was offered for sale.

Not all collaborators considered habitat loss as a factor negatively affecting migrant landbirds on their islands. Seven of the 24 collaborators reported various means by which the rate of habitat loss is decreasing or, in a few instances, establishment of suitable migrant habitat is on the increase. For example, in Cuba, historically increased and widespread habitat loss has negatively affected landbird migrants (O. Garrido, in lett.). However, largely because of a recent surge in public environmental awareness, not only has deforestation greatly diminished, reforestation measures are being conducted throughout the island by various state and local groups. Parks and other natural areas are being set aside nationwide. In the Dominican Republic, although deforestation under past presidential administrations was rampant even in designated national parks, President Joaquin Balaguer has declared a moratorium on all cutting and burning within the country (A. Dod, in lett.). Many areas, especially within parks, could be reforested in the near future.

Puerto Rico and its satellites are prime examples of islands which historically experienced almost total deforestation mainly through agriculture and development, but recently have begun to recover lost forested areas largely because of a shift from an agrarian to an industrialized society. Most forests in Puerto Rico and its satellites had been clear-cut by 1912 for the planting of sugarcane and other agricultural crops (Murphy 1916). Today, only about 0.2% of Puerto Rico's original forests remain. However, an estimated 40% of the island is now covered with natural secondary forests (Schmidt 1982). Density of migrant landbirds is often moderate to high within coastal secondary forest (Robbins et al. 1987; Arendt, unpubl. data). The increase of secondary forests on Puerto Rico is having positive effects on migrant forest bird populations. In Dominica, "There is no strong indication at present that North American migrant warblers are adversely affected by habitat loss" (P. Evans, in lett.). Not only does Dominica host the largest expanse of wet and montane forest remaining in the Lesser Antilles, Evans has shown that migrant warblers concentrate in coastal areas such as the Cabritz Peninsula adjacent to a swamp and dry scrub woodland, often near rubbish dumps which attract insects, the warblers' primary prey.

RESERVES AND OTHER PROTECTED AREAS. Eight collaborators reported that landbird migrants could be affected because few, if any, natural areas were set aside on their respective islands. However, 16 of 24 collaborators reported that the establishment of national parks and other natural areas, coupled with subsequent natural and artificial (human-mediated) reforestation, has helped to recover migrant landbird populations in traditionally forested areas that for the past 400–500 years had been used for agriculture. In Cuba, the entire Sierra Maestra mountain range, the peninsulas of Zapata and Guanahacabibes, have been declared national parks. More than 100 additional reservations of varying sizes have been proposed and are awaiting government approval. In Haiti, the "Direction des Ressources Naturelles" has begun to take an active role in promoting the protection of government lands. Two national parks have been set aside in mountainous areas of the Massif de la Selle and the Massif de la Hotte. Together, they total almost 50,000 ha of protected area (C. Woods, in lett.). In Puerto Rico and the U.S. Virgin Islands, state and federal agencies continue to maintain a large network of forests and other protected areas, thereby assuring migrant landbirds ample natural habitat indefinitely. On St. John, 60% of the landmass is controlled by the National Park Service. On St. Croix the newly formed Virgin Island Natural Heritage Trust (VINHT), a nonprofit land trust corporation, has begun to negotiate for the purchase of key wildlife habitats and is in a position to accept tax-deductible donations of land to be held in perpetuity as green belts and wildlife sanctuaries (F. Sladen, in lett.).

The governments and people of many of the Lesser Antillean islands have seen the need for preserving natural areas. St. Lucia took an early lead in establishing and wisely managing its national forests and other natural areas. Encouragingly, St. Lucia's example has been closely followed by Dominica and St. Vincent, among other islands.

MONOCULTURES. With the destruction of forests throughout the Caribbean region has come the creation of a variety of agricultural and silvicultural monocultures. Historically, virtually all arable lands and areas suitable for development, most of which were covered with prime mangrove, dry, and wet forests, were denuded. Fourteen of the 24 collaborators report that large expanses of monocultural crops such as sugarcane, cotton, bananas, and pineapples, early successional, pioneering species such as acacia, and large single-species plantings of native pines (Pinus spp.) and potential commercial timber

species such as mahogany (Swietenia spp.), teak (Tectona grandis) and mahoe (Hibiscus spp.), that have replaced native vegetation on most islands continue to adversely impact migratory as well as native avifauna. In Jamaica, as forests are converted to monocultures, many forest birds will not be able to adapt to them (Falkenberg et al. 1983). A similar situation exists in Haiti, where exotic tree species such as neem (Melia azadirachta) and leadtree (Leucaena leucocephala) are being used in major reforestation projects (Woods and Ottenwalder 1986). The resultant monocultures are far less suitable as habitat for migrants than was the native vegetation. However, some studies (e.g., Cruz 1987) have shown that if an understory is encouraged, resident as well as migratory species might continue to inhabit monocultures. On Vieques Island, overgrazing by cattle and sheep has resulted in much of the native vegetation having been replaced by monocultures of Acacia and Prosopis spp., thus greatly reducing the diversity of natural vegetation and adversely impacting migrant landbird populations (B. Sorrie, in lett.).

On many Lesser Antillean islands, areas once cleared for the traditional monocultural crops such as sugarcane and cotton are now being planted to bananas and plantains. Bananas and plantains are currently St. Lucia's (and many of its neighbors') principal cash and export crops. On St. Vincent, the most rapid conversion to agricultural lands is occurring on the island's windward side (M. Kelsey, in lett.). Similarly, much of the Ministry of Forestry's reforestation efforts on St. Lucia, St. Vincent, and neighboring islands involves the planting of exotic tree species, often varieties of mahoe. Therefore, although the quantity of forested lands might be holding steady or even increasing, the quality (in terms of vegetational diversity) is in fact decreasing. In the southern Lesser Antilles, of the approximate 42,897 ha of tillable land remaining in Barbados, about 16,187 ha (38%) are planted in sugarcane, a monoculture definitely not conducive to migrant (or resident) bird populations (M. Hutt, in lett.).

SPECIES ADAPTABILITY. Land development and the preservation of "protected areas" of suitable habitat for migrant landbirds do not have to be mutually exclusive. Eight collaborators noted that the planting of gardens, ornamental trees, and fruit-tree orchards, as well as the creation of "manicured" grounds, and golf courses that accompany much agricultural and urban development actually enhance populations of some migrant species. In Haiti, flocks of several hundred individuals of migrant landbirds are regularly observed in disturbed second growth and especially agricultural areas (Woods and Ottenwalder 1983).

It is encouraging that landbird migrants in general are found in a mosaic of habitat types throughout the

Caribbean islands (Table 2). This is especially true for the most common transients and seasonal residents, many of which include species of paruline warblers. Collaborators reporting on three islands (Jamaica, Hispaniola–Dominican Republic, and St. Croix) separated migrant landbirds by habitat type. In Jamaica, large percentages of 56 common landbird migrants, including many species of warblers, were found in 10 major habitats (Table 3) (R. Sutton and others, in lett.). On St. Croix, large percentages of 49 species of landbird migrants (9 paruline warbler species) were found in six major habitats: urban (59% of the species); wetlands (57%); coast (57%) dry (41%); mesic (41%); riparian (3%) (F. Sladen, in lett.). The low percentage of migrant warblers in riparian habitats reflects the fact that there is little riparian habitat remaining on St. Croix, *not* that migrants are avoiding this prime migrant habitat.

In the Dominican Republic, during an intensive two-year study (Arendt, unpubl. data), large percentages of 20 species of migrant warblers frequented six major habitat types: riparian (95% of the species); urban (75%); wetlands (75%); mesic (55%); dry (55%); coast (50%) (see Table 4 for an analysis by species).

TABLE 3.   Habitat use by North American migrant landbirds in Jamaica

Habitat type	No. species	%	Status of habitat
Coast	31	56	decreasing
Mangrove	16	29	decreasing
Dry forest	39	70	decreasing
Wet forest	20	36	decreasing
Elfin woodland	13	23	decreasing
Wetlands	22	40	decreasing
Littoral	13	23	decreasing
Forest edge	22	39	increasing
Open areas	19	35	increasing
Urban areas	30	55	increasing
Riparian	21	38	decreasing
Woodland	21	38	increasing

NOTE: Percentages are the fractional number of species (out of total number of species) inhabiting each habitat and the column total exceeds 100% for all types because several species occur in more than one habitat .

TABLE 4.   Habitat associations of 20 paruline warbler species observed in the Dominican Republic (1976–1978)

Species[a]	Strand vegetation	Coconut palm	Mangrove	Scrub	Disturbed dry forest	Riparian	Urban	Pine forest	Disturbed wet forest	Mesic forest	Wet forest
AMRE	1		17	17	9	20	17		5	8	6
CMWA	1		11	12	14		9	20		19	11
COYE	2		7	53	13	6	10			9	
NOPA				19	19	23	5	2	3	10	19
BAWW	2		26	3		40	14		11		4
OVEN			3	4	12	48	12		5		16
YPWA	4		5	8	3	38	31	2	2		7
PRAW			55	9	4	13	17		2		
BLPW			2	10	14	41	24				9
NOWA	14		82			4					
LOWA			1			49	17		5		28
YTWA	18	64	3	3		8	4				
MYWA	2		4	46	6	28	11	3			
BTBW			5		14	12	11		20	12	26
MAWA	10		5	15		20	50				
BTNW						23			77		
HOWA					10	30	60				
PROW			83					17			
BWWA						(1)[b]					
WIWA						(1)[b]					

NOTE: Numbers represent percentage of individuals observed in each habitat type.

a. Species codes are those used by the U.S. Bird Banding Lab.

b. Represents a single observation.

Use of mature mangrove forest and its importance as suitable habitat for a number of landbird migrants (particularly paruline warblers) should not be underestimated (see Cawkell 1964, ffrench 1966, Johnston 1975, Lack 1976, Cruz 1977, Gochfeld 1985). In a three-year study (1984–1986) to evaluate the importance of mangrove forest to migrants during their nonbreeding seasons (W. Arendt, unpubl. data), 362 individuals of 12 species of Neotropical migrants (11 species of paruline warblers and the Gray-cheeked Thrush) were found in this often overlooked habitat: Northern Waterthrush (75%), Black-and-white Warbler (12%), American Redstart (5%), Worm-eating Warbler (3%), and seven species comprising 1% or less of the captures: Ovenbird, Common Yellowthroat, Northern Parula, Black-throated Blue, Yellow-rumped, Prothonotary, and Prairie warblers. Species recaptured at the study site included: Northern Waterthrush, Northern Parula, Black-and-white, and Worm-eating warblers. There is evidence (Arendt, unpubl. data) that the migrants, especially American Redstarts, are limiting the spatial distributions of the resident Yellow Warbler within mangrove vegetation during the migrants' presence. Yellow Warblers were observed foraging at all levels of black and red mangrove in the absence of migrants, but were limited to the lower strata when migrants were present. However, in forests of black mangrove (*Avicennia germinans*) in Puerto Rico and Grand Cayman, Bennett (1980, Table 4a.) did not observe such a vertical compression of the Yellow Warbler's foraging zone with the arrival of migrant warblers.

Historically, the inherent adaptability of many migrant landbird species to a diversity of habitats might have saved them from extirpation as Caribbean islands were developed over the past few hundred years. This inherent adaptability might also prove to be a major factor in diminishing future extirpations as island development and urbanization continue.

HUNTING. Hunting was reported by 11 of the 24 collaborators as a significant negative factor affecting migratory landbirds. Migrants, together with native species, are constantly taken by rural people on many islands as a supplementary protein source. In Jamaica, the effects of hunting are locally severe (R. Sutton and others, in lett.). Hunting laws are not well enforced and it is probable that game and nongame migrants alike are shot year-round. In Haiti, small peasant children often hunt with slingshots, and a significant number of wintering migrants is taken (C. Woods, in lett.). In the Dominican Republic, small children using slingshots kill many migrant warblers (Arendt, pers. obs.). As an example, in 1981 a Blackpoll Warbler banded during migration in Wisconsin was killed with a slingshot in northwestern (Manzanillo) Dominican Republic (Arendt, unpubl.

data). Many migrants on Hispaniola die each year from such hunting practices, but go unreported.

In the French West Indies, the impact of hunting on migrants as well as native birds is substantial (E. Benito-Espinal, in lett.). There are between 2,000 and 2,500 legal hunters in Guadeloupe alone, not including illegal poachers. In Dominica, "The killing of birds and their harassment by children is not to be underestimated. I have observed a number of birds killed or injured as a consequence of slingshots and stone throwing by youngsters." (P. Evans, in lett.).

Hunting pressure on some islands has actually diminished in recent years. Thus, four of the 24 collaborators considered that reduced hunting pressure would have a positive effect on migrants. In Cuba, hunting is currently almost nonexistent (O. Garrido, in lett.). In Jamaica, although hunting with slingshots is having a negative impact on migrants (M. Gochfeld, in lett.), the hunting ban in effect from 1974 to 1981 (Downer 1981) was effective. Populations of several species of pigeons and doves increased dramatically. However, as Gochfeld points out, "with shooting legalized once again, there is grave concern about the taking of migrants and protected species by hunters unable to, or uninterested in, distinguishing these species from the legal game birds." In the Dominican Republic, populations of the migratory gamebird, the White-crowned Pigeon, increased when a five-year hunting ban was declared for the species (Arendt et al. 1979). However, wildlife protection laws have not been enforced, especially in recent years. Thus, once again, the species might be in jeopardy. In St. Lucia, with the establishment, and more importantly, the stringent enforcement of the Wildlife Protection Act of 1980, migrants and resident birds are fully protected. There is very little killing of migrants or birds of any kind on the island (C. Cox, in lett.; Arendt, pers. obs.).

CLIMATE. In addition to the hazards of inclement weather, which often devastate migratory birds during their long flight between breeding and wintering grounds, is the variable climate found on many Caribbean islands. Ten of the 24 collaborators cited climate, especially hurricanes and droughts, as having a significant negative impact on landbird migrants. Hurricanes can kill migrants outright or indirectly as a result of depleting food supplies and cover by complete or partial defoliation of island vegetation. As Garrido (in lett.) points out, hurricanes can kill a large proportion of migrants in the Greater Antilles because the most severe storms often occur from August through November, the months when many migrants are passing through or setting up seasonal residency in Cuba and other islands.

Periodic droughts, especially of long duration, can significantly reduce migrant populations, particularly on the low, dry islands of the Caribbean region. In the

Turks and Caicos Islands (Greater Antilles), annual rainfall is only about 64 cm, with marked seasonal fluctuations. Fewer landbird migrants remain during dry "winters" (B. Aldridge, in lett.). On Antigua and Barbuda, as a result of the severe and extended drought of 1983 (heavy rains did not come to alleviate drought conditions until the fall of 1984) resident and migratory bird populations declined dramatically (W. Spencer, in lett.; J. Fuller, pers. comm.). During the drought, the Potsworks Reservoir, Antigua's main water source, dried up completely. The "winter" of 1984–85 showed a marked decrease of all birds, including migrant landbirds. Since 1985, migrant landbird numbers have begun to increase, but have not reached previous levels (W. Spencer, in lett.).

In the Caribbean, regional rainfall is associated with the El Niño Southern Oscillation (ENSO). Unusual drought and flood conditions were reported throughout the Caribbean during the 1982–1983 ENSO event (Norton 1983). Thus, climate can have both negative and positive effects on migrant birds as it relates to food resources during their seasonal residency in the West Indies.

ENVIRONMENTAL AWARENESS. Unfortunately, because of a poor economic base shared by many people throughout the Caribbean region, concern for the natural environment is often lacking and is largely responsible for the indiscriminate habitat destruction, development of natural areas, and hunting practices discussed above. Nine of the 24 collaborators cited this factor as negatively impacting migrant landbirds. However, four collaborators reported an increased environmental awareness in at least some sectors of the human population which is positively affecting migrant landbirds in Haiti, the Dominican Republic, St. Croix, and St. Lucia. In Haiti, a new conservation association, the Society Audubon d'Haiti pour la Protection de l'Environnment, has begun to promote an environmental awareness in many of its inhabitants, especially those living in rural areas where human impact on the environment is the strongest (Woods, in lett.). In the Dominican Republic, mainly through the efforts of Annabelle Stockton de Dod and a few others, Dominicans are learning the importance of conserving their natural resources (Keith, in lett.).

In St. Croix, members of two environmental groups, the St. Croix Chapter of the Virgin Island Conservation Society, an affiliate member of the National Wildlife Federation, and the recently formed Virgin Islands Natural Heritage Trust are working closely with governmental planning agencies, developers, and entrepreneurs to develop ways of protecting natural areas so vital to migrants and other wildlife (F. Sladen, in lett.).

A notable exception to the general lack of environmental concern found throughout the Caribbean region is the island of St. Lucia. There, a widespread environmental awareness has come about primarily through the efforts of officers in the Forestry Department and Ministry of Agriculture. An islandwide environmental education campaign was mounted, with the help of government and international funding agencies.

ENVIRONMENTAL POLLUTION. The economy of the larger Caribbean islands, and many of their adjacent satellites, continues to change from an agricultural to an industrial one. Consequently, air and water pollution are on the increase on these islands and pose a major threat to the biota, including landbird migrants. Three collaborators reported negative effects of environmental pollutants on two large islands and one small satellite island. In Jamaica, pesticides, including products banned islandwide (but still in use) such as DDT and dieldrin, are negatively impacting populations of migrant and resident forest birds (R. Sutton and others, in lett.). Pesticide residues in human foods also have been reported (A. Mansingh, pers. comm.). In Puerto Rico, there has been a recent discovery of exceedingly high levels of mercury in seabirds nesting on Culebra and adjacent keys (J. Burger and M. Gochfeld, pers. comm.). These chemical residues threaten, and could already be affecting, the health and reproductive potential of the many rapacious migrants such as hawks and falcons that pass through or reside seasonally in these areas and feed on birds associated with wetlands and marine ecosystems.

On St. Lucia, to enhance the growing tourist industry, many freshwater and estuarine wetlands are being sprayed with uncontrolled levels of dangerous pesticides and herbicides, with the intent of eradicating or at least controlling insect pests, diseases spread by arboviruses, and nonnative vegetation affecting estuarial ecosystems (C. Cox, in lett.; Arendt, pers. obs.). Already, there are reports of massive die-offs of freshwater and wetlands vegetation, particularly mangrove forest, and their respective faunas, which include migrant and resident landbirds and the vertebrate and invertebrate animals upon which they feed. Some of the wetlands areas hardest hit are in the vicinities of Gros Islet and Vieux Fort, all of which offer major habitat for transient and seasonally resident migrant land- and waterbirds (Faaborg and Arendt 1985). Visiting tankers, tourist ships, yachts, speed-boats, and many other types of commercial and pleasure craft are fouling beaches, tidal mangrove forests, and other coastal wetlands areas by discharging excess ballast, oil, and sewage, and by throwing discarded rubbish and garbage overboard (C. Cox, in lett.; Arendt, pers. obs.). As a consequence, estuarine vegetation and its fauna are adversely affected.

COMPETITION FROM EXOTICS. Exotic plants and animals have direct and indirect effects on migrant bird populations. In the Caribbean region, introduced rats (*Rattus* spp.) and the Small Indian Mongoose (*Herpestes auropunctatus*) have adversely affected the resident faunas, contributing to the extinction of native species on some islands (Westermann 1953, Bond 1961). In Jamaica, the disappearance of native birds has been attributed to the mongoose (Seaman 1952). The mongoose might have contributed to the extinction of the Jamaican Pauraque (*Siphonorhis americanus*) (Bond 1961), although it is thought by some to have been eradicated by introduced rats before the introduction of the mongoose (Westermann 1953). Mongooses and rats probably take an unknown quantity of understory and ground-foraging migrant landbirds in addition to the indigenous fauna. In Puerto Rico, in the Luquillo Experimental Forest (Caribbean National Forest), where the mongoose is common, it is a potential predator on the small, but regular, seasonal populations of the Louisiana Waterthrush, which frequent the understory and feed along numerous streams and major highways in the forest.

COMPETITION FROM NATIVE SPECIES. With the alteration of natural vegetation on Caribbean islands, comes the potential for a commensurate range expansion and increased abundance of certain native species which could compete with migrants for food and other resources. For example, Bond (Checklist of birds of the West Indies Supplement 22, 1978) wrote that the spread of the native Yellow Warbler (*Dendroica petechia*) on Barbuda, after the cutting of dry forests for agriculture, attributed to the subsequent reduction in numbers of another native paruline species, the Adelaide's Warbler (*D. adelaidae*), and thus could potentially affect populations of migrant parulines adapted to similar habitats.

DISEASE AND PARASITES. Migrant birds have been shown to transport arboviruses from North America to southern latitudes (Stamm and Newman 1963, Lord and Calisher 1970). Three collaborators reported that disease and parasites negatively affect migrant landbirds on their islands. Zoonotic and arboviral diseases and parasites in birds have been documented in Jamaica (Belle et al. 1964, Bennett et al. 1980), Haiti (McLean et al. 1979), and from the Caribbean Basin in general (Beatty 1938, 1944, O'Connor and Beatty 1938, Bequaert 1940, Spence et al. 1968, Kocan and Sprunt 1971). In coastal scrub and dry forest in southwestern Puerto Rico, pox lesions have been found in resident species (Post 1981) and two North American migrant species (American Redstart and Black-and-white Warbler) (Arendt and Faaborg unpubl. data). Scaly-leg, a disease caused by *Cnemidocoptes* mites (Herman et al. 1962), has been ob-

served (Arendt and Faaborg unpubl. data) in the Ovenbird. In the Dominican Republic, at a mangrove banding site near Sanchez in the Samaná Bay, about 1% of the captured Northern Waterthrushes exhibited swollen and discolored tarso-metatarsal joints of an as yet undetermined disease (Arendt unpubl. data). Infested migrants could infect other migrants either on their nonbreeding grounds, breeding grounds upon their return, or during migration if they come into close contact.

Some species of landbird migrants in the Caribbean tend to frequent areas with high concentrations of insects and thus are more susceptible to arboviral infections and parasitic diseases. Sewage settling tanks and animal waste ponds around animal husbandry facilities, such as dairies, pig farms, cattle, chicken, and horse ranches, are all examples of sites where migrant parulines tend to concentrate. Cape May Warblers and American Redstarts captured in the vicinity of animal waste ponds at cattle ranches and pig farms in the Dominican Republic and Puerto Rico occasionally harbored unidentified larvae in their foot pads (Arendt unpubl. data), presumably contracting the larvae from direct contact with livestock excrement. Thus, infectious diseases and parasitic infestations could lower migrant bird numbers on both their breeding and nonbreeding grounds, with the potential being even greater in human-influenced environments.

UNKNOWN FACTORS. Christmas Bird Counts (CBCs) conducted in the Caribbean region might be an adequate means by which to monitor populations of migrants. For example, results of CBCs for the 12 most common landbird migrant species conducted over 16 years (1973–1988) in Cabo Rojo, Puerto Rico show that at least three species (Osprey, Peregrine Falcon, and Black-and-white Warbler) appear to be increasing. For the two raptorial species, the increase might be due, in part, to disuse of harmful pesticides, stricter laws regulating the protection of raptors, and the all-out recovery efforts launched by conservation agencies and universities to restore populations of both species. Numbers of one migrant species (Belted Kingfisher) have remained generally stable over the years. Intriguingly, four species of paruline warblers (Northern Parula, Cape May, American Redstart, and Northern Waterthrush) show a bimodal distribution with peaks at each end of the sampled period and a depression during the hurricane years of 1979 and following years. One species (Palm Warbler) shows an irruptive pattern of occurrence, with three peaks during the sampled period. Unaccountably, unlike other migratory populations of Prairie Warbler which appear to be declining in the Caribbean region (see below), numbers reported during CBCs at Cabo Rojo, Puerto Rico increased almost sixfold during the last three years of the sampled period. Prairie Warbler numbers averaged six per year for the first 13 years, then increased to an average of 34 for 1986 to 1988.

NEED FOR LONG-TERM BANDING STATIONS

Christmas Bird Counts are merely indices for monitoring bird populations. Also, there are many weaknesses inherent in CBCs, such as yearly variability in weather, area coverage, numbers of observers, and observer expertise. More quantitative results obtained by resident ornithologists at long-term banding sites suggest that populations of other migrant species might be declining. For example, in Jamaica at the long-established (40 years) banding station in the Green Hills, although 26 species of landbird migrants appear to be stable, with populations of two species actually increasing, populations of seven species (White-crowned Pigeon, Yellow-bellied Sapsucker, Tree Swallow, Gray Catbird, Tennessee Warbler, Prairie Warbler, and Indigo Bunting) are declining (R. Sutton and others, in lett.). Habitat alteration and overhunting were offered as probable factors. Collaborators report that, although no apparent decline has been noticed in the paruline warblers, populations of the eight most common species (American Redstart, Ovenbird, Black-and-white, Worm-eating, Yellow, Swainson's, Black-throated Blue, and Prairie warblers) undergo wide fluctuations in the number of individuals captured each year. Such severe fluctuations could be disastrous for these small island populations. As a case-in-point, the Prairie Warbler, which is showing population declines on both its breeding and nonbreeding grounds (Robbins et al. 1989), shows the widest population fluctuations of all eight species. At a long-term banding site in southwestern Puerto Rico, migrant paruline warblers show similar wide population fluctuations (Faaborg and Arendt 1984, 1989).

What is causing the population fluctuations of small island bird populations reported at long-term banding stations? Existing information indicates that climate and habitat disturbances play major roles. As an example, Faaborg et al. (1984) found that resident bird populations declined in response to prolonged droughts. Frugivores and nectarivores were most adversely affected. By contrast, however, marked population declines of resident and migrant insectivores were not observed. Similar results were observed following two recent hurricanes (Arendt 1990, Wunderle et al. 1989, Wunderle 1990). Although Faaborg et al. (1984) did not find a decline in migrant insectivores following severe drought conditions, populations of at least four species of Neotropical landbird migrants (Northern Parula, Ovenbird, Cape May, and Prairie warblers) appear to be on a continual decline (see Faaborg and Arendt, this volume). Presently, there are no obvious explanations for these declines, unless these normally insectivorous species are eating, and relying heavily upon, fruits in their nonbreeding quarters.

These studies show that stochastic factors such as periodic storms and climatic fluctuations can significantly impact the persistence of some species, most of which are represented by small populations at these banding sites. More long-term monitoring sites are needed on Jamaica, Puerto Rico, and throughout the region, especially in the western Caribbean where larger populations of warblers spend the nonbreeding season.

Conclusions

The two most important conclusions resulting from this regional survey are that (1) the status, distribution, and habitat use of migratory landbirds are not well known in many parts of the Caribbean, especially in the Lesser Antilles, and (2) the few existing long-term avian population studies suggest population declines in some migrant species. In two species (Cape May and Prairie warblers) most individuals spend the nonbreeding season in the Caribbean region. If the decline of the Guánica, Puerto Rico, populations of these two species is not due to site-specific factors, which does not appear to be the case as shown by stable or even increasing populations of other migrant and resident species, these two species might be in trouble.

SYNTHESIS OF COLLABORATORS' RECOMMENDATIONS

The biota of each Caribbean island is diverse, but many of the factors affecting their management and conservation are shared, either on a regional level or among subsets of islands possessing common (and often interrelated) inherent characteristics such as: SIZE AND LOCATION (Greater and Lesser Antillean islands, leeward and windward islands). TOPOGRAPHY (high- vs. low-relief islands). CULTURE (e.g., Netherlands and French Antilles, U.S. and British Virgin Islands, each harboring people with varying ethnic backgrounds and perspectives on the use and value of natural resources). ECONOMY (historically, Caribbean island people have been sustained largely through a strong agriculture. High-relief islands with a wider range of temperatures and diverse vegetation and edaphic conditions have exhibited a stronger economy with more exports than small, low-relief islands which, by necessity, have had to import many goods. Also, islands that depend on a tourist industry will affect natural resources in ways very different from those emphasizing an agrarian economy). ENVIRONMENTAL AWARENESS (because of weak economies, many island governments, especially those of small islands, have not included environmental education as part of the teaching curriculum. As a result, on many islands, appreciation, and thus wise use, of natural resources is often lacking.

When the 24 collaborators offered recommendations for conserving North American landbird migrants, and hence resident fauna and flora on Caribbean islands, the above-cited inherent characteristics of the islands and their inhabitants became immediately obvious. Eighteen major recommendations provided by the collaborators can be grouped into four main categories relating either directly or indirectly to migrant habitat, its establishment, management, legal protection, and research within natural areas, all of which vary in relevance among the various subsets of islands.

NATURAL AREAS. Several collaborators expressed an urgent need to establish national parks and other natural areas. Invariably, emphasis was placed on the preservation of native vegetation, often the most resilient to natural and human-induced disturbance, in the most inaccessible areas of the high-relief islands. From a regional perspective, the larger islands of the Greater Antilles with strong economies already have, and manage, more natural reserves than the smaller islands of the Lesser Antilles. However, through a concerted effort by local governments and international funding agencies, national parks are being proposed and established on the smaller, high-relief islands of the Lesser Antilles, such as St. Lucia and Montserrat. Elsewhere in the Lesser Antilles, the need for natural preserves is especially critical on high-relief islands where active timber industries exist and remaining interior forests are being threatened by a growing demand for lumber and living space (e.g., on Dominica and St. Vincent).

SILVICULTURAL AND OTHER RESOURCE MANAGEMENT METHODS. Virtually all the collaborators advocated much stronger programs in reforestation and restoration of degraded habitats on a regional scale. Management prescriptions should include the establishment of line plantings and plantations on natural forest peripheries and along already existing corridors, highways, for example, where the interspersion of marketable tree species in natural forests would better maintain the continuity and diversity of native vegetation and its birdlife. The most often quoted adverse effect of monocultures—the loss of biodiversity—could be mitigated by providing for vegetational diversity in the understory of monocultures as well as in areas of severe habitat alteration. On several low-relief islands throughout the region monocultures, such as acacia woodland in coastal areas, have replaced the original and more diverse dry forest vegetation (e.g., many of the arid British and U.S.

Virgin Islands, northern and southern Netherlands Antillean islands, Antigua, and Barbados).

Associated with several arid, low-relief islands, which once contained extensive coastal dry forests, is the need to (1) ameliorate frequently occurring, severe climatic fluctuations by constructing permanent water sources in drought-prone habitats and (2) limit livestock browsing and grazing in traditionally forested areas.

Many Caribbean islands, regardless of location or topography, once harbored large wetlands areas, often including ample tracts of tidal mangrove forest, prime migrant and resident bird habitat. Today, because of increasing urban development, many wetlands are disappearing. Thus, the need for more control of wetlands draining was often cited.

A few collaborators stressed the minimization of environmental pollution through the control of pesticides and development of a better rapid-transit system, both of which directly or indirectly affect migrant as well as resident fauna. Although having relevance on a regional level, this recommendation is most applicable on the larger, more industrialized islands such as Puerto Rico and Guadeloupe, and islands with a strong agrarian economy such as Cuba and Hispaniola.

NATURAL RESOURCES LEGISLATION AND ENVIRONMENTAL EDUCATION. To enhance the conservation of migrant and resident bird populations, the introduction of more wildlife and wildlands protection legislation and better regulation of hunting through stricter law enforcement measures were recommended by several collaborators. These needs are most critical on islands with weak economies, for example, Hispaniola, Antigua-Barbuda, St. Kitts-Nevis, a few of the smaller islands in the Netherlands and French Antilles, Grenada, and the Grenadines. Not surprisingly, the collaborators writing for many of these same islands expressed the need for improvement of public awareness by increasing the number and intensity of public education courses in schools, universities, and civic centers. On a local level, progress in these areas could be greatly enhanced if commensurate steps were taken to increase and improve human population control measures.

From an international perspective, some collaborators emphasized that the minimization of the impact on migrants caused by introduced plants and animals could be achieved through more regional cooperation by entering and upholding international treaties and conventions (e.g., CITES) formed to control the exotics trade.

MIGRANT BIRD RESEARCH. Several collaborators proposed long-term migrant bird population monitoring via a network of banding stations on the major Caribbean islands. Concomitant with population monitoring is the immediate need for more research on the ecology and behavior of Caribbean landbird migrants to assess more quantitatively the impacts of continual habitat alteration, urban development, and environmental pollution, all of which are on the increase in the region.

FUTURE OF CARIBBEAN LANDBIRD MIGRANTS

Nine of the 24 collaborators concluded that, contingent upon the perpetuity of suitable habitat, populations of landbird migrants will continue to sustain themselves on their respective islands (Cuba, Caymans, Turks and Caicos, Dominican Republic, Puerto Rico, St. Croix, northern and southern Netherlands Antilles, Trinidad and Tobago). Six collaborators noted that because of the current rate of habitat loss, coupled with other negative factors, population declines among migrant landbirds will continue in the future on their respective islands (Jamaica, Haiti, Vieques, St. John, St. Vincent, Barbados). Two collaborators did not feel that sufficient information was available to predict the future of migrant landbirds on their respective islands (St. Lucia and the French West Indies).

Upon review of Table 1, it is evident that some species might actually be increasing their nonbreeding season ranges farther east in the Caribbean as habitat continues to dwindle on the more westerly islands. Observations of seasonally resident White-eyed Vireos have increased in recent years in the U.S. Virgin Islands (R. Norton, in lett.). In nearby Puerto Rico, three White-eyed Vireos (one each Spring from 1985 to 1987) have been observed singing in different sections of the Luquillo Experimental Forest (Arendt, pers. obs.).

Many species of Neotropical landbird migrants are now known to be long-lived, with the Caribbean's seasonal populations showing a high degree of philopatry on different islands (Downer 1972, Diamond and Smith 1973, Faaborg and Arendt 1984, 1989). These attributes will help preserve these species and their various populations in the future as long as suitable habitat remains available on their breeding and nonbreeding grounds and along their migratory routes.

Before the future of North American migrant landbirds can be ensured in the Caribbean region, more research and long-term monitoring studies are needed. However, commensurate with research, the general public on all major Caribbean islands must show a genuine concern for their natural heritage, including resident and migratory birds, by protecting the natural environment. Encouragingly, in recent years, the number and scope of environmental education programs have increased on several islands in response to increased attention and funding by international conservation agencies.

Acknowledgments

I and my collaborators thank J. Hagan, D. Johnston, A. Cruz, and an anonymous reviewer for insightful suggestions for improving the manuscript. In addition to the 24 collaborators who have offered their information, perspectives, and expertise, I would like to thank their respective supporting agencies, universities, and governments. In support of my studies, I thank the U.S. Peace Corps (Dominican Republic), World Wildlife Fund–U.S., U.S. Agency for International Development, and especially the U.S. Forest Service for financial and logistic support.

Literature cited

Aldrich, J.W., and A.J. Duvall. 1958. Distribution and migration of races of the Mourning Dove. *Condor* 60:108–128.

Aldridge, B.M. 1987. Sampling migratory birds and other observations on Providenciales Islands B.W.I. *N. Am. Bird Bander* 12:13–18.

American Ornithologists' Union. 1983. *Check-list of North American Birds.* 6th ed. Washington: American Ornithologists' Union.

Arendt, W.J. 1990. Impact of Hurricane Hugo on the Montserrat Oriole, other forest birds, and their habitats. Unpubl. Rept. to WWF-US, RARE Center, Montserrat Government and National Trust, and USDA Forest Service. USDA For. Ser., Inst. Trop. Forest., So. For. Exp. Stat., Call Box 25000, Rio Piedras, Puerto Rico 00928-2500.

Arendt, W.J., T.A. Vargas Mora, and J.W. Wiley. 1979. White-crowned Pigeon: Status rangewide and in the Dominican Republic. *Proc. Ann. Conf. S.E. Assoc. Fish Wildl. Agencies* 33:111–122.

Barlow, J.C. 1978. Records of migrants from Grand Cayman Island. *Bull. Brit. Ornithol. Club* 98:144–146.

Beatty, H.A. 1938. *Filariasis* of Ground Doves in St. Croix, Virgin Islands. *Trans. Royal Soc. Trop. Med. Hyg.* 31:407–412.

———. 1944. The endoparasites of St. Croix, V.I. *J. Agric., Univ. Puerto Rico* 28:107–110.

Belle, E.A., L.S. Grant, and W.A. Page. 1964. The isolation of St. Louis encephalitis virus from *Culex nigripalpus* mosquitos in Jamaica. *Am. J. Trop. Med. Hyg.* 13:452–454.

Benito-Espinal, E. 1990. *Birds of the West Indies.* Saint-Barthélemy, F.W.I.: Editions du Latanier.

Bennett, G.F., H. Witt, and E.M. White. 1980. Blood parasites of some Jamaican birds. *J. Wildl. Dis.* 16:129–138.

Bennett, S.E. 1980. Interspecific competition and the niche of the American Redstart (*Setophaga ruticilla*) in wintering and breeding communities. Pages 319–335 in *Migrant Birds in the Neotropics: Ecology, Behavior, Distribution and Conservation,* A. Keast and E.S. Morton, eds. Washington: Smithsonian Institution Press.

Bequaert, J. 1940. Notes on Hippoboscidae. 17. The Hippoboscidae of the Antilles. *Memor. Soc. Cubana Hist. Nat.* 14:307–327.

Blake, C.H. 1973–1981. Christmas Bird Counts, West Indies region. *Am. Birds* Vols. 27–40.

Bond, J. 1956–1982. *Checklist of the Birds of the West Indies* and 24 supplements. Acad. Nat. Sci. Philadelphia.

———. 1957. North American Warblers in the West Indies. Pages 208–212 in *The Warblers of North America*, L. Griscom and A. Sprunt, Jr., eds. New York: Devin-Adair.

———. 1961. Extinct and near extinct birds of the West Indies. *Pan. Am. Internatl. Council Bird Preserv. Res. Report* 4:1–6.

———. 1970. *Native and Winter Resident Birds of Tobago*. Philadelphia: Livingston Publ. Co.

Bradley, P.E. 1985. *Birds of the Cayman Islands*. Tampa, Fla.: World-wide Printing.

Brewer, A.D. 1977. First occurrence of the Golden-winged Warbler in Trinidad. *Am. Birds* 31:234.

Brodkorb, P. 1950. Geographical variation in the Gray Kingbird, *Tyrannus dominicensis*. *Auk* 67:333–344.

Buden, D.W. 1987. *The birds of the Southern Bahamas*. Brit. Ornithol. Union, Check-list No. 8, London.

Cawkell, E.M. 1964. Use of mangroves by African birds. *Ibis* 106:251–253.

Clark, A.H. 1905. Birds of the Southern Lesser Antilles. *Proc. Boston Soc. Nat. Hist.* 32:203–312.

Cory, C.B. 1909. The birds of the Leeward Islands, Caribbean Sea. *Field Mus. Nat. Hist. Publ. Ornithol.* 1:192–255.

Cruz, A. 1977. The use of mangroves by birds in Jamaica. *Gosse Bird Club Broadsheet* 29:4–5.

———. 1987. Avian community organization in a mahogany plantation on a neotropical island. *Carib. J. Sci.* 23:286–296.

Danforth, S.T. 1930. Notes on the birds of St. Martin and St. Eustatius. *Auk* 47:44–47.

———. 1935. *The birds of Saint Lucia*. Monogr. Univ. Puerto Rico, B, No. 3.

———. 1936. The birds of St. Kitts and Nevis. *Trop. Agric.* 13:213–217.

———. 1939. The birds of Guadeloupe and adjacent islands. *J. Agric., Univ. Puerto Rico* 23:9–46.

Dathe, H., and W. Fischer. 1979. Contributions to the ornithology of Cuba. *Beitr. Vogelkd.* 25:171–203.

Devas, R.P. 1970. *Birds of Grenada, St. Vincent and the Grenadines*. St. George's, Grenada: Carenage Press.

Diamond, A.W. 1972. Transients and scarce winter visitors trapped in Jamaica in 1970–1971. *Gosse Bird Club Broadsheet* 18:11.

Diamond, A.W., and R.W. Smith. 1973. Returns and survival of banded warblers wintering in Jamaica. *Bird-Banding* 44:221–224.

Diamond, A.W., P. Black, and R.W. Smith. 1977. Weights and fat condition of some migrant warblers in Jamaica. *Wilson Bull.* 89:456–465.

Dod, A.S. 1978. *Las aves de la Republica Dominicana*. Santo Domingo: Museo Nac. Hist. Nat.

———. 1981. *Guia de Campo para las aves de la Republica Dominicana*. Santo Domingo: Museo Nac. Hist. Nat.

Downer, A.C. 1972. Longevity records of Indigo Buntings wintering in Jamaica. *Bird-Banding* 43:287.

———. 1981. Note: Breaches of the wildlife protection law. *Gosse Bird Club Broadsheet* 36:3–4.

Downer, A.C., and R. Sutton. 1990. *Birds of Jamaica*. New York: Cambridge University Press.

Eaton, S.W. 1953. Wood warblers wintering in Cuba. *Wilson Bull.* 65:169–174.

Eyre, L.A. 1986. Deforestation in Jamaica: Its rate and implications. Unpubl. Rep. University West Indies, Kingston, Jamaica.

Faaborg, J. 1982. Avian population fluctuations during drought conditions in Puerto Rico. *Wilson Bull.* 94:20–30.

Faaborg, J., and W.J. Arendt. 1984. Population sizes and philopatry of winter resident warblers in Puerto Rico. *J. Field Ornithol.* 55:376–378.

———. 1985. *Wildlife Assessments in the Caribbean*. USDA For. Ser., Inst. Trop. Forest., So. For. Exp. Stat., Call Box 25000, Rio Piedras, Puerto Rico 00928-2500.

———. 1989. Longevity estimates of Puerto Rican Birds. *N. Am. Bird Bander* 14:11–13.

Faaborg, J., W.J. Arendt, and M.S. Kaiser. 1984. Rainfall correlates of bird population fluctuations in a Puerto Rican dry forest: A nine year study. *Wilson Bull.* 96:557–595.

Falkenberg, W.P., C. Robinson, and J.K. Maynard. 1983. Will the birds of Jamaica live in pine plantations? *Gosse Bird Club Broadsheet* 40:1–7.

ffrench, R.P. 1966. The utilization of mangroves by birds in Trinidad. *Ibis* 108:423–424.

———. 1980. *A Guide to the Birds of Trinidad and Tobago*. Wynnewood, Pa.: Livingston Publ. Co.

———. 1985. Changes in the avifauna of Trinidad. Pages 986–991 in *Neotropical Ornithology*, P.A. Buckley, E.S. Morton, R.S. Ridgely, and F.G. Buckley, eds. Ornithol. Monogr. 36.

Fisher, A.K., and A. Wetmore. 1931. Report on birds recorded by the Pinchot Expedition of 1929 to the Caribbean and Pacific. *Proc. U.S. Natl. Mus.* 79:1–66.

Fletcher, J. 1983. Note: Myrtle Warbler. *Gosse Bird Club Broadsheet* 41:15.

Food and Agriculture Organization. 1981. *Food and Agriculture Organization/United Nations Environment Program Tropical Forest Assistance Project (GEMS): Tropical Africa, Tropical Asia, Tropical America* (4 vols.), Rome.

Garrido, O.H. 1985. Cuban endangered birds. Pages 992–999 in *Neotropical Ornithology*, P.A. Buckley, E.S. Morton, R.S. Ridgely, and F.G. Buckley, eds. Ornithol. Monogr. 36.

Garrido, O.H., and F. Garcia Montaña. 1975. *Catalogo de las aves de Cuba*. Havana: Academia de Ciencias de Cuba.

Gochfeld, M. 1974. Status of the genus *Vermivora* (Aves, Parulidae) in the Greater Antilles with new records from Jamaica and Puerto Rico. *Carib. J. Sci.* 14:177–181.

———. 1979. Wintering ranges of migrant warblers of eastern North America. *Am. Birds* 33:742–745.

———. 1985. Numerical relationship between migrant and resident bird species in Jamaican woodlands. Pages 654–662 in *Neotropical Ornithology*, P.A. Buckley, E.S. Morton, R.S. Ridgely, and F.G. Buckley, eds. Ornithol. Monogr. 36.

Gosse Bird Club. 1986. *A Checklist of Birds in Jamaica*. Kingston, Jamaica: Gosse Bird Club.

Gruber, S. 1984. Cannabis avifauna. *Gosse Bird Club Broadsheet* 43:9–10.

Guth, R.W. 1971. New bird records from Guadeloupe and its dependencies. *Auk* 88:180–182.

Herman, C.M., L.N. Locke, and G.M. Clark. 1962. Foot abnormalities of wild birds. *Bird-Banding* 33:191–198.

Holland, C.S., and J.M. Williams. 1978. Observations on the birds of Antigua. *Am. Birds* 32:1095–1105.

Johnston, D.W. 1975. Ecological analysis of the Cayman Island avifauna. *Bull. Fla. State Mus.* 19:235–300.

Kocan, R.M., and A. Sprunt, IV. 1971. The White-crowned Pigeon a fruit-eating pigeon as a host for *Trichomonas gallinae*. *J. Wildl. Dis.* 7:217–218.

La Bastille, A. 1973. Birds and mammals of Anegada Island, British Virgin Islands. *Carib. J. Sci.* 13:91–109.

Lack, D. 1976. *Island Biology*. Berkeley: University of California Press.

Lack, D., and A. Lack. 1973. Birds on Grenada. *Ibis* 115:53–59.

Lack, D., and P. Lack. 1972. Wintering warblers in Jamaica. *Living Bird* 11:129–153.

Lack, D., E. Lack, P. Lack, and A. Lack. 1972. Transients in Jamaica, 1970–1971. *Gosse Bird Club Broadsheet* 18:1–5.

Lindo, L.S. 1968. The effect of hurricanes on the forests of British Honduras. *[Proc.] IX Commonwealth Forestry Conference, India*. Govt. Print. Dept. Belize.

Lord, R.D., and C.H. Calisher. 1970. Further evidence of southward transport of arboviruses by migratory birds. *Am. J. Epidemiol.* 92:73–78.

Lovejoy, T.E. 1983. Tropical deforestation and North American migrant birds. Pages 126–128 in *Bird Conservation, 1*, S.A. Temple, ed. Madison: University of Wisconsin Press.

Lugo, A.E., M. Applefield, D.J. Pool, and R.B. McDonald. 1983. The impact of Hurricane David on the forests of Dominica. *Can. J. Forestry* Res. 13:201–211.

Mayfield, H.F. 1972. Winter habitat of Kirtland's Warbler. *Wilson Bull.* 84:347–349.

McCandless, J.B. 1961. Bird life in southwestern Puerto Rico. I. Fall migration. *Carib. J. Sci.* 1:3–12.

McLean, R.G., H.A. Trevino, and G.E. Sather. 1979. Prevalence of selected zoonotic diseases in vertebrates from Haiti, 1972. *J. Wildl. Dis.* 15:327–330.

Molinares, A. 1980. A second record for Black-throated Green Warbler in Puerto Rico. *Am. Birds* 34:868.

Moore, A.G. 1985. Winter status of birds on Grand Cayman Island. *Bull. Brit. Ornithol. Club* 105:8–17.

Murphy, L.S. 1916. *Forests of Porto Rico, Past, Present, and Future, and Their Physical and Economic Environment*. U.S. Dept. Agric. Bull. No. 354.

Neumann, C.J., G.W. Gry, E.L. Caso, and B.R. Jarvian. 1978. *Tropical Cyclones of the North Atlantic Ocean, 1871–1977*. Asheville, N.C.: Natl. Clim. Cent.

Nicoll, M.J. 1904. On a collection of birds made during the cruise of the 'Valhalla', R.Y.S., in the West Indies (1903–4). *Ibis* 4:555–591.

Nisbet, I.C.T. 1970. Autumn migration of the Blackpoll Warbler: Evidence for a long flight provided by regional survey. *Bird-Banding* 41:207–240.

Norton, R.L. 1979. New records of birds for the Virgin Islands. *Am. Birds* 33:145–146.

———. 1981. Additional records and notes of birds in the Virgin Islands. *Am. Birds* 35:144–147.

———. 1982–1988. Christmas Bird Counts, West Indies region. *Am. Birds* Vols. 41–47.

———. 1983. [Check-list] *Birds of the Virgin Islands National Park*. Philadelphia: Eastern Monuments Assoc.

Norton, R.L., and G.A. Seaman. 1985. Post-fledging distribution of White-crowned Pigeons banded in St. Croix, Virgin Islands. *J. Field Ornithol.* 56:416–418.

O'Connor, F.W., and H.A. Beatty. 1938. *Filariasis* of ground doves in St. Croix, Virgin Islands. *Trans. Roy. Soc. Trop. Med. Hyg.* 31:407–412.

Pashley, D.N. 1988a. Warblers of the West Indies I. The Virgin Islands. *Carib. J. Sci.* 24:11–22.

———. 1988b. Warblers of the West Indies II. The Western Caribbean. *Carib. J. Sci.* 24:112–126.

Paynter, R.A., Jr. 1956. Birds of the Swan Islands. *Wilson Bull.* 68:103–110.

Perez-Rivera, R.A. 1980. Algunas Notas sobre migracion de aves en Puerto Rico. *Science-Ciencia* 7:123–126.

Perez-Rivera, R.A., and G. Bonilla. 1983. Nuevos informes y comentarios sobre las aves de la Isla de Mona. *Science-Ciencia* 10:97–101.

Post, W. 1981. The prevalence of some ectoparasites, diseases, and abnormalities in the Yellow-shouldered Blackbird. *J. Field Ornithol.* 52:16–22.

Raffaele, H.A. 1973. Assessment of Mona Island avifauna. Pages 1–32 in *Las islas de Mona y Monito: Una evaluacion de sus recursos naturales e historicos*. San Juan: Environ. Qual. Board, Commonwealth of Puerto Rico.

———. 1981. New records of bird species for Puerto Rico and one for the West Indies. *Am. Birds* 35:142–143.

———. 1983. *A guide to the birds of Puerto Rico and the Virgin Islands*. San Juan, Puerto Rico: Fondo Educativo Interamericano.

Rappole, J.H., and E.S. Morton. 1985. Effects of habitat alteration on a tropical avian forest community. Pages 1013–1021 in *Neotropical Ornithology*, P.A. Buckley, E.S. Morton, R.S. Ridgely, and F.G. Buckley, eds. Ornithol. Monogr. 36.

Rappole, J.H., E.S. Morton, T.E. Lovejoy, III, and J.L. Ruos. 1983. *Nearctic Avian Migrants in the Neotropics*. Washington: U.S. Fish and Wildlife Service.

Riley, J.H. 1905. Catalogue of a collection of birds from Barbuda and Antigua, British West Indies. *Smithson. Misc. Coll.* 47:2477-2491.

Robbins, C.S., B.A. Dowell, D.K. Dawson, J. Colón, F. Espinoza, J. Rodriguez, R. Sutton, and T. Vargas. 1987. Comparison of Neotropical winter bird populations in isolated patches versus extensive forest. *Acta Oecol.: Oecol. Gen.* 8:285–292.

Robbins, C.S., J.R. Sauer, R.S. Greenberg, and S. Droege. 1989. Population declines in North American birds that migrate to the neotropics. *Proc. Natl. Acad. Sci.* 86:7658–7662.

Robertson, W.B., Jr. 1962. Observations on the birds of St. John, Virgin Islands. *Auk* 79:44–76.

Russell, S.M., J.C. Barlow, and D.W. Lamm. 1979. Status of some birds on Isla San Andres and Isla Providencia, Colombia. *Condor* 81:98–100.

Schmidt, R. 1982. Forestry in Puerto Rico. Pages 69–71 in *Forestry in the Caribbean*, A.E. Lugo and S. Brown, eds. U.S. Man and the Biosphere Report No. 7. Washington, D.C.

Schwartz, A. 1969. Land birds of Isla Saona, Dominican Republic. *Quart. J. Fla. Acad. Sci.* 32:291–306.

Schwartz, A., and R.F. Klinikowski. 1963. Observations on West Indian birds. *Proc. Acad. Nat. Sci. Phila.* 115:53–77.

———. 1965. Additional observations on West Indian birds. *Proc. Acad. Nat. Sci. Phila. Not. Nat.* 376:1–16.

Seaman, G.A. 1952. The mongoose and Caribbean wildlife. *Proc. Trans. N. Am. Wildl. Conf.* 17:188–197.

Serrao, J. 1985. Decline of forest songbirds. *Records of New Jersey Birds* 11:5–9.

Siegel, A. 1983. *Birds of Montserrat.* Montserrat, West Indies: Montserrat National Trust.

Snow, D.W., and B.K. Snow. 1960. Northern Waterthrushes returning to the same winter quarters in successive winters *Auk* 77:351–352.

Sorrie, B.A. 1975. Observations of the birds of Vieques Island, Puerto Rico. *Carib. J. Sci.* 15:89–103.

Spence, L., A.H. Jonkers, and L.S. Grant. 1968. Arboviruses in the Caribbean Islands. *Progr. Med. Virol.* 110:415–486.

Spendelow, P. 1985. Starvation of a flock of Chimney Swifts on a very small Caribbean Island. *Auk* 102:387–388.

Stamm, D.D., and R.J. Newman. 1963. Evidence of southward transport of arboviruses from the U.S. by migratory birds. *Ann. Microbiol.* 11:123–133.

Terborgh, J.W., and J. Faaborg. 1980. Factors affecting the distribution and abundance of North American migrants in the eastern Caribbean region. Pages 145–155 in *Migrant Birds in the Neotropics: Ecology, Behavior, Distribution and Conservation,* A. Keast and E.S. Morton, eds. Washington: Smithsonian Institution Press.

Thompson, D.A. 1983. Effects of hurricane Allen on some Jamaican forests. *Commonw. For. Rev.* 62:107–115.

Van der Werf, P.A., J.S. Zaneveld, and K.H. Voous. 1958. Field observations on the birds of the Islas Las Aves in the southern Caribbean Sea. *Ardea* 46:37–58.

Vaurie, C. 1961. List of and notes on the birds of the Iles des Saintes, French West Indies. *Auk* 78:57–62.

Vogt, W. 1970. The avifauna in a changing ecosystem. Pages 8–16 in *The Avifauna of Northern Latin America,* H.K. Buechner and J.H. Buechner, eds. Smithsonian Contrib. Zool. 26.

Voous, K.H. 1983. *Birds of the Netherlands Antilles.* Utrecht: De Walburg Press.

Wadsworth, F.H., and G.W. Englerth. 1959. Effects of the 1956 hurricane on forests in Puerto Rico. *Carib. For.* 20:38–51.

Wells, J.G. 1902. The birds of the island of Carriacou. *Auk* 19:343–349.

Westermann, J.H. 1953. *Nature Preservation in the Caribbean,* Vol. 9. Utrecht: Found. Sci. Res. Surinam Nether. Antill.

Wilcove, D.S., and J.W. Terborgh. 1984. Patterns of population decline in birds. *Am. Birds* 38:10–13.

Wiley, J.W. 1985. Bird conservation in the United States Caribbean. Pages 107–159 in *Bird Conservation,* 2, S.A. Temple, ed. Madison: University of Wisconsin Press.

Wiley, J.W., and G.P. Bauer. 1985. Site guide—Caribbean National Forest, Puerto Rico. *Am. Birds* 39:12–18.

Williams, E.H., Jr., and L.B. Williams. 1985. A new bird record for Puerto Rico: The Yellow-throated Vireo from Vieques. *Carib. J. Sci.* 21:187.

Woods, C.A. 1975. Banding and recapture of wintering warblers in Haiti. *Bird-Banding* 46:344–346.

Woods, C.A., and J.A. Ottenwalder. 1983. The montane avifauna of Haiti. *Proc. Jean Delacour/IFCB Symp.* 576–590, 607–622.

———. 1986. *The Birds of the National Parks of Haiti.* Port au Prince: USAID/Haiti.

Wunderle, J.M., Jr. 1990. The effect of Hurricane Hugo on bird populations in a Puerto Rican rain forest. [Abstract] Wilson Ornithol. Soc. and Assn. of Field Ornithol. Meeting, Norton, Massachusetts.

Wunderle, J.M., Jr., R.B. Waide, and D.J. Lodge. 1989. The effect of Hurricane Gilbert on the avifauna of Jamaica. [Abstract] American Ornithologists' Union 107th Stated Meeting, Pittsburg, Pennsylvania.

APPENDIX 1. Names of those who contributed information in this paper (some collaborators reported on more than one island)

Collaborator	Island(s)
Beverlea M. Aldridge	Turks and Caicos
Wayne J. Arendt	Hispanida (Domican Republic), Puerto Rico, Mona, Culebra, St. Lucia, St. Vincent
Eduoard Benito-Espinal	French West Indies (Guadeloupe and satellites, Martinique)
Patricia Bradley	Cayman Islands
Christopher Cox	St. Lucia
Annabelle Stockdon de Dod	Hispaniola (Dominican Republic)
Audrey Downer	Jamaica
Peter Evans	Dominica
Richard ffrench	Trinidad and Tobago
Orlando H. Garrido	Cuba
Michael Gochfeld	Jamaica
Karen D. Harvey	Jamaica
Ann M. Haynes	Jamaica
Maurice B. Hutt	Barbados
Allan Keith	Hispaniola (Dominican Republic) and St. Lucia
Martin G. Kelsey	St. Vincent
Earle Kirby	St. Vincent
Robert L. Norton	St. John
Fred W. Sladen	St. Croix
Bruce A. Sorrie	Vieques
William Spencer	Antigua
Robert Sutton	Jamaica
Karel H. Voous	Northern and southern Netherlands Antilles
Charles A. Woods	Hispaniola (Haiti)

The nonbreeding season

RUSSELL GREENBERG
Smithsonian Migratory Bird Center
National Zoological Park
Washington, D.C. 20008

The nonbreeding season: Introduction

The tropical areas in Mesoamerica, the Caribbean, and South America provide the winter habitat for a massive number of birds that retreat each year from their temperate zone breeding areas. At the same time, the face of the region is changing with almost unbelievable speed as forest is cleared farther up seemingly inaccessible slopes and into the farthest reaches of inhospitable lands.

The scale of change is both so rapid and so enormous that the process has overwhelmed the ability of tropical biologists and geographers to monitor the effects. However, it is a fundamental tenet of avian ecology that the association between habitat and bird distribution is a tight one. We can assume that we are watching a drastic change in the avifaunas of the northern Neotropics, both migrant and resident.

Historical geography and paleobiology have uncovered previous episodes of large-scale settlement and deforestation in the region, particularly in Mexico and Mesoamerica. However, we will probably never know precisely what these agricultural landscapes looked like. We will almost certainly not know the detailed effects on communities and populations of small birds. From a purely academic perspective, the current wave of deforestation provides the first opportunity for scientific monitoring of widescale habitat change of a large terrestrial regions.

In addition, research on migratory bird populations may play a strategic role in the design and support of measures to mitigate habitat destruction. The Neotropical migratory bird system involves perhaps 5–10 billion birds of over 150 species, and covers the land masses of the Caribbean, Mesoamerica and much of South America as well. However, the greatest diversity, density and relative density (migrants/total birds) is found in the northern Neotropics, particularly Mexico and the Greater Antilles. These regions have either already experienced the greatest extent of deforestation, or are in the process of losing the remaining forest cover to rural colonization. Even in the seemingly less threatened northern South American region, the greatest diversity and abundance of migrants occurs at the elevational band in the Andes that supports the greatest rural human populations as well. In many of the most endangered areas, Mexico, Guatemala, Costa Rica, Panama, the last large tracts of forest have already been set aside in reserves. The success of these reserves depends upon the ability of governments to manage this land in the face of political and economic pressures for development. However, for largely political reasons some gaps in even this theoretical system of protected lands remain, particularly in Honduras, Nicaragua, and large portions of the Andean slope. These are also the regions where the greatest geographical voids in research can be found.

Recently, there has been a gradual awakening to the realpolitik of habitat conservation in the northern Neotropics. If optimistic estimates that as much as 10% of forest land managed in reserves can be realized, this still leaves at least 90% of the land in a settled, cultivated, or regenerating state. The fate of migratory bird populations may have a stronger link to the way these lands are used and managed than the preservation of these small amounts of wildernes in the region. Surprisingly little research has been conducted on how various patterns of land use differentially affect migratory birds. In many areas where forest loss approaches critical levels, we need to explore "better-than-nothing" efforts involving small forest reserves and the conservation of natural vegetation in the developed countryside. There is much evidence that even the smallest efforts will increase the carrying capacity for migratory birds. However, more research is needed on how minimal conservation efforts might benefit insects, trees, other wildlife, as well as provide resources for rural human populations.

The face of the northern Neotropics will be dramatically different in the next 10–15 years. In many areas, we face the imminent possibility of losing undisturbed "control" areas to study bird populations. The next few years represent the time frame for establishing research that will (1) investigate the role of migratory birds in naturally functioning ecosystems, (2) monitor the rate and extent of changes in the face of increasing deforestation, and (3) determine possible ways of enhancing anthropogenic habitats to mitigate the effects of long-term changes.

The papers in this section represent the healthy diversity of approaches and new tools to tackle these questions. There has been a shift in emphasis. Compared to the field in 1977, when the National Zoo symposium was held, we see an increase in interest in developing a quantitative assessment of the geographic and habitat distribution of migratory birds. We also see the increased interest both in long-term studies and in demography, which comprise the data that, when developed, will allow the assessment of fitness consequences

of habitat use and migration strategies. New tools for investigating the relationship between migratory birds and their winter habitats include the use of remote sensing data, quantitative (mist-net free) regional surveys, detailed demographic studies with color-marked populations, and radiotelemetry to monitor the fate of individual migrants.

The year 1977 seemed like the beginning of a renaissance in research on migratory birds in the Neotropics, a flowering that might involve a general increase in research on tropical birds, and, indeed, tropical ecosystems. While there has been some increased interest in Neotropical migrants in the past few years, the increase has come primarily in topics of forest fragmentation in the temperate zone, a topic that was not formally addressed in the 1977 symposium. There seems to be a modest and constant effort going into the types of ecological studies of Neotropical birds that will be the underpinning for our understanding of migratory bird ecology.

Recent concern over population declines in Neotropical migrants will probably be translated into considerably more research on the conservation biology of these species. Already a bold new federal program is being spearheaded by the Fish and Wildlife Service, the National Forest Service, and the National Fish and Wildlife Foundation. While I laud these efforts, I hope that the rush to provide information to "managers" does not overshadow the need for basic research on natural history. Natural history studies provide two major benefits. First, they strengthen the interest and curiosity that people have about migratory birds. The more details we know about the role that individual species have in tropical communities, the less abstract the migratory system will become and the more these birds and their tropical habitats will be appreciated for what they are. Second, it is often the serendipitously recorded details that lend insight into factors that determine bird distribution.

An emphasis on developing data solely for "management" is dangerous because studies that focus on obtaining standardized census data may be designed specifically to ignore much of the complexities of the systems that will ultimately provide critical insight. For example, in an attempt to standardize between sites, census work may be conducted over short mid-winter periods. However, understanding seasonal changes in populations and in resource use may be critical to understanding what limits populations in a critical area. Tropical ecosystems can be highly seasonal, even within the period that migrants are present. In many parts of Mesoamerica, migrants arrive during the wettest months of the year and persist through some of the driest months. During this period, foliage insect populations are declining and alternative food resources provided by fruiting and flowering trees are used. It is possible that these alternative resources are critical to the successful overwintering of a number of species. Furthermore, by focusing on periods of stable population levels, the importance of habitat and resources to transients is missed. The lack of any focus on stop-over ecology in the tropics is not surprising considering the incipient nature of study of habitat quality of critical sites for North America. The impressive density and diversity of migrants found during late September and October in many sites in the northern Neotropics combined with low resource levels suggest that this may be a period of serious food or habitat limitation in these species. Many South American migrants have long periods of transition through more northern areas in Latin America, where they appear to key in on particular fruiting plants. This heightens the possibility that critical dependencies on particular resources exist.

In general, single species or community level studies that depend on correlating abundance with a particular standardized set of habitat measurements may miss the importance of specific resources. And this does not refer only to frugivores or nectarivores. The dependence of some species of migrants on particular microhabitats, such as dead leaf clusters, is well established.

A second way that migratory bird studies may become too narrow is in the lack of a clear and interesting organizing paradigm. A strictly management oriented paradigm will examine population levels and dynamics in a number of alternative habitats and relate this to patterns and rates of deforestation. However, most previous work on migratory birds was based on several questions related to the evolution of migration systems: what is the role of competition between migratory and resident species or populations? what factors mediate competition between closely related migrant species? what adaptive tradeoffs are associated with occupying tropical and temperate habitats? While the emphasis on competition and adaptation may strike some avian ecologists as naive and narrow, these questions, no matter how they are reframed, still remain unanswered. For example, how is it that the density of insectivorous birds can often double within a period of a few weeks during a resource-poor time of year. Attempting to answer some of the more theoretical questions concerning the migration system may shed considerable light on the more narrowly focused conservation questions.

I am arguing that the success of future conservation and research on Neotropical migratory birds will depend upon how broadly based are the approaches. The conservation of forest-dependent migratory birds provides a powerful tool for developing a cooperative international network for habitat conservation. The success of migratory bird conservation will depend on how well it is integrated with broader concerns for the preservation of biodiversity. Similarly, research on migratory birds will remain fragmented and uninteresting, perhaps unable to answer even the most fundamental questions necessary for conservation, unless it is integrated into studies of tropical ecology in general.

JAMES F. LYNCH
Smithsonian Environmental Research Center
P.O. Box 28
Edgewater, Maryland 21037

Distribution of overwintering Nearctic migrants in the Yucatan Peninsula, II: Use of native and human-modified vegetation

Abstract. Point counts and mist-netting surveys showed that overwintering Nearctic migratory landbirds are both diverse and numerous in virtually all natural and disturbed vegetation types in the Yucatan Peninsula. Migrants accounted for an average of 41% of the individual birds encountered in point counts conducted in habitats ranging from open fields and early second growth to mature tropical forest. Migrants and residents showed approximately the same tendency to utilize highly disturbed or successional vegetation, and had similar habitat niche breadths. Some migratory species reached their maximum abundance in agricultural fields and pastures, but others were associated mainly with tropical forest. Although some forest-associated migrants avoided highly disturbed habitats, none were restricted to mature tropical forest. A few habitat generalists occurred commonly across the entire successional continuum.

Traditional milpa agriculture, which involves shifting cultivation of small plots, presently poses no threat to any migrant species in the Yucatan, and is beneficial to migrants that prefer open habitats. More recent forms of land use (e.g., mechanized agriculture, large-scale cattle ranching), which destroy large areas of forest and prevent regeneration of woody second growth, are harmful to most species of Nearctic migrants. In the Mexican state of Quintana Roo, traditional milpa agriculture is gradually dying out, and the growth of cattle ranching is by far the major threat to the remaining forest. However, a positive development for migrants is a newly implemented system of sustainable forestry, which will soon protect about 90% of the remaining forest in the southern half of Quintana Roo.

Sinopsis. Conteos puntuales y censos con redes de niebla han mostrado que las aves migratorias neárticas invernantes en la Península de Yucatán son tanto diversas como numerosas en virtualmente todos los tipos de vegetación natural y perturbada. Las migratorias representaron en promedio el 41% de las aves individuales encontradas en conteos puntuales llevados a cabo en habitats que variaron desde campos abiertos y crecimiento secundario temprano hasta bosque tropical maduro. Las migratorias y las residentes mostraron aproximadamente la misma tendencia a utilizar vegetación altamente perturbada o vegetación sucesional y tuvieron amplitudes de habitat y nicho similares. Algunas especies migratorias alcanzaron sus abundancias máximas en campos agrícolas y de pastoreo, pero otras estuvieron asociadas principalmente con bosque tropical. Aunque algunas migratorias asociadas al bosque evitaron habitats altamente perturbados, ninguna estuvo restringida a bosque tropical maduro. Unos pocos generalistas de habitat se encontraron comúnmente a través de todo el continuo sucesional.

La agricultura tradicional de milpa, que consiste en el cultivo rotativo de pequeñas parcelas, actualmente no representa una amenaza para ninguna especie migratoria en Yucatán y es benéfica para las migratorias que prefieren habitats abiertos. Formas mas recientes de uso de la tierra (e.g. agricultura mecanizada, ganadería a gran escala) que no solamente destruyen extensas áreas de bosque sino que además impiden la regeneración de bosque secundario, son perjudiciales para la mayoría de especies migratorias neárticas. En el estado mexicano de Quintana Roo, la agricultura tradicional de milpa está desapareciendo gradualmente y el desarrollo de la ganadería es con seguridad la mayor amenaza para el bosque remanente. Sin embargo, un desarrollo positivo para las migratorias es un sistema forestal sostenible recientemente implantado que pronto protegerá aproximadamente el 90% de los bosques remanentes en la mitad sureña de Quintana Roo.

Forest destruction is proceeding at an accelerating pace in most of the American tropics (Bolin 1977, Myers 1980, 1988, Fearnside 1986, Powell and Rappole 1986, Estrada and Coates-Estrada 1988, Sader and Joyce 1988, Gradwohl and Greenberg 1988). In Middle America as much as 80% of the original forest already may have been destroyed (Powell and Rappole 1986). These relatively few regions which, like the Yucatan Peninsula, retain large areas of relatively undisturbed native vegetation, are assuming increasing importance as refugia for forest-dependent wildlife, including the many Nearctic migratory bird species that occur in tropical forests during winter (Rappole et al. 1983, Powell and Rappole 1986, Lynch 1989, Askins et al. 1990). The Yucatan is especially important to conservationists because much of the peninsula's extant native vegetation is tropical dry forest (sensu Holdridge 1967). It is this forest type, rather than the more highly publicized "rain forest," that constitutes the most endangered major habitat type in the New World tropics (Janzen 1988).

As remaining areas of natural vegetation in Middle America are reduced to isolated remnants, the significance of human-modified vegetation to conservation will increase (Janzen 1988, Uhl 1988). Indeed, the only wild animal species that will thrive in Middle America over the coming decades will be those that can tolerate human-modified landscapes. Comparative studies of the use of disturbed vegetation by different species are imperative if we are to understand the impact of current land-use practices on wildlife.

The Yucatan Peninsula, a mosaic of cropland, pastures, regenerating old-fields, and native forest, is an especially favorable area for such studies. In an earlier paper (Lynch 1989), I described general distributional patterns and habitat requirements of migrant and resident birds in the Yucatan region, based on field work conducted there between 1982 and 1987. The purpose of the present paper is to examine the results of this and other recent studies of overwintering migrants in the Yucatan (Lynch et al. 1985, Green et al. 1987, Lopez Ornat et al. 1989, Lopez Ornat and Lynch 1991) in relation to human-induced and natural disturbance of native vegetation. I have attempted to provide the reader with a broad historical and cultural context within which to consider conservation issues. This reflects my belief that biologists who are serious about addressing the plight of migrant birds in the tropics also must deal with the societal factors that are determining the fate of tropical landscapes.

Methods

Information on the natural environment and human history of the Yucatan has been gathered from literature sources and from personal experience in the region over the past 10 years. Data on current land-use and population trends in Quintana Roo are extracted from a series of unpublished reports to the World Wildlife Fund–U.S. by Sanchez (1988, 1989) and Zugasty and Sanchez (1987), and from a quantitative analysis of LANDSAT satellite data (Green et al. 1987). The data base for Nearctic migratory birds consists of (1) approximately 1,000 point counts that I performed in the Yucatan Peninsula between 1982 and 1987 (Lynch 1989), (2) capture information from mist-netting studies that were conducted at 20 sites in the Mexican states of Quintana Roo and Yucatan from 1984 to 1988 (Lynch 1989, Lopez Ornat and Lynch 1991), and (3) intensive studies of the habitat requirements of the Hooded Warbler (*Wilsonia citrina*), the most abundant overwintering migrant species in wooded sections of the northern Yucatan Peninsula (Lynch et al. 1985, Morton et al. 1987). Details regarding methodology can be found in the cited publications. Scientific names of all bird species are given in Appendix 1.

Results and discussion

GEOLOGY, CLIMATE, AND NATIVE VEGETATION OF THE STUDY REGION

Field work was conducted throughout the 240,000-km² Yucatan Peninsula (Lynch 1989), but the present analysis concerns mainly the northern portion of the peninsula (the Mexican states of Campeche, Yucatan, and Quintana Roo), an area of some 140,000 km2 (Fig. 1). In the northern Yucatan, a NW–SE transition is found from arid thorn scrub, through several categories of deciduous and semideciduous forests, to mainly evergreen forest. This gradient reflects an increase in annual rainfall from ca. 500 mm on the northwestern coast of Yucatan state to ca. 1,500 mm in southern Quintana Roo (Garcia 1965). The climate features a 4–6 month winter dry season which is both longer and more severe (i.e., with a smaller proportion of the annual precipitation falling outside the "wet" months) in the northwest. Almost the entire northern half of the peninsula falls within Holdridge's (1967) "Very Dry" or "Dry" Tropical Forest life zones.

Most underlying bedrock is porous, geologically young limestone which allows little or no retention of surface water, even during the rainy season. As a result, soil development in the northern Yucatan is generally so poor that mechanized agriculture or profitable ranching have proven all but impossible. There are no mineral resources except the limestone itself.

Another highly distinctive feature of the study area was forcibly highlighted in September 1988, when Hurricane Gilbert struck the coast of northern Quintana Roo with record high winds of more than 280 km per hour: the Yucatan Peninsula lies squarely across the main track for westward-moving cyclonic storms which originate in the eastern Caribbean (Jauregui et al. 1980). Some 300,000 ha of habitat, mainly semievergreen tropical forest, were either directly damaged by Hurricane Gilbert, or destroyed by the uncontrolled wildfires that raged through the area during the summer following the storm. This represents 10–15% of the remaining forest in Quintana Roo.

The cycles of hurricane damage followed by devastating wildfires that have recurred in the eastern Yucatan over at least the past century (Jauregui et al. 1980, Perez Villegas 1980) account for much of the large-scale patchiness of the region's vegetation. Although lightning-caused fires occasionally occur, almost all major wildfires in recent times appear to have been the intentional or accidental result of human activities (Perez Villegas 1980). Whatever the relative importance of natural vs. human factors in explaining the frequency and extent of storm- and fire-related disturbance in the eastern Yucatan, it is evident that migratory birds and

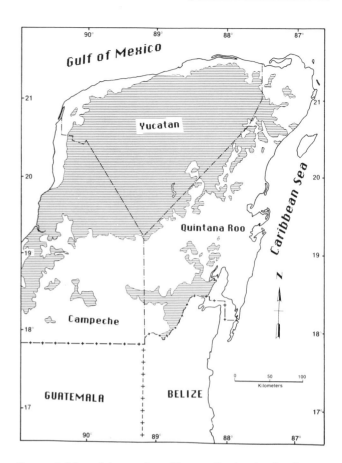

FIGURE 1. Map of the northern Yucatan Peninsula, showing areas of disturbed (cross-hatched) and undisturbed (open) vegetation as of 1976. Data extracted from LANDSAT-based vegetation map prepared by the Direccion del Territorio Nacional, Mexico City (1981).

other wildlife in the area have long been exposed to repeated cycles of habitat destruction and regeneration.

HISTORICAL LAND-USE PATTERNS

The Yucatan Peninsula was the heart of the lowland Maya culture, the first traces of which appeared in the region more than 3,000 years ago. The "Classic" phase of Maya culture (ca. A.D. 300–900), which was characterized by the construction of stone pyramids, stelae, and other monuments, had faded hundreds of years before the 16th century Spanish conquest. Nevertheless, at the time of European contact, the peninsula supported a Maya population of many hundreds of thousands, perhaps millions (Thompson 1966, 1970).

The Classic Maya made use of elaborate irrigation and terracing schemes in the humid southern sections of the Yucatan (Flannery 1982). By the 16th century, however, this technology had died out, and the *conquistadores* encountered an indigenous culture sustained by the cultivation of corn, beans, squash, and other crops in small (1–4 ha) temporary plots called "milpas." In the Yucatan a given milpa produces a useful yield for only 2–3 years, after which time it is abandoned and a new area of forest is cleared. The milpa system has continued to be the basis of the rural economy throughout the Yucatan Peninsula until the past decade or two (see below).

Creation of pastures was not necessary in precolonial Maya society because of the absence of large domesticated animals. The hunting of peccary, deer, and numerous other forest-dwelling mammals and birds was (and continues to be) a major source of protein, and the forest has also been the source of an impressively large number of native plants which are used for food, fiber, construction materials, dyes, and medicine. Gutierrez (1983) lists more than 120 species of native plants which are still used by present-day Maya in one small section of central Quintana Roo. Given the many uses made of the forest, together with the shifting pattern of agriculture, the landscape in traditional Maya society probably retained areas of both old-growth and regenerating forest.

The collapse of the Classic Maya civilization coincided with a major population decline in the ninth and tenth centuries A.D., and the arrival of Europeans signaled an even more catastrophic period of depopulation, mainly because of introduced Old World diseases. Although we lack exact figures, the best evidence indicates that the human population of the Yucatan Peninsula plummeted by as much as 90–95% in the mid-16th century (Thompson 1970). Depopulation allowed forests to regenerate in many areas that previously had been disturbed by human settlement, particularly in the east and south (Quintana Roo, southern Campeche, Belize, the Peten region of Guatemala). Although Maya settlements were larger and more numerous in the eastern Yucatan during the 1520s and 1530s than they are at present, contemporary Spanish chronicles make it clear that most of the eastern and southern Yucatan already was forested at the time of European contact. In subsequent centuries the heavily forested eastern Yucatan became a notorious refuge for "renegade" Maya who waged intermittent warfare against the authorities, whose center of authority was the northwestern portion of the peninsula, in the state of Yucatan. Except for a few coastal settlements, most of the present state of Quintana Roo was avoided by outsiders until the late 1960s and early 1970s. In contrast, the northwestern Yucatan was densely populated and heavily agricultural when the Spanish first traversed the area in the 1520s. Despite the ravages of disease and warfare, this area has maintained a large Maya population throughout the postconquest period. However, only within the past two to three decades has the human population of the entire Yucatan Peninsula approached preconquest levels.

Summarizing, for at least half a millenium (and probably much longer) overwintering migratory birds in the Yucatan region have been exposed both to a well-marked NW-SE gradient in rainfall and native vegetation, and to historically and geographically variable gradients in the intensity of human and storm-related disturbance (Fig. 1). The complex interaction of climatic, geologic, socioeconomic, and historical factors helps to explain why a relatively high proportion of native forest has survived in the eastern and southern Yucatan (Lynch et al. 1985: Fig. 3). Even the densely populated northwest, from which all primary forest was long ago removed, presently supports extensive second growth. The landscape of this region is a patchwork of cultivated fields, pastures, henequen plantations, stands of successional scrub ("acahuales"), and secondary deciduous and semideciduous woodland. To the south and east, the previously extensive old-growth forests of Quintana Roo and southern Campeche have been seriously encroached upon by cattle ranching and agriculture since the 1960s.

PRESENT LAND-USE PATTERNS AND PROJECTED TRENDS

This section emphasizes conditions in Quintana Roo (5.08 million ha), where most of the remaining forest in the northern half of the Yucatan Peninsula is concentrated. Most of our field work on Nearctic migrants has been conducted in Quintana Roo, and reviews of land-use practices and economic trends in the state recently have been completed (Sanchez 1988, 1989; Zugasty and Sanchez 1987).

AGRICULTURE. Traditional milpa agriculture is still widespread in the densely populated northwest region of the Yucatan Peninsula (Yucatan state and northern Campeche), but in the thinly populated state of Quintana Roo corn production has fallen sharply since about 1980. This decline reflects a general depression in the economy of subsistence farming, and many rural people have left their land to take higher-paying jobs in the construction and tourism industry along the Caribbean coast. The area devoted to milpa agriculture in Quintana Roo in 1986 was estimated at only about 65,000 ha (Sanchez 1988). This figure has since declined, and milpa agriculture is likely to continue to dwindle in the foreseeable future (F. Sanchez, pers. comm.).

In the mid-1970s the Mexican government attempted to establish modern mechanized cultivation of rice and sugarcane in areas of southern Quintana Roo where soils are deep enough to permit mechanical tillage. Rice cultivation, which at its peak covered about 16,000 ha, had declined to less than 1,800 ha by 1986, and production had all but ceased by 1989. Approximately 20,000 ha are presently devoted to the cultivation of sugarcane. However, continued production is dependent on government subsidies, and cane production is not expected to expand significantly in the near future. Thus, the combined area devoted to milpa and "modern" agriculture in Quintana Roo is modest (ca. 90,000 ha), and probably is declining due to adverse economic trends and basically unfavorable physical conditions.

FORESTRY. Tropical forests originally covered about 80% of Quintana Roo's 5 million ha. Valuable tropical hardwoods, notably mahogany (*Swietenia macrophylla*) and native "cedar" (*Cedrela odorata*) have long been extracted from the humid forests of Quintana Roo and neighboring Belize. Logging for precious hardwoods continues today, although on a reduced scale. Other hardwood species are cut for use as railroad ties and for the local lumber industry. Smaller trees, including palms, are much used for construction of traditional homes.

Because no market exists for most of the hundreds of tree species that co-occur with mahogany and cedar, logging is invariably selective, and forest disturbance is accordingly localized. Such small-scale disturbance of the forest currently appears to pose no threat to the survival of any forest-associated species of Nearctic migrants, and is probably beneficial to the many species that preferentially occur in clearings and second growth (see below).

The other major product extracted from the Yucatan's forests in modern times is the milky sap ("chicle") of the zapote tree (*Manilkara zapota*), the base for chewing gum. Starting about 1917, "chicleros" routinely tapped virtually every mature zapote tree in the eastern and southern Yucatan. By imparting the living forest with a significant market value, the chicle business has been a force for forest conservation, much as the rubber-tapping business has been in Amazonia. In recent decades, however, inexpensive artificial substitutes have nearly eliminated the chicle industry. As a result, zapote trees that in the past would have been left standing, even where the surrounding forest was cleared for farming or ranching, now are bulldozed and burned, or cut for timber. Very recently, the modern taste for "natural" foods has extended even to chewing gum, and the new international market that is developing for chicle might again impart cash value to the intact forest.

CATTLE RANCHING. With local exceptions (notably, western Campeche), poor pasture quality has kept cattle production and profitability very low throughout most of the Yucatan Peninsula. This general economic failure of ranching stands in marked contrast to what is seen to the south and west, in the Mexican states of Tabasco, Chiapas, and Veracruz. There, higher rainfall and deep

soils have allowed the establishment of productive pasturelands, and cattle ranching has been the main force driving deforestation.

Despite the unprofitability of cattle in most of the Yucatan region, extensive areas of forest continue to be cleared for the creation of new pastures. In Quintana Roo, government subsidies have been used to finance destruction of as much as 40% of the 4.0–4.5 million ha of forest that was standing in 1960 (Zugasty and Sanchez 1987). Much of the poor-quality pastureland created in the 1970s and 1980s already has been abandoned, but clear-cutting of forest continues. Some 650,000 ha of forest were destroyed between 1980 and 1987. The total area nominally devoted to cattle ranching in the state is more than 2 million ha (Zugasty and Sanchez 1987). Even if official estimates of the amount of land currently in active pasture prove to be somewhat exaggerated, cattle ranching is by far the most serious threat to the remaining large tracts of tropical forest in Quintana Roo.

COASTAL DEVELOPMENT. Prior to the 1970s, the main human disturbance to the Yucatan's coast had been the commercial cultivation of coconut palms (*Cocos nucifera*) in plantations ("cocales") along the northern and eastern shores. This industry has practically disappeared since 1980 because of a massive die-off of coconut palms following the introduction of an exotic viral disease from Florida. The demise of the cocales has been overshadowed, however, by the most significant economic and demographic event that has occurred in the entire Yucatan Peninsula for at least the past 50 years: the meteoric emergence of Cancun, Quintana Roo as a major international center for Caribbean tourism. In 1950, the entire state of Quintana Roo had only about 27,000 inhabitants, most of them rural villagers, and by 1963 the population had only increased to about 61,000. Since the mid-1970s, when Cancun was established as a resort, the population of Quintana Roo has mushroomed at the almost unbelievable rate of 20% *per year*. The state's population reached 850,000 in 1989, 85% of which now reside in Cancun and a few other coastal towns (Sanchez 1989). Thus, in a single generation Quintana Roo has made the transition from a virtually unpopulated territory to a highly urbanized state.

Coastal development already has spread southward from Cancun, and within the next decade the entire 150 km stretch of coast between Cancun and Punta Allen is expected to be dotted with hotels, condominiums, and vacation homes. Although the area that will be directly impacted by coastal development is relatively limited (ca. 40,000–50,000 ha), the coastal population also makes very large demands on the interior of Quintana Roo for food, fuel, building materials, and other products. Moreover, the narrow strip of coastal dune vegetation is extremely fragile, and supports a highly distinctive flora (Moreno-Casasola and Espejel 1986) and bird community (Lopez Ornat et al. 1989, Lopez Ornat and Lynch 1991). From the standpoint of Nearctic migrants, probably the main significance of the coastal dune strip is its use by large numbers of fall and spring transients, notably Eastern Kingbirds and Purple Martins (Lopez Ornat and Lynch 1991).

OCCURRENCE OF NEARCTIC MIGRANTS IN NATIVE AND DISTURBED VEGETATION

Recent studies have confirmed and extended earlier indications (e.g., Paynter 1955, Tramer 1974, Waide 1980, Waide et al. 1980) that the Yucatan Peninsula is a major overwintering area for migrant landbirds. Based on point counts and mist-netting, Lynch (1989) documented the occurrence of 42 species of overwintering migrants, and showed that migrants are abundant over essentially the entire available range of natural and human-modified vegetation types. During the September–April overwintering period, from 30 to 58% ($\bar{X}$ = 41%) of the total individuals, and from 29 to 54% ($\bar{X}$ = 37%) of the total species encountered in point counts conducted within 11 major natural and disturbed habitat types were Nearctic migrants (Lynch 1989).

During winter, cattle pastures and milpas tend to be numerically dominated by Nearctic migrants and by resident species with ecologically similar congeners in the North Temperate Zone (Table 1). In Quintana Roo, migrants constituted 17% of the 101 species tallied in point counts conducted in open fields and pastures, but 29% of the 34 commonest species were migrants (Lynch 1989). The high prevalence of migrants was not confined to fields and pastures, as migrants were also disproportionately represented among the commonest species in acahuales and forests (Table 1).

Lynch (1989) divided the overwintering migratory species in the Yucatan region into five groups, based on their tendency to occur in highly modified vs. undisturbed vegetation. In the present analysis, this classification has been simplified to only three very general habitat associations, and residents as well as migrants have been included (Table 2). "Field species" are arbitrarily defined as those whose rate of occurrence in point counts was more than four times as high in milpas, pastures less than one year into abandonment or early old-fields (acahuales) as they were in "dry" (= semideciduous), "moist" (= semievergreen), or "wet" (= evergreen) forest. Migrants that qualify by this criterion as field species in the northern Yucatan Peninsula include Common Yellowthroat, Yellow-throated Warbler, Palm Warbler, Yellow Warbler, and Indigo Bunting. Common resident species in this category include Tropical Mockingbird, Melodious Blackbird, Red-billed Pi-

geon, Tropical Kingbird, White-collared Seedeater, Common Ground-Dove, and Hooded Oriole.

"Field/forest species" are here defined as those showing less than a fourfold difference between their occurrence rates in forest vs. fields, pastures, and/or acahuales. Among migrants, the commonest field/forest species were Least Flycatcher, Gray Catbird, White-eyed Vireo, Magnolia Warbler, and Hooded Warbler (Table 2). Resident field/forest species included Plain Chachalaca, Cinnamon Hummingbird, Buff-bellied Hummingbird, Yellow-lored Amazon, Golden-fronted Woodpecker, Boat-billed Flycatcher, Social Flycatcher, Dusky-capped Flycatcher, Spot-breasted Wren, Brown Jay, Yucatan Jay, Blue-gray Gnatcatcher, Mangrove Vireo, Rufous-browed Peppershrike, Rose-throated Tanager, and Blue Bunting.

Finally, occurrence rates of birds classed as "forest species" were at least four times as high in one or more types of forest as in fields or acahuales. Migrants in this group included Wood Thrush, Kentucky Warbler, American Redstart, Black-and-white Warbler, Black-throated Green Warbler, and Ovenbird. Common residents in this category included Keel-billed Toucan, Pale-billed Woodpecker, White-bellied Emerald, Olivaceous Woodcreeper, Bright-rumped Attila, Northern Bentbill, Stubtailed Spadebill, Tropical Gnatcatcher, Lesser Greenlet, and Red-throated Ant-tanager (Table 2).

This three-way classification is more conservative in assigning species to "specialist" status than was the earlier (Lynch 1989) five-way system. As a result, a few species (e.g., Hooded Warbler) that had been classified as "forest generalists" are now simply termed "generalists." Nevertheless, the results of the two systems are highly conformable.

Interspecific differences in habitat association, although highly significant statistically (Lynch 1989), were not absolute. Thus, even those migrant species most characteristic of open fields (e.g., Common Yellowthroat, Indigo Bunting) occasionally occurred in treefall gaps or other small disturbed sites within the interior of forest. Conversely, forest-associated migrants (e.g., Wood Thrush, Kentucky Warbler) were sometimes observed or mist-netted in early second growth. In all, 32 of the 36 commonest migratory landbirds in the Yucatan (the 22 species listed in Table 2, plus Ruby-throated Hummingbird, Golden-winged Warbler, Swainson's Warbler, Worm-eating Warbler, Black-throated Blue Warbler, Cape May Warbler, Wilson's Warbler, Yellow-breasted Chat, Northern Waterthrush, Louisiana Waterthrush, Painted Bunting, Blue Grosbeak, Summer Tanager, Orchard Oriole) occurred at least occasionally in mature tropical forest. For 21 of the 36 migrant species (58%), forest was the main habitat.

The occurrence in point counts of overwintering migrants in relation to old-field succession in the northern

TABLE 1. Occurrence rates (OR) of the commonest bird species observed from October through April in the northern Yucatan Peninsula in three successional habitats, based on point counts

	Milpa and pasture			Acahual			Forest	
Rank	Species	OR	Rank	Species	OR	Rank	Species	OR
*1	Common Yellowthroat	54	*1	Magnolia Warbler	36	*1	Hooded Warbler	69
2.5	Mangrove Vireo	30	*2	Common Yellowthroat	35	*2	Magnolia Warbler	57
2.5	Tropical Mockingbird	30	*3	Hooded Warbler	33	*3	American Redstart	47
*5	Least Flycatcher	28	*4	White-eyed Vireo	29	*4	White-eyed Vireo	31
*5	Magnolia Warbler	28	5	Mangrove Vireo	28	5	Lesser Greenlet	30
5	Melodious Blackbird	28	6	Melodious Blackbird	24	*6	Black-and-white Warbler	28
7	Red-billed Pigeon	24	*7.5	Least Flycatcher	21	6	Red-throated Ant-tanager	28
*8	Indigo Bunting	22	*7.5	Gray Catbird	21	8	Brown Jay	27
9.5	Tropical Kingbird	21	9.5	Tropical Kingbird	18	9	Spot-breasted Wren	19
9.5	Golden-fronted Woodpecker	21	*9.5	Indigo Bunting	18	10	Keel-billed Toucan	18
*11.5	Gray Catbird	17	11.5	Tropical Mockingbird	17	*11	Wood Thrush	17
11.5	Social Flycatcher	27	11.5	Golden-fronted Woodpecker	17	*12	Black-throated Green Warbler	16
*13.5	White-eyed Vireo	15	13	Hooded Oriole	14	*13	Kentucky Warbler	15
13.5	Yellow-lored Amazon	15	14	Fork-tailed Emerald	12	14	Rose-throated Tanager	14
15	Brown Jay	15	*17	Yellow Warbler (migratory races)	11	16.5	Dusky-capped Flycatcher	12
16	White-collared Seedeater	14	17	Buff-bellied Hummingbird	11	16.5	Buff-bellied Hummingbird	12
17	Boat-billed Flycatcher	12	17	Red-billed Pigeon	11	16.5	Carolina Wren	12
*20	Northern Parula	11	17	Blue Bunting	11	16.5	Northern Bentbill	12
20	Common Ground-Dove	11	17	Cinnamon Hummingbird	11	20	Stub-tailed Spadebill	10
20	Northern Cardinal	11	21.5	Rufous-browed Peppershrike	10	*20	Gray Catbird	10
20	Fork-tailed Emerald	11	21.5	Spot-breasted Wren	10	20	Golden-fronted Woodpecker	10
20	Blue-gray Gnatcatcher	11	21.5	Northern Cardinal	10	22.5	Ferruginous Pygmy-Owl	9
23	Spot-breasted Wren	10	21.5	Social Flycatcher	10	22.5	Yellow-lored Amazon	9
*25	Yellow-throated Warbler	9	25	Black-headed Saltator	8	24.5	Tropical Gnatcatcher	8
25	Buff-bellied Hummingbird	9	25	Orange Oriole	8	24.5	Pale-billed Woodpecker	8
*25	Rose-breasted Grosbeak	9	*25	American Redstart	8			
Mean no. migrant occurrences/point		1.9			2.1			2.7

NOTE: Entries are the percent of point counts in which each species occurred in milpas and pastures (n=92), 4–8 year-old acahuales (n=72) and mature semi-evergreen forest (n=404)

*Nearctic migrants

TABLE 2. Habitat use by 58 common migratory and resident landbirds in the Yucatan Peninsula

Species	Coastal scrub	All other habitats
Field species		
Migrants		
1. Common Yellowthroat	35	FP(54), Ac(35), DF(10), MF(1)
2. Indigo Bunting	3	FP(22), Ac(18), DF(3), MF(2), WF(2)
3. Yellow-throated Warbler	5	FP(9), Ac(4)
4. Palm Warbler	3	FP(8), Ac(8)
5. Yellow Warbler	18	Ac(11), FP(5)
Residents		
1. Tropical Mockingbird	65	FP(30), Ac(17), DF(4), MF(2)
2. Melodious Blackbird	3	FP(28), Ac(24), MF(4)
3. Red-billed Pigeon	2	FP(24), Ac(11), MF(3)
4. Tropical Kingbird	10	FP(21), Ac(18), DF(5), MF(2), WF(3)
5. White-collared Seedeater	7	FP(14), Ac(4), WF(2)
6. Common Ground-Dove	5	FP(11), Ac(4), DF(1)
7. Hooded Oriole	23	Ac(14), FP(10), DF(3), MF(1)
Field/Forest species		
Migrants		
1. Least Flycatcher	7	FP(28), DF(24), Ac(21), MF(11)
2. Yellow-rumped Warbler	10	FP(10), DF(7)
3. Northern Cardinal	7	FP(11), Ac(10), DF(3), MF(1)
4. Rose-breasted Grosbeak	–	FP(8), Ac(6), DF(2), MF(1)
5. Gray Catbird	12	Ac(21), FP(17), MF(9), DF(2)
6. Northern Parula	2	DF(12), FP(11), Ac(7), MF(6), WF(3)
7. White-eyed Vireo	12	DF(52), MF(32), Ac(29), FP(15), WF(9)
8. Magnolia Warbler	2	MF(54), WF(36), Ac(36), DF(32), FP(28)
9. Hooded Warbler	–	MF(73), DF(46), WF(42), Ac(33), FP(4)
Residents		
1. Mangrove (=Scrub) Vireo	30	FP(30), Ac(28), DF(24), MF(7), WF(2)
2. Golden-fronted Woodpecker	5	FP(21), Ac(17), MF(12), DF(5)
3. Yellow-lored Amazon	2	FP(15), Ac(7), MF(7), DF(2)
4. Boat-billed Flycatcher	–	FP(12), DF(7), WF(4), MF(3)
5. Cinnamon Hummingbird	25	Ac(11), DF(8), FP(4), MF(2)
6. Blue Bunting	–	Ac(11), DF(3), MF(3), WF(2), FP(2)
7. Social Flycatcher	8	DF(18), FP(17), Ac(10), MF(7)
8. Blue-gray Gnatcatcher	–	DF(15), FP(11), Ac(10), MF(1)
9. Yucatan Jay	–	DF(9), FP(), Ac(7), MF(6)
10. Fork-tailed Emerald	3	DF(12), Ac(12), FP(11), MF(8)
11. Rufous-browed Peppershrike	2	DF(11), Ac(10), MF(3), FP(2)
12. Brown Jay	–	MF(18), F(15), Ac(6), FP(2)
13. Plain Chachalaca	5	MF(6), FP(6), Ac(3), DF(3), WF(3)
14. Rose-throated Tanager	2	MF(13), Ac(6), DF(3), WF(2), FP(1)
15. Spot-breasted Wren	–	MF(18), DF(11), FP(10), Ac(10)
16. Buff-bellied Hummingbird	5	WF(14), MF(13), Ac(11), FP(9), DF(5)
17. Dusky-capped Flycatcher	–	MF(10), WF(9), DF(9), Ac(6), WF(4), FP(2)
Forest species		
Migrants		
1. Black-throated Green Warbler	–	DF(23), MF(14), WF(6), FP(4), Ac(1)
2. American Redstart	–	MF(44), DF(24), WF(22), Ac(8), FP(2)
3. Black-and-white Warbler	3	MF(24), DF(17), WF(3), Ac(3)
4. Ovenbird	–	MF(19), DF(11), Ac(3), FP(1)
5. Yellow-throated Vireo	–	MF(5), DF(2)

TABLE 2—*Continued next page*

TABLE 2—*Continued*

Species	Coastal scrub	All other habitats
Forest species (*continued*)		
Migrants (*continued*)		
6. Blue-winged Warbler	–	MF(3), WF(2), DF(1)
7. Kentucky Warbler	–	WF(31) MF(13), DF(1)
8. Wood Thrush	–	WF(33), MF(11)
Residents		
1. Carolina Wren	8	DF(12), MF(8), FP(1)
2. Ferruginous Pygmy Owl	–	DF(8), MF(7), WF(2), FP(2)
3. Red-throated Ant-tanager	–	MF(22), WF(9), DF(4), Ac(3), FP(2)
4. White-bellied Emerald	–	MF(4), WF(2), FP(2), Ac(1)
5. Northern Bentbill	–	MF(12), WF(9), Ac(3), FP(1)
6. Bright-rumped Attila	–	MF(7), WF(5), DF(2)
7. Lesser Greenlet	–	MF(19), WF(8)
8. Keel-billed Toucan	–	WF(16), MF(11), Ac(3), FP(2)
9. Olivaceous Woodcreeper	–	WF(12), MF(6), DF(2)
10. Stub-tailed Spadebill	–	WF(9), MF(8), DF(1)
11. Pale-billed Woodpecker	–	WF(9), MF(5)
12. Tropical Gnatcatcher	–	WF(5), MF(3)

NOTE: Entries are percentages of point counts within a given habitat in which a species was detected. See text for definitions of habitat categories and associations. For each species, the occurrence rate in native coastal scrub is given, followed by occurrence rates for all other occupied habitats, in descending order. Number of point counts for each habitat: acahual (Ac) = 72; coastal scrub = 60; field and pasture (FP) = 92; dry forest (DF) = 184; moist forest (MF) = 424; wet forest (WF) = 64.

Yucatan is summarized in Figure 2. For a few species, (e.g., Wood Thrush), mist-netting data have been used to confirm the occasional presence of species in disturbed habitats where they were not detected in point counts. Only the common species that occur along the generalized field-forest successional continuum in the northern Yucatan are included. Thus, migrants whose Yucatan distribution is exclusively southern (e.g., Wilson's Warbler, Louisiana Waterthrush) are omitted, as are uncommon species for which we lack sufficient distributional data (e.g., Golden-winged Warbler, Swainson's Warbler, Worm-eating Warbler, Black-throated Blue Warbler), and species whose primary habitat in the Yucatan is coastal scrub (Yellow-rumped Warbler, Palm Warbler, Blue Grosbeak).

Some salient features of this generalized successional sequence are: (1) 57% (12 of 21) of the commonest migrant species in the northern Yucatan were more frequent in highly disturbed milpas and early successional scrub, than in forest or late successional growth, (2) 38% (8 of 21) occurred more frequently in late second growth and mature forest than in highly disturbed vegetation and, (3) 43% (9 of 21) of the commonest migrant species occurred regularly across the entire successional continuum, from cultivated fields and active pastures to mature tropical forest.

No consistent tendency was found for forest-associated migrants to be either more or less abundant (as judged by point count frequencies) in their main habitat than field-associated species were in theirs. If niche breadth is defined in terms of the tendency to use six major habitat types (field, acahual, coastal scrub, dry forest, moist forest, wet forest) in proportion to their availability, no significant difference was found in the median niche breadths of migrant vs. resident species (Table 3). Thus, these two groups are similar in their general patterns of habitat use, even though migrants tend to differ from residents in being smaller in size and more highly insectivorous (Willis 1980).

RELATIVE ABUNDANCE OF MIGRANTS AND RESIDENTS IN DIFFERENT HABITATS

A traditional view of overwintering Nearctic migrants is that they "fit in" to crowded tropical bird communities mainly by occupying disturbed, marginal or ephemeral habitats that are not extensively used by permanently resident tropical species (e.g., Slud 1960, Willis 1966, Fitzpatrick 1980, Stiles 1980, Rappole and Warner 1980). If such a scenario is valid, one should observe a negative correlation between the abundance of migrants and residents across a range of habitats. Instead,

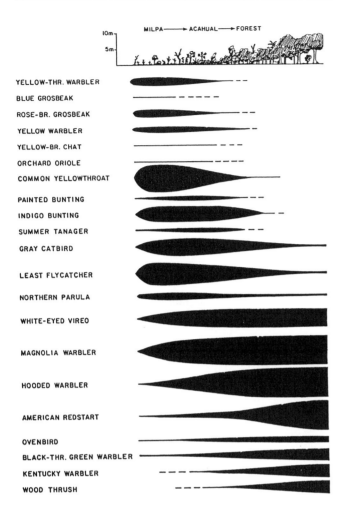

FIGURE 2. Diagrammatic representation of the occurrence of 21 species of Nearctic migrants along a generalized successional gradient in Quintana Roo, based on point count data. Thickness of the blackened area is proportional to the percentage of point counts in which the species was detected. Dashed lines represent occurrence rates < 1%. In a few cases occurrence has been inferred from mist-net captures.

TABLE 3. Distribution of estimated habitat niche breadths for the 68 commonest resident and migratory landbird species in the northern Yucatan Peninsula, based on occurrences in point counts that were conducted in six major habitat types

Niche breadth*	Number of Species	
	Migrants ($n = 18$)	Residents ($n = 50$)
1.6—1.9	2	4
2.0—2.3	1	4
2.4—2.7	3	7
2.8—3.1	2	8
3.2—3.5	3	6
3.6—3.9	3	7
4.0—4.3	2	6
4.4—4.7	–	3
4.8—5.1	1	4
5.2—5.5	1	–
5.6—5.9	–	1
Median niche breadth	3.4	3.2

NOTE: Sample sizes for point counts in each habitat are given in Table 2. Niche breadth reaches its maximum (exp [H'] = K = number of habitats) when a species occurs at the same frequency in all habitats. Migrants and residents do not differ significantly in their distribution of niche breadths ($P > 0.9$; Wilcoxon two-sample test).

* exp [H'] = exp $(- \sum P_i \ln P_i)$; P_i = proportion of point counts in i^{th} habitat in which a species was detected (K = 6 habitats).

however, one finds a highly significant ($P < 0.001$) *positive* correlation between the occurrence rates of migrants and residents in the Yucatan in individual point counts (Fig. 3). Habitats favorable for migrants as a group also appear to be favorable for residents as a group, and the ratio of migrant species to resident species remains approximately constant across the entire successional continuum (see above). A positive correlation between migrant and resident abundance also was found in Waide's (1980) mist-netting study of five sites in Campeche, and in Hutto's (1980, this volume) point surveys of migrants and residents in western Mexico.

The traditional view that many migrants occur in marginal and disturbed habitats does, however, contain

some truth. The diversity and abundance of migrants (including many species that are restricted to closed-canopy forest on their temperate breeding grounds) in what can be characterized as "scruffy" successional vegetation is impressive (Tables 1, 2; Fig. 1). However, it is not generally realized (but see Willis 1980) that these same disturbed habitats are also used by many resident species as well.

MIST-NET DATA

Capture data for migrants in northeastern Quintana Roo are presented in Table 4. It is well known that mist-net capture rates produce biased estimates of species abundance and community composition, due both to the placement of nets in the ground-shrub zone and to the inability of nets of a given mesh size to capture all bird species (Lynch 1989). There is a fairly low, but statistically significant, correlation ($r = 0.5$; $P < 0.05$) between mist-net capture rates and point count frequencies for

188 • James F. Lynch

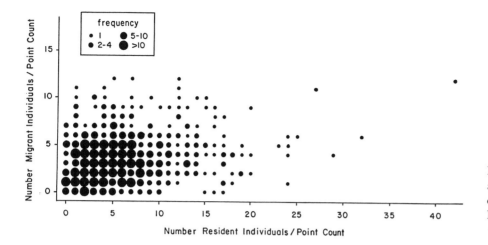

FIGURE 3. Relationship between the abundance of migrant and resident individuals in 978 point counts. The Pearson correlation coefficient (r) = +.26 ($P < 0.001$).

TABLE 4. Daily capture rates (DCR = 100 × number of individuals netted per net-morning) for common Nearctic migrants in three successional habitats in northeastern Quintana Roo

Field/Pasture		Acahual		Mature forest	
Species	DCR	Species	DCR	Species	DCR
1. Indigo Bunting	41	Gray Catbird	14	Hooded Warbler	4
2. Common Yellowthroat	11	White-eyed Vireo	12	Ovenbird	4
3. Gray Catbird	7	Ovenbird	8	Wood Thrush	3
4. White-eyed Vireo	6	Wood Thrush	8	White-eyed Vireo	2
5. Least Flycatcher	5	Common Yellowthroat	7	Black-and-white Warbler	2
6. Painted Bunting	4	Hooded Warbler	6	Kentucky Warbler	2
7. Magnolia Warbler	3	Magnolia Warbler	5	Magnolia Warbler	1
9. Yellow-breasted Chat	3	Indigo Bunting	4		
10. American Redstart	2	Yellow Warbler	2		
11. Ovenbird	2	Northern Parula	2		
12. Summer Tanager	2	Painted Bunting	2		
13. Northern Waterthrush	2	Kentucky Warbler	2		
14. Northern Parula	1	Yellow-breasted Chat	2		
15. Orchard Oriole	1	American Redstart	1		
16. Black-and-white Warbler	1	Summer Tanager	1		
17. Blue Grosbeak	1	Worm-eating Warbler	1		
18. Blue-winged Warbler	1				
All other migrant species	< 1		2		1.5
TOTAL MIGRANT DCR	96+		85		19.5

migrants, but no significant correlation for resident species (Lynch 1989). Even with these caveats in mind, it is striking that capture data from Quintana Roo showed substantially higher total abundance and 30–40% higher species diversity (corrected to equal numbers of captures) for both migrants and residents within small areas (1–3 ha grids) of successional vegetation than in equivalent areas of semievergreen forest (Lynch 1989). Although true diversity undoubtedly differs from estimates derived from mist-netting, it is clear

that both forest and second-growth vegetation are extensively used by migrant and resident birds in the Yucatan. Having said this, one must also recognize that individual species differ greatly in their tendency to use disturbed vs. undisturbed vegetation. Moreover, the relative ratio of disturbed vs. undisturbed vegetation in a given landscape may determine the mixture of species observed at any given site (Askins et al. 1987). That is, small old-fields within an extensive matrix of forest might be readily used by forest-associated species that would not occur in similar old-fields within a deforested landscape. Another important question is whether the overwinter survivorship of individual migrants is as high (or even higher) in open, disturbed habitats as in forest. Russell Greenberg's studies in central Quintana Roo (this volume) are addressing this crucial issue of the relative "quality" of disturbed vs. undisturbed habitats.

SOURCE OF THE AVIFAUNA ASSOCIATED WITH DISTURBED VEGETATION

In the Yucatan Peninsula, the native vegetation type where many field-associated bird species reached their greatest abundance was coastal dune scrub (Table 2). For four migratory species (Yellow Warbler, Yellow-throated Warbler, Palm Warbler, Blue Grosbeak), coastal scrub was virtually the only natural habitat used in the study area, although other native vegetation (e.g., pine savanna) may be used elsewhere in Middle America and in the Caribbean region. Two other field-associated migrants (Yellow-rumped Warbler, Common Yellowthroat) were encountered more frequently in coastal scrub than in any other type of native vegetation, but also were observed occasionally in semideciduous forest. Five migratory species (Least Flycatcher, Gray Catbird, White-eyed Vireo, Northern Parula, Magnolia Warbler) classified by Lynch (1989) as habitat generalists made some use of coastal scrub, but occurred at higher frequencies in other types of native vegetation (Table 2). Of the nine migratory species classified as "forest-associated" (Lynch 1989), only the Black-and-white Warbler occurred more than very rarely in coastal scrub.

A similar tendency to occur commonly in coastal scrub holds for resident species that are common in highly disturbed vegetation (Table 2). The seven commonest resident "field species" all occurred regularly in coastal dune scrub, as did 10 of the 17 commonest "field/forest" generalists. In contrast, only one of the 12 commonest resident "forest species" (Carolina Wren) was encountered in point counts conducted in coastal scrub. Coastal dune scrub was the type of native vegetation in which such characteristic milpa/acahual species as Common Ground-Dove, Cinnamon Hummingbird, Tropical Mockingbird, Tropical Kingbird, White-collared Seedeater, and Hooded Oriole reached their highest apparent densities (Table 2).

These data support the hypothesis that, before the advent of widespread human-caused habitat disturbance, the narrow fringe of coastal scrub might have been the primary Yucatan habitat for a number of migrants (e.g., Common Yellowthroat, Yellow-throated Warbler, Yellow-rumped Warbler, Palm Warbler) and residents (e.g., Cinnamon Hummingbird, Common Ground-Dove, Tropical Kingbird, Tropical Mockingbird,

Hooded Oriole) that today are characteristic of milpas, pastures, and acahuales. The primordial Yucatan habitat for several other common field-associated migrants (e.g., Least Flycatcher, Gray Catbird, White-eyed Vireo, Magnolia Warbler, Northern Parula, Indigo Bunting, Painted Bunting, Rose-breasted Grosbeak) and residents (e.g., Yellow-lored Amazon, Red-billed Pigeon, Golden-fronted Woodpecker, Social Flycatcher, Brown Jay, Mangrove Vireo, Melodious Blackbird) was presumably forest, particularly semideciduous forest, where all of these species occur commonly.

RESPONSE OF THE AVIFAUNA TO HURRICANE GILBERT: THE ROLE OF MAJOR NATURAL DISTURBANCES

Hurricane Gilbert, which passed through the region in September 1988, had a major effect on the region's avifauna. At our study site near Puerto Morelos, all trees were defoliated, and all fruits and flowers were blown from the forest canopy. Although the mean number of bird species detected per point count declined from 8.6 (composite value for two winters before the hurricane) to 5.1 five months after the hurricane, the dominance/diversity pattern of the community was virtually unchanged after the storm (Table 5). Rarefaction analysis showed that a random sample of 100 detections would contain 43 (SD = 3) species before the hurricane, vs. 41 (SD = 3) species afterward. There were, however, some marked changes in the relative abundance of individual species. The Hooded Warbler remained the most frequently detected species after the storm, but hummingbirds (all species combined) dropped from second to 12th rank. Two frugivores (Keel-billed Toucan and Wood Thrush) that had ranked among the 10 most frequent species before Hurricane Gilbert were completely absent from point counts five months later. Conversely, the ranked abundance of White-eyed Vireo increased from 12th to 3d after the storm.

Capture data from 396 net hours of mist-netting conducted in a tract of semievergreen forest five months after the hurricane were compared with pre-hurricane data from the same forested site, and from an adjacent acahual that was five to seven years into secondary succession (Table 6). The overall capture rate at the forest site more than doubled after the hurricane (29.0 vs. 11.9/100 net hr), although the post-hurricane capture rate in the forest was less than the very high pre-hurricane capture rate (41.3/100 net hr) for the acahual. The high post-hurricane capture rate might be due to an absolute influx of birds into the storm-affected area, or might simply reflect a downward vertical movement of canopy-dwelling species to ground level in response to the post-hurricane increase in the density of the shrub layer. Given the mixture of old-field and forest-canopy

TABLE 5. Pre-hurricane (February 1987–March 1988) and post-hurricane (March 1989) comparison of point count data for medium-height semievergreen forest in the vicinity of Puerto Morelos, Quintana Roo

Variable	Pre-hurricane counts (n = 52)		Post-hurricane counts (n = 45)	
Total species detected		69		59
Mean no. species/point		8.6		5.1
Estimated species/100 detections, mean(SD)[a]		43.2(2.8)		41.2(2.7)
Most frequent species:	*1	Hooded Warbler	*1	Hooded Warbler
	2	all hummingbirds	*2	Magnolia Warbler
	3	Brown Jay	*3	White-eyed Vireo
	*4	Magnolia Warbler	*4	American Redstart
	5	Red-throated Ant-tanager	*5	Black-and-white Warbler
	*6.5	Wood Thrush	6	Rose-throated Tanager
	*6.5	American Redstart	7.5	Stub-tailed Spadebill
	8	Lesser Greenlet	7.5	Lesser Greenlet
	9	Stub-tailed Spadebill	9	Spot-breasted Wren
	10	Keel-billed Toucan	10	Brown Jay
	11	Dusky-capped Flycatcher	11	Northern Bentbill
	14	Golden-fronted Woodpecker	13	all hummingbirds
	14	Carolina Wren	13	Golden-fronted Woodpecker
	*14	Black-and-white Warbler	13	Pale-billed Woodpecker
	*14	White-eyed Vireo		
	14	Rose-throated Tanager		

*Nearctic migrants

a. The predicted mean number of species per 100 detections (standard deviation in parentheses) was determined by rarefaction (Simberloff 1978).

species that were netted after the hurricane, both factors were probably involved. Unlike the point count data, which did not indicate that the hurricane changed the dominance/diversity profile of the forest bird community, the estimated species richness per 100 mist-net captures (based on rarefaction analysis) increased significantly ($P < 0.05$) from 30 before the hurricane to 41 afterward (Table 5). The latter figure is nearly identical to the pre-hurricane value estimated for the acahual site (Table 5).

These admittedly biased and preliminary mist-net data indicate a partial convergence of the post-hurricane forest bird community with the acahual community in terms of total abundance, dominance/diversity relationships, and species composition. One of the most dramatic species-specific effects of the hurricane was a 30-fold increase in capture rate of White-eyed Vireos after the storm (pre-storm = 0.1/100 net hr; post-storm = 3.3/100 net hr), an increase that was also evident in the point count data. The post-storm capture rate for White-eyed Vireo compares with the pre-hurricane

figure (2.9/100 net hr) at the acahual site. Other migrants that were normally associated with field/acahual habitats but commonly netted in the forest after Hurricane Gilbert included Indigo Bunting, Painted Bunting, and Orchard Oriole (Table 6). Several ecologically generalized migrant species (e.g., Magnolia Warbler, Hooded Warbler) were common in the forest both before and after the hurricane, as were a number of forest specialists. Thus, the hurricane apparently produced a kind of hybrid bird community which combined characteristics of both forest and scrub assemblages. The longevity of this effect is not known, and is under study.

Areas disturbed by hurricanes and subsequent wildfires, as well as areas covered by native coastal scrub, might have been major historical reservoirs of habitat for the many migratory and resident species that today are associated with fields, pastures, and early successional regrowth. Lugo (1988) suggested that the flora and fauna of the Caribbean region might be unusually resilient to human disturbance, due in large part to the adaptations of this biota to the effects of fre-

TABLE 6. Pre-hurricane and post-hurricane mist-net capture data for bird communities in a tract of medium-height, semievergreen forest and an adjacent 5–7 year-old "acahual" near Puerto Morelos, Quintana Roo

Variable	Forest		Acahual
	Pre-hurricane	Post-hurricane	Pre-hurricane
Net-hours	4,313	396	1,346
Captures	527	130	612
Hourly capture rate[a]	11.9	29.0	41.3
Est. species/100 captures, (SD)[b]	30.4(2.5)	40.9(1.8)	40.4(3.1)
Most frequently captured species:	1 Red-throated Ant-tanager	*1 White-eyed Vireo	*1 Gray Catbird
	2 Ruddy Woodcreeper	2 Red-throated Ant-tanager	2 Blue Bunting
	*3 Hooded Warbler	3 Ivory-billed Woodcreeper	*3 White-eyed Vireo
	*4 Ovenbird	4 Olivaceous Woodcreeper	4 Olivaceous Woodcreeper
	*5 Wood Thrush	*5 Magnolia Warbler	5.5 Black Catbird
	*6.5 Kentucky Warbler	*7.5 Hooded Warbler	*5.5 Wood Thrush
	6.5 Tawny-crowned Greenlet	7.5 Stub-tailed Spadebill	*7 Ovenbird
	8 Ivory-billed Woodcreeper	*7.5 Indigo Bunting	8 Caribbean Elaenia
	*9 Black-and-white Warbler	*7.5 Orchard Oriole	*9 Common Yellowthroat
	10 Wedge-tailed Sabrewing	11 Spot-breasted Wren	10 White-bellied Wren
		11 Tawny-crowned Greenlet	11 Mangrove (= Scrub) Vireo
		11 Orange Oriole	*12 Hooded Warbler

NOTE: Pre-hurricane data were gathered during October–March between February 1984 and February 1988 (the acahual could not be re-sampled after the hurricane because it was converted to an orchard in 1986).

a. Hourly capture rate = 100 × number of new individuals per net hr.

b. Estimated by rarefaction (Simberloff 1978) of total data to 100 captures.

quent hurricanes. In this context, the responses of Quintana Roo's birds to hurricane damage might help us to understand at least some of the avifauna's reactions to ranching and farming. Although we must be cautious about extrapolating these results from the Caribbean area to other geographic regions where large-scale natural disturbances are rare, recent research has made it clear that massive natural disruptions, especially fire, have occurred with previously unexpected frequency even in such "stable" tropical regions as the Amazon basin (Uhl 1988).

EFFECTS ON MIGRANTS OF TRADITIONAL VS. CURRENT LAND-USE PATTERNS

Historically, the dominant land-use pattern for most of the peninsula has consisted of small, shifting milpas and acahuales in an extensive matrix of forest. Even within active milpas, some canopy trees and clumps of brush are usually left standing. Because the roots of felled trees are not always killed, sprouting by some species is rapid following abandonment. The brushy second growth that quickly invades abandoned milpas includes many fruit-bearing plant species used by birds, and mist-net capture rates and diversity indices in 1–8-year-old acahuales are higher than in any other habitats that were studied in Quintana Roo (Lynch 1989) and Campeche (Waide 1980). The apparent richness of acahuales as habitat for migrants and residents might reflect biases inherent in mist-netting at the ground-shrub level, because a lower proportion of the total species pool is netted in tall forest than in low vegetation. Nevertheless, point count data confirm that brushy second growth is readily used by a large group of migrant (as well as resident) species. A similar pattern appears to hold true in lowland habitats elsewhere in Mexico (Hutto 1980, Rappole and Morton 1985). Older (i.e., sapling-stage and pole-stage) second growth also is favorable habitat for a variety of migrants and residents, including forest-associated species in the Yucatan region (Lynch 1989) and elsewhere in Middle America (Martin 1985).

Because virtually all forest-associated migrant species in the Yucatan are capable of using relatively young (5–7-year-old) second-growth habitat, traditional milpa agriculture probably was not highly detrimental to most forest-associated Nearctic migrants, except in areas where human populations were so high that the usual 25–50-year fallow period was drastically shortened. The latter situation has long existed in the heavily populated northwestern portion of the Yucatan Peninsula (Yucatan state), where the fallow period for old-fields is commonly less than 10 years, and where little mature forest survives (Lynch 1989).

Rather than milpa agriculture, it is the post-1960 spread of large-scale cattle ranching that presently poses the major threat to forest-dependent migratory and resident species. Long-term, intensive ranching entails not only the initial destruction of large tracts of forest, but also the continued suppression of woody second growth. Despite the fact that it has not been possible to establish an economically viable cattle industry in Quintana Roo, millions of hectares have been deforested for ranches because of government subsidization of forest clearance. To make matters even worse, almost none of the trees that are felled to make pastures are utilized in any way—they are simply burned or left to rot. It is fortunate for migratory birds that in Quintana Roo some of the worst effects of deforestation have been mitigated by the rough-and-ready style of ranching that is typically practiced. There, stocking levels are low, and ranches tend to be so short-lived that most cattlemen do not bother trying to eradicate every tree and patch of shrubs from their pastures. Even the smallest remnant clumps of trees and bushes, as well as invading woody species that are unpalatable to cattle, often shelter "forest" migrants (e.g., American Redstart, Magnolia Warbler, Black-throated Green Warbler, Hooded Warbler), although typically at lower densities than are observed in forests (Lynch 1989, Askins et al. 1990).

The countrywide economic depression that has crippled Mexico in recent years has forced a virtual halt to government-subsidized forest-clearing projects in the Yucatan Peninsula. However, there is no guarantee that a future economic upswing or a change in the political winds might not spur another episode of wasteful forest destruction.

ALTERNATIVES TO DEFORESTATION IN QUINTANA ROO

The establishment of pristine reserves should always be among the major goals of conservationists, because without such undisturbed sites we can never fully understand the impacts of human activities on the biosphere. Nevertheless, political realities in Mexico and many other countries dictate that conservationists also should concern themselves with lands that do not enjoy protected status. Partially disturbed vegetation can harbor many plant and animal species that are of concern to conservationists, and can serve as corridors for animals dispersing between remnants of native vegetation. However much conservationists may bemoan the fact, most lowland forest in Middle America already has been "developed," and all but a tiny fraction of the remainder is certain to be disturbed by human activity within the next few years. Nevertheless, there is a wide range of possible economic uses to which these remaining wild areas might be subjected, ranging from complete deforestation for ranching or farming, to relatively benign forest-based industries (e.g., chicle extraction, highly selective logging), or even ecotourism.

In most of the forested sections of the Yucatan Peninsula, the welfare of migratory and resident bird species, not to mention the rural human population, would be much better served if sustainable forestry could be substituted for cattle-ranching as the cornerstone for rural economic development. Such a program, the "Plan Piloto Forestal" (PPF), has in fact been instituted in southern Quintana Roo by a group of West German and Mexican foresters under the aegis of Mexico's Subsecretariat of Forestry and Wildlife (SARH). The stated objective of the legal association (Sociedad Civil) formed by the 10 original communities that agreed to participate in the PPF is: "To preserve natural forests in a permanent way as an ecological alternative to other land uses, to promote integral forest use, to manage more species and make the best use of each log" (Sanchez 1989). The basic geographic-political units within which local forestry plans are being developed are the *ejidos*. These are communally owned rural townships which, in Quintana Roo, contain anywhere from a few dozen to several thousand people and might encompass many thousands of hectares.

Beginning in 1985, residents of several ejidos in central and southern Quintana Roo have compiled forest inventories, planned cutting schedules, carried out logging operations, manufactured lumber and secondary wood products, and controlled the business aspects of their forestry operations. Logging is highly selective as to the size and species of tree, and each ejido is subdivided into 25 zones, only one of which is selectively logged in a given year. Fires are actively and effectively suppressed, instead of being allowed to burn unchecked as happened in northern Quintana Roo in the wake of Hurricane Gilbert (see above). Illegal tree-cutting is rigorously prevented. Finally, and perhaps most surprising to some observers, several ejidos have spontaneously created natural reserves that are off-limits to any logging. In some communities, land that previously had been devoted to cattle pasture now has been designated for reforestation, and an active research program is planned to study tree propagation techniques, natural regeneration, growth rates, and mortality factors. In marked contrast to many other forestry programs, the PPF does not involve introduction of exotic tree species, nor will there be any attempt to establish monoculture plantations of selected native species.

By late 1989, 26 ejidos, whose lands encompass more than 525,000 ha, were enrolled in the PPF program. In 1989, the state government of Quintana Roo formed a statewide "Plan Forestal Estadal" which embraces the same management principles enunciated by the original PPF. The state plans to add 425,000 ha of land to the program, which will bring the total area to 950,000 ha.

This constitutes about 90% of the remaining forest in the southern half of the state (the "mahogany zone"), or 40% of the total extant forest in Quintana Roo. At present, the officially stated policy of Quintana Roo is that sustainable forestry, not cattle ranching, will be the economic basis for future rural development in the state.

It is too soon to know whether or not the eastern Yucatan Peninsula will be spared the destruction which has obliterated most of the original tropical forest that once cloaked the Middle American lowlands. However, conservationists can now point to a program for sustainable tropical forestry that is ecologically and economically sound, and which functions profitably at a regional scale. The rural people of Quintana Roo, with the support of their government, have enthusiastically embraced a development plan that may enable them to retain both their forests and their traditional independence, while still promoting economic progress. That migratory birds also stand to reap great benefits from the success of the PPF and similar forestry programs is perhaps a coincidence, but one for which all avian conservationists should be grateful.

Acknowledgments

It is a pleasure to acknowledge those who have helped with the field work in Mexico over the past decade: Ed Balinsky, Mauro Berlanga, Edgar Cabrera, Gilberto Chavez, Laurie Greenberg, Russ Greenberg, Jamie Harms, Burt Jones, Arturo Lopez, Bill Mayher, Patricia Mehlhop, Gene Morton, Martita Van der Voort, and Dennis Whigham. The development work of Felipe Sanchez and Patricia Zugasty has been an inspiration, and their careful research on farming, ranching, and forestry in Quintana Roo was critical to the preparation of this paper. Alfredo Careaga and Enrique Carillo, former directors of the Centro de Investigaciones de Quintana Roo (CIQRO), encouraged our research in that state. Margaret McWethy prepared the figures, and Meridel Jellifer did her usual careful job in preparing the manuscript. Financial support was provided by World Wildlife Fund-U.S. and the Smithsonian Institution. Finally, I thank Curt Freese for encouraging me to address conservation issues head-on.

Literature cited

American Ornithologists' Union. 1983. *Check-list of North American Birds.* 6th ed. Washington: American Ornithologists' Union.

Askins, R.A., J.F. Lynch, and R. Greenberg. 1990. Population declines in migratory birds in eastern North America. *Current Ornithol.* 7:1–57.

Askins, R.A., M.J. Philbrick, and D.S. Sugeno. 1987. Relationship between the regional abundance of forest and the composition of forest bird communities. *Biol. Conserv.* 39:129–152.

Bolin, B. 1977. Changes of land biota and their importance for the carbon cycle. *Science* 196:613–615.

Estrada, A., and R. Coates-Estrada. 1988. Tropical rainforest conservation and perspectives in the conservation of wild primates (*Alouatta* and *Ateles*) in Mexico. *Am. J. Primatology* 14:315–327.

Fearnside, P.M. 1986. Spatial concentration of deforestation in the Brazilian Amazon. *Ambio* 1986:74–81.

Fitzpatrick, J.W. 1980. Wintering of North American tyrant flycatchers in the Neotropics. Pages 67–78 in *Migrant Birds in the Neotropics: Ecology, Behavior, Distribution and Conservation,* A. Keast and E.S. Morton, eds. Washington: Smithsonian Institution Press.

Flannery, K.V. (ed.) 1982. *Maya Subsistence: Studies in Memory of Dennis E. Puleston.* New York: Academic Press.

Garcia, E. 1965. *Distribucion de la precipitacion en la Republica Mexicana.* Publ. Geogr. Univ. Nac. Mexico, Vol. 1.

Gradwohl, J., and R. Greenberg. 1988. *Saving the Tropical Forests.* London: Earthscan Publ. Ltd.

Green, K.M., J.F. Lynch, J. Sircar, and L.Z. Greenberg. 1987. Use of Landsat remote sensing to assess habitat for migratory birds in the Yucatan Peninsula. *Vida Silv. Neotrop.* 1(2):27–38.

Gutierrez Gonzalez, E. 1983. Aspectos etnobotanicos de le reserva de la biosfera de Sian Ka'an. Pages 145–179 in *Sian Ka'an: Estudios preliminares de una zona en Quintana Roo propuesta como Reserva de la Biosfera.* Puerto Morelos, Quintana Roo, Mexico: Centro de Investigaciones de Quintana Roo.

Holdridge, L.R. 1967. *Life Zone Ecology.* San Jose, Costa Rica: Tropical Science Center.

Hutto, R.L. 1980. Winter habitat distribution of migratory land birds in western Mexico with special reference to small, foliage-gleaning insectivores. Pages 181–204 in *Migrant Birds in the Neotropics: Ecology, Behavior, Distribution and Conservation,* A. Keast and E.S. Morton, eds. Washington: Smithsonian Institution Press.

Janzen, D.H. 1988. Tropical dry forests: The most endangered major tropical ecosystem. Pages 130–137 in *Biodiversity,* E.O. Wilson, ed. Washington: National Academy Press.

Jauregui, E., J. Vidal, and F. Cruz. 1980. Los ciclones y tormentas tropicales en Quintana Roo durante el period 1871–1978. Pages 47–64 in *Quintana Roo: Problematica y perspectivas.* Mexico City: Centro de Investigaciones de Quintana Roo and Universidad Nacional Autonoma de Mexico.

Lopez Ornat, A., and J.F. Lynch. 1991. Landbird communities of the coastal dune scrub in Yucatan and Quintana Roo, Mexico. *Fauna Silvetre Neotropical* 2:21–31.

Lopez Ornat, A., J.F. Lynch, and B.M. de Montes. 1989. New and noteworthy records of birds from the eastern Yucatan Peninsula. *Wilson Bull.* 101:390–409.

Lugo, A.E. 1988. Estimating reductions in the diversity of tropical forest species. Pages 58–70 in *Biodiversity,* E.O. Wilson, ed. Washington: National Academy Press.

Lynch, J.F. 1989. Distribution of overwintering Nearctic migrants in the Yucatan Peninsula, I: General patterns of occurrence. *Condor* 91:515–544.

Lynch, J.F., E.S. Morton, and M.E. Van der Voort. 1985. Habitat segregation between the sexes of wintering Hooded Warblers (*Wilsonia citrina*). *Auk* 102:714–721.

Martin, T.E. 1985. Selection of second-growth woodlands by frugivorous migrating birds in Panama: An effect of fruit size and density? *J. Trop. Ecol.* 1:157–170.

Moreno-Casasola, P., and I. Espejel. 1986. Classification and ordination of coastal sand dune vegetation along the Gulf and Caribbean Sea of Mexico. *Vegetatio* 66:147–182.

Morton, E.S., J.F. Lynch, K. Young, and P. Mehlhop. 1987. Do male Hooded Warblers exclude females from nonbreeding territories in tropical forest? *Auk* 104:133–135.

Myers, N. 1980. *Conversion of Tropical Moist Forests.* Washington: National Academy of Sciences.

———. 1988. Tropical forests and their species: Going, going . . . ? Pages 28–35 in *Biodiversity,* E.O. Wilson, ed. Washington: National Academy Press.

Paynter, R.A., Jr. 1955. The ornithogeography of the Yucatan Peninsula. *Peabody Mus. Nat. Hist. Yale University Bull.* 9:1–347.

Perez Villegas, G. 1980. El clima y los incendios forestales en Quintana Roo. Pages 65–80 in *Quintana Roo: Problematica y perspectivas.* Mexico City: Centro de Investigaciones de Quintana Roo and Universidad Nacional Autonoma de Mexico.

Powell, G.V.N., and J.H. Rappole. 1986. The Hooded Warbler. Pages 827–853 in *The Audubon Wildlife Report 1986.* A. Eno, ed. New York: National Audubon Society.

Rappole, J.H., and E.S. Morton. 1985. Effects of habitat alteration on a tropical avian forest community. Pages 1013–1021 in *Neotropical Ornithology,* P.A. Buckley, E.S. Morton, R.S. Ridgely, and F.G. Buckley, eds. Ornithol. Monogr. 36.

Rappole, J.H., and D.W. Warner. 1980. Ecological aspects of migrant bird behavior in Veracruz, Mexico. Pages 353–394 in *Migrant Birds in the Neotropics: Ecology, Behavior, Distribution and Conservation,* A. Keast and E.S. Morton, eds. Washington: Smithsonian Institution Press.

Rappole, J.H., E.S. Morton, T.E. Lovejoy, III, and J.L. Ruos. 1983. *Nearctic Avian Migrants in the Neotropics.* Washington: U.S. Fish and Wildlife Service.

Sader, S.A., and A.T. Joyce. 1988. Deforestation rates and trends in Costa Rica, 1940–1983. *Biotropica* 20:11–19.

Sanchez Roman, F. 1988. Unpublished report to World Wildlife Fund–U.S. on natural resources in Quintana Roo.

———. 1989. Rural development and conservation of natural resources in the state of Quintana Roo, Mexico. Unpublished report to World Wildlife Fund–U.S.

Simberloff, D. 1978. Use of rarefaction and related methods in ecology. Pages 150–165 in *Biological Data in Water Pollution Assessment.* K.L. Dickson, J. Cairns, and R.J. Livingston, eds. Philadelphia: Amer. Soc. Testing Materials.

Slud, P.R. 1960. The birds of finca "La Selva": A tropical wet forest locality. *Bull. Amer. Mus. Nat. Hist.* 121:49–148.

Stiles, F.G. 1980. Evolutionary implications of habitat relations between permanent and winter resident landbirds in Costa Rica. Pages 421–436 in *Migrant Birds in the Neotropics: Ecology, Behavior, Distribution and Conservation,* A. Keast and E.S. Morton, eds. Washington: Smithsonian Institution Press.

Thompson, J.E.S. 1966. *The Rise and Fall of Maya Civilization.* 2d ed. Norman: University Oklahoma Press.

———. 1970. *Maya History and Religion.* Norman: University Oklahoma Press.

Tramer, E. 1974. Proportions of wintering North American birds in disturbed and undisturbed dry tropical habitats. *Condor* 76:460-464.

Uhl, C. 1988. Restoration of degraded lands in the Amazon basin. Pages 326–332 in *Biodiversity,* E.O. Wilson, ed. Washington: National Academy Press.

Waide, R.B. 1980. Resource partitioning between migrant and resident birds: The use of irregular resources. Pages 337–352 in *Migrant Birds in the Neotropics: Ecology, Behavior, Distribution and Conservation,* A. Keast and E.S. Morton, eds. Washington: Smithsonian Institution Press.

Waide, R.B., J.T. Emlen, and E.J. Tramer. 1980. Distribution of migrant birds in the Yucatan Peninsula: A survey. Pages 165–171 in *Migrant Birds in the Neotropics: Ecology, Behavior, Distribution and Conservation,* A. Keast and E.S. Morton, eds. Washington: Smithsonian Institution Press.

Willis, E.O. 1966. The role of migrant birds at swarms of army ants. *Living Bird* 5:187–231.

———. 1980. Ecological roles of migratory and resident birds on Barro Colorado Island, Panama. Pages 205–226 in *Migrant Birds in the Neotropics: Ecology, Behavior, Distribution and Conservation,* A. Keast and E.S. Morton, eds. Washington: Smithsonian Institution Press.

Zugasty Towle, P. and F. Sanchez Roman. 1987. Use of intensive forage production to reduce forest destruction in Quintana Roo, Mexico. Unpubl. Progress Report to World Wildlife Fund–U.S.:1–14.

APPENDIX 1.   Species mentioned in the text, figures, and tables. Scientific and common names and the order of families follow the A.O.U. check-list (1983) (+ = resident population also present; * = Nearctic migrants)

Black-shouldered Kite (*Elanus leucurus*)
Plain Chachalaca (*Ortalis vetula*)
Black-throated Bobwhite (*Colinus nigrogularis*)
Red-billed Pigeon (*Columba flavirostris*)
Common Ground-Dove (*Columbina passerina*)
White-winged Dove (*Zenaida asiatica*)
Yellow-lored Amazon (*Amazona xantholora*)
Ferruginous Pygmy-Owl (*Glaucidium brasiliensis*)
*Ruby-throated Hummingbird (*Archilochus colubris*)
Cinnamon Hummingbird (*Amazilia rutila*)
Buff-bellied Hummingbird (*Amazilia yucatanensis*)
White-bellied Emerald (*Amazilia candida*)
Fork-tailed Emerald (*Chlorostilbon caniveti*)
Wedge-tailed Sabrewing (*Campylopterus curvipennis*)
Keel-billed Toucan (*Ramphastos sulfuratus*)
Pale-billed Woodpecker (*Campephilus guatemalensis*)
Golden-fronted Woodpecker (*Melanerpes aurifrons*)
Olivaceous Woodcreeper (*Sittasomus griseicapillus*)
Ivory-billed Woodcreeper (*Xiphorhynchus flavigaster*)
Ruddy Woodcreeper (*Dendrocincla homochroa*)
*Least Flycatcher (*Empidonax minimus*)
*Eastern Kingbird (*Tyrannus tyrannus*)
Bright-rumped Attila (*Attila spadaceus*)
Tropical Kingbird (*Tyrannus melancholicus*)
Boat-billed Flycatcher (*Megarhynchus pitangua*)
Social Flycatcher (*Myiozetetes similis*)
Dusky-capped Flycatcher (*Myiarchus tuberculifer*)
Stub-tailed Spadebill (*Platyrhynchus mystaceus*)
Northern Bentbill (*Oncostoma cinereigulare*)
*Purple Martin (*Progne subis*)
Brown Jay (*Cyanocorax morio*)
Yucatan Jay (*Cyanocorax yucatanicus*)
Carolina Wren (*Thryothorus ludovicianus*)
Spot-breasted Wren (*Thryothorus maculipectus*)
White-bellied Wren (*Uropsila leucogastra*)
Blue-gray Gnatcatcher (*Polioptila caerulea*)
Tropical Gnatcatcher (*Polioptila plumbea*)
*Wood Thrush (*Hylocichla mustelina*)
*Gray Catbird (*Dumetella carolinensis*)
Black Catbird (*Melanoptila glabirostris*)
Tropical Mockingbird (*Mimus gilvus*)
Lesser Greenlet (*Hylophilus decurtatus*)

Tawny-crowned Greenlet (*Hylophilus ochraceiceps*)
*White-eyed Vireo (*Vireo griseus*)
Mangrove (= Scrub) Vireo (*Vireo pallens*)
*Yellow-throated Vireo (*Vireo flavifrons*)
Rufous-browed Peppershrike (*Cyclarhis gujanensis*)
*Black-throated Blue Warbler (*Dendroica caerulescens*)
*Black-throated Green Warbler (*Dendroica virens*)
*Cape May Warbler (*Dendroica tigrina*)
*Magnolia Warbler (*Dendroica magnolia*)
*Palm Warbler (*Dendroica palmarum*)
+*Yellow Warbler (*Dendroica petechia*)
*Yellow-throated Warbler (*Dendroica dominica*)
*Yellow-rumped Warbler (*Dendroica coronata*)
*Common Yellowthroat (*Geothlypis trichas*)
*Worm-eating Warbler (*Helmitheros vermivorus*)
*Yellow-breasted Chat (*Icteria virens*)
*Swainson's Warbler (*Limnothlypis swainsonii*)
*Black-and-white Warbler (*Mniotilta varia*)
*Kentucky Warbler (*Oporornis formosus*)
*Northern Parula (*Parula americana*)
*Louisiana Waterthrush (*Seiurus motacilla*)
*Northern Waterthrush (*Seiurus noveboracensis*)
*Ovenbird (*Seiurus aurocapillus*)
*American Redstart (*Setophaga ruticilla*)
*Hooded Warbler (*Wilsonia citrina*)
*Wilson's Warbler (*Wilsonia pusilla*)
Bananaquit (*Coereba flaveola*)
*Summer Tanager (*Piranga rubra*)
Red-throated Ant-tanager (*Habia fuscicauda*)
Red-crowned Ant-tanager (*Habia rubica*)
*Blue Grosbeak (*Guiraca caerulea*)
*Indigo Bunting (*Passerina cyanea*)
*Painted Bunting (*Passerina ciris*)
*Rose-breasted Grosbeak (*Pheucticus ludovicianus*)
Blue Bunting (*Cyanocampsa parellina*)
Northern Cardinal (*Cardinalis cardinalis*)
Black-headed Saltator (*Saltator atriceps*)
White-collared Seedeater (*Sporophila torqueola*)
*Orchard Oriole (*Icterus spurius*)
Hooded Oriole (*Icterus cucullatus*)
Orange Oriole (*Icterus auratus*)
Melodious Blackbird (*Dives dives*)

ROBERT A. ASKINS
Department of Zoology
Connecticut College
New London, Connecticut 06320

DAVID N. EWERT
The Nature Conservancy
East Lansing, Michigan 48823

ROBERT L. NORTON
British Virgin Islands National Parks Trust
Ministry of Natural Resources and Labor
Road Town, Tortola, British Virgin Islands

Abundance of wintering migrants in fragmented and continuous forests in the U.S. Virgin Islands

Abstract. Populations of winter-resident birds were surveyed on St. John and St. Thomas, two adjacent islands in the U.S. Virgin Islands. Because a large proportion of St. John is included in Virgin Islands National Park, only 12% of the island is developed. In contrast, 62% of St. Thomas is covered with urban and suburban areas. We used fixed-radius point counts to survey birds at 218 points on the two islands. We also analyzed the structure of the vegetation at each survey point. Warblers (Parulinae) accounted for 99% of the individual winter residents recorded during point surveys. Most of the 13 species of wintering warblers were found primarily in moist forest and the adjacent moist forest/dry woodland ecotone. Both the density and species richness of migratory warblers were significantly higher in moist forest than in either dry woodland or gardens. Moreover, the average number of species and individuals per survey point was significantly higher in the extensive tracts of moist forest on St. John than in the small remnant patches of moist forest on St. Thomas. In fact, all habitats on St. John had significantly higher densities of migrants than comparable habitats on St. Thomas. The relatively low density of migrants on St. Thomas might be the result of widespread degradation and destruction of forest on this island.

Sinopsis. Se censaron las poblaciones de aves residentes de invierno en dos islas adyacentes en las Islas Vírgenes de los Estados Unidos: St. John y St. Thomas. Puesto que una gran proporción de St. John está incluída en el Parque Nacional de las Islas Vírgenes, solamente el 12% de la isla está intervenido. Por el contrario, el 62 % de St. Thomas está cubierto de áreas urbanas y suburbanas. Nosotros usamos conteos puntuales de radio fijo para censar las aves en 218 puntos en las dos islas. Igualmente, analizamos la estructura de la vegetación en cada sitio de censo. Las Parulinae representaron el 99% de los individuos residentes de invierno registrados durante censos puntuales. La mayoría de las 13 especies de Parulinae invernantes se encontraron primariamente en bosque húmedo y el ecotono bosque húmedo-matorral seco adyacente. Tanto la densidad como la riqueza de especies de las Parulinae migratorias fué significativamente mayor en bosque húmedo que en matorral seco o en jardines. Además, el número promedio de especies e individuos por punto de censo fue significativamente mayor en los extensos tramos de bosque húmedo en St. John que en los pequeños parches remanentes de este tipo de bosque en St. Thomas. De hecho, todos los habitats de St. John tuvieron densidades de migratorias significativamente superiores que habitats comparables en St. Thomas. La densidad relativamente baja de migratorias en St. Thomas podría ser el resultado de la extensiva degradación y destrucción de los bosques en esta isla.

The effect of tropical forest destruction on migratory songbirds is a growing concern (Terborgh 1980, Rappole et al. 1983, Morton and Greenberg 1989, Askins et al. 1990). In many tropical regions only small, isolated patches of forest remain. Small remnants of both temperate-zone deciduous forest and tropical rain forest have a relatively low density and diversity of breeding forest-interior birds (Ambuel and Temple 1983, Blake and Karr 1984, Lovejoy et al. 1984, Askins et al. 1987, Diamond et al. 1987, Robbins et al. 1989). However, a similar pattern has never been documented for overwintering Neotropical migrants, even though many of these species tend to be less abundant in small forest remnants than in large tracts of forest during the breeding season (Blake and Karr 1984, Askins et al. 1987). In fact, Robbins et al. (1987) reported that many species of wintering migrants were equally common in small (5–50 ha) and large (> 1000 ha) woodlands in Venezuela, Costa Rica, and the West Indies. Only two species of migrants (Gray-cheeked Thrush *Catharus minimus* and Louisiana Waterthrush *Seiurus motacilla*) were found exclusively in extensive forests. Also, in Quintana Roo, Mexico, Greenberg (this volume) detected forest-dwelling winter residents more frequently in small clumps of trees than in the surrounding 3–5-year-old scrub, which indicates that some migrants can use even tiny forest remnants. Other studies have shown that some species of migrants that nest in forest may spend the winter in shrubby second-growth habitats (Hutto 1989; Lynch 1989; Waide and Wunderle, unpubl. data). In the Bahamas, Robert Waide and Joseph Wunderle (pers. comm.) found high densities of wintering warblers in residential areas with ornamental plantings. Apparently, at least some species of migrants do not require extensive areas of tropical forest during the winter.

It is notable, however, that the island of St. John, which has relatively large tracts of tropical moist forest and dry evergreen woodland, apparently has a higher

density and diversity of winter-resident warblers than do nearby islands in the Virgin Islands group (Robertson 1962, Norton 1979, Pashley and Martin 1988). Several species of wintering warblers reported on Christmas bird counts on St. John have never been reported during counts on the more heavily developed islands of St. Thomas and St. Croix (Pashley and Martin 1988). This indicates that extensive destruction and degradation of forest on the latter two islands might have resulted in reduced diversity of winter residents.

The primary goal of our project was to determine whether extensive tracts of forest in the Virgin Islands have higher densities of winter residents than remnant patches of forest or artificial habitats (gardens and residential areas). A second goal was to determine the specific types of vegetation that are used most frequently by winter residents on these islands.

Methods

BIRD SURVEYS

We assessed avian abundance using fixed-radius point counts (Hutto et al. 1986). We recorded all birds detected within 25 m of each survey point during a 10-minute period. Recorded "spishing" noises (Smith 1975) were broadcast for one minute during the second minute and again during the sixth minute of the observation period. A copy of the same recording (on a loop tape) was used during all surveys, and the volume of the tape recorder was adjusted so that the tape was barely audible (to us) 50 m away. During a study in the Yucatan, Lynch (1989) found that winter residents showed a positive response to recordings of warbler call notes and imitations of distress calls and Ferruginous Pygmy-Owl (*Glaucidium brasilianum*) calls. They approached significantly more closely than in the absence of recordings, a pattern confirmed when we used "spishing" tapes during our initial observations in the Virgin Islands.

The duration of surveys was established on the basis of a series of 32 preliminary surveys in moist forest and dry evergreen woodland. Each of these surveys lasted 20 min (Hutto et al. 1986), with the "spishing" tape played once every five min. After 10 min we detected an average of 84% (range: 50–100%, SD = 0.34) of the winter-resident species and individuals that were detected during the entire 20 min (Fig. 1). The pattern was similar for the number of species and individuals of all birds (permanent and winter residents): 79% (SD = 0.18) and 78% (SD = 0.17), respectively (Fig. 1). In a similar analysis, Robert Waide and Joseph Wunderle (pers. comm.) detected an average of 79% of the migrant species during the first 10 min of 20-min preliminary point counts in Puerto Rico. Like Hutto et al. (1986) and Waide and Wunderle, we decided to conduct 10-min

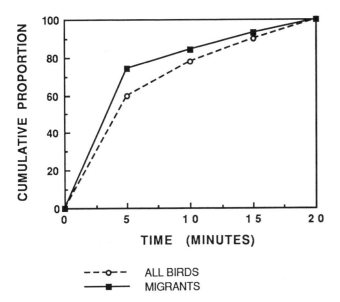

FIGURE 1. Cumulative proportion of the total number of individual birds detected during 32 preliminary point surveys on St. John.

surveys; a longer period would yield only a small number of additional species per survey point and would reduce the number of survey points we could sample. The 10-min period was extended for a maximum of five additional minutes if a mixed foraging flock entered the survey plot and all participants had not been identified at the end of the period. This happened during only two surveys.

Surveys were conducted between 0630 and 0930, the period when birds were most active. On St. John we conducted surveys between 31 October and 3 December 1987, which was after the period when most passage migrants stop in the Virgin Islands (Robert Norton, pers. obs.). Surveys on St. Thomas were completed between 5 and 19 December 1987. Adjacent survey points were separated by at least 150 m, and all points were at least 100 m from any obvious habitat edge.

In 1987 the total annual precipitation in the Virgin Islands was somewhat higher than normal: 114 cm for St. John, which is 3 cm more than the long-term average for 1951 to 1988, and 137 cm for St. Thomas, which is 26 cm more than the long-term average (National Oceanic and Atmospheric Administration 1987). The three months preceding the initiation of the study were drier than normal, however. The total rainfall for August, September, and October was 19–21 cm less than

normal for St. John and St. Thomas. Rainfall was heavy in November (15 cm above normal on St. John and 22 cm above normal on St. Thomas), and nearly normal in December.

HABITAT TYPES

We surveyed birds at 218 points in moist forest, dry evergreen woodland, and ecotone (areas that are transitional between these two), as well as in gardens and residential areas, on St. Thomas and St. John. The two islands are separated by a 3-km-wide channel. Their topography and climate are similar. The maximum elevation is 474 m for St. Thomas and 387 m for St. John, and both islands are characterized by steep slopes cut by deep valleys. St. Thomas is larger than St. John (71 km^2 vs. 50 km^2). The most conspicuous difference between the islands, however, is that most parts of St. Thomas are heavily developed, whereas large areas of natural habitat are protected in Virgin Islands National Park on St. John.

Almost all of the forest and woodland on the islands has become re-established since the 19th century when plantation agriculture was abandoned (Rogers and Teytaud 1988). Moist forest is found on the highest slopes of the islands and in ravines and coastal basins (Woodbury and Weaver 1987). The canopy is 10–30 m high, two or three tree strata are present, and more than 70% of the trees are evergreen. Introduced tree species are common in some stands. Dry evergreen woodland is the dominant vegetation on steep, dry slopes. The canopy is only 5–10 m high and two tree strata are typically present (Woodbury and Weaver 1987). Most of the trees are small-leaved and thorny. In dryer, more windswept locations, this woodland grades into a low (< 5 m high) thicket or scrub dominated by cacti and thorny, deciduous shrubs. Woodbury and Weaver (1987) list the dominant species for each of these vegetation types.

We determined the extent of various habitat types on the two islands using U.S. Geological Survey topographical maps (1:24,000; photorevised in 1982), aerial photographs (National Ocean Service, NOAA; 1:30,000; 1981), and, for St. John, the vegetation map in Woodbury and Weaver (1987). Moist forests are taller and have a less open canopy than dry woodland, so they appear distinctly darker on aerial photographs. The other major habitat types are indicated on topographical maps. The area of forest patches was determined using the scientific measurement program Sigma Scan (Jandel Scientific). A "forest patch" was defined as an area of continuous forest uninterrupted by openings wider than 10 m (e.g., major roads or powerlines). The area of a patch includes the total area of moist forest, dry evergreen woodland, moist forest/dry woodland ecotone, and mangrove swamp.

VEGETATION SURVEYS

We analyzed the structure of vegetation on a circular plot centered at each bird survey point. A 22-m-diameter plot was defined by running two tape measures perpendicularly from the center in the four cardinal directions. The height of the tallest tree in each of the resulting quadrants was measured using a rangefinder and clinometer. The average height for these four trees was used as a measure of canopy height. Percent cover was determined for four strata: litter (dead leaves and branches on the forest floor), herb (< 0.5 m), shrub (0.5–4 m), and tree (> 4 m). To evaluate percent cover, we sighted into each stratum with a piece of PVC tubing (2.7 cm diameter, 5.5 cm long). The proportion of the field of view covered by leaves was categorized as follows for each stratum: 0 (0%), 1 (1–25%), 2 (25–50%), 3 (50–75%), 4 (75–100%). This process was repeated 25 times at approximately 2-m intervals along each of the crossed tapes (James F. Lynch, pers. comm.). In extremely dense thorn scrub these readings were taken along two 22-m-long transects running parallel on opposite sides of a trail instead of on perpendicular transects. The sum of the 25 readings for each stratum yielded the overall percent cover. We also determined the elevation and aspect of each vegetation plot, and we counted the number of both columnar cacti and palms that were > 10 cm dbh.

The vegetation type for each survey point on St. John was assigned according to the vegetation map in Woodbury and Weaver (1987). Our moist forest category included the upland, gallery, and basin moist forest categories of Woodbury and Weaver, and our dry evergreen woodland category included their dry evergreen woodland, dry evergreen thicket, and thorn-and-cactus categories. Survey points on St. Thomas were assigned to vegetation type on the basis of our experience on St. John. The similarity of sites assigned to the same habitat type on the two islands was assessed later by comparing data on vegetation structure.

Results

SPECIES OF WINTER RESIDENTS

We detected a total of 15 species of warblers and one species of vireo during point surveys on the two islands (Table 1). They accounted for 55% of the species recorded on point surveys. Four additional species of warblers, Chestnut-sided Warbler (*Dendroica pensylvanica*), Palm Warbler (*D. palmarum*), Kentucky Warbler (*Oporornis formosus*), and Common Yellowthroat (*Geothlypis trichas*), were observed after 10 November at times when we were not doing point counts. The Kentucky Warbler was observed on St. Thomas and the other three species were on St. John.

Blackpoll Warblers were not detected after 6 November, and they are known to be late passage migrants in the Virgin Islands (Raffaele 1989; Robert Norton, pers. obs.), so they were not included in the analysis of winter residents. Also, Yellow Warblers were assumed to be permanent residents because permanent and winter residents are not easily distinguished in the field, and only the resident subspecies has been recorded in the Virgin Islands (Pashley 1988).

COMPARISON OF HABITATS

Dry evergreen woodland is the most abundant natural habitat on St. John and St. Thomas (Table 2). Moist forest is considerably less extensive and mangrove, which is an important winter habitat for some migrants (Lynch 1989), is restricted to small patches. The most distinct difference between the two islands is the much higher proportion of developed land on St. Thomas than on St. John (Table 2).

Winter residents were much more abundant in moist forest and (on St. John) in moist/dry ecotone than in dry evergreen woodland or gardens (Table 1, Fig. 2). Analysis of variance showed that on both islands the average number of individuals per survey point was significantly different in different habitats (St. John: $F = 16.6$, $P < 0.0001$; St. Thomas: $F = 3.9$, $P < 0.02$). The average number of species per survey point also differed significantly among habitats (St. John: $F = 16.4$, $P < 0.0001$; St. Thomas: $F = 3.9$, $P < 0.02$). Multiple range testing (Least Significant Difference; Snedecor and Cochran 1967) showed that both the number of individuals and the number of species of winter residents was significantly higher ($P < 0.05$) in moist forest than in either dry woodland or gardens on each of the two islands.

Multiple regression analysis using vegetation characteristics as independent variables confirmed this pattern; the number of individuals and the number of species of winter residents per survey point were positively correlated with percent tree cover on St. John ($P < 0.0001$ in both cases) and with canopy height on St. Thomas ($P < 0.01$ in both cases). These variables had their highest values in moist forest.

Most of the common species of winter residents occurred at least occasionally in dry woodland and gardens (Table 1), but all Hooded Warblers and almost all American Redstarts were recorded in moist forest or ecotone.

Migrants accounted for a high proportion of the individual birds detected at survey points in moist forest on both St. John and St. Thomas, and in the ecotone on St. John (Table 1). The proportion of migrants was much lower in dry woodland and gardens. This was partly because of the larger number of residents per survey point detected in dry woodlands and gardens than in moist

TABLE 1. Comparison of bird distributions in the major habitats on St. John and St. Thomas, U.S. Virgin Islands

Species	St. John				St. Thomas			
	Moist[a]	Ecotone[b]	Dry[c]	Gardens[d]	Moist	Ecotone	Dry	Gardens
No. of survey points	55	11	46	23	37	12	13	21
Individual species								
Yellow-throated Vireo (*Vireo flavifrons*)	1							
Blue-winged Warbler (*Vermivora pinus*)	2							
Northern Parula (*Parula americana*)	46	4	6	5	12		1	2
Yellow Warbler (*Dendroica petechia*)			8	1			3	
Magnolia Warbler (*D. magnolia*)	3	1						
Cape May Warbler (*D. tigrina*)	3	1	1					
Black-thr. Blue Warbler (*D. caerulescens*)					2			
Black-thr. Green Warbler (*D. virens*)					2			
Prairie Warbler (*D. discolor*)	1	5	5	4				
Blackpoll Warbler (*D. striata*)	1	1						
Black-and-white Warbler (*Mniotilta varia*)	17	1	1		2			
American Redstart (*Setophaga ruticilla*)	12		1					
Worm-eating Warbler (*Helmitheros vermivorus*)	2		1		1			
Ovenbird (*Seiurus aurocapillus*)	6	2	3		1			
Northern Waterthrush (*S. noveboracensis*)				2	4		1	
Hooded Warbler (*Wilsonia citrina*)	8	1			1			
Average no. of winter-resident individuals	1.9	1.4	0.5	0.6	0.6	0.1	0.1	0.1
Average no. permanent-resident individuals	3.7	3.8	5.0	4.9	2.5	3.0	4.6	3.2
Percentage of winter residents in total sample	33.9	26.9	9.1	10.9	19.4	3.2	2.1	3.0

NOTE: Number of individuals detected during point counts in each habitat on each island is listed for all species of warblers (Parulinae) and vireos (Vireonidae).

a. Moist forest.
b. Transition zone between moist forest and dry woodland.
c. Dry evergreen woodland.
d. Residential areas, hotel grounds and other artificial habitats.

TABLE 2. Total area of major habitats on St. John and St. Thomas, U.S. Virgin Islands, and number of separate tracts of forest containing each of the three types of forest

Habitat type[a]	St. John		St. Thomas	
	Area (ha) (% total area)	No. of patches	Area (ha) (% total area)	No. of patches
Dry evergreen woodland	3380 (67)	10	2317 (33)	22
Moist forest	925 (18)	5[b]	321 (5)	14[c]
Mangrove	52 (1)	4	42 (< 1)	2
Rock pavement	64 (1)		13 (< 1)	
Salt pond	19 (< 1)		6 (< 1)	
Development	575 (12)		4440 (62)	
TOTAL	5015		7139	

a. Categories for natural vegetation are derived from Woodbury and Weaver (1987). "Development" includes urban and suburban areas, towns, resort complexes, and similar artifical habitats.
b. 1 of the 5 patches is <10 ha.
c. 7 of the 14 tracts are <10 ha.

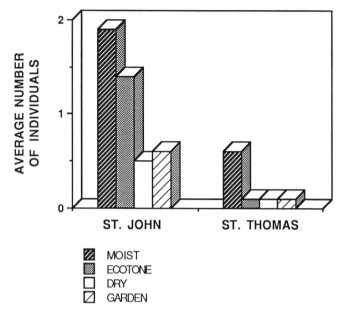

FIGURE 2. Average number of individual winter residents per survey point in different habitats on St. John and St. Thomas.

forest (Table 1; St. John: $F = 3.6, P < 0.02$; St. Thomas: $F = 7.8, P < 0.001$).

COMPARISON OF MIGRANT ABUNDANCE AND DIVERSITY ON THE TWO ISLANDS

The average number of individual winter residents per survey point was greater on St. John than on St. Thomas for all habitats (Fig. 2). These differences were significant (Student's t-test: $P < 0.001$ for moist forest, $P < 0.03$ for dry woodland, ecotone and gardens). The average number of species of winter residents per survey point was also greater on St. John for moist forest ($\bar{X} = 1.6$ for St. John and 0.6 for St. Thomas; $t = 4.2, F = 90, P < 0.001$) and the other habitats ($P < 0.03$ for dry woodland, and $P < 0.02$ for ecotone and gardens). The two most abundant species of winter residents, Northern Parula and Black-and-white Warbler, were significantly more frequent at survey points on St. John than on St. Thomas (t-test: $P < 0.001$ and 0.01, respectively).

Moist forest and gardens on St. John not only had more winter residents than similar habitats on St. Thomas, but also more permanent residents (Table 1; t-test: $P < 0.05$ for both number of species and number of individuals per survey point). However, no significant differences were found between the two islands in the

number of permanent residents in dry woodland or ecotone.

The surveys on St. John were completed earlier in the season than those on St. Thomas, so the difference in migrant density might have been due to the greater frequency of passage migrants on St. John. This is unlikely, however, because no significant difference was found in either the average number of migrant individuals or migrant species per survey point during the first half of the period on St. John (31 October–16 November) and the second half of the period (17 November–3 December) (t-test: $P > 0.4$ in both comparisons), which indicates that the number of migrants had stabilized by the time our study began.

Except for the patchy distribution of natural habitat on St. Thomas, the vegetation on the two islands was similar. The mean values for five of the six vegetation variables (canopy height; tree, shrub and herb cover; and number of columnar cacti) were not significantly different for moist forest sites or for ecotonal sites on the two islands ($P > 0.05$). However, for both habitats the average percent cover of leaf litter was lower on St. Thomas (t-test: $P < 0.001$). Moreover, dry woodland sites on St. Thomas had significantly greater percent cover for both the tree and shrub layers, and garden sites on St. Thomas had greater average values for canopy height and litter cover ($P < 0.05$ in all cases).

We also used factor analysis to compare vegetation structure on the two islands. We determined factors using oblimin rotation (SPSS Inc. 1986) for all vegetation variables for all survey points on the two islands. Factor 1 was positively correlated with canopy height and tree cover, and negatively correlated with the density of columnar cacti; thus, it separated moist and dry sites. Factor 2 is positively correlated with shrub cover and negatively correlated with herb and litter cover. Factor 1 accounted for 48% of the variation in the original variables and Factor 2 accounted for an additional 19%.

Scores for Factor 1 were not significantly different between the two islands for moist forest, ecotone or dry evergreen woodland, but they were significantly different for gardens (t-test: $P < 0.001$). Gardens on St. Thomas had higher scores because they tended to have taller trees. Mean scores for Factor 2 were significantly higher on St. Thomas than on St. John for moist forest and ecotone ($P < 0.02$ in both cases), indicating that sites on St. Thomas tended to have less leaf litter and perhaps a sparser shrub layer. Factor 2 accounted for relatively little of the variation in vegetation variables, however, and it is unlikely that the minor differences in the vegetation of the natural environments on the two islands accounted for the distinct differences in the abundance and diversity of migrants. In contrast, the vegetation of gardens and other artificial habitats was substantially different for the two islands. Because winter residents were most abundant in moist forest, one would expect that the more forest-like structure of gardens on St. Thomas compared to St. John (as indicated by their mean scores for Factor 1) would result in a higher density of winter residents on St. Thomas. However, the density of winter residents was higher on St. John.

RELATIONSHIP BETWEEN FOREST AREA AND THE NUMBER OF MIGRANTS

Tracts of continuous forest were significantly smaller on St. Thomas ($\bar{X}$ = 82 ha) than on St. John ($\bar{X}$ = 435 ha; t = 2.7, d.f. = 41, P < 0.01). Hence, a negative relationship between forest area and density of winter residents could account for the relatively low frequency of winter residents on St. Thomas. We used linear regression to test this hypothesis. Because most winter residents occurred in moist forest, we only included survey points in moist forest in this analysis. We could not analyze the relationship between forest area and the density of winter residents for St. John because all of the moist forest points were in two large patches of continuous forest (Fig. 3). Moreover, we only found seven forest patches on St. Thomas with large enough areas of moist forest to accommodate survey points (Fig. 3). The regression of the number of winter residents with forest area for these patches was not significant (F = 0.6, P = 0.47). Given the small number of patches with moist forest on each island, our results concerning the relationship between forest area and winter-resident density were not conclusive.

Discussion

HABITAT PREFERENCES OF WINTER RESIDENTS

Both the abundance and species richness of winter residents were significantly higher in moist forest than in other habitats on both St. John and St. Thomas. Of the 13 species of wintering warblers, all except the Prairie Warbler were found primarily in moist forest and adjacent moist forest/dry woodland ecotone (Table 1). Although overall densities of warblers were lower in dry woodland and scrub than in forests in Jamaica (Lack and Lack 1972) and Hispaniola (Terborgh and Faaborg 1980), studies in many other areas of the West Indies and on the Yucatan Peninsula have shown that high densites of wintering warblers occur in dry woodland, dry scrub, gardens, and tree plantations (Lack and Lack 1972, Post 1978, Waide et al. 1980, Lynch 1989). The apparent difference in habitat use between these areas and the Virgin Islands is probably due to the disproportionate abundance in the Virgin Islands of warbler species that tend to winter in forests, and the near ab-

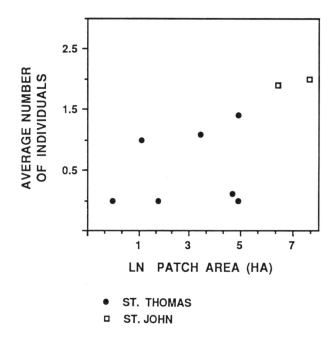

FIGURE 3. Relationship between the natural logarithm (ln) of the area of forest patches and the average number of individual winter residents per survey point within the patches. Only data from survey points in moist forest were used to calculate the average number of winter residents.

sence of species that winter primarily in arid scrub or disturbed habitats. The five most common species of warblers in the Virgin Islands (Northern Parula, Black-and-white Warbler, American Redstart, Ovenbird, and Hooded Warbler) are found in arid scrub and dry forest in Puerto Rico (Post 1978, Faaborg and Arendt 1984). However, in the Yucatan, where Lynch (1989) has systematically compared migrant densities in different habitats, the first four species occur at higher densities in forest than in coastal scrub or disturbed habitats. Only the Northern Parula was found to be equally frequent in forested and non-forested habitats.

Palm Warbler, Yellow-throated Warbler (*Dendroica dominica*), Yellow-rumped Warbler (*D. coronata*), Cape May Warbler, and Common Yellowthroat are infrequent in the Virgin Islands (Pashley 1988, Raffaele 1989). These are the common species in arid habitats in some other regions of the Caribbean Basin (Lack and Lack 1972, Emlen 1977, Post 1978, Waide 1980, Lynch 1989). The low density of these species largely accounts for the low density of winter residents in arid woodlands in the Virgin Islands. Similarly, the relatively low density of warblers in Virgin Islands gardens might be due partially to the scarcity of Cape May Warblers, a common species in park-like areas in Jamaica (Lack and Lack 1972).

COMPARISON OF WINTER-RESIDENT DENSITIES IN THE VIRGIN ISLANDS AND OTHER REGIONS IN THE CARIBBEAN BASIN

Although arid and artificial habitats in the Virgin Islands have relatively few winter residents, moist forests (especially on St. John) support an impressive density and diversity of wintering warblers. On St. John 34% of the individual birds detected in moist forest were wintering migrants (Table 1). This is in the same range as the percentage of wintering migrants in a variety of forest types in Jamaica and Hispaniola (Terborgh 1980, Gochfield 1985) and in semievergreen forest on the Yucatan Peninsula (Waide et al. 1980, Lynch 1989). The percentage of migrants is generally higher for sites in the Bahamas (Emlen 1980) and western Mexico (Hutto 1980), and lower in the Lesser Antilles (Terborgh and Faaborg 1980) and in Costa Rica, Panama, and South America (Terborgh 1980). Comparisons of the percentage of winter residents in the total bird population have become standard, but their meaning is unclear because the percentages reflect the abundance of permanent residents as well as the abundance of winter residents. As Robertson (1962) points out, the moist forests on St. John typically have a low density and diversity of resident birds. This might be due to the more arid conditions in the West Indies during the last glacial period; until the end of the Pleistocene, most of the islands were probably covered with arid scrub and savanna, with little or no moist forest (Pregill and Olson 1981, Faaborg 1985). Also, many resident species of forest birds might have been extirpated when most of St. John was converted to sugarcane, cotton, and coffee plantations in the 18th century (Robertson 1962, Tyson 1987). Whatever the reason for the low density of residents in the moist forests of the Virgin Islands, the result is that migrants are proportionately very important in the winter bird community.

Recently point surveys have been used to survey wintering migrants in several studies, which provides an opportunity for a more direct comparison of migrant densities in different regions of the tropics. Waide and Wunderle (unpubl. data) and Hutto (1989) counted birds within the same distance of survey points (25 m) and for the same period of time (10 min) as we did, but they did not use recordings of "spishing" or other aural stimuli to attract winter residents. Lynch (1989) used recordings to attract migrants, but he counted all birds detected from a point regardless of distance during a 10–12 min period. Clearly, comparisons of the density of migrants in different regions of the tropics would be more conclusive if the same survey methods had been used in different studies, but general comparisons can still be made.

Waide and Wunderle (pers. comm.) found that the average number of migrants per survey point was less than 1.5 for a variety of forest types in the Bahamas, the Dominican Republic, and Puerto Rico. The comparable value for moist forest on St. John (1.9 migrants per survey point) is somewhat higher. However, the "spishing" tapes might have attracted more migrants in the Virgin Islands surveys. In undisturbed tropical deciduous forest in western Mexico, Hutto (1989) recorded an average of 1.7 winter residents per survey point without using aural stimuli, which is similar to the average for moist forests on St. John. Moist forests on the Yucatan Peninsula appear to have substantially higher densities of winter residents; Lynch (1989) recorded an average of 3.8 individual winter residents per survey point. Although Lynch counted all birds detected from a survey point regardless of distance, his results indicate that winter-resident densities are higher on the Yucatan Peninsula than in the Virgin Islands. Moreover, an analysis of Christmas Count data by Pashley and Martin (1988) indicates that the total abundance of warblers on St. John and St. Thomas is high compared to sites in Puerto Rico, the Dominican Republic, and Jamaica, but lower than for most sites in the Bahamas and many sites in eastern Mexico.

COMPARISON OF MIGRANT DISTRIBUTIONS ON ST. JOHN AND ST. THOMAS

Winter residents were more abundant in moist forest on St. John than in moist forest on St. Thomas. Moist forest was structurally similar on the two islands, but the distribution of this habitat differed markedly: on St. John, relatively large areas of moist forest were embedded in extensive tracts of dry woodland in Virgin Islands National Park, whereas on St. Thomas, moist forest was limited to relatively small, isolated patches along steep ravines and on mountain tops. Hence, the low density of winter residents on St. Thomas might be due to the reduction of their preferred habitat to remnant patches. The small number of tracts with moist forest on each island precluded a conclusive analysis of the relationship between forest area and winter-resident density, but the distinct difference in the abundance of winter residents in continuous forest tracts on St. John and in remnant patches on St. Thomas suggests that forest fragmentation has had an effect on these birds. All habitats, including gardens, had lower densities of winter residents on St. Thomas than on St. John despite the structural similarity of plant communities on the two islands. This indicates that the large-scale destruction and fragmentation of natural habitats on St. Thomas has generally reduced the abundance of winter-resident birds on this island.

In the temperate-zone breeding areas, the density of many of the species that are regular winter residents in the Virgin Islands (Northern Parula, Black-and-white Warbler, American Redstart, Worm-eating Warbler, Ovenbird, and Hooded Warbler) is positively correlated with forest area and negatively correlated with isolation from other forests (Blake and Karr 1984, Lynch and Whigham 1984, Askins et al. 1987, Robbins et al. 1989), indicating that they are affected negatively by forest fragmentation during the breeding season. Our results imply that forest fragmentation might have a negative impact on these species in their wintering areas as well. However, Robbins et al. (1987) found that most species of winter residents had equally high densities in small and large forests in 12 regions in Puerto Rico, the Dominican Republic, Jamaica, Costa Rica, and Venezuela. Also, Greenberg (this volume) found higher densities of migrants that winter primarily in forests in small, isolated groups of trees than in the surrounding scrubland. These studies indicate that at least some species of forest-dwelling migrants can winter in small forest patches. Perhaps the regional configuration of forest is important in determining whether relict patches are occupied. No large tracts of forest remain on St. Thomas, and the greater isolation of the relict patches on St. Thomas compared to those studied by Robbins et al. (1987) and Greenberg (this volume) might have resulted in low densities of warblers. Small patches were within 5–10 km of large forests in the study of Robbins et al. (1987) and within 1 km of extensive forest in Greenberg's study (Russell Greenberg, pers. comm.). No extensive moist forests remain on St. Thomas; the largest continuous tract is only 109 ha.

To maintain populations of a diversity of migratory birds in the Virgin Islands, it would be judicious to protect the areas where they are most abundant: the largest remaining patches of moist forest on St. Thomas and the large, continuous areas of moist forest on St. John. Because the density of winter residents is so low in relict patches of forest on St. Thomas, fragmentation of the larger tracts should be avoided. The largest tract of moist forest on St. Thomas, which stretches from Crown Mountain to Signal Hill, was undergoing development at the time of our surveys. In fact, the area where we found the highest density and diversity of warblers on St. Thomas, an expanse of moist forest immediately west of Signal Hill, had recently been subdivided for house lots. On St. John some of the largest areas of moist forest, such as those in Reef Bay Gut and Fish Bay Gut, are protected in Virgin Islands National Park. Other continuous tracts of moist forest at Bordeaux

Mountain and Adrian are within the park boundary, but have become increasingly disrupted by roads and houses associated with private land holdings. Given the evidence for low densities of winter residents on the heavily developed island of St. Thomas, preservation of these continuous forest tracts is important for sustaining populations of some species of migratory songbirds.

Acknowledgments

This research was supported by the National Geographic Society and the World Nature Association. We were given permission to work in Virgin Islands National Park, and John Miller and Caroline Rogers of the park staff helped in many ways. We also received a permit for the project from the U.S. Virgin Islands Department of Planning and Natural Resources. Ann Swanbeck and David Nellis of the U.S.V.I. Division of Fish and Wildlife gave us invaluable assistance in finding study sites on St. Thomas. Kirsten Canoy provided facilities at the Virgin Islands Ecological Research Station. Michael Canoy, Gary Owen, and Edward Towle helped us locate study sites and information. Richard Hutto and Jim Lynch advised us on survey techniques, and Phillip Barnes gave us advice on statistical analysis. John Faaborg and an anonymous reviewer gave helpful suggestions on revising this paper.

Literature cited

Ambuel, B., and S.A. Temple. 1983. Area-dependent changes in the bird communities and vegetation of southern Wisconsin forests. *Ecology* 64:1057–1068.

Askins, R.A., J.F. Lynch, and R. Greenberg. 1990. Population declines in migratory birds in eastern North America. *Current Ornithol.* 7:1–57.

Askins, R.A., M.J. Philbrick, and D.S. Sugeno. 1987. Relationship between the regional abundance of forest and the composition of forest bird communities. *Biol. Conserv.* 39:129–152.

Blake, J.G., and J.R. Karr. 1984. Species composition of bird communities and the conservation benefit of large versus small forests. *Biol. Conserv.* 30:173–187.

Diamond, J.M., K.D. Bishop, and S. Van Balen. 1987. Bird survival in an isolated Javan woodland: Island or mirror? *Conserv. Biol.* 1:132–142.

Emlen, J.T. 1977. *Land Bird Communities of Grand Bahama Island: The Structure and Dynamics of an Avifauna.* Ornithol. Monogr. 24.

———. 1980. Interactions of migrant and resident land birds in Florida and Bahama pinelands. Pages 133–143 in *Migrant Birds in the Neotropics: Ecology, Behavior, Distribution and Conservation,* A. Keast and E.S. Morton, eds. Washington: Smithsonian Institution Press.

Faaborg, J. 1985. Ecological constraints on West Indian bird distributions. Pages 621–653 in *Neotropical Ornithology,* P.A.

Buckley, E.S. Morton, R.S. Ridgely, and F.G. Buckley, eds. Ornithol. Monogr. 36.

Faaborg, J., and W.J. Arendt. 1984. Population sizes and philopatry of winter resident warblers in Puerto Rico. *J. Field Ornithol.* 55:376–378.

Gochfield, M. 1985. Numerical relationships between migrant and resident bird species in Jamaican woodlands. Pages 654–662 in *Neotropical Ornithology*, P.A. Buckley, E.S. Morton, R.S. Ridgely, and F.G. Buckley, eds. Ornithol. Monogr. 36.

Hutto, R.L. 1980. Winter habitat distribution of migratory land birds in western Mexico, with special reference to small foliage-gleaning insectivores. Pages 181–203 in *Migrant Birds in the Neotropics: Ecology, Behavior, Distribution and Conservation*, A. Keast and E.S. Morton, eds. Washington: Smithsonian Institution Press.

———. 1989. The effect of habitat alteration on migratory land birds in a west Mexican tropical deciduous forest: a conservation perspective. *Conserv. Biol.* 3:138–148.

Hutto, R.L., S.M. Pletschet, and P. Hendricks. 1986. A fixed-radius point count method for nonbreeding and breeding season use. *Auk* 103:593–602.

Lack, D., and P. Lack. 1972. Wintering warblers in Jamaica. *Living Bird* 11:129–153.

Lovejoy, T.E., J.M. Rankin, R.0. Bierregaard, Jr., K.S. Brown, Jr., L.H. Emmons, and M.E. Van de Voort. 1984. Ecosystem decay of Amazon forest remnants. Pages 295–325 in *Extinctions*, M.E. Nitecki, ed. Chicago: University of Chicago Press.

Lynch, J.F. 1989. Distribution of overwintering Nearctic migrants in the Yucatan Peninsula, I: General patterns of occurrence. *Condor* 91:515–544.

Lynch, J.F., and D.F. Whigham. 1984. Effects of forest fragmentation on breeding bird communities in Maryland, U.S.A. *Biol. Conserv.* 28:287–324.

Morton, E.S., and R. Greenberg. 1989. The outlook for migratory songbirds: "Future shock" for birders. *Am. Birds* 43:178–183.

National Oceanic and Atmospheric Administration. 1987. *Climatological Data Annual Summary. Puerto Rico and the Virgin Islands.* Vol. 33, No. 13. Asheville, North Carolina: National Climatic Data Center.

Norton, R.L. 1979. New records of birds for the Virgin Islands. *Am. Birds* 33:145–146.

Pashley, D.N. 1988. Warblers of the West Indies. I. The Virgin Islands. *Carib. J. Sci.* 24:11–22.

Pashley, D.N., and R.P. Martin. 1988. The contribution of Christmas bird counts to knowledge of the winter distribution of migratory warblers in the tropics. *Am. Birds* 42:1164–1176.

Post, W. 1978. Social and foraging behavior of warblers wintering in Puerto Rican coastal scrub. *Wilson Bull.* 90:197–214.

Pregill, G.K., and S.L. Olson. 1981. Zoogeography of West Indian vertebrates in relation to Pleistocene climatic cycles. *Ann. Rev. Ecol. Syst.* 12:75–98.

Raffaele, H.A. 1989. *A Guide to the Birds of Puerto Rico and the Virgin Islands.* Rev. ed. Princeton: Princeton University Press.

Rappole, J.H., E.S. Morton, T.E. Lovejoy, III, and J.L. Ruos. 1983. *Nearctic Avian Migrants in the Neotropics.* Washington: U.S. Fish and Wildlife Service.

Robbins, C.S., D.K. Dawson, and B.A. Dowell. 1989. *Habitat Area Requirements of Breeding Forest Birds of the Middle Atlantic States.* Wildl. Monogr. 103.

Robbins, C.S., B.A. Dowell, D.K. Dawson, J. Colón, F. Espinoza, J. Rodriguez, R. Sutton, and T. Vargas. 1987. Comparison of Neotropical winter bird populations in isolated patches versus extensive forest. *Acta Oecol.: Oecol. Gen.* 8:285–292.

Robertson, W.B, Jr. 1962. Observations on the birds of St. John, Virgin Islands. *Auk* 79:44–76.

Rogers, C.S., and R. Teytaud. 1988. *Marine and Terrestrial Ecosystems of the Virgin Islands National Park and Biosphere Reserve.* Biosphere Report No. 29, U.S. National Park Service and Island Resources Foundation, St. Thomas, U.S. Virgin Islands.

Smith, N.G. 1975. "Spshing" noise; Biological significance of its attraction and nonattraction by birds. *Proc. Nat. Acad. Sci.* 72:1411–1414.

Snedecor, G.W., and W.G. Cochran. 1967. *Statistical Methods.* 6th ed. Ames: Iowa State University Press.

SPSS Inc. 1986. *SPSS User's Guide.* 2d ed. New York: McGraw-Hill.

Terborgh, J.W. 1980. The conservation status of neotropical migrants: Present and future. Pages 21–30 in *Migrant Birds in the Neotropics: Ecology, Behavior, Distribution and Conservation*, A. Keast and E.S. Morton, eds. Washington: Smithsonian Institution Press.

Terborgh, J.W., and J.R. Faaborg. 1980. Factors affecting the distribution and abundance of North American migrants in the eastern Caribbean region. Pages 145–155 in *Migrant Birds in the Neotropics: Ecology, Behavior, Distribution and Conservation*, A. Keast and E.S. Morton, eds. Washington: Smithsonian Institution Press.

Tyson, G.F., Jr. 1987. *Historic Land Use in the Reef Bay, Fish Bay and Hawknest Bay Watersheds, St. John, U.S. Virgin Islands: 1718–1950.* Biosphere Reserve Research Report No. 19, VIRMC/NPS.

Waide, R.B. 1980. Resource partitioning between migrant and resident birds: The use of irregular resources. Pages 337–352 in *Migrant Birds in the Neotropics: Ecology, Behavior, Distribution and Conservation*, A. Keast and E.S. Morton, eds. Washington: Smithsonian Institution Press.

Waide, R.B., J.T. Emlen, and E.J. Tramer. 1980. Distribution of migrant birds in the Yucatan Peninsula: A survey. Pages 165–171 in *Migrant Birds in the Neotropics: Ecology, Behavior, Distribution and Conservation*, A. Keast and E.S. Morton, eds. Washington: Smithsonian Institution Press.

Woodbury, R.0., and P.L. Weaver. 1987. *The Vegetation of St. John and Hassel Island, U.S. Virgin Islands.* U.S. National Park Service Research/Resources Management Report SER-83, Southeast Regional Office, Atlanta, Georgia.

CHANDLER S. ROBBINS
BARBARA A. DOWELL
DEANNA K. DAWSON
Patuxent Wildlife Research Center
Laurel, Maryland 20708

JOSÉ A. COLÓN
Box 5887
Puerta de Tierra, Puerto Rico 00906

ROSAMOND ESTRADA
Apdo. Postal 176
San Andres Tuxtla, Veracruz 02975, Mexico

ANN SUTTON
ROBERT SUTTON
P.O. Box 58
Mandeville, Jamaica

DORA WEYER
Rt. 8, Box 218A
Fayetteville, Arkansas 72701

Comparison of Neotropical migrant landbird populations wintering in tropical forest, isolated forest fragments, and agricultural habitats

Abstract. Neotropical migrant bird populations were sampled at 76 sites in seven countries by using mist nets and point counts during a six-winter study. Populations in major agricultural habitats were compared with those in extensive forest and isolated forest fragments. Certain Neotropical migrants, such as the Northern Parula, American Redstart, and the Black-throated Blue, Magnolia, Black-and-white, and Hooded warblers, were present in arboreal agricultural habitats such as pine, cacao, citrus, and shade coffee plantations in relatively large numbers. Many north temperate zone shrub-nesting species, such as the Gray Catbird, White-eyed Vireo, Tennessee Warbler, Common Yellowthroat, and Indigo Bunting, also used agricultural habitats in winter, as did resident hummingbirds and migrant orioles. Ground-foraging migrants, such as thrushes and Kentucky Warblers, were rarely found in the agricultural habitats sampled. Although many Neotropical migrants use some croplands, this use might be severely limited by overgrazing by cattle, by intensive management (such as removal of ground cover in an orchard), or by heavy use of insecticides, herbicides, or fungicides.

Sinopsis. Se mostrearon poblaciones de aves terrestres neotropicales migratorias en 76 sitios de siete países usando redes de niebla y conteos puntuales durante un estudio de seis inviernos. Las poblaciones de habitats agrícolas principales se compararon con aquellas de bosques extensos y de fragmentos forestales aislados. Ciertas migratorias neotropicales, como *Parula americana, Setophaga ruticilla, Dendroica caerulescens, D. magnolia, Mniotilta varia* y *Wilsonia citrina*, estuvieron presentes en números relativamente grandes en habitats agrícolas arbóreos tales como plantaciones de pinos, cacao, cítricos y cafetales de sombrío. Muchas especies de la zona templada del norte anidantes en arbustos, como *Dumetella carolinensis, Vireo griseus, Vermi-*

vora peregrina, Geothlypis trichas y *Passerina cyanea,* igualmente usaron habitats agrícolas en invierno, como también lo hicieron los colibrís residentes y los *Icterus* migratorios. Migratorias que se alimentan en el piso, como los *Catharus* spp. y *Oporornis formosus,* se encontraron raramente en los habitats agrícolas mostreados. Aunque muchas migratorias neotropicales usan algunas tierras de cultivo, este uso podría estar seriamente limitado por el sobrepastoreo de ganado, el manejo intensivo (como por ejemplo la remoción de cobertura del suelo en una arboleda) o por el uso masivo de insecticidas, herbicidas o fungicidas.

In January 1984, the U.S. Fish and Wildlife Service (USFWS) began a cooperative study of use of tropical forest habitats by migratory songbirds during the northern winter. This study was prompted by concern that tropical deforestation was causing population declines in some species of northern songbirds that winter in the Neotropics. The Food and Agriculture Organization of the United Nations (1986) has reported the number of hectares of forested land in each nation in 1974–1976 and in 1984. In Mexico, for example, forested land declined 10.7% (from 51,150,000 to 45,700,000 ha); in Guatemala, 14.3% (4,933,000 to 4,230,000 ha); in Honduras, 16.3% (4,470,000 to 3,740,000 ha); in Nicaragua, 20.0% (5,050,000 to 4,040,000 ha); in Costa Rica, 29.1% (2,200,000 to 1,560,000 ha); but in Cuba an increase of 5.5% was reported (1,838,000 to 1,940,000 ha). The concern over tropical deforestation presented an opportunity to establish long-term cooperative studies in the tropics as a followup to month-long migratory bird workshops conducted for Latin American biologists under auspices of the USFWS Office of International Affairs. After four winters of comparing bird populations in isolated or fragmented tropical forests with those in nearby extensive undisturbed forest, the emphasis changed to evaluating the use of various agricultural habitats by wintering passerine migrants. With the rapid conversion of native tropical forest to cropland and pasture, it became increasingly important to know which species were able to use habitats to which forests were being converted. Little information had been available on use of agricultural habitats by either Neotropical migrants or resident species.

We conducted field work in Venezuela, Costa Rica, Belize, Mexico, Jamaica, Dominican Republic, and Puerto Rico. We placed the greatest emphasis on the Greater Antilles, Mexico, and Belize, because we found that the proportion of North American migrants was highest in these countries. Terborgh (1989: 77–78) presents a summary of the proportion of North American migrants at 76 sites in the Neotropics.

Focusing on those countries for which we have data on agricultural habitats, extensive forest, and forest fragments permits a three-way comparison. This allows us to assess habitat use in the original forest and the effects of forest fragmentation and of conversion to agriculture.

Methods

During midwinter (January and February) of 1984–1987, we used mist nets and point counts to sample bird populations in 16 pairs of tropical study sites in mature extensive forest (> 1,000 ha) and in small isolated patches (5–50 ha) of similar forest. Most sites were studied in only one or two winters, but one pair of sites in Jamaica was studied in three consecutive winters. During the winters of 1987–1989, we conducted similar counts at 32 sites in seven different agricultural habitats to learn which species could use various manmade habitats and which could not. We compare the habitat distributions of common migratory forest species based on the first year of netting and census results at these 64 sites. We also make some reference to data from 12 other sites, including early successional habitats, pastures, and crops such as cashew (*Anacardium occidentale*) and commercial banana (*Musa* sp.) that were used by very few birds.

SELECTION OF STUDY SITES. Finding extensive tracts of undisturbed tropical forest accessible from all-weather roads was seldom easy. The majority of extensive tracts that we used were in national parks or preserves. Small isolated tracts also were a challenge to locate. In some instances we could make a random selection. More frequently it was a matter of selecting the one candidate site that was the best match in terms of proximity (generally < 5 km), elevation (< 100 m difference), vegetation, and isolation from neighboring woodland. Other constraints were the size range of 5–50 ha, satisfactory shape (avoiding long, narrow tracts), uniformity, lack of present disturbance, accessibility, and ability to obtain landowner permission.

With early successional habitats, and with some of the agricultural habitats, it was possible to make a random selection from among candidate sites. Starting in 1989, candidate sites were selected from satellite imagery when available. Then, study sites were selected from the largest accessible uniform areas of habitat as identified on the imagery. These sites were then ground-truthed for uniformity, shape, size, proximity of edge, and disturbance.

NETTING OPERATIONS. Our chief method of determining bird use of different habitats was through the use of mist nets. Unbaited nets were erected at the same height in all habitats, and caught birds flying within 2 m of the ground. In most agricultural habitats, 16 nets could be placed systematically in a grid. In national parks, preserves, and other places where cutting vegetation was not permitted and on very steep slopes, nets had to be placed along existing trails. We used 12-m, 4-shelf nets, with 36 mm (75%), and 30 mm (25%) mesh. Nets were generally operated for three days per site, from shortly before sunrise until about sunset, but were closed whenever heavy rain or high winds occurred. Furthermore, nets that became exposed to full sunlight were closed temporarily when the safety of birds was in question. Net hours were recorded. Birds captured were banded, aged and sexed, and wing chord, fat, weight, time of day, and net and shelf number recorded.

In January and February, the number of new birds per 100 net hours declined rapidly with each day of netting. About 73% of the birds captured in five days of netting were caught in the first two days, and 86% by the third day. Therefore, we use the number of birds captured in three days as our netting standard for habitat comparisons rather than the number of birds per 100 net hours.

POINT COUNTS. At each site two (occasionally three) 5-min point counts were made at each of 10 flagged locations spaced at least 100 m apart throughout the netting area. Separate counts were made of birds observed within 30 m and beyond 30 m. Activity and estimated height above ground were recorded for each bird seen. Residents as well as migrants were counted. The method is similar to that used by Hutto et al. (1986).

VEGETATION SAMPLING. In forested sites, we modified the method of James and Shugart (1970); our circles (three or more randomly selected at each site) each had an area of 0.02 ha, instead of 0.04, because of the very dense foliage. We also took four density board readings (Noon 1981) and 20 vertical foliage sightings (Schemske and Brokaw 1981) in each circle. Where possible, a resident botanist identified the tree species. In arboreal agricultural habitats such as coffee and citrus plantations, we used rectangular vegetation plots, 20 × 20 m. The vegetation data for pairs of extensive forest and forest fragment sites were compared initially to assure that the sites were structurally comparable. More detailed analyses are planned for relating habitat descriptions to satellite imagery.

Results

In prior studies in the tropics, we banded 2,766 birds in 10,358 net hours in forest fragments, and 2,913 in 10,704 net hours in extensive forest (Robbins et al. 1987 and in press). In the agricultural habitats summarized

here, we banded 5,008 birds in 11,989 net hours.

In cropland habitats there were 14 Neotropical migrant species for which captures exceeded 40 individuals. To show the range of croplands used by these common migrants, their mean 3-day banding totals for the major agricultural habitats are shown in Table 1. Of 5,008 birds banded at the 32 sites summarized in Table 1, 1,250 (25%) were North American migrants.

Table 1 includes the major habitats for which at least three sites were sampled; the rice field was also included because of the large number of birds captured in that habitat. The first four columns of the table show West Indian habitats. Birds that winter primarily in the West Indies (e.g., Black-throated Blue Warbler) would be largely restricted to these columns, regardless of habitat requirements. Similarly, catbirds, orioles, and some of the warblers would be restricted to the Central American columns on the right. The citrus and cacao plantations stand out as supporting a wide variety of Neotropical migrants, as well as relatively high abundance.

A comparison of banding totals and point count totals for the species most commonly detected in agricultural habitats is presented in Table 2. Data represent the habitat and country in which the largest numbers were banded or counted. When the highest point count was from a different habitat, the second habitat is also listed. For most species the banding results yielded much larger counts than did the point counts (Table 2), so banding totals form the primary basis for comparison of habitat use. The point count totals tended to confirm the same habitats as being important, although not necessarily in the same sequence of relative abundance as suggested by the banding data. The chief values of the point counts were to reveal the presence of birds that were feeding above the 2-m height of nets, to detect large species such as raptors, jays, and toucans, that were not readily captured in nets, and to provide additional comparisons of relative abundance of common species. Except for the Blue-gray Gnatcatcher, which was slim enough to slip through the nets without being captured, the Gray Catbird and Northern Rough-winged Swallow were the only common passerines in agricultural habitats to be detected in larger numbers on point counts than by netting.

Agricultural habitats varied greatly in amount of bird use (Fig. 1). Even plantations of the same crop in the same geographic location varied greatly in bird species composition, probably as a function of age of crop, blooming or fruiting condition, time of season when birds were sampled, type and proximity of nearby habitats, and management practices, including type and density of ground cover, pruning regime, and use of chemicals. Much more work will be required to evaluate these various influences.

The percentage of migrants, as estimated from the

TABLE 1. Mean 3-day banding totals, rounded to nearest whole number, of Neotropical migrants by habitat (number of sites in parentheses)

Species	Puerto Rico		Jamaica		Belize					Costa Rica
	Shade (3)	Sun (3)	Coffee (3)	Citrus (3)	Citrus (5)	Cacao (4)	Mango (3)	Rice (1)	Pine (4)	Citrus (3)
Gray Catbird	–	–	–	–	7	4	+	1	8	–
Tennessee Warbler	–	–	+	–	6	10	–	–	–	3
Northern Parula	3	4	+	2	1	2	–	–	–	–
Magnolia Warbler	–	–	+	1	6	11	4	–	3	+
Black-thr. Blue Warbler	6	1	7	1	–	–	–	–	–	–
Black-and-white Warbler	4	2	2	3	12	12	5	–	3	1
American Redstart	2	+	2	2	8	9	2	–	5	+
Ovenbird	1	1	5	8	2	4	+	–	4	4
Northern Waterthrush	+	–	–	1	2	6	–	3	–	3
Common Yellowthroat	–	–	2	3	3	1	+	21	2	–
Hooded Warbler	–	–	–	–	1	3	1	–	5	+
Indigo Bunting	–	+	+	1	10	5	–	98	–	–
Orchard Oriole	–	–	–	–	7	3	–	2	–	–
Northern Oriole	–	–	–	–	6	4	–	–	–	1
Total banded	564	467	389	1014	787	1022	50	303	226	186
Total North American	55	27	93	97	316	300	41	127	146	48
% North American	10	6	24	10	40	29	82	42	65	26
Total net hours	1431	1461	1656	1542	1543	1609	1268	229	1944	1234
Migrant species	9	8	15	15	30	25	9	7	15	16
Total species	26	31	36	47	81	64	14	15	36	39

NOTE: + = present but < 0.5. Scientific names given in Table 2.

TABLE 2. Comparison of banding and point count totals in major agricultural habitats used by common migrants

Species	Mean number		Habitat	Country
	Banded[a]	Pt. count[b]		
Least Flycatcher *Empidonax minimus*	2	1	Citrus/Cacao	Belize
Northern Rough-winged Swallow *Stelgidopteryx serripennis*	0	6	Grazed pasture	Belize
Blue-gray Gnatcatcher *Polioptila caerulea*	0	1	Cacao	Belize
Gray Catbird *Dumetella carolinensis*	8	11	Pine/Citrus	Belize
Tennessee Warbler *Vermivora peregrina*	10	1	Cacao/Citrus	Belize
Northern Parula *Parula americana*	4	1	Sun coffee/Cacao	Puerto Rico
Magnolia Warbler *Dendroica magnolia*	11	6	Cacao/Citrus	Belize
Black-throated Blue Warbler *D. caerulescens*	7	1	Coffee	Jamaica
Prairie Warbler *D. discolor*	5	+	Coffee	Jamaica
Black-and-white Warbler *Mniotilta varia*	12	3	Citrus/Cacao	Belize
American Redstart *Setophaga ruticilla*	9	6	Cacao/Pine	Belize
Worm-eating Warbler *Helmitheros vermivorus*	3	+	Cacao	Belize
Ovenbird *Seiurus aurocapillus*	8	+	Citrus	Jamaica
Northern Waterthrush *S. noveboracensis*	6	1	Cacao	Belize
Common Yellowthroat *Geothlypis trichas*	21	7	Rice/Citrus	Belize
Hooded Warbler *Wilsonia citrina*	5	1	Pine	Belize
Indigo Bunting *Passerina cyanea*	98	6	Rice/Grazed pasture	Belize
Orchard Oriole *Icterus spurius*	7	+	Citrus	Belize
Northern Oriole *I. galbula*	6	2	Citrus	Belize

a. Mean of the 3-day banding totals for the stated habitat and country.
b. Mean of the highest totals for 10 point count positions in the stated habitat and country.

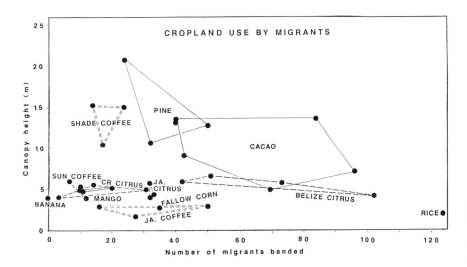

FIGURE 1. Number of migrant songbirds banded in three days of mist netting in agricultural habitats as a function of canopy height.

banding totals for each habitat, also varied within and among habitats as well as among countries (Table 3). We have assumed that relative vulnerability to capture of migrants and residents remained constant among habitats, but this may not have been true in fallow rice (*Oryza sativa*). The number of individuals of migrant birds captured in fallow rice far exceeded that in any other habitat even though the number of migratory species in rice was the second lowest of any habitat sampled. The actual number of migrants present was much larger than the 127 birds banded. The banders caught so many birds in the rice field that some nets were never set; furthermore, dozens of Indigo Buntings that came to roost at dusk were released unbanded so the nets could be closed before the arrival of bats.

The highest percentage of migrant individuals was in mango (*Mangifera indica*) plantations, but this was the poorest habitat in total number of birds captured. The two most productive agricultural habitats for Neotropical migrants, in both number of species and number of individuals (excluding fallow rice), were citrus (*Citrus* spp.) groves and cacao (*Theobroma cacao*) plantations. For comparison with the use of agricultural habitats by migrants (Table 3), the average use of native forest habitats, both in extensive forest and forest fragments, is summarized by country in Table 4. When individual species are not considered, but only percent of migrants in a population, use of forest fragments compared favorably with extensive forest. The percentage of migrants was especially high in Belize forests (52% and 55%), far

TABLE 3. Mean number of birds captured, percent of migrants, and number of migrant species in agricultural habitats, arranged by decreasing number of migrant species

Habitat	Country	Mean birds captured		Percent migrants	Migrant species
		All species	Migrants		
Citrus	Belize	157	63	40	30
Cacao	Belize	256	75	29	25
Hurricane Coffee[a]	Jamaica	130	31	24	15
Citrus	Costa Rica	62	16	26	16
Citrus	Jamaica	338	32	10	15
Planted pine	Belize	56	36	65	15
Mango	Belize	17	14	82	9
Cashew	Belize	30	10	33	9
Shade Coffee	Puerto Rico	188	18	10	9
Sun Coffee	Puerto Rico	156	9	6	8
Rice	Belize	303	127	42	7
Fallow corn	Belize	117	33	28	6

a. Former shade coffee whose shade trees were destroyed by hurricane.

TABLE 4. Percent of migrant birds in native forest habitats based on banding totals

Country and habitat	Number of sites	Total banded	Total migrants	Percent migrants
Venezuela E	2	311	4	1
Venezuela F	2	207	7	3
Costa Rica E	2	213	3	1
Costa Rica F	2	165	10	6
Belize E	2	348	182	52
Belize F	2	238	132	55
Mexico E	2	187	22	12
Mexico F	2	244	75	31
Jamaica E	4	458	75	16
Jamaica F	4	584	90	15
Dominican Republic E	2	254	62	24
Dominican Republic F	2	233	45	19
Puerto Rico E	4	414	135	33
Puerto Rico F	4	351	101	29

NOTE: E = Extensive forest; F = Forest fragment < 50 ha.

TABLE 5. Comparison of agricultural habitats with native extensive forest, by country, based on banding totals

Country	Native forest		Agricultural habitats	
	Total migrants	Percent migrants	Total migrants	Percent migrants
Costa Rica	3	1	48	26
Belize	243	42	930	39
Mexico	22	12	—	—
Jamaica	75	16	190	14
Dominican Republic	62	24	—	—
Puerto Rico	135	33	83	8
TOTAL	540	25.6	1251	16.8

exceeding the percentage found in any agricultural habitat sampled. As has been noted by other investigators (Rappole et al. 1983, Terborgh 1989), the percentage of Neotropical migrants in tropical forests was much lower in Venezuela and Costa Rica than in Belize, Mexico, and the Greater Antilles.

When percentage of migrants (total individuals) is computed for each country for all native forest habitats and all agricultural habitats studied (Table 5), the percentage of migrants using agricultural habitats in Belize compares favorably with the percentage using native forest. A further comparison, summarizing the number of migrant and resident species (rather than individuals) netted in each habitat is presented in Appendix 1. The number of species with which migrants

must compete for resources in just the lower two meters of some wintering habitats is truly impressive, reaching 70 or more species.

In Puerto Rico the percentage of migrants in agricultural habitats was low because coffee was the only agricultural habitat sampled there. The total numbers of migrants in Table 4 cannot be compared between native forest and agricultural habitats because the number of sites differed. Also, because Table 4 includes only matched extensive forest sites and fragments, the total number of migrants there was fewer than the number in Table 5. The total number of Neotropical migrants captured in the 32 agricultural sites was 1,250, as compared with 537 found in 16 extensive forest sites.

Habitat use by six species of north temperate zone

FIGURE 2. Relative abundance of the Northern Parula, *Parula americana*, a habitat generalist, in the winter habitats in which it was captured in largest numbers. Here and in the figures to follow, extensive mature forest habitats are shown at the center of each graph, in decreasing importance from left to right. When a habitat is listed as "Tie" in the last position at the right, two or more habitats in third place had the same small number of individuals. Forest data are available for all countries, but we have agricultural data for the same region only for Belize, Jamaica, and Puerto Rico. See Robbins et al. 1987 and in press for details of the forest habitats.

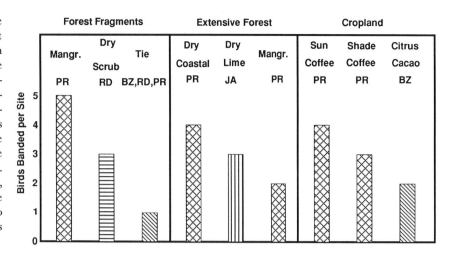

FIGURE 3. Relative abundance of the Black-throated Blue Warbler, *Dendroica caerulescens*, a habitat generalist, in the winter habitats in which the largest numbers were captured.

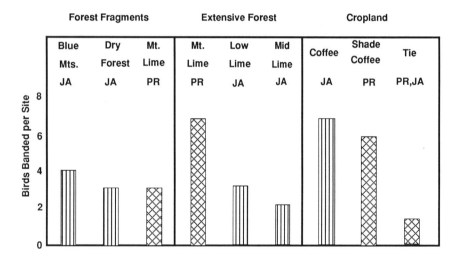

forest-breeding birds that winter in several agricultural habitats as well as extensive forest and forest fragments is summarized in Figures 2–7. We discuss each of these six species briefly, and then we discuss winter habitat use by some typical ground-feeding and brush-nesting species.

Data from the 64 sites were condensed as follows: (1) data from similar agricultural sites in the same country were combined into a single mean; (2) when a site was visited in multiple years only the data from the first year were used; and (3) within each category (extensive forest, isolated forest patches, and agricultural sites), only the three habitats in which a species was most common are included on the graphs.

SPECIES ACCOUNTS

The Northern Parula (Fig. 2) (see Table 2 for scientific names), which Raffaele (1989) calls the "most common wintering warbler" in Puerto Rico and the Virgin Islands, was as common in cropland as in native forest, and was the only warbler regularly captured in sun coffee plantations.

The Black-throated Blue Warbler (Fig. 3), a typical West Indian wintering species, was frequently captured in shade coffee plantations in Puerto Rico and in hurricane-damaged coffee plantations in Jamaica, but averaged no more than one bird per site in other agricultural habitats.

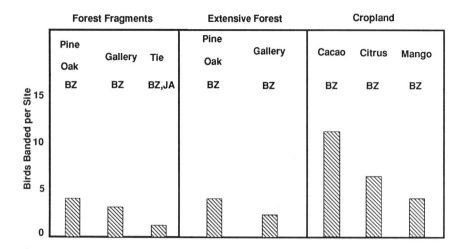

FIGURE 4. Relative abundance of the Magnolia Warbler, *Dendroica magnolia*, a habitat generalist, in the winter habitats in which the largest numbers were captured.

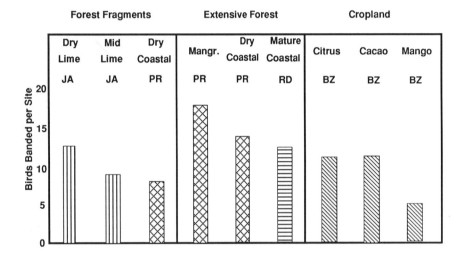

FIGURE 5. Relative abundance of the Black-and-white Warbler, *Mniotilta varia*, a habitat generalist, in the winter habitats in which the largest numbers were captured.

The Magnolia Warbler (Fig. 4) is an example of a species that apparently has adapted to orchard habitats (cacao, citrus, and mango). It was found in all arboreal agricultural habitats we sampled within its winter range.

The Black-and-white Warbler (Fig. 5) is a widely distributed species that was encountered in almost all of our study sites. It was not only widespread geographically, but in most agricultural habitats it was among the three most common species captured, and was the most common migrant encountered during the study.

The American Redstart (Fig. 6) is an example of a warbler that is widely distributed geographically and uses a wide variety of agricultural habitats. In addition to the cacao, citrus, and pine plantations shown here,

smaller numbers were found in mango and in both shade and sun coffee plots.

The Hooded Warbler (Fig. 7), on the other hand, was more restricted both geographically and ecologically. It was found regularly in pine plantations, and in cacao, but was scarce or absent in other agricultural habitats.

Species that feed on the forest floor, such as the Ovenbird and especially waterthrushes and thrushes, appear to be less adaptable to habitat change, based on our results. The Ovenbird, a very common and widespread species, was found in small numbers in many agricultural habitats. The Northern Waterthrush (Fig. 8) is a mangrove and floodplain specialist and was rarely found in cropland, not even the extensive rice field.

The Wood Thrush (*Hylocichla mustelina*, Fig. 9) is a

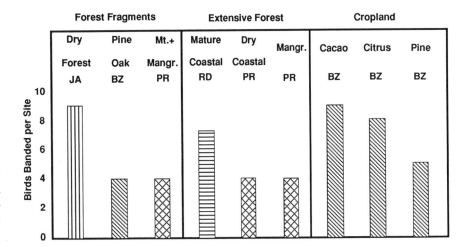

FIGURE 6. Relative abundance of the America Redstart, *Setophaga ruticilla*, a habitat generalist, in the winter habitats in which the largest numbers were captured.

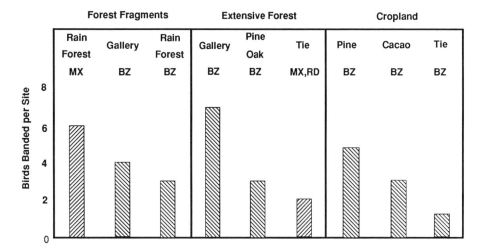

FIGURE 7. Relative abundance of the Hooded Warbler, *Wilsonia citrina*, a habitat generalist, in the winter habitats in which the largest numbers were captured.

mature forest specialist that was almost never recorded in agricultural habitats. The Gray-cheeked Thrush (*Catharus minimus*) was never encountered in winter anywhere except in extensive forest.

The Kentucky Warbler (*Oporornis formosus*, Fig. 10) is another ground forager that requires forest. Some were found in early successional habitats, but only an occasional bird was captured in pine woods or agricultural habitats.

Scrub-nesting species of the north temperate zone tended to be common in one forest habitat, but much scarcer in a variety of other habitats, including agricultural habitats. The Gray Catbird (Fig. 11), for example, showed a strong preference for gallery forest in the tropics, but also used arboreal cropland (pine, citrus, ca-

cao). The White-eyed Vireo (*Vireo griseus*, Fig. 12) required a dense understory, and was fairly common in pine-oak savanna; however, no more than one individual was found in any cropland habitat. The Prairie Warbler (Fig. 13) was encountered most commonly in dry limestone forest in Jamaica, but averaged only two or three individuals in other habitats, including agricultural habitats. The Common Yellowthroat (not figured) was, by far, most common in the rice plantation, with citrus plots the second most common habitat choice.

Nectar feeders, especially migratory orioles and resident hummingbirds, were common or abundant in citrus and cacao plantations, far exceeding their abundance in forested habitats. And finally, the Indigo Bunting was a rice-field specialist in our study. Its num-

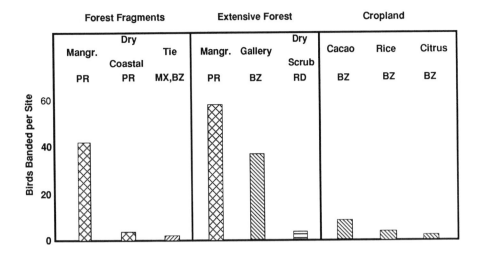

FIGURE 8. Relative abundance of the Northern Waterthrush, *Seiurus noveboracensis*, a ground feeder, in the winter habitats in which the largest numbers were captured.

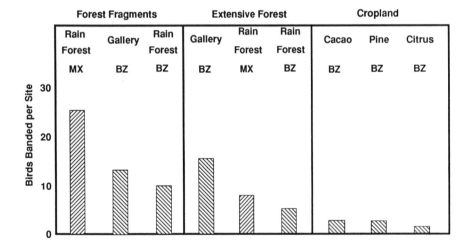

FIGURE 9. Relative abundance of the Wood Thrush, *Hylocichla mustelina*, a ground feeder, in the winter habitats in which the largest numbers were captured.

bers in a fallow rice field (98 banded) far exceeded the abundance of any other migratory species found in any habitat. Crease (1989) reported netting 682 Indigo Buntings in February-March 1989 at the Big Falls Rice Farm in Belize, but commented: "The numbers at BFF are unquestionably down now that rice production has ceased and so much of the farm is overgrown. It seems likely that only 50% of the total of ca. 2000 birds estimated to be using the area in 1986 (Triggs 1987) now find sufficient food to sustain them there throughout the northern winter."

We did not conduct netting in pasture habitats, so direct comparisons with other habitats cannot be made. Point counts in pastures, however, confirmed our gener-

al observations that closely cropped pastures contained very few birds. On the other hand, hedgerows adjacent to pastures or along roadsides often were used by migrants. Many migrants were seen in banana plants growing in small patches or scattered throughout other habitats; but when a large commercial banana plantation was examined, no arthropods could be found in the litter, and no birds were seen. Clearly more work needs to be done to evaluate bird use of these habitats.

Our results indicate that some Neotropical migrant species appear to be restricted to forested habitats in the tropics, whereas other species are present in early successional and agricultural habitats as well as in forests. They also show that some agricultural habitats

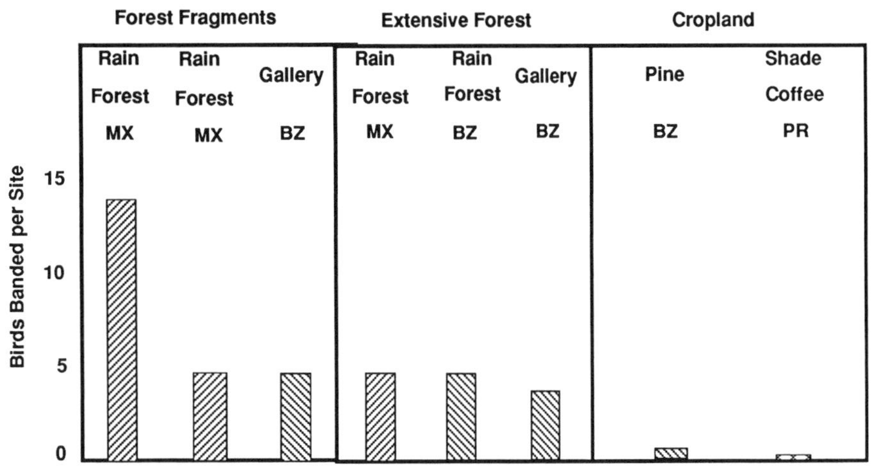

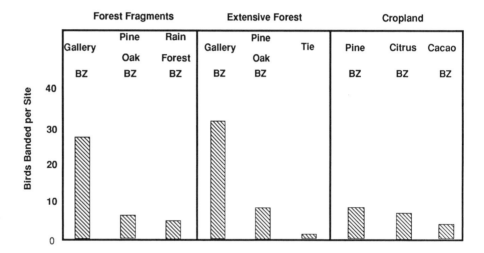

FIGURE 10. Relative abundance of the Kentucky Warbler, *Oporornis formosus,* a ground feeder, in the winter habitats in which the largest numbers were captured.

FIGURE 11. Relative abundance of the Gray Catbird, *Dumetella carolinensis,* a brush nester, in the winter habitats in which the largest numbers were captured.

contain a wide variety of migrant species, but that others support very few birds.

Discussion

This study was originally designed to assess the occurrence of Neotropical migrants in extensive and fragmented native tropical forests. When we found that many species of migrants were also using some of the agricultural habitats during the mid-winter season, we began sampling bird populations in major agricultural habitats also, while continuing to sample in nearby woodlands.

It became apparent early in the study that many

Neotropical migrant species were using isolated forest fragments during the northern winter, and that their density in these fragments was comparable with that in extensive forest. Furthermore, in isolated forest fragments, as well as in extensive forest, we found a high return rate (up to 50%) for banded migrants in successive years, indicating that birds were surviving and returning to established territories (Robbins et al. 1987). On the other hand, some species of migrants (especially thrushes and Louisiana Waterthrushes, *Seiurus motacilla*) and many resident species (especially suboscines) were not found in isolated forest patches.

When bird populations in agricultural habitats are compared with those in woodland from which the crop-

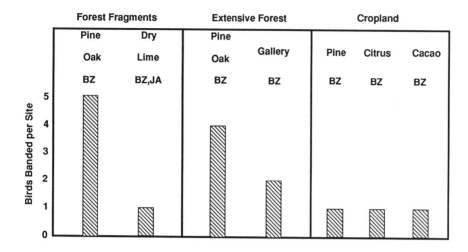

FIGURE 12. Relative abundance of the White-eyed Vireo, *Vireo griseus,* a brush nester, in the winter habitats in which the largest numbers were captured.

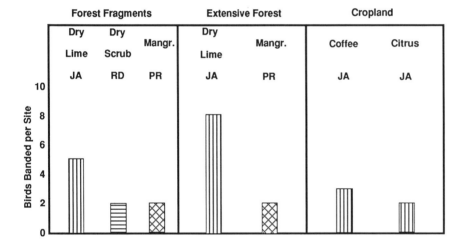

FIGURE 13. Relative abundance of the Prairie Warbler, *Dendroica discolor,* a brush nester, in the winter habitats in which the largest numbers were captured.

land was carved, the differences are more striking, as would be expected. The number of species captured in rice and fallow corn fields was very small, even though the total number of individuals was fairly high (Table 3). With shrub and tree crops, the bird species composition and density varied greatly depending on the crop. In general, a high avian diversity was associated with a high plant diversity; the outstanding exception was mature citrus groves, which supported a high avian diversity and density.

It is important to consider that 2-m-high mist nets come much closer to sampling the whole bird population in agricultural habitats than in mature forest with a high canopy. Direct comparisons can be made between extensive forest and isolated forest fragments because each pair of sites was selected for comparability, but point counts confirmed that few canopy-feeding forest species were captured in the nets. Therefore, although use of agricultural habitats might be compared among structurally similar crop habitats, netting efficiency is much higher in low-stature habitats than in high-canopy forest.

Cacao (under a canopy of *Erythrina*) and shade coffee plantations came closest to matching bird populations of native broadleaf forest, but ground-feeding birds such as thrushes and the Kentucky Warbler were scarce or absent in these agricultural habitats. Pine plantations were used by many species, a high percentage of which were migrants, but avian densities there were always low.

Mature citrus groves were especially attractive to Neotropical migrants (Tables 1–3), and avian densities were high, except in Costa Rica which is too far south to have a high density of migrants. The number of resident species found in citrus groves was low, suggesting that citrus might not provide desirable nesting habitat for many tropical species.

So far, only one agricultural study site (a cacao plantation) has been sampled in two winters, so we do not yet know how regularly migrants are using these agricultural habitats throughout the winter, or returning in subsequent years. Neither do we know whether these habitats fulfill all the needs of these birds during the winter season, or whether some of the birds spend part of their time in neighboring habitats. Furthermore, we have not been able to evaluate effects of fungicides, herbicides, and other chemicals that are used in croplands.

Thus, this rather optimistic report on the occurrence of many migrant species in a variety of agricultural habitats in the tropics must be tempered until we have more information on the extent to which various cropland habitats fulfill the requirements of birds using them. These habitats cannot serve as a haven for either migrants or resident species if toxic pesticides threaten the birds' condition directly, or indirectly through their food supply.

If we are to prevent the further loss of birds, we must not only conserve forest habitats, but we must also find ways to assure that agricultural habitats provide safe and productive alternatives for migratory birds. Other recommendations would be to encourage the retention of corridors of native vegetation, especially along streams, and to promote intercropping rather than extensive monocultures.

Acknowledgments

We thank our many Latin American and Caribbean colleagues who helped with logistics and with location of study sites, and who worked long days with us in the field. In particular, we acknowledge the collaboration of Tomas Vargas in the Dominican Republic and Kathleen Anderson in Belize; they both proved to be indispensable in many aspects of the study. We thank Brian Johns of the Canadian Wildlife Service, and the following volunteers from the United States, who assisted with the field work one or more years: Steve Baird, Marty Barron, Dan Boone, Margaret and Morrill Donnald, Walter Ellison, Andy Hicks, Linda Hollenberg, David Holmes, Doug Inkley, David Johnston, José Laborde, Bob Leberman, Wendy Lee, Henry Louie, Bob Lyon, Nancy Martin, Bruce Miller, Carolyn Miller, Bob Mulvihill, Dan Niven, Charlotte Pryor, Chris Rimmer, David Rimmer, Jane Robbins, Barbara Ross, John Sauer, Ed Smith, Susan Strange, Max Thompson, Rick West, and Eugene Young. The Dorothy Blake Martin Fund of the Maryland Ornithological Society covered field expenses for several of the volunteers, and the late Jonnie Fisk and the Vermont Institute of Natural Science helped with expenses for some of the others. We also thank the many volunteers from the host countries. In addition, we thank the many government officials who facilitated the field work, and the land owners who graciously granted permission for us to work on their properties. The Office of International Affairs (USFWS) sponsored the research for the first three winters. We appreciate the constructive criticisms of John Sauer, Matthew Perry, R. Michael Erwin, Sarah E. Mabey, and an anonymous reviewer.

Literature cited

Crease, A.J. 1989. Exercize King Vulture III, the British Army Bird Watching Society expedition to Belize February–March 1989. Unpubl. Rept.

Food and Agricultural Organization. 1986. *1985 FAO Production Yearbook*. Vol. 39, FAO Statistics Series No. 70. Rome: FAO.

Hutto, R.L., S.M. Pletschet, and P. Hendricks. 1986. A fixed-radius point count method for nonbreeding and breeding season use. *Auk* 103:593–602.

James, F.C., and H.H. Shugart, Jr. 1970. A quantitative method of habitat description. *Aud. Field Notes* 24(6): 727–736.

Noon, B.R. 1981. Techniques for sampling avian habitats. Pages 42–52 in *The use of multivariate statistics in studies of wildlife habitat*, D.E. Capen, ed. USDA For. Serv. Gen. Tech. Rep. RM-87.

Raffaele, H.A. 1989. *A Guide to the Birds of Puerto Rico and the Virgin Islands*. Rev. ed. Princeton: Princeton University Press.

Rappole, J.H., E.S. Morton, T.E. Lovejoy, III, and J.L. Ruos. 1983. *Nearctic Avian Migrants in the Neotropics*. Washington: U.S. Fish and Wildlife Service.

Robbins, C.S., B.A. Dowell, D.K. Dawson, J. Colón, F. Espinoza, J. Rodriguez, R. Sutton, and T. Vargas. 1987. Comparison of Neotropical winter bird populations in isolated patches versus extensive forest. *Acta Oecol.: Oecol. Gen.* 8:285–292.

Robbins, C.S., B.A. Dowell, D.K. Dawson, R. Coates-Estrada, J. Colón, F. Espinoza, J. Rodriguez, R. Sutton, T. Vargas, and D. Weyer. In press. Comparaciones de populaciones invernales de aves en los bosques extensos neotropicales contra fragmentos aislados. *Proc. 3d Neotrop. Congr. Ornithol.* Cali, Colombia.

Schemske, D.W., and N. Brokaw. 1981. Treefalls and the distribution of understory birds in a tropical forest. *Ecology* 62:938–945.

Terborgh, J. 1989. *Where Have All the Birds Gone?* Princeton: Princeton University Press.

Triggs, P. 1987. The Royal Air Force Kinloss Expedition to Belize, March 1987. *RAFOS [Royal Air Force Ornith. Soc.] Newsletter* 45:3–7.

APPENDIX 1. Numbers of migrant and resident species netted in study sites, by habitat

Country and habitat	Year	Number of migrant species	Number of resident species
Puerto Rico, USA			
Mangrove swamp (2 sites)	1984	9	12
Mt. serpentine forest (2)	1984	7	16
Dry coastal limestone (2)	1985	11	20
Haystack hills (2)	1987	2	10
Sun coffee (3)	1988	8	24
Shade coffee (3)	1988	9	17
Dominican Republic			
Mature coastal limestone (2)	1984	6	18
Thorn scrub (2)	1984	11	22
Jamaica			
Montane forest (2)	1986	7	21
Mid-level limestone (2)	1984	6	30
Low-level limestone (2)	1985	7	28
Arid limestone (2)	1984	9	19
Hurricane-damaged coffee (3)	1989	16	20
Citrus (3)	1989	15	32
Mexico			
Veracruz rain forest (3)	1987	17	47
Oaxaca rain forest[a] (2)	1987	16	35
Belize			
Gallery forest (2)	1987	17	47
Pine-oak savanna (2)	1987	16	35
Mature rain forest (1)	1989	3	25
Second-growth broadleaf (3)	1989	15	46
Caribbean pine (4)	1989	15	21
Citrus (3)	1988 & 1989	24	36
Fallow rice[a] (1)	1989	7	8
Fallow corn[a] (1)	1989	6	16
Mango (3)	1989	7	8
Cacao (4)	1987 & 1988	28	42
Costa Rica			
Mature rain forest (4)	1984	7	64
Citrus (3)	1989	16	23
Venezuela			
Mid-level semideciduous (2)	1985	2	27
Low-level semideciduous (2)	1985	3	31

a. Substandard netting effort in this habitat

RICHARD L. HUTTO
Division of Biological Sciences
University of Montana
Missoula, Montana 59812

Habitat distributions of migratory landbird species in western Mexico

Abstract. I conducted point counts within a variety of habitat types and geographic locations west of the Continental Divide from Sinaloa south to Chiapas, Mexico. By categorizing each of 36 sites into one of four general habitat types (tropical deciduous forest, thornforest, cloud forest, and pine-oak-fir forest), I was able to describe and compare the patterns of habitat use among resident and migratory landbirds. The relative distribution of detections across the four habitat types differed between migrants and residents, with the mean number of migratory species detections per site being greatest in the cloud forest habitat, and the mean number of resident species detections per site being greatest in the tropical deciduous forest habitat. The mean habitat breadth of migratory species was significantly greater than that of the resident species.

Patterns of habitat distribution for four migratory species and 14 resident species differed significantly between a northern group of 23 sites and a southern group of 13 sites, indicating that generalizations about habitat requirements cannot be drawn safely from data limited in geographic scope.

The relative detection rates of most species differed significantly between disturbed (second-growth) and undisturbed topical deciduous forest near Chamela, Jalisco. As a group, migrants were detected relatively more often in the disturbed than in the undisturbed habitats (33.2% vs. 29.0%), and the majority of migratory species (63%) was either restricted to, or more often detected in, the second-growth habitat. Nonetheless, the remaining migratory species were restricted to, or more abundant in, the undisturbed forest. Thus, even though the "average" migratory species might differ from the "average" resident species in the range of habitats it uses during the nonbreeding season, or in its response to habitat disturbance, those averages conceal considerable variation among species within both groups. Because of this variation, migrants as a whole do not comprise a useful management group for the purposes of planning conservation action.

Sinopsis. Yo realicé conteos puntuales en una variedad de tipos de hábitat y localidades geográficas en México al occidente de la divisoria continental desde Sinaloa hacia el sur hasta Chiapas. Asignando cada uno de los 36 sitios a una de cuatro categorías generales de habitat (bosque tropical deciduo, bosque espinoso, bosque nublado y bosque de pino-roble-abeto), pude describir y comparar los patrones de uso habitacional de las aves terrestres residentes y migratorias. La distribución relativa de las detecciones a través de los cuatro tipos de habitat difirieron entre migratorias y residentes, siendo máximo el número promedio de detecciones por sitio de especies migratorias en el habitat de bosque nublado y el de especies residentes en el habitat de bosque deciduo tropical. La amplitud promedio de habitat de las especies migratorias fue significativamente mayor que la de las especies residentes.

Los patrones de distribución habitacional de cuatro especies migratorias y 14 residentes difirieron significativamente entre un grupo norteño de 23 localidades y un grupo sureño de 13, indicando que las generalizaciones sobre los requerimientos de habitat no pueden extraerse confiadamente de datos limitados en su cobertura geográfica.

Las tasas relativas de detección de la mayoría de las especies fueron significativamente diferentes en bosques tropicales deciduos perturbados (desarrollo secundario) y no perturbados cerca a Chamela, Jalisco. Como grupo, las migratorias fueron detectadas relativamente con mayor frecuencia en los habitats perturbados que en los no perturbados (33.2% vs. 29.0%) y la mayoría de las especies migratorias (63%) estuvo restringida o al menos fue detectada con mayor frecuencia en el habitat de desarrollo secundario. No obstante, las especies migratorias restantes estuvieron restringidas o fueron mas abundantes en el bosque no perturbado. Por lo tanto, aunque la "especie migratoria promedio" podría diferir de la "especie residente promedio" en el número de habitats que utiliza por fuera de la época de cría, o en su respuesta a la perturbación de habitat, dichas interpretaciones esconden una variación considerable entre especies dentro de cada grupo. Por tal variación, las migratorias como un todo no comprenden un grupo utilizable de manejo para fines de planeación de acciones conservacionistas.

Despite a growing concern about the negative effects of tropical deforestation on migratory landbird populations (Terborgh 1980, Ambuel and Temple 1982, Lovejoy 1983, Rappole et al. 1983, Hall 1984, Robbins et al. 1989), biologists are in a poor position to verify such effects (Hutto 1988). This is because specific predictions require knowledge of both the extent of a species' habitat and geographic distribution, and the densities and mortality rates in each habitat or location (Lynch 1989).

Unfortunately, details of the geographic distribution of wintering landbirds in the Neotropics are sketchy because they have been derived primarily from published and unpublished museum collection records, which might be geographically biased. Moreover, we have virtually no information on the relative abundance of any species throughout the various parts of its range, even though information on the relative abundance of migratory landbirds in various locations and habitats in win-

ter should be integral to conservation of those species. It is only through such information that one can judge the cumulative effect of development in a particular place and habitat type. How, for example, can one evaluate the overall effect of habitat alteration in a riparian wash near Chamela, Jalisco, on Lucy's Warbler without knowing whether that is its exclusive wintering location and habitat?

Most of what we know about patterns of habitat use in winter has been derived from local studies, museum specimens, and casual field observations. The only systematic surveys of habitat use by wintering migrants throughout sizable areas are those of Hutto (1980) in western Mexico, and Lynch (1989) in the Yucatan Peninsula.

Western Mexico is probably the exclusive wintering location for the majority of western North American long-distance migratory landbirds (Barlow 1980, Fitzpatrick 1980, Hutto 1985). From an earlier study, Hutto (1980) suggested that, in western Mexico, both the absolute number and relative proportion of migratory species are greatest in the lowland habitats, and greater in disturbed than in undisturbed habitats (especially in the lowlands). In an effort to examine the same questions using a different census methodology, and to provide additional baseline data on habitat use by the migratory landbird species of western Mexico, I conducted a new series of censuses within a variety of habitats and geographic locations throughout the region. I use these new data to describe the patterns of habitat use by all landbird species that I encountered in western Mexico, and to measure the extent to which patterns of habitat use by migrants are similar to one another and distinctive relative to residents.

Methods

STUDY SITES AND HABITAT CLASSIFICATIONS. I conducted standardized bird counts in each of 36 study sites that were widely distributed west of the Continental Divide from southern Sinaloa to southern Oaxaca (Fig. 1). The location, elevation, vegetation type, and date(s) of visitation for each study site are presented in Appendix 1. Most sites were disturbed to some extent by cattle grazing or selective cutting but, with one exception, not such that overall vegetation structure was altered noticeably. Therefore, all but one site could be readily classified into one of four major habitat types: tropical deciduous forest, thornforest, cloud forest, or pine-oak-fir forest. These types correspond with the vegetation types labeled bosque espinoso, bosque tropical caducifolio y subcaducifolio, bosque mesófilo de montaña, and bosque de *Quercus* y de coníferas, respectively, of Rzedowski (1983). The exceptional site consisted of second-growth vegetation which had regenerated following the aban-

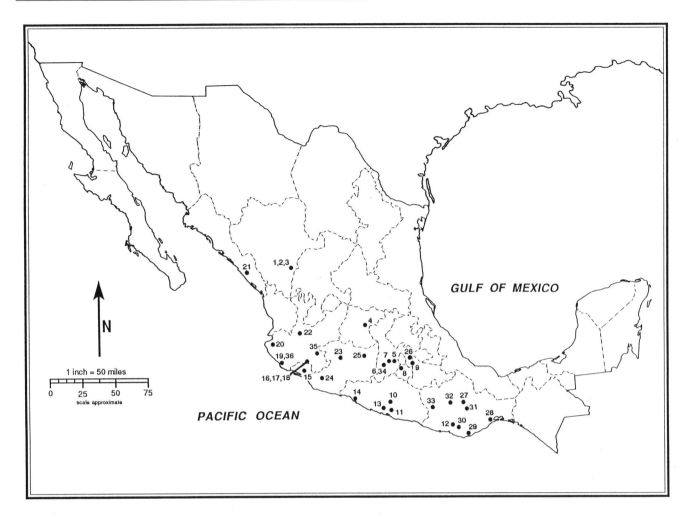

FIGURE 1. Location of the 36 study sites in western Mexico. Numbers correspond with site numbers given in Appendix 1

donment of cleared tropical deciduous forest (described in Hutto 1989). For the analysis of habitat use by individual species, I created a fifth habitat category for this disturbed vegetation type. Otherwise, this site was classified as tropical deciduous forest.

LATITUDE CLASSIFICATION. I divided the 36 study sites into a northern group (those 23 sites situated north of the transvolcanic belt, or about 19°N latitude) and a southern group (the remaining 13 sites) for the purposes of analysing the relationship between latitude and pattern of habitat use.

BIRD COUNTS. To estimate bird abundances, I used a point count technique that was developed in western Mexico for the purpose of across-habitat comparisons of bird densities (Hutto et al. 1986). Each point was located at least 200 m from other points within a single site, and the positions of points were determined by the location of permanent access trails (where passage through

the habitat was otherwise impossible) or randomly directed straight-line transects (in the more open sites). At each point, I recorded (1) the number of individuals of each species detected (excluding flyovers, nocturnal species, and aerially feeding species) within a 25-m radius, and (2) the presence of any other species that was detected beyond 25 m but still within the habitat of interest. Birds moving to within the 25-m radius during the count were recorded as detections within 25 m. All counts were conducted between 0700 and 1100, and each lasted 10 min.

BIRD NOMENCLATURE. The taxonomic arrangement and English names for all species mentioned in the text were taken from the A.O.U. Check-list (A.O.U. 1983 and supplements). Scientific and English names are given in Table 2.

MIGRATORY STATUS. A bird species was categorized as a migrant if individuals were not known to breed in Mexico. The information on breeding distribution was obtained from the A.O.U. Check-list (A.O.U. 1983), and from my own censuses conducted during July, 1975 and 1976. All other species were categorized as residents, even though individuals from the northernmost populations of some of those species (so-called partial migrants) are known to migrate south in winter. Thus, the wintering populations of some resident species might have included individuals that migrated from the northern parts of their breeding distribution. The effect of classifying the partial migrants as residents instead of migrants is discussed wherever the result of an analysis is sensitive to the method of classification.

ANALYSIS. I used the unlimited-radius point count data for all my analyses. For most species, this increased the number of detections beyond that obtained from the fixed-radius data alone, and permitted the inclusion of many species that were rarely or never detected within 25 m. Use of the unlimited-radius data does not affect information on relative detection rates among habitats for a given species because density estimates based on fixed-radius data are highly correlated with abundance estimates based on unlimited-radius data (Hutto et al. 1986, Hutto 1989).

Although the multiple counts within a site were positioned far enough apart to be independent of one another for most species, they are really "pseudoreplicates" (Hurlbert 1984) of a particular habitat type; only multiple sites within a single habitat constitute true replicates for the comparison of a species' abundance among habitat categories. Therefore, statistical comparisons of detection frequencies and migrant proportions among habitat types were based on the study site (not the point count) as a single sample. Nonetheless, for the purposes of comparing the distribution of points where a species was detected to the distribution of overall census effort, I treated each point count as an independent sample of the habitat within which it was conducted.

To determine whether the number of detections for a species was independent of habitat type, I first had to control for differences in effort among habitats by weighting (dividing) the actual numbers of birds detected in a given habitat type by the percentage of point counts conducted in that habitat type. This resulted in an index of abundance per unit effort (a detection rate) for each species in each habitat, and generated a distribution of detections that would be expected if effort were equal among habitat types. Then, knowing the relative detection rates among habitats for a species, I used Levins's (1968) measure of niche breadth ($B = 1/\Sigma p_i^2$) to rank the species according to degree of specialization. A species with a distribution of detections across the four habitat types that matched the distribution of number of point counts across habitats had the broadest possible habitat breadth ($B = 4.0$), whereas a species restricted to any one of the four habitat types had the narrowest possible habitat breadth ($B = 1.0$).

Results

SUMMARY STATISTICS FOR MIGRANTS AND RESIDENTS. The number of study sites was not evenly distributed across the four habitat types (Table 1). This is largely a reflection of the proportionate distribution of each of the four habitat types in Mexico west of the Continental Divide and south of Sonora, which is roughly 30%, 4%, 1%, and 60% for tropical deciduous forest, thornforest, cloud forest, and pine-oak-fir forest habitats, respectively (see habitat maps in Leopold 1959, Rzedowski 1983). Consequently, the majority (64.3%) of the 1,649 point counts conducted during the two winters were positioned within pine-oak-fir forest habitat, and most of the remaining counts (28.2%) fell within tropical deciduous forest habitat (Table 1).

The number of species detected varied from 48 in the cloud forest habitat to 157 in the pine-oak-fir forest habitat (Table 1). This variation can be best explained on the basis of census effort, as evidenced by the significant correlation between number of species detected and number of point counts conducted in a given habitat ($r = 0.98$; $n = 4$). The vast majority (80.5%) of the 241 species detected were residents, although 36 of these were actually partial migrants, and might have included some migratory individuals from the north temperate zone. Therefore, over all point counts, migratory landbird species comprised between 20% and 34% of those detected, depending on how one chooses to classify the partial migrants.

Overall, the mean number of migratory species detected per site was 8.8, and did not vary significantly among habitat types ($F_{3,32} = 1.3$; NS). In contrast, the mean number of resident species per site was 33.9 overall, and did vary significantly among habitat types ($F_{3,32} = 3.0$; $P < 0.05$). The lowest mean resident species richness per site was associated with the thornforest habitat (21.3) and the greatest mean (40.5) with the tropical deciduous forest habitat (Table 1). Although I conducted 30–40 point counts in most sites, two sites (1 and 19) received more intense effort (about 100 counts each). Thus, the mean richness values for the tropical deciduous forest and pine-oak-fir forest might have been biased upward. After recalculating species richness for these two sites on the basis of a randomly selected subsample of 40 points each, the mean richness values for neither migrants nor residents differed significantly among habitats.

The mean percentage of migratory species detected within a site differed significantly among habitat types ($F_{3,32} = 4.4$; $P < 0.05$) and ranged from 15% in tropical

TABLE 1. Summary statistics for each of the four major habitat types, including the distribution of census effort, cumulative numbers of species and species detections, mean number of species per site, mean number of species per count, mean percentages of migratory species and migratory species detections per site, and mean detection frequencies per site

Statistic	Tropical deciduous	Thorn forest	Cloud forest	Pine-oak-fir forest	All habitats combined	P [a]
No. study sites	6	3	2	25	36	
No. point counts	465	80	43	1,061	1,649	
Cumulative no. species detected:						
Migrants[b]	22	14	14	30	47	
Residents	94	52	34	127	194	
All species	116	66	48	157	241	
Mean species richness per site:						
Migrants[b]	7.3	5.7	11.0	9.3	8.8	NS
Residents	40.5	21.3	24.0	34.6	33.9	*
All species	47.8	27.0	35.0	43.9	42.6	NS
Mean percentage migratory species present in a site:						
Partial migrants not included	15.0	21.7	31.3	20.2	20.1	**
Partial migrants included	37.2	46.4	43.4	42.5	42.0	NS
Cumulative no. species detections:						
Migrants[b]	410	48	112	1,514	2,084	
Residents	3,757	325	160	6,199	10,441	
All species	4,167	373	272	7,713	12,525	
Mean species richness per count:						
Migrants[b]	1.5	1.1	2.9	2.0	1.9	**
Residents	6.7	4.0	3.9	5.8	5.7	**
All species	7.5	4.6	6.5	7.3	7.1	**
Mean percentage migratory species detections in a site:						
Partial migrants not included	11.3	13.3	41.9	21.2	20.0	**
Partial migrants included	30.2	51.8	54.3	43.7	42.7	NS
Mean percentage of counts within a site on which any given species was detected:						
Migrants[b]	12.1	10.8	26.5	18.0	16.9	*
Residents	17.4	19.6	16.1	17.7	17.7	NS
All species	16.8	17.5	19.3	17.6	17.6	NS

a. Significance of F-statistic from ANOVA; * = $0.01 < P < 0.05$; ** = $P < 0.01$, NS = not significant.

b. These numbers are conservative estimates for the migratory species because individuals of some species classified as residents might have been migrants from the north temperate zone.

deciduous forest to 31.3% in cloud forest (Table 1). This statistic should be unaffected by differences in sampling intensity among habitat types because greater numbers of both migrants and residents should have been detected in the more heavily sampled habitats. If I had classified the partial migrants as migrants instead of residents, the overall mean percentage of migratory species would have been 42%, and would not have differed sig-

nificantly among habitat types ($F_{3,32} = 0.7$; NS).

The cumulative number of species detections over all point counts was 12,525, with roughly five times more resident than migrant species detections recorded (Table 1). Again, the variation in total number of detections among habitat types is largely a reflection of the differences in sampling intensity among habitats ($r = 0.99$; $n = 4$).

Unlike the mean species richness per site, the mean species richness per count differed significantly among habitat types ($F_{3,32} = 6.9$; $P < 0.01$). The highest average richness per count (7.5) was recorded in tropical deciduous forest and the lowest (4.6) was recorded in thornforest (Table 1). Mean richness per count also differed significantly among habitat types for the migrant and resident species subgroups. Moreover, the distribution of average richness across habitat types differed significantly between migrants and residents (two-way ANOVA, $F_{3,64} = 5.7$; $P < 0.01$); the number of migrant species detected per count was relatively high in the cloud forest, whereas the number of resident species detected per count was relatively high in the tropical deciduous forest (Table 1). Consequently, the mean proportion of migratory species detections within a site also differed significantly ($F_{3,32} = 6.9$; $P < 0.01$) among habitats, with proportionately more migrant detections in the cloud forest than in the other habitat types (Table 1). As with the number of species detected, the distribution of detections per count for the migrant subgroup is sensitive to whether partial migrants are classified with them; if migrants and partial migrants are grouped together, significant differences were found in neither species richness per count among the four habitat types ($F_{3,32} = 2.2$; NS), nor in the distribution of means across habitat types between migrants and residents (two-way ANOVA, $F_{3,64} = 2.8$; NS).

The abundance of an "average" migratory or resident species was estimated by calculating the percentage of counts within a site on which each species was detected, averaged over all species within the group (Table 1). Those percentages differed significantly among habitat types ($F_{3,32} = 3.5$; $P < 0.05$) for migrants, but not for residents ($F_{3,32} = 0.4$; NS) or for all species combined ($F_{3,32} = 0.1$; NS). The average migratory species was detected on as many as 26.5% of all point counts (in the cloud forest habitat), and as few as 10.8% of all counts (in the thornforest habitat). Across all habitats, the average migratory species was no more or less frequently detected than the average resident species (two-way ANOVA, group effect, $F_{3,64} = 0.4$; NS); they were each detected on about 17% of the counts within a site (Table 1). The differences in detection rates among habitats for both migrants and residents were nonsignificant with the partial migrants classified as migrants, and the average migrant and resident were still equally abundant.

HABITAT DISTRIBUTIONS OF INDIVIDUAL SPECIES. The distribution of detections per unit effort across the four minimally disturbed and one heavily disturbed habitat types varied widely among species (Table 2); most tended to be restricted to only one or two of the five habitat types. I categorized each species into one of three groups, depending on its breadth of habitat use: (1) habitat specialists were restricted (or nearly so) to one of the five habitat types, as indicated by their index of habitat breadth (≤ 1.3); (2) two-zone generalists were more broadly distributed than the specialists, and had an index of habitat breadth between 1.3 and 2.3; and (3) broad generalists had indices of habitat breadth ≥ 2.3, indicating their relatively even occurrence across more than two habitat types (Table 2). Overall, 66% of the landbird species were classified as habitat specialists, and 59% were detected in only a single habitat type— proportions that did not differ significantly between migrants and residents (G-tests; NS). If those species with fewer than 30 detections were omitted from the analysis, however, a significantly ($G = 5.9$; $P < 0.05$) greater proportion of residents than migrants (49% vs. 13%; $n = 100$) was restricted to a single habitat type. Again, omitting the species with fewer than 30 detections, the mean habitat breadth of migrants ($B = 1.93$) was also significantly greater than that of residents ($B = 1.55$; $t = 3.11$; $P < 0.01$). These trends are independent of whether the partial migrants are grouped with the migrants or residents.

HABITAT DISTRIBUTION ACROSS LATITUDE. The distribution of detections (adjusted for effort) across habitat types varied significantly with latitude for 18 of 40 species that met two criteria: sample size of at least 30 detections, and presence in both northern and southern sites (Table 2). Four of the 18 species that revealed significant differences in habitat distribution with latitude were migrants, and all four migratory species (Nashville, Black-throated Gray, Black-and-white, and Wilson's warblers) were, on average, three times more likely to be detected in tropical deciduous forest in northern than in southern sites. Thus, the picture of habitat use for a species might depend to some extent on where the data are collected.

EFFECTS OF HUMAN-RELATED HABITAT DISTURBANCE. The only disturbed condition for which I obtained a sufficient number of point counts for comparison with an undisturbed condition was lowland second growth. I conducted point counts within a number of disturbed patches located near a large tract of undisturbed tropical deciduous forest in Chamela, Jalisco. With partial migrants classified as residents, the proportion of migratory species detections was independent of disturbance level ($G = 1.5$; NS). With partial migrants classified as migrants, a significantly ($G = 5.5$; $P < 0.05$) greater proportion of migrant species detections (33.2% vs. 29.0%) was recorded in the disturbed than in the undisturbed sites (Table 3). For this particular analysis I feel that the partial migrants are best grouped with migrants because previous counts conducted during two

TABLE 2. Habitat distributions of migratory and resident landbirds during the nonbreeding season in western Mexico. Numbers represent the percentage of detections within each category weighted by the numbers of counts conducted in each habitat category (see Methods). A species that was equally detectable in all four habitats would have an equal percentage of detections per unit effort (20%) within each habitat type. Species were classified as single-habitat specialists if their habitat breadth was ≤1.3, two-zone specialists if between 1.3 and 2.3, and broad generalists if ≥2.3. (TDF = tropical deciduous forest; DDF = disturbed deciduous forest (second growth); THF = thornforest; CLF = cloud forest; POF = pine-oak-fir forest; + = significant (G-test; $P < .05$) difference in habitat distribution between northernmost and southernmost sites; NS = no difference; blank = either insufficient breadth in geographic distribution, or insufficient sample size for analysis)

Species	(N)	Habitat type					Habitat breadth[a]	Latitude change
		TDF	DDF	THF	CLF	POF		
A. Tropical deciduous forest specialists								
Migrants:								
Least Flycatcher (*Empidonax minimus*)	2	100	—	—	—	—	1.00	
Black-capped Vireo (*Vireo atricapillus*)	1	100	—	—	—	—	1.00	
Yellow-throated Vireo (*Vireo flavifrons*)	1	100	—	—	—	—	1.00	
Magnolia Warbler (*Dendroica magnolia*)	2	100	—	—	—	—	1.00	
Ovenbird (*Seiurus aurocapillus*)	3	100	—	—	—	—	1.00	
Summer Tanager (*Piranga rubra*)	24	100	—	—	—	—	1.00	
Painted Bunting (*Passerina ciris*)	1	100	—	—	—	—	1.00	
Residents:								
Wagler's Chachalaca (*Ortalis poliocephala*)	142	87	13	—	—	—	1.29	
White-fronted Parrot (*Amazona albifrons*)	39	98	—	—	—	2	1.04	NS
Lesser Ground-Cuckoo (*Morococcyx erythropygus*)	1	100	—	—	—	—	1.00	
Groove-billed Ani (*Crotophaga sulcirostris*)	26	100	—	—	—	—	1.00	
Cinnamon Hummingbird (*Amazilia rutila*)	65	100	—	—	—	—	1.00	
Plain-capped Starthroat (*Heliomaster constantii*)	1	100	—	—	—	—	1.00	
Citreoline Trogon (*Trogon citreolus*)	49	100	—	—	—	—	1.00	
Gila Woodpecker (*Melanerpes uropygialis*)	7	95	—	—	—	5	1.11	
Pale-billed Woodpecker (*Campephilus guatemalensis*)	94	100	—	—	—	—	1.00	
Ivory-billed Woodcreeper (*Xiphorhynchus flavigaster*)	49	100	—	—	—	—	1.00	
Nutting's Flycatcher (*Myiarchus nuttingi*)	5	100	—	—	—	—	1.00	
Brown-crested Flycatcher (*Myiarchus tyrannulus*)[b]	117	100	—	—	—	—	1.00	
Flammulated Flycatcher (*Deltarhynchus flammulatus*)	2	100	—	—	—	—	1.00	
Great Kiskadee (*Pitangus sulphuratus*)	1	100	—	—	—	—	1.00	
Thick-billed Kingbird (*Tyrannus crassirostris*)	68	100	—	—	—	—	1.00	
Rufous-naped Wren (*Campylorhynchus rufinucha*)	10	100	—	—	—	—	1.00	
White-bellied Wren (*Uropslia leocogastra*)	83	100	—	—	—	—	1.00	
Black-capped Gnatcatcher (*Polioptila nigriceps*)	6	100	—	—	—	—	1.00	
White-lored Gnatcatcher (*Polioptila albiloris*)	42	100	—	—	—	—	1.00	
Rufous-backed Robin (*Turdus rufopalliatus*)	15	98	—	—	—	2	1.05	
Golden Vireo (*Vireo hypochryseus*)	10	100	—	—	—	—	1.00	
Tropical Parula (*Parula pitiayumi*)	130	100	—	—	—	—	1.00	
Yellow Warbler (*Dendroica petechia*)[b]	10	100	—	—	—	—	1.00	
Common Yellowthroat (*Geothlypis trichas*)[b]	2	100	—	—	—	—	1.00	
Yellow-breasted Chat (*Icteria virens*)[b]	5	100	—	—	—	—	1.00	
Red-breasted Chat (*Granatellus venustus*)	10	100	—	—	—	—	1.00	
Scrub Euphonia (*Euphonia affinis*)	39	100	—	—	—	—	1.00	
Red-crowned Ant-Tanager (*Habia rubica*)	1	100	—	—	—	—	1.00	
Rosy Thrush-Tanager (*Rhodinocichla rosea*)	1	100	—	—	—	—	1.00	
Grayish Saltator (*Saltator coerulescens*)	12	100	—	—	—	—	1.00	

a. Habitat breadth = $1/\Sigma p_i{}^2$, where p_i = proportion of weighted detections in habitat i.
b. Partially migratory species.

TABLE 2—*Continued next page*

TABLE 2—*Continued*

Species	(N)	TDF	DDF	THF	CLF	POF	Habitat breadth[a]	Latitude change
Northern Cardinal (*Cardinalis cardinalis*)	3	100	—	—	—	—	1.00	
Pyrrhuloxia (*Cardinalis sinuatus*)	1	100	—	—	—	—	1.00	
Blue Bunting (*Cyanocompsa parellina*)	50	100	—	—	—	—	1.00	
Blue Grosbeak (*Guiraca caerulea*)[b]	7	100	—	—	—	—	1.00	
Olive Sparrow (*Arremonops rufivirgatus*)	2	100	—	—	—	—	1.00	
Blue-black Grassquit (*Volatina jacarina*)	13	100	—	—	—	—	1.00	
White-collared Seedeater (*Sporophila torqueola*)	1	100	—	—	—	—	1.00	
Stripe-headed Sparrow (*Aimophila ruficauda*)	42	100	—	—	—	—	1.00	
Brown-headed Cowbird (*Molothrus ater*)[b]	1	100	—	—	—	—	1.00	
Altamira Oriole (*Icterus gularis*)	8	100	—	—	—	—	1.00	
Yellow-winged Cacique (*Cacicus melanicterus*)	165	100	—	—	—	—	1.00	

B. Disturbed tropical deciduous forest (second-growth) specialists

Migrants:

Species	(N)	TDF	DDF	THF	CLF	POF	Habitat breadth[a]	Latitude change
Bell's Vireo (*Vireo bellii*)	18	2	98	—	—	—	1.03	
Grasshopper Sparrow (*Ammodramus savannarum*)	8	—	100	—	—	—	1.00	

Residents:

Species	(N)	TDF	DDF	THF	CLF	POF	Habitat breadth[a]	Latitude change
Common Ground-Dove (*Columbina passerina*)	77	7	93	—	—	—	1.15	
Vermilion Flycatcher (*Pyrocephalus rubinus*)	11	—	99	—	—	1	1.02	
Orchard Oriole (*Icterus spurius*)[b]	4	—	97	—	—	3	1.06	

C. Thornforest specialists

Migrants:

Species	(N)	TDF	DDF	THF	CLF	POF	Habitat breadth[a]	Latitude change
Gray Flycatcher (*Empidonax wrightii*)	3	—	—	100	—	—	1.00	
Western Kingbird (*Tyrannus verticalis*)	12	—	—	100	—	—	1.00	
Brewer's Sparrow (*Spizella breweri*)	2	—	—	100	—	—	1.00	

Residents:

Species	(N)	TDF	DDF	THF	CLF	POF	Habitat breadth[a]	Latitude change
Chihuahuan Raven (*Corvus cryptoleucus*)	13	—	—	100	—	—	1.00	
Verdin (*Auriparus flaviceps*)	1	—	—	100	—	—	1.00	
Cactus Wren (*Campylorhynchus brunneicapillus*)	27	—	—	100	—	—	1.00	
Black-tailed Gnatcatcher (*Polioptila melanura*)	7	—	—	100	—	—	1.00	
Curve-billed Thrasher (*Toxostoma curvirostre*)	10	—	—	98	—	2	1.04	
Loggerhead Shrike (*Lanius ludovicianus*)[b]	7	—	—	100	—	—	1.00	
Rusty-crowned Ground-Sparrow (*Melozone kieneri*)	1	—	—	100	—	—	1.00	
Black-chested Sparrow (*Aimophila humeralis*)	2	—	—	100	—	—	1.00	
Black-chinned Sparrow (*Spizella atrogularis*)[b]	1	—	—	100	—	—	1.00	
Black-throated Sparrow (*Amphispiza bilineata*)	1	—	—	100	—	—	1.00	
Black-vented Oriole (*Icterus wagleri*)	2	—	—	100	—	—	1.00	
House Finch (*Carpodacus mexicanus*)	36	—	—	89	—	11	1.24	NS

D. Cloud forest specialists

Migrants:

Species	(N)	TDF	DDF	THF	CLF	POF	Habitat breadth[a]	Latitude change
Black-throated Green Warbler (*Dendroica virens*)	8	—	—	—	96	4	1.08	
Worm-eating Warbler (*Helmitheros vermivorus*)	1	—	—	—	100	—	1.00	
MacGillivray's Warbler (*Oporornis tolmiei*)	30	—	—	4	91	5	1.21	
Rose-breasted Grosbeak (*Pheucticus ludovicianus*)	4	—	—	—	100	—	1.00	

Residents:

Species	(N)	TDF	DDF	THF	CLF	POF	Habitat breadth[a]	Latitude change
Violet Sabrewing (*Campylopterus hemileucurus*)	1	11	—	—	89	—	1.23	
Stripe-tailed Hummingbird (*Eupherusa eximia*)	1	—	—	—	100	—	1.00	
Collared Trogon (*Trogon collaris*)	4					—	1.00	
Gray-crowned Woodpecker (*Piculus auricularis*)	1					—	1.00	

a. Habitat breadth = $1/\Sigma p_i^2$, where p_i = proportion of weighted detections in habitat i.
b Partially migratory species.

TABLE 2—*Continued*

Species	(N)	TDF	DDF	THF	CLF	POF	Habitat breadth[a]	Latitude change
Streak-headed Woodcreeper (*Lepidocolaptes souleyetii*)	6	2	—	—	98	—	1.05	
Green Jay (*Cyanocorax yncas*)	14	—	—	—	100	—	1.00	
Flame-colored Tanager (*Piranga bidentata*)	7	—	—	—	91	9	1.20	
Audubon's Oriole (*Icterus graduacauda*)	4	—	—	—	96	4	1.08	
E. Pine-oak-fir forest specialists								
Migrants:								
Ruby-throated Hummingbird (*Archilochus colubris*)	6	—	—	—	—	100	1.00	
Black-chinned Hummingbird (*Archilochus alexandri*)	1	—	—	—	—	100	1.00	
Calliope Hummingbird (*Stellula calliope*)	1	—	—	—	—	100	1.00	
Broad-tailed Hummingbird (*Selasphorus platycercus*)	16	—	—	—	—	100	1.00	
Rufous Hummingbird (*Selasphorus rufus*)	2	—	—	—	—	100	1.00	
Red-naped Sapsucker (*Sphyrapicus nuchalis*)	29	—	—	—	—	100	1.00	
Williamson's Sapsucker (*Sphyrapicus thyroideus*)	2	—	—	—	—	100	1.00	
Hammond's Flycatcher (*Empidonax hammondii*)	9	—	—	—	—	100	1.00	
Water Pipit (*Anthus spinoletta*)	1	—	—	—	—	100	1.00	
Cedar Waxwing (*Bombycilla cedrorum*)	8	—	—	—	—	100	1.00	
Red-faced Warbler (*Cardellina rubrifrons*)	44	—	—	—	—	100	1.00	
Lazuli Bunting (*Passerina amoena*)	1	—	—	—	—	100	1.00	
White-crowned Sparrow (*Zonotrichia leucophrys*)	2	—	—	—	—	100	1.00	
Cassin's Finch (*Carpodacus cassinii*)	1	—	—	—	—	100	1.00	
Residents:								
Crested Guan (*Penelope purpurascens*)	4	—	—	—	—	100	1.00	
Wild Turkey (*Meleagris gallopavo*)	2	—	—	—	—	100	1.00	
Montezuma Quail (*Cyrtonyx montezumae*)	3	—	—	—	—	100	1.00	
Band-tailed Pigeon (*Columba fasciata*)[b]	101	—	—	—	—	100	1.00	
Military Macaw (*Ara militaris*)	1	—	—	—	—	100	1.00	
Yellow-headed Parrot (*Amazona oratrix*)	1	—	—	—	—	100	1.00	
Green Violet-ear (*Colibri thalassinus*)	21	—	—	—	—	100	1.00	
White-eared Hummingbird (*Hylocharis leucotis*)	222	—	—	—	—	100	1.00	
Violet-crowned Hummingbird (*Amazilia violiceps*)	1	—	—	—	—	100	1.00	
Green-fronted Hummingbird (*Amazilia viridifrons*)	1	—	—	—	—	100	1.00	
Amethyst-throated Hummingbird (*Lampornis amethystinus*)	2	—	—	—	—	100	1.00	
Blue-throated Hummingbird (*Lampornis clemenciae*)[b]	6	—	—	—	—	100	1.00	
Magnificent Hummingbird (*Eugenes fulgens*)[b]	54	—	—	—	—	100	1.00	
Bumblebee Hummingbird (*Atthis heloisa*)	2	—	—	—	—	100	1.00	
Mountain Trogon (*Trogon mexicanus*)	68	—	—	—	—	100	1.00	
Elegant Trogon (*Trogon elegans*)	7	—	—	—	—	100	1.00	
Hairy Woodpecker (*Picoides villosus*)	73	—	—	—	—	100	1.00	
Strickland's Woodpecker (*Picoides stricklandi*)	123	—	—	—	—	100	1.00	
Northern Flicker (*Colaptes auratus*)	324	2	—	11	—	88	1.29	NS
Lineated Woodpecker (*Dryocopus lineatus*)	5	—	—	—	—	100	1.00	
White-striped Woodcreeper (*Lepidocolaptes leucogaster*)	91	—	—	—	—	100	1.00	
Pileated Flycatcher (*Xenotriccus mexicanus*)	2	—	—	—	—	100	1.00	
Pine Flycatcher (*Xenotriccus mexicanus*)	28			—	—	100	1.00	
Buff-breasted Flycatcher (*Empidonax fulvifrons*)[b]	6			—	—	100	1.00	
Black-crowned Tityra (*Tityra inquisitor*)	2			—	—	100	1.00	
Steller's Jay (*Cyanocitta stelleri*)	200			—	—	100	1.00	

a. Habitat breadth = $1/\Sigma p_i^2$, where p_i = proportion of weighted detections in habitat *i*.

b. Partially migratory species.

TABLE 2—*Continued next page*

TABLE 2—*Continued*

Species	(N)	TDF	DDF	THF	CLF	POF	Habitat breadth[a]	Latitude change
Gray-breasted Jay (*Aphelocoma ultramarina*)	200	—	—	—	—	100	1.00	
Mexican Chickadee (*Parus sclateri*)	208	—	—	—	—	100	1.00	
Bridled Titmouse (*Parus wollweberi*)	55	—	—	—	—	100	1.00	
White-breasted Nuthatch (*Sitta carolinensis*)	263	—	—	—	—	100	1.00	
Pygmy Nuthatch (*Sitta pygmaea*)	78	—	—	—	—	100	1.00	
Brown Creeper (*Certhia americana*)	151	—	—	—	—	100	1.00	
Gray-barred Wren (*Campylorhynchus megalopterus*)	41	—	—	—	—	100	1.00	
Canyon Wren (*Catherpes mexicanus*)	7	—	—	—	—	100	1.00	
Bewick's Wren (*Thryomanes bewickii*)	5	—	—	—	—	100	1.00	
Golden-crowned Kinglet (*Regulus satrapa*)	30	—	—	—	—	100	1.00	
Eastern Bluebird (*Sialia sialis*)[b]	11	—	—	—	—	100	1.00	
Western Bluebird (*Sialia mexicana*)	143	—	—	—	—	100	1.00	
Townsend's Solitaire (*Myadestes townsendi*)	1	—	—	—	—	100	1.00	
Slate-colored Solitaire (*Myadestes unicolor*)	4	—	—	—	—	100	1.00	
Russet Nightingale-Thrush (*Catharus occidentalis*)	13	—	—	—	—	100	1.00	
Black Robin (*Turdus infiscatus*)	4	—	—	—	—	100	1.00	
American Robin (*Turdus migratorius*)[b]	274	—	4	—	—	96	1.08	
Phainopepla (*Phainopepla nitens*)	40	—	—	—	—	100	1.00	
Hutton's Vireo (*Vireo huttoni*)	132	—	—	—	—	100	1.00	
Chestnut-sided Shrike-Vireo (*Vireolanius melitophrys*)	1	—	—	—	—	100	1.00	
Red Warbler (*Ergaticus ruber*)	90	—	—	—	—	100	1.00	
Painted Redstart (*Myioborus pictus*)[b]	136	—	—	—	—	100	1.00	
Golden-crowned Warbler (*Basileuterus culicivorus*)	2	—	—	—	—	100	1.00	
Golden-browed Warbler (*Basileuterus belli*)	10	—	—	—	—	100	1.00	
Olive Warbler (*Peucedramus taeniatus*)[b]	218	—	—	—	—	100	1.00	
Blue-hooded Euphonia (*Euphonia elegantissima*)	9	—	—	—	—	100	1.00	
Common Bush-Tanager (*Chlorospingus opthalmicus*)	2	—	—	—	—	100	1.00	
Rufous-capped Brush-Finch (*Atlapetes pileatus*)	18	—	—	—	—	100	1.00	
Green-striped Brush-Finch (*Atlapetes virenticeps*)	11	—	—	—	—	100	1.00	
Collared Towhee (*Pipilo ocai*)	24	—	—	—	—	100	1.00	
Rufous-sided Towhee (*Pipilo erythrophthalmus*)	76	—	—	—	—	100	1.00	
Cinnamon-bellied Flowerpiercer (*Diglossa baritula*)	19	—	—	—	—	100	1.00	
Striped Sparrow (*Oriturus superciliosus*)	31	—	—	—	—	100	1.00	
Yellow-eyed Junco (*Junco phaeonotus*)	237	—	—	—	—	100	1.00	
Eastern Meadowlark (*Sturnella magna*)	2	—	—	—	—	100	1.00	
Red Crossbill (*Loxia curvirostra*)	51	—	—	—	—	100	1.00	
Pine Siskin (*Carduelis pinus*)	53	—	—	—	—	100	1.00	
Black-headed Siskin (*Carduelis notata*)	24							
Evening Grosbeak (*Coccothraustes vespertinus*)	5	—	—	—	—	100	1.00	
House Sparrow (*Passer domesticus*)	1	—	—	—	—	100	1.00	

F. Two-zone (deciduous forest and second growth) generalists

Residents:

Species	(N)	TDF	DDF	THF	CLF	POF	Habitat breadth[a]	Latitude change
Red-billed Pigeon (*Columba flavirostris*)	15	80	20	—	—	—	1.48	
Inca Dove (*Columbina inca*)	52				9	—	1.36	
White-tipped Dove (*Leptotila verreauxi*)	236				71	1	1.82	+
Lilac-crowned Parrot (*Amazona finschi*)	171				69	4	1.83	
Broad-billed Hummingbird (*Cynanthus latirostris*)[b]	50				23	6	1.76	NS
Golden-cheeked Woodpecker (*Melanerpes chrysogenys*)	218				45	—	2.14	NS

a. Habitat breadth = $1/\Sigma p_i^2$, where p_i = proportion of weighted detections in habitat i.

b. Partially migratory species.

TABLE 2—*Continued*

Species	(N)	TDF	DDF	THF	CLF	POF	Habitat breadth[a]	Latitude change
N. Beardless Tyrannulet (*Camptostoma imberbe*)	139	35	64	—	—	1	1.88	NS
Western Flycatcher (*Empidonax difficilis*)[b]	118	65	21	—	11	2	2.08	++
Bright-rumped Attila (*Attila spadiceus*)	55	57	31	—	11	1	2.30	
Sinaloa Wren (*Thryothorus sinaloa*)	44	30	70	—	—	—	1.74	
Orange-breasted Bunting (*Passerina leclancherii*)	76	15	69	16	—	—	1.90	+
Hooded Oriole (*Icterus cucullatus*)[b]	15	27	65	—	—	8	2.00	
G. Two-zone (deciduous forest and thornforest) generalists								
Migrants:								
Virginia's Warbler (*Vermivora virginiae*)	4	29	—	66	—	5	1.92	
Residents:								
Orange-fronted Parakeet (*Aratinga canicularis*)	46	53	—	40	—	7	2.23	+
Golden-fronted Woodpecker (*Melanerpes aurifrons*)	34	70	—	30	—	—	1.73	+
Magpie Jay (*Calosaitta colliei* and *formosa*)	38	65	—	35	—	—	1.83	+
Yellow Grosbeak (*Pheucticus chrysopeplus*)	11	69	—	31	—	—	1.75	
H. Two-zone (deciduous forest and cloud forest) generalists								
Migrants:								
Swainson's Thrush (*Catharus ustulatus*)	6	37	—	—	63	—	1.88	
Wilson's Warbler (*Wilsonia pusilla*)	176	22	2	—	71	5	1.78	+
Western Tanager (*Piranga ludoviciana*)	59	14	6	—	77	3	1.62	NS
Residents:								
Fork-tailed Emerald (*Chlorostilbon canivettii*)	42	83	—	—	17	—	1.40	
Rose-throated Becard (*Pachyramphus aglaiae*)	14	24	—	—	68	8	1.91	
Masked Tityra (*Tityra semifasciata*)	22	52	—	—	47	1	2.03	
White-throated Robin (*Turdus assimilis*)	25	12	—	—	85	3	1.35	
I. Two-zone (deciduous forest and pine-oak-fir forest) generalists								
Migrants:								
Black-throated Gray Warbler (*Dendroica nigrescens*)	110	56	—	—	—	44	1.98	+
Residents:								
Gray-collared Becard (*Pachyramphus major*)	4	49	—	—	—	51	2.00	
Rufous-crowned Sparrow (*Aimophila ruficeps*)	3	85	—	—	—	15	1.33	
J. Two-zone (second-growth and thornforest) generalists								
Migrants:								
Lucy's Warbler (*Vermivora luciae*)	14	4	76	19	—	—	1.61	
Vesper Sparrow (*Pooecetes gramineus*)	5	—	16	84	—	—	1.38	
Lincoln's Sparrow (*Melospiza lincolnii*)	3	—	42	54	—	4	2.14	
Residents:								
American Kestrel (*Falco sparverius*)[b]	66	—	62	30	—	8	2.08	NS
Ruddy Ground-Dove (*Columbina talpacoti*)	8	—	24	75	—	1	1.61	
Dusky Hummingbird (*Cynanthus sordidus*)	4	7	26	66	—	—	1.94	
Tropical Kingbird (*Tyrannus melancholicus*)	25	—	81	19	—	—	1.46	
Northern Mockingbird (*Mimus polyglottos*)	23	—	60	40	—	—	1.93	
Lark Sparrow (*Chondestes grammacus*)[b]	9	—	70	29	—	1	1.75	
Lesser Goldfinch (*Carduelis psaltria*)	4			—	—	3	1.77	
K. Two-zone (thornforest and cloud forest) generalists								
Resident:								
Rusty Sparrow (*Aimophila rufescens*)	3			—	49	—	2.00	
L. Two-zone (thornforest and pine-oak-fir forest) generalists								
Migrants:								
Yellow-rumped Warbler (*Dendroica coronata*)	335			3	—	62	2.07	NS

a. Habitat breadth = $1/\Sigma p_i^2$, where p_i = proportion of weighted detections in habitat i.
b. Partially migratory species.

TABLE 2—*Continued next page*

TABLE 2—*Continued*

Species	(N)	TDF	DDF	THF	CLF	POF	Habitat breadth[a]	Latitude change
Residents:								
Mourning Dove (*Zenaida macroura*)[b]	57	3	6	81	—	10	1.49	+
Cassin's Kingbird (*Tyrannus vociferans*)[b]	10	8	—	73	—	19	1.75	
Common Raven (*Corvus corax*)	149	1	—	31	—	68	1.81	NS
Bushtit (*Psaltriparus minimus*)	55	—	—	33	—	67	1.80	NS
Spotted Wren (*Campylorhynchus gularis*)	14	—	—	50	—	50	2.00	NS
House Wren (*Troglodytes aedon*)[b]	116	—	—	37	—	63	1.88	NS
Brown Towhee (*Pipilo fuscus*)	30	—	—	80	—	20	1.47	
Chipping Sparrow (*Spizella passerina*)[b]	44	—	—	49	—	51	2.00	NS
Scott's Oriole (*Icterus parisorum*)[b]	19	—	—	61	—	39	1.91	NS
M. Two-zone (cloud forest and pine-oak-fir forest) generalists								
Migrants:								
Ruby-crowned Kinglet (*Regulus calendula*)	505	—	—	7	8	85	1.37	NS
Hermit Thrush (*Catharus guttatus*)	57	—	—	—	58	42	1.95	
Townsend's Warbler (*Dendroica townsendi*)	114	—	—	—	62	38	1.89	
Hermit Warbler (*Dendroica occidentalis*)	81	—	—	—	24	76	1.56	
Residents:								
Berylline Hummingbird (*Amazilia beryllina*)	7	—	—	—	80	20	1.46	
Acorn Woodpecker (*Melanerpes formicivorus*)	258	—	—	—	37	63	1.87	
Tufted Flycatcher (*Mitrephanes phaeocercus*)	89	—	—	—	36	64	1.86	
Greater Pewee (*Contopus pertinax*)[b]	126	—	—	—	45	55	1.98	
Brown-backed Solitaire (*Myadestes obscurus*)	184	—	—	—	83	17	1.40	
Gray Silky-Flycatcher (*Ptilogonys cinereus*)	235	—	—	4	34	63	1.97	NS
Crescent-chested Warbler (*Parula superciliosa*)	57	—	—	—	31	69	1.74	
Grace's Warbler (*Dendroica graciae*)[b]	139	—	—	—	72	28	1.68	
Slate-throated Redstart (*Myioborus miniatus*)	117	—	—	—	39	61	1.91	
Hepatic Tanager (*Piranga flava*)[b]	89	—	—	—	22	78	1.52	
N. Broad generalists								
Migrants:								
Orange-crowned Warbler (*Vermivora celata*)	84	10	60	5	—	25	2.31	NS
Nashville Warbler (*Vermivora ruficapilla*)	179	30	17	5	45	3	3.08	+
Black-and-white Warbler (*Mniotilta varia*)	69	27	4	5	52	12	2.73	+
Northern Oriole (*Icterus galbula*)	40	—	8	10	56	26	2.51	NS
Residents:								
White-winged Dove (*Zenaida asiatica*)[b]	90	17	27	38	—	18	3.58	+
Squirrel Cuckoo (*Piaya cayana*)	12	31	47	20	—	2	2.77	
Ladder-backed Woodpecker (*Picoides scalaris*)	18	14	13	32	30	12	4.19	NS
Dusky-capped Flycatcher (*Myiarchus tuberculifer*)	282	58	7	3	28	5	2.37	+
Ash-throated Flycatcher (*Myiarchus cinerascens*)[b]	209	25	27	47	—	1	2.78	+
San Blas Jay (*Cyanocorax sanblasianus*)	53	50	34	16	—	—	2.56	
Happy Wren (*Thryothorus felix*)	39	10	14	18	55	3	2.72	
Blue-gray Gnatcatcher (*Polioptila caerulea*)[b]	330	27	38	19	16	1	3.64	+
Blue Mockingbird (*Melanotis caerulescens*)	16	34	—	—	48	18	2.63	
Solitary Vireo (*Vireo solitarius*)[b]	79	28	—	—	51	21	2.61	NS
Warbling Vireo (*Vireo gilvus*)[b]	110	41	13	13	16	18	3.91	+
Rufous-capped Warbler (*Basileuterus rufifrons*)	31	—	—	41	39	20	2.77	+
Black-headed Grosbeak (*Pheucticus melanocephalus*)[b]	25	12	21	26	—	42	3.36	
Varied Bunting (*Passerina versicolor*)	60	37	50	13	—	1	2.51	+
Streak-backed Oriole (*Icterus pustulatus*)	117	31	32	37	—	1	3.03	NS

a. Habitat breadth = $1/\Sigma p_i^2$, where p_i = proportion of weighted detections in habitat i.

b. Partially migratory species.

breeding seasons (Hutto 1980) revealed no partial migrants breeding in heavily disturbed habitats. Therefore, it is likely that individuals of the partially migratory species detected in the disturbed sites were migrants.

The significant difference in proportion of migrant detections between the disturbed and undisturbed sites could result from relatively few migratory or resident species contributing a disproportionate number of detections. Therefore, I considered every species, regardless of the number of times it was detected, and tallied the proportion of species that had the greater number of detections per unit effort in the disturbed areas. The same trend was evident (Table 4): a significantly ($G = 5.0; P < 0.05$) greater proportion of migrants (including partial migrants) than residents showed a higher rate of detection in the disturbed tropical deciduous forest habitat (63% vs. 40% for migrants and residents, respectively). Perhaps most notably, a large number of species (51 of 98) were detected in either the disturbed or undisturbed conditions, but not in both; they were restricted either to disturbed or undisturbed conditions (Table 5).

Discussion

WITHIN-HABITAT PATTERNS. In comparison with other geographic locations in the Neotropics, western Mexico has been labeled unique in terms of the relatively high proportion of migratory species wintering in most of the available habitat types (Hutto 1980, in press; Rappole et al. 1983). Data from the present study are consistent with that suggestion; on average, 20% of the species in a single study site were migrants (42%, if the partial migrants are included). In comparison, Lynch (1989) found that migrants comprised 37% of the species, averaged over numerous sites in the Yucatan. Progressively smaller percentages of migrants occur in wintering sites as one moves south in the Neotropics (Terborgh 1980). The proximity of wintering grounds to breeding grounds in western North America is probably the factor that contributes most to the unique community composition, as discussed by Terborgh (1980) and Hutto (1980, in press).

In contrast with the Yucatan, where Lynch (1989) found that migrants comprised a larger percentage of the more common species than they represented overall, migrants in western Mexico comprised a somewhat lower percentage (13.9%) of the commonest 100 species than they comprised overall (19.5%). In addition, the average abundances (frequencies of detection) of the migrants and residents did not differ significantly in western Mexico; species in both groups were detected on about 17% of the point counts in a site, on average (Table 1). The commonness of migrants relative to residents in Lynch's study might be a product of the fact

TABLE 3. Number of independent migrant and resident species detections from point counts conducted within a single undisturbed lowland site in comparison with point counts taken from heavily disturbed, second-growth areas surrounding the site

Status	Relative intensity of land use			
	Heavily disturbed		Undisturbed	
Migrant	77		276	
Partial migrant	211	} 33.2%	502	} 29.0%
Resident	579	66.8%	1907	71.0%
TOTAL	867		2685	

NOTE: Migrant vs. resident: G = 1.5; NS. Migrant and partial migrant vs. resident: G = 5.5; P < .05.

TABLE 4. Distribution of migrant and resident species according to the condition (disturbed or undisturbed tropical deciduous forest) under which they had their highest frequency of detection

Status	Relative intensity of land use		
	Heavily disturbed	Undisturbed	Total
Migrant	8 (44%)	10 (56%)	18
Partial migrant	16 (80%) } 63.2%	4 (20%) } 36.8%	20
Resident	24 (40%)	36 (60%)	60

NOTE: Migrant vs. resident: G = 0.18; NS. Migrant and partial migrant vs. resident: G = 5.0; P < .05.

that the proportion of disturbed and early successional areas in his survey was greater than in my study, or due to the fact that he used tape playbacks, which attract migrants more than residents. Alternatively, the ratio of migrant to resident individuals in habitats of any given type might be greater in eastern than in western Mexico. Because our habitat classifications and census methods are not strictly comparable, it is difficult to interpret this difference in our results.

PATTERNS OF HABITAT USE BY LONG-DISTANCE MIGRANTS. Both the mean proportion and the mean abundance (frequency of detection) of migratory species were significantly higher in the cloud forest habitat than in the other three habitat types. Nonetheless, because these results are sensitive to the way partial migrants are classified, the biological significance of such a pattern should not be overstated. In addition, the high proportion of migratory species in the cloud forest is probably an indirect consequence of disturbance to the understo-

TABLE 5. Species listed according to whether they were more abundant in disturbed (second-growth) or undisturbed tropical deciduous forest near Chamela, Jalisco. Species with asterisks were restricted to habitat type indicated

Status	Disturbed habitat	Undisturbed habitat
Migrant	Bell's Vireo Orange-crowned Warbler* Lucy's Warbler Yellow-rumped Warbler* Vesper Sparrow* Grasshopper Sparrow* Lincoln's Sparrow* Northern Oriole*	Least Flycatcher* Swainson's Thrush* Black-capped Vireo* Nashville Warbler Black-throated Gray Warbler* Black-and-white Warbler Ovenbird* Wilson's Warbler Summer Tanager* Western Tanager
Partial migrant	American Kestrel* White-winged Dove Mourning Dove Broad-billed Hummingbird Ash-throated Flycatcher Blue-gray Gnatcatcher American Robin* Yellow Warbler* Common Yellowthroat Yellow-breasted Chat* Black-headed Grosbeak Blue Grosbeak Lark Sparrow* Brown-headed Cowbird* Orchard Oriole* Hooded Oriole*	Western Flycatcher Brown-crested Flycatcher Solitary Vireo* Warbling Vireo
Resident	Inca Dove Common Ground-Dove Ruddy Ground-Dove* Squirrel Cuckoo Groove-billed Ani Dusky Hummingbird* Ladder-backed Woodpecker N. Beardless Tyrannulet Vermilion Flycatcher* Great Kiskadee* Tropical Kingbird* Thick-billed Kingbird Sinaloa Wren Happy Wren Northern Mockingbird* Grayish Saltator Pyrrhuloxia* Varied Bunting Orange-breasted Bunting Blue-black Grassquit*	Chachalaca Red-billed Pigeon White-tipped Dove Orange-fronted Parakeet* Lilac-crowned Parrot Lesser Ground-Cuckoo* Fork-tailed Emerald* Cinnamon Hummingbird Plain-capped Starthroat* Citreoline Trogon* Golden-cheeked Woodpecker Pale-billed Woodpecker Ivory-billed Woodcreeper* Bright-rumped Atilla Dusky-capped Flycatcher Nutting's Flycatcher* Flammulated Flycatcher* Gray-collared Becard* Rose-throated Becard* Masked Tityra*

TABLE 5—*Continued*

Status	Disturbed habitat	Undisturbed habitat
Resident—*cont.*	White-collared Seedeater*	San Blas Jay
	Stripe-headed Sparrow*	White-bellied Wren
	Streak-backed Oriole	Black-capped Gnatcatcher*
	Lesser Goldfinch*	White-lored Gnatcatcher
		White-throated Robin*
		Rufous-backed Robin*
		Blue Mockingbird*
		Golden Vireo
		Tropical Parula
		Red-breasted Chat*
		Scrub Euphonia
		Red-crowned Ant-Tanager*
		Rosy Thrush-Tanager*
		Yellow Grosbeak*
		Blue Bunting
		Yellow-winged Cacique

ry through land conversion for the production of coffee beans. Is the proportion of migrants abnormally high as a result of this disturbance, or is the proportion of residents abnormally low, or both? I suspect that the disturbance affects resident species more negatively than it affects migratory species positively. This follows from the fact that the mean migratory species richness per site did not vary significantly among habitats, whereas the mean resident species richness per site was significantly less in the cloud forest than in the other two forested habitats (presumably because of disturbance). In any case, migrant species richness appears to be similar in all forested habitats. It is difficult to understand the habitat distributions of migrants and residents independent of disturbance effects without sampling a large number of sites to control statistically for those effects. Nonetheless, one generalization that seems to emerge from this study is that migrants (no matter how restrictively or liberally defined) tend to be broader in their habitat use than residents, which are more often restricted to a single habitat type. Even though the difference is insensitive to the classification of partial migrants, it underscores the limitation of such summary statistics because some migratory species were just as specialized as the most specialized resident species (see Table 2, parts A through D).

EFFECT OF HABITAT DISTURBANCE. Several migratory species detected in the undisturbed tropical deciduous forest at Chamela went undetected not only in nearby second-growth habitat, but in all other study sites as

well. These include Least Flycatcher, Black-capped Vireo, Ovenbird, and Summer Tanager. In western Mexico, these species are probably restricted to undisturbed tropical deciduous forest, and would, therefore, be especially sensitive to deforestation in the lowlands. The migratory and partially migratory species that were restricted to disturbed second growth were also detected in relatively undisturbed native habitats of other types censused elsewhere (American Kestrel; Orange-crowned and Yellow-rumped warblers; Vesper, Lincoln's, Grasshopper, and Lark sparrows; and Northern, Orchard, and Hooded orioles), or were detected in riparian forests, which I did not census formally during the present study, but did census in connection with an earlier study (Bell's Vireo, Lucy's and Yellow warblers, and Yellow-breasted Chat). Thus, no migratory species appears to be restricted to disturbed lowland second growth, even though the abundances of many were relatively high therein. The migratory species of western Mexico can, therefore, be viewed as integral parts of relatively undisturbed habitat at *some* point in space, but several species must also be viewed as integral parts of disturbed forests, where they might attain their greatest abundance.

I hasten to add that the absence of census data from a more complete spectrum of disturbance levels and habitat types makes it impossible to generalize about the degree to which a given migratory species is restricted to a particular set of environmental conditions. Unfortunately, even the scope of a single multiyear study, such as the present one, or that of Lynch (1989), is too narrow for the generation of average values for a complete habitat by disturbance matrix. Only if future research efforts are designed to fill in the information gaps will we gain a better understanding of the habitat "needs" of migrants.

IMPLICATIONS FOR CONSERVATION. Individual migratory species differ markedly from one another in their patterns of habitat use, and they overlap completely the patterns of habitat use exhibited by resident species. Consequently, we cannot distinguish migrants from residents with respect to their patterns of habitat use. Some migratory species are as broadly distributed as the most broadly distributed residents (Table 2, part K), and others are as specialized as the most specialized residents (Table 2, parts A through D). Moreover, some migratory species are as common as the most common residents (e.g., Wilson's Warbler) and others are as rare as the rarest residents (e.g., Black-capped Vireo). And some migratory species fare well under disturbed conditions (e.g., Bell's Vireo) while others do not (e.g., Summer Tanager). We can no longer afford to ignore this variation among migratory species by grouping them in writing and conversation as if they were ecologically identical. The conservation of migrants cannot be achieved by characterizing what they do, on average, or by monitoring migrants as a group (Hutto 1989, this study). Clearly, we must begin to build recognition of the uniqueness of these (and other) species into our conservation programs.

In addition, most migratory bird species probably use a broad range of habitats across their winter range, and their pattern of habitat use might vary geographically (Table 2). Consider a comparison of my data on habitat distribution of some migrants with Lynch's (1989) data from the Yucatan: Black-and-white Warbler was classified as a forest specialist in the Yucatan, but was classified as a broad generalist in western Mexico; Least Flycatcher and Black-throated Green Warbler were classified as a habitat generalists in the Yucatan, but were forest specialists in western Mexico; Wilson's Warbler was classified an extreme specialist on dense tropical forests in the Yucatan, but is an understory generalist in western Mexico. Although some of these differences are undoubtedly artifacts of small sample sizes or differences in habitat classification schemes, it is important to recognize the possibility that habitat use might vary geographically. If true (and further study is needed to verify the presence of such patterns), conservation strategies for long-distance migratory landbirds that are built around recommendations from studies in single localities, no matter how detailed those studies might be, will fail to meet the needs of migrants in other locations.

From a conservation perspective, then, we are faced with the same dilemma facing the U.S. Forest Service and other federal agencies responsible for maintaining viable populations of all vertebrate species in all parts of their historic ranges (Salwasser et al. 1984, Norse et al. 1986): Is there a short-cut to having to monitor them all? As I noted earlier, it would be meaningless to monitor migrants as a group because of the tremendous variation in geographic and habitat distribution among species. If one were to subdivide the migratory species into a slightly larger number of "management guilds" (Verner 1984) to cover all habitats and all geographic locations, the situation would not be much improved because of the diversity of habitat and geographic distributions exhibited by migrants.

For any given species, it will only be through a coupling of detailed studies of mortality rates with estimates of relative abundance in all possible combinations of habitats and disturbance levels that we can hope to predict the effects of a changing landscape. Although this makes the situation seem hopeless, it is not. A productive start would be to catalogue relative abundances of *all* species detected (through simple presence-absence information) in each of the major habitat types and disturbance conditions. Then, knowledge of the rates of change in areal coverage of the land types would allow reasonable first estimates of effects. For example, if Mexico consisted of 80% land type A and 20% land type B, and a species were equally common in both, the gradual conversion of A to B would not be expected to affect the species, assuming mortality rates are equal in both land types. Alternatively, a species more abundant in A would probably be negatively affected, and a species more abundant in B would probably be benefitted. With the aid of satellite imagery (Green et al. 1987, Palmeirim 1988), data on rates of conversion of land types could be calculated; we lack only the descriptive information on relative abundances of bird species in each of the land types over a broad geographic area.

We could also focus conservation attention toward the preservation of locations within which the majority of species reside, as suggested by the "gap analysis" approach of Scott et al. (1987). This might prove to be a satisfactory strategy for deciding which areas to save first, but it will not be a successful stand-alone conservation strategy, as evidenced by the ongoing debate about whether saving a few large or several small reserves is a better long-term conservation strategy (Simberloff and Abele 1976a,b, Diamond 1976, Terborgh 1976, Whitcomb et al. 1976). In addition to the ecological problems associated with putting all our eggs in only a few baskets (Simberloff 1982, Simberloff and Abele 1982, Lahti and Ranta 1985, McLellan et al. 1986, Soulé and Simberloff 1986), there is the more subtle sociological question of whether establishment of a few geographically isolated "gap preserves" will promote a change in public attitude toward conservation in general. A truly successful conservation strategy must promote a change in human values toward respect for the land (Leopold 1949), but the creation of a small number of isolated, zoo-like biological preserves might unintentionally reinforce the view that humans are largely separate from the "natural" world. An alternative that seems to hold considerable promise is a habitat-based approach (Norton 1986, Hutto et al. 1987, Noss 1987, Thomas and Salwasser 1989). The short-term goal under a habitat-based approach would be to preserve as much land in as broad a range of geographic locations and habitats as possible. In the long run, we would at least be saving the greatest possible variety of ecological conditions. In so doing, we would be more effective at educating the public about the importance and value of local habitats, and less prone to forcing all our conservation attention toward relatively few, species-rich locations. If a habitat-based strategy promoted a change in public attitude about the importance of preserving the modicum of remaining undisturbed land, we might even end up with more land and more species than that ultimately saved by a gap approach alone.

Results from the present study suggest that each combination of geographic location and habitat type is most critical to *some* species or another. Therefore, success in conservation might be best measured by the geographic breadth of places preserved. Let us not attempt, then, to find the "place" that needs conservation attention; instead, let us attempt to clarify for the public the uniqueness of every place and every habitat.

Acknowledgments

I appreciate the generous financial support provided by the World Wildlife Fund–U.S., the Smithsonian Institution, and the University of Montana. Housing, and other forms of logistical support were provided by the Instituto de Ecología for work at the La Michilía Biosphere Reserve, and by the Universidad Nacional Autónoma de México for work at the Estación de Biología Chamela. I am most grateful to the people associated with these organizations for their support, and to Robert Bennetts, Paul Hendricks, Margaret Hillhouse, Philip Hooge, Sandra Pletschet, and Susan Reel, who assisted so expertly in the field.

Literature cited

Ambuel, B., and S.A. Temple. 1982. Songbird populations in southern Wisconsin forests: 1954 and 1979. *J. Field Ornithol.* 53:149–158.

American Ornithologists' Union. 1983. *Check-list of North American Birds.* 6th ed. Washington: American Ornithologists' Union.

Barlow, J.C. 1980. Patterns of ecological interactions among migrant and resident vireos on the wintering grounds. Pages 79–107 in *Migrant Birds in the Neotropics: Ecology, Behavior, Distribution and Conservation,* A. Keast and E.S. Morton, eds. Washington: Smithsonian Institution Press.

Diamond, J.A. 1976. Island biogeography and conservation: Strategy and limitations. *Science* 193:1027–1029.

Fitzpatrick, J.W. 1980. Wintering of North American tyrant flycatchers in the Neotropics. Pages 67–78 in *Migrant Birds in the Neotropics: Ecology, Behavior, Distribution and Conservation,* A. Keast and E.S. Morton, eds. Washington: Smithsonian Institution Press.

Green, K.M., J.F. Lynch, J. Sircar, and L.S.Z. Greenberg. 1987. Use of Landsat remote sensing to assess habitat for migratory birds in the Yucatan Peninsula. *Vida Silv. Neotrop.* 1(2):27–38.

Hall, G.A. 1984. Population decline of neotropical migrants in an Appalachian forest. *Am. Birds* 38:14–18.

Hurlbert, S.H. 1984. Pseudoreplication and the design of ecological field experiments. *Ecology* 54:187–211.

Hutto, R.L. 1980. Winter habitat distribution of migratory land birds in western Mexico, with special reference to small, foliage-gleaning insectivores. Pages 181–203 in *Migrant Birds in the Neotropics: Ecology, Behavior, Distribution and Conservation,* A. Keast and E.S. Morton, eds. Washington: Smithsonian Institution Press.

———. 1985. Habitat selection by nonbreeding, migratory landbirds, Pages 455–476 in *Habitat Selection in Birds,* M.L. Cody, ed. New York: Academic Press, Inc.

———. 1988. Is tropical deforestation responsible for the reported declines in neotropical migrant populations? *Am. Birds* 42:375–379.

———. 1989. The effect of habitat alteration on migratory land birds in a west Mexican tropical deciduous forest: A conservation perspective. *Conserv. Biol.* 3:138–148.

———. In press. Some ornithologically unique aspects of western Mexico. In *The Endangered Vertebrates of Mexico,* G. Ceballos and D. Navarro L., eds.

Hutto, R.L., S.M. Pletschet, and P. Hendricks. 1986. A fixed-radius point count method for nonbreeding and breeding season use. *Auk* 103:593–602.

Hutto, R.L., S. Reel, and P.B. Landres. 1987. A critical evaluation of the species approach to biological conservation. *Endang. Spec. Update* 4:1–4.

Lahti, T., and E. Ranta. 1985. The SLOSS principle and conservation practice: An example. *Oikos* 44:369–370.

Leopold, A. 1949. *A Sand County Almanac.* New York: Oxford University Press.

Leopold, A.S. 1959. *Wildlife in Mexico.* Berkeley: University of California Press.

Levins, R. 1968. *Evolution in Changing Environments.* Princeton: Princeton University Press.

Lovejoy, T. 1983. Tropical deforestation and North American migrant birds. *Bird Conserv.* 1:126–128.

Lynch, J.F. 1989. Distribution of overwintering Nearctic migrants in the Yucatan Peninsula, I: General patterns of occurrence. *Condor* 91:515–544.

McLellan, C.H., A.P. Dobson, D.S. Wilcove, and J.F. Lynch. 1986. Effects of forest fragmentation on New- and Old-World bird communities: Empirical observations and theoretical implications. Pages 305–313 in *Wildlife 2000: Modeling Habitat Relationships of Terrestrial Vertebrates,* J. Verner, M.L. Morrison, and C.J. Ralph, eds. Madison: University of Wisconsin Press.

Norse, E.A., K.L. Rosenbaum, D.S. Wilcove, B.A. Wilcox, W.H. Romme, D.W. Johnston, and M.L. Stout. 1986. *Conserving Biological Diversity in Our National Forests.* Washington: The Wilderness Society.

Norton, B.G. 1986. Epilogue. Pages 268–283 in *The Preservation of Species,* B.G. Norton, ed. Princeton: Princeton University Press.

Noss, R.F. 1987. From plant communities to landscapes in conservation inventories: A look at the Nature Conservancy (USA). *Biol. Conserv.* 41:11–37.

Palmeirim, J.M. 1988. Automatic mapping of avian species habitat using satellite imagery. *Oikos* 52:59–68.

Rappole, J.H., E.S. Morton, T.E. Lovejoy, III, and J.L. Ruos. 1983. *Nearctic Avian Migrants in the Neotropics.* Washington: U.S. Fish and Wildlife Service.

Robbins, C.S., J.R. Sauer, R.S. Greenberg, and S. Droege. 1989. Population declines in North American birds that migrate to the neotropics. *Proc. Natl. Acad. Sci.* 86:7658–7662.

Rzedowski, J. 1983. *Vegetación de México.* Mexico, D.F.: Editorial Limusa.

Salwasser, H., S.P. Mealey, and K. Johnson. 1984. Wildlife population viability: A question of risk. *Trans. N. Am. Wildl. and Natur. Resources Conf.* 49:421–439.

Scott, J.M., B. Csuti, J.D. Jacobi, and J.E. Estes. 1987. Species richness: A geographic approach to protecting future biological diversity. *BioScience* 37:782–788.

Simberloff, D. 1982. Big advantages of small refuges. *Nat. History* 94:6–14.

Simberloff, D.S., and L.G. Abele. 1976a. Island biogeography theory and conservation practice. *Science* 191:285–286.

———. 1976b. Island biogeography and conservation: Strategy and limitations. *Science* 193:1032.

———. 1982. Refuge design and island biogeography theory: Effects of fragmentation. *Am. Nat.* 120:41–50.

Soulé, M.E., and D. Simberloff. 1986. What do genetics and ecology tell us about the design of nature reserves? *Biol. Conserv.* 35:19–40.

Terborgh, J. 1976. Island biogeography and conservation: Strategy and limitations. *Science* 193:1029–1030.

———. 1980. The conservation status of neotropical migrants. Pages 21–30 in *Migrant Birds in the Neotropics: Ecology, Behavior, Distribution and Conservation,* A. Keast and E.S. Morton, eds. Washington: Smithsonian Institution Press.

Thomas, J.W., and H. Salwasser. 1989. Bringing conservation biology into a position of influence in natural resource management. *Conserv. Biol.* 3:123–127.

Verner, J. 1984. The guild concept applied to management of bird populations. *Environ. Manage.* 8:1–14.

Whitcomb, R.F., J.F. Lynch, P.A. Opler, and C.S. Robbins. 1976. Island biogeography and conservation: Strategy and limitations. *Science* 193:1030–1032.

APPENDIX 1. Location, elevation, vegetation type, and dates of visitation for each of the study sites.

1. LA MICHILIA INTERNATIONAL BIOSPHERE RESERVE: 45 km southwest of Vicente Guerrero, Durango (23°30' N, 104°15' W); 2,500 m; dry, pine-oak forest; 1/4–26/1984, 1/9–19/1985.

2. LA MICHILIA II: 45 km southwest of Vicente Guerrero, Durango (23°30' N, 104°15' W); 2,500 m; heavily disturbed portions of pine-oak forest, including agricultural fields, forest edges, and ejidos; 1/4–26/1984.

3. SUCHIL OAK WOODLAND: 35 km southwest of Vicente Guerrero, Durango (23°37' N, 104°10' W); 2,400 m; dry, pure oak woodland; 1/19–23/1984.

4. SAN MIGUEL: 5 km north of San Miguel de Allende, Guanajuato (21°00' N, 100°45' W); 2,000 m; *Acacia-Prosopis* thornscrub; 1/28/1984.

5. NEVADO TOLUCA: 70 km south of Toluca, Mexico (19°10' N, 99°48' W); pure pine forest off the road to Nevado de Toluca; 3,700 m; 1/29/1984.

6. VALLE DE BRAVO I: 2 km south of the lake at Valle de Bravo, Mexico (19°10' N, 100°10' W); tall pine-oak forest with some riparian canyons; 2,000 m; 1/30/1984.

7. SW TOLUCA: 30 km southwest of Toluca, Mexico (19°10' N, 99°58' W); tall, selectively cut pine-fir forest with thick understory of flowering perennials; 3,000 m; 1/30/1984.

8. CUERNAVACA: 41.5 km south of Mexico, D.F., and 3.5 km west of old Highway 95 (19°10' N, 99°15' W); pine-oak forest with bunchgrass understory; 2,300 m; 2/4–5/1984.

9. PASO DE CORTEZ: on the pass between the volcanoes Iztaccihuatl and Popocatepetl, Mexico (19°10' N, 98°40' W); pure pine forest with bunchgrass understory; 3,650 m; 2/6/1984.

10. CHILPANCINGO: west of Highway 95, 4.5 km north of Chilpancingo, Guerrero (17°35' N, 99°30' W); *Acacia* thornforest; 1,100 m; 2/7/1984.

11. EL RINCON: 3 km west of Highway 95 at El Rincon, Guerrero (17°20' N, 99°30' W); dry, pine-oak forest; 1,000 m; 2/8/1984.

12. SAN JUAN LACHAO: 70 km north of Puerto Escondido, Oaxaca (16°20' N, 97°05' W); cloud forest with understory of scattered coffee plants; 2,000 m; 2/10/1984.

13. EL PARAISO: 75 km northwest of Acapulco, Guerrero (17°25' N, 100°20' W); cloud forest with much of the understory converted to coffee plants; 2,000 m; 2/12/1984.

14. IXTAPA: 2 km north of Highway 200 between Zihuatanejo and Ixtapa, Guerrero (17°40' N, 101°40' W); tropical deciduous forest; 20 m; 2/13/1984.

15. LOS GOLONDRINAS: 1 km west of Highway 110, 10 km south of Colima, Colima (19°15' N, 103°45' W); *Acacia* thornforest; 500 m; 2/16/1984.

16. VOLCAN FUEGO: on the road up the Volcan de Colima, Jalisco (19°30' N, 103°35' W); heavily cut pine-oak woodlands with well developed understory; 2,500 m; 2/18/1984.

17. NIEVE COLIMA I: end of the road to the Volcan de Nieve, Jalisco (19°35' N, 103°35' W); pure pine forest up to timberline; 3,400 m; 2/19/1984.

18. NIEVE COLIMA II: at a lower elevation on the road to the Volcan de Nieve, Jalisco (19°35' N, 103°35' W); pine-oak-fir forest; 3,000 m; 2/20/1984.

19. CHAMELA I: 10 km south of Chamela, Jalisco, at the Estación de Biología Chamela (19°30' N, 105°03' W); undisturbed tropical deciduous forest; 30 m; 2/21–28/1984, 11/15–12/10/1984, 2/18–28/1985.

20. VALLARTA: 40 km south of Puerto Vallarta, Jalisco (20°10' N, 105°17' W); pine-oak forest; 500 m; 2/29/1984.

21. EL QUELITE: 60 km north of Mazatlan, Sinaloa, north of road to El Quelite (23°30' N, 106°30' W); heavily cut tropical deciduous forest; 100 m; 1/3–4/1985.

22. EL BOSQUE PRIMAVERA: 20 km west of Guadalajara, Jalisco, and 10 km south of Highway 15 (20°40' N, 103°32' W); uncut pine-oak forest; 1,600 m; 1/21/1985.

23. CARAPAN: 10 km south of Carapan, Michoacan (19°46' N, 102°02' W); pine-oak forest; 2,200 m; 1/22–23/1985.

24. COALCOMAN: 10 km northeast of Coalcoman, Michoacan (18°50' N, 103°05' W); heavily cut pine-oak forest; 2,000 m; 1/26–27/1985.

25. MORELIA: 25 km east of Morelia, Michoacan, south of Highway 15 on dirt road to Pino Real (19°40' N, 101°00' W); selectively cut pine-oak forest; 2,200 m; 1/28/1985.

26. RIO FRIO: 45 km east of Mexico City and 5 km northwest of Rio Frio, Mexico, north of Highway 190 (19°20' N, 98°40' W); pine-oak forest; 2,600 m; 1/31/1985.

27. OAXACA: 50 km northeast of Oaxaca, Oaxaca, south of Highway 175 (17°10' N, 96°35' W); pine-oak forest; 2,100 m; 2/4/1985.

28. TEHUANTEPEC: 20 km west of Tehuantepec, Oaxaca, south of Highway 190 (16°25' N, 95°25' W); tropical deciduous forest; 700 m; 2/9/1985.

29. PUERTO ANGEL: 40 km northeast of Puerto Angel, Oaxaca, north of Highway 200 (15°50' N, 96°10' W); 150 m; 2/10/1985.

30. LOXICHA: 40 km northwest of Puerto Angel, Oaxaca, west of Highway 175 on road to Loxicha (16°00' N, 96°30' W); pine-oak forest; 2,000 m; 2/11/1985.

31. CUAJIMALOYA: 40 km east-northeast of Oaxaca, Oaxaca, on road between Cuajimaloya and Buenavista (17°10' N, 96°20' W); pine-oak-fir forest; 2,500 m; 2/12/1985.

32. HERRADURA: 40 km northwest of Oaxaca, Oaxaca, south of Highway 190 at La Herradura (17°20' N, 97°00' W); pine-oak forest; 2,200 m; 2/13/1985.

33. TLAXIACO: 120 km west of Oaxaca, Oaxaca, east of Highway 125 (17°20' N, 97°40' W); pine-oak forest; 2,000 m; 2/14/1985.

34. VALLE DE BRAVO II: 10 km north of Valle de Bravo, Mexico (19°15' N, 100°08' W); pine-oak forest; 2,300 m; 2/16/1985.

35. LAS CABANAS: 30 km northeast of Tamazula, Jalisco (19°50' N, 103°05' W); pine-oak forest; 2,000 m; 2/17/1985.

36. CHAMELA II: several locations along Highway 200 within 20 km of Chamela, Jalisco (19°30' N, 105°05' W); early successional second-growth from what was tropical deciduous forest; 50 m; 2/22–24/1985.

JOHN C. KRICHER
Wheaton College
Norton, Massachusetts 02766

WILLIAM E. DAVIS, JR.
Boston University
Boston, Massachusetts 02215

Patterns of avian species richness in disturbed and undisturbed habitats in Belize

Abstract. Two disturbed sites and one undisturbed moist forest site in the immediate proximity of a Kekchi-Mayan Indian village in southern Belize supported different resident and Neotropical migrant avian assemblages. Migrants occurred commonly in mature moist forest, but were more abundant in early successional stages. Compared with resident species, species richness of migrants was higher in disturbed areas than in undisturbed forest. Kekchi-Mayan Indians, practicing milpa agriculture, have created a mosaic of habitats which support different bird assemblages. Conservation efforts directed toward maximizing avian species richness should include preservation (or continual creation) of disturbed areas, thus creating a mosaic of habitats that support diverse assemblages of resident and migrant species. Such a mosaic should be directly accessible from mature forest because 57% of species utilizing successional sites are edge or forest-border species. Mature forest seems essential to much of the avian species richness of disturbed sites.

Sinopsis. Dos sitios perturbados y un área de bosque primario en la proximidad inmediata de un poblado indígena Kekchi-Maya en el sur de Belize mantuvieron diferentes conjuntos de aves residentes y migratorias neotropicales. Las migratorias se encontraron comúnmente en bosque húmedo maduro, pero fueron mas abundantes en estadios sucesionales tempranos. En comparación con la riqueza de especies residentes, aquella de migratorias fue mayor en áreas perturbadas que en bosque intacto. Los indígenas Kekchi-Maya, al practicar agricultura de milpa han creado un mosaico de habitats que mantiene distintos conjuntos de aves. Los esfuerzos de conservación dirigidos a maximizar la riqueza de especies de aves deben incluír la preservación (o la creación continua) de áreas perturbadas que mantengan un mosaico de habitats que pueda contener dichos conjuntos diferentes de aves residentes y migratorias. Tales mosaicos deben ser directamente accesibles desde zonas de bosque maduro puesto que un 57% de las especies que utilizan sitios sucesionales son propias de borde de bosque. El bosque maduro parece ser esencial para una buena parte de la riqueza de especies de aves en los sitios perturbados.

The combination of accelerated cutting and habitat conversion of Neotropical forest (Myers 1980) plus a noted decline in some species of long-distance migrant songbirds (Wilcove and Whitcomb 1983, Wilcove and Terborgh 1984, Robbins et al. 1989, Askins et al. 1990) has stimulated interest in the composition of wintering Neotropical avian assemblages (Keast and Morton 1980, Rappole et al. 1983). We report here the results of a study conducted in southern Belize, the objectives of which were to (1) inventory, using both observations and mist-netting, all resident and Neotropical migrant bird species on three study sites in the vicinity of a Mayan Indian village, and (2) compare avian species richness among areas of recent disturbance with undisturbed moist forest.

Study area

Belize is located on the southern part of the Yucatan Peninsula, bordered on the south and west by Guatemala, and on the north by Mexico. The distribution of birds in Belize was described by Russell (1964). Paynter (1955), Tramer (1974), Waide et al. (1980), and Lynch (1989) have discussed the distribution of birds in the Yucatan Peninsula.

The present study was undertaken near Blue Creek Village, in the Toledo District of Belize (16°30' N, 89°03' W, 100 m elevation) for 10-day periods in January of 1982–1984 (Kricher and Davis 1986). The area is located southeast of the Maya Mountains in Belize and receives approximately 4,000 mm of annual precipitation supporting tropical moist forest (as defined by Holdridge et al. 1971). January is the end of the rainy season, but the three-month-long dry season does not begin until March. Blue Creek Village, a small settlement of approximately 170 Kekchi-Mayan Indians, is one of many villages of the agrarian Mopan Maya which are scattered throughout the region. Shifting cultivation, chiefly of corn, is the normal practice, with the landscape divided into cultivated milpas (plots). Blue Creek Village, typical of the villages of the region, is surrounded by successional areas in various degrees of vegetative regrowth, and is immediately adjacent to mature, uncut, moist forest.

Three sites, each distinct in its degree of disturbance and recovery and within 1 km of the village, were selected for study (Kricher and Davis 1986). The most recently disturbed area, termed Indian Village (IV), represents an early successional old field, and consists of dense tangles of herbaceous and some woody vegetation with much vine growth, the canopy averaging about 2–3 m tall. Emergent *Cecropia* and *Orbignya* and several leguminous trees are common on the 34-ha site. Pig Alley (PA), cut 20–25 years ago, represents a later successional stage. This 18-ha site is a young forest of dense woody and some herbaceous vegetation ranging from 4 to 12 m in height. In addition to the disturbed sites, a 45-ha Field Station (FS) plot was chosen within mature moist forest, where the forest had a canopy of 35–40 m and supported dense epiphytic and vine growth typical of lush, moist forests.

Methods

Species richness was determined by combining observations with the results of mist-netting. Observations occurred throughout the day, but because of the demands of extensive mist-netting, no attempt was made to quantify abundances, and only presence of species was recorded. Mist nets were placed in essentially, often exactly, the same locations in each year of the study. All netted birds (except hummingbirds) were fitted with U.S. Fish and Wildlife Service bands and released at the net where captured.

Mist nets were mostly standard 12 × 2.6 m nylon, with 36-mm mesh. Several 20-m-long nets were used in 1983 and 1984. Eight nets were set at IV (total net length 172 m), 8 at PA (total length 128 m), and 12 nets were set at FS (total length 176 m). Several nets in IV and PA were within 10 m of the habitat edge, but all nets in FS were located beyond 10 m of the forest edge. Nets were opened at 0630, closed from approximately 1200 to 1430, reopened, and then closed for the day at 1700.

Coefficients of similarity were calculated to compare the three study sites using the formula given by Beals (1960). A coefficient of 1.0 indicates that two data sets are essentially identical, and a coefficient of 0 that no species are held in common.

Results

SPECIES RICHNESS. Among the three sites 157 species were recorded including 31 North American migrants (19.7%) (Table 1). IV and PA, the two successional sites, were nearly identical in species richness and both somewhat exceeded the richness of FS, the uncut forest. The percentages of total species netted among the three sites were lowest for FS and highest for IV (Table 1). Of the 157 species, 57% are described as forest border or edge species (Peterson and Chaliff 1973, Ridgely 1976), and the percentage of forest border or edge species was similar (56–58%) among the three sites. The coefficients of similarity between sites, based on presence or

TABLE 1.   Summary of species richness, comparing total species richness (observed plus netted) with netting data alone, and comparing resident richness with migrant species richness at Indian Village, Pig Alley, and Field Station study sites

Variables	Indian Village	Pig Alley	Field Station	Total
Total species richness	102	98	87	
Number of species netted	60	56	45	
% netted of total	58.8	57.1	51.7	
Total individuals netted	241	258	343	842
Total resident richness	80	75	70	
Number resident species netted	44	40	37	
% netted of total	55.0	53.3	52.9	
Total individuals netted	168	179	283	630
Total migrant richness	22	23	17	
Number migrant species netted	16	16	8	
% netted of total	72.7	69.6	47.1	
Total individuals netted	73	79	60	212
Number of exclusive species	24	12	29	65
% exclusive species	23.5	12.2	33.3	
Number resident exclusive	20	11	25	
Resident %	25.0	14.9	35.7	
Number migrant exclusive species	4	1	4	
Migrant %	18.1	4.3	23.5	

NOTE: Exclusive species are those found only in one study area (i.e. 24 species were found only in Indian Village, of which 20 were residents, and 4 were migrants).

TABLE 2.   Resident and migrant species distributions among study sites based upon both observational and netting data

Site	Residents			Migrant	
	Sp.	(Exp.)	%	Sp.	%
All sites	32	(40.6)	25.6	10	32.2
Indian Village	20	(16.3)	16.0	4	12.9
Pig Alley	11	(4.0)	8.8	1	3.2
Field Station	25	(16.3)	20.0	4	12.9
Indian Village and Pig Alley	22	(32.5)	17.6	8	25.8
Pig Alley and Field Station	10	(16.3)	8.0	4	12.9
Indian Village and Field Station	6	(0)	4.8	0	0.0

NOTE: χ^2 analysis indicated significant differences ($P < .001$) from migrant distribution. Numbers in parentheses are expected values, if resident distribution was proportionally identical to migrant distribution. For instance, had resident and migrant distributions been identical, one would expect 40.6 (41) species of residents to have been found at all three sites.

absence of each species in a particular habitat (Beals 1960), were as follows: IV/PA = 0.701; PA/FS = 0.568; IV/FS = 0.473. Predictably, coefficients of similarity were most similar between the two successional areas and least similar between the early successional area (IV) and the uncut forest (FS).

Each site included species found in neither of the other two sites (Table 1, exclusive species) and, overall, 41.4% of the species occurred at only one of the three sites. Although FS had the lowest species richness, it contained the largest percentage (33.3%) of exclusive species. PA, the mid-successional site, had the smallest percentage (12.2%) of exclusive species. Forty-two species (26.8%) were observed at all three sites.

NEOTROPICAL MIGRANTS. North American migrant species richness was highest in the two disturbed sites (Table 1). A smaller percentage of migrants was netted at FS relative to the total of observed migrant species (Table 1). This was due to the high canopy at that site, where many species were observed but not netted.

Migrant distribution among the sites differed significantly (χ^2 = 373, 6 d.f., P < 0.001, Sokal and Rohlf 1969) from that of residents (Table 2). More resident species (44.8%) were exclusive to one site than were migrants (29.0%). Of the 31 migrant species, 8 were found both in IV and PA, 10 species occurred in all three sites, and only 4 species occurred exclusively at FS. Thus, migrant species were more common in disturbed sites than in undisturbed forest.

NETTING RESULTS. A total of 842 individual birds were netted (not including recaptures and recoveries) of which 630 (74.8%) were residents and 212 (25.2%) were migrants. Overall, 30.1% of the netted individuals and 26.7% of the species were migrants at IV; 30.6% of the individuals and 28.6% of the species were migrants at PA; and 17.5% of the individuals and 17.7% of the species were migrants at FS. Curves for each study site showing the cumulative number of species netted from 1982 through 1984 (Fig. 1) indicate by their flattening that most species that could be captured were, in fact, captured. It should be noted, however, that each of the three curves, although approaching asymptotic, is also well below the total number of species observed at each of the sites (Table 1) indicating that netting alone is not adequate to sample all species. Four migrant species, Wood Thrush (*Hylocichla mustelina*) (36 netted), Kentucky Warbler (*Oporornis formosus*) (33), Ovenbird (*Seiurus aurocapillus*) (32), and Gray Catbird (*Dumetella carolinensis*) (27) accounted for 60.4% of the total number of migrants netted.

NETTING COMPARISONS BETWEEN YEARS. For each site, coefficients of similarity, based on numbers of each

Cumulative Number of Species Netted

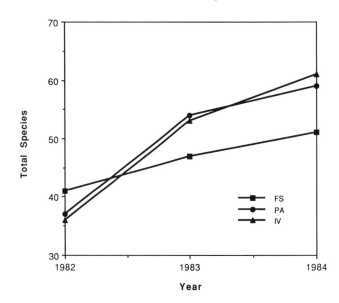

FIGURE 1. Cumulative number of species netted through the duration of the study. For abbreviations, see text.

TABLE 3. Coefficients of similarity of study sites between years and between study sites per year

	1982–83	1983–84	1982–84	$\bar{x}$
Between years:				
Indian Village	.61	.62	.65	.63
Pig Alley	.68	.60	.59	.62
Field Station	.74	.72	.71	.72
Between sites:				
Indian Village and Pig Alley	.59	.57	.55	.57
Pig Alley	.48	.40	.39	.42
Indian Village and Field Station	.43	.55	.50	.49

species netted in each habitat (Beals 1960), varied little from year to year (Table 3). Although the moist forest site (FS) consistently had the highest between-year similarity, indicating the least change in the avian community among years, no statistical significance (all χ^2, P > 0.05) was found for any year to year differences among the sites. Coefficients ranged from 0.59 to 0.74, indicating that substantial year to year variation existed among all sites.

NETTING COMPARISONS BETWEEN SITES. For each year, coefficients of similarity (calculated from numbers of individuals netted per species) showed the highest similarity between IV and PA (Table 3). Similarity quotients between FS and IV averaged slightly higher than those comparing FS with PA. However, no trends among differences between sites were statistically significant (all χ^2, $P > 0.05$). Similarity quotients indicated that substantial differences existed among the sites during all years of the study.

Discussion

Blue Creek Village could aptly be described as the nucleus of an array of anthropogenic landscape patches (Forman and Godron 1986), each of which is relatively physiognomically distinct and in direct contact with contiguous moist forest. Such a patch array, at least in the temperate zone, maximizes the potential for edge effect to enhance bird species richness (Galli et al. 1976). In the present study disturbed, successional areas contain high species richness of both residents and migrants. Mayan farming practices, insofar as they contribute to the creation of such areas, can promote species richness. In the Blue Creek area, Kekchi farmers typically abandon their milpas after as brief a period as two or three years (F. Dodd, pers. comm.). Although the native farmers have a negative impact upon large bird species such as guans (Cracidae), which are hunted, human activity in Blue Creek Village probably has promoted rather than reduced avian species richness. The results of our study support the view that "moderate levels of tropical forest disturbance might benefit a considerable number of Nearctic migrant species that utilize edge habitats and successional vegetation" even though some have suggested that this view has been "largely discredited" (see Lynch 1989:526).

The overall species richness of this area might be highly dependent upon access to forest. The FS site used in this study is not a forest island but is part of an extensive, continuous forest system which extends, with limited disturbance, throughout the Maya Mountain region. Given the high percentage of edge and forest border species encountered at each of the disturbed sites, we hypothesize that had IV and PA not been in close proximity to forest, it is doubtful that species richnesses would have been as high. Further, Pig Alley is itself a young forest. Old field succession can be quite rapid in the tropics, especially during its initial stages (Knight 1975, Bazzaz and Pickett 1980, Ewel 1980). As long as succession occurs without disruption, forests throughout much of Central America regenerate following disturbance, providing suitable habitats for birds throughout the successional process.

Bird abundance in this study was quantified only with mist-net data, and mist-netting is subject to a number of biases (Lovejoy 1974), Karr 1981, Remsen and Parker 1983, Levey 1988, Lynch 1989). Mist-netting is most effective in lower strata, least in high strata. The composition of the avifauna in forest canopy is undoubtedly undersampled by mist-netting. Data collected by mist-netting require cautious interpretation.

Percentage of migrant species netted compared with those observed, differed from one site to another (Table 1). Had netting data alone been considered, migrant species richness in the moist forest would have been considerably underestimated (47% of the migrant species were netted—Table 1), compared with that of the successional areas, where higher percentages of migrant species were captured. On the other hand, some resident species such as Bare-crowned Antbird (*Gymnocichla nudiceps*), Speckled Mourner (*Lanicera rufescens*), White-throated Spadebill (*Platyrinchus mystaceus*), and Northern Bentbill (*Oncostoma cinereigulare*) were rarely or never observed other than by mist-netting. Observations alone might underestimate the presence of some of these species. The combined use of both observations and netting is probably necessary to detect all species, at least in habitat types sampled in this study.

Lloyd-Evans (1984) reported on netting studies conducted in central Belize from 1 February to 15 April, 1983 and 1984. In that study, relative migrant abundance (individual birds) was 42% in savanna scrub, 43% in pine-oak, 37% in gallery forest, and 22% in hardwood forest. However, some of the birds recorded were probably not winter residents but were migrating northward. Tramer (1974) estimated relatively low migrant percentages (3–36%) based on numbers of individuals in a series of successional stages in northwestern Yucatan. For the central Yucatan Peninsula, Waide (1980) found that migrants made up approximately 50% of the individuals in successional areas, and up to one-third of the forest avian communities. Lynch (1989) reported similar percentages from Yucatan and northern Belize.

Neotropical migrants comprised a numerically important component of the winter avifauna at Blue Creek. Migrant sampling by netting was probably most accurate at IV and PA where vegetation was generally low. At these sites, migrants represented approximately 30% of the individuals captured. In terms of total species richness (observed and/or netted), migrants represented approximately 20% of all species at each site. Lynch (1989) reported migrant species richness to be 24% based on point counts and 25.3% based on netting for successional habitats, such as IV, throughout the Yucatan Peninsula. He also found that 18% of the species in late successional and mature, medium-stature semievergreen forests were migrants. At FS, the migrants captured were those typically associated with understory—Wood Thrush, Ovenbird, Kentucky Warbler, and Northern Waterthrush (*Seiurus noveboracensis*). Migrants such as Black-and-white Warbler (*Mniotilta varia*) and Magnolia Warbler (*Dendroica magnolia*), both of which were netted at IV and PA, and Black-throated

Green Warblers (*Dendroica virens*) were never netted at FS but were observed in the canopy, frequently in association with mixed-species flocks of Neotropical residents. Although migrants were underrepresented in netting data at FS, they still represented 17.7% of the individuals captured, largely because of the abundance of Wood Thrushes, Ovenbirds, and Kentucky Warblers. Migrants generally occupied habitats structurally similar to those of their breeding grounds: Yellow-breasted Chats (*Icteria virens*), Common Yellowthroats (*Geothlypis trichas*), and Gray Catbirds favored successional sites whereas Wood Thrushes and Kentucky Warblers were most frequently netted in the moist forest. Ovenbirds were most frequently netted at IV, although they were also captured at PA and FS.

The present study indicates that migrant species were most numerous in the two successional sites. Typical forest species such as Wood Thrush, Hooded Warbler (*Wilsonia citrina*), Magnolia Warbler, Ovenbird, and Worm-eating Warbler (*Helmitheros vermivorus*) were netted at IV and/or PA. Migrant species differed from resident species in that migrant species were more apt to occur at more than one site. Some migrants might be floaters, passing through habitats but not occupying territories (Rappole and Morton 1985, Rappole et al. 1989). Lynch (1989) considered the Wood Thrush and Kentucky Warbler to be "forest specialists." However, in southern Belize, we recaptured and/or recovered these two species at IV, the early successional site (Kricher and Davis 1986).

Our results suggest that resident species, though perhaps somewhat more specialized in habitat choice (44.8% of the resident species were found at just one site), are also dynamic. Similarity in community composition among years (Table 3) suggests that avian assemblages at all sites differed substantially from one year to the next. Other studies (e.g., Karr and Freemark 1983) have noted localized small-scale temporal changes within tropical forest avian assemblages.

Human-generated successional areas form important habitats for many resident and migrant species. The presence of substantial numbers of species associated with forest edge and successional habitats suggests that the distribution (and, by implication, the evolutionary history) of Belizean landbirds has been strongly affected by continued disturbance and regeneration of forest. The nonequilibrium concept of tropical forest tree diversity (Connell 1978, Hubbell and Foster 1986) is perhaps reflected by the bird species richness patterns at Blue Creek. Kekchi Indians continually create disturbed sites, and providing that forest is permitted to regrow on these sites, probably promote the patterns observed for bird species richness found in our study. This is a very old practice and should not be confused with permanent pasture or large-scale mechanized agriculture.

Emerging conservation policies for Central America should consider this distinction.

Acknowledgments

We wish to thank all of the Earthwatch volunteers who aided us in the field and The Center for Field Research, which sponsored our project during its three years. We are also indebted to Frederick J. Dodd and to the Bowman family for their logistical support. Wayne R. Petersen and Melinda Welton were invaluable associates in the field. One anonymous reviewer provided very helpful criticism and editorial suggestions, for which we are most grateful.

A complete list of species from each study site is available from the senior author.

Literature cited

Askins, R.A., J.F. Lynch, and R. Greenberg. 1990. Population declines in migratory birds in eastern North America. *Current Ornithol.* 7:1–57.

Bazzaz, F.A., and S.T.A. Pickett. 1980. Physiological ecology of tropical succession: A comparative review. *Ann. Rev. Ecol. Syst.* 11:287–310.

Beals, E.W. 1960. Forest bird communities of the Apostle Islands of Wisconsin. *Wilson Bull.* 72:156–181.

Connell, J.H. 1978. Diversity in tropical rain forests and coral reefs. *Science* 199:1302–1310.

Ewel, J. 1980. Tropical succession: Manifold routes to maturity. Pages 2–7 in *Tropical Succession*, supplement to Biotropica 12.

Forman, R.T.T., and M. Godron. 1986. *Landscape Ecology.* New York: John Wiley and Sons.

Galli, A.E., C.F. Leck, and R.T.T. Forman. 1976. Avian distribution patterns in forest islands of different sizes in central New Jersey. *Auk* 93:356–364.

Holdridge, L.R., W.C. Grenke, W.H. Hatheway, T. Laing, and J.A. Tosi. 1971. *Forest Environments in Tropical Life Zones.* New York: Pergamon Press.

Hubbell, S.P., and R.B. Foster. 1986. Biology, chance, and history and the structure of tropical rain forest tree communities. Pages 314–330 in *Community Ecology*, J. Diamond and T.J. Case, eds. New York: Harper and Row.

Karr, J.R. 1981. Surveying birds with mist nets. Pages 62–67 in *Estimating Numbers of Terrestrial Birds*, C.J. Ralph and M.J. Scott, eds. Studies in Avian Biology No. 6.

Karr, J.R., and K.E. Freemark. 1983. Habitat selection and environmental gradients: Dynamics in the "stable" tropics. *Ecology* 64:1481–1494.

Keast, A., and E.S. Morton, eds. 1980. *Migrant Birds in the Neotropics: Ecology, Behavior, Distribution, and Conservation.* Washington: Smithsonian Institution Press.

Knight, D.H. 1975. A phytosociological analysis of species rich tropical forest on Barro Colorado Island, Panama. *Ecol. Monogr.* 45:259–284.

Kricher, J.C., and W.E. Davis, Jr. 1986. Returns and winter-site fidelity of North American migrants banded in Belize, Central America. *J. Field Ornithol.* 57:48–52.

Levey, D.J. 1988. Tropical wet treefall gaps and distribution of understory birds and plants. *Ecology* 69:1076–1089.

Lloyd-Evans, T. 1984. Banding and census results. Manomet Bird Observatory, August: 7–9.

Lovejoy, T. 1974. Bird diversity and abundance in Amazon forest communities. *Living Bird* 13:127–191.

Lynch, J.F. 1989. Distribution of overwintering Nearctic migrants in the Yucatan Peninsula, I: General patterns of occurrence. *Condor* 91:515–544.

Myers, N. 1980. *Conversion of Tropical Moist Forests.* Washington: National Academy of Sciences.

Paynter, R.A., Jr. 1955. The ornithogeography of the Yucatan Peninsula. Peabody Mus. Nat. Hist., Yale Univ. Bull. 9:1–347.

Peterson, R.T., and E.L. Chaliff. 1973. A Field Guide to Mexican Birds. Boston: Houghton Mifflin Co.

Rappole, J.H., and E.S. Morton. 1985. Effects of habitat alteration on a tropical avian forest community. Pages 1013–1021 in *Neotropical Ornithology,* P.A. Buckley, E.S. Morton, R.S. Ridgely, and F.G. Buckley, eds. Ornithol. Monogr. 36.

Rappole, J.H., E.S. Morton, T.E. Lovejoy, III, and J.L. Ruos. 1983. *Nearctic Avian Migrants in the Neotropics.* Washington: U.S. Fish and Wildlife Service.

Rappole, J.H., M.A. Ramos, and K. Winker. 1989. Wintering wood thrush movements and mortality in southern Veracruz. *Auk* 106:402–410.

Remsen, J.V., Jr., and T.A. Parker III. 1983. Contribution of river created habitats to bird species richness in Amazonia. *Biotropica* 15:223–231.

Ridgely, R.S. 1976. A Field Guide to the Birds of Panama. Princeton: Princeton University Press.

Robbins, C.S., J.R. Sauer, R.S. Greenberg, and S. Droege. 1989. Population declines in North American birds that migrate to the neotropics. *Proc. Natl. Acad. Sci.* 86:7658–7662.

Russell, S.M. 1964. *A Distributional Study of the Birds of British Honduras.* Ornithol. Monogr. 1.

Sokal R.R., and F.J. Rohlf. 1969. *Biometry.* San Francisco: W.H. Freeman and Co.

Tramer, E.J. 1974. Proportions of wintering North American birds in disturbed and undisturbed dry tropical habitats. *Condor* 76:460–464.

Waide, R.B. 1980. Resource partitioning between migrant and resident birds: The use of irregular resources. Pages 337–352 in *Migrant Birds in the Neotropics: Ecology, Behavior, Distribution and Conservation,* A. Keast and E.S. Morton, eds. Washington: Smithsonian Institution Press.

Waide, R.B., J.T. Emlen, and E.J. Tramer. 1980. Distribution of migrant birds in the Yucatan Peninsula: A survey, Pages 165–171 in *Migrant Birds in the Neotropics: Ecology, Behavior, Distribution and Conservation,* A. Keast and E.S. Morton, eds. Washington: Smithsonian Institution Press.

Wilcove, D.S., and J.W. Terborgh. 1984. Patterns of population decline in birds. *Am. Birds* 38:10–13.

Wilcove, D.S., and R.F. Whitcomb. 1983. Gone with the trees. *Nat. History* 92:82–91.

DANIEL R. PETIT
LISA J. PETIT
KIMBERLY G. SMITH
Department of Zoology
University of Arkansas
Fayetteville, Arkansas 72701

Habitat associations of migratory birds overwintering in Belize, Central America

Abstract. During winter 1988–89, mist nets were used to sample understory bird populations in five nonagricultural vegetation types in Belize, Central America to determine effects of disturbance and vegetation structure on migrant habitat use. Early successional growth, pine-savanna, and broadleaved forest edge, the most disturbed habitats, had higher species diversity and abundance of migrants than did broadleaved forest interior and pine forest. Two biotic elements purported to influence habitat use by overwintering migrants, food abundance and competition with residents, could not explain the distribution of migrants as a group. This was due to species-specific responses to the environment and highlights the improbability of a single explanation accounting for the distribution of all migrants in the Neotropics. For example, Wood Thrushes, Kentucky Warblers, and Hooded Warblers in Belize usually were associated with interiors or edges of tall broadleaved forests, whereas Yellow-breasted Chats, Gray Catbirds, Common Yellowthroats, Ovenbirds, and White-eyed Vireos were found disproportionately in pine-savanna and/or early successional scrub. Because migratory (and resident) species differ in their use of habitats, it is not sufficient to preserve only one vegetation type. Knowledge of the distribution and ecology of species in all habitats is crucial if conservationists are to manage for both diversity and rarity. Such knowledge can be gained best by both synecological and single-species demographic studies of North American migrant birds in their winter quarters.

Sinopsis. Durante el invierno de 1988–1989, se usaron redes de niebla para muestrear poblaciones de aves de sotobosque en cinco tipos de vegetación no agrícola en Belize, América Central, para determinar los efectos de la perturbación y de la estructura de la vegetación sobre el uso de habitat por las migratorias. Los habitats mas perturbados (estadios sucesionales tempranos, comunidad pino-sabana y borde de bosque tropical), tuvieron diversidades de especies y abundancias mayores de migratorias que el interior de bosque tropical y de pinos. Dos elementos bióticos que supuestamente afectan el uso de habitat por las migratorias invernantes, la abundancia de alimento y la competencia con aves residentes, no permitieron explicar la distribución de las migratorias como grupo. Esto se debió a las respuestas específicas de especies particulares a su medio y resalta la improbabilidad de una explicación única para la distribución de todas las migratorias en el neotrópico. Por ejemplo, *Hylocichla mustelina, Oporornis formosus* y *Wilsonia citrina* en Belize estuvieron asociadas con el interior o los bordes de bosques tropicales, mientras que *Icteria virens, Dumetella carolinensis, Geothlypis trichas, Seiurus aurocapillus* y *Vireo griseus* se encontraron desproporcionadamente en pino-sabana y/o matorral sucesional temprano. Puesto que las especies migratorias (y residentes) difieren en su uso habitacional, no es suficiente preservar solamente un tipo de vegetación. El conocimiento sobre la distribución y la ecología de las especies en todos los habitats es crucial si los conservacionistas pretenden manejar tanto la diversidad como la rareza. Tal conocimiento puede conseguirse mejor mediante estudios sinecológicos y demográficos monoespecíficos de aves migratorias norteamericanas en sus cuarteles de invierno.

For thousands of years, tropical landscapes have been a dynamic mosaic of undisturbed and disturbed patches of vegetation, the latter a result of both natural and human-related events (Karr 1976a, Myers 1980. During the 20th century, however, the presence of mechanized societies and increased burning of forests to provide pastures have skewed the distribution of tropical habitats toward more early successional, fragmented, and edge-dominated states (Myers 1980). Recently, avian ecologists have attempted to quantify effects of deforestation on tropical bird populations which have evolved along with natural changes in the environment for many millenia, but which now must persist in landscapes that are undergoing drastic, rapid changes. However, some uncertainty exists concerning the effects of habitat alteration on migrant and resident bird species (Hutto 1988). For example, Karr (1976b), Hutto (1980), and Martin (1985) found that migrants were most common in early successional habitats, whereas Lack and Lack (1972), Tramer (1974), and Lynch (1989) detected few noticeable differences in abundance of migrants among a series of successional stages. The search for definitive trends in the distribution of migrant birds is further complicated by variation among individual species in their preferences for undisturbed or disturbed habitats (Terborgh 1980). Thus, our basic understanding of habitat requirements of migrant birds overwintering in the Neotropics is incomplete, and improved knowledge of habitat needs of individual species is critically needed (Greenberg 1986).

Belize is a small Caribbean-basin country bordering the southern Yucatan Peninsula in Central America and contains a diverse array of naturally occurring vegeta-

tion types. Many North American migrants overwinter in Belize, but few ornithologists have studied habitat use of migrant birds there. In 1988, we initiated a study to assess the distribution of migratory and resident bird species across a group of disturbed and undisturbed vegetation types in Belize. In this paper, we report observed trends and relate those data to previously published reports on migrant use of selected habitats in Latin America.

Study sites

Within a 500-km² area of central Belize, 20 sites, representing five major vegetation types, were chosen (Appendix 1). This area encompasses two ecological life zones (Holdridge 1947): subtropical moist forest and the transition zone between subtropical moist and subtropical wet forest (Hartshorn et al. 1984). Habitat types were distinguished based on vegetation structure and composition, although those measures varied among plots within any given habitat type. Five vegetation types defined in this study are: (1) EARLY SUCCESSIONAL GROWTH: milpas (small-scale agricultural land) or pastures abandoned approximately two to five years previously, characterized by short (generally 1–3 m), dense (milpa), or patchy (pasture) vegetation. The four sites (elevation 30–40 m) were located within more extensive semievergreen broadleaved forest, often with a conspicuous cohune palm (*Orbignya cohune*) element. Common woody plants were *Coccoloba, Cecropia, Acacia, Mimosa, Piper, Solanum,* and *Pithecellobium.* (2) PINE-SAVANNA: relatively open, lowland (30 m) habitat of grasses and sedges with frequent dense patches of small broadleaved trees, shrubs (e.g., *Byrsonima, Curatella, Miconia, Quercus,* and *Crescentia*), and palms (*Paurotis* and *Schippia*). The overstory comprised scattered pines (*Pinus caribaea*) 10–22 m tall. A conspicuous component of the lowland savanna habitats is susceptibility to fire, which thins the understory vegetation several times each decade. (3) BROADLEAVED FOREST INTERIOR: semievergreen to semideciduous secondary forests with canopies from 12 to > 30 m tall and well-developed understories. Characteristic tree species included *Swietenia, Manilkara, Brosimum, Drypetes, Dialium, Terminalia, Orbignya, Dendropanax, Lonchocarpus, Zanthoxylum,* and *Ficus.* All four forest interior plots were situated > 50 m (usually > 200 m) from an edge, which was defined as a break of > 1000 m² in the canopy. Elevation ranged from 40 to 440 m ($\bar{X}$ = 270 m). One plot was situated within a tract only 20 ha in size, but all others were > 100 ha. Understories were disturbed only slightly by trails or small-scale collecting of firewood or palm fronds for roof thatching by local people. (4) BROADLEAVED FOREST EDGE: fairly similar to broadleaved forest interior in tree species composition and vegetation structure. Birds were surveyed on the four plots within 25 m of a forest edge (always along a road cut > 20 m in width). In addition to some forest interior plants, *Cecropia, Bursera, Spondias, Protium, Psychotria,* and *Piper* were often present on these relatively low elevation (40–120 m) sites. Forest edges represented highly disturbed habitats with abrupt openings in the forest canopy and consequent changes in vegetation because of increased sunlight (see Lovejoy et al. 1986). (5) PINE FOREST: four plots were located in the Mountain Pine Ridge area (elevation 500 m) where > 500 km² of forest is managed by the Belize Forestry Department for small-scale harvesting of *Pinus caribaea* and *P. oocarpa.* The 15–25-m-tall pine canopy overlaid a patchy, often dense, understory of 1–3-m-tall trees and shrubs, such as *Quercus* and *Miconia,* with low sedges and grasses forming a dense ground cover. Although evidence of fire and selective cutting were apparent in the pine forest, sites chosen for this study had not been disturbed substantially for at least 5–10 years.

Methods

Birds were mist-netted using 9 × 2-m nylon mist nets (32- and 38-mm mesh) between 15 October 1988 and 11 March 1989. Four to 15 nets were run on any given day, depending on weather conditions and habitat type. Nets were usually placed in groups of two to four, parallel or perpendicular to a single transect route bisecting the study plot. To avoid reduced capture rates associated with operating mist nets in the same area on consecutive days, we usually did not net on a study plot more than once per week. We did not strictly limit our diurnal netting schedule, but most of our work was conducted between sunrise (approximately 06:00) and 11:00, especially in the more exposed habitats (i.e., early second growth, pine-savanna, and forest edge). We did not net during windy or prolonged rainy weather. Captured birds were banded with unique combinations of U.S. Fish and Wildlife Service aluminum bands and color bands (resident species received only the latter), measured, weighed, and released within 100 m of the capture site. Multiple captures of the same individual on the same day were ignored. However, because < 10% of all captures were of individuals netted earlier in the winter, we included these captures in our analysis. Capture rates were determined by dividing total number of captured individuals by total net hours (1 net hr = 1 net open for 1 hr).

Karr (1981) outlined several problems associated with using mist nets to census bird communities, the most important of which are biases associated with comparisons across habitat types and among different

species. We acknowledge these potential sources of error in estimating relative bird abundances, and our results and conclusions should be viewed in that light. Nevertheless, mist netting can be a valuable technique for estimating the relative use of habitats by small (5–100 g) species which spend a large proportion of their active hours 0–2 m above ground (Karr 1979). Although interpretation of relative abundances of species across habitat types, as determined by mist netting, is more dubious than simple presence/absence determinations (Karr 1981), netting often provides some indication of relative abundances of understory species (e.g., Waide et al. 1980, Karr 1981, Karr and Freemark 1983, Lynch 1989).

Because analyses at the community level can detect only broad trends in patterns of bird distribution and provide scant detail of how individual species respond to certain environmental factors, we performed additional, single-species analyses on migrants whose capture rates and disproportionate use of the low vegetation strata would allow us to statistically compare their distributions across habitat types. We focused on species that (1) were represented by > 20 captures, and (2) were seen foraging below 3 m over 80% of the time in *all* habitats in which they were sighted. This latter restriction was based on data from a contemporaneous study of migrant foraging behavior (D.R. Petit, unpubl. data) and was used to confine analyses to species that nearly always foraged low in vegetation, regardless of habitat type, making interhabitat comparisons justifiable. For each species, a goodness-of-fit G test (Zar 1984) was used to test for significant departures from uniform distribution across the five habitat types. Because unequal sampling effort (i.e., net hours) was expended among habitat types, we could not simply calculate expected number of captures ($E[c_i]$) for each habitat, i, as $E(c_i) = C/5$, where C equals total number of captures for a given species. Rather, we standardized expected values based on number of net hours (h_i) spent sampling habitat $_i$. Thus, $E(c_i) = C \cdot h_i / H_T$, where $H_T = \Sigma h_i$.

To describe the habitat breadth of each species, we used Levins's (1968) measure of niche breadth: $B = 1/\Sigma p_i^2$, where p_i is the proportion of all captures of a given species that were made in habitat i. In this analysis, B values could range from 1, when a species was found in only one vegetation type, to 5, when it was equally distributed among all habitats. We arbitrarily categorized species as habitat specialists ($B < 2$), moderate generalists ($2 < B < 3.5$), or generalists ($B > 3.5$).

Results

OVERALL HABITAT USE. More than 70 days and 4200 net hours were spent netting birds, consisting of 9 to 22 days and 500 to 1,200 net hours in each habitat type (Table 1). The 1,542 captures included 92 resident and 29 migrant species. Nearly two-thirds of all individuals captured were residents, a proportion that was consistent across all habitats except pine-savanna, where migrants slightly outnumbered residents. Resident species made up three-fourths of all species captured in most vegetation types, although this value approached only 60% in pine-savanna (Table 1).

More migrant species were captured in pine-savanna, early successional growth, and broadleaved forest edge than in pine forest and the interior of broadleaved forest (Table 1). However, this apparent preference for more disturbed habitats might have been distorted by unequal sampling in each of the five habitat types. To address that possibility, we constructed species-effort curves to determine if total net hours for each habitat type was sufficient to describe the number of migrant (and resident) species occupying the 0–2-m zone. The number of migrant species in each habitat increased rapidly over the first several hundred net hours, then leveled off after 200–400 sampling hours (Fig. 1). Resident species continued to increase throughout the sampling period in most habitat types. A plateau might have been reached only in broadleaved forest interior and pine-savanna (Fig. 1). Although the accumulation of resident species clearly slowed in the other three vegetation types, an average of four new resident species per 100 net hours was still being added during the last three days of netting in each habitat. Thus, our netting efforts adequately quantified the presence or absence of "nettable" (see Methods) migrant species, but not resident species.

Analysis of capture rates indicates that migrants occupying low strata of vegetation are more abundant in pine-savanna, early successional growth, and broadleaved forest edge than in pine forest and interiors of broadleaved forest (Fig. 2). Abundance, as measured by capture rates, is tightly correlated with species richness across habitats (Spearman's rho, $r_s = 0.98$). Capture rates of residents were relatively high in early successional growth and forest edge, moderate in broadleaved forest interior and pine-savanna, and low in pine forest (Fig. 2). Species richness was not significantly correlated with abundance (capture rates) for resident species ($r_s = 0.40$), a fact which might reflect less complete sampling of resident populations compared to migrants.

DISTRIBUTIONS OF INDIVIDUAL SPECIES. All eight understory species analyzed here responded differently to different vegetation types (Fig. 3a-b). Ovenbirds (*Seiurus aurocapillus*; $G = 19.3$, $P < 0.001$) and Gray Catbirds (*Dumetella carolinensis*; $G = 34.9$, $P < 0.001$) were captured most frequently in pine-savanna and early successional scrub, respectively, whereas White-eyed Vireos (*Vireo griseus*; $G = 32.5$, $P < 0.001$), Common Yellowthroats (*Geothlypis trichas*; $G = 105.6$, $P < 0.001$), and Yellow-breasted Chats (*Icteria virens*; $G = 45.8$, $P < 0.001$) were captured most frequently in both habitats. Wood Thrushes (*Hylocichla mustelina*; $G = 33.9$, $P < 0.001$), Kentucky Warblers (*Oporornis formosus*; $G = 61.7$, $P < 0.001$), and Hooded Warblers (*Wilsonia citrina*; $G = 24.5$, $P < 0.001$) were netted most often in broadleaved forest interior and edge habitats.

All eight migrants showed nonrandom use of the five habitats, but all species were found in > 1 vegetation

TABLE 1. Summary of mist-netting data collected from five habitat types in central Belize during winter, 1988–89

Variable	Habitat type				
			Broadleaved forest		
	Early successional growth	Pine-savanna	Interior	Edge	Pine forest
Days netting	9	22	21	9	12
Net-hours	669.0	870.5	1186.5	501.3	1026.7
Captures					
residents	321	149	209	199	100
(%)	(70.5)	(42.3)	(66.6)	(70.6)	(71.9)
migrants	134	203	105	83	39
(%)	(29.5)	(57.7)	(33.4)	(29.4)	(28.1)
Species					
residents	44	26	44	41	31
(%)	(72.1)	(59.1)	(78.6)	(70.7)	(73.8)
migrants	17	18	12	17	11
(%)	(27.9)	(40.9)	(21.4)	(29.3)	(26.2)

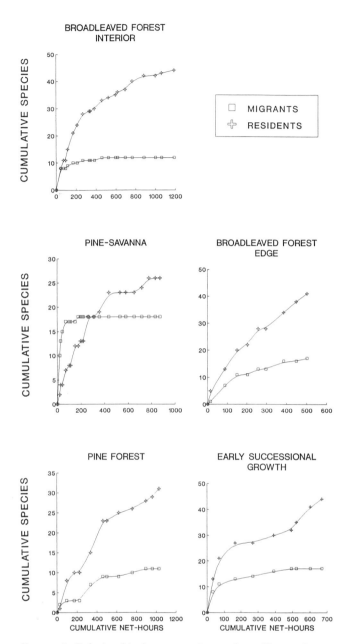

FIGURE 1. Relationship between mist-netting effort and species richness for migrant and resident species inhabiting five habitat types in Belize during winter. Note that axes are scaled differently for each habitat.

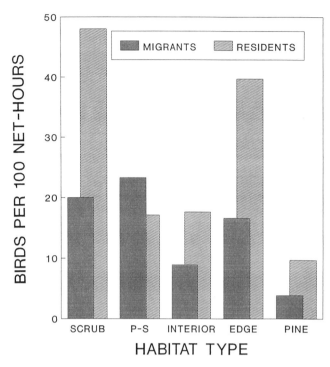

FIGURE 2. Capture rates (birds/100 net hours) of migrant and resident birds in five habitats in Belize during winter. Scrub = early successional growth, P-S = pine-savanna, interior = broadleaved forest interior, edge = broadleaved forest edge, pine = pine forest.

type; on average, each species was netted in 3.75 (± 1.16 SD, range = 2–5) vegetation types. Based on niche breadths, Wood Thrush (B = 1.85), Common Yellowthroat (1.91), and Kentucky Warbler (1.86) were habitat specialists; White-eyed Vireo (2.58), Yellow-breasted Chat (2.68), and Hooded Warbler (3.39) were moderate generalists; and Ovenbird (3.81) and Gray Catbird (4.16) were habitat generalists.

Discussion

HABITAT USE BY MIGRANT BIRDS

Our results are consistent with previous reports showing greater use of disturbed (as opposed to undisturbed) vegetation by migrant landbirds overwintering in the Neotropics (e.g., Karr 1976b, Hutto 1980, Waide 1980, Willis 1980, Martin 1985, Lynch 1989). Early successional scrub, pine-savanna, and forest edge habitats all had higher species richness and capture rates of migrants than the two less disturbed habitats (broadleaved forest interior and pine forest). The causative factor(s) of that relationship are unclear, but have been widely suggested to include food resources (e.g., Willis 1966, Karr 1976b, Hutto 1980) and past or present interspecific interactions (e.g., Emlen 1980, Hutto 1980). The present study supports neither of these hypothesis for migrants *as a group*. For example, our study recorded a positive relationship between resident and migrant capture rates among all habitats (r_s = 0.40) but an inverse relationship would be more likely if residents and migrants were competing groups. Likewise, it is improbable that

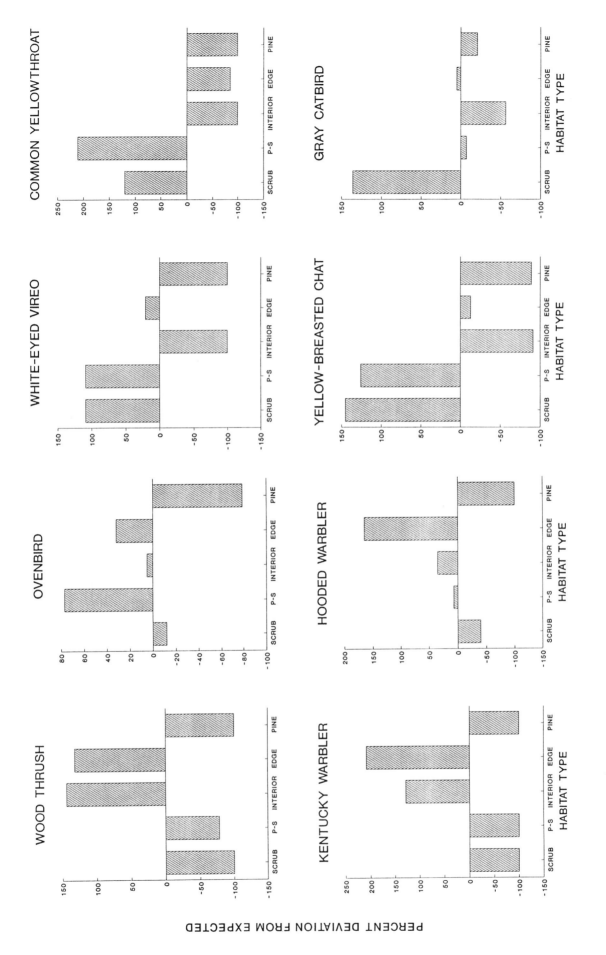

FIGURE 3. Habitat preferences of eight migratory bird species overwintering in Belize based on mist-netting data. Preferences were calculated based on the deviation of total number of captures of a species from that expected if a species was distributed uniformly across all five vegetation types (see text). Scrub = early successional growth, P-S = pine-savanna, interior = broadleaved forest interior, edge = broadleaved forest edge, pine = pine forest.

migrants, as a group, responded strictly to arthropod abundances because densities of understory arthropods were relatively high in the interior of broadleaved forests—where the understory migrant bird populations were relatively depauperate—and relatively low in pine forests, where migrants were equally uncommon (Petit 1991).

In Belize, migrants as a group revealed clear deviations from random use of habitats, but the general pattern of habitat use by migrants was composed of numerous, species-specific distributions. A single explanation for the distribution of all migrants in the Neotropics probably is unattainable if investigators examine migrants as a group rather than on a single species or guild basis (see Hutto 1980, 1989; Petit 1991).

Based on a review of published descriptions of habitat use on breeding grounds (D.R. Petit, unpubl. data), the eight species for which we collected detailed data showed general similarities between winter and summer seasonal use of vegetation types. In addition, the degree of habitat generalization/specialization of most migrant species in Belize was qualitatively comparable to those reported for breeding populations of the same species. Only the Ovenbird, a moderate habitat specialist on the breeding grounds, but a habitat generalist in Belize during the winter, departed from the overall trend. Others (e.g., Brosset 1968, Keast 1980) have noted that some migrant species exhibit interseasonal consistency in habitat use, but the trend is not universal and has gained little acceptance as an explanation of habitat use by overwintering birds in the tropics (see Petit 1991). The variable use of vegetation types by different species has obvious implications for the conservation of Neotropical migrant landbirds.

CONSERVATION OF MIGRANT LANDBIRDS ON WINTERING GROUNDS

Widespread deforestation of the Neotropics and one of its obvious outcomes—the wholesale extinction of plant and animal species—are not new revelations (Myers 1980). The actual effects of alteration of native vegetation on overwintering migrant populations are largely unknown because of the difficulties in monitoring abundances of species that range over millions of square kilometers and because of the early stages of deforestation (Askins et al. 1990). However, based on our current knowledge of winter habitat requirements of Neotropical migrants, avian ecologists have offered empirically based predictions regarding the fate of migratory bird populations. Those prognoses are almost entirely species- or group-specific and few broad generalizations can be made (e.g., Keast and Morton 1980, Rappole and Morton 1985, Hutto 1989, Lynch 1989, Robbins et al.

1989). Results of this study support those concepts. For example, clearing of moist, closed-canopied forests in Belize would have a differential impact on local populations: Wood Thrushes, Kentucky Warblers and, to some extent, Hooded Warblers, would most likely undergo local extinctions or substantial population loss. Concurrently, the fate of other species would depend on exactly what became of the former forest. If it were felled simply for wood, then, within several years, White-eyed Vireos, Common Yellowthroats, Gray Catbirds, Yellow-breasted Chats, and Ovenbirds would thrive within the site. If, on the other hand, the site were converted to agricultural or pasture land, few of those species would be present, or would be present only in low densities (Saab and Petit in press). Thus, it is important to know both the extent of the perturbation and the future use of the converted forest in projecting the direction and magnitude of population change for individual species.

The most imminent threat to Belize's natural ecosystems is large- and small-scale agriculture. Although Belize has remained largely in a natural state in comparison to other Central American countries, forest habitats there are coming under increasing pressure from developers and small-scale farmers (Hartshorn et al. 1984; pers. obs.). The highest priority should be to preserve broadleaved forests, because those vegetation types require relatively extensive periods of time to reach their former states after cutting, and because many migratory and especially, resident, bird species are dependent solely upon that successional stage (see also Terborgh 1980, Willis 1980, Lynch 1989). The notoriety given to tropical broadleaved forests should not, however, lessen the importance of preserving other habitat types. For example, the broadleaved understory of pine forests in the Mountain Pine Ridge area provides food, particularly fruit, during winter to a number of resident species whose reported distributions within the country (Wood et al. 1986) supposedly do not include pine forests (D.R. Petit, unpubl. data). The ecological significance of this bird/habitat relationship remains unclear.

FUTURE RESEARCH

Because species exhibit individual responses to habitats encountered in their wintering area, research aimed at describing ecological attributes of entire migrant bird communities overwintering in the Neotropics might prove to be difficult at best. Nevertheless, synecological (as opposed to species-specific) approaches to deciphering trends such as that described here might be necessary simply because autecological studies might not be generalizable for more than a few species. At this time of rapid tropical deforestation when critical decisions must be made quickly based on very limited scientific data, well-founded arguments can be made for the value of studies of entire communities, as opposed to in-depth examinations of single species (Diamond 1986: 501–502). We advocate more studies of the habitat use and behavioral ecology of entire overwintering bird communities or guilds, combined with simultaneous measurements of environmental factors, such as arthropods, fruit, and vegetation structure and composition. These largely correlational studies, although clearly limited in their ability ultimately to isolate ecologically and evolutionarily important elements (e.g., Karr 1983), would permit formulation of empirically supported hypotheses, which then can be evaluated more critically.

In this way, present-day knowledge of tropical bird communities is similar to what it was for temperate bird communities in the 1950s and 1960s; that is, present-day tropical avian ecologists, as were temperate-based ecologists 30 years ago, are just beginning to understand some of the factors that might influence the presence or absence of bird species within local communities. At present, we simply do not have enough information on migrant (let alone resident) species' basic behavioral ecology to generate justifiable hypotheses. For example, ecologists have yet to produce "a quantitative survey of habitat relations of individual migrant species" (Greenberg 1986:302) wintering in the Neotropics. So, if one were interested in testing the prediction that migrants occupy similar habitats year round, how could it be done? This does not, however, lessen the need for more detailed demographic study of single species on their wintering grounds (e.g., Greenberg 1984, Holmes et al. 1989). As with all research, ecologists must justify their approach based upon the goals of their study.

Acknowledgments

This research has been generously supported by grants from the National Science Foundation (BSR-88-06117), Fulbright Program of the U.S. Information Agency, Wilson Ornithological Society, Sigma Xi, and Department of Biological Sciences and J. William Fulbright College of Arts and Sciences, University of Arkansas. Much appreciation is extended to C.J. Amlaner, Jr., Biological Sciences Department chairman, for supporting L.J. Petit's contribution to this study. In Belize, O. Rosado, R. Belisle, and M. Windsor of the Department of Forestry, and W. Craig and V. Gonzalez of the Belize Audubon Society, were very helpful in obtaining permits for our research. J. Northup ably assisted with mist netting. D. Weyer, Parrots' Wood Biological Station, aided greatly in our efforts to establish a research program, and she, along with D. James, improved our understanding of bird/habitat relationships in Belize. J.M. Hagan, D.W. Johnston, T.E. Martin, K.E. Petit, J.H. Rappole, and an anonymous reviewer suggested numerous ways to improve this manuscript.

Literature cited

Askins, R.A., J.F. Lynch, and R. Greenberg. 1990. Population declines in migratory birds in eastern North America. *Current Ornithol.* 7:1–57.

Brosset, A. 1968. Localisation ecologique des oiseaux migrateurs dans la foret equatoriale du Gabon. *Biol. Gabon.* 4:211–216.

Diamond, J. 1986. The design of a nature reserve system for Indonesian New Guinea. Pages 485–503 in *Conservation Biology: The Science of Scarcity and Diversity*, M.E. Soulé, ed. Sunderland, Mass.: Sinauer Associates Inc.

Emlen, J.T. 1980. Interactions of migrant and resident land birds in Florida and Bahama pinelands. Pages 133–144 in *Migrant Birds in the Neotropics: Ecology, Behavior, Distribution and Conservation*, A. Keast and E.S. Morton, eds. Washington: Smithsonian Institution Press.

Greenberg, R. 1984. The winter exploitation systems of Bay-breasted and Chestnut-sided warblers in Panama. *Univ. Calif. Publ. Zool.* 116:1–107.

———. 1986. Competition in migrant birds in the nonbreeding season. *Current Ornithol.* 3:281–307.

Hartshorn, G., et al. 1984. *Belize Country Environmental Profile.* San Jose, Costa Rica: Trejos Brothers.

Holdridge, L.R. 1947. Determination of world plant formations from simple climatic data. *Science* 105:367–368.

Holmes, R.T., T.W. Sherry, and L. Reitsma. 1989. Population structure, territoriality and overwinter survival of two migrant warbler species in Jamaica. *Condor* 91:545–561.

Hutto, R.L. 1980. Winter habitat distribution of migratory land birds in western Mexico with special reference to small, foliage-gleaning insectivores. Pages 181–204 in *Migrant Birds in the Neotropics: Ecology, Behavior, Distribution and Conservation*, A. Keast and E.S. Morton, eds. Washington: Smithsonian Institution Press.

———. 1988. Is tropical deforestation responsible for the reported declines in neotropical migrant populations? *Am. Birds* 42:375–379.

———. 1989. The effect of habitat alteration on migratory land birds in a west Mexican tropical deciduous forest: A conservation perspective. *Conserv. Biol.* 3:138–148.

Karr, J.R. 1976a. Within- and between-habitat avian diversity in African and neotropical lowland habitats. *Ecol. Monogr.* 46:457–481.

———. 1976b. On the relative abundance of migrants from the north temperate zone in tropical habitats. *Wilson Bull.* 88:433–458.

———. 1979. On the use of mist nets in the study of bird communities. *Inland Bird-Banding* 51:1–10.

———. 1981. Surveying birds with mist-nets. Pages 62–67 in *Estimating Numbers of Terrestrial Birds*, C.J. Ralph and M.J. Scott, eds. Studies in Avian Biology No. 6.

————. 1983. Commentary. Pages 403–410 in *Perspectives in Ornithology*, A.H. Brush and G.A. Clark, Jr., eds. New York: Cambridge University Press.

Karr, J.R., and K.E. Freemark. 1983. Habitat selection and environmental gradients: Dynamics in the "stable" tropics. *Ecology* 65:1481–1494.

Keast, A. 1980. Spatial relationships between migratory parulid warblers and their ecological counterparts in the neotropics. Pages 109–130 in *Migrant Birds in the Neotropics: Ecology, Behavior, Distribution and Conservation*, A. Keast and E.S. Morton, eds. Washington: Smithsonian Institution Press.

Keast, A., and E.S. Morton, eds. 1980. *Migrant Birds in the Neotropics: Ecology, Behavior, Distribution, and Conservation*. Washington: Smithsonian Institution Press.

Lack, D., and P. Lack. 1972. Wintering warblers in Jamaica. *Living Bird* 11:129–153.

Levins, R. 1968. *Evolution in Changing Environments*. Princeton: Princeton University Press.

Lovejoy, T.E., R.O. Bierregaard, Jr., A.B. Rylands, J.R. Malcolm, C.E. Quintela, L.H. Harper, K.S. Brown, Jr., A.H. Powell, G.V.N. Powell, H.O.R. Schubard, and M.B. Hays. 1986. Edge and other effects of isolation on Amazon forest fragments. Pages 257–285 in *Conservation Biology: The Science of Scarcity and Diversity*, M.E. Soulé, ed. Sunderland, Mass.: Sinauer Associates Inc.

Lynch, J.F. 1989. Distribution of overwintering Nearctic migrants in the Yucatan Peninsula, I: General patterns of occurrence. *Condor* 91:515–544.

Martin, T.E. 1985. Selection of second-growth woodlands by frugivorous migrating birds in Panama: An effect of fruit size and plant density? *J. Trop. Ecol.* 1:157–170.

Myers, N. 1980. *Conversion of Tropical Moist Forests*. Washington: National Academy of Sciences.

Petit, D.R. 1991. Habitat associations of migratory birds wintering in Belize, Central America: Implications for theory and conservation. Ph.D. Dissertation, University of Arkansas, Fayetteville.

Rappole, J.H., and E.S. Morton. 1985. Effects of habitat alteration on a tropical avian forest community. Pages 1013–1021 in *Neotropical Ornithology*, P.A. Buckley, E.S. Morton, R.S. Ridgely, and F.G. Buckley, eds. Ornithol. Monogr. 36.

Robbins, C.S., J.R. Sauer, R.S. Greenberg, and S. Droege. 1989. Population declines in North American birds that migrate to the neotropics. *Proc. Natl. Acad. Sci.* 86:7658–7662.

Saab, V.A., and D.R. Petit. In press. Impact of pasture development on winter bird communities in Belize, Central America. *Condor*.

Terborgh, J.W. 1980. The conservation status of neotropical migrants: Present and future. Pages 21–30 in *Migrant Birds in the Neotropics: Ecology, Behavior, Distribution and Conservation*, A. Keast and E.S. Morton, eds. Washington: Smithsonian Institution Press.

Tramer, E. 1974. Proportions of wintering North American birds in disturbed and undisturbed dry tropical habitats. *Condor* 76:460–464.

Waide, R.B. 1980. Resource partitioning between migrant and resident birds: The use of irregular resources. Pages 337–352 in *Migrant Birds in the Neotropics: Ecology, Behavior, Distribution and Conservation*, A. Keast and E.S. Morton, eds. Washington: Smithsonian Institution Press.

Waide, R.B., J.T. Emlen, and E.J. Tramer. 1980. Distribution of migrant birds in the Yucatan Peninsula: A survey. Pages 165–171 in *Migrant Birds in the Neotropics: Ecology, Behavior, Distribution and Conservation*, A. Keast and E.S. Morton, eds. Washington: Smithsonian Institution Press.

Willis, E.O. 1966. The role of migrant birds at swarms of army ants. *Living Bird* 5:187–231.

Willis, E.O. 1980. Ecological roles of migratory and resident birds on Barro Colorado Island, Panama. Pages 205–225 in *Migrant Birds in the Neotropics: Ecology, Behavior, Distribution and Conservation*, A. Keast and E.S. Morton, eds. Washington: Smithsonian Institution Press.

Wood, D.S., R.C. Leberman, and D. Weyer. 1986. *Checklist of the Birds of Belize*. Carnegie Mus. Nat. Hist. Special Publ. No. 12.

Zar, J.H. 1984. *Biostatistical Analysis*. Englewood Cliffs, New Jersey: Prentice Hall.

APPENDIX 1. Locations of the 20 study sites in Belize.

EARLY SUCCESSIONAL GROWTH

1. South side of ("new") Western Hwy. between mile 40.8 and 41.8; 17°16' N, 88°42' W.
2. Along dirt road leading to village of Cotton Tree Bank, ca. 1.5 km north of intersection with Western Hwy.; 17°17' N, 88°43' W.
3. Along dirt road leading to village of Cotton Tree Bank, ca. 4 km north of intersection with Western Hwy.; 17°19' N, 88°44' W.
4. North side of Western Hwy. between mile 45.5 and 46.5; 17°17' N, 88°46' W.

PINE-SAVANNA

1. Ca. 1 km east of "new" Western Hwy. on "old" Western Hwy. and runs south to several hundred meters past Colonel English Creek; 17°21' N, 88°33' W.
2. Ca. 1.5 km east of "new" Western Hwy. on "old" Western Hwy. and runs north to ca. 100 m of "new" Western Hwy.; 17°22' N, 88°32' W.
3. Ca. 3 km east of "new" Western Hwy. on "old" Western Hwy. and runs northeast; 17°22' N, 88°31' W.
4. North side of Western Hwy. at mile 28.5; 17°22' N, 88°33' W.

BROADLEAVED FOREST INTERIOR

1. Guanacaste Park at intersection of Western and Hummingbird hwys.; 17°16' N, 88°47' W.
2. Blue Hole National Park, 4 km southeast of Caves Branch on Hummingbird Hwy.; 17°09' N, 88°41' W.
3. Rio Frio Nature Trail, 1 km west of Augustine; 16°58' N, 89°00' W.
4. Ca. 2 km northwest of Augustine, near Guatemala Caves area; 16°59' N, 89°00' W.

BROADLEAVED FOREST EDGE

1. Southeast along Hummingbird Hwy. beginning near entrance of Blue Hole National Park (southwest side of road); 17°09' N, 88°41' W.
2. Southeast along Hummingbird Hwy. ca. 3.5 km from Blue Hole National Park (southwest side of road); 17°08' N, 88°39' W.
3. Southeast along Hummingbird Hwy. ca. 5 km south of intersection with Western Hwy. (southwest side of road); 17°12' N, 88°46' W.
4. Along north side of Western Hwy. between mile markers 44 and 45; 17°15' N, 88°45' W.

PINE FOREST

1. Three km southeast of Augustine on Inner Circle Road, ca. 2.5 km east of intersection with Chiquibul Road; 16°57' N, 88°58' W.
2. One km north of Augustine on Hydram Road, ca.0.5 km north of intersection with Chiquibul Road; 16°59' N, 88°59' W.
3. Three km east of Augustine on Anderson Road, ca. 0.5 km southeast of intersection with Chiquibul Road; 16°58' N, 88°58' W.
4. Five km northeast of Augustine on Navel Road, ca. 2.5 km east of intersection with Chiquibul Road; 16°59'N, 88°57'W.

JOHN G. BLAKE
BETTE A. LOISELLE
Natural Resources Research Institute
Center for Water and the Environment
University of Minnesota
Duluth, Minnesota 55811

Habitat use by Neotropical migrants at La Selva Biological Station and Braulio Carrillo National Park, Costa Rica

Abstract. We examined the distribution and abundance of Neotropical migrants in second growth (2 sites at approx. 50 m elevation) and primary forest (5 sites, 50 to 2,000 m) over a five-year period (1985–1989) in northeastern Costa Rica. A total of 38 migrant species were either captured in mist nets (32 species) or recorded during point-counts (24 species). Common migrants included Wood Thrush, Swainson's Thrush, Chestnut-sided Warbler, Ovenbird, and Kentucky Warbler. More species were recorded in young (approx. 5–10 yr) second growth than in any other habitat. Overall recapture rates were greatest in lowland primary forest (38%) and least in primary forest at 1,000 m (7%). Recaptures (both within and between winters) of common winter residents exceeded 40%; mean distance between successive captures of the same individuals was less than 75 m. Individuals often were captured in the same net in more than one winter; site fidelity was demonstrated in primary forest and second-growth habitats. We used discriminant function analysis (DFA) to describe features of the habitat associated with net sites where birds were captured versus sites where birds were not or infrequently captured in lowland primary forest and second growth. Habitat models correctly classified over 80% of capture sites. Habitat variables selected by DFA to characterize capture sites of one habitat rarely matched those used to characterize capture sites in another habitat.

Sinopsis. Durante un período de cinco años (1985–1989), examinamos la distribución y abundancia de migratorias neotropicales en bosques secundarios (dos sitios a aproximadamente 50 m de elevación) y bosques primarios (cinco sitios, 50 a 2000 m) en el nordeste de Costa Rica. Un total de 38 especies migratorias fueron capturadas en redes de niebla (32 especies) o registradas durante conteos puntuales (24 especies). Las migratorias mas comunes fueron *Hylocichla mustelina*, *Catharus ustulatus*, *Dendroica pensylvanica*, *Seiurus aurocapillus* y *Oporornis formosus*. Se registraron mas especies en bosque secundario joven (de aproximadamente

5–10 años) que en cualquier otro habitat. Las tasas de re-captura totales mayores se obtuvieron en bosque primario de zonas bajas (38%) y las menores en bosque primario a 1,000 m (7%). Las recapturas de residentes de invierno comunes excedieron el 40% (tanto en cada invierno como entre inviernos). La distancia promedio entre sitios de capturas sucesivas de los mismos individuos fue inferior a 75 m. Frecuentemente se capturaron individuos en las mismas redes en mas de un invierno; la fidelidad al sitio se demostró en habitats tanto primarios como secundarios. Usando análisis de función discriminante (AFD), describimos las características del habitat asociadas con sitios de redes en donde se capturaron aves versus sitios con éxito de captura bajo o nulo en bosques primarios de zonas bajas y en bosques secundarios. Los modelos de habitat clasificaron correctamente mas del 80% de los sitios de captura. Las variables de habitat seleccionadas por el AFD para caracterizar los sitios de captura de un hábitat raramente concordaron con aquellos usados para la caracterización en otro habitat.

Many biologists have expressed concern over apparent declines in populations of many species of birds that breed in temperate North America and winter in the tropics (Neotropical migrants hereafter) (e.g., Briggs and Criswell 1979, Askins et al. 1990). Debate exists over whether survival of such migrants is more dependent on conditions on breeding, migrating, or wintering grounds (e.g., Morse 1980, Holmes and Sherry 1988, Hutto 1988). Destruction of tropical habitats (e.g., Myers 1984) has led to the suggestion that loss of suitable nonbreeding habitat, particularly tropical forest, is a major factor causing declines in breeding populations of Neotropical migrants (e.g., Terborgh 1980, Ambuel and Temple 1982, Rappole et al. 1983, 1989). Continued conversion of tropical forest to other types of habitat will continue to have enormous deleterious effects on many species (Erwin 1988, Raven 1988), yet direct evidence for adverse effects on Neotropical migrants generally is lacking (Holmes and Sherry 1988, Hutto 1988, Wilcove 1988). Exceptions include specific case studies that have documented loss of migrants with loss of habitat in specific tropical wintering areas (e.g., Rappole and Morton 1985). Loss of individuals from tropical sites, however, has not been tied directly to declines in abundance of specific breeding populations in North America.

A major component missing in debates over the potential effects of loss or alteration of tropical habitats is detailed information on winter habitat requirements and preferences for many Neotropical migrants. An earlier symposium on Neotropical migrants (Keast and Morton 1980) highlighted this question. Despite those and more recent studies (e.g., Rappole and Morton

1985, Martin 1985, Martin and Karr 1986, Hutto 1989), much debate continues on habitat requirements of most species during nonbreeding seasons because wintering migrants occupy many habitats. Densities often are high in disturbed or successional habitats and some authors have suggested that migrants, as a rule, prefer such habitats (Martin 1985 and references therein, Hutto 1989). Others have stressed that migrants depend on primary forest (e.g., Stiles 1980, Terborgh 1980, Rappole et al. 1989). In this paper, we describe the distribution of several common Neotropical migrants in second growth and primary forests of northeastern Costa Rica.

Study area

We conducted our research at Estación Biológica La Selva, located in the lowlands (approx. 35 to 100 m elevation) of northeastern Costa Rica, near Puerto Viejo de Sarapiqui, Provincia Heredia (10°25' N, 84°01' W), and at four elevations (500, 1,000, 1,500, and 2,000 m) on the Atlantic slopes of the Cordillera Central in Parque Nacional Braulio Carrillo (Fig. 1). La Selva encompass-

FIGURE 1. Location of major study sites at Estación Biológica La Selva and Parque Nacional Braulio Carrillo, Costa Rica. *YSG* = young second growth; *OSG* = old second growth.

es approximately 1,510 ha, of which approximately 64% is primary forest. The south boundary of La Selva borders Braulio Carrillo and continuous forest cover exists from 40 m to over 2,900 m elevation on Volcan Barva (10°24' N, 84°00' W). The station also supports anthropogenic successional habitats in various stages of regrowth. Braulio Carrillo encompasses approximately 44,099 ha, most (> 90%) of which is primary forest. Life zones characteristic of our study sites were tropical wet forest (50 m), tropical wet, cool transition forest (500 m), premontane rain forest (1,000 m), and lower montane rain forest (1,500 m, 2,000 m) (Holdridge 1967).

Study sites at La Selva were in young (approximately 5 yr postabandonment pasture in 1985) and old (approximately 30 to 35 yr) successional habitats and in undisturbed primary forest. The young successional site was within an approximately 40-ha tract of former pasture bordered by older second growth. Vegetation in this study site averaged 5 to 8 m tall; scattered tall trees (e.g., *Ficus* sp.) also were present. The older successional site was located on a tract of approximately 20 to 25 ha bordered by primary forest and younger second growth. Trees averaged 15 to 20 m over much of the plot. Two lowland primary forest study sites, one established in 1985 and one in 1988, were within the main block of undisturbed forest at La Selva, where canopy height reached 30 to 40 m. All study sites in Braulio Carrillo were in primary forest. Canopy heights were approximately 35 to 40 m (500-m site), 30 to 35 m (1,000-m site), 17 to 25 m (1,500-m site), and 20 m (2,000-m site) (Hartshorn and Peralta 1988).

Rainfall at La Selva averages 3,877 mm/yr (1958–1988, Organization for Tropical Studies, unpublished data). The dry season typically lasts from January or February to March or April with a second, less pronounced dry season in September and October. Although few climatic data are available from higher elevations along the La Selva–Volcan Barva transect, Hartshorn and Peralta (1988) reported mean annual rainfall ranging from 3,268 mm at 2,260 m elevation to 5,096 mm at 970 m elevation in areas adjacent to this transect. The seasonal pattern of rainfall in Braulio Carrillo is similar to that at La Selva, but the dry season is shorter and less pronounced. Rain or mist and clouds occur almost daily at higher (> 1,000 m) elevations. More detailed descriptions of these forests are in Hartshorn (1983), Pringle et al. (1984), and Hartshorn and Peralta (1988).

Methods

Our study included most of 1985 and December–April during 1986–1989. Study sites were sampled every five to six weeks starting in early 1985 (two second-growth sites and primary forest sites at 50 m, 500 m, and 1,000 m elevation), 1987 (forest site at 1,500 m), or 1988 (second lowland primary forest site and forest site at 2,000 m). We did not sample the older second-growth site after April 1987. Samples were divided into dry season (late December through April) and wet season (September–November, 1985 only). We do not include data from May–August 1985 because few Neotropical migrants were present.

NETTING

Mist nets (12-m, 4-shelf, 36-mm mesh) were used to sample birds occurring in the lower levels of each habitat below 1,500 m. We did not use nets at 1,500 m or at 2,000 m because of too frequent rain, mist, and cold weather. In each lowland habitat, we arranged 30 nets, set approximately 40 m apart, in a grid that covered approximately 4.8 ha. The first lowland primary forest plot was expanded to 54 nets (approximately 9 ha) in September 1985. Thirty nets, set 40 m apart along a narrow trail, were used to sample the second lowland primary forest site. Total area covered by nets was approximately 4.8 ha. Each net was operated for only two days/sample (i.e., every 5–6 weeks). Nets were open from dawn to approximately 1300, or as close to 7 hr/day as possible. We operated 20 nets, placed 30 m apart along narrow trails, for two to three days/sample in primary forest at 500 m and 1,000 m elevations. Total forest area sampled was approximately 3 ha at each of these sites. Nets were left open until approximately 1600, except during heavy rain. Captured birds were banded, weighed, sexed and aged if possible, and held for collection of fecal samples. Birds were released at the point of capture.

Ground-level nets effectively sample most birds, especially passerines, that occur in the understory (i.e., below about 3 m; e.g., Karr 1979, 1981, Blake 1989, Loiselle and Blake 1990, 1991). Mist nets operated at ground level do not provide a sample of the entire avifauna but do provide a quantitative sample of birds using a defined stratum of the habitat (Levey 1988, Karr 1990, Loiselle and Blake 1991). Higher capture rates in second-growth habitats are partially, but not completely, a consequence of the shorter stature of the vegetation; mist nets in primary forest sample a smaller proportion of the vegetation. As with any sampling technique, mist nets are subject to biases (Lovejoy 1974, Karr 1981, Remsen and Parker 1983, Loiselle and Blake 1990).

Throughout this paper, "captures" refers to captures of all birds, including recaptures. Birds recaptured within one hour of the initial capture were not counted. "Individuals" refers to number of individual birds (i.e., excluding recaptures). "Recaptured birds" include those recaptured during the same sample period or season ("repeats" in banding terminology) and those recaptured in subsequent winters ("returns," with an intervening migration to and from breeding grounds).

Species represented in mist net samples (and recorded during point-counts [below]) included winter residents at La Selva and Braulio Carrillo as well as transients. "Transients" refers to birds that pass through Costa Rica during migration but generally do not winter there. Most sampling was conducted before the peak of spring migration, so captures (and observations) of "resident" species were composed primarily of residents. The spring migration typically is less pronounced than fall migration at La Selva because more migrants tend to move north along the coast rather than inland (Stiles 1983).

POINT-COUNTS

We established six sample points per site in our first lowland forest and young second-growth sites and eight points per site in the remaining sites (lowland to montane forest) in December 1987. Points were approximately 200 m apart. Each point was visited for 10 min during a count and all birds seen or heard were recorded. Distance to each bird was estimated. Birds flying over the canopy were not included. All counts started at dawn (approximtely 0600) and lasted until approximately 0800. Four to five 2-hr counts (6-8 points/count) were conducted at study sites during each sample. Each site was sampled three times from December 1987 to April 1988, and twice from December 1988 to April 1989.

HABITAT

Vegetation was sampled in two transects (3 × 12.5 m each) located parallel to each side of each mist net in second-growth and lowland primary forest sites. We recorded and measured the diameter at 1.5 m (dbh: diameter at breast height) of all woody stems with a diameter ≥ 2 cm (hereafter referred to as trees); palms (Arecaceae; ≥ 2 cm dbh) were recorded separately. Lianas ≥ 2 cm thick were counted and measured, as were all woody stems < 2 cm dbh and 1.5 m tall (palm stems counted separately), nonwoody plants (≥ 1.5 m) (e.g., *Renealmia*: Zingiberaceae; *Heliconia*: Heliconiaceae), and vines (< 2 cm thick). Fruits were sampled in two transects (2 × 12.5 m each) located parallel to and 1 m distant from each side of each net. During each sample, all plants with fruit displayed below 10 m were identified and ripe and unripe fruits were counted (Blake et al. 1990).

Canopy cover was measured at all sites with a spherical densiometer (Lemmon 1956). Four readings, one in each compass direction, were taken at each end and at the middle of each net lane (12 readings/net).

STATISTICAL ANALYSES

All variables used in statistical analyses were tested for normality (Wilk-Shapiro test) and equality of variances (Bartlett's test) and were transformed (e.g., logarithmic) when needed (Sokal and Rohlf 1981). Nonparametric tests were used when necessary. Specific tests are indicated in the text as appropriate.

We used numbers of birds captured per 100 mist-net hours (mnh; 1 mist net open 1 hr = 1 mist-net hr) as an index of bird activity. Number of captures was compared among sites using chi-square goodness-of-fit tests. Tests were based on actual numbers of captures, not capture rates, and expected values for such tests were based on relative sample effort (mnh) at each site.

Habitat data were analyzed with both univariate and multivariate techniques. One-way analysis of variance (Kruskal-Wallis tests) was used to compare habitat variables among sites. Stepwise discriminant function analysis (DFA) was used to determine if characteristics of the vegetation (Appendix 1) associated with net sites where common species were captured differed statistically from vegetation at net sites where the species was not captured (i.e., were species associated with specific characteristics of the vegetation in different habitats). Groups for DFA of different species were defined on the basis of number of captures per net, with each net constituting one sample unit. We assumed that species were captured more often at net sites characterized by preferred microhabitat (vegetation) characteristics than at other net sites. Movement rate and, therefore, probability of capture, might vary depending on different aspects of the vegetation. Hence, capture frequency might not always adequately represent habitat use. Nonetheless, within a given habitat type, frequency of capture at different net sites provides an indication of the level of activity in that part of the habitat.

We used two-group DFA to describe "used" (1 or more captures) versus "unused" (no captures) habitat (net sites). Because "non-use" of a site is difficult to establish, groups might also be viewed as representing net sites where bird activity (capture rate) was low or net sites where birds were more active (high capture rate). For bird species that were captured frequently, two-group DFA was used to compare infrequently used (0–2 captures) versus commonly used (3 or more captures) net sites. Prior probabilities for classification analyses were set equal to the relative number of net sites at which a species was captured. Classification ability was evaluated by comparing percent correctly classified relative to that expected based on prior probabilities. Transformations (logarithmic, square root) were used to assure multivariate normality and to improve the equality of the variance-covariance matrices among groups.

Multivariate analyses were conducted on all migrants with a minimum number of 15 captures at a given study site; each of the three major lowland habitats was analyzed separately. We used all data from the two second-growth sites because the same number of nets were used in each year. Data from the dry season in 1985 in the lowland primary forest were omitted because only 30 nets were operated during that period. Subsequently, 54 nets were used, which formed the basis of the DFA.

Results

HABITAT STRUCTURE

The three primary study sites at La Selva differed with respect to most habitat variables (Table 1). The youngest site had a relatively open canopy, many shrubs, and much fruit. Small to medium-sized trees ($\leq$ 25 cm dbh) were most common on the older second-growth site, as were small lianas and vines. Primary forest had more large (> 25 cm diameter) trees, palms of all sizes, and large lianas. Canopy cover was most complete in primary forest.

Canopy cover was greater in primary forest from 50 to 500 m than in forest from 1,000 to 2,000 m, or in second growth (Fig. 2). The more open canopy at higher el-

TABLE 1. Habitat structure (means $\pm$ 1 S.E.) at study sites at La Selva; vegetation sampled at net sites during 1986

Variable	Young second growth ($n = 30$)	Old second growth ($n = 30$)	Primary forest ($n = 54$)	χ^2
Trees				
2–3 cm dbh	4.2 $\pm$ 0.65	7.5 $\pm$ 0.69	5.8 $\pm$ 0.36	15.3 * * * *
>3–5 cm dbh	2.1 $\pm$ 0.41	4.5 $\pm$ 0.58	2.7 $\pm$ 0.20	11.1 * * *
>5–10 cm dbh	4.9 $\pm$ 0.64	6.4 $\pm$ 0.68	2.9 $\pm$ 0.25	21.8 * * * *
>10–15 cm dbh	2.2 $\pm$ 0.33	3.2 $\pm$ 0.42	1.3 $\pm$ 0.14	17.3 * * * *
>15–25 cm dbh	0.7 $\pm$ 0.20	2.5 $\pm$ 0.32	0.9 $\pm$ 0.13	24.8 * * * *
>25–50 cm dbh	0.2 $\pm$ 0.11	0.4 $\pm$ 0.11	1.1 $\pm$ 0.13	20.0 * * * *
>50 cm dbh	0.0	0.1 $\pm$ 0.06	0.4 $\pm$ 0.09	6.5 * *
Palm trees				
2–3 cm dbh	0.0	0.3 $\pm$ 0.11	2.2 $\pm$ 0.29	21.6 * * * *
>3–5 cm dbh	0.0	0.0	1.1 $\pm$ 0.16	
>5–10 cm dbh	0.0	0.0	0.6 $\pm$ 0.10	
>10 cm dbh	0.0	0.0	1.3 $\pm$ 0.15	
Lianas				
2–3 cm dbh	0.5 $\pm$ 0.20	3.4 $\pm$ 0.61	1.6 $\pm$ 0.38	21.0 * * * *
>3–5 cm dbh	0.1 $\pm$ 0.07	0.4 $\pm$ 0.11	0.6 $\pm$ 0.13	6.2 * *
>5 cm dbh	0.0	0.0	0.4 $\pm$ 0.11	
Shrubs				
Woody stems	61.2 $\pm$ 3.73	44.4 $\pm$ 2.26	34.8 $\pm$ 1.93	38.5 * * * *
Palm stems	0.0	1.9 $\pm$ 0.50	19.1 $\pm$ 1.46	49.0 * * * *
Non-woody	16.7 $\pm$ 3.87	9.3 $\pm$ 2.38	9.3 $\pm$ 2.51	4.9 *
Vines	16.0 $\pm$ 3.18	21.6 $\pm$ 2.91	4.4 $\pm$ 0.52	49.0 * * * *
Canopy (% open)	26.3 $\pm$ 1.55	13.0 $\pm$ 0.63	4.5 $\pm$ 0.17	93.2 * * * *
Fruiting plants[a]	14.7 $\pm$ 1.41	3.8 $\pm$ 0.49	3.6 $\pm$ 0.50	52.0 * * * *
Fruits[b]	2234.0 $\pm$ 304.4	336.0 $\pm$ 92.4	749.0 $\pm$ 150.9	36.1 * * * *

NOTE: All values are per 75 m^2, except fruit and fruiting plants (per 50 m^2), and canopy cover (% of open sky above net, 12 readings/net). Comparisons among habitats are based on Kruskal-Wallis analysis of variance. **** = $P < 0.001$; *** = $P < 0.005$; ** = $P < 0.05$; * = $P < 0.10$.

a. Maximum number of fruiting plants/net site/sample.

b. Sum of ripe and unripe fruits over all samples.

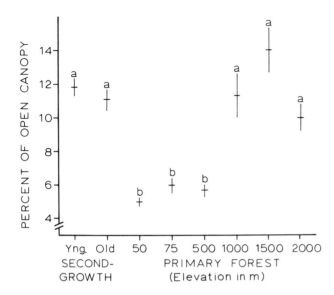

FIGURE 2. Percent of open canopy ($\bar{X} \pm$ 1 S.E.) at study sites in Costa Rica. All samples are from 1989 except the old second-growth sample, which is from 1986. Means not sharing the same letter are significantly different ($P < 0.05$; Scheffé multiple comparison among means test).

evations resulted from shorter trees and the prevalence of branch and tree falls. Canopy cover increased on the young second-growth site over time (compare Table 1 and Fig. 2) and by 1989 was similar to that found at higher elevations.

MIGRANT COMPOSITION

NETTING. Thirty-two species of Neotropical migrants were captured in mist nets (Appendix 2). The number of species captured in different habitats ranged from 31 at the youngest site (only Veery not captured), to seven species in primary forest at 500 m elevation (Table 2). The most frequently captured species were Wood Thrush (328 captures), Swainson's Thrush (225), Ovenbird (121), and Kentucky Warbler (117). All but the Swainson's Thrush were winter residents. These four most frequently captured species accounted for 72% of all captures (Fig. 3). Nine species (28%) were represented by only one or two captures, and together accounted for < 2% of all captures.

TABLE 2. Summary of netting results by season (e.g., Dry 85 = dry season 1985)

Habitat	Dry 85	Wet 85	Dry 86	Dry 87	Dry 88	Dry 89	Total
Young second growth							
Mist-net hours (mnh)	1671	825	1233	1240	1188	805	6962
Number of captures	133	145	126	97	69	41	611
Captures/100 mnh	7.9	17.6	10.2	7.8	5.8	5.1	8.8
Number of species	18	21	15	13	12	8	31
Old second growth							
Mist-net hours (mnh)	1499	399	1227	1228			4353
Number of captures	36	33	36	39			144
Captures/100 mnh	2.4	8.3	2.9	3.2			3.3
Number of species	15	15	8	12			16
Primary forest (50–75 m)							
Mist-net hours (mnh)	1540	1044	2169	3306	3488	2396	13,943
Number of captures	35	25	28	35	66	31	220
Captures/100 mnh	2.3	2.4	1.3	1.1	1.9	1.3	1.6
Number of species	5	7	1	5	3	6	11
Primary forest (500 m)							
Mist-net hours (mnh)	379	596	834	877	1057	518	4261
Number of captures	5	12	17	15	34	9	92
Captures/100 mnh	1.3	2.0	2.0	1.7	3.2	1.7	2.2
Number of species	2	4	4	3	4	2	7
Primary forest (1,000 m)							
Mist-net hours (mnh)	354	649	1137	931	1175	648	4894
Number of captures	9	10	3	4	5	1	32
Captures/100 mnh	2.5	1.5	0.3	0.4	0.4	0.3	0.7
Number of species	1	7	2	2	2	1	11

NOTE: Only Neotropical migrants are included. "Captures" includes all captures of birds, including recaptures. Both sites in lowland primary forest are combined.

Overall capture rate of Neotropical migrants was higher in the young second growth than in any other habitat (paired t-tests; $t > 3.7$, $P < 0.02$, all comparisons) when comparisons were based on seasonal capture rates (Table 2). Capture rates in primary forest were similar at 50 and 500 m elevations ($t = -0.9$, $P < 0.40$), but lower at 1,000 m (50 vs. 1,000 m forest: $t = 3.29$, $P < 0.05$; 500 vs. 1,000 m forest: $t = 1.96$, $P < 0.11$; Table 2). Capture rates in lowland habitats were higher during the wet season than in the dry season, but the same was not true for higher elevations (Table 2).

Capture rates of most species (23 of 32; Table 3) were greatest in the youngest site. This was true both for ground and low understory foraging species (e.g., Ovenbird, Mourning Warbler), as well as for species that forage relatively higher in the vegetation (e.g., Chestnut-sided Warbler, Great Crested Flycatcher). Eleven species (34%) were captured only in young second growth. Eight species (25%) were captured at four or five of the sites (Table 3). Among species captured both in old second-growth and primary forest habitats, capture rates for nine species were highest in the old second growth, with only the Wood Thrush evidencing a higher capture rate in primary forest (Table 3). Wood Thrush capture rates were highest in primary forest at 500 m, but declined sharply by 1,000 m.

TABLE 3. Capture rates (birds captured/1,000 mnh) of Neotropical migrants in second growth and primary forest habitats, 1985–1989. Results from both sites in lowland primary forest (50 to 75m) are combined

Species	Second growth		Primary forest		
	Young	Old	50–75m	500m	1000m
Eastern Wood-Pewee	0.3				
Yellow-bellied Flycatcher	0.4	0.2	0.1		
Acadian Flycatcher	2.4	2.8	0.8	0.2	0.6
"Traill's" Flycatcher[a]	3.3	0.2			
Great Crested Flycatcher	1.4				
Eastern Kingbird	1.3				
Veery		0.2			
Gray-cheeked Thrush	2.3	0.7	0.2	0.5	
Swainson's Thrush	15.7	9.9	2.5	4.9	3.5
Wood Thrush	12.4	5.5	11.3	13.6	0.6
Gray Catbird	7.6				
Yellow-throated Vireo	0.1				
Red-eyed Vireo	0.1	0.2			
Blue-winged Warbler	0.4				
Golden-winged Warbler	0.4				0.2
Chestnut-sided Warbler	5.9	1.6	0.1	0.2	
Magnolia Warbler	0.1				
Blackburnian Warbler	0.1				0.2
Bay-breasted Warbler	0.3		0.1		
Black-and-white Warbler	0.3				0.2
Worm-eating Warbler	2.2	1.4			
Ovenbird	15.8	2.3			0.2
Northern Waterthrush	0.7	0.2			
Louisiana Waterthrush	0.1		0.2		0.2
Kentucky Warbler	10.6	6.2	0.4	1.9	0.4
Mourning Warbler	1.7				
Hooded Warbler	0.6				
Canada Warbler	0.3	0.5	0.1		0.2
Summer Tanager	0.3	0.9	0.1	0.2	0.2
Scarlet Tanager	0.1	0.2			
Rose-breasted Grosbeak	0.1				
Northern Oriole	0.1				

a. Likely includes both *Empidonax alnorum* and *E. traillii*.

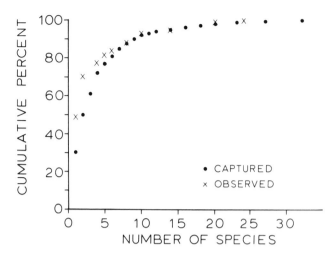

FIGURE 3. Cumulative percent of total captures or observations, all sites combined, plotted against cumulative number of species.

POINT-COUNTS. Twenty-four species of migrants were recorded during one or more counts (Appendix 2, Table 4). As with netting data, more species and individuals were seen or heard in young second growth than in primary forest. Relatively few species and individuals were recorded in primary forest, especially at higher elevations (1,500 and 2,000 m). Among primary forest sites, mean number of birds recorded per count was highest in forest at 500 m and lowest in forest at 1,500 m.

The species accumulation curve based on point-counts was similar to that based on netting data (Fig. 3). Many species (42%) were represented by only one or two records; two species, Chestnut-sided Warbler (165 counted) and Wood Thrush (72), accounted for 71% of all birds seen or heard. Chestnut-sided Warblers accounted for a relatively constant percentage (46 to 53%) of observations at all sites below 1,500 m. By contrast,

TABLE 4. Migrants recorded during point-counts ([birds/point] × 10) December 1987–March 1989 in young second growth and primary forest (+ = < 0.05)

Species	Young second growth	Primary forest				
		50–75 m	500m	1000m	1500m	2000 m
Chuck-wills-widow			0.1			
Olive-sided Flycatcher				0.1	0.1	
Eastern Wood-Pewee	0.1					
Acadian Flycatcher	0.5	+				
"Traill's" Flycatcher[a]	0.4					
Great Crested Flycatcher	0.8	0.6				
Swainson's Thrush	0.3		0.3			
Wood Thrush	2.0	1.1	2.7			
Yellow-throated Vireo	0.1					
White-eyed Vireo	0.2					
Philadelphia Vireo		0.1				
Red-eyed Vireo	0.9					
Golden-winged Warbler	0.1			0.2		
Chestnut-sided Warbler	8.7	2.0	2.5	0.3		
Magnolia Warbler	0.2					
Black-throated Green Warbler				0.2		
Blackburnian Warbler				0.2		
Bay-breasted Warbler	0.2					
Black-and-white Warbler				0.1		
Kentucky Warbler	1.5					
Mourning Warbler	0.2					
Wilson's Warbler						0.2
Summer Tanager	0.2	+				
Northern Oriole	0.6					
Total species	17	6	4	6	1	1
Total birds	172	93	52	14	1	4
Mean number/point (× 10)	16.9	3.9	5.4	1.1	0.1	0.2

a. Likely includes both *Empidonax alnorum* and *E. traillii*

the Wood Thrush accounted for 26 to 50% of migrants recorded in primary forests below 1,000 m, but only 12% in the youngest second-growth site.

RECAPTURES OF MIGRANTS. Recaptured individuals (including repeats and returns, but excluding transient species) accounted for from 25 to 38% of all captures at study sites below 1,000 m, but only 7% of captures in primary forest at 1,000 m (Table 5). Most recaptures were of birds captured within the same winter (dry season). Recaptures (returns) from one winter to the next accounted for 21 to 24% of all recaptures in lowland habitats (Table 5). Distribution of recaptures (repeats and returns) versus nonrecaptures did not differ among sites below 1,000 m ($\chi^2 = 5.9$, d.f. = 3, $0.20 > P > 0.10$).

Swainson's Thrush was one of the most commonly captured species overall, but only four individuals (2%) were recaptured (Appendix 2) and only one recapture was between winters. Swainson's Thrushes primarily are transients at La Selva, remaining in the same area for only brief periods. In contrast, Gray-cheeked Thrushes, although also transients in Costa Rica, were recaptured (repeats) more frequently within the same sample period, indicating that individuals of that species remained in the same location slightly longer than did Swainson's Thrushes. Other species with high recapture rates included Acadian Flycatcher, Wood Thrush, Gray Catbird, Worm-eating Warbler, Ovenbird, and Kentucky Warbler, all winter residents at La Selva.

A greater proportion of Wood Thrushes were recaptured (repeats and returns) in old second growth and lowland primary forest than in young second growth or higher elevation forests ($\chi^2 = 8.8$, d.f. = 3, $P < 0.05$). Returns, however, accounted for similar proportions (24 to 30%) of recaptured Wood Thrushes in each lowland habitat (Table 5). Mean distance between successive captures of individual Wood Thrushes was only slightly less in primary forest and old second growth than in young second growth (Table 6). At all three lowland sites, most Wood Thrush returns were in the same or closely adjacent net sites.

Over half of all Ovenbird captures in young second growth were recaptured individuals (Table 5); returns accounted for about 20% of all recaptures. Mean distance between successive between-winter captures was less than within-winter mean capture distance ($t = 2.26$, d.f. = 59, $P < 0.05$). More than half of all returns were to the same net site.

Kentucky Warblers also showed high recapture rates in second-growth habitats (Table 5). Mean distance between captures was lower in old second growth than in young second growth, but not significantly.

TABLE 5. Total recaptures (and % of total captures) and number of recaptures (and % of total recaptures) at different intervals between captures for all resident species combined and, separately, for Wood Thrush, Ovenbird, and Kentucky Warbler (– = old second growth only sampled 3 years)

Species	Habitat	Total recaptures and (%)	Winters		
			Same	Next	>Next
All species	Young second growth	147 (33)	116 (79)	22 (15)	9 (6)
	Old second growth	25 (25)	19 (76)	6 (24)	–
	Forest: 50–75m	69 (38)	53 (77)	12 (17)	4 (6)
	500m	20 (29)	19 (95)	1 (5)	0
	1000m	1 (7)	1 (100)	0	0
Wood Thrush	Young second growth	19 (22)	14 (74)	3 (16)	2 (10)
	Old second growth	10 (42)	7 (70)	3 (30)	–
	Forest: 50–75m	62 (40)	47 (76)	12 (19)	3 (5)
	500m	17 (29)	16 (94)	1 (6)	0
	1000m	0 (0)	0	0	0
Ovenbird	Young second growth	61 (56)	48 (79)	8 (13)	5 (8)
	Old second growth	0 (0)	0	0	–
Kentucky Warbler	Young second growth	36 (49)	30 (83)	5 (14)	1 (3)
	Old second growth	11 (41)	8 (73)	3 (27)	–
	Forest: 50–75m	1 (17)	1 (100)	0	0
	500m	2 (25)	2 (100)	0	0
	1000m	1 (50)	1 (100)	0	0

TABLE 6. Mean distance (m) between successive captures within winters (repeats) and between winters (returns; last capture in one winter to first capture in subsequent winter) for three common winter residents at La Selva

Species	Habitat	Repeats			Returns		
		n	$\bar{x}$	S.E.	n	$\bar{x}$	S.E.
Wood Thrush	Young second growth	14	74	11.2	5	62	19.5
	Old second growth	7	70	26.7	3	43	41.5
	Forest (50–75m)	47	63	6.6	15	50	9.5
Ovenbird	Young second growth	48	56	6.1	13	28	7.4
Kentucky Warbler	Young second growth	30	55	7.1	6	49	20.4
	Old second growth	8	31	13.2	3	0	0.0
	Forest (50–75m)	1	40				

TABLE 7. Discriminant function analysis of bird habitat use in lowland (50–75 m elevation) primary forest and old second growth in La Selva

Species	Discriminating variables	Wilks' lambda	χ^2	d.f.	$P <$	Groups Capt.	n	%
Primary forest								
Wood Thrush	Open canopy (–); lianas (–); vines (+); >3–5 cm dbh trees (–); palm shrubs (–); >5–10 cm dbh trees (–)	0.68	18.8	6	0.005	0–2	33	88
						≥3	21	57
Swainson's Thrush	Herbaceous shrubs (+); >15–25 cm dbh trees (+); >25 cm dbh trees (+); lianas (–); woody shrubs (+); >5–10 cm dbh trees (+)	0.69	18.5	6	0.005	0	38	92
						≥ 1	16	50
Old second growth								
Wood Thrush	Fruit (+); lianas (–); >5–10 cm dbh trees (+); >25 cm dbh trees (–); woody shrubs (+)	0.45	20.6	5	0.001	0	15	87
						≥1	15	87
Swainson's Thrush	Palm shrubs (–); >15–25 cm dbh trees (–); fruiting plants (+); 2–3 cm dbh trees (–)	0.56	14.6	5	0.02	0	10	60
						≥1	20	90
Kentucky Warbler	Open canopy (+); palm shrubs (+); herbaceous shrubs (+); 2–3 cm dbh trees (–)	0.67	10.4	5	0.07	0	17	88
						≥1	13	62

NOTE: Discriminating variables are listed in order of correlation with function. Number of net sites in each group and percentage (%) of net sites correctly classified are shown. Mean values of discriminating variables characteristic of sites where species was captured most often ("used" habitat group) are indicated as being larger (+) or smaller (–) than values characteristic of sites where the species was captured rarely, if ever (n = number of net sites).

HABITAT USE BY MIGRANTS. Only two species, Wood Thrush (a winter resident) and Swainson's Thrush (a transient), were captured in sufficient numbers in lowland forest to be included in discriminant analyses of habitat use (Table 7). Wood Thrushes were captured more often at net sites characterized by a relatively closed canopy and open understory (i.e., few small trees, palms, or lianas). In contrast, Swainson's Thrushes used sites characterized by well-developed understory (i.e., many herbaceous and woody shrubs) and medium to large trees (> 15 cm dbh).

Three species (Wood Thrush, Swainson's Thrush, and Kentucky Warbler) were captured so frequently in old

second-growth woodland that habitat use could be examined (Table 7). Wood Thrushes found in old second growth avoided sites with substantial liana growth, paralelling results from primary forest. However, capture locations of Wood Thrushes in old second growth, in contrast to sites in lowland primary forest, were characterized by well-developed understory and abundant fruit. Swainson's Thrushes used sites characterized by abundant fruit and few understory palms or small to medium-sized trees. No statistically significant habitat model was generated to describe habitats used by Kentucky Warblers ($P < 0.07$). However, Kentucky Warblers tended to use habitats with a more open canopy and a dense lower understory of palms and other herbaceous shrubs (Table 7).

We examined patterns of habitat use of nine species captured in young second growth (Table 8). Captures of three species (Acadian Flycatcher, Chestnut-sided Warbler, and Worm-eating Warbler) were not associated with specific attributes of the habitat. Results of DFA were not significant ($P > 0.20$) and are not discussed further.

Capture sites of Wood Thrushes in young second growth were characterized by well-developed, relatively open understory, as indicated by the number of herbaceous shrubs and small trees (rather than woody shrubs and vines). Both species of *Catharus* thrushes selected dense understory sites characterized by well-developed woody and herbaceous shrub cover, and abundant fruit (Swainson's Thrush) or lianas (Gray-cheeked Thrush). Catbirds preferred sites with relatively open canopy, dense shrubby growth, and abundant fruit. Kentucky Warblers also used areas of relatively open canopy, but chose areas with fewer small trees and more lianas than

sites used by catbirds. Ovenbirds used areas with open canopy and well-developed woody understory supporting many small to medium-sized trees.

Discussion

Many Neotropical migrants use a variety of habitats and different elevations in Costa Rica (this study, Slud 1964, Stiles 1980). In this study, 15 species (40%) were found only in one habitat (12 species) or at one elevation (3 species). We recorded more migrants in second growth, particularly young (< 10 yr old) second growth, than in primary forest. Undoubtedly, the abundance of migrants in young second growth was biased because there was a greater likelihood that canopy species would be captured or observed in that habitat than in older second growth or primary forest (Stiles 1980). We feel, however, that greater migrant abundance in younger second-growth habitat was not simply a result of sampling bias, but reflected real differences in distribution (see also Martin 1985). Of 11 species that commonly

TABLE 8. Discriminant function analysis (see Table 7) of bird habitat use in young second-growth woodland in La Selva

Species	Discriminating variables	Wilks' lambda	χ^2	d.f.	$P<$	Capt.	n	%
Wood Thrush	2–3 cm dbh trees (+); >3–5 cm dbh trees (+); herbaceous shrubs (+); >5–10 cm dbh trees (+)	0.47	19.8	4	0.001	0–2	16	88
						≥3	14	86
Swainson's Thrush	Herbaceous shrubs (+); open canopy (+); >5–10 cm dbh trees (+); >3–5 cm dbh trees (+); 2–3 cm dbh trees (+); woody shrubs (+); >10–16 cm dbh trees (–); fruiting plants (+); fruit (+); vines (+)	0.22	34.9	10	0.001	0–2	10	80
						≥3	20	100
Gray-cheeked Thrush	Lianas (+); herbaceous shrubs (+); vines (–); >15 cm dbh trees (–); woody shrubs (+); >10–15 cm dbh trees (–)	0.59	13.0	6	0.05	0	18	83
						≥1	12	67
Gray Catbird	>10–15 cm dbh trees (–); >5–10 cm dbh trees (+); open canopy (+); herbaceous shrubs (+); fruit (+); woody shrubs (+); vines (+); lianas (+)	0.29	29.8	8	0.001	0	14	86
						≥1	16	100
Kentucky Warbler	Open canopy (+); >3–5 cm dbh trees (–); fruiting plants (–); >10–15 cm dbh trees (–); fruit (+); lianas (+); >5–10 cm dbh trees (–)	0.40	22.2	7	0.01	0–1	9	78
						≥2	21	95
Ovenbird	Woody shrubs (+); 2–3 cm dbh trees (+); lianas (+); >15 cm dbh trees (–); vines (–); open canopy (+); >5–10 cm dbh trees (+)	0.30	29.0	8	0.001	0–2	12	83
						≥3	18	94

forage at mist-net levels in all habitats (e.g., thrushes, catbird, several warblers), seven had higher capture rates in the young second-growth study site, whereas only the Wood Thrush was captured most often in undisturbed forest (at 500 m elevation). Three species were captured too rarely to categorize.

From a conservation standpoint, critical questions that need further investigation include: the degree of habitat selection by migrants during winter (i.e., how dependent are species on particular types of habitat); factors that influence habitat selection; and effects of habitat selection on probability of winter survival. For example, do species actually "prefer" second-growth habitats or only use second growth because all preferred forest sites are occupied (Rappole et al. 1989). Except for interactions at army ant swarms (Willis 1966) or at fruiting trees (Martin 1982), there currently is little or no evidence to indicate that residents exclude Neotropical migrants from forest habitats (Waide 1981). Moreover, many Neotropical migrants establish intraspecific winter territories and exhibit aggressive behavior toward conspecifics (Rappole et al. 1983, 1989).

Birds select habitats (breeding or wintering) based on a variety of factors, such as suitable nest-site location, effects of direct and diffuse competition, predation risk, abiotic conditions, and food resources (e.g., Cody 1985, Hutto 1985, Martin 1985). Selection of habitats is constrained by a species' morphology and foraging behavior (Robinson and Holmes 1982, Sherry and Holmes 1985). Birds must balance opposing influences when selecting wintering habitats. For example, the abundant food resources present in young second-growth habitats relative to those found in undisturbed forests (Martin 1985, Levey 1988, Loiselle and Blake 1990, Blake and Loiselle 1991) might be outweighed by the greater risk of predation at such sites. The relative costs and benefits of different factors likely change with forest type and geographic location.

High energy demands make food acquisition a primary factor influencing habitat use by migrants during spring and fall migration (Martin 1985). For example, migrating birds frequently use more habitats and a greater size range of forest patches than are used during other seasons (Stiles 1980, Blake 1986, Blake and Karr 1987); migrant abundance often is correlated with food abundance (Hutto 1985, Blake and Hoppes 1986, Pyke and Recher 1988). Swainson's Thrushes, transients rather than winter residents in our study region in Costa Rica, were captured in a variety of habitats. Nonetheless, these thrushes selected sites with dense shrub understory in all habitat types—areas likely to be rich in insect and fruit resources.

Habitats used by a species throughout its winter range probably vary because of differences in habitat availability, density of conspecifics, abundance of preda-

tors, and perhaps because of intra-population differences (see Holmes et al. 1989). Some migrants might be more specific in habitat selection than others (Greenberg 1984). For example, Wood Thrushes prefer undisturbed lowland and foothill forest (< 1,000 m elevation) (e.g., Rappole and Warner 1980, Stiles 1983, Lynch 1989, this study). In contrast, Ovenbirds, Kentucky, and Worm-eating warblers prefer wet forests in Mexico (Rappole and Warner 1980, Lynch 1989), but young second growth in Costa Rica. In Panama, Kentucky Warblers occur both in old forests (Karr 1976, Willis 1980) and young second growth (Martin 1985). Ovenbirds occur in young forests in Panama (Willis 1980, Martin 1985) and scrub forest in Puerto Rico and Jamaica (Terborgh 1980; R.T. Holmes, pers. comm.). These species appear to establish winter territories, or at least show winter site fidelity, at all locations. High recapture rates of Ovenbirds and Kentucky Warblers at our young second-growth site indicate that they preferred second-growth habitats over undisturbed forests in Costa Rica.

To date, few studies of migrants on their wintering grounds have quantified species-habitat relationships in detail. Species may select habitats on the basis of specific components of the vegetation that are similar throughout the winter range, despite geographic variation in habitat types used and habitats available. Moreover, we need to determine if species show consistent habitat preferences throughout their annual range. Habitat models generated for migrants in Costa Rica show some agreement with those produced for the same species on their breeding grounds (see Noon 1981, Blake and Karr 1987).

To better understand habitat distribution of migrants requires more information on survival rates in various habitats during winter, such as provided by Rappole et al. (1989) for Wood Thrushes in Mexico and by Holmes et al. (1989) for Black-throated Blue Warblers (*Dendroica caerulescens*) and American Redstarts (*Setophaga ruticilla*) in Jamaica. Lower recapture rates of Wood Thrush in young second growth than in primary forest observed during our study may indicate (1) a more transient population or (2) a lower winter survival rate. Rappole et al. (1989) demonstrated that nonterritorial Wood Thrushes in Mexico not only frequented second-growth areas more often than did territorial individuals, but also had a lower survival rate.

Clearly we need species-specific studies that examine habitat selection, survival rates, winter-site fidelity, and food abundance throughout a species' winter range. Further, we need to determine wintering and breeding locations for specific populations to understand where migrants are most limited. Given that annual variation in biotic and abiotic conditions influence bird populations, studies are needed that examine patterns of habitat use over more than one year. Only after such studies are completed and integrated with breeding season studies will we be able to formulate adequate conservation plans for Neotropical migrants.

Acknowledgments

We are grateful to F.G. Stiles, R. Holmes, G. Powell, and H. Powell for many discussions on migrants in Costa Rica. J. Hagan, D. Johnston, J. Rappole, and C. Robbins provided many suggestions for improving this manuscript. We thank the Organization for Tropical Studies, particularly David and Deborah Clark, for permission to work at Estación Biológica La Selva and Servicio de Parques Nacionales, particularly F. Cortés and J. Doblez, for permission to work in Parque Nacional Braulio Carrillo. Our research has generously been funded by the National Geographic Society; J.S. Noyes Foundation; University of Wisconsin, Dept. Zoology, Guyer Fellowship; Douroucouli Foundation; National Academy of Sciences, J. Henry Fund; Wilson Ornithological Society, Stewart Award; and Northeastern Bird Banding Association.

Literature cited

Ambuel, B., and S.A. Temple. 1982. Songbird populations in southern Wisconsin forests: 1954 and 1979. *J. Field Ornithol.* 53:149–158.

Askins, R.A., J.F. Lynch, and R. Greenberg. 1990. Population declines in migratory birds in eastern North America. *Current Ornithol.* 7:1–57.

Blake, J.G. 1986. Species-area relationship of migrants in isolated woodlots in east-central Illinois. *Wilson Bull.* 98:291–296.

———. 1989. Birds of primary forest undergrowth in western San Blas, Panama. *J. Field Ornithol.* 60:178–189.

Blake, J.G., and W.G. Hoppes. 1986. Resource abundance and microhabitat use by birds in an isolated east-central Illinois woodlot. *Auk* 103:328–340.

Blake, J.G., and J.R. Karr. 1987. Breeding birds of isolated woodlots: Area and habitat relationships. *Ecology* 68:1724–1734.

Blake, J.G., and B.A. Loiselle. 1991. Variation in resource abundance affects capture rates of birds in three lowland habitats in Costa Rica. *Auk* 108:114–130.

Blake, J.G., B.A. Loiselle, T.C. Moermond, D.J. Levey, and J.S. Denslow. 1990. Quantifying abundance of fruits for birds in tropical habitats. Pages 73–79 in *Avian Foraging: Theory, Methodology, and Applications*, M.L. Morrison, D.J. Ralph, J. Berner, and J.R. Jehl, Jr., eds. Studies in Avian Biology No. 13.

Briggs, S.A., and J.H. Criswell. 1979. Gradual silencing of spring in Washington. *Atlantic Nat.* 32:19–26.

Cody, M.L. 1985. An introduction to habitat selection in birds. Pages 4–56 in *Habitat Selection in Birds*, M.L. Cody, ed. Orlando, Fla.: Academic Press.

Erwin, T.L. 1988. The tropical forest canopy—the heart of biotic diversity. Pages 123–129 in *Biodiversity*, E.O. Wilson, ed. Washington: National Academy Press.

Greenberg, R. 1984. Neophobia in the foraging-site selection of a neotropical migrant bird: An experimental study. *Proc. Nat. Acad. Sci.* 81:3778–3780.

Hartshorn, G.S. 1983. Plants: Introduction. Pages 118–157 in *Costa Rican Natural History*, D.H. Janzen, ed. Chicago: University Chicago Press.

Hartshorn, G.S., and R. Peralta. 1988. Preliminary description of primary forests along the La Selva-Volcan Barva altitudinal transect, Costa Rica. Pages 281–296 in *Tropical Rainforests: Diversity and Conservation*, F. Almeda and C.M. Pringle, eds. San Francisco: California Academy of Sciences.

Holdridge, L.R. 1967. *Life Zone Ecology.* Rev. ed. San Jose, Costa Rica: Tropical Science Center.

Holmes, R.T., and T.W. Sherry. 1988. Assessing population trends of New Hampshire forest birds: Local vs. regional patterns. *Auk* 105:756–768.

Holmes, R.T., T.W. Sherry, and L. Reitsma. 1989. Population structure, territoriality and overwinter survival of two migrant warbler species in Jamaica. *Condor* 91:545–561.

Hutto, R.L. 1985. Habitat selection by nonbreeding, migratory land birds. Pages 455–476 in *Habitat Selection in Birds*, M.L. Cody, ed. Orlando, Fla.: Academic Press.

Hutto, R.L. 1988. Is tropical deforestation responsible for the reported declines in neotropical migrant populations? *Am. Birds* 42:375–379.

Hutto, R.L. 1989. The effect of habitat alteration on migratory land birds in a west Mexican tropical deciduous forest: A conservation perspective. *Conserv. Biol.* 3:138–148.

Karr, J.R. 1976. On the relative abundance of migrants from the north temperate zone in tropical habitats. *Wilson Bull.* 88:433–458.

———. 1979. On the use of mist nets in the study of bird communities. *Inland Bird Banding* 51:1–10.

———. 1981. Surveying birds with mist nets. Pages 62–67 in *Estimating Numbers of Terrestrial Birds*, C.J. Ralph and M.J. Scott, eds. Studies in Avian Biology No. 6.

———. 1990. The avifauna of Barro Colorado Island and the Pipeline Road, Panama. Pages 183–198 in *Four Neotropical Rainforests*, A. Gentry, ed. New Haven: Yale University Press.

Keast, A., and E.S. Morton, eds. 1980. *Migrant Birds in the Neotropics: Ecology, Behavior, Distribution, and Conservation.* Washington: Smithsonian Institution Press.

Lemmon, P. 1956. A spherical densiometer for estimating forest overstory density. *Forest Sci.* 2:314–319.

Levey, D.J. 1988. Spatial and temporal variation in Costa Rican fruit and fruit-eating bird abundance. *Ecol. Monogr.* 58:251–269.

Loiselle, B.A., and J.G. Blake. 1990. Diets of understory fruit-eating birds in Costa Rica: Seasonality and resource abundance. Pages 91–103 in *Avian Foraging: Theory, Methodology, and Applications*, M.L. Morrison, D.J. Ralph, J. Berner, and J.R. Jehl, Jr., eds. Studies in Avian Biology No. 13.

———. 1991. Resource abundance and temporal variation in fruit-eating birds along a wet forest elevational gradient in Costa Rica. *Ecology* 72:180–193.

Lovejoy, T. 1974. Bird diversity and abundance in Amazon forest communities. *Living Bird* 13:127–191.

Lynch, J.F. 1989. Distribution of overwintering Nearctic migrants in the Yucatan Peninsula, I: General patterns of occurrence. *Condor* 91:515–544.

Martin, T.E. 1982. Frugivory and North American Migrants in a Neotropical Second-growth Woodland. Ph.D. dissertation, Univ. Illinois, Champaign, Illinois.

———. 1985. Selection of second-growth woodlands by frugivorous migrating birds in Panama: An effect of fruit size and plant density? *J. Trop. Ecol.* 1:157–170.

Martin, T.E., and J.R. Karr. 1986. Temporal dynamics of neotropical birds with special reference to frugivores in second-growth woods. *Wilson Bull.* 98:38–60.

Morse, D.H. 1980. Population limitation: Breeding or wintering grounds? Pages 437–453 in *Migrant Birds in the Neotropics: Ecology, Behavior, Distribution and Conservation*, A. Keast and E.S. Morton, eds. Washington: Smithsonian Institution Press.

Myers, N. 1984. *The Primary Source: Tropical Forests and Our Future.* New York: W.W. Norton and Co.

Noon, B.R. 1981. The distribution of an avian guild along a temperate elevational gradient: The importance and expression of competition. *Ecol. Monogr.* 51:105–124.

Pringle, C., I. Chacon, M. Grayum, H. Greene, G. Hartshorn, G. Schatz, G. Stiles, C. Gomez, and M. Rodriguez. 1984. Natural history observations and ecological evaluation of the La Selva Protection Zone, Costa Rica. *Brenesia* 22:189–206.

Pyke, G.H., and H.F. Recher. 1988. Seasonal patterns of capture rate and resource abundance for honeyeaters and silver eyes in heathland near Sydney. *Emu* 88:33–42.

Rappole, J.H., and E.S. Morton. 1985. Effects of habitat alteration on a tropical avian forest community. Pages 1013–1021 in *Neotropical Ornithology*, P.A. Buckley, E.S. Morton, R.S. Ridgely, and F.G. Buckley, eds. Ornithol. Monogr. 36.

Rappole, J.H., and D.W. Warner. 1980. Ecological aspects of migrant bird behavior in Veracruz, Mexico. Pages 353–394 in *Migrant Birds in the Neotropics: Ecology, Behavior, Distribution and Conservation*, A. Keast and E.S. Morton, eds. Washington: Smithsonian Institution Press.

Rappole, J.H., E.S. Morton, T.E. Lovejoy, III, and J.L. Ruos. 1983. *Nearctic Avian Migrants in the Neotropics.* Washington: U.S. Fish and Wildlife Service.

Rappole, J.H., M.A. Ramos, and K. Winker. 1989. Wintering wood thrush movements and mortality in southern Veracruz. *Auk* 106:402–410.

Raven, P.H. 1988. Our diminishing tropical forests. Pages 119–122 in *Biodiversity*, E.O. Wilson, ed. Washington: National Academy Press.

Remsen, J.V., Jr., and T.A. Parker, III. 1983. Contribution of river-created habitats to bird species richness in Amazonia. *Biotropica* 15:223–231.

Robinson, S.K., and R.T. Holmes. 1982. Foraging behavior of forest birds: The relationships among search tactics, diet, and habitat structure. *Ecology* 63:1918–1931.

Sherry, T.W., and R.T. Holmes. 1985. Dispersion patterns and habitat responses of birds in northern hardwoods forests. Pages 283–310 in *Habitat Selection in Birds*, M.L. Cody, ed. Orlando, Fla.: Academic Press.

Slud, P. 1964. The Birds of Costa Rica. *Bull. Amer. Mus. Nat. Hist.* 125:1–430.

Sokal, R.R., and F.J. Rohlf. 1981. *Biometry: The Principles and Practice of Statistics in Biological Research.* 2d ed. San Francisco: W.H. Freeman and Co.

Stiles, F.G. 1980. Evolutionary implications of habitat relations between permanent and winter resident landbirds in Costa Rica. Pages 421–436 in *Migrant Birds in the Neotropics: Ecology, Behavior, Distribution and Conservation*, A. Keast and E.S. Morton, eds. Washington: Smithsonian Institution Press.

———. 1983. Birds: Introduction. Pages 502–530 in *Costa Rican Natural History*, D.H. Janzen, ed. Chicago: University of Chicago Press.

Terborgh, J.W. 1980. The conservation status of neotropical migrants. Pages 21–30 in *Migrant Birds in the Neotropics: Ecology, Behavior, Distribution and Conservation*, A. Keast and E.S. Morton, eds. Washington: Smithsonian Institution Press.

Waide, R.B. 1981. Interactions between resident and migrant birds in Campeche, Mexico. *Trop. Ecol.* 22:134–154.

Wilcove, D.S. 1988. Changes in the avifauna of the Great Smoky Mountains: 1947–1983. *Wilson Bull.* 100:256–271.

Willis, E.O. 1966. The role of migrant birds at swarms of army ants. *Living Bird* 5:187–231.

———. 1980. Ecological roles of migratory and resident birds on Barro Colorado Island, Panama. Pages 205–225 in *Migrant Birds in the Neotropics: Ecology, Behavior, Distribution and Conservation*, A. Keast and E.S. Morton, eds. Washington: Smithsonian Institution Press.

APPENDIX 1.   Habitat variables used in discriminant function analyses (DFA) of lowland habitats at La Selva

Habitat variable	Used in DFA of		
	Primary forest	Old second growth	Young second growth
Number of trees/75 m^2			
2–3 cm dbh	×	×	×
>3–5 cm dbh	×	×	×
>5–10 cm dbh	×	×	×
>10–15 cm dbh	×	×	×
>15–25 cm dbh	×	×	
>25 cm dbh	×	×	
>15 cm dbh			×
Palm trees/75 m^2			
2–3 cm dbh	×		
>3–5 cm dbh	×		
5 cm dbh	×		
Lianas (≥2 cm)/75 m^2	×	×	×
Woody shrubs/75 m^2	×	×	×
Palm shrubs/75 m^2	×	×	×
Herbaceous shrubs/75 m^2	×	×	×
Vines/75 m^2	×	×	×
Fruiting plants/50 m^2	×	×	×
Ripe and unripe fruits/50 m^2	×	×	×
Percent open canopy	×	×	×

APPENDIX 2.   English and scientific names of all birds captured in nets or observed during point-counts. Total number captured and recaptured) is shown. Species that are primarily transients at La Selva and Braulio Carrillo are indicated with an asterisk

| Species | | Netted | | Observed |
		Captured	Recaptured	
Chuck-will's-widow	*Caprimulgus carolinensis*			1
Olive-sided Flycatcher	*Contopus borealis*			2
Eastern Wood-Pewee*	*Contopus virens*	2		1
Yellow-bellied Flycatcher	*Empidonax flaviventris*	5		
Acadian Flycatcher	*Empidonax virescens*	44	8	6
"Traill's" Flycatcher*	*Empidonax* spp.[a]	24		4
Great Crested Flycatcher	*Myiarchus crinitus*	10		23
Eastern Kingbird*	*Tyrannus tyrannus*	9		
Veery	*Catharus fuscescens*	1		
Gray-cheeked Thrush	*Catharus minimus*	24	8	
Swainson's Thrush	*Catharus ustulatus*	225	4	4
Wood Thrush	*Hylocichla mustelina*	328	120	72
Gray Catbird	*Dumetella carolinensis*	53	9	
Yellow-throated Vireo	*Vireo flavifrons*	1		1
White-eyed Vireo	*Vireo griseus*			2
Philadelphia Vireo	*Vireo philadelphicus*			2
Red-eyed Vireo*	*Vireo olivaceus*	2		9
Blue-winged Warbler*	*Vermivora pinus*	3	1	
Golden-winged Warbler	*Vermivora chrysoptera*	4	1	3
Chestnut-sided Warbler	*Dendroica pensylvanica*	50	6	165
Magnolia Warbler*	*Dendroica magnolia*	1		2
Black-throated Green Warbler	*Dendroica virens*			3
Blackburnian Warbler	*Dendroica fusca*	2		3
Bay-breasted Warbler*	*Dendroica castanea*	3		2
Black-and-white Warbler*	*Mniotilta varia*	3	1	1
Worm-eating Warbler	*Helmitheros vermivorus*	21	10	
Ovenbird	*Seiurus aurocapillus*	121	61	
Northern Waterthrush	*Seiurus noveboracensis*	6	1	
Louisiana Waterthrush	*Seiurus motacilla*	5	1	
Kentucky Warbler	*Oporornis formosus*	117	51	15
Mourning Warbler	*Oporornis philadelphia*	12	3	2
Wilson's Warbler	*Wilsonia pusilla*			4
Hooded Warbler*	*Wilsonia citrina*	4	1	
Canada Warbler*	*Wilsonia canadensis*	6		
Summer Tanager	*Piranga rubra*	9		3
Scarlet Tanager*	*Piranga olivacea*	2		
Rose-breasted Grosbeak	*Pheucticus ludovicianus*	1		
Northern Oriole	*Icterus galbula*	1		6

a. Likely includes both *Empidonax alnorum* and *E. trailli*.

RUSSELL GREENBERG
Smithsonian Migratory Bird Center
National Zoological Park
Washington, D.C. 20008

Forest migrants in non-forest habitats on the Yucatan Peninsula

Abstract. Most species of migrant landbirds overwintering on the northeastern Yucatan Peninsula were more common in forest than early stages of second growth. However, these forest migrants were often found in fields that had been left fallow for several years since clearing. During the winter declines of forest migrants were most pronounced in cleared and second-growth habitats. Arthropod abundance also decreased during the winter, and the decline in large arthropods was significant for the second-growth but not the forest habitat. Nevertheless, substantial numbers of forest migrants overwintered in second growth. Forest migrants found in these "acahuales" were of comparable body condition (as determined by fat class estimates) to those found in forest. Forest-dependent migrants were found primarily in association with small patches of trees. At least two species were strongly associated with particular types of trees: Black-throated Green Warblers (*Dendroica virens*) were found in areas containing leguminous trees with compound leaves and small leaflets (e.g., *Acacia*), and White-eyed Vireos (*Vireo griseus*) were associated with fruiting *Bursera*. These results indicate that even small efforts toward maintaining tree cover in an agricultural landscape could increase the wintering carrying capacity for certain forest migrants.

Sinopsis. La mayoría de especies de aves terrestres migratorias invernantes en el nordeste de la Península de Yucatán fueron mas comunes en bosques que en estadios tempranos de desarrollo secundario. Sin embargo, estas migratorias de bosque se encontraron frecuentemente en campos abandonados por varios años después de la tala. Durante el invierno la disminución de las migratorias de bosque fue mas pronunciada en habitats abiertos y secundarios. La abundancia de artrópodos también decreció durante el invierno y la disminución de artrópodos grandes fue significativa para el habitat secundario pero no para el de bosque. No obstante, números sustanciales de migratorias de bosque invernaron en habitat secundario. Las migratorias de bosque encontradas en estos "acahuales" estaban en condición corporal (determinada por estimativos de clase de grasa) comparable a la de las presentes en el bosque. Las migratorias que dependen del bosque se encontraron primariamente en asociación con pequeños parches de árboles. Por lo menos dos especies estuvieron fuertemente asociadas con tipos particulares de árboles:

Dendroica virens se encontró en áreas con leguminosas arbóreas de hojas compuestas y pequeñas hojuelas (e.g. *Acacia*) y *Vireo griseus* estuvo asociado con *Bursera* en fructificación. Estos resultados indican que incluso pequeños esfuerzos que tiendan a mantener cobertura arbórea en paisajes agrícolas podrían incrementar la capacidad de carga de invernada para ciertas migratorias de bosque.

Because of its proximity to North America and subtropical climate, the Yucatan Peninsula is an important wintering area for migratory birds. The forest cover that naturally dominates the landscape of the Yucatan Peninsula is rapidly being converted to pasture, agricultural fields, and young shrubby regrowth known locally as "acahuales." Major tracts of forest remain only in portions of Quintana Roo and southeastern Campeche. This rapid change in habitat might have profound effects on the carrying capacity for overwintering migrants and the distribution of migrants in disturbed, and pristine vegetation has been the focus of several studies (Tramer 1974, Waide 1980, Lynch 1989). The latter two studies, particularly the extensive survey work by Lynch, have shown for the Yucatan Peninsula what a number of studies have established for other parts of Mexico (Hutto 1989) and the Caribbean Basin as a whole (Rappole and Warner 1980; Robbins et al., this volume; Waide and Wunderle, pers. comm.): early attempts to generalize about the habitat distribution of migrants are misleading because of considerable interspecific variation. Species tend to specialize on different successional seres. Furthermore, the problem as is classically stated, "how do migratory birds respond to forest clearing?," might offer a false dichotomy. Forest-dependent migrants are often found in secondary scrub and small isolated patches of trees, characteristic of much of the deforested tropical countryside. Recently, research has focused increasingly on the response of individual species or groups of ecologically similar species to the full range of land use. At the core of the problem is the assessment of relative value of different habitats to populations of migratory birds. The few attempts to assess which species are most dependent on mature forest generally have used a single measure of habitat quality: the relative density of a particular species found in habitats at two or more stages of succession (Tramer 1974, Waide 1980, Lynch 1989, Hutto 1989). However, other habitat features might mitigate or exacerbate the change in bird density caused by forest clearing.

The most important additional parameter is individual "success." Because migratory birds do not breed on their tropical wintering grounds, success is defined by the probability of surviving the winter. Rappole and Morton (1985) suggested that, beyond being less common on recently cleared forest land, some migratory birds lead a transitory life in the less optimal habitat, staying only until they locate available patches of preferred habitat. Further studies of one forest migrant, the Wood Thrush (*Hylocichla mustelina*), by Rappole et al. (1989) suggest that some individuals that perhaps are excluded from forest survive more poorly during their nomadic wandering through acahuales.

These observations lead to the general question—are the reduced populations of forest migrants in non-forest habitats viable, or are they comprised of individuals that do not survive the winter or survive in poor condition? In the studies of the Wood Thrush (Rappole et al. 1989), a great effort went into following the fate of radio-tagged birds. Another approach is to test the hypothesis of differential survivorship more indirectly through the use of repeated censuses. Although the possibility that some individuals are not locally resident will make it difficult to track the fate of particular birds, the carrying capacity of a particular patch of land is crucial. If the overall pool of individuals of a particular species of migrants in a suboptimal habitat declines, then the number of individuals that are available for censusing in a particular tract of that habitat will also decline. Declines in numbers might also reflect regional movements. This can be evaluated by comparing rates of decline among habitats.

It is possible that in addition to initial differences in habitat quality, habitats change in their relative quality over the winter. Food availability, measured by arthropod abundance and the availability of fruit and flower crops, generally have been shown to change throughout the winter in Neotropical sites (e.g., in Campeche, Waide 1981). In particular, insect densities often decline, which should have major impact on migrants, because most species are largely insectivorous. However, this should only affect the relative quality of habitats if the severity of the decline in arthropods differs between habitats. In an environment such as the Yucatan Peninsula, which experiences a severe dry season, possibly scrub habitats lack the climatic buffering that large tree canopy provides in the forest. Scrub might experience greater overall desiccation in the dry season, which in turn creates harsher conditions for herbivorous insects. As logical as this argument is, differential seasonality in insect biomass or abundance has rarely been demonstrated (but see Schoener and Janzen 1968).

In addition to differential disappearance rates of birds, other factors that could indicate qualitative differences among habitats include variation in sex-age ratios (Lynch et al. 1985; Lopez Ornat and Greenberg 1990; Wunderle, this volume; Winker et al. 1990) as well as the nutritional condition (Rappole et al. 1989, Holmes et al. 1989) of overwintering birds.

The present study was conducted at the Sian Ka'an

Biosphere Reserve, a large undeveloped area in central Quintana Roo. It focused on the following questions related to the effects of forest clearing on populations of forest migrants: (1) Which species are predominantly forest-wintering? (2) Do forest-wintering species show significantly greater declines when wintering in second-growth than in mature forest habitats? (3) Do migrant species that winter most commonly in forests show a significant difference in nutritional condition between forest and non-forest? and finally (4) Can we identify features of second-growth habitat that promote successful overwintering of forest migrants?

Study site

The Sian Ka'an Biosphere Reserve, Quintana Roo, Mexico, protects approximately 500,000 ha, of which approximately one-third is intact or regenerating forest. In addition, most of the adjacent land is forested and managed primarily for selective logging. This study focused on noninundated forest and its post-clearing successional stages. Based on the moderate rainfall (1,200 mm/year), which falls primarily in a distinct wet season (June-Dec.), the upland forest in this region is classified as Subtropical Dry Forest in the Holdridge System. The entire area is underlain by a limestone substrate, and soil-moisture holding capacity is low. There are two types of upland forest, medium-stature subdeciduous and medium-stature subperennial forest (Rzedowski 1978) which differ in their stature and degree of leaf loss during the dry season (I. Olmsted, pers. comm.). The two forest types were included in this study and they differ significantly, not only in species composition but in structure as well (Table 1). The most conspicuous difference was that the subperennial forest had a substantially higher canopy (10–19 m, $\bar{X}$ = 13.2 versus 8–10 m , $\bar{X}$ = 10.2) than the subdeciduous forest as well as a more open understory (0.9 versus 1.5 stems/m²). The differences were reflected in differences in the resident avifauna as well. A number of species occurred only in the taller forest including: Collared Trogon (*Trogon collaris*), White-necked Puffbird (*Notharchus macrorhynchos*), Thrush-like Manakin (*Schiffornis turdinus*), Sulphur-rumped Flycatcher (*Myiobius sulphureipygius*), Yellow-olive Flycatcher (*Tolmomyias sulphurescens*), Red-crowned Ant-tanager (*Habia rubica*), and Golden-crowned Warbler (*Basileuterus culicivorus*). Because Sian Ka'an was recently established, the reserve contains large areas of abandoned cattle pasture, smaller tracts of abandoned farm plots, as well as active pastures.

Methods

TRANSECT CENSUSES. In 1987–1988, five 1-km transects were established: two in forest, two in 5–7-yr-old second

growth, and one in pasture with an additional transect through 1000 m of milpa (small farm). The last 250 m of the milpa transect extended into a freshly cleared sheep pasture. These transects were censused in the winter of 1988–89. Transects were 40 m wide, 20 m each side of a narrow trail, and were flagged every 50 m. Bird sightings were recorded by transect unit (each 40 × 20 m section) to allow for analysis of the spatial distribution of bird sightings. Censuses were conducted between 0600 and 0845 by walking slowly along the transect at a rate of approximately 300–500 m/hr. Starting time was adjusted by up to 1/2 hr to compensate for changing day lengths. Each transect was censused weekly, alternating the starting point from either end.

OBSERVER CONSISTENCY. Visual and auditory censuses are occasionally criticized because of the lack of standardization resulting from observer variability. Two different sets of observers were used each year. As much as possible, observers were alternated on individual transects in two-week blocks. To determine if a 4–6--week training period resulted in repeatable census results, I calculated the correlation between the two main observers in the average number of individuals/species seen per week. The resulting correlations were 0.99 for both years with intercepts of 0 and slopes of 0.98 and 0.99. This indicates that in both years, the different observers were equivalent in their overall estimation of numbers of migrants. I compared the average of the total number of individuals/species per week for the two seasons (over an equivalent time period 25 October–25 March) and found an overall correlation of 0.95 indicating that both the abundance of birds and the ability of the observers were similar for the two years.

Differential detectability between habitats remains a major source of bias for visual and auditory censuses. I compared the detection distance for the common migrants and found them to be similar between habitats. This was tested statistically by comparing scrub and forest habitat means with a *t*-test with the null hypothesis set as u_1-u_2 = 1 m (that is, the mean detection distance was not more than 1 m different between habitats within a species). The mean detection distance for migrants was 10.1 m (0.01 SE, n = 988) for forest transects, 10.4 m (0.01 SE, n = 892) for acahual transects, and 9.9 m (0.02 SE, n = 305) for pasture and milpa. I conducted pair-wise tests on detection distances between habitats within the seven most common species. In no case was there a significant difference.

HABITAT DESCRIPTION OF TRANSECTS. The six transects were established in a range of habitats from active cattle pasture to mature forest. Three basic habitats were censused: recently cleared land, 5–7-yr-old regrowth, and mature forest (see Table 1 for characteristics). Each

TABLE 1. Vegetation characteristics of the transects

Transect	Time since clearing	Mean canopy ht.	Mean trees/unit[a]	Stems/m² per dbh class				Common trees and shrubs[b]
				Total	< 2.5 cm	2.5–5.0 cm	> 5 cm	
Subperennial forest	50–100 yr	13.2 (0.3)	60–80 approx.	0.88 (0.07)	0.45 (0.06)	0.34 (0.02)	0.09 (0.01)	Manilkara zapota, Caesalpinia gaumeri, Coccoloba spicata, Esenbeckia berlandieri, Vitex gaumeri, Pseudobombax gaumeri, Alseis yucatanensis
Subdeciduous forest	50–100 yr	10.2 (0.2)	80–100 approx.	1.94 (0.10)	1.04 (0.09)	0.86 (0.02)	0.04 (0.01)	Eugenia sp., Bursera simarouba, Caesalpinia gaumeri, Metopium brownei, Croton sp., Sebastiania adrenophora
Grazed acahual	5–7 yr	3.2 (0.2)	14.5+ (2.1)	0.58 (0.05)	0.47 (0.05)	0.10 (0.01)	0.01 (+)	Hempea trilobata, Pithecellobium albicans, Mimosa bahamensis, Lysiloma latisiliqua, Metopium brownei
Ungrazed acahual	5–7 yr	3.5 (0.2)	11.6 (1.9)	0.65 (0.06)	0.54 (0.05)	0.10 (0.02)	< 0.01 (+)	Eugenia axillaris, Croton niveus, Cordia curassavica, Metopium brownii, Randia aculeata
Pasture	1–2 yr	2.5 (0.2)	0.2 (+)	0.44 (0.03)	0.44 (0.03)	0 (–)	0 (–)	Eugenia axillaris, Croton niveus, Hampea trilobata, Lysiloma latisiliqua
Milpa	0–1 yr	0 (–)	0.2 (+)	0 (–)	0 (–)	0 (–)	0 (–)	

NOTE: Standard error in parentheses.
a. 50 × 40 m Transect Unit
b. I. Olmsted, pers. comm.

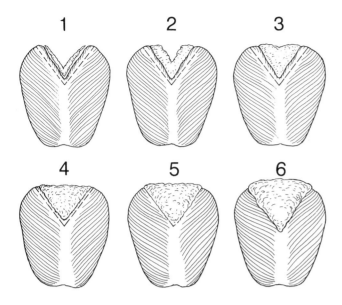

FIGURE 1. Schematic diagram for furcular fat indices (*1-6*, 0 fat not depicted).

of these major habitat types had two replicate transects that passed through distinct forms of that habitat: the recently cleared habitat included an unseeded pasture (cleared and burned), and a small farm planted in corn and beans; the second growth included one actively grazed and one ungrazed area; the forest transects were established on the two major forest types. The two acahuales had a similar mixture of shrubs with patches of trees. The grazed acahual was part of a 5-km² area that supported approximately 150 head of cattle and horses. Because this transect was along a major cow trail, grazing pressure was particularly heavy. The primary vegetative differences were that ground cover (predominantly ferns) was greatly reduced on the grazed site, and that the most common shrubs and trees were all browse-resistant legumes (i.e., *Acacia*) and euphorbs. The ungrazed site had a greater diversity of shrubs and trees (I. Olmsted, pers. comm.). In addition to its greater stature, the tall forest differed from the short forest in its reduced stem density and greater diversity of trees, particularly those characteristic of moist forests. Quantitative measures (Table 1) were taken at 10 systematically selected points per transect unit (20 × 40-m transect unit, 100 points per transect). Five points were sampled at 10-m intervals along the transect, alternating between 1, 10, and 20 m from the transect. Variables include the diameter at breast height (dbh) of trees and shrubs within a 2-m radius circle, as well as maximum canopy height and estimated ground cover. In addition, I counted the number of trees (> 5 m height) in each 40–50-m transect unit.

MIST NETTING ALONG TRANSECTS. Lines of 25–30 mist nets were run for three days along each of the acahual and forest transects during the fall and late winter each year. During the first winter, nets were run from 20 October to 10 November and from 10 February to 10 March. During the second year the fall netting period was conducted from 10 November to 5 December because census numbers showed that populations of local winter residents (particularly Common Yellowthroats, *Geothlypis trichas*) had not stabilized until early November. Nets were run from 0545 to 1000 or 1100 in acahuales, depending upon conditions and from 0545 to 1645 in the forest transects. I used a different daily schedule for the two habitats because capture rates declined drastically in the second growth with the heat and windy conditions during mid-day and afternoon. Furthermore, captured birds are endangered from exposure to such conditions.

Each migrant was banded with a unique combination of two plastic color bands and one numbered metal band. An important aspect of the project was assessing overall nutritional condition using visible fat reserves. Because wintering migrants generally have lighter fat stores than those in migration, we developed a visual index to furcular fat that is more finely graded than the standard system used at banding stations (Fig. 1). The internal consistency of the system was established by repeated simultaneous scoring by all of the banders. After a day of field work, the average rank correlation between observers was very high (0.95–1.0).

SEASONALITY IN FOLIAGE ARTHROPOD ABUNDANCE. For each bird census, we conducted a corresponding foliage insect census along transects perpendicular to the bird census transects. We recorded the number of arthropods found on the first 2,500 leaves located within arm's length. Starting points were located every 100 m on the transect, advancing 100 m each week. Starting direction was alternated left and right 90°. In addition to numbers of arthropods, we recorded their body length, general coloration, order (or family in Orthoptera), and leaf surface.

FORAGING OBSERVATIONS. Observations of foraging behavior were gathered along transects and while on expeditions to different parts of the Sian Ka'an Reserve. This prevented oversampling of the same set of individuals along the transects. Target species were selected on any given day, and an effort was made to gather foraging information from all individuals of those species. Details of foraging observations will be presented elsewhere. In this paper I will only discuss the proportion of individuals observed feeding on or in certain plants. For these data we have recorded only one observation per individual.

Results

WHICH SPECIES ARE FOREST MIGRANTS? The two census years produced nearly identical habitat associations of species. I considered the correlation between years for the cell values in Table 2 (the mean number of birds per habitat per species) sufficiently high ($r = 0.92$, d.f. = 95, $P < 0.001$) to test the significance of the patterns on year one data alone. Ten of the 16 most common migrants were significantly more common in forest than in earlier successional stages. This was tested by aposteriori contrasts based on a one-way Anova (Systat 1987, MGLH module). Most of these species showed consistent increases from clearing to acahual and from acahual to forest. I tested the significance of a pattern of increase across the successional gradient with the polynomial profile procedure (Systat 1987, MGLH module). Using the different census weeks as multiple observations, the profile procedure tested for a pattern of increased bird numbers with habitat rank. Habitat rank, based on successional stage, is an ordinal, independent variable in the analysis. In all six species (where one or fewer habitat cells had no observations), a significant first-order polynomial showed consistent increases from clearing to forest habitats (Table 2). Similarly, three of the six species which were significantly more common in pasture and second-growth transects showed a monotonic decrease from recently cleared land to forest.

I classified a number of rare species by habitat based on the total number of observations for forest and second growth (Table 2). Of the species classified, 16 were forest and 14 were non-forest migrants. All differences between forest and non-forest were significant based on a binomial test and an expected value of 33% of the total observations occuring along forest transects. To evaluate the repeatability of census results, I established replicate transects in distinct phases of the same habitat (e.g., grazed and ungrazed acahual). Each phase showed major structural and floristic differences from its counterpart. Nonetheless, the correlations of the abundances of forest migrants between the two phases of each habitat were high. The Pearson's r correlation coefficient for the two forest types was 0.95 and for the two acahual types was 0.81 (the r value for milpa and pasture was not calculated because forest migrants were too rare). These high correlations indicate that the census results are quite robust for these habitat types in the Sian Ka'an area.

Correlations for numbers of all migrant species (not just forest migrants) were high for the two forest transects (0.92) and the pasture and milpa (0.89). The cor-

relation was lower for the two acahual transects (0.72). Significant differences (Mann-Whitney U, $P < 0.05$) in abundance of forest migrants between the two acahuales were found for the Hooded Warbler (*Wilsonia citrina*), Black-throated Green Warbler (*Dendroica virens*), and White-eyed Vireo (*Vireo griseus*). The largest differences in abundance were in the non-forest migrants; the grazed acahual had significantly more Least Flycatchers (*Empidonax minimus*) and Common Yellowthroats.

I conducted similar analyses for the most common resident species observed along the 42 transect surveys per habitat for comparison with migrant species. Despite that Yucatan forests are of relatively low stature and are often described as "scrubby," the list of common resident birds of forests was almost completely nonoverlapping in species composition for the various cleared and secondary shrub habitats censused. The mean overlap between farm, pasture, grazed and ungrazed acahuales was 0.80 (shared species/20). The overlap of species composition between the low and high stature forest was 0.50, and the overlap between scrub and forest habitats averaged 0.02 (only the Yucatan Jay [*Cyanocorax yucatanicus*] and Fawn-breasted Hummingbird [*Amazilia yucatanensis*] were found commonly along both second-growth and forested transects). The actual correlations (Pearson's r) between the 30 most common species between the pasture and the two acahual censuses were 0.79–0.85, but were lower between milpa and the other disturbed habitats ($\bar{X} = 0.4$). The 30 most common species were used in the correlation analysis to ensure that all species would appear on the lists for different habitats.

WHICH FOREST MIGRANTS OCCUR IN NON-FOREST HABITAT? The most common forest migrants in second-growth habitats were predators on foliage insects in the upper levels of the forest (White-eyed Vireo, American Redstart [*Setophaga ruticilla*], Magnolia Warbler [*Dendroica magnolia*], and Black-throated Green Warbler). Hooded Warbler, a foliage insectivore of the understory, was the only exception to this generalization. The less common forest migrants in second growth included those that forage in aerial leaf litter (Worm-eating Warbler [*Helmitheros vermivorus*] and Blue-winged Warbler [*Vermivora pinus*], Greenberg 1987), terrestrial leaf litter or herbaceous ground cover (Ovenbird [*Seiurus aurocapillus*] and Kentucky Warbler [*Oporornis formosus*]) and on bark (Black-and-white Warbler [*Mniotilta varia*]).

I found a strong correlation ($r = 0.88$, $n = 10$, $P < 0.01$) between the abundance of a forest migrant on the forest transects and on the non-forest transects. By contrast, resident forest bird abundance on non-forest transects was not correlated ($r = 0.21$, $n = 20$, NS) with abundance on forest transects. In fact, many of the most

Table 2. Mean number of individuals of 16 common migratory species sighted per census on the six transects. Mean and (standard error) for year 1 of study, 21 censuses/transect

Species	Cleared Pasture	Cleared Milpa[a]	Acahual Grazed	Acahual Ungrazed	Forest Subdeciduous	Forest Subperennial	ANOVA Forest vs. non-forest[b]	ANOVA	Polynomial profile[c]
I. CLEARING SCRUB SPECIES[d]									
Gray Catbird (Dumetella carolinensis)	0.3 (+)	1.7 (0.2)	2.3 (0.2)	0.4 (+)	0.8 (0.1)	0.2 (+)	$P < 0.05$	13.6	$P < 0.01$
Least Flycatcher (Empidonax minimus)	4.0 (0.5)	3.4 (0.4)	3.9 (0.2)	2.6 (0.3)	1.7 (0.2)	0.6 (0.1)	$P < 0.001$	52.1	$P < 0.001$
Northern Parula (Parula americana)	0.9 (0.2)	1.6 (0.2)	2.7 (0.3)	0.8 (0.2)	0.6 (0.1)	1.1 (0.1)	$P < 0.05$	2.9	NS
Yellow-throated Warbler (Dendroica dominica)	0.2 (+)	0.2 (0.2)	0.1 (+)	0.2 (0.2)	0.0 (0.1)	0.0 (0.2)	$P < 0.01$	NA	
Palm Warbler (Dendroica palmarum)	0 (0)	0.2 (+)	0 (0)	0 (+)	0 (0)	0 (0)	$P < 0.05$	NA	
Common Yellowthroat (Geothlypis trichas)	7.6 (0.7)	8.7 (0.5)	6.3 (0.4)	3.1 (0.4)	0 (0)	0.4 (+)	$P < 0.001$	156.2	$P < 0.001$
II. FOREST SPECIES[e]									
White-eyed Vireo (Vireo griseus)	0.4 (+)	0 (0)	0.4 (+)	1.4 (0.1)	4.8 (0.5)	4.6	$P < 0.001$	65.7	$P < 0.001$
Yellow-throated Vireo (V. flavifrons)	0 (0)	0 (0)	0 (0)	0 (0)	0.3 (+)	1.5 (+)	$P < 0.001$	NA	
Black-and-white Warbler (Mniotilta varia)	0.4 (+)	0.1 (+)	0.1 (+)	0.1 (+)	1.7 (0.3)	1.7 (0.3)	$P < 0.001$	81.9	$P < 0.001$
Blue-winged Warbler (Vermivora pinus)	0 (0)	0 (0)	0 (0)	0 (0)	0.4 (+)	0.6 (+)	$P < 0.05$	NA	
Magnolia Warbler (Dendroica magnolia)	0.2 (+)	1.2 (+)	2.0 (0.2)	2.0 (0.2)	4.3 (0.5)	4.9 (0.5)	$P < 0.001$	123.2	$P < 0.001$
Black-thr. Green Warbler (Dendroica virens)	0 (0)	0 (0)	0.6 (0.2)	0.3 (0.2)	0.9 (0.2)	1.3 (0.2)	$P < 0.001$	57.5	$P < 0.001$
Hooded Warbler (Wilsonia citrina)	0.1 (+)	+ (+)	1.5 (0.2)	2.1 (0.2)	4.0 (0.4)	3.1 (0.3)	$P < 0.001$	151.3	$P < 0.001$
Kentucky Warbler (Oporornis formosus)	0 (0)	0 (0)	0 (0)	0 (0)	0.5 (+)	0.9 (+)	$P < 0.05$	NA	
Ovenbird (Seiurus aurocapillus)	0 (0)	0 (0)	0.1 (+)	+ (0)	0.8 (0.1)	0.4 (+)	$P < 0.01$	NA	
American Redstart (Setophaga ruticilla)	0.5 (+)	1.5 (0.2)	2.3 (0.3)	2.1 (0.3)	5.1 (0.4)	6.3 (0.6)	$P < 0.001$	158.7	$P < 0.001$

a. Milpa figures were corrected for year 1 when transect was only 750 m.

b. A posteriori contrast (Systat 1987) for one-way ANOVA in the general linear model program.

c. F ratio for first-order polynomial profile testing for monotonic increase or decrease across successional stages.

d. Additional uncommon species classified as clearing-scrub species with the ratio of clearing and scrub observations: Ruby-throated Hummingbird (Archilochus colubris) (0:21), Eastern Wood-Pewee (Contopus virens) (0:13), Blue-gray Gnatcatcher (Polioptila caerulea) (505:0), Yellow Warbler (Dendroica petechia) (0:37), Yellow-breasted Chat (Icteria virens) (0:19), Orchard Oriole (Icterus spurius)(0:53), Rose-breasted Grosbeak (Pheucticus ludovicianus) (0:9), Blue Grosbeak (Guiraca caerulea) (0:20), Indigo Bunting (Passerina cyanea) (0:53). An unknown proportion of the Blue-gray Gnatcatchers are probably the migratory subspecies (Polioptila caerulea).

e. Additional uncommon species classified as forest migrants (as above): Great Crested Flycatcher (Myiarchus crinitus) (6:0), Wood Thrush (Hylocichla mustelina) (10:0), Swainson's Thrush (Catharus ustulatus) (9:0), Red-eyed Vireo (Vireo olivaceus) (5:0), Worm-eating Warbler (Helmitheros vermivorus) (8:0), Chestnut-sided Warbler (Dendroica pensylvanica) (5:1).

f. Tests for significance of increasing or decreasing trend with successional stage. NA (not applied) refers to species with more than one habitat cell containing no observations.

TABLE 3. Regression statistics for number of forest migrants observed as a function of date in forest and acahual transects in year 1.

Species	Forest				Non-forest			
	r	slope	intercept	change	r	slope	intercept	change
All forest migrants	-0.39	-0.49	52.3	-0.9	-0.65*	-0.54	27.0	-2.0
White-eyed Vireo	-0.28	-0.15	9.5	-1.6	-0.55*	-0.17	4.8	-3.5
Magnolia Warbler	+0.44*	+0.14	7.6	+1.8	-0.15	-0.05	4.7	-1.1
Hooded Warbler	-0.25	-0.10	8.0	-1.2	-0.48*	-0.15	4.7	-2.8
American Redstart	-0.19	-0.11	12.5	-0.9	-0.67*	-0.31	10	-3.1

*$P < 0.05$.

TABLE 4. Percentage of individuals marked during fall netting that were observed at least one month after capture (n)

Species	Forest	Acahual
Wood Thrush	6 (17)	0 (10)
White-eyed Vireo	39 (13)	44 (18)
Black-and-white Warbler	17 (12)	25 (4)
Blue-winged Warbler	100 (1)	100 (1)
Magnolia Warbler	17 (6)	44 (16)
Black-thr. Green Warbler	—	66 (3)
Hooded Warbler	55 (31)	29 (31)
Ovenbird	22 (23)	8 (12)
American Redstart	10 (10)	24 (33)
TOTAL	29 (113)	29 (125)

common understory species, including the woodcreepers and Red-throated Ant-Tanager, were never observed or captured on the non-forest transects.

OVER-WINTER POPULATION DECLINES IN FOREST MIGRANTS IN AND OUT OF FOREST. Forest migrants declined significantly during the course of the first winter ($r = -0.57$, $n = 21$, $P < 0.05$), but not the second winter ($r = -0.20$, $n = 21$, NS). During the first winter the decline of forest migrants in non-forest habitat was 2.0 birds/week compared to 0.9 birds/week for forest habitats (Table 3). Only the regression for non-forest habitat was significantly less than zero. During the first winter, three of the four most common forest migrants showed significant declines only in the second-growth habitats; the fourth species, Magnolia Warbler, showed a significant increase in the forest habitat and a nonsignificant decline in non-forest habitats.

SEASONALITY OF ARTHROPOD ABUNDANCE. Based on a regression between the number of arthropods/2,500 leaves and week number, foliage arthropods declined significantly in the first winter but not during the sec-

ond winter. The decline for the forest habitat in the first winter is described by the equation $Y = 26.6 - 0.46 X$ ($n = 23$, $r = -0.56$, $P = 0.006$) and for non-forest $Y = 47.5 - 1.2 X$ ($n = 23$, $r = -0.41$, $P = 0.05$). This corresponds to a 1.8% and 2.6% decline per week, respectively. The difference in the magnitude of decline was greater when only arthropods greater than 5 mm were analyzed. Because of the exponential relationship between mass and length of arthropods, this larger size class should account for most of the biomass. The equation for the decline in large arthropods in forest was $Y = 4.6 - 0.03X$ ($P = 0.67$) and for non-forest was $Y = 13.7 - 0.58X$ ($P = 0.04$). The decline was approximately 4.2%/week for nonforest and 0% for forest.

RESIDENCY. Habitat density prevented efficient resighting of color-banded birds in the vicinity of transects. A crude index of the degree of residency was calculated based on the percentage of individuals color-banded that were observed at least one month after initial capture. The pooled value for all forest migrants was not statistically different (χ^2) between the acahual (29%, $n = 125$) and forest habitats (29%, $n = 113$) (Table 4). Species differed in their probability of resighting. Wood Thrushes were almost never resighted (6/27), whereas both Hooded Warblers and White-eyed Vireos were commonly resighted near the same transect point over the entire winter and occasionally between winters. The biggest difference between habitats was found in the Hooded Warbler, the American Redstart, and the Magnolia Warbler. The difference in the Hooded Warbler probably reflects a real difference in residency because Hooded Warblers (55% vs. 29%, χ^2, $P < 0.05$) are readily captured in ground nets. A large difference was found between the two acahuals, where 37% of the netted birds were resighted or recaptured in the ungrazed and only 8% of the birds were similarly resighted or recaptured in the grazed acahual (χ^2, $P < 0.05$). The differ-

TABLE 5. Mean condition scores, with possible range of 1–6, based on visible furcular fat deposits for forest and non-forest migrants (n, S.E.)

Sample (species, time)	Forest netting	Non-forest netting
Forest[a]: early winter, year 1	2.3 (55, 0.1)	2.3 (40, 0.1)
late winter, year 1	2.5 (36, 0.1)	2.5 (26, 0.1)
Forest: early winter, year 2	2.8 (26, 0.2)	2.8 (26, 0.2)
late winter, year 2	3.2 (26, 0.2)	2.8 (36, 0.2)
Forest (pooled)	2.7 (143, 0.1)	2.6 (128, 0.1)
Wood Thrush	3.3 (18, 0.2)	3.4 (20, 0.2)
White-eyed Vireo	2.5 (22, 0.1)	2.8 (30, 0.1)
Magnolia Warbler	2.0 (5, 0.4)	2.4 (20, 0.2)
Hooded Warbler	2.4 (46, 0.1)	2.6 (38, 0.1)
American Redstart	1.2 (28, 0.1)	1.8 (7, 0.2)
Ovenbird	3.1 (20, 0.2)	3.4 (11, 0.2)

a. Only species less than 20g included in pooled forest and non-forest samples.

ence found between forest and acahual in the American Redstart and Magnolia Warbler was more likely an artifact of the greater abundance and lower probability of capturing or accurately sighting birds in the forest habitat than the acahuals.

FAT SCORES FOR FOREST MIGRANTS CAPTURED IN FOREST AND SCRUBBY SECOND GROWTH. Average fat condition did not differ for forest migrants netted in acahual versus forest (Mann-Whitney U, Table 5). In both habitats, forest migrants showed more visible fat in the late winter than the fall and in year 2 versus year 1 (Mann-Whitney U-test, $P < 0.05$) Furthermore, there was no difference in fat class between forest ($\bar{X} = 2.6 \pm 0.1$, $n = 128$) and non-forest ($\bar{X} = 2.8 \pm 0.2$, $n = 74$) migrants (species under 20 g) in the acahuales. Individual species comparisons (pooled for year and season) showed no significant differences between forest and acahuales (Mann-Whitney U-test with alpha level correct for multiple comparisons).

FINE-SCALE DISTRIBUTION OF FOREST MIGRANTS IN ACAHUALES. Forest migrants were patchily distributed along the acahual transects with nearly one-half (45%) of the sightings in the upper quartile of the 20×40-m transect units. This is significantly greater than the 33% value for the forest transects (χ^2, $P < 0.01$). I tested the hypothesis that the distribution of forest migrants is related to the presence of small patches of trees within the acahuales. The correlation between the number of trees per unit and the number of sightings of forest migrants was significant for both years and for both acahuales ($r = 0.68$, 0.57 in ungrazed acahual and $r = 0.59$, 0.58 in grazed acahual) (Fig. 2). No significant cor-

relation was found between these variables for non-forest migrants. The relationship appears to be one with a threshold: units with 8–10 or more small trees (these are the respective medians for the ungrazed and grazed) had nearly three times the number of forest migrant sightings (Table 6). Non-forest migrants did not show this relationship. Forest migrant species for which I had enough observations in the acahuales show considerable variation in their dependence on areas with patches of trees: the White-eyed Vireo was the most specialized (88% of 55 sightings in transect plots with greater than the median number of trees) followed by the Hooded Warbler (78%, 150), the Magnolia Warbler (65%, 150), and the American Redstart (55%, 197).

OCCURRENCE OF MIGRANTS IN TREES IN ACAHUALES. Concentration in patches of trees does not necessarily mean that the migrant was found in trees (Table 7). Relative use of trees by different forest migrant species ranged from 1 to 82% and was similar to the use of trees by non-forest migrants (median is 58% for forest and 40% for non-forest migrant species, NS by Mann-Whitney test). Therefore, in addition to the species that depend upon trees in patches to support their activity (forest migrants), several species of non-forest migrants, such as Northern Parula (*Parula americana*), were found in isolated trees.

DEPENDENCE OF MIGRANTS ON SPECIFIC FOOD PLANTS. The only forest-dwelling migrant that consumed considerable fruit was the White-eyed Vireo. Thirty-five percent of late winter foraging observations involved the use of *Bursura*.

Frugivory was most common in the migrants in ac-

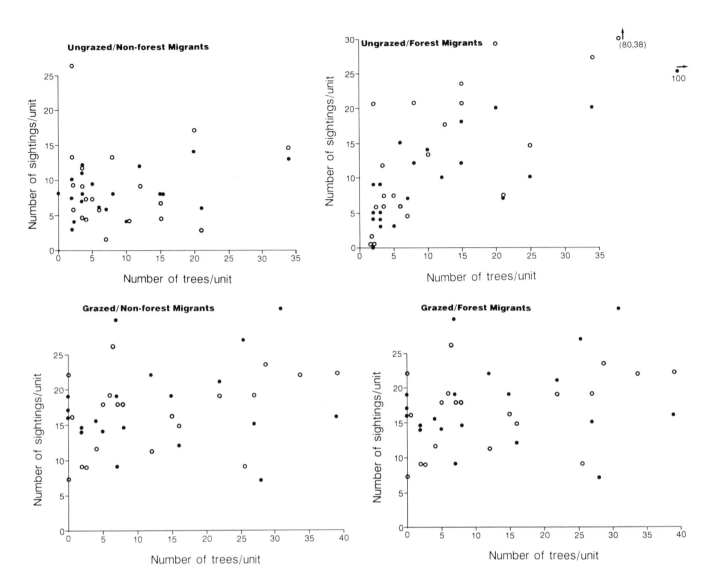

FIGURE 2. Relationship between total sightings of forest or non-forest migrants per transect unit and tree density on grazed and ungrazed acahuales. *Open circles*, data from year 2; *solid circles*, data from year 1.

TABLE 6. Median of the number of total sightings of forest and non-forest migrants per transect unit along the acahual transects comparing the units with below and above the median number of trees (year 1/year2)

	Below median	Above median
Grazed acahual		
Forest migrants	4/7	12/13*
Non-forest migrants	18/11	18/11
Ungrazed acahual		
Forest migrants	6/5	14/13*
Non-forest migrants	7/7	9/6

NOTE: Median number of trees is 10 for grazed and 8 for ungrazed acahual.
*Significant difference between units with below and above median number of trees, $P < 0.001$.

TABLE 7. Percentage of individuals of different migrant species located in trees along the acahual transects

Species	Number	Percent
Forest Migrants		
White-eyed Vireo	40	50
Magnolia Warbler	90	61
American Redstart	112	58
Hooded Warbler	15	0
Black-thr. Green Warbler	18	82
MEDIAN		58
Other Migrants		
Ruby-thr. Hummingbird	15	40
Least Flycatcher	94	44
Gray Catbird	36	33
Northern Parula	102	56
Common Yellowthroat	85	2
Yellow-breasted Chat	10	0
Orchard Oriole	17	56
MEDIAN		40

ahuales, predominantly the Gray Catbird (*Dumetella carolinensis*) and Yellow-breasted Chat (*Icteria virens*). Direct observation was rare, but 33% of the chat and 25% of the catbird feces collected in cleaned bird bags contained seeds corresponding to the common fruiting plants of the acahuales. In October, chats and catbirds ate *Eugenia axillaris* (Myrtaceae) and in November they were found primarily with seeds of *Cordia curassavica* (Boraginaceae).

Flowers were also exploited primarily in acahuales by the Northern Parula, the Orchard Oriole (*Icterus spurius*) and the Ruby-throated Hummingbird (*Archilochus colubris*) (Table 8) during the late winter (Jan.–Mar.). Most of the flowers visited were small white flowers, including *Chiococca alba* (Rubiaceae) and *Hampea trilobata* (Malvaceae). Nectarivory was found predominantly in the scrub habitats. One exception was the Northern Parula which foraged on a small vine (Rubiaceae) in the canopy of the tall forest in February and March. Although not dependent upon them as a food plant, Black-throated Green Warblers occur in mimosoid trees (with small leaflets) well out of proportion to their abundance in the forest. They were observed in these trees 51% of 80 observations compared to 10–25% for all other foliage gleaning migrants including American Redstart (14%,*n* = 101), White-eyed Vireo (24%, 111), Magnolia Warbler (20%, 121), and Northern Parula (17%, 128). Black-throated Green Warblers were found significantly more often in legumes with leaflets than the other four

species ($\chi^2, P < 0.05$). Mimosoid trees comprise approximately 10–20% of the canopy cover in the Sian Ka'an forests (I. Olmsted, pers. comm.)

Discussion

IMPORTANCE OF FOREST TO MIGRANTS AT SIAN KA'AN. Most species of migratory landbirds of the Sian Ka'an Reserve winter most commonly in the closed canopy forest. The small numerical dominance of forest wintering migrants was also reported by Waide (1981) and Lynch (1989). This provides a prima facie case that as land is cleared for ranching and agriculture, the populations of many migratory bird species should decline. However, it is likely that important differences exist between habitat distributions on the Yucatan Peninsula and other, wetter areas of the Caribbean lowlands of Mexico and Central America. Recent declines found in Neotropical migrants censused by the North American Breeding Bird Survey are consistent with this prediction (Robbins et al. 1989). Species that winter most commonly in the forests of Sian Ka'an showed a consistent decline in their population trends (a decrease in the slope of the trend line), whereas species of pasture and scrubby second growth displayed increases in their population trends over the past 10 years. However, individuals of most forest migrant species, particularly the most common species (i.e., American Redstart, White-eyed Vireo, Hooded Warbler, Magnolia Warbler), were found in recently cleared land and young second growth. Given the inevitability of continued forest clearing in the Yucatan, these disturbed habitats might be a reservoir for reduced forest migrant populations (Lynch 1989). For this reason, I focused on the status of forest migrants in secondary habitats.

USE OF ACAHUALES BY FOREST MIGRANTS. Most, but not all, forest wintering migrants were found regularly in non-forest habitats. Clearly, the lack of certain resources, such as large limbs, moist leaf litter, and hanging dead curled leaves, will limit the abundance of forest migrants in second growth. Further, the significant correlation between abundance of a species in forest and the numbers seen in non-forest habitats suggests that factors making it difficult for forest migrants to occupy dry forest are even more severely limiting in dry forest second growth. For example, dry forests support few dead-leaf-foraging birds, including migrants such as the Worm-eating Warbler. This is presumably because birds occupying the large-leafed canopy, the source for much of the aerial leaf litter in a tropical forest, are rare in tropical dry forests (pers. obs.). They are relatively rarer in the scrub associated with dry forest, and dead-leaf-foraging birds are virtually absent. This correlation

TABLE 8. Percentage of feeding records involving non-arthropod food items for commonly omnivorous species

Species	Number	October–December	January–March	Common items	% observ.[a]
Ruby-thr. Hummingbird	18	0	100	*Chioccoca* flowers *Cordea* flowers	
Gray Catbird	36	25	0	*Eugenia* fruit *Trema* fruit *Cordea* fruit	
White-eyed Vireo	199	12	35	*Bursera* fruit	91
Northern Parula	185	4	46	*Chioccoca* flowers	82
				Caesalpinia gaumeri flowers *Hampea trilobata* flowers	15
Yellow-breasted Chat	30	33	0	*Eugenia* fruit *Cordea* fruit	
Orchard Oriole	17	0	92	legume flowers	

a. The percentage of frugivorous or nectarivorous observations within species for particular plant species.

could also result from a spillover effect: more common species have a greater source pool of individuals that can occupy suboptimal habitats.

Three of the four common forest migrants in second growth showed a distinct sexual segregation in habitat use (Lopez Ornat and Greenberg 1990). With the exception of the Northern Parula, females had lower densities in these non-forest habitats than males in the forest. The unbalanced sex ratios in forest and second growth should result in a shift in the overall operational sex ratio as the balance between forest and cleared land changes. It is unclear what effect low levels of habitat alteration might have on a population. It is possible that as forest is cleared on the wintering grounds, females will become a less limiting resource for males in the breeding season. However, if overall habitat alteration is severe, it is also possible that declines in the forest-limited sex (males) might excacerbate a general population decline.

DEPENDENCE OF FOREST MIGRANTS ON PATCHES OF TREES IN ACAHUALES. The few forest migrants found in acahuales tend to concentrate their activities in small patches of trees; the degree of concentration varies between species from the specialized White-eyed Vireo and Hooded Warbler to the less restricted Magnolia Warbler and American Redstart. Robbins et al. (1987) reported that large forest fragments (approx. 100 ha) supported forest migrant densities comparable to those of extensive tracts. In this study, I found that the size threshold of patches of trees used by forest migrants was very low.

It is interesting to note that the number of non-forest migrants observed was not negatively related to local tree density, as might be expected. Therefore, the greatest density and diversity of migrants in acahuales was found in and around patches of trees.

The dependence on patches of trees can be largely, but not wholly, explained by the fact that the forest migrants are largely arboreal and require trees for feeding. In acahuales, forest migrants were located in trees approximately 58% of the time as opposed to 40% for non-forest migrants, but some notable exceptions occurred. Orchard Orioles and Northern Parula were found in trees over 50% of the time. These sets of data combined underscore the need for the preservation of trees in agricultural areas. In addition to the set of forest migrants requiring patches of trees are species that depend upon trees regardless of whether they occur in such patches. By these combined criteria, of the 16 most common migrants, only the Common Yellowthroat and Gray Catbird show no clear relationship with the presence of trees.

In addition to mimicking forest structure, patches of trees might provide specific resources for arboreal migrants. The largest differences in abundance of forest migrants between the two acahuales were found in the Black-throated Green Warbler and White-eyed Vireo. Both species have been associated with particular plants characterizing the acahuales where they are most common. Black-throated Green Warblers in all habitats occurred primarily in small-leafed legume trees, such as *Acacia* (perhaps because they are structurally similar to short-needled conifers, cf. Morse 1980). These trees dominate the heavily grazed acahual (I. Olmsted, unpubl. data), but are rare in the ungrazed acahual where the Black-throated Green Warbler was also rare. Similarly, observations of White-eyed Vireos in the forest showed they commonly eat the fruit of *Bursera simaruba*. They appear to visit specific *Bursera* fruit daily to test for ripe capsules. Like the White-eyed Vireo, *Bursera* is considerably more numerous in the ungrazed acahual than the grazed acahual (I. Olmsted, unpubl. data). White-eyed Vireos were frequently seen visiting *Bursera* in patches of trees in scrubby areas.

STATUS OF POPULATIONS OF FOREST MIGRANT BIRDS IN ACAHUALES. The evaluation of the status of forest migrant populations in non-forest habitats was mixed. Declines in forest migrants observed during the first winter of the study were most pronounced in the non-forest habitats. This winter represented an end of a three-year drought. Foliage insect samples revealed a significant decline, with a particularly sharp decline in large arthropods in second-growth habitats. This suggests that foliage arthropod biomass, which is most strongly correlated with density of larger arthropods, declined most rapidly in second-growth habitats.

However, even during the winter when forest migrants experienced significant declines, common forest migrants maintained their sparse populations in second growth throughout the winter. Our resighting and recapturing of marked birds indicated that the proportion of birds resident in acahuales is comparable to what we found in forest.

Finally, I was unable to detect any significant difference in fat class for forest migrants in forest and acahual habitats. I was also unable to distinguish fat levels of forest from non-forest migrants in acahuales.

POTENTIAL VALUE OF SMALL FOREST PATCHES, HEDGEROWS, AND LONG FALLOW CYCLES FOR FOREST-DEPENDENT MIGRANTS. Young second-growth vegetation, even under heavy grazing, might support populations of forest migrants. Given the abundance and proximity of forest to the acahual transects, it is probably best to regard these results as an optimistic evaluation of the value of acahuales to forest migrants. This is particularly true in light of the spill-over effect suggested by a strong correlation between the abundance of forest migrants in forest and in acahuales. Apparently, however, only the most common forest wintering migrants can be found in acahuales. Furthermore, it appears that during winters when populations decline, the declines are more severe in acahuales than in forests. Even so, these sparse populations might become critical reservoirs as forest clearing continues throughout the Yucatan Peninsula. A strategy for maintaining populations of forest migrants

in the face of the current wave of deforestation would, first, involve the conservation of large tracts of forests; second, promote the protection and establishment of small patches of native wooded vegetation in the agricultural landscape; and finally, promote practices that increase interclearing fallow periods.

The latter two conservation practices might have considerably less effect on the resident forest birds of the Yucatan Peninsula. Many common forest residents do not occur in acahuales, even in large patches of trees. In this sense, although the rubrics "migrant" and "resident" obscure considerable ecological diversity (Hutto 1989), forest migrant birds might present a distinct and complementary conservation problem to those faced by resident birds. The latter might require large forest preserves to prevent extinctions of localized species. Forest migrant populations also can be expected to decline with shrinking forest area. However, these declines can be mitigated through seemingly small changes in agricultural practices that preserve more trees and allow longer fallow periods.

Acknowledgments

I would like to thank Mercedes Foster for her support during the entire project. The project depended upon the competence and enthusiasm of a number of field assistants: Dana Bradley, Mauro Berlanga, Jill Heath, David Heath, Dan Niven, and Rosa Maria Vidal. Ingred Olmsted provided help on botanical problems. Jacalyn Bernstein and Ann Chaney helped with analyses. James Lynch and Arturo Lopez Ornat shared a wealth of information on the land use history and ecology of the Sian Ka'an Reserve. Barbara McKinnon de Montes was an invaluable supporter of the project. I thank the Secretariat de Desarrollo Urbano y Ecologia (SEDUE) and the Centro de Investigaciones de Quintana Roo (CIQRO) for providing me access to the facilities at Sian Ka'an. The research was supported by contract from the National Ecology Center of the U.S. Fish and Wildlife Service. Reconnaissance was suppported by the World Wildlife Fund–U.S. I thank the Ohio State Cooperative Research unit for logistical support.

Literature cited

Greenberg, R. 1987. Seasonal foraging specialization in the Worm-eating Warbler. *Condor* 89:158–168.

Holmes, R.T., T.W. Sherry, and L. Reitsma. 1989. Population structure, territoriality and overwinter survival of two migrant warbler species in Jamaica. *Condor* 91:545–561.

Hutto, R.L. 1989. The effect of habitat alteration on migratory land birds in a west Mexican tropical deciduous forest: A conservation perspective. *Conserv. Biol.* 3:138–148.

Lopez Ornat, A., and R. Greenberg. 1990. Sexual segregation

by habitat in migratory warblers in Quintana Roo, Mexico. *Auk* 107:539–543.

Lynch, J.F. 1989. Distribution of overwintering Nearctic migrants in the Yucatan Peninsula, I: General patterns of occurrence. *Condor* 91:515–544.

Lynch, J.F., E.S. Morton, and M.E. Van der Voort. 1985. Habitat segregation between the sexes of wintering Hooded Warblers (*Wilsonia citrina*). *Auk* 102:714–721.

Morse, D.H. 1980. Foraging and coexistence of spruce-woods warblers. *Living Bird* 18:7–25.

Rappole, J.H., and E.S. Morton. 1985. Effects of habitat alteration on a tropical avian forest community. Pages 1013–1021 in *Neotropical Ornithology*, P.A. Buckley, E.S. Morton, R.S. Ridgely, and F.G. Buckley, eds. Ornithol. Monogr. 36.

Rappole, J., and D.W. Warner. 1980. Ecological aspects of migrant bird behavior in Veracruz, Mexico. Pages 297–309 in *Migrant Birds in the Neotropics: Ecology, Behavior, Distribution and Conservation*, A. Keast and E.S. Morton, eds. Washington: Smithsonian Institution Press.

Rappole, J.H., M.A. Ramos, and K. Winker. 1989. Wintering wood thrush movements and mortality in southern Veracruz. *Auk* 106:402–410.

Robbins, C.S., B.A. Dowell, D.K. Dawson, J. Colón, F. Espinoza, J. Rodriguez, R. Sutton, and T. Vargas. 1987. Comparison of Neotropical winter bird populations in isolated patches versus extensive forest. *Acta Oecol.: Oecol. Gen.* 8:285–292.

Robbins, C.S., J.R. Sauer, R.S. Greenberg, and S. Droege. 1989. Population declines in North American birds that migrate to the neotropics. *Proc. Natl. Acad. Sci.* 86:7658–7662.

Rzedowski, J. 1983. *Vegetación de México*. Mexico, D.F.: Editorial Limusa.

Schoener, T., and D. Janzen. 1968. Notes on environmental determinants of tropical versus temperate insect size patterns. *Amer. Nat.* 102:207–224.

Systat Inc. 1987. *SYSTAT Manual*. Winston, Ill.

Tramer, E. 1974. Proportions of wintering North American birds in disturbed and undisturbed dry tropical habitats. *Condor* 76:460-464.

Waide, R.B. 1980. Resource partitioning of migrant and resident birds: The use of irregular resources. Pages 331–352 in *Migrant Birds in the Neotropics: Ecology, Behavior, Distribution and Conservation*, A. Keast and E.S. Morton, eds. Washington: Smithsonian Institution Press.

———. 1981. Interactions between resident and migrant birds in Campeche, Mexico. *Trop. Ecol.* 22:134–154.

Winker, K., J. Rappole, and M.R. Ramos. 1990. Population dynamics of the wood thrush in southern Veracruz, Mexico. *Condor* 92:444–460.

GEORGE V.N. POWELL
National Audubon Society
115 Indian Mound Trail
Tavernier, Florida 33070

JOHN H. RAPPOLE
Conservation and Research Center
National Zoological Park
Smithsonian Institution
Front Royal, Virginia 22630

STEVEN A. SADER
School of Forestry
University of Maine
Orono, Maine 04469

Neotropical migrant landbird use of lowland Atlantic habitats in Costa Rica: A test of remote sensing for identification of habitat

Abstract. The rapid rate of conversion of broadleaf evergreen forests in the Neotropics to open, herbaceous-dominated habitats has led to concern over potential negative impacts on wintering Neotropical migrant birds. In this study, we tested the use of remote sensing to quantify major habitat types (primarily seral stages and agricultural uses) which we then sampled for migrant use.

A Landsat Thematic Mapper image taken on 6 February 1989 was analyzed with unsupervised classification. Ground truthing at 80 random points indicated the successful classification of forest, open habitats, second growth, and agricultural crops with high standing crop (i.e., banana, palm, bamboo). However, the analysis could not distinguish disturbed from pristine forest, nor could it separate some perennial crops (i.e., citrus, yucca, coffee) from second growth.

Migrant use of the habitats identified with remote sensing was quantified through point censusing and mist netting on randomly selected sites. Twenty-eight migrant species were recorded. Of the 20 species that were sufficiently common to determine habitat use, 12 were found in the three major seral stages identified (forest; second growth; open, herbaceous) by Landsat. Two species were found in forest and second growth, two species were found exclusively in open habitats, two species were restricted to second growth, and two species were restricted to forest. Species recorded exclusively in forest—Acadian Flycatcher (*Empidonax virescens*) and Wood Thrush (*Hylocichla mustelina*)—are considered to be highly vulnerable to deforestation. However, with two exceptions—Yellow Warbler (*Dendroica petechia*) and Common Yellowthroat (*Geothlypis trichas*)—species found in the open habitat category were foraging in trees that were remnants of recently cleared forests. With time, we predict that open Neotropical habitats will decline in value for migrant birds because of the gradual loss of remnant trees.

Sinopsis. La alta tasa de conversión de bosques neotropicales en habitats abiertos dominados por herbáceas ha suscitado la preocupación acerca de los impactos potencialmente negativos de esta práctica sobre las aves migratorias neotropicales invernantes. En este estudio, nosotros examinamos el uso de imágenes de satélite para cuantificar los tipos principales de habitat (principalmente bosque primario, etapas serales y de usos agrícolas), los cuales muestreamos posteriormente para cuantificar el uso por aves migratorias.

Una imagen de Mapeador Temático Landsat tomada el 6 de febrero de 1989 fué analizada con clasificación no supervisada. La verificación de 80 puntos en el terrene, tomados al azar, indicó la clasificación exitosa de bosques, habitats abiertos, áreas de crecimiento secundario y plantaciones agrícolas de cultivos permanentes (i.e. banano, palma, bambú). Sin embargo, el análisis no pudo diferenciar entre bosque pristino y bosque perturbado ni entre algunos cultivos perennes (i.e. cítricos, yuca, café) y áreas de crecimiento secundario.

El uso por aves migratorias de los habitats identificados con imágenes de satélite fue cuantificado mediante censos puntuales y capturas con redes de niebla en sitios seleccionados al azar. Veintiocho especies migratorias fueron registradas. De las 20 especies que fueron suficientemente comúnes como para determinar su uso del habitat, 12 se encontraron en las tres etapas sucesionales mayores identificadas mediante Landsat (bosque, áreas de crecimiento secundario, habitat abierto, herbáceo). Dos especies se encontraron en bosque y áreas de crecimiento secundario, dos exclusivamente en habitats abiertos, dos estuvieron restringidas a áreas de crecimiento secundario y dos restringidas al bosque. Estas últimas (*Empidonax virescens* y *Hylocichla mustelina*) se consideran altamente vulnerables a la deforestación. Sin embargo, con dos excepciones, *Dendroica petechia* y *Geothlypis trichas*, las especies encontradas en la categoría de habitat abierto estuvieron alimentándose principalmente en árboles dejados as talar el bosque.

Nosotros predecimos que con el tiempo los habitats abiertos Neotropicales declinarán en su valor para aves migratorias a causa de la pérdida gradual de estos árboles remanentes.

Broadleaf evergreen forests in the tropics are being rapidly destroyed through conversion to open landscapes dominated by grasslands and agriculture (Myers 1980, Keogh 1984). Recent rates of conversion from forest to open habitats in the Wet Life Zones (sensu Holdridge 1967) have been highest on the Atlantic side of Costa Rica (Sader and Joyce 1988). Analyses, using satellite imagery, have documented that more than 78% of the forest in the Tropical Wet Life Zone has been lost. An estimated 9% of the forest in Costa Rica was destroyed between 1976 and 1983 (Sader and Joyce 1988). Hartshorn et al. (1983) predicted that by the end of the decade, based on present deforestation rates of 60,000–70,000 ha/yr, no unprotected forest would be left in the country. Although that prediction proved to be slightly excessive, it is likely to be fulfilled in the 1990s.

The impact of forest conversion on wintering Neotropical migrants has been the subject of extensive debate (Willis 1966, Karr 1976, Hutto 1980, Rappole and Warner 1980, Terborgh 1980, Powell and Rappole 1986, Lynch 1989, Morton and Greenberg 1989). The disagreement among researchers exists in large part because an absence of reliable data on habitat requirements of migrants in the Neotropics has precluded a quantitative assessment of the impacts of habitat loss. In the absence of these data, opposing hypotheses have been generated to predict the impact of forest loss on migrant populations. One hypothesis is predicated on the premise that migrants are habitat generalists and are, therefore, largely unaffected by habitat conversions (Slud 1960, Willis 1966, Karr 1976). An opposing hypothesis presumes that wintering migrants have specific habitat requirements that restrict them to a single or limited array of habitats (Terborgh 1980, Rappole and Morton 1985, Morton and Greenberg 1989). Those taking the latter position predict that migrant populations are sensitive to habitat changes. Accordingly, species with limited distributions that are restricted to primary forest will be negatively affected by the extensive forest destruction presently occurring in the Neotropics.

The objectives of this study were twofold: to assess the habitat specificity of migrants wintering in the Atlantic lowlands in Costa Rica, and to use ground truthing to test the efficacy of using remote sensing to quantify and monitor the changing distribution of habitats used by migrants. To achieve the latter goal, it is necessary to demonstrate that the satellite imagery analysis depicts habitat types conforming to specific migrant habitat-use patterns.

Methods

A Landsat Thematic Mapper (TM) image taken on 6 February 1986 was processed by a computer-aided technique (unsupervised classification) to generate habitat (land cover) categories. In this technique, the computer searches the TM image and assigns each pixel in the data set to units that "look alike" on the basis of multispectral reflectance characteristics. An image analyst then assigns each unit to descriptive habitat categories. The analysis of the 6 February image produced 10 habitat categories (Table 1). The TM scene used for this

TABLE 1. Habitat categories derived from the Landsat Thematic Mapper. The February 1986 image was analyzed by unsupervised blind classification

Category	Description	Percent coverage
1	Water, pavement	0.6
2	Mature forest	3.2
3	Mature forest	23.6
4	Mature forest	23.0
5	Young second growth (1–5 y)/perennial crops	12.5
6	Disturbed forest/old second growth (> 15 y)	8.5
7	Forest edge	4.8
8	Middle second growth (5–15 y)	3.5
9	Pasture and other herbaceous-dominated areas (open)	16.2
10	Perennial crops	3.7

FIGURE 1. Study area (*bold outline*) on Atlantic slopes of Costa Rica. *Dark area:* national parks, wildlife refuges, and private sanctuaries.

study covers 2,016 km² of the Sarapiqui region of Costa Rica extending from the central valley (Meseta Central) across the Continental Divide into the Atlantic lowlands (Fig. 1). Included within this area is Braulio Carillo National Park and La Selva Biological Station, a complex of protected natural areas which extends from peaks of 2,600 m down to 50 m elevation. In this study we limited our analysis of habitat and migrant use to areas less than 1,000 m in elevation on the Atlantic slope. We deliberately elected to analyze an area consisting primarily of wet life zones (Tosi 1969) to avoid the need to distinguish among climax communities. This allowed us to concentrate on differences between primary forest and seral stages created by human land-use practices.

The accuracy of the habitat classification algorithm was tested by visiting random points and comparing actual habitat with TM predicted habitat. Sample locations to be used for quantifying vegetation characteristics were selected within each of the two most abundant habitat types, mature forest areas and open areas dominated by herbaceous plants, using a computer-generated stratified random sample. A small sample of second-growth sites was selected for a more limited analysis of that habitat type. All selected areas were at least 5 ha in size. Vegetation was characterized using a procedure adapted from James and Shugart (1970). Five points, randomly selected within the site, were used as foci for sample circles 22.5 m in diameter. Within the sample areas, the dbh of all stems greater than 7.6 cm was measured. Along east-west and north-south transects

that intersected at the center of each circle, all stems within 1 m of the transects and taller than 1.5 m were counted. Ground cover and canopy cover along each transect were estimated based on 10 sample points. Canopy height was estimated to the nearest 5 m by visual inspection.

Two methods were used to quantify migrant presence at the sample sites. A variable circular-plot (VCP) census method developed by Reynolds et al. (1980) was used at up to 12 points 200 m apart at all sites. All migrants detected visually or acoustically within a 50-m radius of the center point were recorded along with their distance from the observation point. Also recorded was the vegetation structure in which the bird was observed (short herbaceous, riparian, second growth, edge or forest remnant tree) and whether or not a mixed-species flock was present. If a mixed-species flock was encountered during a census, the flock was followed for an extended period (up to 2 hr) to ensure that all flock members were detected. Although flock members were not individually marked, this continuous monitoring interval made it possible to determine whether migrants were following the flocks.

The second sampling method used a 1-ha grid of 13 12-m mist nets. Nets were set up in five rows 25 m apart. Odd rows had three nets each spaced at 50-m intervals; even rows had two nets spaced at 50-m intervals but with a 25-m offset from odd rows. Nets were operated throughout daylight for a total of 19 hours or 250 net hours. Neotropical migrants were banded with U.S. Fish and Wildlife Service bands; all other individuals were marked by clipping an outer tail feather. Field work was carried out during November 1987 and 1988 and February 1988 and 1989. The primary forest censuses were conducted on four large tracts: La Selva, Starkeys Woods, Rara Avis, and Lake Hule; open habitat censuses were collected at 12 random locations.

Results

VEGETATIONAL DATA

The area represented by each of the 10 habitat categories derived from the Landsat image of the region below 1,000 m elevation ranged from a few percent to 23.6% coverage of the study area (Table 1). Three habitat categories, primary forest, second growth, and open, herbaceous-dominated areas covered 78.5% of the scene. Primary forest, which fell into three classes on the basis of differences in elevation and topography, accounted for 49.8% of the area included within the TM scene. Open, herbaceous-dominated habitat (category 9) accounted for an additional 16.2%. The third most abundant habitat, young second growth (category 5), accounted for 12.5% of the area. Perennial crops with a large standing crop (category 10), primarily banana and palm, accounted for 3.7% of the area within the scene. The remaining four categories were represented by low coverage (Table 1).

Eighty randomly generated points less than 1,000 m elevation were visited to determine the relative accuracy of the remote satellite sensing classification in identifying major habitat types. All points identified as forest from the imagery were forested ($n = 20$). However, the image analysis technique did not separate disturbed forest from undisturbed forest (Table 2). The imagery analysis successfully separated extensive banana and palm plantations into a unique category (Table 1, category 10). Open, herbaceous-dominated habitats (Table 1, category 9) were successfully classified and distinguished from second growth more than five years old and perennial crops with large standing crops. Second-growth areas without a complete canopy, however, were confused with some perennial crops and agricultural sites containing short perennial crops such as pineapple and yucca, or less dense tree crops such as young citrus and coffee tended to be misclassified as open, herbaceous-dominated or young second-growth habitats (Table 2).

The detailed analyses of vegetational data collected, following James and Shugart (1970), illustrated consistent differences among the three major habitat types distinguished in the TM scene (Table 3a). Primary forest was characterized by nearly complete canopy cover, incomplete ground cover, and a uniform representation of larger trees (dbh > 50 cm). The presence of large trees was the distinguishing factor between primary forest and both the open habitat and the young second-

TABLE 2. Agreement of Thematic Mapper classification in predicting habitats based on 80 random points that were visually ground truthed. Entries are the number of random sites in each of the major habitat categories

Thematic Mapper Category	Ground Truth Category										
	Open		Open with scattered trees	Mature forest		Riparian	Second growth			Perennial crops	
	grazed	ungrazed		undisurbed	disturbed		Old (11–15 y)	Med (6–10y)	Yng (1–5y)	large	small
Mature forest				10	10		2				
Second growth 5–15 y						1	1	4			4
1–5 y		3	1			1			4		10
Open	13	2									3
Perennial crops										11	
TOTAL	13	5	1	10	10	2	3	4	4	11	17

TABLE 3a.   Habitat classification procedure (after James and Shugart 1970) for the three major habitat types in the study area

Habitat	Tree DBH (cm)								Ground cover (%)	Canopy		
	≤ 15	≤ 22	≤ 37	≤ 52	≤ 67	≤ 82	≤100	>100		Cover (%)	Height (m)	No. of shrubs
Open (n=9)	0.33	0.16	0.24	0.02	0	0.02	0	0	94	6	8	16
Second growth (≈ 5 y) (n=2)	16.3	3.2	1.7	0.1	0	0	0	0	49	73	18	255
Mature forest Undisturbed (n=3)	11.2	4.1	2.3	1.1	0.7	0.4	0.4	0.5	49	94	35	235
Disturbed (n=7)	13.4	7.4	3.6	1.5	0.9	0.4	0.2	0.3	35	87	31	245

TABLE 3b.   Structural characteristics of open habitat. Sites were randomly selected by stratified random selection.

Site number	Tree DBH (cm)								Ground cover (%)	Canopy		
	7 < x ≤ 15	≤ 22	≤ 37	≤ 52	≤ 67	≤ 82	≤ 100	>100		Cover (%)	Height (m)	No. of shrubs*
109	0.6	0	0.2	0	0	0	0	0	100	12	9	13 (1)
110	0.2	0	0.6	0	0	0.2	0	0	90	8	15	3.6(1)
107	0.8	0.8	0	0.2	0	0	0	0	100	6	4	6.6(2)
101	0	0	0.2	0.2	0	0	0	0	92	5	11	0
108	0.2	0.6	0.4	0	0	0	0	0	100	17	13	97 (5)
14	0.2	0	0	0	0	0	0	0	100	0	5	20 (5)

*Parenthetical number denotes number of subplots of 5 that had shrubs.

growth habitats. The second-growth sites had canopy and ground cover values that were similar to the forests, but lacked larger trees and had a shorter canopy; the open areas lacked canopy and had complete ground cover. As with the Landsat imagery, it was not possible to distinguish between individual undisturbed and disturbed forest tracts on the basis of the data generated by the James and Shugart procedure. However, on average, undisturbed forest tracts had fewer small trees (dbh < 82 cm) and more large trees (dbh > 99 cm) than did disturbed tracts (Table 3).

The habitat category classified as open, herbaceous-dominated proved to be very heterogeneous as demonstrated by the vegetation data collected with each VCP census (Table 4). Eighty percent of the 0.79-ha plots surveyed at 12 random open habitat locations (approx.

10 replicates at each location) contained trees. One half of all sample plots contained a mean of 5.9 (± 6.5, SD) large forest remnants or isolated second-growth trees. Those trees were generally forest remnants with a mean height of 20.2 (± 9.2) m. Another 33% of the VCP open habitat plots had stands of second growth that occurred as riparian habitat (10%), hedgerow (10%), or as young tree and shrub clusters (13%) (Table 4). Only 20% of the open habitat plots were limited exclusively to herbaceous cover.

MIGRANT DATA: MACROHABITAT USE

We conducted 127 VCP censuses in primary forest and 125 censuses in open, herbaceous-dominated plots.

TABLE 4. Vegetational structure of circular plots with 100 m diameters. At least 10 plots were sampled at each of 12 randomly selected sites (n=125).

	Number of plots
Herbaceous only (< 2 m)	21
Trees only	61
Mixed second growth	16
Riparian	13
Hedgerow	12
Edge	2
Number of trees per plot (n = 125)	
0	36
1 ≤ 5	40
6 ≤ 10	14
11 ≤ 15	6
16 ≤ 20	3
21 ≤ 25	4
Mean height of trees (m) per plot (n = 69)	
≤ 5	5
6 ≤ 10	16
11 ≤ 15	7
16 ≤ 20	12
21 ≤ 25	1
26 ≤ 30	28

Eighteen species of migrants were detected during these censuses (Table 5). The detection of migrants within the census area appeared to be uniform in the forest, but declined between 40- and 50-m distance from the observer in the open habitat (Table 6). Therefore, the VCP censuses were effectively sampling a radius of 40 m or an area of 0.5 ha in the open habitats. The forest censuses, which were probably less effective overall, did not show differences within the 50-m radius or an area of 0.79 ha. In general, migrant species were rare, with the nine most common species accounting for 79% of recorded migrant individuals (n = 300). Only one species, the Chestnut-sided Warbler (scientific names in Tables 5 and 7), was common in both the field and forest habitats (Table 5). Several species, including Tennessee Warbler, Common Yellowthroat, and Northern Oriole, were relatively common in field habitats, and less common in forests (Table 5). Two species, Acadian Flycatcher and Wood Thrush, were relatively common in forest and absent from field habitats. Another group of species, when detected in forest censuses, was usually in the presence of mixed-species flocks. These species, including Yellow-throated Vireo, Black-and-white, Blue-winged, and Tennessee warblers along with the Chestnut-sided Warbler, were persistent flock followers asso-

TABLE 5. Frequency of migrants detected in variable circumference points in 2 major habitat types and with and without mixed species flocks in forest.

Species	Open (n=125)	Forest (n=127)	Flock (n=34)[a]	No Flock (n=103)
Eastern Wood-Pewee (Contopus virens)	0.15	0.03	0.03	0.02
Acadian Flycatcher (Empidonax virescens)	0	0.11	0.06	0.09
Great Crested Flycatcher (Myiarchus crinitus)	0.02	0.06	0	0.06
S. Rough-winged Swallow (Stelgidopteryx ruficollis)	0.28	?	—	—
Wood Thrush (Hylocichla mustelina)	0	0.10	0.06	0.08
Yellow-throated Vireo (Vireo flavifrons)	0.05	0.05	0.05	0
Blue-winged Warbler (Vermivora pinus)	0	0.02	0.06	0
Golden-winged Warbler (V. chrysoptera)	0.02	0.02	0.06	0
Tennessee Warbler (V. peregrina)	0.30	0.08	0.30	0.08
Yellow Warbler (Dendroica petechia)	0.14	0	—	—
Chestnut-sided Warbler (D. pensylvanica)	1.0	0.38	1.26	0.11
Bay-breasted Warbler (D. castanea)	0.02	0.02	0.06	0
Black-and-white Warbler (Mniotilta varia)	0	0.05	0.15	0
Louisiana Waterthrush (Seiurus motacilla)	0	0.03	0.06	0.01
Kentucky Warbler (Oporornis formosus)	0	0.03	0.03	0.01
Common Yellowthroat (Geothlypis trichas)	0.19	0	—	—
Summer Tanager (Piranga rubra)	0.09	0	—	—
Northern Oriole (Icterus galbula)	0.70	0.05	0.15	0

a. Includes 10 observations of flocks deliberately located for study as opposed to randomly encountered.

TABLE 6. Number of migrants detected visually or acoustically by distance during variable circular-plot censuses in two major habitat types

Habitat type	Distance from center (m)				
	≤10	≤20	≤30	≤40	≤50
Open	26	31	42	21	15
Forest	1	16	24	9	25

NOTE: Maximum radius was 50 m.

ciating with such permanent residents as the White-lined Tanager (*Tachyphonis rufus*) and Lesser Greenlet (*Hylophilus decurtatus*). Based on the extended following of mixed flocks that were detected during VCP censuses, it appeared that migrant species were consistently present with the flocks throughout the observation periods indicating that they were moving with the flocks. During the 127 VCP censuses, 24 mixed-species flocks were encountered. Because each VCP census covered 0.79 ha of forest, the calculated density of mixed-species flocks was approximately 0.24 flocks per ha. To enlarge the sample size for analyzing migrant participants in mixed-species flocks, an additional 10 flocks were deliberately located and monitored, bringing the total number of flocks to 34. The Chestnut-sided Warbler was present in 26 (76%) of the flocks, and the Tennessee Warbler was present in nine of the 34 flocks (26%). All other migrant species were considerably less common (Table 5).

The inconspicuousness of understory migrants led us to adopt the use of mist-nets to insure that species, such as Kentucky Warbler, Worm-eating Warbler (*Helmitheros vermivorus*), Ovenbird, Northern Waterthrush (*Seiurus noveboracensis*) and Hooded Warbler (*Wilsonia citrina*) were not escaping detection. We netted on 13 primary forest sites, three second-growth sites and five open, herbaceous sites for a total of 5,250 mist-net hours. The Wood Thrush was the only Neotropical migrant that was consistently captured in forest habitats. Netting at six forest locations between 50 m and 300 m elevation yielded a mean of 4.5 (± 2.9 SD) Wood Thrushes per 250 net hours, and single individuals of three additional migrant species (Table 7). Netting at four sites between 500 and 750 m yielded similar results: $\bar{X} = 3.0$ (± 1.4 SD) Wood Thrushes per 250 net hours, one Ovenbird at each of two sites, and a single Yellow-bellied Flycatcher. Netting at swamp forest sites below 50 m yielded different results in that no Wood Thrushes were captured at three sites. The only migrant species captured in 750 hours of netting at the three swamp forest sites was a single Swainson's Thrush.

Species captured in mist nets on the five open sites were similar to those recorded during VCP censuses in open sites. Fifteen migrant species were captured at the five open sites with the two most common being Chestnut-sided Warbler ($\bar{X} = 1.2 \pm 0.8$ SD) and Tennessee Warbler ($\bar{X} = 2.0 \pm 2.9$ SD). The remaining species were present in low numbers (Table 7). In contrast to the overlap between mist-net and VCP results in open habitats, virtually no overlap was found between species captured on the forest grids and those captured on the five open sites. Notable was the complete absence of the Wood Thrush from open habitats (Table 7).

Considerable variation was found in both the number of species and individuals captured in 250 mist-net hours in the open habitats. Site 14, which had both the greatest numbers of species (11) and individuals (15), was the only open site with a hedgerow. That hedgerow accounted for seven individuals representing six of the species that were captured. However, even with the hedgerow birds removed from the sample, Site 14 still had twice the species richness of the other field sites. Site 14 also had one of the greatest shrub covers with 20 (± 14 SD) stalks greater than 1.5 m tall encountered along each 20 m of transect within the five sample plots. The other site with high shrub cover (Site 4) had the second highest number of species captured (4), but few individuals of each.

The greatest number of migrant individuals and species were captured in the second-growth sites (Table 7). Species composition in second growth overlapped considerably with species netted in open habitats (Table 7). Six of the 12 species captured in second growth were also captured in open sites, whereas only one of the second-growth species was captured in forest but not open areas. However, at least in part, this difference reflects the failure of mist nets to sample the canopy. For example, the most frequently captured species in open areas and second growth, the Chestnut-sided Warbler, was also common in the forest but never captured there. Of the two other commonly captured second-growth species, the Mourning Warbler was captured at one of the open sites and the Ovenbird was captured at two of four forest sites above 700 m. The Wood Thrush, the only migrant consistently captured in primary forest, and Acadian and Yellow-bellied flycatchers were absent from the second-growth samples.

MIGRANT DATA: MICROHABITAT USE

The technique used during the VCP censuses to record each migrant's foraging substrate made it possible to examine the specific types of habitat structures being

TABLE 7. Migrants captured in mist-nets during 250 mist-net hours per site.

Species	Mature forest													Second growth				Open			
	< 20 m			50 m–250 m						500 m–800 m											
	1	2	3	1	2	3	4	5	6	1	2	3	4	1	2	3	14	107	108	110	109
Eastern Wood-Pewee																	1				
Yellow-bellied Flycatcher										1											
Empidonax flaviventris																					
Acadian Flycatcher					1																
Swainson's Thrush		1			1																
Catharus ustulatus																					
Wood Thrush				5	10	3	2	3	4	4	3	1	4								
Gray Catbird																2	1				
Dumetella carolinensis																					
Red-eyed Vireo																			1		
Vireo olivaceus																					
Golden-winged Warbler														1							
Tennessee Warbler																1	2	7	1		
Yellow Warbler																1	1	1			
Chestnut-sided Warbler														4	7	5	2	1	2		
Magnolia Warbler															1					1	
D. magnolia																					
Black-and-white Warbler															1						
American Redstart																1					
Setophaga ruticilla																					
Ovenbird										1			1	4	9	4					
Seiurus aurocapillus																					
Louisiana Waterthrush																	1				
Kentucky Warbler							1								1						
Mourning Warbler														4		4	2		1		
O. philadelphia																					
Common Yellowthroat																	1				
Summer Tanager																	1				
Rose-breasted Grosbeak															2						
Pheucticus ludovicianus																					
Orchard Oriole																	2				
Icterus spurius																					
Northern Oriole																	1				
TOTAL SPECIES	0	1	0	1	3	1	2	1	1	3	1	1	2	4	7	7	11	3	4	1	0
TOTAL INDIVIDUALS	0	1	0	5	12	3	3	3	4	6	3	1	5	13	22	18	15	9	5	1	0

NOTE: Thirteen 12-m nets were set in 1-ha grids. Open sites were randomly selected by stratified random selection; for some mature forest sites (on La Selva Field Station), we were restricted to selecting within designated-use areas. See Table 3b for vegetational characteristics of open sites.

TABLE 8. Microhabitat use by migrants in habitats classified as open by Thematic Mapper

Species	Grass	Hedgerow	Second growth	Edge	Riparian	Forest remnant	Total
Eastern Wood-Pewee						6	6
Acadian Flycatcher						1	1
Great Crested Flycatcher					1		1
Yellow-throated Vireo					1		1
Blue-winged Warbler		1					1
Golden-winged Warbler					1	1	2
Tennessee Warbler		3	2	1	2	5	13
Yellow Warbler	6	1					7
Chestnut-sided Warbler		11	6	2	10	20	49
Common Yellowthroat	12	2					14
Summer Tanager		1			1	3	5
Northern Oriole		2				12	14
TOTAL INDIVIDUALS	18	21	8	3	16	48	114

NOTE: Data collected during variable circular-plot censuses on 12 randomly selected sites. See Table 4 for vegetational characteristics.

used by migrants within the open sites (Table 8). Only two migrant species, Common Yellowthroat and Yellow Warbler, which accounted for 16% of migrants recorded, consistently used the herbaceous cover in the open habitat category; all other species were recorded in woody vegetation (Table 8). Forty-two percent of migrants were in forest remnants, 32% were in hedgerows or wooded stream edges.

Discussion

The TM imagery proved to be a valuable tool with which to quantify habitat within the wet tropical region of Costa Rica. Interpretation of the imagery by unsupervised blind classification provided an accurate quantification and distribution of major seral stages. The classification successfully identified (1) primary forest, (2) open, herbaceous-dominated areas, (3) agricultural crops with large biomass (such as banana plantations), and (4) areas with limited standing crop. However, the classification could not reliably distinguish between second growth and mixed agricultural systems with low biomass, nor could it separate older second growth or disturbed forest with a complete canopy from undisturbed forest. Further manipulations of the satellite classification algorithms are necessary to distinguish better among these habitats.

The rapid rate at which Neotropical forests are being converted to open agricultural and pasture habitats presents a potential threat to forest-dependent species, in-

cluding Neotropical migrants which are seasonally dependent on Neotropical habitats. Habitat conversion rates in Costa Rica since 1940 have been quantified through the combined analysis of maps derived from satellite imagery and low-level aerial photography (Sader and Joyce 1988). According to their analysis, between 1940 and 1961, most clearing of forest occurred in the Tropical Moist Life Zone (Holdridge 1967) on the Pacific side of the country. After 1961, wetter forests became the primary target for clearing as Moist and Dry Life Zone forests were practically eliminated. Between 1961 and 1977, the Tropical and Premontane Wet forests on lower Pacific slopes, and to a lesser extent Atlantic slopes, were most heavily impacted. From 1977 through 1983, the remaining large tracts of Tropical Wet forest were deforested.

Although Costa Rica has an exemplary system of national parks and sanctuaries, it is still experiencing an extremely rapid rate of forest destruction (Hartshorn et al. 1983, Sader and Joyce 1988). Comparable data do not exist for other parts of Central America, but indications are that conversion rates throughout the region are also high (Myers 1980). Food and Agriculture Organization data indicate more than 70% of forests in Central America were removed by 1980 (F.A.O. 1984). The ecological implications of these trends are heightened by the heavy bias toward deforestation at low elevation (< 1,000 m). In our study area, which represented an altitudinal range of 30 m to 2,600 m, 45% of the remaining forest was above 1,000 m. Even though a breakdown of remaining forest by elevation does not exist for all of Costa Rica, observations of current forest distributions indicate that proportionally greater loss of lowland forest has occurred nationwide (Sader and Joyce 1988).

This trend is likely to worsen because little lowland Atlantic forest is protected. Although approximately 8.5% of Costa Rica is protected in national parks, biological reserves, and wildlife sanctuaries, only one-third of this is lowland wet habitat and only about one-fourth is in the Atlantic zone (Fig. 2). Only about 130,000 ha in the lowland Atlantic zone are currently in parks, biological reserves, and wildlife refuges, with little likelihood that the area protected will be substantially expanded. The distribution of forest reserves, which are being rapidly deforested, shows an even greater bias toward high elevations (Hartshorn et al. 1983) with only about 20% consisting of lowland habitats and less than 4% or about 20,000 ha in the Atlantic zone (Fig. 2). Currently only about 15,000 km^2 of Atlantic forest are legally protected in all of Central America (IUCN 1982) and much of that area continues to be impacted by clearing and timbering.

The significance of forest conversion rates to migrant population dynamics will depend on the extent to which wintering migrants are habitat specific and dependent on primary forest. The controversy over niche and habitat specificity of wintering migrants is being gradually resolved with habitat-use data accumulated through species-specific studies (Rappole and Warner 1980; Greenberg 1984, 1987; Lynch et al. 1985; Holmes et al. 1989; Rappole et al. 1989). These intensive studies revealed that most migrant passerines are habitat specialists with stable home ranges and that some show a strong dependency on primary forest.

Our study revealed interspecific variability in dependency on tropical primary forest. Some species, including the Yellow Warbler and Common Yellowthroat, were found exclusively in grassland habitats and, therefore, would be expected to have expanding populations as a result of forest conversion. Even these two species required the proximity of woody vegetation (Yellow Warbler) or marsh vegetation (Common Yellowthroat). Other species present in open habitats were dependent on trees within those habitats for their foraging substrate (Table 8). Most trees in open habitats were remnants of forests that had been recently eliminated. Smaller second-growth trees in hedgerows and riparian strips were heavily used by migrants, but these habitats were less common than forest remnants (20% vs. 54% of samples). Most of the 5.9 trees per ha that currently typify open habitats survive as remnant individuals that will not be replaced after they die. Thus, as remnant trees are lost through attrition and human manipula-

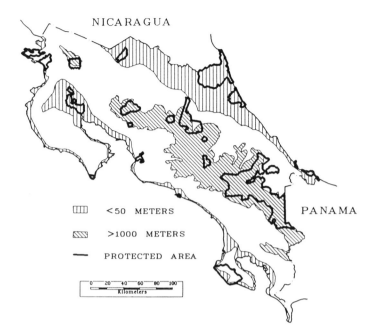

FIGURE 2. Distribution of Costa Rican national parks, wildlife refuges, and private sanctuaries (*bold outlines*) with respect to elevation.

tion, the value of these open habitats to most migrant species will be diminished. The implication of this decline is that the total impact of forest conversion to open habitat will not be realized for decades after a forest is cleared. Currently, no data are available on the life expectancy of forest remnants, so it is impossible to estimate when the final carrying capacity of open habitat for Neotropical migrants will be reached.

A second set of migrant species that was recorded during the VCP censuses was present exclusively in primary forest. These species tended to be present either in the understory (Wood Thrush, Louisiana Waterthrush, Kentucky Warbler) or lower canopy level (Acadian and Yellow-bellied flycatchers). The mist-net capture data corroborated these VCP census data. The Wood Thrush, the most consistently captured forest migrant, was absent from field and young second-growth (less than 10 years old) sites. This restricted habitat distribution supports the prediction that some migrant species are vulnerable to tropical forest conversion because of their dependency on forest for wintering habitat. This vulnerability would be exacerbated if the species has a restricted geographic range. The Wood Thrush, for example, winters in wet, broadleaf forest between extreme southern Mexico and Panama (Rappole et al. 1983) where it is primarily restricted to forests below 1,000 m (Winker 1989; Blake and Loiselle, this volume; C.S. Robbins, pers. comm.). Our capture data from three sites in wet forest below 20 m indicated the species was rare or absent from that elevation. Forests below 20 m on the Atlantic side of Costa Rica are essentially swamp forests with poor drainage and extensive areas of standing water. The extensive submergence or saturation of the soils in these forests probably are responsible for the absence of the predominantly ground-foraging Wood Thrush. If these low-lying forests are not appropriate habitat for Wood Thrushes, as is indicated by the mist-net data, then available habitat for the species is even more limited than originally recognized. Excluding areas below 50 m lowers the amount of protected forest within the Wood Thrush's primary range (50–1,000 m) to less than 10,000 ha of protected habitat in the Atlantic zone (the Wood Thrush also winters at lower densities in moist and wet forests on the Pacific lowlands [Site 19] where little forest remains).

Habitat limitations resulting from deforestation are probably relevant for other forest understory species such as the Kentucky Warbler and Louisiana Waterthrush, as well as the Wood Thrush, but the VCP census and mist-net data are too limited to determine their habitat specificity. Furthermore, the migrant species detected in open habitats were, with few exceptions, foraging in trees within the open sites. The savanna-type habitat characterized by grassland and scattered trees in the wet tropics is entirely an artifact of human modification of closed forest. Given continued human maintenance of pasture and cropland in the region through burning and chopping, the habitat will continue toward an endpoint of treelessness, which our data indicate will have habitat value for a very limited number of migrant species. To the extent that landowners can be convinced to maintain forest buffers along streams and between pastures, a larger component of the migrant community will find suitable habitat. In the absence of habitat heterogeneity, we should ultimately expect a much reduced carrying capacity for the majority of Neotropical migrants that winter in wet habitats in Central America.

Acknowledgments

Our field expenses for this study were supported by U.S. Fish and Wildlife Service Contract #14-16-0009-87-961; the institutions of Rappole and Powell generously provided salary throughout the study. We gratefully acknowledge field assistance from Rafa Flores, Harriett Powell, and Dave Swanson, and the tireless and enthusiastic editorial and secretarial support of Nancy Paul.

Literature cited

Food and Agriculture Organization. 1984. *FAO Production Yearbook 1983*. Vol. 37. FAO Statistics Series No. 55, FAO, Rome, Italy.

Greenberg, R. 1984. The winter exploitation systems of Bay-breasted and Chestnut-sided warblers in Panama. *Univ. Calif. Publ. Zool.* 116:1–107.

———. 1987. Seasonal foraging specialization in the Worm-eating Warbler. *Condor* 89:158–168.

Hartshorn, G., L. Hartshorn, A. Atmella, L.D. Gomez, A. Mata, L. Mata, R. Morales, R. Ocampo, D. Pool, C. Quesada, C. Solera, R. Solorzano, G. Stiles, J. Tosi, Jr., A. Umana, C. Villalobos, and R. Wells. 1983. *Costa Rica: Community Environmental Profile: A Field Study*. San Jose, Costa Rica: Trejos.

Holdridge, L.R. 1967. *Life Zone Ecology*. Rev. ed. San Jose, Costa Rica: Tropical Science Center.

Holmes, R.T., T.W. Sherry, and L. Reitsma. 1989. Population structure, territoriality and overwinter survival of two migrant warbler species in Jamaica. *Condor* 91:545–561.

Hutto, R.L. 1980. Winter habitat distribution of migratory land birds in western Mexico, with special reference to small, foliage-gleaning insectivores. Pages 181–203 in *Migrant Birds in the Neotropics: Ecology, Behavior, Distribution and Conservation*, A. Keast and E.S. Morton, eds. Washington: Smithsonian Institution Press.

IUCN. 1982. *International Union for Conservation of Nature Directory of Neotropical Protected Areas*. Dublin: Tycooly Inter Publishing LTD.

James, F.C., and H.H. Shugart. 1970. A quantitative method of habitat description. *Am. Birds* 24:721–736.

Karr, J.R. 1976. On the relative abundance of migrants from the north temperate zone in tropical habitats. *Wilson Bull.* 88:433–458.

Keogh, R.M. 1984. Changes in the forest cover of Costa Rica through history. *Turrialba* 34:325–331.

Lynch, J.F. 1989. Distribution of overwintering Nearctic migrants in the Yucatan Peninsula, I: General patterns of occurrence. *Condor* 91:515–544.

Lynch, J.F., E.S. Morton, and M.E. Van der Voort. 1985. Habitat segregation between the sexes of wintering Hooded Warblers (*Wilsonia citrina*). *Auk* 102:714–721.

Morton, E.S., and R. Greenberg. 1989. The outlook for migratory songbirds: "Future shock" for birders. *Am. Birds* 43:178–183.

Myers, N. 1980. *Conversion of Tropical Moist Forests*. Washington: National Academy of Sciences.

Powell, G.V.N., and J.H. Rappole. 1986. The Hooded Warbler. Pages 827–854 in *Audubon Wildlife Report 1986*, R. DiSilvestro, ed. New York: National Audubon Society.

Rappole, J.H., and E.S. Morton. 1985. Effects of habitat alteration on a tropical avian forest community. Pages 1013–1021 in *Neotropical Ornithology*, P.A. Buckley, E.S. Morton, R.S. Ridgely, and F.G. Buckley, eds. Ornithol. Monogr. 36.

Rappole, J.H., and D.W. Warner. 1980. Ecological aspects of migrant bird behavior in Veracruz, Mexico. Pages 353–393 in *Migrant Birds in the Neotropics: Ecology, Behavior, Distribution and Conservation,* A. Keast and E.S. Morton, eds. Washington: Smithsonian Institution Press.

Rappole, J.H., E.S. Morton, T.E. Lovejoy, III, and J.L. Ruos. 1983. *Nearctic Avian Migrants in the Neotropics.* Washington: U.S. Fish and Wildlife Service.

Rappole, J.H., M.A. Ramos, and K. Winker. 1989. Wintering Wood Thrush (*Hylocichla mustelina*) movements and mortality in southern Veracruz. *Auk* 106:402–410.

Reynolds, R.T., J.M. Scott, and R.A. Nussbaum. 1980. A variable circular-plot method for estimating bird numbers. *Condor* 82:309-313.

Sader, S.A., and A.T. Joyce. 1988. Deforestation rates and trends in Costa Rica, 1940–1983. *Biotropica* 20:11–19.

Slud, P.R. 1960. The birds of finca "La Selva": A tropical wet forest locality. *Bull. Amer. Mus. Nat. Hist.* 121:49–148.

Terborgh, J.W. 1980. The conservation status of neotropical migrants: Present and future. Pages 21–30 in *Migrant Birds in the Neotropics: Ecology, Behavior, Distribution and Conservation,* A. Keast and E.S. Morton, eds. Washington: Smithsonian Institution Press.

Tosi, J.A. 1969. *Mapa ecologico de Costa Rica.* San Jose, Costa Rica: Tropical Science Center.

Willis, E.O. 1966. The role of migrant birds at swarms of army ants. *Living Bird* 5:187–231.

Winker, K. 1989. The Wood Thrush (*Catharus mustelinus*) on its wintering grounds in southern Veracruz, Mexico. M.S. thesis, University of Minnesota, Minneapolis, Minnesota.

JOSEPH M. WUNDERLE, JR.*
Department of Biology
University of Puerto Rico
Cayey, Puerto Rico 00633

Sexual habitat segregation in wintering Black-throated Blue Warblers in Puerto Rico

Abstract. Sexual habitat segregation by Black-throated Blue Warblers (*Dendroica caerulescens*) wintering in Puerto Rico appears to be related to the canopy height and successional stage of montane forests. A stepwise discriminant function analysis was based upon altitude and 13 vegetation variables measured at warbler capture sites in three study areas. Female capture sites differed from those of males by having smaller trees, more foliage at 0–2 m and 4–6 m above the ground, and less foliage at 12–15 m above the ground. Using a classificatory discriminant function analysis with four vegetation variables it was possible to classify correctly 60 of 64 warbler capture sites in three study areas. Thus female Black-throated Blue Warblers were most common in the younger, shrubby-sapling stages at high altitude and males were most common in the older, taller forests of lower altitude. Forests of intermediate canopy height and age had an equal mix of males and females. The possibility that the observed habitat segregation is maintained by behavioral dominance and/or intrinsic "preferences" is discussed.

Sinopsis. La segregación sexual de habitat de *Dendroica caerulescens* invernantes en Puerto Rico parece estar relacionada con la altura del dosel y el estadio sucesional de los bosques montanos. Se realizó un análisis de función discriminante STEPWISE basado en altitud y 13 variables de vegetación medidas en sitios de captura de *D. caerulescens* en tres áreas de estudio. Los sitios de captura de hembras difirieron de aquellos de los machos por tener árboles mas pequeños, mas follaje a 0–2 m y 4–6 m por encima del suelo y menos follaje a 12–15 m. Usando un análisis clasificatorio de función discriminante con cuatro variables de vegetación fue posible clasificar correctamente 60 de 64 sitios de captura de *D. caerulescens* en tres áreas de estudio. Así, las hembras fueron mas comunes en los estadios arbustivos mas jóvenes en elevaciones altas y los machos en los bosques mas maduros y altos de elevaciones bajas. Bosques con edades y alturas de dosel intermedias tuvieron

*Current address: Institute of Tropical Forestry, Southern Forest Experiment Station, USDA Forest Service, P.O. Box B, Palmer, PR 00721.

una mezcla proporcional de ambos sexos. La posibilidad de que la segregación de hábitat observada sea mantenida por dominancia conductual y/o "preferencias" intrínsecas es discutida.

Competition theory has provided potential mechanisms for explaining variation in migration patterns and nonbreeding distributions of birds (e.g., Salomonsen 1955, Cox 1968, Lack 1968, Fretwell 1972, 1980, Gauthreaux 1978, 1982). Despite the attractiveness of these theories, little current evidence indicates that competition is important in determining winter distributions within or among migrant species (Greenberg 1986). Evidence for past or present intraspecific competition on the wintering grounds includes geographic separation, habitat segregation, territoriality, dominance hierarchies, and foraging differences. Some of these patterns, such as geographic separation, might indicate past competition between sex or age classes which no longer occurs on the wintering grounds. Other patterns, such as habitat segregation and foraging differences, might also indicate past competition, which now might be completely or partially extant. Evidence for current competition includes intraspecific territoriality or dominance hierarchies on wintering grounds.

The level of documentation of the evidence for intraspecific competition on the wintering grounds is highly variable. For example, geographic separation of sex or age classes has been demonstrated for waterfowl (e.g., Bellrose et al. 1961, Nichols and Haramis 1980), raptors (e.g., Belopol'skij 1972, Mead 1973, Mueller et al. 1977), shorebirds (e.g., Myers 1981), woodpeckers (Howell 1953), finches (King et al. 1965, Ketterson and Nolan 1976, Balph 1977), tanagers (Pearson 1980), and blackbirds (Dolbeer 1982, James et al. 1984). However, factors other than intraspecific competition could explain these distributions (e.g., Myers 1981, Gauthreaux 1982, Ketterson and Nolan 1983, Greenberg 1986). Foraging differences between sexes within the same habitat have been well documented for many species (e.g., Pitelka 1950, Kilham 1965, Selander 1966, Storer 1966, Morse 1968, Williamson 1971, Peters and Grubb 1983). Intraspecific territoriality is common and widespread among various wintering migrants ranging from raptors, shorebirds, woodpeckers, hummingbirds, to a variety of passerines (e.g., Rappole and Warner 1980, Greenberg 1985, Myers et al. 1979). Also, dominance relationships have been documented among wintering migrants, particularly within social species (see Gauthereaux 1978, for review), but the ecological importance of these relationships as an indicator of intraspecific competition (i.e., whether they produce reduced fitness in

subordinates) remains controversial (e.g., Ketterson and Nolan 1983).

Only a few examples of intersexual habitat segregation have been found for migrant passerines wintering in the tropics. In Malaysia, overwintering Oriental Reed Warblers (*Acrocephalus orientalis*) display habitat segregation by sex (Nisbet and Medway 1972). Females were most common in Phragmites swamps, which were similar in structure to the reed beds used on the breeding grounds, but males were most abundant in scrub habitats. In the Yucatan Peninsula of Mexico, wintering male and female Hooded Warblers (*Wilsonia citrina*) segregated on the basis of habitat structure (Lynch et al. 1985). Female Hooded Warblers were found mostly in open low vegetation whereas males occupied the closed-canopy forests of moderate to tall stature. In Haiti, field observations and netting results indicated that female Black-throated Blue Warblers (*Dendroica caerulescens*) were most abundant in montane regions while males were most abundant in lowland forests (Woods 1975).

My preliminary observations of Black-throated Blue Warblers throughout Puerto Rico indicated that males occupy tall-stature montane forests and woodlands and that females occur in brushy (sapling stage) low-stature secondary woodlands in montane regions. Montane areas with intermediate stature forests contained both males and females. To test the hypothesis that the sexes of wintering Black-throated Blue Warblers occupy different habitats in Puerto Rico, I quantified altitude and vegetation characteristics in the sites where the birds were captured or observed.

Study areas

Three study areas were selected where different sex ratios of wintering Black-throated Blue Warblers had been observed. These three areas (El Verde, Palo Hueco, and Carite) are still in use as part of an ongoing study of Black-throated Blue Warbler demography and population ecology. Two other localities (Cedro and Big Tree Trail) were used for transect samples to verify observations made on the three intensive study areas. These two localities were selected because of their vegetation characteristics and altitude, without prior knowledge of warbler sex ratios.

EL VERDE. The El Verde Field Station is located in the Luquillo Experimental Forest in eastern Puerto Rico. Warblers were captured over an area of about 25 ha around the field station. The forest at El Verde is classified as subtropical wet forest in the Holdridge system and is a broad-leaved evergreen forest (Odum and Pigeon 1970, Ewel and Whitmore 1973, Brown et al. 1983). The study area is approximately 350 m in elevation (range 312–472 m) with moderately sloping topography. The dominant tree, tabonuco (*Dacryodes excelsa*) comprises as much as 35% of the forest canopy (Wadsworth 1951), but species in the genera *Sloanea*, *Inga*, *Sapium*, *Alchorneopsis*, *Manilkara*, *Guarea*, *Cecropia*, and *Didymopanix* are also common. Three tree strata include: a discontinuous upper canopy layer (at 24 m), a second continuous canopy (at 20 m), and a sparsely vegetated, open understory (foliage height profiles in Wunderle et al. 1987).

PALO HUECO. The study area (about 23 ha) at approximately 515 m elevation is 1.2 km southwest of El Verde in the Luquillo Experimetal Forest. The slightly sloping area is within the lower montane wet forest zone in the Holdridge system and was originally a broad-leaved evergreen forest (Ewel and Whitmore 1973). The site has been extensively disturbed by man, and presently consists of a heterogenous mix of native secondary forest, brushy edge and field, and an overgrown plantation of *Callophylum brasiliense*. The western boundary along highway 186 is a brushy mix of dense fern thickets, bamboo, and diverse second-growth trees and saplings, particularly *Cecropia* and *Didymopanix*, as well as numerous shrubs in the Melastomatacea, Piperacea, and Rubiacea. Remnant second-growth forest is scattered along the east and southern boundaries and contains a mix of trees in the genera *Cyrilla*, *Buchenavia*, *Micropholis*, *Ocotea*, *Magnolia*, *Tabebuia*, *Dacryodes*, *Inga*, and *Ficus*. The remnant secondary forest has a relatively closed canopy at 15–20 m with several indistinct layers below, including a thick understory of shrubs, palms, and ferns.

CARITE. The Carite study area (38 ha) is located approximately 33 km to the southwest of the Palo Hueco area in the Sierra de Cayey in southeastern Puerto Rico. It has a mean elevation of 720 m (range 640–768 m) with variable topography. The area lies within the lower montane wet forest zone of the Holdridge system and was originally broad-leaved forest (Ewel and Whitmore 1973). It is covered with a patchwork of abandoned farmland and partially cut forests which has resulted in a scattered mix of dense thickets of ferns and razor grass (*Scleria canescens*), shrubby edges, sapling thickets, and patches of secondary palm and broadleaf forest. The ridges and upper slopes are shrubby with widely scattered trees of the genera *Cecropia*, *Didymopanix*, *Micropholis*, *Ocotea*, *Ormosia*, *Alchornea*, *Buchenavia*, *Tabebuia*, and the palm *Prestoea montana*. These trees form a closed canopy (15–20 m) in the stream valleys. Shrubs in the Melastomatacea, Piperacea, and Rubiacea are abundant throughout the area. The brushy edge and sapling areas of Carite resemble those of Palo Hueco.

BIG TREE TRAIL TRANSECT. The 500-m transect was situated on the Big Tree Trail, located at approximately 518 m

in the Luquillo Experimental Forest. This area was selected because it represented tall-stature, mature forest at a relatively high altitude. The tabonuco (*Dacryodes excelsa*) forest along the trail is similar in structure and composition to the El Verde forest.

CEDRO TRANSECT. The 600-m transect was located at approximately 508 m elevation along a dirt road running east, 3 km from the town of Cedro in the Sierra de Cayey. The area was selected because it represented short-stature, brushy, second-growth woodland at an altitude lower than Carite. The transect ran through the bottom of a valley, surrounded by overgrown farmland. Trees here were generally of lower stature than those of Palo Hueco, but the species composition appeared similar.

Methods

Black-throated Blue Warblers were located and captured with tape recordings played on a Sony TCM 5000 tape recorder as described in Holmes et al. 1989. The tapes consisted of a mixture of primary song (LP record by Borror and Gunn, no date) and aggressive "chip" notes recorded in Carite in October 1988. Once a responsive individual was found, the tape recorder was turned off and a 12-m mist net was set-up within the birds' area of activity. A speaker was placed on the ground, under the middle of the net, and operated remotely by a hidden observer located 6 m from the net. Songs and call notes were played at a natural rate with variations in volume until the focal bird was captured or until 1–2 hr had passed without success. In addition to the songs, a mount of a male Black-throated Blue Warbler, placed on a 1.5-m upright stick alongside the net was used for the last 80% of the captures (total captures = 64). Both sexes responded readily to the recordings alone or to the mount and recordings together.

Birds were captured with playback during all daylight hours almost every morning from 21 October 1988 through 31 March 1989. However, 64% of the captures occurred during October and November when the warblers appeared to be most responsive to song. We attempted to capture all birds encountered, and occasionally (27% of 64 birds) we returned to a site, following an earlier failure, to capture a specific individual. Eleven birds (six males; five females) were impossible to capture and thus were not marked. Once an individual was captured, the capture site was marked with colored plastic flagging and the locality indicated on a map. For each captured warbler, we obtained standard measurements and banded it with three plastic color bands and an aluminum U.S. Fish and Wildlife Service band.

In addition to captures of individual warblers by playback in the three study areas we ran transects with playback to locate Black-throated Blue Warblers along the

Big Tree Trail (4 February 1989) and in Cedro (7 February 1989). The transects represent an independent test of the sexual habitat segregation observations made on the three study areas. Trails or dirt roads were used to pass through each habitat in a relatively straight line. The observer walked slowly through the habitat with a tape playback of warbler song and calls. When an individual responded to the recording, the location where the bird was first observed was indicated with flagging and then marked on a map. Each transect was terminated after a predetermined, arbitrary number of individuals ($n = 8$) were located.

From 13 to 28 April 1989, we returned to the sites where individuals had been observed along the two transects and to the capture sites of each bird on the other three study areas to measure altitude and vegetation features. We established the center of each vegetation plot 15 m from the site of initial observation along the transect or 15 m from the capture site in the direction from which the bird approached the playback, as noted earlier when first encountered. An altimeter was used to take altitude readings in the center of each plot. From the center, four 8-m radius transects were established in the N, S, E, W compass directions. Vegetation features measured within each 0.02-ha circular plot were:

1. Shrub density at breast height was counted along two radial transects by an observer counting all vertical woody stems (< 3 cm diameter) touching his outstretched arms. The number of deciduous shrubs (i.e., broadleaf), palms, and ferns was recorded separately.

2. We measured the diameter at breast height (dbh) of all saplings and standing trees with diameters greater than 3 cm. Trees were classified as either standing dead, palm, broadleaf, or tree fern.

3. Canopy height of the 10 highest canopy trees extending over each plot was measured with a range finder.

4. We measured foliage height profiles by using a method modified after that of Schemske and Brokaw (1981). Profiles were determined at 20 points (every 1.6 m) along north-south and east-west transects in each plot. A 3-m vertical pole, marked at 0.5-m intervals, was placed at each point to record the intervals in which vegetation touched the pole. For height intervals above 3 m we sighted along the pole into the canopy and counted the presence of vegetation in estimated height intervals in meters (3–4, 4–6, 6–8, 8–10, 10–12, 12–15, 15–20, and 20–25). We recorded only the presence or absence of a leaf contact in each height category and not the total number of contacts per category. Therefore for each height category a maximum of 20 touches could be obtained, because each height class was sampled at 20 points along the transects within each plot.

Information from these measurements was summarized for discriminant function analysis into: shrub density of broadleaf stems (< 3 cm dbh); total broadleaf stems > 3 cm dbh; mean dbh of the five largest trees; mean canopy height; and number of points with the presence of at least one broadleaf contact in the height classes of 0–2 m, 2–4 m, 4–6 m, 6–8 m, 8–10 m, 10–12 m, 12–15 m, 15–20 m, and 20–25 m. Emphasis was placed on the structure of broadleaf plants because this is the most commonly used substrate for foraging (Wunderle, unpubl.).

The first level of analysis consisted of a stepwise discriminant function analysis (Tabachnick and Fidell 1983) using SAS software version 6.03 (SAS Institute Inc. 1988). Each vegetation plot at the capture site of 64 birds in the three study areas was classified apriori as either "male" or "female" based on the gender of the bird at the capture site. We then used the stepwise procedure to indicate which vegetation variables contributed most to the differentiation of the two habitat classes. Once the habitat variables with the greatest discriminatory power were identified, they were then used in a classificatory discriminant analysis (Tabachnick and Fidell 1983) to classify habitats as "male" or "female." This procedure permitted the identification of "incorrectly" classified sites (capture sites or transect sites), thus providing an indication of the ability of the discriminant function to correctly describe male and female habitat.

Results

Captures of Black-throated Blue Warblers indicated significantly different ($\chi^2 = 21.22$, d.f. = 2, $P < 0.001$) sex ratios in the three study areas: 83% females in Carite ($n = 24$); 50% females in Palo Hueco ($n = 20$); and 15% females in El Verde ($n = 20$). The eight warblers located using playback along the Cedro transect were females; on the Big Tree Trail transect eight males were encountered.

Of the 64 warblers captured in the three study sites, 49 (77%) were observed again during the winter months. Of those observed again, 37 (76%) were found within 50 m of their original capture site. Maps of locations of these individuals indicated that these birds were mostly inhabiting exclusive areas (with the exception of some overlap between male and female habitat use discussed below). In addition, their consistent aggressive behavior (i.e., chases and "chip" notes) within a relatively limited area implies that these birds were territorial, as documented for Black-throated Blue Warblers in Jamaica (Holmes et al. 1989). However, 12 (seven males, five females) of the re-sighted birds were found in different parts of the study area at distances greater than 100 m from the original capture site. Seven of these birds were observed more than once in wide-

TABLE 1 Summary of the stepwise discriminant function analysis on 64 capture sites of males ($n = 31$) and females ($n = 33$) with 14 original variables

Variable	Step	Partial r^2	F statistic	P
Mean dbh of five largest trees	1	0.574	83.679	0.0001
Foliage class 0–2 m	2	0.251	20.464	0.0001
Foliage class 12–15 m	3	0.199	14.933	0.0003
Foliage class 4–6 m	4	0.081	5.167	0.0270
Altitude	5	0.012	0.705	0.4047
Shrub density	5	0.011	0.636	0.4285
Canopy height	5	0.002	0.101	0.7514
Foliage class 2–4 m	5	0.001	0.048	0.8275
Foliage class 6–8 m	5	0.001	0.020	0.8891
Foliage class 8–10 m	5	0.003	0.186	0.6681
Foliage class 10–12 m	5	0.002	0.130	0.7200
Foliage class 15–20 m	5	0.022	1.302	0.2585
Foliage class 20–25 m	5	0.001	0.048	0.8269
Total stems	5	0.006	0.342	0.5607

ly scattered localities throughout the study area. Such birds could not be predictably relocated, and were generally found outside known territories. These birds were usually silent, were never observed chasing conspecifics and were probably nonterritorial floaters. This analysis is based upon the capture sites of all 64 warblers and thus includes the habitats used by both territorial and floater individuals.

The results of the stepwise discriminant function analysis were consistent with my previous field observations of habitat segregation by sex. The analysis found that four of the original 14 variables (1 altitude and 13 vegetation) had significant discriminatory power (Table 1). Female capture sites differed from those of males by having smaller trees (mean dbh of five largest trees, $\bar{X}$ = 19.3 cm vs. $\bar{X}$ = 29.4 cm), more foliage in the 0–2-m and 4–6-m height classes ($\bar{X}$ = 12.7 vs. $\bar{X}$ = 7.7, and $\bar{X}$ = 13.3 vs. $\bar{X}$ = 5.7), and less foliage in the 12–15-m height class ($\bar{X}$ = 3.4 vs. $\bar{X}$ = 14.1). Differences in foliage height profiles of male and female capture sites were apparent in Carite and Palo Hueco, but not in El Verde (Fig. 1).

Using a classificatory discriminant function analysis with these four variables alone it was possible to classify correctly 60 of the 64 capture sites in the three study areas. Two of the misclassified sites were in Palo Hueco where one male capture site was classified as a female site and one female site classified as a male site. In El Verde, two female capture sites were incorrecly classified as male sites. When all 14 of the original variables were used to construct a discriminant function, all 64 capture sites were correctly classified.

To test the 4-variable discriminant function I used it

to classify independently male and female sites on the Cedro and Big Tree transects. Fifteen of the 16 activity sites along the two transects were correctly classified. One male on the Big Tree transect was incorrectly classified. All of the transect birds were classified correctly by the 14-variable discriminant function.

Black-throated Blue Warblers might spatially segregate based on altitude alone, whereby females predominate at higher altitudes (i.e., Carite) and males at lower altitude (i.e., El Verde). Observed habitat differences between the sexes might then reflect the relationship between vegetation and altitude. Indeed, significant ($P < 0.05$) positive correlations were found between altitude and individual variables such as shrub density ($r = 0.51$), total stems ($r = 0.81$), and the 2–4-m ($r = 0.65$), 4–6-m ($r = 0.75$), 6–8-m ($r = 0.79$), 8–10-m ($r = 0.47$) foliage classes, whereas significant negative correlations existed between altitude and individual variables such as canopy height ($r = -0.81$), mean dbh of the five largest trees ($r = -0.67$), and the 12–15-m ($r = -0.67$), 15–20-m ($r = -0.74$), 20–25-m ($r = -0.61$) foliage classes. Nevertheless, several results indicate that the sexes are not segregated on the basis of altitude alone. In the Palo Hueco area where male and female capture sites showed no significant differences in altitude ($t = 0.406$, $P = 0.689$), 90% of the sites were properly classified by the discriminant function analysis using only four vegetation variables. Furthermore, accurate discrimination of male and female sites using only vegetation variables was possible from sites along the two transects in which mean altitude did not differ significantly ($t = 1.838$, $P = 0.087$). Thus, it appears that male and female Black-throated Blue Warblers in our study sites segregated

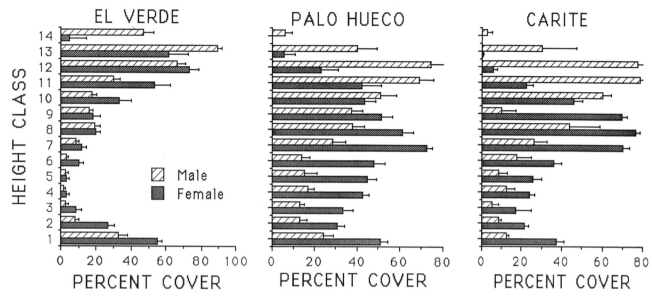

FIGURE 1. Foliage height profiles from capture sites of male and female Black-throated Blue Warblers in El Verde ($n = 3$ females, $n = 17$ males), Palo Hueco ($n = 10$ females, $n = 10$ males), and Carite ($n = 20$ females, $n = 4$ males), Puerto Rico. Percent cover represents percentage of sample points with live vegetation present in a given height interval. Height intervals in meters: $1 = 0–0.5$, $2 = 0.5–1.0$, $3 = 1.0–1.5$, $4 = 1.5–2.0$, $5 = 2.0–2.5$, $6 = 2.5–3.0$, $7 = 3.0–4.0$, $8 = 4.0–6.0$, $9 = 6.0–8.0$, $10 = 8.0–10.0$, $11 = 10.0–12.0$, $12 = 12.0–15.0$, $13 = 15.0–20.0$, $14 = 20.0–25.0$.

mostly on the basis of vegetation structure. However, because many of these characteristics (e.g., tree size and foliage height profiles) also vary with altitude, females will probably predominate at high altitude (because of low stature vegetation) whereas males predominate at low altitude (because of high stature vegetation) in undisturbed locations.

Discussion

There are two alternative hypotheses regarding the proximate mechanisms responsible for the maintenance of intersexual habitat segregation on the wintering grounds. The behavioral dominance hypothesis suggests that the behaviorally dominant sex excludes the subordinate sex from the preferred habitat (Lynch et al. 1985). The other, an intrinsic hypothesis, proposes that females and males each have an intrinsic "preference" for the different habitats in which they are found (Morton et al. 1987). These two hypotheses are not necessarily mutually exclusive. This study was not designed to test either of these hypotheses, but some observations are consistent with an intrinsic hypothesis and others are consistent with a behavioral dominance hypothesis, possibly indicating that a complex mechanism is responsible for Black-throated Blue Warbler habitat segregation.

Observations and preliminary results from El Verde appear to be consistent with the intrinsic preference hy-

pothesis. For example, in El Verde males spent most of their time in the uppermost canopy and only infrequently came down to within a meter of the ground in gaps (i.e., openings in the canopy). Although males were sometimes captured in treefall gaps and a powerline opening, they were never captured in the forest understory during a one-year netting study in El Verde (Wunderle et al. 1987). Only with song playback were we able to attract males down from the canopy into the understory at El Verde. The absence of Black-throated Blue Warblers in the El Verde forest understory can probably be attributed to the relative absence of broadleaf foliage in the first 10 m from the ground (e.g., Fig. 1). This absence of understory foliage most likely explains the absence of females, which are known to forage primarily in the lower foliage strata on both the breeding grounds (mean foraging height = 3.3 m, Holmes 1986) and on the wintering grounds in Puerto Rico (Wunderle, unpubl. data). Thus, if females "prefer" the lower foliage strata, they would be absent from habitats lacking such strata.

Further evidence from El Verde, consistent with the intrinsic hypothesis, is the similarity of sex ratios among transients or floaters (defined as individuals never recaptured or resighted) and territorial individuals. After the passage of Hurricane Hugo on September 1989, we initiated a general netting program in El Verde following the methods of Wunderle et al. (1987). Twenty-four 12-m nets were opened for two days at two or three week intervals (October 1989–April 1990) in the center of the study site. We captured and color-banded 27 individuals, of which 15 individuals were transients or floaters. Of these transient/floaters 80% were males as compared to 83% of territorial individuals ($n = 12$) recordered during November 1989. Thus, males established territories at El Verde in approximately the same proportions as nonterritorial warblers moving through the forest—a finding consistent with an intrinsic habitat preference explanation. If males were always dominant to females, then females should be more common among the transient/floaters than among territory holders at El Verde, a prediction that was not supported by the data.

These observations do not refute the importance of behavioral dominance as a proximate explanation for sexual habitat segregation in Puerto Rico. The evidence for dominance based on morphology is mixed. For example, the significant difference ($t = 2.25$, $P = 0.03$) in average body weight of males (9.8 g + 0.4 SE, $n = 33$) and females (9.5 g + 0.3 SE, $n = 31$) in October–December was so slight (3%) that it probably has little or no effect on the outcome of aggressive interactions. Yet Black-throated Blue Warblers of all ages are sexually dichromatic throughout the year, and such plumage differences can be important in dominance relationships (Rohwer 1975, 1977). Studies in Jamaica (Holmes et al. 1989) and in Puerto Rico (Wunderle, unpubl. data) show that dominance interactions might be common. For example, these warblers are highly territorial, within and between sexes, although aggressive interactions appear to be greater within than between sexes. Males and females fight using highly stereotyped displays. Also, I found three territories (two in El Verde, one in Palo Hueco) that were initially occupied by females but in the second year were occupied by males. Yet females and males often have overlapping territories and sometimes forage in close proximity. Age too, is likely to be important in these dominance relationships, because juveniles are commonly displaced by older birds, at least within the same sex (Wunderle, unpubl. data). Consistent with the complexity of these dominance interactions is an explanation suggested by Sherry (pers. comm.) in which females tend to be outcompeted for preferred habitat and/or microhabitat on average, but some females (older?) hold their own against some males. Other females coexist with males by deferring to male dominance with very localized (microhabitat) segregation while maintaining high overlap of territories spatially.

Behavioral dominance might reinforce sexual habitat preferences if males tend to be dominant in habitats with high foliage strata and females dominate in habitats with low foliage strata. The overlap of male and female territories might occur only when both "male" and

"female" strata occur together. Therefore, if the strength of an aggressive response is related to the strength of a preference for a foraging site (e.g., vegetation strata) then habitat segregation might become more marked. A test of this hypothesis requires observations of males losing a disproportionate number of territorial interactions in "female" habitat and females losing a disproportionate number in "male" habitat. Presently, such data are unavailable for any of the species known to show habitat segregation.

Sexual habitat segregation spreads Black-throated Blue Warblers across several habitats in montane regions and presumably reduces the likelihood of intraspecific competition. It is probable that the diets of males and females differ in their corresponding habitats. Dietary preferences might actually drive the segregation, but which is the cause and which is the effect is currently unknown. Diet differences occur in the three study sites (Wunderle, unpubl. data). Females commonly fed on the abundant melastome fruits in Carite whereas in El Verde the abundance of small fruits is limited and males rarely fed on fruit. Thus sexual habitat segregation might produce (or be a result of) dietary differences, which in turn might have differential effects on dispersion patterns, social behavior, and survivorship of males and females.

Habitat segregation between male and female Black-throated Blue Warblers might be difficult to detect in areas with forests of intermediate stature with a wide range of foliage height strata. Studies in such forests are likely to find an equal mix of males and females. This might be why habitat segregation was not found in Jamaica on the sites intensively studied by Holmes et al. (1989), or in surveys of migrants (Waide, Wunderle, and Lodge, unpubl. data) in a diversity of Jamaican habitats during the winter 1987–88. However, a survey in Jan. 1989 by Waide, Wunderle, and Lodge following Hurricane Gilbert showed a preponderance of females in montane forests in the Blue Mountains. Additional surveys of migrants by the same workers were conducted in a diversity of habitats in the Dominican Republic, and failed to detect habitat segregation in this species. In these cases, male and female habitat segregation might not have been detected because only intermediate stature forests were surveyed and not the extremes of "female" or "male" habitats. Also, tall-stature forest, in which males are expected to predominate, is now rare in the Caribbean region as a result of deforestation.

Finally, the observed pattern of habitat segregation may exist only under certain population densities relative to the availability of male and female habitats. If density-dependent habitat selection occurs on the wintering grounds, then reduction or elimination of the favored habitat of one sex could force the displaced sex into the remaining habitats. If the displaced sex moved into habitats occupied by the opposite sex, the pattern of habitat segregation would disappear. This too, might contribute to differential mortality depending on the behavioral dominance relationships of the sexes. For example, if the displaced sex was behaviorally subordinate, it would likely suffer higher mortality. However, if the displaced sex were dominant it might, in turn, displace some of the subordinate sex from the remaining habitat and contribute to higher mortality of subordinates.

Rangewide changes in land use, such as deforestation or reforestation, might upset existing patterns of sexual habitat segregation. In Puerto Rico, the land area covered by natural forest has been increasing in the past 30 years from a minimum of 6% of the island in the 1940s to a current level of approximately 32% (Birdsey and Weaver 1982). Thus, Black-throated Blue Warblers overwintering in Puerto Rico might have passed through a habitat and population bottleneck in the past and now find a more equitable mix of male and female habitats which permits or drives habitat segregation. However, deforestation is currently the norm throughout the rest of this warbler's Caribbean wintering grounds, and in these areas individuals of the displaced sex (males, in the case of Black-throated Blue Warblers) are likely to flood the habitat of the other sex. This process could obscure or eliminate sexual habitat segregation.

Acknowledgments

The cooperation, assistance, and suggestions provided by Richard T. Holmes have been most helpful to this work. I thank Oscar Diaz and Susan MacVean for their field assistance. I am grateful for the valuable assistance regarding the design and statistical analysis of this work provided by Andy Gillespie. Also, Andy Wilson and Jorgé Pérez-Coffie provided valuable help with the analysis. Finally, the manuscript benefited from the constructive comments provided by Wayne Arendt, Andy Gillespie, Richard Holmes, Jean Lodge, James Lynch, Thomas Sherry, Juan Torres, Marcia Wilson, an anonymous reviewer, and the editors.

Literature cited

Balph, M.H. 1977. Winter social behavior of Dark-eyed Juncos: Communication, social organization, and ecological implications. *Anim. Behav.* 25:859–884.

Bellrose, F.C., T.G. Scott, A.S. Hawkins, and J.B. Low. 1961. Sex ratios and age ratios in North American ducks. *Illinois Nat. Hist. Surv. Bull.* 27:293–329.

Belopol'skij, L.O. 1972. Ecological peculiarities in *Accipter nisus* (L.) migrations. *Ekologiya* 3:58–63. (Translated in *Soviet J. Ecol.* 3:138–142, 1972).

Birdsey, R.A., and P.L. Weaver. 1982. The forest resources of Puerto Rico. *For. Serv. Res. Bull.* SO-85, New Orleans, La., So. For. Exp. Sta. USDA.

Borror, D.J., and W.W.H. Gunn (no date). Songs of warblers of eastern North America. Sounds of Nature Series, Vol 4. Federation of Ontario Naturalists, Don Mills, Ontario.

Brown, S., A.E. Lugo, S. Silander, and L. Liegel. 1983. *Research History and Opportunities in the Luquillo Experimental Forest.* USDA Forest Service, Gen. Tech. Rep. SO-44.

Cox, G.W. 1968. The role of competition in the evolution of migration. *Evolution* 22:180–189.

Dolbeer, R.A. 1982. Migration patterns for age and sex classes of blackbirds and starlings. *J. Field Ornithol.* 53:28–46.

Ewel, J.J., and J.L. Whitmore. 1973. *The Ecological Life Zones of Puerto Rico and the U.S. Virgin Islands.* USDA Forest Service, Research Paper ITF-18.

Fretwell, S. 1972. *Populations in a Seasonal Environment.* Princeton: Princeton University Press.

———. 1980. Evolution of migration in relation to factors regulating bird numbers. Pages 517–529 in *Migrant Birds in the Neotropics: Ecology, Behavior, Distribution and Conservation*, A. Keast and E.S. Morton, eds. Washington: Smithsonian Institution Press.

Gauthreaux, S. 1978. The ecological significance of behavioral dominance. Pages 17–54 in *Perspectives in Ornithology*, P.P.G. Bateson and P.H. Klopfer, eds. New York: Plenum.

———. 1982. The ecology and evolution of avian migration systems. Pages 93–167 in *Avian Biology*, Vol. 6, D.S. Farner and J.R. King, eds. New York: Academic Press.

Greenberg, R. 1985. The social behavior and feeding ecology of neotropical migrants in the non-breeding season. *Acta 18th Internat. Ornithol. Cong.* (Moscow): 648–653.

———. 1986. Competition in migrant birds in the nonbreeding season. *Current Ornithol.* 3:281–307.

Holmes, R.T. 1986. Foraging patterns of forest birds: Male-female differences. *Wilson Bull.* 98:196–213.

Holmes, R.T., T.W. Sherry, and L. Reitsma. 1989. Population structure, territoriality and overwinter survival of two migrant warbler species in Jamaica. *Condor* 91:545–561.

Howell, T.R. 1953. Racial and sexual differences in migration in *Sphyrapicus varius. Auk* 70:118–126.

James, F.C., R.T. Engstrom, C. Nesmith, and R. Laybourne. 1984. Inferences about population movements of Redwinged Blackbirds from morphological data. *Am. Midl. Nat.* 111:319–331.

Ketterson, E.D., and V. Nolan, Jr. 1976. Geographic variation and its climatic correlates in the sex ratio of eastern-wintering Dark-eyed Juncos (*Junco hyemalis*). *Ecology* 57:679–693.

———. 1983. The evolution of differential migration. *Current Ornithol.* 1:357–402.

Kilham, L. 1965. Differences in the feeding behavior of male and female Hairy Woodpeckers. *Wilson Bull.* 77:134–145.

King, J.R., D.S. Farner, and L.R. Mewaldt. 1965. Seasonal sex and age ratios in populations of the White-crowned Sparrows of the race *gambelii. Condor* 67:489–504.

Lack, D. 1968. Bird migration and natural selection. *Oikos* 19:1–9.

Lopez Ornat, A., and R. Greenberg. 1990. Sexual segregation by habitat in migratory warblers in Quintana Roo, Mexico. *Auk* 107:539–543.

Lynch, J.F., E.S. Morton, and M.E. Van der Voort. 1985. Habitat segregation between the sexes of wintering Hooded Warblers (*Wilsonia citrina*). *Auk* 102:714–721.

Mead, C.J. 1973. Movements of British raptors. *Bird Study* 20:259–286.

Morse, D.H. 1968. A quantitative study of foraging male and female spruce-woods warblers. *Ecology* 49:779–784.

Morton, E.S., J.F. Lynch, K. Young, and P. Mehlhop. 1987. Do male Hooded Warblers exclude females from nonbreeding territories in tropical forest? *Auk* 104:133–135.

Mueller, H.C., D.D. Berger, and G. Allez. 1977. The periodic invasions of Goshawks. *Auk* 94:652–663.

Myers, J.P. 1981. A test of three hypotheses for latitudinal segregation of the sexes in wintering birds. *Can. J. Zool.* 59:1527–1534.

Myers, J.P., P.G. Connors, and F.A. Pitelka. 1979. Territoriality in non-breeding shorebirds. Pages 231–246 in *Shorebirds in Marine Environments*, F.A. Pitelka, ed. Studies in Avian Biology No. 2.

Nichols, J.D., and G.M. Haramis. 1980. Sex-specific differences in winter distribution patterns of Canvasbacks. *Condor* 82:406–416.

Nisbet, I.C.T., and L. Medway. 1972. Dispersion, population ecology and migration of Eastern Great Reed Warblers *Acrocephalus orientalis* wintering in Malaysia. *Ibis* 114:451–494.

Odum, H.T., and R.F. Pigeon. 1970. A tropical rain forest: A study of irradiation and ecology at El Verde, Puerto Rico, U.S. Atomic Energy Commission. N.T.I.S., Springfield, Virginia.

Peters, W.D., and T.C. Grubb. 1983. An experimental analysis of sex-specific foraging in the Downy Woodpecker, *Picoides pubescens. Ecology* 64:1437–1443.

Pearson, D. 1980. Bird migration in Amazonian Ecuador, Peru, and Bolivia. Pages 273–285 in *Migrant Birds in the Neotropics: Ecology, Behavior, Distribution and Conservation*, A. Keast and E.S. Morton, eds. Washington: Smithsonian Institution Press.

Pitelka, F.A. 1950. Geographic variation and the species problem in the shore bird genus *Limnodromus. Univ. Calif. Publ. Zool.* 50:1–108.

Rappole, J.H., and D.W. Warner. 1980. Ecological aspects of migrant bird behavior in Veracruz, Mexico. Pages 353–394 in *Migrant Birds in the Neotropics: Ecology, Behavior, Distribution and Conservation*, A. Keast and E.S. Morton, eds. Washington: Smithsonian Institution Press.

Rohwer, S. 1975. The social significance of avian winter plumage variability. *Evolution* 29:593–610.

———. 1977. Status signaling in Harris' Sparrows: Some experiments in deception. *Behaviour* 61:107–129.

Salomonsen, F. 1955. The evolutionary significance of bird-migration. *Dan. Biol. Medd.* 22:1–61.

SAS Institute. 1988. *SAS User's Guide: Statistics.* Cary, N.C.: SAS Institute.

Schemske, D.W., and N. Brokaw. 1981. Treefalls and the distribution of understory birds in a tropical forest. *Ecology* 62:938–945.

Selander, R.K. 1966. Sexual dimorphism and differential niche utilization in birds. *Condor* 68:113–151.

Storer, R.W. 1966. Sexual dimorphism and food habits in three North American accipiters. *Auk* 83:423–436.

Tabachnick, B.G., and L.S. Fidell. 1983. *Using Multivariate Statistics.* New York: Harper and Row.

Wadsworth, F.H. 1951. Forest management in the Luquillo Mountains. I. The setting. *Carib. For.* 12:93–114.

Williamson, P. 1971. Feeding ecology of the Red-eyed Vireo (*Vireo olivaceus*) and associated foliage-gleaning birds. *Ecol. Monogr.* 41:129–152.

Woods, C.A. 1975. Banding and recapture of wintering warblers in Haiti. *Bird-Banding* 46:344–346.

Wunderle, J.M., A. Diaz, I. Velazquez, and R. Scharron. 1987. Forest openings and the distribution of understory birds in a Puerto Rican rainforest. *Wilson Bull.* 99:22–37.

NOTE ADDED IN PROOF: Lopez and Greenberg (1990) have recently documented sexual segregation by habitat in five species of migrant warblers wintering in Mexico. In these cases, males were most common in the mature stages of succession and females most common in the earlier stages.

CYNTHIA A. STAICER*
Department of Zoology
University of Massachusetts
Amherst, Massachusetts 01003

Social behavior of the Northern Parula, Cape May Warbler, and Prairie Warbler wintering in second-growth forest in southwestern Puerto Rico

Abstract. The behavior of wintering individuals of three migratory parulines (*Parula americana, Dendroica tigrina, and D. discolor*) was studied to identify factors of importance to the maintenance of wintering populations. Most individuals of all three species exhibited strong site fidelity both within and among winter seasons, but spacing systems varied at the levels of species, individual, and sex. Birds usually moved about independently within overlapping home ranges, although sometimes moved in small cohesive flocks. Some individuals defended exclusive areas, using vocal and visual displays to advertise their presence. Most Cape May Warblers clearly maintained exclusive intraspecific territories and also chased other species. The Northern Parula, the most abundant warbler species in the winter community, exhibited the most plastic spacing behaviors, from territorial to gregarious to wandering, with males being more aggressive than females. Prairie Warblers appeared to adopt a behavioral strategy of avoidance of other warbler individuals, being less aggressive, less vocal, and moving more rapidly and widely than the other migrant species.

The flexibility in social systems apparent among and within individuals in this study has important implications for the conservation of wintering migrants. Observed variability in spacing behavior suggests that species and individuals respond to details of their environment in different ways. The persistence of a sedentary nature in the absence of territoriality in many individuals suggests that familiarity with feeding sites or other attributes of an area is advantageous to a winter resident, even if exclusive use is not achieved. It follows that displacement of sedentary individuals because of habitat destruction would negatively affect their survival probabilities. The features of the surrounding habitat can also be a critical factor affecting the use of a site by migrants. Winter residents often left their restricted daytime home ranges to roost in mixed-species

*Current address: Department of Biology, Dalhousie University, Halifax, NS, Canada B3H 4J1.

flocks in adjacent habitats. This behavioral strategy reveals an inherent plasticity in response to environmental conditions and indicates that second-growth habitats can be deficient in important ways. The spatial distribution of second-growth habitats should be considered in future studies, and especially in the conservation of nonbreeding season habitat.

Sinopsis. Se estudió el comportamiento de individuos invernantes de tres parulinos migratorios (*Parula americana, Dendroica tigrina* y *D. discolor*) para identificar factores de importancia para el mantenimiento de poblaciones invernantes. La mayoría de individuos de las tres especies exhibió una marcada fidelidad al sitio tanto durante una misma estación como entre distintos inviernos, pero los sistemas de espaciamiento variaron al nivel de especie, de individuo y de sexo. Las aves usualmente se desplazaron independientemente dentro de ámbitos domésticos traslapados, aunque algunas veces se movieron en pequeñas bandadas cohesivas. Algunos individuos defendieron áreas exclusivas usando despliegues visuales y vocales para anunciar su presencia. La mayoría de las *D. tigrina* claramente mantuvieron territorios intraespecíficos exclusivos y también persiguieron a otras especies. La especie de Parulinae mas abundante en la comunidad invernante, *P. americana,* exhibió los comportamientos de espaciamiento mas plásticos, desde territorial hasta gregaria o hasta errática, siendo los machos mas agresivos que las hembras. Las *D. discolor* aparentemente adoptaron una estrategia conductual de eludir a otros individuos de Parulinae, siendo menos agresivos, menos vocales y moviéndose mas rápida y ampliamente que las otras especies migratorias. La flexibilidad aparente, tanto intra como inter-individual, de los sistemas sociales en este estudio, tiene implicaciones importantes para la conservación de migratorias invernantes. La variabilidad observada de la conducta de espaciamiento sugiere que las especies y los individuos responden a detalles de su medio ambiente en formas diferentes. La persistencia de una naturaleza sedentaria y la ausencia de territorialidad en muchos individuos indica que la familiaridad con sitios de alimentación u otros atributos de un área es ventajosa para un residente de invierno, incluso si no se consigue su uso exclusivo. Por lo tanto, el desplazamiento de individuos sedentarios como consecuencia de la destrucción de habitat afectaría sus probabilidades de supervivencia. Las características del habitat en los alrededores puede ser también un factor crítico que afecta el uso de un sitio por migratorias. Las aves residentes de invierno frecuentemente abandonan su ámbito doméstico diurno restringido para descansar en bandadas mixtas en los habitats adyacentes. Esta estrategia conductual revela una plasticidad inherente en respuesta a condiciones medioambientales e indica que los habitats de desarrollo secundario pueden ser deficientes de manera importante. La distribución espacial de los habitats secundarios deben considerarse en estudios futuros y especialmente en la conservación de habitat para la estación no reproductiva.

Knowledge of avian social behavior has played an integral role in our understanding of the ecology and evolution of birds (e.g., Orians 1961). More recently, information on the social behavior of Nearctic migrants wintering in the Neotropics has been recognized as crucial to the conservation of those species (Keast and Morton 1980). The effect of habitat alteration on a wintering population likely will depend on the degree to which individuals are sedentary and the survival advantage of maintaining access to resources (Rappole et al. 1989). Spacing systems have been chronicled for several species of wood-warblers wintering in the Neotropics (e.g., Schwartz 1964, Rappole and Warner 1980, Greenberg 1984, Holmes et al. 1989, Rappole et al. 1989), and the responses of social systems to resource availability and habitat structure have been identified as important factors (Morton 1980).

The Northern Parula (*Parula americana*), Cape May Warbler (*Dendroica tigrina*), and Prairie Warbler (*D. discolor*) are among the many Neotropical migrant species that have declined in abundance in recent years in breeding areas (Robbins et al. 1989) and in wintering areas (Faaborg and Arendt, this volume). These species winter mainly in the Caribbean (Rappole et al. 1983) where they are common on many islands and frequently coexist in the same habitat (e.g., Eaton 1953, Lack and Lack 1972, Post 1978). Recent studies of these species have described much variation in habitat preferences and social behavior across various wintering locations (Faaborg and Arendt 1984; Arendt, this volume; Askins et al., this volume; Robbins et al., this volume). To understand the mechanisms underlying this variation, it is necessary to examine how individual birds respond to one another and their environment. To date no studies have been made on the winter spacing behavior of marked individuals of these species.

The present investigation was undertaken to fill this gap in knowledge of migrant winter ecology. Field work was conducted at a site in Puerto Rico where numbers of warbler individuals literally quadruple each fall with the influx of wintering migratory parulines of a dozen species (unpubl. data). The study focused on the three most common of these species, the Northern Parula, the Prairie Warbler, and the Cape May Warbler. The presence of the permanently resident Adelaide's Warbler (*Dendroica adelaidae*) at this site afforded the opportunity to observe interactions between residents and migrants. This paper describes the social behavior of known individuals of the three migrant species and examines microhabitat relations and social interactions among migrants and residents. This approach might aid in understanding mechansims and identifying factors important to the maintenance of wintering warbler populations.

Study site and methods

STUDY SITE. This study was conducted at the Cabo Rojo National Wildlife Refuge (CRNWR), located on the low coastal plain at the southwestern tip of Puerto Rico (17°59' N, 67°10' W). The area, relatively undisturbed for the last 20 years, had a previous history of agriculture. The second-growth habitat was heterogeneous and included components of thorn scrub, seasonal deciduous forest, and savanna. A low (mostly < 10 m), open canopy of deciduous trees was characterized by the introduced *Prosopis juliflora*, *Pithecellobium dulce*, *Parkinsonia aculeata*, and *Tamarindus indica* and the native *Bucida buceras*, believed to have dominated the original vegetation. A dense understory, 1–2 m in height, consisted of shrubs (mainly *Lantana* sp.) and grasses (dominated by *Panicum maximum*). Vines (*Tournefortia volubilis* and *Stigmaphyllon periplocifolium*) occurred from ground to canopy and contributed to dense thickets of vegetation. In areas where tree density was low, often a single vertical layer of vegetation was found. Data for tree density were available from a vegetation study made on the grid in the summer of 1985 (Henry Zuill, unpubl. report to the CRNWR), but no data were available for shrub density.

A grid marked at 50-m intervals encompassed 8 ha of second-growth habitat at the northern edge of CRNWR. Maps of the grid and surrounding areas, drawn with the aid of aerial photos, facilitated pinpointing particular trees, other landmarks, and ultimately, bird locations. The grid was the site of the most intensive behavioral observations and where most individuals were netted, but adjacent areas were searched regularly for the presence of banded birds. Similar habitat was adjacent on two sides of the grid and included trails marked at 50-m or 100-m intervals. The grid was bounded on the other two sides by habitat used for grazing and farming, dotted by a few large isolated trees.

DATA COLLECTION. Data were collected over five winter seasons, in all months when migrants were regularly present (September–April), for a total of 54 weeks between March 1984 and December 1987. Each winter season (the period September through April of the following year) observations were made over a period of one to four months, either at the beginning, middle, or end of the season, but never at both the beginning and end of the same season. Preliminary observations and mist-netting began March–April 1984. Birds were color-marked (two or three colored plastic leg bands plus an aluminum USFWS band) and detailed observations of social behavior were made with the aid of several trained assistants, January–April 1985 and 1986, September 1986–January 1987 and December 1987. A total of 1752 net hr was accumulated over 82 days scat-tered throughout the study period. Net numbers and sizes varied, but on average six nets (32-mm mesh) of a combination of lengths (6 m, 9 m, 12 m, and 13 m) were placed about 25 m apart, at various angles to one another, to cover an area of about 1 ha. Nets were usually moved to another location > 100 m away after one or two days because of declining net site capture rates. Birds were banded within an area of 50 ha, although most were captured within 100 m of the grid.

To collect behavioral data, the observer moved through the habitat until encountering a warbler, then observed it for up to 5 min and recorded the following: date, time, location, species, bands, sex, number of seconds observed, distance the bird moved, vocalizations, posture, nearby birds (species and distance), behavioral interactions, height of bird in the vegetation, and vegetation type. Vocalization types recognized were "tseep" and "chip" (e.g., Morton 1980), and posture was either "normal" (wings folded on back with tips above tail) or "wing droop" (wingtips held below level of base of tail) (e.g., Rappole and Warner 1980). No further data were taken from the same individual for ≥ 1 hr. The observer then moved until encountering another individual and repeated the procedure. Each encounter with an individual (average duration of 106 sec) was represented by a single datum for each variable. Although foraging data were not collected specifically, most individuals foraged during the observation period. Additional sightings of marked birds were accumulated while attending to other projects on the study area.

DATA ANALYSIS. Nonparametric tests of significance were used because few data conformed to a normal distribution. Two-tailed Mann-Whitney U-tests were used to compare two groups in the case of continuous variables (distance from capture site, height, and rate of movement). For categorical variables, G-tests, that is, row by column tests of independence, were used to compare frequencies in the different categories of two variables. Goodness of fit tests (which also report the G statistic) were used to compare observed with expected frequencies of categories within a given variable (Sokal and Rohlf 1981). Much variation was found within individuals, and samples were obtained from as many individuals as possible (no individual contributed more than 4% of the data points). Data from different individuals were pooled for analyses in the following sections: social aggregations, social displays, aggressive interactions, and microhabitat use.

TERMINOLOGY. The following terms had specific meanings in this study. *Winter* was the lengthy period of six or more months during the nonbreeding season in which migrants reside at a particular Neotropical location. A *wintering individual* was a resident during its nonbreeding season. A bird returned for a *second season* if the bird was present during the following winter, that is, after an intervening breeding season (summer). A *home range* was the area in which a bird spent most of the day, feeding and resting. (Often birds moved off their home range to roost, and such movements were excluded when mapping the home range of an individual.) A *territory* was the portion, if any, of the home range that the individual actively defended, attempting to exclude other individuals by using aggressive territorial displays, including postures, call notes, and chases. A bird could have a very restricted home range and be nonterritorial.

Results

RETURN RATE

At least one half of all migrants banded returned to the site the subsequent year (Fig. 1). Data are included for all migrants ($n = 98$) banded at least three seasons previous to the last and within 100 m of the grid. Most marked individuals (86/98 or 87.8% of all three species combined) remained through the banding season. One half (45/98 or 49.9%) of all marked migrants were recorded again in their second season (the winter season following the banding season), but only 14.3% (14/98) were recorded their third season (Fig. 1). If return rates are calculated based on the number of marked birds sighted the previous year (instead of the number originally banded), then 52% (45/86) returned in the second and 31% (14/45) returned in the third season. The lower rates of return in the third season are likely an artifact of less field time in what corresponded to the third season for most birds (December 1987).

The three migrant species showed a similar pattern of return rate among successive seasons (Fig. 1). Of the banded Northern Parulas, 91% were seen the season of banding, 49% the second season, and 14% the third. Of the banded Prairie Warblers, 84% were seen the season of banding, 40% the second season, and 16% the third. Of the banded Cape May Warblers, 75% were seen the season of banding, 38% the second season, and 13% the third. Apparently lower rates of return for the less numerous species in the second season (Prairie and especially Cape May warblers) might be an artifact of smaller sample sizes. Some Prairie Warbler returns probably went undetected because it was more difficult to read leg bands in this species.

More than five times as many returns were detected using the resighting technique than by recapturing birds in mist nets. Of the 156 migrants that were color-banded, 121 (78%) were seen after the banding date, and 54 (35%) in a subsequent season. Only 14% of 190 individuals banded were recaptured, 6% in a subsequent season; only nine birds were recaptured twice, and none

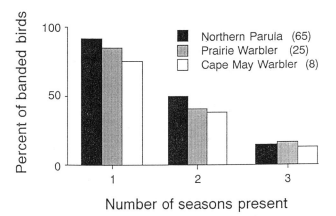

FIGURE 1. Year-to-year site fidelity for migrants (number of different individuals in parentheses) banded between spring 1984 and spring 1986 at Cabo Rojo NWR. Bars represent percentage of total number of individuals banded that were observed in each winter season. Banding occurred in different calendar years for different birds, but for all birds season 1 is the banding season. Bars for season 1 represent percentage of birds banded and resighted the same season. Bars for season 2 represent percentage of birds banded the previous season that were resighted during the second season. Bars for season 3 represent percentage of birds banded two seasons previous that were resighted during the third season. A few individuals banded (4 Northern Parulas, 4 Prairie Warblers, 1 Cape May Warbler) were not resighted until a subsequent season. These birds were assumed to have been present and are included in percentages present the previous season.

were netted more frequently. It should be noted, however, that considerably more time was spent searching for banded birds than netting, and that the area sampled by netting is much smaller.

SITE FIDELITY

Individuals of the three migrant species appeared to be resident throughout the winter period. In a given year, previously banded birds were among the first individuals of a given species to return and the last to leave the study location. Earliest arrival dates (fall 1986) and latest departure dates (spring 1985) of marked winter residents (different birds in fall and spring) were as follows: Northern Parula, 11 October and 25 April; Cape May Warbler, 11 November and 21 April; Prairie Warbler, 8 September and 9 April. The record duration held by a Northern Parula individual was arrival by 13 October and departure after 22 April.

Individuals showed a high degree of site fidelity both within and among years. Most (78%) sightings ($n = 880$) of marked migrants ($n = 122$ individuals) occurred within 100 m of the original capture site (Fig. 2). Each datum represents, for an individual on a given day, the

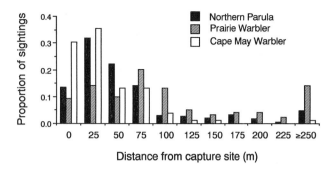

FIGURE 2. Within-season site fidelity. Data pooled for 81 birds and all years. Each sighting ($n = 880$) represents maximum distance at which an individual was encountered on a given day in relation to its original capture site.

TABLE 1. Classification of spacing behavior for 80 marked Northern Parula individuals wintering in second-growth dry forest at the Cabo Rojo WNR, southwestern Puerto Rico, March 1984–December 1987

	Number of sedentary individuals[a]			Number of wandering individuals[e]
	Territorial[b]	Gregarious[c]	Other[d]	
Males	10	6	15	15
Females	5	9	15	5

a. Typically observed within a small area (≤ 50 m radius).
b. Defended area against conspecifics, frequently used aggressive displays.
c. Rarely aggressive, often observed ≤ 5 m from conspecifics, sometimes in cohesive flocks.
d. Too few data or no clear trends for territorial vs. gregarious behavior in these individuals.
e. Sightings of these individuals tended to be more infrequent and far (> 100 m) apart.

sighting most distant from the original capture site. Data from all years were combined because there was little or no difference in distances among years for individuals. These distance data, which provide a measure of site fidelity, are conservative because the capture site often was not central to a bird's range. Many birds were apparently captured when moving to or from their roosts or in the more peripheral portions of their home range.

The three species differed in how far they ranged in relation to their original capture site. Cape May Warblers tended to be seen closer to, and Prairie Warblers farther from, their capture site than Northern Parulas. The Prairie Warbler differed significantly in mean distance from the Northern Parula ($P < 0.01$) and the Cape May Warbler ($P < 0.05$, two-tailed Mann-Whitney U-tests, each individual contributing one data point). Thus, Prairie Warblers had significantly larger home ranges than the other two migrants. The overall median distances per individual from resighting location to capture site were as follows: Northern Parula, 56 m ($n = 81$); Prairie Warbler, 88 m ($n = 33$); Cape May Warbler, 34 m ($n = 8$).

SPACING OF INDIVIDUALS

Much individual variation was found in the spacing of Northern Parulas (Table 1). Most marked individuals (75%) were quite sedentary but only 25% of these were observed to defend territories actively. The home range of an individual typically overlapped substantially from year to year, often including the same trees each year, whether or not the bird defended a territory (Fig. 3). Some birds, for example male S/Bb (Fig. 3A) and female S/Ob (Fig. 3B), clearly defended a territory smaller than their home range. These territorial birds used displays ("chip" vocalizations and wing droop posture) and chased intruders in defense of the canopy in their

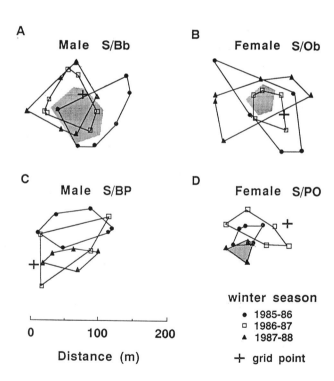

FIGURE 3. Home ranges and territories of four sedentary Northern Parula individuals during three winter seasons. Areas defended by each bird are shaded. Grid point is the same reference point throughout figure and indicates spatial relationships among these individuals. Defended area of Male S/Bb (A) shifted slightly between years, apparently in response to blow down of a tall mesquite, whose canopy he defended; shown is the composite area defended across the study.

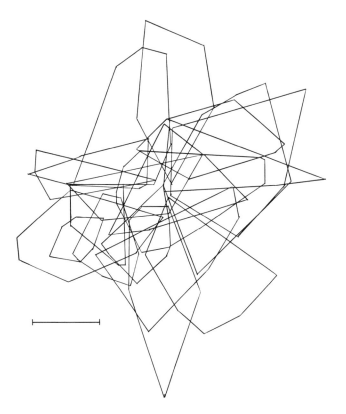

FIGURE 4. Overlapping home ranges of sedentary Northern Parulas. Maps of home ranges of 10 marked males and 10 marked females in most densely vegetated portion of grid, mid-January to late-April 1986. Though some of these individuals defended part of their home range (5 males and 3 females), most of the area encompassed by these 20 home ranges was not defended as exclusive territories. Other birds, including unmarked individuals, also were present and some defended territories in this area. Bar scale = 50 m.

home range. When in other portions of their home range, territorial individuals were typically silent and tolerant of other individuals.

By contrast, many Northern Parulas with home ranges just as restricted, such as male S/BP (Fig. 3C), were basically nonaggressive (Table 1). These nonterritorial individuals frequently associated with conspecifics and sometimes moved in small cohesive flocks. These birds were sedentary, nonterritorial individuals whose home ranges overlapped and encompassed largely undefended areas (Fig. 4). One female, S/PO (Fig. 3D), was sedentary all three years but did not exhibit territorial behavior until her third year, when she defended a dense shrub thicket. One fourth of all Northern Parulas appeared to wander more widely (Table 1), based on very infrequent sightings near their banding site or scattered sightings > 100 m apart. Sedentary nonterritorial individuals were more often female and territorial individuals were more often males (Table 1), but the re-

lationship between territorial tendency and sex was not significant. Densities of wintering parulas were high, ca. 6/ha, but only certain areas were defended and territories were not necessarily contiguous.

Cape May Warblers were highly territorial and defended exclusive areas, usually the canopies of *Prosopis*, which produce abundant nectar. Individuals frequently chased and supplanted conspecifics, and both sexes appeared equally territorial. Heterospecifics were tolerated in the shrub understory below, and sometimes within the same canopy. Individuals that returned for a subsequent season held virtually identical territories each year (< 50 m apart). During the spring of 1986 at least eight individuals (including unmarked birds) defended exclusive territories on the grid, though territories were not contiguous, giving a winter density of ≥ 1/ha. A few unmarked individuals appeared to participate in mixed species flocks.

No clear evidence of territoriality was obtained for the Prairie Warbler. The secretive habits and quick movements of Prairie Warblers made them more difficult to observe than the other species. Most individuals ranged more widely and rarely appeared to interact aggressively, suggesting either that territories were larger or that territorial defense was less common in this species. At least some individuals, however, gave aggressive displays, vocalizations and postures, suggestive of territorial defense. Winter territorial defense might be common but more subtle in this species. More work is needed to characterize individual variation in spacing behavior. Wintering densities were similar to that of the resident Adelaide's Warbler, ≥ 2/ha.

ROOSTING BEHAVIOR

Each evening birds moved en masse from the grid to adjacent areas. Encounters with marked sedentary individuals > 100 m from their home range occurred when birds were en route to or from a roost. During the hour before sunset, migrants moved off the grid singly or in small mixed species flocks to roost communally. Movement to and from the roost was qualitatively different from movement within the home range, and was suggestive of migratory flocks, including more rapid movement and use of "tseep" calls among birds moving together. Upon arrival at the roost site, much flying, chasing, and vocalizing ensued as individuals appeared to vie for roost positions. After sunrise migrants moved rapidly back to their home ranges and then engaged in bouts of interspecific "chipping," in which several individuals of migrant and resident warbler species uttered "chips" for periods of ≥ 1 min.

Roosting habitat differed from the grid habitat in the presence of taller, older trees, particularly *Bucida buceras* and *Hymenaea courbaril*, with broader canopies and

TABLE 2. Proportions of sightings where a subject was solitary, or in different types of associations with other birds

Species (n)[a]	Solitary	Association type[b] (birds < 10 m apart)				
		C	H	B	UW	N
Northern Parula (583)	0.41	0.25	0.20	0.05	0.04	0.06
Prairie Warbler (199)	0.41	0.10	0.35	0.05	0.04	0.07
Cape May Warbler (80)	0.28	0.08	0.43	0.11	0.06	0.05
Adelaide's Warbler (128)	0.27	0.35	0.27	0.02	0.01	0.10

a. n is the number of observations per species; tests of independence revealed a significant relationship between species and whether birds were solitary vs. associating ($G = 12.9$, df = 3, $P < 0.005$), and between species and whether associations were conspecific vs. heterospecific ($G = 34.2$, df = 3, $P < 0.001$).

b. Other individual(s) present included: C, conspecific(s) only; H, heterospecific(s) only; B, both conspecific(s) and heterospecific(s); UW, unidentified warbler species; N, non-warbler species.

denser foliage. Roost trees were surrounded by recent second-growth scrub or were isolated in cattle pastures or cultivated fields, and were not used by large numbers of migrants during the day. Sometimes an individual migrant warbler would roost on the grid and would "chip" the next morning before the others had arrived. The resident Adelaide's Warblers roosted on their territories and sang before sunrise throughout the year. Some resident species which fed on the grid during the day, however, roosted elsewhere during the nonbreeding season, such as the year-round territorial Gray Kingbird *Tyrannus dominicensis* (unpubl. data).

SOCIAL AGGREGATIONS

Overall, birds were more often observed in association with other individuals (< 10 m apart) than alone (Table 2). Such associations were noted in 60% of all observations, in which the average distance to the nearest other bird was 4.8 m. The migrants did not follow territorial residents (Adelaide's Warblers or other species) as they moved about their territory. Cohesive flocks of birds that followed one another closely contained only migrants, typically two to four individuals of one or more species, and usually not more than one male per species. Relatively few of the migrant individuals ob-

served in associations, however, were actually members of cohesive flocks. Rather, migrants usually appeared to move about their home ranges largely independently, forming temporary social aggregations, as described in previous studies as "collections" (Lack and Lack 1972) or stationary flocks (Post 1978). Migrant individuals that were otherwise territorial joined nonterritorial individuals to feed or rest in areas of dense vegetation that were not actively defended. In these areas, relatively little aggression was observed among migrants and between migrants and residents, even when individuals were ≤ 1–2 m apart.

Species varied in their tendency to associate with conspecifics or heterospecifics (Table 2). Cape May and Adelaide's warblers were more likely to form associations than the other species. Conspecific migrant associations were most frequent in the most abundant species, the Northern Parula, and least frequent in the least abundant species, the Cape May Warbler. Resident Adelaide's Warblers, which maintained long-term pair bonds (unpubl. data), were most often observed in conspecific associations. The frequency with which a given migrant individual associated solely with Adelaide's Warblers differed among species ($G = 7.2$, d.f. = 2, $P < 0.05$), with Prairie Warblers associating with the resident more often (16% of observations) and Northern

TABLE 3. Relative frequencies of social displays observed for each of the migrant species

Species	Vocalization				Wing posture		
	(n)[a]	Silent	"Tseep"	"Chip"	(n)	Normal	Droop
Northern Parula	(605)	0.64	0.13	0.24	(540)	0.79	0.21
Prairie Warbler	(199)	0.77	0.03	0.20	(178)	0.87	0.13
Cape May Warbler	(74)	0.57	0.23	0.20	(67)	0.76	0.24

a. n is the number of observations per species; tests of independence revealed a significant relationship between species and vocalization type ($G = 31.7$, df = 4, $P < 0.001$), and between species and wing posture ($G = 6.9$, df = 2, $P < 0.05$).

TABLE 4. Number of aggresive interactions (chases plus supplants) in which the aggressor (chaser) or subject (bird chased) was determined, and the proportion of known conspecific interactions

Aggressor	Subject of aggression					Proportion conspecific
	NP	PW	CM	AW	U	
Northern Parula (NP)	37	4	1	1	8	0.86
Prairie Warbler (PW)	1	2	0	1	2	0.50
Cape May Warbler (CM)	25	6	9	3	12	0.21
Adelaide's Warbler (AW)	12	11	1	2	1	0.08
unidentified warbler (U)	6	1	0	0	8	—

NOTE: A test of independence between the four species and their roles in aggressive interactions revealed a significant relationship ($G = 27.8$, df = 3, $P < 0.001$).

Parulas associating with the resident less often (6% of observations) than expected.

SOCIAL DISPLAYS

The three migrant species differed in their tendencies to vocalize (Table 3). The Prairie Warbler was silent most often and the territorial Cape May Warbler was vocal most often. Overall, migrants were silent during the majority of observations (66%). Warblers were significantly more likely to "chip" when solitary and to "tseep" when associating ($G = 4.3$, d.f. = 1, $P < 0.05$). If birds vocalized while associating with other individuals, they were twice as likely to give "tseep" calls if near conspecifics. No significant relationships were found, however, between tendency to vocalize (silent vs. vocalizing) and to associate (solitary vs. associating), or between association type (conspecific vs. heterospecific) and vocalization type ("tseep" vs. "chip"). Within species, sexual differences in tendency to vocalize were found only in the Northern Parula, with males vocalizing with "chips" twice as frequently as females ($G = 20.0$, d.f. = 2, $P < 0.001$).

The extent to which migrants used the agonistic wing droop display differed among the species (Table 3). Wing position was significantly associated with a tendency to vocalize ($G = 37.2$, d.f. = 1, $P < 0.001$) and type of vocalization, "tseep" or "chip" ($G = 6.8$, d.f. = 1, $P < 0.01$). Normal posture was observed three times more frequently when birds were silent than when vocalizing. Birds giving "chips" used wing droop display twice as frequently as birds giving "tseeps." No significant relationship was found between wing position and tendency to associate.

AGGRESSIVE INTERACTIONS

Species differed in their aggressive tendencies (Table 4). Frequencies of aggressive interactions per species

differed from those expected based on relative species abundances ($G = 57.9$, d.f. = 3, $P < 0.001$). Cape May Warblers, the largest of the migrants, were involved in more aggressive interactions than expected, whereas Prairie and Adelaide's warblers, the smallest of the warblers, were involved in less aggressive interactions than expected. A significant association was found between species and role (aggressor or subject of aggression) played in an encounter (Table 4). Cape May and Adelaide's warblers were more likely to be aggressors, whereas Northern Parulas and Prairie Warblers were more likely to be the subject of aggression. Prairie Warblers, perhaps because of their small size, were often chased by the other warbler species. During the first two weeks that Prairie Warblers were present in September 1986, many individuals were chased by Adelaide's Warblers, but thereafter, chasing was infrequent. No peaks in interspecific aggression were noted after the arrival of any other migrant warbler species.

Aggressive encounters, chases or supplants, occurred in about 10% of all observations, although the species or individuals involved were not always identified (Table 4). In 1985, when the numbers of interactions observed per hour were recorded, the overall rate of aggressive interactions was 0.97/hr. Males tended to be involved in more aggressive interactions than females in all except the Cape May Warbler, in which females outnumbered males. In the Northern Parula, males were significantly more aggressive than females ($G = 6.8$, d.f. = 1, $P < 0.01$), initiating aggressive interactions three times more often.

MICROHABITAT USE

Six major types of vegetation, the four most common tree species plus shrubs and vines, were identified as being the units of vegetation used most frequently by the four warbler species. Patterns of vegetation type use for each bird species were determined by the relative pro-

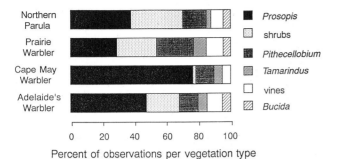

Northern Parula
Prairie Warbler
Cape May Warbler
Adelaide's Warbler

■ *Prosopis*
▨ shrubs
▨ *Pithecellobium*
▨ *Tamarindus*
□ vines
▨ *Bucida*

0   20   40   60   80 100

Percent of observations per vegetation type

FIGURE 5. Use of different types of vegetation by warbler species. Subjecting this data to a test of independence between warbler species ($n = 4$) and type of vegetation ($n = 6$) resulted in a significant relationship: $G = 75.6$, d.f. = 15, $P < 0.001$. See text for more details. Number of observations per species were: Parula, 458; Prairie, 160; Cape May, 60; Adelaide's, 119.

portions of observations in each vegetation type. Each warbler species tended to use these vegetation types to different extents (Fig. 5). The Cape May exhibited the most distinct pattern, avoiding the shrubs used by the other warbler species. Between-species comparisons showed that the Cape May differed significantly from each of the other warbler species ($21.6 \leq G \leq 50.5$, d.f. = 3, $P < 0.001$, categories of the three least common vegetation types combined because of small cell totals for Cape May Warblers). The Northern Parula and Prairie Warblers differed significantly in their patterns of vegetation use ($G = 17.1$, d.f. = 5, $P < 0.005$), and the Adelaide's differed significantly from the Prairie Warbler ($G = 12.2$, d.f. = 5, $P < 0.05$) but not from the Northern Parula ($G = 10.1$, d.f. = 5, $0.05 < P < 0.10$).

Each warbler species tended to prefer different tree species (Fig. 5). Use of the four most common tree species was compared to tree availability as measured by basal areas (*Prosopis* 1.47, *Pithecellobium* 0.74, *Tamarindus* 0.14, *Bucida* 0.20 m²/ha). Only the Northern Parula used the four tree species according to availability, whereas tree use for the other species differed significantly from that predicted by chance. The Cape May ($G = 20.4$, d.f. = 3, $P < 0.001$) and Prairie ($G = 13.1$, d.f. = 3, $P < 0.005$) differed most from expected, the Adelaide's barely differed from expected ($G = 8.1$, d.f. = 3, $P < 0.05$), and the Northern Parula did not differ from expected ($G = 4.1$, d.f. = 3, $0.10 < P < 0.50$). *Prosopis* was preferred by all but the Prairie Warbler which avoided this species, whereas *Pithecellobium* was preferred by the Prairie Warbler and avoided by the others. *Tamarindus* was preferred by the Prairie and Adelaide's warblers, and *Bucida* was avoided by the Cape May Warbler.

Foraging height distributions differed significantly for

all species pairs except the Northern Parula and Adelaide's Warbler. Cape May Warblers used greatest heights (median = 5 m) and differed most from the other species ($P < 0.001$, all comparisons). Prairie Warblers used lowest heights (median = 2.5 m) and differed significantly from Northern Parulas ($P < 0.01$) and Adelaide's Warblers ($P < 0.05$) (median for both = 3 m). Also a significant difference ($P < 0.001$) was found between male (3 m) and female (2.5 m) foraging height for the Northern Parula.

Rates of movement through the habitat differed among the warbler species. The ratio of distance moved to amount of time observed provided a measure of rate of movement. The Prairie Warbler moved more rapidly (median = 0.1 m/sec) than the Northern Parula (0.07 m/sec), Adelaide's Warbler (0.07 m/sec) and Cape May Warbler (0.06 m/sec). The only significant species differences, however, were found between the Prairie Warbler and the other two migrants ($P < 0.05$). The sexes did not differ in rate of movement for any species.

Discussion

Northern Parulas, Prairie, and Cape May warblers wintering at the CRNWR showed a high degree of site fidelity from year to year. Of the marked birds that exhibited site fidelity, 54% of Northern Parulas, 48% of Prairie Warblers, and 50% of Cape May Warblers returned the year after banding. These figures correspond well with the recent estimates that return rates of migrant parulines to wintering sites are about 50% (Holmes and Sherry, this volume). If annual survival is closer to 60% for parulines (Roberts 1971), some marked individuals might survive but winter at a different site. Most sightings of marked individuals in the present study were within 100 m of their original capture site, and it was common to observe repeatedly a given individual in the same trees or shrubs during the banding season as well as in subsequent years. The degree of within-season site fidelity found was comparable to that shown for other warbler species wintering in Jamaica (Holmes et al. 1989).

A mist-netting study conducted at the Guánica Forest only 50 km away concluded that the Northern Parula, Prairie, and Cape May warblers were neither territorial nor part of the regular winter bird community of Puerto Rico, but were "opportunistic species" whose populations varied greatly year to year and which showed little evidence of site fidelity (Faaborg and Arendt 1984). Disparity in these results might be due, in part, to differences in methodology, habitat, and sample sizes. Conclusions of the present study would have been very different if based on mist-netting data rather than observations of marked birds, because so few were recaptured. The open canopy apparently made it possible for warblers to detect and avoid nets. Recaptures of resident warblers were also quite low, although some resident species that foraged below the canopy were recaptured frequently. The vegetation at the Guánica forest was denser, less disturbed, dominated by native species, and lacked a distinct grass or shrub layer. Abundances of the three migrant species at Guánica were lower and have declined in recent years (Faaborg and Arendt, this volume). Because of the variation often observed in migrant behavior in different habitats and under different migrant densities (e.g., Mabey and Morton, this volume; R. Waide and J. Wunderle, unpubl. data), spacing of individuals of the same species might in fact differ between CRNWR and Guánica.

Sedentary individuals often left their daytime foraging sites to roost communally in mixed species assemblages in adjacent habitat. Similar roosting behavior has been noted only at one other location, also in Puerto Rico (C. Leck, pers. comm.). That this behavior has not been described for sedentary migrant parulines elsewhere suggests a response to particular characteristics of the study site habitat. The openness of the habitat, especially during drought periods, probably made good roost sites difficult to find. The densest thickets often contained nests of roof rats (*Rattus rattus*), which were frequently observed sleeping in the daytime and moving along branches at dawn. Birds moved to the roosts long before darkness curtailed foraging, an observation that Morton (1980) suggested is evidence that roost sites are limiting.

The three migrant species differed significantly from one another in simple measures of microhabitat use. Microhabitat preferences and foraging behavior were generally similar to those described for the same species wintering in Jamaica (Lack and Lack 1972). Cape May Warblers used the highest stratum, but interestingly avoided the tallest tree species, *Bucida,* instead preferring *Prosopis,* an important nectar source. Prairie Warblers used the lowest stratum, foraging at heights similar to those used during the breeding season (Nolan 1978), and avoided tree species preferred by the other warbler species. The Northern Parula and resident Adelaide's Warbler used intermediate heights and were more similar to one another in vegetation type use. The Northern Parula was the only species that used tree types in proportion to their abundance, suggesting little species-specificity for microhabitats. This observation corroborates the finding that wintering Northern Parulas are habitat generalists in the Yucatan (Lynch 1989) and as well as among Caribbean Islands (Arendt, this volume).

Within a particular Neotropical bird community, migrant and resident paruline species tend to be rather similar ecologically, although specific foraging tactics generally differ between any two paruline species (e.g.,

Howell 1971, Keast 1980, Waide 1981). Although the three migrants studied appeared well separated from one another in microhabitat use, their overlap with the resident warbler was more substantial. The Prairie Warbler was more similar to the resident Adelaide's Warbler than to the other migrants in microhabitat use, and the Northern Parula and Adelaide's Warbler were very similar to each other in microhabitat use and foraging height. Qualitative observations suggest that further differences between residents and migrants would probably be found if foraging maneuvers, efficiency of prey capture, or diet were quantified. The Northern Parula and Adelaide's Warbler, however, were observed near one another less frequently than expected by chance, suggesting the two species might actively avoid one another.

Differences in male and female foraging behavior in the breeding season, particularly foraging height, has been explained by an economic argument in which both sexes benefit (e.g., Morse 1968, Nolan 1978). In the nonbreeding season, however, the more dominant sex might exclude the other from preferred microhabitats (Desrochers 1989). Sexual differences in aggression might be in part responsible for the habitat segregation by sex found in many species of wintering parulines, including the Northern Parula (Ornat and Greenberg 1990). In the present study, male Northern Parulas were more aggressive (initiated more chases), more vocal (chipped more frequently), foraged higher in the vegetation, and were more likely to defend territories than females. Holmes et al. (1989) also found sexual differences in aggression of wintering parulines.

In contrast to a number of species that winter at mainland sites such as Panama (Greenberg 1984), migrants in this study did not join mixed-species flocks. In dry lowland forests in the Antilles, residents rarely form mixed-species flocks (Lack and Lack 1972, Post 1978) and thus nuclear species (e.g., Powell et al., this volume) are lacking. Nonetheless, the three migrant species sometimes formed small cohesive flocks among themselves and with other migrants, such as the less abundant American Redstart (*Setophaga ruticilla*) and Black-and-white Warbler (*Mniotilta varia*). Cohesive flocks of migrants were, however, uncommon, perhaps because many of the migrants were territorial. Individuals observed in proximity to one another usually were not moving together and thus were not members of a cohesive flock. More typically, birds formed temporary aggregations, moving to and from an area largely independently of one another. Similar descriptions of a temporary aggregation of migrants have been called a "collection" in Jamaica (Lack and Lack 1972) and a "stationary flock" at a nearby site in Puerto Rico (Post 1978). In Cuba, Eaton (1953) reported that Northern Parula and Prairie Warblers tended to occur in flocks, but it is not clear whether all groups observed were cohesive flocks. In the Virgin Islands, especially in fragmented habitats, these species are reported to form flocks frequently (Ewert and Askins in press). Methodological differences among studies, including criteria used for determining whether birds are part of a flock, might be responsible for some of the differences reported. It would seem desirable to distinguish between cohesive and stationary flocks because these might imply different spacing patterns and perhaps home range sizes of participating individuals.

Migrant individuals used vocal and visual displays to advertise their presence and defend territories. "Chips" and wing droop displays, as described for other winter territorial species (Morton 1980, Rappole and Warner 1980, Holmes et al. 1989), were common and tended to occur together. In contrast to many previous studies (e.g., Morse 1976, Post 1978, Greenberg 1984, Tramer and Kemp 1980, but see Chipley 1976), chases and supplants were slightly more common between heterospecifics than conspecifics. Dominance relationships among the migrants were directly related to size (see also Post 1978), although the resident Adelaide's, the smallest species, tended to dominate the migrants (see also Greenberg 1984).

Several lines of evidence suggest that the Prairie Warbler adopts a winter strategy of avoidance of other warblers. Lack and Lack (1972) reported the Prairie preferred open habitats where mimosaceous trees predominate, and Nolan (1978) regarded it as a habitat generalist with a plastic feeding strategy. In addition, recent studies have concluded the Prairie, as well as the Parula, are habitat generalists in winter (Arendt, this volume; Askins et al., this volume). Yet in this study the Prairie avoided the dominant mimosaceous tree, *Prosopis,* which was preferred by the other warbler species. In addition, it moved more rapidly, ranged greater distances and was silent more often than the other species. Upon arrival in fall, as the first migrant species to occupy the habitat, it was chased by the resident Adelaide's. Thereafter, although the Prairie was involved in relatively few aggressive interactions, it was more often the subject of aggression than the aggressor and was chased by the other warbler species. These observations suggest that the behavior of the Prairie Warbler might be tailored to avoiding the other warbler species.

The Cape May Warbler was the most aggressive and territorial of the three migrant species. Males and females were equally aggressive and maintained exclusive intraspecific territories, and often chased away other warbler species. The Cape May Warbler was the species least often observed near conspecifics and most often observed near heterospecifics, which might explain why most aggressive encounters initiated by Cape Mays

were interspecific. In the study area, the synchronous flowering and even dispersion of *Prosopis* blossoms likely made a sedentary, territorial strategy profitable for the Cape May. In Cuba, Eaton (1953) noted that, while he did not observe active defense, Cape May Warblers usually fed alone, around trees in flower. A number of reports have described individuals of this species defending clumped food resources, such as nectar, against other parulines outside of the breeding season (Kale 1967, Leck 1972, Emlen 1973, Sealy 1989).

Mixed strategies in spacing behaviors were evident among Northern Parulas. Some individuals defended territories, while other individuals, no less restricted in their movements, did not. Territorial individuals had a higher probability of returning in subsequent years than nonterritorial individuals (67% of territorial and 50% of nonterritorial birds returned). Territorial individuals typically defended only a portion (usually $\leq$ 500 m^2) of their home range, and usually a specific unit of vegetation (i.e., tree canopy or shrub thicket). Defense of a larger area might not have been feasible under the pressure of high densities of conspecifics, or food might not have been abundant or predictable enough to make defense economically feasible. It is also possible that food was abundant enough that defense was unnecessary (Brown 1964). In other parts of their home range, territorial individuals were gregarious, joining temporary mixed-species aggregations to forage or rest, often in dense tangles of vegetation. Nonterritorial individuals were more gregarious and sometimes moved together in small flocks. Most had home ranges identical in size to territorial individuals, though some ranged more widely and were considered wanderers. Nonterritorial, wandering individuals also have been found in other wintering migrant species exhibiting territoriality (Rappole and Warner 1980, Holmes et al. 1989).

The present study has shown that site fidelity is not necessarily associated with territory defense, and that individuals that do not defend territories are not necessarily wanderers. Although the distinction between territoriality and nonaggressive sedentary behavior has been emphasized in the present study, the individual variation in spacing behavior observed is probably best represented as a continuum between these two strategies. As more studies focus on the behavior of banded individuals, similar variability in the spacing of individuals might be found in other wintering paruline species. Variability in spacing behavior among individuals, and within the same individual at different times of day, is common among shorebird species (Myers et al. 1979), but has not been previously reported in wintering parulines. Most studies of wintering migrants have focused on whether individuals defend territories outside of the breeding season (e.g., Rappole and Warner 1980, Greenberg 1984), though some variation in territorial behavior has been noted in relation to resource distribution (Morton 1980, Tramer and Kemp 1980, Holmes et al. 1989).

Familiarity with an area and its inhabitants might be advantageous, regardless of exclusive use (Fretwell 1980). A proposed disadvantage of territorial defense in small insectivorous species is that it limits the range of an individual to a small defendable area (Greenberg 1984). The present study found that Northern Parula individuals tended to limit their range of movement, whether or not they defended a territory, suggesting that sedentary behavior might confer an advantage. Such advantages may include increased feeding efficiency based on better knowledge of resources, and improved predator avoidance through familiarity with the activity patterns of local predators and the reactions of other residents to predators. Possible social advantages to a sedentary individual might include site-related dominance (Wiley and Wiley 1980) and the ability to assess more accurately the outcomes of interactions with known individuals.

The sedentary nature of Neotropical migrant landbirds in winter has important implications for conservation. Destruction of winter habitat is likely to displace sedentary individuals from their familiar home ranges. In view of recent findings that wanderers suffer higher mortality than sedentary indviduals (Rappole et al. 1989), habitat destruction might result in decreased probabilities that experienced sedentary individuals, displaced from their home ranges, will survive the winter season. Whether individuals do indeed suffer higher mortality after loss of their home ranges is an important question that has yet to be answered.

A recurring theme among studies of habitat preferences and spacing systems of Neotropical migrants is that their social behavior is remarkably flexible and responsive to habitat conditions. For example, Northern Parulas tended to form flocks more often on islands with more fragmented habitats (Ewert and Askins in press). The extent of variation in habitat quality on different islands might also explain why habitat segregation by sex is found in some areas (Wunderle, this volume) but not in others (Holmes et al. 1989). In habitats that support higher wintering densities of conspecifics, aggressive behavior among conspecifics is more frequent (Mabey and Morton, this volume). To be able to predict how a species will respond to changes in its environment, it will be crucial to understand more fully the mechanisms responsible for this variation. In particular it will be important to determine the limits of behavioral flexibility of a particular species in responding to changing habitats.

Some behavioral strategies of warblers wintering at the CRNWR are likely responses to features of this particular second-growth habitat. Although the grid habitat was obviously rich in foraging sites, apparently it contained few safe roost sites because migrants usually left their home ranges each afternoon to roost communally in adjacent habitats. The adoption of this unusual behavioral strategy, reported to date only for migrant warblers in Puerto Rico, reveals an inherent plasticity in migrant responses to their environment. Moreover, this finding suggests that while second-growth habitats often support high abundances of Neotropical migrants, these areas might be deficient in important ways, such as lacking in roost sites. Results such as these underline the importance of the spatial distribution of habitats in the ecology and conservation of migrant landbirds.

In summary, the socioecology of Neotropical migrant warblers wintering in a second-growth habitat in southwestern Puerto Rico was surprisingly complex. Whereas all species exhibited high site fidelity, they varied in their response to the habitat and to other warbler species. Territorial behavior differed among species and individuals, as well as between sexes. Strategies adopted by an individual typically persisted from year to year, although some individuals became more sedentary or territorial in later years. Although the resource base was not quantified, obvious seasonal changes in resource availability were cued to rainfall (e.g., abundance of lepidopteran larvae and amount of cover afforded by the deciduous foliage). If resource availability affects spacing systems, seasonal variation is also likely to occur in the spacing behavior of individuals. More work is needed to determine why individuals adopt a particular behavioral strategy, including information on resource availability over space and time, and the dynamics of social interactions among individuals through the season.

Acknowledgments

This study would not have been possible without the generous help of several able and enthusiastic field assistants. For their long hours in the field I thank E. Carey, C. Cutler, C. Hill, T. Blodgett, P. Hark, G. Jongejan, K. Frey, P. Rodewald, and R. Minear. As manager of CRNWR, S. Furniss provided the permission, facilities, equipment, and necessary permits to conduct the study. Plant specimens were identified by S. Silander, G. Proctor, and P. McKensie. For their assistance and hospitality, I am indebted to the USFWS personnel of the CRNWR and others, including J. Collazo, R. DiRosa, M. Rodriguez, P. Geer, M. Conser, D. Mignon, S. Rice, and especially, S. and M. Furniss. For their continued support through various phases of this study I also thank A. Pinder, D. Kroodsma, G. Drake, D. Spector, T. Highsmith, and B. Freedman. I am grateful to T. Sherry, R. Holmes, R. Greenberg, D. Kroodsma, D. McKinnon, two anonymous reviewers, and the editors for their insightful and instructive comments on this paper. Financial assistance was provided by a Bergstrom Memorial Research Award from the Association of Field Ornithologists and a grant from P. Geer of Boqueron.

Literature cited

Brown, J.L. 1964. The evolution of diversity in avian territorial systems. *Wilson Bull.* 76:160–169.

Chipley, R.M. 1976. The impact of wintering migrant wood warblers on resident insectivorous passerines in a subtropical Colombian oak woods. *Living Bird* 15:119–141.

Desrochers, A. 1989. Sex, dominance, and microhabitat use in wintering Black-capped Chickadees: A field experiment. *Ecology* 70:636–645.

Eaton, S.W. 1953. Wood warblers wintering in Cuba. *Wilson Bull.* 65:169–174.

Emlen, J.T. 1973. Territorial aggression at Bahama Agave blossoms. *Wilson Bull.* 85:71–74.

Ewert, D.N., and R.A. Askins. In press. Flocking behavior of migratory warblers in winter in the Virgin Islands. *Condor.*

Faaborg, J., and W.J. Arendt. 1984. Population sizes and philopatry of winter resident warblers in Puerto Rico. *J. Field Ornithol.* 55:376–378.

Fretwell, S. 1980. Evolution of migration in relation to factors regulating bird numbers. Pages 517–527 in *Migrant Birds in the Neotropics: Ecology, Behavior, Distribution and Conservation,* A. Keast and E.S. Morton, eds. Washington: Smithsonian Institution Press.

Greenberg, R. 1984. The winter exploitation systems of Bay-breasted and Chestnut-sided Warblers in Panama. *Univ. Calif. Publ. Zool.* 116:1–107.

Holmes, R.T., T.W. Sherry, and L. Reitsma. 1989. Population structure, territoriality and overwinter survival of two migrant warbler species in Jamaica. *Condor* 91:545–561.

Howell, T.R. 1971. An ecological study of the birds of the lowland pine savanna and adjacent rain forest in northeastern Nicaragua. *Living Bird* 10:185–242.

Kale, H.W., II. 1967. Aggressive behavior by a migrating Cape May Warbler. *Auk* 84:120–121.

Keast, A. 1980. Spatial relationships between migratory parulid warblers and their ecological counterparts in the neotropics. Pages 109–130 in *Migrant Birds in the Neotropics: Ecology, Behavior, Distribution and Conservation,* A. Keast and E.S. Morton, eds. Washington: Smithsonian Institution Press.

Keast, A., and E.S. Morton, eds. 1980. *Migrant Birds in the Neotropics: Ecology, Behavior, Distribution, and Conservation.* Washington: Smithsonian Institution Press.

Lack, D., and P. Lack. 1972. Wintering warblers in Jamaica. *Living Bird* 11:129–153.

Leck, C.F. 1972. Observations of birds at Cecropia trees in Puerto Rico. *Wilson Bull.* 84:498–500.

Lynch, J.F. 1989. Distribution of overwintering Nearctic migrants in the Yucatan Peninsula, I: General patterns of occurrence. *Condor* 91:515–544.

Morse, D.H. 1968. A quantitative study of foraging of male and female spruce-woods warblers. *Ecology* 49:779–784.

———. 1976. Hostile encounters among spruce-woods warblers (Dendroica, Parulidae). *Anim. Behav.* 24:764–771.

Morton, E.S. 1980. Adaptations to seasonal changes by migrant land birds in the Panama Canal Zone. Pages 437–476 in *Migrant Birds in the Neotropics: Ecology, Behavior, Distribution and Conservation,* A. Keast and E.S. Morton, eds. Washington: Smithsonian Institution Press.

Myers, J.P., P.G. Connors, and F.A. Pitelka. 1979. Territoriality in non-breeding shorebirds. Pages 231–246 in *Shorebirds in Marine Environments,* F.A. Pitelka, ed. Studies in Avian Biology No 2.

Nolan, V., Jr. 1978. *The Ecology and Behavior of the Prairie Warbler* Dendroica discolor. Ornithol. Monogr. 26.

Orians, G.H. 1961. The ecology of blackbird (*Agelaius*) social systems. *Ecol. Monogr.* 31:285–312.

Ornat, A.L., and R. Greenberg. 1990. Sexual segregation by habitat in migratory warblers in Quintana Roo, Mexico. *Auk* 107:539–543.

Post, W. 1978. Social and foraging behavior of warblers wintering in Puerto Rican coastal scrub. *Wilson Bull.* 90:197–214.

Rappole, J.H., and D.W. Warner. 1980. Ecological aspects of migrant bird behavior in Veracruz, Mexico. Pages 353–393 in *Migrant Birds in the Neotropics: Ecology, Behavior, Distribution and Conservation,* A. Keast and E.S. Morton, eds. Washington: Smithsonian Institution Press.

Rappole, J.H., E.S. Morton, T.E. Lovejoy, III, and J.L. Ruos. 1983. *Nearctic Avian Migrants in the Neotropics.* Washington: U.S. Fish and Wildlife Service.

Rappole, J.H., M.A. Ramos, and K. Winker. 1989. Wintering Wood Thrush movements and mortality in southern Veracruz. *Auk* 106:402–410.

Robbins, C.S., J.R. Sauer, R.S. Greenberg, and S. Droege. 1989. Population declines in North American birds that migrate to the neotropics. *Proc. Natl. Acad. Sci.* 86:7658–7662.

Roberts, J.O. 1971. Survival among some North American wood warblers. *Bird-Banding* 42:165–184.

Sealy, S.G. 1989. Defense of nectar sources by migrating Cape May Warblers. *J. Field Ornithol.* 60:89–93.

Schwartz, P. 1964. The Northern Waterthrush in Venezuela. *Living Bird* 3:169–184.

Sokal, R.R., and F.J. Rohlf. 1981. *Biometry: The Principles and Practice of Statistics in Biological Research.* 2d ed. San Francisco: W.H. Freeman and Co.

Tramer, E.J., and T.R. Kemp. 1980. Foraging ecology of migrant and resident warblers and vireos in the highlands of Costa Rica. Pages 285–296 in *Migrant Birds in the Neotropics: Ecology, Behavior, Distribution and Conservation,* A. Keast and E.S. Morton, eds. Washington: Smithsonian Institution Press.

Waide, R.B. 1981. Interactions between resident and migrant birds in Campeche, Mexico. *Trop. Ecol.* 22:134–154.

Wiley, R.H., and M.S. Wiley. 1980. Territorial behavior of a blackbird: Mechanisms of site-dependent dominance. *Behaviour* 73:130–154.

DAVID A. WIEDENFELD*
Department of Biological Science
Florida State University
Tallahassee, Florida 32306-2043

Foraging in temperate- and tropical-breeding and wintering male Yellow Warblers

Abstract. Migratory "Yellow" forms of *Dendroica petechia* breed in North America. In winter they occur in mangrove woodlands along with resident "Mangrove" Warblers, another form of the same species but distinguishable by plumage and morphology. I studied foraging behavior of males during the breeding season in Colorado, Montana, and Ontario, and in winter at three sites in Panama and one in Yucatan, Mexico. On their wintering grounds, "Yellow" Warblers shift their foraging behavior from their breeding pattern toward that of "Mangrove" Warblers. This shift is not complete, and occurs primarily in their selection of tree height or distance from canopy edge, features only indirectly related to prey capture. Foraging rate and perch-to-perch attack distance remain largely unchanged. If the shift in foraging behavior in the Yellow Warbler can be generalized to other species, birds might be able to adjust their foraging behavior for small changes in habitat physiognomy. However, results from this study on *Dendroica petechia* suggest that birds might not be able to accommodate large, rapid shifts in habitat structure, such as those caused by human destruction of primary habitats.

Sinopsis. Las formas "amarillas" migratorias de *Dendroica petechia* anidan en Norteamérica. En invierno se encuentran en bosques de manglar junto con "reinitas mangleteras" residentes, otra forma de la misma especie distinguible de la anterior por plumaje y morfología. Yo estudié el comportamiento de forrajeo de los machos durante la estación reproductiva en Colorado, Montana y Ontario y en invierno en tres sitios en Panamá y uno en Yucatán, México. En sus zonas de invernada las "reinitas amarillas" cambian su patrón de forrajeo de la época de cría por el de las "reinitas mangleteras". Este cambio no es completo e incluye primariamente la altura de los árboles o la distancia del borde del dosel, características relacionadas solamente de manera indirecta con la captura de presas. La tasa de forrajeo y la distancia de ataque de percha a percha permanecen casi sin alteraciones. Si el cambio en el comportamiento de forrajeo de *D. petechia* puede generalizarse a otras especies, las aves podrían ser entonces capaces de ajustar su comportamiento alimentario a pequeños cambios en la fisionomía del habitat. Sin embar-

*Current address: Museum of Natural Science, Room 119, Foster Hall, Louisiana State University, Baton Rouge, LA 70803.

go, los resultados de este estudio sugieren que las aves tal vez no serían capaces de acomodarse a grandes y rápidos cambios en la estructura del habitat, tales como los causados por la destrucción de habitats primarios.

Ornithologists expect bird species to use different foraging techniques in different parts of their geographic ranges, at least partly because habitat structure and food sources vary from place to place. Because resources vary, the techniques birds use to obtain food are expected to vary also. This expectation has seldom been examined or verified quantitatively, and in particular, few comparisons have been made between the tropics and the temperate zone. Understanding differences and similarities in foraging behavior, both its prey-capture and microhabitat choice aspects, in a migrant species between its temperate-zone breeding and tropical wintering areas adds to understanding the species' ecology. Differences and similarities in foraging behavior between a migrants' breeding and wintering areas also can have important conservation implications, allowing us to understand how changes in habitats could affect the bird's populations.

Although many studies have considered foraging behavior of migrant birds, particularly New World warblers, in the tropics (e.g., Lack and Lack 1972, Post 1978, Greenberg 1979), and community-oriented studies of niche overlap between migrants and residents in the tropics (e.g., Baker and Baker 1973, Bennett 1980, Hutto 1981), few comparisons have been made of the foraging behavior of a single species in both its breeding and wintering ranges (Rabenold 1980, Mallory 1981, and Greenberg 1987b). In none of these studies was there a standard against which the shift in the migratory birds' behavior could be compared to that of a permanent tropical resident. Although these studies could identify a shift in foraging behavior, the direction and magnitude of the shift could not be assessed. This study, then, addresses these two questions: (1) when it is in the tropics, does a migrant's foraging become more like that of a similar but tropical bird, or does it shift in some other direction? and (2) if the migrant's foraging becomes more like that of a tropical bird, can it forage completely as a tropical bird, or does it continue foraging partially as a temperate-zone bird?

Few choices of passerine species allow us to make these comparisons; even most widespread migratory species do not have tropical-breeding populations. One of the few that does is the Yellow Warbler (*Dendroica petechia*). Within this single species, it is possible to determine how the temperate-breeding populations shift their foraging behavior on the wintering grounds in relation to that of birds that live in the tropics year-round.

The Yellow Warbler has the largest breeding range of any wood-warbler species, breeding from near the Arctic Circle to the equator. Breeding populations in the northern temperate zone are all migratory. Because tropical-breeding populations are not known to migrate, the migratory and nonmigratory forms can occur in the same habitat in winter. The Yellow Warbler has the added advantage that the two forms that come together have distinct plumages. In fact, the two forms were once considered to be two species. The form that breeds in North America was called the "Yellow" Warbler, and the nonmigratory, tropical-breeding form was called the "Mangrove" Warbler. The "Yellow" Warbler is referred to in the A.O.U. Check-list (A.O.U. 1983) as the *Dendroica petechia aestiva* subspecies group; the "Mangrove" Warbler as the *D. p. erithachorides* subspecies group. These two groups were lumped because there are intermediate forms, mostly on islands in the Caribbean (Lowery and Monroe 1968). Although the species' common name is now Yellow Warbler, for clarity in this paper, I shall use the old names: "Yellow Warbler" will refer to the population that breeds in the U.S. and Canada and winters in the Neotropics, and "Mangrove Warbler" will designate the permanent resident tropical forms.

"Mangrove" Warblers, as the name suggests, occur almost strictly in mangrove woodlands along the coasts of Mexico, Central America, and northern South America (Lowery and Monroe 1968). They rarely occur even a few hundred meters from mangrove woods. In winter, "Yellow" Warblers also occur in mangrove woods, although many of them winter inland away from the mangroves (Wetmore et al. 1984; pers. obs.). My observations suggest that about one-sixth of the individuals in the mangrove swamps at my field sites are "Yellow" Warblers, and the rest are "Mangrove" Warblers.

Methods

Only males will be considered in this paper, because females of the two forms are nearly indistinguishable in the field. Many subspecies have been described (Lowery and Monroe 1968), but I will just compare the two major plumage types, ignoring subspecies designations.

STUDY SITES

I observed "Yellow" and "Mangrove" warblers foraging at seven study sites, three in North America and four in Middle America (Fig. 1). At the Middle American study sites I obtained information on both wintering "Yellow" Warblers and on "Mangrove" Warblers; in North America, of course, there were only breeding "Yellow" Warblers. A brief description of each site follows.

1. Queen's University Biological Station, Ontario,

FIGURE 1. Seven study sites where foraging behavior data were collected. *A*, Queen's University Biological Station, Ontario; *B*, Townsend, Montana; *C*, Graneros Creek, Colorado; *D*, Celestún, Yucatan, Mexico; *E*, Isla Galeta, Canal Zone, Panama; *F*, Playa El Agallito, Prov. Herrera, Panama; *G*, Río Juan Díaz, Prov. Panamá, Panama.

Canada (76°21' W, 44°33' N). This site is near the town of Chaffey's Locks, and about 30 km north of Kingston, Ontario. The study area is mostly old field and edge. Beech (*Fagus* sp.) and oak (*Quercus* sp.) trees predominate, although some willows (*Salix* sp.) occur along water courses. More conifers occur here than at the other sites. I observed 109 foraging events at the Station from 2 through 17 June 1986.

2. Townsend, Montana, U.S.A. (111°32' W, 46°21' N). This site includes habitat along the Missouri River at the south end of Canyon Ferry Lake. The habitat consists almost solely of willows near the water and cottonwood trees (*Populus deltoides*) farther back from it. I observed 152 foraging events at this site from 16 June through 4 July 1987.

3. Graneros Creek, near Rye, Colorado, U.S.A. (104°52' W, 37°55' N). The Yellow Warbler habitat along the creek is more linear than at the two previous sites, being confined mostly to a band about 75 m wide, beyond which is open grassland. Trees at the site are primarily low scrub oaks, usually less than 5 m high, with a few willows and cottonwoods. I obtained data on 98 foraging events between 24 May and 10 June 1987.

4. Celestún, Yucatan, Mexico (90°23' W, 20°52' N). This study site lies along the western shore of Estero

Celestún, a shallow, tidal lagoon. The habitat at this and the other tropical sites is almost exclusively mangrove woodlands, composed of a fairly even mixture of red mangrove (*Rhizophora mangle*) and black mangrove (*Avicennia nitida*). Here the mangroves are in a strip usually not more than about 100 m wide along the banks of the lagoon. I observed 18 foraging events on "Yellow" and 40 foraging events on "Mangrove" warblers here from 26 January through 22 February 1988.

5. Isla Galeta, Canal Zone, Panama (79°52' W, 9°24' N). Isla Galeta is just east of the Caribbean entrance to the Panama Canal. The site includes large areas of low red mangroves, with some strips of low black mangroves along the road from Coco Solo. I observed 23 foraging events on "Yellow" and 58 events on "Mangrove" warblers at this site, from 16 March through 2 April 1986 and 29 January through 7 February 1987.

6. Playa El Agallito, Prov. Herrera, Panama (80°22' W, 8°0' N). This site is on the east coast of the Azuero Peninsula, about 5 km east of the town of Chitré. The habitat is primarily medium-height black mangroves. I obtained foraging data mainly on "Mangrove" Warblers (76 foraging events; only five on "Yellow" Warblers) on 9 and 10 April 1986 and 19 through 23 January 1987.

7. Mouth of the Río Juan Díaz, Prov. Panamá, Panama (79°27' W, 9°1' N). This site is at the eastern edge of Panama City. It is a large area composed almost exclusively of tall black mangroves. As at the Playa El Agallito site, I saw mainly "Mangrove" Warblers here. I collected data (118 foraging events on "Mangrove" Warblers; only seven on "Yellow" Warblers) here from 4 through 7 April 1986 and 8 through 16 February 1987.

FORAGING BEHAVIOR ANALYSIS

The species takes its prey by two methods. In perch actions, the bird captures prey while standing on its perch. This is the way many wrens and warblers commonly catch their prey. In aerial actions, the *bird* itself is flying when it captures the food item. In this latter category I have combined three techniques used by Yellow Warblers that are distinguished by Fitzpatrick (1980): hover-gleaning, outward-striking, and aerial-hawking. Aerial actions are commonly used by flycatchers when obtaining their prey.

I recorded the first prey-capture event each time that I located a "Yellow" or "Mangrove" warbler, and tried not to record any other event on the same bird until at least the next day. Morrison (1984) and Tacha et al. (1985) found that recording a single event on each bird, rather than recording a sequence of events on the same bird, tends to miss some rare events. However, recording a single event avoids the problem of autocorrelation inherent in sequence data. Wagner (1981) determined that sequences are biased toward visible locations, and single event records are biased toward information on perch selection. Because neither technique is always preferable, I used the single-event method, to reduce the need to treat the data for autocorrelation. It is not difficult to avoid using the same bird repeatedly, because even the migrant "Yellow" Warblers are territorial in winter (Morton 1976, 1980, Hutto 1981, Wetmore et al. 1984), and I could avoid seeing a bird again by walking out of its territory.

At each prey-capture event, I recorded three characters that are directly related to a bird's prey capture. First, I recorded the action used by the bird to catch its prey (Perch or Aerial action), but made no attempt to determine whether the attack was successful or not. Next, I measured the amount of time from the attack to, but not including, the next attack, as a measure of foraging rate, using an electronic metronome which clicked at 1-sec intervals. For the aerial actions I also recorded the distance the bird flew to its prey item, and the distance beyond to its next perch. These distances, added together, provide a perch-to-perch attack distance, a measure of the agility and ability of the bird to maneuver within the foliage.

I also used five measurements of the microhabitat choice of the bird; these are only indirectly related to the bird's prey capture: (1) height (m) of the bird, (2) height (m) of tree, (3) proportional height of bird to height of the tree, (4) distance (m) of bird from canopy edge, and (5) estimate of foliage density within a 1/2-m radius sphere around the foraging bird (0 = no leaves to 5 = no light visible from beyond the bird). I measured distances with an extension ruler (for tree height, bird height, etc.), or by estimating numbers of warbler-lengths for short attack distances. I made no attempt to characterize the entire habitat, but only to see what part of it the birds selected.

I used the chi-squared statistic to compare the frequencies of use of the foraging action categories. Most of the remaining characters had highly skewed distributions; all other comparisons were made using the Mann-Whitney U-test. Significance levels for all tests were adjusted for multiple comparisons using the Bonferroni correction (Harris 1985).

Results

WITHIN THE TEMPERATE ZONE. No differences were found among the three North American study sites for any of the three direct or five indirect foraging characters, except for a significantly shorter perch-to-perch attack distance between the Ontario and Colorado sites (Table 1). Therefore, although the sites were widely spaced, little difference was found among the "Yellow" Warblers' foraging behavior, in either its prey capture or microhabi-

TABLE 1. Percentages of actions and median values for foraging and microhabitat characters of "Yellow" Warblers at three North American sites

Characters	Ontario ($n=109$)	Montana ($n=152$)	Colorado ($n=98$)
Prey-capture Characters			
Action (%)			
Perch actions	58	59	70
Aerial actions	43	40	29
Perch-to-perch attack	0.6	0.8	0.9
distance (m)	(0–1.8)	(0–24.6)	(0–9.5)
Foraging rate (sec)	14	11	14
	(3–66)	(3–41)	(4–175)
Microhabitat Characters			
Height of bird (m)	4.0	4.3	6.1
	(0.5–14.9)	(0–14.6)	(0.3–12.5)
Height of tree (m)	7.9	6.7	7.5
	(0.5–15.3)	(0.3–16.8)	(1.5–15.3)
Proportional height	0.71	0.73	0.81
	(0.14–1)	(0–1)	(0.08–1)
Distance from edge	0.2	0.3	0.2
of canopy (m)	(0–4.6)	(0–3.7)	(0–4.9)
Foliage density (0–5)	2.0	2.0	2.5
	(0–4)	(0–4)	(0–5)

NOTE: n = the number of foraging events observed. Range of values indicated in parentheses. Tests of all pairs showed no significant differences except in perch-to-perch attack distance between Montana and Colorado ($P < 0.05$).

tat aspects, even though prey species and plant species probably vary from site to site.

WITHIN THE TROPICS. Sample sizes of "Yellow" Warblers from each study site in the tropics were too small for separate analysis. However, for "Mangrove" Warblers, the samples were sufficiently large for comparison among the sites. Among the three Panamanian study sites there were few significant differences in the "Mangrove" Warblers (medians in Table 2, tests in Table 3). All of the differences among these sites were in habitat characters. Foraging behavior of warblers at the Isla Galeta and Playa El Agallito sites was similar, although they are on opposite coasts of Panama. The foraging behavior of the birds at Playa El Agallito and Río Juan Díaz, both on the Pacific coast of Panama, was more different than either was from the Isla Galeta site, on the Caribbean coast.

The Celestún, Mexico, site is more than 1500 km from any of the Panamanian sites. Not surprisingly, more differences in foraging behavior were found between the Celestún and Panamanian sites than among the Panamanian sites. Again, however, the differences

TABLE 2. Percentages of actions and median values for foraging and microhabitat characters of "Mangrove" Warblers at four Middle American sites

Characters	Isla Galeta (n=58)	Río Juan Díaz (n=118)	Playa El Agallito (n=76)	Celestún (n=40)
Prey-capture characters				
Action (%)				
Perch actions	73	76	81	75
Aerial actions	28	24	20	26
Perch-to-perch attack distance (m)	1.1	1.1	1.2	0.8
	(0–3.2)	(0–11.1)	(0–4.0)	(0–4.0)
Foraging rate (sec)	14	15	14	10
	(3–100)	(3–58)	(2–61)	(3–17)
Microhabitat characters				
Height of bird (m)	4.3	6.1	5.5	8.4
	(0–11.6)	(0–18.3)	(0–15.3)	(2.4–16.8)
Height of tree (m)	9.2	13.7	8.8	9.9
	(1.5–13.7)	(1.2–19.8)	(0.5–16.8)	(3.1–18.9)
Proportional height	0.50	0.45	0.72	0.88
	(0–1)	(0–0.92)	(0–1)	(0.53–1)
Distance from edge of canopy (m)	0.9	2.4	0.6	0.3
	(0–10.1)	(0–19.7)	(0–9.2)	(0–4.9)
Foliage density (0–5)	2.0	2.0	2.0	2.0
	(0–4)	(0–5)	(0–3)	(0–4)

NOTE: Range of values indicated in parentheses.

TABLE 3. Tests between locality pairs, for four tropical sites ("Mangrove" Warblers only)

Character	Gal. vs. RJD	Gal. vs. Pla.	RJD vs. Pla.	Pla. vs. Cel.	RJD vs. Cel.	Pla. vs. Cel.
Prey-capture characters						
Action	+	+	+	+	+	+
Perch-to-perch attack distance	+	+	+	+	+	+
Foraging rate	+	+	+	0.27	**0.01**	+
Microhabitat characters						
Height of bird	0.24	+	+	**< .01**	**0.05**	**0.01**
Height of tree	**< .01**	+	**< .01**	+	**0.01**	**< .01**
Proportional height	+	0.16	**< .01**	**< .01**	**< .01**	**< .01**
Distance from edge of canopy	+	0.32	**< .01**	**0.01**	**< .01**	+
Foliage density	+	+	+	+	+	**< .01**

NOTE: Tests as in Table 2; bold-faced values are significant ($P < 0.05$, corrected for multiple tests). Locality abbreviations are: Gal.= Isla Galeta; RJD= Río Juan Díaz; Pla.= Playa El Agallito; Cel.= Celestún, Mexico.

are mostly in the characters indirectly related to foraging rather than in the ones directly related to prey capture (Tables 2, 3). "Mangrove" Warblers at Celestún attack prey at shorter intervals than do birds from the Río Juan Díaz, but not more than birds from Isla Galeta or Playa El Agallito.

BETWEEN THE TROPICS AND THE TEMPERATE ZONE. For comparison of foraging behavior in the tropics and temperate zone, I have combined data from birds from all three sites in North America and all four sites in Middle America. The "Yellow" Warblers from the temperate zone are one group (temperate "Yellow" Warblers), "Yellow" Warblers from the tropical sites are a second group (tropical "Yellow" Warblers), and the "Mangrove"

Warblers are a third group.

Temperate "Yellow" Warblers are significantly different from "Mangrove" Warblers in six of the eight characters (medians in Table 4, tests in Table 5). Temperate "Yellow" Warblers used aerial foraging actions more than did "Mangrove" Warblers, but flew a shorter perch-to-perch attack distance. The two forms foraged at the same rate (no statistical significance, Table 5). Temperate "Yellow" Warblers chose a proportionately higher position in the tree, although they were absolutely lower and in shorter trees than were "Mangrove" Warblers. They also foraged nearer to the edge of the trees' canopy. Temperate "Yellow" Warblers used areas with about the same foliage density as "Mangrove" Warblers.

The "Yellow" Warblers do not drastically shift their foraging behaviors in the tropics. A comparison of temperate "Yellow" Warblers with tropical "Yellow" Warblers shows no significant differences in any character except distance from canopy edge (Table 5); tropical "Yellow" Warblers foraged farther beneath the canopy than did temperate "Yellow" Warblers. However, there was some shift in the "Yellow" Warblers' foraging behavior from the temperate zone to the tropics, because tropical "Yellow" Warblers also are not significantly different from "Mangrove" Warblers in any character (except proportional height, Table 5). Because "Mangrove" and temperate "Yellow" Warblers differ in most characters, the distribution of values for tropical "Yellow" Warblers must be intermediate to, or overlap, distributions of temperate "Yellow" Warblers and "Mangrove" Warblers. This indicates a shift in foraging behavior from the temperate "Yellow" Warbler type toward the "Mangrove" Warbler type when "Yellow" Warblers migrate south. However, the shift is not the same across all characters. Examination of the medians of the characters directly associated with prey capture shows that temperate "Yellow" Warblers and tropical "Yellow" Warblers have not shifted in foraging rate or attack distance, only in proportions of actions used in capturing prey. The medians of the indirect characters, however, show both "Mangrove" and tropical "Yellow" Warblers in the tropics to be similar to each other and both different from the temperate "Yellow" Warblers.

Discussion

Differences between foraging birds in the temperate zone and birds in the tropics were much greater than any differences within the two regions. This is not a sur-

TABLE 4. Percentages of actions and median values for foraging and microhabitat characters in the three major groups of *Dendroica petechia*

Characters	Temperate "Yellow" Warblers ($n = 373$)	Tropical "Yellow" Warblers ($n = 53$)	"Mangrove" Warblers ($n = 292$)
Prey-capture characters			
Action (%)			
Perch actions	62	81	76
Aerial actions	38	19	23
Perch-to-perch attack distance (m)	0.8	0.7	1.1
	(0–24.6)	(0–1.8)	(0–11.1)
Foraging rate (sec)	12	12	15
	(3–175)	(3–67)	(2–100)
Microhabitat characters			
Height of bird (m)	4.9	6.4	6.1
	(0–14.9)	(0.5–16.5)	(0–18.3)
Height of tree (m)	7.5	9.8	10.7
	(0.3–16.8)	(1.2–18.3)	(0.5–19.8)
Proportional height	0.75	0.77	0.63
	(0–1)	(0.08–1)	(0–1)
Distance from edge of canopy (m)	0.2	1.2	1.2
	(0–4.9)	(0–6.7)	(0–19.7)
Foliage density (0–5)	2.0	2.0	2.0
	(0–5)	(0–4)	(0–5)

NOTE: Range of values given in parentheses.

TABLE 5. Statistical tests between group pairs, for three major groups

Characters	Temp. "Yellow" vs. "Mangrove"	Temp. "Yellow" vs. Trop. "Yellow"	Trop. "Yellow" vs. "Mangrove"
Prey-capture characters			
Action	**0.01**	0.12	+
Perch-to-perch attack distance	**< .01**	+	+
Foraging rate	+	+	+
Microhabitat characters			
Height of bird	**0.01**	0.25	+
Height of tree	**< .01**	0.15	+
Proportional height	**< .01**	+	**0.02**
Distance from edge of canopy	**< .01**	**< .01**	+
Foliage density	+	+	+

NOTE: Tests as in Table 2; bold-faced values are significant ($P < 0.05$, corrected for multiple tests).

prising result because the two regions obviously have a number of major differences. The warblers foraging in mangrove woodlands in the tropics are not only exposed to a different climate from those foraging in the temperate zone, but also must forage in different species of trees, usually in an area with very low plant species diversity (usually the only plants are mangrove trees themselves), on different prey species, and in a coastal, salt-water habitat not encountered by the birds in the temperate zone.

For this species, the results above provide the answers to the two questions stated earlier. The migrant warblers' foraging behavior shifts to become like that of their year-round tropical-resident counterparts, but that shift is not complete.

Most of the shift in foraging behavior was made in characters indirectly related to prey capture, that is, in the habitat characters such as tree height or distance from edge of canopy. These characters are probably partially dependent on habitat structure and tree species. Because habitats are different between the tropics and temperate zone as described above, the five indirect characters should be the ones most likely to change when the birds migrate from their breeding grounds to the wintering areas.

Several reasons potentially explain the partial shift in "Yellow" Warblers' foraging behavior. If their morphology is adapted for foraging on their breeding grounds or to migration, those adaptations might restrict the birds' foraging abilities when on their wintering grounds. Wiedenfeld (1988) showed that "Yellow" and "Mangrove" Warblers have different wing shapes and different abilities to hover, and those differences can affect foraging abilities.

A nonexclusive alternative is that "Yellow" Warblers cannot shift their foraging behavior completely because

of constraints from innate and/or learned behavior differences. The *Dendroica petechia erithachorides* and *D. p. aestiva* subspecies groups have different phylogenetic histories. Work by Greenberg (1984a,b, 1987a,b) on other species of *Dendroica* and the Worm-eating Warbler (*Helmitheros vermivorus*) showed innately controlled as well as learned aspects to the birds' foraging behavior. These factors could at least partially determine the "Yellow" Warblers abilities to shift their behavior.

Knowledge of additional dimensions of foraging, such as diet, can probably add greatly to our understanding of the foraging behavior shift. The varied environments encountered by a migrating warbler present difficult problems to it, and we are only beginning to sort out how birds solve those problems.

CONSERVATION IMPLICATIONS

The Yellow Warbler will probably never be threatened by forest clearing in the tropics the way some other species might be. The species is quite at home in anthropogenous habitats. The migrant form can be common in mango (*Mangifera indica*) orchards, or in ornamental trees planted in towns, as well as several natural open habitats, such as dry scrub, savanna, and marshlands (ffrench 1973). Although the "Mangrove" Warblers in this study are restricted primarily to mangrove habitats, other nonmigratory forms, occurring principally on islands of the Caribbean, also occupy dry scrub and acacia savanna (Bond 1971, Voous 1983). However, if the foraging behavior flexibility and shift in foraging behavior in migrants seen in the Yellow Warbler can be generalized to other species, there are implications to conservation of those species.

Although there is some flexibility in "Yellow" Warblers' foraging behavior, most of that flexibility is in characters related to habitat. Thus, one would expect any individual warbler to be able to adapt to a forest that is physiognomically similar to its "natural" habitat. Destruction of a primary forest and replacement of it with a physiognomically similar second growth therefore might not severely affect the birds' foraging behavior. The warblers' foraging flexibility has limits, however, and changing the forest too much would at some point shift its physiognomy beyond the warblers' ability to cope on a nonevolutionary time scale. Of course, a change in the forest without a large change in its physiognomy might cause a change in the prey species available, a change to which the warblers might not be able to adjust. I have not addressed questions of diet and prey availability in this paper. Because the warblers' foraging behavior flexibility is limited, however, the birds might be unable to adjust to large-scale, rapid, manmade changes in their environment.

Acknowledgments

Support for this project came from many sources. A Smithsonian Tropical Research Institute Short-term Fellowship supported much of the fieldwork in Panama. Other fieldwork was supported by Ducks Unlimited–Mexico, Montana Department of Fish, Wildlife, and Parks, Queen's University Biological Station, and the Josselyn Van Tyne Memorial Fund. Melissa G. Wiedenfeld provided material and immaterial support. Frances C. James and Joseph R. Wunderle read and commented on the manuscript.

Literature cited

American Ornithologists' Union. 1983. *Check-list of North American Birds*. 6th ed. Washington: American Ornithologists' Union.

Baker, M.C., and A.E. Baker. 1973. Niche relationships among six species of shorebirds on their wintering and breeding ranges. *Ecol. Monogr.* 43:193–212.

Bennett, S.E. 1980. Interspecific competition and the niche of the American Redstart (*Setophaga ruticilla*). Pages 319–335 in *Migrant Birds in the Neotropics: Ecology, Behavior, Distribution and Conservation*, A. Keast and E.S. Morton, eds. Washington: Smithsonian Institution Press.

Bond, J. 1971. *Birds of the West Indies*. Boston: Houghton Mifflin Co.

ffrench, R. 1973. *A Guide to the Birds of Trinidad and Tobago*. Wynnewood, Penn.: Livingston Publ. Co.

Fitzpatrick, J.W. 1980. Foraging behavior of Neotropical tyrant flycatchers. *Condor* 82:43–57.

Greenberg, R. 1979. Body size, breeding habitat, and winter exploitation systems in *Dendroica*. *Auk* 96:756–766.

———. 1984a. Differences in feeding neophobia in the tropical migrant wood warblers *Dendroica castanea* and *D. pensylvanica*. *J. Comp. Psychol.* 98:131–136.

———. 1984b. Neophobia in the foraging-site selection of a Neotropical migrant bird: An experimental study. *Proc. Natl. Acad. Sci.* 81:3778–3780.

———. 1987a. Development of dead leaf foraging in a tropical migrant warbler. *Ecology* 68:130–141.

———. 1987b. Seasonal foraging specialization in the Wormeating Warbler. *Condor* 89:158–168.

Harris, R.J. 1985. *A Primer of Multivariate Statistics*. 2d ed. New York: Academic Press.

Hutto, R. 1981. Seasonal variation in foraging behavior in some migratory western wood warblers. *Auk* 98:765–777.

Lack, D., and P. Lack. 1972. Wintering warblers in Jamaica. *Living Bird* 11:129–153.

Lowery, G.H., and B.L. Monroe. 1968. Family Parulidae. Pages 3–93 in *Check-list of Birds of the World*, R.A. Paynter, ed. Cambridge, Mass.: Museum of Comparative Zoology.

Mallory, E.P. 1981. Ecological, behavioral, and morphological adaptations of a migratory shorebird, the Whimbrel (*Numenius phaeopus*) in its different environments. Ph.D. Dissertation, Dartmouth College, Hanover, New Hampshire.

Morrison, M.L. 1984. Influence of sample size and sampling design on analysis of avian foraging behavior. *Condor* 86:146–150.

Morton, E.S. 1976. The adaptive significance of dull coloration in Yellow Warblers. *Condor* 78:423.

———. 1980. Adaptations to seasonal changes by migrant land birds in the Panama Canal Zone. Pages 437–453 in *Migrant Birds in the Neotropics: Ecology, Behavior, Distribution and Conservation*, A. Keast and E.S. Morton, eds. Washington: Smithsonian Institution Press.

Post, W. 1978. Social and foraging behavior of warblers wintering in Puerto Rican coastal scrub. *Wilson Bull.* 90:197–214.

Rabenold, K.N. 1980. The Black-throated Green Warbler in Panama: Geographical and seasonal comparison of foraging. Pages 297–307 in *Migrant Birds in the Neotropics: Ecology, Behavior, Distribution and Conservation*, A. Keast and E.S. Morton, eds. Washington: Smithsonian Institution Press.

Tacha, T.C., P.A. Vohs, and G.C. Iverson. 1985. A comparison of interval and continuous sampling methods for behavioral observations. *J. Field Ornithol.* 56:258–264.

Voous, K.H. 1983. *Birds of the Netherlands Antilles*. Zutphen, Netherlands: Walberg Pers.

Wagner, J.L. 1981. Visibility and bias in avian foraging data. *Condor* 83:263–264.

Wetmore, A., R.F. Pasquier, and S.L. Olson. 1984. *The Birds of the Republic of Panama, Part 4, Passeriformes: Hirundinidae (Swallows) to Fringillidae (Finches)*. Washington: Smithsonian Institution Press.

Wiedenfeld, D.A. 1988. Ecomorphology and foraging behavior of the Yellow Warbler (*Dendroica petechia*). Ph.D. Dissertation, Florida State University, Tallahassee, Florida.

SARAH E. MABEY*
Department of Zoology
University of Maryland
College Park, Maryland 20742

EUGENE S. MORTON
Department of Zoological Research
National Zoological Park
Smithsonian Institution
Washington, D.C. 20008

Demography and territorial behavior of wintering Kentucky Warblers in Panama

Abstract. Wintering Kentucky Warblers (*Oporornis formosus*) are both territorial and dependent upon moist lowland forest throughout their Neotropical nonbreeding range, making them particularly vulnerable to deforestation. We studied the behavioral ecology of Kentucky Warblers in two populations in Panama to determine their densities, over-winter survival, and site fidelity. Densities of Kentucky Warblers differed between sites and both were relatively lower than those reported for Veracruz, Mexico. The Panamanian populations also differed in the rate of natural territorial interactions and in time-to-response to playback, which might be related to differences in density. Over-winter survival, based on 34 color-banded individuals, was estimated to be from 25 to 59%. However, resighting and recapturing birds was extremely difficult, and the data on survivorship within and between winters are not conclusive. Based on variation in territorial behavior and population density, a comparative study of the Kentucky Warbler throughout its winter range is recommended.

Sinopsis. Durante la invernada, *Oporornis formosus* es territorial y dependiente de bosques húmedos de tierras bajas a lo largo de todo su areal de distribución neotropical no reproductiva, lo cual lo hace muy vulnerable a la deforestación. Nosotros estudiamos la ecología conductual de *O. formosus* en dos poblaciones en Panamá para determinar su densidad, supervivencia de invernada y fidelidad al sitio. Las densidades de esta especie difirieron entre los dos sitios y ambas fueron relativamente mas bajas que aquellas reportadas para Veracruz en México. Las poblaciones panameñas también difirieron en la tasa natural de interacciones territoriales y en su tiempo de respuesta a grabaciones, lo cual podría estar relacionado con diferencias en densidad poblacional. La supervivencia invernal, basada en 34 individuos marcados con anillos de color, fue estimada entre el 25 y el 59%. Sin embargo, el avistaje y la recaptura de aves marcadas fue extremadamente difícil y los datos sobre supervivencia dentro y entre inviernos no son concluyentes. Con base en la variación encontrada en el comportamiento territorial y la densidad, se recomienda un estudio de *O. formosus* a través de toda su área de invernada.

*Current address: Division of Natural Heritage, Department of Conservation and Recreation, 1500 E. Main Street, Richmond, VA 23219.

For most of the year, Kentucky Warblers (*Oporornis formosus*) are residents in the understory of moist, lowland tropical forests from southern Mexico to northern Colombia (Rappole et al. 1983, American Ornithologists' Union 1983). Recently, Lynch (1989) classified this species in the Yucatan as a "forest specialist" found only in tall and medium height semievergreen forests. Morton (1980) found them mainly concentrated in the moist forests of central and Atlantic Panama rather than on the drier Pacific side. Willis (1980) also reported finding Kentucky Warblers only in forest areas at least 50 years old on Barro Colorado Island in Panama, and Lovejoy (1983) pointed out that this species depends "very much on mature tropical forest." Thus, the Kentucky Warbler might be particularly vulnerable to tropical deforestation (Lynch 1989, Rappole and Morton 1982).

Previous attempts to determine migrant population fluctuations and their relationships to habitat disturbance have focused on determining trends in breeding populations (Temple and Temple 1976, Whitcomb et al. 1981, Robbins et al. 1986) or migrating populations (Jones 1986; Stewart 1987). These studies provide information that primarily addresses problems of North American habitat changes (but see Robbins et al. 1989). They do not, however, directly answer questions of winter survival rates, nor do they investigate environmental and ecological pressures that birds experience during the nonbreeding season. For example, Kentucky Warblers base their nonbreeding social system on individual territoriality (Morton 1980, Rappole and Warner 1980, E.O. Willis, pers. comm.). References to banded Kentucky Warblers returning to the same site in successive winters are common (Karr 1971, Ely 1973, Ely et al. 1977, Loftin 1977, Rappole and Warner 1980, J.R. Karr, pers. comm.), which indicates stable and sedentary local populations. These behavioral characteristics might compound the birds' sensitivity to tropical deforestation for at least two reasons. First, the number of individuals within a certain area is limited by the minimum size of territories. Second, site fidelity and territory maintenance for the entire nonbreeding season might interfere with an individual's ability to move to a new location if its home habitat is in some way altered.

Only a few studies have shown the relationship between behavior and survival during the nonbreeding season (Lynch et al. 1985, Morton et al. 1987, Holmes et al. 1989, Rappole et al. 1989). It is clear that behavior, as well as demography and ecology, should be considered in assessing the effects of environmental alteration on birds (Morton and Greenberg 1989).

Here, we investigate winter territoriality of Kentucky Warblers in relation to density, local distribution, site fidelity and over-winter survival near the southern end of their winter range.

Methods

Field work was conducted during late winter and early winter over two years: 14 February–14 March, 1988 (mid dry season); November 1988 (late wet season); 5 February–4 April, 1989 (denoted as study periods DS88, WS88, and DS89, respectively). Kentucky Warblers are common in Panama by October, settled on territories by November, and begin spring migration in late March (Mabey and Morton, pers. obs.).

STUDY SITES. Field work was conducted in central Panama on Barro Colorado Island (BCI, 14.8 km^2) in Gatun Lake and 7 km away in the Parque Nacional Soberania, along the first 7 km of the Pipeline Road (PIR). (For detailed descriptions of the two areas, see Bennett 1963, Karr 1971, Hespenheide 1980, Willis 1980, and Leigh et al. 1982.) The forest on the northeast side of BCI is about 60–90 years old, and that on the southwest side is over 100 years old (Willis 1980).

The flora of the Pipeline Road area is more diverse than that of BCI, with a greater number of canopy and understory species (R. Foster, pers. comm.). The Pipeline Road is about 10 m across, running approximately northwest for 17 km through mostly mature forest. Although the road is enclosed by overhanging branches of canopy trees for long stretches, the growth along its edges (occasionally up to 25 meters deep) tends to be younger, even scrubby in some patches, with fast growing second-growth tree species such as *Cochlospermum* and *Cecropia*.

Three sections of PIR were marked as transects during the DS88 study period as TI (2.1 km), TII (2.0 km), and TIII (1 km). Transects were chosen arbitrarily, without regard to the vegetation, and only TIII was chosen specifically for its steep slopes. In addition, one nontransect section of approximately 100 m at the intersection with the Rio Frijoles Road, was well studied.

Trails on BCI are marked every 100 m and were used as transects. The transect length on BCI was increased from 7 km to 15 km in successive study periods to increase sample size. Most of our study was conducted on the northwest side of the island.

SURVEY AND TERRITORY LOCATION PROCEDURE. To locate Kentucky Warblers quickly, we conducted playback surveys. An average of 30 sec of recorded Kentucky Warbler vocalizations (a mixture of mainly chips with some song/chip sequences) was played every 50 m from a Realistic cassette player attached to a Realistic amplified speaker at an amplitude slightly louder than normal to increase its range. Playback was broadcast over 360° to ensure even coverage and was not used during heavy rain or wind. Kentucky Warblers responded from as far away as 75–100 m away. Human listeners confirmed a

75-m radius coverage for playback in the field. Each playback was followed by a minimum 3-min silent observation interval to detect a response. Because we were also moving slowly along transects, this gave us ample time to detect the presence of Kentucky Warblers. The locations and, when possible, the band combinations of responding Kentucky Warblers were noted. These surveys helped us locate the majority of the individuals studied. Some birds, however, were located during other field activities as they responded to playback or vocalized independently. All surveys were conducted between 0600 and 1200 EST. Estimates of population density were calculated as the total number of birds detected over area surveyed (breadth of survey coverage = 150 m based on conservative estimates of playback coverage and our ability to hear Kentucky Warblers). Population density estimates were then standardized to birds per 10 ha.

Sites of response are considered to be part of a "territory" defined as a stationary or mobile area of "space-related dominance" (Kaufmann 1983), and are referred to as territories hereafter. Most sites of response were revisited at least once and many were revisited on four or more occasions during each study period (DS88, WS88, DS89) to check for Kentucky Warbler presence. Particular attention was given to response sites that had been occupied by marked individuals in previous study periods. A territory was considered empty after no response was detected on at least three thorough searches with playback on separate days.

CAPTURING, BANDING, AND BEHAVIORAL OBSERVATIONS. Individuals were captured using 8 × 2-m or 12 × 2-m mist nets usually set in the estimated center of the territory. When territory boundaries were unknown, we set our nets near the site of response to previous playback and assumed we were on the bird's territory. Recorded vocalizations were played from the net area to attract the presumed resident bird. Presence and activity of the target individual were noted before an attempt. Elapsed time between playback and vocal response was recorded during each trial. Vocalizations were the only consistently reliable means of determining response to playback because of dense vegetation and the shyness of Kentucky Warblers. Comparable data were collected during real territorial encounters whenever possible. All behavioral observations and capture attempts were made between 0600 and 1800 EST, but most before 1400 EST.

Once captured, the bird was banded with a numbered U.S. Fish and Wildlife Service aluminum band and two plastic color bands in a unique combination for field identification. Each bird was sexed and aged following Pyle et al. (1987) combined with the assumption that females are not likely to have gray-tipped crown feathers,

a characteristic Mabey determined from museum specimens and breeding birds of known sex. Wing length, body fat, weight, feather/molt condition, and skull ossification (WS88 only) were noted. The bird was released within 10 m of its capture site.

Results

SEX AND AGE OF BIRDS. Forty-three Kentucky Warblers were banded during the three study periods: 26 along the PIR and 17 on BCI. There was no noticeable skew in the sex ratio of birds captured, with 24 males, 18 females, and one of undetermined sex. Fourteen juveniles (first yr.) and 17 adults (after-first yr.) were classified during WS88 and DS89. The ages of the 11 birds captured in DS88 were not determined.

The mean weight of 23 males was 14.39 g (± 0.81 SD), whereas 18 females had a mean weight of 13.89 g (± 0.80 SD) (not significant by t-test). Wing length averaged 71.5 mm for 20 males and 68.9 mm for 11 females, but because wing length was used, in part, to determine sex, it could be a biased association.

RETURN RATES AND OVER-WINTER SITE FIDELITY. Of 34 individuals banded during DS88 and WS88, five were resighted during later study periods (WS88: PIR = 1, BCI = 1; DS89: PIR = 2, BCI = 2), which includes one that was banded in DS88 and seen in both of the subsequent periods. Including the individual present during the entire study, four were seen within 50 m of their original capture sites. One bird, banded in November, was seen in February 1989 about 300 m from its original capture site (and in place of another individual also banded in WS88).

One resighting is particularly intriguing: bird A-G was caught and marked on territory 29 on PIR, 13 March 1988. On 4 November 1988, a new bird, A-BG, was caught and marked on the same territory. Neighbors on both sides of territory 29 were also marked within the same week. A year later, on 6 March 1989, an unbanded individual was observed vocalizing in response to playback within territory 29 and was assumed to be the current occupant. On 30 March 1989, A-G was recaptured on territory 29. A-G apparently had not remained resident on territory 29 for the entire winter.

Despite intensive effort, we located only about one-half (19 out of 34) of the birds that were marked during a previous study period. For example, we spent nearly 30 person-hours trying to see a Kentucky Warbler we suspected was banded. The dark, dense habitat and the bird's shyness made this effort unsuccessful. However, replacement of banded individuals from wet season to dry season (within a single winter) was found to occur at a higher frequency than persistence of the same individual on the same territory. A breakdown of resightings of

TABLE 1. Persistence of marked Kentucky Warblers on territories within a single winter

Territory occupant	BCI	PIR
WS88 Occupants[a]		
Unidentified occupant	2(6.2%)	2(5.3%)
Unbanded	22(68.8%)	19(50%)
Banded	8(25%)	17(44.7%)
DS89 Occupants[b]		
Same occupant	1(12.5%)	1(5.9%)
Banded replacement	1(12.5%)	1(5.9%)
Unbanded replacement	2(25.0%)	4(23.5%)
Unidentified occupant	2(25.0%)	9(52.9%)
Unoccupied	2(25.0%)	2(11.8%)

a. Total territories WS88: BCI=32, PIR=38.

b. Only those dry season territories that were held by banded individuals during the previous wet season.

the WS88 marked individuals during the DS89 period can be found in Table 1. No more than two banded individuals were resighted during any single period at either site and only two individuals were known to return for the second winter.

POPULATION DENSITY. Population densities varied between the two sites and between study periods. Kentucky Warblers were more frequently encountered along the Pipeline Road than on BCI. Density estimates, based on actual numbers of birds encountered, ranged from 3.9 to 5.5 Kentucky Warblers/10 ha along the Pipeline Road during our study and only 0.8 to 1.6 birds/10 ha on BCI (Table 2). All areas surveyed are included in these estimates. It would not be easy to factor out uninhabited portions of the transects (i.e., TIII on PIR and some of the outer trails on BCI, Figs. 1, 2), particularly for BCI. Territory size was not determined because individuals were difficult to follow. Lower densi-

ties on BCI do not necessarily indicate larger territory size as well.

Kentucky Warblers were not evenly distributed throughout each study site (Figs. 1, 2). At PIR, TI and TII contained almost the entire study population, while no birds were detected along TIII where the road was cut into a steep hill (Fig. 1). A comparison of the 37 DS89 territories to a Poisson distribution showed that the distribution of birds on TI and TII did not differ from random ($\chi^2 = 0.3388$, $n = 42$ 100-m sections of the two transects) (Simpson et al. 1960). On BCI, large tracts were uninhabited by Kentucky Warblers, and territories appear to be clumped in a few areas (Fig. 2). These uninhabited areas could not be classified by age of forest or topography and did not appear to share any characteristics different from the inhabited areas. Most territories held occupants for more than one study period (Fig. 1, 2). However, during each study period, Kentucky Warblers were only detected once on some sites, despite explorations with playback on at least two more occasions. These "single-encounter territories" made up 13–35% of the total number of territories (DS88: BCI = 8/23 or 35%; WS88: PIR = 5/38 or 13%, BCI = 11/32 or 34%; DS89: PIR = 13/42 or 31%, BCI = 6/20 or 30%).

BEHAVIORAL RESPONSE TO PLAYBACK. Kentucky Warblers responded much more quickly to playback and were more readily caught on PIR than on BCI. The average time to response for 27 PIR birds was 1.02 ± 1.98 min., whereas the average time to response for 32 BCI birds was 4.10 ± 6.23 min. ($P < 0.005$, one-tailed t-test). Responsiveness to playback (a measure of territorial defense behavior) varied significantly between the two sites. An F-test for variance (Sokal and Rohlf 1987) shows that response was significantly less consistent on BCI than PIR ($F_{31,26} = 9.90$, $P < 0.005$). Within a given site, seasonal difference in time to response was not significant, although our data indicate quicker reponse during the wet season. For BCI, the mean time to response in WS88 was 1.93 ± 3.14 min. ($n = 23$), but was

TABLE 2. Population densities for the two study sites

Season	BCI			PIR		
	Birds[a] n	Area[b] (ha)	Density[c] (n/10 ha)	Birds[a] n	Area[b] (ha)	Density[c] (n/10 ha)
DS88	24	195	1.2	30	78	3.9
WS88	32	195	1.6	38	78	4.9
DS89	20	255	0.8	43	78	5.5

a. Total number of birds detected.

b. Total area covered during each study period.

c. Conversion to birds/10 ha.

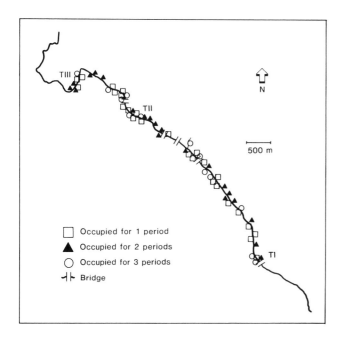

FIGURE 1. Locations of Kentucky Warbler territories along the Pipeline Road, showing their distribution during three study periods: DS88, WS88, DS89 (see text). A warbler located within 50 m of a previous territory during an earlier study period is categorized as on the same territory.

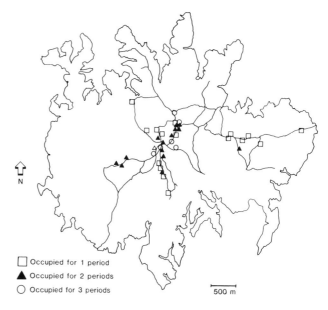

FIGURE 2. Locations of Kentucky Warbler territories on Barro Colorado Island during three study periods. For description of criterion used see Figure 1.

9.66 ± 8.34 min. in DS89 ($n = 9$) ($P < 0.1$, two-tailed t-test). Likewise, there was no significant difference for the comparable values for PIR (WS88: 0.97 ± 2.06 min., $n = 21$; DS89: 1.17 ± 1.64 min., $n = 6$, $P > 0.1$).

Vocal activity prior to capture attempts was equally frequent at both sites. Despite this, more Kentucky Warblers were netted at PIR than on BCI, and more incidents of "no response" after playback occurred on BCI than at PIR (Table 3).

Another measure of the degree of agonistic territorial behavior at each site was the number of real (between individuals) interactions we encountered. We found nearly twice as many natural interactions per field hour

along PIR than on BCI. During 178.5 hr of observation at the PIR site and 201 hr of observation on BCI for the WS88 and DS89 period, 14 interactions (0.078/hr) were recorded for PIR and nine (0.044/hr) for BCI. For each site most of those interactions were recorded for the wet season period in the early winter (PIR: $n = 14$, 64% in WS88, $\chi^2 = 1.24$, d.f. = 1, $P < 0.5$; BCI: $n = 9$, 89% in WS88, $\chi^2 = 13.78$, d.f. = 1, $P < 0.005$). Natural encounters often involved chases, and lasted from 1 to 12 min, with one participant often dropping out of the vocal exchange two to three minutes before the other(s).

Discussion

Kentucky Warblers wintering in Panama were found in varying local densities with expression of territorial be-

TABLE 3. Comparison of responses to playback during capture attempts

Behavioral response	BCI	PIR	χ^2	$P <$
Active before trial[a]	60.8%	58.1%	0.65	0.500
No response[b]	37.3%	27.9%	1.66	0.250
Active and no response	19.6%	02.0%	22.28	0.005
Caught	19.6%	39.5%	2.18	0.250

NOTE: BCI: $n=52$; PIR: $n=43$.

a. Includes birds that were vocal in area prior to trial.

b. Includes vocal response and/or approach.

havior, through response to playback and natural encounters, less common on BCI where densities were lowest.

Our data offer only suggestive evidence about the degree of site fidelity and tenacity within a population of Kentucky Warblers in the southern end of their winter range. Perhaps the territories where Kentucky Warblers were encountered only once represent a wandering portion of the population or, alternately, mobile territories. Although individuals of many Neotropical migratory species clearly demonstrate site attachment throughout the nonbreeding season, floaters have also been reported. Using radiotelemetry, Rappole et al. (1989) found wanderers among a sedentary population of Wood Thrushes (*Hylocichla mustelina*), and Holmes et al. (1989) used techniques similar to ours to detect a high level of site fidelity with American Redstarts (*Setophaga ruticilla*) and Black-throated Blue Warblers (*Dendroica caerulescens*) in Jamaica. Hooded Warblers (*Wilsonia citrina*) show similar territorial tenacity (Morton et al. 1987). Indeed, Rappole and Warner (1980) defined territoriality to include both site tenacity and defensiveness, and found that Kentucky Warblers wintering in Veracruz, Mexico satisfied these two requirements.

Measuring the degree of site tenacity is essential for a strong estimate of over-winter survival of territorial individuals. We can extrapolate from our resighting data (Table 1) to make extreme estimates of survival. If all the unidentified individuals belonged to the "same occupant" category, then the highest possible proportion of individuals surviving from wet season to dry season for BCI is 37.5% (3 individuals) and for PIR is 58.8% (10 individuals). However, if all the unidentified individuals belonged to the "unbanded replacement" category, then at least 50% (4 individuals) of the BCI population were lost to mortality or emigration during the winter and 76.4% (13 individuals) were lost from PIR. If we assume that the population consisted mainly of sedentary, territorial individuals, then there appears to be low over-winter survival (Greenberg 1980, Holmes et al. 1989, Rappole 1989). Alternatively, the low number of territories occupied by the same individual may indicate a low degree of site attachment. If this is the case, we cannot accurately assess individual survival with our data.

For at least two reasons, detecting the survival and site fidelity of individual, territorial Kentucky Warblers might have been complicated by the requisite use of playback to locate and identify birds. First, we might have been attracting individuals from surrounding areas, especially when playback time was long, or when playback was used on a territory edge. Second, birds might have rapidly habituated to the playback, reducing

our ability to recapture and identify them. Despite our greater efforts in territories that had been occupied by banded birds, rarely could we follow individuals or catch them after they had been captured once. There were several occasions when we knew from previous activity that a Kentucky Warbler was present but remained vocally unresponsive to playback. Only once, however, did we observe a bird approach silently in response to playback.

Behavioral differences between the two sites seem to reflect the dissimilarity in the population densities. Kentucky Warblers of PIR consistently responded to playback more rapidly than those on BCI. Although it is possible that this is a side effect of higher densities on PIR, resulting in more individuals near a speaker at any given time, individuals at both sites had the same frequency of activity before playback was begun (Table 3). In over half the cases for both sites the target individual was known to be present (i.e., within hearing distance) before a trial. Greater territorial pressure from more neighbors at PIR might have influenced the heightened reaction to playback and the higher frequency of natural territorial interactions at that study site. Titus and Haas (1990) found evidence that higher densities of American Robin (*Turdus migratorius*) territories were correlated with higher singing rates and increased reaction to playback. Rappole et al. (1989) found a difference in behavior between territorial and wandering individuals within the same population of Wood Thrushes: wandering individuals displayed less agonistic behavior, were chased more often, and were less site-faithful than sedentary individuals. We were unable to determine if our study populations contained both wandering and territorial individuals and therefore cannot speculate on the relative importance of site attachment to the observed behavioral differences of the PIR and BCI Kentucky Warblers.

Habitat variation is probably an important factor in both the variation of population density and, hence, behavior. The uneven distribution of Kentucky Warblers and their consistent reuse of most territories indicate that, within and between our sites, some areas are more frequently selected. The Pipeline Road is an extensive forest light gap. This fact might have biased our findings for the PIR site if Kentucky Warblers are attracted to light gaps, especially since most of our work was done in the early morning when the extra light provided by the road may have been beneficial for foraging. Although no apparent difference was found in foraging behavior or the use of PIR and BCI habitats, the importance of the habitat's structural elements, such as roost sites and tree fall gaps, for survival of wintering Kentucky Warblers could be more thoroughly investigated if radiotelemetry were used. Based on a qualitative assessment, it is interesting to note that there was no segregation of sexes into distinct habitat types as reported for Hooded Warblers (Morton et al. 1987, Morton 1990).

Geographic location might be an important factor influencing observed densities. Low densities of Kentucky Warblers at our study sites might be the result of their location at the southern fringe of the species' winter range. Our highest density estimates of 5.5 birds/10 ha in Panama are substantially lower than the 30 birds/10 ha extrapolated from the territory size estimated by Rappole and Warner (1980) for Veracruz, Mexico, at the northern limit of the Kentucky Warbler's winter range. These density differences suggest that Veracruz might be a preferable area for wintering, perhaps because of its proximity to the breeding range. It is even possible that geographical differences between the two Panamanian sites are relevant. It would not be surprising if fewer Kentucky Warblers used or found BCI because it is a small island (Whitcomb et al. 1981).

Although lower relative densities might be caused by poor habitat, they presumably are associated with greater movement and variable use of habitat by individuals, making the study of territoriality difficult. Social behavior might also contribute to the observed pattern of territoriality (Figs. 1, 2), but it is probably not a substantial determinant of densities in these two populations. The random distribution of territories along PIR seems to indicate that individuals are neither particularly attracted to nor repelled by each other, as a highly clumped or evenly spread distribution might suggest.

It appears that there are substantial behavioral differences between the PIR and BCI populations, which are related to density. The question of how these differences affect survival of Kentucky Warblers is still open. Information on the degree of over-winter site attachment, territorial behavior and survival in northern populations of wintering Kentucky Warblers would be valuable for comparison. We might then be able to look for patterns in the relationships among density, territoriality, and survival throughout the Kentucky Warblers' winter range.

Acknowledgments

Funding for this research was provided by the Friends of the National Zoo and Manomet Bird Observatory's Kathleen Anderson Award. This research would not have been possible without the permission and support of INRENARE and the Smithsonian Tropical Research Institute. We would like to express our appreciation to Jan Blew and Mary Victoria McDonald for assistance in the field and in preparation of this manuscript. R. Foster, J.R. Karr, E.G. Leigh Jr., A.S. Rand, K. Sieving, N.G. Smith, and R. Urriola gave generously of their time to help facilitate our work in Panama. Two anonymous reviewers helped strengthen this paper and L-A. Hayek provided statistical advice.

Literature cited

American Ornithologists' Union. 1983. *Check-list of North American Birds*. 6th ed. Washington: American Ornithologists' Union.

Bennett, C.F. 1963. A phytophysiognomic reconnaissance of Barro Colorado Island, Canal Zone. *Smithsonian Misc. Coll.* 146(7):1–8.

Ely, C.A. 1973. Returns of North American birds to their wintering grounds in southern Mexico. *Bird-Banding* 44:228–229.

Ely, C.A., P.J. Latas, and R.N. Lohoenfoner. 1977. Additional returns and recoveries of North American birds banded in Southern Mexico. *Bird-Banding* 48:275–276.

Greenberg, R. 1980. Demographic aspects of long-distance migrations. Pages 493–504 in *Migrant Birds in the Neotropics: Ecology, Behavior, Distribution and Conservation*, A. Keast and E.S. Morton, eds. Washington: Smithsonian Institution Press.

Hespenheide, H.A. 1980. Bird community structure in two Panama forests: Residents, migrants and seasonality during the non-breeding season. Pages 227–237 in *Migrant Birds in the Neotropics: Ecology, Behavior, Distribution and Conservation*, A. Keast and E.S. Morton, eds. Washington: Smithsonian Institution Press.

Holmes, R.T., T.W. Sherry, and L. Reitsma. 1989. Population structure, territoriality and overwinter survival of two migrant warbler species in Jamaica. *Condor* 91:545–561.

Jones, T.E. 1986. The passerine decline. *North American Bird Bander* 11:74.

Karr, J.R. 1971. Wintering Kentucky Warblers (*Oporornis formosus*) and a warning to banders. *Bird-Banding* 42:299.

Kaufmann, J.H. 1983. On the definitions and functions of dominance and territoriality. *Biol. Rev.* 58:1–20.

Loftin, H. 1977. Returns and recoveries of banded North American birds in Panama and the tropics. *Bird-Banding* 48:253–258.

Leigh, E.G. Jr., A.S. Rand, and D.M. Windsor, eds. 1982. *The Ecology of a Tropical Forest*. Washington: Smithsonian Institution Press.

Lovejoy, T.E. 1983. Tropical deforestation and North American migrant birds. Pages 126–128 in *Bird Conservation*, 1, S.A. Temple, ed. Madison: University of Wisconsin Press.

Lynch, J.F. 1989. Distribution of overwintering Nearctic migrants in the Yucatan Peninsula, I: General patterns of occurrence. *Condor* 91:515–544.

Lynch, J.F., E.S. Morton, and M.E. Van der Voort. 1985. Habitat segregation between the sexes of wintering Hooded Warblers (*Wilsonia citrina*). *Auk* 102:714–721.

Morton, E.S. 1980. Adaptations to seasonal changes by migrant land birds in Panama, Canal Zone. Pages 437–453 in *Migrant Birds in the Neotropics: Ecology, Behavior, Distribution and Conservation*, A. Keast and E.S. Morton, eds. Washington: Smithsonian Institution Press.

———. 1990. Habitat segregation by sex in the Hooded Warbler: Experiments on proximate causation and discussion of its evolution. *Am. Nat.* 135:319–333.

Morton, E.S., and R. Greenberg. 1989. The outlook for migratory songbirds: "Future shock" for birders. *Am. Birds* 43:178–183.

Morton, E.S., J.F. Lynch, K. Young, and P. Mehlhop. 1987. Do male Hooded Warblers exclude females from nonbreeding territories in tropical forest? *Auk* 104:133–135.

Pyle, P., S.N.G. Howell, R.P. Yunick, and D.F. DeSante. 1987. *Identification Guide to North American Passerines*. Bolinas, Calif.: Slate Creek Press.

Rappole, J.H., and E.S. Morton. 1985. Effects of habitat alteration on a tropical avian forest community. Pages 1013–1021 in *Neotropical Ornithology*, P.A. Buckley, E.S. Morton, R.S. Ridgely, and F.G. Buckley, eds. Ornithol. Monogr. 36.

Rappole, J.H., and D.W. Warner, 1980. Ecological aspects of migrant bird behavior in Veracruz, Mexico. Pages 353–393 in *Migrant Birds in the Neotropics: Ecology, Behavior, Distribution and Conservation*, A. Keast and E.S. Morton, eds. Washington: Smithsonian Institution Press.

Rappole, J.H., E.S. Morton, T.E. Lovejoy, III, and J.L. Ruos. 1983. *Nearctic Avian Migrants in the Neotropics*. Washington: U.S. Fish and Wildlife Service.

Rappole, J.H., M.A. Ramos, and K. Winker, 1989. Wintering

Wood Thrush movements and mortality in Southern Veracruz. *Auk* 106:402–410.

Robbins, C.S., D. Bystrak, and P.H. Geissler. 1986. *The Breeding Bird Survey: Its First Fifteen Years, 1965–1979*. U.S. Fish and Wildlife Serv. Resource Pub. 157.

Robbins, C.S., J.R. Sauer, R.S. Greenberg, and S. Droege. 1989. Population declines in North American birds that migrate to the neotropics. *Proc. Natl. Acad. Sci.* 86:7658–7662.

Simpson, G.G., A. Roe, and R.C. Lowentin. 1960. *Quantitative Zoology*. New York: Harcourt, Brace and Co.

Sokal, R.R., and F.J. Rohlf. 1987. *Introduction to Biostatistics*. New York: W.H. Freeman and Co.

Stewart, P.A. 1987. Decline in numbers of wood Warblers in spring and autumn migrations through Ohio. *North American Bird Bander* 12:58–59.

Temple, S.A., and B.L. Temple. 1976. Avian population trends in central New York state, 1935–1972. *Bird-Banding* 47:238–257.

Titus, R.C., and C.A. Haas. 1990. Singing behavior of American robins in linear and non-linear habitats. *Wilson Bull.* 102:325-328.

Whitcomb, R.F., C.S. Robbins, J.F. Lynch, B.L. Whitcomb, M.K. Klimkiewicz, and D. Bystrak. 1981. Effects of forest fragmentation on the avifauna of the eastern deciduous forest. Pages 125–205 in *Forest Island Dynamics in Man-dominated Landscapes*, R.L. Burgess and D.M. Sharpe, eds. New York: Springer-Verlag.

Willis, E.O. 1980. Ecological roles of migratory and resident birds on Barro Colorado Island, Panama. Pages 205–225 in *Migrant Birds in the Neotropics: Ecology, Behavior, Distribution and Conservation*, A. Keast and E.S. Morton, eds. Washington: Smithsonian Institution Press

JOHN H. RAPPOLE
Conservation and Research Center
National Zoological Park
Smithsonian Institution
Front Royal, Virginia 22630

EUGENE S. MORTON
Department of Zoological Research
National Zoological Park
Smithsonian Institution
Washington, D.C. 20008

MARIO A. RAMOS
World Wildlife Fund–U.S.
1250 24th Street NW
Washington, D.C. 20009.

Density, philopatry, and population estimates for songbird migrants wintering in Veracruz

Abstract. Populations of migrants wintering in the Tuxtla Mountain region of southern Veracruz were monitored through the use of netting, color-marking, recaptures, and observation. We examined habitat use and intraseasonal philopatry in lowland rain forest and second growth. We combined these data with information from earlier studies on territory size to calculate densities, and to make some predictions concerning population changes for these species as habitat alteration practices continue. Several species, among them the Kentucky Warbler and Wood Thrush, are likely to show significant declines throughout their range within the next decade.

Sinopsis. Poblaciones de aves migratorias invernantes en la región de la montaña de Tuxtla en el sur de Veracruz fueron monitoreadas mediante capturas con redes, marcaje de color, recapturas y observación. Nosotros examinamos uso habitacional y filopatría intraestacional en bosque lluvioso de zonas bajas y en bosque secundario. Combinamos estos datos con información de estudios precedentes sobre tamaño territorial para calcular densidades y hacer algunas predicciones concernientes a cambios poblacionales de estas especies a medida que las prácticas de alteración de habitat continúan. Varias especies, entre ellas *Oporornis formosus* e *Hylocichla mustelina*, probablemente mostrarán declinaciones significativas a través de su área de distribución dentro de la próxima década.

The role of migratory species in tropical communities during the nonbreeding season has been debated for some time. MacArthur (1972:135), Leck (1972:848), Karr (1976:456), Robinson et al. (1988:2306), Hutto (1980:198), and others have questioned whether migratory species can occupy niches in stable tropical environments (see review in Rappole et al. 1983). In particular, these authors questioned whether migrants that breed in North America are capable of functioning in undisturbed tropical forests where specialized resident birds presumably fill all available niches. The Old World literature is nearly unanimous in this view of wintering migrants as interlopers into tropical avian communities. Beginning with the work of Morel and Bourlière (1962), several papers have indicated that migratory species wintering in Paleotropical environments are characterized as wandering infiltrators into these communities (summarized in Leisler 1990).

In the present paper we summarize data from studies performed at different sites in the Tuxtla Mountains of southern Veracruz. We address three primary questions: (1) Do Neotropical migrants inhabit undisturbed tropical forests? (2) Is there evidence of intraseasonal philopatry of migrants to primary forest sites? (3) What are the relative densities of understory migrants in primary forest and young second growth as determined by mist nets? We use our data on density of territories of migrants in tropical forest, and information on deforestation in the Tuxtla Mountains, to assess population trends in the region from pre-Columbian times to the present.

Study area

The Tuxtla Mountains of southern Veracruz, Mexico are located roughly 90 km southeast of Veracruz City along the coast of the Gulf of Mexico (Fig. 1) and comprise about 3,000 km² of rugged peaks and steep-sided valleys, all of which was forested prior to European colonization.

Work at three localities is reported in this paper: (1) Motel Playa Escondida—undisturbed primary rain forest bordered by 1–5-yr-old second growth during our initial visit in 1973; it has since been largely cleared (Rappole and Morton 1985), (2) La Peninsula de Moreno (110 m elevation)—primary rain forest located on steep slopes along the Coxcoapan River, (3) the most remote of our study areas, located in the vast crater of Volcan Santa Martha. The crater itself was 5 km in diameter with vertical walls up to 500 m in height separating the interior from surrounding areas. Except for the steepest parts of the wall, the interior of the crater was covered with rain forest and cloud forest at elevations of 500–1,700 m. The nearest areas of human disturbance were 3–5 km away.

Methods

Our field work was begun in the Tuxtla Mountains in August 1973 and has been conducted annually through 1988 except for years 1976–1979. Most of the work has been done during the winter months, November–March. The primary method of investigation has been placement of grids of mist nets (12 × 2.6 m; 30-mm, 36-mm, and 61-mm mesh) in forested sites for capturing understory birds. The grids covered areas rang-

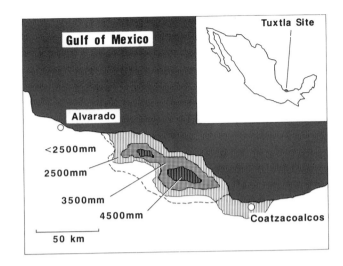

FIGURE 1. Map of the Tuxtla Mountains region showing rainfall isobars.

ing from 1 to 8.75 ha in size with one net every 35 to 50 m. Grids were also placed in adjacent second growth and pasture at Site 1. Captive birds were sexed, aged, checked for molt and subcutaneous fat, banded with U.S. Fish & Wildlife Service bands and color bands, and released. Wood Thrushes (*Hylocichla mustelina*) and individuals of some other species were tagged with radio transmitters from 1983 to 1988.

Data on intraseasonal philopatry are presented for two sites: Playa Escondida for the field season from 10 December 1974 to 15 March 1975, and La Peninsula from 2 October 1982 to 1 May 1983 and 2 November 1983 to 28 April 1984.

Data on relative use of primary forest and second growth were obtained at Site 1. Capture data for the two main habitat types (lowland rain forest and 1–5-yr-old second growth) are presented as birds/net hour (total birds captured within a given habitat type divided by the total number of net hours accumulated for each habitat). Recaptures/net hour were used as a measure of philopatry. We accumulated 16,883 net hours in rain forest habitat on a 10-ha study area at Site 1 from 1 November 1974 to 15 March 1975. These data are compared with netting data for 1–5-yr-old second growth at Site 1 on a 2-ha plot. A total of 381 net hours were accumulated on this site with a 12-net grid from 27 January to 15 March 1975; 858 in November 1980; and 330 in November 1981 for a total of 1,569 net hours in young second growth.

Procedures used during the expedition to the Santa Martha crater were, of necessity, quite different. We hiked to the northeast rim of the crater on 4 March 1985 where we established a base camp. We stayed on the rim until 20 March 1985, making excursions into

TABLE 1.   Neotropical migrants recorded in undisturbed rain forest and cloud forest of the Santa Martha crater

Species	Comments
Swainson's Hawk (*Buteo swainsoni*)	Flocks of migrating birds seen between 1145 and 1410 on 12 and 13 March: 8 groups of 23, 29, 48, 36, 52, 22, 29, and 18 birds
Vaux's Swift (*Chaetura vauxi*)	Large flocks daily flying through deep gorge of crater
Yellow-bellied Sapsucker (*Sphyrapicus varius*)	One seen on 15 March
Eastern Phoebe (*Sayornis phoebe*)	One seen and heard (Type A song) at base camp (elev. 700 m), 13–15 March
Yellow-bellied Flycatcher (*Empidonax flaviventris*)	Several daily at 500–700 m
Gray Catbird (*Dumetella carolinensis*)	Two seen (14, 15 March) in dense second growth along stream bank
Wood Thrush (*Hylocichla mustelina*)	One or two daily along river flood plain at 500 m or below. One bird netted on 16 March
Blue-gray Gnatcatcher (*Polioptila caerulea*)	Several daily in canopy
White-eyed Vireo (*Vireo griseus*)	One seen at crater interior camp site (500 m)
Solitary Vireo (*Vireo solitarius*)	Several daily
Yellow-throated Vireo (*Vireo flavifrons*)	One bird seen on 20 March near Rio Suchiapa
Tennessee Warbler (*Vermivora peregrina*)	A single bird netted near base camp (700 m) on 19 March
Nashville Warbler (*Vermivora ruficapilla*)	A single bird netted near base camp (700 m) on 8 March; a second bird seen on 11 March
Black-throated Green Warbler (*Dendroica virens*)	Seen daily from 500–1,000 m
Magnolia Warbler (*Dendroica magnolia*)	Call notes heard several times daily at 500–1,000 m
Black-and-white Warbler (*Mniotilta varia*)	Seen daily below 700 m
Louisiana Waterthrush (*Seiurus motacilla*)	Seen daily along streams and rivers below 700 m
Ovenbird (*Seiurus aurocapillus*)	Two birds netted, 13 and 18 March respectively

the crater itself and to neighboring river valleys to survey for Neotropical migrants (Rappole and Ramos 1985, Howe 1989). We surveyed rain forest and cloud forest areas from 500 m to 1,700 m (top of Santa Martha), noting presence and abundance of Neotropical migrants, and supplemented this activity with mist netting. Two mist nets were run for a total of 95 net hours on the rim of the crater, and 16 nets were run from 9 to 19 March for a total of 830 net hours in the Rio Suchiapa Valley, 500 m north of the rim.

Further detail on study areas, materials, and methods are contained in Rappole and Warner (1980), Rappole and Morton (1985), Rappole et al. (1989), and Winker et al. (1990a).

Results

MIGRANT USE OF UNDISTURBED TROPICAL HABITATS. During the Santa Martha expedition, a total of 135 party hours was spent in walking surveys, and 925 net hours were accumulated. We recorded a total of 22 migrant species in this remote area of primary rain forest and cloud forest (Table 1).

At least one of these species was probably a transient over or through the area, viz., the Swainson's Hawk (*Buteo swainsoni*), which winters primarily in scrub, grassland, and savanna habitats, and is an early spring transient (March) along the western Gulf coast. The Vaux's Swift (*Chaetura vauxi*) might also fit in this category.

Most of the migratory species recorded, however, were winter residents. Captured birds showed only the small amount of furcular fat characteristic of sedentary, wintering individuals (Rappole and Warner 1980). Behavior of individuals (calling, chasing) further indicated winter residency in the forest. Most observations of migrants were made by locating calling birds. These call notes are used by individuals of many species to defend winter territories (Rappole and Warner 1980).

INTRASEASONAL PHILOPATRY OF MIGRANTS. Recapture and resighting data on seven species of migrants from Sites 1 (Playa Escondida) and 2 (La Peninsula) are presented in Table 2. These seven species represent those Neotropical migrants most likely to be captured at mistnet height (0–2.6 m). We recaptured or resighted a total of 62 Wood Thrushes two or more days after original

TABLE 2. Intraseasonal philopatry for Neotropical migrants at study sites in the Tuxtla Mountains of Veracruz

Species	Earliest arrival[a]	Latest departure[a]	Total days[b]	Longest tenure[c]
Wood Thrush (*Hylocichla mustelina*)	6 Nov	6 Apr	150	145
Black-and-white Warbler (*Mniotilta varia*)	15 Nov	4 Mar	109	71
Worm-eating Warbler (*Helmitheros vermivorus*)	7 Nov	6 Apr	150	136
Ovenbird (*Seiurus aurocapillus*)	7 Nov	11 Mar	124	117
Kentucky Warbler (*Oporornis formosus*)	2 Oct	5 Apr	185	143
Hooded Warbler (*Wilsonia citrina*)	2 Oct	23 Mar	172	111
Wilson's Warbler (*Wilsonia pusilla*)	2 Nov	26 Apr	175	148

a. Earliest arrival date/latest departure date for a known territory holder, not necessarily for the same individual.
b. Total days from earliest arrival date to latest departure date, not necessarily for the same individual.
c. Earliest arrival date to latest departure date for a single individual.

capture over three seasons, two at La Peninsula, and one at Playa Escondida. The average observed length of stay on site was 23.5 days. The actual length of stay for Neotropical migrants on a given site was much longer; the probability of recapturing or resighting a given individual, even if resident, is fairly low. This point is illustrated by the example of Wood Thrush PE 72, originally captured in net C6 on the Playa Escondida study site on 16 November 1973, and recaptured on 10 December 1973 and again on 3 January 1974. It was not seen or captured again despite intensive netting and observations in the area until 25 January 1975, when it was recaptured within 50 m of its original capture point. It seems probable that this bird was on the site during the remainder of the 1973–74 winter season, and throughout the entire 1974–75 season as well. This case is by no means aberrant for Wood Thrushes, or any of the other species in Table 2. A second example of philopatry is illustrated by Black-and-white Warbler LP 474, originally captured on 27 January 1983. It was not seen or recaptured again until 6 February 1984, although the bird was probably present throughout both seasons. A third example is that for Wilson's Warbler LP 913, originally captured in net 36 on 28 April 1983, recaptured in net 36 on 6 April 1984, and recaptured again in net 36 on 6 March 1985.

A more accurate picture of the residency status of these birds is represented by the longest documented period on site for a given individual of a species (Table 2), and the total residency period based on earliest and latest dates documented for resident individuals of a species (Table 2), where "resident" is defined as a bird with a documented stay of greater than 30 days on site. These methods show an on-site residency of up to 185 days (for the Kentucky Warbler, Table 2); an arrival in early October, and a departure in early April. Residency periods of about 150 days (e.g., Wood Thrush and

Worm-eating Warbler), representing arrivals in early November and departures in early April, are typical for several species of Neotropical migrants in the Tuxtla Mountains.

RELATIVE DENSITIES OF UNDERSTORY MIGRANTS IN PRIMARY FOREST AND YOUNG SECOND GROWTH. Based on captures/net hr and recapture rates, understory migrants in rain forest and second growth appear to fall into three, fairly distinct categories (Table 3). The first group, including the Yellow-bellied Flycatcher, Wood Thrush, Black-and-white Warbler, Worm-eating Warbler, Ovenbird, and Louisiana Waterthrush, are essentially forest birds that were occasionally found in second growth. The second group, including the Least Flycatcher, Gray Catbird, Yellow-breasted Chat, Common Yellowthroat, Orange-crowned Warbler, and Indigo Bunting, are scrub, thicket, and savanna species that were seldom found in forest. The third group includes species that are found commonly in both forest and second growth. This group includes the Hooded Warbler, Kentucky Warbler, and several species not included in Table 3 because, although they were netted commonly in second growth, they foraged mostly above net height in forest—namely Wilson's Warbler (*Wilsonia pusilla*), White-eyed Vireo (*Vireo griseus*), and Magnolia Warbler (*Dendroica magnolia*).

Discussion

USE OF UNDISTURBED PRIMARY, TROPICAL FOREST BY NEOTROPICAL MIGRANTS. Our survey work in the Santa Martha crater indicates that Neotropical migrant passerines are a significant component of undisturbed, isolated, primary rain forest and cloud forest communities in the Tuxtla Mountains. Virtually all components of the avian community, residents as well as migrants, in the large block of isolated forest were similar to those found on our less remote, forested sites (Tables 1–3; also Rappole and Warner 1980, Rappole and Morton 1985). This result is not surprising because the habitats were similar except for elevation. Winker et al. (1990b) compared the vegetation at the Santa Martha and La Peninsula sites, and found them to be structurally comparable.

INTRASEASONAL PHILOPATRY OF MIGRANTS TO PRIMARY RAIN FOREST. In this study, we documented intraseasonal tenure for several migrant inhabitants of tropical rain forest understory (cf. Table 2). Individuals of these species arrive early (early October to early November, depending on the species), and remain on the same site, generally within 50 m of their original point of capture, throughout the entire season (late March to late April). These data do not support the hypothesis that migratory species differ fundamentally from tropical resident species in terms of resource and habitat use, as has been proposed by several authors (summarized in Leisler 1990); rather our data indicate that several species of Neotropical migrants can use stable resources in primary tropical communities for extended periods. Holmes et al. (1989) document similar over-winter tenacity to territories for Black-throated Blue Warblers (*Dendroica caerulescens*) and American Redstarts (*Setophaga ruticilla*) in various forest types in Jamaica.

DENSITY OF NEOTROPICAL MIGRANTS IN WINTER HABITATS. Mist netting provides an index to habitat use for understory species, and recapture and resighting rates for these birds provide documentation of intraseasonal philopatry. In addition to the data presented here, interseasonal site fidelity to winter quarters has been documented for 50 species of Neotropical migrants (summarized in Rappole et al. 1983:17–21). Neotropical migrant habitat use has been documented as well by many researchers using various types of walking censuses (Rappole et al. 1983:7). However, none of these methods furnishes the key piece of information, that is, the average density of individuals within a given habitat type. Winker (1989) determined by radio-tracking at Site 2 (La Peninsula) that the density of Wood Thrush territories was 2.4/ha or 21 birds for the 8.75-ha site. Yet an average of 72.3 (± 23.6) Wood Thrushes was captured on this site during the winters (Nov.–Feb.) of 1982–83, 1983–84, and 1984–85 or 8.2 birds/ha. Is the actual density of Wood Thrushes in Tuxtla rain forest closer to 2.4 or 8.2 birds/ha? Based on our radio-tracking work (Rappole et al. 1989), we conclude that it is closer to 2.4 birds/ha. Most birds comprising the difference between 2.4 and 8.2 are floaters, that is, nonterritorial, nonphilopatric individuals that moved over large areas daily. They also shifted rapidly between habitat types, roosting in second growth or edge and moving into primary forest in an apparent search for undefended sites suitable for territory establishment. We found

TABLE 3. Birds/10,000 net hours for understory Neotropical migrants in forest and second growth

Species	Rain forest[a]		Second growth[b]	
	Captures /net hr[c]	Recaptures[d] /net hr	Captures /net hr	Recaptures /net hr
Yellow-bellied Flycatcher (*Empidonax flaviventris*)	11.8	5.3	6.3	0.0
Least Flycatcher (*Empidonax minimus*)	1.0	0.0	127.0	31.8
Wood Thrush (*Hylocichla mustelina*)	52.1	23.0	0.0	0.0
Gray Catbird (*Dumetella carolinensis*)	7.1	1.0	95.6	38.2
Orange-crowned Warbler (*Vermivora celata*)	0.0	0.0	19.1	12.7
Black-and-white Warbler (*Mniotilta varia*)	16.0	6.5	0.0	0.0
Worm-eating Warbler (*Helmitheros vermivorus*)	11.3	4.7	6.3	0.0
Ovenbird (*Seiurus aurocapillus*)	4.7	1.8	6.3	0.0
Louisiana Waterthrush (*Seiurus motacilla*)	1.8	1.2	0.0	0.0
Kentucky Warbler (*Oporornis formosus*)	19.5	7.1	19.1	6.7
Common Yellowthroat (*Geothlypis trichas*)	0.5	0.0	12.7	6.4
Hooded Warbler (*Wilsonia citrina*)	17.0	11.8	44.0	12.7
Yellow-breasted Chat (*Icteria virens*)	0.5	0.0	63.7	25.4
Indigo Bunting (*Passerina cyanea*)	1.0	0.5	159.3	0.0

a. Rain forest net hours = 16,883.

b. Second growth net hours = 1,569.

c. Ratios are presented as birds/net hour × 10,000.

d. Does not include multiple captures of the same individual.

similarly high numbers of floaters among Wilson's Warblers in second growth at Site 1 (Playa Escondida) where 13 individuals were captured on a 1-ha area on which only two territorial birds were known. Most birds disappeared 24–48 hr after capture (Rappole and Morton 1985).

The relative numbers of individual Neotropical migrants in different habitats is a point of critical interest, both from an ecological and a conservation point of view. As pointed out by Lynch (1989) and many others (and this paper), several species of Neotropical migrants appear to occur in much higher numbers in tropical second growth than in primary forest, even among those species known to defend territories in primary forest throughout the winter. However, two questions must be answered regarding these birds before any conclusions can be reached concerning their habitat needs on the wintering grounds: first—what is the relative rate of movement by individuals of these species in the different habitat categories? and second—what is their relative survivorship? Unfortunately, these questions cannot be answered by any sort of visual census or single-visit netting procedure.

We have made some progress toward answering these questions for the Wood Thrush in which we have found that movement rates are much higher and survivorship lower for individuals in tropical second growth versus mature habitats (Rappole et al. 1989). Intraseasonal banding and recapture data for the Wilson's Warbler and Magnolia Warbler indicate that the same phenomenon may occur in these species; they show much higher capture rates, and much lower recapture rates in second growth than in mature tropical rain forest. We hypothesize that in these species many of the birds using second growth are floaters, using resources in these sites while searching for available territories in mature forest sites—perhaps because of greater stability of resources in mature forest or decreased vulnerability to predators. The fact that, throughout the winter, deceased territorial individuals in mature forest sites are replaced by new territory owners (Rappole and Warner 1980, Holmes et al. 1989) indicates that such a pool of floaters exists.

Forest losses in the Tuxtla Mountains are shown in Figure 2. The entire Tuxtla Mountain region was forested at the time of European colonization in 1532 (Medel y Alvarado 1963). Roughly 50% was still forested in 1960, when Andrle (1964) was working on the biogeography. In 1975, about one third of the forest remained (Rappole and Warner 1980), and in 1985, less than 15% of the original forest remained (Winker 1989:3).

We estimated the number of resident birds/km² for several of the common migrants that are primarily rain forest species in the Tuxtla Mountains (Table 4) based on color-marking, observation, and radio-tracking (Rap-

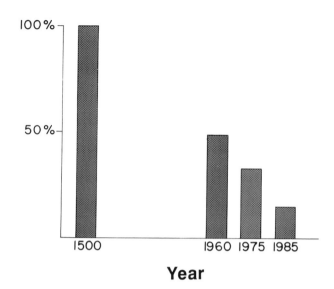

FIGURE 2. Decline in percentage of forested land in the Tuxtla Mountains of Veracruz from 1500 to 1985.

pole and Warner 1980, Rappole and Morton 1985, Rappole et al. 1989). This table shows the population declines predicted to have occurred in the region as a result of forest loss, assuming density to be equal to number of resident birds/ha in rain forest, and near zero in pasture. We know that neither of these assumptions is precisely correct. However the trends indicated probably are correct, not only for the Tuxtla Mountains, but for most of the lowland forest biome in Central America where forest conversion rates range from 2 to 4% annually and where 50–90% has already been cleared, depending on the country (Myers 1980, Sader and Joyce 1988).

POPULATION TRENDS IN FOREST-RELATED MIGRANTS. Questions concerning the densities of forest-related migrants in forest and second growth are becoming largely academic. They serve to improve understanding of Neotropical migrant ecology, but they cloud the conservation picture because in many parts of the tropics, including the Tuxtla Mountains, the forests are being replaced by pasture, not second growth (Fig. 3). In some forms of pasture, that is, those with extensive hedgerows of second growth, forest-related migrants can still be found, but generally at low densities.

Recent studies of Neotropical migrant populations indicate a distinct decline for a number of long-distance migrants that winter in the tropics. These trends have been attributed to forest fragmentation by a number of authors (see summary in Robbins et al. 1989). Fragmentation of breeding habitat probably plays a role in declines of some species, as might other factors related to

TABLE 4. Estimated decline in populations of Neotropical migrants in the Tuxtla Mountains of southern Veracruz

Species	Density[b]/km²	Est. pop. (× 1,000)			
		1500	1960	1975	1985
Yellow-bellied Flycatcher (*Empidonax flaviventris*)	40	60	30	20	9
Wood Thrush (*Hylocichla mustelina*)	150	225	112	74	34
Black-and-White Warbler (*Mniotilta varia*)	40	60	30	20	9
Worm-eating Warbler (*Helmitheros vermivorus*)	40	60	30	20	9
Ovenbird (*Seiurus aurocapillus*)	40	60	30	20	9
Louisiana Waterthrush (*Seiurus motacilla*)	40	60	30	20	9
Kentucky Warbler (*Oporornis formosus*)	70	105	53	35	16
Hooded Warbler (*Wilsonia citrina*)	60	90	45	30	14

a. These densities are based on estimated territory size and number/ha from earlier studies (Rappole and Warner 1980, Rappole and Morton 1985, Winker 1989).

breeding season habitat changes, for example, human disturbance (Johnston and Winings 1987) or the effects of white-tailed deer (*Odocoileus virginianus*) populations on vegetation understory structure and productivity (Alverson et al. 1988, Baird 1990). However, populations of many species have shown declines despite the lack of apparent change in breeding habitat structure or composition (Briggs and Criswell 1979, Johnston and Winings 1987, Marshall 1988, Morton and Greenberg 1989). We suggest that the magnitude of forest conversion in the major tropical wintering areas for many species of North American, forest-related migrants is a significant factor contributing to declines observed in these species. As forest is converted to pasture, no alternatives are available for forest-related migrants, and even many of the species that winter in scrub, savanna, and thicket habitats of the tropics are likely to show declines.

Acknowledgments

We thank K. Winker, J. Klicka, S. Stucker, S. Barrios, J.L. Alcantara, M. Neri F., E. Inigo E., E. Gongora A., M. Aranda, S. Barrios, J. Vega R., I. Carmona, M. Van der Voort, E. Fisk, F. Gonzalez, and N. Tsipoura.

Literature cited

Alverson, W.S., D.M. Waller, and S.L. Solheim. 1988. Forests too deer: Edge effects in northern Wisconsin. *Conserv. Biol.* 2:348–358.

Andrle, R. 1964. A biogeographical investigation of the Sierra de Tuxtla in Veracruz, Mexico. Ph.D. Dissertation, Louisiana State University, Baton Rouge, Louisiana.

Baird, T.H. 1990. Changes in breeding bird populations between 1930 and 1985 in the Quaker Run Valley of Allegany State Park, New York. *New York State Mus. Bull.* 477:1–41.

Briggs, S.A., and J.H. Criswell. Gradual silencing of spring in Washington. *Atlantic Nat.* 32:19–26.

Holmes, R.T., T.W. Sherry, and L. Reitsma. 1989. Population structure, territoriality and overwinter survival of two migrant warbler species in Jamaica. *Condor* 91:545–561.

Howe, J. 1989. Carmela's toucan. *Margin* 8:69–82.

Hutto, R. 1980. Winter habitat distribution of migratory land birds in western Mexico, with special reference to small foliage-gleaning insectivores. Pages 181–203 in *Migrant Birds in the Neotropics: Ecology, Behavior, Distribution and Conservation*, A. Keast and E.S. Morton, eds. Washington: Smithsonian Institution Press.

FIGURE 3. Looking northward from Cerro El Vigia at the rainforest–pasture interface at the Biology Station of the University of Mexico, January 1988.

Johnston, D.W., and D.I. Winings. 1987. Natural history of Plummers Island, Maryland. XXVII. The decline of forest breeding birds on Plummers Island, Maryland, and vicinity. *Proc. Biol. Soc. Wash.* 100:762–768.

Karr, J. 1976. On the relative abundance of migrants from the north temperate zone in tropical habitats. *Wilson Bull.* 88:433–458.

Leck, C.F. 1972. The impact of some North American migrants at fruiting trees in Panama. *Auk* 89:842–850.

Leisler, B. 1990. Habitat selection and utilization of wintering migrants. Pages 156–174 in *Bird Migration—Physiology and Ecophysiology,* E. Gwinner, ed. Berlin: Springer-Verlag.

Lynch, J.F. 1989. Distribution of overwintering Nearctic migrants in the Yucatan Peninsula, I: General patterns of occurrence. *Condor* 91:515–544.

MacArthur, R.A. 1972. *Geographical Ecology.* New York: Harper and Row.

Marshall, J.T. 1988. Birds lost from a giant sequoia forest during fifty years. *Condor* 90:359–372.

Medel y Alvarado, L. 1963. *Historia de San Andres Tuxtla.* Mexico, D.F.: Editorial Citlatepetl.

Morel, G., and F. Bourlière. 1962 Relations ecologiques des avifaunes sedentaire et migratrice dans une savane sahelienne du bas Senegal. *La Terre et la Vie* 4:371–393.

Morton, E.S., and R. Greenberg. 1989. The outlook for migratory songbirds: "Future shock" for birders. *Am. Birds* 43:178–183.

Myers, N. 1980. *Conversion of Tropical Moist Forests.* Washington: National Academy of Sciences.

Rappole, J.H., and E.S. Morton. 1985. Effects of habitat alteration on a tropical avian forest community. Pages 1013–1021 in *Neotropical Ornithology,* P.A. Buckley, E.S. Morton, R.S. Ridgely, and F.G. Buckley, eds. Ornithol. Monogr. 36.

Rappole, J.H., and M.A. Ramos. 1985. The current status of threatened rain forest habitats of the Tuxtla Mountains of southern Veracruz with special emphasis on endangered birds and mammals. Pages 397–411 in *Primer Simposium Internacional de Fauna Silvestre,* L. Blankinship, ed. Mexico City: Sec. Desarollo Urbano y Ecologia.

Rappole, J.H., and D.W. Warner. 1980. Ecological aspects of avian migrant behavior in Veracruz, Mexico. Pages 353–393 in *Migrant Birds in the Neotropics: Ecology, Behavior, Distribution and Conservation,* A. Keast and E.S. Morton, eds. Washington: Smithsonian Institution Press.

Rappole, J.H., E.S. Morton, T.E. Lovejoy, III, and J.L. Ruos. 1983. *Nearctic Avian Migrants in the Neotropics.* Washington: U.S. Fish and Wildlife Service.

Rappole, J.H., M.A. Ramos, and K. Winker. 1989. Wintering Wood Thrush movements and mortality in southern Veracruz. *Auk* 106:402–410.

Robbins, C.S., D.K. Dawson, and B.A. Dowell. 1989. *Habitat Area Requirements of Breeding Forest Birds of the Middle Atlantic States.* Wildl. Monogr. 103.

Robinson, S.K., J. Terborgh, and J.W. Fitzpatrick. 1988. Habitat selection and relative abundance of migrants in southeastern Peru. *Acta 19th Internat. Ornithol. Cong.* (Ottawa): 2298–2307.

Sader, S.A., and A.T. Joyce. 1988. Deforestation rates and trends in Costa Rica, 1940–1983. *Biotropica* 20:11–19.

Winker, K. 1989. The Wood Thrush (*Catharus mustelinus*) on its wintering grounds in southern Veracruz, Mexico. M.S. thesis, University of Minnesota, Minneapolis.

Winker, K., J.H. Rappole, and M.A. Ramos O. 1990a. Population dynamics of the Wood Thrush in southern Veracruz, Mexico. *Condor* 92:444–460.

———. 1990b. Within-forest preferences of Wood Thrushes wintering in the rainforest of southern Veracruz. *Wilson Bull.* 102:715–720.

FRANK R. MOORE
Department of Biological Sciences
University of Southern Mississippi
Hattiesburg, Mississippi 39406-5018

TED R. SIMONS
National Park Service
Gulf Islands National Seashore
3500 Park Road
Ocean Springs, Mississippi 39564

Habitat suitability and stopover ecology of Neotropical landbird migrants

Abstract. The availability of suitable en route habitats where passage migrants can safely and rapidly deposit energy reserves is critical to a successful migration, especially for migrants that must cross geographic barriers. Existing evidence suggests that passage migrants select habitats during stopover and that differences in length of stopover and the rate of fat deposition during stopover are related to the intrinsic suitability of the habitat. Yet, the availability of suitable habitats during migration might be limited in the absolute sense, or effectively so, because migrants cannot search for the "best" stopover site. We discuss the importance of intrinsic (within-habitat) factors that determine the favorability of stopover habitat, and the influence of extrinsic (extra-habitat) factors on the opportunity to select habitats during migration.

Sinopsis. La disponibilidad de habitats adecuados en la ruta, en donde las migratorias de paso pueden rápida y seguramente acumular reservas energéticas, es crítica para una migración exitosa, especialmente para migratorias que deben atravesar barreras geográficas. La evidencia existente sugiere que las migratorias de paso seleccionan habitats durante sus paradas y que las diferencias en la duración de estas y la tasa de deposición de grasa durante las mismas, están relacionadas con la calidad intrínseca del habitat. Sin embargo, la disponibilidad de habitats adecuados durante la migración podría ser limitada en un sentido absoluto, o efectivamente porque las migratorias no pueden buscar el "mejor" sitio de parada. Nosotros discutimos la importancia de factores intrínsecos (dentro del habitat) que determinan la favorabilidad del habitat de parada y la influencia de factores extrínsecos (extra-habitat) sobre la oportunidad de seleccionar habitats durante la migración.

Approximately two-thirds of the breeding bird species of eastern United States forests migrate to tropical wintering areas in the Caribbean, Mexico, and Central and South America (Keast and Morton 1980). The benefits of that migration, regardless of whether they accrue through increased survivorship by overwintering in the tropics, increased productivity by breeding in temperate areas, or both, must be balanced against the increased cost experienced during migration (Fretwell 1972, Greenberg 1980, Gauthreaux 1982). Mortality during migration is difficult to estimate, but could be substantial (Lack 1946, Moreau 1972, Ketterson and Nolan 1982) because migrants face several problems during migration. For example, when a Red-eyed Vireo (*Vireo olivaceus*) stops en route, it might be in unfamiliar surroundings when energy demands are likely to be high (e.g., Loria and Moore 1990, Martin and Karr 1990). It might be necessary to resolve conflicting demands between predator avoidance and food acquisition (e.g., Metcalfe and Furness 1984, Lindstrom 1989, Lindstrom 1990), to compete with other migrants and resident birds for limited resources (e.g., Hutto 1985b, Lindstrom et al. 1990, Moore and Wang 1991), or to cope with unpredictable weather (e.g., Gauthreaux 1971, Alerstam 1990, Moore 1990). These problems are magnified when long-distance migrants must negotiate a geographical barrier (see Alerstam 1981, Loria and Moore 1990).

How well migrants offset the costs of migration, that is, satisfy energy demands and meet en route contingencies, depends not only on the intrinsic suitability of stopover habitat, but also on the time and energy available for selecting among alternative habitats, the relative availability of more suitable habitats, and the probability of survival during migration. In this paper, we focus on the stopover ecology of Neotropical landbird migrants following spring trans-Gulf migration and consider, first, the various factors that determine the intrinsic (within-habitat) suitability of stopover habitat and then ask how extrinsic (extra-habitat) factors might affect the opportunity to select favorable habitats during migration.

Trans-Gulf migration

The movement of birds across the Gulf of Mexico each spring and fall is a prominent feature of the Nearctic-Neotropical bird migration system (Lowery 1946, Buskirk 1980, Gauthreaux 1971, 1972, Able 1972, Rappole et al. 1983, Ramos 1988). From early April through mid-May, the day-to-day consistency of migration across the Gulf of Mexico is rarely interrupted, and then only when strong cold fronts are positioned over the southern Gulf of Mexico (Gauthreaux 1971). Migrants sometimes occur at very high densities in coastal habitats in response to weather that is unfavorable for continued migration (Gauthreaux 1971, 1972, Moore and Kerlinger 1987). Even with favorable weather, migrants use coastal habitats in large numbers (Moore and Simons,

unpubl. data).

The coastal woodlands and narrow barrier islands that lie scattered along the northern coast of the Gulf of Mexico probably provide important stopover habitat for Neotropical landbird migrants (Moore et al. 1990). They represent the last possible stopover before fall migrants make a nonstop flight (18–24 hr) of greater than 1,000 km, and the first possible landfall for birds returning north in spring (e.g., Rappole and Warner 1976, Moore and Kerlinger 1987). Unfortunately, the loss of coastal habitat suitable for forest-dwelling migrants is accelerating due to the extensive development of coastal regions. Between 1960 and 1985, the population living within 50 miles of the U.S. coast increased from 92.7 million people to 125 million people—52% of the population in the coterminous United States (U.S. Department of Commerce 1988). As stopover habitat is transformed or degraded, the cost of migration increases and the potential for a successful migration is jeopardized.

Intrinsic habitat suitability

Largely correlative evidence indicates that landbird migrants select among available habitats on the basis of factors intrinsic to the habitat (sensu Hutto 1985a). For example, Lindstrom and Alerstam (1986) interpreted the reoriented autumn migrations of Chaffinches (*Fringilla coelebs*) and Bramblings (*F. montifringilla*) along the southern coast of Sweden as flights to more suitable, inland habitats where fat deposits could be safely and rapidly deposited (Alerstam 1978, Sandberg et al. 1988). Later, Lindstrom (1990) suggested that habitat changes among Bramblings at more inland sites in southern Sweden depended on the ratio between habitat-specific rates of predation and fat deposition. When Bairlein (1983) mist netted Palearctic migrants in several habitats during autumn migration, he reported species-specific habitat associations, speculated that the patterns were related to "dietary preferences," and further suggested that observed preferences were innate because hatching-year individuals displayed the same pattern as adult migrants. Martin (1980) studied the distribution of spring migrants among shelterbelts (habitat "islands") on the Great Plains and suggested that migrants dispersed among the islands in relation to available food supply. The abundance of fruit in relation to energetic needs was responsible for attracting frugivorous migrants to second-growth woodlands in Panama (Martin 1985). When Hutto (1985b) examined the distribution and abundance of insectivorous migrants in southeastern Arizona, seasonal changes in bird density over different habitat types closely matched changes in food availability.

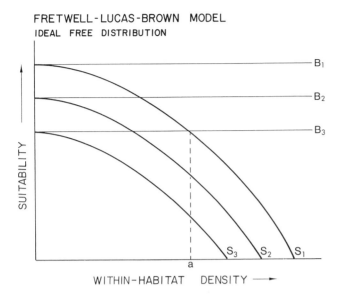

FRETWELL-LUCAS-BROWN MODEL
IDEAL FREE DISTRIBUTION

FIGURE 1. The ideal-free pattern of habitat selection given three hypothetical habitat types. See text for explanation.

EN ROUTE HABITAT SELECTION

Presumably, migrants select particular habitats to enhance their fitness. The Fretwell-Lucas-Brown model of habitat selection (Brown 1969, Fretwell and Lucas 1970, Fretwell 1972) provides a theoretical framework for studying habitat use by migrating birds. The model predicts that at low densities, a migrant should settle where it can achieve the highest fitness, that is, the highest rate of consumption of resources. As density increases, the rate of food consumption declines in the preferred habitat until a point is reached where the next arrivals will do just as well or better by settling in the next best habitat, and so on with additional habitats (Fig. 1).

According to the "ideal-free" pattern (Fretwell and Lucas 1970), the distribution of individuals in relation to habitat suitability results in each individual experiencing the same rate of acquisition of resources. In the situation depicted in Figure 1, intrinsic suitability (B) varies among three habitats in such a way that migrants would be expected to settle first in habitat 1 until density reduced the suitability of the preferred habitat to the intrinsic suitability of the second habitat (B_2), and so on until migrants are settling in all three habitats (point a on the abscissa). If the settlement pattern is "ideal-free," the relative suitabilities would be equal across the three habitats ($S_1 = S_2 = S_3$) and all migrants, irrespective of habitat choice, achieve the same fitness, even though the preferred habitats support the highest population density.

Alternatively, the opportunity to settle in a preferred habitat might be constrained by migrants already present, so that later arrivals are forced to occupy less suitable habitat. As a consequence of the "ideal-despotic" distribution, an individual's fitness would vary in relation to the intrinsic suitability of the habitat occupied, although all individuals within the same habitat would experience the same success (Fretwell and Lucas 1970, Fretwell 1972). The ideal-free and ideal-despotic models of habitat selection have not been applied to the use of habitat by passage migrants, although density-dependent patterns of settlement have been observed during migration (Viega 1986).

We examined the distribution of spring trans-Gulf migrants among five plant habitats on Horn Island, a barrier island off the northern coast of the Gulf of Mexico (Moore et al. 1990), and found that the distribution of migrants deviated from that expected based on the availability of habitats (Fig. 2). This result was consistent with habitat selection, that is, the differential, non-random use of alternative habitats. Migrants settled most frequently in Scrub-Shrub, Forest, and Relic Dune habitats. Whereas Scrub-Shrub comprised 14% of available habitat, it was characterized by the greatest number of species, the highest species diversity, and the largest number of individuals. More than twice the number of individuals ($n = 682$) were seen in Scrub-Shrub than any other habitat, and three times more than the number expected if migrants were distributed independently of habitat type. Of the 46 species observed, 94% were seen in Scrub-Shrub, 78% in Forest, 60% in Relic Dune, and only 37% of the species were seen in Marsh-Meadow and Primary Dune. Yet, only six or seven species should have been found in Scrub-Shrub habitat if they were distributed independently of habitat type. If the observed use of habitats on Horn Island was in accord with the ideal-free distribution, relative suitabilities among Scrub-Shrub, Forest, and Relic Dune habitats would be equivalent when all three habitats were occupied, and we would not expect fitness, or some fitness surrogate (e.g., rate of fat deposition), to differ among habitat types. On the other hand, if habitat selection were despotic, we would expect rates of fat deposition to differ among the three habitats.

Although we can only speculate why certain habitats were attractive to migrants on Horn Island, two observations suggest that shortly after migrants arrived on Horn Island they "ranked" alternative habitats during an initial exploratory phase: (1) When migrants arrived they appeared to "stream" through habitats in loose mixed-species groups, and seldom fed. Shortly thereafter, they were usually found foraging alone or in small single-species flocks. (2) The difference in habitat use between morning and afternoon observations is consistent with an initial exploratory phase. The distribution

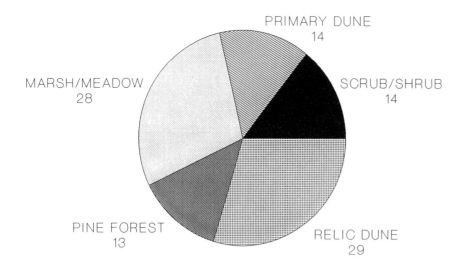

FIGURE 2a. Relative availability (percent occurrence) of different habitat types on Horn Island. See Moore et al. 1990 for habitat descriptions.

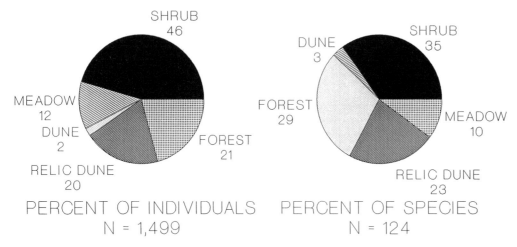

FIGURE 2b. Percent use of habitat types on Horn Island by individuals and species in spring 1987.

of migrants among habitat types was consistent with a pattern of random settlement in the afternoon. Because most trans-Gulf migrants arrive over the northern Gulf coast after 1000 (Gauthreaux 1971, 1972) and because many of the birds that stopped during the day left the island the evening of their arrival (see also Moore and Kerlinger 1987), migrants observed during afternoon censuses were likely to be birds that arrived that day, whereas birds observed during the morning censuses were birds that spent at least one day on the island. An initial "exploratory phase" to habitat selection might be adaptive if the availability of highly suitable habitat is unpredictable, as it probably would be for a passage migrant (see Hutto 1985a).

FOOD AVAILABILITY

Differences in habitat suitability might include differences in food abundance, competition, and shelter

against predators or adverse weather. Possibly the single most important constraint during migration is to acquire enough food to meet energetic requirements, especially for long-distance migrants which must overcome geographic barriers (Wood 1982, Bairlein 1985, Biebach et al. 1986, Moore and Kerlinger 1987, Safriel and Lavee 1988, Loria and Moore 1990). Individuals in migratory disposition (sensu Berthold 1975) become hyperphagic and deposit lipid stores which are mobilized to meet the energetic requirements of migration. Intercontinental migrants that must cross geographic barriers deposit fat on the average of 30–50% of their live mass (Berthold 1975, Blem 1980), whereas the fat reserves of short- and middle-distance migrants average only 13–25% (King and Farner 1965, Yarbrough and Johnston 1965). As lipid stores are depleted during migration, some free-ranging birds are capable of rapidly rebuilding reserves in a few days at rates approaching 10% of body mass/day (e.g., Dolnik and Blyumental

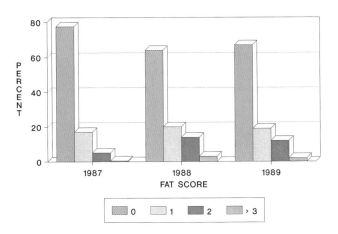

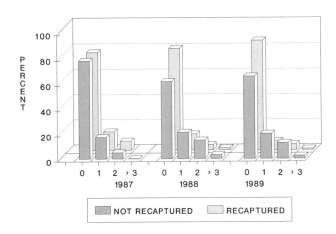

FIGURE 3a. Distribution of fat scores for spring trans-Gulf migrants captured 19 km off the Mississippi Gulf coast on East Ship Island in 1987 (*n* = 874), 1988 (*n* = 3,352) and 1989 (*n* = 3,122). Fat scoring after Helms and Drury (1960).

FIGURE 3b. Distribution of fat scores of migrants recaptured on E. Ship Island and migrants never recaptured in 1987, 1988, and 1989.

1967, Bairlein 1985, Biebach et al. 1986, Moore and Kerlinger 1987).

Birds mobilize stored lipid for energy when crossing the Gulf of Mexico, so many individuals arrive on the northern coast of the Gulf of Mexico in a fat-depleted condition (Moore and Kerlinger 1987; Fig. 3a). There are several consequences of arriving in such poor condition. Lean, fat-depleted birds remain longer at stopover sites than birds in better energetic condition (Cherry 1982, Bairlein 1985, Pettersson and Hasselquist 1985, Biebach et al. 1986, Moore and Kerlinger 1987). Trans-Gulf migrants recaptured during stopover were leaner than birds that departed the day of their arrival (i.e., were never recaptured) (Fig. 3b). Longer stopover periods could lead to delayed arrival on the breeding grounds (Lavee and Safriel 1989), and a migrant that arrives late on the breeding grounds might jeopardize opportunities to secure a territory or a mate (Francis and Cooke 1986). Migrants in poor condition are also more susceptible to predators (Metcalfe and Furness 1984) and the effects of adverse weather on food supplies.

Although it would be difficult to measure directly the effect of en route habitats on survival or reproductive success, it is possible to evaluate the immediate consequences in relation to how effectively migrants satisfy energy demands during migration. The availability of food in relation to energetic condition, for example, could be expected to influence how long passage migrants stay during stopover and the rate at which migrants replenish energy stores. The combination of having little reserve fat coupled with a high probability of building reserves should inhibit migratory activity (Gwinner et al. 1985, Terrill 1988). Conversely, low fat

combined with a low probability of replenishment should stimulate migration and the search for more suitable stopover habitat (Rappole and Warner 1976, Graber and Graber 1983, Lindstrom and Alerstam 1986, Sandberg et al. 1988).

Site-specific differences in the rate at which migrants deposit energy during stopover is probably correlated with food supply, although few studies have explicitly examined food abundance or resource availability (sensu Wiens 1984). Bibby and Green (1983) found that Sedge Warblers (*Acrocephalus schoenobaenus*) and Reed Warblers (*A. scirpaceus*) gained mass during fall passage at a French marshland near Le Migron, but failed to do so at a second stopover site near Passay, France. They related those differences to the abundance of plum-reed aphids (*Hyalopterus pruni*) at one of the sites. Sedge Warblers gained 0.40 and 0.55 g/day in 1973 and 1975, respectively, in the French marshland, but only 0.05 g/d when aphid abundance was very low in 1974 (Bibby et al. 1976). Sedge Warblers shortened their stay in 1974 when the likelihood of gaining mass was lower (Bibby et al. 1976). In central Spain, Pied Flycatchers (*Ficedula hypoleuca*) gained 0.11 g/day at one locality and 0.23 g/day at a second locality (Viega 1986). Because comparisons were made between different years, the differences in the rate at which Pied Flycatchers rebuilt reserves could be attributed to year-to-year variation in habitat suitability. Adult Pied Flycatchers at one locality, for example, gained 0.35 g/day in 1983 and only 0.16 g/day in 1984. In a third study, Mehlum (1983b) reported year-to-year differences in the rate of mass change among European Robins (*Erithacus rubecula*) at an island stopover site during fall migration: –0.32 g/day in 1975 vs. –0.72 g/day in 1976, although differences could not

TABLE 1. Mass change (g/day) and stopover length (SL) for trans-Gulf migrants at East Ship Island and Peveto Woods, two study sites along the northern coast of the Gulf of Mexico, in 1988

Species	East Ship Island				Peveto Woods				t	χ^2
	g/day $\bar{x} \pm 1$SE	SL $\bar{x} \pm 1$SE	n	% lost mass	g/day $\bar{x} \pm 1$SE	SL $\bar{x} \pm 1$SE	n	% lost mass	P	P
White-eyed Vireo *Vireo griseus*	0.00 ± 0.08	3.4 ± 0.6	30	56.7	0.33 ± 0.08	3.4 ± 0.6	33	18.2	<.01	<.01
Red-eyed Vireo *V. olivaecus*	−1.07 ± 0.09	1.9 ± 0.4	29	96.6	−0.19 ± 0.13	2.0 ± 0.3	36	58.3	<.01	<.01
Prothonotary Warbler *Protonotaria citrea*	−0.01 ± 0.04	8.4 ± 1.9	8	62.5	0.26 ± 0.29	4.2 ± 1.4	6	16.7	NS	NS
Black-and-white Warbler *Mniotilta varia*	−0.12 ± 0.11	1.6 ± 0.3	14	50.0	0.15 ± 0.07	2.5 ± 0.4	33	33.3	<.05	<.01
Worm-eating Warbler *Helmitheros vermivorus*	0.23 ± 0.21	2.2 ± 0.5	9	33.3	0.31 ± 0.09	3.7 ± 0.5	37	21.6	NS	NS
Swainson's Thrush *Catharus ustulatus*	−0.74 ± 0.35	1.6 ± 0.3	12	83.3	−0.05 ± 0.21	1.6 ± 0.1	41	43.9	NS	<.05
Gray-cheeked Thrush *C. minimus*	0.19 ± 0.23	2.6 ± 0.7	11	27.2	−0.27 ± 0.21	2.8 ± 0.5	24	58.3	NS	NS
Summer Tanager *Piranga rubra*	−1.61 ± 0.54	1.8 ± 0.5	8	87.5	0.22 ± 0.52	1.8 ± 0.2	19	42.0	<.05	NS
Orchard Oriole *Icterus spurius*	0.55 ± 0.16	1.9 ± 0.3	19	21.1	0.26 ± 0.49	2.5 ± 0.2	11	45.5	NS	NS
Indigo Bunting *Passerina cyanea*	−0.10 ± 0.26	3.5 ± 0.7	31	54.8	0.12 ± 0.09	3.1 ± 0.8	29	31.0	NS	NS

NOTE: Mass change and stopover length calculated according to Moore and Kerlinger (1987). Percent of migrants losing mass during stopover is given. Two sample t-test performed on rate of mass change. One-tailed probabilities given, though pattern of statistical significance is the same for two-tailed probabilities. Contingency chi-square performed on frequency losing mass during stopover at the two sites.

be related to food availability. The spring arrival of wood-warblers (Parulinae) in southern Illinois coincided with irruptions of lepidopteran larvae in 1979–1981, with peak numbers of birds present in arboreal habitats at or near the peak of larvae population (Graber and Graber 1983). The rate of food consumption by passage warblers in Illinois varied in relation to the supply of larvae. Finally, at two sites along the U.S. Gulf coast that varied in food abundance, fat-depleted birds experienced a higher probability of replenishing energy reserves at the more favorable site (Kuenzi 1989; Moore and Simons, unpubl. data; Table 1).

The availability of food resources and the rate at which migrants replenish energy reserves should be influenced by the density of migrants using stopover habitat (sensu Fretwell and Lucas 1970). Regardless of whether food is actually limited, we would expect competition during stopover because migrants with similar food requirements and heightened energy demands are concentrated in a small area (e.g., Hutto 1985b). Observations of territoriality among transients (e.g., Rappole and Warner 1976, Bibby and Green 1980, Mehlum 1983a, Sealy 1988, 1989), density-dependent patterns of settlement during migration (Viega 1986), and reports that migrants "track" habitats in relation to food availability (Hutto 1985b, Martin 1985, Martin and Karr 1986) are consistent with the occurrence of resource-based competition. If competition does occur during stopover, we would expect a decrease in the rate at which migrants replenish energy reserves (gain mass) either because the availability of food is depressed (Moore and Wang 1991) or because migrants have a direct effect on each other's intake rates (Goss-Custard 1984). Even when food availability is not depressed sufficiently to affect rates of mass gain, resource depression increases search time which could conflict with migration timing (cf. Safriel and Lavee 1988).

Factors other than migrant density might constrain food availability and affect habitat suitability. The physical structure of habitat is an important selective force in determining patterns of locomotion, foraging behavior, and resource exploitation. Habitat structure, including plant species composition and foliage structure, affects how birds move through the habitat and how they see and capture prey (Holmes and Robinson 1981, Robinson and Holmes 1982, 1984) and could affect the rate at which migrants replenish energy reserves.

Habitat extent or "patchiness" also contributes to habitat suitability and could influence the stopover ecology of migrants. Bird species require different threshold levels of habitat area below which they find habitat unsuitable (Cody 1985, Robbins et al. 1989a). Although usually discussed in the context of breeding success, sensitivity to area might affect habitat use during migration and the rate at which migrants replenish energy

reserves. Habitats along the northern coast of the Gulf of Mexico, for example, are fragmented, and many woodlands average only a few hectares in area. Development in the coastal zone is likely to continue the fragmentation of stopover habitat in the future.

PREDATION

The habitats used during migration also influence a migrant's vulnerability to predators. Lindstrom (1989) found that Chaffinch and Brambling flocks on migration through southern Sweden were repeatedly attacked by raptors and estimated that predation might be responsible for as much as 10% of the mortality among finches during autumn migration. Our observations of Neotropical migrants at study sites along the northern coast of the Gulf of Mexico revealed that birds are heavily preyed upon at some stopover sites (Moore et al. 1990) and indicated that predation pressure is positively correlated with migrant density. Kerlinger (1989) speculated that hawks migrate along coasts because of the concentration of potential prey, notably energetically stressed birds which might be easy prey.

Avoidance of predators must be balanced with energetic demands (e.g., Lima 1985). For example, the "trade-off" between foraging and predator avoidance is affected by the migrant's energetic condition (e.g., Metcalfe and Furness 1984). Fat-depleted migrants should be more willing to "trade off" the risk of predation to meet energetic requirements than birds that arrive with unmobilized fat in reserve (cf. Godin and Sproul 1988). Bramblings, for example, normally forage in fields of Summer Rape (Brassica napus) stubble where their rate of food intake is high, in spite of a high rate of predation, and switch to beech forest where the predation rate is lower in years of good beech mast crops (Lindstrom 1990).

Extrinsic effects on habitat suitability

Hutto (1985a) recognized that during migration, factors which affect the accessibility of suitable habitat can sometimes override ranking of habitats based solely on intrinsic (within-habitat) criteria such as food availability (Table 2). Favorable en route habitat is probably limited for migrants (see Sprunt 1975, Hutto 1985b, Martin and Karr 1986), or effectively so because migrants often cannot search extensively for the "best" stopover site. For example, if fatigue and low energy reserves are the primary causes for trans-Gulf migrants landing at coastal stopover sites (Rappole and Warner 1976, Moore and Kerlinger 1987), the opportunity to search for more suitable habitats will be circumscribed by more immediate energetic needs. For a fat-depleted migrant, unfamiliar with the availability of favorable habitat, the

TABLE 2. Intrinsic (within-habitat) and extrinsic (extra-habitat) constraints on habitat use in relation to geographic scale

Geographic scale or distance between habitats	Factors contributing to the costs and benefits of habitat use	
	Intrinsic[a]	Extrinsic[b]
Broad Scale, Distant	Unimportant	Important
Local Scale, Close	Important	Unimportant

NOTE: Modified from Hutto (1985a).
a. Food abundance, habitat structure, habitat patchiness, Competition, predation.
b. Habitat availability, energetic state, weather, time.

benefits of rejecting suboptimal habitats might be out-weighed by the cost of finding a more suitable site. Habitat selection during migration is time-limited, if not by energetic constraints then by travel-time constraints (Alerstam and Lindstrom 1990). Consequently, rejection of suboptimal habitats (greater discrimination among alternative habitats) will depend upon the relative abundance of optimal and inferior habitats, the time available to search for optimal habitats, the migrant's searching efficiency, and the probability of survival during migration (cf. Ward 1987). The latter factor is likely to be age-dependent (Greenberg 1980, Gauthreaux 1982, Ketterson and Nolan 1983), thus leading us to expect different habitat use between yearling and adult birds.

Weather, for example, is an extrinsic factor that affects the likelihood of a migrant's staying at a stopover site and the probability of its settling there in the first place. The peak of trans-Gulf migration occurs over the latter half of April through early May and coincides with a period of predictable southerly airflow and infrequent frontal activity (Buskirk 1980). Nevertheless, unfavorable weather associated with frontal activity (i.e., northerly winds and precipitation) occasionally extends south to the Gulf coast and into the Gulf of Mexico, forcing migrants to "fallout" when and where they might not otherwise stop (Lowery 1955, Gauthreaux 1971, 1972). Migrants encountering weather unfavorable for migration stop in large numbers along the Gulf coast regardless of the intrinsic suitability of stopover habitats. When Moore and Kerlinger (1987) looked at the energetic condition of migrants in relation to weather, more lean birds and fewer fat migrants ceased mi-

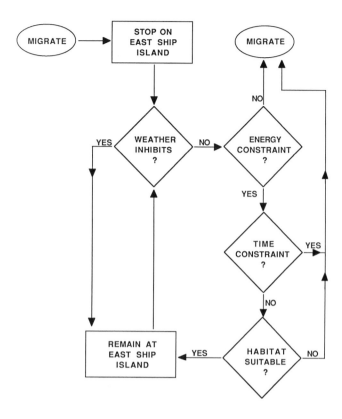

FIGURE 4. Flowchart summarizing possible "decisions" made by a spring trans-Gulf migrant during stopover following a flight across the Gulf of Mexico.

grating on clear days when winds were favorable for migration.

Discussion

Habitat use during migration has profound consequences for a bird's (1) ability to satisfy energy requirements, (2) vulnerability to predators, and (3) exposure to environmental stress. Although the intrinsic suitability of stopover habitat will determine the response of passage migrants to en route problems, it is not the only factor that determines whether and how long the bird interrupts its migration. Figure 4 depicts the set of "decisions" a hypothetical migrant might make when it stops following a trans-Gulf flight. Although it is convenient to represent those "decisions" sequentially, the reality of the process is more complex. For example, Gauthreaux (1971) argued that weather is largely an inhibitory influence on the nightly initiation of passerine migration. His radar studies along the coast of Louisiana revealed that birds initiated migration under a wide variety of weather conditions and that the day-to-day constancy of spring trans-Gulf migration and subsequent departure from coastal stopover areas was rarely interrupted. In the absence of adverse weather such as rain and head winds, only lean migrants are likely to stay (Moore and Kerlinger 1987). Even among lean birds the probability of staying is dependent on intrinsic suitability, including food availability and predation pressure, and subject to time constraints (Alerstam and Lindstrom 1990). The time allocated to migration affects the likelihood of finding a better habitat and might override a "decision" based simply on the relative abundance of superior habitat.

It is also important to recognize that the opportunity to select high quality habitats might be constrained by factors extrinsic to the habitat itself. When adverse weather conditions are encountered while aloft, for example, a migrant might be forced to land in habitat it would otherwise bypass. If energy reserves are depleted, stopover "options" are more narrowly circumscribed (i.e., the probability that stopover habitat will be accepted varies with the energetic state of the migrant).

If the persistence of migrant populations depends on the bird's ability to find favorable conditions for survival throughout the annual cycle (Morse 1980a, Keast and Morton 1980, Rappole et al. 1983, Robbins et al. 1989b, Terborgh 1989, Askins et al. 1990), factors associated with the en route ecology of migrants must figure in any analysis of population change and in the development of a comprehensive conservation "strategy" for Neotropical wintering landbird migrants. Yet, their conservation is complicated by the very life history characteristic that permits them to exploit seasonal environments, namely migration (Morse 1980b, Myers et al. 1987, Hutto 1988, Holmes and Sherry 1988, Gradwohl and Greenberg 1989). For a representative intercontinental landbird migrant, such as a Red-eyed Vireo or Magnolia Warbler (*Dendroica magnolia*), choice of habitat must be made in Neotropical wintering quarters, in temperate breeding areas, and repeatedly during migration. Each of the habitats encountered during the migrant's annual cycle faces different threats of degradation and destruction. Unfortunately we still know little about the status of the stopover habitats upon which migratory birds depend. Although habitats represent a crucial link in the annual cycle of these birds, we do not know what types of habitat are most important, where they occur, and how their distribution and abundance are changing as a result of development and land conversion.

We are reminded that "if little is known about the contingencies facing migrants on their wintering grounds, even less is known about the challenges that they face along their migratory lanes" (Morse 1980a). That statement remains as true today as it was a decade ago, and we still know almost nothing about stopover habitats. Unless habitat requirements during migration are met, conservation measures which focus on temperate breeding grounds and/or Neotropical wintering areas will be compromised.

Acknowledgments

Research on the stopover biology of Neotropical migrants has been funded by the University of Southern Mississippi Research Council, the National Geographic Society, the Department of Interior (National Park Service), and the State of Mississippi Heritage Program. P. Kerlinger and A. Kuenzi contributed to the development of this manuscript.

Literature cited

Able, K.P. 1972. Fall migration in coastal Louisiana and the evolution of migration patterns in the Gulf region. *Wilson Bull.* 84:231–242.

Alerstam, T. 1978. Reoriented bird migration in coastal areas: Dispersal to suitable resting grounds? *Oikos* 30:405–408.

———. 1981. The course and timing of bird migration. Pages 9–54 in *Animal Migration*, D.J. Aidley, ed. Soc. Exp. Biol. Seminar Series 13, Cambridge: Cambridge University Press.

———. 1990. Ecological consequences of bird orientation. *Experientia* 46:405–415.

Alerstam, T., and A. Lindstrom. 1990. Optimal bird migration: The relative importance of time, energy, and safety. Pages 331–351 in *Bird Migration—Physiology and Ecophysiology*, E. Gwinner, ed. Berlin: Springer-Verlag.

Askins, R.A., J.F. Lynch, and R. Greenberg. 1990. Population declines in migratory birds in eastern North America. *Current Ornithol.* 7:1–57.

Bairlein, F. 1983. Habitat selection and associations of species in European passerine birds during southward, post-breeding migrations. *Ornis Scand.* 14:239–245.

———. 1985. Body weights and fat deposition of Palaearctic passerine migrants in the central Sahara. *Oecologia* 66:141–146.

Berthold, P. 1975. Migration: Control and metabolic physiology Pages 77–128 in *Avian Biology*, Vol. 5, D.S. Farner and J.R. King, eds. New York: Academic Press.

Bibby, C.F., and R.E. Green. 1980. Foraging behavior of migrant pied flycatcher, *Ficedula hypoleuca*, on temporary territories. *J. Anim. Ecol.* 49:507–521.

———. 1983. Food and fattening of migrating warblers in some French marshlands. *Ringing and Migration* 4:175–184.

Bibby, C.F., R.E. Green, G.R.M. Pepler, and P.A. Pepler. 1976. Sedge warbler migration and reed aphids. *Brit. Birds* 69:384–399.

Biebach, H., W. Friedrich, and G. Heine. 1986. Interaction of body mass, fat, foraging and stopover period in trans-Sahara migrating passerine birds. *Oecologia* 69:370–379.

Blem, C.R. 1980. The energetics of migration. Pages 175–224

in *Animal Migration, Orientation, and Navigation*, S.A. Gauthreaux, Jr., ed. New York: Academic Press.

Brown, J.L. 1969. Territorial behavior and population regulation in birds. *Wilson Bull.* 81:293–329.

Buskirk, W.H. 1980. Influence of meteorological patterns and trans-Gulf migration on the calendars of latitudinal migrants. Pages 485-491 in *Migrant Birds in the Neotropics: Ecology, Behavior, Distribution and Conservation*, A. Keast and E.S. Morton, eds. Washington: Smithsonian Institution Press.

Cherry, J.D. 1982. Fat deposition and the length of stopover of migrant white-crowned sparrows. *Auk* 99:725–732.

Cody, M.L. 1985. An introduction to habitat selection in birds. Pages 3–56 in *Habitat Selection in Birds*, M.L. Cody, ed. New York: Academic Press, Inc.

Dolnik, V.R., and T.I. Blyumental. 1967. Autumnal premigratory and migratory periods in the Chaffinch (*Fringilla coelebs coelebs*) and some other temperate zone birds. *Condor* 69:435–468.

Francis, C.M., and F. Cooke. 1986. Differential timing of spring migration in wood warblers (Parulinae). *Auk* 103:584–556.

Fretwell, S. 1972. *Populations in a Seasonal Environment*. Princeton: Princeton University Press.

Fretwell, S.D., and H.L. Lucas, Jr. 1969. On territorial behavior and other factors influencing habitat distribution in birds. I. Theoretical development. *Acta Biotheor.* 19:16–36.

Gauthreaux, S.A., Jr. 1971. A radar and direct visual study of passerine spring migration in southern Louisiana. *Auk* 88:343–365.

———. 1972. Behavioral responses of migrating birds to daylight and darkness: A radar and direct visual study. *Wilson Bull.* 84:136–148.

———. 1982. The ecology and evolution of avian migration systems. Pages 93–167 in *Avian Biology*, Vol. 6. D.S. Farner and J.R. King, eds. New York: Academic Press.

Godin, J.-G.J., and C.D. Sproul. 1988. Risk taking in parasitized sticklebacks under threat of predation: Effects of energetic need and food availability. *Can. J. Zool.* 66:2360–2367.

Goss-Custard, J.D. 1984. Intake rates and food supply in migrating and wintering shorebirds. Pages 233–270 in *Behavior of Marine Animals*, Vol. 6, J. Burger and B.L. Olla, eds. New York: Plenum Press.

Graber, J.W., and R.R. Graber. 1983. Feeding rates of warblers in spring. *Condor* 85:139–150.

Gradwohl, J., and R. Greenberg. 1989. Conserving nongame migratory birds: A strategy for monitoring and research. Pages 297–328 in *Audubon Wildlife Report 1989/1990*. W.J. Chandler et al., eds. New York: Academic Press.

Greenberg, R. 1980. Demographic aspects of long-distance migration. Pages 493–504 in *Migrant Birds in the Neotropics: Ecology, Behavior, Distribution and Conservation*, A. Keast and E.S. Morton, eds. Washington: Smithsonian Institution Press.

Gwinner, E., H. Biebach, and I. Kreis. 1985. Food availability affects migratory restlessness in Garden Warblers (*Sylvia borin*). *Naturwissenshaften* 72:51–52.

Helms, C.W. and W.H. Drury. 1960. Winter and migratory weight and fat: Field studies on some North American buntings. *Bird-Banding* 31:1–40.

Holmes, R.T., and S.K. Robinson. 1981. Tree species preferences of foraging insectivorous birds in a northern hardwoods forest. *Oecologia* 48:31–35.

Holmes, R.T., and T.W. Sherry. 1988. Assessing population trends of New Hampshire forest birds: Local vs. regional patterns. *Auk* 105:756–768.

Hutto, R.L. 1985a. Habitat selection by nonbreeding, migratory landbirds. Pages 455–476 in *Habitat Selection in Birds*, M.L. Cody, ed. New York: Academic Press, Inc.

———. 1985b. Seasonal changes in the habitat distribution of transient insectivorous birds in southeastern Arizona: Competition mediated? *Auk* 102:120–132.

———. 1988. Is tropical deforestation responsible for the reported declines in neotropical migrant populations? *Am. Birds* 42:375–379.

Keast, A., and E.S. Morton, eds. 1980. *Migrant Birds in the Neotropics: Ecology, Behavior, Distribution, and Conservation*. Washington: Smithsonian Institution Press.

Kerlinger, P. 1989. *Flight Strategies of Migrating Hawks*. Chicago: University of Chicago Press.

Ketterson, E.D., and V. Nolan, Jr. 1982. The role of migration and winter mortality in the life history of a temperate-zone migrant, the Dark-eyed Junco, as determined from demographic analyses of winter populations. *Auk* 99:243–259.

———. 1983. The evolution of differential bird migration. *Current Ornithol.* 1:357–402.

King, J.R., and D.S. Farner. 1965. Studies of fat deposition in migratory birds. *Ann. N.Y. Acad. Sci.* 131:422–440.

Kuenzi, A.J. 1989. Stopover biology of Nearctic-Neotropical passerine migrants on East Ship Island, Mississippi. M.S. thesis, Southern Mississippi University, Hattiesburg.

Lack, D. 1946. Do juvenile birds survive less well than adults? *Brit. Birds* 32:258–264.

Lavee, D., and S. Safriel. 1989. The dilemma of cross-desert migrants—stopover of skip a small oasis? *J. Arid Environ.* 17:69–81.

Lima, S.L. 1985. Maximizing feeding efficiency and minimizing time exposed to predators: A tradeoff in the Black-capped Chickadee. *Oecologia* 66:60–67.

Lindstrom, A. 1989. Finch flock size and risk of hawk predation at a migratory stopover site. *Auk* 106:225–232.

———. 1990. The role of predation risk in stopover habitat selection in migrating Bramblings, *Fringilla montifringilla*. *Behav. Ecol.* 1:102–106.

Lindstrom, A., and T. Alerstam. 1986. The adaptive significance of reoriented migration of Chaffinches *Fringilla coelebs* and Bramblings *F. montifringilla* during autumn in southern Sweden. *Behav. Ecol. Sociobiol.* 19:417–424.

Lindstrom, A., D. Hasselquist, S. Bensch, and M. Grahn. 1990. Asymmetric contests over resources for survival and migration: A field experiment with bluethroats. *Anim. Behav.* 40:453–461.

Loria, D., and F.R. Moore. 1990. Energy demands of migration on Red-Eyed Vireos, *Vireo olivaceus*. *Behav. Ecol.* 1:24–35.

Lowery, G.H. 1946. Evidence of trans-Gulf migration. *Auk* 63:175–211.

———. 1955. *Louisiana Birds*. Baton Rouge: Louisiana State University Press.

Martin, T.E. 1980. Diversity and abundance of spring migratory birds using habitat islands on the Great Plains. *Condor* 82:430-439.

————. 1985. Selection of second-growth woodlands by frugivorous migrating birds in Panama: An effect of fruit size and plant density. *J. Trop. Ecol.* 1:157–170.

Martin, T.R., and J.R. Karr. 1986. Patch utilization by migrating birds: Resource oriented? *Ornis Scand.* 17:165–174.

————. 1990. Behavioral plasticity of foraging maneuvers of migratory warblers: Multiple selection periods for niches? Pages 353–359 in *Avian Foraging: Theory, Methodology, and Applications,* M.L. Morrison, D.J. Ralph, J. Berner, and J.R. Jehl, Jr., eds. Studies in Avian Biology 13.

Mehlum, F. 1983a. Weight changes in migrating Robins (*Erithacus rubecula*) during stop-over at the island of Store Faerder, Outer Oslofjord, Norway. *Fauna Norv.* Ser. C, Cinclus 6:57–61.

————. 1983b. Resting time in migrating Robins (*Erithacus rubecula*) at Store Faerder, Outer Oslofjord, Norway. *Fauna Norv.* Ser. C, Cinclus 6:62–72.

Metcalfe, N.B., and R.W. Furness. 1984. Changing priorities: The effect of pre-migratory fattening on the trade-off between foraging and vigilance. *Behav. Ecol. Sociobiol.* 15:203–206.

Moore, F.R. 1990. Evidence of redetermination of migratory direction following wind displacement. *Auk* 107:425–428.

Moore, F.R., and P. Kerlinger. 1987. Stopover and fat deposition by North American wood-warblers (Parulinae) following spring migration over the Gulf of Mexico. *Oecologia* 74:47–54.

Moore, F.R., P. Kerlinger, and T.R. Simons. 1990. Stopover on a Gulf coast barrier island by spring trans-Gulf migrants. *Wilson Bull.* 102:487–500.

Moore, F.R., and Wang Yong. 1991. Intercontinental bird migrants compete for food resources during stopover. *Behav. Ecol. Sociobiol.* 28:85–90.

Moreau, R.E. 1972. *The Palearctic-African Bird Migration System.* New York: Academic Press.

Morse, D.H. 1980a. Population limitations: Breeding or wintering grounds? Pages 437–453 in *Migrant Birds in the Neotropics: Ecology, Behavior, Distribution and Conservation,* A. Keast and E.S. Morton, eds. Washington: Smithsonian Institution Press.

————. 1980b. *Behavioral Mechanisms in Ecology.* Cambridge: Harvard University Press.

Myers, J.P., R.I.G. Morrison, P.Z. Antas, B.A. Harrington, T.E. Lovejoy, M. Sallaberry, S.E. Senner, and A. Tarak. 1987. Conservation strategy for migratory species. *Am. Scientist* 75:19–26.

Pettersson, J., and D. Hasselquist. 1985. Fat deposition and migration capacity of Robins *Erithacus rubecula* and Goldcrest *Regulus regulus* at Ottenby, Sweden. *Ringing and Migration* 6:66–75.

Ramos, M.A. 1988. Eco-evolutionary aspects of bird movements in the northern Neotropical region. *Acta 19th Internat.* *Ornithol. Cong.* (Ottawa): 251–293.

Rappole, J.H., and D.W. Warner. 1976. Relationships between behavior, physiology and weather in avian transients at a migration stopover site. *Oecologia* 26:193–212.

Rappole, J.H., E.S. Morton, T.E. Lovejoy, III, and J.L. Ruos. 1983. *Nearctic Avian Migrants in the Neotropics.* Washington: U.S. Fish and Wildlife Service.

Robbins, C.S., D.K. Dawson, and B.A. Dowell. 1989a. *Habitat Area Requirements of Breeding Forest Birds of the Middle Atlantic States.* Wildl. Monogr. 103.

Robbins, C.S., J.R. Sauer, R.S. Greenberg, and S. Droege. 1989b. Population declines in North American birds that migrate to the neotropics. *Proc. Natl. Acad. Sci.* 86:7658–7662.

Robinson, S.K., and R.T. Holmes. 1982. Foraging behavior of forest birds: The relationships among search tactics, diet, and habitat structure. *Ecology* 63:1918–1931.

————. 1984. Effects of plant species and foliage structure on the foraging behavior of forest birds. *Auk* 101:672–684.

Safriel, U.N., and D. Lavee. 1988. Weight changes of cross-desert migrants at an oasis—do energetic considerations alone determine the length of stopover? *Oecologia* 76:611–619.

Sandberg, R., J. Pettersson, and T. Alerstam. 1988. Why do migrating robins, *Erithacus rubecula,* captured at two nearby stop-over sites orient differently? *Anim. Behav.* 36:865–876.

Sealy, S.G. 1988. Aggressiveness in migrating Cape May Warblers: Defense of an aquatic food source. *Condor* 90:271–274.

————. 1989. Defense of nectar resources by migrating Cape May Warblers. *J. Field Ornithol.* 60:89–93.

Sprunt, A. 1975. Habitat management implications of migration. Pages 81–86 in *Proc. Symp. on Management of Forest and Range Habitats for Non-game Birds.* USDA Forest Service, GTR WO-1.

Terborgh, J. 1989. *Where Have All the Birds Gone?* Princeton: Princeton University Press.

Terrill, S.B. 1988. The relative importance of ecological factors in bird migration. *Acta 19th Internat. Ornithol. Cong.* (Ottawa): 2180–2190.

Viega, J.P. 1986. Settlement and fat accumulation by migrant Pied Flycatchers in Spain. *Ringing and Migration* 7:85–98.

Ward, S.A. 1987. Optimal habitat selection in time-limited dispersers. *Am. Nat.* 129:568–579.

Wiens, J. 1984. Resource systems, populations and communities. Pages 397–436 in *A New Ecology,* P.W. Price, W.S. Gaud, and C.N. Slobodchikoff, eds. New York: Wiley.

Wood, B. 1982. The trans-Saharan spring migration of yellow wagtails (*Motacilla flava*). *J. Zool., London* 197:267–283.

Yarbrough, C.G., and D.W. Johnston. 1965. Lipid deposition in wintering and premigratory Myrtle Warblers. *Wilson Bull.* 77:175–191.

FRANZ BAIRLEIN*
Physiological Ecology Section
Department of Zoology
University of Cologne
5000 Cologne 41, F.R.G.

Morphology-habitat relationships in migrating songbirds

Abstract. During migration, birds are faced with a large variety of habitats from which they might derive energy for migratory fat deposition. In the present study, birds were investigated during their migratory stopover, at one site in SW-Germany during fall migration and at another on the Louisiana coast following spring trans-Gulf migration. The analysis was based on standard mist netting, and the frequency distribution of captures was used as an index of habitat use. External morphological variables of the functional complexes "flying," "pedal locomotion," and "bill" were related to variation in the species-specific patterns of habitat use. At both study sites, habitat selection was related to the morphological features of the flying apparatus and the hind limb. Long-distance migrants that relied on their wings for foraging chose open habitats with vegetation gaps, or tended to minimize flight while behaving in their habitats during migratory stopover. Because body morphology is one important feature related to habitat selection, detailed ecomorphological work could provide important information about habitat selection in the birds' annual cycle, and consequently, about the impact of land use, and about habitat preservation and management.

Sinopsis. Durante la migración, las aves se enfrentan a una gran variedad de habitats de los cuales podrían obtener energía para la deposición de grasa. En este trabajo, se estudiaron aves migratorias durante sus paradas de descanso en dos áreas: una en el suroeste de Alemania en el transcurso de la migración otoñal y la otra en la costa de Louisiana después de la migración a través del Golfo de México en primavera. El análisis se basa en capturas regulares con redes de niebla y la frecuencia de captura se toma como un índice del uso habitacional. Variables morfológicas externas de los complejos funcionales "vuelo", "locomoción pedal" y "pico" se relacionan con la variación en los patrones específicos de uso habitacional de cada especie. En los dos estudios, la selección de habitat estuvo relacionada con las características morfológicas del aparato de vuelo y las extremidades posteriores. Las migratorias de larga distancia dependientes de sus alas para alimentarse escogieron habitats abiertos con claros en la vegetación, o tendieron a minimizar el vuelo durante su permanencia en dichos habitats durante la parada migratoria.

*Current address: "Vogelwarte Helgoland," An der Vogelwarte 21, 2940 Wilhelmshaven, West Germany.

Puesto que la morfología corporal es una característica importante en relación con la selección de habitat, trabajos ecomorfológicos detallados podrían proveer información importante sobre dicha selección en el transcurso del ciclo anual del ave y, por lo tanto, sobre el impacto del uso de la tierra y la preservación y manejo del habitat sobre la selección del mismo.

Migration is one of the most energy-demanding processes for birds. Many migrant songbirds, for example, accumulate much fat prior to or even during migration at particular stopover sites with body mass gains of up to 100% above nonmigratory levels (Bairlein 1978, Berthold 1975, Blem 1980). To meet the physiological preparation for migration, species depend on adequate food supplies and foraging conditions. Therefore, availability of habitats and appropriate habitat use during migratory stopover are prerequisites for successful migration.

During migration, migrants are often faced with variable habitat conditions and food supplies. Habitat selection of migrants during migration, however, is less well known (Hutto 1985a). Among the factors involved in habitat use, much attention is given to the roles of food availability and vegetation structure (Hutto 1985a). Intrinsic factors, by contrast, are less often considered. Aside from possible physiological constraints (Walsberg 1985), a bird's morphology is important in understanding the exploitation of available resources (Winkler and Leisler 1985). Morphological characters can predispose birds to occupy a given habitat or to use a particular foraging mode (Lederer 1984, Leisler and Winkler 1985). Therefore, knowledge of the morphological characters of species and their functions might contribute to the understanding of ecological segregation of species, and might help to evaluate predictions about ecological and behavioral patterns of resource partitioning within an avian community. As pointed out by Leisler and Winkler (1985), the study of ecomorphology addresses interrelationships between morphological variation in birds and the corresponding variation in ecology in a more general sense, rather than dealing with the adaptive significance of certain morphological features.

The objectives of this paper are to show two case studies in which migrants were investigated at stopover sites and to relate external morphological variation between species to variation in habitat use. The first study was conducted on Palearctic passerines during their fall southward migration in central Europe; the second was conducted on Nearctic passerine migrants during their spring northward migration in coastal Louisiana.

Methods

STUDY SITES. The European study was carried out within a long-term capture program on 36 bird species during their fall migration at a trapping station at the west end of Lake Constance/South-Germany (Berthold and Schlenker 1975). From late June to early November, 52 6-m nets were placed continuously in eight different habitats ranging from a dense bushy thicket (habitat A in Fig. 1) to a dense reed bed at the lake shore (habitat H in Fig. 1).

The study of North American passerines was conducted at a coastal Louisiana stopover site during their northward migration in 1988 (see Moore and Kerlinger 1987). Twenty-two 12-m and four 6-m nets were continuously used in a small woodland near the shore from the end of March to mid-May. Four of the 12-m nets were set up in canopy gaps 3 m above ground. Although the Louisiana study site might represent only one habitat type, a woodland, there was an obvious mosaic of different microhabitats which were used to classify habitat selection. The netting sites matched these microhabitats quite well.

DATA COLLECTION. The analyses in both studies were based on captures of migrants at their stopover sites and on measurements of external morphological characters in the field.

In both studies birds were caught, without flushing, using mist nets placed at the same locations and heights throughout the study. Patterns of habitat use were derived from these capture locations. For each bird we recorded the number of the net (which indicated its location of capture), and the number of the net panel (each net was divided into four panels, each 0.5 m in height) in which it was caught. For further analysis, the species-specific percentage distributions of specimens caught among the nets or net levels were used as an index of habitat use and stratification, respectively. Although some biases may exist by using netting operations to derive habitat use because of different trapabilities in different habitats (e.g., open versus dense habitats), its suitability as an index of habitat use is proven. Both comparisons of observational data and concurrent netting results, and the analysis of the patterns of habitat association of recaptures in relation to birds caught for the first time did not show significant biases using nets (Bairlein 1981).

In addition to analysis of patterns of habitat use during migratory stopover, morphological characters were measured to identify relationships between morphological variation and habitat selection. The morphology of the 32 European species investigated (Table 1) was de-

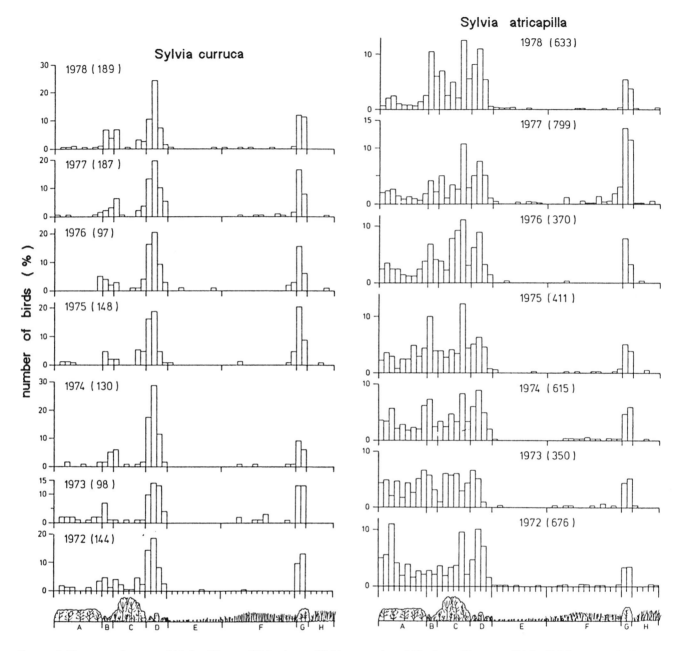

FIGURE 1: Patterns of captured birds of Lesser Whitethroat (*Sylvia curruca*) and Blackcap (*S. atricapilla*) in SW-Germany during autumn migration in seven successive years. Bars show number of captured birds (first time) in one mist net within the migratory season. Habitats covered by mist netting: *A*, bushy thicket; *B*, sparse bushes; *C*, wood, *D*, grassy open scrub with small trees; *E*, sedges; *F*, dry reeds; *G*, bank with bushes; *H*, flooded reeds. Number of trapped birds within a season in parentheses (after Bairlein 1981).

scribed by 36 external variables: 14 variables are related to the flying apparatus (wing and tail; Table 2), 11 to hind limb (tarsus and foot), and 11 to the feeding apparatus (bill structure and bristles). With few exceptions, 20 specimens of each species were measured in the field.

For North American songbirds, I measured 22 external morphological characters, and derived three from ratios (see Tables 6–8). Of the total 681 specimens measured from 41 species, only 26 wood-warbler species had appropriate sample sizes to be included in the analysis (see Table 5). This taxonomic group is well suited for a

TABLE 1. The 32 bird species measured during fall migration in Europe

1. European Blackbird (*Turdus merula*)
2. Bluethroat (*Luscinia svecica*)
3. Blue Tit (*Parus caeruleus*)
4. Whinchat (*Saxicola rubetra*)
5. Common Whitethroat (*Sylvia communis*)
6. Great Reed Warbler (*Acrocephalus arundinaceus*)
7. Grasshopper Warbler (*Locustella naevia*)
8. Willow Warbler (*Phylloscopus trochilus*)
9. Garden Warbler (*Sylvia borin*)
10. Redstart (*Phoenicurus phoenicurus*)
11. Icterine Warbler (*Hippolais icterina*)
12. Spotted Flycatcher (*Muscicapa striata*)
13. Black Redstart (*Phoenicurus ochruros*)
14. Dunnock (*Prunella modularis*)
15. Whitethroat (*Sylvia curruca*)
16. Great Tit (*Parus major*)
17. Blackcap (*Sylvia atricapilla*)
18. Red-backed Shrike (*Lanius collurio*)
19. Red Bunting (*Emberiza schoeniclus*)
20. Savi's Warbler (*Locustella luscinoides*)
21. European Robin (*Erithacus rubecula*)
22. Sedge Warbler (*Acrocephalus schoenobaenus*)
23. Aquatic Warbler (*Acrocephalus paludicola*)
24. Songthrush (*Turdus philomelos*)
25. Firecrest (*Regulus ignicapillus*)
26. Marsh Warbler (*Acrocephalus palustris*)
27. Reed Warbler (*Acrocephalus scirpaceus*)
28. Pied Flycatcher (*Ficedula hypoleuca*)
29. Wryneck (*Jynx torquilla*)
30. Goldcrest (*Regulus regulus*)
31. Wren (*Troglodytes troglodytes*)
32. Chiffchaff (*Phylloscopus collybita*)

TABLE 2. Principal component analysis of 36 external characters of 32 species of European songbirds

Character	Principal component			
	I	II	III	IV
Flight characters				
Wing chord		0.56		
Wing width	0.51			
Wing area				
Wing span				
Wing tip to primary 10		0.81		
Wing tip to secondary 1		0.91		
Notch on inner web of second primary				
Tail length				
Graduation of tail[a]	-0.93			
Wing load[b]				
Wing slenderness[c]		0.75		
Wing length/tail length				
Wing length/tarsus length				
Wing width/wing span		-0.87		
Bill structure				
Bill length (skull)			0.83	
Bill depth			-0.75	
Bill width/nostril			-0.59	
Bill width/base		0.61		
Number of rictal bristles	0.82			
Rictal bristle length	0.75			
Bill length/bill width			0.91	
Bill length/bill depth			0.93	
Bill width/bill depth				
Bill length/wing length			0.70	
Bill length/tarsus length				
Hind limb				
Foot span	-0.64			
Foot span with claws				0.60
Hind toe				
Inner toe				
Middle toe				
Outer toe	-0.62			0.57
Hind claw				0.57
Inner claw				0.90
Middle claw				0.89
Outer claw				0.94
Tarsus length			0.59	
PERCENTAGE OF TOTAL VARIANCE	34.4	15.4	12.8	9.3
CUMULATIVE PERCENTAGE OF VARIANCE	34.4	49.8	62.6	71.9

SOURCE: Bairlein et al. 1986.

NOTE: Only signifcant PC loadings are shown.

a. Distance between shortest and longest tail feather (positive value in convex tails, negative in concave tails).

b. Body mass/wing area.

c. (Wing span)^2/wing area

detailed ecomorphological analysis as proposed by Lederer (1984) who suggested that such analyses be restricted to similar species. Wood-warblers are thought to be a morphological homogeneous group with regard to their foraging mode, even though some species do not follow the general pattern of foliage-gleaners (Morse 1985). In addition, even though all of the wood-warblers are migrants, their migratory distances are quite different. The migratory distances used in the analysis were derived from information provided in the A.O.U. Check-list (1983), and they were estimated as the distances between the species-specific centers of breeding and wintering grounds.

STATISTICAL METHODS. To identify groups of species with similar patterns of capture and characters in morphology, cluster analysis (average linkage) based upon a matrix of Euclidean distances was used as an index of dissimilarity between the species (Sneath and Sokal 1973).

For analyses of morphological data and relationships to ecological data, I used multivariate statistical methods. These methods enabled the simultaneous use of many variables and, thus, included more information, although their analytical sophistication might be rather low (Miles and Ricklefs 1984, Leisler and Winkler 1985). Prior to analysis, the original variables were adjusted to body size differences among the species (Miles and Ricklefs 1984, Leisler and Winkler 1985).

The structure of the morphological space occupied by a given species was investigated using principal component analysis (PCA). The PCA technique makes it possible to consider all of the original variables simultaneously and to extract combinations of original variables, the principal components (PC), that account for the greatest amount of variation in the original data matrix (Morrison 1976). Graphs of the PC derived variables (axes) provide insights into morphological segregation of species.

Canonical correlation analysis (CCA) was used to describe quantitatively the relationships between the morphological data set and corresponding ecological data, To reduce the morphological character set (Leisler and Winkler 1985), the morphological data were first subjected to a PCA, and the derived principal components were then used in the CCA. The correlations of the derived canonical axes (canonical variates), both with the variables of the data sets and between the data sets, provide a useful basis for interpretation.

In all multivariate analyses, interpretation of the derived components is based upon their correlation to the original variables and the known functional correlates (reviewed, for example, in Leisler 1980, Lederer 1984, Leisler and Winkler 1985).

Results

ECOMORPHOLOGY IN PALEARCTIC PASSERINE MIGRANTS

HABITAT DISTRIBUTION. Caught individuals of each species were not equally distributed across a habitat gradient; rather, they were associated with certain habitats (Fig. 1). Each species was characterized by a species-specific distribution of captures within each habitat type, which was highly consistent between years, thus reflecting strong species-specific patterns of habitat use.

Distinct groups of species were identified by cluster analysis (Fig. 2). These groups were characterized by similar habitat use because of their specific spatial patterns of capture. Two highly dissimilar groups were identified which divided birds of reed beds (the lower cluster) from birds of scrub and woods (upper cluster). Within these groups, further clusters of species emerged. Among the reed bed species, Bluethroats, Reed Buntings, and Grasshopper Warblers occurred more in drier areas whereas the others (Savi's Warbler to Sedge Warbler) preferred the dense wet reed zone. The entire sample of shrub and woodland species was differentiated into species preferring dense scrub and woodland, and species of open, savanna-like scrubs. Similar differentiation into groups of species with similar habits were found regarding the vertical distribution of species within habitats, as derived from analysis of the species-specific distributions of captures across vertical net levels (Bairlein 1981). These data clearly demonstrate that migrants differ in their patterns of habitat use during migratory stopover.

Some species change habitat use between breeding and stopover sites. Blue Tits, for example, typically inhabit woodlands during the breeding season (Perrins 1979), while they are abundant in reed beds during migration. Furthermore, some species shift their habitat selection at one particular study site within the same migratory season or even within a day (Bairlein 1981), even though availabilty of habitats did not change. Chiffchaffs, for example, particularly occurred in scrub until the end of August with only 10% of captures in reed beds, but increasingly invaded reed beds from September onward (26% in September and 44% in October, respectively).

MORPHOLOGICAL FEATURES. The most important morphological features derived by PCA from the 36 variables were characters relating to flight abilities (Table 2). Whereas PC I represents mainly graduation of tail, roundedness of wing, foot size, and number and length of rictal bristles, PC II indicates long, pointed wings combined with relatively broad bills. Species scoring high in PC I are maneuverable flyers with short feet, with the ability to capture flying prey; those scoring high in PC II have long pointed wings, which facilitates high performance flight enabling them to sally for insect prey. PC III ordinates species primarily with respect to slenderness of bill, and PC IV is positively correlated with lengths of claw, representing increasing clinging ability.

In the following canonical correlation analysis, these four principal components, explaining almost 72% of the total variance within the morphological characters, were related to data on habitat (net) distribution and stratification (vertical net levels, Bairlein et al. 1986). This analysis yielded two significant sets of correlations (Table 3). The first canonical axis was negatively correlated both with PC I and net panel, indicating a strong correlation between size of foot, graduation of tail, and length of rictal bristles, and vertical stratum selection (Fig. 3). Thus, species captured near the ground were mainly characterized by morphological features typical of pedal locomotion. The second significant canonical axis was correlated with PC II and habitat distribution of captures (Table 3). It represents a significant relationship between flight characteristics and habitat use. This important relationship is particularly obvious if a separate PCA of the 14 characters relating to flying is conducted (Table 4). PC I represents mainly a long pointed wing, and separates relatively long-winged species from shorter-winged species. Functionally, higher values along that axis are associated with an increase

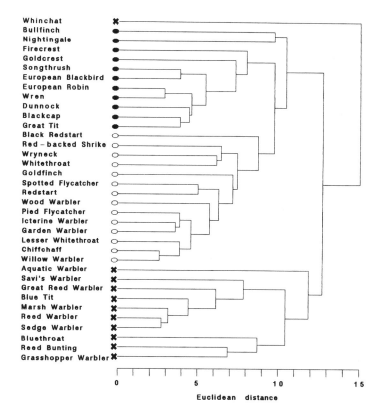

FIGURE 2: Dendrogram for 36 habitat distributions of species investigated during migratory stopover in SW-Germany. *Open ovals*, birds caught in dense scrub and woodlot; *closed ovals*, birds caught in open savanna-like scrub; *x*, birds caught in reed beds (after Bairlein 1983).

TABLE 3. Canonical correlation analysis of morphology and ecology of 32 bird species during migratory stopover

	Correlation with canonical variate	
	I	II
Morphology		
PC I (decreasing graduation of tail, small foot, increasing rictal bristles length)	-0.92	0.30
PC II (increasing wing pointedness, broader bills)	-0.25	-0.78
PC III (longer, slender bill)	0.28	0.29
PC IV (increasing clinging)	-0.09	-0.47
Ecology		
Net location (habitat)[a]	0.26	-0.97
Net level (stratum)	-0.99	-0.08
CANONICAL CORRELATION	0.61	0.38
	$P < 0.001$	$P < 0.01$

NOTE: Morphological data are the PCA scores from Table 2.
a. cf. Figure 1.

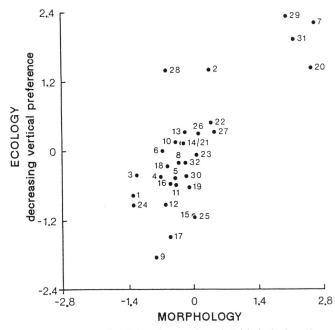

FIGURE 3: First canonical correlation between two ecological characters and four principal component scores derived from 36 morphological characters in 32 bird species (see Tables 2 and 3 for further details) studied during their fall stopover in SW-Germany. Numbers refer to species code noted in Table 1 (from Bairlein et al. 1986).

in the ability for high performance flights, typical of long-distance migrants (Leisler and Winkler 1985). PC II is correlated with characters representing rounded wings and is related to maneuverability. Consequently, in the space spanned by these two PC-axes (Fig. 4), the upper right species combine long pointed wings with maneuverable wings indicating that these species are particularly adapted to foraging on flying insects by sallying. The relationship between the ordination of species in that morphological space and the pattern of habitat selection which emerged from cluster analysis reveals that species with this particular morphological combination were typically found in open, savanna-like scrub. Birds inhabiting reed beds, by contrast, generally scored low in PC II. Species caught mainly in the dense scrub are morphologically characterized by short, maneuverable wings which are adapted for living in thickets.

ECOMORPHOLOGY OF MIGRATING WOOD-WARBLERS IN SPRING

HABITAT USE. From cluster analysis of habitat use (distribution of captures across the various nets), five distinct groups of species emerged (Fig. 5). They differ significantly (χ^2 tests, $P < 0.05$) with respect to capture rates in canopy gaps, in nets located in open understory

TABLE 4. Principal component analysis of 14 morphological flight characters of 33 species of European songbirds

Character	Principal component		
	I	II	III
Wing chord	0.77	0.54	-0.28
Wing width	0.04	0.86	-0.38
Wing area	0.39	0.53	0.63
Wing span	0.65	0.67	-0.15
Wing tip to primary 10	0.86	0.11	-0.03
Wing tip to secondary 1	0.97	0.01	-0.01
Notch on inner web of second primary	-0.22	0.94	-0.02
Tail length	0.33	0.30	-0.16
Graduation of tail[a]	-0.12	-0.74	0.07
Wing load[b]	-0.10	-0.28	0.94
Wing slenderness[c]	0.65	-0.25	0.52
Wing length/tail length	0.37	0.21	-0.10
Wing length/tarsus length	0.55	0.47	0.25
Wing width/wing span	-0.81	0.38	-0.33
PERCENTAGE OF TOTAL VARIANCE	38.7	27.0	11.8
CUMULATIVE PERCENTAGE OF VARIANCE	38.7	65.7	77.5

SOURCE: Bairlein 1981.

NOTE: In addition to the set of species in Table 1, data on Moustached Warbler (*Acrocephalus melanopogon*) are included.

a. Distance between shortest and longest tail feather (positive value in convex tails, negative in concave).

b. Body mass/wint area.

c. (Wing span)^2/wing area.

TABLE 5. Taxonomic list of the warbler species (with their acronyms and sample size) measured during spring migration in Louisiana

Species	Sample size	Species	Sample size
Prothonotary Warbler (PRWA) *Protonaria citrea*	13	Prairie Warbler (PIWA) *Dendroica discolor*	1*
Blue-winged Warbler (BWWA) *Vermivora pinus*	20	Bay-breasted Warbler (BBWA) *Dendroica castanea*	21
Golden-winged Warbler (GWWA) *Vermivora chrysoptera*	20	Blackpoll Warbler (BPWA) *Dendroica striata*	11
Brewster Warbler (BRWA) *Vermivora pinus x chrysoptera*	1*	Yellow Warbler (YEWA) *Dendroica petechia*	20
Tennessee Warbler (TEWA) *Vermivora peregrina*	20	Mourning Warbler (MOWA) *Oporornis philadelphia*	2*
Orange-crowned Warbler (OCWA) *Vermivora celata*	5	Kentucky Warbler (KEWA) *Oporornis formosus*	20
Nashville Warbler (NAWA) *Vermivora ruficapilla*	1*	Canada Warbler (CAWA) *Wilsonia canadensis*	14
Northern Parula (NOPA) *Parula americana*	8	Hooded Warbler (HOWA) *Wilsonia citrina*	50
Black-and-white Warbler (BAWW) *Mniotilta varia*	20	Worm-eating Warbler (WEWA) *Helmitheros vermivorus*	20
Cerulean Warbler (CRWA) *Dendroica cerulea*	20	Swainson's Warbler (SWWA) *Limnothlypis swainsonii*	16
Blackburnian Warbler (BKWA) *Dendroica fusca*	15	Ovenbird (OVEN) *Seiurus aurocapillus*	20
Chestnut-sided Warbler (CHSD) *Dendroica pensylvanica*	20	Louisiana Waterthrush (LOWA) *Seiurus motacilla*	8
Magnolia Warbler (MGWA) *Dendroica magnolia*	20	Northern Waterthrush (NOWA) *Seiurus noveboracensis*	21
Yellow-rumped Warbler (YRWA) *Dendroica coronata*	22	Common Yellowthroat (COYE) *Geothlypis trichas*	10
Black-throated Green Warbler (BTGW) *Dendroica virens*	19	American Redstart (AMRE) *Setophaga ruticilla*	20
Yellow-throated Warbler (YTWA) *Dendroica dominica*	2*		

* = not in analysis because of small sample size.

beneath a dense canopy, in nets located in dense undergrowth with canopy, and in nets set up in dense scrub with only a few taller trees.

MORPHOLOGY. The structure of the external morphology of the 26 warbler species is best revealed by separate PCAs of the functional complexes of wing, foot, and bill, respectively.

Regarding wing and tail, most significant variation among species is related to features of wings adapted to high-performance flights (Table 6). Species scoring high in this component (Fig. 6) showed relatively long, pointed wings with considerable wing-load. Highest scores were attained by some of the canopy species (Fig. 5).

Moreover, PC I is strongly correlated with migration distance (Fig. 7). PC II is correlated with broader wings, longer tails, and deeper feather notches, and characterizes more maneuverable fliers. Along that axis the highest scores are attained by species that hawk for food.

Foot size is the major feature derived from PCA of the 10 hind limb characters, followed by length of the hind and inner toes, and tarsus length (Table 7). Within the space spanned by components I and III, some species or groups of species are well separated (Fig. 8). Species with large feet and long tarsi are adapted to cling to vertical surfaces, whereas large feet and short tarsi are characteristic of species that creep along trunks. Worm-eating Warblers and Swainson's Warblers

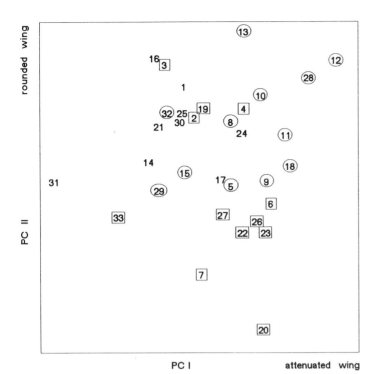

FIGURE 4: Plot of first two component axes in a principal component analysis of 14 external forelimb characters of 33 European migratory bird species. Center of species code gives position of the species in that space. For species codes see Table 1. *Numbers without symbol*, species caught in dense scrub and woodlot; *numbers circled*, species caught in open scrub; *numbers boxed*, species caught in reed beds (after Bairlein 1981).

Discussion

Habitat selection of migrants during stopover appears to be most related to morphological structure of the flying apparatus and the leg and foot. Bill structure plays a minor role, although it influences both the size of the prey taken and the foraging behavior (e.g., probing, pecking).

Habitat use of migratory bird species seems to be particularly constrained by the morphology necessary for migration. Long, pointed wings seem to be a prerequisite for high-performance flights in long-distance migration (Leisler and Winkler 1985). Consequently, wing shape is strongly correlated with migratory distance. Long-distance migrants appear to be somewhat restricted in habitat selection; they either use habitats in which they rely on pedal locomotion, or they chose open habitats with vegetation gaps which facilitate flight.

Waterthrushes and Ovenbirds, which are adapted to their migration by quite attenuated wings, were caught mainly in the dense understory where they forage by walking or hopping. The European long-distance migratory *Acrocephalus* and *Locustella* species, which are particularly adapted for long-distance migration, are reluctant to use their wings while in reed habitats (Leisler and Winkler 1985). Consequently, these species are well adapted in their hind-limb morphology to cling to vertical and horizontal surfaces, including the ground (see also Leisler and Winkler 1985). Other long-distance migrants, such as the old-world *Sylvia* warblers which need their wings also for foraging in shrub habitats, were found in the open savanna-like habitats of the study site. Similar results were derived from the wood-warbler study. Some of the *Dendroica* warblers with attenuated wings (Fig. 6) were caught principally in canopy gaps. These observations are consistent with the many observations from the tropical wintering grounds where migrants often occupy drier open habitats and forest gaps, rather than dense forest (for examples, see Moreau 1972, Keast and Morton 1980, Curry-Lindahl 1981, Buckley et al. 1985, Cody 1985, Levey 1988, Leisler 1990). In turn, thicket habitats with dense understory or even dense canopy, which would require rounded, maneuverable wings for flights, can be exploited by species that do not migrate long distances. Examples include the Common Yellowthroat, Northern Parula, or Orange-crowned Warbler in the Nearctic, and the Bullfinch, European Wren, or tits in the Palearctic. Thus, it appears that morphology is intimately involved in habitat selection and resource partitioning even during migratory stopover (Hutto 1985b).

Fine-tuned interactions between morphology and habitat use are obvious in observed within-season habitat shifts of some European species at a particular

might be characterized as species that walk on horizontal structures. Ground-dwellers ordinated low in PC I.

The third functional complex studied was the foraging apparatus. PCA extracted two components of interest (Table 8). PC I shows a positive correlation with longer bills and shorter rictal bristles. PC II correlates with bill width. Ordination of species in that morphological space (Fig. 9) reveals a major group of warblers with relatively short bills, representing their general foliage-gleaning habits. Some other groups are well separated. The Hooded Warbler and American Redstart, with relatively short, broad bills and long rictal bristles, are adapted to hawking insects. The Tennessee Warbler, Orange-crowned Warbler, and Northern Waterthrush have thin bills, possibly adapted to foliage-gleaning on less mobile prey. The long narrow bills of Prothonotary Warblers, Worm-eating Warblers, Blue-winged Warblers, and Swainson's Warblers appear to be adapted to probing for prey and/or to closing their bills more rapidly (Greenberg 1981).

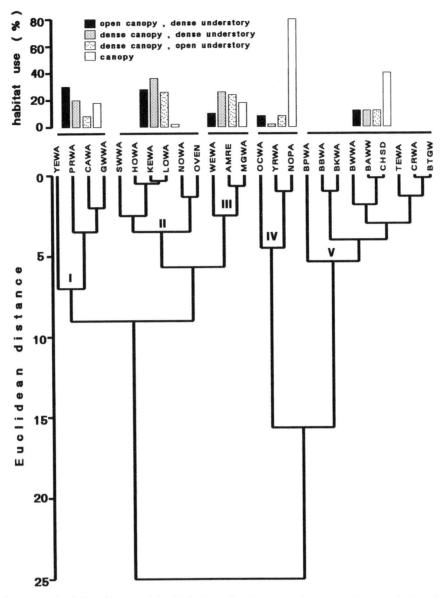

FIGURE 5: Dendrogram (Euclidian distances) for 25 habitat distributions of wood-warblers studied during spring stopover at Louisiana Gulf coast in 1988. Figures above dendrogram show percentages of specimens of each cluster trapped in the four most prominent habitat categories. For species acronyms see Table 5. Roman numbers within the derived clusters are used for further cluster identification.

stopover site. These local habitat shifts might be best explained by changes in food availabilities between habitats. The scrubby sites in the European study, for example, provide much food until defoliation occurs in early fall, whereupon reed beds exhibit a relatively better food supply (Bairlein 1981). Although food availability might be the proximate factor in such shifts (Hutto 1985a), morphology seems to predispose a species' ability to change habitats opportunistically. From the few data available, it appears that the only species able to

use very different habitats depend on morphological features adapted to function efficiently in several types of habitat. The Chiffchaff, for example, which lives mainly in shrub habitats, but invades into reed beds during migratory stopover, exhibits hind-limb character variation tending toward the typical reed bed species (Bairlein 1981, Leisler and Winkler 1985).

Even large-scale (geographical) habitat shifts and changes in foraging behavior in a species' annual cycle might be related to morphological structure.

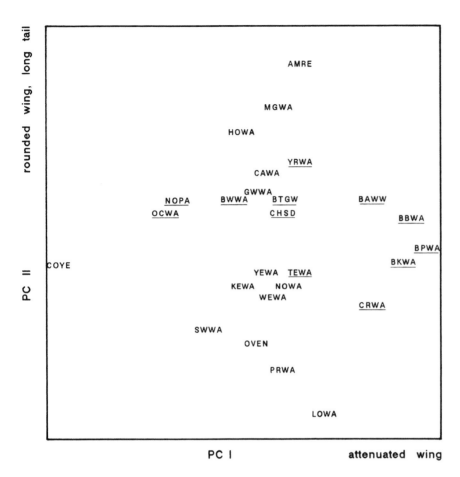

FIGURE 6: Plot of first two component axes in a principal component analysis of 11 external forelimb characters of 26 wood-warblers (cf. Table 6). Center of species acronym gives position of the species in that space. For species acronyms see Table 5. Underlined species were found mainly in the canopy (clusters IV and V in Fig. 5), the others in the understory (clusters I–III in Fig. 5).

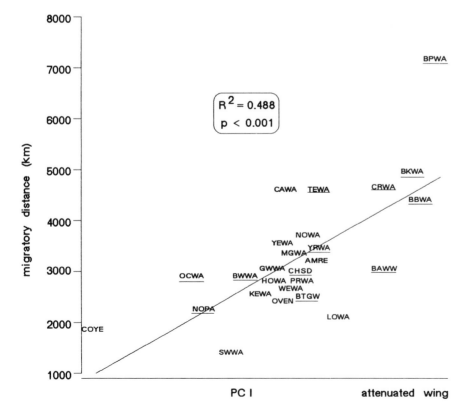

FIGURE 7: Relationship between migratory distance and flight performance (principal component I in Table 6) in 26 wood-warbler species. Center of species acronym gives position of the species in that space. For species acronyms see Table 5.

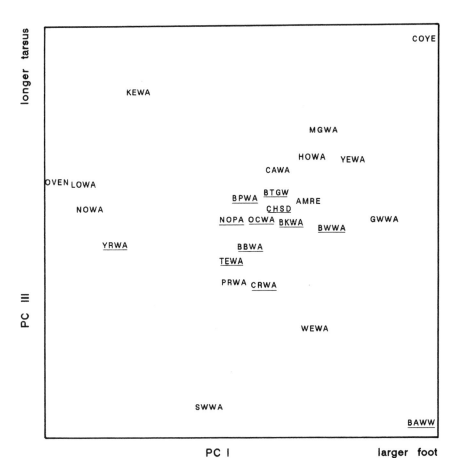

FIGURE 8: Plot of principal component axes I and III in a principal component analysis of 10 external hind limb characters of 26 wood-warblers. For further explanations see Fig. 6.

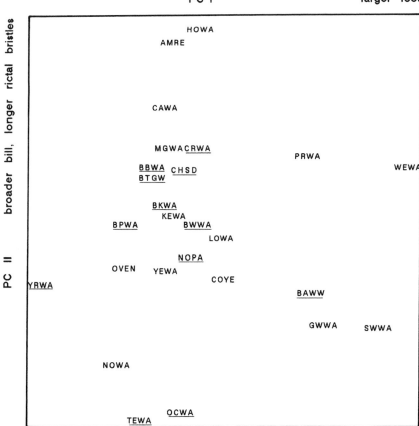

FIGURE 9: Plot of first two component axes in a principal component analysis of four external bill characters of 26 wood-warblers. For further explanations see Fig. 6

TABLE 6. Correlations of the principal components with the original characters in a PCA of 11 forelimb characters of 26 wood-warblers

Character	Principal component	
	I	II
Wing chord	0.992[c]	0.026
Wing width	0.310	0.856[c]
Wing area	0.833[c]	0.058
Wing span	0.993[c]	-0.013
Wing tip to primary 10	0.971[c]	0.182
Wing tip to secondary[a]	0.844[c]	-0.479
Notch on inner web of second primary	0.211	0.545[c]
Tail length	0.308	0.857[c]
Wing load[a]	-0.521	-0.672[c]
Wing slenderness[b]	0.465	-0.792[c]
Wing width/wing span	-0.640[c]	0.715[c]
PERCENTAGE OF TOTAL VARIANCE	49.6	32.9
CUMULATIVE PERCENTAGE OF VARIANCE	49.6	82.5

a. Body mass/wing area
b. (Wing span)^2/wing area
c. Coefficients used for interpretation

TABLE 7. Correlations of the principal components with the original characters in a PCA of 10 hind limb characters of 26 wood-warblers

Character	Principal component		
	I	II	III
Foot span with claws	0.883*	0.336	-0.263
Hind toe	0.706*	0.559*	0.086
Inner toe	0.689*	0.691*	-0.123
Middle toe	0.863*	-0.169	0.065
Outer toe	0.842*	-0.099	-0.311
Hind claw	0.839*	-0.485	0.047
Inner claw	0.860*	-0.350	0.178
Middle claw	0.861*	-0.433	0.180
Outer claw	0.841*	0.061	-0.208
Tarsus length	0.340	0.333	0.853*
PERCENTAGE OF TOTAL VARIANCE	62.2	15.7	10.3
CUMULATIVE PERCENTAGE OF VARIANCE	62.2	77.9	88.2

* = coefficients used for interpretation.

TABLE 8. Correlations of the principal components with the original characters in a PCA of 4 bill characters of 26 wood-warblers

Character	Principal component	
	I	II
Bill length (skull)	0.738*	0.504
Bill depth	0.905*	0.251
Bill width/base	-0.277	0.916*
Rictal bristle length	-0.865*	0.400
PERCENTAGE OF TOTAL VARIANCE	54.7	32.9
CUMULATIVE PERCENTAGE OF VARIANCE	54.7	87.6

* = coefficients used for interpretation.

Worm-eating Warblers, which live in broad-leaved forests and forage on live foliage during the breeding season, invade moist forests to forage on dead leaves on their tropical wintering grounds (Greenberg 1987). Their short tarsi, combined with a relatively large foot and the long bill, might be adaptations for flexibility in variable resource use during their annual cycle (Greenberg 1987).

Considerable similarities in ecomorphological features have been found in the few studies carried out during migratory stopover (Bairlein 1981), even though studies varied in habitat type, scale of habitat (macrohabitats versus microhabitats), and in avian guild composition. Even if these similarities indicate more general principles of habitat use by migrants and possible morphological constraints, more data on ecological variables are needed for a refined analysis and interpretation, and to draw general conclusions regarding factors that determine habitat use in migrants, both during migration stopover and in tropical wintering habitats (Leisler 1990). Such detailed ecomorphological studies based on a wide variety of morphological and ecological characters, however, might enable us to evaluate hypotheses on the ecological structure and dynamics of avian communities, even during stopover, much better than relying on simple physical habitat features (Winkler and Leisler 1985). In this context, multivariate statistical methods permit simultaneous use of many characters and identification of interesting correlates. In turn, these techniques could help to identify the ecological and behavioral features of a species, within a guild or even a community (for example, Karr and James 1975, Holmes et al. 1979, Ricklefs and Travis 1980, Miles and Ricklefs 1984). To my knowledge, ecomorphology has not been applied to conservation efforts. Nevertheless, refined ecomorphological studies in avian communities might be of particular interest for wildlife conservationists and others concerned about the effects of human-land use on wildlife species. Such studies might provide identification of ecological requirements of a guild in critical need of preservation through habitat management. Moreover, these studies are likely to allow predictions on the impact of habitat alterations or even clearing of vegetation on wildlife (e.g. Rappole and Morton 1985).

Acknowledgments

I thank F.R. Moore for providing the opportunity to study the ecomorphology of Nearctic passerines on the Louisiana Gulf coast during spring migration in 1988, and for reading a first draft of this manuscript. The study was further supported by the Deutsche Forschungsgemeinschaft. The study of the European songbirds was carried out at the Vogelwarte Radolfzell, Max-Planck-Institute for Ethology. Moreover, I gratefully acknowledge further comments on the manuscript by J.M. Hagan, D.W. Johnston, B. Leisler, C.J. Ralph, and an anonymous reviewer.

Literature cited

American Ornithologists' Union. 1983. *Check-list of North American Birds.* 6th ed. Washington: American Ornithologists' Union.

Bairlein, F. 1981. Ökosystemanalyse der Rastplätze von Zugvögeln. *Ökol. Vögel* 3:7–137.

———. 1983. Habitat selection and associations of species in European passerine birds during southward, post-breeding migrations. *Ornis Scand.* 14:239–245.

———. 1987. The migratory strategy of the garden warbler: A survey of field and laboratory data. *Ringing and Migration* 8:59–72.

Bairlein, F., B. Leisler, and H. Winkler. 1986. Morphologische Aspekte der Habitatwahl von Zugvögeln in einem SW-deutschen Rastgebiet. *J. Ornithol.* 127:463–473.

Berthold, P. 1975. Migration: Control and metabolic physiology Pages 77–128 in *Avian Biology*, Vol. 5, D.S. Farner and J.R. King, eds. New York: Academic Press.

Berthold, P., and R. Schlenker. 1975. Das "Mettnau-Reit-Illmitz-Programm"—ein langfristiges Vogelfangprogramm der Vogelwarte Radolfzell. *Vogelwarte* 28:97–123.

Blem, C.R. 1980. The energetics of migration. Pages 175–224 in *Animal Migration, Orientation, and Navigation*, S.A. Gauthreaux, ed. New York: Academic Press.

Buckley, P.A., M.S. Foster, E.S. Morton, R.S. Ridgely, and F.G. Buckley, eds. 1985. *Neotropical Ornithology.* Ornithol. Monogr. 36

Cody, M.L., ed. 1985. *Habitat Selection in Birds*, New York: Academic Press, Inc.

Curry-Lindahl, K. 1981. *Bird Migration in Africa.* London: Academic Press.

Greenberg, R. 1981. Dissimilar bill shapes in New World tropical versus temperate forest foliage-gleaning birds. *Oecologia* 49:143–147.

———. 1987. Seasonal foraging specialization in the Worm-eating Warbler. *Condor* 89:158–168.

Holmes, R.T., R.E. Bonney, Jr., and S.W. Pacala. 1979. Guild structure of the Hubbard Brook bird community: A multivariate approach. *Ecology* 60:512–520.

Hutto, R.L. 1985a. Habitat selection by nonbreeding, migratory landbirds. Pages 455–476 in *Habitat Selection in Birds*, M.L. Cody, ed. New York: Academic Press, Inc.

———. 1985b. Seasonal changes in the habitat distribution of transient insectivorous birds in southeastern Arizona: Competition mediated? *Auk* 102:120–132.

Karr, J.R., and F.C. James. 1975. Eco-morphological configurations and convergent evolution in species and communities. Pages 258–291 in *Ecology and Evolution of Communities*, M.L. Cody, ed. Cambridge: Belknap.

Keast, A., and E.S. Morton, eds. 1980. *Migrant Birds in the Neotropics: Ecology, Behavior, Distribution, and Conservation.* Washington: Smithsonian Institution Press.

Lederer, R.J. 1984. A view of avian ecomorphological hypotheses. *Ökol. Vögel* 6:119–126.

Leisler, B. 1980. Morphological aspects of ecological specialization in bird genera. *Ökol. Vögel* 2:199–220.

———. 1990. Habitat selection and utilization of wintering migrants. Pages 156–174 in *Bird Migration—Physiology and Ecophysiology*, E. Gwinner, ed. Berlin: Springer-Verlag.

Leisler, B., and H. Winkler. 1985. Ecomorphology. *Current Ornithol.* 2:155–186.

Levey, D.J. 1988. Tropical wet forest treefall gaps and distributions of understory birds and plants. *Ecology* 69:1076–1089.

Miles, D.B., and R.E. Ricklefs. 1984. The correlation between ecology and morphology in deciduous forest passerine birds. *Ecology* 65:1629–1640.

Moore, F., and P. Kerlinger. 1987. Stopover and fat deposition by North American wood-warblers (Parulinae) following spring migration over the Gulf of Mexico. *Oecologia* 74:47–54.

Moreau, R.E. 1972. *The Palaearctic-African Bird Migration Systems.* London: Academic Press.

Morrison, D.F. 1976. *Multivariate Statistical Methods.* Tokyo: McGraw-Hill Kogakusha.

Morse, D.H. 1985 Habitat selection in North American parulid warblers. Pages 131–157 in *Habitat Selection in Birds*, M.L. Cody, ed. New York: Academic Press, Inc.

Perrins, C.M. 1979. *British Tits.* London: Collins.

Rappole, J.H., and E.S. Morton. 1985. Effects of habitat alteration on a tropical avian forest community. Pages 1013–1021 in *Neotropical Ornithology*, P.A. Buckley, E.S. Morton, R.S. Ridgely, and F.G. Buckley, eds. Ornithol. Monogr. 36.

Ricklefs, R.E., and J. Travis. 1980. A morphological approach to the study of avian community organization. *Auk* 97:321–338.

Sneath, P.H.A., and R.R. Sokal. 1973. *Numerical Taxonomy.* San Francisco: Freeman.

Walsberg, G.E. 1985. Physiological consequences of microhabitat selection. Pages 389–413 in *Habitat Selection in Birds*, M.L. Cody, ed. New York: Academic Press, Inc.

Winkler, H., and B. Leisler. 1985. Morphological aspects of habitat selection in birds. Pages 415–434 in *Habitat Selection in Birds*, M.L. Cody, ed. New York: Academic Press, Inc

ROSA MARÍA VIDAL-RODRIGUEZ
Asociacion Mexicana Pro-Conservacion
de la Naturaleza (PRONATURA)
Apdo 219 San Cristobal de las Casas
29200, Chiapas, Mexico

Abundance and seasonal distribution of Neotropical migrants during autumn in a Mexican cloud forest

Abstract. Transect censuses were conducted during the autumn of 1987 in an isolated cloud forest near San Cristobal de las Casas, Chiapas, Mexico. The censuses were conducted on an almost daily basis to delineate the seasonal pattern of occurrence. Three western migrant species comprised over 90% of the observations. This core migrant fauna consisted of two canopy and one understory species. Approximately 70% of the total migrant individuals observed were of the two common canopy species, Townsend's (*Dendroica townsendi*) and Audubon's Warbler (*D. coronata auduboni*). Aggressive interactions were observed among and between members of the two canopy species. Fifteen additional species were mostly uncommon transients, and over two-thirds had a boreal or eastern U.S. breeding distribution. The volume of migration increased from August and September to October and November. Most species were observed sporadically throughout the fall. Sightings of several species were concentrated in short periods. The three most common migrants were present throughout the fall (and presumably through the winter), but showed strong peaks within the migration period.

Sinopsis. Durante el otoño de 1987, se llevaron a cabo censos de transecto en un bosque nublado aislado cerca de San Cristóbal de Las Casas, Chiapas, México. Los censos se efectuaron casi diariamente para delinear el patrón estacional de ocurrencia. Más del 90% de las observaciones estuvieron representadas por tres especies migratorias occidentales. Esta avifauna migratoria nuclear consistió de dos especies de dosel y una de sotobosque. Aproximadamente el 70% del total de individuos migratorios observados pertenecían a las dos especies comunes del dosel, *Dendroica townsendi* y *D. coronata auduboni*. Se observaron interacciones agresivas dentro y entre las dos especies de dosel. Quince especies adicionales fueron en su mayoría transeúntes poco comunes y más de dos tercios tienen una distribución de cría boreal o al este de los Estados Unidos. El volumen de la migración incrementó desde agosto y septiembre hasta octubre y noviembre. La mayoría de las especies fueron observadas esporádicamente durante todo el otoño. Las observaciones de varias especies estuvieron concentradas en períodos cortos. Las tres migratorias más comunes estuvieron presentes durante todo el otoño (y presumiblemente durante el invierno), pero mostraron fuertes picos dentro del período de migración.

The Mexican state of Chiapas is strategically located to support migratory and wintering populations from both eastern and western North America. Because of this, 190 species of migratory birds have been reported from the state (Alvarez del Toro 1971). However, the deforestation rate in Chiapas is also among the highest in Latin America; 160,000 ha of forest are cleared annually in tropical Mexico (Lanley 1981). Despite its clear importance as a migratory pathway, relatively little work has been done on the volume, distribution, and timing of migration in Mexico (but see Loetscher 1955, Coeffey 1960, Andrle 1966, Ely et al. 1977, Rappole et al. 1979, Ramos and Warner 1980, Ramos 1983), and in Chiapas in particular.

The highlands in Chiapas are among the economically poorest parts of Mexico. They are heavily settled by Mayan agronomists who are by and large culturally and linguistically isolated from people in other parts of Mexico. The land is generally farmed or grazed in small plots, and the landscape is highly fragmented. Much of the land area is being actively farmed (29.8%) or grazed (29.5%) (Parra Vasquez 1989). An additional 16.7% is secondary scrub, only 21.7% is covered by forest, and old growth forest accounts for less than 9%. Chiapas is of critical conservation importance because of the diversity of habitats, some of which are quite restricted (Toledo 1988). In particular, Chiapas is a stronghold for humid high elevation (cloud) forest, a forest type that covered less than 0.5% of the Mexican territory (Leopold 1950). In the central highlands of Chiapas, significant patches of cloud forest are restricted to the highest, most inaccessible peaks such as Huitepec and Tzontehuitz. In this paper I report on a study of the seasonal abundance patterns of migratory birds in a cloud forest in the highlands of Chiapas.

Study area

The study was conducted at 2,500 m altitude in the PRONATURA-Huitepec reserve located 3.5 km northwest of San Cristobal de las Casas in the central highlands of Chiapas. This 50-ha patch of cloud forest is surrounded by a second-growth pine-oak woodland. The cloud forest is foggy most of the year and receives

1,500–2,000 mm of rainfall each year, primarily during a rainy season that lasts from May to November. The canopy is dominated by *Quercus crassifolia, Q. candicans, Q. crissipipilis, Styrax ramirezii, Clereya theaoides, Prunus serotina,* and *Arbutus xalapensis,* with *Parathesis leptopa, Sauraviaoreophila, Oreophanax xalapensis,* and *Cestrum guatemalense* in the understory. The forest supports an abundance of bromeliads and epiphytic ferns.

Methods

Censuses were conducted between 0630 and 1030, five days a week from 1 August through 30 November 1987. I recorded all individual migrants located within 10 m of a 3.4-km transect. Visual and auditory transect surveys were used after trying mist netting during the previous spring and finding few of the most common canopy species represented in the nets. I also recorded the foraging height each time an individual was sighted in a different tree and all agonistic interactions involving migrant species. Distribution patterns were classified based on ranges outlined in the A.O.U check-list (1983). Breeding ranges were classified, based on the predominant distribution, as western (montane regions of western North America), northeastern (boreal and northern hardwood forests of U.S. and Canada), eastern (eastern U.S.), and southeastern (southeastern U.S.). Winter ranges were classified based on whether most of the species population winters in (1) Mexico (and north), (2) Central America and Mexico, (3) South America, (4) West Indies, or (5) over 2, 3, and 4 combined.

Results

RELATIVE ABUNDANCE OF MIGRANT SPECIES. I recorded a total of 1,731 observations of migrants during 296 field hr. After 21 August, when the first migrant was observed, an average of 7.6 individuals per km were observed per census. Although I recorded 18 species, observation totals were dominated by only a few (Table 1). Townsend's Warbler comprised 59%, and together with Audubon's and Wilson's warbler, they comprised 91% of the total observations.

BREEDING DISTRIBUTION OF MIGRANTS. Of the 18 species of migrants, seven species have a predominantly Western Cordilleran distribution in North America, nine occur primarily in eastern U.S. or northeastern U.S. and the boreal zone of Canada, and two have a southeastern breeding range (Table 1). However, the three most common migrants (winter residents) and 80% of the five most common species have a primarily western breeding distribution. In the case of the Wilson's Warber, all three subspecies have been identified among the netted

TABLE 1. Species recorded during the autumn of 1987 in a cloud forest of Chiapas, Mexico

Species	Date	Number observed	Breeding distribution[a]	Winter distribution[b]
Yellow-bellied Sapsucker *Sphyrapicus varius*	Oct. 23	2	NE	1
Eastern Wood-Pewee *Contopus virens*	Aug 21–Sept 4	12	E	3
Acadian Flycatcher *Empidonax virescens*	Aug 28–Sept 11	12	SE	2
Gray Catbird *Dumetella carolinensis*	Oct 16	2	E	1
Solitary Vireo *Vireo solitarius*	Oct 22, Nov 27	4	?	1
Black-throated Blue Warbler *Dendroica caerulescens*	Oct 28, Nov 17–30	5	NE	4
Audubon's Warbler *Dendroica coronata auduboni*	Oct 16–Nov 30	180	W	1
Blackburnian Warbler *Dendroica fusca*	Nov 9, 10	2	NE	3
Hermit Warbler *Dendroica occidentalis*	Sept 11–29	10	W	1
Townsend's Warbler *Dendroica townsendi*	Aug 22–Nov 30	1013	W	1
Black-and-white Warbler *Mniotilta varia*	Aug 27–Nov 30	12	E	5
MacGillivray's Warbler *Oporornis tolmiei*	Sept 16–Nov 24	14	W	1
Louisiana Waterthrush *Seiurus motacilla*	Sept 16–29	2	SE	5
Northern Waterthrush *Seiurus noveboracensis*	Aug 27	2	NE	5
Tennessee Warbler *Vermivora peregrina*	Oct 22–29	35	NE	2
Wilson's Warbler *Wilsonia pusilla*	Sept 4–Nov 30	367	W?	1
Rose-breasted Grosbeak *Pheucticus ludovicianus*	Nov 3–30	7	NE	3
Western Tanager *Piranga ludoviciana*	Nov 17–30	22	W	1

a. NE = boreal and northern hardwoods biome of U.S. and Canada, E = eastern U.S., SE = southeastern U.S., W = mountains of western U.S.
b. 1 = Mexico (and north), 2 = Central America and Mexico, 3 = South America, 4 = West Indies, 5 = broad tropical (over 2, 3, + 4 combined).

individuals (A. Phillips, pers. comm.). I have classified Wilson's Warbler as a western migrant because the species has a predominantly western breeding range. The subspecific identity and, therefore, the breeding range of the Solitary Vireos was not known. One-half of the migrant species observed at Huitepec winter in Mexico or the United States. A smaller number of species winter mainly in Central America ($n = 2$),

South America ($n = 3$), West Indies ($n = 1$) or have a broad tropical distribution ($n = 3$). Again, the three most common migrants and 80% of the five most commonly observed species winter primarily in Mexico and points north. The five Black-throated Blue Warbler observations are noteworthy because this West Indian wintering species has rarely been reported in Chiapas (Hunn 1973).

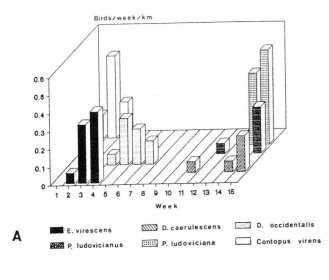

Birds/week/km

A

- ■ E. virescens
- ▨ P. ludovicianus
- ▧ D. caerulescens
- ▦ P. ludoviciana
- ▤ D. occidentalis
- □ Contopus virens

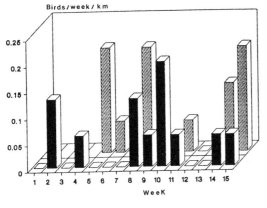

Birds/week/km

B

- ■ Mniotilta varia
- ▨ Oporornis tolmiei

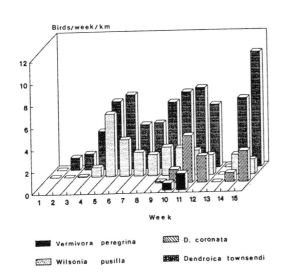

Birds/week/km

C

- ■ Vermivora peregrina
- ▨ D. coronata
- ▨ Wilsonia pusilla
- ▨ Dendroica townsendi

FIGURE 1. Seasonal distribution of sightings of migratory birds at Huitepec Cloud forest in fall 1987. *A,* six species with few sightings concentrated in short periods; *B,* two species of few sightings scattered throughout the fall; *C,* four common species.

SEASONAL PATTERN OF OCCURRENCE. The first migrants were observed in late August. The average number of migrants/km seen per census increased from 1.0 in August to 7.1 in September and reached a plateau in October and November of 10.5 and 11.5, respectively. The cumulative number of species observed per month paralleled this pattern, increasing from four in August to seven in September, seven in October, and eight in November.

Among the species for which I obtained more than five observations (Table 2), I discerned three temporal patterns of occurrence (Fig. 1). Group I species, including Eastern Wood-Pewee, Acadian Flycatcher, and Hermit Warbler, occurred in relatively short periods. Group II species, including Black-and-white Warbler and MacGillivray's Warbler, were observed sporadically throughout the autumn. Group III species, Townsend's, Wilson's, and Audubon's warblers, were common winter residents, showing increasing numbers as the autumn progressed. These species showed considerable variation in abundance across the autumn which indicates that censused individuals were migrating (Fig. 1). Strong peaks in abundance occurred in late September for Wilson's Warbler, late October for Audubon's Warbler, and in late September, late October and late November for Townsend's Warbler. I tested the significance of the seasonal patterns against a null hypothesis of an even temporal distribution using the weekly proportions of total observed seasonally (Kolmogorov-Smirnof single sample test, Snedecor and Cochran 1967). The seasonal heterogeneity in all three common species was significant.

FORAGING HEIGHT OF COMMON MIGRATORY SPECIES. The common migratory species (Table 3) include three canopy dwellers (Audubon's, Hermit, and Townsend's warblers), two low understory species (Wilson's and MacGillivray's warblers) and four mid-level species (Acadian Flycatcher, Solitary Vireo, Black-and-white Warbler, and Tennessee Warbler). Although the different species were approximately equally distributed among the three strata, over two-thirds (69%) of the individuals were observed in the canopy. This is because two of the most common species, Townsend's and Audubon's warblers, were found primarily in this stratum. Aggression was frequently observed both within and between migrants. The interspecific chases were found most commonly between the two common canopy species, Audubon's and Townsend's warblers (16/30 total recorded chases). Interestingly, the 10 chases observed in October and early November involved Townsend's Warblers chasing Audubon's Warblers. However, all six chases from mid-November on were the reverse of this.

TABLE 2. Average daily number of migrants/kilometer each week of sampling. Mean (S.E.) of 5 censuses/week

Species	August		September					October				November			
	1	2	3	4	5	6	7	8	9	10	11	12	13	14	15
Eastern Wood-Pewee	0.13 (0.07)	0.46 (0.15)	0.20 (0.18)	0	0	0	0	0	0	0	0	0	0	0	0
Acadian Flycatcher	0	0.06 (0.06)	0.33 (0.13)	0.40 (0.11)	0	0	0	0	0	0	0	0	0	0	0
Tennessee Warbler	0	0	0	0	0	0	0	0	0	0.66 (0.36)	1.54 (0.58)	0	0	0	0
Black-throated Blue Warbler	0	0	0	0	0	0	0	0	0	0	0.06 (0.06)	0	0	0.06 (0.06)	0.20 (0.07)
Black-and-White Warbler	0	0.13 (0.07)	0	0.06 (0.06)	0	0	0	0.13 (0.07)	0.06 (0.06)	0.20 (0.07)	0.06 (0.06)	0	0	0.06 (0.06)	0.06 (0.06)
Audubon's Warbler	0	0	0	0	0	0	0	0	0.13 (0.12)	1.22 (0.42)	4.26 (0.66)	2.40 (0.25)	0	0.83 (0.36)	2.80 (0.91)
Hermit Warbler	0	0	0	0.06 (0.13)	0.26 (0.24)	0.20 (0.12)	0.13 (0.12)	0	0	0	0	0	0	0	0
Townsend's Warbler	0	1.40 (0.63)	1.46 (0.58)	3.46 (0.73)	6.13 (0.68)	6.73 (0.47)	4.00 (0.82)	4.13 (0.75)	6.00 (0.72)	6.90 (0.52)	7.26 (1.49)	5.73 (0.50)	0	6.26 (0.81)	10.41 (1.10)
MacGillivray's Warbler	0	0	0	0	0.20 (0.07)	0.06 (0.06)	0	0.20 (0.07)	0.06 (0.06)	0	0.06 (0.06)	0	0	0.13 (0.12)	0.20 (0.18)
Wilson's Warbler	0	0	0.06 (0.06)	0.86 (0.33)	5.66 (0.99)	3.33 (0.44)	2.16 (0.22)	1.93 (0.43)	2.60 (0.25)	2.50 (0.16)	2.00 (0.31)	1.80 (0.22)	0	1.08 (0.16)	1.33 (0.37)
Rose-breasted Grosbeak	0	0	0	0	0	0	0	0	0	0	0	0.06 (0.06)	0	0	0.26 (0.11)
Western Tanager	0	0	0	0	0	0	0	0	0	0	0	0	0	0.40 (0.21)	0.53 (0.15)
TOTAL INDIVIDUALS/KM	0.1	2.0	2.0	4.8	12.2	10.3	6.3	6.4	8.8	11.5	15.2	10.0	0	8.8	15.8
TOTAL SPECIES	1	4	4	5	4	4	3	4	5	5	7	4	0	7	8

NOTE: Week 1 indicates 15–21 Aug, the first week of sightings. No censuses were performed during week 13. Week 15 was extended to include 30 Nov.

TABLE 3. Vertical distribution (mean height and standard deviation) of Neotropical migrants in the Highlands, Chiapas

Species	Mean ht (m), (SD)	Observations
Acadian Flycatcher	3.9 (1.3)	25
Solitary Vireo	5.5 (0.85)	27
Hermit Warbler	6.1 (2.7)	26
Black-and-white Warbler	3.5 (1.7)	28
MacGillivray's Warbler	1.5 (1.5)	26
Tennessee Warbler	5.1 (1.4)	31
Audubon's Warbler	8.3 (2.1)	89
Townsend's Warbler	6.9 (3.7)	327
Wilson's Warbler	2.4 (2.2)	212

Discussion

The cloud forests of the highlands of Chiapas supported high densities of both transient and overwintering migratory birds. Three species of western migrants, Townsend's, Audubon's, and Wilson's warblers, comprised approximately 90% of the migrants observed. Based on their abundance at the end of the study in late November, it appears that these three species were the core winter residents. These three species also dominated similar habitats in the Sierra Madre of western Mexico as well (Hutto 1980). The high density of the two *Dendroica* in the canopy suggests the possibility of competition during peak migration periods. The observation of aggressive interactions suggest an area for further study. However, the adjacent Caribbean lowlands support a migratory fauna of predominantly eastern North American species. Of the common species at San Cristobal, only the Wilson's Warbler is common in the Lacandon Forest (Gonzales-Garcia 1988). The transition up the Caribbean slope of Chiapas appears to represent a contact zone for the distinct western and eastern migratory bird faunas outlined by Hutto (1980, 1985). In addition to breeding in eastern North America, most of the common species observed in the autumn were those that winter primarily in North America. This, combined with the observation that the migrant numbers remained high through the mid to late fall, suggests that the cloud forest at Huitepec is more important in supporting winter resident migratory birds than waves of transients.

This study clearly demonstrates the use of cloud forest habitat by Neotropical migrants from both eastern and western North America. Further research in other habitats is needed to evaluate the consequence of further forest clearing in the highlands. Although the degree to which the migrant species in this study are

found in secondary versus old-growth forests is unclear, most of these species occur predominantly in woodlands or forest and are uncommon in the milpas and pastures that cover most of the countryside in the highlands of Chiapas.

Acknowledgments

This study was supported by CONACYT and the Instituto Nacional de Investigaciones sobre Recursos Bioticos (INIREB). PRONATURA, A.C. allowed me to work at the Biological Station at the Huitepec Reserve. I thank Romeo Dominguez Barradas, Jacalyn Speicher, Russell Greenberg, and Kevin Winker for their comments and assistance. I dedicate this paper to my parents.

Literature cited

Alvarez del Toro, M. 1971. Las Aves de Chiapas. Tuxtla Gutierrez. Gob del Estado.

American Ornithologists' Union. 1983. *Check-list of North American Birds.* 6th ed. Washington: American Ornithologists' Union.

Andrle, R.F. 1966. North American migrants in the Sierra de Tuxtla of southern Veracruz, Mexico. *Condor* 68:177–184.

Coffey, B.B., Jr. 1960. Late North American spring migrants in Mexico. *Auk* 77:288–297.

Ely, C.A., P.J. Latas, and R.R. Lohoefener. 1977. Additional returns and recoveries of North American birds banded in southern Mexico. *Bird-Banding* 48:275–276.

Gonzales-Garcia, F. 1988. Inventario avifaunistico de la Reserva de la Biosfera Montes Azules. Selva Lacandona. INIREB. Chiapas.

Hunn, E. 1973. Noteworthy bird observations from Chiapas, Mexico. *Condor* 75:483.

Hutto, R.L. 1980. Winter habitat distribution of migratory landbirds in western Mexico with special reference to small, foliage-gleaning insectivores. Pages 181–203 in *Migrant Birds in the Neotropics: Ecology, Behavior, Distribution and Conservation,* A. Keast and E.S. Morton, eds. Washington: Smithsonian Institution Press.

———. 1985. Habitat selection by nonbreeding, migratory landbirds. Pages 455–476 in *Habitat Selection in Birds,* M.L. Cody, ed. New York: Academic Press, Inc.

Lanly, J.P., ed. 1981. *Tropical forest resources assessment project (GEMS), tropical Africa, tropical Asia, tropical America.* Rome: FAO/UNEP.

Leopold, A. 1950. Vegetation zones of Mexico. *Ecology* 28:274-280.

Loetscher, J.R. 1955. North American migrants in the state of Veracruz: A summary. *Auk* 72:14–54.

Parra Vasquez. 1989. *El subdesarrollo agricola en los Altos de Chiapas.* Texcoco, Mexico: Universidad Autonoma de Chapingo.

Ramos, M.A., and D.W. Warner. 1980. Analysis of North American subspecies of migrant birds, wintering in Los Tuxtlas southern Veracruz, Mexico. Pages 177–180 in *Migrant Birds in the Neotropics: Ecology, Behavior, Distribution and Conservation*, A. Keast and E.S. Morton, eds. Washington: Smithsonian Institution Press.

Ramos, M.A. 1983. Seasonal movements of birds populations in the neotropical region of southern Veracruz, Mexico. Ph.D. Dissertation, University of Minnesota, Minneapolis.

Rappole, J., M.A. Ramos, R.J. Oehlenschlager, D.W. Warner, and C.P. Barkan. 1979. Timing of migration and route selection in North American songbirds. Pages 199–214 in *Proc. First Welder Wildlife Foundation Symposium*, D. Lynn Drane, ed. Sinton, Tex.: Welder Wildlife Foundation.

Snedecor, G.W., and W.G. Cochran. 1967. *Statistical Methods*. Ames: University of Iowa Press.

Toledo, V.M. 1988. La diversidad biologica de Mexico. *Ciencia y Desarrollo* 81:14.

JONATHAN L. ATWOOD
Manomet Bird Observatory
P.O. Box 1770
Manomet, Massachusetts 02345

Inferred destinations of spring migrant Common Yellowthroats based on plumage and morphology

Abstract. Investigations of migration ecology and behavior would be enhanced by knowing the ultimate destinations of migrant individuals. Based on specimen measurements of breeding Common Yellowthroats (*Geothlypis trichas brachydactylus*) from nine geographic regions in northeastern North America, I used discriminant function analysis (DFA) to estimate the destinations of spring migrants captured in coastal Massachusetts and Toronto, Ontario. Migrants in Massachusetts were classified as belonging to breeding populations in New England or coastal areas of northeastern Canada, whereas those in Toronto, Ontario were classified as belonging to southcentral and southeastern Ontario breeding populations. These results are consistent with the expectation that spring migrants at these two northerly localities are headed for destinations generally north of each site. Multivariate classification techniques such as DFA could be used more extensively as a means of identifying the approximate destinations of migrant birds.

Sinopsis. Las investigaciones de la ecología y el comportamiento de la migración mejorarían si se conociera el destino último de individuos migratorios. Con base en medidas de especímenes de *Geothlypis trichas brachydactylus* anidantes de nueve regiones geográficas en el nordeste de Norteamérica, realicé un análisis de función discriminante (AFD) para estimar los destinos de migratorias primaverales obtenidas en las costas de Massachusetts y en Toronto, Ontario. Las migratorias de Massachusetts se clasificaron como pertenecientes a poblaciones reproductivas de New England o áreas costeras del nordeste de Canada, mientras que aquellas de Toronto se clasificaron como propias de poblaciones de cría del sureste y centro-sur de Ontario. Estos resultados son consistentes con la hipótesis de que las migratorias de primavera en estas dos localidades norteñas se dirigen hacia destinos aun mas al norte de cada sitio. Las técnicas de clasificación multivariada tales como el AFD podrían usarse mas extensivamente como medios de identificación de la destinación aproximada de aves migratorias.

Detailed studies of migration are often hindered by the fact that the ultimate destinations of migrating birds are usually known only in a general sense, if at all. For example, research on the physiological ecology of migration is confounded because samples of migrants from a single locality might include individuals that are both close to and far from their final destination (Bairlein 1985, Moore and Kerlinger 1987). In-depth studies of migration timing (Phillips 1951, Francis and Cooke 1986), behavior during stopover (Rappole and Warner 1976), or orientation (Helbig et. al 1989) are similarly affected by this problem. Conclusions regarding population trends based on counts of migrant birds (Hussell 1981; Hagan et al., this volume) might be inaccurate because annual fluctuations in numbers might reflect year-to-year differences in the geographic composition of a sample of migrants, rather than increases or decreases in a population. Finally, knowledge of the geographic origin of migrants might be of importance as biologists attempt to identify and protect wintering grounds or migration pathways used by specific breeding populations (Ramos and Warner 1980).

Unfortunately, for most North American passerine species, same-year recoveries of banded, migrant individuals at their breeding or wintering destinations, or at different points along their migratory route, occur very rarely. For example, of 70,880 Common Yellowthroats (*Geothlypis trichas*) banded in the United States during April and May from 1955 through 1988, only nine were recovered during the same year at either their probable breeding destination or elsewhere along their northward migratory pathway (Atwood, unpubl. data, based on records of U.S. Fish and Wildlife Service, Bird Banding Laboratory). Such sparse data provide little useful information on within-year movements of migrants.

An alternative approach is to use subspecific identification to locate the source of populations represented by migrants. J.T. Marshall noted that "races constitute whole [marked] populations. . . . By carefully identifying a bird to race, we can tell from which general breeding area of the species it originated, just as surely as if it were banded" (Phillips et al. 1964). However, only a few studies in North America have used morphological variation in research on migration ecology or behavior (Phillips 1951, 1975a,b, Storer 1951, Raveling 1965, Raveling and Warner 1978, Harrington and Morrison 1979, Ramos and Warner 1980, James et al. 1984). This has been at least partly because of the frequent difficulty of making accurate subspecific identifications, especially of live birds. Without considerable expertise in traditional avian systematics, and the ability to compare an individual migrant directly with adequate reference material, identification of poorly differentiated races is often impossible. And, as noted by Storer (1982), "the 'typological' view of subspecies has blinded many workers to the possibilities of statistical methods of analysis," whereby multivariate techniques might permit discovery of geographic differentiation within monotypic species (Zink and Remsen 1986), or within a widely distributed subspecies. Such approaches have become common in studies of avian systematics (Johnson 1980, Zink 1986, Atwood 1988), but use of multivariate morphometrics remains rare in investigations of migration ecology.

In this paper I explore the usefulness of discriminant function analysis in evaluating the destinations of migrant Common Yellowthroats in spring. First, I calculate a discriminant function based on morphological measurements of museum specimens representing nine breeding populations in northeastern North America. Then, by weighting measurements of migrants obtained in Massachusetts and Ontario according to the equation separating the breeding populations, I predict the breeding destinations of migrants at each of these two sites. Finally, I evaluate the effectiveness of this approach by comparing the putative breeding destinations of migrants from Massachusetts with those of migrants from Ontario.

Methods

BREEDING POPULATION SAMPLES. Morphological analysis of northeastern North American breeding populations was accomplished by measuring study skins of 194 males obtained from U.S. and Canadian collections. Specimens were deemed to represent breeding individuals based on recorded testis condition or date of collection (mid-June through July); birds showing excessive feather wear were excluded from analysis. Nine geographic groupings were constructed on the basis of available sample sizes (Fig. 1); specific localities and sample sizes included in each of these groupings are provided in Appendix 1.

Six morphological characters were measured on each specimen: (1) exposed culmen (BL), (2) bill width (BW)—the distance from one tomium to the other taken at the position of the nostril's midpoint, (3) tarsus length (TA), (4) unflattened wing chord (WL), (5) tail length (TL), and (6) width of black face mask (BK)—distance along the median axis of the crown from anterior edge of mask at the unfeathered base of the maxilla to posterior margin of mask. Except where noted, measurements followed those described in Baldwin et al. (1931). Measurements were taken to 0.01 mm, and then rounded to the nearest 0.1 mm for BL, BW, TA, and TL, to the nearest 1.0 mm for WL, and to the nearest 0.5 mm for BK.

MIGRANT SAMPLES. Two samples of male, spring migrant Common Yellowthroats were included in the analysis.

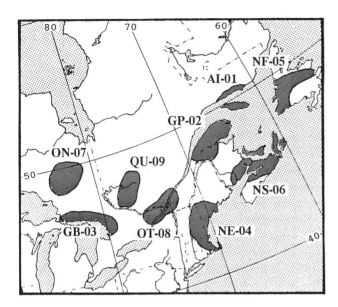

FIGURE 1. Location of northeastern North American breeding populations of the Common Yellowthroat used in analyses of geographic variation. Specific sample localities included in each area are provided in Appendix 1.

During 1988–1989, 69 individuals were captured in mist nets at Manomet Bird Observatory (MBO), located on the western side of Cape Cod Bay, Plymouth Co., Massachusetts (41°50' N, 70°30' W). Nets were operated annually from 15 April through 15 June, thereby covering fully the species' migration period through New England (Eaton 1914, Forbush 1929, Palmer 1949, Hill 1965, Laughlin and Kibbe 1985). Because Common Yellowthroats breed locally at MBO and I wished to consider only migrant individuals, any birds with enlarged cloacal protuberances were eliminated from the analysis. As a further means of conservatively selecting only migrants, I excluded males captured after 29 May, the calculated date by which 90% of all spring captures of this sex had occurred during the years 1973–1989.

The second sample of migrant Common Yellowthroats consisted of 22 study skins obtained from tower kills near Toronto, Ontario (43°35' N, 79°28' W) during 1970–1985. Because these specimens were killed while flying at night, I assumed all to be migrating individuals rather than birds that had established breeding territories. Morphological measurements of both migrant samples were obtained as described above.

To evaluate differences between measurements of live birds and prepared specimens, 18 small passerines were collected, measured within one hour of death, and then prepared as study skins. Species were selected on the basis of availability and morphological similarity to Common Yellowthroats; included were: *Geothlypis trichas*, n = 3; *Dendroica coronata*, n = 3; *Mniotilta varia*, n = 2;

Dendroica caerulescens, n = 2; *Regulus calendula*, n = 1; *Vireo philadelphicus*, n = 1; *Vermivora ruficapilla*, n = 1; *Vermivora pinus*, n = 1; *Dendroica magnolia*, n = 1; *Dendroica petechia*, n = 1; *Setophaga ruticilla*, n = 1; *Wilsonia pusilla*, n = 1. After being dried and stored for six months, these specimens were measured again. Paired *t*-tests showed significant (*P* < 0.05) differences for WL, BW and BL, with dried specimens exhibiting shrinkage in BL and BW and lengthening in WL (possibly due to flattening of the wing's camber). Consequently, I applied correction factors to data from live birds based on the mean values of a character's study skin measurement divided by that character's mean live measurement. These corrections were as follows: WL = live measurement × 1.02; BL = live measurement × 0.97; BW = live measurement × 0.95. Although cognizant of the potential inaccuracies caused by differences in feather wear between samples obtained largely in May vs. those collected in June or July (Cooke and Wood 1989), I felt that application of further correction factors would be inappropriate, given the degree of uncertainty already introduced by the need to transform fresh measurements to their museum specimen equivalents.

STATISTICAL ANALYSES. Analyses were performed using SAS (Version 5.18) procedures MEANS, GLM, FREQ, STEPDISC, CLUSTER, and DISCRIM (SAS Institute 1985). All measurements were log 10 transformed to improve normality of distribution.

Results

Univariate analyses of specimens representing nine breeding populations showed significant (*P* < 0.05) differences among sample areas in only three characters: WL, TL, and BK (Table 1). Variation in all characters was slight; for example, the range of mean wing length (WL) across all sample areas was only 1.6 mm. There were no obvious clines or other geographic patterns of variation among the characters.

Stepwise discriminant analysis was used to identify those characters most effective in separating samples from each breeding area. All six variables (BK, TL, WL, BW, TA and BL) contributed to the discrimination model (*P* = 0.15; Costanza and Afifi 1979). Using these characters, multivariate analysis of variance (MANOVA) showed significant differences (*P* = 0.0001) among breeding localities.

Cluster analysis (UPGMA, unweighted pair-group method using arithmentic averages) defined two major groups of phenetically similar populations (Fig. 2). One cluster consisted primarily of birds from northeastern sample localities bordering the Gulf of St. Lawrence (AI-01, GP-02, NS-06, NF-05), whereas the other was composed mainly of birds from southwestern areas in

TABLE 1.   Univariate statistics describing geographic variation in northeastern North American breeding populations of the Common Yellowthroat (males)

Area[b]	n	Character means[a]					
		Bill length BL	Bill width BW	Wing length WL	Tarsus length TA	Tail length TL	Black width BK
AI-01	11	10.26 (0.36)	3.15 (0.23)	54.82 (1.41)	20.45 (0.78)	50.15 (1.81)	6.18 (0.78)
GP-02	15	10.59 (0.45)	3.24 (0.20)	54.31 (1.14)	19.60 (0.76)	49.03 (2.04)	5.97 (0.53)
GB-03	27	10.65 (0.45)	3.28 (0.18)	55.48 (1.31)	19.87 (0.55)	49.46 (1.90)	5.50 (0.90)
NE-04	16	10.55 (0.44)	3.32 (0.31)	55.24 (2.39)	19.91 (0.69)	48.21 (1.90)	5.37 (1.14)
NF-05	20	10.57 (0.59)	3.21 (0.19)	55.20 (1.74)	19.91 (0.92)	50.33 (2.12)	6.15 (1.06)
NS-06	35	10.58 (0.48)	3.20 (0.16)	54.34 (1.49)	19.76 (0.68)	50.28 (2.44)	6.15 (0.67)
ON-07	17	10.42 (0.43)	3.18 (0.12)	55.88 (1.11)	19.84 (0.58)	49.98 (1.69)	5.38 (0.65)
OT-08	30	10.40 (0.46)	3.30 (0.23)	54.73 (1.41)	19.78 (0.71)	49.10 (1.41)	5.65 (0.73)
QU-09	21	10.40 (0.46)	3.33 (0.22)	54.90 (1.73)	19.70 (0.62)	48.77 (2.14)	6.00 (0.55)
P[c]		0.23	0.09	0.02	0.17	0.01	< 0.01

a. $\bar{x}$ in mm (SD). characters as defined in Methods.
b. Geographic regions as described in Fig. 1 and Appendix A.
c. P values based on analysis of variance (ANOVA).

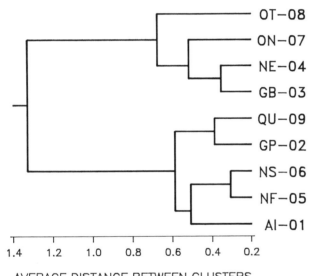

AVERAGE DISTANCE BETWEEN CLUSTERS

FIGURE 2. UPGMA cluster analysis of geographic variation in northeastern North American breeding populations of Common Yellowthroat (males). Characters included in analysis: BL, BW, TA, TL, WL, and BK. Sample area abbreviations as indicated in Figure 1.

New England and the interior of Canada (OT-08, ON-07, GB-03, NE-04). The western Quebec sample (QU-09), which was geographically intermediate to ON-07 and OT-08, was phenetically more similar to samples from areas near the Gulf of St. Lawrence. All populations showed little geographic differentiation on the basis of characters measured here, as expected, considering that only one subspecies, *G. t. brachydactylus*, breeds

within the species' range in northeastern America (A.O.U. 1957).

A quadratic discriminant function, again using the six variables, was calculated from the within-group covariance matrices of the nine breeding localities (Kendall and Stuart 1961, SAS Institute 1985). This equation was then applied to the two samples of migrants. Of 69 male Common Yellowthroats captured in coastal Massachusetts during the spring migrations of 1988 and 1989, 55 (79.7%) were classified as belonging either to the New England breeding population (NE-04) or to populations located north and east of the capture site (AI-01, GP-02, NF-05, NS-06) (Fig. 3). By contrast, the same classification algorithm placed 18 of 22 (81.8%) migrant Common Yellowthroats obtained in Toronto as belonging to breeding populations located west of New England.

Discussion

Discriminant function analysis (DFA) of spring migrant Common Yellowthroats from two widely separated localities produced geographically "logical" results that conform to a basically north-south pattern of movement. Most migrants in coastal Massachusetts were classified as belonging to breeding populations of New England or coastal areas of northeastern Canada, whereas most birds migrating through Ontario were assigned to breeding localities in southern Ontario and southwestern Quebec. I am unable to confirm that such results in fact reflect the true destinations of these birds. However, had the analyses shown an opposite pat-

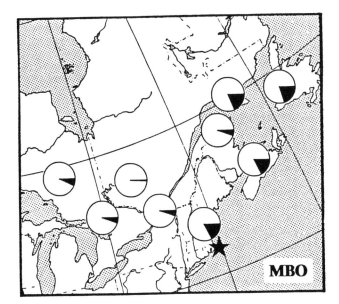

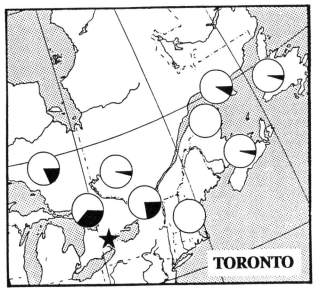

FIGURE 3. DFA classification of migrant Common Yellowthroats into northeastern North American breeding populations. *Stars*, locations where samples of migrants were obtained. Blackened portions of pie charts show percent of migrant sample from each individual site (MBO, n = 69; Toronto, n = 22) that was classified into indicated breeding areas.

tern, namely that Massachusetts migrants were destined for breeding areas in western Ontario, or that Toronto migrants belonged to breeding populations of Nova Scotia, the usefulness of this approach might have been called into serious question. At least at this broad geographic level, I suggest that DFA is a valuable technique for determining the destinations of spring migrant Common Yellowthroats. Furthermore, use of tra-

ditional subspecific identification would have been less informative than the results of this statistical treatment. All of the migrant individuals considered here would merely have been described as belonging to a single subspecies, *G. t. brachydactylus*, that breeds widely throughout much of North America east of 100° W and north of 35° N (A.O.U. 1957).

Spring migrant Common Yellowthroats in Toronto primarily represented breeding populations of southern Ontario and southwestern Quebec, while birds migrating through eastern Massachusetts belonged mainly to breeding populations of New England or coastal areas of northeastern Canada. Thus population indices based on counts of spring migrants from relatively high latitude sites probably reflect trends in regions directly to the north of a sampling area rather than throughout a species' overall range. Effective population monitoring of species with breeding distributions that extend across southern Canada might be accomplished by a strategically placed network of banding stations located across the United States at approximately 45° N; such stations might be expected to sample, during spring migration, breeding populations associated with areas immediately to the north. Further information is needed regarding whether fall migration counts from high latitude sites reflect regional or more widespread population trends. However, results presented here do suggest caution in interpretation of correlations between population indices derived from longitudinally extensive Breeding Bird Survey strata and migration counts obtained at single stopover sites (Hagan et al., this volume).

The "discovery" that spring migrant Common Yellowthroats from Massachusetts and Toronto have destinations generally north of these areas is, admittedly, somewhat tautological. Nonetheless, this approach offers a method that under different circumstances might provide less intuitive results. For example, can breeding populations be assigned to specific migration routes or wintering areas? Such information would be valuable in assessing whether habitat loss along migratory pathways or in wintering areas might be associated with regional population changes of a species. Similarly, knowledge of source populations would permit analysis of more detailed topics concerning migration ecology, such as whether the timing of migration is correlated with breeding latitude, or whether fat levels of migrants are related to their remaining travel distance. Application of discriminant function analysis or similar statistical treatments as a way of identifying source populations of migrant or wintering birds could thus provide a more efficient method of addressing these types of questions than the slow accumulation of banding recoveries.

However, this technique also has various limitations. Because it is based on quantitative comparison of morphological differences, species showing little geographic variation are not amenable to analysis. Accumulation of adequate specimen material representing a wide geographic range of breeding populations might be difficult, depending on the species. And, because freshly molted fall birds would predictably have different measurements for characters such as wing or tail length than breeding individuals with moderately worn plumage, such characters would be inappropriate for classifying fall migrants or wintering birds as to their breeding population.

In 1980 Ramos and Warner also discussed the value of a population-level approach to Neotropical migrant conservation issues, and used subspecies identifications as a means of identifying the source populations of migrants wintering in Veracruz, Mexico. Ten years later our knowledge of North American migrants generally continues to lack precise data regarding the migratory movements and wintering distributions of specific breeding populations. Clearly there are limitations to studies based on the natural "marking" systems of geographic variation, using either traditional methods of subspecific identification or statistical techniques of multivariate analysis. Nonetheless, considering the importance of information gained from specific knowledge of migrant destinations, use of such techniques merits further exploration.

Acknowledgments

I wish to thank the many volunteers, assistants, students and staff who have contributed to Manomet Bird Observatory's bird-banding program; although too many to name individually, this work would have been impossible without their help. Curators of the following collections kindly made available specimen material under their care: Academy of Natural Sciences, Philadelphia; Dickey Collection, University of California, Los Angeles; Field Museum of Natural History, Chicago; Los Angeles County Museum of Natural History; Los Angeles; Museum of Comparative Zoology, Harvard University; Boston; Museum of Natural History, University of Kansas, Lawrence; Museum of Natural Science, Louisiana State University; Baton Rouge; Museum of Vertebrate Zoology, University of California, Berkeley; National Museum of Canada, Ottawa; Peabody Museum, Yale University, New Haven; Royal Ontario Museum, Toronto; National Museum of Natural History, Washington, D.C. Danny Bystrak (Bird Banding Laboratory, U.S. Fish and Wildlife Service) provided data concerning Common Yellowthroat banding and recoveries. Barbara Hamilton assisted in data recording and entry, and gave encouragement during preparation of the manuscript. Trevor L. Lloyd-Evans made useful comments on an earlier draft of the manuscript; the final version was improved by criticisms by Frances C. James, John M. Hagan, David W. Johnston and an anonymous reviewer. Manomet Bird Observatory's land-bird banding program is supported financially by the membership and by generous grants from several sources, including the Malcolm Oakes Memorial Fund, the William Wharton Trust, the George Coleman Fund, Crawford H. Greenewalt, and several anonymous donors.

Literature cited

American Ornithologists' Union. 1957. *Check-list of North American Birds.* 5th ed. Baltimore: American Ornithologists' Union.

Atwood, J.L. 1988. *Speciation and geographic variation in Black-tailed Gnatcatchers.* Ornithol. Monogr. 42.

Bairlein, F. 1985. Body weight and fat deposition of Palearctic passerine migrants in the central Sahara. *Oecologia* (Berlin) 66:141–146.

Baldwin, S.P., H.C. Oberholser, and L.G. Worley. 1931. Measurements of birds. *Sci. Publ. Cleveland Mus. Nat. Hist.*, Vol. II.

Costanza, M.C., and A.A. Afifi. 1979. Comparison of stopping rules in forward stepwise discriminant analysis. *J. Am. Statistical Assoc.* 74:777–785.

Eaton, E.H. 1914. *Birds of New York.* Albany: New York State Museum, Memoir 12. Vol. 2.

Forbush, E.H. 1929. *Birds of Massachusetts and Other New England States.* Vol. 3. Boston: Massachusetts Department of Agriculture.

Francis, C.M., and F. Cooke. 1986. Differential timing of spring migration in wood warblers (Parulinae). *Auk* 103:548–556.

Francis, C.M., and D.S. Wood. 1989. Effects of age and wear on wing length of sood warblers. *J. Field Ornithol.* 60:495–503.

Harrington, B.A., and R.I.G. Morrison. 1979. Semipalmated Sandpiper migration in North America. *Stud. Avian Biology* 2:83–100.

Helbig, A.J., P. Berthold, and W. Wiltschko. 1989. Migratory orientation of Blackcaps *(Sylvia atricapilla)*: Population-specific shifts of direction during the autumn. *Ethology* 82:307–315.

Hill, N.P. 1965. *The Birds of Cape Cod, Massachusetts.* New York: William Morrow and Co.

Hussell, D.J.T. 1981. The use of migration counts for detecting population levels. Pages 92–102 in *Estimating Numbers of Terrestrial Birds*, C.J. Ralph and M.J. Scott, eds. Studies in Avian Biology No. 6.

James, F.C., R.T. Engstrom, C. Nesmith, and R. Laybourne. 1984. Inferences about population movements of Red-winged Blackbirds from morphological data. *Am. Midl. Nat.* 111:319–331.

Johnson, N.K. 1980. Character variation and evolution of sibling species in the *Empidonax difficilis-flavescens* complex (Aves: Tyrannidae). *Univ. Calif. Publ. Zool.* 112:1–151.

Kendall, M.G., and A. Stuart. 1961. *The Advanced Theory of Statistics.* Vol. 3. London: Charles Griffin and Co., Ltd.

Laughlin, S.B., and D.P. Kibbe. 1985. *The Atlas of the Birds of Vermont.* Hanover, N.H.: University Press of New England.

Moore, F., and P. Kerlinger. 1987. Stopover and fat deposition by North American wood-warblers (Parulinae) following spring migration over the Gulf of Mexico. *Oecologia* (Berlin) 74:47–54.

Palmer, R.S. 1949. Maine birds. *Bull. Mus. Comp. Zool.* 102.

Phillips, A.R. 1951. Complexities of migration: A review. *Wilson Bull.* 63:129–136.

———. 1975a. Semipalmated Sandpiper: Identification, migrations, summer and winter ranges. *Am. Birds* 29:799–806.

———. 1975b. Why neglect the difficult? *Western Birds* 6:69–86.

Phillips, A., J. Marshall, and G. Monson. 1964. *The Birds of Arizona.* Tucson: University of Arizona Press.

Ramos, M.A., and D.W. Warner. 1980. Analysis of North American subspecies of migrant birds wintering in Los Tuxtlas, southern Veracruz, Mexico. Pages 173–180 in *Migrant Birds in the Neotropics: Ecology, Behavior, Distribution and Conservation,* A. Keast and E.S. Morton, eds. Washington: Smithsonian Institution Press.

Rappole, J.H., and D.W. Warner. 1976. Relationships between behavior, physiology and weather in avian transients at a migration stopover site. *Oecologia* 26:193–212.

Raveling, D.G. 1965. Geographic variation and measurements of Tennessee Warblers killed at a TV tower. *Bird-Banding* 36:89–101.

Raveling, D.G., and D.W. Warner. 1978. Geographic variation of Yellow Warblers killed at a TV tower. *Auk* 95:73–79.

SAS Institute Inc. 1985. *SAS User's Guide: Statistics, Version 5 Edition.* Cary, N.C.: SAS Institute Inc.

Storer, R.W. 1951. Variation in the Painted Bunting *(Passerina ciris),* with special reference to wintering populations. *Occas. Pap. Mus. Zool. Univ. Michigan* No. 532.

———. 1982. Subspecies and the study of geographic variation. *Auk* 99:599–601.

Zink, R.M. 1986. *Patterns and Evolutionary Significance of Geographic Variation in the* schistacea *Group of the Fox Sparrow* (Passerella iliaca). Ornithol. Monogr. 40.

Zink, R.M., and J.V. Remsen. 1986. Evolutionary processes and patterns of geographic variation in birds. *Current Ornithol.* 4:1–69.

APPENDIX 1. Collection localities of breeding specimens used in analysis of geographic variation

For each sample area, the number of specimens examined is provided for each specific collecting locality. Alphanumeric codes for sample areas as indicated in Figure 1.

Anticosti Island (AI-01)

QUEBEC: Anticosti Island (6); Saguenay, Baie de Moîsie (4); Saguenay, Havre-St.-Pierre (1).

Gaspé Peninsula (GP-02)

NEW BRUNSWICK: Gloucester Co., Miscou Island (1); Madawaska Co., St. Leonard (2); QUEBEC: Bonaventure Co., Maria (2); Bonaventure Co., Reserve de Port-Daniel (1); Grande Rivière (1); Matane Co., Les Boules (1); Percé (5); Rivière-du-Loup (3).

Georgian Bay (GB-03)

ONTARIO: Algoma Dist., Laird (2); Biscotasing (3); Bracebridge (2); Bruce Co., Howden Vale (1); Gravenhurst (2); Iron Bridge (5); Mindemoya (1); Muskoko Co., Kilworthy (1); Port Sydney (3); Torrance (5); Washago (2).

New England (NE-04)

MAINE: Oakland (1); Oxford Co., Upton (2); Sebec Lake (2); Small Point (1); MASSACHUSETTS: Essex Co., Plum Island (2); Essex Co., W. Newbury (1); Gloucester (1); Middlesex Co., Cambridge (1); Wareham (1); Woods Hole (1); NEW HAMPSHIRE: Concord (2); Coos Co. (1).

Newfoundland (NF-05)

NEWFOUNDLAND: Badger (1); Bonavista Bay (1); Cape Ray (1); Doyles (13); Princeton (1); Pushthrough (1); St. Georges (1); St. Andrews (1).

Nova Scotia (NS-06)

NEW BRUNSWICK: Kings Co., Anagance (2); Kings Co., Head Of Millstream (2); Kings Co., Waterford (4); King's Co. (1); Moncton (1); NOVA SCOTIA: Baddeck (2); Cape Breton Island (1); Inverness Co., Orangedale (1); Inverness Co., Strathlorne (8); N. Sydney (2); Richmond Co., Sporting Mtn. (1); Richmond Co., Thibeauville (1); Wolfville (1); PRINCE EDWARD ISLAND: East Lake (1); Hermanville (4); Mt. Stewart (1); Souris (1); St. Peters (1).

Ontario (ON-07)

ONTARIO: Chapleau (3); Cochrane Dist., Fauquier (1); Cochrane Dist., Hearst (2); Cochrane Dist., 68 km SE Moosonee (1); Fraserdale (5); Genier (5).

Ottawa (OT-08)

ONTARIO: Grenville Co., Kemptville Cr. (1); Kemptville (5); North Gower (2); Ottawa-Carleton, Gloucester (1); Ottawa-Carleton, Osgoode (2); Ottawa-Carleton, Ottawa (1); Vernon (1); Winchester (2); QUEBEC: Bonaventure Co., St.-Pié X (1); Châteauguay Co., Sherrington (1); St.-Maurice Co., St.-Mathieu (2); Duplessis Co., St. Augustin (1); Gatineau Co., Messine (1); Huntingdon Co., Huntingdon (2); Iberville Co., Mont-Johnson (1); Pontiac Co., Fraser Landing (1); Pontiac Co., Shawville (1); Rouville Co., Mont-St.-Hilaire (2); Shefford Co., Mont-Shefford (2).

Quebec (QU-09)

ONTARIO: Renfrew Co., Petawawa (1); QUEBEC: Abitibi Co., Belcourt (1); Abitibi Co., Obaska (1); Abitibi Co., Senneterre (3); Amos (2); Lac St.-Jean Ouest Co., Lac Baillarge (1); Lac St.-Jean Ouest Co., Lac Patterson (3); Laviolette Co., Lac Jean-Pierre (1); Rapides-des-Joachims (4); Villemontel (4).

KEVIN WINKER
DWAIN W. WARNER
Bell Museum of Natural History
University of Minnesota
Minneapolis, Minnesota 55455

A.R. WEISBROD
Bell Museum of Natural History
University of Minnesota
Minneapolis, Minnesota 55455
and
Spring Creek Field Laboratory
St. Croix National Riverway
Marine On St. Croix, Minnesota 55047

The Northern Waterthrush and Swainson's Thrush as transients at a temperate inland stopover site

Abstract. Transient nocturnal migrants were netted on daily stopover during three years (1984–1986) through the peaks of spring and autumn passage for a total of over 135,000 net hours in five habitat types in the St. Croix River Valley, Minnesota, USA. Two species illustrate seasonal and heterospecific differences in habitat use: Swainson's Thrush (Muscicapidae: Turdinae: *Catharus ustulatus*) and the Northern Waterthrush (Emberizidae: Parulinae: *Seiurus noveboracensis*). Molting waterthrushes showed greater likelihood of remaining at the site for more than a day, and recaptured Swainson's Thrushes in molt showed loss of mass, while those not molting showed a gain. Although these observations suggest basic physiological differences among conspecifics, condition (mass/wing length) differences between these groups were not present at initial capture. For autumn thrushes and spring waterthrushes, recaptured birds tended to be leaner upon initial capture than nonrecaptured individuals. We found substantial gains in mass through the daylight hours in spring and autumn in both species. Recaptured birds did not show gains of similar magnitude. On average, spring Swainson's Thrushes appeared to accumulate enough mass during the day for an entire night of flying. Capture data suggested considerable use of small (1–3 ha) habitat patches by migrating individuals. Capture rates among habitats showed species-specific patterns and a seasonal shift in habitat use (both species). Migratory routes, strategies of migration, and conservation considerations are discussed.

Sinopsis. Aves migratorias de tránsito nocturno fueron capturadas con redes durante sus paradas diurnas durante tres años (1984–1986) a través de los períodos de máximo tránsito primaveral y otoñal para un total de mas de 135,000 horas-red en cinco tipos de habitat en el Valle del Río St. Croix, Minnesota, USA. Dos especies ilustran diferencias estacionales y heteroespecíficas en su uso del habitat: *Catharus ustulatus* y *Seiurus noveboracensis*. Durante la muda, individuos de S. noveboracensis presentaron una mayor probabilidad de permanecer en un sitio durante mas de un día e individuos de *C. ustulatus* recapturados en muda presentaron pérdida de masa, mientras que los que no estaban mudando tuvieron una ganancia. Aunque estas observaciones sugieren diferencias fisiológicas básicas entre conespecíficos, no se encontraron diferencias de condición (masa/longitud alar) entre dichos grupos en la primera captura. Comparando *C. ustulatus* de otoño y de invierno, las aves recapturadas tendieron a ser mas livianas en la captura inicial que los individuos no recapturados. Encontramos ganancias de masa sustanciales a través de las horas de luz en primavera y otoño para ambas especies. Las aves recapturadas no presentaron ganancias de magnitud similar. En promedio, los individuos primaverales de *C. ustulatus* aparentemente acumularon suficiente masa durante el día para una noche entera de vuelo. Las tasas de captura entre habitats mostraron patrones particulares por especie y una deriva estacional en el uso del habitat (ambas especies). Se discuten las rutas y estrategias de migración y consideraciones conservacionistas.

Fat provides the energy needed for migration in birds (Berthold 1975, Dawson et al. 1983). Many long-distance migrant passerines do not or cannot carry enough fat reserves to allow them to migrate the full distance between their breeding and wintering areas (e.g., Nisbet et al. 1963, Nisbet and Medway 1972, Berthold 1975, Bairlein 1987). Fat reserves are accumulated through intensive feeding bouts prior to and during migration (King and Farner 1965). Thus, many long-distance migrant passerines depend on food resources located between breeding and wintering grounds. The importance of stopover sites is only beginning to be investigated (e.g., Nisbet et al. 1963, Parnell 1969, Hutto 1985, Bairlein 1983, 1987, Biebach et al. 1986, Berthold 1989). Much work on transient migrants has focused on areas near natural ecological barriers, such as deserts or large bodies of water (e.g., Nisbet et al. 1963, Mueller and Berger 1966, Luleeva and Luleev 1985, Yablonkevich et al. 1985a,b, Biebach et al. 1986, Moore and Kerlinger 1987, Safriel and Lavee 1988). Some of these studies have shown that resources at suitable sites allow migrants to deposit sufficient fat for successful crossing of major ecological barriers (e.g., Nisbet et al. 1963, Bairlein 1988). For contrast, we examine habitat use and general stopover ecology of transients at an inland North American stopover site far from ecological barriers.

Our approach was that, first, if fat is required to complete semiannual migrations, how and where resources are acquired will illuminate specific migration strategies and identify geographic areas where resources needed for migration are available. Second, if there is selective pressure on transient migrants to use available woodlands to their advantage, differential habitat use should occur. Our specific questions were: (1) do transient, woodland-associated nocturnal migrants add to their fat reserves at a stopover site in east-central Minnesota? (2) do these migrants show differential distribu-

tions among available wooded habitat types? (3) if habitat selection is occurring, does it change between spring and autumn? finally, (4) how do data from our site contribute to an understanding of specific migration strategies over a broad geographic range? Migrant passerines at stopover sites in southern Minnesota could experience selective pressure from food availability and predation pressure. Because of the difficulties in examining the food resources available to particular woodland species, we did not examine this factor directly, but instead examined habitat use and mass changes of captured birds for inference. The role of predation was not investigated.

For this paper, *stopover site* is defined as: *any site at which transient nocturnal migrants occur during the day in migration.* A stopover site that provides substantial resources might be considered a *staging area: stopover site at which an individual remains for some period of time, using local resources to deposit fat for migration and/or survival if resources become scarce near the end of the migration.* In some species energetic costs at stopover sites can include molt (this study; D.F. Parmelee, pers. comm.), increasing the potential for individual differences in energy demand and relative success in fat deposition. For conservation considerations, the importance of a stopover site might be assessed by determining the percentage of transients using the site as a staging area, or, alternately, simply by the numbers of individuals occurring at the site in migration. Myers et al. (1985) noted the locations of three staging areas important to migrant Sanderlings (*Calidris alba*) using the latter criterion. Comparable staging areas have not been documented for woodland passerines, perhaps because of differences between "flyway" and "broad-front" migrants. The questions of stopover site use are no less important for broad-front migrants, but are probably more difficult to answer, given the relative availability of potentially suitable stopover sites. As we will show, the use of a site by woodland-associated migrant passerines can vary at the individual and species levels, and can differ between spring and autumn.

We present data on Swainson's Thrush (*Catharus ustulatus*) and the Northern Waterthrush (*Seiurus noveboracensis*), because (1) their breeding and wintering ranges are similar (Fig. 1), thus their migratory status and physiology at our site might initially be hypothesized as similar; (2) their stopover ecology is distinct and species-specific; and (3) both species forage primarily on or near the ground and are suitably sampled using mist nets.

Methods

STUDY SITE. The study area was near Afton, Minnesota, in the St. Croix River Valley (44°55' N, 92°48' W), approximately 2 km from the river. The region consisted

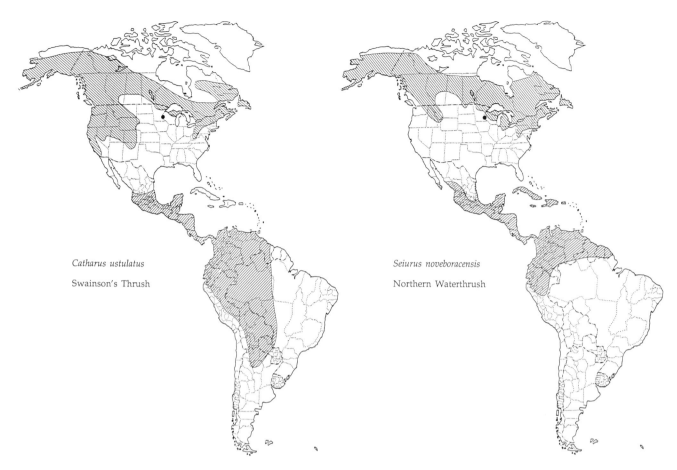

FIGURE 1. Breeding and wintering ranges of Swainson's Thrush (*Catharus ustulatus*) and the Northern Waterthrush (*Seiurus noveboracensis*), after Bond (1936), Dunning (1982), and A.O.U. (1983). Study site is located in east central Minnesota (*solid circle*), approximately 150–200 km from the regular breeding range of both species.

of a mosaic of suburban-residential, agricultural, and wooded tracts. Local topography included low undulating hills, with occasional steep ravines; net sites were on flat terrain. Valley Creek, a small stream, flowed near three of our net habitats. The site was not near an ecological barrier (e.g., desert, large body of water, large mountains), nor was it an island of wooded habitat. The wooded sites we sampled were relatively discrete habitats which could be considered islands of particular vegetation assemblages; together these habitats constituted a cross-section of the native woodlands in the area. These habitats were called Floodplain, Swamp, Upland, Willows, and Oaks. Upland and Oaks were well-drained sites, whereas Swamp, Floodplain, and Willows were moister (with occasional shallow pools of surface water) and were close to flowing water. Floodplain was a moderately open woodland dominated by *Salix nigra, Ulmus* sp., and *Acer saccharinum,* with a mean height of 13.1 m. Swamp was a wet area with little canopy cover and dense thickets of *Alnus rugosa* and *Cornus* sp. with a mean height of 4.8 m. Upland was a closed-canopy woodland dominated by *Quercus alba, Q. borealis, Populus tremuloides,*

and *Betula papyrifera,* with a mean height of 16.8 m. Willows was a relatively closed-canopy woodland with a *Salix nigra* and *Populus tremuloides* overstory and *Rhamnus catharticus* understory, with a mean height of 15.2 m. Oaks was dominated by *Quercus macrocarpa* and *Q. borealis* with a *Rhamnus catharticus* understory, and had a mean height of 14.5 m. The Oaks habitat was the least sampled and was treated in less depth than the others. Habitat patches were approximately 1–3+ ha; Oaks was smallest, Floodplain and Upland largest. Each habitat was a component of broken, semicontiguous woodlands.

FIELD METHODS. Standard nylon mist nets (12 × 2.6 m) of 30-mm and 36-mm mesh were placed in lanes 30 m apart at 30-m intervals (30-m grid, one net at each grid point). The number of nets placed in each habitat varied according to habitat patch size: Floodplain (18), Swamp (12), Upland (18), Willows (12), Oaks (10). Nocturnal captures were rare, and nets were closed only for inclement weather or personnel limitations. Capture effort (net hours) was recorded daily (one net hour is one net open for one hour). When nets were open all day, net hours were calculated based on sunrise-to-sunset time plus 0.5 hr. Nets were operated during the following periods: 1 May–27 May, 9 August–24 September (1984); 29 April–29 May, 14 August–22 September (1985); 28 April–28 May, 17 August–23 September (1986). These dates span the time of spring and autumn passage of most long-distance migrant passerines at this location (unpubl. data). Captured birds were removed 130–820 m to a central location for banding. Measurements included mass (to the nearest 0.1 g on Ohaus triple-beam balances), and flattened wing (Pyle et al. 1987:5). Also recorded were time and specific net of capture, and age in autumn, based upon presence (immature) or absence (adult) of unpneumatized or unossified regions in the skull (McClure 1984:307). Swainson's Thrushes with pinhole "windows" in autumn were designated as adult unless they possessed juvenal coverts. In 1985–1986 molt was assessed and assigned a value (1–9) based on the locations of growing feathers (0 = none). We did not examine sexual differences because Swainson's Thrush and the Northern Waterthrush are sexually monochromatic, and a large proportion of our birds could not be sexed by wing length.

BODY FAT. Fat content causes most of the variation in body mass among samples of migrant passerines, and, when standardized for body size, an individual's mass is a reasonable predictor of its fat content (Odum 1960, Connell et al. 1960, Rogers and Odum 1964, Rogers and Odum 1966). We employed this relationship by using mass/wing length as an index of body condition, rather than using (subjective) fat classes, as is more frequently done (e.g., Cherry 1985, Bairlein 1987, Moore and Kerlinger 1987). Possible error in percent body fat estimates (see Fig. 4) from the presence of gut contents was calculated to be approximately 1–5% for an average fat-free Swainson's Thrush (data from Rogers and Odum 1966). Analyses of net casualties showed that while material is usually present, full guts (proventriculus, ventriculus, intestines, cloaca) are rare. All analyses on body condition are made using mass/wing length.

RECAPTURES. Stopover duration for a given bird is a minimum estimate, obtained by subtracting date of first capture from date of last capture (after Cherry 1982). Because capture and handling is stressful (Rogers and Odum 1966, Nisbet and Medway 1972), we ignored same-day recaptures for analyses and did not "correct" mass to a particular hour of day (Cherry 1982, cf. Moore and Kerlinger 1987).

CAPTURE ANALYSES. Relative abundance indices were calculated as birds captured/net hr × 1000 (birds/1000 net hr). Analyses of habitat distributions were based on captures from days when habitats were sampled simultane-

ously, because daily abundance during migration is highly variable. Capture rate calculations include only the initial captures of individuals (excludes recaptures) to satisfy the assumption of independence in statistical tests. Unless otherwise noted, *significant* indicates the results of statistical analyses where $\alpha \leq 0.05$.

STOMACH CONTENTS. Specimens dying from predators, nets, or handling were examined for evidence of recent feeding. "Active" digestive tracts were those with food material in the proventriculus, ventriculus, and/or intestines. Alimentary canals with small chitinous insect parts in the folds of the stomach lining without other material in the proventriculus/ventriculus or intestines were considered inactive.

MASS CHANGES AMONG FIRST CAPTURES. To estimate net daily (24 hr) mass gains from the diurnal gains apparent in linear regressions of condition on time of day, we estimated gross diurnal gains for individuals of average size (wing, in mm) and mass (g) and subtracted estimated nocturnal losses (see Table 6). Estimates of fat used in nocturnal metabolism were made following Mueller and Berger (1966) for an average Swainson's Thrush and scaled for body size to an average Northern Waterthrush using field metabolic rates (FMR) for passerines (Nagy 1987), and average fat-free body mass for size (Swainson's Thrush: 25.26 g; Northern Waterthrush: 13.92 g). In each case, resting cost for an 8-hr night was approximately 24% of total daily costs (using Nagy 1987). This cost (kJ) was scaled to an average day-night cycle during the period of netting, and the resultant loss in mass was calculated using an energy content of 39.8 kJ/g of fat (Nisbet et al. 1963).

Results

Although captures varied between years, many birds of both species used our site on stopover in both spring and autumn (Table 1). Annual variation in numbers did not seem to be caused by closing nets during inclement weather. Over all years, Swainson's Thrushes (SWTH) showed a general trend of more birds in autumn than in spring, while Northern Waterthrushes (NOWA) showed the opposite (Fig. 2). Linear regression of wing length on date showed significant negative slopes for spring in both species (SWTH: $P < 0.00005$; NOWA: $P < 0.00005$), suggesting sexual segregation in spring passage. Differences in timing between the sexes in spring has also been demonstrated by Ramos (1983; southern Veracruz, México) and Annan (1962; Chicago, IL). No relationship was found between wing length and date in autumn.

Wing lengths differed significantly between seasons in both species (Table 2), but shorter wings in spring are

TABLE 1. Sample effort (net hr) and captures (1), banded releases (2), and recaptures (3) of Swainson's Thrush and the Northern Waterthrush

Year	Net hours		Swainson's Thrush						Northern Waterthrush					
	Spring	Autumn	Spring			Autumn			Spring			Autumn		
			1	2	3	1	2	3	1	2	3	1	2	3
1984	17,708	22,971	224	213	3	115	113	9	175	173	30	77	77	28
1985	25,720	24,999	73	69	0	359	353	25	162	162	22	86	83	21
1986	7,023	17,829	49	47	1	189	187	13	94	89	15	72	70	17
TOTAL	70,451	65,799	346	329	4	663	653	47	431	424	67	235	230	66

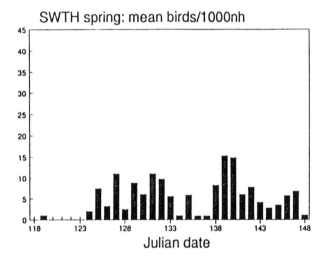

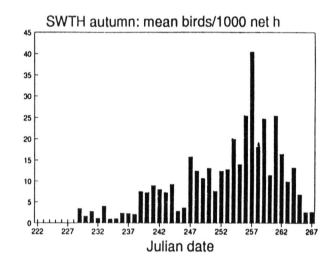

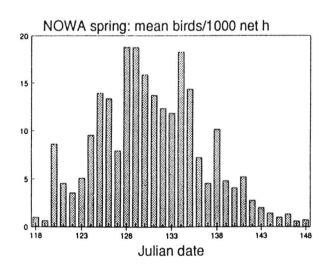

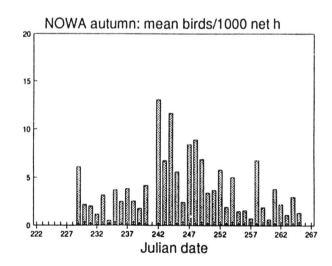

FIGURE 2. Summary of captures through time showing relative abundance and timing during spring and autumn migration. Values represent mean birds per 1000 net hours for specific days during the three-year study. Day 244 = 1 September and Day 135 = 15 May (in non-leap years).

probably due to primary wear rather than to possible racial or sexual differences. Swainson's Thrushes showed a significantly higher proportion of immatures in autumn 1984 than in either 1985 or 1986 (*G*-test with Williams's correction, $G > 13.7$, $P < 0.001$; Table 3). Northern Waterthrushes showed no variation in age composition among autumns (Table 3). A higher proportion of immature Northern Waterthrushes was recaptured relative to individuals not recaptured (Table 3, $G = 5.25$, $0.05 > P > 0.025$). Swainson's Thrushes did not show this difference.

Cherry (1985) noted that some Swainson's Thrushes leave their breeding areas either before molting or while they are still in the early stages of prebasic molt. We found many Swainson's Thrushes and Northern Waterthrushes in prebasic (postnuptial) molt. Of 548 autumn Swainson's Thrushes whose molt was recorded upon first capture, 30.8% were molting to some degree, and 7.3% were molting extensively. Of 157 Northern Waterthrushes, 11.5% were molting to some degree and only one was molting extensively. Differences in the percentage of molting birds between the two age classes were not significant, although adults were more likely to

be molting in the humeral, alar, or caudal tracts (i.e., extensively). Molting birds made up a disproportionately large percentage of recaptures (31.6%) in the Northern Waterthrush ($G = 5.63$, $0.025 > P > 0.01$), but in Swainson's Thrush no difference was found in the proportion of molting birds between recaptured and nonrecaptured birds. Also, no difference was apparent in condition (mass/wing length) between molting and nonmolting birds upon initial capture in either species (Mann-Whitney *U*-test, $z < 1.3$, $P > 0.18$).

WHAT FUEL RESERVES ARE NEEDED TO MAKE THE BIANNUAL JOURNEYS? In assessing the demand that individuals might place on the food resources at a site, one might ask how far these individuals could travel relative to their eventual goal based on their fuel reserves at first capture. Bairlein (1987) applied this approach to the autumn migration of Garden Warblers (*Sylvia borin*) across a north African desert. Based on data from nearly 60 stopover sites north of the Sahara, he found few birds with a body mass sufficiently high to complete a nonstop Saharan crossing (also see Baggott 1986).

We estimated the potential flight ranges of Swain-

TABLE 2. Means and standard deviations of mass (g) and flattened wing length (mm) by season for Swainson's Thrush and the Northern Waterthrush

Season	Swainson's Thrush				Northern Waterthrush			
	Mass		Wing		Mass		Wing	
	Mean	SD	Mean	SD	Mean	SD	Mean	SD
Spring	35.0	3.61	99.0	3.22	17.8	2.23	75.1	2.89
Autumn	30.1	2.75	99.5	3.44	17.8	2.20	75.7	2.91

TABLE 3. Ages of autumn migrant Swainson's Thrushes and Northern Waterthrushes: overall, and with recaptured and nonrecaptured individuals compared

	Swainson's Thrush			Northern Waterthrush		
	adults	immatures	U	adults	immatures	U
1984	30 (28.3)[a]	76	9	21 (28.4)	53	3
1985	206 (57.5)	152	1	20 (23.5)	65	1
1986	118 (64.4)	65	6	29 (42.0)	40	3
TOTALS:	354 (54.7)	293	16	70 (30.7)	158	7
Recaptured[b]	26 (57.8)	19	1	15 (20.8)[c]	57	1
Nonrecaptured[b]	294 (60.2)	194	6	54 (35.8)	97	6

NOTE: Numbers in parentheses represent percent of sample composed of adults.

a. Significantly different from other years, $P < 0.001$.

b. Years showing no significant difference in overall age composition are combined: Swainson's Thrush: 1985 and 1986; Northern Waterthrush: 1984–1986.

c. Higher proportion of immatures recaptured, $0.05 > P > 0.025$.

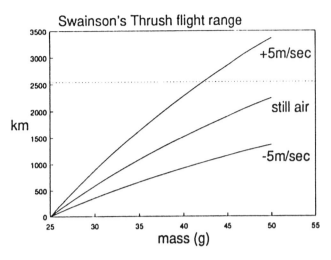

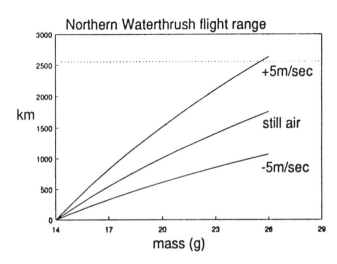

FIGURE 3. Theoretical flight ranges of Swainson's Thrush and the Northern Waterthrush in relation to body mass (g), calculated after Tucker (1974). Potential range varies with fat load and wind condition; shown are still air, tailwinds (+5m/sec), and headwinds (–5m/sec). Dotted lines indicate minimum flight distance from Minnesota study site to a very northerly point in the normal wintering range (Tampico, Tamaulipas, México).

son's Thrush and the Northern Waterthrush using the formulae of Tucker (1974) and the average fat-free body mass for each species in Rogers and Odum (1966). These calculations (Fig. 3) show that under still air conditions neither species can carry enough fat to make a nonstop flight from our site to a point near the northern edge of the species' regular wintering ranges (ca. 2,500 km). Only a very fat bird flying with a tail wind could make this journey nonstop, and, since this is the shortest distance between our site and suitable wintering habitat (Fig. 1), most autumn migrants of these species would be forced to feed at stopover sites between our site and their wintering destinations. Similarly, most birds arriving at our site in spring would probably have had to consume resources at sites along the route. If very fat birds arrive at our site in spring, then presumably feeding occurred near our latitude.

Most of the individuals at our site in autumn seem dependent on resources at stopover sites between our site and their wintering grounds (Fig. 4). Because of our proximity to the breeding range and the unknown quantity of fat needed to survive possible periods of resource uncertainty on the breeding grounds, we can say nothing about the resource needs of spring migrants. Very few spring migrants are lean, however. Swainson's Thrushes carried more fat in spring than in autumn, as indicated by an interseasonal comparison of mass/wing length on first capture (Table 2; t-test on mass/wing length [normality verified], separate variance estimate; $t = 21.85$, d.f. $= 472$, $P < 0.00005$; Fig. 4). Northern Waterthrushes showed no difference in this regard (Table 2; $t = 1.51$, d.f. $= 367$, $P = 0.13$; Fig. 4).

RECAPTURED INDIVIDUALS. An average of 1.2% of Swainson's Thrushes captured in spring, and 7.2% of those captured in autumn, were recaptured after the day of first capture (Table 1). This proportion did not vary significantly between years. The recapture rate was greater in autumn than in spring (G-test, $G = 18.02$, $P < 0.005$), but the number of individuals remaining on the site for more than one night seemed low (Table 1), and very few appeared to remain two or more nights (Fig. 5B). The proportion of Northern Waterthrushes recaptured one night or more after first capture also did not vary significantly between years. An average of 15.8% of individuals captured in spring, and 28.7% of individuals captured in autumn, were recaptured one night or more following first capture (Table 1). Pooling all years, a higher percentage of individuals was recaptured during autumn migration (G-test, $G = 9.57$, $P < 0.005$), suggesting that the site was being used for more than a single day by a higher percentage of stopover migrants during this season. In comparing the two species, a greater percentage of Northern Waterthrushes remained at the site for more than one day in both spring (G-test, $G = 48.8$, $P < 0.001$) and autumn ($G = 45.7$, $P < 0.001$) than did Swainson's Thrushes. This comparison assumes equal capture probabilities for the two species.

Recaptured Swainson's Thrushes in autumn were leaner at initial capture than individuals not recaptured (mass/wing length, Wilcoxon Rank sum: $z = 2.54$, $P = 0.011$). Spring Northern Waterthrush recaptures were also leaner than nonrecaptured birds ($z = 2.03$, $P = 0.042$). Autumn Northern Waterthrush recaptures did

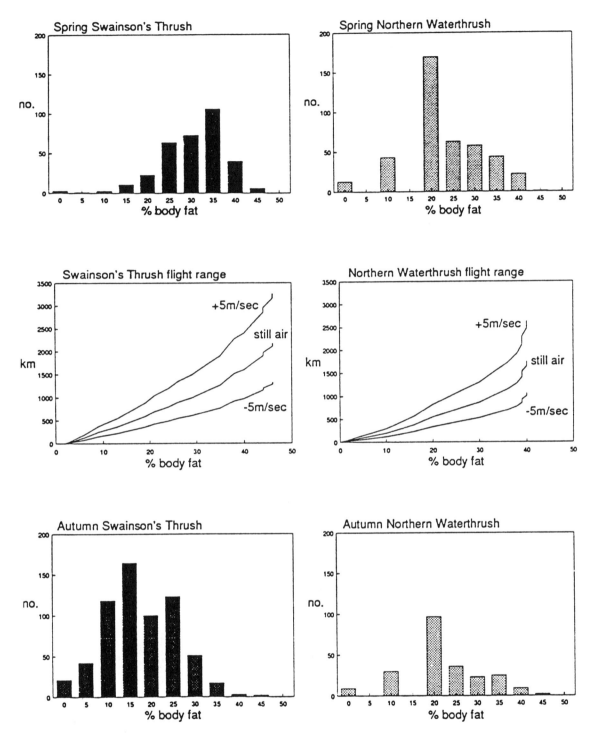

FIGURE 4. Seasonal comparison of birds captured to theoretical flight ranges. To standardize for size variation among individuals, estimates of percent body fat (body fat as a percentage of total body mass) are given. These estimates were made by applying a summary of fat extraction data for both species (Rogers and Odum 1966, Odum et al., unpubl. data) to field measurements. Theoretical flight ranges are converted from a mass base to one of estimated percent body fat (from Fig. 3). Swainson's Thrush shows significant seasonal difference in fat reserves, whereas Northern Waterthrushes do not.

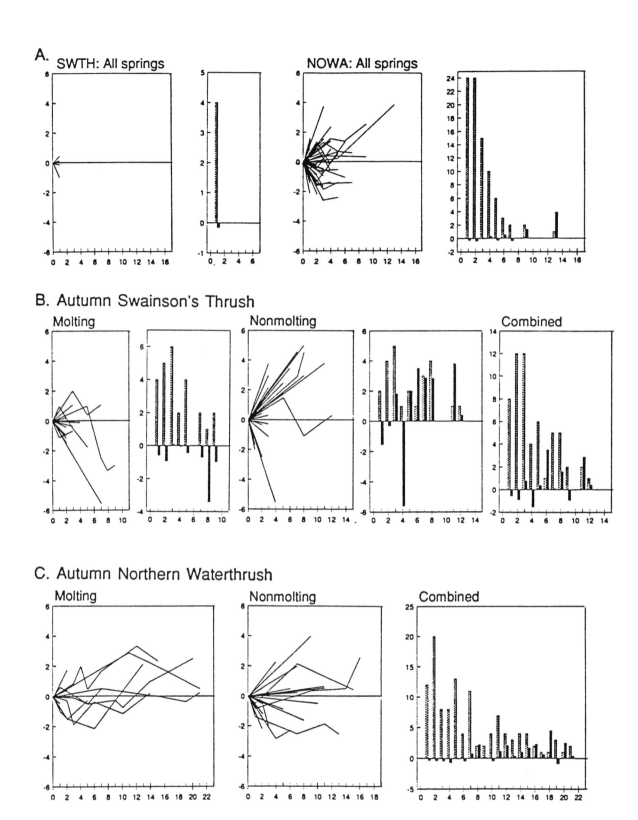

Days Following First Capture

FIGURE 5. Mass changes (g) and minimum length of stay (days) in recaptured Swainson's Thrushes (SWTH) and Northern Waterthrushes (NOWA). Line diagrams show mass changes through time for individuals whose mass at first capture is set to zero. Bar diagrams show number of individuals captured *x* days following initial capture (*light bars*), and the mean change in body mass for this group of individuals (*dark bars*). Individuals may be represented more than once in bar diagrams. Vertical axes in bar diagrams indicate number of individuals and change in body mass (g). *A* includes all spring recaptures for both species. *B* illustrates significant differences between molting and nonmolting autumn Swainson's Thrushes (1985 and 1986) and shows mass changes in all autumn recaptures combined. *C* shows recaptured Northern Waterthrushes; molting birds were recaptured more times (no difference in mass change). Line diagrams in *C* include 1985 and 1986, whereas the bar chart shows all autumns combined.

TABLE 4. Comparison of individuals recaptured one night or more following first capture

Species (season)	n	Mean days present	Mean g/d[a] A	B	Nonmolting[b] n	avg.Δg	Molting[b] n	avg.Δg	t[c]	P[c]
Swainson's Thrush (spring)	4	1.0	-0.15	–	–	–	–	–	–	–
Northern Waterthrush (spring)	67	3.0	0.07	0.14	–	–	–	–	–	–
Swainson's Thrush (autumn)	47	4.1	0.12	0.26	22	1.06	16	-0.83	2.57	0.01
Northern Waterthrush (autumn)	66	7.6	0.05	0.09	25	-0.02	12	0.76	-1.13	0.26

NOTE: Seasonal differences in mean number of days present are significant (within species).

a. Mean change in mass per day of all recaptured birds over entire capture history: A: relative to mass at first capture, and B: relative to mean 2-day post first–capture low.

b. Includes only birds from 1985 and 1986.

c. Results of t-test examining differences in mass change between recaptured molting and nonmolting individuals.

not show this difference ($z = 0.94, P = 0.35$).

For recaptures, the average minimum number of days present did not differ significantly between years, and overall means are considered here (Table 4). During autumn, molting Northern Waterthrushes were recaptured with greater frequency than would be predicted by their representation in the overall sample. Their change in mass while at the site showed no difference, however, from recaptures that were not molting (Fig. 5C). In fact, mass change in molting Northern Waterthrushes tended to be greater than in nonmolting conspecifics (Table 4). This trend was not significant, but molting birds were recaptured more times during their residence than nonmolting birds (Mann-Whitney U-test, $z = 3.06, P = 0.02$), even though there was no difference between the groups in days present ($z = 1.13, P = 0.26$). Recaptured Swainson's Thrushes showed the opposite trend; molting birds had a lower rate of mass change than nonmolting birds (Table 4).

DIURNAL MASS CHANGES. Few Swainson's Thrushes appeared to remain and use local resources (Table 1). Conceivably, birds might only be resting, waiting for night and/or favorable weather for renewed flight. Rapole and Warner (1976) found that transients at a site in Texas were frequently in a state of Zugstimmung (flyers), not dependent on the food resources of an area (perhaps not feeding). Bairlein (1987) determined that fat birds on stopover in the Sahara tended to be active only at night, and that in the day they rested in shade (also see Biebach et al. 1986, Biebach 1988). Observations of birds at our site during the day suggest that feeding was common (Winker, unpubl. data). Analyses of specimens acquired as net casualties support these observations. All Northern Waterthrush specimens ($n = 12$) had food material in the alimentary canals, as did 92% ($n = 27$) of Swainson's Thrushes (combined spring and autumn). In general, transients at our site had active digestive tracts (95.1% of 144 specimens). Similarly, Brensing (1977) found that large amounts of invertebrates were eaten by many migrants in Germany.

If birds at our site were not feeding, they would show a loss in mass during daylight hours due to normal metabolic activity. Regression of mass/wing length on time of day (24-hr clock) for first captures suggests that captured birds were feeding (Figs. 6, 7). For both species in both seasons these regressions yielded significant positive slopes (Table 5). The daily rate of increase for Swainson's Thrushes was significantly higher in spring than in autumn ($F = 42.14$, d.f. = 2,26, $P > 0.001$; comparison of slopes after Weisberg [1985]). Northern Waterthrushes showed no seasonal differences in daily rate of mass gain.

Increase in mass during the day is expected in feeding birds, with this gain usually being reversed during the night as undigested food material is excreted from the alimentary canal and fat is used to fuel nocturnal metabolism (Baldwin and Kendeigh 1938, Mueller and Berger 1966). The amount of daily gain due to fat deposition depends on several variables. We follow Nisbet et al. (1963) and assume that water loss in a migrating individual is negligible, although in less hospitable climes this assumption is probably invalid (see Biebach 1988). Food material in the alimentary tract is probably a primary factor in individual daily mass variation (Baldwin and Kendeigh 1938). These investigators found an average daily variation of 4.5% of total body mass in free-living birds during the breeding season (primarily small passerines, probably not depositing significant fat reserves). We used two estimates of nightly loss: one was 4.5% of body mass alone; the second added to this value the fat used in nocturnal metabolism. There are valid reasons for considering both estimates (see Baldwin and Kendeigh 1938:418, 429). Applying these mass correc-

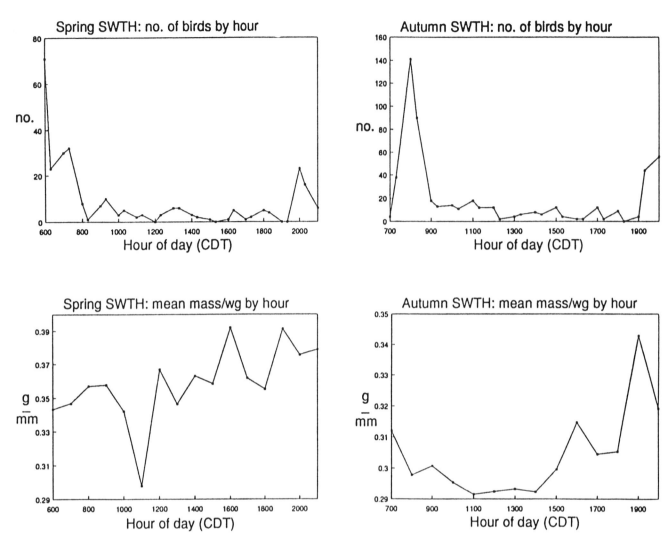

FIGURE 6. Distribution and mean condition (body mass/wing length) of first captures of Swainson's Thrush by hour of day. Change through day is positive and significant. Gains suggest population-wide feeding in all cases.

tions for "average" individuals to the linear regressions in Table 5 suggests fat gains of 1.4–8.9% of total body mass per day in birds captured at our site (Table 6). The estimated flying times that these gains would allow vary from 1.9 to 11.8 hr (Table 6, calculated after Tucker 1974).

As King (1972) noted, examination of daily variation in total body mass gives only a "semi-quantitative" estimate of variation in fat reserves. We have attempted to subtract major nonfat and metabolized fat losses from apparent daily gains to estimate average fat gains, and consider that, although the figures are not exact (thus the presentation of a range of possible gains), treatment of data sets in this fashion allows assessment of samplewide trends and comparison of these trends between seasons. Because of individual variability in daily

mass fluctuation (Baldwin and Kendeigh 1938, King 1972), these calculations should only be applied to large samples.

Included in Table 6 are estimates based on data in Mueller and Berger (1966:93) for autumn Swainson's Thrushes in Wisconsin. A regression of mass by hour (24 hr clock) results in a similar linear equation to those in Table 5 ($m = 0.00137$ g/hundredth-hr, $b = 28.76$, $F = 99.9$, $P < 0.0005$). Using changes in fat class rather than mass, these authors estimated a net fat gain of 0.0–0.61 g/day (averaging about 0.34 g/day), an estimate that is close to ours based on their mass data alone. Mueller and Berger recaptured 19.6% of their original captures, a significantly larger proportion than our 7.2% ($G = 53.17$, $P < 0.001$). Estimates of fat gain in our birds exceeded estimates for Mueller and Berg-

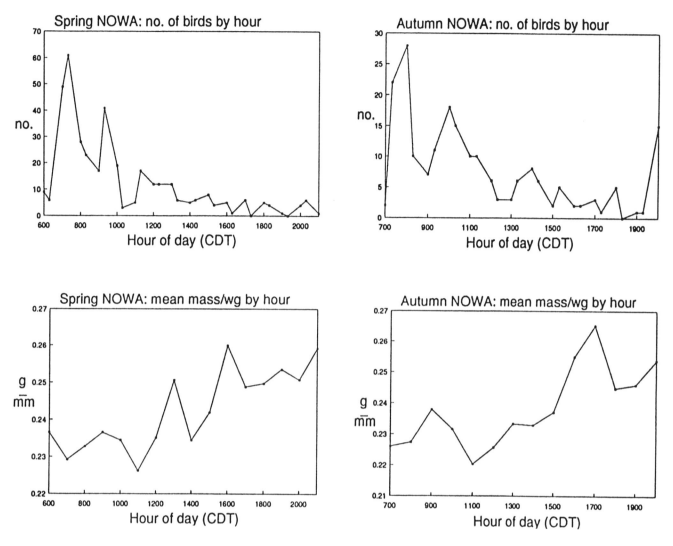

FIGURE 7. Distribution and mean condition (body mass/wing length) of first captures of Northern Waterthrush by hour of day. Change through day is positive and significant. Gains suggest population-wide feeding in all cases.

TABLE 5. Summary of linear regressions for daily change in mean condition (mass/wing length = y) by hour of day (x) in first captures

Species (season)	m	b	r^2	F	P	g/mm per day[a]
Swainson's Thrush (spring)	0.0000274	0.32	0.34	7.27	0.017	0.0406
Swainson's Thrush (autumn)	0.0000182	0.28	0.29	4.92	0.047	0.0245
Northern Waterthrush (spring)	0.0000182	0.22	0.65	26.71	0.00005	0.0270
Northern Waterthrush (autumn)	0.0000234	0.21	0.57	15.98	0.0018	0.0315

NOTE: The equations have the form $y = mx + b$, where m is the slope (grams per hundredth-hour) and b the y intercept. r^2 gives the proportion of the total variability of mean condition accounted for by time of day, while the F statistic and its corresponding P value serve to test how well the regression model fits the data. For $P < 0.05$, we accept the hypothesis that there is a positive, nonzero relationship between the two variables.

a. Gain in mass over full day (by mm of wing length) based on linear model.

TABLE 6. Application of linear regressions to average individuals in the transient populations to estimate average net daily increases in fat reserves

Species (season)	Mean mass	Gross Δg/day[a]	Nocturnal loss[b]	4.5% mass	Net gain/day[c] A	Net gain/day[c] B	Increase as % of mass	Hours of flight[d]
Swainson's Thrush (spring)	34.9	4.02	0.54	1.57	2.45	1.91	5.5–7.0	8.1–10.3
Swainson's Thrush (autumn)	30.1	2.43	0.64	1.35	1.08	0.44	1.4–3.6	1.9–4.6
Swainson's Thrush (autumn[e])	30.0	1.85	0.60	1.35	0.50	-0.10	-0.3–1.7	0.0–2.1
Northern Waterthrush (spring)	17.8	2.03	0.34	0.80	1.22	0.88	4.9–6.9	6.6–9.2
Northern Waterthrush (autumn)	17.6	2.36	0.41	0.79	1.57	1.16	6.6–8.9	8.7–11.8

NOTE: Included for comparison are data from Mueller and Berger (1966) on autumn Swainson's Thrushes in Wisconsin. Units are grams, except for final column.

a. Diurnal mass gain (g/d), calculated directly from linear model in Table 5, using average wing lengths of: Swainson's Thrush 99 mm, Northern Waterthrush 75 mm, except for *e* (see text).

b. Fat used in nocturnal metabolism (g), calculated for an average individual of each species. Entry under Swainson's Thrush (autumn[e]) is Mueller and Berger's (1966) own estimate; see text.

c. Net mass gain in 24–hr period after subtracting night losses estimated as A: 4.5% of body mass; and B: 4.5% body mass *and* nocturnal fat loss due to metabolism; see text.

d. Hours of flight possible if net gain is all fat. Calculated after Tucker (1974:306), whereby fat is lost at 0.237g/h (Swainson's Thrush) and 0.133g/h (Northern Waterthrush) in flight.

e. Derived from Mueller and Berger (1966); see text.

er's sample (Table 6). If mass gains influence individual decisions on whether to migrate or remain at a stopover site, this is the predicted relationship: lower samplewide mass gains would result in more individuals remaining to be recaptured (when daily mass gains are greater than zero).

HABITAT SELECTION. Despite the relatively small size (1–3 ha) of our sampled habitats, many transients used them. Autumn Swainson's Thrushes and Northern Waterthrushes in both seasons showed no significant among-year variation in habitat distribution. Both species showed significant differences between seasons (Fig. 8). Spring Swainson's Thrushes showed no differences among habitats in capture rate (the entire habitat group forms one subset), whereas in spring Northern Waterthrushes, Swamp and Floodplain showed a higher capture rate than Willows and Upland. Similarly, for autumn Northern Waterthrushes, Floodplain showed a significantly higher capture rate than Willows and Upland, and Swamp showed a higher capture rate than Upland. For spring Swainson's Thrushes, between-year variation in habitat distribution was significant among springs (two-way ANOVA, testing two-way interactions between habitat and year: $F = 2.45$, $P = 0.025$). Examination of Swainson's Thrush distribution each spring (one-way ANOVA) revealed that no habitat or group of habitats was used more than another ($P > 0.05$). Although analyses performed at the level $\alpha = 0.10$ did show differential use, these differences were

not consistent among years. All spring Swainson's Thrushes were combined in Figure 8 to illustrate significant differences between seasons. These habitat use profiles (Fig. 8) were developed using 168–497 individual captures over 57 days (autumn) and 69 days (spring) of simultaneous netting (Table 7).

The Oaks habitat was thoroughly netted only in spring 1986 and autumn 1985. Given the between-year variation evident among springs in apparent habitat use by Swainson's Thrush, we include this habitat with the caution that the capture rates during these seasons might not accurately reflect the overall ranking of Oaks among the available habitats when averaged among several years. Within the respective seasons, Oaks was directly comparable to Upland in both species; differences between the two habitats in the two seasons were not significant ($P > 0.10$). These habitat analyses show that the waterthrushes preferred the wetter habitats (Swamp, Floodplain, Willows; Fig. 8) and that seasonal shifts in distribution occurred among these habitats. Swainson's Thrushes, on the other hand, showed a shift from drier sites (Upland, Oaks) in spring toward wetter sites (Floodplain, Willows) in autumn (Fig. 8).

Discussion

HABITAT SELECTION. Habitat selection of migrating passerines has been documented for only a few species at a few sites (e.g., Parnell 1969, Berthold et al. 1976, Bairlein 1983, Hutto 1985, Berthold 1989, this study),

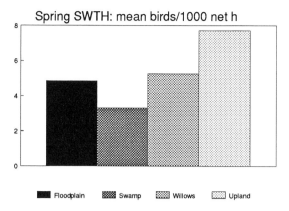

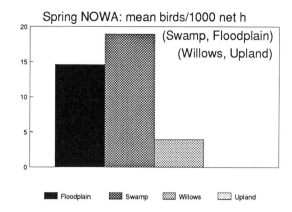

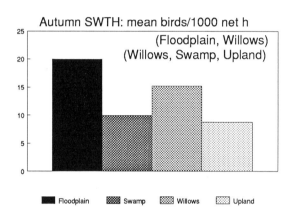

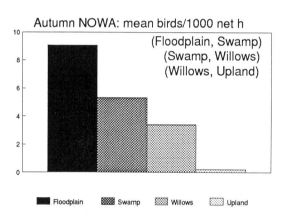

FIGURE 8. Distribution of individuals as reflected by mean capture rates on days when nets in four habitats were open simultaneously. Parenthetical groups denote homogeneous subsets as determined through one-way ANOVA; absence of a particular habitat type from any parenthetical subset indicates a significant difference between it and that subset's members.

and demonstrations of seasonal shifts in use are rare (Jones 1895, Hutto 1985, this study). Significant between-year, within-season variability in habitat distribution, as found at our site in spring Swainson's Thrushes, does not seem to have been described. Swainson's Thrushes showed a broad distribution among available habitats in spring. Wider availability of resources or wider "tolerance" of available habitat types during the vernal migration might cause broad habitat use. Another factor might be our narrow array of habitat types. Although Bairlein (1983) and Berthold (1989) described relatively constant between-year distributions among habitats, our data suggest that at a finer scale (i.e., within woodlands, rather than between wood, savanna, bush, etc.) annual shifts can occur.

MOLT. As Cherry (1985) noted, it is generally assumed that long-distance migrants undergo a prebasic molt be-

fore migration. Few studies have documented molt in transient long-distance migrant passerines (e.g., Cherry 1985, Rappole and Ballard 1987, Rimmer 1988), but it appears to be a phenomenon restricted to stopover sites near the breeding ranges of the respective species. Northerly stopover sites can thus provide autumn migrants both fuel for continued migration and resources to complete feather growth. Data from recaptured Swainson's Thrushes imply that these two energetic demands cannot be met simultaneously among all individuals, and that basic physiological differences exist between conspecifics at our site. Although Northern Waterthrush recaptures suggest that some individuals overlap these activities without sacrificing mass gain, a lower percentage of the waterthrushes were molting flight feathers, and molting birds showed a greater likelihood of recapture. These observations suggest that the two energetically demanding phenomena are in some

TABLE 7. Numbers of days of simultaneous netting in Floodplain, Swamp, Willows, and Upland by season and year, together with total net hours and numbers of individuals used in establishing profiles of habitat selectivity. The Oaks habitat is considered separately.

Season	Year	Days[a]	Net hours[b]	Swainson's Thrush[c]	Northern Waterthrush[c]
Spring	1984	15	13,560	205	202
	1985	28	24,923	77	184
	1986	26	22,510	40	111
TOTAL SPRING		69	60,993	322	497
Autumn	1984	25	18,945	122	73
	1985	24	18,636	324	70
	1986	8	5,564	66	25
TOTAL AUTUMN		57	43,145	512	168
Oaks[d]	1986	26	26,213	93	111
	1985	22	19,657	377	67

a. Number of days on which all habitats considered were sampled for a similar period during the day. Days with > 12% difference among habitats in the portion of day sampled were excluded from the analysis. Top section of table considers Floodplain, Swamp, Willows, and Upland. Oaks section considers all five habitat types.

b. Total from all habitats considered on simultaneously sampled days.

c. Number of individuals captured during simultaneous sampling; includes only first captures.

d. Considered separately because of lower sample effort in this fifth habitat. This habitat was netted thoroughly in spring 1986 and autumn 1985.

manner "juggled" by migrating individuals (also see Berthold 1975), and that adaptations enabling individuals to reproduce, molt, and migrate successfully probably differ among northerly breeding long-distance migrant passerine species.

MIGRATION STRATEGY. Most investigations at stopover sites focus on data from recaptured individuals (e.g., Rappole and Warner 1976, Moore and Kerlinger 1987, Safriel and Lavee 1988), yet these individuals usually represent a minority of the birds occurring at a site. It is difficult to use data from birds that are encountered only once, but the method used here (modified from Mueller and Berger 1966; see also Collins and Bradley 1971, Shimov 1985, Yablonkevich et al. 1985a,b) suggests that other conclusions regarding the use of stopover resources might be drawn if only recaptures are examined. Few Swainson's Thrushes remained at our site in spring (Fig. 5A). Insofar as those that remained did not acquire substantial mass gains, the vernal resources at this site are clearly not used in a "staging" fashion. If only recaptures are examined, resources at this site would appear to be unimportant for this species during spring migration. Examination of the captured group as a whole, however, yields a very different picture (Figs. 6, 7; Table 6). When considered on a samplewide basis, spring migrant Swainson's Thrushes

seemed to be feeding prodigiously throughout the day, and their average daily gains might be sufficient for a night's flight.

Ramos (1983) found a median date of passage of 12 May for Swainson's Thrushes in southern Veracruz, México. The median date of individual passage at our site over all springs was 18 May (Day 138). These dates suggest rapid spring passage for the species between southern México and southern Minnesota: approximately 480 km/day in a straight-line direction, 520 km/day by land (minimum distance). Recapture rates of Swainson's Thrushes in spring are low: Rappole and Warner (1976) recaptured 5.7% of their sample in south Texas; Galindo et al. (1963) showed 5.2% recaptured in Panamá. Both of these are significantly higher than the spring recapture rate at our site ($G > 7.5, P < 0.01$), but are not significantly different from each other. Unless there are unknown staging areas where birds deposit substantial amounts of fat, the fast rate of spring migration must be sustained largely by refueling during single-day stopovers. Our data support this concept. Based on the magnitude of the daily mass gains in spring Swainson's Thrushes (Table 6), the few recaptures (Table 1), and the fat loads carried (Fig. 4), the species may follow a "feed-by-day, fly-by-night" strategy during spring migration in central North America, whereby sufficient fat reserves are accumulated by day to allow a full (or a ± near-full) night's flight. This strategy would minimize the time required to complete a migration (since nights would not be "wasted" on stopover), but would necessitate adequate resources being available on daily stopovers.

Peak efficiency in pursuing this strategy would require rapid assessment of local habitats for suitable daytime feeding areas. Cochran et al. (1967) noted that migrant thrushes landing in darkness do not select their diurnal habitat until dawn. These authors also noted that some spring migrant thrushes were able to migrate on two consecutive nights in Illinois. We might predict that many of the spring Swainson's Thrushes at our site could also do so (Fig. 4), but that they could not make successive-night flights and maintain the fat loads observed without daily feeding on an impressive scale (e.g., Table 6). This strategy would require hyperphagia to persist through the migration period, and there is evidence for this in some migrant species (King 1961, Berthold 1976). The lesser mass gains shown by recaptured Swainson's Thrushes in autumn, and in Northern Waterthrush recaptures at both seasons, suggest that this daily cycle is not followed in both seasons, nor in equivalent-distance migrants.

GEOGRAPHIC FAT DEPOSITION PATTERNS. Transient Swainson's Thrushes exhibit geographic variation in body mass, suggesting different patterns of fat deposition. Geographic coverage is incomplete, however, with spotty coverage in North America and a lack of data south of Panamá. Child (1969) found a relatively low mean mass in Panamá in spring, which was also the case in spring in southern Veracruz, México ($\bar{X}$ = 28.76, SD = 4.27, n = 179; specimens in the Bell Museum of Natural History, Minneapolis, MN), and on the northern Gulf coast (Child 1969). Fatter birds at our site in spring than in autumn suggests that fat is deposited between the Gulf coast and the breeding grounds, despite an apparently rapid northward passage. In autumn, birds seem to accumulate fat between our site and the northern Gulf region, such that at our site a "heavier spring, leaner autumn" relationship exists, whereas in the Gulf region the opposite relationship appears (Child 1969). Autumn migrants largely miss southern Veracruz (see Rappole et al. 1979; very small specimen sample), and although Child's (1969) data suggest a minor "heavier autumn, leaner spring" relationship in Panamá, Rogers and Odum (1966) showed that this relationship is small or nonexistent. Child (1969) found no significant differences in wing length (as a size indicator) among his sites, and Ramos (1983) found no mensural differences between races of Swainson's Thrushes, which lends credence to direct mass comparisons of this sort.

These latitudinal comparisons suggest a migratory strategy for birds passing through Minnesota whereby

fat is accumulated in the continental United States both in spring and autumn. In both seasons birds are approaching an ecological barrier: one of a physical nature in the case of the Gulf of México in autumn, and of a temporal nature as they approach the breeding grounds in spring (given time, resources will become available). The median date of spring passage in Panamá appears to be from 21 to 27 April (Galindo and Méndez 1965), so the rapid rate of Swainson's Thrushes' passage between Veracruz and Minnesota is not maintained throughout spring migration. Also, the "heavier spring, leaner autumn" relationship at our site does not appear in migrant Swainson's Thrushes in western Pennsylvania (Clench and Leberman 1978). Further geographic comparisons are impeded by failing to recognize racial differences. Ramos (1983) found five races passing through Veracruz in spring (*swainsoni, incanus, almae, ustulatus,* and *appalachiensis* [Phillips 1991:90]); we recorded two (*incanus* and *swainsoni*) and by geography western Pennsylvania should have two or three (*swainsoni-clarescens* and *appalachiensis*). Ramos (1989) presented evidence suggesting that comparisons of migration strategies will have to be made between population subunits (including races), and Moreau and Dolp (1970:112) noted that neighboring breeding populations might differ in regard to migratory fat. Karlsson et al. (1988) found differences in fat deposition suggesting different migration strategies between two populations of Robins (*Erithacus rubecula*) in Sweden. The difference in spring versus autumn mass relationships in Swainson's Thrushes between western Pennsylvania and Minnesota imply that further understanding of North American fat deposition patterns in this species will require consideration of the breeding grounds of individuals in passage.

Little is known of body mass in migrating Nearctic species in South America and Central America outside of Panamá, and sufficient data on body mass in the Northern Waterthrush were unavailable for broad geographic comparisons. Our finding of similar mass between spring and autumn, however, suggests that this species follows a different annual migration strategy than Swainson's Thrush.

ROUTE SELECTION. Fewer Northern Waterthrush captures in autumn, when greater numbers are expected due to summer recruitment, suggest seasonal migratory route differences. Rappole at al. (1979) described an easterly route for the species in autumn based on abundance records for two sites on the Gulf of México (Texas and Veracruz). Our data suggest that this autumn easterly trend is present far north of the Gulf of México. Banding in western Pennsylvania (Clench and Leberman 1978) showed the expected trend of more birds in autumn than spring, and supports the concept of the eastwardly autumn route. Given the breeding range of the species, however (Fig. 1), a westerly route is also followed by some members of the species (*S. n. notabilis* and *linnaeus* by the nomenclature of McCabe and Miller 1933). Swainson's Thrushes showed no consistent pattern of seasonal abundance at our site (Table 1). The species appears to migrate along a very broad front. The presence of *incanus* at our site in spring suggests that some birds do not follow a minimum-distance route to their breeding grounds, unless a spring trans-Caribbean flight is made by some, which seems unlikely, given the spring presence of the race in southern Veracruz (Ramos 1983).

CONSERVATION CONSIDERATIONS. Seasonal distributions of birds among our habitats suggest that individuals of these two species prefer certain wooded habitats over others. No single habitat was used above all others, however. In addition, both species showed seasonal shifts in distribution, which we interpret as a shift in preference. Although species with broad habitat use might show few effects from the loss of some habitat types, seasonal shifts in habitat preference suggest that an array of habitats is desirable.

The effects on migrants that the loss of available stopover sites would have depends on several factors: the rate of habitat change, the size of the bird, and the species' pattern of habitat use. Perhaps the most recent example of extreme stopover habitat loss is the change that has occurred in North Africa. Two million to 4,000 years ago the eastern Sahara underwent periods of rainfall that caused a degree of surface water buildup sufficient to form a network of river and stream channels (McCauley et al. 1982). Human habitation in the region covered a period 200,000–4,000 years ago (Szabo et al. 1989). The deterioration of the region from "savanna-like" to uninhabited, hyperarid desert (see McCauley et al. 1982) implies loss of potential stopover sites to long-distance Palearctic migrants, including species migrating across the region today. Passerines continue to migrate across this 1,500–2,000-km ecological barrier (Biebach et al. 1986, Biebach 1988), showing that some species can accommodate these changes when they occur over a long period. If current Nearctic barriers were to expand to 1,500–2,000 km, however, calculations of energetics (after Tucker 1974) show that species such as the Ruby-throated Hummingbird (*Archilochus colubris*) and the smaller paruline warblers would be unable to carry enough fat to successfully complete a crossing, making them dependent on resources available in transit. Research at oases in the Sahara (Bairlein 1985, 1988, Biebach et al. 1986) suggests that some Palearctic migrants use resources at suitable desert stopover sites, but it is uncertain what role these resources play in the overall migration strategy of en-

tire species (Bairlein 1985). A decrease in suitable stopover sites would probably force individual and specific strategies of migration to change. The daily refueling strategy indicated for spring Swainson's Thrushes would be less likely to succeed as daily encounters with suitable feeding sites diminished.

At our site the concept of staging area applied to only a few Northern Waterthrushes that remained for a considerable period of time using resources primarily to complete the prebasic molt. Few remaining birds of either species deposited substantial fat reserves when considered on a gain-per-day basis. The average recapture showed little mass gain, which might imply that this site was not important to these transients. Daily mass gains of the overall captured sample suggest otherwise, however. These seemingly contradictory observations are confusing, and may be caused by the many differences noted between recaptured and nonrecaptured individuals, that is, molt status, fat reserves, age, and, least investigated, handling effects. The differences between individuals "dropping out" of migration and those continuing need further investigation. Our data suggest that dramatic differences might exist between these two groups with regard to their daily resource consumption, and that a majority of transients are depositing fat.

The strategies used in spring migration seem to differ between Swainson's Thrush and the Northern Waterthrush, as suggested by the seasonal difference in stopover site use by Swainson's Thrushes and the virtual lack of difference on the part of the Northern Waterthrush (apart from numbers). Comparisons at this level are difficult, however, since seasonal route differences and probable racial differences hinder a species-level understanding of migration strategies and the role of stopover sites.

The role of specific habitat types in this overall picture has not been examined thoroughly here. Stomach contents, daily gains in mass in the overall sample, and seasonal shifts in distribution among habitats all imply that food resources in the vicinity of our study site were being used in migration by both species. Differences between seasons in apparent habitat use and inferred feeding rates (e.g., Swainson's Thrush daily mass change) underscore the fact that a woodland stopover site's importance varies both with species and with season. Further progress on this subject will demand investigation on two levels: (1) broader geographic coverage, and (2) more intense local analyses, especially of factors not considered here (e.g., social, racial, intraseasonal).

Acknowledgments

We gratefully acknowledge support from the James Ford Bell Foundation and the U.S. National Park Service. We also extend thanks and appreciation to Mr. and Mrs. Charles Bell; without their interest in songbirds this project would not have occurred. Chris Rimmer pointed out the importance of prebasic molt and enabled more thorough examination of birds in the field. The manuscript benefitted from discussions with B.A. Fall, G.E. Nordquist, H.B. Tordoff, and M. Sorenson, and from critical reading by J.T. Klicka, T.L. Lloyd-Evans, F. McKinney, D.F. Parmelee, an anonymous reviewer, and the editors. D.F. Parmelee allowed free access to specimens in the ornithological collection of the Bell Museum of Natural History. E.P. Odum sent summaries of fat extraction data. We thank the numerous field assistants whose tireless efforts allowed us to keep the nets open. Finally, we thank Marie Ward for her help, support, and good-natured tolerance of those semiannual invasions of her domain.

Literature cited

Annan, O. 1962. Sequence of migration, by sex, age, and species, of thrushes of the genus *Hylocichla*, through Chicago. *Bird-Banding* 33:130–137.

American Ornithologists' Union. 1983. *Check-list of North American Birds.* 6th ed. Washington: American Ornithologists' Union.

Baggott, G.K. 1986. The fat contents and flight ranges of four warbler species on migration in North Wales. *Ringing and Migration* 7:25–36.

Bairlein, F. 1983. Habitat selection and associations of species in European passerine birds during southward, postbreeding migrations. *Ornis Scand.* 14:239–245.

———. 1985. Body weights and fat deposition of palearctic passerine migrants in the central Sahara. *Oecologia* 66:141–146.

———. 1987. The migratory strategy of the Garden Warbler: A survey of field and laboratory data. *Ringing and Migration* 8:59–72.

———. 1988. How do migratory songbirds cross the Sahara? *Trends Ecol. Evol.* 3:191–194.

Baldwin, S.P., and S.C. Kendeigh. 1938. Variations in the weights of birds. *Auk* 55:416–467.

Berthold, P. 1975. Migration: Control and metabolic physiology Pages 77–128 in *Avian Biology*, Vol. 5, D.S. Farner and J.R. King, eds. New York: Academic Press.

———. 1976. Über den Einfluß der Fetdeposition auf die Zugunruhe bei der Gartengrasmücke *Sylvia borin*. *Vogelwarte* 28:263–266.

———. 1989. The control of migration in European warblers. *Acta 19th Internat. Ornithol. Cong.* (Ottawa): 215–249.

Berthold, P., F. Bairlein, and U. Querner. 1976. Über die Verteilung von ziehenden Kleinvögeln in Rastbiotopen und den Fangerfolg von Fanganlagen. *Vogelwarte* 28:267–273.

Biebach, H. 1988. Ecophysiology of resting Willow Warblers (*Phylloscopus trochilus*) crossing the Sahara. *Acta 19th Internat. Ornithol. Cong.* (Ottawa): 2162–2168.

Biebach, H., W. Friedrich, and G. Heine. 1986. Interaction of body mass, fat, foraging and stopover period in trans-Sahara migrating passerine birds. *Oecologia* 69:370–379.

Bond, J. 1936. *Birds of the West Indies.* Philadelphia: Academy Natural Science.

Brensing, D. 1977. Nahrungsökologische Untersuchungen an Zugvögeln in einem südwestdeutschen Durchzugsgebiet während des Wegzuges. *Vogelwarte* 29:44–57.

Cherry, J.D. 1982. Fat deposition and length of stopover of migrant White-crowned Sparrows. *Auk* 99:725–732.

———. 1985. Early autumn movements and prebasic molt of Swainson's Thrushes. *Wilson Bull.* 97:368–370.

Child, G.I. 1969. A study of nonfat weights in migrating Swainson's Thrushes (*Hylocichla ustulata*). *Auk* 86:327–338.

Clench, M.H., and R.C. Leberman. 1978. Weights of 151 species of Pennsylvania birds analyzed by month, age, and sex. *Bull. Carnegie Mus. Nat. Hist.* 5:1–87.

Cochran, W.W., G.G. Montgomery, and R.R. Graber. 1967. Migratory flights of *Hylocichla* thrushes in spring: A radiotelemetry study. *Living Bird* 6:213–225.

Collins, C.T., and R.A. Bradley. 1971. Analysis of body weights of spring migrants in Southern California. *Western Bird Bander* 46:48–51.

Connell, C.E., E.P. Odum, and H. Kale. 1960. Fat-free weights of birds. *Auk* 77:1–9.

Dawson, W.R., R.L. Marsh, and M.E. Yacoe. 1983. Metabolic adjustments of small passerine birds for migration and cold. *Amer. J. Physiol.* 245:R755–R767.

Dunning, J.S. 1982. *South American Land Birds.* Newtown Square, Pa.: Harrowood Books.

Galindo, P., and E. Méndez. 1965. Banding of thrushes and catbirds at Almirante, Panama. Second year of observations. *Bird-Banding* 36:233–239.

Galindo, P., E. Méndez, and A.J. Adames. 1963. Banding of migrant thrushes in Almirante, Panamá. *Bird-Banding* 34:202–209.

Godfrey, W.E. 1951. A new northwestern Olive-backed Thrush. *Can. Field Nat.* 65:172–174.

Hutto, R.L. 1985. Seasonal changes in the habitat distribution of transient insectivorous birds in southeastern Arizona: Competition mediated? *Auk* 102:120–132.

Jones, L. 1895. Bird migration at Grinnell, Iowa. II. Fall migration. *Auk* 12:231–237.

Karlsson, L., K. Persson, J. Pettersson, and G. Walinder. 1988. Fat-weight relationships and migratory strategies in the Robin *Erithacus rubecula* at two stopover sites in south Sweden. *Ringing and Migration* 9:160–168.

King, J.R. 1961. The bioenergetics of vernal premigratory fat deposition in the White-crowned Sparrow. *Condor* 63:128–142.

———. 1972. Adaptive periodic fat storage by birds. *Proc. 15th Internat. Ornithol. Cong.* (The Hague): 200–217.

King, J.R. and D.S. Farner. 1965. Studies of fat deposition in migratory birds. *Annals N.Y. Academy Science* 131:422–440.

Luleeva, D.S., and V.I. Luleev. 1985. [Body weight and fat of small passerine birds at the oasis in south Kyzilkum desert during spring 1973 and 1981]. *Tr. Zool. Inst. Akad. NAUK SSSR* 137:60–68.

McCabe, T.T., and A.H. Miller. 1933. Geographic variation in the Northern Water-thrushes. *Condor* 35:192–197.

McCauley, J.F., G.G. Schaber, C.S. Breed, M.J. Grolier, C.V. Haynes, B. Issawi, C. Elachi, and R. Blom. 1982. Subsurface valleys and geoarcheology of the eastern Sahara revealed by shuttle radar. *Science* 218:1004–1020.

McClure, H.E. 1984. *Bird Banding*. Pacific Grove, Calif.: Boxwood Press.

Moore, F.R. and P. Kerlinger. 1987. Stopover and fat deposition by North American wood-warblers (Parulinae) following spring migration over the Gulf of Mexico. *Oecologia* 74:47–54.

Moreau, R.E., and R.M. Dolp. 1970. Fat, water, weights and wing-lengths of autumn migrants in transit on the northwest coast of Egypt. *Ibis* 112:209–228.

Mueller, H.C., and D.D. Berger. 1966. Analyses of weight and fat variations in transient Swainson's Thrushes. *Bird-Banding* 37:83-112.

Myers, J.P., J.L. Maron, and M. Sallaberry. 1985. Going to extremes: Why do Sanderlings migrate to the neotropics? Pages 520–535 in *Neotropical Ornithology*, P.A. Buckley, E.S. Morton, R.S. Ridgely, and F.G. Buckley, eds. Ornithol. Monogr. 36.

Nagy, K. 1987. Field metabolic rate and food requirement scaling in birds and mammals. *Ecol. Monogr.* 57:111–128.

Nisbet, I.C.T. and Lord Medway. 1972. Dispersion, population ecology and migration of Eastern Great Reed Warblers *Acrocephalus orientalis* wintering in Malaysia. *Ibis* 114:451–494.

Nisbet, I.C.T., W.H. Drury, Jr., and J. Baird. 1963. Weight loss during migration. Part I: Deposition and consumption of fat in the Blackpoll Warbler *Dendroica striata. Bird-Banding* 34:107–139.

Odum, E.P. 1960. Lipid deposition in nocturnal migrant birds. *Proc. 12th Internat. Ornithol. Cong.* (Helsinki): 563–576.

Parnell, J.F. 1969. Habitat relations of the Parulidae during spring migration. *Auk* 86:505–521.

Phillips, A.R. 1991. *The Known Birds of North and Middle America, Part II.* Denver: A.R. Phillips.

Pyle, P., S.N.G. Howell, R.P. Yunick, and D. DeSante. 1987. *Identification Guide to North American Passerines.* Bolinas, Calif.: Slate Creek Press.

Ramos, M.A. 1983. Seasonal movements of bird populations at a neotropical study site in southern Veracruz, México. Ph.D. Dissertation, University of Minnesota, Minneapolis.

———. 1988. Eco-evolutionary aspects of bird movements in the northern Neotropical region. *Acta 19th Internat. Ornithol. Cong.* (Ottawa): 251–293.

Rappole, J.H. and K. Ballard. 1987. Postbreeding movements of selected birds in Athens, Georgia. *Wilson Bull.* 99:475–480.

Rappole, J.H. and D.W. Warner. 1976. Relationships between behavior, physiology and weather in avian transients at a migration stopover site. *Oecologia* 26:193–212.

Rappole, J., M.A. Ramos, R.J. Oehlenschlager, D.W. Warner, and C.P. Barkan. 1979. Timing of migration and route selection in North American songbirds. Pages 199–214 in *Proc. First Welder Wildlife Foundation Symposium*, D. Lynn Drane, ed. Sinton, Tex.: Welder Wildlife Foundation.

Rimmer, C.C. 1988. Timing of the definitive prebasic molt in Yellow Warblers at James Bay, Ontario. *Condor* 90:141–156

Rogers, D.T., Jr., and E.P. Odum. 1964. Effect of age, sex, and level of fat deposition on major body components in some wood warblers. *Auk* 81:505–513.

———. 1966. A study of autumnal postmigrant weights and vernal fattening of North American migrants in the tropics. *Wilson Bull.* 78:415–433.

Safriel, U.N., and D. Lavee. 1988. Weight changes of cross-desert migrants at an oasis—do energetic considerations alone determine the length of stopover? *Oecologia* 76:611–619.

Shimov, S.V. 1985. [Body weight and fat of the birds netted at Sorbulak Lake during spring migration.] *Tr. Zool. Akad. NAUK SSSR* 137:164–180.

Szabo, B.J., W.P. McHugh, G.G. Schaber, C.V. Haynes, Jr., and C.S. Breed. 1989. Uranium-series dated authigenic carbonates and acheulian sites in southern Egypt. *Science* 243:1053–1056.

Tucker, V.A. 1974. Energetics of natural avian flight. Pages 298–328 in *Avian Energetics*, R.A. Paynter, Jr., ed. Cambridge, Mass.: Nuttall Ornithol. Club.

Weisberg, S. 1985. *Applied Linear Regression.* New York: J. Wiley and Sons.

Yablonkevich, M.L., K.V. Bolshakov, V.N. Buliuk, D.O. Eliseev, V.D. Efremov, and A.K. Shamuradov. 1985a. [Body weight and fat of birds passing across the middle Asia deserts in spring.] *Tr. Zool. Inst. Akad. NAUK SSSR* 137:11–59.

Yablonkevich, M.L., A.V. Bardin, K.V. Bolshakov, E.A. Popov, and A.P. Shapoval. 1985b. [Body weight and fat of small passerine birds passing over the middle Asia deserts in autumn.] *Tr. Zool. Inst. Akad. NAUK SSSR* 137:69–97.

The breeding season

SCOTT K. ROBINSON
Illinois Natural History Survey
607 East Peabody Drive
Champaign, Illinois 61820

The breeding season: Introduction

The papers in this section make a convincing case that factors associated with the breeding season contribute to population changes in Neotropical migrants. During the nonbreeding portions of their life cycle, the major problem faced by migrants is survival. During the breeding season, however, migrants face additional demands of finding enough food to feed young and of protecting their nests against predators and brood parasites. Changes in food supply, predator pressure, and climate affect population dynamics directly through their impact on the recruitment of young. The most compelling demonstration of the importance of these factors comes from Sherry and Holmes's (this section) study of a declining population of American Redstarts (*Setophaga ruticilla*) in the relatively unfragmented forests of central New Hampshire. The population changes in redstarts over the last ten years correlate most closely with recruitment of young males, which is significantly related to fledging success the previous summer. Fledging success, in turn, was largely a function of nest predation. Sherry and Holmes also found that weather-related starvation of young correlated with recruitment rates and population trends in redstarts. Blake et al. (this section) argue that the severe midwestern drought of 1986–1988 may have caused the declines of many Neotropical migrants in Wisconsin and Michigan during this period. Similarly, the population declines documented by Robinson (this section) in Illinois during the late 1980s may be at least partly related to the same drought. The relationship between climatic extremes and productivity implied in these studies merits greater attention, especially in light of global climate change. These papers show that factors associated with the breeding season can cause long- and short-term population declines even in the absence of recent human disturbance. How, then, might human activities be contributing to the problems faced by breeding Neotropical migrants?

One of the most characteristic features of human-dominated landscapes is the fragmentation of remaining habitats. Fragmented landscapes consist of small, often isolated patches of habitat dominated by edges. As Freemark and Collins (this section) and many others have demonstrated, small forest fragments lack most area-sensitive species and are dominated by "edge" species. Bollinger and Gavin (this section) show that area-sensitivity also characterizes at least some grassland species. Freemark and Collins also, however, found that area-sensitivity varies regionally, apparently in response to the extent of habitat fragmentation. In extremely fragmented landscapes, birds appear to be more area-sensitive than in more forested landscapes. The papers by both Freemark and Collins and Villard et al. (this section) argue that the increased area-sensitivity of birds in highly fragmented landscapes results from the lack of nearby large forest tracts with correspondingly higher migrant bird populations. Large tracts can provide a relatively stable source of immigrants to recolonize populations in small patches that "wink out." Without nearby large tracts, immigration must occur over great distances and recolonization events are likely to be fewer. Increasing habitat fragmentation can lead to regional population declines if large tracts are lost. Alternatively, regional populations can recover if once-isolated forest patches become connected to larger tracts (Askins et al. 1987).

The papers by Freemark and Collins and Villard et al. use metapopulation models to describe the population dynamics of migrants in fragmented landscapes. Metapopulation models assume that regional population changes are determined by the dynamics of subpopulations linked by dispersal. Pulliam (1988) has expanded these models to include the concept of population "sources," which produce a surplus of young, and "sinks," in which reproduction is insufficient to compensate for adult mortality. Sink populations can only be maintained by dispersal from source populations. If habitat fragmentation increases the ratio of sink to source populations, then regional populations may decline.

The paper by Robinson (this section) illustrates the factors that can cause highly fragmented woodlots to become population sinks. In an archipelago of small (< 65 ha) woodlots in a sea of corn and soybeans in central Illinois, Robinson found that breeding success of Neotropical migrants was almost too low to measure. Nest predation and brood parasitism were so severe that there was little recruitment of young; the populations of Neotropical migrants likely depend upon immigration from sources outside the study area. Gibbs and Faaborg (1990) also found that most Ovenbird (*Seiurus aurocapillus*) males defending territories in small Missouri woodlots were unmated. If this proves to be a general phenomenon, then the viability of Neotropical mi-

grant populations in highly fragmented landscapes might be even less than we currently suspect. These studies, and related work by Temple and Cary (1988), provide an indication of the possible mechanisms through which habitat fragmentation can cause regional population declines.

Fragmentation is not the only way that human activities can affect Neotropical migrant populations. Bollinger and Gavin's study (this section) shows how changes in the management of forage crops prevent successful reproduction in Bobolinks (*Dolichonyx oryzivorus*), a rapidly declining Neotropical migrant. Litwin and Smith (this section) argue that most of the changes in populations of breeding birds in Sapsucker Woods, New York, reflect changes in vegetation structure due to regrowth following past episodes of logging and grazing. Litwin and Smith emphasize that studies of population trends need to take into account local changes in vegetation structure as well as landscape-level characteristics such as fragmentation, a concern shared by Holmes et al. (1986). Martin (this section) concludes from his own work and an exhaustive review of the literature that the availability of safe nest sites is more likely to regulate populations than food availability. Martin argues that active management to increase available nest sites might be an effective practice for declining species in areas of intense predation pressure.

Future research needs

Virtually all of the authors in this section agree that we know far too little about what factors regulate populations of Neotropical migrants in fragmented or in unfragmented landscapes. Before metapopulation models can be evaluated, we need far more studies of avian productivity across landscapes of differing degrees and types of fragmentation, and in different geographical regions. We know that fragmentation can create severe problems for Neotropical migrants, especially when carried to the extremes seen in central Illinois (Robinson, this section). But, we do not yet know if fragmentation is one of the primary causes of continentwide population declines or if it is only a factor in some regional population declines.

Until we understand the scope on which metapopulations interact, it will be difficult to design conservation strategies to reverse population losses. It is possible, for example, that birds breeding in central Illinois disperse from great distances. The Wood Thrush (*Hylocichla mustelina*), for example appears to reproduce very little in small midwestern woodlots where it suffers nearly 100% parasitism rates by Brown-headed Cowbirds (*Molothrus ater*) (Robinson this section, unpublished data; C.L. Trine, unpublished data). Yet, the Wood Thrush is only rarely parasitized farther east, even in small woodlots (C.S. Robbins, pers. comm.). It is possible that Wood Thrushes breeding in midwestern woodlots are produced farther east where productivity is apparently greatest. Perhaps genetic markers will help shed light on the origins of birds breeding in population sinks. Meanwhile, intensive single-species studies that measure productivity across different landscapes are mostly likely to shed light on metapopulation dynamics.

Martin (this section) also makes a plea for more studies of basic life history characteristics of migrant birds species. Until the nest site requirements and foraging microhabitats of each species are known, we cannot devise effective management strategies. Bollinger and Gavin (this section), for example, can recommend the optimal rotational age and cutting schedule for hayfields based on their knowledge of the Bobolink's nesting cycle and nest site selection. Forestry practices that promote a particular kind of understory might reduce predation on a locally threatened Neotropical migrant by increasing the number of places where it can hide its nests (Martin, this section). In general, however, we know very little about the impacts of forestry practices on the productivity of Neotropical migrants; this question should be a high research priority for land management agencies.

The role of the Brown-headed Cowbird in causing population declines merits further attention. Cowbirds have shouldered much of the blame for population declines of many Neotropical migrants that accept cowbird eggs (Mayfield 1977, Brittingham and Temple 1983, May and Robinson 1985). Nevertheless, we know little about the extent to which cowbird parasitism contributes to mortality. Martin (this section) even makes the intriguing suggestion that the amount of mortality due to cowbird parasitism might be overestimated because the effects of nest predation have not been considered fully. Nor do we understand what makes some landscapes more favorable than others for cowbirds. Until we have experimentally manipulated cowbird populations and studied cowbird movements in different landscapes, it might be premature to use large-scale cowbird control to reverse regional population declines.

Conclusions

The last symposium (Keast and Morton 1980) dealt only with migrant birds in the nonbreeding season. Since 1977, when that symposium was held, it has become clear that migrant birds face major conservation problems in both the nonbreeding and breeding seasons. We now realize that habitat fragmentation on the breeding grounds can be added to the list of probable causes of population declines along with tropical deforestation and the loss of migratory stopover sites. As Sherry and Holmes (this section) state, if nest predation drives population trends in relatively unfragmented landscapes, then its impact should be even greater in predator and parasite-saturated fragmented landscapes. Any conservation plan for Neotropical migrants will have to include provisions for studying breeding productivity as well as winter survivorship.

Literature cited

Askins, R.A., M.J. Philbrick, and D.S. Sugeno. 1987. Relationship between the regional abundance of forest and the composition of forest bird communities. *Biol. Conserv.* 39:129–152.

Brittingham, M.C., and S.A. Temple. 1983. Have cowbirds caused forest songbirds to decline? *BioScience* 33:31–35.

Gibbs, J.P., and J. Faaborg. 1990. Estimating the viability of Ovenbird and Kentucky Warbler populations in forest fragments. *Conserv. Biol.* 4:193–196.

Holmes, R.T., T.W. Sherry, and F.W. Sturges. 1986. Bird community dynamics in a temperate deciduous forest: Long-term trends at Hubbard Brook. *Ecol. Monogr.* 50:201–220.

Keast, A., and E.S. Morton, eds. 1980. *Migrant Birds in the Neotropics: Ecology, Behavior, Distribution, and Conservation.* Washington: Smithsonian Institution Press.

May, R.M. and S.K. Robinson. 1985. Population dynamics of avian brood parasitism. *Am. Nat.* 126:475–494.

Mayfield, H. 1977. Brown-headed Cowbird: Agent of extermination. *Am. Birds* 31:107–113.

Pulliam, H.R. 1988. Sources, sinks, and population regulation. *Am. Nat.* 132:652–661.

Temple, S.A., and J.R. Cary. 1988. Modeling dynamics of habitat-interior bird populations in fragmented landscapes. *Conserv. Biol.* 2:340–347.

SCOTT K. ROBINSON
Illinois Natural History Survey
607 East Peabody Drive
Champaign, Illinois 61820

Population dynamics of breeding Neotropical migrants in a fragmented Illinois landscape

Abstract. Several lines of evidence suggest that an archipelago of small (< 70 ha) woodlots in central Illinois is a population sink for most breeding Neotropical migrants. Although the three intensively studied woodlots were small (14–65 ha), they contained several species that are considered area-sensitive elsewhere in their range, including the Worm-eating Warbler (*Helmitheros vermivorus*) and Ovenbird (*Seiurus aurocapillus*). Populations of six Neotropical migrants declined by at least 50% and none increased by more than 10% during the five years (1985–1989) of the study. Mist-net data suggest very low (ca. 15%) return rates of adults between years with only a small core of adults returning year after year. Data on nesting success indicate that most nests fail because of high predation rates (ca. 80% of open cup nests) and brood parasitism (ca. 76% of nests of Neotropical migrants) by the omnipresent, abundant Brown-headed Cowbird (*Molothrus ater*). Parasitized nests with more than one cowbird egg were the rule rather than the exception, and contained an average of 3.3 cowbird eggs for Neotropical migrants. Wood Thrush (*Hylocichla mustelina*) nests averaged nearly four times as many cowbird eggs as host eggs (4.6 vs. 1.2). Ground-nesting species such as the Ovenbird and Kentucky Warbler (*Oporornis formosus*) appear to be less susceptible to brood parasitism than shrub-nesting species. Midsummer mist-net data also showed little evidence of reproduction by Neotropical migrants as hatching year:adult ratios averaged 0.1 compared with ratios of > 1.0 for many year-round residents and short-distance migrants. Populations of most Neotropical migrants in the Shelbyville area might be maintained by immigrants, possibly from source populations over 200 km away.

Sinopsis. Varias líneas de evidencia sugieren que un archipiélago de pequeños (< 70 ha) lotes de bosque en el centro de Illinois es un sitio de drenaje poblacional para la mayoría de migratorias neotropicales anidantes. Aunque los tres parches de bosque intensivamente estudiados fueron pequeños (14–65 ha), contenían varias especies que son consideradas sensibles al área en otros sitios de su distribución geográfica, incluyendo a *Helmitheros vermivorus* y a *Seiurus aurocapillus*. Las poblaciones de seis migratorias neotropicales declinaron en al menos 50% y ninguna incrementó en mas de un 10% durante los cinco años (1985-1989) del estudio. Los datos de capturas con redes de niebla sugieren tasas de retorno muy bajas (ca. 15%) para adultos entre años con solamente un pequeño núcleo de adultos retornando un año tras otro. Los datos de éxito de anidación indican que la mayoría de nidos fallan debido a las altas tasas de predación (ca. 80% de los nidos de copa abierta) y parasitismo de cría (ca. 76% de los nidos de migratorias neotropicales) por parte del omnipresente y abundante *Molothrus ater*. Nidos parasitados con mas de un huevo de *M. ater* fueron muy comunes y contenían un promedio de 3.3 huevos del parásito para las migratorias neotropicales. Los nidos de *Hylocichla mustelina* tuvieron en promedio cerca de cuatro huevos de *M. ater* por cada huevo del huésped (4.6 vs. 1.2). Las especies anidantes del piso tales como *S. aurocapillus* y *Oporornis formosus* parecen ser menos susceptibles al parasitismo de cría que las especies anidantes en arbustos. Los datos de anidación de mediados del verano también mostraron escasa evidencia de reproducción de migratorias neotropicales puesto que las tasas eclosión anual:adultos promediaron 0.1 en comparación con tasas >1.0 para muchas residentes permanentes y migratorias de distancia corta. Las poblaciones de la mayoría de migratorias neotropicales en el área de Shelbyville podrían estar mantenidas por inmigrantes, posiblemente provenientes de poblaciones distantes mas de 200 km.

There is an emerging consensus that both habitat fragmentation in North America and tropical deforestation have played a role in the population declines and area sensitivity exhibited by forest-interior songbirds (reviewed in Whitcomb et al. 1981; Askins et al. 1990; Robbins et al. 1989a; Terborgh, this volume). The last 15 years have seen an increasing awareness of the problems faced by Neotropical migrants attempting to breed in fragmented landscapes (reviewed in Harris 1984, Howe 1984, Robinson 1988, Yahner 1988, Wilcove and Robinson 1990). Birds nesting in small edge-dominated habitat patches suffer from abnormally high levels of brood parasitism by Brown-headed Cowbirds (scientific names given in Appendix 1) (Gates and Gysel 1978, Chasko and Gates 1982, Brittingham and Temple 1983), nest predation (Gates and Gysel 1978, Wilcove 1985, Wilcove et al. 1986, Yahner and Cypher 1987, Ratti and Reese 1988, Yahner and Scott 1988, Temple and Cary 1988), and competition from nonforest species such as Common Grackles that invade small forest patches (Wilcove and Robinson 1990). Temple and Cary (1988) found a nearly fourfold increase in reproductive success of birds nesting in the interior of larger forest tracts compared with those nesting near edges; they hypothesized that fragmented landscapes consist of population "sources" which produce a surplus of young and

"sinks" maintained by immigration from those sources (see also Pulliam 1988).

Robinson (1988) and Wilcove and Robinson (1990) reported preliminary results from a study of forest bird nesting success in a series of small (14–65 ha) woodlots with extensive edges isolated in a sea of corn and soybean fields in central Illinois. In this extraordinarily fragmented landscape, reproductive success appeared to be very low due to high levels of nest parasitism (> 60% of all nests) and nest predation (> 75% of all open-cup nests). Nevertheless, these woodlots contained populations of many species normally restricted to much larger tracts in the Midwest (Kendeigh 1982; Ambuel and Temple 1983; Blake and Karr 1987) and in the eastern U.S. (reviewed in Robbins et al. 1989a). These results indicated that such small, isolated woodlots might act as ecological "traps" (sensu Gates and Gysel 1978) which attract dispersing birds that do not reproduce successfully because of predation and brood parasitism. This paper expands on the results presented in Robinson (1988) and Wilcove and Robinson (1990) by further documenting reproductive failure in Neotropical migrants in these small woodlots and by examining recent changes in population densities.

Study area

All study sites border Lake Shelbyville in Moultrie and Shelby counties, central Illinois (39° N 88° W). An archipelago of small habitat patches (upland oak/hickory and old pastures undergoing succession) was bordered by open water on one side and corn, soybeans, and pastures on the other (Fig. 1). The majority of woodlots were on slopes too steep for row crops but used as wooded pastures and selectively logged as recently as 20 years ago. All habitat patches were small (the largest woodlot is 65 ha) and contained abundant edge (Fig. 1). In no woodlot could birds nest more than 250 m from an edge. The woodlots bordering Lake Shelbyville were extremely isolated; the nearest woodlots of > 1000 ha were at least 200 km away in southern Illinois, west-central Indiana, and southeastern Missouri. Nevertheless, the aggregate area of woodlots bordering Lake Shelbyville exceeded 1500 ha.

This paper used data from three of the widest (> 400 m) woodlots in the Shelbyville area. All three consist of oak-dominated upland forest (Table 1); the deeper ravines where more mesic streamside forest exist were flooded when the lake was formed. All study sites have similar topography and vegetation structure except for the following details. Pogue Woods, the smallest (14 ha) site, was never pastured; it is dominated by closely spaced, large White Oaks (*Quercus alba*). Unlike the other two sites, Pogue Woods has no steep ravines or intermittent streams. Railroad Woods is also small (25 ha)

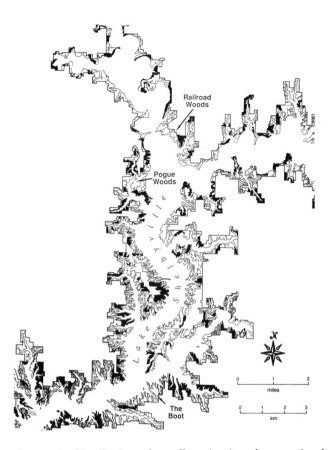

FIGURE 1. Distribution of woodlots (*gray*) and successional thickets (*black*) in land managed by the U.S. Corps of Engineers along a portion of Lake Shelbyville (*white*).

and contains a steep ravine with heavy flood damage near the lake. The ridge tops were pastured and consist of large White Oaks scattered among dense young (8–30 cm dbh) oaks and hickories (*Carya* spp.). The largest (65 ha) woodlot, the "Boot," is dissected by numerous intermittent streams and has vegetation structure similar to that of Railroad Woods.

Methods

Unless otherwise stated, I present data only on Neotropical migrant passerines that occupy the forest interior. I excluded such edge species as the Indigo Bunting and Blue-gray Gnatcatcher, but included the Kentucky Warbler, Rose-breasted Grosbeak, and Summer Tanager. The latter three species preferred edges in Illinois but also forage at least 100 m into the forest interior (Robinson, unpubl. data).

BIRD CENSUSING. Spot-mapping (Kendeigh 1944) constituted the primary census method. Observers walked fixed routes through each study site from 1 June to 10 July, 1985–1989. Each plot was visited at least three times per year. The largest plot, the Boot, was censused at least seven times per breeding season. All censuses were conducted by Scott Robinson, (1985–1988) and Dave Enstrom (1989 only). An attempt was made to census each woodlot in its entirety, including the perimeter. During morning (0600–1000) censuses, observers stopped every 150 m at permanent census points and recorded the distance and compass angle of each bird heard during a 6-min period. All simultaneous registrations of conspecifics (countersinging) were noted. Birds heard between census points, during censuses of edges, and during other activities (e.g., nest searching

TABLE 1. Vegetation characteristics of the three major study areas based on the methods of James and Shugart (1970)

Characteristics	Study area		
	Boot	Railroad Woods	Pogue Woods
Points sampled	26	9	9
Size (ha)	65	25	14
Canopy height (m)	22–28	23–27	26–30
Canopy cover (%)	87	87	86
Basal area/point	$1.1m^2$	$1.2m^2$	$1.4m^2$
Dominance values of trees			
White Oak	41	49	69
Red Oak	16	3	3
Black Oak	11	12	5
Shagbark Hickory	6	9	14
Woody stems/ha	27,260	35,416	39,107
Ground cover (%)	54	78	50

and mist netting) were mapped on separate sheets. All records for each species were summarized on maps to calculate population density estimates based on number of defended territories.

Because Brown-headed Cowbird populations contain a mixture of territorial and nonterritorial females (A. Raim, pers. comm.), spot-mapping was not used for this species. Instead, I used the number of separate individuals or groups (a female accompanied by 1–5 males) per point recorded during 6-min samples as an index of relative abundance.

MATED STATUS. A special attempt was made to determine the mated status of several Neotropical migrants, especially the Ovenbird. During searches for nests, selected territories were checked for evidence of females or other activities suggesting nest defense. If no females were found and the territorial males sang frequently and moved extensively, the territory was assumed to be occupied by an unmated male.

YEAR-TO-YEAR RETURNS. Mist-net data from two consecutive years on the same net line were used to estimate population turnover between 1985 and 1986 in the Boot. Mist nets were strung end to end along a 1-km net line in 1985 and 1986. Each of the 75 nets was opened at least four mornings (0600–1200 hr) during the breeding season (5 June to 20 July). The percentage of individuals caught in 1985 that was also caught in 1986 is used as an index of return rates. Because the total number of net mornings differed between years (376 in 1985, 300 in 1986), return rates are probably underestimated. Other limitations of these data are discussed below (see Results).

NESTING SUCCESS. When a nest was located, its contents were checked. When possible these nests were monitored two or three times per week to determine their fate. The sample included in the present paper differs from that in Robinson (1988) and Wilcove and Robinson (1990) because it excludes nests found outside the three major study areas and includes nests located in 1987 and 1988. The Mayfield (1975) index was used to measure daily survival rates. In general, sample sizes were too small to calculate predation rates at different stages of the nest cycle and for statistical comparisons of different species.

HATCHING-YEAR:ADULT RATIOS. The ratio of hatching-year (HY) to after-hatching-year (AHY) adults in mist-net samples from 25 June through 19 July, 1985 and 1986, was used as an index of local reproductive success for each forest species. These dates were chosen to represent the period after which fledglings of all species began to appear and before the arrival of fall migrants.

Because post-fledging behavior differs among species, interspecific statistical comparisons were not made.

Results

SPECIES COMPOSITION AND POPULATION TRENDS. Although the three woodlots were small, they contained several species that are usually considered area-sensitive, including the Worm-eating Warbler, Ovenbird, and Kentucky Warbler (Appendix 2). At least in some years, population densities of Neotropical migrants in Shelbyville woodlots (Appendix 2) were similar to those reported from much larger upland forest tracts in Wisconsin (cf. Bond 1957, Ambuel and Temple 1983). The Boot (the largest tract) had more forest interior migrant species (e.g., Ovenbird, Worm-eating Warbler) than the other sites (Appendix 2). The increased diversity was at least in part due to the Boot's well-developed ravine system, which provided habitat for Worm-eating Warblers (steep slopes), Acadian Flycatchers (mesic ravines), and Louisiana Waterthrushes (streams), which were absent from the smallest tract. Otherwise, the species composition of the three tracts was generally similar.

Even during the five years of this study, evidence of population declines, or at least of fluctuations, were found in seven of the Neotropical migrant species (Fig. 2). Populations of four species in all three woodlots combined declined significantly, including the Kentucky Warbler (slope = –3.1, R^2 = 0.94, P = 0.007), Worm-eating Warbler (slope = – 1.1, R^2 = 0.92, P = 0.011), Louisiana Waterthrush (slope = –1.4, R^2 = 0.93, P = 0.009), and Acadian Flycatcher (slope = –2.1, R^2 = 0.90, P = 0.015). Most of the declines were in the Boot, which initially had the highest populations of all four species (Appendix 2). Four other species showed steep but not significant declines: the Red-eyed Vireo (slope = –1.5, R^2 = 0.73, P = 0.065), which declined only in Pogue Woods (Appendix 2), the Rose-breasted Grosbeak (slope = –2.3, R^2 = 0.67, P = 0.09), which declined in both the Boot and Pogue Woods (Appendix 2), the Wood Thrush (slope = –4.2, R^2 = 0.66, P = 0.10), which declined in all three woodlots (Appendix 2), and Ovenbird (slope = –3.1, R^2 = 0.48, P = 0.20), which declined only in the Boot (Appendix 2). By contrast, populations of only five species remained relatively stable: the Eastern Wood-Pewee (slope = –1.0, R^2 = 0.02, P = 0.58), Yellow-throated Vireo (slope = – 0.30, R^2 = 0.125, P = 0.56), Scarlet Tanager (slope = +0.7, R^2 = 0.272, P = 0.37), Summer Tanager (slope = – 0.3, R^2 = 0.04, P = 0.75), and Great Crested Flycatcher (slope = –0.2, R^2 = 0.02, P = 0.81). Summer Tanager populations fluctuated from two to eight territories per year but showed no evidence of a consistent decline.

Populations of some species fluctuated considerably within woodlots (Appendix 2). Ovenbirds, for example,

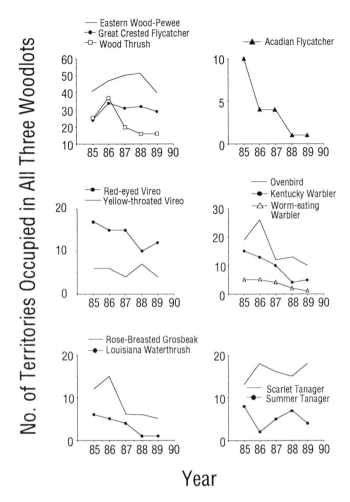

FIGURE 2. Population trends of Neotropical migrants in the three woodlots combined. See Appendix 2 for complete data.

TABLE 2. Recaptures in 1986 of birds banded in 1985 on the same net line in the Boot

Species	Number of adults caught in 1985	Percentage recaptured in 1986
Great Crested Flycatcher	21	9.5
Eastern Wood-Pewee	9	22.2
Acadian Flycatcher	6	16.7
Wood Thrush	26	19.2
Red-eyed Vireo	2	0.0
Kentucky Warbler	22	18.2
Worm-eating Warbler	4	25.0
Ovenbird	18	16.7
Louisiana Waterthrush	4	0.0
Rose-breasted Grosbeak	3	0.0
Scarlet Tanager	4	50.0
TOTAL	119	15.1

absent in Railroad Woods the first year of the study but present the next four years, disappeared from Pogue Woods in 1989. Kentucky Warblers and Red-eyed Vireos disappeared from Pogue Woods and Summer Tanagers were present in Railroad Woods only in some years.

MATED STATUS. A high percentage of the territories of several forest species appeared to be occupied by unmated males. Only 58% of 59 Ovenbird territories contained evidence of breeding pairs; the remaining territories were occupied by apparently unmated males. One color-banded unmated male Ovenbird defended two territories of 6 ha approximately 200 m apart in 1985. By 1988, only five mated pairs were left in the Boot. Other species in which unmated males were found in the Boot included Kentucky Warblers (at least 5 of 17 territories in 1985 and 1986), Worm-eating Warbler (at least 2 of 10 territories in 1985 and 1986), and Acadian Flycatch-

er (at least 2 of 11 territories in 1985 and 1986). The only records of Hooded Warblers were three unmated males observed for only 1–3 days.

YEAR-TO-YEAR RETURNS. Only 15% of the 119 adult Neotropical migrants caught in 1985 in the Boot net line were recaptured the following year (Table 2). These results indicate a high population turnover between years. This high turnover rate is especially apparent in the Wood Thrush, which had only a 19% return rate (Table 2) even though the nets caught an estimated 79% and 67% of all adults in the Boot in 1985 and 1986, respectively. Return rates from net lines, however, should be considered cautiously because small shifts in territories between years can substantially reduce the chances of recapture. Similarly, the reduced effort (300 net mornings in 1986 versus 376 in 1985) undoubtedly contributed to the low estimate of return rate of birds caught in 1985 (Table 2). Acquired net shyness might also reduce proportional recapture rates. The return rates presented in Table 2, therefore, probably have been underestimated.

NEST PREDATION. Data on the 55 open cup nests monitored during the study indicate that nest predation rates were very high (Table 3). Assuming a 25-day average nest cycle and a 0.938% daily survival probability, an average nest has only a 20% chance of escaping predation. If the resident Northern Cardinal and short-distance migrant Rufous-sided Towhee are excluded, the daily survival probability for only the Neotropical mi-

TABLE 3. Predation of forest birds that build open cup nests

Species	Nests found	Exposure days	Daily probability of survival[a]	Probability of survival[b]
Eastern Wood-Pewee	2	18	.944	.21
Acadian Flycatcher	2	36	.972	.46
Wood Thrush	15	111	.928	.18
Kentucky Warbler	3	16	.937	.22
Ovenbird	4	39	.949	.30
Northern Cardinal	17	146	.925	.18
Rose-breasted Grosbeak	3	22	.955	.35
Rufous-sided Towhee	4	59	.966	.45
Scarlet Tanager	2	16	.937	.21
Summer Tanager	3	22	.909	.10
TOTAL (all species)	55	485	.938	
TOTAL (Neotropical migrants)	34	280	.939	

a. Calculated using the Mayfield (1975) index.
b. Calculated using the average nest cycle length (23–27 days) for each species (Robinson, unpubl. data).

TABLE 4. Yearly and among-site variation in the relative abundance of cowbirds

Site	Number of cowbird registrations/10 census points (number of point censuses)				
	1985	1986	1987	1988	1989
Boot	9.1 (93)	8.2 (71)	6.7 (45)	15.8 (31)	11.9 (85)
Pogue Woods	10.6 (14)	8.6 (17)	10.0 (8)	12.5 (4)	12.5 (12)
Railroad Woods	8.9 (44)	5.9 (17)	13.3 (10)	10.0 (10)	7.0 (30)

grants remains essentially the same (0.939%). The data are too few to allow interspecific comparisons, but no indications of pronounced differences in survival probabilities were found among ground nesters (Ovenbird, Kentucky Warbler, and Rufous-sided Towhee), shrub/sapling nesters (Acadian Flycatcher, Wood Thrush, and Northern Cardinal), and canopy nesters (Eastern Wood-Pewee, Rose-breasted Grosbeak, Scarlet Tanager, and Summer Tanager).

BROOD PARASITISM. Brown-headed Cowbirds were abundant throughout the three woodlots, although populations fluctuated among years (Table 4). In 1985 and 1986 when census data were most complete, cowbirds were recorded at least once at every one of the 35 permanent census points. Cowbird populations in the three tracts were similar (Table 4). There is also no evidence that cowbird populations varied according to changes in host population densities. Populations of cowbirds were high in the Boot and in Pogue Woods in 1988 and 1989, for example, although most host populations were very low (see Appendix 2). Cowbird pressure might, therefore, vary somewhat between years; unfortunately too

few data on frequency of parasitism (see below) are available to analyze each year separately.

Most species of Neotropical migrants were parasitized frequently by cowbirds (Table 5). Over two-thirds of the 73 nests were parasitized, including 75.5% of the 49 nests of Neotropical migrants that accept cowbird eggs. Multiple parasitism was the rule in nests found during the incubation period, with an overall average of 3.3 cowbird eggs/parasitized nest. Wood Thrushes were most heavily parasitized, with nearly four times more cowbird eggs than host eggs. The 15 Wood Thrush nests found during the incubation period produced only a single host fledgling. Scarlet and Summer tanagers were nearly as heavily parasitized in the small sample of nests we found (Table 5). Although sample sizes are too small for interspecific comparisons, Ovenbirds and Kentucky Warblers might suffer less from parasitism than other species. Both species hide their nests well; in spite of intensive efforts, we found only 11 nests of these two species in four years. In fact, ground nesters generally suffered less parasitism (41% of 17 nests) than shrub, sapling, and canopy nesters (75% of 56 nests).

TABLE 5. Frequencies of nest parasitism of forest birds which build open cup nests and accept cowbird eggs for all three woodlots combined. Data include nests that were not monitored for predation (Table 3)

Species	Nests[a]	Percentage parasitized	Average number of host eggs/nest (nest (n)[b]	Average number of cowbird eggs/nest (n)[c]	Average number of cowbird eggs/parasitized nests (n)
Eastern Wood-Pewee	3	67	2.0 (1)	2.0 (1)	2.0 (1)
Acadian Flycatcher	2	50	2.0	1.0	1.0 (1)
Wood Thrush	19	100	1.2 (15)	4.6 (15)	4.6 (15)
Kentucky Warbler	6	33	3.5 (4)	0.8 (4)	3.0 (1)
Ovenbird	5	40	3.6 (5)	1.0 (5)	2.0 (2)
Louisiana Waterthrush	2	50	–	–	–
Northern Cardinal	20	55	2.4 (16)	1.2 (16)	1.7 (11)
Rose-breasted Grosbeak	2	0	3.5 (2)	0.0 (2)	–
Rufous-sided Towhee	4	50	3.0 (4)	1.5 (4)	3.0 (2)
Scarlet Tanager	4	75	2.0 (2)	2.5 (2)	5.0 (1)
Summer Tanager	6	100	1.5 (4)	3.8 (4)	3.8 (4)
TOTAL	73	67.1			3.3 (38)

a. Total number of nests found.
b. n = number of nests with eggs.
c. n = number of parasitized nests.

Data from fledged families provide additional evidence of high parasitism rates (Table 6). All five Wood Thrush families observed in the Boot had at least one cowbird fledgling; only one had a host fledgling. Six of seven Scarlet Tanager families had at least one cowbird fledgling; only two had host young. All three Red-eyed Vireo families and the only Yellow-throated Vireo family contained only cowbirds, indicating that canopy-nesting vireos were also heavily parasitized. By contrast, only one of four Kentucky Warbler and one of four Ovenbird families had cowbird fledglings. Only two of seven Northern Cardinal families contained cowbird fledglings, a finding which suggests that the sample in Table 5 is biased toward parasitized nests or that Northern Cardinals are poor hosts for cowbirds. In general, however, the parasitism rates of fledged families and nests (Table 5) were similar; these data indicate that the sample of nests we found was not strongly biased toward conspicuous nests which are easy for both cowbirds and humans to find.

HY:AHY RATIOS. Midsummer mist-net samples provided evidence of poor reproduction by Neotropical migrants (Table 7). Only 10 of 123 Neotropical migrants caught in 1985 and 1986 were in their hatching-year. By contrast, HY:AHY ratios from much larger tracts in the Shawnee National Forest in southern Illinois for the same species range from 0.4 (Wood Thrush, Eastern Wood-Pewee) to over 1.0 (Worm-eating Warbler, Kentucky Warbler) (S. Robinson, unpubl. data). Year-round

residents also had HY:AHY ratios suggesting much greater reproductive success, including the Northern Cardinal (1.3; 43 caught), Tufted Titmouse (1.8; 42 caught), Blue Jay (0.8; 24 caught), and Downy Woodpecker (1.9; 32 caught).

Discussion

SHELBYVILLE WOODLOTS AS POPULATION SINKS. The data presented in this paper indicate that the three woodlots studied are population sinks (sensu Pulliam 1988) for many Neotropical migrants. With 80% nest predation rates and 76% parasitism rates, it is difficult to imagine how most species could be producing enough young to replace the adult population. Based on HY:AHY ratios, local reproductive success was almost too low to measure (Table 7), and population turnover between years was high (Table 2). Wood Thrushes, in particular, are unlikely to be producing enough young to replace the adult population because of 100% parasitism rates, multiple parasitism, and a very high (ca. 90%) nest-predation rate (Table 3).

Given the lack of reproductive success, it is interesting that these woodlots contain so many Neotropical migrants. Woodlots of comparable sizes in Missouri, east-central Illinois, and in the eastern U.S. generally lack Kentucky and Worm-eating warblers and Ovenbirds (Kendeigh 1982, Ambuel and Temple 1983, Blake and Karr 1987, Robbins et al. 1989a). Isolated archipelagos of small habitat patches, such as those surrounding

TABLE 6. Composition of recently fledged families found in the three wooded study sites, 1985–1988

Species	Host young only	Host and cowbird young	Cowbirds only
Eastern Wood-Pewee	2		2
Acadian Flycatcher			1
Wood Thrush		1	4
Yellow-throated Vireo			1
Red-eyed Vireo			3
Kentucky Warbler	3		1
Ovenbird	3	1	
Louisiana Waterthrush	1		1
Northern Cardinal	5	2	0
Rose-breasted Grosbeak	1		
Rufous-sided Towhee	2	1	1
Scarlet Tanager	1	1	5
TOTAL	18	6	19

NOTE: Percent families containing cowbirds: 58 (n = 43); percent Neotropical migrant families with cowbirds: 66 (n = 32)

TABLE 7. Hatching year (HY): Adult (AHY) ratios in mist-net samples from 25 June through 15 July, 1985–1986, in the Boot and Railroad Woods

Species	Forest interior Neotropical migrants	
	HY:AHY ratio	Total (HY and AHY) captured
Great Crested Flycatcher	0.1	19
Eastern Wood-Pewee	0.2	12
Acadian Flycatcher	0.0	5
Wood Thrush	0.1	46
Red-eyed Vireo	0.0	2
Kentucky Warbler	0.3	14
Worm-eating Warbler	0.0	4
Ovenbird	0.0	11
Louisiana Waterthrush	0.5	3
Scarlet Tanager	0.0	7
TOTAL HY:TOTAL AHY	0.1	123

Lake Shelbyville, might be especially attractive to dispersing adults because there are no other large (> 500 ha) upland forest tracts within a 200-km radius. Alatalo et al. (1988) and Slagsvold et al. (1988) showed that Pied Flycatchers (*Ficedula hypoleuca*) experience costs searching for mates because of rapidly deteriorating reproductive condition and often settle for less than optimal mates. Neotropical migrants might be similarly constrained by the short nesting season when searching for a territory, thus limiting how far and wide they can search. The lack of local alternatives might cause dispersers to concentrate in the largest habitat patches available, which become "ecological traps" (sensu Gates and Gysel 1978) and are too small to offer protection from nest predators and cowbirds, which avoid the interior of larger tracts (Brittingham and Temple 1983).

If all similarly small, isolated woodlots in central Illinois are population sinks, then immigrants to this region must be coming from source populations at least 200 km away, a far greater distance than migrants are generally thought to disperse (Whitcomb et al. 1981). Temple and Cary (1988) also hypothesized that source populations in northern Wisconsin might supply immigrants to maintain population sinks in central and southern Wisconsin. Interestingly, both Worm-eating and Kentucky warblers, which occupy uncharacteristically small woodlots in the Shelbyville area, appear to be nesting successfully in large tracts in the Shawnee National Forest ca. 200 km to the south (S. Robinson, unpubl. data). Immigrants from this source population

might supply the numerous small woodlots of central Illinois with dispersing first-year birds searching for (apparently) suitable unoccupied habitats.

POPULATION TRENDS IN "SINKS". The high between-year turnover of individuals within populations (Table 2) coupled with low local reproductive success (Table 7) indicate that population changes within woodlots reflect fluctuations in the availability of immigrants. The declining populations of many Neotropical migrants in these woodlots (Fig. 2) may therefore result from declining productivity in distant source populations. It might be significant that of the most variable populations some species are at or near the edges of their breeding ranges (Kentucky Warbler, Rose-breasted Grosbeak, Acadian Flycatcher, Worm-eating Warbler, Summer Tanager). The supply of dispersers in these species might fluctuate because they depend on just a few source populations. By contrast, some of the species that fluctuated the least have large ranges that include most of the Midwest (Great Crested Flycatcher, Eastern Wood-Pewee, Yellow-throated Vireo, Red-eyed Vireo, Scarlet Tanager). The supply of dispersers in these species might be more stable because the Shelbyville area is surrounded by potential source populations. Variations in the reproductive success within any one source population are, therefore, less likely to cause population fluctuations in sink populations.

Wood Thrushes, however, have declined considerably even though Shelbyville is well within the central core of its breeding range. The only data on reproductive success elsewhere in the Midwest show that they might suffer from extremely high cowbird parasitism rates throughout the region. Brittingham and Temple (1983), for example, found > 80% of the Wood Thrush nests parasitized, even in the forest interior of Wisconsin. Similarly, S. Robinson and C. Trine (unpubl. data) found > 90% parasitism frequencies > 300 m from the forest edge in large (> 1,000 ha) tracts in southern Illinois. Wood Thrushes might, therefore, be in the early stages of a major regional population decline (see also Robbins et al. 1989b).

MULTIPLE PARASITISM. The parasitism frequencies in the Lake Shelbyville area are among the highest ever recorded (May and Robinson 1985). Most parasitized nests contained two or more cowbird eggs; one Wood Thrush nest had 12 cowbird eggs (Robinson 1988). Clearly, cowbirds have saturated the Shelbyville area and only species that conceal their nests well (e.g., Kentucky Warbler, Ovenbird) can regularly escape parasitism. The only other areas with comparable community-wide levels of multiple parasitism are in the Kansas tallgrass prairie (Elliott 1978) and in the Shawnee National Forest of southern Illinois (S. Robinson, unpubl. data). Interestingly, all three areas are well within the historical range of the Brown-headed Cowbird (Mayfield 1965). The apparent lack of resistance to cowbird parasitism by most host species suggests that the intensity of parasitism might be much greater now than in the past (cf. Brittingham and Temple 1983). Long-term nest monitoring programs such as the Ontario Nest Records Scheme (Peck and James 1983) might reveal increases in parasitism rates as cowbird populations continue to grow.

CAVEATS. Two of the problems in this study, and many others like it, are small sample sizes and the indirect nature of much of the data used to estimate population dynamics. Traditional spot-mapping can lead to population overestimates because many males may be unmated. Population trends must be measured for long periods to separate true declines from short-term fluctuations, but interpreting population trends is complicated by inevitable changes in vegetation structure, climate, and food availability over time (Holmes et al. 1986; Blake et al., this volume). Estimates of population turnover from net lines (Table 2) are particularly subject to biases, but mapping each color banded bird year after year is labor-intensive. Direct measurements of nesting success are also preferable to HY:AHY ratios (Table 7), but nests are difficult to find and monitor in the numbers necessary to examine each species separately. As a result, most studies rely on either artificial nests (e.g., Wilcove 1985) or composite data from nests of many species from many years (e.g., Brittingham and Temple 1983, Temple and Cary 1988, Robinson 1988). Even studies of nests are subject to potential biases because the nests researchers find might be those that predators and brood parasites also find. The only way to avoid these problems is to select a species to study, color band local populations, find every nest, and monitor population dynamics and reproductive success for several consecutive years with large field crews. In the absence of those ideal conditions, however, researchers must generalize cautiously from indirect estimates and indices such as those presented here. Nevertheless, the consistency of several independent lines of evidence (parasitism and predation rates, year-to-year returns, and HY:AHY ratios) indicate that Neotropical migrants breeding in these small Illinois woodlots suffer sufficiently high levels of both nest predation and parasitism that reproduction probably does not compensate for adult mortality, a result consistent with the population declines observed at the site.

Acknowledgments

This study benefited from the work of many expert field assistants. Dave Enstrom ably continued the census work in 1989 when I was occupied elsewhere and helped with statistical analyses. Arlo Raim directed all mist-netting efforts and was helped by Renee Wheeler. Brian Lane, Kent Jones, and Katie Sieving found the majority of nests and Jean Adams was in charge of nest monitoring. Others who assisted in various phases of the project include Dale Droge, Bill Iko, Paul Brewer, and Mike Nelson. Bill Severinghaus and Dave Tazik initiated the project and provided much assistance throughout the study as did Glen C. Sanderson of the Illinois Natural History Survey. This research was funded initially by the U.S. Army Corps of Engineers (DACW 88-85-D-0004-06 and DACA 88-86-0001-013). Dave Enstrom, Dan Niven, Jim Herkert, Kris Bruner, Miguel Marini, John Faaborg, Tom Sherry, Glen C. Sanderson, and Cheryl Trine reviewed the manuscript and provided many helpful comments.

Literature cited

Alatalo, R.V., A. Carlson, and A. Lundberg. 1988. The search cost in mate choice of the Pied Flycatcher. *Anim. Behav.* 36:289–291.

Ambuel, B., and S.A. Temple. 1983. Area-dependent changes in the bird communities and vegetation of southern Wisconsin forests. *Ecology* 64:1057–1068.

Askins, R.A., J.F. Lynch, and R. Greenberg. 1990. Population declines in migratory birds in eastern North America. *Current Ornithol.* 7:1–57.

Blake, J.G., and J.R. Karr. 1987. Breeding birds in isolated woodlots: Area and habitat relationships. *Ecology* 68:1724–1734.

Bond, R.R. 1957. Ecological distribution of breeding birds in the upland forests of southern Wisconsin. *Ecol. Monogr.* 27:351–384.

Brittingham, M.C., and S.A. Temple. 1983. Have cowbirds caused forest songbirds to decline? *BioScience* 33:31–35.

Chasko, G., and J. Gates. 1982. *Avian Habitat Suitability Along a Transmission-Line Corridor in an Oak-Hickory Forest Region.* Wildl. Monogr. 82.

Elliott, P.F. 1978. Cowbird parasitism in the Kansas tallgrass prairie. *Auk* 95:161–167.

Gates, J.E., and L.W. Gysel. 1978. Avian nest dispersion and fledgling success in field-forest ecotones. *Ecology* 59:871–883.

Harris, L.D. 1984. *The Fragmented Forest.* Chicago: University of Chicago Press.

Holmes, R.T., T.W. Sherry, and F.W. Sturges. 1986. Bird community dynamics in a temperate deciduous forest: Long-term trends at Hubbard Brook. *Ecol. Monogr.* 50:201–220.

Howe, R.W. 1984. Local dynamics of bird assemblages in small forest habitat islands in Australia and North America. *Ecology* 65:1585–1601.

James, F.C., and H.H. Shugart. 1970. A quantitative method of habitat description. *Aud. Field Notes* 24:727–736.

Kendeigh, S.C. 1944. Measurement of bird populations. *Ecol. Monogr.* 14:67–106.

———. 1982. *Bird Populations in East Central Illinois: Fluctuations, Variations, and Development over a Half-century.* Ill. Biol. Monogr. 52.

May, R.M., and S.K. Robinson. 1985. Population dynamics of avian brood parasitism. *Am. Nat.* 126:475–494.

Mayfield, H. 1965. The Brown-headed Cowbird, with old and new hosts. *Living Bird* 4:13–28.

———. 1975. Suggestions for calculating nest success. *Wilson Bull.* 87:456–466.

Peck, G.K., and R.D. James. 1983. *Breeding Birds of Ontario: Nidiology and Distribution, Vol. 2: Passerines.* Toronto: Royal Ontario Museum.

Pulliam, H.R. 1988. Sources, sinks, and population regulation. *Am. Nat.* 132:652–661.

Ratti, J.T., and K.P. Reese. 1988. Preliminary test of the ecological trap hypothesis. *J. Wildl. Manage.* 52:484–491.

Robbins, C.S., D.K. Dawson, and B.A. Dowell. 1989a. *Habitat Area Requirements of Breeding Forest Birds of the Middle Atlantic States.* Wildl. Monogr. 103.

Robbins, C.S., J.R. Sauer, R.S. Greenberg, and S. Droege. 1989b. Population declines in North American birds that migrate to the neotropics. *Proc. Natl. Acad. Sci.* 86:7658–7662.

Robinson, S.K. 1988. Reappraisal of the costs and benefits of habitat heterogeneity for nongame wildlife. *Trans. N.A. Wildl. Nat. Res. Conf.* 53:145–155.

Slagsvold, J., J.T. Litjeld, G. Stenmark, and T. Breiehagen. 1988. On the cost of searching for a mate in female Pied Flycatchers *Ficedula hypoleuca. Anim. Behav.* 36:433–442.

Temple, S.A., and J.R. Cary. 1988. Modeling dynamics of habitat-interior bird populations in fragmented landscapes. *Conserv. Biol.* 2:340–347.

Whitcomb, R.F., C.S. Robbins, J.F. Lynch, B.L. Whitcomb, M.K. Klimkiewicz, and D. Bystrak. 1981. Effects of forest fragmentation on the avifauna of the eastern deciduous forest. Pages 125–205 in *Forest Island Dynamics in Man-dominated Landscapes,* R.L. Burgess and D.M. Sharpe, eds. New York: Springer-Verlag.

Wilcove, D.S. 1985. Nest predation in forest tracts and the decline of migratory songbirds. *Ecology* 66:1211–1214.

Wilcove, D.S., and S.K. Robinson. 1990. The impact of forest fragmentation on bird communities in eastern North America. Pages 319–331 in *Biogeography and Ecology of Forest Bird Communities,* A. Keast, ed. SPB Academic Publishers, The Hague, Netherlands.

Wilcove, D.S., C.H. McLellan, and A.P. Dobson. 1986. Habitat fragmentation in the temperate zone. Pages 237–256 in *Conservation Biology: The Science of Scarcity and Diversity,* M.E. Soulé, ed. Sunderland, Mass.: Sinauer Associates Inc.

Yahner, R.H. 1988. Changes in wildlife communities near edges. *Conserv. Biol.* 2:333–339.

Yahner, R.H., and B.L. Cypher. 1987. Effects of nest location on depredation of artificial arboreal nests. *J. Wildl. Manage.* 51:178–181.

Yahner, R.H., and D.P. Scott. 1988. Effects of forest fragmentation on depredation of artificial nests. *J. Wildl. Manage.* 52:158–161

APPENDIX 1. Scientific names of birds mentioned in this paper.

Common name	Scientific name
Downy Woodpecker	*Picoides pubescens*
Great Crested Flycatcher	*Myiarchus crinitus*
Eastern Wood-Pewee	*Contopus virens*
Acadian Flycatcher	*Empidonax virescens*
Blue Jay	*Cyanocitta cristata*
Tufted Titmouse	*Parus bicolor*
Blue-gray Gnatcatcher	*Polioptila caerulea*
Wood Thrush	*Hylocichla mustelina*
Yellow-throated Vireo	*Vireo flavifrons*
Red-eyed Vireo	*V. olivaceus*
Kentucky Warbler	*Oporornis formosus*
Hooded Warbler	*Wilsonia citrina*
Worm-eating Warbler	*Helmitheros vermivorus*
Ovenbird	*Seiurus aurocapillus*
Louisiana Waterthrush	*S. motacilla*
Rose-breasted Grosbeak	*Pheucticus ludovicianus*
Northern Cardinal	*Cardinalis cardinalis*
Indigo Bunting	*Passerina cyanea*
Rufous-sided Towhee	*Pipilo erythrophthalmus*
Common Grackle	*Quiscalus quiscula*
Scarlet Tanager	*Piranga olivacea*
Summer Tanager	*P. rubra*
Brown-headed Cowbird	*Molothrus ater*

APPENDIX 2. Populations and population densities of forest Neotropical migrants, 1985–1989

Species, by woodlot	Territories (Territories/40 ha)				
	1985	1986	1987	1988	1989
Boot (65 ha)					
Great Crested Flycatcher	19 (11.7)	24 (14.8)	22 (13.5)	20 (12.3)	21 (12.9)
Eastern Wood-Pewee	23 (14.2)	32 (19.7)	30 (18.5)	28 (17.2)	23 (14.2)
Acadian Flycatcher	8 (4.9)	3 (1.8)	4 (2.5)	0	0
Wood Thrush	18 (11.1)	25 (15.4)	13 (8.0)	10 (6.2)	11 (6.8)
Yellow-throated Vireo	4 (2.5)	5 (3.1)	2 (1.2)	5 (3.1)	3 (1.8)
Red-eyed Vireo	10 (6.2)	10 (6.2)	10 (6.2)	7 (4.3)	8 (4.9)
Kentucky Warbler*	8 (4.9)	9 (5.5)	8 (4.9)	3 (1.8)	4 (2.5)
Worm-eating Warbler	5 (3.1)	5 (3.1)	4 (2.5)	2 (1.2)	1 (0.6)
Ovenbird	18 (11.1)	20 (12.3)	7 (4.3)	8 (4.9)	7 (4.3)
Louisiana Waterthrush	5 (3.1)	4 (2.5)	3 (1.8)	1 (0.6)	1 (0.6)
Rose-breasted Grosbeak*	7 (4.3)	11 (6.8)	5 (3.1)	4 (2.5)	4 (2.5)
Scarlet Tanager	9 (5.5)	12 (7.4)	12 (7.4)	10 (6.2)	12 (7.4)
Summer Tanager*	6 (3.7)	2 (1.2)	3 (1.8)	5 (3.1)	4 (2.5)
TOTAL	140 (86.3)	162 (99.9)	123 (75.8)	103 (63.5)	99 (61.0)
Railroad Woods (25 ha)					
Great Crested Flycatcher	5 (8.3)	5 (8.3)	5 (8.3)	7 (11.7)	5 (8.3)
Eastern Wood-Pewee	8 (13.3)	8 (13.3)	10 (16.7)	11 (18.3)	12 (20.0)
Acadian Flycatcher	1 (1.7)	1 (1.7)	0	1 (1.7)	0
Wood Thrush	2 (3.3)	4 (6.7)	2 (3.3)	2 (3.3)	1 (1.7)
Yellow-throated Vireo	2 (3.3)	1 (1.7)	2 (3.3)	2 (3.3)	1 (1.7)
Red-eyed Vireo	4 (6.7)	3 (5.0)	2 (3.3)	2 (3.3)	4 (6.7)
Kentucky Warbler*	4 (6.7)	3 (5.0)	1 (1.7)	0	0
Ovenbird	0	5 (8.3)	4 (6.7)	3 (5.0)	4 (6.7)
Louisiana Waterthrush	1 (1.7)	1 (1.7)	1 (1.7)	0	0
Rose-breasted Grosbeak*	1 (1.7)	2 (3.3)	1 (1.7)	2 (3.3)	1 (1.7)
Scarlet Tanager	2 (3.3)	3 (5.0)	2 (3.3)	3 (5.0)	3 (5.0)
Summer Tanager	2 (3.3)	0	2 (3.3)	2 (3.3)	0
TOTAL	32 (53.3)	36 (60.0)	32 (53.3)	35 (58.3)	31 (51.6)
Pogue Woods (14 ha)					
Great Crested Flycatcher	5 (15.4)	5 (15.4)	4 (12.3)	5 (15.4)	3 (9.2)
Eastern Wood-Pewee	10 (30.8)	7 (21.7)	10 (30.8)	12 (39.0)	4 (12.3)
Wood Thrush	5 (15.4)	7 (21.7)	5 (15.4)	4 (12.3)	2 (6.2)
Red-eyed Vireo	3 (9.2)	2 (6.2)	3 (9.2)	1 (3.1)	0
Kentucky Warbler*	3 (9.2)	1 (3.1)	1 (3.1)	1 (3.1)	0
Ovenbird	1 (3.1)	3 (9.2)	1 (3.1)	2 (6.2)	0
Rose-breasted Grosbeak*	4 (12.3)	2 (6.2)	0	0	0
Scarlet Tanager	2 (6.2)	3 (9.2)	2 (6.2)	2 (6.2)	3 (6.2)
TOTAL	33 (101.6)	30 (92.4)	26 (80.1)	27 (83.1)	12 (36.9)

* Including territories on edge of the plot.

JOHN G. BLAKE*
GERALD J. NIEMI
JOANN M. HANOWSKI
Natural Resources Research Institute
Center for Water and the Environment
University of Minnesota
Duluth, Minnesota 55811

Drought and annual variation in bird populations

Abstract. We examined annual variation in abundance of bird species over a five-year period (1985–1989) in northern Wisconsin and Upper Peninsula Michigan. Abundances of most common species varied in parallel in both states, indicating that most species were influenced by the same or similar factors. During a period of moderate to extreme drought (1986 to 1988), eight of 11 long-distance migrant species examined in Wisconsin and eight of 13 in Michigan significantly declined in abundance. Annual variation in abundance of long-distance migrants was correlated with drought. Moreover, the patterns of correlations indicated that species breeding in upland deciduous habitats (e.g., Ovenbird, *Seiurus aurocapillus;* Red-eyed Vireo, *Vireo olivaceus*) were most affected by the drought. Long-distance migrants might have been more affected by drought than other species because most long-distance migrants nested in June when effects of drought were severest. For the most part, short-distance migrants and permanent residents did not show the same pattern of declines.

Sinopsis. Durante un período de cinco años (1985–1989), examinamos la variación anual en abundancia de especies de aves en el norte de Wisconsin y la Península Superior en Michigan. Las abundancias de las especies mas comunes variaron paralelamente en ambos estados, indicando que la mayoría de las especies fueron influenciadas por factores iguales o muy similares. Durante un período de sequía moderada a extrema (1986 a 1988), ocho de 11 especies migratorias de larga distancia examinadas en Wisconsin y ocho de 13 en Michigan, declinaron significativamente en abundancia. La variación anual en abundancia de migratorias de larga distancia estuvo correlacionada con la sequía. Mas aún, los patrones de correlaciones indicaron que las especies que anidan en habitats deciduos de zonas altas (e.g., *Seiurus aurocapillus* y *Vireo olivaceus*) fueron las mas afectadas por la sequía. Las migratorias de larga distancia podrían haber estado mas afectadas por la sequía que otras especies ya que la mayoría de las migratorias transcontinentales anidaron en junio cuando los efectos de la sequía fueron mas severos. En su mayoría, las migratorias de distancias cortas y las residentes permanentes no mostraron el mismo patrón de disminución.

*Current address: Department of Biology, University of Missouri–St. Louis, 8001 Natural Bridge Road, St. Louis, MO 63121.

Annual fluctuations in bird populations have been attributed to many factors, including changes in resource abundance (Holmes et al. 1986, Loiselle 1987, 1988), alteration in habitat (e.g., Järvinen and Väisänen 1978, Holmes and Sherry 1988), and weather (e.g., Graber and Graber 1979, Holmes et al. 1986, Holmes and Sherry 1988). Recent attention has focused on apparent declines in breeding populations of species that winter in the tropics and breed in temperate regions (e.g., Hutto 1988, 1989, Askins et al. 1990). Population declines have been linked to forest fragmentation on breeding grounds (e.g., Leck et al. 1988, Temple and Cary 1988), adverse weather during migration or winter (e.g., Holmes and Sherry 1988), loss of migratory stop-over points (e.g., Myers 1989), and loss of winter habitat (Askins et al. 1990, and below).

Extensive alteration of tropical habitats has occurred over the past several decades (e.g., Myers 1984) and provides a compelling argument that loss of winter habitat, particularly tropical forests, has been and continues to be a major factor contributing to declines of some species (e.g., Morse 1980, Rappole et al. 1983, Rappole and Morton 1985, Askins et al. 1990). Unfortunately, except for relatively local effects (Rappole and Morton 1985), direct evidence that loss of winter habitat is causing declines in long-distance migrants is lacking (Holmes and Sherry 1988, Hutto 1988, Wilcove 1988).

Here we examine annual variation in abundance of birds in northern Wisconsin and Michigan over a five-year period (1985–1989). We consider the possibility that drought might have contributed to observed patterns of variation in abundance. We present evidence that (1) conditions on the breeding grounds might cause declines in migrant populations and that (2) differences in the extent of annual variation in abundance among migratory groups might relate to factors other than loss of winter habitat. We stress, however, that our results do not preclude the possibility that habitat change in tropical regions will affect (or has already affected) migrant populations over a longer time scale than considered here.

Earlier, Blake et al. (1989) noted that declines in breeding populations of long-distance migrants in northern Wisconsin and Upper Peninsula Michigan were not matched by similar declines in populations of short-distance migrants and permanent residents. Similar patterns have been noted previously (Briggs and Criswell 1978), and have been taken as evidence that events in the tropics influenced breeding populations of many species (see review in Askins et al. 1990). However, population declines in northern Wisconsin and Michigan generally coincided with a series of dry years in the study region. If populations of long-distance migrants were, for whatever reason(s), more susceptible to drought-induced effects, this pattern (i.e., declines in long-distance migrants not matched by declines in other groups) also might emerge, irrespective of events elsewhere. If drought was largely responsible for population declines, populations should eventually return to pre-drought levels if moisture levels return to "normal." Recovery might not, however, be immediate if the drought had long-term effects on populations levels or habitat (Grant 1986). Speed of recovery might further depend on whether birds assess habitat quality based on short-term weather conditions (e.g., current rainfall) or more long-term conditions (e.g., underlying drought severity). No recovery would be expected if, on the other hand, loss of winter habitat was responsible for observed declines.

Our data are based on a study designed to test for effects of the United States Navy's extremely low frequency (ELF) communications systems on bird populations. We do not discuss potential effects of the antenna system here (see Blake et al. 1989 for a recent summary of results) but it is important to note the following. First, the Wisconsin facility began operation in 1969 and has been in operation throughout this study. We have not detected any difference in annual trends in bird populations between control (areas not affected by the antenna) and treatment (areas affected by the antenna) study sites (Hanowski et al. 1991). Hence, changes in bird populations among years are not likely related to antenna operation. Second, although the antenna in Michigan was not fully operational during this study, it was tested at less than full strength from 1987 to 1989. Although it is possible that testing the antenna had some effect on birds, our study has not detected any consistent effects (i.e., differences in bird populations between treatment and control sites).

Study areas and methods

STUDY AREAS. Birds were sampled at sites in northwestern Wisconsin (Ashland, Bayfield, and Sawyer counties) and in Upper Peninsula Michigan (Dickinson and Marquette counties), approximately 240 km apart. Primary habitats in both regions included upland and lowland forests (deciduous, coniferous, and mixed deciduous-coniferous). Principal tree species include sugar maple (*Acer saccharum*), balsam fir (*Abies balsamea*), birch (*Betula papyrifera* and *B. lutea*), red maple (*Acer rubrum*), black ash (*Fraxinus nigra*), aspen (*Populus tremuloides* and *P. grandidentata*), black spruce (*Picea mariana*), cedar (*Thuja occidentalis*), and red pine (*Pinus resinosa*).

BIRD SAMPLES. We established 20, randomly selected 4.35-km transects, including 10 in Michigan and 10 in Wisconsin. Detailed descriptions of selection procedures are in Blake et al. (1989) and in Hanowski et al. (1990). Transects were distributed over approximately 860 km² in Wisconsin and 1,500 km² in Michigan. Thus, the data are representative of the region and do not reflect purely local effects. Each 4.35-km transect consisted of eight 500-m segments arrayed in a single line; segments were separated by a 50-m buffer. We tested the independence of adjacent 500-m segments using runs tests and correlation tests (Hanowski et al. 1990). Most analyses (> 90%) indicated that adjacent segments were independent (P < 0.05).

We counted birds on each 500-m segment (80/state) once during June from 1985 to 1989. Time constraints precluded sampling each segment more than once, given the number of transects sampled, the time required, delays caused by rain, and our desire to control for seasonal and observer effects. We decided it was better to obtain a greater number of samples (80 replicates/region) rather than sample a smaller number of sites repeatedly (for further discussion see Gates 1981, Hanowski et al. 1991). Counts were started about 0.5 hr before sunrise and lasted up to 4.5 hr after sunrise on days with little wind (< 15 km/hr) and little or no precipitation. Two transects (8 segments/transect) were sampled per day, with counts conducted simultaneously. Each observer walked at a rate of 1 km/hr and recorded each bird detected (by sight or sound) within 100 m of the transect center line.

Birds were classified by migratory status (long-distance migrant: generally winter in the tropics; short-distance migrants: generally winter south of study region but north of tropics; permanent resident in study region) and preferred breeding habitat. We based our classifications on published information (e.g., Terres 1982, A.O.U. 1983, Ehrlich et al. 1988) and personal observations. (See Lynch [1987] for comments on the consistency among researchers in assigning such categories.)

ANALYSES. We eliminated from all analyses those segments where logging affected at least 25% of the segment (three in Wisconsin; eight in Michigan). We also eliminated data collected in 1986 by one observer who was significantly more conservative than other observers in estimating the number of birds present.

We used total number of birds recorded per 500-m segment as our estimate of abundance (Hanowski et al. 1990). We compared means for total individuals, individuals in different migratory groups, and individuals of "common" species among years. A species was considered "common" if we recorded, on average, at least 1 bird/km in at least two years. Many species were recorded too infrequently to justify analyzing trends in abundance. Although arbitrary, we felt this level of abundance represented a reasonable level for inclusion in

analyses. Variables were tested for assumptions of normality (Wilk-Shapiro test) and equality of variances (Bartlett's test) (Sokal and Rohlf 1981) and were transformed (e.g., square root, logarithmic) when necessary.

We used Järvinen's ratio (Järvinen 1979, Brawn et al. 1987; ratio of the sum of individual species abundance variances to total sample variance) to examine population fluctuations at the community level. Järvinen's ratio indicates parallel (ratio < 1.0), reciprocal (ratio > 1.0), or independent (ratio near 1.0) fluctuations in abundance. Parallel changes in abundance suggest that species were responding to the same factor or set of factors. We followed Brawn et al. (1987; after James and Boecklen 1984) in performing covariance analyses. In addition, correlation analyses were used in pairwise comparisons of abundances of common species in each state. High positive correlations indicate parallel and high negative values reciprocal changes in abundance. Because multiple comparisons (e.g., correlations) are not statistically valid, we use these data primarily for descriptive purposes.

WEATHER. Climate data were obtained from the National Climatic Data Center, National Oceanic and Atmospheric Administration (NOAA 1988, updated to 1989). Two drought indices that incorporate information on moisture and temperature were used to describe moisture conditions in the study regions. The Palmer Drought Severity Index is a meteorological index that expresses the severity of a wet or dry spell by incorporating past and present conditions. As such, it is less sensitive to monthly departures from prolonged drought or wet spells. The Palmer "Z" or Moisture Anomaly Index is a measure of the departure from normal of the moisture climate for a particular month. It can reflect above normal precipitation even during a general drought period, and vice versa. The two indices provide different information on moisture conditions: long-term trends (drought severity) and current conditions (moisture anomaly).

Correlation analyses were used to relate bird abundances to the drought indices. However, because monthly values for the drought severity index are not independent, we used only May values in correlation analyses. By contrast, the monthly moisture anomaly values are independent (at least to the extent that weather in any month is independent of the previous month). Consequently, we used values for April, May, and/or June in analyses. Because our sample sizes (number of years) are small (5 yr), correlations should be viewed primarily as indicative of possible patterns. Population levels during the breeding season might be influenced by events during the preceding year (e.g., reproductive success). Hence, we also used drought indices from 1984 to 1988 in correlations with bird data from 1985 to 1989 (i.e., with a time lag of one year). June values were used as that is when most young were being hatched or fed.

Results

VARIATION IN ABUNDANCE: MIGRATORY GROUPS. Extent and direction of annual changes in abundance differed among migratory groups (Fig. 1). Long-distance migrants varied in abundance in both states (Wisconsin: Kruskal-Wallis [KW] analysis of variance, $\chi^2 = 167.2$, d.f. = 4, $P < 0.001$; Michigan: $F_{4,355} = 28.5$, $P < 0.001$). Long-distance migrants increased in abundance from 1988 to 1989 in Wisconsin but not in Michigan. Short-distance migrants varied in abundance in Wisconsin ($F_{4,350} = 11.6$, $P < 0.001$), but the overall pattern of variation differed from that displayed by long-distance migrants (r = 0.13 between groups). Total abundance of short-distance migrants declined from 1987 to 1988 in Wisconsin, which paralleled results of long-distance migrants. Abundance of short-distance migrants did not vary in Michigan (KW: $\chi^2 = 2.5$, d.f. = 4, $P < 0.65$). Few permanent residents were present, but abundance of those species fluctuated over time in both states (Wisconsin: F = 5.4, $P < 0.001$; Michigan: F = 15.3, $P < 0.001$). Fluctuations were more pronounced in Michigan.

Total bird abundance varied among years in Wisconsin (KW: $\chi^2 = 143.3$, d.f. = 4, $P < 0.001$) and Michigan ($F_{4,355} = 26.0$, $P < 0.001$) (Fig. 1). Because most individuals recorded during bird counts were long-distance migrants, changes in total abundance largely reflected changes in abundance of those species, particularly in Michigan. Changes in total abundance were particularly pronounced in Michigan between 1985 and 1986 (25% decline) and between 1987 and 1988 in Wisconsin (40% decline).

VARIATION IN ABUNDANCE: INDIVIDUAL SPECIES. Twenty-two species in Wisconsin and 19 in Michigan were sufficiently common (i.e., ≥ 1 bird/km in at least two years) to examine for annual variation in abundance (Appendix 1). Eight of 11 common, long-distance migrants varied in abundance among years in Michigan (Table 1). Overall, numbers tended to be greatest in 1985 (six of eight species whose numbers varied over time). Most species declined in abundance over time, particularly from 1985 to 1986 (eight species) and from 1987 to 1988 (eight species). In no case, however, were changes in abundance significant between adjacent years (multiple comparison among means tests). Eight of 13 long-distance migrants varied in abundance in Wisconsin (Table 2). All species (13) declined in abundance from 1987 to 1988. Seven species increased in abundance from 1988 to 1989 in Wisconsin. Changes between adjacent years were significant only in three cases (Table 2). Six of the 10 species that were common in both states varied

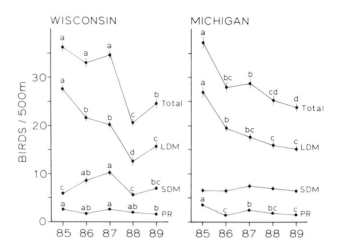

FIGURE 1. Mean (± 1 SE) number of individuals/500 m from June 1985 to 1989 in Wisconsin and Michigan for all species (*Total*), long-distance migrants (*LDM*), short-distance migrants (*SDM*), and permanent residents (*PR*). Means (for each group) not sharing the same letter are significantly different at $P < 0.05$ (Scheffé multiple comparison among means tests). For example, mean total abundance in Wisconsin did not differ significantly from 1985 to 1987 (all values have same letter *a*); mean abundance for 1988 and for 1989 differed significantly from each other (letters *c* and *b*) and each differed from 1985 to 1987. N = 72/yr in Michigan; n = 77/yr in Wisconsin, except 1986 when n = 47 (see text).

significantly in abundance in both states.

Four of eight short-distance migrants and permanent residents in Michigan and seven of nine in Wisconsin varied significantly in abundance among years (Table 3). Only three species (Blue Jay, Golden-crowned Kinglet, Hermit Thrush) varied in both states. Patterns of variation differed among species and, generally, from those of long-distance migrants. For example, no short-distance migrant or permanent resident steadily declined in abundance from 1985 to 1989 in either state. In Wisconsin, six of seven species showed some increase from 1985 to 1986, in direct contrast to long-distance migrants. All seven species, however, that varied over time in Wisconsin declined in abundance from 1987 to 1988, a pattern also observed for most long-distance migrants.

CORRELATIONS IN ABUNDANCE BETWEEN SPECIES. Covariance analyses indicated that population fluctuations tended to be parallel among species. Järvinen ratios were small and comparable between groups and states (Table 4). Furthermore, the sums of individual species variances were at least 300 (Michigan) or 400 (Wisconsin) standard deviations less than the estimated total variance for each group, indicating large positive covariance terms for each state. These parallel changes in

TABLE 1. Mean (± 1 SE) number of individuals/500 m of common long-distance migrants in Michigan. Results of Kruskal-Wallis analysis of variance (among years) are shown

Species	1985	1986	1987	1988	1989	χ^2	$P <$
Species showing significant variation among years:							
Black-throated Green Warbler	2.2 ± 0.24	1.4 ± 0.21	1.3 ± 0.21	1.2 ± 0.19	1.2 ± 0.18	16.1	0.003
Chestnut-sided Warbler	3.1 ± 0.46	1.5 ± 0.32	1.3 ± 0.28	1.1 ± 0.23	0.9 ± 0.19	11.3	0.05
Least Flycatcher	1.1 ± 0.20	1.1 ± 0.31	1.0 ± 0.32	0.9 ± 0.32	0.7 ± 0.26	17.7	0.002
Mourning Warbler	1.0 ± 0.21	0.4 ± 0.12	0.5 ± 0.10	0.2 ± 0.06	0.3 ± 0.08	17.8	0.002
Nashville Warbler	4.0 ± 0.49	2.5 ± 0.37	2.2 ± 0.30	2.4 ± 0.30	2.2 ± 0.24	10.4	0.05
Ovenbird	6.1 ± 0.46	4.7 ± 0.35	3.9 ± 0.30	3.4 ± 0.28	3.7 ± 0.31	26.2	0.001
Red-eyed Vireo	4.2 ± 0.46	2.5 ± 0.33	2.2 ± 0.26	1.8 ± 0.25	1.5 ± 0.19	24.0	0.001
Rose-breasted Grosbeak	1.0 ± 0.14	1.1 ± 0.17	0.6 ± 0.11	1.0 ± 0.13	0.7 ± 0.14	10.4	0.05
Species without significant variation:							
Black-and-white Warbler	0.8 ± 0.12	0.6 ± 0.11	0.7 ± 0.15	0.6 ± 0.10	0.4 ± 0.08	7.1	0.13
Veery	0.4 ± 0.09	0.6 ± 0.15	0.5 ± 0.14	0.4 ± 0.10	0.5 ± 0.11	0.8	0.94
Yellow-bellied Flycatcher	0.6 ± 0.18	0.6 ± 0.15	0.3 ± 0.10	0.4 ± 0.09	0.3 ± 0.09	4.6	0.33

TABLE 2. Mean (± 1 SE) number of individuals/500 m of common long-distance migrants in Wisconsin. Results of Kruskal-Wallis analysis of variance (among years) are shown. Significant between-year differences (multiple comparison among means tests) are indicated with an asterisk (*) between values for appropriate years

Species	1985	1986	1987	1988	1989	χ^2	$P <$
Species showing significant variation among years:							
Blackburnian Warbler	0.2 ± 0.05	0.5 ± 0.12	0.6 ± 0.14	0.2 ± 0.06	0.4 ± 0.10	12.6	0.02
Black-throated Green Warbler	2.7 ± 0.25*	1.3 ± 0.27	1.9 ± 0.23	1.2 ± 0.14	1.3 ± 0.19	29.7	0.001
Common Yellowthroat	0.8 ± 0.18	0.5 ± 0.14	0.8 ± 0.15	0.6 ± 0.11	0.3 ± 0.07	10.0	0.05
Least Flycatcher	1.3 ± 0.27	0.7 ± 0.25	0.6 ± 0.18	0.4 ± 0.13	0.5 ± 0.24	18.1	0.002
Nashville Warbler	3.7 ± 0.44	3.7 ± 0.55	3.0 ± 0.31*	1.2 ± 0.17	1.7 ± 0.26	41.5	0.001
Ovenbird	6.5 ± 0.48	5.3 ± 0.59	3.8 ± 0.39	2.6 ± 0.30	3.6 ± 0.33	45.7	0.001
Red-eyed Vireo	4.6 ± 0.37*	3.0 ± 0.40	2.2 ± 0.22	1.5 ± 0.17	2.3 ± 0.26	51.8	0.001
Rose-breasted Grosbeak	0.4 ± 0.09	0.4 ± 0.12	0.6 ± 0.09	0.3 ± 0.07	0.3 ± 0.07	10.4	0.05
Species not showing significant variation							
Black-and-white Warbler	0.8 ± 0.12	0.7 ± 0.13	0.9 ± 0.14	0.6 ± 0.10	0.6 ± 0.10	4.5	0.35
Chestnut-sided Warbler	1.5 ± 0.24	1.9 ± 0.33	1.9 ± 0.24	1.5 ± 0.24	1.4 ± 0.23	5.5	0.24
Mourning Warbler	0.7 ± 0.14	0.4 ± 0.14	0.6 ± 0.10	0.4 ± 0.07	0.6 ± 0.11	4.2	0.38
Northern Parula	0.4 ± 0.10	0.6 ± 0.16	0.5 ± 0.12	0.4 ± 0.08	0.3 ± 0.10	4.0	0.41
Yellow-bellied Flycatcher	1.1 ± 0.20	0.8 ± 0.19	1.0 ± 0.15	0.7 ± 0.12	0.7 ± 0.12	2.1	0.72

abundance indicate that most species were influenced by the same or similar factor(s). Similar results were obtained when pairwise correlations analyses were examined. Abundances of most of the common species fluctuated in parallel in both states; 86% (199 of 231) of pairwise correlations were positive in Wisconsin whereas 67% (115 of 171) were positive in Michigan. In both states, the number of positive correlations exceeded that expected by chance (i.e., 50:50 ratio; $\chi^2 > 10$, $P < 0.001$, both states).

DROUGHT INDICES. Drought indices indicated that moisture levels were normal to slightly below normal in 1984 and normal to slightly above normal in 1985 (Table 5) in both states. By contrast, drought conditions generally have prevailed since 1986. Rainfall was closer to normal in 1989 in Wisconsin, as indicated by moisture anomaly data, but was still insufficient to recharge groundwater. May 1989 was relatively wet, with rainfall in 1989 more than twice that of 1988. By contrast, rainfall during April through June 1989 in Michigan was still below

TABLE 3. Mean (± 1 SE) number of individuals/500 m of common short-distance migrants and two permanent residents (Black-capped Chickadee, Blue Jay). Results of Kruskal-Wallis analysis of variance (among years) are shown. Significant between-year differences (multiple comparison among means tests) are indicated with an asterisk (*) between values for appropriate years

Species	1985	1986	1987	1988	1989	χ^2	$P <$
Michigan							
American Robin	0.8 ± 0.13	0.7 ± 0.12	0.8 ± 0.14	0.5 ± 0.10	0.5 ± 0.12	8.8	0.07
Black-capped Chickadee	1.1 ± 0.17*	0.2 ± 0.07	0.5 ± 0.11	0.6 ± 0.14	0.5 ± 0.12	29.3	0.001
Blue Jay	0.7 ± 0.10	0.5 ± 0.11	0.9 ± 0.15	0.6 ± 0.10	0.4 ± 0.09	13.2	0.01
Golden-crowned Kinglet	0.4 ± 0.11	0.6 ± 0.17	0.9 ± 0.18	0.9 ± 0.16	0.8 ± 0.16	13.8	0.008
Hermit Thrush	1.1 ± 0.15*	0.4 ± 0.08	0.7 ± 0.12	0.8 ± 0.13	0.9 ± 0.12	21.7	0.001
White-throated Sparrow	1.4 ± 0.20	1.2 ± 0.22	1.1 ± 0.23	1.2 ± 0.21	1.1 ± 0.19	3.0	0.60
Winter Wren	0.4 ± 0.09	0.3 ± 0.08	0.7 ± 0.13	0.4 ± 0.09	0.4 ± 0.09	4.2	0.40
Yellow-rumped Warbler	0.2 ± 0.09	0.3 ± 0.08	0.3 ± 0.11	0.5 ± 0.12	0.3 ± 0.08	6.6	0.17
Wisconsin							
American Robin	0.5 ± 0.11	0.4 ± 0.15*	0.6 ± 0.10*	0.2 ± 0.05	0.2 ± 0.06	22.0	0.001
Black-capped Chickadee	0.6 ± 0.09	0.4 ± 0.12	0.5 ± 0.12	0.5 ± 0.10	0.5 ± 0.10	2.8	0.60
Blue Jay	0.6 ± 0.11	0.7 ± 0.16	1.0 ± 0.14	0.6 ± 0.10	0.5 ± 0.12	13.9	0.008
Golden-crowned Kinglet	0.1 ± 0.05*	0.6 ± 0.17	0.6 ± 0.14	0.2 ± 0.07	0.5 ± 0.10	23.6	0.001
Hermit Thrush	0.8 ± 0.11	0.9 ± 0.16	1.4 ± 0.18	0.8 ± 0.14*	1.5 ± 0.18	14.0	0.008
Song Sparrow	0.2 ± 0.08	0.6 ± 0.19	0.6 ± 0.13	0.4 ± 0.10	0.3 ± 0.09	12.2	0.02
White-throated Sparrow	1.0 ± 0.17*	2.7 ± 0.39	2.9 ± 0.36*	1.2 ± 0.18	1.2 ± 0.26	35.5	0.001
Winter Wren	0.5 ± 0.11	0.7 ± 0.19	0.9 ± 0.14*	0.4 ± 0.09	0.8 ± 0.14	16.5	0.003
Yellow-rumped Warbler	0.3 ± 0.10	0.2 ± 0.10	0.3 ± 0.10	0.3 ± 0.06	0.3 ± 0.08	2.6	0.64

TABLE 4. Results of covariance analyses (following Brawn et al. 1987) based on all common (see text) species and common long-distance migrants

	All common species	Common long-distance migrants
Wisconsin		
Number of species	22	12
Järvinen ratio[a]	0.178	0.206
Michigan		
Number of species	19	11
Järvinen ratio	0.161	0.169

a. Järvinen ratio = sum est. species variances / est. total sample variance.

normal, although a wetter latter half of 1988 had alleviated drought conditions more than in Wisconsin.

DROUGHT AND BIRD ABUNDANCE. Bird abundance appeared to be influenced by drought or drought related factors because declines in abundance (Fig. 1) were most widespread from 1987 to 1988, the year of the most severe drought, especially in Wisconsin. The pronounced drop from 1985 to 1986 in Michigan coincided with an extremely dry May (Table 5). Correlations between bird abundance and drought indices within a year (i.e., without a time lag) generally were stronger for long-distance migrants than for other groups (Table 6). Short-distance migrants, by contrast, often were negatively correlated with drought, perhaps as a result of milder winters. Correlations usually were higher in Michigan than in Wisconsin when based on April and May moisture anomaly values (i.e., short-term moisture conditions) but not when correlations were based on drought severity indices (i.e., long-term conditions). Differences between groups were more pronounced when a one-year time lag was introduced (Table 6), suggesting that reproductive activities (or lack thereof) of long-distance migrants were more affected than in other groups.

TABLE 5. Palmer drought indices (moisture anomaly and drought severity; see text) for study areas in Wisconsin and Michigan

State	Year	Moisture anomaly[a]			Drought severity[b]		
		April	May	June	April	May	June
Michigan	1984	1.18	-2.16**	-0.59	-0.39	-1.07	-1.16
	1985	2.25	0.05	-0.81	1.77	1.61	1.17
	1986	-1.96*	-5.68**	-1.48*	-0.65	-2.48*	-2.72*
	1987	-3.12**	-0.79	-3.27**	-4.05**	-3.90**	-4.59**
	1988	-2.57**	-3.65**	-3.96**	-1.45	-2.52*	-3.58**
	1989	-1.44*	-1.34*	1.83	-0.73	-1.10	-0.38
Wisconsin	1984	0.71	-1.67*	-0.21	0.28	-0.56	-0.57
	1985	-0.20	-0.04	-0.02	1.27	1.12	1.00
	1986	-0.62	-4.74**	-0.44	-0.35	-1.90	-1.85
	1987	-3.20**	-2.10**	-3.36**	-2.48*	-2.91*	-3.73**
	1988	-2.17**	-4.02**	-4.15**	-2.43*	-3.52**	-4.54**
	1989	-1.17	0.48	-0.85	-2.77*	-2.33*	-2.37*

NOTE: * = moderate drought values; ** = severe or extreme drought values.

a. Absolute values <1.29 indicate normal, 1.29–1.99 mild to moderate, 2–2.74 severe, and >2.74 extreme wet (positive) or dry (negative) conditions.

b. Absolute values <1.00 indicate normal, 1–1.99 mild, 2–2.99 moderate, 3–3.99 severe, and >3.99 extreme wet (positive) or dry (negative) conditions.

TABLE 6. Correlations between migratory groups and drought indices (Table 5). Correlations between abundance and June drought indices with a 1-year time lag (June–1 yr) also are shown

Group	Moisture anomaly				Drought severity	
	April	May	June	June–1 yr	May	June–1 yr
Michigan						
Long-distance migrants	0.82	0.32	0.06	0.80	0.71	0.53
Short-distance migrants	-0.42	0.39	-0.69	0.08	-0.52	-0.47
Permanent residents	0.73	0.78	-0.10	0.46	0.61	-0.08
Wisconsin						
Long-distance migrants	0.52	0.24	0.66	0.84	0.87	0.77
Short-distance migrants	-0.49	-0.21	-0.12	0.48	-0.32	0.34
Permanent residents	-0.26	0.40	-0.12	0.49	0.43	0.14

Abundances of many common species in Michigan and Wisconsin were correlated with drought indices (Tables 7, 8). (We used moisture anomaly indices for April and May in Michigan and for May and June in Wisconsin because Michigan was sampled in the first week of June and Wisconsin in the third.) Most correlations were positive (lower abundance as drought severity increased) except for a few species (e.g., Golden-crowned Kinglet, Yellow-rumped Warbler). Unlike most species, the kinglet increased in abundance in Michigan

from a low in 1985 to a high in 1988 and showed a strong negative correlation with drought. When data from both states were combined in one analysis, correlations for many species tended to be less, suggesting that patterns of variation differed between the two regions.

Introduction of a one-year time lag did not substantially alter the results (Table 7, 8). Correlations were stronger in some cases but not in others when compared to results without the time lag. Effects of a time lag tended to be more pronounced in Wisconsin.

TABLE 7. Correlations (>0.50) between individual species and moisture anomaly indices (see text, Table 5). Correlations between abundance and June drought indices with a 1-year time lag (June–1 yr) also are shown

Species	Michigan			Wisconsin		
	April	May	June–1yr	May	June	June–1yr
American Robin			0.95			0.82
Black-and-white Warbler			0.83			0.73
Black-capped Chickadee	0.84	0.74		0.89		
Black-throated Green Warbler	0.93		0.71	0.51		0.57
Blue Jay		0.52				0.68
Chestnut-sided Warbler	0.90		0.73	-0.68		0.72
Common Yellowthroat						0.68
Golden-crowned Kinglet	-0.88		-0.68			
Hermit Thrush	0.65	0.76				
Least Flycatcher			0.96		0.73	0.63
Mourning Warbler	0.85	0.60	0.71	0.88		
Nashville Warbler	0.95		0.59		0.62	0.94
Northern Parula				-0.69		0.70
Ovenbird	0.88		0.79		0.82	0.75
Red-eyed Vireo	0.84		0.81		0.80	0.60
Rose-breasted Grosbeak		-0.57				0.75
Song Sparrow				-0.67		
White-throated Sparrow	0.95		0.54			0.58
Winter Wren		0.50				
Yellow-bellied Flycatcher	0.58		0.70			0.72
Yellow-rumped Warbler	-0.62	-0.51	-0.70	0.79		

TABLE 8. Correlations (>0.50) between species and drought severity indices (see text, Table 5). Correlations with a 1-year time lag (June–1 yr) also are shown

Species	Michigan		Wisconsin	
	May	June–1yr	May	June–1yr
American Robin		0.64		0.55
Black-capped Chickadee	0.84			
Black-throated Green Warbler	0.79		0.84	
Chestnut-sided Warbler	0.75			0.66
Golden-crowned Kinglet	-0.76	-0.70	-0.53	
Hermit Thrush	0.76	-0.52		
Least Flycatcher		0.70	0.98	0.59
Mourning Warbler	0.67		0.65	
Nashville Warbler	0.87		0.67	0.92
Northern Parula				0.78
Ovenbird	0.71	0.64	0.91	0.79
Red-eyed Vireo	0.68		0.99	0.60
Rose-breasted Grosbeak	-0.54	0.57		0.55
Veery		0.62		
White-throated Sparrow	0.89			0.52
Winter Wren	-0.52			
Yellow-bellied Flycatcher		0.83	0.71	
Yellow-rumped Warbler		-0.80		-0.53

Discussion

Bird populations in northern Wisconsin and Upper Peninsula Michigan have varied in abundance from 1985 to 1989. Populations of many species have declined, resulting in approximately 35% fewer birds recorded in 1989 than in 1985. Despite the widespread occurrence of population variation, and the fact that populations of different species tended to fluctuate in parallel, important differences were noted among species, particularly with respect to migratory strategy. Species that winter in the tropics made up the majority of breeding birds and accounted for most declines. Species wintering in temperate regions showed less change; some increased in abundance during part of the study. The fact that many species in two states were affected and the fact that species with different ecological requirements varied in similar ways, suggest that observed fluctuations in abundance were in response to a single factor or combination of related factors. Less widespread, consistent patterns would be expected if population variation was a consequence of species-specific factors or interactions. For example, we found little evidence for reciprocal changes in abundance among species.

Moderate to extreme drought conditions have prevailed over many parts of the upper midwest during the past two to three years (NOAA 1988, Clark 1989, Droege and Sauer 1989). The severe drought in 1988 was accompanied by above average temperatures as well. Droege and Sauer (1989) suggested that the hot, dry spring and summer of 1988 was responsible for many declines in bird populations in the midwest, and several lines of evidence indicate that drought was a major factor causing or promoting declines in bird abundance in northern Wisconsin and Michigan.

First, major declines in abundance of many species often corresponded with those years when drought was particularly severe. In Michigan, an extremely dry May in 1986 coincided with a sharp decline in breeding populations in June. Drought conditions continued through 1989 and populations of many species did not show any recovery. In Wisconsin, declines also were noted from 1985 to 1986, again coinciding with a dry May; a second, pronounced decrease in bird abundances occurred from 1987 to 1988, during a period of extreme drought. Significant declines were not, however, noted in all species when severe drought conditions prevailed, as in Michigan in 1988, indicating that other factors influenced populations as well. However, the influence of drought in Wisconsin, where the 1988 drought was more severe, was evident because all birds declined in abundance (long-distance migrants, short-distance migrants, and permanent residents).

Second, abundances of many birds were highly correlated with regional, independently derived measures of drought severity. Furthermore, correlations, particularly in Wisconsin, often were stronger when a one-year time lag was introduced, indicating that poor reproductive success might have affected populations. Populations of long-distance migrants breeding in drier habitats (e.g., upland deciduous areas) tended to be more strongly correlated with drought indices than those of other species.

Although not related to changes in bird abundance, evidence from other studies in Upper Peninsula Michigan indicated that effects of the drought were sufficient to affect vertebrate populations. Concurrent studies on chipmunks (*Tamias striatus*) and deermice (*Peromyscus maniculatus*) in the Michigan study sites demonstrated that populations of these species crashed during 1986, with declines continuing at least into 1987 (Beaver et al. 1988). Declines were attributed to increased mortality from disease, probably induced by stress due to the drought in 1986.

Detrimental effects of drought on bird populations have been noted previously (Welty 1982). An extreme drought in 1977, for example, caused large declines in bird populations in northern Utah (Smith 1982); particularly affected were birds breeding in aspen (*Populus tremuloides*) stands. Birds breeding in coniferous habitats were less affected. Similarly, Hicks (1935, *fide* Smith 1982) reported a sharp decline in species breeding in a deciduous forest in Ohio during a drought year. In both studies, population levels returned to normal or near normal in 1–2 years. In our study, drought conditions have continued for several years and population levels might require more time to return to predrought levels. Grant (1986) noted that populations of Darwin's finches (*Geospiza*) did not immediately return to predrought levels, even though rainfall returned to normal. The time lag was related to mortality of major food plants and the recovery time of those food sources.

Drought or other disturbances (e.g., treefalls, landslips, fire) do not affect all species equally. In this study, differences among migratory groups in direction and extent of population variation were noted. In particular, long-distance migrants were apparently affected more than other groups. Time of breeding might have influenced the response of birds to the drought. Most short-distance migrants and permanent residents commence breeding long before most long-distance migrants arrive in northern Wisconsin and Michigan (i.e., in April and May). Effects of the drought were less severe early in the year when temperatures were mild and moisture from winter snowfall was present. Thus, early breeding species would have faced less stressful conditions. In contrast, long-distance migrants that arrive in mid-to-late May would be nesting and caring for young (mid-to-late June) when drought conditions were severe. Although food may at times be superabundant on breeding grounds (e.g., Holmes et al. 1986), at other times food may be limiting or nearly so (Martin 1987). Increased stress or decreased resource abundance that increases time required to find and deliver food to nestlings may limit reproductive success or increase mortality of young. Similarly, birds may not breed if conditions are not suitable. Declines in bird abundance also might have reflected declines in singing intensity associated with increased need for foraging and/or decreased reproductive activities.

Destruction or alteration of tropical habitats may cause long-term declines in long-distance migrants, as many have suggested. Although destruction of tropical forests and conversion to pasture and cropland has had and will continue to have (with increasingly detrimental effects) adverse impacts on many species (e.g., Erwin 1988, Raven 1988), direct evidence for such effects on long-distance migrants is limited, as pointed out by Holmes and Sherry (1988) and Hutto (1988). Several points indicate that loss of winter habitat probably was not a major factor causing the population changes we observed from 1985 to 1988. First, population declines were relatively abrupt (up to a 40% decline from one year to the next), whereas conversion of tropical habitats occurs at a much slower rate (generally < 5–10%/year; Rappole et al. 1983, Sader and Joyce 1988), although that rate may be increasing. Tropical deforestation might have as strong (or stronger) an effect on bird populations as other factors (e.g., drought), but that effect is more likely to be felt over a longer time scale than that observed here. It is entirely possible, of course, that any effects of drought might have been exacerbated by loss or alteration of wintering or breeding habitats. If true, we would expect declines to persist over the long term, even if rainfall returns to normal.

Second, declines were noted among species wintering in a variety of habitats (early successional to primary forest) and in a variety of locations. Species that experienced severe declines included the Ovenbird, Red-eyed Vireo, and Black-throated Green Warbler, among others. The Ovenbird winters primarily in younger habitats (second growth, scrub) on islands in the Caribbean region and in Central America; the vireo winters in primary forests of northern South America; and the Black-throated Green Warbler winters in higher elevation forests in Central America (Rappole et al. 1983; Ehrlich et al. 1988; R. Holmes, pers. comm.; Blake and Loiselle, this volume, pers. obs.). It is unlikely that loss or alteration of these different habitats and regions was sufficiently extensive or rapid enough to account for the changes observed in Wisconsin and Michigan. Furthermore, although many individuals return to the same

wintering site year after year (references in Rappole et al. 1983; Blake and Loiselle, this volume, unpubl. data), birds from a particular breeding area might not all winter in the same area. Certainly, different species that breed in the same area often winter in different locations (e.g., Ovenbird, Red-eyed Vireo). Thus, it appears unlikely that some event in the tropics would have been widespread enough to affect so many species and to have influenced breeding populations in both Wisconsin and Michigan.

Furthermore, not all species that winter in the tropics declined in abundance (e.g., Black-and-white Warbler, Yellow-bellied Flycatcher), and declines in some species were noted in one state but not in the other (e.g., Chestnut-sided Warbler, Mourning Warbler). Declines were noted, however, in abundances of some short-distance migrants and permanent residents, particularly when the drought was most severe in Wisconsin.

Finally, at least in Wisconsin, a partial recovery of populations was noted in 1989; such a recovery, especially if it continues, would not be expected if habitat loss in the tropics was the sole cause of the declines. Lack of recovery in Michigan might reflect habitat mediated differences between the two regions, differences in regional rainfall patterns, or other factors (e.g., variation in resource abundance). Rainfall remained below normal during April-June 1989 in Michigan but not in Wisconsin.

Short-term responses of birds to drought do not mean that migrants and nonmigratory tropical residents will not be (or have not been) adversely affected by alteration of tropical habitats. Many species may survive in altered habitats for some time even though long-term survival is reduced. Effects of habitat changes can be indirect and might not necessarily be confined to specific wintering or breeding habitats. If tropical deforestation is contributing to global warming, with consequent effects on habitat and weather, then breeding populations might be affected (e.g., by increased frequency and severity of droughts). Over a five-year study, we noted substantial variation in bird populations in northern Michigan and Wisconsin. Yet, even five years is inadequate to assess population trends and obtain conclusive results. The need for long-term monitoring (on the order of decades) data has never been more clear, especially as scientists attempt to separate the effects of changing weather conditions and changes in both breeding and wintering habitats on migratory birds.

Acknowledgments

We thank A. Lima for her help with all aspects of the analyses and P. Collins for conducting many of the bird counts. This paper has been improved by the comments of E.K. Bollinger, D. Heinemann, and B.A. Loiselle.

This study was funded by the United States Navy, sub-contract number EO6549-84-011. This is contribution number 65 of the Center for Water and the Environment, University of Minnesota.

Literature cited

Askins, R.A., J.F. Lynch, and R. Greenberg. 1990. Population declines in migratory birds in eastern North America. *Current Ornithol.* 7:1–57.

American Ornithologists' Union. 1983. *Check-list of North American Birds.* 6th ed. Washington: American Ornithologists' Union.

Beaver, D.L., R.W. Hill, and J.H. Asher, Jr. 1988. ELF communications system ecological monitoring program: Small vertebrates—the Michigan study site, tasks 5.6, small mammals, and 5.12A, nesting birds. Annual Report 1987, Subcontract No. E06549-84-C-006. *In* Compilation of 1987 Annual Reports of the Navy ELF Communications System Ecological Monitoring Program, Technical Report E06595-2, Contract No. N00039-88-C-0065, Part G, pp. 1–119. Chicago: IIT Research Institute.

Blake, J.G., J.M. Hanowski, and G.J. Niemi. 1989. ELF communications system ecological monitoring program: Bird species and communities. Annual Report 1988, Subcontract No. EO6595-88-011. *In* Compilation of 1988 Annual Reports of the Navy ELF Communications System Ecological Monitoring Program, Technical Report EO6595-2, Contract No. NO0039-89-C-0065, Part G, pp. 1–98. Chicago: IIT Research Institute.

Brawn, J.D., W.J. Boecklen, and R.P. Balda. 1987. Investigations of density interactions among breeding birds in ponderosa pine forests: Correlative and experimental evidence. *Oecologia* 72:348–357.

Briggs, S.A., and J.H. Criswell. 1978. Gradual silencing of spring in Washington. *Atlantic Nat.* 32:19–26.

Clark, J.S. 1989. The forest is for burning. *Nat. History* 1989 (Jan):51–52.

Droege, S., and J.R. Sauer. 1989. *North American Breeding Bird Survey: Annual Summary 1988.* U.S. Fish and Wildlife Service Biol. Rept. 89(13).

Ehrlich, P.R., D.S. Dobkin, and D. Wheye. 1988. *The Birder's Handbook: A Field Guide to the Natural History of North American Birds.* New York: Simon and Schuster.

Erwin, T.L. 1988. The tropical forest canopy—the heart of biotic diversity. Pages 123–129 in *Biodiversity*, E.O. Wilson, ed. Washington: National Academy Press.

Gates, C.E. 1981. Optimizing sampling frequency and number of transects and stations. Pages 399–404 in *Estimating Numbers of Terrestrial Birds*, C.J. Ralph and M.J. Scott, eds. Studies in Avian Biology No. 6.

Graber, J.W., and R.R. Graber. 1979. Severe winter weather and bird populations in southern Illinois. *Wilson Bull.* 91:88–102.

Grant, P.R. 1986. *Ecology and Evolution of Darwin's Finches.* Princeton: Princeton University Press.

Hanowski, J.M., J.G. Blake, G.J. Niemi, and P.T. Collins. 1991. ELF communications system ecological monitoring program: Wisconsin bird studies—Final report. Technical Report EO6628-2, Contract No. N00039-88-C-0065. Chicago: IIT Research Institute.

Hanowski, J.M., G.J. Niemi, and J.G. Blake. 1990. Statistical perspectives and experimental design when counting birds with line transects. *Condor* 92:328–337.

Hicks, L.E. 1935. A ten year study of a bird population in central Ohio. *Am. Midl. Nat.* 16:177–186.

Holmes, R.T., and T.W. Sherry. 1988. Assessing population trends of New Hampshire forest birds: Local vs. regional patterns. *Auk* 105:756–768.

Holmes, R.T., T.W. Sherry, and F.W. Sturges. 1986. Bird community dynamics in a temperate deciduous forest: Long-term trends at Hubbard Brook. *Ecol. Monogr.* 50:201–220.

Hutto, R.L. 1988. Is tropical deforestation responsible for the reported declines in neotropical migrant populations? *Am. Birds* 42:375–379.

———. 1989. The effect of habitat alteration on migratory land birds in a west Mexican tropical deciduous forest: A conservation perspective. *Conserv. Biol.* 3:138–148.

James, F.C., and W.J. Boecklen. 1984. Interspecific morphological relationships and the densities of birds. Pages 458–477 in *Ecological Communities: Conceptual Issues and the Evidence*, D.R. Strong, Jr., D. Simberloff, L.G. Abele, and A. Thistle, eds. Princeton: Princeton University Press.

Järvinen, O. 1979. Geographical gradients of stability in European land bird communities. *Oecologia* 38:51–69.

Järvinen, O., and R.A. Väisänen. 1978. Recent changes in forest bird populations in northern Finland. *Ann. Zool. Fennici* 15:279–289.

Leck, C.F., B.G. Murray, Jr., and J. Swinebroad. 1988. Long-term changes in the breeding bird populations of a New Jersey forest. *Biol. Conserv.* 46:145–157.

Loiselle, B.A. 1987. Migrant abundance in a Costa Rican lowland forest canopy. *J. Trop. Ecol.* 3:163–168.

———. 1988. Bird abundance and seasonality in a Costa Rican lowland forest canopy. *Condor* 90:761–772.

Lynch, J.F. 1987. Responses of breeding bird communities to forest fragmentation. Pages 123–140 in *Nature Conservation: The Role of Remnants of Native Vegetation*, D.A. Saunders, G.W. Arnold, A.A. Burbridge, and A.J.M. Hopkins, eds. Australia: Surrey Beatty and Sons Pty Ltd.

Martin, T.E. 1987. Food as a limit on breeding birds: A life-history perspective. *Ann. Rev. Ecol. Syst.* 18:453–487.

Morse, D.H. 1980. Population limitation: Breeding or wintering grounds? Pages 437–453 in *Migrant Birds in the Neotropics: Ecology, Behavior, Distribution and Conservation*, A. Keast and E.S. Morton, eds. Washington: Smithsonian Institution Press.

Myers, J.P. 1989. Delaware Bay: A spectacle of spring passage. *Nat. Conserv. Mag.* 39:14–18.

Myers, N. 1984. *The Primary Source: Tropical Forests and Our Future.* New York: W.W. Norton and Co.

National Oceanic and Atmospheric Administration. 1988. Time bias corrected divisional temperature-precipitation-drought index. Unpub. rept. TD-9640. Washington: NOAA.

Rappole, J.H., and E.S. Morton. 1985. Effects of habitat alteration on a tropical avian forest community. Pages 1013–1021 in *Neotropical Ornithology*, P.A. Buckley, E.S. Morton, R.S. Ridgely, and F.G. Buckley, eds. Ornithol. Monogr. 36.

Rappole, J.H., E.S. Morton, T.E. Lovejoy, III, and J.L. Ruos. 1983. *Nearctic Avian Migrants in the Neotropics*. Washington: U.S. Fish and Wildlife Service.

Raven, P.H. 1988. Our diminishing tropical forests. Pages 119–122 in *Biodiversity*, E.O. Wilson, ed. Washington: National Academy Press.

Sader, S.A., and A.T. Joyce. 1988. Deforestation rates and trends in Costa Rica, 1940–1983. *Biotropica* 20:11–19.

Smith, K.G. 1982. Drought-induced changes in avian community structure along a montane sere. *Ecology* 63:952–961.

Sokal, R.R., and F.J. Rohlf. 1981. *Biometry: The Principles and Practice of Statistics in Biological Research*. 2d ed. San Francisco: W.H. Freeman and Co.

Temple, S.A., and J.R. Cary. 1988. Modeling dynamics of habitat-interior bird populations in fragmented landscapes. *Conserv. Biol.* 2:340–347.

Terres, J.K. 1982. *The Audubon Society Encyclopedia of North American Birds*. New York: Alfred A. Knopf.

Welty, J.C. 1982. *The Life of Birds*. 3d ed. New York: Sanders College Publ.

Wilcove, D.S. 1988. Changes in the avifauna of the Great Smoky Mountains: 1947–1983. *Wilson Bull.* 100:256–271.

APPENDIX 1. Bird species used in analyses of annual variation

English name	Scientific name	Status[a]
Yellow-bellied Flycatcher	*Empidonax flaviventris*	Long-distance migrant
Least Flycatcher	*Empidonax minimus*	Long-distance migrant
Blue Jay	*Cyanocitta cristata*	Permanent resident
Black-capped Chickadee	*Parus atricapillus*	Permanent resident
Winter Wren	*Troglodytes troglodytes*	Short-distance migrant
Golden-crowned Kinglet	*Regulus satrapa*	Short-distance migrant
Veery	*Catharus fuscescens*	Long-distance migrant
Hermit Thrush	*Catharus guttatus*	Short-distance migrant
American Robin	*Turdus migratorius*	Short-distance migrant
Red-eyed Vireo	*Vireo olivaceus*	Long-distance migrant
Nashville Warbler	*Vermivora ruficapilla*	Long-distance migrant
Northern Parula	*Parula americana*	Long-distance migrant
Chestnut-sided Warbler	*Dendroica pensylvanica*	Long-distance migrant
Yellow-rumped Warbler	*Dendroica coronata*	Short-distance migrant
Black-throated Green Warbler	*Dendroica virens*	Long-distance migrant
Blackburnian Warbler	*Dendroica fusca*	Long-distance migrant
Black-and-white Warbler	*Mniotilta varia*	Long-distance migrant
Ovenbird	*Seiurus aurocapillus*	Long-distance migrant
Mourning Warbler	*Oporornis philadelphia*	Long-distance migrant
Common Yellowthroat	*Geothlypis trichas*	Long-distance migrant
Rose-breasted Grosbeak	*Pheucticus ludovicianus*	Long-distance migrant
Song Sparrow	*Melospiza melodia*	Short-distance migrant
White-throated Sparrow	*Zonotrichia albicollis*	Short-distance migrant

THOMAS W. SHERRY
Department of Ecology, Evolution,
and Organismal Biology
Tulane University
New Orleans, Louisiana 70118

RICHARD T. HOLMES
Department of Biological Sciences
Dartmouth College
Hanover, New Hampshire 03755

Population fluctuations in a long-distance Neotropical migrant: Demographic evidence for the importance of breeding season events in the American Redstart

Abstract. Demographic studies of American Redstarts (*Setophaga ruticilla*) were conducted in the Hubbard Brook Experimental Forest, New Hampshire, during the decade 1981–1990 to assess the importance of breeding season ecological events on population dynamics in this long-distance migratory passerine. Our results show that (1) breeding abundances in an unfragmented forest landscape declined; (2) this decline was due in part to low yearling male recruitment (defined as the number of yearlings present one year as a percent of total males present the previous year), which varied from 17–52%; and (3) recruitment of yearling males into the breeding population was strongly and significantly related to fledging success the previous summer. Fledging success depended primarily on nest depredation, but also on weather-related starvation in three seasons. These results show that nesting success of birds breeding in a relatively unfragmented forest landscape was the major influence on recruitment of yearlings, and was also an important influence on long-term fluctuations in population numbers. If this link between nesting success and yearling recruitment may be generalized to redstart or other migrant species populations elsewhere in North America, then our data provide the strongest evidence yet available that the continentwide declines documented in many of these migrants are caused by the increased nest predator and brood parasite populations resulting from human activity on the breeding grounds.

Sinopsis. Estudios demográficos de *Setophaga ruticilla* se llevaron a cabo en el Bosque Experimental de Hubbard Brook, New Hampshire, durante la década 1981–1990 para determinar la importancia de eventos ecológicos de la temporada de cría sobre la dinámica poblacional en este passerino migratorio de larga distancia. Nuestros resultados muestran que (1) las abundancias reproductivas en un paisaje forestal no fragmentado declinaron; (2) esta declinación se debió en parte al bajo reclutamiento de machos de un año (definido como el número de aves de un año de edad presentes en un año como porcentaje de todos los machos presentes el año previo), el cual varió entre 17 y 52%; y (3) el reclutamiento de machos de un año de edad en la población de cría estuvo fuerte y significativamente relacionado con el éxito de volantones del verano precedente. El éxito de los volantones dependió principalmente de la predación de nidos, pero también de inanición relacionada con el clima durante tres estaciones. Estos resultados muestran que el éxito de anidación de aves reproduciéndose en un paisaje forestal relativamente no fragmentado fue la mayor influencia sobre el reclutamiento de aves de un año de edad e igualmente influyó de manera importante sobre las fluctuaciones a largo plazo del tamaño poblacional. Si este eslabón entre el éxito de anidación y reclutamiento de aves de un año de edad puede generalizarse a poblaciones de *S. ruticilla* u otras especies migratorias en otros sitios en Norteamérica, entonces nuestros datos proveen la mas fuerte evidencia disponible de que las declinaciones poblacionales documentadas a nivel continental para muchas de estas especies migratorias son causadas por el incremento en las poblaciones de predadores y parásitos de cría resultante de la actividad antrópica en las áreas de cría.

Ornithologists have become increasingly concerned that populations of songbirds that migrate between North America and the Neotropics are declining (e.g., Robbins et al. 1989; Gauthreaux, this volume). However, the specific locations and causes of these population declines are poorly understood because of multiple potential causes of the decline (Holmes et al. 1986, Robbins et al. 1989, Terborgh 1989, Askins et al. 1990), and because of the difficulty of studying populations of these birds on the international scales which they traverse annually. A number of authors have proposed that tropical deforestation has caused declines, presumably by reducing adult survival (for recent reviews see Hutto 1988, Robbins et al. 1989, Terborgh 1989, Askins et al. 1990). A high degree of winter territoriality and high site tenacity where some populations of these birds winter (Holmes et al. 1989; Rappole et al. 1989; Holmes and Sherry, this volume) reinforces the possibility that deteriorating habitat quality in winter could force birds to search for new habitats in which they might face lower survival.

More abundant evidence supports the alternative hypothesis that habitat degradation where these migrants breed in North America has caused observed population declines, presumably by decreasing reproductive success. Populations of open-cup nesting species that migrate to the Neotropics have declined alarmingly in re-

cent decades within North American landscapes where breeding habitat has become fragmented into small forested islands surrounded by agricultural and suburban areas (Robbins 1979, Whitcomb et al. 1981, Wilcove et al. 1986; see reviews by Terborgh 1989, Askins et al. 1990). Populations of nest predators are higher in fragmented landscapes than in continuous forest (Wilcove 1985, Andrén and Angelstam 1988, Small and Hunter 1988, Yahner and Scott 1988; review in Askins et al. 1990). Brown-headed Cowbirds (*Molothrus ater*) have increased dramatically during the 20th century in eastern North America, particularly in agricultural landscapes, and have increased frequencies of nesting failure in a variety of host species (Mayfield 1978; Brittingham and Temple 1983; Walkinshaw 1983; Robinson 1988, this volume). Additional evidence that conditions during the breeding period are important to these birds comes from the observations that long-distance migratory songbird populations have not declined alarmingly in heavily forested landscapes (Holmes and Sherry 1988, Wilcove 1988, Askins et al. 1990), and populations in a Connecticut forest increased again when the landscape subsequently became more forested (Askins and Philbrick 1987).

To date most of our knowledge about the dynamics and regulation of songbird populations comes from long-term studies of nonmigratory species, especially European hole nesters (e.g., O'Connor 1980, Ekman 1984, Nilsson 1987). Explicit treatment of the population regulation of migratory passerines is rare (but see Fretwell 1986, O'Connor 1981, 1985, Nolan 1978). Population dynamics and regulatory mechanisms of Neotropical migrants are poorly understood despite their dominance in north temperate deciduous forest avifaunas (MacArthur 1959, Herrera 1978). Knowledge of year-round demographic processes and their ecological bases are needed to pinpoint the cause(s) of declining long-distance migrant populations.

In the present study we used a long-term demographic approach to address the hypothesis that ecological events in the breeding season are a major factor causing population fluctuations, particularly declines, of a long-distance migrant, the American Redstart (*Setophaga ruticilla*). This hypothesis predicts that annual variations in population parameters such as total abundance and yearling recruitment result from variable annual ecological circumstances during previous or present breeding seasons. Specifically, we asked (1) does recruitment of yearling males into a local breeding population depend on the previous year's nesting success, and what ecological factors influence nesting success? (2) Does total adult male redstart abundance depend on yearling male recruitment into the populations? We discuss implications of the results for scale of demographic processes and conservation in Neotropical migrants.

Study species

The American Redstart is a particularly useful species for such a demographic study for several reasons. First, redstarts reoccupy a broad geographic area of the northern United States and southern Canada each spring, encountering a variety of ecological circumstances within their breeding and wintering ranges. They comprise the most abundant breeding species, on average, in the northern hardwoods forests in New Hampshire (Holmes et al. 1986), where this study was conducted. Second, their numbers have declined in human-disturbed landscapes outside of New England within recent decades (Robbins 1979, Whitcomb et al. 1981, Johnston and Winings 1987), and their nesting success in some landscapes is potentially affected by cowbird parasitism—based on their susceptibility to cowbird parasitism (Baker 1944, Ficken 1961, Brittingham and Temple 1983). Thus, evidence bearing on the possible causes of population declines in this species is desirable. Third, redstart abundances and population age structure can be measured readily. Redstarts have conspicuous plumage and postures associated with stereotyped song and flight displays (Ficken 1962 1963, Ficken and Ficken 1967, Ickes and Ficken 1970) and a conspicuous yearling male plumage resembling that of females (Ficken and Ficken 1967, Rohwer et al. 1983), characteristics which facilitated our censusing male population age structure across large forested study areas. Redstarts have high adult site fidelity both in winter and summer (Holmes and Sherry, this volume), but low natal site fidelity, facts which helped us assess causes and scale of annual population changes (see Discussion).

Study site

Our study site in the Hubbard Brook Experimental Forest, West Thornton, New Hampshire consisted of unbroken northern hardwoods, mixed in some places with small patches of coniferous vegetation (Bormann and Likens 1979). The 1 × 3-km study site on generally south-facing slopes (400–600 m elevation) was surrounded by continuous, largely unfragmented forest both within the Hubbard Brook basin and adjacent areas of the White Mountain National Forest. Within this area we established a total of 10 km of belt transects, arranged in four parallel lines 200 m apart (Sherry and Holmes 1985). These transects were flagged at 25 m intervals to facilitate locating bird observations on maps. We refer to this area henceforth as the "transect" or "180-ha area," which is the total area censused by 100 m wide belts centered on each line in addition to the area between adjacent lines.

The vegetation was predominantly old second-growth northern hardwoods (Bormann and Likens 1979), dominated by American beech (*Fagus grandifolia*), sugar maple (*Acer saccharum*), and yellow birch (*Betula alleghaniensis*), with occasional white ash (*Fraxinus americana*), red spruce (*Picea rubra*), and eastern hemlock (*Tsuga canadensis*). Canopy height ranged generally between 20 and 30 m, and was taller in the stream valleys and shorter on ridges. Subcanopy vegetation was dominated by saplings of the dominant tree species as well as striped and mountain maples (*A. pensylvanicum* and *A. spicatum*, respectively). See Holmes et al. (1986) and Sherry and Holmes (1985) for additional descriptions of the study area vegetation.

Methods

In 1981–1982, redstarts were censused on the 180-ha area at Hubbard Brook, using the timed-census method of Holmes and Sturges (1975), in which we walked at a rate of 50 m/6 min along the 10 km of 100 m wide belt transects. Censusers recorded on field maps all birds detected, especially by their counter-singing behavior, and movements. Censuses were conducted four times during June, the peak breeding period of redstarts. In these two years, all territorial bird species were recorded, but effort was made to identify yearling and older male redstarts as well.

From 1983 to 1990 we made at least one complete census of the 180-ha area (and 1–2 recensuses of more densely occupied areas) during the first three weeks of June. Instead of walking at a timed rate along the center of a belt transect, we adopted the more intensive method of mapping individual territories (Holmes and Sturges 1975), which was necessary to see and age all territorial males and obtain more accurate maps of their territories. We walked systematically along transect lines, moving as necessary up to 100 m perpendicularly away from the flagged transect line. We could usually identify individual males by their distinctive breast plumage patterns (Ficken 1963), thus facilitating mapping of territorial boundaries. We spent at least 40 min/100 m of belt transect to avoid overlooking infrequently singing males (e.g., during the incubation and nestling-feeding stages of the breeding cycle), and more than 60 min/100 m wherever redstarts were abundant. Territory boundaries were estimated from data compiled onto transparent overlay sheets, by encompassing all observations of identifiable individuals, and by drawing boundaries along lines of territorial contests, or between counter-singing records or individual birds of different plumage. We searched throughout the nesting period and throughout our Hubbard Brook study area to find as many redstart nests each season as possible (relatively few nests were found in 1981–82 because of less search effort). Care was taken not to touch or otherwise

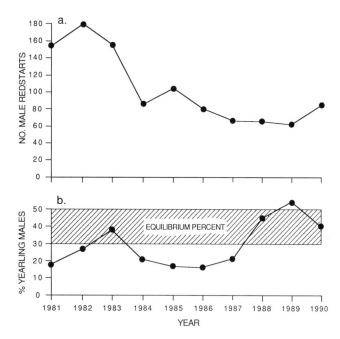

FIGURE 1. Changes in (*a*) total male American Redstart abundance and (*b*) percentage of the male population comprised of yearling individuals on the 180-ha study site in the Hubbard Brook Experimental Forest from 1981 to 1990. Equilibrium percent of yearling males is estimated from a model of a hypothetical population characterized by no annual changes in abundance, stable-age-distribution, average annual survival bounded by 50% and 70%, and maximum longevity of seven years (see text).

the modal length of combined incubation and nestling periods in redstarts (see Table 1). Nests were included in these analyses regardless of age of male (yearling vs. older male), time of the season at which found, and habitat. Nests were excluded from analyses for any of three reasons: (1) Nest failures prior to start of incubation, (2) evidence of human disturbance, or (3) outcome of nest not known. A nest was assumed to have been depredated if the entire contents of the nest disappeared between nest checks, or the nest became inactive before young had sufficient time to fledge. Nestling starvation was identified by dead nestlings (along with confirmation as often as possible that at least one parent was still alive), but its frequency was probably underestimated both because of the difficulty of examining high nests (we checked these using ladders whenever possible) and of detecting starvation of part of a brood (= "partial starvation"). A nest was considered successful if at least one young fledged. Tests of hypotheses about mean nesting success per year were based on the methods of Sauer and Williams (1989), and were conducted using the computer program "Contrast" (J.E. Hines and J.R. Sauer software, and unpubl. software documentation).

Results

American Redstart abundances, as assessed by the number of territorial males on the 180-ha study area at Hubbard Brook, have fluctuated dramatically since 1981 (Fig. 1a). However, the net trend is a strong decline beginning in 1983, and continuing until 1989. The population showed three years of increase, including a 35% increase between 1989 and 1990. The abundance of redstarts measured on only 10 ha of the 180-ha area showed similar fluctuations (Holmes et al. 1986). Moreover, redstart fluctuations on this 10-ha area were significantly correlated with abundances throughout the state of New Hampshire from Breeding-Bird Survey (BBS) data (Holmes and Sherry 1988).

Age ratios of redstarts also fluctuated during the past decade (Fig. 1b), although no net long-term trend was evident in the data. In sections that follow we explore the details and possible causes of such temporal variation in redstart abundances and age ratios.

ANNUAL VARIATION IN REDSTART AGE RATIOS

Yearling redstart males comprised from 17% to 52% of all breeding males during this study (Fig.1b), but this percentage generally remained near 20% except for four years (1983, 1988–1990) in which it was near or above 40%. To assess the significance of these fluctuations in yearling male percentages we have elsewhere (Sherry and Holmes in press) estimated that yearling

disturb the immediate surroundings of the nest site, particularly for low nests. Nests were checked every day to every few days, depending on the stage at which found (for example, a nest was checked every day if found in mid incubation, so as to determine as nearly as possible the hatch date). Nest stage was observed directly, often using a convex mirror on a telescoping pole for low nests (1–12 m), or using cues from the parents' behavior in the case of occasional high nests (12–30 m). Incubation was assumed to begin on the day the penultimate egg of the clutch was laid, or whenever the female was observed to begin sitting. Nest exposure days, and mean nest survival probabilities per day were calculated according to the methods of Mayfield (1961, 1975; see also Hensler and Nichols 1981) with modifications as described below. We quantified nesting success by what we refer to subsequently as "fledging success," that is, the probability that a nest survived the entire incubation plus nestling periods. We calculated fledging success from the average daily survival rate of nest contents. This rate was raised to the power 20, which was

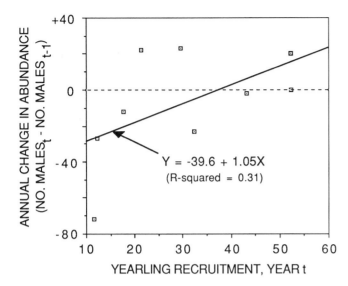

FIGURE 2. Annual changes in American Redstart population at Hubbard Brook from year t–1 to year t as a function of yearling recruitment in year t (i.e., number of yearling recruits into the population this year, as a percentage of total males in the population last year).

males should comprise 30–50% of all breeding males, as indicated by the hatched area in Fig. 1b. This range of 30–50% yearlings is based on a hypothetical ideal population characterized by a constant abundance, and constant annual survival and longevity similar to those of Hubbard Brook redstarts. Percent of yearling males was calculated from the ratio of yearlings to older males, which was itself easily calculated since frequency of males in all age classes older than yearlings could be expressed as the average annual survival probability raised to the power of the number of years survived past the first year. Annual percentage survival was estimated to lie within a range of 50–70% for males one year old or older (Sherry and Holmes in press; see also Nichols et al. 1981; Holmes and Sherry, this volume), and maximum observed longevity was seven years. The observed percentage of yearlings, however, was often lower than this range of 30–50% (Fig. 1b), suggesting that an insufficient number of yearling male redstarts was being recruited most years into the Hubbard Brook breeding population (Fig. 1b), and indeed, this total male population tended to decline between 1983 and 1987, a period when yearling recruitment was particularly low (Fig. 1a).

We next asked whether or not yearling recruitment each spring was responsible for observed changes in the total male population. In other words, was yearling recruitment an important enough influence on population dynamics to exceed the influences of other factors such

as older male dispersal or survival from year to year? We predicted that yearling recruitment and population changes would be related if either yearling males dominated the total population, which they did not in most years (Fig. 1b), or if adult survival were correlated with yearling recruitment, that is, with survival of birds to the start of the first potential breeding season. To examine effects of yearling recruitment on total population change, we first defined yearling recruitment operationally as the number of yearling males entering the population each spring expressed as a percentage of the number of adults present the preceeding year:

$$\frac{N_{YEARLING,t}}{N_{TOTAL,t-1}} \cdot 100.$$

We use the term "recruitment" here, even though yearlings returning to the study area were not generally fledged there, because we assume that rates of immigration to our study area approximately equalled emigration rates, for all age classes of males. Yearling recruitment, calculated with the above expression, was highly correlated with the percentage of yearlings in the male population (Pearson's product-moment correlation, $r = 0.91$, $P < 0.05$, 6 d.f.). We next looked at the regression of changes in the breeding male population from one year to the next, that is, the number of total males in a particular year minus the number the previous year (= $N_{TOTAL,t} - N_{TOTAL,t-1}$), against yearling male recruitment into the population in year t. Results of this analysis (Fig. 2) show weak, but not statistically significant, support for the predicted correlation of total population density changes as a function of yearling recruitment ($r = 0.56$, $P > 0.05$, 7 d.f.). We note that the two quantities in this regression are not statistically independent because they both contain the term "$N_{TOTAL,t-1}$", and so we expected them to be correlated. The fact that these two quantities were not more significantly correlated means that either we were not able to measure them accurately in the field, or that other factors (such as dispersal among populations) were obscuring the relationship (see Discussion).

ECOLOGICAL BASIS FOR ANNUAL VARIATION IN AGE RATIOS

Analyses of redstart fledging success measured in each breeding season since 1981 allowed us to evaluate the hypothesis that recruitment of yearling males into the redstart population each spring was dependent upon nesting success the previous summer. The pooled statistics from all years indicate that the probability of a given nesting attempt surviving the 20-day (average combined incubation and nestling) exposure period was close to 0.5 (Table 1), typical of many species of temperate passerines (e.g., Martin, this volume). Our figure of

TABLE 1. Nesting and fledging success statistics of American Redstarts in the Hubbard Brook Experimental Forest, New Hampshire, 1981–1989

Year	Mean nest success rates: Daily (1 S.E.)[a]	Mean nest success rates: 20 days[b]	Exposure-days[a] (Number of nests)	Percent nest losses attributable to predators[c] (Number nests lost)
1981	0.964 (0.0176)	0.480	112.0 (10)	100.0 (4)
1982	0.976 (0.0098)	0.615	245.0 (16)	100.0 (6)
1983	0.922 (0.0142)	0.197	357.0 (42)	96.4 (28)
1984	0.961 (0.0091)	0.451	459.5 (33)	55.6 (18)
1985	0.943 (0.0134)	0.309	299.0 (33)	100.0 (17)
1986	0.973 (0.0069)	0.578	548.5 (46)	86.7 (15)
1987	0.977 (0.0076)	0.628	388.5 (35)	100.0 (9)
1988	0.985 (0.0061)	0.739	396.0 (35)	100.0 (6)
1989	0.968 (0.0095)	0.522	339.5 (29)	100.0 (11)
All years	0.964 (0.0033)	0.480	3145.0 (279)	90.4 (114)

NOTE: A nest was considered successful if at least one egg or nestling survived the period under consideration.

a. Mayfield estimates of mean daily nest success rate $\pm$ 1 S.E. (= square root of variance), based on Hensler and Nichols (1981; see also Mayfield 1961, 1975). Exposure days are summed over incubation period (beginning on penultimate day of egg-laying, when most females began incubation) and nestling period.

b. The 20-day nest-success rate, i.e. fledging success, is the daily rate raised to the power 20 ($= e^{20 \cdot \log_e S}$), where S is the mean daily nest-survival rate, and e is the base of natural logarithms). Twenty days were chosen as the typical period of redstart exposure of eggs and nestlings, based on the modal values for combined incubation period (11–12 days) and nestling period (8–9 days) (T.W. Sherry and R.T. Holmes, unpubl. data).

c. Any additional losses were due to total starvation (i.e., loss of all nestlings—additional cases of partial starvation, i.e. part of brood found dead on nest, were not included in any of these figures).

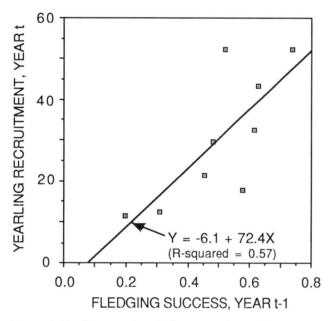

FIGURE 3. Yearling American Redstart recruitment in year t as a function of fledging success in year t–1 in the Hubbard Brook Experimental Forest, 1981–1990. Yearling recruitment is the number of yearlings returning each year, expressed as a percentage of total males in the breeding population the previous year; fledging success each year is the Mayfield estimate of mean daily nesting success raised to the power 20, giving the probability that a particular nest survived the 20-day combined incubation and nestling periods (see Table 1).

0.5 would probably be lower if we included nest failures prior to the start of incubation. Of greater significance is the fact that redstart fledging success was highly variable from year to year, ranging from 0.2 to 0.7 (Table 1). This variation was statistically significant ($\chi^2 = 23.9$, $P < 0.003$, 8 d.f.). Calculating annual fledging probabilities as the daily nesting success rate raised to the power 20 (see Table 1 and Methods) assumes that these daily probabilities were statistically independent and constant throughout the 20-day period within a particular year. In support of the latter assumption, we found no statistically significant differences of nest content survival rates during incubation vs. nestling stages, whether data were analyzed separately by year or pooled over all years (T.W. Sherry, unpubl. data).

Yearling recruitment varied from about 10% (1 yearling male entering a spring population for every 10 males in the population the previous year) to about 55%. Moreover, yearling recruitment in a given year (t) was strongly and significantly related to fledging success the previous year (t–1), with almost 60% of the variance in recruitment explained by fledging success ($R^2 = 0.57$, $P < 0.05$; Fig. 3). The likelihood that we measured these population parameters accurately is reinforced by details of the regression relationship (Fig. 3). Specifically, the y-intercept of –6.1 indicates that some minimum amount of fledging success is necessary for any measurable recruitment (i.e., recruitment > zero), which is consistent with the very reasonable notion that some birds inevitably die sometime between the time they fledge the nest and return to the breeding grounds the following spring. This regression equation predicts, in fact, that the fledging success necessary to offset this mortality exactly (the x-intercept) is 0.085, that is, more than 8.5% of nests must fledge young on average to produce any returning yearlings at all.

Causes of redstart nest failures varied annually, just as did abundance and age structure of the population. The proportion of nests whose young all died of starvation varied from 0% in most years to almost 50% in 1984. We observed partial starvation of nestlings only four times in all years of this study (three of these cases were in 1984), but the frequency of partial starvation was probably underestimated (see Methods). We included as "starvation" in Table 1 only those cases in which all nestlings starved because these cases were easier to detect than partial starvation. A probable cause of the widespread nestling starvation in 1984 was a series of heavy rainstorms during the late nestling period that year that depressed insect abundances, or reduced foraging time or success, or both. However, high rates of nestling starvation were recorded in Black-throated Blue Warblers (*Dendroica caerulescens*) at Hubbard Brook in 1984, as well as 1983 and 1985, all years of relatively low caterpillar abundance (Rodenhouse 1986), suggesting that both food abundance and weather were important causes of nestling starvation. Because of our inclusion of only those nests in which incubation had begun (see Methods), we clearly underestimated in Table 1 cases of weather-related nest losses, which tended to occur each summer early in the season, when the females made their first nest-building attempts in late May (T.W. Sherry and R.T. Holmes, unpubl. data). Despite our likely underestimation of partial starvation and weather-related nest losses early in the season, our data indicate that nest predation was the predominant cause of nest failure in most, if not all, years (Table 1).

Nest parasitism by cowbirds is rare in the forest at Hubbard Brook, and thus cannot account for any significant annual decrease in nesting success there. Of the many hundreds of nests and fledged family groups we have examined since bird studies began in 1969, we have never seen a cowbird egg in the nest of any bird species, and we have observed a host parent feeding a fledgling cowbird only twice: A female Black-throated Blue Warbler was observed feeding a cowbird along a dirt road only a few hundred meters from our study area in July 1975 (S.K. Robinson, pers. comm.); and a Yellow-rumped Warbler (*Dendroica coronata*) fed a cowbird in a forested plot on the slopes of Mount Moosilauke, within 250 m of a paved road in 1990 (D.J. North,

pers. comm.). We have rarely seen adult cowbirds in the Hubbard Brook forest during the breeding season (only during late July or August, and only in years with high caterpillar abundance—see Holmes and Sturges 1975). The distance of our study areas from non-forested habitats preferred by cowbirds probably accounts for the near absence of cowbirds there (see Brittingham and Temple 1983), although cowbirds are observed frequently in the agricultural and residential areas in surrounding valleys.

Discussion and conclusions

Our results demonstrate that the population of redstarts breeding in the Hubbard Brook Experimental Forest declined during the 1980s. This decline occurred simultaneously throughout New Hampshire (Holmes and Sherry 1988), and throughout the United States (Robbins et al. 1989) beginning about 1978. Our data also show that variation in nesting success was correlated with yearling recruitment and population dynamics of American Redstarts breeding in New Hampshire. We thus suggest that breeding season events have contributed significantly to the observed decline. Both redstarts and other avian populations at Hubbard Brook have fluctuated widely since monitoring efforts began there in 1969, and ecological conditions during the breeding period have contributed to these fluctuations (Holmes et al. 1986, in press b). Many of these population changes were correlated with long-term fluctuations in ecological conditions that were independent of human activity (see below). Declines in populations of redstarts and of other long-distance migrants that breed in less forested parts of North America than New Hampshire are alarming, however, because such declines appear to be caused by wide-scale habitat deterioration associated with human activities (Terborgh 1989, Askins et al. 1990).

In the following discussion we evaluate the relative importance of different mechanisms by which breeding season events might have operated, assess the geographic scale of their impact, and then consider methodological and conservation implications of our findings.

CAUSES OF VARIATION IN DEMOGRAPHIC PARAMETERS

The particular ecological variables influencing recruitment of yearling males into the Hubbard Brook redstart population include fledging success (Fig. 3) and, at least in some years, weather conditions and food availability during the nestling period, as suggested by the large proportion of failed nesting attempts because of starvation in 1984 (Table 1; see also Rodenhouse 1986). The strength of the relationship in Figure 3 indicates that fledging success (and thus primarily nest predators) had a stronger effect most years on yearling recruitment than did post-fledging survival or any other ecological variable in summer. Nest predation is often the primary cause of nesting failure (Martin, this volume). Other studies have found weather to have a strong negative effect on nesting success (e.g., Hejl et al. 1988; Blake et al., this volume).

Who were the nest predators? A large pool of mammals and birds preys on passerine birds' nests at Hubbard Brook (Reitsma et al. 1990), and it is not yet clear which, if any, of these predator species accounts for the majority of depredated redstart nests. That many mammal species have varied greatly in abundance from year to year (R.T. Holmes and T.W. sherry, unpubl. data) suggests that the large annual variation in nest predation rates (Table 1) resulted because total nest predator populations fluctuated in abundance. Nest parasitism was almost nonexistent in our study, unlike the situation in many other forests or forest fragments (e.g., Robinson, this volume).

Results of the present study are important because they establish a link between one ecological variable—nesting success in summer—and subsequent changes in population age-structure. To our knowledge the only other data showing that fledging success influences recruitment of yearlings into a population of long-distance migratory birds comes from Nolan's study (1978) of the Prairie Warbler (*Dendroica discolor*). He found that the percentage of females one summer was significantly correlated with the annual production of fledglings the previous summer ($R^2 = 0.69$, $n = 6$ years; p. 468). Black-throated Blue Warblers at Hubbard Brook also show a strong correlation between nesting success one year and yearling recruitment the next (Holmes et al. in press a), but more years of study are needed to be sure of this result. At extremely low levels of fledging success yearling recruitment ought to be related to fledging success the previous year, since no young can return as yearlings if they are not produced in at least some habitats or geographic areas. High fledging success, however, does not in theory guarantee high recruitment of yearling birds, because other sources of mortality could be important (e.g., mortality during the post-fledging period prior to autumn migration, autumn migration itself, winter territorial establishment, winter in the Neotropics, and spring return migration) and could vary annually independently of fledging success. That these potential sources of mortality were relatively unimportant in redstarts is suggested by the fact that almost 60% of the variation in yearling recruitment was explained by fledging success (Fig. 3). Our finding that recruitment of yearlings is highly correlated with fledging success is of added interest because it contrasts with the situation in year-round resident bird populations. In

several European species, for example, survival of young after fledging and in winter, rather than fledging success *per se*, had a dominant effect on their subsequent level of recruitment into breeding populations (e.g., Great Tit, *Parus major* —Perrins 1980; Willow Tit, *Parus montanus*—Ekman 1984; European Nuthatch, *Sitta europaea*—Nilsson 1987). More migratory and resident species must be studied, however, to generalize about similarities or differences of population processes.

Much work at Hubbard Brook suggests that food availability is also important to avian population dynamics. Greater caterpillar abundance during summer was correlated with population increases of various avian species breeding there (Holmes and Sturges 1975, Holmes et al. 1986 and in press b). Birds depleted available caterpillar resources during certain parts of the breeding season and in some years (Holmes et al. 1979), indicating that such food was not superabundant and could potentially limit production of offspring. Higher breeding season food abundance resulted in more frequent double clutching, increased nestling growth rates, and higher annual productivity of fledglings in Black-throated Blue Warblers (Rodenhouse 1986, Holmes et al. in press b). Food limitation during the breeding season is widespread in birds (Martin 1987). In redstarts we know that food is potentially important at least in some years, as indicated by the starvation recorded in 1984 (Table 1). However, the absence of double clutches in redstarts (T.W. Sherry, unpubl. data) allows less opportunity for food to influence total annual productivity of fledglings, since frequency of double-clutching in species such as the Black-throated Blue Warbler is strongly dependent on caterpillar abundance (Rodenhouse 1986, Holmes et al. in press a,b). At present we are unable to distinguish between the relative effects of nest predation and food abundance on subsequent yearling recruitment. Moreover, nest predation and food abundance might interact in complex ways (for example, high food abundance could help support nest-predator populations such as Blue Jays [*Cyanocitta cristata*] and various mammals, which could lead to a *positive relationship* between food abundance and nest predation). The problem at Hubbard Brook (and elsewhere) has been to establish not only how food or nest predators affect populations, but also to relate these effects directly to subsequent changes in population demography or abundance.

Factors other than yearling recruitment must have affected the total male redstart population, because these two variables were not significantly correlated. Our data indicate the possibility of "source-and-sink" dynamics of local populations in the White Mountains of New Hampshire (e.g., Pulliam 1988). This model proposes that populations in some habitats or areas ("sinks") are maintained by immigration from other populations producing a surplus of individuals ("sources"). Since we began in 1984 to color-band nearly all male redstarts on a 34-ha part of our study area, as many as 50% of the two-year-and-older males defending territories have been unbanded birds (T.W. Sherry and R.T. Holmes, unpubl. data), indicating considerable immigration from wherever these birds displayed territories and/or nested the previous summer. A related factor is that over 50% of yearling male redstarts present each summer have remained unmated throughout the summer (Sherry and Holmes 1989; T.W. Sherry, unpubl. data), and some newly arriving two-year-and-older male redstarts on our study area each summer might represent birds that were unmated yearlings the previous summer. Elsewhere in North America, habitats or regions with abnormally high rates of nest losses because of either high nest predation or brood parasitism appear to be habitat sinks for susceptible, especially open-cup nesting, migrant populations, whereby such populations are maintained by continual input from heavily forested areas (Temple and Cary 1988; Leck et al. 1988; Robinson, this volume).

SCALE OF ESTIMATING POPULATION PARAMETERS

The relationship we have documented between yearling recruitment and nesting success the previous year might have been possible largely because we could obtain estimates of these two parameters that were both sufficiently accurate and broadly representative of surrounding regions. We base this argument on four observations: (1) Yearlings recruited onto our study area must have come from nests in a region far larger than our study area, based on the low percentages of nestlings banded on the study area that returned as yearlings. Of the 161 redstart nestlings we banded between 1983 and 1988, we recorded only one individual (0.6%) returning to our study area, and other studies on migratory passerines have recorded similarly low levels of 1–10% annual returns on banded nestlings (Nolan 1978, Drilling and Thompson 1988, Wolf et al. 1988). (2) At least some population parameters in these highly vagile migratory birds are spatially replicable even on study areas an order of magnitude smaller than our 180-ha study area: Total abundances of redstarts, and of the majority of other migratory passerines breeding on a 10-ha study area at Hubbard Brook, were significantly correlated with estimates of their abundances throughout New Hampshire over the period 1969–1986 (Holmes and Sherry 1988). This observation indicates that individuals within a redstart population are vagile enough to be distributed evenly among all suitable habitat each season. Thus these birds appear to have evolved efficient (optimal?) ability to find suitable nest-

ing habitat each season. (3) If different age classes are vagile enough to distribute themselves among suitable habitat patches, just as the entire population appears to be, then our 180-ha study area was certainly large enough to obtain a reliable estimate of yearling relative abundance in our population each year, and thus of yearling recruitment. Males compete vigorously for relatively preferred, deciduous habitats (Sherry and Holmes 1989, unpubl. data), and this competition via territorial behavior probably provides the mechanism by which individuals become widely dispersed across suitable habitat within a region. Our estimates of male age structure were spatially repeatable within each year even among subsets of our total study area (Sherry and Holmes in press). (4) Nesting success estimated by our samples of nests might also have been broadly representative of conditions prevailing in surrounding northern New England forests each summer (see Nolan 1978, p. 469, for a similar argument in Prairie Warblers). Nesting success is overwhelmingly influenced by nest predators in these migratory birds (Ricklefs 1969; Martin, this volume), and the probability a nest was depredated probably depended far more on the abundances of nest predators than on changing food demand by the same total population of predators or on the ability of particular birds to find safe nesting sites. The kinds of ecological factors that influence nest predator populations (winter weather, mast seed crops of tree species), moreover, are typically broadly regional in scale. One limitation of our study is that we quantified redstart age structure using only males, and we cannot yet evaluate how applicable our male findings might have been to females. We do not yet have an efficient means of catching and aging females in large enough numbers to give us meaningful results.

Some evidence from wintering populations of redstarts supports the conclusion that population parameters estimated within a particular year are broadly representative over a large region. Redstarts wintering in Jamaica are highly territorial (Holmes et al. 1989; Holmes and Sherry, this volume), providing a mechanism by which redstarts could become widely dispersed across suitable habitat, and percentages that yearling males comprised of total males were relatively similar within years in the various Jamaican study sites studied (R.T. Holmes and T.W. Sherry, unpubl. data). We note a fascinating correlation between Faaborg and Arendt's (this volume) redstart spring abundances in Guánica, Puerto Rico, and our 180-ha study area at Hubbard Brook during the nine years, 1981–1989 (Pearson's product-moment correlation $r = 0.84$, $P < 0.01$, 7 d.f.). It is unlikely that this correlation is coincidental. Rather, we argue that the data might instead reflect very broad regional declines of redstart populations, although the ecological causes of the declines apparently vary from one region of the redstart breeding range to another (see below).

CONSERVATION IMPLICATIONS

Our results provide strong evidence for a link between poor nesting success in migrant songbirds, that is, between breeding season events and subsequent population declines. First, we have documented such a correlation within a heavily forested landscape where habitat fragmentation has not occurred to any significant extent. Our results thus provide independent corroboration for the widely cited correlation between population declines and decreased nesting success in fragmented landscapes (Whitcomb et al. 1981, Wilcove 1985; reviews in Terborgh 1989, Askins et al. 1990). In the forested Hubbard Brook landscape, however, we envision the redstart population decline as a result of natural long-term fluctuations in nest predator abundances and weather conditions, rather than as any direct manifestation of human activities.

Second, and more importantly, our results help establish a cause-and-effect relationship between many of these population declines recently documented elsewhere in North American migratory passerines and poor nesting success. Habitat fragmentation and certain agricultural practices have resulted in increased nest parasitism by Brown-headed Cowbirds (Mayfield 1978, Brittingham and Temple 1983), and several species have experienced reduced nesting success attributable to cowbird parasitism (e.g., Probst 1986; Robinson, this volume). Redstarts are susceptible to both cowbird parasitism (Baker 1944, Ficken 1961, Brittingham and Temple 1983) and to nest predation because their nests are open cups, often near the ground. Redstart populations have declined in landscapes of fragmented forest (Robbins 1979, Whitcomb et al. 1981, Johnston and Winings 1987, Robbins et al. 1989). We have documented here for the Hubbard Brook study site a relationship in redstarts between poor nesting success in several years and low availability of yearling birds to maintain the population in the subsequent years. If we extrapolate this relationship to other regions of North America, and assume only that yearling recruitment is generally proportional to nesting success the previous year, then the declines elsewhere than Hubbard Brook must be the result at least in part of sustained periods of reduced nesting success. Reduced nesting success has not been documented to our knowledge in redstarts that breed in fragmented forest landscapes, but has been documented in a variety of migratory species occupying edge habitats or isolated forest patches (Mayfield 1978; Brittingham and Temple 1983; Temple and Carey 1988; Robinson, this volume), and in numerous artificial nest

experiments (e.g., Wilcove 1985, Andrén and Angelstam 1988, Small and Hunter 1988, Yahner and Scott 1988). Low yearling recruitment in regions with fragmented breeding habitat (Leck et al. 1988; Temple and Cary 1988; Robinson, this volume) also support the idea that poor reproduction in such areas contributes to population declines. Admittedly, more data are needed to assess the generality of these findings to other regions and species. What data are available nonetheless allow us to conclude that deterioration or loss of suitable nesting habitat in North America must be considered an important cause of redstart and other migrant population declines. The implication of this conclusion is that preservation of North American breeding habitats is necessary to maintain populations of migratory forest passerines.

Our findings do not rule out the possibility that habitat loss or deterioration elsewhere than the breeding grounds has not also contributed to migratory bird population declines. Deforestation in the Neotropics where many migrants spend the winter also appears to be causing significant declines of some forest-inhabiting migrants (reviewed by Robbins et al. 1989, Terborgh 1989, Askins et al. 1990), and ecological conditions along the Gulf of Mexico, where these migrants make landfall in spring may also be important (Moore 1990, Moore and Yong 1991). In Jamaica, where redstarts are abundant during winter (Holmes et al. 1989), they are widely distributed in different habitats, as are most other migrant bird populations there, and appear to be nearly as abundant in many human-disturbed habitats as in old-growth forests (A. Sliwa, unpubl. data). Thus, to the extent that deforestation has occurred in Jamaica to date, it appears to have had less effect on redstart populations than loss of suitable breeding habitat in North America. Other regions where redstarts winter might have experienced severe enough habitat deterioration to have affected local populations.

Acknowledgments

For their invaluable help studying redstarts in the field over the years we thank Rob Brumfield, Mario Cohn-Haft, Randall Detmers, Walter Ellison, Laura Greffenius, Irby Lovette, Kevin Omland, Ken petit, Elizabeth Proctor-Gray, Leonard Reitsma, George Roderick, Daniel Schell, Scott Schwenk, Robert Secunda, Carl Seielstad, Michael Serio, Franklin W. Sturges, Carol Von Dolan, Ginger Wallis, Elizabeth Webb, Todd Wilkinson, and Peter Yaukey. Tom Martin made helpful suggestions concerning anlyses of nesting success. John Hagan, David Johnston, Doug Levey, Val Nolan, and an anonymous reviewer made numerous helpful suggestions on the manuscript. We gratefully acknowledge Robert Pierce and Wayne Martin of the Northeast Forest Experiment Station, United States Forest Service, for their continued logistic support and cooperation in the Hubbard Brook Experimental Forest over the many years of this study. Our research has been financially supported by grants from the National Science Foundation to Dartmouth College and Tulane University.

Literature cited

Andrén, H., and P. Angelstam. 1988. Elevated predation rates as an edge effect in habitat islands: Experimental evidence. *Ecology* 69:544–547.

Askins, R.A., J.F. Lynch, and R. Greenberg. 1990. Population declines in migratory birds in eastern North America. *Current Ornithol.* 7:1–57.

Askins, R.A., and M.J. Philbrick. 1987. Effect of changes in regional forest abundance on the decline and recovery of a forest bird community. *Wilson Bull* 99:7–21.

Baker, B.W. 1944. Nesting of the American redstart. *Wilson Bull.* 56:83–90.

Bormann, F.H., and G.E. Likens. 1979. *Pattern and Process in a Forested Ecosystem.* New York: Springer-Verlag.

Brittingham, M.C., and S.A. Temple. 1983. Have cowbirds caused forest songbirds to decline? *BioScience* 33:31–35.

Drilling, N.E., and C.F. Thompson. 1988. Natal and breeding dispersal in House Wrens (*Troglodytes aedon*). *Auk* 105:480–491.

Ekman, J. 1984. Density-dependent seasonal mortality and population fluctuations of the temperate-zone willow tit (*Parus montanus*). *J. Anim. Ecol.* 53:119–134.

Ficken, M.S. 1961. Redstarts and cowbirds. *Kingbird* 11:83–85.

———. 1962. Maintenance activities of the American Redstart. *Wilson Bull.* 74:153–165.

———. 1963. Courtship of the American redstart. *Auk* 80:307–317.

Ficken, M.S., and R.W. Ficken. 1967. Age specific differences in the breeding behavior and ecology of the American Redstart. *Wilson Bull.* 79:188–199.

Fretwell, S. 1986. Distribution and abundance of the Dickcissel. *Current Ornithol.* 4:211–242.

Hejl, S.J., J. Verner, and R.P. Balda 1988. Weather and bird populations in true fir forests of the Sierra Nevada, California. *Condor* 90:561–574.

Hensler, G.L., and J.D. Nichols. 1981. The Mayfield method of estimating nesting success: A model, estimators and simulation results. *Wilson Bull.* 93:42–53.

Herrera, C.M. 1978. On the breeding distribution patterns of European migrant birds: MacArthur's theme reexamined. *Auk* 95:496–509.

Holmes, R.T., J.C. Schultz, and P. Nothnagle. 1979. Bird predation on forest insects: An exclosure experiment. *Science* 206:462–463.

Holmes, R.T., and T.W. Sherry. 1988. Assessing population trends of New Hampshire forest birds: Local vs. regional patterns. *Auk* 105:756–768.

Holmes, R.T., and F.W. Sturges. 1975. Bird community dynam-

ics and energetics in a northern hardwoods ecosystem. *J. Anim. Ecol.* 44:175–200.

Holmes, R.T., T.W. Sherry, P.P. Marra, and K.E. Petit. In press a. Multiple-brooding, nesting success, and annual productivity of a Neotropical migrant, the Black-throated Blue Warbler (*Dendroica caerulescens*), in an unfragmented temperate forest. *Auk.*

Holmes, R.T., T.W. Sherry, and L. Reitsma. 1989. Population structure, territoriality and overwinter survival of two migrant warbler species in Jamaica. *Condor* 91:545–561.

Holmes, R.T., T.W. Sherry, and F.W. Sturges. 1986. Bird community dynamics in a temperate deciduous forest: Longterm trends at Hubbard Brook. *Ecol. Monogr.* 50:201–220.

———. In press b. Numerical and demographic responses of temperate forest birds to annual fluctuations in their food resources. *Proc. 20th Intern. Ornithol. Cong.*

Hutto, R.L. 1988. Is tropical deforestation responsible for the reported declines in neotropical migrant populations? *Am. Birds* 42:375–379.

Ickes, R.A., and M.S. Ficken. 1970. An investigation of territorial behavior in the American Redstart utilizing recorded songs. *Wilson Bull.* 82:167–176.

Johnston, D.W., and D.I. Winings. 1987. Natural history of Plummers Island, Maryland. XXVII. The decline of forest breeding birds on Plummers Island, Maryland, and vicinity. *Proc. Biol. Soc. Wash.* 100:762–768.

Leck, C.F., B.G. Murray, Jr., and J. Swinebroad. 1988. Longterm changes in the breeding bird populations of a New Jersey forest. *Biol. Conserv.* 46:145–157.

MacArthur, R.H. 1959. On the breeding distribution patterns of North American migrant birds. *Auk* 76:318–325.

Martin, T.E. 1987. Food as a limit on breeding birds: A life history perspective. *Ann. Rev. Ecol. Syst.* 19:453–487.

Mayfield, H.F. 1961. Nesting success calculated from exposure. *Wilson Bull.* 73:255–261.

———. 1975. Suggestions for calculating nesting success. *Wilson Bull.* 87:456–466.

———. 1978. Brood parasitism: Reducing interactions between Kirtland's Warblers and Brown-headed Cowbirds. Pages 85–91 in *Endangered Birds: Management Techniques for Preserving Threatened Species*, S.A. Temple, ed. Madison: University of Wisconsin Press.

Moore, F.R., and W. Yong. 1991. Evidence of food-based competition among passerine migrants during stopover. *Behav. Ecol. Sociobiol.* 28:85–90.

Moore, F.R., P. Kerlinger, and T.R. Simons. Stopover on a gulf coast barrier island by spring trans-gulf migrants. *Wilson Bull.* 102:487–500.

Nichols, J.D., B.R. Noon, S.L. Stokes, and J.E. Hines. 1981. Remarks on the use of mark-recapture methodology in estimating avian population size. Pages 121–136 in *Estimating Numbers of Terrestrial Birds*, C.J. Ralph and M.J. Scott, eds. Studies in Avian Biology No. 6.

Nilsson, S.G. 1987. Limitation and regulation of population density in the nuthatch *Sitta europaea* (Aves) breeding in natural cavities. *J. Anim. Ecol.* 56:921–937.

Nolan, V., Jr. 1978. *The ecology and behavior of the Prairie Warbler Dendroica discolor.* Ornithol. Monogr. 26.

O'Connor, R.J. 1980. Population regulation in the Yellowhammer *Emberiza citrinella*. Pages 190–200 in *Bird Census Work and Nature Conservation*, H. Oelke, ed. [International Conference on Bird Census Work.] Lengede, FRG: Dachverbandes Deutscher Avifaunisten.

———. 1981. Comparisons between migrant and non-migrant birds in Britain. Pages 167–195 in *Animal Migration*, D.J. Aidley, ed. Soc. Exp. Biol. Seminar Series 13, Cambridge: Cambridge University Press.

———. 1985. Behavioural regulation of bird populations: A review of habitat use in relation to migration and residency. Pages 105–142 in *Behavioural Ecology: Ecological Consequences of Adaptive Behavior*, R.M. Sibly and R.H. Smith, eds. Oxford: Blackwell Scientific Publications.

Perrins, C.M. 1980. Survival of young Great Tits, *Parus major. Acta 17th Internat. Ornithol. Cong.* (Berlin): 159–174.

Probst, J.R. 1986. A review of factors limiting the Kirtland's Warbler on its breeding grounds. *Am. Midl. Nat.* 116:87–100.

Pulliam, H.R. 1988. Sources, sinks, and population regulation. *Am. Nat.* 132:652–661.

Rappole, J.H., M.A. Ramos, and K. Winker. 1989. Wintering Wood Thrush movements and mortality in southern Veracruz. *Auk* 106:402–410.

Reitsma, L.R., R.T. Holmes, and T.W. Sherry. 1990. Effects of removal of red squirrels, *Tamiasciurus hudsonicus*, and eastern chipmunks, *Tamias striatus*, on nest predation in a northern hardwood forest: An artificial nest experiment. *Oikos* 57:375–380.

Ricklefs, R.E. 1969. *An Analysis of Nesting Mortality in Birds*. Smithsonian Contrib. Zool. 9.

Robbins, C.S. 1979. Effect of forest fragmentation on bird populations. Pages 33–48 in *Management of Northcentral and Northeastern Forests for Non-game Birds*, R.M. DeGraaf and K.E. Evans, eds. North Central Forest Exp. Stn. Publ. U.S. Forest Service, Minnesota.

Robbins, C.S., J.R. Sauer, R.S. Greenberg, and S. Droege. 1989. Population declines in North American birds that migrate to the neotropics. *Proc. Natl. Acad. Sci.* 86:7658–7662.

Robinson, S.K. 1988. Reappraisal of the costs and benefits of habitat heterogeneity for nongame wildlife. *Trans. N.A. Wildl. Nat. Res. Conf.* 53:145–155.

Rodenhouse, N.L. 1986. Food limitation for forest passerines: Effects of natural and experimental food reductions. Ph.D. Dissertation, Dartmouth College, Hanover, New Hampshire.

Rohwer, S., W.P. Klein, Jr., and S. Heard. 1983. Delayed plumage maturation and the presumed prealternate molt in American Redstarts. *Wilson Bull.* 95:199–208.

Sauer, J.R., and B.K. Williams. 1989. Generalized procedures for testing hypotheses about survival or recovery rates. *J. Wildl. Manage.* 53:137–142.

Sherry, T.W., and R.T. Holmes. 1985. Dispersion patterns and habitat responses of birds in northern hardwoods forests. Pages 289–309 in *Habitat Selection in Birds*, M.L. Cody, ed. New York: Academic Press, Inc.

———. 1989. Age-specific social dominance affects habitat use by breeding American redstarts (*Setophaga ruticilla*): A removal experiment. *Behav. Ecol. Sociobiol.* 25:327–333

———. In press. Population age-structure of long-distance migratory passerine birds: Variation in time and space. *Proc. 20th Internat. Ornithol. Cong.*

Small, M.F., and M.L. Hunter. 1988. Forest fragmentation and avian nest predation in forested landscapes. *Oecologia* 76:62–64.

Temple, S.A., and J.R. Cary. 1988. Modelling dynamics of habitat-interior bird populations in fragmented landscapes. *Conserv. Biol.* 2:340–347.

Terborgh, J. 1989. *Where Have All the Birds Gone?* Princeton: Princeton University Press.

Walkinshaw, L.H. 1983. *The Kirtland's Warbler.* Bloomfield Hills, Mich.: Cranbrook Institute of Science.

Whitcomb, R.F., C.S. Robbins, J.F. Lynch, B.L. Whitcomb, M.K. Klimkiewicz, and D. Bystrak. 1981. Effects of forest fragmentation on the avifauna of the eastern deciduous forest. Pages 125–205 in *Forest Island Dynamics in Man-dominated Landscapes*, R.L. Burgess and D.M. Sharpe, eds. New York: Springer-Verlag.

Wilcove, D.S. 1985. Nest predation in forest tracts and the decline of migratory songbirds. *Ecology* 66:1211–1214.

Wilcove, D.S. 1988. Changes in the avifauna of the Great Smoky Mountains: 1947–1983. *Wilson Bull.* 100:256–271.

Wilcove, D.S., C.H. McLellan, and A.P. Dobson. 1986. Habitat fragmentation in the temperate zone. Pages 237–256 in *Conservation Biology: The Science of Scarcity and Diversity*, M.E. Soulé, ed. Sunderland, Mass.: Sinauer Associates Inc.

Wolf, L., E.D. Ketterson, and V. Nolan, Jr. 1988. Paternal influence on growth and survival of Dark-eyed Junco young: Do parental males benefit? *Anim. Behav.* 36:1601–1618.

Yahner, R.H. and D.P. Scott. 1988. Effects of forest fragmentation on depredation of artificial nests. *J. Wildl. Manage.* 52:158–161

KATHRYN FREEMARK
BRIAN COLLINS
Environment Canada
Canadian Wildlife Service
Ottawa, Ontario, Canada K1A 0H3

Landscape ecology of birds breeding in temperate forest fragments

Abstract. We compared bird species numbers in a range of forest sizes (1.8–65 ha) replicated among two study areas in Ontario, and one each in Missouri and Illinois, to examine the importance of differences in landscape context of their forests. Regression parameters for numbers of edge species against forest size were not significantly different among study areas. Regression slopes were not significantly different for numbers of interior-edge species against forest size, but the 3-ha regression estimate was significantly lower for the study area with the most forest cover. Few forest-interior species, many of which overwinter in the Neotropics, were found in small-sized forests (particularly those < 10 ha) in any study area. At least one-half of the regional pool of area-sensitive species was observed in 54–65-ha forests annually. The study area with the most forest cover had the highest number of area-sensitive species per forest, and the greatest increase in numbers of forest-interior species as forest size increased. Differences in numbers of area-sensitive or forest-interior species per forest among the other study areas in relation to landscape context were not clear. A better understanding of the relation between landscape structure and the distribution and survival of species is an important prerequisite for developing and implementing effective conservation plans for birds breeding in temperate forest fragments.

Sinopsis. Nosotros comparamos números de especies de aves en una variedad de tamaños de bosques (1.8–65 ha) replicados en dos áreas de estudio en Ontario, una en Missouri y una en Illinois para examinar la importancia de diferencias en el contexto del paisaje de sus bosques. Los parámetros de regresión para los números de especies de borde contra el tamaño del bosque no fueron significativamente diferentes de aquellos de especies de interior contra la misma variable, pero los estimativos de regresión para 3 ha fueron significativamente mas bajos para el área de estudio con el máximo de cobertura de bosque. Pocas especies de interior de bosque, muchas de las cuales invernan en el Neotrópico, fueron encontradas en bosques de tamaño pequeño (particularmente aquellos < 10 ha) en cualquier área de estudio. Por lo menos la mitad del conjunto regional de especies sensitivas al área fue observado en bosques de 54–65 ha anualmente. El área de estudio con el máximo de cobertura de bosque tuvo el número mas alto de especies sensitivas al área por bosque y el mayor incremento en números de especies de interior a medida que aumentaba el área de bosque. Las diferencias en los números de especies sensitivas al área o especies de interior por bosque entre las otras áreas de estudio en relación con el contexto del paisaje no fueron claras. Una mejor comprensión de la relación entre la estructura del paisaje y la distribución y supervivencia de las especies es un prerrequisito importante para el desarrollo y la implementación de planes de conservación efectivos para aves anidantes en fragmentos de bosques templados.

Landscape ecology is the study of spatial patterns and how they develop through natural or human influences (Naveh and Leiberman 1984, Risser et al. 1984, Forman and Godron 1986, Moss 1988). The distribution and local abundance of birds in fragments of eastern deciduous forest in North America have been especially well studied (reviewed by Robbins et al. 1989, Askins et al. 1990). Forest size is generally a primary correlate with the species richness and composition of breeding bird assemblages. Smaller forest fragments contain a nonrandom subset of the species pool found in larger forests. Many bird species that are uncommon in smaller forests (i.e., are area sensitive) overwinter in the Neotropics, and/or typically breed only in forest-interior habitats. Habitat characteristics of forests, although correlated with the density of individual species, are generally secondarily important to the richness, composition, and total density of forest-interior or Neotropical migrant species. Several studies have suggested that the richness of area-sensitive species is correlated with the proportion of forest nearby, or the proximity to larger forests (i.e., the landscape context). Their results were inconclusive because most of the measures of forest isolation were correlated with forest size, confounding statistical analyses of their relative importance.

In this paper, we examine the relationship between bird species richness and composition, and forest size and landscape context. We compare linear regressions of bird species number on forest sizes replicated between two study areas in eastern Ontario which differed in the extent and isolation of their forests. Data reported in the literature were reanalyzed for one area. Because of the survey methods used and the observed similarity in regional bird species composition, differences in regression parameters between study areas were judged to reflect differences in landscape context of forests rather than differences in forest size, habitat heterogeneity, or the bird species pool (Martin 1981). Published data on birds in fragmented deciduous forests

in Missouri and Illinois were reanalyzed and compared with those from our study areas in order to increase the sample of landscape contexts.

Methods

ONTARIO. We compared the distribution of forest birds between two study areas, 40 km apart and west of Ottawa, Ontario, Canada (approximately 45° N, 76° W). Muchoki (1988) characterized the landscape context for a sample of 3–220-ha forest fragments in each area (Table 1). The study area with more agriculture, hereafter ON(A), had less forest, of which about one-half was extensive forest. Forest fragments were more numerous, farther apart, and had fewer hedgerow connections. The farmland was primarily cropped for corn. Data for 16 forests (3–7,620 ha) studied by Freemark and Merriam (1986) were reanalyzed for ON(A). The study area with more forest, hereafter ON(F), had less agriculture, and about three-quarters of its forest cover as extensive forest. The farmland was primarily cropped for hay. We studied 13 forests (3–8,600 ha) in ON(F). In both ON(A) and ON(F), only mature upland deciduous or mixed forests (presence of trees > 36 cm dbh) were studied. Each forest fragment had a relatively continuous canopy, well-developed understory, low perimeter-to-area ratio, was relatively undisturbed, and usually separated from other forests by at least 100 m (but occasionally by as little as 20 m).

Birds were sampled using unlimited-distance point counts conducted twice during the breeding season (late May–early July) (details in Freemark and Merriam 1986). Sampling effort increased with forest size as follows: one 30-min count for 3–8-ha forests; two 20-min counts for 13–14-ha forests; three 20-min counts for 16–23-ha forests; four 15-min counts for 27–44-ha forests; five 15-min counts for 58–79-ha forests; six 15-min counts for forests > 79 ha. The total number of species was accumulated across points within a forest in each year. Data were reanalyzed for forests in ON(A) surveyed in 1980–1981 by Freemark and Merriam (1986). We surveyed forests in ON(F) in 1984 and 1988–1989.

ILLINOIS. Blake (1983) and Blake and Karr (1982, 1984, 1987) studied birds in 15 forests (1.8–600 ha) located in Champaign, Macon, McLean and Piatt counties in east-central Illinois during the 1979–1981 breeding seasons. Forest cover averaged 2.1% (range 1.4–2.4) for these counties in 1985 (calculated from Iverson et al. 1989). These forests were separated by many kilometres of cropland and fields. Both upland forests dominated by sugar maple (*Acer saccharum*) and bottomland forests dominated by silver maple (*A. saccharinum*) were included. The occurrence of oaks (*Quercus* spp.), shagbark

TABLE 1. Landscape context of forest fragments in study areas near Ottawa, Ontario, Canada

	ON (F)	ON(A)
STUDY AREA (km^2)	400	450
FARMLAND[a]		
Corn (%)	16	34
Small grains (%)	6	15
Hay (%)	28	18
Total (%)	50	67
FOREST		
Total (%)[a]	30	19
Proportion as extensive[b] forest[a]	0.73	0.58
Distance between extensive[b] forest[a]	3	16
No. isolated[b] forests[a]	17	54
Distance between forests[c] (m, mean ± SD)	256±74	401±170
Hedgerows abutting forest[c] (m, mean ± SD)	585±486	449±375

SOURCE: Muchoki 1988.

a. Measured from LANDSAT TM imagery encompassing 4–220-ha forests in ON(A) and 3–175-ha forests in ON(F).

b. Undefined.

c. Measured from gridded overlays on air photos of 8 forests of 4–220-ha in ON(A) and 3–175-ha in ON(F).

hickory (*Carya ovata*), hawthorn (*Crataegus* spp.) and cherry (*Prunus serotina*) varied significantly among forests. Each forest had a mature canopy, a well-developed understory, and was relatively undisturbed. Differences in habitat that existed among and within forests were not closely related to forest size (Blake and Karr 1987). Birds were surveyed at least three times each year using 15-min point counts at a sampling intensity similar to our study in Ontario. The total number of species was accumulated across points within a forest in each year.

MISSOURI. Hayden (1985) and Hayden et al. (1985) studied birds in 15 forests (1.2 to > 1,000 ha) located in Audrain, Boone, and Callaway counties in central Missouri during the 1983–1984 breeding seasons. Forest cover averaged 22% for these counties in 1984 (Giessman et al. 1986). The forests studied were separated by cropland or pasture. Distances between forests were usually > 200 m. Relatively mature, undisturbed upland deciduous forests dominated by oak (*Quercus* spp.) and hickory (*Carya* spp.) were studied. Birds were surveyed by systematically traversing the interior and edge of forests at least three times each year. Mist netting was also used in some forests but added only one species not observed during traverse surveys.

OTHER AREAS. Studies by Askins et al. (1987) in Connecticut and Whitcomb et al. (1981), Robbins et al.

(1989), and Lynch and Whigham (1984) in Maryland and adjacent states were not included because of low sampling intensity in larger forests. The study by Howe (1984) in Wisconsin was not included because of the small size and restricted size-range of forest fragments studied. Studies by Ambuel and Temple (1983) and Temple (1986) in Wisconsin, and Galli et al. (1976), and Forman et al. (1976) in New Jersey were not included because data were not readily available.

BIRD SPECIES COMPOSITION. We included all bird species heard or seen (except those only flying over forests) in Ontario comparisons. We excluded the following in comparisons with Missouri and Illinois: raptors, nocturnal species, crepuscular species, aerial insectivores (e.g. swifts, swallows), crows, shorebirds, and waterfowl.

We categorized bird species according to habitat use, area sensitivity, and migratory strategy (Appendix 1). While habitat use and area sensitivity of species may vary from one region to another, we used a single designation in each category for each species to examine relationships among study areas with different landscape characteristics (primarily forest cover).

Habitat use was based on spot-mapping and point-count data (Whitcomb et al. 1981; Blake and Karr 1984, 1987; Hayden et al. 1985; Freemark and Merriam 1986; Askins et al. 1987) and was defined as follows: (1) forest-interior species nest only within the interior of forests and rarely occur near the edge; (2) interior-edge

TABLE 2. Composition of forest birds compared between study areas in Ontario for all forest sizes combined. See Appendix 1 for details on bird species

Composition	Mean no. species per year (± SD)		Mean annual % species different (±SD)
	ON(F)	ON(A)	
Total species pool	65.3 (2.5)	62.5 (2.1)	11.2 (1.2)
Habitat use			
Forest–Interior	24.3 (1.2)	19.5 (0.7)	14.1 (2.6)
Interior–Edge	17.0 (1.0)	17.0 (0.0)	7.8 (4.0)
Edge	24.0 (1.7)	26.0 (1.4)	10.6 (2.2)
Area sensitivity			
Sensitive	24.0 (1.0)	22.0 (0.0)	5.1 (1.7)
Insensitive	22.0 (1.0)	24.5 (2.1)	7.5 (2.2)
Unknown	19.3 (2.3)	16.0 (0.0)	23.7 (3.1)
No. Forests studied	13	16	–
Size Range (ha)	3–8600	3–7620	–
Median size (ha)	17.0	24.5	–
No. Years	3	2	–
Forest Cover	30	19	–

species have territories located entirely within the forest, but can also utilize forest edge, or in some cases, can extend a single territory across more than one forest fragment; (3) edge species typically use forest perimeters, nearby fields, or large clearings within a forest during the breeding season. Of the 91 species included in comparisons among all study areas, only two forest-interior, four interior-edge, and one edge species were classified differently among the references used (Appendix 1).

Area sensitivity has been determined by statistical analyses (e.g., chi-square, logistic regression) of a species distribution across a size range of forests during the breeding season (Blake and Karr 1987, Hayden et al. 1985, Temple 1986, Askins et al. 1987, Robbins et al. 1989) and is defined as follows: (1) sensitive species occur more frequently or increase in density as forest size increases; (2) insensitive species are as likely to occur in small forests as larger forests; (3) unknown species have not had sufficient sample sizes to determine their area sensitivity. Of the 69 species included in comparisons among all study areas and for which information on area sensitivity was available, 11 sensitive and 5 insensitive species were classified differently among the references used (Appendix 1).

Biological explanations for differences in a species classification in the existing literature (including the types of factors we are examining) require further study. In the interim, we resolved discrepancies based on the number of studies with the same designation. When the number of studies with different designations was equal, the species was categorized in order to introduce the least potential bias in the analyses (e.g., categorizing a species as area sensitive when perhaps it was not).

Migratory strategy was categorized as reported for each study area and is defined as follows: (1) resident species remain in the study area throughout the year, with, at most, small-scale movements; (2) short-distance species winter south of the study area but north of the tropics; (3) Neotropical migrant species winter in tropical and subtropical regions of Central and South America.

STATISTICAL ANALYSES. We evaluated species-area relationships among study areas by analysis of variance using the GLM procedure (SAS Institute 1988). Forest area was log transformed to reduce skewness. Comparisons were restricted to 1.8–65-ha forest fragments because the number and size of fragments in this size range were similar among study areas, had the most rapid increase in total species number, and, therefore, were most likely to reflect differences in landscape context.

The data were analyzed using a linear model with terms for study area, log(forest size) and their interaction term after we determined that averaging data across years for individual forest fragments did not affect our results. The slope and number of bird species for a 3-ha forest were estimated from the regression for each study area. The number of bird species for a 3-ha forest was calculated because it was the smallest fragment size common to all study areas and therefore provided a more precise estimate than extrapolating to the y-intercept. Multiple comparisons of regression parameters among study areas were done using the stepwise Bonferonni *t*-test (Miller 1981) using a 5% significance level.

Results

ONTARIO. The mean numbers of bird species detected annually were similar between study areas with generally less than a 14% difference in species composition (Table 2). About one-half of the 27 forest-interior species observed overwinter in the Neotropics (Appendix 1). About 60% of the area-sensitive species observed typically nest in forest-interior habitats, and about 75% overwinter in the Neotropics. Information on area sensitivity was lacking for many species in Ontario.

The total number of bird species increased with forest size in both study areas (Fig. 1A). Regression parameters were not significantly different. The number of edge species was not significantly related to forest size in either study area and regression parameters were not significantly different (Fig. 1B). The number of interior-edge species increased with forest size in both study areas (Fig. 1C). Regression slopes were not significantly different, but the 3-ha regression estimate for ON(A) was significantly higher than that for ON(F). The number of forest-interior species also increased significantly with forest size in both study areas (Fig. 1D). The 3-ha regression estimates were not significantly different. Few forest-interior species were found in smaller forests, particularly those less than 10 ha, in either study area. Regression slopes were significantly different between study areas. The number of forest-interior species increased more quickly as forest size increased in ON(F), the landscape in which forests were more extensive and less isolated.

The number of area-sensitive species increased significantly with larger forest size in both study areas (Fig. 1E). Regression slopes were not significantly different. The significant difference in the 3-ha estimate indicated that forest fragments in ON(F) had more area-sensitive species than those in ON(A). In both study areas, about 66% of the regional pool of area-sensitive species was observed in the largest forest fragment (54–58 ha) annually.

COMPARISONS WITH MISSOURI (MO) AND ILLINOIS (IL). MO and IL had smaller species pools than ON(F) and ON(A), particularly of forest-interior species (Table 3). Twenty of the 30 forest-interior species reported overwinter in the Neotropics (Appendix 1). Twenty of the 33 area-sensitive species typically nest in forest interiors, and 26 overwinter in the Neotropics.

The total number of bird species increased with forest size in all study areas (Fig. 2). The 3-ha regression

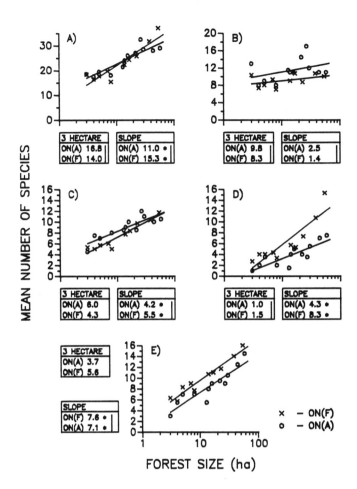

FIGURE 1. Comparisons of linear regressions of mean number of (*A*) all bird species, (*B*) edge species, (*C*) interior-edge species, (*D*) forest-interior species, and (*E*) area-sensitive species on forest size for study areas ON(F) and ON(A) near Ottawa, Ontario, Canada. Regression slopes are given in the *SLOPE* box. Regression estimates for a 3-ha forest are given in the *3 HECTARE* box. In each box, a solid line joins regression values which are not significantly different ($P > 0.05$); * denotes nonzero regression slope ($P < 0.05$).

estimates were not significantly different. Regression slopes for ON(F) and IL were significantly higher than the slope for MO.

The number of edge species was not significantly related to forest size in ON(F), ON(A) or MO but increased with forest size in IL (Fig. 3). Despite this, regression parameters were not significantly different. The number of interior-edge species increased significantly with forest size in all study areas (Fig. 4). Regression slopes were not significantly different but the 3-ha regression estimates for IL and MO were significantly higher than the estimate for ON(F). The number of forest-interior species increased significantly

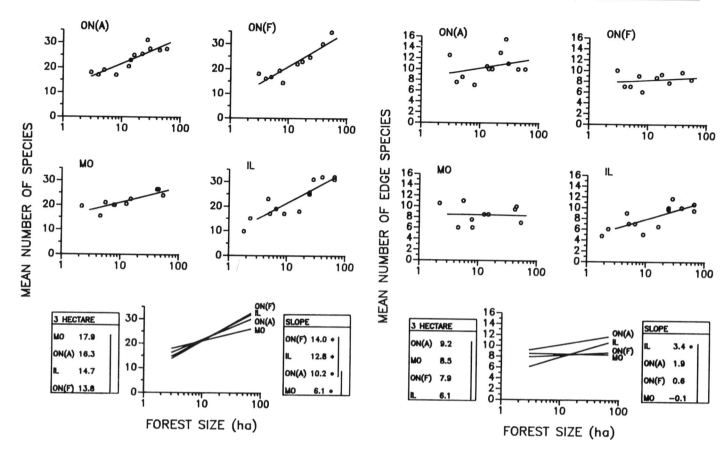

FIGURE 2. Comparisons of linear regressions of mean number of all bird species on forest size for study areas in Ontario (ON(F) and ON(A)), Missouri (MO), and Illinois (IL). See Figure 1 for additional explanation.

FIGURE 3. Comparisons of linear regressions of mean number of edge species on forest size for study areas in Ontario (ON(F) and ON(A)), Missouri (MO), and Illinois (IL). See Figure 1 for additional explanation.

TABLE 3. Composition of forest birds compared among study areas in Ontario (ON(F), ON(A)), Illinois (IL) and Missouri (MO) for all forest sizes combined. See Appendix 1 for details on bird species

Composition	Mean no. species per year (± SD)				All study areas/years combined
	ON(F)	ON(A)	MO	IL	
Total species pool	59.3 (1.2)	58.5 (0.7)	43.5 (0.7)	47.7 (2.1)	91
Habitat use					
Forest-Interior	22.3 (0.6)	19.0 (0.0)	7.5 (2.1)	11.0 (1.0)	30
Interior-Edge	15.7 (0.6)	16.0 (0.0)	20.5 (0.7)	20.0 (1.0)	27
Edge	21.3 (0.6)	23.5 (0.7)	15.5 (2.1)	16.7 (2.1)	34
Area sensitivity					
Sensitive	22.0 (1.0)	20.0 (0.0)	15.5 (2.1)	19.0 (1.0)	33
Insensitive	21.7 (0.6)	24.0 (1.4)	25.0 (1.4)	27.0 (2.6)	36
Unknown	15.7 (1.2)	14.5 (0.7)	3.0 (1.4)	1.7 (0.6)	22
No. Forest studied	13	16	15	15	–
Size Range (ha)	3–8600	3–7620	1.2–1000	1.8–600	–
Median size (ha)	17.0	24.5	12.6	24.0	–
No. Years	3	2	2	1–3	–
Forest Cover (%)	30	19	22	2	–

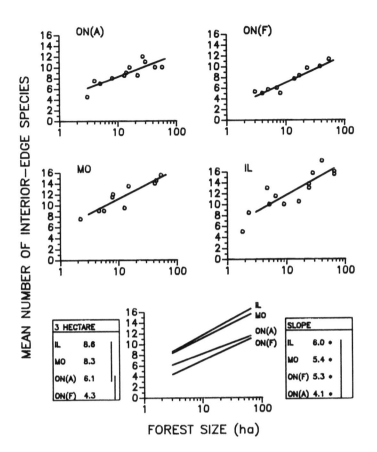

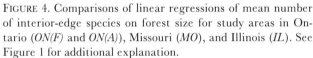

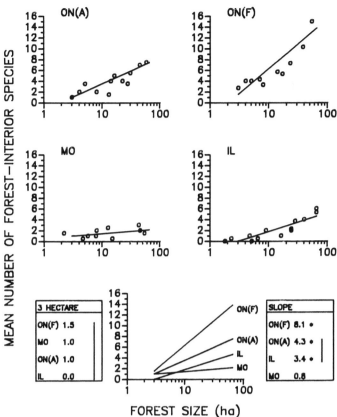

FIGURE 4. Comparisons of linear regressions of mean number of interior-edge species on forest size for study areas in Ontario (*ON(F)* and *ON(A)*), Missouri (*MO*), and Illinois (*IL*). See Figure 1 for additional explanation.

FIGURE 5. Comparisons of linear regressions of mean number of forest-interior species on forest size for study areas in Ontario (*ON(F)* and *ON(A)*), Missouri (*MO*), and Illinois (*IL*). See Figure 1 for additional explanation.

with forest size in all study areas except MO (Fig. 5). The 3-ha regression estimates were not significantly different. Few forest-interior species were found in smaller forest fragments in any study area. The number of forest-interior species increased most quickly with forest size in ON(F), the study area which had the most forest cover. The regression slopes for ON(A) and IL were statistically similar and significantly higher than the slope for MO.

The number of area-sensitive species increased significantly with forest size in all study areas (Fig. 6). Forests in ON(F) usually had the greatest number of area-sensitive species, although regression parameters were only significantly higher than IL (for 3-ha estimate) and MO (for slope). In ON(F), ON(A) and IL, about 65% of the regional pool of area-sensitive species was observed in the largest forest fragment (54–65 ha) annually. In MO, only 48% of the regional pool of area-sensitive species was observed in the largest fragment (54 ha) annually.

Discussion

LANDSCAPE ECOLOGY OF TEMPERATE FOREST BIRDS

Our results are consistent with the findings of Robbins et al. (1989) that small forest fragments (particularly those under 10 ha) in eastern North America support few, if any, area-sensitive species or forest-interior species, many of which overwinter in the Neotropics. However, small forest fragments were particularly important to interior-edge species where forest cover was reduced (cf. Arnold 1983, Blake and Karr 1987). Our results further suggest that differences in the landscape context of forest fragments also affect the distribution of bird species, independent of forest size.

In our comparisons, numbers of area-sensitive species were highest, and numbers of forest-interior species increased most rapidly with forest size in the study area with the greatest overall forest cover. Contrary to our expectations, bird species distributions among forest

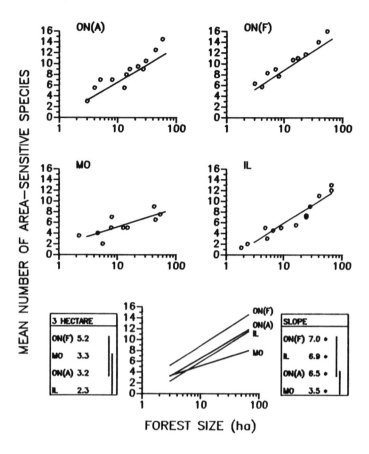

FIGURE 6. Comparisons of linear regressions of mean number of area-sensitive species on forest size for study areas in Ontario (*ON(F)* and *ON(A)*), Missouri (*MO*), and Illinois (*IL*). See Figure 1 for additional explanation.

fragments in Illinois were similar to those in the more-intensively farmed study area in Ontario. Forest fragments in Missouri were used the least by forest-interior and area-sensitive bird species. Aspects of landscape context other than total forest cover might account for these differences. For example, the size distribution, shape and connectivity (e.g., distance between forests, hedgerow corridors) of forests should also be quantified. Investigations of dispersal characteristics of forest birds in relation to inter-patch distance and "resistance" of the intervening habitats are also needed (Urban and Shugart 1986, Askins et al. 1990).

Several factors other than landscape context could also explain differences in the distribution of species among study areas. Certain species might be absent from small forest fragments because small populations have an increased probability of local extinction because of stochastic changes in population size (Shaffer 1981, Wright and Hubbell 1983, but see Ambuel and Temple 1983). Although stochastic population processes

might affect the probability of occurrence of some bird species in smaller fragments, it is unlikely that these processes accounted for the observed differences in species distribution because the number and size range of forest fragments were replicated among study areas.

Although we selected forests in Ontario to be as similar in habitat as possible, differences in species distribution in relation to habitat cannot yet be fully evaluated. Habitat differences among study areas might be important in determining numbers of area-sensitive species (Robbins et al. 1989) and/or their probabilities of local extinction (Whitcomb et al. 1981, Karr 1982, Karr and Freemark 1983), once the effect of forest size has been removed.

Observational and experimental evidence as well as simulation modelling suggest that many bird species (particularly single-brooded, low-nesting Neotropical migrants) might be absent from smaller forest fragments or forests with little core habitat (i.e., habitat > 100 m from an edge) because of more intense competition and higher rates of predation and nest parasitism associated with edge habitat (Ambuel and Temple 1983, Wilcove 1985, Temple 1986, Robinson 1988, Temple and Cary 1988). These authors argue that more intense biotic interactions lead to lower reproductive success and reduced rates of return by adult birds. Our results are consistent with the biotic-interaction model because more edge and interior-edge species, and few forest-interior species were found in smaller forest fragments in all study areas. In our comparisons, numbers of interior-edge species were lowest in the study area with the greatest overall forest cover. The observed differences in distributions of forest-interior and area-sensitive species among the study areas could have been, at least in part, a result of differences in the intensity of biotic interactions within forest fragments.

The spatial distribution of at least some species within and between years likely depends upon population dynamics at a variety of spatial and temporal scales, such as biotic interactions (e.g., territoriality, predation, nest parasitism) within individual forest fragments, dispersal of birds among fragment populations, and configuration of fragment populations into metapopulations (Merriam 1988a). Landscape pattern, coupled with the behavioral ecology (e.g., dispersal characteristics) of species, might affect the number of fragment populations that can interact, the size of those populations, their temporal variability, and ultimately, the survival of the metapopulation (Shaffer 1985; Urban and Shugart 1986; Merriam 1988a,b; Hanski 1989). Few field data are yet available to test the validity of the metapopulation model for patchily distributed species (but see Villard et al., this volume).

CONSERVATION IMPLICATIONS

Understanding the relationship between landscape structure and the distribution and probability of local extinction of species is an important prerequisite for developing and implementing effective conservation plans (Opdam et al. 1985, Merriam 1988a). Conservation of forest bird diversity will depend on the ability of managers to maximize the abundance and size of forests within and among landscapes. Providing different habitats and minimizing edge will also be important. The value of improving connectivity of forests is unclear at present.

Few studies have identified the number and size of forests needed to conserve area-sensitive bird species within agricultural landscapes. Forest fragments under 10 ha are unsuitable for many forest-dwelling Neotropical migrant species. Robbins et al. (1989) conclude that 3,000 ha is the minimum forest size that might be expected to retain all species of the forest-interior avifauna of eastern North America. They estimate that the probability of detecting even one-half of all of the area-sensitive species in a 50-ha forest is very low although several 50-ha forests can contain the species complement of a single, 3,000-ha forest. By contrast, we found that at least one-half of the regional pool of area-sensitive species was detected annually in a single 54–65-ha forest in each of the four study areas compared.

Robbins et al. (1989) also found that the probability of occurrence for many area-sensitive species appeared to be unrelated to forest size when more than 33% forest was within 2 km of the bird survey point. In our comparisons, numbers of area-sensitive species within forests, and the rate of increase in forest-interior species richness with larger forest size were highest in the Ontario study area which had about 30% forest cover. Quantifying relationships between spatial distributions of area-sensitive species and overall forest cover warrants further study.

A better understanding of metapopulations is needed in order to address the design of landscapes for conservation of forest-interior and area-sensitive bird species (Shaffer 1985, Merriam 1988a, Hanski 1989). Metapopulation theory provides a potential framework for developing conservation strategies for temperate forest birds based on networks of reserves within landscapes (Hanski 1989). For example, management actions that reduce the abundance and size of forests might lead to the regional extirpation of a species even if habitat of suitable quality remains. Effective conservation of patchily distributed species might require the preservation of suitable but intermittently unoccupied habitat (Shaffer 1985).

Relationships between landscape structure and the distribution of species in more extensively forested landscapes have been studied much less (Freemark 1989). Additional research is needed to investigate potential differences in the response of forest species to landscape structure along a fragmentation gradient from farmland to extensive forest. Studies of the relationship between landscape structure and the distribution and survival of forest species will be particularly important for Canada if boreal forests become reduced and fragmented by the effects of global warming (Rizzo and Wiken 1989).

About three-quarters of the forest-interior or area-sensitive species in forests of eastern North America overwinter in the Neotropics. Conservation efforts for these species at temperate latitudes will be moot if conditions for their survival are unsuitable in their overwintering areas as a result of factors such as habitat loss and habitat fragmentation. A better understanding of the relation between landscape structure and the distribution and survival of species is an important prerequisite for developing and implementing effective conservation plans for birds breeding in temperate forests.

Acknowledgments

We thank H. Boyd, A. Gaston, A. Keith, G. Merriam, M.-A. Villard, two anonymous reviewers and the editors for their comments on earlier drafts. J. Faaborg was particularly helpful in providing information for Missouri.

Literature cited

Ambuel, B., and S.A. Temple. 1983. Area-dependent changes in the bird communities and vegetation of southern Wisconsin forests. *Ecology* 64:1057–1068.

Arnold, G.W. 1983. The influence of ditch and hedgerow structure, length of hedgerows, and area of woodland and garden on bird numbers on farmland. *J. Appl. Ecol.* 20:731–750.

Askins, R.A., J.F. Lynch, and R. Greenberg. 1990. Population declines in migratory birds in eastern North America. *Current Ornithol.* 7:1–57

Askins, R.A., M.J. Philbrick, and D.S. Sugeno. 1987. Relationship between the regional abundance of forest and the composition of forest bird communities. *Biol. Conserv.* 39:129–152.

Blake, J.G. 1983. Ecological relationships of breeding birds in isolated forest patches in east-central Illinois. Ph.D. Dissertation, University of Illinois, Urbana, Illinois.

Blake, J.G., and J.R. Karr. 1982. *Ecology of Forest Island Bird Communities in East-central Illinois.* Laurel, Md.: U.S. Fish and Wildlife Service Contract Report No. 14-16-0009-79-023.

———. 1984. Species composition of bird communities and

the conservation benefit of large versus small forests. *Biol. Conserv.* 30:173–187.

———. 1987. Breeding birds of isolated woodlots: Area and habitat relationships. *Ecology* 68:1724–1734.

Forman, R.T.T., and M. Godron. 1986. *Landscape Ecology.* New York: J. Wiley and Sons.

Forman, R.T.T., A.E. Galli, and C.F. Leck. 1976. Forest size and avian diversity in New Jersey woodlots with some land use implications. *Oecologia* 26:1–8.

Freemark, K. 1989. Landscape ecology of forest birds in the northeast. Pages 7–12 in *Is Forest Fragmentation a Management Issue in the Northeast?*, R. DeGraaf and W. Healy, comps. USDA Forest Service, Northeastern Forest Experiment Station, Gen. Tech. Rep. NE-140.

Freemark, K., and H.G. Merriam. 1986. Importance of area and habitat heterogeneity to bird assemblages in temperate forest fragments. *Biol. Conserv.* 36:115–141.

Galli, A.E., C.F. Leck, and R.T.T. Forman. 1976. Avian distribution patterns in forest islands of different sizes in central New Jersey. *Auk* 93:356–364.

Giessman, N.F., T.W. Barney, T.L. Haithcoat, J.W. Myers, and R. Massengale. 1986. Distribution of forestland in Missouri. *Trans. Mo. Acad. Sci.* 20:5–14.

Hanski, I. 1989. Metapopulation dynamics: Does it help to have more of the same? *Trends Res. Ecol. Evol.* 4:113–114.

Hayden, T.J. 1985. Minimum area requirements of some breeding bird species in fragmented habitats in Missouri. M.A. Thesis, University of Missouri, Columbia, Missouri.

Hayden, T.J., J. Faaborg, and R.L. Clawson. 1985. Estimates of minimum area requirements for Missouri forest birds. *Trans. Mo. Acad. Sci.* 19:11–22.

Howe, R.W. 1984. Local dynamics of bird assemblages in small forest habitat islands in Australia and North America. *Ecology* 65:1585–1601.

Iverson, L.R., R.L. Oliver, D.P. Tucker, P.G. Risser, C.D. Burnett and R.G. Rayburn. 1989. *The forest resources of Illinois: An atlas and analysis of spatial and temporal trends.* Champaign: Illinois Nat. Hist. Survey Spec. Publ. 11.

Karr, J.R. 1982. Population variability and extinction in the avifauna of a tropical land bridge island. *Ecology* 63:1975–1978.

Karr, J.R., and K.E. Freemark. 1983. Habitat selection and environmental gradients: Dynamics in the "stable" tropics. *Ecology* 64:1481–1494.

Lynch, J.F., and D.F. Whigham. 1984. Effects of forest fragmentation on breeding bird communities in Maryland, U.S.A. *Biol. Conserv.* 28:287–324.

Martin, T.E. 1981. Species-area slopes and coefficients: A caution on their interpretation. *Am. Nat.* 118:823–837.

Merriam, G. 1988a. Landscape dynamics in farmland. *Trends Res. Ecol. Evol.* 3:16–20.

———. 1988b. Landscape ecology: The ecology of heterogeneous systems. Pages 43–50 in *Landscape Ecology and Management*, M.R. Moss, ed. Montreal: Polyscience Publications.

Miller, R.G., Jr. 1981. *Simultaneous Statistical Inference.* New York: Springer-Verlag.

Moss, M.R., ed. 1988. *Landscape Ecology and Management.* Montreal: Polyscience Publications.

Muchoki, C.H.K. 1988. Remotely sensed relationships between wooded patch habitats and agricultural landscape type: A basis for ecological planning. Pages 85–94 in *Landscape Ecology and Management*, M.R. Moss, ed. Montreal: Polyscience Publications.

Naveh, Z., and A.S. Lieberman. 1984. *Landscape Ecology: Theory and Application.* New York: Springer-Verlag.

Opdam, P., G. Rijsdijk, and F. Hustings. 1985. Bird communities in small woods in an agricultural landscape: Effects of area and isolation. *Biol. Conserv.* 34:333–352.

Risser, P.G., J.R. Karr, and R.T.T. Forman. 1984. *Landscape Ecology: Directions and Approaches.* Champaign: Illinois Nat. Hist. Survey Spec. Publ. 2.

Rizzo, B. and E. Wiken. 1989. Assessing the sensitivity of Canada's ecosystems to climatic change. Pages 94–111 in *Discussion Report on Fenno-Scandian Regions, Conference on Landscape-Ecological Impacts of Climatic Change.* The Netherlands: Agricultural University of Wageningen.

Robbins, C.S., D.K. Dawson, and B.A. Dowell. 1989. *Habitat Area Requirements of Breeding Forest Birds of the Middle Atlantic States.* Wildl. Monogr. 103.

Robinson, S.K. 1988. Reappraisal of the costs and benefits of habitat heterogeneity for nongame wildlife. *Trans. N.A. Wildl. Nat. Res. Conf.* 53:145–155.

SAS Institute. 1988. *SAS/STAT Users' Guide, Release 6.03.* Cary, N.C.: SAS Institute Inc.

Shaffer, M.L. 1981. Minimum population sizes for species conservation. *BioScience* 31:131–134.

———. 1985. The metapopulation and species conservation: The special case of the Northern Spotted Owl. Pages 86–99 in *Ecology and Management of the Spotted Owl in the Pacific Northwest*, R.J. Gutiérrez and A.B. Carey, eds. Portland, Oreg.: USDA Forest Service Gen. Tech. Rept. PNW-185.

Temple, S.A. 1986. Predicting impacts of habitat fragmentation on forest birds: A comparison of two models. Pages 301–304 in *Wildlife 2000: Modeling Habitat Relationships of Terrestrial Vertebrates*, J. Verner, M.L. Morrison, and C.J. Ralph, eds. Madison: University of Wisconsin Press.

Temple, S.A., and J.R. Cary. 1988. Modelling dynamics of habitat-interior bird populations in fragmented landscapes. *Conserv. Biol.* 2:340–347.

Urban, D.L., and H.H. Shugart, Jr. 1986. Avian demography in mosaic landscapes: Modeling paradigm and preliminary results. Pages 273–279 in *Wildlife 2000: Modeling Habitat Relationships of Terrestrial Vertebrates*, J. Verner, M.L. Morrison, and C.J. Ralph, eds. Madison: University of Wisconsin Press.

Whitcomb, R.F., C.S. Robbins, J.F. Lynch, B.L. Whitcomb, M.K. Klimkiewicz, and D. Bystrak. 1981. Effects of forest fragmentation on the avifauna of the eastern deciduous forest. Pages 125–205 in *Forest Island Dynamics in Man-dominated Landscapes*, R.L. Burgess and D.M. Sharpe, eds. New York: Springer-Verlag.

Wilcove, D.S. 1985. Nest predation in forest tracts and the decline of migratory songbirds. *Ecology* 66:1211–1214.

Wright, S.J., and S.P. Hubbell. 1983. Stochastic extinction and reserve size: A focal species approach. *Oikos* 41:466–476.

APPENDIX 1. Classification of forest bird species for study areas in Ontario (ON(F),ON(A)), Missouri (MO) and Illinois (IL) according to: area sensitivity (I, insensitive; S, sensitive; U, unknown), habitat use (I, forest interior; I/E, Interior and edge; E, edge), migratory strategy (R, resident; SD, short distance; NT, neotropical migrant). N/A denotes species not included in comparisons with MO and IL. See Methods for additional details

Species	Area sensitivity	Habitat use	Migratory strategy			
			ON(F)	ON(A)	MO	IL
Sharp-shinned Hawk, *Accipiter striatus*	U	I/E	SD		N/A	N/A
Cooper's Hawk, *Accipiter cooperii*	U	I	SD		N/A	N/A
Red-shouldered Hawk, *Buteo lineatus*	S	I/E	SD	SD	N/A	N/A
Broad-winged Hawk, *Buteo platypterus*	U	I	NT	NT	N/A	N/A
Red-tailed Hawk, *Buteo jamaicensis*	I	E	SD	SD	N/A	N/A
American Kestrel, *Falco sparverius*	U	E	SD	SD	N/A	N/A
Ruffed Grouse, *Bonasa umbellus*	U	I/E	R	R	R	
Wild Turkey, *Meleagris gallopavo*	U	I/E			R	
Northern Bobwhite, *Colinus virginianus*	I	E			R	
American Woodcock, *Scolopax minor*	U	E	SD	SD	N/A	N/A
Mourning Dove, *Zenaida macroura*	I	E	SD	SD	SD	SD
Black-billed Cuckoo, *Coccyzus erythropthalmus*	I	I/E[a]	NT		NT	NT
Yellow-billed Cuckoo, *Coccyzus americanus*	I[a]	I/E			NT	NT
Barred Owl, *Strix varia*	U	I	R		N/A	N/A
Ruby-thr. Hummingbird, *Archilochus colubris*	I	E	NT	NT		NT
Red-headed Woodpecker, *Melanerpes erythrocephalus*	I	E			R	R
Red-bellied Woodpecker, *Melanerpes carolinus*	S	I/E			R	R
Yellow-bellied Sapsucker, *Sphyrapicus varius*	U	I/E	SD	SD		
Downy Woodpecker, *Picoides pubescens*	I[a]	I/E	R	R	R	R
Hairy Woodpecker, *Picoides villosus*	S	I	R	R	R	R
Northern Flicker, *Colaptes auratus*	I	I/E	SD	SD	R	SD
Pileated Woodpecker, *Dryocopus pileatus*	S[a]	I[a]	R	R	R	
Olive-sided Flycatcher, *Contopus borealis*	U	I	NT			
Eastern Wood-Pewee, *Contopus virens*	I	I/E	NT	NT	NT	NT
Acadian Flycatcher, *Empidonax virescens*	S	I			NT	NT
Alder Flycatcher, *Empidonax alnorum*	U	E	NT			
Least Flycatcher, *Empidonax minimus*	S	E	NT	NT		
Eastern Phoebe, *Sayornis phoebe*	U	I/E	SD	SD	SD	
Great Crested Flycatcher, *Myiarchus crinitus*	S[a]	I/E	NT	NT	NT	NT
Eastern Kingbird, *Tyrannus tyrannus*	I	E	NT	NT		
Tree Swallow, *Tachycineta bicolor*	U	E	NT		N/A	N/A
Blue Jay, *Cyanocitta cristata*	I	I/E	R	R	R	R
American Crow, *Corvus brachyrhynchos*	S	E	R	R	N/A	N/A
Common Raven, *Corvus corax*	U	I	R		N/A	N/A
Black-capped Chickadee, *Parus atricapillus*	I[a]	I/E	R	R	R	R
Tufted Titmouse, *Parus bicolor*	S[a]	I/E			R	R
Red-breasted Nuthatch, *Sitta canadensis*	U	I	R	R		
White-breasted Nuthatch, *Sitta carolinensis*	S	I[a]	R	R	R	R
Brown Creeper, *Certhia americana*	S[a]	I	R	R		R
House Wren, *Troglodytes aedon*	I[a]	E[a]			SD	SD
Winter Wren, *Troglodytes troglodytes*	U	I	SD	SD		
Golden-crowned Kinglet, *Regulus satrapa*	U	I	SD	SD		
Blue-gray Gnatcatcher, *Polioptila caerulea*	S	I/E			NT	NT
Eastern Bluebird, *Sialia sialis*	I	E			SD	
Veery, *Catharus fuscescens*	S	I	NT	NT		NT
Swainson's Thrush, *Catharus ustulatus*	U	I	NT	NT		
Hermit Thrush, *Catharus guttatus*	S	I	SD			
Wood Thrush, *Hylocichla mustelina*	S	I/E	NT	NT	NT	NT
American Robin, *Turdus migratorius*	I	E	SD	SD	SD	SD

a. Classified differently among references reviewed. See Methods for details.

APPENDIX 1—*Continued next page*

APPENDIX 1—*Continued*

Species	Area sensitivity	Habitat use	Migratory strategy			
			ON(F)	ON(A)	MO	IL
Gray Catbird, *Dumetella carolinensis*	I[a]	I/E[a]	SD	SD	SD	SD
Northern Mockingbird, *Mimus polyglottos*	I	E			SD	
Brown Thrasher, *Toxostoma rufum*	I	E	SD	SD	SD	SD
Cedar Waxwing, *Bombycilla cedrorum*	I	E	SD	SD	SD	R
European Starling, *Sturnus vulgaris*	I	E		R	R	R
White-eyed Vireo, *Vireo griseus*	I	I/E			NT	NT
Yellow-throated Vireo, *Vireo flavifrons*	S[a]	I/E	NT		NT	NT
Warbling Vireo, *Vireo gilvus*	U	E	NT	NT	NT	
Red-eyed Vireo, *Vireo olivaceus*	S[a]	I/E	NT	NT	NT	NT
Blue-winged Warbler, *Vermivora pinus*	U	E			NT	
Nashville Warbler, *Vermivora ruficapilla*	U	E	NT	NT		
Northern Parula, *Parula americana*	S	I/E[a]	NT	NT	NT	NT
Yellow Warbler, *Dendroica petechia*	U	E	NT	NT		
Chestnut-sided Warbler, *Dendroica pensylvanica*	S[a]	E	NT	NT		
Magnolia Warbler, *Dendroica magnolia*	I	I	NT	NT		
Black-thr. Blue Warbler, *Dendroica caerulescens*	S	I	NT	NT		
Yellow-rumped Warbler, *Dendroica coronata*	U	I	SD			
Black-thr. Green Warbler, *Dendroica virens*	S[a]	I	NT	NT		
Blackburnian Warbler, *Dendroica fusca*	U	I	NT	NT		
Yellow-throated Warbler, *Dendroica dominica*	U	I				NT
Pine Warbler, *Dendroica pinus*	I	I	SD	SD		
Cerulean Warbler, *Dendroica cerulea*	S	I				NT
Black-and-white Warbler, *Mniotilta varia*	S	I	NT	NT		
American Redstart, *Setophaga ruticilla*	S	I	NT	NT	NT	NT
Worm-eating Warbler, *Helmintheros vermivorus*	S	I			NT	
Ovenbird, *Seiurus aurocapillus*	S	I	NT	NT	NT	NT
Northern Waterthrush, *Seiurus noveboracensis*	S	I	NT	NT		
Louisiana Waterthrush, *Seiurus motacilla*	S	I			NT	
Kentucky Warbler, *Oporornis formosus*	S[a]	I			NT	NT
Mourning Warbler, *Oporornis philadelphia*	S	E	NT	NT		
Common Yellowthroat, *Geothlypis trichas*	I	I/E[a]	SD	SD	SD	SD
Hooded Warbler, *Wilsonia citrina*	S[a]	I				NT
Canada Warbler, *Wilsonia canadensis*	S	I	NT	NT		
Yellow-breasted Chat, *Icteria virens*	I	E				NT
Summer Tanager, *Piranga rubra*	S	I/E			NT	
Scarlet Tanager, *Piranga olivacea*	S	I	NT	NT		NT
Northern Cardinal, *Cardinalis cardinalis*	I	I/E			R	R
Rose-breasted Grosbeak, *Pheucticus ludovicianus*	S[a]	I/E	NT	NT	NT	NT
Indigo Bunting, *Passerina cyanea*	I	E	NT	NT	NT	NT
Rufous-sided Towhee, *Pipilo erythrophthalmus*	I	I/E			SD	SD
Chipping Sparrow, *Spizella passerina*	U	E	SD	SD		SD
Field Sparrow, *Spizella pusilla*	I	E			SD	SD
Song Sparrow, *Melospiza melodia*	I	E	SD	SD		SD
Swamp Sparrow, *Melospiza georgiana*	U	E	SD			
White-throated Sparrow, *Zonotrichia albicollis*	U	E	SD	SD		
Bobolink, *Dolichonyx oryzivorus*	U	E	NT	NT		
Red-winged Blackbird, *Agelaius phoeniceus*	I	E	SD	SD	SD	SD
Common Grackle, *Quiscalus quiscula*	I	E	SD	SD	SD	SD
Brown-headed Cowbird, *Molothrus ater*	I	E	SD	SD	SD	SD
Northern Oriole, *Icterus galbula*	I	E	NT	NT	NT	NT
Purple Finch, *Carpodacus purpureus*	U	I/E	R	R		
American Goldfinch, *Carduelis tristis*	I	E	SD	SD	SD	SD
House Sparrow, *Passer domesticus*	I	E		R		R

a. Classified differently among references reviewed. See Methods for details.

THOMAS E. MARTIN
U.S. Fish and Wildlife Service
Arkansas Cooperative Fish
and Wildlife Research Unit
University of Arkansas
Fayetteville, Arkansas 72701

Breeding productivity considerations: What are the appropriate habitat features for management?

Abstract. Habitat requirements of species are often assayed by correlating bird abundance with features of occupied habitat. Such correlations might not identify appropriate features for management efforts; appropriate features are those that most directly influence fitness components (reproduction, survival). Choice of habitat features that increase reproductive output should be favored over evolutionary time, and management of such features should exert the greatest effects on population recruitment over shorter periods. Nesting success and sources of mortality were reviewed for 32 species of passerines that migrate to the Neotropics. Nest predation was the primary source of nesting mortality for all but four species and nest predation is an important influence on habitat choices and demography. The low amount of mortality caused by starvation may not reflect the influence of food on populations because food limitation may be expressed through reduced clutch sizes or fewer breeding attempts rather than mortality. Cowbird parasitism also varied in importance as a source of mortality. The amount of mortality attributable to parasitism may be overestimated because predation causes losses that are not fully recognized. Thus, cowbird removal can cause less response than expected. However, removal of cowbirds or predators represents only stop-gap responses. Long-term solutions depend on identifying and manipulating habitat features that reduce the limiting nature of these processes. An abundance of the nesting substrates and microhabitats used by coexisting species can reduce probability of predation and increase densities. Nesting microhabitats can differ from foraging microhabitats and both resources are needed to sustain populations. We lack information on specific microhabitat requirements for nesting and foraging for most species and we still lack basic life history data for many species. Future study needs are identified.

Sinopsis. Los requerimientos de habitat de las especies normalmente se detectan al correlacionar la abundancia de aves con características del habitat ocupado. Tales correlaciones a lo mejor no identifican características apropiadas para los esfuerzos de manejo; las características apropiadas son aquellas que influencian de una manera mas directa las componentes de eficacia biológica (reproducción, supervivencia). La escogencia de características de habitat que incrementan el éxito reproductivo deben estar favorecidas en el tiempo evolutivo y su manejo debería ejercer los mayores efectos sobre el reclutamiento poblacional en períodos mas cortos. El éxito de anidación y las causas de mortalidad de 32 especies de passeriformes que migran al neotrópico fueron examinadas. La predación de nidos fue la causa primaria de mortalidad de anidación para todas las especies excepto cuatro y constituye una influencia importante sobre la escogencia de habitat y la demografía. La baja proporción de mortalidad debida a la falta de alimento podría no reflejar la influencia de este recurso sobre las poblaciones puesto que la limitación alimentaria puede expresarse en tamaños de postura reducidos o menos intentos de cría en vez de mortalidad en si misma. El parasitismo por *Molothrus* también varió en importancia como causa de mortalidad. La proporción de muertes atribuíble al parasitismo puede estar sobreestimada puesto que la predación causa pérdidas que no son completamente reconocibles. Por lo tanto, la remoción de *Molothrus* o de predadores solamente representa respuestas momentáneas. Las soluciones a largo plazo dependen de la identificación y la manipulación de características del habitat que reducen la naturaleza limitante de estos procesos. La abundancia de sustratos de anidación y de microhabitats usados por especies coexistentes pueden reducir la probabilidad de predación e incrementar densidades. Los microhabitats de anidación pueden diferir de los microhabitats de forrajeo y ambos recursos son necesarios para mantener las poblaciones. Carecemos de la información de requerimientos específicos de microhabitat para la anidación y el forrajeo de la mayoría de especies y aún carecemos de la historia natural básica de especies. Se identifican trabajos futuros.

Conservation of Neotropical migrant birds requires an understanding of habitat requirements necessary for population maintenance. Usually, the presence or abundance of species are correlated with measured habitat features (e.g., foliage profiles, densities of stems of different size classes or taxa and basal area) under the assumption that correlations reflect suitability of habitats. Yet, species might be present or even more abundant in marginal or unsuitable habitats because of limited availability of preferred habitat, social interactions, or other influences (Van Horne 1983, Pulliam 1988). Correlations based on presence or abundances can then misrepresent suitability of habitats. Appropriate habitat features (those that most directly influence reproduction or survival) might not even be measured because

most habitat studies seek to describe habitat associations of species rather than identify features that affect the success of populations. For example, multivariate habitat studies of coexisting species (e.g., James 1971, Anderson and Shugart 1974, Whitmore 1975, 1977, Smith 1977, James and Warner 1982) indicate habitat features associated with species, but are the biologically important features identified? For example, are the 2–4-cm stems associated with a given species really important to the success of that species or are such habitat features merely indirectly correlated with the actual features influencing choice of habitat and success of the population?

Indirect and correlative tests are difficult to avoid in field studies because of the complex and often intractable nature of ecological systems. Yet, even under such methods, the relevance of habitat features for management goals and ecological study can be improved by testing hypotheses about their effects on fitness components (Martin 1986). Fitness components are important metrics for three reasons. First, fitness components provide insight into the evolutionary bases of habitat requirements and choices. Second, fitness components are traits that exert direct effects on population recruitment and demography on shorter (ecological) time scales. Third, study of fitness components provides needed information on the life history of species and allows identification of critical periods (bottlenecks) for management.

Habitat features can affect fitness by providing resources, and quality and abundance of those resources are influenced by the evolved physiology, morphology, and behavior of a species (Partridge 1978, Karr and Freemark 1983, Robinson and Holmes 1982, 1984, Toft 1985, Martin 1986 and references therein). Moreover, biological processes (e.g., competition, predation, parasitism) can modify availability or quality of resources and simultaneously influence populations through the effects of coexisting species on each other (Fretwell 1972, Lawlor and Maynard Smith 1976, Holt 1977, 1984, Rosenzweig 1981, 1985, Pimm and Rosenzweig 1981, Werner et al. 1983a,b, Martin 1986, 1988b,c). Thus, effective management practices require: (1) identification of specific habitat features and associated resources that directly influence reproduction or survival and (2) simultaneous consideration of the consequences of those features for coexisting species and any interacting effects species have on one another (biodiversity approach). In this paper, I examine the contribution of various mortality factors to reproductive success to gain insight into processes that might be important to demography of Neotropical migrants. Then, I examine the possible consequences of those mortality factors to the identification of appropriate habitat features for species management.

Nest success and mortality in Neotropical migrants

Data on nesting success and causes of nest mortality were obtained for as many open-nesting passerines that winter in the Neotropics as data were available. I define a Neotropical migrant as any species that centers its winter range south of the continental U.S. border. I present only information from studies that included a minimum of 15 nests *and* information on causes of mortality. Nesting success might be overestimated where some nests were found after the egg-laying period and nesting success is estimated by the fraction (proportion) of surviving nests; consequently, Mayfield methods provide a better estimate of actual nest success (Mayfield 1961, 1975, Johnson 1979, Hensler and Nichols 1981). However, even some current studies do not include such information. Thus, success was calculated in three ways. (1) Nest loss: I report the fraction of nests that were successful (fledged at least one young) relative to the total number of nests studied. (2) Egg loss: When possible, success was calculated per egg laid rather than per nest because effects of parasitism and starvation usually caused only partial nest losses. (3) Mayfield estimates: In some cases, investigators also reported the Mayfield estimate of nesting success. Estimates for both fraction and Mayfield methods are reported when possible. I also report the relative contribution of predation, parasitism, addling (nonhatch), starvation, and weather to mortality of nesting attempts. Because these parameters are percentages, I used an arcsin transformation prior to testing for significant differences with t-tests.

Data for 32 species from 35 different studies or locations were obtained (Table 1). The data reveal the inadequacy of our knowledge about the biology of migrant passerines, because only a small fraction have had nesting success and causes of nesting mortality described. I provided the data for seven of the species in Table 1; only 25 migrant species were described previously. For some species I studied, basic life history information, such as clutch size and duration of incubation and nestling periods, were unknown. In addition to such gaps in basic breeding biology, most nesting success studies do not include analysis of habitat characteristics that influence nesting mortality. Moreover, comparisons of nesting success within a single species under different habitat management regimes are lacking. Thus, information on life history, nesting mortality, and habitat influences on mortality is urgently needed for Neotropical migrants.

The data for the 32 species reviewed here, nonetheless, provide a substantially larger data base than contained in earlier works (e.g., Lack 1954, 1968, Nice 1957, Ricklefs 1969). Nesting success averaged 44.0% based on fraction estimates (Table 1). Nesting success was similar (42%) for 17 species under the Mayfield method. However, fraction estimates ($\bar{X} \pm$ SE = 0.518 $\pm$ 0.044) were significantly higher ($P < 0.05$) than Mayfield estimates (0.422 $\pm$ 0.042) when only species providing both sets of information were compared ($n = 16$, Table 1). These results reconfirm that the fraction method overestimates nesting success. If the differences exhibited by these 16 species are used to adjust fraction estimates of all 32 species, the resulting estimate of nesting success is 35.8%, which is lower than traditionally accepted rates of about 45% based on smaller samples (Lack 1954, Nice 1957, Ricklefs 1969). Yet, these results are comparable to data for 59 species/locations of non- or short-distance migratory species that build open nests (Martin, unpubl. data).

Nest predation is the only mortality factor found in every study, and it caused mortality in 42.8% of all active nests initiated (Table 1). This estimate is conservative because many studies did not incorporate the more realistic Mayfield estimates of nest success. Yet, predation accounted for 77% of the total mortality incurred by these species. In fact, predation was the primary mortality agent in all cases except the Bell's Vireo (scientific names in Appendix 1), Black-capped Vireo, Solitary Vireo, and Common Yellowthroat where parasitism by Brown-headed Cowbirds was the primary mortality agent. Parasitism was also significant (> 10% mortality) for the Ovenbird, Kirtland's Warbler, Prairie Warbler, Indigo Bunting, and Dickcissel (Table 1). Together, predation and parasitism accounted for 86% of all mortality (Table 1).

Weather was a frequent cause of some nesting mortality, but weather-induced mortality was usually relatively low (2–4%), except for Western Kingbird, Eastern Kingbird, and Gray Catbird (Table 1). Mortality from eggs not hatching because of addling or other causes was common but relatively low (2–4%). Mortality from starvation was the least common mortality agent, and accounted for very little mortality when it did occur (Table 1). Nest mortality was greater during incubation than in the nestling stage in 22 of 28 cases (Table 1), thus indicating that much mortality occurs during a stage (egg) when food limitation contributes little to nest mortality.

In summary, predation was the primary cause of nest mortality and accounted for most of the mortality across a diversity of species, geographic locations, and habitat types. Parasitism was also a significant source of mortality in some cases.

TABLE 1. Nesting success and sources of mortality for open-nesting passerines that winter in the Neotropics

Species (references)[a]	n[b]	Nest Succc	Mayf Est[d]	Nest Pred[e]	Cowb Para[f]	Non-Hatc[g]	Strv[h]	Weath[i]	Survival Egg	Survival Inc	Survival Nestl	Hab[j]	Location
[†]Acadian Flycatcher (1)	(319)	.574		.279	.044	.044	.000	.000		.677	.847	3	Michigan
[§]Willow Flycatcher (2)	(268)	.369		.522	.015	.034	.015	.034		.548	.664	6	Ohio
[§]Least Flycatcher (3)	303	.414	.358	.533	.008		.011	.077	.854	.662	.628	1	Manitoba
[†]Cassin's Kingbird (4)	(209)	.287		.426	.000	.057	.005	.072				4,7	Arizona
[†]Western Kingbird (4)	(660)	.202		.376	.000	.079	.011	.211				4,7	Arizona
[†]Eastern Kingbird (5)	109		.470	.349	.000	.021		.136				1	Kansas, New York
[§]Gray Catbird (6)	56	.518	.445	.437	.000	.060				.570	.780	4	Iowa
[§]Gray Catbird (7)	(137)	.591	.570	.215	.000	.046	.008	.115		.730	.840	6	Iowa
[§]Gray Catbird (8)	(74)	.487		.351	.000	.108				.635	.766	6	Iowa
[§]Wood Thrush (9)	(276)	.333		.525	.000	.029		.062		.514	.648	1	Delaware
[§]Bell's Vireo (10)	(79)	.114		.114	.646			.127				6	Kansas
[§]Black-capped Vireo (11)	(225)	.191		.124	.542	.062				.422	.453	8	Oklahoma, Texas
[†]Warbling Vireo (12)	55	.618	.550	.450	.000		.000	.000	.950	.721	.817	3	Arizona
[†]Red-eyed Vireo (13)	(98)	.602		.357	.000	.041						3	Ontario
[‡]Solitary Vireo (14)	(209)	.453		.180	.333					.693	.654	2	Colorado
[‡]Orange-crowned Warbler (12)	90	.667	.501	.499	.000		.000	.000	.800	.806	.768	3	Arizona
[‡]Virginia's Warbler (12)	26	.692	.580	.420	.000		.000	.000	1.000	.766	.787	3	Arizona
[§]Yellow Warbler (15)	225	.453		.342	.089	.049	.005	.031	.877	.658	.703	1	Manitoba
[§]Black-thr. Blue Warbler (16)	151	.609	.477	.428	.000		.017			.760	.750	1	New Hampshire
[†]Yellow-rumped Warbler (12)	29	.621	.468	.532	.000				.692	.814	.814	3	Arizona
[§]Kirtland's Warbler (17)	(427)	.300	.201	.458	.168					.390	.656	6	Michigan
[§]Prairie Warbler (18)	400	.223		.618	.139	.039	.000	.015	.600	.500	.667	6	Indiana
[‡]Ovenbird (19)	(155)	.452		.245	.187	.039	.000	.000		.639	.707	1	Michigan
[‡]Common Yellowthroat (20)	(152)	.520		.145	.197	.054				.658	.790	6,8	Minnesota, Michigan
[§]Yellow-breasted Chat (21)	(152)	.197		.669	.054		.000	.016		.281	.698	6	Indiana
[§]MacGillivray's Warbler (12)	71	.507	.384	.616	.000		.000	.000	.699	.718	.797	3	Arizona
[‡]Wilson's Warbler (22)	63	.603		.349	.000		.000	.048		.907	.641	6	California
[‡]Red-Faced Warbler (12)	30	.600	.518	.482	.000		.000	.000	.877	.734	.759	3	Arizona
[‡]American Redstart (23)	278	.583	.470	.480	.000		.050	.000				1	New Hampshire
[†]Western Tanager (12)	26	.538	.389	.611	.000		.000	.000	.772	.676	.734	3	Arizona
[†]Rose-breasted Grosbeak (6)	18	.500	.333	.667	.000		.000	.000		.450	.730	4	Iowa
[†]Black-headed Grosbeak (12)	13	.769	.743	.257	.000	.000	.000	.000	.855	1.000	.827	3	Arizona

TABLE 1—*Continued*

Species (references)[a]	n[b]	Nest Succ[c]	Mayf Est[d]	Nest Pred[e]	Cowb Para[f]	Non-Hatc[g]	Strv[h]	Weath[i]	Survival Egg	Survival Inc	Survival Nestl	Hab[j]	Location
†Black-headed Grosbeak (24)	29	.552		.448	.000							1	New Mexico
§Indigo Bunting (6)	26	.077	.013	.533	.247	.000				.180	.070	4	Iowa
§Dickcissel (25)	401	.200	.168	.576	.224				.682	.380	.629	6	Kansas
Eastern Meadowlark (26)	(507)	.385		.536		.022				.479	.802	8	Illinois
Mean		.440	.419	.428	.090	.049	.006	.043	.814	.618	.698		
Standard Error		.032	.042	.027	.028	.012	.003	.012	.033	.036	.029		
Number of species		32	17	33	32	16	19	22	13	27	27		

NOTE: ‡ = ground-nesters, § = shrub or understory-nesters, † = sub-canopy or canopy-nesters.

a. References = (1) Walkinshaw 1966; (2) Holcomb 1972; (3) Briskie and Sealy 1987, 1989a, 1989b; (4) Blancher and Robertson 1985; (5) Murphy 1983; (6) Best and Stauffer 1980; (7) Johnson and Best 1980; (8) Zimmerman 1963; (9) Longcore and Jones 1969; (10) Barlow 1962; (11) Graber 1961; (12) Martin, unpubl. data; (13) Lawrence 1953; (14) Marvil and Cruz 1989; (15) Goossen and Sealy 1982; (16) Rodenhouse 1986; (17) Mayfield 1960; (18) Nolan 1978; (19) Hahn 1937; (20) Hofslund 1957, 1959; (21) Thompson and Nolan 1973; (22) Stewart et al. 1978; (23) Sherry and Holmes 1990; (24) Hill 1988; (25) Zimmerman 1982, 1983, 1984; (26) Roseberry and Klimstra 1970;

b. Sample size in terms of number of nests (or number of eggs if in parentheses).

c. Nesting success as a fraction of the number of nests (or number of eggs if sample size is in parentheses).

d. Mayfield estimate of nesting success.

e. Proportion of nests or eggs lost to nest predation.

f. Proportion of nests or eggs lost to cowbird parasitism. Percentage of nests parasitized can be markedly higher; I only report failures (mortality) attributed to parasitism.

g. Proportion of eggs that did not hatch due to addling or other causes.

h. Proportion of nestlings lost to starvation.

i. Proportion of nests or eggs lost due to severe weather (wind, rain, snow).

j. Nest or egg survival during the egg-laying, incubation, and nestling stages.

k. Habitat Types: 1 = deciduous forest, 2 = coniferous forest, 3 = mixed coniferous-deciduous forests, 4 = riparian forest, 5 = forest edge, 6 = shrublands, 7 = desert, 8 = grasslands, 9 = marsh/cattail.

TABLE 2. Nest success and reproductive mortality from nest predation and Brown-headed Cowbird parasitism among vegetation layers and habitat types

Nesting layer	All species	Forest habitats	Scrub habitats
Nest success			
Ground	0.548 ± 0.052 (7)[a]	0.603 ± 0.054 (4)	0.474 ± 0.090 (3)
Understory/shrub	0.325 ± 0.047 (13)	0.463 ± 0.046 (5)	0.238 ± 0.052 (8)
Subcanopy/canopy	0.513 ± 0.044 (11)	0.513 ± 0.044 (11)	
Nest predation			
Ground	0.371 ± 0.050 (7)	0.412 ± 0.058 (4)	0.317 ± 0.092 (3)
Understory/shrub	0.456 ± 0.050 (13)	0.489 ± 0.047 (5)	0.436 ± 0.077 (8)
Subcanopy/canopy	0.422 ± 0.040 (12)	0.422 ± 0.040 (12)	
Brown-headed Cowbird parasitism			
Ground	0.079 ± 0.037 (7)	0.047 ± 0.047 (4)	0.122 ± 0.061 (3)
Understory/shrub	0.151 ± 0.060 (13)	0.019 ± 0.017 (5)	0.233 ± 0.085 (8)
Subcanopy/canopy	0.031 ± 0.028 (12)	0.031 ± 0.028 (12)	

a. Mean ± Standard error (sample size)

Nest mortality among vegetation layers and habitat types

The data included in Table 1 allow crude comparisons of nesting mortality among vegetation layers, assuming that differences in geographic locations do not overly bias results. I use fraction estimates of nest success because they are available for more studies, and I assume that any biases are in a similar direction for all studies. The results show that nesting success of shrub-nesting birds is lowest, ground-nesting birds highest, and tree-nesting birds are intermediate (Table 2). These results are contrary to the long-standing dogma that ground-nesting birds have the lowest nesting success (e.g., Ricklefs 1969, Whitcomb et al. 1981, Wilcove 1985, Terborgh 1989), but the results must be viewed with some caution because of small sample sizes and geographic variation. However, these results parallel those for species coexisting on my study sites in Arizona where habitat and geographic location are held constant (Martin, unpubl. data).

The greater nest success of ground nesters than understory or shrub nesters holds in both forest and scrub habitats (Table 2). The lower nest success of shrub nesters is due in part to higher nest predation than for ground or tree nesters, but also because cowbird parasitism is substantially higher for shrub nesters, particularly in the scrub habitat (Table 2). The data suggest that nest predation is similar or somewhat lower in scrub than forest habitat, but overall nesting success is lower in scrub because of a much higher incidence of mortality from cowbird parasitism. However, the effect of cowbird parasitism varies among species even in scrub habitat. These data support the widely held recog-

nition that cowbird pressures are generally much greater in more open or disturbed habitats (e.g., see Airola 1986), although Robinson (this volume) found extensive cowbird parasitism within forest islands in Illinois.

Selection potential and demographic consequences of nesting mortality

The primary role of predation in nesting mortality implies that selection should favor choice of nesting habitats that minimize risk of predation and a variety of evidence confirms such evolutionary effects (see below). Predation can also potentially affect population sizes/maintenance on shorter time scales by reducing recruitment to the population. A review of studies of ground-nesting waterfowl shows that removal of predators results in marked decreases in nesting mortality and increased population sizes (Martin in press a). Rates of nesting success and predation in the waterfowl studies are similar to those for the Neotropical migrant species examined here, suggesting predation can exert similar effects on migrants. Sherry and Holmes (this volume) found that nesting mortality in the preceding season explained 70% of the variation in number of first-year recruits in American Redstarts at Hubbard Brook, with nest predation the major cause of nesting mortality.

Nesting mortality is not the only influence on number of young potentially recruited to a population; number of nesting attempts also influences breeding productivity. In fact, high mortality rates can be offset to some extent by persistent renesting attempts and multiple

TABLE 3. Nesting success and reproductive mortality attributable to predation and parasitism by Brown-headed Cowbirds as compared to percentage of nests parasitized. Information sources are provided in Table 1

Species	Nest success	Nest predation	% of Nests parasitized	Parasitism mortality
Acadian Flycatcher	.574	.279	.207	.044
Bell's Vireo	.114	.114	.686	.646
Black-capped Vireo	.191	.124	—	.542
Solitary Vireo	.487	.180	.487	.333
Yellow Warbler	.453	.342	.256	.089
Kirtland's Warbler	.201	.458	.547	.168
Prairie Warbler	.223	.618	.274	.139
Ovenbird	.452	.245	.520	.187
Common Yellowthroat	.520	.145	.385	.197
Dickcissel	.168	.576	.600	.224

brood efforts by successful pairs. As a result, nesting mortality can sometimes underestimate the importance of other limiting factors to natural selection or demographic constraints. For example, starvation is uncommon and accounts for little mortality (Table 1). Yet, birds commonly reduce clutch sizes or number of nesting attempts in response to food limitation, rather than producing young that starve (Rodenhouse 1986, Martin 1987, Simons and Martin 1990). Species that depend on unpredictable food types, such as birds that forage on flying insects are an exception; such species often show higher mortality from weather effects (Table 1, Martin 1987). Thus, food limitation might constrain populations and reduce the reproductive component of fitness even though mortality (starvation) from food limitation is low.

In contrast, the consequences of cowbird parasitism to nesting mortality and demography can be easily overestimated. First, the percentage of nests parasitized does not necessarily indicate the mortality induced by parasitism; the actual mortality induced relative to the percentage of nests parasitized varies widely among species (Table 3). This variance partly reflects variation in the response of species to parasitism; some species eject and other species accept cowbird eggs or abandon the nest (Rothstein 1975, 1982, Rohwer and Spaw 1988). Also, the effect of a cowbird nestling on mortality of host nestlings varies among host species and is often related to size differences. Mortality actually caused by cowbirds also varies with the incidence of other mortality agents, as demonstrated in the Kirtland's Warbler.

Early work on the Kirtland's Warbler indicated that about 55% of the nests were parasitized and parasitized nests had about 78% mortality (Mayfield 1960; also Tables 1, 3). Consequently, parasitism was viewed as the primary limitation on population productivity, and cowbird control efforts were initiated in the early 1970s. Nesting success then increased from 20% to 33%, thus stopping a long-term decline in the population (Walkinshaw 1983). However, the population did not fully recover; removal of cowbirds only stabilized the population, leading to speculation that the population was limited on the wintering grounds. Given the high incidence of parasitism (55%) and the high mortality induced by parasitism (78%), cowbird-induced mortality should have been 43% (55% × 78%). As a consequence, cowbird removal was expected to have a great effect. So, why did cowbird removal only cause a 13% increase in nesting success?

Predation caused mortality in about one-half of parasitized and unparasitized nests (Table 3) and, although not immediately obvious, was the primary source of nesting mortality. Parasitism mortality was irrelevant for one-half of the parasitized nests because they would be lost to predation anyway. Once the 78% parasitism mortality is adjusted by the proportion of nests parasitized (54.7%) and nests surviving predation (46.4%) and surviving other mortality agents (85%), the actual rate of mortality from parasitism was only 16.8%. Removal of cowbirds will not cause recovery of all cowbird-induced mortality because some mortality was due to abandonment following parasitism. About one-half of the nests that were not abandoned following cowbird removal would be lost to predation. Thus, the observed 13% increase in nesting success is almost exactly that expected once the consequences of predation are considered.

The primary role of predation in nesting mortality of Kirtland's Warbler generates the question of whether population recovery might occur following removal of predators. The stabilization of the population following cowbird removal indicates that processes acting on the breeding grounds exert at least some influence on population size. Removal of predators might illustrate such breeding constraints further by potentially yielding additional recovery of the Kirtland's Warbler population. Yet, both cowbird and predator removal are merely stop-gap measures that are continuously costly and that treat symptoms rather than provide long-term solutions. Long-term solutions rest on determining the environmental causes of increases in population sizes of cowbirds and predators and identification of habitat conditions that can minimize such intrusion pressures.

Throughout the rest of this paper I will focus on possible habitat influences on nest predation and breeding productivity. Although I will include some discussion of food, the focus will be on nest predation because it is usually the primary cause of nesting mortality and because it has been given less attention than food. Moreover, some of the potential consequences of nest predation for coexistence of species still remain largely unrecognized.

Identification of appropriate habitat features: The case of foliage density

Natural selection can potentially favor the ability of organisms to identify and choose habitat features influencing nest success and/or adult survival. Manipulation of such habitat features should then exert the greatest and most direct effects on population recruitment. Birds choose nest sites nonrandomly; nesting microhabitats generally differ among coexisting species (MacKenzie et al. 1982, Stauffer and Best 1986, Martin in press b, unpubl. data). Also, nest sites generally differ from unused sites within the same habitat or even territory (e.g., MacKenzie and Sealy 1981, Clark et al. 1983, Petersen and Best 1985, Bekoff et al. 1987, Martin and Roper 1988, Petit et al. 1988). The influence of such choices on the probability of nest predation has been investigated less often, however. Nevertheless, the evidence indicates that birds can respond to predation in their choice of territories and nest sites. Prior experience with predation can influence subsequent nest site choice; Goldeneyes (Dow and Fredga 1983), Tengmalm's Owls (Sonerud 1985), Great Tits (Harvey et al. 1979), Eastern Bluebirds (Pinkowski 1979), Mountain Bluebirds (Herlugson 1981), Stonechats (Greig-Smith 1982), Reed Warblers (Catchpole 1972) and Pinyon Jays (Marzluff 1988) chose nest sites that were spatially distant from previously depredated sites. Also, birds chose nest sites with characteristics that reduced risk of predation (Martin and Roper 1988, Marzluff 1988). In addition, territory occupancy by Eastern Kingbirds was negatively related to predation risk on the territories

(Blancher and Robertson 1985). Thus, birds can choose habitat conditions that reduce risk of nest predation.

Given that birds choose habitat features that increase chances of nesting success, identification of such features is critical for effective management. Identification is facilitated by testing specific predictions generated by hypotheses about the operation of general processes, such as nest predation. A good example is provided by the common association of bird species with vegetation density (see references in Martin 1988a). This association suggests that management of habitats to increase vegetation density can increase the diversity and abundances of birds using the habitat. However, to accomplish such a management goal, we need to know if birds are responding to the density of any specific types of foliage and the spatial scales at which responses occur. Moreover, we need to know the basis for such responses; results can be extended more easily to other habitats and geographic locations by understanding the influence of general processes on habitat choices.

EFFECTS OF NEST PREDATION ON HABITAT QUALITY AT DIFFERENT SPATIAL SCALES

NEST SITE. Foliage density around the nest can be important in concealing the nest. Nest concealment by foliage often decreases the rate of nest predation in both grassland/marsh and shrub/woodland habitats and across a diversity of species (Table 4). In some cases, the lack of a relationship between nest concealment and probability of nest predation might reflect investigator-caused biases; Westmoreland and Best (1985) found that visits to nests by humans increased the probability of nest predation and negated an association between nest concealment and nest predation for Mourning Doves in woodland habitat. Certainly, biases are not always strong given the large number of studies that have found an association between nest concealment and nest predation (see Table 4). Thus, these studies suggest that dense foliage next to the nest reduces the probability of nest predation.

NEST PATCH. Nest concealment is important, but complex habitat in the patch surrounding a nest might reduce predator search efficiency even for poorly concealed nests. Nesting success and population sizes of waterfowl increased in habitats with denser and taller foliage (Kirsch 1969, Oetting and Cassel 1971, Duebbert and Kantrud 1974, Higgins, 1977). Moreover, experimental removal of vegetation caused increased predation and reduced nesting success of waterfowl (e.g., Bengston 1972), although such effects might reflect responses of predators to vegetation disturbance (e.g., Lenington 1979). However, nesting success of White-winged Doves was greater at heights where foliage was

TABLE 4. Number of cases in which frequency of predation was or was not reduced by nest concealment from foliage cover

Taxonomic group	Habitat	Reduced	Not reduced
Artificial nests	Grassland/Marsh	6	0
	Shrub/Woodland	3	1
Anatinae	Grassland/Marsh	8	1
Phasianidae, Columbidae	Grassland/Marsh	1	0
	Shrub/Woodland	4	1
Passeriformes	Grassland/Marsh	1	2
	Shrub/Woodland	6	2
TOTALS	Grassland/Marsh	16	3
	Shrub/Woodland	13	4

SOURCES: References for artificial nests: Dwernychuk and Boag 1972, Jones and Hungerford 1972, Schranck 1972, Picozzi 1975, Gottfried and Thompson 1978, Baker 1979, Boag et al. 1984, Sugden and Beyersbergen 1986, 1987, Storaas 1988; Anatinae: Jarvis and Harris 1971, Oetting and Cassel 1971, Bengston 1972, Schranck 1972, Byers 1974, Duebbert and Kantrud 1974, Livezey 1981, Hines and Mitchell 1983, Hill 1984; Phasianidae, Columbidae: Chesness et al. 1972, Wallestad and Pyrah 1974, Butler 1977, Keppie and Herzog 1978, Erikstad et al. 1982, Westmoreland and Best 1985; Passeriformes: Nice 1937, Caccamise 1977, Knapton 1978, Best 1978, Nolan 1978, Wray and Whitmore 1979, Best and Stauffer 1980, Murphy 1983, Conner et al. 1986, Marzluff 1988, Martin and Roper 1988.

denser; nests above or below the strata of densest foliage suffered higher predation rates (Butler 1977). Also, nest predation was greater in Cassin's Kingbird in open riparian habitat than in denser riparian habitat (Blancher and Robertson 1984). More directly, Bowman and Harris (1980) showed that raccoon (*Procyon lotor*) foraging efficiency decreased, search time increased, and fewer clutches of eggs were found as understory foliage density was artificially increased.

These studies suggest that dense foliage in the nest patch might impede probability of predation. Yet, increases in total foliage are not always beneficial (Belles-Isles and Picman 1986, Li and Martin 1991). Thus, birds may choose patches with the greatest total foliage or with habitat features that are simply correlated with vegetation density. For example, a quantitative model of predator foraging (Martin, in prep.) predicts that predators can increase their foraging efficiency when searching for prey (e.g., nests) that are sedentary on specific vegetation types by first searching for these vegetation types (potential nest sites). Increases in the number of these potential nest sites can reduce the probability that predators discover the one containing the nest (Martin 1988c). Hermit Thrushes almost always nest in small white firs (*Abies concolor*) in central Arizona (Martin and Roper 1988). Predation rates were lower at nests with greater numbers of potential nest sites (small white firs) in the surrounding patch, as pre-

dicted by the potential nest site hypothesis (Martin and Roper 1988, Martin in press b, unpubl. data). In contrast, predation rates did not differ among nests with different densities of total foliage, indicating total foliage density was not important to predation probability (Martin and Roper 1988, Martin in press b, unpubl. data). Similar results exist for other species in Arizona and other locations (Martin in press b, unpubl. data). Identification of these habitat features (potential nest sites) that directly affect nesting success then represent critical habitat features for management.

TERRITORY. Nest sites of open-nesting birds have been neglected as a basis for territory choice because sites are typically thought to be abundant rather than limiting (e.g., Ricklefs 1969, Lack 1971). However, such conclusions have been based only on the microsites in which nests are located. If nest sites are characterized by both the site and the surrounding habitat patch, then suitable nest sites might not be as abundant as conventionally thought. Probability of predation may decrease with increasing numbers of patches that must be searched, similar to the response to number of potential nest sites in the nest patch (see above). An abundance of suitable nest patches also is needed within a territory to provide options for renesting attempts; three to five renesting attempts are not uncommon for open-nesting birds (e.g., Nice 1937, Nolan 1978, Martin, unpubl.

data). Once a nest has been found, predators might revisit a general area around the nest, potentially explaining the tendency of birds to move a substantial distance following predation (e.g., Catchpole 1972, Harvey et al. 1979, Greig-Smith 1982, Dow and Fredga 1983, Sonerud 1985) and making dispersion of nest patches within territories important. Such effects might extend between seasons; nest sites of open-nesting species that have previously been depredated have a higher probability of being attacked than previously successful nest sites for Eastern Kingbirds (Blancher and Robertson 1985) and Pinyon Jays (Marzluff 1988). Thus, quality of territories should be influenced by the number and dispersion of nest patches such that some minimum number of nest patches might be required for a territory to be suitable for occupancy. Some studies have shown that female choice of males or territories may be based on availability of quality nest sites (see Pleszczynska and Hansell 1980, Garson 1980, Askenmo 1984, Alatalo et al. 1986, Slagsvold 1986, Hill 1988).

The use of a conceptual model (predator search strategy) based on the hypothesized action of a general process (predation) allowed specific predictions about habitat features to be tested. Results from this approach can be easily extended to other habitats or geographic locations; birds can be examined in any geographic location to determine whether they choose nest patches and territories with an abundance of nesting substrates.

FOOD ABUNDANCE VS. NEST SUBSTRATES AS DETERMINANTS OF HABITAT QUALITY

Elimination of alternative hypotheses favoring the same pattern is needed for clear evaluation of the importance of habitat features. For example, nest patches with dense foliage might be chosen because of associated increases in abundance of foods (Conner et al. 1986). Such alternatives can be tested. The food limitation hypothesis generates the prediction that foliage used for foraging should be greater in chosen nest patches or territories than in unoccupied areas. In the case of the Hermit Thrush, this alternative can be eliminated because Hermit Thrushes forage on the ground away from small white firs (i.e., nesting patches) (Martin and Roper 1988, Martin, unpubl.).

Separation of foraging and nesting habitat features is not as easy for many other species. For example, Least Bell's Vireo used the same plant species and heights for both foraging and nesting and they chose territories with dense foliage at those heights (Franzreb 1989). Similarly, Northern Cardinals chose territories with more foliage at the height at which they both foraged and nested, and successful nests were in territories with significantly more foliage at those heights (Conner et al. 1986). However, such analyses do not necessarily

identify the specific habitat features being chosen or the basis for the choice, that is, were the birds actually choosing general foliage density or some other habitat feature (density of foraging or nesting substrates) associated with general foliage density? Were choices based on nest predation, which favors choice of nesting substrates, or food limitation, which favors choice of foraging substrates? Answers to such questions aid habitat management.

Importance of different resources to habitat choices can be indicated by whether the fitness components affected were those expected under the hypothesized process. For example, Conner et al. (1986) showed that successful territories of Northern Cardinals had more foliage and associated insect food. These results could be interpreted to favor the food limitation hypothesis. Yet, actual effects of food on choice were not examined; their results showed that successful territories had more food, along with other potential resources, but they did not show that food affected reproductive success. Birds commonly increase the size or number of clutches in response to increased food and they can choose territories with more food (reviewed in Martin 1987). So, examination of the prediction that larger or more clutches occur in territories with more food (foliage) provides a clearer test of food limitation as the basis for choice of these territories. Such reproductive information was not reported by Conner et al. (1986) and, thus, food limitation effects could not be examined. However, causes of nesting mortality were reported; nest predation and parasitism were the cause of all nest failures. Failed nests were in territories with less foliage at nesting height. Therefore, nests lost to predators and parasites must have existed in territories with significantly less foliage at nest height than successful nests. Such results suggest that choice of territories with dense foliage was influenced by nest predation and parasitism. Moreover, the birds might have chosen territories with more foliage of the specific types used as nesting substrates, and density of these specific habitat features may merely be correlated with measured foliage density. However, such specific features were not measured by Conner et al. (1986).

Indications that predation is important to territory choices does not mean that food might not also be important. Birds using substrates that differ for nesting as compared to foraging undoubtedly choose territories and habitats that supply both resources. In fact, nest sites and food can be limiting simultaneously. A clear example is provided by cavity-nesting birds; cavities are commonly limiting (Balda 1975, Slagsvold 1978, Scott 1979, Mannan et al. 1980, Village 1983, Raphael and White 1984), but so is food (Martin 1987). Thus, different processes (e.g., food limitation vs. nest predation) can cause different habitat features to be simultaneously important. Effective management requires incorporation of each critical feature, but inclusion of critical features in the management plan first requires their identification; identification is facilitated by testing alternative hypotheses that address *why* the features might be important.

Studies of foraging sites provide a good example of the lack of information on specific habitat features needed by bird species. Foraging behavior is commonly studied, but the specific foliage types and microhabitat conditions associated with actual foraging sites are rarely described. Yet, some studies have shown that birds can exhibit plant species preferences because of morphological constraints and/or food availability differences (Morse 1976, Holmes and Robinson 1981, Wiens and Rotenberry 1981, Rotenberry 1985, Whelan 1987, Knopf et al. 1990). The suitability of any particular foraging substrate can vary depending on characteristics of the surrounding microhabitat, either in terms of exposure to sun or shade, effect of soil nutrients on plant chemicals, or influence of surrounding vegetation on insect production or vulnerability to predators. Yet, patch characteristics associated with foraging sites are rarely studied. More importantly, the influence of foraging substrates and surrounding habitat on fitness components are unstudied.

Population-level perspectives in breeding vs. winter seasons

Variation in abundance and quality of resources (e.g., nest sites and food) can favor choice of habitat patches with more of these resources. At larger spatial scales, variation in these resources can affect numbers of individuals (density) choosing a habitat. For example, increases in the density of potential nest sites can allow an increase in density of birds without increased risk of predation (Martin 1988a, unpubl. ms). Indeed, artificial or natural changes in numbers of preferred nesting sites is positively associated with changes in population sizes of open-nesting species (Kilgore 1971, Best 1972, Dwernychuk and Boag 1972, Evans 1978, Castrale 1982, Munkejord et al. 1985, Martin 1988a). Artificial increases in nest sites in heavily managed forests produced significant increases in population sizes of some open-nesting species (Pfeifer 1963). In addition, nest sites are commonly limiting in salt marshes (Post 1974) and desert habitats (Tomoff 1974, Finch 1985).

When both food and nest sites become limiting, changes in abundances of either should cause changes in population sizes within habitats. For example, understory brush removal did not affect the numbers of nest sites available to American Robins and Western Wood-Pewees, but did increase availability of foraging sites; consequently, these two species subsequently increased

following shrub removal (Kilgore 1971). Yet, shrub removal reduced numbers of available nest sites for ground- and shrub-nesting species and three of these species declined in abundance or disappeared following shrub removal (see Kilgore 1971).

In short, changes in abundance of nest sites or food can cause temporal changes in population sizes. Changes in abundance of resources can occur from habitat degradation, or natural processes. Holmes et al. (1986) showed that most bird species at Hubbard Brook Experimental Forest in New Hampshire significantly decreased in abundance over 16 years, and suggested the decline for many foliage-gleaning species was due to a general decrease in abundance of defoliating Lepidoptera. Food limitation caused by natural fluctuations in an unpredictable food source might have caused these long-term population declines, although succession caused some changes in vegetation structure and these successional changes could have contributed to declines of some species (Holmes and Sherry 1988).

The population declines of migrants at Hubbard Brook are also seen in a variety of Neotropical migrants throughout eastern North America (Robbins et al. 1989). Holmes and Sherry (1988) provided a variety of convincing evidence as to why the declines at Hubbard Brook cannot be attributed to deforestation on tropical wintering areas, although Holmes et al. (1989) point out that events affecting survival on the wintering grounds might also affect demography. Robbins et al. (1989) recognized the potential influence of problems on both wintering and breeding grounds to long-term population declines of migrants, but concluded that tropical deforestation exerted a more direct impact than forest losses and fragmentation in North America. They based their conclusions on results indicating that forest-wintering species generally showed long-term population declines, whereas scrub-wintering species did not show general population declines. They carefully based their wintering habitat classifications on data, but the data were from a single site (Quintana Roo, Yucatan, Mexico) and they acknowledged that habitat data from other locations in the Neotropics were needed. This caution was lost by the strength of their conclusions which stated that tropical deforestation is at the root of migrant population declines. Yet, many migrant species vary their habitat use patterns in different parts of their wintering ranges (see below). As a result, the strength of negative population trends in forest- as compared to scrub-wintering migrants can differ among winter sites.

First, some species that were characterized as primarily forest-wintering by Robbins et al. (1989) included White-eyed Vireo, Chestnut-sided Warbler, Ovenbird, and Kentucky Warbler. All four species exhibited negative population trends from 1978 to 1987 (Robbins et al. 1989), but all four species were more abundant and frequently recaptured (indicating preference for the sites) in second-growth habitats in Belize (Petit et al., this volume), Costa Rica (Blake and Loiselle, this volume), and Panama (Martin and Karr 1986). Given that these species show population declines, can we conclude that tropical second-growth areas are limiting and disappearing? Second, Petit et al. (this volume) provided data on habitat preferences of eight migrant species wintering in Belize. Four of these species were more abundant in scrub habitat and three showed significant population declines based on data in Robbins et al. (1989), whereas only two of the four species that were more abundant in forest had significant population declines (although one species also had a nonsignificant negative trend). Finally, Lynch (1989) provided winter habitat associations for migrant species over a large portion of the Yucatan Peninsula and, thereby, provided strong replication of species habitat patterns. Population trend data for these species, using Lynch's classification, indicated that 50% ($n = 6$ species) of early succession species, 60% ($n = 5$) of generalist species, and only 27% ($n = 11$) of forest species had significantly negative population trends. Thus, these three examples indicate that population declines are not more marked among forest-wintering migrants. Although the study by Lynch (1989) provided the most extensive geographic coverage of any existing study, these examples still suffer from the same problem as that of Robbins et al. (1989): habitat associations of species in the locations examined might not be typical of the species throughout their winter ranges. Unfortunately, we cannot characterize habitat-use patterns of most migrants throughout their winter ranges because insufficient data are available for (1) different locations and (2) different habitat types within locations using both netting and visual censuses and including recapture data to examine suitability.

These three examples suggest that habitat loss problems on the wintering grounds may include not only forest but also woody second growth. However, these examples may also indicate that population trends arise from processes acting elsewhere. James et al. (this volume) show that long-term population trends of the eight most common wood warbler species in the southeastern United States differ in lowland as compared to upland forest habitats. Such differences among conditions on the breeding grounds suggest breeding season influences on demography. That evidence, added to the variety of evidence in this paper documenting the importance of the breeding season to demographic trends, should raise caution in attributing the primary cause of migrant population declines to tropical deforestation alone; migrants might be constrained during breeding, migration, or winter (Martin and Karr 1990), and alternative

hypotheses focused on these different seasons need study before concluding that wintering grounds are the major source of population problems (Holmes and Sherry 1988, Hutto 1988). Of course, such conclusions do not diminish the need for immediate conservation of tropical forests.

Habitat quality/degradation and coexistence of species

Given that habitat conditions on the breeding grounds are influencing demographies, then attention to habitat degradation on the breeding grounds is necessary. Moreover, habitat conditions might not simply influence the demography of individual species but also affect coexistence of species, and interactions among these coexisting species may even contribute to population problems. Thus, considerations of the impacts of habitat degradation need to include entire species assemblages.

Habitat degradation can be caused by fragmentation, a subject which has received much attention, or by grazing, logging, or understory removal, which have received somewhat less attention. Fragmentation of habitats often occurs because of replacement of portions of forests or other natural habitats with agricultural or pasture lands. Decreased area of forest tracts generally leads to a decrease in total numbers of coexisting species and a disproportionate increase in abundance of species that feed on the additional food supplied by the surrounding landscape (Martin 1981, Ambuel and Temple 1983, Blake 1983). As a result, bird density is disproportionately increased in small forest islands (Martin 1981). I have argued elsewhere and provided experimental evidence that predators respond to the cumulative density of all species with similar nest sites (Martin 1988b,c). Increases in density of various bird species because of food augmentation by the surrounding landscape in small islands causes an increase in occupied nest sites relative to potential sites and can then cause an increase in predation probability, yielding the prediction of increased predation in smaller islands. Experiments indicate that smaller forest tracts have higher rates of nest predation than larger tracts (Wilcove 1985, Small and Hunter 1988). This result is usually attributed to increased densities of nest predators by the disturbed surrounding landscape and, indeed, increased predator densities should cause increased predation rates. Yet, the possible added attraction of high nest density might contribute to the increased predation rates. However, such effects have not been recognized or studied.

Predators are thought to be particularly abundant along forest edges and cause increased predation pressure there, thus creating an "ecological trap." Gates and Gysel (1978) suggested that birds are attracted to the increased vegetative density and heterogeneity of edges, but are then subject to greater predation rates because of increased densities and activity of predators along the edge. However, experimental tests of this proposition did not yield evidence of increased predation rates at edges as compared to forest interiors (e.g., Yahner and Wright 1985, Angelstam 1986, Ratti and Reese 1988, Small and Hunter 1988). Increased vegetation density and heterogeneity along edges increases the number of potential nest sites and might offset the increase in predator abundance. Indeed, Small and Hunter (1988) examined forest islands in Maine that did not have edges adjacent to agricultural or other food supplies that might augment predator populations, and they found predation actually increased with distance from the edge. If foliage density was greater along the edge, then decreased predation there might reflect the increased density of potential nest sites.

Such interactions also need to be considered for Brown-headed Cowbird parasitism. Cowbird parasitism is thought to be inversely density-dependent, where parasitism frequency decreases with increased host density (Fretwell 1977). However, possible effects of cumulative densities of coexisting host species and vegetation structure have not been examined. For example, Zimmerman (1983) examined parasitism on Dickcissels in prairie (low density) and old field (high density) habitats and found lower frequency of parasitism in old fields consistent with the higher density of Dickcissels there. Yet, Zimmerman (1983) noted that only a few individuals of one alternate host species occurred in old-field sites, but several alternate hosts occurred in prairie sites (also see Elliot 1978). Thus, cumulative nest density of all hosts might actually be higher in the prairie habitat. Moreover, the old-field habitat provided a structurally more complex habitat. The potential interacting effects of habitat complexity and cumulative host density on parasitism needs study.

Habitat complexity and heterogeneity can also be important by providing the habitat requirements for greater numbers of species. The increase in numbers of species with increased habitat complexity is usually thought to reflect the need for partitioning of foraging space because of food-based competition (references in Martin 1986, 1988a). However, nest predation can favor microhabitat differences among coexisting species; predators might respond to the cumulative density of coexisting species that use similar nesting sites and thereby favor coexistence of species with different nesting sites (Martin 1988b,c, in press b). Indeed, bird species commonly differ in their nest site requirements (Martin in press b, unpubl. data). Thus, the increase in numbers of species with foliage density and habitat heterogeneity might reflect availability of suitable nest sites instead of or in addition to foraging sites (Martin 1988a,b,c). Consequently, reduction in diversity of nest

sites by habitat degradation can cause increased overlap in nest site use among coexisting species and, thereby increase predation risk (Martin, unpubl. data) or cause elimination of species.

Cattle can reduce understory vegetation when allowed to graze within forests and cause a reduction in numbers of coexisting bird species (Martin 1984). Cattle grazing can also lead to an increase in cowbirds and thus create additional problems for remaining species. Forestry practices, such as single-tree selection and understory removal techniques, cause a reduction in the diversity and density of potential nest sites, which can cause an increase in predation and/or direct loss of species (see Martin 1988a). Also, fragmentation might cause a change in the structure of vegetation because of potential consequences for the amount of sunlight or wind that enters the habitat after fragmentation. Forest area often influences the diversity of microhabitats present, which can then influence the types of birds present (e.g., Johnson 1975, Lynch and Whigham 1984). Area of forest fragments usually predicts numbers of species, but the presence and abundance of individual species within fragments are usually better predicted by habitat features than area (Robbins 1980, Ambuel and Temple 1983, Lynch and Whigham 1984, Blake and Karr 1987). Approaches that identify specific habitat needs of species and the loss of such habitat features from fragments need study.

Fragmentation is commonly thought to affect many Neotropical migrants because many are ground- or near-ground nesters which are thought to be more susceptible to predation, and because most are thought to produce only a single brood per year (see Whitcomb et al. 1981, Wilcove 1985, Robbins et al. 1989, Terborgh 1989). Yet, the evidence examined here (Tables 1, 2) calls into question the long-standing dogma that ground-nesting birds are more susceptible to predation. Moreover, ground-nesting warblers have larger clutches than off-ground nesters (Martin 1988d). Thus, ground-nesting migrants might have higher nesting success and larger clutches as compared to off-ground nesters. Of course, the differences in clutch size could be offset by differences in numbers of broods (ground nesters might have fewer broods per year), thereby yielding similar or even lower annual productivity in ground nesters. Such patterns cannot be addressed at present because information on numbers of broods is particularly rare. Yet, detailed studies of species such as Black-throated Blue Warbler (Rodenhouse 1986), Prairie Warbler (Nolan 1978), Least Bell's Vireo (Franzreb 1989), and Black-capped Vireo (Tazik and Cornelius 1989) indicate that double-brooding might be common among migrants previously thought to be single-brooded. Of course, the number of successful broods attempted by Neotropical migrants may still be less than many resident or short-

468 • Thomas E. Martin

distance migrants. More life-history studies are needed before many generalizations can be made. Data are particularly lacking for western U.S. species where such basic information as duration of incubation and nestling periods is unknown for some species.

Conclusions and management implications

The specific habitat features that have a direct effect on reproduction or survival represent the appropriate and critical features that need to be identified for management plans. Predation can make nest sites a critical resource because nest sites vary in their vulnerability to nest predation and nest predation is commonly the primary source of nesting mortality (Table 1). Two separate factors might influence risk of predation (and possibly parasitism): (1) density and types of vegetation substrates that provide potential nest sites and (2) density of predators (or nest parasites). Both factors are modified by land use practices; grazing, logging, and understory removal can affect potential nest sites (Martin 1988a) and, as already recognized, the type of land use practices surrounding a habitat fragment can influence predator populations and predation rates (Wilcove 1985, Small and Hunter 1988). Such effects apply to cowbirds as well; the amount of habitat that is suitable for cowbirds needs to be examined relative to host habitat as a measure of "cowbird pressure" (McGeen 1972) because total abundance of cowbirds undoubtedly influences cowbird pressure and impact.

A number of studies have shown that loss of individual species with decreasing area of habitat fragments is more strongly related to changes in habitat than area (see earlier). Such results emphasize the importance of identifying the critical habitat features influencing success of species. Population declines require immediate action, but such action can be inappropriate if we are not managing or saving the appropriate environmental conditions. Indeed, surveys of the abundance or presence of species must be viewed cautiously as a measure of habitat suitability because species might be present in habitat conditions in which the population is sustained by immigration rather than breeding productivity (e.g., see Pulliam 1988; Robinson, this volume; Martin in press b). Also, studies of the same species need to be conducted in a variety of geographical and habitat settings because general physiognomy of preferred habitat might remain similar, but actual floristics and habitat breadth might vary over the range of a species (James et al. 1984, Rotenberry 1985, Knopf et al. 1990).

I focused on nest predation and food limitation, but other factors could also be important in influencing habitat choices. For example, the quality of a nest site is probably influenced by effects of habitat features on the microclimate (Calder 1973). Effects of macroclimate

might also be important given the common loss of nests as a result of inclement weather (Table 1). Similarly, specific habitat features might influence the probability of nest discovery by cowbirds and thereby affect parasitism rates, but examination of microhabitat influences on parasitism are lacking. Also, parasitism could increase with cumulative density of all potential hosts, but again such effects have not been studied. This neglect occurs for several endangered species (e.g., Kirtland's Warbler, Black-capped Vireo, Least Bell's Vireo) that are strongly affected by parasitism (Table 1). Such studies are needed.

Examination of the evidence that habitat losses on the wintering grounds are the main cause of declines in migrant populations indicates that such conclusions may be hasty; alternative hypotheses, such as habitat losses on the breeding grounds, also need further testing (Holmes and Sherry 1988, Hutto 1988). Evidence provided here and elsewhere indicates that constraints on reproductive success strongly influence population sizes. I emphasized the importance of fitness components because of their potential consequences for natural selection and population dynamics. Such approaches are also needed on the wintering grounds; examination of survival or recapture rates in different habitat types is needed to determine quality of habitat types (e.g., see Blake and Loiselle, this volume). Moreover, population declines of migratory species could be caused by decreased survival on the wintering grounds as a result of habitat loss or caused by decreased nesting success resulting from habitat degradation on the breeding grounds. Examination of both reproductive success and survival is needed to pinpoint relative contribution of these causes to population declines.

Demography of a population is a consequence of life history traits that evolve as a function of ecological traits of species (e.g., the type of nest site or habitat used by species). Thus, many migrant species have evolved traits (e.g., clutch size, numbers of nesting attempts) that allow maintenance of the population even under nest mortality rates of about 50 to 60% (Table 1). However, additional increases in nesting mortality from nest predation or other sources (e.g., cowbird parasitism) because of habitat degradation might increase mortality to levels that cannot be compensated and thereby form an important constraint on population sizes. More studies of life history traits are needed to identify such effects. Moreover, examination of breeding season constraints have not been experimentally studied for passerines, although such studies are possible. Experimental removal of predators in studies of nesting game birds have provided clear evidence of increased reproductive success and population sizes (see earlier). Such studies have not been conducted with passerines, but could provide important information on the limiting nature of predation. Removal of predators, however, is a means of studying the potential limiting influence of such factors on population sizes; predator removal is not advocated as a management tool. When factors such as predation or parasitism are significant threats to populations, such as Kirtland's Warblers or Black-capped Vireos, they are almost undoubtedly symptoms of a larger problem caused by habitat degradation. Identification of habitat features that directly impede the effectiveness of predators and parasites at finding nests and reduction of land use practices that augment predator or omnivore populations form the long-term solution to such problems. We need to begin to identify such features in our attempts at conservation of species.

Acknowledgments

I greatly appreciate comments by R. Goforth, J.M. Hagan, D.W. Johnston, F.L. Knopf, D.R. Petit, L.J. Petit, and T.W. Sherry on early drafts. My work on effects of nest predation and habitat selection has been supported by the National Science Foundation (grants BSR-8614598 and BSR-9006320).

Literature cited

Airola, D.A. 1986. Brown-headed Cowbird parasitism and habitat disturbance in the Sierra Nevada. *J. Wildl. Manage.* 50:571–575.

Alatalo, R.V., A. Lundberg, and C. Glynn. 1986. Female Pied Flycatchers choose territory quality and not male characteristics. *Nature* 323:152–153.

Ambuel, B., and S.A. Temple. 1983. Area-dependent changes in the bird communities and vegetation of southern Wisconsin forests. *Ecology* 64:1057–1068.

Anderson, S.H., and H.H. Shugart. 1974. Habitat selection of breeding birds in an east Tennessee deciduous forest. *Ecology* 55:828–837.

Angelstam, P. 1986. Predation on ground-nesting birds' nests in relation to predator densities and habitat edge. *Oikos* 47:365–373.

Askenmo, C.E.H. 1984. Polygyny and nest site selection in the Pied Flycatcher. *Anim. Behav.* 32:972–980.

Baker, B.W. 1979. Ecological factors affecting wild turkey nest predation on south Texas rangelands. *Proc. Ann. Conf. S.E. Assoc. Fish and Wildl. Agencies* 32:126–136.

Balda, R. 1975. Vegetation structure and breeding bird diversity. Pages 59–80 in *Proc. Symp. Manage. For. Range Habitats for Non-game Birds.* USDA Forest Service GTR WO-1.

Barlow, J.C. 1962. Natural history of the Bell Vireo, *Vireo bellii* Audubon. *Univ. Kans. Publ. Mus. Nat. Hist.* 12:241–296.

Bekoff, M., A.C. Scott, and D.A. Conner. 1987. Nonrandom nest-site selection in Evening Grosbeaks. *Condor* 89:819–829.

Belles-Isles, J.C., and J. Picman. 1986. Nesting losses and nest site preferences in House Wrens. *Condor* 88:483–486.

Bengston, S.A. 1972. Reproduction and fluctuations in size of duck populations at lake Myvatn, Iceland. *Oikos* 23:35–58.

Best, L.B. 1972. First-year effects of sagebrush control on two sparrows. *J. Wildl. Manage.* 36:534–544.

———. 1978. Field Sparrow reproductive success and nesting ecology. *Auk* 95:9–22.

Best, L.B., and D.F. Stauffer. 1980. Factors affecting nesting success in riparian bird communities. *Condor* 82:149–158.

Blake, J.G. 1983. Trophic structure of bird communities in forest patches in east-central Illinois. *Wilson Bull.* 95:416–430.

Blake, J.G., and J.R. Karr. 1987. Breeding birds in isolated woodlots: Area and habitat relationships. *Ecology* 68:1724–1734.

Blancher, P.J., and R.J. Robertson. 1984. Resource use by sympatric kingbirds. *Condor* 86:305–313.

Blancher, P.J., and R.J. Robertson. 1985. Site consistency in kingbird breeding performance: Implications for site fidelity. *J. Anim. Ecol.* 54:1017–1027.

Boag, D.A., S.G. Reebs, and M.A. Schroeder. 1984. Egg loss among Spruce Grouse inhabiting lodgepole pine forests. *Can. J. Zool.* 62:1034–1037.

Bowman, G.B., and L.D. Harris. 1980. Effect of spatial heterogeneity on ground-nest depredation. *J. Wildl. Manage.* 44:806–813.

Briskie, J.V., and S.G. Sealy. 1987. Responses of Least Flycatchers to experimental inter- and intraspecific brood parasitism. *Condor* 89:899–901.

———. 1989a. Determination of clutch size in the Least Flycatcher. *Auk* 106:269–278.

———. 1989b. Nest-failure and the evolution of hatching asynchrony in the Least Flycatcher. *J. Anim. Ecol.* 58:653–665.

Butler, W.I., Jr. 1977. A White-winged Dove nesting study in three riparian communities on the Lower Colorado River. M.S. Thesis, Arizona State University, Tempe, Arizona.

Byers, S.M. 1974. Predator-prey relationships on an Iowa nesting area. *Trans. N. Am. Wildl. Nat. Resour. Conf.* 39:223–229.

Caccamise, D.F. 1977. Nesting success and nest site characteristics in the Red-winged Blackbird. *Wilson Bull.* 89:396–403.

Calder, W.A. 1973. Microhabitat selection during nesting of hummingbirds in the Rocky Mountains. *Ecology* 54:127–134.

Castrale, J. 1982. Effects of two sagebrush control methods on nongame birds. *J. Wildl. Manage.* 46:945–952.

Catchpole, C.K. 1972. A comparative study of territory in the reed warbler (*A. schoenobaenus*). *J. Zool.* (London) 166:213–231.

Chesness, R.A., M.M. Nelson, and W.H. Longley. 1972. The effect of predator removal on pheasant reproductive success. *J. Wildl. Manage.* 32:683–697.

Clark, L., R.E. Ricklefs, and R.W. Schreiber. 1983. Nest-site selection by the Red-tailed Tropicbird. *Auk* 100:953–959.

Conner, R.N., M.E., Anderson, and J.G. Dickson. 1986. Relationships among territory size, habitat, song, and nesting success of Northern Cardinals. *Auk* 103:23–31.

Dow, H., and S. Fredga. 1983. Breeding and natal dispersal of the Goldeneye, *Bucephala clangula. J. Anim. Ecol.* 52:681–695.

Duebbert, H.F., and H.A. Kantrud. 1974. Upland duck nesting related to land use and predator reduction. *J. Wildl. Manage.* 38:257–265.

Dwernychuk, L.W., and D.A. Boag. 1972. How vegetative cover protects duck eggs from egg-eating birds. *J. Wildl. Manage.*

36:955–958.

Elliot, P.F. 1978. Cowbird parasitism in the Kansas tallgrass prairie. *Auk* 95:161–167.

Erikstad, K.E., R. Blom, and S. Myrberget. 1982. Territorial Hooded Crows as predators on Willow Ptarmigan nests. *J. Wildl. Manage.* 46:109–114.

Evans, E.W. 1978. Nesting responses of Field Sparrows (*Spizella pusilla*) to plant succession on a Michigan old field. *Condor* 80:34–40.

Finch, D.M. 1985. Multivariate analysis of early and late nest sites of Abert's Towhees. *Southwest. Nat.* 30:427–432.

Franzreb, K.E. 1989. *Ecology and Conservation of the Endangered Least Bell's Vireo.* U.S. Fish and Wildlife Service Biological Rept. 89.

Fretwell, S. 1972. *Populations in a Seasonal Environment.* Princeton: Princeton University Press.

———. 1977. Is the Dickcissel a threatened species? *Am. Birds* 31:923–932.

Garson, P.J. 1980. Male behaviour and female choice: Mate selection in the wren? *Anim. Behav.* 28:491–502.

Gates, J.E., and L.W. Gysel. 1978. Avian nest dispersion and fledgling success in field forest ecotones. *Ecology* 59:871–883.

Goossen, J.P., and S.G. Sealy. 1982. Production of young in a dense nesting population of Yellow Warblers, *Dendroica petechia*, in Manitoba. *Can. Field-Nat.* 96:189–199.

Gottfried, B.M., and C.F. Thompson. 1978. Experimental analysis of nest predation in an old-field habitat. *Auk* 95:304–312.

Graber, J.W. 1961. Distribution, habitat requirements, and life history of the Black-capped Vireo (*Vireo atricapilla*). *Ecol. Monogr.* 31:313–336.

Greig-Smith, P.W. 1982. Dispersal between nest-sites by stonechats *Saxicola torquata* in relation to previous breeding success. *Ornis Scand.* 13:232–238.

Hahn, H.W. 1937. Life history of the Ovenbird in southern Michigan. *Wilson Bull.* 49:145–237.

Harvey, P.H., P.J. Greenwood, and C.M. Perrins. 1979. Breeding area fidelity of Great Tits (*Parus major*). *J. Anim. Ecol.* 48:305–313.

Hensler, G.L., and J.D. Nichols. 1981. The Mayfield method of estimating nesting success: A model, estimators and simulation results. *Wilson Bull.* 93:42–53.

Herlugson, C.J. 1981. Nest site selection in Mountain Bluebirds. *Condor* 83:252–255.

Higgins, K.F. 1977. Duck nesting in intensively farmed areas of North Dakota. *J. Wildl. Manage.* 41:232–242.

Hill, D.A. 1984. Factors affecting nest success in the Mallard and Tufted Duck. *Ornis. Scand.* 15:115–122.

Hill, G.E. 1988. Age, plumage brightness, territory quality, and reproductive success in the Black-headed Grosbeak. *Condor* 90:379–388.

Hines, J.E., and G.J. Mitchell. 1983. Gadwall nest-site selection and nesting success. *J. Wildl. Manage.* 47:1063–1071.

Hofslund, P.B. 1957. Cowbird parasitism of the northern Yellow-throat. *Auk* 74:42–48.

———. 1959. A life history study of the Yellowthroat, *Geothlypis trichas*. *Proc. Minn. Acad. Sci.* 27:144–174.

Holcomb, L.C. 1972. Nest success and age-specific mortality in Traill's Flycatcher. *Auk* 89:837–841.

Holmes, R.T., and S.K. Robinson. 1981. Tree species preferences by foraging insectivorous birds in a northern hardwoods forest. *Oecologia* 48:31–35.

Holmes, R.T., and T.W. Sherry. 1988. Assessing population trends of New Hampshire forest birds: Local vs. regional patterns. *Auk* 105:756–768.

Holmes, R.T., T.W. Sherry, and L. Reitsma. 1989. Population structure, territoriality and overwinter survival of two migrant warbler species in Jamaica. *Condor* 91:545–561.

Holmes, R.T., T.W. Sherry, and F.W. Sturges. 1986. Bird community dynamics in a temperate deciduous forest: Long-term trends at Hubbard Brook. *Ecol. Monogr.* 50:201–220.

Holt, R.D. 1977. Predation, apparent competition and the structure of prey communities. *Theor. Pop. Biol.* 12:197–229.

———. 1984. Spatial heterogeneity, indirect interactions, and the coexistence of prey species. *Am. Nat.* 124:377–406.

Hutto, R.L. 1988. Is tropical deforestation responsible for the reported declines in neotropical migrant populations? *Am. Birds* 42:375–379.

James, F.C. 1971. Ordination of habitat relationships among breeding birds. *Wilson Bull.* 83:215–236.

James, F.C., and N.O. Wamer. 1982. Relationships between temperate forest bird communities and vegetation structure. *Ecology* 63:159–171.

James, F.C., R.F. Johnston, N.O. Wamer, G.J. Niemi, and W.J. Boecklen. 1984. The Grinnellian niche of the Wood Thrush. *Am. Nat.* 124:17–47.

Jarvis, R.L., and S.W. Harris. 1971. Land-use patterns and duck production at Malheur National Wildlife Refuge. *J. Wildl. Manage.* 35:767–773.

Johnson, D.H. 1979. Estimating nest success: The Mayfield method and an alternative. *Auk* 96:651–661.

Johnson, E.J., and L.B. Best. 1980. Breeding biology of the Gray Catbird in Iowa. *Iowa State J. Res.* 55:171–183.

Johnson, N.K. 1975. Controls of number of bird species on montane islands in the Great Basin. *Evolution* 29:545–567.

Jones, R.E., and K.E. Hungerford. 1972. Evaluation of nesting cover as protection from magpie predation. *J. Wildl. Manage.* 36:727–732.

Karr, J.R., and K.E. Freemark. 1983. Habitat selection and environmental gradients: Dynamics in the "stable" tropics. *Ecology* 64:1481–1494.

Keppie, D.M., and P.W. Herzog. 1978. Nest site characteristics and nest success of Spruce Grouse. *J. Wildl. Manage.* 42:628–632.

Kilgore, B.M. 1971. Response of breeding bird populations to habitat changes in a giant sequoia forest. *Am. Midl. Nat.* 85:135–152.

Kirsch, L.M. 1969. Waterfowl production in relation to grazing. *J. Wildl. Manage.* 33:821–828.

Knapton, R.W. 1978. Breeding ecology of the Clay-colored Sparrow. *Living Bird* 17:137–138.

Knopf, F.L., J.A. Sedgwick, and D.B. Inkley. 1990. Regional correspondence among shrubsteppe bird habitats. *Condor* 92:45–53.

Lack, D. 1954. *The Natural Regulation of Animal Numbers.* Oxford: Oxford University Press.

———. 1968. *Ecological Adaptations for Breeding in Birds.* Oxford: Oxford University Press.

———. 1971. *Ecological Isolation in Birds.* Cambridge: Harvard University Press.

Lawlor, L.R., and J. Maynard Smith. 1976. The coevolution and stability of competing species. *Am. Nat.* 110:79–99.

Lawrence, L.K. 1953. Nesting life and behavior of the Red-eyed Vireo. *Can. Field-Nat.* 67:47–77.

Lenington, S. 1979. Predators and blackbirds: The "uncertainty principle" in field biology. *Auk* 96:190–192.

Li, P., and T.E. Martin. 1991. Nest site selection and nesting success of cavity-nesting birds in high elevation forest drainages. *Auk* 108:405–418.

Livezey, B.C. 1981. Duck nesting in retired croplands at Horicon National Wildlife Refuge, Wisconsin. *J. Wildl. Manage.* 45:27–37.

Longcore, J.R., and R.E. Jones. 1969. Reproductive success of the Wood Thrush in a Delaware woodlot. *Wilson Bull.* 81:396–406.

Lynch, J.F. 1989. Distribution of overwintering Nearctic migrants in the Yucatan Peninsula, I: General patterns of occurrence. *Condor* 91:515–544.

Lynch, J.F., and D.F. Whigham. 1984. Effects of forest fragmentation on breeding bird communities in Maryland, U.S.A. *Biol. Conserv.* 28:287–324.

MacKenzie, D.I., and S.G. Sealy. 1981. Nest site selection in Eastern and Western Kingbirds: A multivariate approach. *Condor* 83:310–321.

MacKenzie, D.I., S.G. Sealy, and G.D. Sutherland. 1982. Nest-site characteristics of the avian community of the dune-ridge forest, Delta Marsh, Manitoba: A multivariate approach. *Can. J. Zool.* 60:2212–2223.

Mannan, R.W., E.C. Meslow, and H.M. Wight. 1980. Use of snags by birds in douglas-fir forests, western Oregon. *J. Wildl. Manage.* 44:787–797.

Martin, T.E. 1981. Limitation in small habitat islands: Chance or competition? *Auk* 98:715–733.

———. 1984. Impact of livestock grazing on birds of a Colombian cloud forest. *Tropical Ecol.* 25:158–171.

———. 1986. Competition in breeding birds: On the importance of considering processes at the level of the individual. *Current Ornithol.* 4:181–210.

———. 1987. Food as a limit on breeding birds: A life-history perspective. *Ann. Rev. Ecol. Syst.* 18:453–487.

———. 1988a. Habitat and area effects on forest bird assemblages: Is nest predation an influence? *Ecology* 69:74–84.

———. 1988b. Processes organizing open-nesting bird assemblages: Competition or nest predation? *Evol. Ecol.* 2:37–50.

———. 1988c. On the advantage of being different: Nest predation and the coexistence of bird species. *Proc. Natl. Acad. Sci.* 85:2196–2199.

———. 1988d. Nest placement: Implications for selected life-history traits, with special reference to clutch size. *Am. Nat.* 132:900–910.

———. In press a. Food limitation in breeding birds: Is that all there is? *Proc. 20th Internat. Ornithol. Cong.*

———. In press b. Nest predation, nest sites, and birds: New perspectives on old patterns. *BioScience.*

Martin, T.E., and J.R. Karr. 1986. Temporal dynamics of neotropical birds with special reference to frugivores in second-growth woods. *Wilson Bull.* 98:38–60.

———. 1990. Behavioral plasticity of foraging maneuvers of migratory warblers: Multiple selection periods for niches? Pages 353–359 in *Avian Foraging: Theory, Methodology, and Ap-plications,* M.L. Morrison, D.J. Ralph, J. Berner, and J.R. Jehl, Jr., eds. Studies in Avian Biology No. 13.

Martin, T.E., and J.J. Roper. 1988. Nest predation and nest site selection of a western population of the Hermit Thrush. *Condor* 90:51–57.

Marvil, R.E., and A. Cruz. 1989. Impact of Brown-headed Cowbird on the reproductive success of the Solitary Vireo. *Auk* 106:476–480.

Marzluff, J.M. 1988. Do Pinyon Jays alter nest placement based on prior experience? *Anim. Behav.* 36:1–10.

Mayfield, H. 1960. *The Kirtland's Warbler.* Bloomfield Hills, Mich.: Cranbrook Inst. Sci.

———. 1961. Nesting success calculated from exposure. *Wilson Bull.* 73:255–261.

———. 1975. Suggestions for calculating nest success. *Wilson Bull.* 87:456–466.

McGeen, D.S. 1972. Cowbird host relationships. *Auk* 89:360–380.

Morse, D.H. 1976. Variables affecting the density and territory size of breeding spruce-woods warblers. *Ecology* 57:290–301.

Munkejord, A., F. Hauge, S. Fokedal, and A. Kvinnesland. 1985. Nest density, breeding habitat and reproductive output in a population of the Hooded Crow *Corvus corone cornix* on Karmoy, SW Norway. *Fauna Norv. Ser. C, Cinclus* 8:1–8.

Murphy, M.T. 1983. Nest success and nesting habits of Eastern Kingbirds and other flycatchers. *Condor* 85:208–219.

Nice, M.M. 1937. Studies in the life history of the Song Sparrow. I. *Trans. Linn. Soc. New York* 4:1–247.

Nice, M.M. 1957. Nesting success in altricial birds. *Auk* 74:305–321.

Nolan, V., Jr. 1978. *The Ecology and Behavior of the Prairie Warbler* Dendroica discolor. Ornithol. Monogr. 26.

Oetting, R.B., and J.F. Cassel. 1971. Waterfowl nesting on interstate highway right-of-way in North Dakota. *J. Wildl. Manage.* 35:774–781.

Partridge, L. 1978. Habitat selection. Pages 351–376 in *Behavioral Ecology,* J.R. Krebs and N.B. Davies, eds. Sunderland, Mass.: Sinauer Associates Inc.

Petersen, K.L., and L.B. Best. 1985. Nest-site selection by Sage Sparrows. *Condor* 87:217–221.

Petit, K.E., D.R. Petit, and L.J. Petit. 1988. On measuring vegetation characteristics in bird territories: Nest sites vs. perch sites and the effect of plot size. *Am. Midl. Nat.* 119:209–215.

Pfeifer, S. 1963. Dichte und dynamik von brutpopulationen zweier deutscher Waldgebiete 1949–1961. *Proc. 13th Internat. Ornithol. Cong.* (Ithaca): 754–765.

Picozzi, N. 1975. Crow predation on marked nests. *J. Wildl. Manage.* 39:151–155.

Pimm, S.L., and M.L. Rosenzweig. 1981. Competitors and habitat use. *Oikos* 37:1–6.

Pinkowski, B.C. 1979. Nest site selection in Eastern Bluebirds. *Condor* 81:435–436.

Pleszczynska, W.K., and R.I.C. Hansell. 1980. Polygyny and decision theory: Testing of a model in Lark Buntings (*Calamospiza melanocorys*). *Am. Nat.* 116:821–830.

Post, W. 1974. Functional analysis of space-related behavior in the Seaside Sparrow. *Ecology* 55:564–575.

Pulliam, H.R. 1988. Sources, sinks, and population regulation.

Am. Nat. 132:652–661.

Raphael, M.G., and M. White. 1984. Use of snags by cavity-nesting birds in the Sierra Nevada. *Wildl. Monogr.* 86.

Ratti, J.T., and K.P. Reese. 1988. Preliminary test of the ecological trap hypothesis. *J. Wildl. Manage.* 52:484–491.

Ricklefs, R.E. 1969. *An Analysis of Nesting Mortality in Birds.* Smithsonian Contrib. Zool. 9.

Robbins, C.S. 1980. Effects of forest fragmentation on breeding populations in the piedmont of the mid-Atlantic region. *Atlantic Nat.* 33:31–36.

Robbins, C.S., J.R. Sauer, R.S. Greenberg, and S. Droege. 1989. Population declines in North American birds that migrate to the neotropics. *Proc. Natl. Acad. Sci.* 86:7658–7662.

Robinson, S.K., and R.T. Holmes. 1982. Foraging behavior of forest birds: The relationships among search tactics, diet, and habitat structure. *Ecology* 63:1918–1931.

———. 1984. Effects of plant species and foliage structure on foraging behavior of forest birds. *Auk* 101:672–684.

Rodenhouse, N.L. 1986. Food limitation for forest passerines: Effects of natural and experimental food reductions. Ph.D. Dissertation, Dartmouth College, Hanover, New Hampshire.

Rohwer, S., and C.D. Spaw. 1988. Evolutionary lag versus bill size constraints: A comparative study of the acceptance of cowbird eggs by old hosts. *Evol. Ecol.* 2:27–36.

Roseberry, J.L., and W.D. Klimstra. 1970. The nesting ecology and reproductive performance of the Eastern Meadowlark. *Wilson Bull.* 82:243–267.

Rosenzweig, M.L. 1981. A theory of habitat selection. *Ecology* 62:327–335.

———. 1985. Some theoretical aspects of habitat selection. Pages 517–540 in *Habitat Selection in Birds*, M.L. Cody, ed. New York: Academic Press, Inc.

Rotenberry, J.T. 1985. The role of vegetation in avian habitat selection: Physiognomy or floristics? *Oecologia* 67:213–217.

Rothstein, S.I. 1975. Evolutionary rates and host defenses against avian brood parasitism. *Am. Nat.* 109:161–176.

———. 1982. Successes and failures in avian egg and nestling recognition with comments on the utility of optimality reasoning. *Am. Zool.* 22:547–560.

Schranck, B.W. 1972. Waterfowl nest cover and some predation relationships. *J. Wildl. Manage.* 36:182–186.

Schrantz, F.G. 1943. Nest life of the eastern Yellow Warbler. *Auk* 60:367–387.

Scott, V.E. 1979. Bird response to snag removal in ponderosa pine. *J. Forestry* 77:26–28.

Simons, L.S., and T.E. Martin. 1990. Food limitation of avian reproduction: An experiment with the Cactus Wren. *Ecology* 71:869–876.

Slagsvold, T. 1978. Competition between the Great Tit *Parus major* and the Pied Flycatcher *Ficedula hypoleuca*: An experiment. *Ornis Scand.* 9:46–50.

———. 1986. Nest site settlement by the Pied Flycatcher: Does the female choose her mate for the quality of his house or himself? *Ornis Scand.* 17:210–220.

Small, M.F., and M.L. Hunter. 1988. Forest fragmentation and avian nest predation in forested landscapes. *Oecologia* 76:62–64.

Smith, K.G. 1977. Distribution of summer birds along a forest moisture gradient in an Ozark watershed. *Ecology*

58:810–819.

Sonerud, G.A. 1985. Nest hole shift in Tengmalm's Owl *Aegolius funereus* as defense against nest predation involving long-term memory in the predator. *J. Anim. Ecol.* 54:179–192.

Stauffer, D.F., and L.B. Best. 1986. Nest-site characteristics of open-nesting birds in riparian habitats in Iowa. *Wilson Bull.* 98:231–242.

Stewart, R.M., R.P. Henderson, and K. Darling. 1978. Breeding ecology of the Wilson's Warbler in the high Sierra Nevada, California. *Living Bird* 16:83–102.

Storaas, T. 1988. A comparison of losses in artificial and naturally occurring Capercaillie Nests. *J. Wildl. Manage.* 52:123–126.

Sugden, L.G., and G.W. Beyersbergen. 1986. Effect of density and concealment on American crow predation of simulated duck nests. *J. Wildl. Manage.* 50:9–14.

Sugden, L.G., and G.W. Beyersbergen. 1987. Effect of nesting cover density on American Crow predation of simulated duck nests. *J. Wildl. Manage.* 51:481–485.

Tazik, D.J., and J. Cornelius. 1989. *The Black-capped Vireo on the Lands of Fort Hood, Texas. Preliminary status report.* Environmental Division, U.S. Army Const. Eng. Res. Lab., Champaign, Illinois.

Terborgh, J. 1989. *Where Have All the Birds Gone?* Princeton: Princeton University Press.

Thompson, C.F., and J. Nolan, Jr. 1973. Population biology of the Yellow-breasted Chat (*Icteria virens* L.) in southern Indiana. *Ecol. Monogr.* 43:145–171.

Toft, C.A. 1985. Resource partitioning in amphibians and reptiles. *Copeia* 1985:1–21.

Tomoff, C.S. 1974. Avian species diversity in desert scrub. *Ecology* 55:396–403.

Van Horne, B. 1983. Density as a misleading indicator of habitat quality. *J. Wildl. Manage.* 47:893–901.

Village, A. 1983. The role of nest-site availability and territorial behavior in limiting the breeding density of kestrels. *J. Anim. Ecol.* 52:635–645.

Walkinshaw, L.H. 1966. Studies of the Acadian Flycatcher in Michigan. *Bird-Banding* 37:227–257.

———. 1983. *Kirtland's Warbler, the Natural History of an Endangered Species.* Bloomfield Hills, Mich.: Cranbrook Inst. Sci.

Wallestad, R., and D. Pyrah. 1974. Movement and nesting of sage grouse hens in central Montana. *J. Wildl. Manage.* 38:630–633.

Werner, E.E., G.G. Mittlebach, D.J. Hall, and J.F. Gilliam. 1983a. Experimental tests of optimal habitat use in fish: The role of relative habitat profitability. *Ecology* 64:1525–1539.

Werner, E.E., J.F. Gilliam, D.J. Hall, and G.G. Mittlebach. 1983b. An experimental test of the effects of predation risk on habitat use in fish. *Ecology* 64:1540–1548.

Westmoreland, D., and L.B. Best. 1985. The effect of disturbance on Mourning Dove nesting success. *Auk* 102:774–780.

Whelan, C.J. 1987. Effects of foliage structure on the foraging behavior of insectivorous forest birds. Ph.D. Dissertation, Dartmouth College, Hanover, New Hampshire.

Whitcomb, R.F., C.S. Robbins, J.F. Lynch, B.L. Whitcomb, M.K. Klimkiewicz, and D. Bystrak. 1981. Effects of forest fragmentation on the avifauna of the eastern deciduous forest. Pages 125–205 in *Forest Island Dynamics in Man-dominated Landscapes*, R.L. Burgess and D.M. Sharpe, eds. New York: Springer-Verlag.

Whitmore, R.C. 1975. Habitat ordination of passerine birds in the Virgin River Valley, southwestern Utah. *Wilson Bull.* 87:65–74.

Whitmore, R.C. 1977. Habitat partitioning in a community of passerine birds. *Wilson Bull.* 89:253–265.

Wiens, J.A., and J.T. Rotenberry. 1981. Habitat associations and community structure of birds in shrub-steppe environments. *Ecol. Monogr.* 51:21–41.

Wilcove, D.S. 1985. Nest predation in forest tracts and the decline of migratory songbirds. *Ecology* 66:1211–1214.

Wray, T., II, and R.C. Whitmore. 1979. Effects of vegetation on nesting success of Vesper Sparrows. *Auk* 96:802–805.

Yahner, R.H., and A.L. Wright. 1985. Depredation on artificial ground nests: Effects of edge and plot age. *J. Wildl. Manage.* 49:508–513.

Zimmerman, J.L. 1963. A nesting study of the Catbird in southern Michigan. Jack-Pine Warbler 41:142–160.

———. 1982. Nesting success of Dickcissels (*Spiza americana*) in preferred and less preferred habitats. *Auk* 99:292–298.

———. 1983. Cowbird parasitism of Dickcissels in different habitats and at different nest densities. *Wilson Bull.* 95:7–22.

———. 1984. Nest predation and its relationship to habitat and nest density in Dickcissels. *Condor* 86:68–72.

APPENDIX 1. Scientific names of species mentioned in the text

Common name	Scientific name
Goldeneye	*Bucephala clangula*
White-winged Dove	*Zenaida asiatica*
Mourning Dove	*Zenaida macroura*
Tengmalm's Owl	*Aegolius funereus*
Western Wood-Pewee	*Contopus sordidulus*
Acadian Flycatcher	*Empidonax virescens*
Willow Flycatcher	*Empidonax traillii*
Least Flycatcher	*Empidonax minimus*
Cassin's Kingbird	*Tyrannus vociferans*
Western Kingbird	*Tyrannus verticalis*
Eastern Kingbird	*Tyrannus tyrannus*
Pinyon Jay	*Gymnorhinus cyanocephalus*
Great Tit	*Parus major*
Reed Warbler	*Acrocephalus scirpaceus*
Stonechat	*Saxicola torquata*
Eastern Bluebird	*Sialia sialis*
Mountain Bluebird	*Sialia currucoides*
Wood Thrush	*Hylocichla mustelina*
American Robin	*Turdus migratorius*
Gray Catbird	*Dumetella carolinensis*
Bell's Vireo	*Vireo bellii*
Least Bell's Vireo	*Vireo bellii pusillus*
Black-capped Vireo	*Vireo atricapillus*
Warbling Vireo	*Vireo gilvus*
Red-eyed Vireo	*Vireo olivaceus*
Solitary Vireo	*Vireo solitarius*
Orange-crowned Warbler	*Vermivora celata*
Virginia's Warbler	*Vermivora virginiae*
Yellow Warbler	*Dendroica petechia*
Black-thr. Blue Warbler	*Dendroica caerulescens*
Yellow-rumped Warbler	*Dendroica coronata*
Kirtland's Warbler	*Dendroica kirtlandii*
Prairie Warbler	*Dendroica discolor*
Ovenbird	*Seiurus aurocapillus*
Common Yellowthroat	*Geothlypis trichas*
Yellow-breasted Chat	*Icteria virens*
MacGillivray's Warbler	*Oporornis tolmiei*
Wilson's Warbler	*Wilsonia pusilla*
Red-faced Warbler	*Cardellina rubrifrons*
American Redstart	*Setophaga ruticilla*
Western Tanager	*Piranga ludoviciana*
Northern Cardinal	*Cardinalis cardinalis*
Rose-breasted Grosbeak	*Pheucticus ludovicianus*
Black-headed Grosbeak	*Pheucticus melanocephalus*
Indigo Bunting	*Passerina cyanea*
Dickcissel	*Spiza americana*
Eastern Meadowlark	*Sturnella magna*
Brown-headed Cowbird	*Molothrus ater*

MARC-ANDRÉ VILLARD
Ottawa-Carleton Institute of Biology
Department of Biology
Carleton University
Ottawa, Ontario, Canada K1S 5B6

KATHRYN FREEMARK
Environment Canada
Canadian Wildlife Service
Ottawa, Ontario, Canada K1A 0H3

GRAY MERRIAM
Ottawa-Carleton Institute of Biology
Department of Biology
Carleton University
Ottawa, Ontario, Canada K1S 5B6

Metapopulation theory and Neotropical migrant birds in temperate forests: An empirical investigation

Abstract. We examined the applicability of metapopulation theory to Neotropical migrant populations in agricultural landscapes. This model predicts a pattern of "winking patches" whereby patch populations become extinct and are recolonized, but with these dynamics stabilized at the higher, metapopulation level. In our main data set, presence or absence of Wood Thrush (*Hylocichla mustelina*), Ovenbird (*Seiurus aurocapillus*), and Scarlet Tanager (*Piranga olivacea*) was determined over two successive breeding seasons in 71 forest patches (1.3–73.1 ha) from five agricultural landscapes near Ottawa, Canada. In these "landscapes," frequencies of local extinctions ranged from 0 to 25% (median = 10%) among species, with frequencies of recolonization varying between 0 and 50% (median = 22.5%). However, this instability in patch occupancy did not result in significant between-year differences in the frequency of occurrence of the species in the corresponding landscapes, because recolonizations balanced local extinctions. For the Wood Thrush and Ovenbird, patches experiencing a local extinction or recolonization were significantly smaller than those remaining occupied, whereas no significant difference was found for Scarlet Tanager. Given this pattern of active year-to-year dynamics in patch occupancy, coupled to stability at the landscape scale, we suggest that the relevant demographic unit for these species in fragmented forests consists of a network of interacting patch populations. This suggestion is supported by long-term data sets from the literature.

Sinopsis. Nosotros examinamos la aplicabilidad de la teoría de la metapoblación a aves migratorias neotropicales en paisajes agrícolas. Este modelo predice un patrón de "parches de parpadeo" en donde las poblaciones se extinguen y son recolonizadas, pero con esta dinámica se estabilizan al nivel metapoblacional mayor. En nuestro conjunto principal de datos, la presencia o ausencia de *Hylocichla mustelina*, *Seiurus aurocapillus* y *Piranga olivacea* fue determinada en dos estaciones reproductivas sucesivas en 71 parches de bosque (1.3–73.1 ha) de cinco ambientes agrícolas cerca a Ottawa, Canada. En estos "paisajes", las

Manomet Symposium 1989

tasas locales de extinción variaron entre 0 y 25% (mediana=10%) entre especies, con tasas de recolonización variables entre 0 y 50% (mediana=22.5%). Sin embargo, esta inestabilidad en la ocupación de parches no representó diferencias significativas entre años en la frecuencia de ocurrencia de las especies en los paisajes correspondientes, puesto que la recolonización compensó las extinciones locales. Aquellos parches que presentaron extinción o recolonización de *H. mustelina* y *S. aurocapillus*, fueron significativamente mas pequeños que los que permanecieron ocupados, mientras que no se encontró ninguna diferencia significativa para *P. olivacea*. Basándonos en este patrón de dinámica activa año a año en ocupación de parches, acoplado con la estabilidad a la escala del paisaje, sugerimos que la unidad demográfica relevante para estas especies en bosques fragmentados consiste de una red de parches de poblaciones interactuantes. Esta sugerencia es apoyada por conjuntos de datos de largo plazo de la literatura.

Under the impetus of Whitcomb et al. (1981), a number of studies have documented the patterns and some of the inferred processes through which temperate forest fragmentation impacts bird populations. Many regional studies have addressed the effects of patch area and habitat on the composition of bird assemblages (e.g., Ambuel and Temple 1983, Lynch and Whigham 1984, Freemark and Merriam 1986, Blake and Karr 1987, Askins et al. 1987), whereas intensive studies have focused on nest predation and brood parasitism (Gates and Gysel 1978; Brittingham and Temple 1983; Wilcove 1985; Andrén and Angelstam 1988; Robinson, this volume).

Between these broad patterns and "subtle" processes, very little attention has been given to the spatio-temporal variations in the distribution of individual species at a scale larger than that of a single habitat patch. These dynamics result from the complex interaction of demographic and environmental stochasticity, natal and breeding dispersal, and mortality. The difficulty of measuring these factors, made even greater by the migratory nature of the species on which we focus, might partly explain the scarcity of explicit models for explaining the spatio-temporal dynamics of Neotropical migrant species breeding in fragmented habitats. To find such models, we have to refer to the theoretical ecology literature. Levins (1970) suggested that populations in patchy habitats function as "metapopulations," a concept nicely defined by Wilson (1975: 107) as "a nexus of patches, each patch winking into life as a population colonizes it, and winking out again as extinction occurs. At equilibrium the rate of winking and the number of occupied sites are constant, despite the fact that the pattern of occupancy is constantly shifting."

The mathematical formulation of the model by Levins (1970) considers a large number of patches of identical size and quality, with patch populations either at zero or carrying capacity. Each patch population goes extinct with a probability e (constant), but the metapopulation persists if the number of patch populations is large enough so that simultaneous extinction is unlikely. Although patch occupancy is dynamic, the proportion of occupied patches will remain stable as long as recolonization events balance the number of local extinctions.

The metapopulation concept was recently rediscovered in studies pertaining to spatio-temporal dynamics of animal populations in fragmented habitats (Merriam 1984, Shaffer 1985, Opdam 1988). However, our empirical knowledge of its component processes has progressed very slowly (Hanski 1989). For example, local extinctions and recolonizations of bird populations are documented mainly through studies of species turnover at single sites (Merriam and Wegner in press). To our knowledge, the only study reporting local extinctions and recolonizations from a large number of habitat patches in successive years is that on Spruce Grouse (*Dendragapus canadensis*) by Fritz (1979).

In this paper, we will evaluate the applicability of metapopulation theory to three Neotropical migrant species breeding in forest patches in agricultural landscapes of eastern Ontario. First, we will calculate the rates of local extinction and recolonization in forest patches. We will then determine whether these events alter the frequency of patch occupancy over a larger spatial scale. Thirdly, we will assess the relative suitability of patches that experienced a population turnover using patch area as a criterion.

Study area and methods

Forest birds were surveyed in agricultural landscapes near Ottawa, Ontario (Canada). Presence-absence data were collected for three Neotropical migrant species in 71 forest patches, 64 of which are spatially clustered in five landscapes. These "landscapes" represent samples of sites from areas of approximately 125 km^2 which differ in their degree of forest fragmentation. The effect of patch isolation on the year-to-year occupancy of forest patches by these species was analyzed elsewhere (Villard 1991).

Two other data sets documenting year-to-year changes in patch occupancy by the target species were used for comparison. One is a subsample of the previous one which comprises 16 forest patches censused in 1987 and 1988. The other is a set of 16 patches surveyed in 1980 and 1981 (Freemark and Merriam 1986), 12 of which are located in one of the landscapes surveyed in 1988–1989.

The species studied were Wood Thrush (*Hylocichla mustelina*), Ovenbird (*Seiurus aurocapillus*), and Scarlet Tanager (*Piranga olivacea*). These species showed presences and absences among small patches in 1980, 1981, and 1987 data sets, making them good candidates for studying temporal dynamics in their spatial distribution in small to medium-sized patches. These species are recognized in the literature as being sensitive to fragmentation of their habitat, at least as it reduces the area of forest patches (Robbins 1979, Hayden et al. 1985, Robbins et al. 1989).

SELECTION OF STUDY SITES

Forest patches in Ontario ranged from 1.3 to 79.0 ha in size. In data sets of 1987, 1988, and 1989, forest patches were selected so as to minimize the variance in vegetation among them. The patches censused by Freemark and Merriam (1986) varied in internal habitat heterogeneity, but independently of patch area. All forest patches were relatively mature deciduous stands dominated by Sugar Maple (*Acer saccharum*), White Ash (*Fraxinus americana*), and Ironwood (*Ostrya virginiana*). A few sites with imperfect to poor drainage were dominated by Red Maple (*Acer rubrum*). Recently disturbed patches were rejected. Three of the 74 patches surveyed in 1988–1989 were not used in the analysis because of some selective clearing between breeding seasons. However, historical perturbations such as grazing and selective cutting could not be avoided. These perturbations caused moderate patchiness in the vertical structure of foliage, but rarely caused changes in species composition of the tree stratum. Most of the vegetation patches interspersed among those we selected were also dominated by deciduous trees. Very few comprised only thickets or shrubbery.

BIRD SURVEYS

We used two techniques for censusing birds. The first was a modified version of the point count method with unlimited distance (see Blondel et al. 1981). This technique was used in the 1980, 1981, and 1987 bird surveys. In 1988, we selected additional study sites around those censused with point counts so as to obtain clusters of sites in each landscape. These additional forest patches were surveyed for presence-absence of each target species based on a *field check* method (Villard 1991). The observers walked slowly along the long axis of the forest patches, recording any contact with a target species. The number of singing males encountered was recorded, which gave us a minimum abundance value. Absences were validated using song playbacks. Playbacks were also used to hasten late morning surveys, when singing rates usually decrease. For both census tech-

niques, three visits were made to each study site between the last week of May and the first week of July, except in 1980 and 1981, when only two visits were made. In patches where absences were noted on the first visit, we made special efforts to survey additional portions of forest during subsequent visits. In cases where three visits were completed, transients, or wandering individuals (sensu Morse 1989) were given special attention. Individuals recorded only on the first visit were considered as transients and, accordingly, an absence was recorded for that species. Most point counts were conducted between sunrise and 09:30, while presence-absence surveys were done mainly between 09:30 and noon.

In 1988, the proportion of forest patches censused with point counts ranged from 33.3 to 46.7% among the five landscapes. In 1989, only one patch per landscape was censused by point counts. All other patches were surveyed with field checks. Regardless of the sampling technique, doubts persist about species absences. Point counts represent a minimum of 60 min. (and up to 300 min.) of censusing in each woodlot. For presence-absence surveys, the duration of censuses varied extensively depending on the ease of detecting the target species. The longest surveys were in those larger patches where one or many target species were missing. Presence-absence surveys generally resulted in less censusing time per unit area than point counts and were conducted later in the morning. However, the use of song playbacks appeared to compensate very well for a lower censusing intensity. In many instances, the playbacks induced a response from individuals which we would have missed during a given visit. These two very different techniques gave reliable presence-absence data for our target species.

Another censusing problem has been identified by Wander (1985). Some forest patches might be inhabited only by males which remained unmated throughout the breeding season. Hence, the presence of the species might not indicate reproductive output. In this study, it was impossible to determine the pairing status or reproductive output of all singing males. We considered that presence represented a potential for reproduction at a given site.

To make comparisons, we compiled local extinctions and recolonizations in two additional data sets from the literature (Table 1). The first included censuses of Ovenbirds in forest patches in an agricultural landscape in New Jersey (Wander 1985). The second comprised complete censuses of forest birds, including all our target species, from various localities within the Great Smoky Mountains National Park in Tennessee and North Carolina (Wilcove 1988). For the latter data set, we restricted our analysis to four localities where censuses were replicated for two successive years. The cor-

TABLE 1.   Distribution of local extinctions and recolonizations among species and study areas

Study area	n	Wood Thrush			Ovenbird			Scarlet Tanager		
		LE	R	%	LE	R	%	LE	R	%
Ontario										
Heckston										
1988–89	13	1	1	15.4	0	0	0	2	1	23.1
Kinburn										
1988–89	12	0	0	0	1	0	8.3	1	2	25.0
1980–81	12	1	1	16.7	1	2	25.0	0	2	16.7
Metcalfe										
1988–89	15	1	2	20.0	0	2	13.3	1	2	20.0
Cumberland										
1988–89	9	1	1	22.2	0	1	11.1	0	0	0
North Gower										
1988–89	15	1	2	20.0	0	1	6.7	1	2	20.0
New Jersey										
1982–83	12	–	–	–	0	2	16.7	–	–	–
1983–84	14	–	–	–	2	1	21.4	–	–	–
Great Smoky Mts.										
1982–83	4	1	1	50.0	0	0	0	0	1	25.0

SOURCES: Data for New Jersey from Wander 1985; data from Great Smoky Mountains from Wilcove 1988.
NOTE: LE = local extinctions; R = recolonizations; % = frequency of population turnovers (see methods).

responding census plots ranged from 4.2 to 11.0 ha in size.

DATA ANALYSIS

From frequencies of local extinctions and recolonizations, we can calculate the frequency of population turnovers (Table 1) by dividing the number of events (extinctions plus recolonizations) by the number of forest patches surveyed.

Because we then lose the information contrasting the number of local extinctions to recolonizations, we present both actual numbers (Table 1) and frequencies (Table 2), calculated from the following equations:

$$\% \text{ Local extinctions} = PA/(PP + PA) \times 100,$$
$$\% \text{ Recolonizations} = AP/(AP + AA) \times 100,$$

where PA is the number of forest patches where the species became extinct the second year (local extinctions), PP is the number of sites where it was present both years, AP is the number of sites where it was recorded only the second year (recolonizations), and AA is the number of sites which remained unoccupied both years.

This information gives us a ratio of the number of sites experiencing an event to the number of sites which could potentially experience it. We restricted our inves-

tigation to successive breeding seasons to reduce the probability that observed turnover is due to large-scale, long-term population fluctuations occurring between the years examined.

Results and discussion

LOCAL EXTINCTIONS AND RECOLONIZATIONS

All three target species exhibited year-to-year dynamics in their distribution in the various landscapes surveyed (Table 1). Such temporal dynamics were also found for Ovenbirds in New Jersey and for Wood Thrush and Scarlet Tanager in the Great Smoky Mountains. These results indicate that local extinctions and recolonizations are not exclusive to habitat patches, but can also be observed in plots located within extensive forest tracts. A similar pattern was seen for species with low abundance in the extensive forests of Bialowieza National Park, Poland (Tomialojác et al. 1984), where local extinctions and recolonizations in 24–33-ha census plots were relatively frequent.

In Ontario, the number of local extinctions and recolonizations varied between 0 and 2 among species and landscapes (Table 1). These numbers appear relatively low, but such raw numbers do not give an accurate picture of the actual importance of these events because

TABLE 2. Frequency of local extinctions and recolonizations in various data sets

Data set	n	Wood Thrush		Ovenbird		Scarlet Tanager	
		%LE	%R	%LE	%R	%LE	%R
M.-A. Villard (1988–89)							
Heckston	13	9.1	50.0	0.0	0.0	18.2	50.0
		(11)	(2)	(13)	(0)	(11)	(2)
Kinburn	12	0.0	0.0	8.3	0.0	25.0	25.0
		(5)	(7)	(12)	(0)	(4)	(8)
Metcalfe	15	12.5	28.6	0.0	0.0	25.0	25.0
		(8)	(7)	(7)	(8)	(5)	(10)
Cumberland	9	25.0	20.0	0.0	16.7	0.0	0.0
		(4)	(5)	(3)	(6)	(2)	(7)
North Gower	15	16.7	22.2	0.0	9.1	25.0	18.2
		(6)	(9)	(4)	(11)	(4)	(11)
All sites							
1988–89	71	13.5	26.5	2.5	16.1	21.4	16.3
95% C.I.		(4.5–28.9)	(12.8–44.6)	(1.1–18.6)	(5.4–33.8)	(8.3–41.0)	(6.8–30.8)
		(37)	(34)	(40)	(31)	(28)	(43)
1987–88	16	7.1	0.0	0.0	50.0	23.1	33.3
		(14)	(2)	(14)	(2)	(13)	(3)
K. Freemark (1980–81)							
Kinburn	12	16.7	16.7	20.0	28.6	0.0	20.0
		(6)	(6)	(5)	(7)	(2)	(10)
All sites	16	12.5	12.5	14.3	33.3	25.0	16.7
		(8)	(8)	(7)	(9)	(4)	(12)
Wander (1985)							
1982–83	12	–	–	0.0	40.0	–	–
				(7)	(5)		
1983–84	14	–	–	18.2	33.3	–	–
				(11)	(3)		

NOTE: LE = local extinctions; R = recolonizations. The denominators used in the calculation of these rates are shown in parentheses (see methods). Confidence intervals (C.I.) are shown for the largest sample.

many sites could not even experience them. For example, although one local extinction and one recolonization were recorded for Wood Thrush in Heckston, only two patches were available for recolonization compared to 11 for local extinction. Furthermore, the occurrence of local extinctions depends partly on recolonizations the year before the data were collected.

To circumvent this problem, we calculated frequencies of local extinction and recolonization (Table 2). These frequencies ranged from 0 to 25% for local extinctions and from 0 to 50% for recolonizations. The frequency of local extinctions tended to be consistently lower than the frequency of recolonizations for the Ovenbird, whereas no such trend was found in the other species.

The principal problem in calculating these frequen-

cies of local extinctions and recolonizations was obtaining a large enough number of sites and minimizing the proportion of sites where a species was consistently absent (AA). Small numbers of sites give doubtful frequencies. For example, we would get a 100% frequency of recolonizations for Wood Thrush in the subset of Wilcove's (1988) data. Frequencies of recolonizations were also affected by the number of study sites where the species was absent both years. These sites might not be suitable to the species for various reasons (patch area, habitat, biotic interactions), thereby leading to an underestimation of the frequencies of recolonizations. Despite these methodological difficulties, we found significant frequencies of local extinctions and recolonizations, which support one of the corollaries of metapopulation theory.

TABLE 3. Frequency of occurrence (%) of three Neotropical migrant species in five agricultural landscapes near Ottawa. Combined frequencies represent the proportion of patches where all three species were present

Landscape	n	Year	Wood Thrush	Ovenbird	Scarlet Tanager	Combined
Heckston	13	1988	84.6	100.0	84.6	76.9
		1989	84.6	100.0	76.9	69.2
Kinburn	12	1980	50.0	41.7	16.7	8.3
		1981	50.0	50.0	33.3	25.0
		1988	41.7	100.0	33.3	33.3
		1989	33.3	91.7	33.3	16.7
Metcalfe	15	1988	53.3	46.7	33.3	26.7
		1989	60.0	60.0	40.0	33.3
Cumberland	9	1988	44.4	33.3	22.2	22.2
		1989	44.4	44.4	22.2	22.2
North Gower	15	1988	40.0	26.7	26.7	13.3
		1989	53.3	33.3	33.3	26.7

PATTERNS AT THE LANDSCAPE SCALE

We can then compare these temporal dynamics at the patch scale to those occurring at the landscape scale.

Even though the pattern of patch occupancy changed as a result of population turnovers, these changes were not reflected in the frequency of occurrence of our target species in the landscapes we surveyed (Table 3). Rather, the only significant difference between years was in the Ovenbird frequencies in Kinburn landscape between 1980–1981 and 1988–1989 (Fisher's exact tests). This difference might be due to the fact that many of the patches surveyed in 1980 and 1981 were not included in the more recent sample. Another explanation for this might be that regional population trends between 1980–1981 and 1988–1989 periods rendered them incomparable.

Hence, we found little change in the proportion of sites that were occupied by a species at the landscape scale despite relatively high frequencies of local extinctions and recolonizations at the patch scale.

EFFECT OF PATCH AREA

Equilibrium biogeography relates island area to population size and extinction probability: the smaller the island, the smaller the population and, thus, the greater the probability of extinction due to demographic stochasticity (MacArthur and Wilson 1967). Opdam and Schotman (1987) have shown a significant decrease in species turnover rates with an increase in patch area for forest birds of the Netherlands. Here, we wanted to determine whether forest patches that experienced a population turnover (PA + AP) were smaller than those where the species was consistently present (PP), and larger than those where the species was never recorded (AA). For that purpose, we used our sample of 71 patches from 1988 to 1989.

For Wood Thrush and Ovenbird, patches that experienced a population turnover were smaller than those where the species remained present, but they were not significantly larger than the sets of patches where each species was never recorded (Kruskal-Wallis tests, Table 4).

This suggests that the empty patches (AA) might actually differ from patches experiencing a population turnover in their internal habitat characteristics, even though these study sites were selected to minimize between-patch differences in vegetation. The lack of significant difference in patch area between these classes might also be explained by a low probability of recolonization of such forest patches over a two-year period. Then, some patches classified as AA might only be recolonized over a longer time scale. In such cases, woodland configuration around a forest patch might be more relevant than internal habitat characteristics.

For the Scarlet Tanager, patches that experienced a population turnover were significantly larger than those remaining empty (Table 4). This indicates that the presence of this species in a patch was dependent on patch size, and that any patch larger than a certain threshold might experience a population turnover, regardless of area in excess of the threshold. Other factors, such as woodland configuration in the neighborhood of a patch, might determine the actual stability of these local tanager populations.

TABLE 4. Results of Kruskal-Wallis tests comparing patch area among three sets of study sites: patches where the species was present both years (PP), patches experiencing a population turnover (PA+AP), and patches where the species remained absent (AA)

Wood Thrush	PA + AP $\bar{x}$= 10.1 ha $n = 14$	AA
PP $\bar{x}$ =31.0 ha $n = 32$	***	***
AA $\bar{x}$ = 9.3 ha $n = 25$	n.s.	—
Ovenbird	PA + AP $\bar{x}$ = 9.7 ha $n = 6$	AA
PP $\bar{x}$ = 27.6 ha $n = 39$	*	***
AA $\bar{x}$ = 8.8 ha $n = 26$	n.s.	—
Scarlet Tanager	PA + AP $\bar{x}$ = 18.8 ha $n = 13$	AA
PP $\bar{x}$ = 33.9 ha $n = 22$	n.s.	***
AA $\bar{x}$ = 10.4 ha $n = 36$	*	—

NOTE: * = $P < 0.05$, *** = $P < 0.001$

From our abundance data, we determined whether the observed local extinctions and recolonizations involved few or many individuals. Table 5 shows a strong tendency for these events to occur within very small patch populations (one or two singing males). Within species, 83 to 100% of local extinctions involved only one singing male, whereas for recolonizations, the proportion was 67 to 86%. Overall, 92% of local extinctions and 76% of recolonizations involved a minimum of one singing male.

Although we have limited confidence in the exactness of our abundance values in large forest patches, it is obvious that very small patch populations were involved in the observed population turnovers. However, when a species was present, it was generally recorded in two or all three visits we made (Table 5). Thus, these individuals were either nesting there or were consistently available for nesting.

Many studies indicate that small forest reserves (< 30 ha) are not buffered against population declines of Neotropical migrants. These declines have been attributed to deforestation in the vicinity (Butcher et al. 1981, Askins and Philbrick 1987), to habitat destruction in the Neotropics (Leck et al. 1988), and to a combination of area and isolation effects (Lynch and Whitcomb 1978). Such relatively small patches represent the bulk of the forest fragments in most agricultural landscapes of eastern North America, which in turn cover a large portion of the breeding range of many Neotropical migrant species. The conservation of these species calls for better knowledge of their ecology in fragmented landscapes, including their spatial and temporal dynamics. This is particularly true if we accept the premise that an accumulation of local extinctions may lead to regional extirpation and, in some cases, global extinction of a species.

Conclusions

We have examined the applicability of metapopulation theory to our system by (1) calculating the rates of local extinction and recolonization; (2) looking at the effect of these events on the proportion of patches occupied at the landscape scale; and (3) determining whether these events may occur in any patch or strictly in marginally suitable habitat patches. Our results are consistent with the "equilibrium" state described by Wilson (1975) whereby the proportion of occupied sites is stable despite the fact that the pattern of patch occupancy shifts between years. We have yet to determine whether local extinction and recolonization rates (winking rate) remain constant over many successive years. Our results depart from the theoretical concept of metapopulation in the distinctive characteristics of the patches that were "winking." For the Wood Thrush and Ovenbird, population turnovers tended to occur in the smaller patches and for all three species, very small subpopulations were involved. This suggests that these patches may represent population sinks (Wiens and Rotenberry 1981, Pulliam 1988) colonized sporadically by surplus individuals from "source" patches.

Metapopulation theory thus appears as a useful framework for analyzing dynamics in the distribution of forest birds in mosaic landscapes. However, a realistic model of forest bird metapopulations must take into account the effect of patch quality on the probability of local extinction. As shown in this study, patch area is an important parameter of patch quality, but at least for

TABLE 5. Abundance shifts associated to population turnovers

	Wood Thrush				Ovenbird				Scarlet Tanager	
	1988	1989			1988	1989			1988	1989
LE	1(2)	—	LE		1(2)	—	LE		2(1,2,3)	—
LE	1(2)	—	R		—	1(1,2)	LE		1(1,2,3)	—
LE	1(1,2,3)	—	R		—	1(2)	LE		1(1,3)	—
LE	1(1,2)	—	R		—	1(1,2)	LE		1(2,3)	—
LE	1(1,2)	—	R		—	1(1,2,3)	LE		1(3)	—
R	—	1(1,2,3)	R		—	2(1,2,3)	LE		1(3)	—
R	—	1(1,2)					R		—	1(1,2)
R	—	1(3)					R		—	1(2,3)
R	—	2(1,2,3)					R		—	1(3)
R	—	1(2,3)					R		—	1(2,3)
R	—	2(1,2,3)					R		—	1(1,2)
R	—	1(2)					R		—	1(1,2,3)
R	—	2(1,2,3)					R		—	2(1,2,3)
R	—	1(1,2)								

NOTE: The minimum number of singing males present is indicated, while the visit(s) (1st, 2nd or 3rd) in which a species was encountered in the forest patch is shown in brackets. LE = local extinction, R = recolonization.

the Scarlet Tanager, other factors seem to be involved and patch isolation might be one of them. In the European Nuthatch (*Sitta europaea*), Verboom et al. (in press) found that the probability of local extinction decreased with forest patch area and the probability of recolonization decreased with patch isolation from surrounding occupied sites.

It would be interesting to examine the consistency of the patterns we observed in our Neotropical migrant species by calculating local extinction and recolonization rates in other parts of the Eastern Deciduous Forest. The next step, which has been neglected too long, would be to collect data on nonmigratory movements of forest birds in agricultural landscapes, as well as those of birds from other landscape mosaics. Such studies might help to identify what Goodman (1987) calls the "circumstances" which expose a species to a series of "bad luck" events that lead to regional extirpation and global extinction.

Acknowledgments

We thank R. Bracken and B. Graham for their assistance in the collection of bird data. J. Wegner, R. Askins, H. Boyd, A. Keith and R. Ricklefs made insightful comments on the manuscript. We also thank all landowners who kindly tolerated our peregrinations in their woods. This research was supported by the National Science and Engineering Research Council of Canada and the University Research Support Fund of the Canadian Wildlife Service.

Literature cited

Ambuel, B., and S.A. Temple. 1983. Area-dependent changes in the bird communities and vegetation of southern Wisconsin forests. *Ecology* 64:1057–1068.

Andrén, H., and P. Angelstam. 1988. Elevated predation rates as an edge effect in habitat islands: Experimental evidence. *Ecology* 69:544–547.

Askins, R.A., and M.J. Philbrick. 1987. Effect of changes in regional forest abundance on the decline and recovery of a forest bird community. *Wilson Bull.* 99:7–21.

Askins, R.A., M.J. Philbrick, and D.S. Sugeno. 1987. Relationship between the regional abundance of forest and the composition of forest bird communities. *Biol. Conserv.* 39:129–152.

Blake, J.G., and J.R. Karr. 1987. Breeding birds of isolated woodlots: Area and habitat relationships. *Ecology* 68:1724–1734.

Blondel, J., C. Ferry, and B. Frochot. 1981. Point counts with unlimited distance. Pages 414–420 in *Estimating Numbers of Terrestrial Birds*, C.J. Ralph and M.J. Scott, eds. Studies in Avian Biology No. 6.

Brittingham, M.C., and S.A. Temple. 1983. Have cowbirds caused forest songbirds to decline? *BioScience* 33:31–35.

Butcher, G.S., W.A. Niering, W.J. Barry, and R.H. Goodwin. 1981. Equilibrium biogeography and the size of nature preserves: An avian case study. *Oecologia* 49:29–37.

Freemark, K.E., and H.G. Merriam. 1986. Importance of area and habitat heterogeneity to bird assemblages in temperate forest fragments. *Biol. Conserv.* 36:115–141.

Fritz, R.S. 1979. Consequences of insular population structure: Distribution and extinction of Spruce Grouse populations. *Oecologia* 42:57–65.

Gates, J.E., and L.E. Gysel. 1978. Avian nest dispersion and fledging success in field-forest ecotones. *Ecology* 59:871–883.

Goodman, D. 1987. The demography of chance extinction. Pages 11–34 in *Viable Populations for Conservation*, M.E. Soulé, ed. Cambridge: Cambridge University Press.

Hanski, I. 1989. Metapopulation dynamics: Does it help to have more of the same? *Trends Ecol. Evol.* 4:113–114.

Hayden, T.J., J. Faaborg, and R.L. Clawson. 1985. Estimates of minimum area requirements for Missouri (USA) forest birds. *Trans. Mo. Acad. Sci.* 19:11–22.

Leck, C.F., B.G. Murray, and J. Swinebroad. 1988. Long-term changes in the breeding bird populations of a New Jersey forest. *Biol. Conserv.* 46:145–157.

Levins, R. 1970. Extinction. Pages 77–107 in *Some Mathematical Questions in Biology*, M. Gerstenhaber, ed. Lectures on mathematics in the life sciences, vol.2. Providence, R.I.: American Mathematical Society.

Lynch, J.F., and D.F. Whigham. 1984. Effects of forest fragmentation on breeding bird communities in Maryland, U.S.A. *Biol. Conserv.* 28:287–324.

Lynch, J.F., and R.F. Whitcomb. 1978. Effects of the insularization of the eastern deciduous forest on avifaunal diversity and turnover. Pages 461–489 in *Classification, Inventory, and Evaluation of Fish and Wildlife Habitat*, A. Marmelstein, ed. U.S. Fish and Wildlife Serv. Pub. OBS-78176.

MacArthur, R.H., and E.O. Wilson. 1967. *The Theory of Island Biogeography*. Princeton: Princeton University Press.

Merriam, G. 1984. Connectivity: A fundamental ecological characteristic of landscape pattern. Pages 5–15 in *Proceedings of the 1st International Seminar on Methodology in Landscape Ecological Research and Planning*. Roskilde, Denmark: International Association for Landscape Ecology.

Merriam, G., and J. Wegner. In press. Local extinctions, habitat fragmentation and ecotones. SCOPE Ecotones Workshop, Paris. Dec. 1988.

Morse, D.H. 1989. *American Warblers*. Cambridge: Harvard University Press.

Opdam, P. 1988. Populations in fragmented landscapes. Pages 75–77 in *Connectivity in Landscape Ecology*. K.-F. Schreiber, ed. Mänster, West Germany: Proceedings of the 2d International Seminar of the International Association for Landscape Ecology.

Opdam, P., and A. Schotman. 1987. Small woods in rural landscape as habitat islands for woodland birds. *Acta Oecol., Oecol. Gener.* 8:269–274.

Pulliam, H.R. 1988. Sources, sinks, and population regulation.

Am. Nat. 132:652–661.

Robbins, C.S. 1979. Effect of forest fragmentation on bird populations. Pages 198–212 in *Management of North Central and Northeastern Forests for Nongame Birds; Workshop Proceedings*, R.M. DeGraaf and K.E. Evans, eds. St. Paul, Minn.: USDA Forest Service Gen. Tech. Rept. NC-51.

Robbins, C.S., D.K. Dawson, and B.A. Dowell. 1989. *Habitat Area Requirements of Breeding Forest Birds of the Middle Atlantic States*. Wildl. Monogr. 103.

Shaffer, M.L. 1985. The metapopulation and species conservation: The special case of the Northern Spotted Owl. Pages 86–99 in *Ecology and Management of the Spotted Owl in the Pacific Northwest*, R.J. Gutiérrez and A.B. Carey, eds. Portland, Oreg.: USDA Forest Service Gen. Tech. Rept. PNW-185.

Tomialojác, L., T. Wesolowski, and W. Walankiewicz. 1984. Breeding bird community of a primaeval temperate forest (Bialowieza National Park, Poland). *Acta Ornithol.* 20:241–310.

Verboom, J., A. Schotman, P. Opdam, and J.A.J. Metz. In press. European Nuthatch metapopulations in a fragmented agricultural landscape. *Oikos* 61.

Villard, M.-A. 1991. Spatio-temporal dynamics of forest bird patch populations on agricultural landscapes. Ph.D. Dissertation, Carleton University, Ottawa, Ontario.

Wander, S.A. 1985. Comparative breeding biology of the ovenbird in large vs fragmented forests: Implications for the conservation of neotropical migrant birds. Ph.D. Dissertation, Rutgers University, New Brunswick, New Jersey.

Wiens, J.A., and J.T. Rotenberry. 1981. Censusing and the evaluation of avian habitat occupancy. Pages 522–532 in *Estimating Numbers of Terrestrial Birds*, C.J. Ralph and M.J. Scott, eds. Studies in Avian Biology No. 6.

Whitcomb, R.F., C.S. Robbins, J.F. Lynch, B.L. Whitcomb, M.K. Klimkiewicz, and D. Bystrak. 1981. Effects of forest fragmentation on the avifauna of the eastern deciduous forest. Pages 125–205 in *Forest Island Dynamics in Man-dominated Landscapes*, R.L. Burgess and D.M. Sharpe, eds. New York: Springer-Verlag.

Wilcove, D.S. 1985. Nest predation in forest tracts and the decline of migratory songbirds. *Ecology* 66:1211–1214.

———. 1988. Changes in the avifauna of the Great Smoky Mountains: 1947–1983. *Wilson Bull.* 100:256–271.

Wilson, E.O. 1975. *Sociobiology*. Cambridge, Mass.: Belknap Press.

THOMAS S. LITWIN*
Laboratory of Ornithology
Cornell University
Ithaca, New York 14850

CHARLES R. SMITH
Laboratory of Ornithology and
Department of Natural Resources
Cornell University
Ithaca, New York 14850

Factors influencing the decline of Neotropical migrants in a northeastern forest fragment: Isolation, fragmentation, or mosaic effects?

Abstract. Breeding bird populations at Sapsucker Woods, Ithaca, NY, were analyzed by comparing vegetation and bird censuses conducted in 1949–50 and 1979–80 for the eastern portion of the Sapsucker Woods. Seventeen censuses conducted between 1957 and 1974 were also analyzed. Declines or local extinctions occurred in 10 Neotropical migrant species between 1949 and 1980. Species richness and abundance of the nonmigratory population increased. Although species turnover rates were highly variable, species richness of the total breeding population remained constant. Pair-wise comparisons of 20 yearly Shannon diversity indices revealed little significant variation. Wide-ranging raptor species nested regularly over a period totaling 35 years.

Observed declines in breeding densities of Neotropical migrants and concurrent increases in resident species can be explained best by patterns of forest successional change affected by land-use history. Land-use history at local and regional scales can have significant effects on patterns of bird distribution and abundance, particularly with respect to the cumulative effects of gap-phase succession resulting from loss of individual canopy trees. To distinguish bird population changes resulting from local successional patterns from other influences, it is essential that vegetation data be collected and analyzed in parallel with bird population data. In this more dynamic context, reported declines in populations of eastern woodland songbirds, attributed to forest fragmentation, insularization, and even tropical deforestation, might need to be qualified.

Sinopsis. Se hizo un análisis de la comunidad de aves anidantes en la porción oriental de Sapsucker Woods, Ithaca, NY, mediante comparación de censos de vegetación y aves realizados en 1949–1950 y 1979–1980. Igualmente, se analizaron 17 censos llevados a cabo entre 1957 y 1974. La riqueza de especies y la abundancia de las poblaciones no migratorias incrementaron. Aunque las tasas de renovación de especies fueron altamente variables, compara-

*Current address: Department of Biological Sciences, Smith College, Northampton, Massachusetts 01063

ciones pareadas de 20 índices de diversidad anuales de Shannon revelaron muy poca variación significativa. Especies de rapaces con amplia distribución anidaron regularmente durante un período total de 35 años.

Las declinaciones observadas de las densidades de cría de migratorias neotropicales e incrementos concurrentes de especies residentes pueden explicarse bien por los patrones de cambio sucesional del bosque afectado por la historia del uso de la tierra. La historia del uso de la tierra a escalas local y regional puede tener efectos significativos sobre los patrones observados de distribuciones y abundancias de aves, particularmente con respecto a los efectos acumulativos de la sucesión de claros resultante de la pérdida de árboles individuales dominantes del dosel del bosque. Para distinguir cambios poblacionales de aves resultantes de patrones sucesionales locales de aquellos producidos por otras influencias es esencial que los datos de vegetación sean colectados y analizados paralelamente con los datos poblacionales de aves. En este contexto mas dinámico, las declinaciones reportadas en las poblaciones orientales de aves canoras de bosque atribuidas a la fragmentación, la insularización e incluso la deforestación tropical, podrían necesitar calificación.

The history of the Sapsucker Woods Sanctuary (SSW), established in 1953 by Arthur A. Allen and Cornell University, illustrates the intimate relationship of land-use activity and preserve design and management. In 1789, the wilderness of New York State was subdivided into 640-acre parcels and distributed to Revolutionary War veterans as compensation for their participation in the war. With land officially recognized as a form of currency, the landscape was rapidly deforested for agricultural purposes. Between 1835 and 1875, from 75% to 87% of the land areas of townships surrounding Sapsucker Woods were cleared of trees (New York Secretary of State 1836, 1846, Lewis 1933). Not since the Wisconsin Glaciation had the eastern deciduous forest been so extensively modified. SSW probably became a forest isolate in the period around 1845 and served as a farm woodlot. This 40-ha woodlot remained forested because its wet soils were better suited to growing trees than seasonal crops.

The ecological value of SSW was first identified in June 1909 by Allen and Louis Agassiz Fuertes, who documented on this visit the first nesting of the Yellow-bellied Sapsucker within the Cayuga Lake Basin. Allen's subsequent preservation efforts were based on the regional uniqueness of the habitat and occurrence in the woods of the Yellow-bellied Sapsucker, Brown Creeper, Canada Warbler, and Northern Waterthrush. After acquiring the woodlot, the primary management actions were the erection of a fence around the perimeter and elimination of all timber harvesting.

Allen initiated two separate SSW breeding bird monitoring efforts. In 1949–1950, Allen and Oliver Owen conducted a detailed bird census and vegetation analysis of the eastern portion of Sapsucker Woods (Owen 1950). The second effort was an annual breeding bird census of SSW conducted between 1956 and 1974 by Allen and colleagues. In 1979–1980, the Owen census was replicated by Litwin (1986).

Using these databases, this study has two primary goals: (1) to describe changes in the Sapsucker Woods breeding bird community over a 30-year period, and (2) to identify the processes that most probably influenced those changes.

Methods

ALLEN BREEDING BIRD CENSUSES, 1956–1981

In 1957, Allen initiated a breeding bird census, using the Williams spot-mapping technique (Williams 1936, Kendeigh 1982, Horn 1985), which was conducted in the early morning during the first half of June, between 1957 and 1980. Only the results from east SSW will be reported in this paper. Additional records document songbird nesting persistence and the nesting of wide-ranging species such as raptors and Pileated Woodpecker. In 1962, Allen formulated the Nesting Birds of Sapsucker Woods that classified nesting persistence for all species (Appendix 1). Although data for raptors were not available for all species in all years, the data were consistent enough to serve as a record of nesting persistence.

The Williams spot-mapping technique was used for both the 1949–50 and 1979–80 breeding bird censuses. Using a 50×50-m grid system, which replicated that of Owen (1950), we conducted 7 censuses in 1979 (5–28 June) and 13 in 1980 (14 May–3 July) between 0600 and 0930. Field data were transferred to standardized composite maps for each species and analyzed according to International Bird Census Committee criteria (Robbins 1970).

For purposes of analysis, bird species were classified into groups according to migratory pattern. Within each group a mean population size for each species was calculated, then converted into a standard birds-per-40-ha value. The 1949–50 and 1979–80 censuses were compared by calculating percent change in density per 40 ha between the two census periods (Table 1).

Species turnover rates were calculated using a modified form of Diamond's (1969) method. Percent turnover rate per time interval equals:

$$\frac{100 \, (E + H)}{C + D - G},$$

where E equals extinctions, H equals colonizations, C equals total number of species recorded the first year, D

TABLE 1. Comparisons of breeding bird species populations in east SSW between the 1949-50 censuses and the 1979–80 censuses. An asterisk (*) indicates an average value less than 0.5 pairs per 40 ha for each pair of years

Species	Mean pairs/40 ha		Percent change
	1949–50	1979–80	
RESIDENTS:			
Black-capped Chickadee (Parus atricapillus)	8.6	14.6	+170
White-breasted Nuthatch (Sitta carolinensis)	3.2	3.7	+16.7
Tufted Titmouse (Parus bicolor)	0	2.2	*
Brown Creeper (Certhia familiaris)	0	11.9	*
Downy Woodpecker (Picoides pubescens)	1.1	5.4	+400
Hairy Woodpecker (Picoides villosus)	2.2	3.2	+50
Pileated Woodpecker (Dryocopus pileatus)	2.2	2.2	0
American Crow (Corvus brachyrhynchos)	*	2.2	*
Blue Jay (Cyanocitta cristata)	1.1	3.8	+250
Ruffed Grouse (Bonasa umbellus)	*	*	0
Barred Owl (Strix varia)	*	*	0
Great Horned Owl (Bubo virginianus)	0	*	*
SHORT-DISTANCE MIGRANTS:			
American Robin (Turdus migratorius)	1.6	4.3	+167
Gray Catbird (Dumetella carolinensis)	0	0.5	*
Eastern Phoebe (Sayornis phoebe)	2.7	0	-100
Common Flicker (Colaptes auratus)	1.1	1.1	0
Brown-headed Cowbird (Molothrus ater)	0	22.7[a]	*
Red-shouldered Hawk (Buteo lineatus)	*	*	0
Cooper's Hawk (Accipiter cooperii)	*	*	0
Belted Kingfisher (Megaceryle alcyon)	0	*	*
NEOTROPICAL MIGRANTS:			
Red-eyed Vireo (Vireo olivaceus)	20.0	5.9	-71
Scarlet Tanager (Piranga olivacea)	6.5	3.2	-50
Rose-breasted Grosbeak (Pheucticus ludovicianus)	0	3.2	*
Wood Thrush (Hylocichla mustelina)	9.7	10.3	+10
Veery (Catharus fuscescens)	13	5.4	-58
Great Crested Flycatcher (Myiarchus crinitus)	4.3	5.9	+38
Eastern Wood-Pewee (Contopus virens)	6.5	7.6	+17
Ovenbird (Seiurus aurocapillus)	14.0	5.4	-62
Northern Waterthrush (Seiurus noveboracensis)	7.6	6.5	-14
Common Yellowthroat (Geothlypis trichas)	0	5.4	+100
Canada Warbler (Wilsonia canadensis)	8.7	0	-100
Black-and-white Warbler (Mniotilta varia)	4.9	0	-100
Black-throated Green Warbler (Dendroica dominica)	5.4	0	-100
Magnolia Warbler (Dendroica magnolia)	2.7	0	-100
Chestnut-sided Warbler (Dendroica pensylvanica)	1.1	0	-100
American Redstart (Setophaga ruticilla)	3.8	0	-100

SUMMARY	Total species 1949–1950	Total mean pairs/40 ha	Total species 1949–1950	Total mean pairs/40 ha	Percent change density
Residents	6	18.4	9	49.1	+267
Short-distance migrants	3	5.4	3	5.9	+10
Neotropical migrants	14	108	10	58.9	-55
Totals and % change density	23	131.8	22	113.9	-14

a. Sightings.

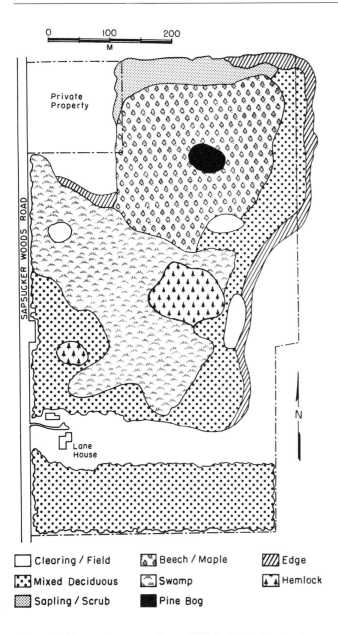

0   100   200
M

Private
Property

SAPSUCKER WOODS ROAD

N

Lane
House

☐ Clearing / Field   [∴] Beech / Maple   ▨ Edge

[∷] Mixed Deciduous   Swamp   ▲ Hemlock

Sapling / Scrub   ● Pine Bog

FIGURE 1. Vegetation map of east SSW in 1950, showing locations of major dominance types (after Owen 1950).

equals the total number of species for the second year, and G equals species introduced by man. Bird species diversity was calculated using the Shannon index (Shannon and Weaver 1949, MacArthur and MacArthur 1961).

SEQUENTIAL ANALYSIS OF LAND USE IN THE SAPSUCKER WOODS VICINITY

To assess the historical context of SSW in the local landscape, a sequential analysis of land-use patterns surrounding SSW was performed using aerial photography for the years 1938, 1954, 1964, 1968, and 1980. Each

year class of photographs was stereoscopically analyzed and digitized using land-use categories modified after Hardy et al. (1971; Appendix 2). The accommodation of the largest breeding bird territory of any species nesting in SSW was the primary criterion for determining the size of the sample area around SSW. The widest-ranging SSW species were the Red-shouldered Hawk and Pileated Woodpecker, whose breeding territory size was estimated at 0.62 km² by Craighead and Craighead (1969) and 0.43 km² by Tanner (1942). The biological criterion was met with a 5-km diameter circular plot having an area of 19.63 km² (1,962 ha), with SSW serving as the center of the circle.

VEGETATION AND SUCCESSIONAL ANALYSIS

In 1950, Owen created a vegetation map of east SSW identifying three major dominance types, Beech/Maple, Elm/Maple/Ash ("Swamp"), and Mixed Deciduous (Fig. 1). To quantify the tree species composition of each of these types, Owen (1950) established a 30.5 m × 30.5 m (100 ft × 100 ft) quadrat in each type. Within each quadrat he measured species abundance and diameter at breast height (dbh = 1.4 m above ground level) for trees having a dbh of 7 cm or over. From these data he derived relative abundance and relative basal area contribution by species.

We replicated Owen's vegetation survey first by identifying disturbances such as the effects of storms, fire, disease, logging, grazing, or release of agricultural land that would affect vegetation patterns. Second, a vegetation map was created independently of Owen's map, again using a dominance-type classification scheme (Whittaker 1978). The map was made by traversing east SSW on three separate occasions, noting changes in tree species composition and distribution, using the grid system for reference.

An intensive survey was conducted using 0.04-ha (0.10 ac) plots (James and Shugart 1970). Sample plot locations were chosen by selecting grid points randomly from within dominance types. A grid point served as the center of each plot. Five sample plots per dominance type was a sufficient sample (James and Shugart 1970). In dominance types where fewer than five plots were available, all suitable points were sampled. For the purpose of comparison, Owen's (1950) 100 ft × 100 ft quadrats were converted to 0.04-ha circular plot statistics, each quadrat equalling 2.32 circular plots.

REGIONAL AVIAN POPULATION ANALYSIS

To assess the possibility that declining population trends of certain SSW breeding birds are a reflection of regional population trends, Breeding Bird Survey (BBS) data were analyzed for strata 16 and 24 of New York

State. The two strata were pooled and a maximum of 35 routes was analyzed for each year of the survey (1967 to 1981). A yearly population index for each species was calculated by dividing the total number of individuals of the species observed on all routes by the total number of routes sampled.

Results

SEQUENTIAL ANALYSIS OF LAND USE IN THE SAPSUCKER WOODS VICINITY

Land use around SSW has changed dramatically since 1938 (Table 2). Openland (OL) has decreased since 1938 (from 74 to 34%) and Brushland (FC) has increased (7 to 23%). Residential Low (RL) development has also increased, from 0 to 12%. Forest (FN) has been relatively stable, increasing from 17% to 21%. The combined totals of Openland, Brushland, and Forest for the five year classes indicate their combined dominance: 1938, 98%; 1954, 92%; 1964, 87%; 1968, 84%; 1980, 78%. Chi-square analysis indicates that distributions of the relative proportions of the various categories are significantly nonrandom among categories ($\chi^2 = 1031.49, P \leq 0.05$, d.f. = 10).

Apparently SSW has not become more fragmented during the period 1938 to 1980, but rather has become consolidated and less isolated from other woodlands. The wooded area which Owen (1950) studied was 18.5 ha. In 1980, the wooded area within the fence of east SSW, which includes Owen's area, was 20.6 ha. The increase in woodland is larger if the second-growth habitat beyond the eastern boundary of east SSW is included. In general, this pattern exists for the entire 1,962 ha land-use study area. Most of the wooded areas lost since 1938 have been relatively small tracts. Concurrently, the remaining larger tracts became consolidated and larger in size, resulting in the stability of total woodlot area from 1938 to 1980 (Table 2). In 1938, brushland frequently intruded into woodlots, causing forest fragmentation. This probably resulted from wood-cutting operations.

Also, between 1938 and 1980, study area woodlots became less isolated from each other because of ecological succession of Openland (OL) to Brushland (FC). In 1980, a bird could travel along a number of woodland/brushland corridors that traverse the study area, without leaving cover. This was not the case in 1938 when woodlots were separated by expanses of agricultural fields. Residential Low (RL) has had little impact on woodlot area since it represents only 12% of the 1980 study area and has largely replaced Openland.

LOCAL BIRD POPULATION ANALYSIS

Since 1949–50 the resident avian population of east SSW has undergone a modest increase in species richness and a substantial increase in density (Table 1). Short-distance migrants have increased by two species, although their density has remained constant. Neotropical migrants, other than warblers, have increased slightly in species richness but have declined nearly one-third in density. The warblers have undergone the greatest decline in density and are the only group to have declined in species richness. Neotropical migrant density has declined 46%. It should be noted that the popula-

TABLE 2. Sequential analysis of land-use types surrounding SSW (5-km dia. study area, total area = 1,962 ha). Upper row of each year class represents percent contribution, lower row represents actual area. Method subject to a 2 % error. See Appendix 2 for a description of classifications

Year	Land-use types—percent contribution and actual area (ha)										
1938	OL(74)	FN(17)	FC(7)	FP(1)	WS(1)	RH(0)	RL(0)	P(0)	A(0)	C(0)	IA(0)
	(1419.4)	(335.5)	(142.9)	(19.2)	(16.9)	(0)	(0)	(0)	(0)	(0)	(0)
1954	OL(62)	FN(20)	FC(10)	RL(3)	FP(2)	A(2)	WS(1)	RH(0)	P(0)	C(0)	IA(0)
	(1223.1)	(383.8)	(183.9)	(56.3)	(31.9)	(38.19)	(16.75)	(0)	(0)	(0)	(0)
1964	OL(52)	FN(22)	FC(13)	RL(7)	FP(2)	A(2)	WS(1)	RH(.50)	P(.20)	C(.10)	A(.20)
	(1003)	(428.1)	(249.79)	(140.4)	(33.8)	(45.54)	(17.19)	(7.67)	(3.6)	(1)	(4)
1968	OL(48)	FN(21)	FC(15)	RL(9)	FP(2)	A(2)	WS(1)	RH(1)	IA(.40)	C(.35)	P(.25)
	(938.4)	(416)	(286.6)	(166.2)	(31.7)	(43.4)	(17.8)	(18.9)	(5.5)	(5.5)	(3.8)
1980	OL(34)	FC(23)	FN(21)	RL(12)	FP(2)	A(2)	RH(2)	WS(1)	IA(1)	C(1)	P(1)
	(664)	(445.5)	(414)	(232.9)	(39.4)	(47.36)	(36.9)	(17.6)	(6.6)	(11.3)	(18.4)

Key: OL = Open land, FN = Forest, FC = Brushland, FP = Forest plantation, WS = River, RH = Residential high, RL = Residential low, P = Public property, A = Airport, C = Commercial, IA = Industrial.

tions of east SSW species were small, and caution should be used when assessing the biological significance of percent change calculations in Table 1.

Despite the species-specific changes that have taken place in the SSW avian community, little change has occurred in total density and species richness over a 30-year period (Table 1). The SSW avian community has declined in density by 14% since 1950. Using 20–25% as a range of predictable variation (Lynch and Whitcomb 1978), the observed changes could be expected due to chance alone. Pair-wise comparisons of diversity indices for the 1949–50 and 1979–80 censuses were not significant (*t*-test, $P \leq 0.05$). Of greater interest are the declines seen for Neotropical migrants. Four species within this group have undergone declines of greater than 25% (Veery, Red-eyed Vireo, Ovenbird, Scarlet Tanager), and six species have become locally extinct (Magnolia, Black-throated Green, Black-and-white, Canada, and Chestnut-sided warblers, and American Redstart). These six species account for most of the 17.8 pairs/40 ha decline in warblers since 1949–50.

ALLEN BREEDING BIRD CENSUSES, 1956–1980

For the 16 years of Allen data, the mean number of species was 26.1 (SD = 2.4). Taking annual variation and the different sampling techniques into consideration, this figure is very close to the 23 and 22 species found in the 1949–50/1979–80 censuses (Table 1). The number of breeding pairs was more variable ($\bar{X}$ = 54.1, SD = 8.3) in the Allen census than in the 1949–50 and 1979–80 censuses. Indications of relative stability in the east SSW bird community are found in the lack of variability between Shannon diversity indices. With the exception of three years (3 of 16, 18.85%), all pair-wise comparisons of yearly indices were not significant (*t*-test, $P \leq 0.05$). A low yearly species turnover rate also indicates a relatively stable bird community. Rates range from 13 to 36% ($\bar{X}$ = 22.6%, SD = 6.7). The turnover rates for the 1949–50 census (10%) and the 1979–80 census (4.8%) are below those of the Allen survey. This is probably an artifact of different sampling methods where the more intensive method would yield lower turnover rates because of excluding nonbreeders.

Of the four declining species (Table 1), only the Veery declined significantly ($P < 0.05$). However, the slope (–0.17) indicates a very modest rate of decline. The correlation coefficients of the Red-eyed Vireo, Ovenbird, and Scarlet Tanager were also negative, but not significant.

Species with large territories have consistently nested in SSW. Minimally, the Barred Owl has nested 26 of 35 years, Red-shouldered Hawk 26 of 35 years, Great Horned Owl 12 of 35 years, Cooper's Hawk 8 of 35 years, and Pileated Woodpecker 19 of 35 years.

When comparing Allen's analysis of the SSW breeding bird community to that of the 1949–50/1979–80 analysis, it is apparent that all species that declined by more than 25% between 1949 and 1980 were found by Allen to be regular nesters (Appendix 1). Those species that became locally extinct between 1949 and 1980, with the exception of the Canada Warbler, were listed by Allen as irregular nesters. Allen's listing of the Canada Warbler as a regular nester is based on its occurrence in west SSW, as it was a sporadic nester in east SSW.

REGIONAL BIRD POPULATION ANALYSIS

Based on an analysis of BBS data for New York State strata 16 and 24 for 1967 through 1981, the regional Veery population began a decline in 1967 which ended in approximately 1974. For the period 1974 to 1981, which encompasses the 1979–80 SSW census, the regional population increased rapidly, whereas the local SSW population continued a steady decline. Generally, the SSW Veery population declined significantly ($P \leq 0.05$), whereas the regional population showed a statistically nonsignificant increasing tendency.

Statistically, local and regional population trends of the Red-eyed Vireo were different. Although the local SSW population showed a nonsignificant negative trend, the regional population exhibited a significant positive trend ($R^2 = 0.78$, $P \leq 0.05$). A similar relationship was found for both the Ovenbird and Scarlet Tanager. Regionally, these species exhibited statistically significant increases from 1967 to 1981. Locally, within east SSW, a nonsignificant negative trend was identified. The American Redstart and Magnolia Warbler showed relatively strong, significant ($P \leq 0.05$) regional population increases. Despite regional trends, these species no longer nest in SSW. The Black-throated Green and Chestnut-sided warblers also showed nonsignificant regional increases ($P \leq 0.05$). In contrast to regional increases, these species have become locally extinct in SSW.

Two species had negative regional declines, the Canada Warbler (significant) and the Black-and-white Warbler (nonsignificant). The Canada Warbler was the only species examined that might be exhibiting parallel trends on the local and regional levels, although the evidence is not strong. The sole supporting evidence is the fact that during the period when the regional population was at its highest level (1967–1971), nesting recurred in east SSW after a six-year nesting hiatus. The Black-and-white Warbler regional population fluctuated between 0.3 and 1.0 mean birds per route, with only a slight indication of a directional trend. Black-and-white Warblers have not nested in east SSW since 1950.

In summary, for the SSW species examined, the regional populations tended to increase while the local

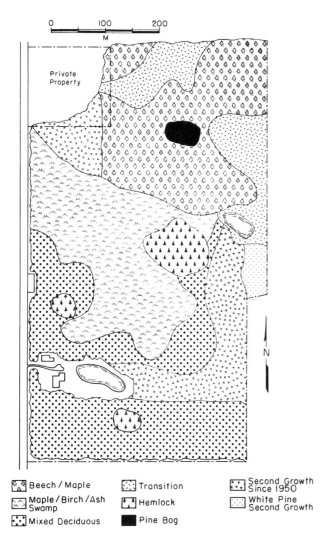

FIGURE 2. Vegetation map of east SSW in 1980, showing locations of major dominance types (Litwin 1986).

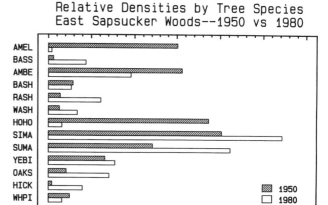

FIGURE 3. Relative percent stem densities of tree species in east SSW, comparing 1950 with 1980. For a more detailed description of species composition, refer to Owen (1950) and Litwin (1986). Abbreviations: *AMEL*—American elm (*Ulmus americana*), *BASS*—basswood (*Tilia americana*), *AMBE*—American beech (*Fagus grandifolia*), *BASH*—black ash (*Fraxinus nigra*), *RASH*—red ash (*Fraxinus pennsylvanica*), *WASH*—white ash (*Fraxinus americana*), *HOHO*—hop hornbeam (*Ostrya virginiana*), *SIMA*—silver maple (*Acer saccharinum*), *SUMA*—sugar maple (*Acer saccharum*), *YEBI*—yellow birch (*Betula lutea*), *OAKS*—includes white oak (*Quercus alba*), swamp white oak (*Quercus bicolor*), mossy-cup oak (*Quercus macrocarpa*), and red oak (*Quercus rubra*), *HICK*—includes shagbark hickory (*Carya ovata*) and pignut hickory (*Carya glabra*), *WHPI*—white pine (*Pinus strobus*), *OTHR*—other species, including eastern hemlock (*Tsuga canadensis*), tuliptree (*Liriodendron tulipifera*), black cherry (*Prunus serotina*), and blue beech (*Carpinus caroliniana*).

SSW populations declined. Two species, the Black-throated Green and Black-and-white warblers appeared to fluctuate, without strong positive or negative trends. The Canada Warbler showed a significant negative trend, but with a modest slope (–0.03).

VEGETATION AND SUCCESSIONAL ANALYSIS

In 1980, the major dominance types identified in east SSW were Maple/Birch/Ash Swamp, Beech/Maple, Mixed Deciduous, Hemlock, White Pine Bog, Transitional, Second Growth since 1950, and White Pine Second Growth (Fig. 2). Several vegetation changes have occurred since 1950 (Fig. 1), particularly in regard to relative stem densities (Fig. 3) and basal area. Basal

area estimates were significantly correlated with relative stem densities ($P \leq 0.0001$).

The impact of Dutch elm disease on American elm in east SSW during the mid-1950s is clear; the species was virtually eliminated from the area (Fig.3). The decline in relative density for American beech can be attributed to the introduction of beech bark disease to the Northeast, including SSW (Houston et al. 1979). Basswood, silver maple, sugar maple, red ash, and white ash have increased in density. Hop hornbeam, an understory species, has declined substantially in relative density. The loss of this early successional/gap-phase species is a clear indicator of canopy closure and successional maturation of SSW since 1950.

Logging and firewood cutting that took place in the

Mixed Deciduous habitat type until approximately 1945 is responsible for the density increases seen in basswood, white ash, and sugar maple. When Owen (1950) analyzed this dominance type, it was being more heavily harvested than surrounding types, allowing for competitive release of basswood, white ash, and sugar maple.

Owen (1950) provides descriptive information characterizing SSW prior to and during his study. He indicates that grazing stopped in east SSW around 1920. This is substantiated by the fact that most of the woods in the area of SSW, including SSW, were burned between 1880 and 1900 to control woody understory growth and promote the growth of grass for grazing. During Owen's study, grazing was reported on the south margin of east SSW. Prior to this time Owen reported that the swamp was fenced to prevent grazing cattle from wandering into that area. Grazing on the eastern margin of SSW caused compaction which restricted the height of herbaceous cover (Owen 1950).

Owen (1950) reported the effects of logging and wood cutting in a variety of ways. He stated, "The presence of old timber trails and rotting stumps of substantial proportions indicate that at one time a fair amount of rather mature timber was removed." The Mixed Deciduous habitat was described as having "a substantial number of trees removed for timber" and "a large number of breaks in the canopy due to trails, scattered cutting operations, windfalls, and lightning strikes." These descriptions are corroborated by the high percentages of basal area removed by logging from the total basal area of each dominance type, as calculated from existing stumps: Maple/Birch/Ash Swamp (60%), Beech/Maple (20%), Mixed Deciduous (37%), Hemlock (70%), White Pine Bog (56%). Logging of softwood species took place in a single event sometime between 1915 and 1930. Hardwood harvesting took place more sporadically between 1922 and 1945.

Owen (1950) used terms to describe the understory, such as "extensive," "impenetrable," and "dense." Based on significant changes in stem densities, basal area, and woodland maturation, the shrub layers of the major dominance types have probably declined since 1950 because of canopy closure. As a result, the east SSW understory in 1980 was relatively open with the exception of occasional shrub patches. The exception is the shrub layer of the Beech/Maple habitat which in 1950 Owen called "practically non-existent." In 1980, the Beech/Maple type contained more shrub stems per hectare than either the Mixed Deciduous or Swamp habitat types (Beech/Maple = 4,866 stems/ha, Mixed Deciduous = 3,921 stems/ha, Swamp = 3,804 stems/ha).

Tree composition and vegetation structure of east SSW has been subjected to a variety of land-use activities including logging, grazing, and cultivation. These activities took place from approximately 1880 to 1956 and created a woodlot that was patchy, heterogeneous in both horizontal and verticle structure, and relatively young in age. With the establishment of the SSW Sanctuary these land-use activities ended, allowing vertical and horizontal successional processes to advance. The general trend within the dominance types is fewer individual trees than 1950, with an equal or increasing amount of biomass concentrated in these fewer individuals (Litwin 1986). A canopy that was broken and relatively open had closed. Canopy closure eliminated early successional tree species and reduced shrub density. Forest gaps created by selective logging and trails have since closed, but others have been created by loss of elm and beech. The woodland edge which was highly variable and showed a good deal of structural gradation, has now been assimilated into the woodland proper, meeting abruptly with adjoining fields and shrublands. In comparison to the woodlot which Owen (1950) surveyed, east SSW is now structurally more homogeneous, less patchy, and exhibits characteristics of a mature woodlot. In assessing which factor might have had the greatest influence on the breeding bird population of east SSW since 1950, internal successional change clearly emerges as a primary influence when compared to external land-use patterns or regional population changes.

Discussion

The decline of Neotropical migrants in forest fragments, as seen in SSW, has been widely reported (Galli et al. 1976, Lynch and Whitcomb 1978, Whitcomb 1977, Whitcomb et al. 1981, Butcher et al. 1981, Ambuel and Temple 1982, Askins et al. 1990). These studies also demonstrate stable or increasing resident populations, as was also the case in SSW (Table 1).

The annual species turnover rates for the 1949–50 (10%) and 1979–80 (4.8%) censuses and 16-year Allen census ($\bar{X}$ = 22%) are also within the same general range found in other studies. Butcher et al. (1981) reported a mean turnover rate of 23% (range = 17.4–29.6%) for their Connecticut study area and Whitcomb (1977) found a mean turnover rate of 10% (range = 7–11%) on their Maryland plot. Lynch and Whitcomb (1978) found the mean annual turnover rate for 15 six-year intervals among their study plots ranged between 8% and 37%. Although these rates can be compared in only a general way, they do indicate an interval of 10 to 37% within which turnover rates fluctuate on similar sized woodlots in the eastern forest.

The turnover rate found between the 1949–50 and 1979–80 SSW censuses (32.5%) draws attention to those species which have become locally extinct, including the Magnolia Warbler, Black-throated Green Warbler,

Black-and-white Warbler, American Redstart, Canada Warbler, and Chestnut-sided Warbler (Table 1). The loss of these species, and a gain in resident species between the 1950 and 1980 censuses were the primary factors contributing to a relatively high turnover when compared to the 1949–50, 1979–80, or Allen census rates. Based solely on the turnover rate calculated from two censuses separated by 30 years, one might assume there is a high degree of instability within the SSW breeding bird community. An examination of the Allen censuses, conducted between 1950 and 1980, indicates this is not the case. Both species richness and density estimates fluctuated within an expected range, and wide-ranging species remained a predictable component of the SSW avian community.

Allen listed all of the species that became locally extinct between 1949 and 1980 as sporadic nesters with very small populations (Appendix 1). What was occurring between 1950 and 1980 was "crypto turnover," the process of repeated colonizations and extinctions (Lynch and Whitcomb 1978, Butcher et al. 1981) that is symptomatic of small forest patch populations (Whitcomb et al. 1981).

In this context, the sporadic nesters that have become locally extinct in SSW (Canada Warbler, Black-and-white Warbler, Black-throated Green Warbler, Magnolia Warbler, Chestnut-sided Warbler, American Redstart) are to be distinguished from a second group, consistent breeders (Red-eyed Vireo, Scarlet Tanager, Veery, Ovenbird, Northern Waterthrush) that are declining. The apparent instability of SSW breeding birds, resulting from the turnover of sporadic nesters, might in fact have little to do with the core members of the SSW breeding bird community. In this regard, SSW appears to be a long-established woodlot whose avian species richness has been stable, but whose species turnover rates have been more dynamic.

It is possible that the Neotropical migrant declines observed in SSW result from the relaxation process that begins after a habitat patch becomes isolated, whereby species loss occurs until a species richness is reached that can be supported by the reduced size of the new isolate (Diamond 1972, Soulé et al. 1979). Since SSW has been a woodland patch for approximately 150 years, and has been subjected to periodic, small-scale disturbances, it is unlikely that relaxation explains changes in avian species composition between 1950 and 1980.

Because of the particular land-use circumstances that comprise the history of SSW, a successional turnover model (Lynch and Johnson 1974) provides a more appropriate explanation for the observed avian population dynamics. The relevance of SSW's changing habitat structure to the bird species that are locally extinct or declining is evident when their habitat preferences are examined. Based on habitat preference, the locally ex-

tinct or declining species of SSW can be categorized in three groups.

Group I contains the Chestnut-sided Warbler that selects open habitats with dense ground cover and moderate to dense understories associated with open woodlands, woodland edges, abandoned agricultural land and young clearcuts (Eaton 1914, Saunders 1936, Kendeigh 1945, Bent 1963, Keller 1980, Collins et al. 1982).

Group II includes the Magnolia Warbler, Black-and-white Warbler, American Redstart, and Canada Warbler. These species are identified with second-growth and forest-edge habitats having a high percentage of shrub or sapling understory and includes such habitats as early second-growth conifer, deciduous or mixed-growth woodlands, old field thickets, wet thickets, clearcuts, and woodland clearings (Eaton 1914, Chapman 1917, Saunders 1936, Bent 1963, Kendeigh 1945, Martin 1960, Keller 1980, Collins et al. 1982, Clark et al. 1983). The birds of Groups I and II regularly use early successional and disturbed habitats, and include all of the SSW bird species which have become locally extinct, with the exception of the Black-throated Green Warbler. These groups also represent those species considered by Allen to be irregular nesters.

Group III includes the Black-throated Green Warbler, Ovenbird, Veery, Red-eyed Vireo, and Scarlet Tanager. The Black-throated Green Warbler is associated with coniferous and coniferous/mixed hardwoods second growth and more mature woods with greater than 75% canopy cover and moderate ground and shrub cover (Eaton 1914, Chapman 1917, Saunders 1936, Bent 1963, Martin 1960, Collins et al. 1982).

The Veery nests in a variety of habitats including 4- to 13-year-old clearcuts, abandoned field shrub/sapling thickets, and early deciduous second growth, but reaches highest densities in intermediate aged hardwoods with developed shrub layers (Saunders 1936, Bertin 1977, Keller 1980, Noon et al. 1980, Sousa 1982, Clark et al. 1983). The Red-eyed Vireo uses a range of habitats from shrublands to older forest (Saunders 1936, Martin 1960), reaching its greatest density in woodlands with intermediate levels of canopy volume and tree densities (Clark et al. 1983). It is associated with selectively cut open woodlands or early second growth having a developed sapling layer, but is also found in abandoned orchards, regenerated burns, and farmland margins (Forbush 1925, Saunders 1936, Martin 1960, Clark et al. 1983). The Scarlet Tanager also tolerates a range of habitats including open woodlands and orchards, reaching highest densities in woodlands with a moderate to well-developed shrub layer (Saunders 1936, Bent 1965, Keller 1980). Similarly, Ovenbirds select young to intermediate aged deciduous second-growth woods with both a moderate amount of undergrowth and areas of clear forest floor, although they nest in earlier seres including 14-year old clearcuts (Chapman 1917, Bent 1963, Keller 1980, Whitcomb et al. 1981, Collins et al. 1982).

The species in Group III include those birds that have declined in east SSW (with the exception of the Black-throated Green Warbler) and corresponds with Allen's category of "regular nesters" (Appendix 1).

When the species of Groups I, II, and III are placed along a successional gradient, Group I is found in the earliest successional stage, Group II occurs in a shrub/early second-growth stage, and Group III occurs from the early second-growth to mature-forest stages. In 1950, the interspersion of these vegetation patch types within SSW permitted the simultaneous occurrence of these groups. With continued maturation of east SSW, those patches supporting Groups I and II declined, reducing the horizontal and vertical heterogeneity of the woods. Local extinctions of sporadic nesters resulted from the ephemeral nature of the habitats they were using, in addition to their very small population sizes. The retention of declining/regular nesters resulted from successional maturation that provided habitat for Group III species at initially higher densities. As SSW continued to mature, declining densities of Group III species can be attributed to the further loss of both vertical and horizontal structural heterogeneity, and the overall decline in productivity associated with forest maturation (Kendeigh 1946, Odum 1950, 1969, Johnston and Odum 1956, Margalef 1958, Karr 1968, Aber 1979, Keller 1980).

As of 1980, the species diversity of east SSW had remained stable since 1950 because of compensatory resident species additions and density increases in existing resident species populations (Table 1). These species (Black-capped Chickadee, White-breasted Nuthatch, Tufted Titmouse, Brown Creeper, Downy Woodpecker, Hairy Woodpecker) most likely benefited from increased foraging and nest site opportunities that resulted from an increase in dead wood associated with maturing woods (Litwin 1986), Dutch elm disease, and beech bark disease. Considering the work of Holmes and Robinson (1981), changing tree species composition and age of trees in SSW might have provided foraging opportunities beneficial to resident and Group III species, but might have been detrimental to species requiring earlier successional habitats. Such patterns are applicable on both local and regional scales.

Observations similiar to those made in SSW have been reported by others. Examining the effects of logging on songbird populations, Webb et al. (1977) surveyed northern hardwoods subjected to 25, 50, 75, and 100% cuts of marketable timber. The densities of the American Redstart, Chestnut-sided Warbler, Veery, Canada Warbler, and Black-and-white Warbler increased with increased cutting. Red-eyed Vireo and

Scarlet Tanager densities remained constant through 75% cutting. Ovenbird and Black-throated Green Warbler densities were constant from uncut to 50% cutting, then declined with cutting beyond that point. In comparing selectively cut forest to mature forest in West Virginia, Maurer et al. (1981) found the Veery, Black-and-white Warbler, Chestnut-sided Warbler, and Canada Warbler occurring in selective cuts, but not mature forest. This was attributed to the release of the shrub and sapling layers in the selectively cut woods, which were used by these species.

Results from a comparison of vegetation and bird composition of a selectively cut woods to an uncut mature woods by Adams and Barrett (1976) were comparable to changes in SSW over a 30-year period. The selectively cut woods had a greater tree species richness distributed over more age classes, a greater absolute tree density, and greater vertical heterogeneity than the mature woods. The selectively cut woods was more heterogeneous in its avian composition, compared with the older woods which had higher densities concentrated in fewer species. The greater species diversity in the cut woods was attributed to the ability of the rarer bird species to make use of the more complex vertical structure. Similarly, Hagar (1960) found increased species diversity and abundance in logged Douglas fir forest, when compared to older growth uncut stands. This was attributed to an increase in the shrub layer and associated increase of food resources. In a second-growth red spruce forest, Hall (1984a) attributed the local extinction of the Chestnut-sided Warbler, and the decline of the Magnolia Warbler, to crown closure and reduction of structural diversity. Hall (1984b) attributed increased abundance of both the Canada and Magnolia warblers in old-growth spruce to their colonizations of gaps resulting from storm-induced blowdowns.

These examples represent specific mechanisms that alter the vertical and horizontal structure of habitats, and are quite similar to the events that have taken place in SSW. Within ecological communities increased habitat heterogeneity has consistently been correlated with increased breeding bird diversity (MacArthur and MacArthur 1961, MacArthur et al. 1962, Karr and Roth 1971, Willson 1974, Pickett and Thompson 1978, Swift et al. 1984). Increased structural heterogeneity creates a more complex three-dimensional habitat space, which results in increased habitat diversity and greater variety of niche exploitation opportunities. With canopy closure, spatial heterogeneity is reduced (primarily due to the decline of the shrub layer), consequently reducing niche diversity (Willson 1974, Roth 1976, Aber 1979, Swift et al. 1984) and the number of species that can exploit the habitat. In this regard, Willson (1974) found the correlation of bird species diversity to vegetation volume of particular significance, emphasizing the importance of the shrub layer. The emergence of the shrub layer as an important component of forest heterogeneity is supported by trends observed in SSW, as well as in a number of other forest situations (Haapanen 1966, Roth 1976, Karr and Roth 1971, Hooper et al. 1973, Swift et al. 1984, Aber 1979, Lynch and Whigham 1984)

Habitat quality and heterogeneity have consistently been important aspects of studies examining species diversity. In numerous studies involving birds, mammals, plants, and invertebrates, habitat heterogeneity has proved to be a stronger explanation for the species diversity observed, when tested against such factors as the geometry of an area or its isolation (Lack 1976, Johnson 1972, 1975, Power 1972, 1975a,b, Harris 1973, Amerson 1975, Picton 1979, Buckley 1982, Dickerson and Robinson 1985). In light of the numerous examples presented, including those of SSW, the concept of habitat as "the template for ecological strategies" (Southwood 1977), or as "the stage set in the ecological theater" (Hutchinson 1965), remains a fundamental element in our understanding of avian community composition at both local and regional scales of geographic resolution.

Conclusions

The avian population and habitat selection patterns found in SSW are not dramatically different from those found in similar studies, covering a wide geographic area. The most widely accepted explanation for the patterns observed (declining Neotropical migrants, stable resident populations, an apparent equilibrial state, "high" turnover rates) is increasing habitat fragmentation and isolation (Forman et al. 1976, Whitcomb 1977, Lynch and Whitcomb 1978, Robbins 1979, Butcher et al. 1981). From these observations it can be concluded that some Neotropical migrant, forest-interior bird species are area sensitive and may not be able to maintain viable nesting populations in fragments below a certain size (Robbins 1979, Whitcomb et al. 1981). These conclusions have contributed to the development of a series of strategies for establishing and managing refuges with the goal of preserving area-sensitive species (Terborgh 1974, 1975, Diamond 1975, Diamond and May 1976, Wilson and Willis 1975, Whitcomb 1977, Forman et al. 1976, Robbins 1979).

Based on the profound influence of historical land-use activity and disease-related tree loss within SSW, it is clear that Neotropical migrant bird management needs to consider these factors as well as those involving fragmentation and isolation. In attempting to evaluate the causes for avian population change in SSW, a number of factors required simultaneous examination. We have demonstrated this approach through examination of ex-

ternal regional influences (land-use change and avian population trends), as related to internal dynamics such as vertical and horizontal vegetation structure and gap-phase successional patterns.

Within the eastern deciduous forest, events that have affected SSW are not unique. Because of the decline of agriculture in the northeastern United States, beginning around 1900, the forest from New Jersey to New England has been increasing in area and age (Brooks 1990). Given the widespread distribution of Dutch elm and beech bark diseases in the eastern and northeastern United States, it is unlikely that many forest fragments, and the birds associated with them, have escaped the effects of these two pathogens (Houston et al. 1979, Sinclair and Campana 1978). In addition, the effects of past events like fire, logging, blowdowns, insect infestations (e.g., gypsy moth), grazing, and browsing by mammalian herbivores (e.g., white-tailed deer) on the structure and composition of plant communities within forest fragments have to be considered explicitly and cannot be underestimated. Mature forest fragments are not static, and the time line for change within them can be extensive; their composition and structure can be significantly affected by the cumulative and interactive effects of these factors. Such considerations are in addition to evaluations of anthropogenic factors affecting the landscape and land-use patterns in areas surrounding the forest fragment.

Interpretations of long-term patterns of change in the distributions and abundances of bird species in the absence of information about vegetation and land-use changes can be misleading, perhaps even wrong. Both the *content* and *context* of the study plot require explicit consideration. Information about bird populations should be assembled in parallel with information about plant community structure and composition, and those factors that shape successional patterns over different spatial and temporal scales.

Acknowledgments

Initiation of the study upon which this paper is based was made possible through the contributions and encouragement of Donald A. McCrimmon, Jr. Robert Askins and David Wilcove provided thoughtful comments which contributed to the development of this paper. We also thank Paul Hamel and an anonymous reviewer for reading an earlier draft of this manuscript and making many helpful suggestions for its improvement. Support for this study was provided by the Research Department of the National Audubon Society, the Cornell Laboratory of Ornithology, the Natalie Peters Webster Trust, and through Hatch Project No. NYC-171401, U.S. Department of Agriculture, to C.R. Smith.

Literature cited

Aber, J.D. 1979. A method for estimating foliage-height profiles in broad-leaved forests. *J. Ecol.* 67:35–40.

Adams, D.L., and G.W. Barret. 1976. Stress effects on bird-species diversity within mature forest ecosystems. *Am. Midl. Nat.* 96:179–194.

Ambuel, B., and S.A. Temple. 1982. Area-dependent changes in the bird communities and vegetation of southern Wisconsin forests. *Ecology* 64:1057–1068.

Amerson, A.B. 1975. Species richness on the nondisturbed northwestern Hawaiian Islands. *Ecology* 56:435–444.

Askins, R.A., J.F. Lynch, and R. Greenberg. 1990. Population declines in migratory birds in eastern North America. *Current Ornithol.* 7:1–57.

Bent, A.C. 1963. *Life Histories of North American Wood Warblers.* Vol. I and II. New York: Dover Publications, Inc.

———. 1965. *Life Histories of North American Blackbirds, Orioles, Tanagers, and Allies.* New York: Dover Publications, Inc.

Bertin, R.I. 1977. Breeding habitats of the Wood Thrush and Veery. *Condor* 79:303–311.

Brooks, R.T. 1990. Timber management and its effects on wildlife. Pages 37–54 in *Proceedings of the 1989 Forest Resources Issues Conf.,* J.C. Finley and M.C. Brittingham, eds. University Park: Pennsylvania State University.

Buckley, R. 1982. The habitat-unit model of island biogeography. *J. Biogeog.* 9:339–344.

Butcher, G.S., W.A. Niering, W.J. Barry, and R.H. Goodwin. 1981. Equilibrium biogeography and the size of nature preserves: An avian case study. *Oecologia* 49:29–37.

Chapman, F.M. 1917. *The Warblers of North America.* New York: D. Appleton and Co.

Clark, E., D. Evler, and E. Armstrong. 1983. Habitat association of breeding birds in cottage and natural areas of central Ontario. *Wilson Bull.* 95:77–96.

Collins, S.L., F.C. James, and P.G. Risser. 1982. Habitat relationships of wood warblers (Parulidae) in north central Minnestoa. *Oikos* 39:50–58.

Craighead, J.J. and F.C. Craighead, Jr. 1969. *Hawks, Owls and Wildlife.* New York: Dover Publications.

Diamond, J.M. 1969. Avifaunal equilibrium and species turnover rates on the Channel Islands of California. *Proc. Natl. Acad. Sci.* 64:57–63.

———. 1972. Biogeographic kinetics: Estimation of relaxation times for avifaunas of Southwest Pacific Islands. *Proc. Natl. Acad. Sci.* 69:3199–3203.

———. 1975. The island dilemma: Lessons of modern biogeographic studies for the design of natural reserves. *Biol. Conserv.* 7:129–146.

Diamond, J.M., and R.M. May. 1976. Island biogeography and the design of nature reserves. Pages 163–186 in *Theoretical Ecology,* R.M. May, ed. Philadelphia: Saunders Co.

Dickerson, J.E., and J.V. Robinson. 1985. Microcosms as islands: A test of the MacArthur-Wilson equilibrium theory. *Ecology* 66:966–980.

Eaton, E.H. 1914. *Birds of New York.* Albany: New York State Museum, Memoir 12. Vol. 2.

Forbush, E.H. 1925. *Birds of Massachusetts and Other New England States.* Vols. I-III. Massachusetts Dept. of Agriculture.

Forman, R.T.T., A.E. Galli, and C.F. Leck. 1976. Forest size and avian diversity in New Jersey woodlots with some land use implications. *Oecologia* 26:1–8.

Galli, A.E., C.F. Leck, and R.T.T. Forman. 1976. Avian distribution patterns in forest islands of different sizes in central New Jersey. *Auk* 93:356–364.

Haapanen, A. 1966. Bird fauna of Finnish forests in relation to forest succession. I. *Ann. Zool. Fenn.* 2:153–196.

Hagar, D.C. 1960. The interrelationships of logging, birds, and timber regeneration in the Douglas fir region. *Ecology* 41:116–125.

Hall, G.A. 1984a. A long-term bird population study in an Appalachian spruce forest. *Wilson Bull.* 96:228–240.

———. 1984b. Population decline of neotropical migrants in an Appalachian forest. *Am. Birds* 38:14–18.

Hardy, E.E., R.L. Shelton, D.J. Belcher, and J.T. Roach. 1971. *New York State Land Use and Natural Resources Inventory: Volume II, Classification and Inventory Methods.* Ithaca, N.Y.: Center for Aerial Photographic Studies, Cornell University.

Harris, M.P. 1973. The Galapagos avifauna. *Condor* 75:265–278.

Holmes, R.T., and S.K. Robinson 1981. Tree species preferences of foraging insectivorous birds in a northern hardwoods forest. *Oecologia* 48:31–35.

Hooper, R.G., B.S. Crawford, and R.F. Harlow. 1973. Bird density and diversity as related to vegetation in forest recreation areas. *J. Forestry* 71:766–769.

Horn, D.J. 1985. Breeding birds of a central Ohio woodlot in response to succession and urbanization. *Ohio J. Sci.* 85:34–40.

Houston, D.R., E.J. Parker, R. Perrin, and K.J. Lang. 1979. Beech bark disease: A comparison of the disease in North America, Great Britain, France, and Germany. *Eur. J. For. Path.* 9:199–211.

Hutchinson, G.E. 1965. *The Ecological Theater and the Evolutionary Play.* New Haven: Yale University Press.

James, F.C., and H.H. Shugart, Jr. 1970. A quantitative method of habitat description. *Aud. Field Notes* 24:727–736.

Johnson, N.K. 1972. Origin and differentiation of the avifauna of the Channel Islands, California. *Condor* 74:295–315.

———. 1975. Controls of number of bird species on montane islands in the Great Basin. *Evolution* 29:545–567.

Johnston, D.W., and E.P. Odum. 1956. Breeding bird populations in relation to plant succession on the Piedmont of Georgia. *Ecology* 37:50–61.

Karr, J.R. 1968. Habitat and avian diversity on strip-mined land in east-central Illinois. *Condor* 70:348–357.

Karr, J.R., and R.R. Roth. 1971. Vegetation structure and avian diversity in several New World areas. *Am. Nat.* 105:423–435.

Keller, J.K. 1980. Species composition and density of breeding birds in several habitat types on the Connecticut Hill Wildlife Management Area. M.S. Thesis, Cornell University, Ithaca, New York.

Kendeigh, S.C. 1945. Community selection by birds on the Helderberg Plateau of New York. *Auk* 62:418–436.

Kendeigh, S.C. 1946. Breeding birds of the beech-maple-hemlock community. *Ecology* 27:226–245.

Kendeigh, S.C. 1982. *Bird Populations in East Central Illinois: Fluctuations, Variations, and Development over a Half-century.* Ill. Biol. Monogr. 52.

Lack, D. 1976. *Island Biology, Illustrated by the Land Birds of Jamaica.* Studies in Ecology 3. Berkeley: University of California Press.

Lewis, A.B. 1933. An economic study of land utilization in Tompkins County, New York. Ph.D. Dissertation, Cornell University, Ithaca, New York.

Litwin, T.S. 1986. Factors affecting avian diversity in a northeastern woodlot. Ph.D. Dissertation, Cornell University, Ithaca, New York.

Lynch, J.F., and N.K. Johnson. 1974. Turnover and equilibria in insular avifaunas with special reference to California Channel Islands. *Condor* 76:370–384.

Lynch, J.F., and D.F. Whigham. 1984. Effects of forest fragmentation on breeding bird communities in Maryland, U.S.A. *Biol. Conserv.* 28:287–324.

Lynch, J.F., and R.F. Whitcomb. 1978. Effects of the insularization of the eastern deciduous forest on avifaunal diversity and turnover. Pages 461–489 in *Classification, Inventory, and Evaluation of Fish and Wildlife Habitat,* A. Marmelstein, ed. U.S. Fish and Wildlife Serv. Pub. OBS-78176.

MacArthur, R.H., and J.W. MacArthur. 1961. On bird species diversity. *Ecology* 42:594–598.

MacArthur, R., J.W. MacArthur, and J. Preer. 1962. On bird species diversity. II. Prediction of bird censuses from habitat measurements. *Am. Nat.* 96:167–174.

Margalaf, D.R. 1958. Information theory in ecology. *General Systems* 3:36–71.

Martin, N.D. 1960. An analysis of bird populations in relation to forest succession in Algonquin Provincial Park, Ontario. *Ecology* 41:126–140.

Maurer, B.A., L.B. McArthur, and R.C. Whitmore. 1981. Effects of logging on guild structure of a forest bird community in West Virginia. *Am. Birds* 35:11–13.

New York Secretary of State. 1836. *Census of the State of New York for 1835.* Albany: Croswell, van Benthuysen, and Burt.

———. 1846. *Census of the State of New York for 1845.* Albany: Carroll and Cook.

Noon, B.R., D. Dawson, D. Inkley, C.S. Robbins, and S.H. Anderson. 1980. Consistency in habitat preference of forest bird species. *Transactions of the North American Wildlife and Natural Resources Conf.* 45:226–244.

Odum, E.P. 1950. Bird populations of the Highlands (North Carolina) Plateau Region in relation to plant succession and avian invasion. *Ecology* 31:587–605.

———. 1969. The strategy of ecosystem development. *Science* 164:262–270.

Owen, O.S. 1950. The Bird community of an elm-maple-ash swamp in central New York. Ph.D. Dissertation, Cornell University, Ithaca, New York.

Pickett, S.T.A., and J.N. Thompson. 1978. Patch dynamics and the design of nature reserves. *Biol. Conserv.* 13:27–37.

Picton, H.D. 1979. The application of insular biogeographic theory to the conservation of large mammals in the northern Rocky Mountains. *Biol. Conserv.* 15:73–79.

Power, D.M. 1972. Numbers of bird species on the California Islands. *Evolution* 26:451–463.

———. 1975a. Avifauna richness on the California Channel Islands. *Condor* 78:394–396.

———. 1975b. Similarity among avifaunas of the Galapagos Islands. *Ecology* 56:616–626.

Robbins, C.S. 1970. An international standard for a mapping method in bird census work. International Bird Census Committee. *Aud. Field Notes* 24:722–726.

———. 1979. Effect of forest fragmentation on bird populations. Pages 198–212 in *Management of North Central and Northeastern Forests for Nongame Birds; Workshop Proceedings,* R.M. DeGraaf and K.E. Evans, eds. St. Paul, Minn.: USDA Forest Service Gen. Tech. Rept. NC-51.

Roth, R.R. 1976. Spatial heterogeneity and bird species diversity. *Ecology* 57:773–782.

Saunders, A.A. 1936. *Ecology of the Birds of Quaker Run Valley, Alleghany State Park, N.Y.* Albany: New York State Museum Handbook 16.

Shannon, C., and W. Weaver. 1949. *The Mathematical Theory of Communication.* Urbana: University of Illinois Press.

Sinclair, W.A., and R.J. Campana, eds. 1978. *Dutch elm disease perspectives after 60 years.* Search Agriculture 8(5). Ithaca: Cornell University Agric. Exp. Sta.

Soulé, M.E., B.A. Wilcox, and C. Holtby. 1979. Benign neglect: A model of faunal collapse in game reserves of East Africa. *Biol. Conserv.* 15:259–272.

Sousa, P.J. 1982. *Habitat Suitability Index Models: Veery.* U.S. Dept. of Interior, FWS/OBS-82/10.22.

Southwood, T.R.E. 1977. Habitat, the templet for ecological strategies? *J. Anim. Ecol.* 46:337–365.

Swift, B.L., J.S. Larson, and R.M. DeGraff. 1984. Relationship of breeding bird density and diversity of habitat variables in forested wetlands. *Wilson Bull.* 96:48–59.

Tanner, J.T. 1942. *The Ivory-billed Woodpecker.* National Audubon Society Res. Rep. No. 1.

Terborgh, J. 1974. Preservation of natural diversity: The problem of extinction prone species. *BioScience* 24:715–722.

———. 1975. Faunal equilibria and the design of wildlife preserves. Pages 369–380 in *Tropical Ecological Systems,* F.B. Galley and E. Medina, eds. New York: Springer-Verlag.

Webb, W.L., D.F. Behrend, and B. Saisorn. 1977. *Effect of Logging on Songbird Populations in a Northern Hardwood Forest.* Wildl. Monogr. 55.

Whitcomb, R.F. 1977. Island biogeography and habitat islands of eastern forests. *Am. Birds* 31:3–5.

Whitcomb, R.F., C.S. Robbins, J.F. Lynch, B.L. Whitcomb, M.K. Klimkiewicz, and D. Bystrak. 1981. Effects of forest fragmentation on the avifauna of the eastern deciduous forest. Pages 125–205 in *Forest Island Dynamics in Man-dominated Landscapes,* R.L. Burgess and D.M. Sharpe, eds. New York: Springer-Verlag.

Whittaker, R.H. 1978. *Dominance-types. Classification of Plant Communities.* The Hague: Dr. W. Junk b.v. Publishers.

Williams, A.B. 1936. The composition and dynamics of a beech-maple climax community. *Ecol. Monogr.* 6:317–408.

Willson, M.F. 1974. Avian community organization and habitat structure. *Ecology* 55:1017–1029.

Wilson, E.O., and E.O. Willis. 1975. Applied biogeography. Pages 522–534 in *Ecology and Evolution of Communities,* M.L. Cody and J.M. Diamond, eds. Cambridge, Mass.: Belknap Press.

APPENDIX 1. Condensed version of A.A. Allen's 1962 Nesting Birds of Sapsucker Woods list

Regular nesters within the fenced area of Sapsucker Woods
   Cooper's Hawk
   Red-shouldered Hawk
   Barred Owl
   Pileated Woodpecker
   Hairy Woodpecker
   Downy Woodpecker
   Eastern Phoebe
   Blue Jay
   Common Crow
   Black-capped Chickadee
   White-breasted Nuthatch
   Brown Creeper
   American Robin
   Wood Thrush
   Veery
   Red-eyed Vireo
   Ovenbird
   Northern Waterthrush
   Common Yellowthroat
   Canada Warbler[1]
   Brown-headed Cowbird
   Scarlet Tanager
   Rose-breasted Grosbeak
Irregular nesters within the fenced area of Sapsucker Woods:
   American Kestrel
   Ruffed Grouse
   Great Horned Owl
   Magnolia Warbler
   Black-and-white Warbler[2]
   American Redstart
   Chestnut-sided Warbler
   Black-throated Green Warbler

1. Regular nester only in west SSW.
2. Nested only during Owen survey (1950).

APPENDIX 2. Land-use classification categories for sequential analysis presented in Table 2. Modified from Hardy et al. 1971

1. Open Land (OL)

Contains both active agricultural land (e.g. dairy, poultry, orchards, croplands, and grazing lands) and inactive agricultural lands (land recently removed from active agriculture but not yet showing advanced signs of old field succession). The amount of woody vegetation in inactive agricultural land does not exceed 10%

2. Brushland (FC)

Areas where successional advancement is actively moving toward forest regeneration. This includes areas having more than 10% woody plant cover, up to and including pole-sized stands (approximately 6-inch diameter at breast height) less than 30 feet in height and 40–50 years of age. These are often former agricultural lands or forests which have been heavily grazed, burned-over, or clear-cut

3. Forest Lands (FN)

Naturally wooded stands where 50% or more of the trees are over 50 years old and over 30 feet tall.

4. Forest Plantation (FP)

Areas artificially stocked with trees of any species, age, or size class

5. Residential High (RH)

Residential areas with housing lots ranging from 0 to 100 feet in frontage. This category also includes apartment houses and trailer parks

6. Residential Low (RL)

Housing units having frontage in excess of 100 feet, but which occur with regularity as a result of established land-use patterns, such as tract housing. This category does not include isolated houses, like those found in rural situations. Isolated houses were included as part of the dominant habitat that surrounded them

7. Commercial (C)

Areas connected with the sale of products or services including stores, shopping centers, strip development, and warehouses

8. Industrial (IA)

Areas devoted to product manufacturing and research, including light and heavy manufacturing, industrial parks, and research facilities

9. Public (P)

Noncommercial facilities which provide public services, including hospitals, schools, churches, and municipal buildings

10. Airport (A)

This category specifically accommodates the Tompkins County Airport

11. River (WS)

This category specifically accommodates Fall Creek

ERIC K. BOLLINGER*
THOMAS A. GAVIN
Department of Natural Resources
Cornell University
Ithaca, New York 14853

Eastern Bobolink populations: Ecology and conservation in an agricultural landscape

Abstract. Populations of Bobolinks (*Dolichonyx oryzivorus*) have declined in the eastern United States since the early 1900s. In this region, hayfields are an important nesting habitat for this species. Bobolink abundance in old hayfields (≥ 8 years since planting) in our New York study site was at least 67% greater than in any other habitat type in this area and four times greater than in midwestern prairies. Bobolink abundance increased exponentially with hayfield size, and was highest in fields with the least alfalfa cover. Several features of current forage crop agriculture are probably contributing to declining populations of Bobolinks, as well as most other grassland birds. These include declining area in hay, increasing use of alfalfa as the primary forage crop, earlier hay-cropping dates, and earlier rotation of hayfields to other crops. Conservation practices designed for Bobolinks should concentrate on creating or maintaining large habitat patches that resemble old hayfields.

Sinopsis. Las poblaciones de *Dolychonyx oryzivorus* han declinado en el oriente de los Estados Unidos desde comienzos del presente siglo. En esta región, los campos de heno son un importante habitat de anidación para esta especie. La abundancia de *D. oryzivorus* en campos viejos de heno (ocho o mas años desde su plantación) en nuestra área de estudio en New York fué por lo menos 67% mayor que en cualquier otro tipo de habitat en esta región y cuatro veces mas grande que en las praderas del medio oeste. La abundancia de *D. oryzivorus* incrementó exponencialmente con el tamaño del campo de heno y alcanzó su máximo en campos con el mínimo de cobertura de alfalfa. Varias características de la agricultura actual de forraje probablemente contribuyen a la disminución de las poblaciones de esta especie y de otras aves de pastizales. Estas incluyen el decrecimiento del área de heno, incremento en el uso de alfalfa como el principal cultivo de forraje, fechas de cosecha del heno mas tempranas y rotación prematura de campos de heno a otros cultivos. Las prácticas de conservación de *D. oryzivorus* que se diseñen, deben concentrarse en crear o antener grandes parches de habitat que se asemejen a campos viejos de heno.

*Current address: Department of Zoology, Eastern Illinois University, Charleston, Illinois 61920

The Bobolink (*Dolichonyx oryzivorus*) is one of the few obligate grassland species that breeds in North America and winters in the Neotropics. To date, much more emphasis has been devoted to forest-nesting Neotropical migrant landbirds (e.g., Keast and Morton 1980), especially with respect to detrimental effects of habitat fragmentation (Robbins 1979, Whitcomb et al. 1981, Wilcove 1985, Robbins et al. 1989). Nevertheless, similar patterns and trends might also hold for grassland species (Johnson and Temple 1986, 1990).

Populations of Bobolinks in the eastern United States have declined since the early 1900s (Griscom and Snyder 1955, Bent 1958, Bull 1974, Leck 1984), and during the past 20 years in several states (S. Droege and J.R. Sauer, unpubl. data; Table 1). This pattern is true for most grassland-nesting species in the eastern United States (Robbins et al. 1986; Table 1). Several explanations for the decline of Bobolinks have been suggested, including farmland abandonment and the decline of hayfield area (Griscom and Snyder 1955, Bent 1958, Laughlin and Kibbe 1985, Andrle and Carroll 1988), earlier and more frequent hay-cropping schedules together with the use of modern mowing and raking equipment (Bent 1958, Andrle and Carroll 1988), and the shift from timothy (*Phleum pratense*) and clover (*Trifolium* spp.) hay crops to alfalfa (*Medicago sativa*) (Campbell 1968).

These potential negative effects of modern forage crop agriculture on Bobolinks are paradoxical. Land clearing for agriculture was largely responsible for the initial population increases and geographical range expansions of many grassland bird species in the eastern United States (Hurley and Franks 1976, Andrle and

Carroll 1988). Today, agricultural practices such as hay-cropping are important for the existence of Bobolinks in this region, because they help prevent the establishment of woody vegetation (Griscom and Snyder 1955, Laughlin and Kibbe 1985). Furthermore, as native prairie habitats are decimated, populations of Bobolinks in eastern states are becoming a significant component of the entire, continent-wide population (Robbins et al. 1986).

We were primarily interested in the effects of modern forage crop agriculture on Bobolinks nesting in eastern hayfields. Our study focused on hayfields because they represent one of the largest blocks of potential nesting habitat for Bobolinks in the eastern United States. Hayfields are generally listed as the preferred habitat of this species (Bent 1958, Graber and Graber 1963, Kantrud 1981, Laughlin and Kibbe 1985).

Methods

STUDY AREA. The study was conducted primarily in northern Madison County, New York during 1984–1988 (Fig. 1). This is one of the largest dairy-producing counties in New York (Nicholson 1985). Our primary study area was divided into two sections based on soil types, topography, and the intensity of dairy farming. The southern Oneida Lake plain (i.e., the northern portion of our primary study area) was considered a low-quality agricultural area because the soils were poorly drained with "poor" or "fair" potential for agriculture (Hanna 1981). Few dairy farms and relatively large amounts of abandoned farmland were in this area. The southern portion of our primary study area was considered a

TABLE 1. Population trends (1966–1988) for six species of grassland birds in 18 northeastern states[a] based on data from the Breeding Bird Survey

Species	Number of states[b]		
	Decreasing	Increasing	No change[c]
Bobolink	5 (38%)[d]	1 (8%)	7
Eastern Meadowlark	12 (80%)	0 (0%)	3
Grasshopper Sparrow	9 (82%)	0 (0%)	2
Henslow's Sparrow	2 (33%)	0 (0%)	4
Savannah Sparrow	6 (46%)	0 (0%)	7
Upland Sandpiper	2 (29%)	0 (0%)	5
TOTALS	36 (55%)	1 (2%)	28

SOURCES: Robbins et al. 1986, S. Droege and J. R. Sauer, unpubl. data.

a. States are CT, DE, IL, IN, ME, MD, MA, MI, MN, NH, NJ, NY, OH, PA, RI, VT, WV, WI.

b. Only state trends based on >10 routes are included.

c. No significant change ($P > 0.05$).

d. % of states (whose trend was based on >10 routes) with a significant decreasing trend, 1966–1986.

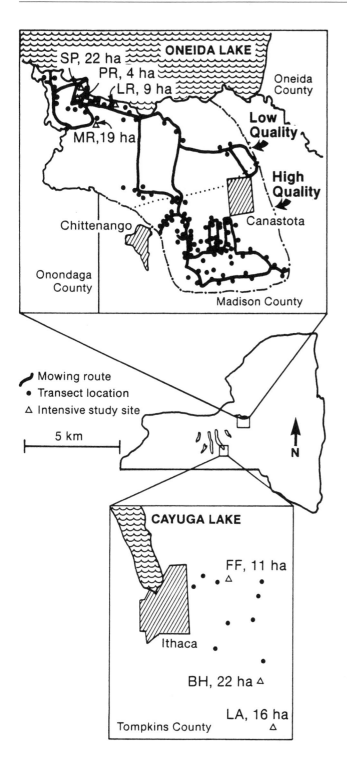

FIGURE 1. Location of study areas in west-central New York. Primary study area in northern Madison County was divided into high- and low-quality agricultural sections based on soil types and land-use practices. Also shown are transect locations of hayfields used for extensive studies as well as locations, abbreviations, and sizes of seven intensive study sites; see Methods for further explanation.

high-quality agricultural area. The soils there were generally well drained with "good" potential for agriculture (Hanna 1981). Dairy farms were common, and abandoned farmland was rare. The remainder of our intensive study sites (3 of 9) and hayfields in our survey (< 10%) were located in Tompkins County, New York, near Ithaca (Fig. 1).

INTENSIVE STUDIES. We intensively monitored Bobolink populations at nine locations (3–7 each year) in 1984–1986 (see Gavin 1984, Bollinger 1988, Bollinger and Gavin 1989 for details). At each site, using mist nets, we captured, banded, and individually color-marked more than 90% of the resident adult Bobolinks. Male territories were mapped primarily using Wiens's (1969) flush technique in late May. We found all or nearly all nests, and monitored them every 1–2 days.

EXTENSIVE STUDIES. We obtained information on almost 300 hayfields through interviews with local farmers. This information included field size, field age (i.e., number of years since planting or reseeding; 1-yr-old fields were in their first full-production year), and original planting mixture (e.g., pure alfalfa, timothy/trefoil [*Lotus corniculatus*] mixture). A hayfield was considered active if it was planted with a perennial forage crop and had been cut for forage at least once a year since planting. From this group of fields, we randomly selected 110 hayfields to sample for vegetation characteristics and Bobolink abundance. We used field age and size as blocking factors such that our sample of hayfields was relatively evenly divided among five age classes (i.e., 1 yr, 2–3 yr, 4–7 yr, 8–15 yr, > 15 yr). These age classes were determined arbitrarily before sampling began. Mean field size did not vary among age classes (Bollinger 1988). In each of these fields, vegetation characteristics were sampled at 10 randomly selected plots (0.25 m²) along a transect line (as in Wiens 1969). We visually estimated percent cover by species in each of the plots, and estimated litter cover, vegetation height, and vertical distribution of vegetation (see Bollinger 1988 for details).

We used line transects (Burnham et al. 1980) to estimate Bobolink abundance in each of the 110 fields. Each transect (one per field) began from a random point at the field edge 100 m or more from any other edge, and extended (to the opposite edge) 154–569 m perpendicular to the starting edge. Bobolinks were counted along the transect line two times per field between 0630 and 0900 EDT, from 29 May to 12 June, before seasonal mowing. We estimated the perpendicular distance of each detected Bobolink from the transect line in 20 m intervals, to a distance of 100 m. For most analyses, male Bobolink abundance (males/100 m of transect) was used as an index of Bobolink density. This index was highly correlated with actual Bobolink density at intensively studied sites (Bollinger et al. 1988). When density estimates were needed, we used the computer program TRANSECT (Laake et al. 1979) and the Fourier series estimator (see Bollinger et al. 1988).

Bobolinks were also counted in open, non-hayfield habitats. These habitats included "lightly grazed" pastures (pastures with abundant tall vegetation that appeared suitable for Bobolinks), "old fields" (mostly open fields dominated by herbaceous vegetation with scattered [< about 25% cover] woody shrubs and saplings), and "fallow fields" (corn or small grain stubble left idle for ≥ 1 yr; see Graber and Graber 1963). Bobolinks were also counted in three open habitat types that appeared to be unsuitable habitat for this species: (1) "heavily grazed" pastures (pastures with most vegetation cropped to approximately ground level), (2) "brushy fields" (fields with many [> about 25% cover] woody shrubs and saplings), and (3) oatfields.

We determined the timing of hay-cropping in our study area in 1984–1986 by driving a 195-km roadside survey route at 4–6-day intervals from early June through mid-July and intermittently thereafter, until at least the middle of August. In 1987, the survey route was completed three times (13 June, 5 July, 20 October). For all fields visible from the road, we recorded the proportion of each hayfield that was mowed. We noted fields that were no longer being mowed, those that were plowed and rotated to another crop, and new hayfields planted along the route.

EFFECTS OF HISTORICAL CHANGES AND CURRENT FORAGE CROP PRACTICES. We assessed the effects of current forage crop practices and trends on Bobolinks in the eastern United States. Information came from a variety of sources, including our mowing survey route and interviews with farmers, discussions with agronomists and forage crop specialists, forage crop statistics, and the literature. Trends were calculated in hayfield area in the eastern United States, along with changes in the types of forage crops planted, stand longevity, mowing dates and hay-cropping equipment, and ways the cut forage is handled (e.g., baling vs. silage).

COMPARISON OF BOBOLINK ABUNDANCE IN EASTERN HAYFIELDS AND MIDWESTERN PRAIRIES. Data on Bobolink densities in mixed- and tall-grass prairie plots were used as reported in the Breeding Bird Census (and previously published in *American Birds*) to compare with our data for eastern hayfields (see Bollinger 1988 for a detailed list of references). Hayfields and prairie plots where Bobolinks were never detected were not used. When a plot or field was censused in more than one year, the mean density for those years in which Bobolinks were present was used. Wetland areas (identified as such in the descriptions of some of the prairie plots) were deleted before calculating densities. Because our line transect counts overestimated Bobolink density (Bollinger et al. 1988), our densities were adjusted based on the strong linear relationship (i.e., $r = 0.93$) between actual and estimated density (Bollinger 1988).

Results

BOBOLINK ABUNDANCE IN HAYFIELDS AND OTHER HABITATS. Bobolinks were most abundant in hayfields with relatively low amounts of total vegetation cover, low alfalfa cover, and low total legume cover but with high litter cover and high grass/legume ratios. Bobolink abundance was significantly correlated with each of these five vegetation variables ($|r| > 0.55$, $P < 0.001$, Fig. 2). These conditions generally occur in older hayfields (Bollinger 1988). If hayfields are arbitrarily divided into "old" (≥ 8 yr since planting) and "young" (< 8 yr) categories, Bobolinks were more abundant in old hayfields (t-test, $P < 0.001$). Furthermore, mean Bobolink abundance in old hayfields (2.5 males/100 m) was greater than in any of the non-hayfield habitat types we sampled ($P < 0.025$, t-tests, Fig. 3). No Bobolinks were detected in five oat fields, and only 0.06 and 0.01 males/100 m were counted in 10 heavily grazed pastures and 10 brushy fields, respectively.

Bobolink abundance increased exponentially with field size (Fig. 4); the correlation ($r = 0.40$, $P < 0.001$) between abundance and (field size)^2 was higher than correlations with field size, ln (field size), or (field size)^3. Finally, Bobolink populations declined significantly after hayfields were abandoned (i.e., not cut, grazed, or otherwise managed). Densities were about 50% lower when fields were resampled three years after abandonment than before abandonment ($n = 10$, $\bar{X} = 1.3$ vs. 2.5 males/100 m, $P < 0.05$, paired t-test). Tree saplings, primarily ash (*Fraxinus* sp.), often became abundant in these fields after abandonment.

Bobolinks appeared to nest in greater densities in our hayfields than in native prairie habitats in the midwestern United States. Densities in prairies were one-third of those in all sampled hayfields and one quarter of those in old hayfields ($P < 0.05$, Table 2).

PHENOLOGY OF BOBOLINK FLEDGING AND TIMING OF HAY-CROPPING. Fledging dates for Bobolinks in our intensive sites ranged from 10 June to 20 July in 1984–1986 (Fig. 5); about 75% fledged by 25 June. Our mowing survey route encompassed 776–841 ha of active hayfields (in 119–134 fields) from 1984 to 1987. Hay-cropping (first cutting) began in late May in all years. About 50–60% of the area in hay had been cut by 1 July (Fig. 6).

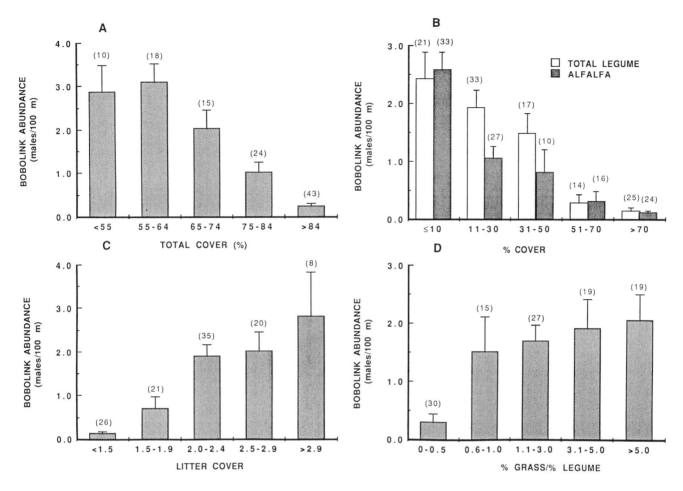

FIGURE 2. Relationships between mean Bobolink abundance (males/100 m ± SE) and the following vegetation characteristics for 110 hayfields in west-central New York: *A*—total vegetation cover (%), *B*—total legume and alfalfa cover (%), *C*—litter cover (litter cover recorded in classes, with 1 = < 5%, 2 = 5–25%, 3 = 26–50%), and *D*—% grass cover/% legume cover. Sample sizes (no. of fields) in parentheses.

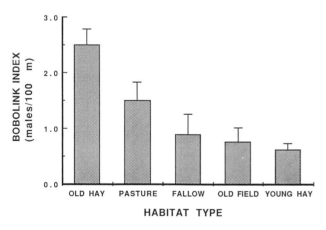

FIGURE 3. Mean Bobolink abundances (males/100 m, ± SE) for various habitat types in west-central New York (*n* = 60, 50, and 10 fields for young hayfields, old hayfields, and each of the other three habitat types, respectively). Pasture denotes "lightly-grazed" pasture only (see text). Bobolink abundance in old hayfields was significantly greater than in other habitats (*t*-tests, *P* < 0.03).

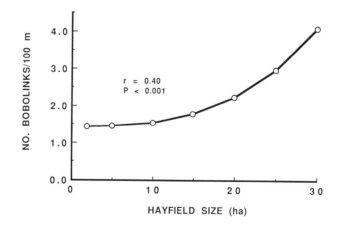

FIGURE 4. Relationship between Bobolink abundance and field size for 110 hayfields in west-central New York. Predicted values of least squares regression line of Bobolink abundance vs. (field size)^2 are shown using field size as x-axis.

TABLE 2. Comparisons of mean Bobolink densities (males/km^2; standard deviation in parentheses) between midwestern tall- and mixed-grass prairies and hayfields in central New York[a]

Habitat type	No. of Sites	Density (males/km^2)
Mixed-grass prairie[b]	12	33 (24) A[c]
Tall-grass prairie[b]	9	26 (19) A
All hayfield	81	91 (70) B
Old hayfield[d]	45	120 (81) B

a. Only sites where Bobolinks were detected were included.
b. Data are from the Breeding Bird Census (see Bollinger 1988 for detailed list of references).
c. Habitat types with the same letter were not significantly different (t-tests, $P > 0.05$).
d. Old hayfields are those ≥ 8 years old. This category was a subset of "all hayfield" and was not compared statistically with it.

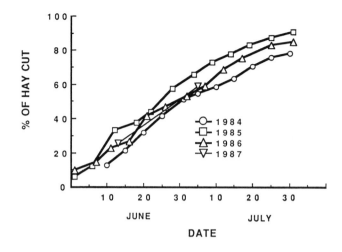

FIGURE 6. Cumulative distribution functions of hay-cropping dates (first cutting) along a 195-km survey route in Madison County, New York, in 1984–1987 ($n \geq 820$ ha).

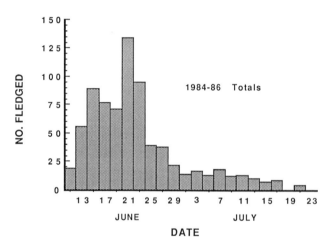

FIGURE 5. Histogram of combined fledging dates for Bobolinks at intensive study sites in west-central New York in 1984–1986 ($n = 752$ fledglings).

CURRENT TRENDS AND PRACTICES IN FORAGE CROP AGRICULTURE. The combined hay acreage for the 18 northeastern states encompassing the breeding range of Bobolinks east of the Mississippi River (see Table 1) has declined from 12.6 million ha in 1940 to 7.1 million ha in 1986 (Fig. 7A). Specifically, hay area has declined by 17% in this area since 1966 (USDA 1967, 1987). Land area devoted to hay crops along our survey route declined from 841 ha to 776 ha between 1984 and 1987. Area losses were greatest in the low-quality agricultural area (24% loss), due primarily to land abandonment, whereas hay area increased slightly in the high-quality area (8% increase).

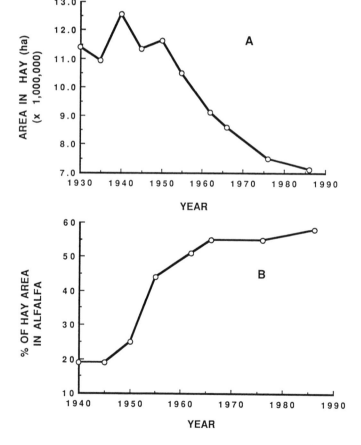

FIGURE 7. Area (ha) in hay (A) and percent of hay that is alfalfa and alfalfa mixtures (B) in 18 northeastern states (see Table 1) from 1930 to 1986. Based on statistics reported in USDA (1936–1987).

Despite these declines, the area devoted to alfalfa and alfalfa mixtures increased more than three times from 1920 to 1960 in northeastern states (Hanson and Barnes 1973). Although the absolute area devoted to alfalfa and alfalfa mixtures has declined since the early 1960s, their proportion of all hay area has continued to increase (from 50 to 58% in the 18 northeastern states, Fig. 7B). Based on seed sales of perennial forage crops in the 12 northeastern states for which data were available, the proportion of all seeds that were alfalfa increased from 25% to nearly 50% from 1953 to 1988 (Johnson and Elston 1959, Fortmann 1974, Pardee 1981, 1988). Thus, farmers have shifted from planting primarily grass-dominated stands (especially timothy/clover mixtures) to planting primarily legume-dominated stands (especially alfalfa; Hanson and Barnes 1973, Metcalfe 1973). Of hayfields used in our study, those planted to pure legumes and legume/grass mixtures were relatively more common among the younger fields, whereas those planted to grass or grass/legume mixtures increased in relative abundance among the older fields (Fig. 8).

Compared with 30–50 years ago, stands of hay are currently cut earlier in the season and more frequently, and are rotated more quickly to other crops. In New York, hay-cropping dates (first cutting) average about one week earlier than they did 20 years ago (W.D. Pardee, pers. comm.) and two to three weeks earlier than 30–40 years ago (C.C. Lowe, pers. comm.; see also Warner and Etter 1989). Surveys of New York farmers indicate that they usually rotate their alfalfa fields after four to six years (Pardee 1985). This crop rotation pattern agrees with our survey route data. For example,

67% of hay rotation occurred before or during the sixth year a field was active in our study area. Thirty to 40 years ago stands were commonly left for over 10 years before rotation (C.C. Lowe, pers. comm.). The median age of hayfields in our study area was four years; < 25% of the fields were ≥ 8 years old. Furthermore, from 1984 to 1987, hay area along the mowing survey route declined most rapidly among fields ≥ 8 years old. Additions to this age-class of hayfields (because of "aging" of younger fields) represented only 44% of the area lost to land abandonment and crop rotation. However, area in fields 1–3 years old changed little. Finally, the equipment used to mow hay and handling of the cut vegetation have also changed. Historically, hay was cut by a horse- or tractor-drawn sickle bar. Today, most hay is cut by either self-propelled or tractor-drawn mower/conditioners that not only cut the hay but also use a rotating rake to pick up lodged vegetation, as well as a conditioner that crushes the vegetation for faster drying. Today most first-cut hay is used for silage (Pardee and Seaney 1976); 30–50 years ago most of the first-cut hay was baled. Silage generally requires at most 2/3 of the field drying time required by baled hay.

Discussion

IMPORTANCE OF HAYFIELDS TO EASTERN BOBOLINK POPULATIONS. Hayfields currently are one of the largest blocks of suitable nesting habitat for Bobolinks in the eastern United States. For example, about 75% of the Bobolinks in our study area nested in hayfields (Bollinger et al. 1990). "Old" hayfields (i.e., fields 8 yr old) were especially preferred by Bobolinks and appear to represent optimum habitat; abundances in these fields were 67% greater than in lightly grazed pastures, and four times greater than in both "young" hayfields and native prairie habitats. However, a variety of trends and current agricultural practices are decreasing the productivity of hayfields for Bobolinks.

EFFECTS OF CURRENT FORAGE CROP AGRICULTURE ON BOBOLINKS. During the early part of this century conditions were probably ideal for Bobolinks over much of the United States east of the Mississippi River. Land area devoted to hay and pasture was at a peak, and the majority of this hay was timothy and timothy/clover mixtures. These stands were commonly left for long periods of time without rotation or reseeding. Bobolinks seem to prefer this type of old, sparse, grass-dominated hay. Little hay-cropping occurred before July, so that most nesting was completed by the time hay-cropping commenced. For example, in our intensive sites, 80–90% of Bobolink nestlings had fledged by 1 July. The machinery used in the early 1900s lacked the rakes and conditioners present today. Most of the hay was baled (rather

Figure 8

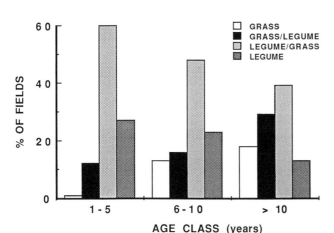

FIGURE 8. Relationship between a field's age and its original planting mixture for hayfields in Madison County, New York, 1984–1987.

than used for silage), so that cut vegetation was generally left on the ground for 2–3 days, allowing more time for young to fledge prior to baling or other field operations.

Since the early 1900s, hay area has declined by about 45%. In addition, much less land is used for permanent pasture. This dramatic decline in nesting habitat is probably an important factor in the decline of Bobolinks (but see Clark et al. 1986). Furthermore, the area devoted to hay has become increasingly dominated by legumes, primarily alfalfa, which is not generally used by Bobolinks: fields with the least alfalfa cover in our study had over 15 times more Bobolinks than did fields with the most alfalfa cover. In our study area, about 85% of the hayfields planted within the last five years were planted with a legume-dominated seed mixture. These fields also tend to be rotated to other crops more quickly than in the past (Baylor and Vough 1985). Although economically sound, rapid rotation prevents fields from developing into the sparse, grass-dominated stands preferred by Bobolinks. We have shown elsewhere (Bollinger 1988) that vegetation in legume-dominated hayfields undergoes successional changes, eventually becoming grass-dominated and much sparser. The shift to legume-dominated stands is expected to continue in the east (Baylor and Vough 1985, Van Keuren and George 1985).

Current patterns of hay-cropping are also detrimental to Bobolink populations. With the shift to alfalfa-dominated stands and the development of new cultivars with faster regrowth, dates of first cutting have advanced to the point where a sizable fraction of nesting production is destroyed, especially in areas of intensive dairy farming. Modern hay-cropping equipment and the current shift to storing first-cut hay as silage assure that nearly all affected nests are destroyed. In our high-quality area, for example, an estimated 40% nest mortality occurred because of hay-cropping and subsequent field operations (Bollinger et al. 1990, see also Frawley 1989). Furthermore, we estimated that mowing-induced nest mortality has increased 2–3 times over the past 50 years because of this trend toward earlier cutting (Bollinger et al. 1990).

RECOMMENDATIONS FOR CONSERVATION OF BOBOLINKS. Thus, modern forage crop agriculture has had a series of negative effects on populations of Bobolinks. If expected trends continue, agricultural habitats, especially hayfields, might shift from optimum habitats to reproductive "sinks" (Sample 1989), and Bobolink populations should continue to decline in the eastern United States. Our results suggest that to conserve this species, landowners, farmers, and conservation agencies should be encouraged to:

(1) Create or maintain patches of relatively sparse, grass-dominated vegetation resembling old hayfields. Scattered, broad-leafed forbs (e.g., *Trifolium*) should be encouraged for nest-site cover. Highly erodable farmlands might be useful candidates for establishment of these types of patches.

(2) Create large patches (> 10–15 ha) whenever possible. Fewer large grassland patches tend to contain more breeding Bobolinks than numerous smaller patches of equal total area. This might be because both nest predation and nest parasitism by Brown-headed Cowbirds (*Molothrus ater*) tend to be higher in small grassland patches (Johnson and Temple 1990).

(3) Hay-crop these patches every 2–3 years to prevent excessive encroachment of woody vegetation. Cutting should occur after the middle of July (and preferably in August) to avoid nest mortality.

PROBABLE EFFECTS ON OTHER GRASSLAND BIRD SPECIES. These practices should also help populations of most other declining grassland species as well (Table 1). For example, in our hayfields, densities of Eastern Meadowlarks (*Sturnella magna*), Upland Sandpipers (*Bartramia longicauda*), Henslow's Sparrows (*Ammodramus henslowii*), and Grasshopper Sparrows (*A. savannarum*) were all significantly positively correlated with Bobolink densities (Bollinger 1988). Furthermore, abundances of all of these species were positively correlated with hayfield age and, except for the Eastern Meadowlark, with hayfield size as well. Nesting seasons for these species usually begin earlier (and never markedly later) than the nesting season of the Bobolink (Frawley 1989, Sample 1989). Thus, we feel that breeding habitat requirements for these species are similar enough to those of the Bobolink for these species to benefit noticeably from the above recommendations.

Acknowledgments

We thank J.L. Forney, director of the Cornell Biological Field Station, for financial and logistical support. We also thank L.V. Grant and H. Smith for use of their hayfields. Field assistance was provided by P.B. Bollinger, P.A. Crane, C.J. Hibbard, J.L. Howe, M. O'Neill, T.M. Steedle, J.J. Strnisa, R.C. Titus, and J.T. Wootton. We are grateful to S. Droege and J.R. Sauer for providing the data from the Breeding Bird Survey and to the many volunteers who collected these data. P.B. Bollinger, D.J. Decker, M.E. Richmond, and D.S. Robson provided constructive criticism of the manuscript. D.S. Robson gave advice on statistics. This study was funded by a Cornell Graduate Research Fellowship, Paul A. Stewart Award, Walter E. Benning

Award, and Sigma Xi research award to EKB, and Hatch grants 147426 and 147429 to TAG. This is contribution 116 of the Cornell Biological Field Station.

Literature cited

Andrle, R.F., and J.R. Carroll. 1988. *The Atlas of Breeding Birds in New York State*. Ithaca, N.Y.: Cornell University Press.

Baylor, J.E., and L.R. Vough. 1985. Hay and pasture seedings for the Northeast. Pages 338–347 in *Forages: The Science of Grassland Agriculture*, M.E. Heath, R.F. Barnes, and D.S. Metcalfe, eds. Ames: Iowa State University Press.

Bent, A.C. 1958. *Life Histories of North American Blackbirds, Orioles, Tanagers, and Allies*. U.S. Natl. Mus. Bull. 211.

Bollinger, E.K. 1988. Breeding dispersion and reproductive success of Bobolinks in an agricultural landscape. Ph.D. Dissertation, Cornell University, Ithaca, New York.

Bollinger, E.K., and T.A. Gavin. 1989. The effects of site quality on breeding-site fidelity in Bobolinks. *Auk* 106:584–594.

Bollinger, E.K., P.B. Bollinger, and T.A. Gavin. 1990. Effects of hay-cropping on eastern populations of the Bobolink. *Wildl. Soc. Bull.* 18:142–150.

Bollinger, E.K., T.A. Gavin, and D.C. McIntyre. 1988. Comparison of transects and circular-plots for estimating Bobolink densities. *J. Wildl. Manage.* 52:777–786.

Bull, J. 1974. *Birds of New York State*. Ithaca, N.Y.: Comstock Publishing.

Burnham, K.P., D.R. Anderson, and J.L. Laake. 1980. *Estimation of Density from Line Transect Sampling of Biological Populations*. Wildl. Monogr. 72.

Campbell, L. 1968. Birds of the Toledo Area. *The Blade*, Toledo, Ohio.

Clark, R.G., P.J. Weatherhead, H. Greenwood, and R.D. Titman. 1986. Numerical responses of Red-winged Blackbirds to changes in regional land-use patterns. *Can. J. Zool.* 64:1944–1950.

Fortmann, H.R. 1974. *Forage Crops Seed Usage in the Northeastern United States*. Pennsylvania State University, College of Agr., Agr. Exp. Sta., Bull. 797.

Frawley, B.J. 1989. The dynamics of nongame bird breeding ecology in Iowa alfalfa fields. M.S. Thesis, Iowa State University, Ames, Iowa.

Gavin, T.A. 1984. Broodedness in Bobolinks. *Auk* 101:179–181.

Graber, R.R., and J.W. Graber. 1963. A comparative study of bird populations in Illinois, 1906–1909 and 1956–1958. *Ill. Nat. Hist. Surv. Bull.* 28:383–528.

Griscom, L., and D.E. Snyder. 1955. *The Birds of Massachusetts*. Portland, Maine: The Anthoensen Press.

Hanna, W.E. 1981. *Soil Survey of Madison County, New York*. USDA Soil Conserv. Service.

Hanson, C.H., and D.K. Barnes. 1973. Alfalfa. Pages 136–147 in *Forages: The Science of Grassland Agriculture*, M.E. Heath, D.S. Metcalfe, and R.F. Barnes, eds. Ames: Iowa State University Press.

Hurley, R.J., and E.C. Franks. 1976. Changes in the breeding ranges of two grassland birds. *Auk* 93:108–115.

Johnson, A.A., and R.C. Elston. 1959. *A Study of Seed Usage for Improved Varieties of Forage Crops in the Northeast—1958 Report*. USDA, Northeast Reg. Publ. No. 40.

Johnson, R.G., and S.A. Temple. 1986. Assessing habitat quality for birds nesting in fragmented tallgrass prairies. Pages 245–249 in *Wildlife 2000: Modeling Habitat Relationships of Terrestrial Vertebrates*, J. Verner, M.L. Morrison, and C.J. Ralph, eds. Madison: University of Wisconsin Press.

———. 1990. Nest predation and brood parasitism of tallgrass prairie birds. *J. Wildl. Manage.* 54:106–111.

Kantrud, H.A. 1981. Grazing intensity effects on the breeding avifauna of North Dakota native grasslands. *Can. Field-Nat.* 95:404–417.

Keast, A., and E.S. Morton, eds. 1980. *Migrant Birds in the Neotropics: Ecology, Behavior, Distribution, and Conservation*. Washington: Smithsonian Institution Press.

Laake, J.L., K.P. Burnham, and D.R. Anderson. 1979. *User's Manual for Program TRANSECT*. Logan: Utah State University Press.

Laughlin, S.B., and D.P. Kibbe. 1985. *The Atlas of Breeding Birds of Vermont*. Hanover, Vt.: University Press of New England.

Leck, C.F. 1984. *The Status and Distribution of New Jersey's Birds*. New Brunswick, N.J.: Rutgers University Press.

Metcalfe, D.S. 1973. Forage Statistics. Pages 64–77 in *Forages: The Science of Grassland Agriculture*, M.E. Heath, D.S. Metcalfe, and R.F. Barnes, eds. Ames: Iowa State University Press.

Nicholson, A.G. 1985. *The development of agriculture in New York State*. Nat. Resources Res. and Ext. Series 23. Cornell University, Ithaca, New York.

Pardee, W.D. 1981. 1981 report. Northeast seed use survey: Small seeded grasses and legumes. Plant Breeding Mimeo No. PB 81–2. Dept. Plant Breeding and Biometry. N.Y. State College of Agr. and Life Sc., Cornell Univ., Ithaca, New York.

———. 1985. Preliminary report: 1984 Farmer alfalfa seed use survey. Plant Breeding Mimeo, Dept. of Plant Breeding and Biometry. N.Y. State College of Agr. and Life Sc., Cornell Univ., Ithaca, New York.

———. 1988. 1987 report: Northeast seed use survey, small seeded grasses and legumes. Plant Breeding Mimeo, Dept. of Plant Breeding and Biometry. N.Y. State College of Agr. and Life Sc., Cornell Univ., Ithaca, New York.

Pardee, W.D., and R.R. Seaney. 1976. Alfalfa use in New York survey results, 1976 report. Plant Breeding Mimeo, Dept. of Plant Breeding and Biometry. N.Y. State College of Agr. and Life Sc., Cornell Univ., Ithaca, New York.

Robbins, C.S. 1979. Effect of forest fragmentation on bird populations. Pages 198–212 in *Management of North Central and Northeastern Forests for Nongame Birds; Workshop Proceedings*, R.M. DeGraaf and K.E. Evans, eds. St. Paul, Minn.: USDA Forest Service Gen. Tech. Rept. NC-51.

Robbins, C.S., D. Bystrak, and P.H. Geissler. 1986. *The Breeding Bird Survey: Its First Fifteen Years, 1965–1979*. U.S. Fish and Wildlife Serv. Resource Pub. 157.

Robbins, C.S., D.K. Dawson, and B.A. Dowell. 1989. *Habitat Area Requirements of Breeding Forest Birds of the Middle Atlantic States*. Wildl. Monogr. 103.

Sample, D.W. 1989. Grassland birds in southern Wisconsin: Habitat preferences, population trends, and response to land use changes. M.S. Thesis, University of Wisconsin, Madison, Wisconsin.

USDA. 1936–1987. *Agricultural Statistics.* U.S. Government Printing Office, Washington, D.C.

Van Keuren, R.W., and J.R. George. 1985. Hay and pasture seedings for the central and lake states. Pages 348–358 in *Forages: The Science of Grassland Agriculture,* M.E. Heath, R.F. Barnes, and D.S. Metcalfe, eds. Ames: Iowa State University Press.

Warner, R.E., and S.L. Etter. 1989. Hay cutting and the survival of pheasants: A long-term perspective. *J. Wildl. Manage.* 53:455–461.

Whitcomb, R.F., C.S. Robbins, J.F. Lynch, B.L. Whitcomb, M.K. Klimkiewicz, and D. Bystrak. 1981. Effects of forest fragmentation on the avifauna of the eastern deciduous forest. Pages 125–205 in *Forest Island Dynamics in Man-dominated Landscapes,* R.L. Burgess and D.M. Sharpe, eds. New York: Springer-Verlag.

Wiens, J.A. 1969. *An Approach to the Study of Ecological Relationships among Grassland Birds.* Ornithol. Monogr. 8.

Wilcove, D.S. 1985. Nest predation in forest tracts and the decline of migratory songbirds. *Ecology* 66:1211–1214.

Hemispheric
perspectives

CHANDLER S. ROBBINS
Patuxent Wildlife Research Center
Laurel, Maryland 20708

Hemispheric perspectives: Introduction

The five chapters in this section focus attention on conservation priorities for Neotropical migrants in the light of global environmental change. Malcolm Hunter sets the stage by explaining the astronomical features that generate glacial periods, with their dramatic changes in plant distribution at intervals of about 100,000 years. He then contrasts the 6,000 to 8,000 year history of present plant communities with some of the changes measured in decades that are causing present concern. He suggests that Neotropical migrants exhibit more behavioral plasticity than do permanent resident species. Although conservation of temperate zone birds should focus primarily on the species in imminent danger of extinction, consideration should also be given to sedentary species that prefer large tracts of old forest, as these birds may be more vulnerable to climatic change than are most Neotropical migrants.

Michael Reed presents the first attempt to rate all North American warblers and vireos according to their susceptibility to extinction. He uses the Rabinowitz (1981) method developed for British flora, which is based on habitat specificity, geographic distribution, and local population size. He gives separate ratings for the breeding and wintering areas. This is a static (point-in-time) system that does not consider rate of habitat loss.

Robert Ricklefs then ties resident tropical birds and resident temperate birds into a megapopulation, linked by the interacting populations of Neotropical migrants that compete with the residents for resources during both breeding and wintering seasons. The life tables of fecundity and mortality reported for tropical, temperate, and migrant species show, however, that there is not complete density-dependent coupling in either season.

Scaling down to an individual species (Cerulean Warbler) Chandler Robbins, John Fitzpatrick, and Paul Hamel discuss constraints facing this species in view of habitat changes taking place on both its temperate breeding grounds and its tropical wintering grounds.

Finally, Richard Holmes and Thomas Sherry consider

site fidelity of individual warblers of two species, comparing summer and winter return rates by age and sex. They suggest that higher site fidelity in winter than in summer means that winter habitats are crucial for survival and that alteration of winter habitats could have a disproportionately severe negative impact on survival of Neotropical migrants.

Comparing these papers with those presented in the symposium a decade ago (Keast and Morton 1980), one notes a shift in geographic scale; largely regional documentary studies are replaced by hemispheric and global concerns about population declines and the need to establish priorities to prevent extinctions. Except for species in imminent danger, however, there is clearly no unanimity of opinion as to which species are most at risk. Reed rates the Cerulean and Golden-winged warblers (declining species) and Blue-wing Warbler (an expanding species) equally, assigning them low priority, whereas Robbins and coauthors would claim greater priority for the Cerulean and Gill (1980) would claim it for the Golden-winged. Hunter even suggests that resident species of the boreal forest may be less adaptable to climatic change than are Neotropical migrants.

At least I feel that we are on the right track. We are beginning to concentrate on certain species that seem to be at greatest risk. We are developing ability to monitor habitat change through satellite imagery. We shall be better prepared to monitor effects of global warming than we were to face the problems related to persistent pesticides or acid precipitation.

We have identified problems and have begun to create the first crude models to predict population change. We are hampered, however, by not having a coordinated program to monitor population changes of Neotropical migrants on any of their wintering grounds or to monitor resident tropical species at any season. There still is pitifully little information relating specific breeding populations to their wintering areas. Greater efforts toward banding Neotropical migrants on their breeding and wintering grounds need to be linked with educational programs to promote reporting of banded birds. Winter mortality rates are unknown for most species, as are mortality rates during the fall and spring migration periods. How many decades will pass before a coordinated program will be launched to place radio transmitters on a thousand known-age Wood Thrushes on their breeding grounds in one season and follow their migration and survival by satellite for the ensuing twelve months? Only then can we realistically hope to make real strides in modeling survival of various segments of the population.

Looking ahead to the next Neotropical Migrant Symposium, I hope for much greater participation by Latin American and Caribbean researchers, and more cooperative papers based on pooled results. The time is ripe for establishing a Neotropical data base to which standardized census and banding data can be contributed. Conservation of Neotropical migrants on their wintering grounds should logically be coordinated with preservation of habitats for resident tropical birds, many of which are at greater risk than the migrants we seek to protect. We must truly adopt a hemispheric perspective in our conservation efforts.

Literature cited

Gill, F.B. 1980. Historical aspects of hybridization between Blue-winged and Golden-winged Warblers. *Auk* 97:1–18.

Keast, A., and E.S. Morton, eds. 1980. *Migrant Birds in the Neotropics: Ecology, Behavior, Distribution, and Conservation.* Washington: Smithsonian Institution Press.

Rabinowitz, D. 1981. Seven forms of rarity. Pages 205–217 in *The Biological Aspects of Rare Plant Conservation*, H. Synge, ed. New York: Wiley.

MALCOLM L. HUNTER, JR.
Department of Wildlife
University of Maine
Orono, Maine 04469

Paleoecology, landscape ecology, and conservation of Neotropical migrant passerines in boreal forests

Abstract. Paleoecological research demonstrates that the geographic ranges of plant taxa shift in highly individualistic patterns because climate changes continuously, and therefore seemingly distinctive ecological communities, such as the boreal forest community, are transitory assemblages. The consequences of climate changes for boreal forest birds that migrate to the Neotropics may be mitigated for two reasons: (1) members of these transitory assemblages have, *de facto*, demonstrated their ability to cope with such changes in the past (if not, they would be extinct); and (2) Neotropical-boreal migrants are probably relatively plastic, as indicated by their ability to survive in both boreal and tropical ecosystems. The prospects of accelerated climate change due to increased levels of CO_2 is certainly cause for concern, but primarily for year-round resident birds and other less plastic and less vagile biota. In most boreal forest landscapes, clearcutting is the major form of manipulation. Clearcuts are a crude analogue of catastrophic fires and other natural disturbances and therefore the broad distribution of fire sizes suggests that there should be many different sizes of clearcuts. To determine a clearcut size distribution, several factors can be considered, such as the maximum size of natural disturbance events, the habitat requirements of species with large home ranges, and the need to avoid fragmenting habitat with many small cuts. Birds that need large areas of old forests are most likely to be sensitive to clearcutting and several resident species fit this description. Conservation of boreal birds should primarily focus on those species that are demonstrably in danger of extinction, such as the Kirtland's Warbler (*Dendroica kirtlandii*). However, consideration should also be given to species that are currently secure, but likely to be sensitive to future habitat change. As a generalization, sedentary, stereotypic species, especially those that prefer large tracts of old forest, are most likely to be vulnerable to change.

Sinopsis. La investigación paleoecológica demuestra que las distribuciones geográficas de taxa vegetales derivan en patrones altamente individualistas porque el clima cambia continuamente y por lo tanto comunidades ecológicas aparentemente disímiles, tales como la comunidad de bosque boreal, son conjuntos transitorios. Las consecuencias de cambios climáticos para las aves de bosques boreales que migran al neotrópico pueden estar mitigadas por dos razones: (1) los miembros de estos conjuntos transitorios han demostrado *de facto* su habilidad para enfrentar tales cambios en el pasado (si no lo hubieran hecho estarían extintos); y (2) las migratorias neotropicales-boreales son probablemente relativamente plásticas como lo indica su habilidad para sobrevivir tanto en ecosistemas boreales como tropicales. El prospecto de cambio acelerado del clima debido a los incrementos en los niveles de CO_2 ciertamente es una causa de preocupación, pero primariamente para aves permanentemente residentes y otra biota menos plástica y menos vágil. En la mayoría de paisajes forestales boreales, la tala es la mayor forma de manipulación. La tala es un análogo crudo de los fuegos catastróficos y otras perturbaciones naturales y por lo tanto la amplia distribución de tamaños de los incendios sugiere que debe haber muchos tamaños diferentes de tala. Para determinar una distribución de tamaño de las talas, deben considerarse varios factores, tales como el máximo tamaño de los eventos de perturbación natural, los requerimientos de habitat de especies con ámbitos domésticos grandes y la necesidad de evitar la fragmentación del habitat con muchos parches de tala pequeños. Las aves que necesitan grandes áreas de bosque maduro son probablemente mas sensibles a la tala y varias especies residentes corresponden a esta descripción. La conservación de aves boreales debe enfocarse primariamente en aquellas especies para las cuales puede demostrarse el peligro de extinción, tales como *Dendroica kirtlandii*. Sin embargo, también deben considerarse especies que están actualmente seguras pero que probablemente serán sensibles a cambios futuros de habitat. Como una generalización, especies sedentarias estereotípicas, especialmente aquellas que prefieren grandes áreas de bosque maduro son probablemente las mas vulnerables al cambio.

Our understanding of many ecological phenomena is constrained by the scales at which we investigate them. Time scales are particularly abbreviated because most research projects last fewer than five years, because quantitative ecology is only a few decades old, and because examination of fossil pollen, bones, and other relics provides only a narrow window on the past. Large spatial-scale studies are curtailed primarily by logistical or financial limitations, making it very difficult to characterize phenomena for a whole landscape or region, except for rather coarse features such as climate and geographic ranges of species.

These same limitations characterize our attempts to understand migrant birds. Even our longest research projects (e.g., Järvinen and Ulfstrand 1980, Ambuel and

Temple 1982, Helle and Järvinen 1986, Robbins et al. 1986) are but an instant on an evolutionary time scale. Similarly, most detailed avian ecological research has taken place on only one or a few plots, plots too small (typically less than 20 ha) to characterize a whole landscape (e.g., Rabenold 1980, Bennett 1980). Even recent research on the effects of forest fragmentation on birds has only extended the size of study plots to a few hundred hectares. From these site-specific projects it is a rather large leap to programs that characterize avifauna at a regional or continental scale (e.g., Kalela 1949, Helle and Järvinen 1986, Robbins et al. 1986).

In this paper I will attempt to circumvent partially these scale limitations and shed new light on some ornithological issues by drawing from two other disciplines, paleoecology and landscape ecology. More specifically, I will first use paleoecology to describe patterns of vegetative response to climate change, and then speculate about the relative ability of Neotropical migrants to respond to these long-term changes. In the second part of the paper, I will examine clearcutting and ancillary spatial issues such as forest fragmentation and, again, speculate about the implications for bird conservation. Because the boreal forest biome has been particularly dynamic at large spatial and temporal scales, it will be the primary focus of this paper.

A paleoecological perspective

It is intuitively obvious that 18,000 years ago, when the climate was much cooler and an ice sheet extended south to New York and Illinois, various community types—tundra, boreal forest, temperate deciduous forest, and others—must have been displaced far south of their current range. This is a well-known and well-documented story because, beginning in the 1930s, paleoecologists have used the stratigraphy of fossil pollen in lake sediments and peat deposits to map long-term changes in the distribution of vegetation. However, the story grew more complex when paleoecologists went beyond reconstructing coarse vegetational patterns to mapping the shifting distribution of individual plant species and genera (Davis 1981a, 1986, Jacobson et al. 1987, Webb 1987) (Fig. 1). This approach revealed that the range expansions and contractions of various plant taxa were highly individualistic responses to changing climate and that the assemblage of plants occupying a given area was in continual flux. Consequently, there are no modern analogues for many of the vegetation communities that existed 18,000 years ago. Only in the last 6,000 to 8,000 years did communities, as we now know them, begin to appear. For example, beech (*Fagus americana*) and hemlock (*Tsuga canadensis*), two major components of the northern hardwood forest of north-

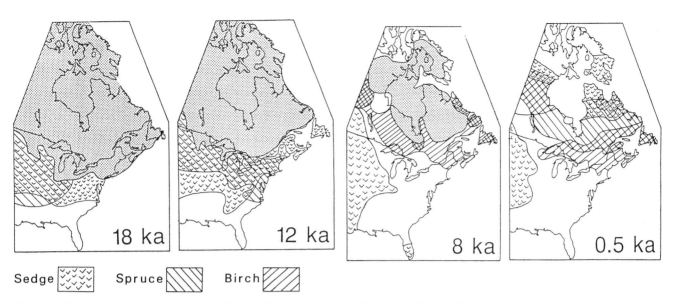

FIGURE 1. Distributions of regions with pollen profiles comprised of 20% spruce (*Picea*), 20% birch (*Betula*), and 5% sedge (*Carex*) at 18,000, 12,000, 8,000, and 500 years ago (*ka* = kiloannum). The Laurentide ice sheet is shown in stippling. Note that patterns of range overlap between species are not stable. For example, 8,000 years ago spruce had a very limited distribution which barely overlapped with that of birch. Redrawn from Plates 1 and 2 in Jacobson et al. 1987.

eastern North America, only developed a substantial range overlap 6,000 years ago (Jacobson et al. 1987).

This story is not unique to the trees of North America. Three small mammals with widely divergent current ranges—eastern chipmunk (*Tamias striatus*), northern bog lemming (*Synaptomys borealis*), and black-tailed prairie dog (*Cynomys ludovicianus*)—shared the same habitat in western Iowa 23,000 years ago (Graham 1986). Furthermore, data on changing plant distributions exist for many areas including tropical South America (Colinvaux 1987), Australia (Walker and Chen 1987), and Africa (Livingstone 1982). The common impression of tropical forests is one of great stability, but paleoecological data, admittedly still sparse for the tropics, has yet to document a single case of a tropical forest community persisting through millenia.

To understand why the responses to climate change are so individualistic, one needs to know two facts about the nature of climate change. First, the last 18,000 years of climate change are just the most recent manifestation of a 2.5 million-year period of substantial fluctuations that experienced more than 20 glacial/ interglacial cycles (Broecker and van Donk 1970). More specifically, the current interglacial period, the Holocene, began about 10,000 years ago and was preceded by nearly 100,000 years of colder climate; such colder climates have characterized about 90% of the last 2.5 million years. Second, these glacial/ interglacial cycles are driven by systematic changes in three of the earth's orbital parameters: (1) eccentricity of the

earth's orbit (periodicity—100,000 years); (2) tilt of the earth's axis of rotation or obliquity (41,000 years); and (3) precession of the equinoxes (19,000 and 23,000 years) (Berger et al. 1984). Together, these three phenomena generate a quasi-periodic cycle with a periodicity of about 100,000 years. Because the overall cyclicity is generated by three different orbital phenomena, some meteorological features vary independently of one another, for example, temperature and moisture regimes (Webb 1986). In other words, as the temperature shifts from glacial to interglacial, climatic regions do not simply contract and expand along a pole-equator axis. Instead, different climate parameters change in different ways and whole new climates are generated (Kutzbach and Guetter 1986). Each plant taxon responds to these new climates in a different manner thus generating the individual range shifts seen in Figure 1.

The idea of plants responding to long-term climatic cycles by shifting their ranges is easier to understand conceptually if one draws an analogy with the annual range shifts migratory animals use to adapt to annual climatic cycles (Huntley and Webb 1989; Fig. 2). In both cases, species respond to periodic climate change by shifting their ranges; the magnitude of the climate change and the distances moved are roughly comparable; only the periodicity, and thus rate of movement, are enormously different. These paleoecological events are also easier to envision when one considers recent changes in the status and distribution of species. In just a few decades, the American chestnut (*Castanea ameri-*

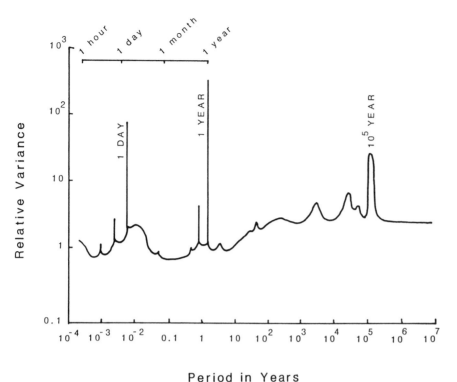

FIGURE 2. Relative variance of climate over a scale from ten million years to one hour shows three distinct peaks corresponding with cycles of a day, a year, and 100,000 years. Some organisms (e.g., plankton) migrate in response to diurnal cycles; some animals (e.g., migratory birds) make annual range shifts; most organisms respond to glacial/ interglacial cycles by changing their ranges.

cana) has all but disappeared from the landscape, whereas the Chestnut-sided Warbler (*Dendroica pensylvanica*), a bird formerly so rare that Audubon encountered it only once in his life (Forbush 1929), is now a common, widespread species. Animal ecologists who have observed the changing distributions of Cattle Egrets (*Bubulcus ibis*), Northern Mockingbirds (*Mimus polyglottos*), and nine-banded armadillos (*Dasypus novemcinctus*) should be particularly attuned to the phenomenon of shifting ranges. Admittedly, the changes cited here might be more related to anthropogenic changes than climate changes, but the point is that many species have the ability to change their ranges quite rapidly. In particular, species can become rare and experience a major range contraction quickly, as has happened recently to many of our endangered species. This has also happened in the past, for example, when hemlocks declined dramatically about 4,800 years ago, presumably because of the advent of a virulent pathogen (Davis 1981b).

Whither the future of climate change? As stated above, climates have been changing in a quasi-periodic fashion for as long as can be detected. However, quantitative analyses of the rates of vegetation change over the last 18,000 years indicate that the past 1,000 years have been a period of particularly substantial change in North America (Jacobson et al. 1987, Grimm and Jacobson in press). Indeed, climate-induced changes of the last 1,000 years might well have been more substantial than the human-induced changes that began with European settlement 500 years ago (Grimm and Jacobson in press), and, therefore, the plant range shifts depicted in Figure 1 might underestimate the current rates of biotic change. Finally, and perhaps most importantly, models of the relationship between climate and carbon dioxide, methane, ozone, and other gases suggest that air pollution might profoundly accelerate climate change by inducing global warming (Pisias and Shackleton 1984, Shands and Hoffman 1987, National Research Council 1988, Cess et al. 1989). This prospect is particularly worrisome in light of some recent evidence about the potential rapidity of climate change. Analyses of heavy stable isotopes, trace elements, and continental dust in deep ice cores collected in Greenland indicate that 10,700 years ago the climate there changed very rapidly (Dansgaard et al. 1989); within a period of 20–50 years there was a 7° C warming, a 50% increase in precipitation, and a decrease in storminess. To summarize, plant distributions shift in species-specific patterns in response to changing climates. Such changes are normal but there are three reasons for concern: (1) we are currently in a 1,000-year-old period of exceptional change; (2) some evidence indicates that extremely dramatic changes can occur in a period of decades; and (3) climate changes might be further amplified by atmospheric pollution.

Changing climates and the adaptability of boreal birds

If the basic message from paleoecology is one of continuing change, and our manipulations of the atmosphere are likely to accelerate these changes, what does this portend for the Neotropical migrants of boreal forests? For example, what would the impact be if spruce trees declined as dramatically in the next 500 years as hemlock did 4,800 years ago? Even though some bird species show a marked preference for using certain species of trees (Franzreb 1978, Hunter 1980, Holmes and Robinson 1981, Benkman 1987a,b), one could still give an optimistic response: extant bird species must have adapted to major habitat changes over the last several millennia and can be expected to continue doing so in the future. We might not know whether they have adapted by shifting their geographic ranges to follow their preferred tree species, or by switching to other types of vegetation, or both, but undoubtedly they have adapted. Unfortunately, we cannot be entirely satisfied with this answer. Recent anthropogenic changes—habitat fragmentation, environmental contaminants, an accelerated rate of habitat loss, for example—undoubtedly hinder the birds' ability to respond to long-term changes effected by climate. Thus, it is important to evaluate further their adaptability. It is difficult to evaluate adaptability in an absolute sense; it would require knowledge of extinction probabilities. Thus I will focus on comparing Neotropical migrants to year-round resident birds of the boreal forest.

MORPHOLOGICAL AND PHYSIOLOGICAL ADAPTATIONS. A key aspect of the adaptability issue is the extent to which birds have evolved specific morphological and physiological adaptations to a boreal environment that might restrict their ability to function in a different habitat. Some nonmigrants show highly specific adaptations; the crossed mandibles of white-winged crossbills (*Loxia leucoptera*) (Benkman 1987a,b) and the digestive systems of spruce grouse (*Dendragapus canadensis*) and blue grouse (*D. obscurus*) (Leopold 1953) are good examples. In contrast, many Neotropical migrants (e.g., boreal warblers, flycatchers, thrushes, and vireos) must make major habitat changes each season moving among their breeding, migration, and winter habitats, and thus they are probably less likely than year-round residents to have very specialized adaptations (Keast 1980b). This said, there are obvious exceptions: migratory hummingbirds are more specialized than resident chickadees, for example. Moreover, it is possible that subtle adaptations might be widespread, but have not been identified by ornithologists. For example, Winkler and Leisler (1985) ascribed differences in the toe pad configurations of Firecrests (*Regulus ignicapillus*) and Goldcrests (*R.*

regulus) to the Goldcrest's association with conifers.

A paucity of specific adaptations to a boreal environment among migrants would not be surprising if one accepts the idea that most Neotropical migrants probably originated in the tropics and thus have adapted to boreal environments only secondarily (Keast 1980a; for an alternative idea about the evolution of Neotropical migrants see Greenberg 1979). For example, Grant (1966) used an analysis of tarsal length and perch stability to imply that the Cape May Warbler (*Dendroica tigrina*) is better adapted to its winter habitat than to its summer habitat.

FORAGING BEHAVIOR RESPONSES. Whereas most morphological and physiological adaptations can change only at an evolutionary pace, behavioral responses to environmental change might be much more rapid. Intuitively, one would expect the foraging behavior of birds migrating among markedly different environments to be quite plastic, especially in terms of habitat selection, and this generalization is widely reported (e.g., Keast 1980b). A well-known example is the fact that many migrants that are primarily insectivorous in the summer, add fruit and nectar to their winter diets (Moreau 1972, Morton 1980). There are two ways in which the foraging behavior of migrants might be relatively plastic: (1) they can be plastic compared to similar, nonmigratory species (either on wintering or breeding grounds) (e.g., Tramer and Kemp 1980) and (2) they can have a relatively broad behavioral repertoire during one season compared to another season (e.g., Rabenold 1980). As with all generalizations, some exceptions are known. Some migrant species, for example the Chestnut-sided Warbler (Greenberg 1979), exhibit fairly specialized foraging behavior, especially foraging maneuvers, in both their summer and winter habitat (Greenberg 1986). Some species might select habitat on both their wintering and breeding grounds that are fairly similar to one another (Fitzpatrick 1980, Lynch 1989), although this option is not really open to boreal birds migrating between needle-leaved and broad-leaved forests. Despite these and other exceptions, one is left with an overall impression that Neotropical migrants exhibit considerable latitude in habitat selection and, to a lesser degree, style of habitat exploitation, primarily foraging behavior. This is not surprising; a boreal forest bird that required a close analog to boreal forest while wintering in the Neotropics would face a difficult prospect.

RESPONSES TO SYMBIONT ASSEMBLAGES. Besides long-term changes in vegetation, there are also likely to be concomitant changes in the assemblages of predators, parasites, pathogens, and competitors to which migrant birds must respond. Some human-induced changes in these assemblages provide good examples of the issues:

mammalian and avian carnivores preying on bird nests near edges (Gates and Gysell 1978, Soulé et al. 1988); Brown-headed Cowbirds (*Molothrus ater*) parasitizing the nests of Kirtland's Warbler (*Dendroica kirtlandii*) and other passerines (Brittingham and Temple 1983); avian malaria and birdpox decimating the avifauna of Hawaii (Warner 1968, Van Riper et al. 1986); European Starlings (*Sturnus vulgaris*) competing for nest sites with Eastern Bluebirds (*Sialia sialis*) and other cavity nesters. Obviously the anthropogenic problems listed are of serious concern, but does the possibility of long-term changes in predator, parasite, pathogen, or competitor assemblages pose a significant additional threat to migrants? Again, the fact that migrants move through many different communities during the course of a year indicates that they might be better able to cope with long-term changes in the composition of symbiont assemblages than year-round residents that only experience one community. Keast (1980b) made a similar speculation, but I know of no evidence to support the idea.

RESPONSES TO CLIMATIC EXTREMES. There is a tendency to think of climate in terms of parameters such as mean annual precipitation or mean July temperature, but from an evolutionary standpoint, climatic means are generally not as important as extreme events, such as prolonged droughts or cold spells. The North American drought of 1988 provides a recent example of a climatic event that might have served as an important evolutionary bottleneck (Droege and Sauer 1989); the impact of the winters of 1962–63 and 1981-82 on Britain's avifauna are well-documented examples (Dobinson and Richards 1964, O'Connor and Cawthorne 1982). Neotropical migrant boreal birds might differ from year-round resident boreal birds in their ability to survive such extreme events. Migrant birds experience a narrower range of temperatures during the course of a year than birds remaining in the north (Kendeigh 1934) and thus are likely to be adapted to the modest temperature fluctuations characterizing tropical environments. This suggests that migrants might be less tolerant of extremes than residents. On the other hand, if migrants are behaviorally plastic, this might allow them to find food during brief periods of adverse weather; Keast (1980b) describes an example of this.

The consequences of precipitation for migrants might present a rather different picture from that of temperature. Many tropical ecosystems have pronounced wet and dry seasons, while water, at least as snow, is available to animals in boreal ecosystems throughout the year. Thus, birds associated with tropical environments might be better adapted to cope with droughts and prolonged periods of rain. This is a complex issue because temperature and water availability are interactive fac-

tors (surviving a heat wave is much easier with unlimited water) and because they affect birds indirectly in many ways such as through food supply. Unusually heavy rains had a pronounced negative effect on populations of Black-throated Green Warblers (*Dendroica virens*) in coastal Maine (Morse 1976), and a very positive effect on Darwin's finches (*Geospiza* spp.) in the arid Galapagos (Gibbs and Grant 1987).

MOBILITY. Mobility might be a critical factor in determining how well various plant and animal species will respond to future climate changes (Jacobson and Hunter, unpubl. ms.). Mobility can be thought of both in terms of the lifetime movements of an individual and the dispersal movements of populations between generations. Clearly, species that are mobile both as individuals and between generations are most likely to adapt to climate change by shifting their ranges. Species such as the Winter Wren (*Troglodytes troglodytes*) and Mourning Warbler (*Oporornis philadelphia*) that both migrate and seek out transitory, early successional ecosystems are good examples, as are species such as crossbills and Cape May Warblers that might move long distances among areas of high cone or budworm (*Choristoneura* spp.) densities. Resident species associated with mature forest ecosystems such as the Spotted Owl (*Strix occidentalis*) and Spruce Grouse might be less likely to change their ranges quickly. These differences in the relative mobility of different bird species seem less important when one realizes that extant trees, which can move their ranges less than a few hundred meters per year (Davis 1986), have survived past climate changes.

SUMMARY. Compared to year-round residents, birds migrating between the Neotropics and the boreal forest appear to exhibit more behavioral plasticity and mobility and probably have evolved fewer specific morphological and physiological traits that tie them to a particular climate, plant taxa, or assemblage of animal symbionts. Thus, the optimistic response to the question posed at the beginning of this section might be reasonable: Neotropical-boreal migrant birds are likely to be relatively adaptable in the face of long-term changes effected by climate. There are some important qualifiers to this statement. First, the statement is a generalization based on an incomplete understanding of these birds and their prospects for survival. This review simply suggests that we need to identify and focus conservation efforts on those species that are least adaptable to long-term change and that such species might be more likely to be found among resident boreal birds than among migrants. Second, the discussion has emphasized the *relative* adaptability of many Neotropical-boreal migrant birds, as compared to resident boreal birds, or even sedentary animals or plants. If profound, very rapid climate changes should occur, the impacts might be most drastic for less mobile biota, but it is possible that the *absolute* adaptability of some migrant birds will be exceeded. Third, Neotropical migrants might be particularly poor at surviving extreme climatic events, notably cold spells, which could serve as critical evolutionary bottlenecks. Finally, the likely ability of many boreal migrants to respond to long-term changes should not be taken to imply that they can readily cope with short-term anthropogenic changes such as habitat fragmentation. In fact, these short-term exigencies could severely inhibit the ability of some bird species to respond to long-term change.

Climate change and conservation

A paleoecological perspective can provide new insights on certain conservation issues. For example, Hunter et al. (1988) recommended that because future climate change will necessitate species shifting their ranges: (1) nature reserves should encompass a wide range of environments, particularly by having a wide altitudinal range (Peters and Darling 1985); (2) reserves should be connected by continental-scale corridors; and (3) most importantly, attention should be focused on wise stewardship and maintenance of biological diversity on entire landscapes, not just reserves.

People concerned with the fate of birds should add their voices to those protesting the overburdening of our atmosphere with carbon dioxide, lest we exacerbate the rate of climate change. Unfortunately, there is so much momentum in the climatic processes now in motion that we will probably experience significant climate change, even if we were to implement major programs to curb emissions (Mintzer 1987). Therefore, it is important to consider mitigating activities such as designing appropriate reserves and corridors, and even intensive population management techniques such as translocation and artificial breeding (Jacobson and Hunter, unpubl. ms.). Also, anything that can lessen other stresses on bird populations—environmental contaminants, habitat fragmentation, overexploitation, for example—make it more likely that populations will have time to adapt to long-term habitat changes. For many bird species these sources of stress are likely to be more critical than long-term changes in habitat effected by climate.

Boreal landscapes as habitats for Neotropical migrant passerines

In recent years many bird conservationists have adopted a landscape perspective because of concern over the effect of forest fragmentation on bird communities, particularly species of Neotropical migrants (e.g., Lynch

and Whigham 1984, Wilcove 1988, Hunter 1990). Some species require large forest patches with sizable areas of forest interior; many species suffer heavy nest losses near the ubiquitous edges characterizing a fragmented forest landscape (Gates and Gysel 1978, Brittingham and Temple 1983, Temple 1986). Virtually all of the research on this topic has been conducted in temperate latitude landscapes where most of the forest has been converted to agriculture and suburban areas. Consequently, it is difficult to distinguish between those impacts due to reduction in forest area versus those due to fragmentation of forest landscapes by roads, timber harvest operations, and other human intrusions. The difference between these processes is important because in most boreal regions forests have been fragmented to varying degrees, but the total area of forest has not been markedly reduced (Haden-Guest et al. 1956, WRI and IIED 1986).

The few studies available from extensively forested landscapes do not provide a consensus on the likely importance of fragmentation issues in boreal regions. Rosenberg and Raphael (1986) studied fragmentation issues for three years in Douglas-fir forests of northwestern California; the landscape was largely forested except that during the preceding 30 years about half the forest had been clearcut. They found some species closely associated with clearcut edges and some that avoided heavily harvested areas, but their general conclusion was that the assemblage of birds and other vertebrates was still very similar in patches varying widely in size and isolation. They speculated that differences might develop in the future as site-faithful individuals die and are not replaced. Indeed, Helle's (1985, 1986) analyses of long-term trends in forest bird populations of northern Finland concluded that fragmentation was responsible for declines of several species, especially cavity-nesting, nonmigratory species. Patterns of predation on bird nests near edges have been investigated in extensively forested landscapes in Maine (Small and Hunter 1988) and Sweden (Angelstam 1986) using artificial nests. In neither study was proximity to edge correlated to predation risk, but in the Maine study, predation risk was significantly negatively correlated to the size of the forest patch. Obviously, boreal forest fragmentation is a topic that merits considerably more research.

The absence of definitive studies on boreal forest fragmentation hinders our ability to assess the likely impacts of people on boreal landscapes, but some predictions can be made. For the foreseeable future, the primary direct impact will probably be through timber harvesting. Specifically, large stands will be clearcut as they reach ages of 40–80 years, roughly the age at which the growth for a given year drops below the mean annual growth in most boreal forests. The resulting land-

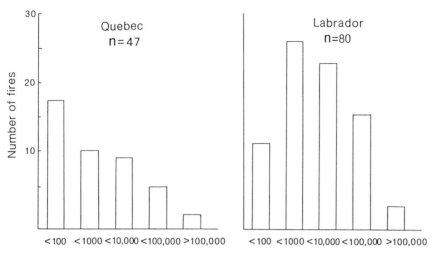

FIGURE 3. *A*, frequency distribution of fires by size class between 1920 and 1984 in northern boreal forests of Quebec (ca. 74–76° W; 55–55°30' N); based on data from Payette et al. (1989). *B*, frequency distribution of fires by size class in southeastern Labrador, 1870–1979, (ca. 53°45'–60° W; 52–53°30' N); based on data from Foster (1983).

scape will be a patchwork of stands of many ages laced by access roads, but this patchwork will be largely devoid of old stands except in remote, inaccessible, or protected areas. Many issues pertinent to bird conservation arise from this scenario—a shortage of old-growth forests and their associated biota (Hunter 1989) and an acceleration of secondary succession through herbicide use (Santillo et al. 1989), for example—but here I will focus on spatial issues by considering the landscape mosaics generated by clearcutting.

CLEARCUTTING BOREAL FOREST LANDSCAPES. Clearcuts are often decried as a travesty for wildlife, but this view needs to be carefully evaluated. First, recently clearcut sites are habitat for American Kestrels (*Falco sparverius*), Eastern Bluebirds, Mourning Warblers, Winter Wrens, and many other bird species, most of which are not considered "undesirable," as are cowbirds and Common Grackles (*Quiscalus quiscula*), for example. Second, large-scale, catastrophic disturbances initiating secondary succession, most notably fires, are common, natural events in many boreal landscapes, and they tend to produce a mosaic of fairly large, even-aged stands (Heinselman 1973, 1981a,b, Foster 1983, Payette et al. 1989). In such a landscape, clearcutting is an effective silvicultural tool and might provide a crude analogue of the natural disturbance regime, especially if some residual snags, logs, and large trees are left (Franklin 1989).

The similarities between clearcuts and natural disturbances are far from perfect (e.g., the type and abundance of residual organic matter is quite different). Moreover, silvicultural alternatives to clearcutting boreal forests are available; for example, uneven-aged harvesting methods such as selection cutting can be successfully used (Burns 1983). These caveats and other

issues such as aesthetics and nutrient loss merit concern, but ultimately, unless strong counter-arguments are developed, short-term financial exigencies will prevail and clearcutting will continue to be the preferred method of harvesting boreal forests.

What should be the size distribution of clearcuts? One possibility is to match the scale of harvest regimes to the scale of natural disturbance regimes, and in Figure 3 two potential models are shown—size-class distributions for natural (uncontrolled) fires in boreal forests in Quebec and in Labrador. This broad distribution of fire sizes (< 50 ha to ca. 118,000 ha) indicates no single optimal size for clearcuts. This is particularly manifest when one considers the broad distribution of the home range area requirements of different organisms; the span from small, sedentary plants and invertebrates to large carnivorous mammals is about 12 orders of magnitude (Hunter 1987, 1990). Although the span of home range sizes for Neotropical-boreal migrant passerines is relatively narrow (ca. 0.5–5 ha, Fig. 4), it still suggests that it would be a mistake to constrain clearcuts to a certain size. This is often the effect of forest harvest regulations; if a law prohibits clearcuts above 25 ha, the vast majority of cuts are likely to be between 20 and 25 ha.

What should be the maximum size of clearcuts? The question can be answered in at least three ways. First, in most types of forest ecosystems, it would be reasonable to let the upper limit be determined by the natural disturbance regime; for example, the limit could be one standard deviation larger than the mean disturbance size. However, in boreal forests that limit is likely to be many thousands of hectares (27,000 ha in the Quebec example), and most people would argue that other considerations (e.g., aesthetics and soil erosion risk) should

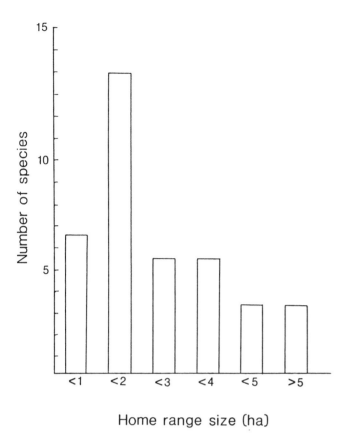

FIGURE 4. Frequency distribution for estimated home range sizes of 35 species of boreal-Neotropical forest passerines. Estimates derived from midpoints of ranges of sampling densities reported in Brown (1985) and DeGraaf and Rudis (1986). They are sensitive to estimates made in suboptimal habitat and unoccupied habitat between ranges and therefore are larger than mean home range sizes.

dictate a much smaller maximum, especially because clearcuts are an imperfect analogue of natural disturbances.

A second approach could consider which animal species have large home ranges and therefore require a large clearcut or the large block of continuous forest which the clearcut will eventually become. Most species with very large home ranges, notably large carnivorous mammals, are habitat generalists and thus unlikely to require large blocks of uniform habitat (Hunter 1990). Smaller carnivores, such as accipiters, owls, and pine martens (*Martes americana*), are more likely to be habitat specialists and thus their home range requirements (typically ca. 50–500 ha) might be more appropriate to consider.

A third approach can be derived from considering forest fragmentation and habitat islands. If the problems associated with temperate zone forest fragmentation (predation and brood parasitism of nests near edges, a dearth of interior forest) are also relevant to boreal landscapes dominated by timber harvesting, this would argue for making clearcuts quite large (Fig. 5; Franklin and Forman 1987). This assertion assumes that the choice is between a few, large cuts and many, small cuts of equal total area; simple geometry dictates that the small cuts will have a higher edge-to-area ratio and proportionately less interior area. Similarly, irregular, elongate cuts will have relatively more edge and less interior than cuts that approximate a circle or square. Furthermore, harvesting from many small cuts is likely to necessitate a larger network of maintained roads, and these might also be an important source of fragmentation and general environmental degradation (Mader

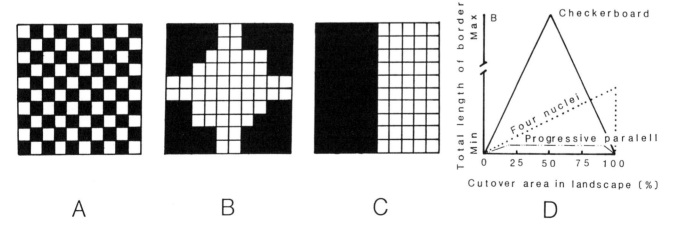

FIGURE 5. Landscape patterns generated by three different cutting regimes: *A*, checkerboard—small, dispersed cuts; *B*, four nuclei—large cuts spreading out from four points; and *C*, progressive parallel—a single large cut moving across the landscape. In each case 50% of the landscape has been cut. *D* shows total edge length for each regime at different levels of cutting; checkerboard cutting generates the most edge except at very high levels of cutting when the individual cuts coalesce. Redrawn from Franklin and Forman (1987).

1984). Therefore, if research in boreal landscapes were to demonstrate that fragmentation is an important issue there, this would argue against having an upper limit on clearcut size and for avoiding irregularly shaped clearcuts.

Despite the negative aspects associated with edges, there probably should not be any minimum limit on the size of clearcuts because different species are likely to find optimal habitat in forests managed at a variety of different scales: clearcuts, patch cuts, group selection cutting, and individual tree selection cutting. For most species, tracts of forest managed by selection cutting are likely to function as contiguous forest despite the small canopy gaps created by harvesting (Hunter 1990). Therefore, if large enough, these stands might also provide unfragmented habitat. However, as noted above, selection cutting is generally not considered the most economical way to manage boreal forests and will usually be employed only on steep slopes, riparian zones, and other sensitive areas.

Which boreal birds are most likely to be sensitive to clearcutting? The general answer is habitat specialists with large home range requirements, particularly those that prefer old forests. Concern for the Spotted Owl and Capercaillie (*Tetrao urogallus*) is well known; concern has also been expressed for Spruce Grouse in New York (Fritz 1979) and Red Crossbills in Newfoundland (Benkman 1989). Indeed, the Newfoundland Red Crossbill (*Loxia curvirostra percna*) is now very rare, having been largely excluded from the main island of Newfoundland by competition from introduced red squirrels (*Tamiasciurus hudsonicus*, Benkman 1989). Many Neotropical migrant passerines prefer old, boreal forests, but none of them have large home ranges (Fig. 4). Their sensitivity to clearcutting might depend largely on the unresolved issue of fragmentation impacts in boreal landscapes.

Conclusions

Some common themes for bird conservation emerge from both the paleoecological and landscape perspectives. Paleoecology suggests that sedentary, stereotypic species are less likely to adapt to climate change than mobile, plastic species. Landscape ecology suggests that the short-term impacts of timber harvesting are likely to affect habitat specialists that need large tracts of old forests. In many cases, these are the same species: raptors such as Spotted Owls, galliforms such as Spruce Grouse, Blue Grouse, and Capercaillie, perhaps some woodpecker, crossbill, and corvid species. Neotropical-boreal migrants for such a list do not come to mind readily, and it is tempting to generalize that collectively they might be of less concern to conservationists than many boreal residents. As explained at several points in this paper, there are important caveats to this general-

ization, and it is worth highlighting a species that illustrates the dangers of such a generalization. The Kirtland's Warbler is one of the rarest Neotropical migrants and one of the rarest boreal birds. It nests on outwash plains of coarse Grayling sand at the southern edge of the jack pine's (*Pinus banksiana*) range in Michigan; it requires both coarse sand and young jack pines (Botkin et al. 1991). If the jack pine's range recedes from Michigan because of climate warming, the Kirtland's Warbler might become extinct simply because it is unable to find suitable habitat elsewhere. Conservationists concerned with boreal forest birds should neglect neither resident nor migratory species, and when priorities must be assigned, first place should be given to species known to be threatened, whatever their life history. The next priority should be given to species that are currently secure, but likely to be sensitive to future habitat change. As a generalization, sedentary, stereotypic species, especially those that prefer large tracts of old forest, are most likely to be vulnerable to changes in their habitat.

Acknowledgments

I thank Craig Benkman, Yrjö Haila, George Jacobson, Tom Martin, Reed Noss, Raymond O'Connor, Elliot Tramer, and Don Whitehead for their advice. Financial support during preparation of this paper came from the Holt Woodlands Research Foundation and McIntire-Stennis Funds. Publication No. 1482 of the Maine Agricultural Experiment Station.

Literature cited

Ambuel, B., and S.A. Temple. 1982. Songbird populations in southern Wisconsin forests: 1954 and 1979. *J. Field Ornithol.* 53:149–158.

Angelstam, P. 1986. Predation on ground-nesting birds' nests in relation to predator densities and habitat edge. *Oikos* 47:365–373.

Benkman, C.W. 1987a. Food profitability and the foraging ecology of crossbills. *Ecol. Monogr.* 57:251–267.

———. 1987b. Crossbill foraging behavior, bill structure, and patterns of food profitability. *Wilson Bull.* 99:351–368.

———. 1989. On the evolution and ecology of island populations of crossbills. *Evolution* 43:1324–1330.

Bennett, S.E. 1980. Interspecific competition and the niche of the American redstart (*Setophaga ruticilla*) in wintering and breeding communities. Pages 319–335 in *Migrant Birds in the Neotropics: Ecology, Behavior, Distribution and Conservation*, A. Keast and E.S. Morton, eds. Washington: Smithsonian Institution Press.

Berger, A., J. Imbrie, J. Hays, G. Kukla, and B. Saltzman (eds.). 1984. *Milankovitch and Climate.* Dordrecht: Reidel.

Botkin, D.B., D.A. Woodby, and R.A. Nisbet. 1991. Kirtland's warbler habitats: A possible early indicator of climatic warming. *Biol. Conserv.* 56:63–78.

Brittingham, M.C., and S.A. Temple. 1983. Have cowbirds caused forest songbirds to decline? *BioScience* 33:31–35.

Broecker, W.S., and J. van Donk. 1970. Insolation changes, ice volumes, and the O-18 record in deep-sea cores. *Reviews of Geophysics and Space Physics* 8:169–197.

Brown, E.R., ed. 1985. *Management of Wildlife and Fish Habitats in Forests of Western Oregon and Washington.* Portland, Oreg.: USDA Forest Service Publ. No. R6-F&WL-192.

Burns, R.M., tech. comp. 1983. *Silvicultural Systems of the Major Forest Types of the United States.* Washington: USDA Forest Service Agriculture Handbook No. 445.

Cess, R.D., G.L. Potter, J.P. Blanchet, G.J. Boer, S.J. Ghan, J.T. Kiehl, H. Le Treut, Z.-X. Li, X.-Z. Liang, J.F.B. Mitchell, J.-J. Morcrette, D.A. Randall, M.R. Riches, E. Roeckner, U. Schlese, A. Slingo, K.E. Taylor, W.M. Washington, R.T. Wetherald, and I. Yagai. 1989. Interpretation of cloud-climate feedback as produced by 14 atmospheric general circulation models. *Science* 245:513-516.

Colinvaux, P. 1987. Amazon diversity in light of the paleoecological record. *Quaternary Science Reviews* 6:93–114.

Dansgaard, W., J.W.C. White, and S.J. Johnsen. 1989. The abrupt termination of the Younger Dryas climate event. *Nature* 339:532-534.

Davis, M.B. 1981a. Quaternary history and the stability of forest communities. Pages 132–153 in *Forest Succession, Concepts and Application,* D.C. West, H.H. Shugart, and D.B. Botkin. eds. New York: Springer-Verlag.

———. 1981b. Outbreaks of forest pathogens in Quaternary history. Pages 216–227 in *Proceedings Fourth International Palynological Conference (1976–77),* Vol. 3. Lucknow, India.

———. 1986. Climatic instability, time lags, and community disequilibrium. Pages 269–284 in *Community Ecology,* J. Diamond and T.J. Case, eds. New York: Harper and Row.

DeGraaf, R.M., and D.D. Rudis. 1986. *New England Wildlife: Habitat, Natural History, and Distribution.* Broomall, Pa.: USDA Forest Serv., N.E. Forest Exp. Sta., Gen. Tech. Rep. NE-108.

Dobinson, H.M., and A.J. Richards. 1964. The effects of the severe winter of 1962/63 on birds in Britain. *Brit. Birds* 57:373–434.

Droege, S., and J.R. Sauer. 1989. *North American Breeding Bird Survey: Annual Summary 1988.* U.S. Fish and Wildlife Service Biol. Rept. 89(13).

Fitzpatrick, J.W. 1980. Wintering of North American tyrant flycatchers in the Neotropics. Pages 67–78 in *Migrant Birds in the Neotropics: Ecology, Behavior, Distribution and Conservation,* A. Keast and E.S. Morton, eds. Washington: Smithsonian Institution Press.

Forbush, E.H. 1929. *Birds of Massachusetts and Other New England States.* Vol. 3. Boston: Massachusetts Department of Agriculture.

Foster, D.R. 1983. The history and pattern of fire in the boreal forest of southeastern Labrador. *Can. J. Bot.* 61:2459–2471.

Franklin, J. 1989. Towards a new forestry. *American Forests* November/December:37–44.

Franklin, J.F., and R.T.T. Forman. 1987. Creating landscape patterns by forest cutting: Ecological consequences and principles. *Landscape Ecol.* 1:5–18.

Franzreb, K.E. 1978. Tree species used by birds in logged and unlogged mixed coniferous forests. *Wilson Bull.* 90:221–238.

Fritz, R.S. 1979. Consequences of insular population structure: Distribution and extinction of spruce grouse populations. *Oecologia* 42:57–65.

Gates, J.E., and L.W. Gysel. 1978. Avian nest dispersion and fledging success in field forest ecotones. *Ecology* 59:871–883.

Gibbs, H.L., and P.R. Grant. 1987. Ecological consequences of an exceptionally strong El Nino event on Darwin's finches. *Ecology* 68:1735–1746.

Graham, R.W. 1986. Response of mammalian communities to environmental changes during the late Quaternary. Pages 300–313 in *Community Ecology,* J. Diamond and T.J. Case, eds. New York: Harper and Row.

Grant, P.R. 1966. Further information on the relative length of tarsus in land birds. *Yale Peabody Mus. Nat. Hist. Postilla* 98:1–13.

Greenberg, R. 1979. Body size, breeding habitat, and winter exploitation systems in *Dendroica. Auk* 96:756–766.

———. 1986. Competition in migrant birds in the nonbreeding season. *Current Ornith.* 3:281–307.

Grimm, E.C., and G.L. Jacobson, Jr. In press. Fossil-pollen evidence for abrupt climate changes during the past 18,000 years in eastern North America. *Climate Dynamics.*

Haden-Guest, S., J.K. Wright, and E.M. Teclaff. 1956. *A World Geography of Forest Resources.* New York: Ronald Press.

Heinselman, M.L. 1973. Fire in the virgin forests of the Boundary Waters Canoe Area, Minnesota. *Quat. Res.* 3:329–382.

———. 1981a. Fire intensity and frequency as factors in the distribution and structure of northern ecosystems. Pages 7–57 in *Fire Regimes and Ecosystem Properties,* H.A. Mooney, T.M. Bonnicksen, N.L. Christensen, J.E. Lotan, and W.A. Reiners, eds. USDA Forest Service Gen. Tech. Rep. WO-26.

———. 1981b. Fire and succession in the conifer forests of northern North America. Pages 374–405 in *Forest Succession: Concepts and Application,* D.C. West, H.H. Shugart, and D.B. Botkin, eds. New York: Springer-Verlag.

Helle, P. 1985. Effects of forest fragmentation on bird densities in northern boreal forests. *Ornis Fenn.* 62:35–41.

———. 1986. Bird community dynamics in a boreal forest reserve: The importance of large-scale regional trends. *Ann. Zool. Fennici* 23:157–166.

Helle, P., and O. Järvinen. 1986. Population trends of North Finnish land birds in relation to their habitat selection and changes in forest structure. *Oikos* 46:107–115.

Holmes, R.T., and S.K. Robinson. 1981. Tree species preferences of foraging insectivorous birds in a northern hardwoods forest. *Oecologia* 48:31–35.

Hunter, M.L., Jr. 1980. Microhabitat selection for singing and other behaviour in great tits, *Parus major*: Some visual and acoustical considerations. *Anim. Behav.* 28:468–475.

———. 1987. Managing forest for spatial heterogeneity to maintain biological diversity. *Trans. North Amer. Wildl. Nat. Resourc. Conf.* 52:60–69.

———. 1989. What constitutes an old-growth stand? *J. Forestry* 87:33–35.

———. 1990. *Wildlife, Forests, and Forestry: Principles of Managing Forests for Biological Diversity.* Englewood Cliffs, N.J.: Prentice-Hall.

Hunter, M.L., Jr., G.L. Jacobson, Jr., and T. Webb, III. 1988. Paleoecology and the coarse-filter approach to maintaining biological diversity. *Conserv. Biol.* 2:375–385.

Huntley, B., and T. Webb III. 1989. Migration: Species response to climatic variations caused by changes in the earth's orbit. *J. Biogeogr.* 16:5–19.

Jacobson, G.L., Jr., T. Webb III, and E.C. Grimm. 1987. Patterns and rates of vegetation change during the deglaciation of eastern North America. Pages 277–288 in *North America and Adjacent Oceans During the Last Deglaciation*, W.F. Ruddiman and H.E. Wright, Jr., eds. Boulder, Colo.: Geological Society of America.

Järvinen, O., and S. Ulfstrand. 1980. Species turnover of a continental bird fauna: Northern Europe, 1950–1970. *Oecologia* 46:186–195.

Kalela, O. 1949. Changes in geographic ranges in the avifauna of northern and central Europe in relation to recent changes in climate. *Bird-Banding* 2:77–103.

Keast, A. 1980a. The ecological basis and evolution of the nearctic-neotropical bird migration system. Pages 561–576 in *Migrant Birds in the Neotropics: Ecology, Behavior, Distribution and Conservation*, A. Keast and E.S. Morton, eds. Washington: Smithsonian Institution Press.

———. 1980b. Migratory parulidae: What can species co-occurrence in the north reveal about ecological plasticity and wintering patterns? Pages 457–476 in *Migrant Birds in the Neotropics: Ecology, Behavior, Distribution and Conservation*, A. Keast and E.S. Morton, eds. Washington: Smithsonian Institution Press.

Kendeigh, S.C. 1934. The role of environment in the life of birds. *Ecol. Monogr.* 4:299–417.

Kutzbach, J.E., and P.J. Guetter. 1986. The influence of changing orbital parameters and surface boundary conditions on climate simulations for the past 18,000 years. *J. Atmos. Sci.* 43:1726–1959.

Leopold, A.S. 1953. Intestinal morphology of gallinaceous birds in relation to food habits. *J. Wildl. Manage.* 17:197–203.

Livingstone, D.A. 1982. Quaternary geography of Africa and the refuge theory. Pages 523–536 in *Biological Diversification in the Tropics*, G.T. Prance, ed. New York: Columbia University Press.

Lynch, J.F. 1989. Distribution of overwintering Nearctic migrants in the Yucatan Peninsula, I: General patterns of occurrence. *Condor* 91:515–544.

Lynch, J.F., and D.F. Whigham. 1984. Effects of forest fragmentation on breeding bird communities in Maryland, U.S.A. *Biol. Conserv.* 28:287–324.

Mader, H.J. 1984. Animal habitat isolation by roads and agricultural fields. *Biol. Conserv.* 29:81–96.

Mintzer, I.M. 1987. *A Matter of Degrees: The Potential for Controlling the Greenhouse Effect*. Washington: World Resources Institute.

Moreau, R.E. 1972. *The Palaearctic-African Bird Migration Systems*. London: Academic Press.

Morse, D.H. 1976. Variables affecting the density and territory size of breeding spruce-woods warblers. *Ecology* 57:290–301.

Morton, E.S. 1980. Adaptations to seasonal changes by migrant land birds in the Panama Canal Zone. Pages 437–453 in *Migrant Birds in the Neotropics: Ecology, Behavior, Distribution and Conservation*, A. Keast and E.S. Morton, eds. Washington: Smithsonian Institution Press.

National Research Council. 1988. *Toward an Understanding of Global Change*. Washington: National Academy Press.

O'Connor, R.J., and R.A. Cawthorne. 1982. How Britain's birds survived the winter. *New Scientist* 93:786–788.

Payette, S., C. Morneau, L. Sirois. and M. Desponts. 1989. Recent fire history of the northern Quebec biomes. *Ecology* 70:656–673.

Peters, R.L., and J.D.S. Darling. 1985. The greenhouse effect and nature reserves. *BioScience* 35:707–717.

Pisias, N.G., and N.J. Shackleton. 1984. Modelling the global climate response to orbital forcing and atmospheric carbon dioxide changes. *Nature* 310:757–759.

Rabenold, K.N. 1980. The black-throated green warbler in Panama: Geographic and seasonal comparison of foraging. Pages 297–307 in *Migrant Birds in the Neotropics: Ecology, Behavior, Distribution and Conservation*, A. Keast and E.S. Morton, eds. Washington: Smithsonian Institution Press.

Robbins, C.S., D. Bystrak, and P.H. Geissler. 1986. *The Breeding Bird Survey: Its First Fifteen Years, 1965–1979*. U.S. Fish and Wildlife Serv. Resource Pub. 157.

Rosenberg, K.V., and M.G. Raphael. 1986. Effect of forest fragmentation on vertebrates in Douglas-fir forests. Pages 263–272 in *Wildlife 2000: Modeling Habitat Relationships of Terrestrial Vertebrates*, J. Verner, M.L. Morrison, and C.J. Ralph, eds. Madison: University of Wisconsin Press.

Santillo, D.J., P.W. Brown, and D.M. Leslie, Jr. 1989. Response of songbirds to glyphosate-induced habitat changes on clearcuts. *J. Wildl. Manage.* 53:64–71.

Shands, W.E., and J.S. Hoffman, eds. 1987. *The Greenhouse Effect, Climate Change, and U.S. Forests*. Washington: Conservation Foundation.

Small, M.F., and M.L. Hunter. 1988. Forest fragmentation and avian nest predation in forested landscapes. *Oecologia* 76:62–64.

Soulé, M.E., D.T. Boulger, A.C. Alberts, R. Sauvajot, J. Wright, M. Sorice, and S. Hill. 1988. Reconstructed dynamics of rapid extinctions of chaparral-requiring birds in urban habitat islands. *Conserv. Biol.* 2:75–92.

Temple, S.A. 1986. Predicting impacts of habitat fragmentation on forest birds: A comparison of two models. Pages 301–304 in *Wildlife 2000: Modeling Habitat Relationships of Terrestrial Vertebrates*, J. Verner, M.L. Morrison, and C.J. Ralph, eds. Madison: University of Wisconsin Press.

Tramer, E.J., and T.R. Kemp. 1980. Foraging ecology of migrant and resident warblers and vireos in the highlands of Costa Rica. Pages 285–296 in *Migrant Birds in the Neotropics: Ecology, Behavior, Distribution and Conservation*, A. Keast and E.S. Morton, eds. Washington: Smithsonian Institution Press.

Van Riper III, C., S.G. Van Riper, M.L. Goff, and M. Laird. 1986. The epizootiology and ecological significance of malaria in Hawaiian landbirds. *Ecol. Monogr.* 56:327–344.

Walker, D., and Y. Chen. 1987. Palynological light on tropical forest dynamics. *Quaternary Science Reviews* 6:77–92.

Warner, R.E. 1968. The role of introduced diseases in the extinction of the endemic Hawaiian avifauna. *Condor* 70:101–120.

Webb, T., III. 1986. Is vegetation in equilibrium with climate? How to interpret late-Quaternary pollen data. *Vegetatio* 67:75–91.

———. 1987. The appearance and disappearance of major vegetational assemblages: Long-term vegetational dynamics in eastern North America. *Vegetatio* 69:177–187.

Wilcove, D.S. 1988. Changes in the avifauna of the Great Smoky Mountains: 1947–1983. *Wilson Bull.* 100:256–271.

Winkler, H., and B. Leisler. 1985. Morphological aspects of habitat selection in birds. Pages 415–434 in *Habitat Selection in Birds,* M.L. Cody, ed. Orlando, Fla.: Academic Press.

World Resources Institute and International Institute for Environment and Development. 1986. *World Resources 1986.* New York: Basic Books.

J. MICHAEL REED*
Department of Zoology
Campus Box 7617
North Carolina State University
Raleigh, North Carolina 27695-7617

A system for ranking conservation priorities for Neotropical migrant birds based on relative susceptibility to extinction

Abstract. I used a method of classifying species rarity to rank Neotropical migrant bird species by their susceptibility to extinction. This method allowed assessment of the relative susceptibility to extinction among species, and assessment of the relative threat to species survival on the breeding vs. wintering grounds. I suggest that species conservation efforts be based on relative susceptibility to extinction, with higher susceptibility having a higher priority. This ranking system is based on habitat specificity, geographic distribution, and local population size.

This system was applied to 47 North American wood-warbler species (Emberizidae) and 10 Neotropical migrant vireo species (Vireonidae). My results show that Neotropical migrant birds are vulnerable both on their breeding and on their wintering grounds, and that threats often differ between the two ranges. Ten (21.3%) species on their breeding grounds and seven (14.9%) species on their wintering grounds had high vulnerability to extinction. Twenty-one (44.7%) species were classified differently on their breeding and wintering grounds; of these, 14 (66.7%) species were found to be more susceptible to extinction on their breeding grounds. These results differ from previous work that has identified the wintering ground as the more vulnerable site for migratory landbird species. This paper provides a framework for organizing and directing conservation and research efforts, and shows that a classification system can be used to address ecological and evolutionary problems associated with migratory bird species.

Sinopsis. En este estudio, yo utilicé un método de clasificación de rareza de especies para ordenar aves migratorias neotropicales por su susceptibilidad de extinción. Este método permitió la determinación de la susceptibilidad relativa a la extinción entre especies y la distinción entre la amenaza relativa a la supervivencia en las zonas de cría vs. aquella en los cuarteles de invierno para cada especie. Sugiero que los esfuerzos para la conservación de especies se basen en su susceptibilidad relativa a la extin-

*Current address: Ecology, Evolution, and Conservation Biology Program, RWF 1000 Valley Road, University of Nevada, Reno, Nevada 89512

ción, teniendo las máximas susceptibilidades una prioridad mas alta. Este sistema de categorización se basa en la especificidad de hábitat, la distribución geográfica y el tamaño local de la población.

El sistema fue aplicado a 47 especies norteamericanas de Parulinae (Emberizidae) y 10 especies neotropicales migratorias de Vireonidae. Mis resultados muestran que las aves migratorias neotropicales son vulnerables tanto en sus zonas de cría como en las de invernada y que las amenazas frecuentemente difieren entre los dos areales. Diez especies (21.3%) en sus zonas de cría y 7 (14.9%) en sus sitios de invernada tuvieron una alta vulnerabilidad a la extinción. Veintiuna especies (44.7%) se clasificaron diferentemente en ambas regiones de su distribución y de éstas, 14 (66.7%) se encontraron mas susceptibles a la extinción en sus sitios de reproducción. Estos resultados difieren de trabajos previos que han identificado las áreas de invernada como los sitios mas vulnerables para las aves terrestres migratorias. Este trabajo provee un marco de referencia para la organización y la dirección de los esfuerzos de investigación y conservación y muestra que un sistema de clasificación puede ser usado enfrentar problemas ecológicos y evolutivos asociados con especies de aves migratorias.

New World migrant birds are of interest to conservation biologists because of the reported population declines of many species (e.g., Aldrich and Robbins 1970, papers in Keast and Morton 1980, Wilcove and Terborgh 1984, Rappole and Morton 1985, Askins and Philbrick 1987, Holmes and Sherry 1988, Hutto 1988, 1989, Morton and Greenberg 1989, Robbins et al. 1989). Habitat loss on the breeding and wintering grounds has received much attention as a primary cause of these declines in woodland species. Habitat loss directly threatens the survival of many woodland species through loss of breeding areas, and habitat fragmentation, which can exacerbate species declines through insularization effects (e.g., Robbins 1979, 1980, Diamond 1984, Askins and Philbrick 1987) and possibly competitive replacement (e.g., Ambuel and Temple 1983, Askins and Philbrick 1987). Breeding habitat fragmentation can also lead to increased rates of nest parasitism by cowbirds (e.g., Mayfield 1977, Brittingham and Temple 1983) and of nest predation (Ambuel and Temple 1983, Wilcove 1985, Wilcove et al. 1986).

Once populations become small, extinction might follow even if habitat destruction is stopped or reversed. This might be due to environmental, demographic and genetic stochasticity, systematic exploitation of the animal or catastrophe (Shaffer 1981, Rabinowitz et al. 1986, Reed 1990). Migratory birds might suffer an even greater risk of extinction over nonmigratory species because migrant birds might be inherently more susceptible to extinction (Pimm et al. 1988).

If habitat loss were the only threat to a species' survival, conservation efforts would be relatively simple—save or create habitat. However, a shortage of habitat might not be the most immediate threat to survival of a given population or species. For example, if the presence of a predator is the most immediate threat to a population's survival, increasing habitat availability might not result in that species' recovery. Because money, time, and other resources are limited, we should identify the most vulnerable species and then the most immediate threats to population survival for those species. We need a species ranking system whereby species may be arranged in order of priority for conservation efforts (Office of Migratory Bird Management 1990). Because some threats to species survival, such as habitat loss or environmental stochasticity, can vary by locale and over time, this system should be sufficiently flexible to account for the variability of specific threats. In addition, because of the controversy surrounding the relative importance of threats on breeding vs. wintering grounds to Neotropical migrant birds (Hutto 1989, Morton and Greenberg 1989, Robbins et al. 1989), the ranking scheme should incorporate the relative comparison of threats between the breeding and wintering areas.

A systematic method is needed that (a) identifies species for which basic data required for assessing susceptibility to extinction are missing, (b) can distinguish the relative threats to species' survival on both the breeding and wintering grounds, (c) can be used to rank species by degree of susceptibility to extinction, and (d) can anticipate threats to survival that might arise because of changes in distribution or population size. My objectives are to (1) use an existing rarity classification scheme to provide the basic framework for a system that meets the above goals, and (2) apply this system with some modification to North American wood-warblers (Emberizidae) and migratory vireos (Vireonidae) on both their breeding and wintering grounds. Management decisions must be made soon for many species. The system I propose uses censuses and general habitat data commonly available for most species, so it will be generally and immediately applicable to many species.

Classification scheme

Species rarity has broad ecological meaning. Biologically, there are many types of rarity, each type differing in which threats are most relevant to survival. Rabinowitz (1981) proposed a method for classifying species using three dichotomous categories: habitat specificity, geographic distribution, and local population size.

Rabinowitz applied her classification scheme to the British flora (Rabinowitz et al. 1986), and discussed how various threats to species survival differentially affected a species within certain rarity categories. This static (point-in-time) classification scheme (Reed 1990) has also been applied to butterflies (Thomas and Mallorie 1985) and mammals (J.P. Hayes unpubl. data). Species falling in only one of the eight categories within Rabinowitz's scheme can be considered "common," that is, those with broad habitat specificity, a wide geographic distribution, having at least one large population; the other categories were considered rare by Rabinowitz et al. (1986). However, not all seven remaining categories are vulnerable to extinction because of rarity. For example, some categories represent species that occur in low density because of large territory requirements.

Other schemes for ranking conservation priority based on rarity have been proposed (Millsap et al. 1990, and op. cit.). However, none of the ranking schemes provided what I felt was needed. Specifically, it must be generally applicable to species with a wide range of natural history characteristics, be sensitive to different biological threats to species survival (particularly to the geographic extent of the threat, explained below), and be applicable despite the minimal data that typify many species. Rabinowitz's (1981) rarity classification scheme provides a basis for a ranking system to assign conservation priorities to Neotropical migrant landbirds. This scheme lacks, however, objective criteria for distinguishing the dividing line within each of the dichotomous categories. Therefore, each category is seen as a segment of a continuum, and no rules exist for placement of the divisions. Here I propose criteria for defining category divisions.

HABITAT SPECIFICITY

Habitat specificity refers to the degree of habitat specialization a species displays in both its breeding and wintering ranges. For example, the Yellow-rumped Warbler (*Dendroica coronata*) is a habitat generalist on its wintering grounds, occurring in most available habitats (Rappole et al. 1983). The Kirtland's Warbler (*Dendroica kirtlandii*), on the other hand, is a habitat specialist on its breeding grounds, requiring young jack pine (*Pinus banksiania*), which is periodically burned to provide nesting habitat. Another specialized habitat is mature forest, even of mixed tree species, and is of particular concern for Neotropical migrants (see above references). For example, in a study in Mexico, Hutto (1989) found three species of migrant warblers that used exclusively mature forest.

The more difficult species to classify are those that use a single habitat most of the time. A great variety of diversity measures can be used to describe habitat use in greater detail (Magurran 1988 and citations therein), and any one of these indices can be used. Nonetheless, decisions on how to distinguish between specialists and generalists would still be arbitrary (e.g., Kotrschal and

Thomson 1986). I define a habitat specialist on the breeding grounds by the following criteria: (1) when birds are at low population densities, all individuals select the same habitat type; (2) at high population densities, surplus individuals select other habitats for nesting (Fretwell and Lucas 1969, O'Connor 1985, O'Connor and Fuller 1985); and (3) habitat specialists nesting in the secondary habitat types contribute insubstantially to population reproduction (Murton and Westwood 1974). These species are habitat specialists from a conservation perspective because loss of the preferred habitat would result in loss of the population. On the wintering grounds, habitat specialists are defined as those that select a single habitat type when the population is at low densities; at high densities, if survival is substantially higher in a single habitat type, the species are also defined as specialists.

GEOGRAPHIC RANGE

Categorizing a species' distribution as broad or narrow is scale-dependent. For example, a species with a limited distribution in North America and a species widely distributed in Nova Scotia are being assessed at different scales. Species vagility should be considered in determining classification of geographic distribution. Relatively mobile species (such as migratory birds) might differ from sessile species in their ability to recolonize. Therefore, a sessile species distributed across the state of Pennsylvania might be considered widely distributed, whereas the breeding range for a bird species that covered the same area would have a narrow geographic distribution.

The definition of a "broad" geographic distribution should be relative to the area over which a threat to species survival can be expected to span. That is, over what geographic range can a threat be expected to have an effect? This is a necessary criterion because conservation biologists are interested in the effect a threat has on species survival. For example, if all species of interest were vulnerable to the destruction resulting from a single fire, none could be considered broadly distributed. In this paper, categorizing a species' distribution as broad or narrow gives information on species vulnerability.

Catastrophe and environmental stochasticity have the potential to cover the greatest area (e.g., hurricane, fire, spread of a disease, drought). An example is the spread of Rinderpest, a disease that affected ungulates during the 1890s in Africa (Dobson and May 1986). In less than 10 years, Rinderpest spread through the ungulate populations across two-thirds the length of Africa. In the first wave of infection, 90% of individuals of some species died. Extreme meteorological and climatalogical conditions can also have wide geographic effects on populations. Severe winters can substantially increase bird mortality across a wide area (e.g., Dobinson and Richards 1964, numerous citations in Gessaman and Worthen 1982). In 1989, hurricane Hugo caused severe habitat destruction in a narrow 10° latitudinal path from Puerto Rico to Virginia. Some Neotropical migrant landbirds winter primarily in the Caribbean Islands, and might be especially vulnerable to hurricanes. Effects of severe weather and disease or parasites might interact to cause widespread avian mortality (MacLean et al. 1973).

The ranking system I present here is flexible because the criteria defining a narrow distribution will change by species depending on the types of threats to survival of the species present. A problem is that the maximum area a threat actually covers might differ from that which is anticipated. Based on the above examples of threats to vertebrates, I suggest the following criteria defining the distribution of Neotropical migrant bird species: if a coastal species breeds (or overwinters) continuously across 10° latitude, or if an interior species is distributed continuously across 765,000 km^2 (a square with each side equal to the distance of 10° longitude at the equator), it has a broad geographic distribution; otherwise it has a narrow distribution. I believe this area is large enough that the entire range of a species will not be affected by the largest conceivable threats, such as hurricanes or drought.

POPULATION SIZE

One method for distinguishing species rarity is to determine whether or not at least one large population exists for the species. Rabinowitz et al. (1986) and Thomas and Mallorie (1985) used subjective estimation to determine if large populations of a species existed locally. I have used the same criterion of "locally abundant" in my classifications. These data are readily attainable for most bird species, and when making a first effort at ranking species susceptibility to extinction, data that can be gathered quickly are paramount.

Hidden within this classification system is a larger issue, which I will introduce (but not develop) here. Ultimately, local abundance is not adequate for assessing population size, and population size must be defined. A range map of distribution is not necessarily a single biological population. Populations are defined by gene flow (Mayr 1966). For a small isolated population it might be reasonable to assume that all individuals have a similar probability of intermating, particularly for most birds. As population size increases, however, gene flow becomes restricted because individuals tend to mate with neighbors rather than randomly with any other individual in the population (Wright 1946). Therefore, population size should be defined using strict criteria based on

the biology of the species. Models are available for determining population size that are based on dispersal distance and breeder density (Wright 1946), and definitions of population size are necessary to determine population viability (e.g., LaCava and Hughes 1984, Reed et al. 1986, 1988). A population should be viable, that is, self-sustaining for an indefinite period of time, before it can be considered large (Reed 1990). However, the criteria for defining viability are complicated, and largely unsettled (Shaffer 1981, Gilpen and Soulé 1986), and the data required to make this assessment are lacking for most species. Therefore, "locally abundant" must suffice as a criterion for large population size until long-term population studies are available. This might be an adequate criterion because local abundance and range can be associated in many noncolonial species (Arita et al. 1990), but it needs to be tested.

To create the classification scheme, then, these categories of habitat specificity, geographic range, and population size are nested to form an 8-celled table (Table 1). For the purposes of this study the hierarchy of habitat specificity and geographic distribution have been reversed from that proposed by Rabinowitz (1981). The species to be categorized in each cell can be susceptible to extinction by different threats.

THREATS TO EXTINCTION

The threats listed below are the mechanisms for species declines, but do not identify what is causing the threat. For example, habitat loss is identified here as a threat, but the causes of the habitat loss are not identified. Each threat is assigned to the category in which it most affects species survival (Reed 1990; Table 1). Threats to species survival include the following:

(1) Human-associated habitat destruction to species with specialized habitat requirements (Temple 1986), particularly to those species found only in small populations (Shaffer 1987).

(2) Demographic stochasticity is an occurrence of chance events in survival and reproductive success of individuals in a population (May 1973). It is manifested through fluctuations in birth rate, sex ratio, death rate, and in who dies (e.g., breeding or nonbreeding male). These events inherently threaten small populations (Lande 1988), because a downward population fluctuation has a greater probability of leading to extinction (Pimm et al. 1988).

(3) Genetic stochasticity results in loss of genetic variability within a population. Genetic loss can result from random drift, founder effect, and inbreeding (Berry 1971, Soulé 1980). This process is a threat to small-population survival (Frankel and Soulé 1981).

(4) Environmental stochasticity is temporal variation of biotic and abiotic factors (May 1973, Shaffer 1981),

TABLE 1.   Categories for rarity classification scheme taken from Rabinowitz (1981)

Population size	Habitat specificity			
	Broad		Restricted	
	Wide[a]	Narrow[a]	Wide[a]	Narrow[a]
Somewhere large	(A) –	(B) ca	(C) hl, es	(D) hl, ca, es
Everywhere small	(E) es, ds, gs	(F) ca, es, ds, gs	(G) hl, es, ds, gs	(H) hl, ca, es, ds, gs

NOTE: Five major threats to species survival are catastrophe (ca), habitat loss (hl), environmental stochasticity (es), demographic stochasticity (ds) and genetic stochasticity (gs). Threats significant to species in each category are listed.

a. Geographic distribution.

affecting reproduction and survival of all individuals of a given age and sex (Lande 1988). These include fluctuations in the relative effects of predators, competitors, pollution, and diseases as part of the local environment. Environmental stochasticity does not include introduction of new predators or pathogens, if they affect a population as would an abiotic catastrophe. Conversely, if a particular catastrophe occurred regularly, it would be defined as environmental stochasticity because it would be a normal part of the environment. Environmental stochasticity differs from catastrophe only by its relative regularity.

Environmental stochasticity can be contrasted with demographic and genetic stochasticity by whether adjacent populations are similarly affected. Environmental stochasticity (e.g., drought) affects populations similarly within a narrow geographic range, that is, each population shows a similar effect from the drought. Demographic and genetic stochasticity affect each population differently, so effects on a population (e.g., sex ratio, age-specific survival) among geographically close populations are uncorrelated.

(5) Catastrophes, such as floods, aperiodic fires, and disease, also threaten species with a narrow geographic range. I suggest that a criterion for distinguishing catastrophe from environmental stochasticity would be that a catastrophe is an environmental event that causes a population effect of ≥ 2 standard deviations below the survival rate or reproductive success of the population mean.

Rabinowitz (1981, Rabinowitz et al. 1986) included systematic exploitation in her list of threats to species survival. I do not distinguish this threat from the threats presented above because low-level exploitation (i.e., a fixed small percentage of individuals harvested) biologically functions as environmental stochasticity, whereas severe exploitation acts as a catastrophe.

It should be noted that categories are not always strictly independent. For example, if a population has high habitat specificity, but this limitation is a result of small population size, conservation efforts should concentrate on the problem of small population size. The classification scheme I present here is a contingency table, and it is not necessary for the classification categories to be independent. The list of threats in Table 1 are only potential threats, and when categories are correlated, species might be vulnerable to only a subset of threats (i.e., some of the potential threats might be spuriously correlated with other threats). This potential lack of independence is important to conservation efforts to institute species protection or recovery plans. If two classification categories are not independent, the conservation effort must address the category that is actively limiting the population, rather than the correlated category.

Recently Arita et al. (1990) analyzed the problem of potential correlations among local abundance and geographic range for Neotropical mammals. They concluded that these traits were not correlated for mammals with the same diet and body size. If this result proves to be a general rule, then the species I analyze here should not show an independence problem for these categories because the birds are all small insectivores.

Ranking species by relative susceptibility to extinction

The criterion I use to answer my original question of "which species do we try to save first?" is "which species are most susceptible to extinction?" The method introduced here is to rank each of the lettered cells in Table 1 based on species' relative susceptibility to extinction. These rankings then act as priority values for species conservation. These ranks are based on my interpretation from the literature of how important each of Rabinowitz's (1981) categories is to a given species' survival.

I used the following rules for assessing risk of extinction. Species that are habitat generalists with broadly distributed, large populations are the least vulnerable to extinction, whereas habitat specialists occurring over a small geographic area with only small populations are the most vulnerable (Rabinowitz et al. 1986). Habitat specialists are at greater risk of extinction than generalists, species with narrow geographic distribution are at greater risk than those with broad distribution, and small populations are at a greater risk of extinction than are large populations. Following these criteria, species in cells D, F, and G are at greater risk of extinction than are species in cells B, C, and E (see Table 1). Assuming habitat specificity imposes greater risk to survival for birds than would a narrow geographic distribution or small population size. Rabinowitz et al. (1986) asserted that a narrow geographic distribution implies that all available habitat is being used by a species, whereas small populations over a broad distribution imply that unused habitat might be available. If this is the case, a narrow distribution (implying limited habitat availability) is a greater threat to survival than is small population size because colonization ability should be a relatively minor problem for birds as potentially mobile as migrants.

Based on these rules, I propose the following relationships for extinction probability of cells in Table 1:

Cell = H > D > G > F > C > B > E > A,
Rank = 1 , 2 , 3 , 4 , 5 , 6 , 7 , 8.

A rank of 1 is the highest risk of extinction. The ranks differ slightly from those suggested earlier (Reed 1990) and are open to criticism. In particular, the assertions of Rabinowitz et al. (1986) might not be correct, and there might be correlations among classification variables which might result in species within a cell being differentially vulnerable to the threats in Table 1. Small populations are threatened on both breeding and wintering grounds, although genetic stochasticity is not a threat in the latter. Because demographic stochasticity might be the greatest threat to small populations (Lande 1988), I believe this ranking order is valid for both breeding and wintering grounds. The specific conservation efforts used to preserve species within a given cell will vary with taxonomic group because of differential vulnerability to specific threats to survival, and conservation efforts will change if the immediacy of a given threat changes (i.e., the severity of habitat destruction increases, or a new pollutant is introduced to a population).

These rankings can serve as a priority system for species conservation efforts: the greater the risk of extinction, the higher the conservation priority. Species for which so little data are available that they cannot be placed within this simple system represent important research priorities because not enough is known about them to formulate even basic conservation plans.

I applied Rabinowitz's classification scheme to 47 species of North American wood-warblers (Emberizidae:

Parulinae) and 10 species of migratory vireos (Vireonidae) (Table 2), and summarize the results (Tables 3 and 4). Most species in Table 2 can be classified as "common" (broad habitat specificity, wide geographic distribution, and presence of at least one large population) on both the breeding and wintering grounds (Tables 3 and 4). In their breeding range, 24 (42%) of the 57 species fall into a "rare" category (all cells except cell A), whereas 20 species (35%) are rare on the wintering grounds. However, not all of the "rare" categories are actually vulnerable to extinction (Rabinowitz et al. 1986). In the ranking system I present here, 10 species are in the four "most-vulnerable" cells (D, F, G, and H) on their breeding ground and seven species are placed in the most-vulnerable cells on their wintering grounds.

Discussion

I have shown that Rabinowitz's (1981) classification scheme can be used to rank conservation priorities for Neotropical migrant birds, and that this scheme fulfills the needs put forth in the introduction. This system requires the type of information typically gathered about a species, is biologically founded, and identifies threats to species survival.

Rappole et al. (1983) identified Neotropical migrant bird species they believed were most vulnerable to extinction. Of these, 23 species overlapped those I classified in Table 2 (denoted by #). The classification scheme of Rappole et al. contained four categories, and the 23 species we analyzed in common were placed into two categories: two species were predicted to become extinct in the near future, and 21 species were predicted to decline in the near future. Rappole et al. (1983) further asserted that all of these species were vulnerable on only their wintering grounds. My classification scheme predicts species vulnerability on both their breeding and wintering ranges, and indicates that more species are vulnerable on their breeding grounds, possibly because of nesting requirements. The 23 species Rappole et al. (1983) placed into two categories fall into seven categories using my system, and only five are in the four most-vulnerable cells (Black-capped Vireo, Bachman's Warbler, Lucy's Warbler, Golden-cheeked Warbler, Kirtland's Warbler). Of these five species, all are vulnerable on both their breeding and wintering grounds. Furthermore, my results indicate species possibly vulnerable to extinction on their wintering grounds but not noted by Rappole et al. (1983), such as the Gray Vireo and Colima Warbler (Table 2). The Hermit and Red-faced warblers are interesting because they were not identified as threatened on their wintering grounds by Rappole et al. (1983) or in this paper, but they are threatened on their breeding grounds (Table 2).

Some species select different habitats on breeding

TABLE 2. Data used for classification of species in the framework provided in Table 1

Species	Range	Habitat specificity	Geographic distribution	Any large populations	Cell[a]	Rank
White-eyed Vireo	BR	B	W	Yes[b]	A	8
Vireo griseus	WI	B	W	Yes	A	8
Bell's Vireo	BR	B	W	No[e]	E*	7
V. bellii	WI	B	W	Yes	A	8
Black-capped Vireo	BR	R	N	No[t]	H	1
V. atricapillus	WI#	R	N	No	H	1
Gray Vireo	BR	B	W	No[b]	E*	7
V. vicinior	WI	R	N	Yes	D	2
Solitary Vireo	BR	B	W	Yes[c]	A	8
V. solitarius	WI	B	W	Yes	A	8
Yellow-throated Vireo	BR	B	W	Yes[d]	A	8
V. flavifrons	WI#	B	W	Yes	A	8
Warbling Vireo	BR	B	W	Yes[d]	A	8
V. gilvus	WI	B	W	Yes	A	8
Philadelphia Vireo	BR	B	W	No[b]	E	7
V. philadelphicus	WI#	B	W	No	E	7
Red-eyed Vireo	BR	B	W	Yes[c]	A	8
V. olivaceus	WI	B	W	Yes	A	8
Black-whiskered Vireo	BR	B	N	No[b]	F*	4
V. altiloquus	WI	B	W	Yes	A	8
Bachman's Warbler	BR	R[r]	N	No[r]	H	1
Vermivora bachmanii	WI#	R	N	No	H	1
Blue-winged Warbler	BR	B[f]	W	No[b]	E*	7
V. pinus	WI#	B	W	Yes	A	8
Golden-winged Warbler	BR	B[f]	W	No[b]	E*	7
V. chrysoptera	WI#	B	W	Yes	A	8
Tennessee Warbler	BR	B[f]	W	Yes[h]	A	8
V. peregrina	WI	B	W	Yes	A	8
Orange-crowned Warbler	BR	B[f]	W	Yes[i]	A	8
V. celata	WI	B	W	Yes	A	8
Nashville Warbler	BR	B[f]	W	Yes[h]	A	8
V. ruficapilla	WI	B	W	Yes	A	8
Virginia's Warbler	BR	B[f]	N	No[b]	F*	4
V. virginiae	WI	B	N	Yes	B	6
Colima Warbler	BR	B[k]	N	No[j]	F	4
V. crissalis	WI	B	N	No	F	4
Lucy's Warbler	BR	R[f]	N	Yes[b]	D*	2
V. luciae	WI#	B	N	No	F	4
Northern Parula	BR	B[g]	W	Yes[f]	A	8
Parula americana	WI	B	W	Yes	A	8
Yellow Warbler	BR	B[f]	W	Yes[c]	A	8
Dendroica petechia	WI	B	W	Yes	A	8
Chestnut-sided Warbler	BR	B[f]	W	Yes[n]	A	8
D. pensylvanica	WI#	B	N	Yes[n]	B	6

TABLE 2—*Continued*

Species	Range	Habitat specificity	Geographic distribution	Any large populations	Cell[a]	Rank
Magnolia Warbler	BR	B[k]	W	Yes[l]	A	8
D. magnolia	WI	B	W	Yes	A	8
Cape May Warbler	BR	B[f]	W	Yes[b]	A*	8
D. tigrina	WI#	B	W	No	E	7
Black-throated Blue Warbler	BR	B[f]	W	Yes[c]	A	8
D. caerulescens	WI#	B	W	Yes	A	8
Yellow-rumped Warbler	BR	B[f]	W	Yes[c]	A	8
D. coronata	WI	B	W	Yes	A	8
Black-throated Gray Warbler	BR	B[f]	W	Yes[b]	A	8
D. nigrescens	WI	B	W	Yes	A	8
Townsend's Warbler	BR	R[k]	W	Yes[b]	C*	5
D. townsendi	WI	B	W	Yes	A	8
Hermit Warbler	BR	R[f]	N	No[j]	H*	1
D. occidentalis	WI	B	N	Yes	B	6
Black-throated Green Warbler	BR	R[q]	W	Yes[c]	C*	5
D. virens	WI#	B[q]	W	Yes	A	8
Golden-cheeked Warbler	BR	B[k]	N	No[j]	F	4
D. chrysoparia	WI#	B	N	No	F	4
Blackburnian Warbler	BR	R[m]	W	Yes[h]	C*	5
D. fusca	WI	B[m]	W	Yes	A	8
Yellow-throated Warbler	BR	B[f]	W	Yes[b]	A	8
D. dominica	WI	B	W	Yes	A	8
Pine Warbler	BR	R[f]	W	Yes[g]	C	5
D. pinus	WI	R	W	Yes	C	5
Kirtland's Warbler	BR	R[s]	N	No[s]	H	1
D. kirtlandii	WI#	R	N	No	H	1
Prairie Warbler	BR	B[o]	W	Yes[o]	A	8
D. discolor	WI	B[o]	W	Yes	A	8
Palm Warbler	BR	B[f]	W	Yes[b]	A	8
D. palmarum	WI	B	W	Yes	A	8
Bay-breasted Warbler	BR	B[f]	W	Yes[n]	A*	8
D. castanea	WI#	B[n]	N	Yes[n]	B	6
Blackpoll Warbler	BR	R[f]	W	Yes	C	5
D. striata	WI	R	W	Yes	C	5
Cerulean Warbler	BR	B[f]	W	No[b]	E*	7
D. cerulea	WI#	B	W	Yes	A	8
Black-and-white Warbler	BR	B[f]	W	Yes[c]	A	8
Mniotilta varia	WI	B	W	Yes	A	8
American Redstart	BR	B[p]	W	Yes[d]	A*	8
Setophaga ruticilla	WI	R[p]	W	Yes	C	5
Prothonotary Warbler	BR	B[c]	W	Yes[g]	A*	8
Protonotaria citrea	WI#	B	N	Yes	B	6
Worm-eating Warbler	BR	B[f]	W	No[b]	E*	7
Helmitheros vermivorus	WI#	B	W	Yes	A	8

TABLE 2—*Continued next page*

TABLE 2—*Continued*

Species	Range	Habitat specificity	Geographic distribution	Any large populations	Cell[a]	Rank
Swainson's Warbler	BR	B[f]	W	No[b]	E*	7
Limnothlypis swainsonii	WI#	B	N	Yes	B	6
Ovenbird	BR	B[f]	W	Yes[h]	A	8
Seiurus aurocapillus	WI#	B	W	Yes	A	8
Northern Waterthrush	BR	B[f]	W	Yes[h]	A	8
S. noveboracensis	WI	B	W	Yes	A	8
Louisiana Waterthrush	BR	B[f]	W	Yes[g]	A	8
S. motacilla	WI#	B	W	Yes	A	8
Kentucky Warbler	BR	B[f]	W	Yes[b]	A	8
Oporonis formosus	WI#	B	W	Yes	A	8
Connecticut Warbler	BR	B[f]	W	No[b]	E	7
O. agilis	WI#	B	W	No	E	7
Mourning Warbler	BR	B[k]	W	Yes[h]	A	8
O. philadelphia	WI	B	W	Yes	A	8
Common Yellowthroat	BR	B[f]	W	Yes[d]	A	8
Geothlypis trichas	WI	B	W	Yes	A	8
Hooded Warbler	BR	B[f]	W	Yes[b]	A	8
Wilsonia citrina	WI#	B	W	Yes	A	8
Wilson's Warbler	BR	B[f]	W	Yes[h]	A	8
W. pusilla	WI	B	W	Yes	A	8
Canada Warbler	BR	B[f]	W	Yes[h]	A	8
W. canadensis	WI	B	W	Yes	A	8
Red-faced Warbler	BR	B[k]	N	No[b]	F*	4
Cardillina rubrifrons	WI	B	W	Yes	A	8
Yellow-breasted Chat	BR	B[f]	W	Yes[d]	A*	8
Icteria virens	WI	R	W	Yes	C	5

SOURCES: Except where otherwise noted, vireo distribution data are from Barlow (1980), and warbler distribution data and winter habitat come from Rappole et al. (1983). Winter population size data are inferred from Rappole et al. (1983).

NOTE: Range: BR = breeding, WI = winter. Habitat specificity: B=broad, R=restricted. Geographic distribution: W=wide, N=narrow. The rank is the relative vulnerability rank, with 1 denoting the greatest vulnerability to extinction and 8 the least vulnerability; see text for an explanation. Some of the assignments are tentative. * in the cell column designates a difference in cell classification between breeding and wintering ground, and # in the range column marks species that were identified as threatened on the wintering grounds by Rappole et al. (1983).

a. Cell letter from Table 1.
b. Robbins et al. (1986).
c. Laughlin and Kibbe (1985).
d. Johnsgard (1979).
e. Rappole and Blacklock (1985)
f. Bent (1953).
g. Wood and Schnell (1984).
h. James et al. (1976).
i. Kessell and Gibson (1978).
j. Inferred by their absence from Robbins et al. (1986).

k. A.O.U. (1983).
l. Tufts (1961).
m. Chipley (1980).
n. Greenberg (1984).
o. Nolan (1978).
p. Bennett (1980).
q. Rabenold (1980).
r. Hamel (1986).
s. Mayfield (1977b).
t. Grzybowsky et al. (1986).

TABLE 3. Number of species from Table 2 falling into each classification category based on their breeding distributions and habits

| Population size | Breeding habitat specificity | | | |
| | Broad | | • Restricted | |
	Wide[a]	Narrow[a]	Wide[a]	Narrow[a]
Somewhere large	34	0	5	1
Everywhere small	9	5	0	4

a. Breeding geographic distribution.

TABLE 4. Number of species from Table 2 falling into each classification category based on their wintering distributions and habits

| Population size | Wintering habitat specificity | | | |
| | Broad | | Restricted | |
	Wide[a]	Narrow[a]	Wide[a]	Narrow[a]
Somewhere large	38	6	4	1
Everywhere small	3	3	0	3

a. Wintering geographic distribution.

and wintering grounds and population trends vary depending on range and habitat selection (Robbins et al. 1989). These species switched between forest and scrub habitat, and loss of forested habitat was proposed to affect population trends. Some species change cell designation, based on Table 1, between their breeding and wintering grounds, and, therefore, change conservation priority rank, between breeding and wintering grounds. This can occur through changes in habitat specificity, as noted by Robbins et al. (1989), or by changing geographic range or population density. Two of the four species noted by Robbins et al. (1989) as habitat switchers also changed vulnerability status from breeding to wintering grounds (Table 2) (Robbins et al. noted other other habitat switchers; these are not included in the species evaluated in this paper). Changes in rank (Table 2) between breeding and wintering grounds provide important information for species conservation. For example, for a species that has a vulnerability rank of 2 (= high conservation priority) on its wintering grounds and a rank of 7 (= low conservation priority) on its breeding grounds (e.g., Gray Vireo), conservation efforts should be concentrated on the wintering grounds. A species that switches vulnerability rank from 7 to 8 (the two lowest priorities) between breeding and wintering

grounds (e.g., Cape May Warbler) is not of immediate conservation concern.

Twenty-one species changed vulnerability status (rank) from breeding to wintering ranges (noted in Table 2 by an *). Of these, 14 are more susceptible to extinction on their breeding grounds. This does not contradict the finding of Robbins et al. (1989) that habitat loss on the wintering range has a greater effect on forest species than does habitat loss on the breeding ground. Habitat loss is only one of many threats to species survival (Table 1), and from my analysis apparently other threats (e.g., insularization, genetic and demographic stochasticity) might be more serious on the breeding grounds. These changes might be a result of breeding requirements, resulting in habitat specialization and species distribution patterns along resource gradients.

This classification scheme can also be used to address ecological questions. For example, an explanation for the changes in vulnerability status between the wintering and breeding ranges might indicate a change in competition pressure. Considerable interest has been generated on the importance of competition in structuring bird communities and affecting geographic ranges of Neotropical migrant birds on the wintering grounds (references in Greenberg 1986). Greenberg (1986) has pointed out that interspecific competition should concentrate individuals of a given species, whereas intraspecific competition should spread out members of a species. These competitive interactions could be manifested in all three species characteristics used in Table 1. The pattern observed for the 21 species that changed vulnerability status between wintering and breeding grounds in this study is that 13 species show a change consistent with increased interspecific competition on their wintering grounds, five species are consistent with an increase in intraspecific competition, whereas three species (Black-whiskered Vireo, Hermit Warbler, and Red-faced Warbler) showed changes consistent with both hypotheses. A problem with using this scheme for identifying ecological shifts is that the categories in Table 1 represent gross changes in species characteristics, so the effect causing the shift would have to be very strong. Therefore, I suggest that this scheme be used only to identify coarse patterns that could be studied in detail. Any explanation for vulnerability status changes needs to be tested for each species. However, this classification scheme indicates the subset of species that show the greatest potential for studying these processes.

It is not my intent to suggest that species with intermediate ranks are not in need of conservation. This scheme identifies threats in each cell, so that if conservation efforts are desired, the cell classification identifies which threats might be addressed. In addition, the classification scheme used assesses species susceptibility to extinction as a rangewide phenomenon. Classifying a species into a low-risk cell does not mean that any given local population has a low risk of extinction. This analytic procedure can be duplicated for species at the local level, although some criteria (e.g., what constitutes a broad geographic range) must be changed to fit different objectives.

Of the vulnerability cells presented in Table 1, the cells of least interest are H and A, which represent the most critically threatened species, and the most common species, respectively. This is not the surprise it first seems. A species classified as a top conservation priority will probably be well known to be endangered, such as Bachman's or Kirtland's warblers. Conversely, a species found in high numbers across a broad range, such as the Red-eyed Vireo, is not an immediate conservation concern. Species placed in the intermediate rarity cells, on the other hand, will be perceived as common or uncommon depending on what part of their ranges are being investigated. Some species will be locally abundant, but occur in very few populations, whereas others will be found in low numbers across a broad range (Rabinowitz et al. 1986). It is for these species that this classification scheme is most useful to conservation biologists. This ranking scheme allows discrimination among these species regarding relative susceptibility to extinction, and identifies potential threats to species survival and how they differ among species.

Although this method for setting conservation priorities is based on species classification, I do not advocate species-centered conservation efforts. As Conner (1988) pointed out, species exist as an integrated part of a community, or ecosystem. Any conservation effort made to protect a single species should be made to protect it in the context of its natural ecosystem. Species-specific efforts are justified only when a species is critically endangered; even then, species should be preserved in the context of a community (essays in Phillips and Nash 1981). For example, Kirtland's Warbler is in the most-threatened category of the classification scheme presented here (Table 2), but conservation efforts in the wild have concentrated on maintaining its ecosystem (Mayfield 1978). In addition, managing a single species without regard to its role in a community can lead to community breakdown and species loss (Conner 1988).

Many of the species in Table 2 are in similar ecological guilds (Verner 1984) (e.g., forest interior species, forest edge species), and the best method for protecting one species often is to establish measures that protect the entire guild, or suite of species, by protecting the entire community of which they are a part (Verner 1984, Conner 1988). Ecosystem conservation has been espoused before (e.g., Graul and Miller 1984, Soulé 1985), and the conservation priority system presented here can be used in concert with this ideal. Once species are ranked by conservation priority, communities that have a suite of threatened species, or species with intermediate priority rankings, should have management priority. A benefit of a community-based conservation approach is efficiency in use of time and money. Efforts to protect communities act to protect all species of concern in that community, not just a single species.

Conclusions

This ranking scheme is biologically based (i.e., is based on characteristics of species abundance and distribution) and can be used to organize research and prioritize species conservation efforts. It can also be integrated with other ranking systems, such as economic considerations involved in decision making processes. This classification scheme provides a framework for classifying potential threats to species survival and directing species conservation efforts. My results stress that Neotropical migrant birds are vulnerable both on their breeding and wintering ranges. Although most previous research has focused on the problem of habitat loss, it becomes apparent that possible threats need to be carefully examined when formulating species conservation plans. This paper represents the first attempt to unify breeding and wintering problems into a framework that can allow organized, systematic research of the many threats to Neotropical migrant bird survival.

Acknowledgments

I thank B. Blackwell, T. Cook, C. Copeyon, J. Hagan, D. Johnston, M. LaBranche, T.H. Martin, L. McKean, R. O'Connor, J. Walters, and an anonymous reviewer for commenting on this manuscript, J. Hagan for discussions during its development, and K. Reed for typing and encouragement. R. O'Connor provided a particularly thorough and helpful review of this manuscript. My research was supported by NSF grant BSR-8717683 to J.R. Walters and P.D. Doerr.

Literature cited

Aldrich, J.W., and C.S. Robbins. 1970. Changing abundance of migratory birds in North America. Pages 17–26 in *The Avifauna of Northern Latin America*, H.K. Buechner and J.H. Buechner, eds. Smithsonian Contrib. Zool. 26.

Ambuel, B., and S.A. Temple. 1983. Area-dependent changes in the bird communities and vegetation of southern Wisconsin forests. *Ecology* 64:1057–1068.

American Ornithologists' Union. 1983. *Check-list of North American Birds.* 6th ed. Washington: American Ornithologists' Union.

Arita, H.T., J.G. Robinson, and K.H. Redford. 1990. Rarity in

Neotropical forest mammals and its ecological correlates. *Conserv. Biol.* 4:181–192.

Askins, R.A., and M.J. Philbrick. 1987. Effect of changes in regional forest abundance on the decline and recovery of a forest bird community. *Wilson Bull.* 99:7–21.

Barlow, J. 1980. Patterns of ecological interactions among migrant and resident vireos on the wintering grounds. Pages 79–108 in *Migrant Birds in the Neotropics: Ecology, Behavior, Distribution and Conservation*, A. Keast and E.S. Morton, eds. Washington: Smithsonian Institution Press.

Bennett, S.E. 1980. Interspecific competition and the niche of the American Redstart (*Setophaga ruticilla*) in wintering and breeding communities. Pages 319–336 in *Migrant Birds in the Neotropics: Ecology, Behavior, Distribution and Conservation*, A. Keast and E.S. Morton, eds. Washington: Smithsonian Institution Press.

Bent, A.C. 1953. *Life Histories of North American Wood Warblers.* U.S. Natl. Mus. Bull. 203.

Berry, R.J. 1971. Conservation aspects of the genetical constitution of populations. Pages 177–206 in *The Scientific Management of Animal and Plant Communities for Conservation*, E.D. Duffey and A.S. Watt, eds. Oxford, England: Blackwell.

Brittingham, M.C., and S.A. Temple. 1983. Have cowbirds caused forest songbirds to decline? *BioScience* 33:31–35.

Chipley, R.M. 1980. Nonbreeding ecology of the Blackburnian Warbler. Pages 309–318 in *Migrant Birds in the Neotropics: Ecology, Behavior, Distribution and Conservation*, A. Keast and E.S. Morton, eds. Washington: Smithsonian Institution Press.

Conner, R.N. 1988. Wildlife populations: Minimally viable or ecologically functional? *Wildl. Soc. Bull.* 16:80–84.

Diamond, J.M. 1984. "Normal" extinctions in isolated populations. Pages 191–246 in *Extinctions*, M.H. Nitecki, ed. Chicago: University of Chicago Press.

Dobinson, H.M., and A.J. Richards. 1964. The effects of the severe winter of 1962/63 on birds in Britain. *Brit. Birds* 57:373–434.

Dobson, A.P., and R.M. May. 1986. Disease and conservation. Pages 345–365 in *Conservation Biology: The Science of Scarcity and Diversity*, M.E. Soulé, ed. Sunderland, Mass.: Sinauer Associates Inc.

Frankel, O.H., and M.E. Soulé. 1981. *Conservation and Evolution.* Cambridge: Cambridge University Press.

Fretwell, S.D., and H.L. Lucas, Jr. 1969. On territorial behavior and other factors influencing habitat distribution in birds. I. Theoretical development. *Acta Biotheor.* 19:16–36.

Gessaman, J.A., and G.L. Worthen. 1982. *The Effect of Weather on Avian Mortality.* Logan: Utah State University.

Gilpen, M.E., and M.E. Soulé. 1986. Minimum viable populations: Processes of species extinction. Pages 19–34 in *Conservation Biology: The Science of Scarcity and Diversity*, M.E. Soulé, ed. Sunderland, Mass.: Sinauer Associates Inc.

Greenberg, R. 1984. The winter exploitation systems of Bay-breasted and Chestnut-sided Warblers in Panama. *Univ. California Publ. Zool.* 116:1–107.

———. 1986. Competition in migrant birds in the nonbreeding season. *Current Ornithol.* 3:281–307.

Graul, W.D., and G.C. Miller. 1984. Strengthing ecosystem management approaches. *Wildl. Soc. Bull.* 12:282–289.

Grzybowsky, J.A., R.B. Clapp, and J.T. Marshall, Jr. 1986. His-

tory and current population status of the Black-capped Vireo in Oklahoma. *Am. Birds* 40:1151–1161.

Hamel, P.B. 1986. *Bachman's Warbler: A Species in Peril.* Washington: Smithsonian Institution Press.

Holmes, R.T., and T.W. Sherry. 1988. Assessing population trends of New Hampshire forest birds: Local vs. regional patterns. *Auk* 105:756–768.

Hutto, R.L. 1988. Is tropical deforestation responsible for the reported declines in neotropical migrant populations? *Am. Birds* 42:375–379.

———. 1989. The effect of habitat alteration on migratory land birds in a west Mexican tropical deciduous forest: A conservation perspective. *Conserv. Biol.* 3:138–148.

James, R.D., P.L. McLaren, and J.C. Barlow. 1976. *Annotated Checklist of the Birds of Ontario.* Toronto: Bryant Press.

Johnsgard, P.A. 1979. *Birds of the Great Plains: Breeding Species and Their Distribution.* Lincoln: University of Nebraska Press.

Keast, A., and E.S. Morton, eds. 1980. *Migrant Birds in the Neotropics: Ecology, Behavior, Distribution, and Conservation.* Washington: Smithsonian Institution Press.

Kessel, B., and D.D. Gibson. 1978. *Status and Distribution of Alaska Birds.* Studies in Avian Biology No. 1.

Kotrschal, K., and D.A. Thomson. 1986. Feeding patterns in eastern tropical Pacific blennioid fishes (Teleostei: Tripterygiidae, Labrisomidae, Chaenopsidae, Blenniidae). *Oecologia* 70:367–378.

LaCava, J., and J. Hughes. 1984. Determining minimum viable population levels. *Wildl. Soc. Bull.* 12:370–376.

Lande, R. 1988. Genetics and demography in biological conservation. *Science* 241:1455–1460.

Laughlin, S.B., and D.P. Kibbe. 1985. *The Atlas of Breeding Birds of Vermont.* Hanover, N.H.: University Press of New England.

MacLean, G.L., R.M. Gous, and T. Bosman. 1973. Effects of drought on the White Stork in Natal, South Africa. *Vogelwarte* 27:134–136.

Magurran, A.E. 1988. *Ecological Diversity and its Measure.* Princeton: Princeton University Press.

May, R.M. 1973. *Stability and Complexity in Model Ecosystems.* Princeton: Princeton University Press.

Mayfield, H.F. 1977. Brown-headed Cowbird: Agent of extermination? *Am. Birds* 31:107–113.

———. 1978. Brood parasitism: Reducing interactions between Kirtland's Warblers and Brown-headed Cowbirds. Pages 85–91 in *Endangered Birds: Management Techniques for Preserving Threatened Species*, S.A. Temple, ed. Madison: University of Wisconsin Press.

Mayr, E. 1966. *Animal Species and Evolution.* Cambridge, Mass.: Belknap Press.

Millsap, B.A., F.A. Gore, D.E. Runde, and S.I. Cerulean. 1990. *Setting priorities for the conservation of fish and wildlife species in Florida.* Wildl. Monogr. 111.

Morton, E.S., and R. Greenberg. 1989. The outlook for migratory songbirds: "Future shock" for birders. *Am. Birds* 43:178–183.

Murton, R.K., and N.J. Westwood. 1974. Some effects of agricultural change on the English avifauna. *Brit. Birds* 67:41–69.

Nolan, V., Jr. 1978. *The Ecology and Behavior of the Prairie Warbler* Dendroica discolor. Ornithol. Monogr. 26.

O'Connor, R.J. 1985. Behavioural regulation of bird populations: A review of habitat use in relation to migration and residency. Pages 105–142 in *Behavioural Ecology: Ecological Consequences of Adaptive Behavior,* R.M. Sibly and R.H. Smith, eds. Oxford: Blackwell Scientific Publications.

O'Connor, R.J., and R.J. Fuller. 1985. Bird population responses to habitat. Pages 197–212 in *Bird Census and Atlas Studies.* K. Taylor, R.J. Fuller, and P.C. Lack, eds. Tring, England: British Trust for Ornithology.

Office of Migratory Bird Management. 1990. *Conservation of Avian Diversity in North America.* Washington: U.S. Fish and Wildl. Serv.

Phillips, D., and H. Nash. 1981. *Captive or Forever Free? The Condor* Question. San Francisco: Friends of the Earth.

Pimm, S.L., H.L. Jones, and J. Diamond. 1988. On the risk of extinction. *Am. Nat.* 132:757–785.

Rabenold, K.N. 1980. The Black-throated Green Warbler in Panama: Geographic and seasonal comparisons of foraging. Pages 297–308 in *Migrant Birds in the Neotropics: Ecology, Behavior, Distribution and Conservation,* A. Keast and E.S. Morton, eds. Washington: Smithsonian Institution Press.

Rabinowitz, D. 1981. Seven forms of rarity. Pages 205–217 in *The Biological Aspects of Rare Plant Conservation,* H. Synge, ed. New York: Wiley.

Rabinowitz, D., S. Cairns, and T. Dillon. 1986. Seven forms of rarity and their frequency in the flora of the British Isles. Pages 182–204 in *Conservation Biology: The Science of Scarcity and Diversity,* M.E. Soulé, ed., Sunderland, Mass.: Sinauer Associates Inc.

Rappole, J.H., and G.W. Blacklock. 1985. *Birds of the Texas Coastal Bank: Abundance and Distribution.* College Station: Texas A & M University Press.

Rappole, J.H., and E.S. Morton. 1985. Effects of habitat alteration on a tropical avian forest community. Pages 1013–1021 in *Neotropical Ornithology,* P.A. Buckley, E.S. Morton, R.S. Ridgely, and F.G. Buckley, eds. Ornithol. Monogr. 36.

Rappole, J.H., E.S. Morton, T.E. Lovejoy, III, and J.L. Ruos. 1983. *Nearctic Avian Migrants in the Neotropics.* Washington: U.S. Fish and Wildlife Service.

Reed, J.M. 1990. The dynamics of Red-cockaded Woodpecker rarity and conservation. Pages 37–56 in *Conservation and Management of Woodpecker Populations,* A. Carlsson and G. Aulén, eds. Uppsala: Swedish University of Agricultural Sciences, Report 7.

Reed, J.M, P.D. Doerr, and J.R. Walters. 1986. Determining minimum population sizes for birds and mammals. *Wildl. Soc. Bull.* 14:255–261.

———. 1988. Minimum viable population size of the Red-cockaded Woodpecker. *J. Wildl. Manage.* 52:385–391.

Robbins, C.S. 1979. Effect of forest fragmentation on bird populations. Pages 198–212 in *Management of North Central and Northeastern Forests for Nongame Birds; Workshop Proceedings,* R.M. DeGraaf and K.E. Evans, eds. St. Paul, Minn.: USDA Forest Service Gen. Tech. Rept. NC-51.

———. 1980. Effect of forest fragmentation on breeding bird populations in the piedmont of the mid-Atlantic region. *Atlantic Nat.* 33:31–36.

Robbins, C.S., D. Bystrak, and P.H. Geissler. 1986. *The Breeding Bird Survey: Its First Fifteen Years, 1965–1979.* U.S. Fish and Wildlife Serv. Resource Pub. 157.

Robbins, C.S., J.R. Sauer, R.S. Greenberg, and S. Droege. 1989. Population declines in North American birds that migrate to the neotropics. *Proc. Natl. Acad. Sci.* 86:7658–7662.

Shaffer, M.L. 1981. Minimum population sizes for species conservation. *BioScience* 31:131–134.

———. 1987. Minimum viable populations: Coping with uncertainty. Pages 69–86 in *Viable Populations for Conservation.* M.E. Soulé, ed. Cambridge: Cambridge University Press.

Soulé, M.E. 1980. Thresholds for survival; maintaining fitness and evolutionary potential. Pages 151–170 in *Conservation Biology: An Evolutionary-Ecological Perspective,* M.E. Soulé and B.A. Wilcox, eds. Sunderland, Mass.: Sinauer.

———. 1985. What is conservation biology? *BioScience* 35:727–734.

Temple, S.A. 1986. The problems of avian extinctions. *Current Ornithol.* 3:453–485.

Thomas, C.D., and H.C. Mallorie 1985. Rarity, species richness and conservation: Butterflies of the Atlas Mountains in Morocco. *Biol. Conserv.* 33:95–117.

Tufts, R.W. 1961. *The Birds of Nova Scotia.* Halifax, Nova Scotia: Rolph-Clark-Stone, Maritimes, Ltd.

Verner, J. 1984. The guild concept applied to management of bird populations. *Environ. Manage.* 8:1–14.

Wilcove, D.S. 1985. Nest predation in forest tracts and the decline of migratory songbirds. *Ecology* 66:1211–1214.

Wilcove, D.S., and J.W. Terborgh. 1984. Patterns of population decline in birds. *Am. Birds* 38:10–13.

Wilcove, D.S., C.H. McLellan, and A.P. Dobson. 1986. Habitat fragmentation in the temperate zone. Pages 237–256 in *Conservation Biology: The Science of Scarcity and Diversity,* M.E. Soulé, ed., Sunderland, Mass.: Sinauer Associates Inc.

Wood, D.S., and G.D. Schnell. 1984. *Distributions of Oklahoma Birds.* Norman: University of Oklahoma Press.

Wright, S. 1946. Isolation by distance under diverse systems of mating. *Genetics* 31:39–59.

ROBERT E. RICKLEFS
Department of Biology
University of Pennsylvania
Philadelphia, Pennsylvania 19104-6018

The megapopulation: A model of demographic coupling between migrant and resident landbird populations

Abstract. A megapopulation is a system of interacting populations that exhibit integrated demographic characteristics arising from mutual adjustments of geographic distribution, habitat selection, and within-habitat resource partitioning. Neotropical migrants potentially link some temperate and tropical resident species of birds into a single megapopulation. This paper presents a model of interactions between migrant and resident populations and tests some of its demographic predictions. The model incorporates the following features: density-dependent limitation of fecundity during the most productive season (summer), density-dependent limitation of survival during the least productive season (winter), and a fraction (m) of birds that migrate from the less seasonal of two regions, where they winter, to the more seasonal region, where they breed. With complete density-dependent coupling, the model predicts that the life tables (fecundity and mortality) of populations in both of the resident communities and the migrant community would be identical when the migrant fraction had achieved a stably regulated equilibrium value ($\hat{m}$). Different life tables reported in the literature for tropical, temperate, and migrant species suggest that their populations are not fully coupled, if at all. The predicted ecological isolation, which has been described in field studies, finds additional support in a discriminant analysis of morphological characters of the three types of species.

Sinopsis. Una megapoblación es un sistema de poblaciones interactuantes que exhiben características demográficas integradas como resultado de los ajustes mutuos de distribución geográfica, selección de habitat y repartición de recursos dentro del habitat. Las aves migratorias neotropicales potencialmente encadenan algunas especies de aves residentes del neotrópico y la zona templada en una sola megapoblación. Este artículo presenta un modelo de interacciones entre poblaciones migratorias y residentes y examina algunas de sus predicciones demográficas. El modelo incorpora las siguientes características: limitación de la fecundidad dependiente de la densidad durante la estación mas productiva (verano), limitación de la supervivencia dependiente de la densidad durante la estación menos productiva (invierno) y una fracción (m) de aves que migran desde la zona menos estacional, donde invernan, hacia la región mas estacional en donde anidan. Con un apareamiento completamente dependiente de la densidad, el modelo predice que las tablas de vida (fecundidad y mortalidad) de las poblaciones tanto en las comunidades residentes como en la comunidad migratoria serían idénticas cuando la fracción migratoria haya alcanzado un valor de equilibrio regulado estable ($\hat{m}$). Las diferentes tablas de vida reportadas en la literatura para especies templadas, tropicales y migratorias sugieren que sus poblaciones no estan completamente apareadas, si es que lo están. El aislamiento ecológico predicho, que ha sido descrito en estudios de campo, encuentra apoyo adicional en un análisis discriminante de características morfológicas de los tres tipos de especies.

Each year, millions of songbirds migrate between wintering grounds in the tropics and breeding grounds in the temperate zone. Populations of these migrants might be limited by factors affecting them in both regions (Fretwell 1972, Keast 1980a, Morse 1980, Alerstam and Högstedt 1982, Holling 1988). In the tropics, they are subject to various mortality factors that determine the number of adults returning to the breeding grounds each spring. Habitat destruction might in part have caused the recent decline in populations of migrant breeding birds in eastern North America (Morse 1980, Lovejoy 1983, Hall 1984, Wilcove and Terborgh 1984, Holmes and Sherry 1988, Robbins et al. 1989). On the breeding grounds, many ecological factors influence the productivity of migrant populations and thus determine the number of individuals leaving each year for their southerly wintering quarters.

On both their wintering and breeding grounds, migrants interact behaviorally and ecologically with other species of permanent resident birds. When these interactions involve competition for limited resources, migrants and residents might influence each others' population processes and play a role in regulating the sizes of populations. In some temperate areas, migrants comprise a large fraction of the breeding avifauna (MacArthur 1959, Herrera 1978a, Morse 1980). In some tropical areas, they also constitute a majority of the wintering populations (Chipley 1976, Karr 1976, Terborgh 1980, Gochfeld 1985). Hence the potential for major impacts is present. Ricklefs (1980) suggested that migrants depressed population sizes of resident birds in the Greater Antilles and East Indies. Competitive release following the annual departure of migrants allowed residents to rear larger broods than do similar species in areas of the tropics with fewer migrants. Most

theories concerning the evolution of migration systems have focussed on ecological interactions, particularly competition for food within and between migrant and resident populations (Cox 1968, 1985; Alerstam and Högstedt 1980, 1982; Fretwell 1980; Keast 1980b; Gauthereaux 1982; O'Connor 1985; Lundberg and Alerstam 1986).

Interactions between migrants and residents might act to couple the populations of resident species in temperate and tropical regions. For example, if migrant populations were limited by access to resources during the winter owing to competition from resident species in the tropics, their impact on resident species in temperate regions would be diminished and, at least, the breeding season productivity of resident species would increase. This coupling could link population dynamics and influence demographic and evolutionary adjustments of populations to one another. Thus, the geographical distribution, habitat occupancy, and niche relations within habitats are molded through interactions of species within a region of sufficient size to encompass these processes. Each of the populations participating in these interactions might be considered a component of a larger megapopulation, which provides the proper context for interpreting its geographic and ecological position. The occurrence of widespread migration involving substantial portions of local faunas greatly increases the geographical boundaries of the megapopulation. In this paper, I explore some consequences of demographic coupling of migrant and resident populations in the hope of gaining insight into the processes that limit their populations and to elucidate the concept of the megapopulation.

A model of demographic coupling

I define two regions, X and Y. Each has resident species whose populations both breed and winter within the region. In addition, populations of migrant species winter in the less seasonal region (i.e., tropical zone) and breed in the more seasonal region (i.e., temperate zone), migrating between the two regions each year.

Population size is determined by resource level in each region during each season in a density-dependent fashion. Thus, adult survival is determined by resource level during the winter period relative to the number of birds present at the beginning of the season. Fecundity is determined by the level of resources during the summer period relative to the number of birds present at the beginning of that season (Fig. 1). These assumptions seem reasonable because, in general, populations of birds track resource abundance rather closely; habitat productivity and bird populations vary seasonally less in the humid tropics than in the seasonally dry tropics, subtropics, and temperate regions (see, for exam-

More seasonal environment (X)

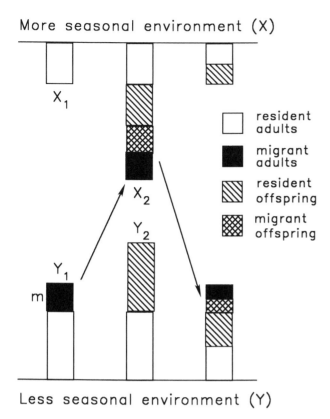

resident adults

migrant adults

resident offspring

migrant offspring

Less seasonal environment (Y)

FIGURE 1. Graphic representation of a model of demographic coupling between resident and migrant populations. X_1 and Y_1 represent the number of individuals that can be supported by resources in the more seasonal region (X) and the less seasonal region (Y), respectively. X_2 and Y_2 represent the capacity of breeding season resources to support individuals. A fraction m of wintering birds in the less seasonal environment migrates to the more seasonal environment to breed. Breeding productivity and adult survival are based on strict density dependence of population processes on both the wintering and breeding grounds.

ple, Morel and Bourlière 1962; Holmes and Sturges 1973, 1975; Nix 1974; Weiner and Glowacinski 1975; Dickson 1978; Willis 1980; Bell 1982; Lack 1987). Likewise, brood size is directly related to the ratio of primary productivity to density of breeding birds (Ricklefs 1980).

I assume that migrant birds compete on an equal basis with ecologically similar residents in both regions when they are present. That is, nothing intrinsic to being a migrant reduces its competitive ability on either the wintering or breeding grounds, even though migration might delay the onset of breeding relative to residents (Murphy 1989). In the model, the number of migrants is allowed to increase or decrease according to their survival and fecundity, until the number comes into equilibrium. The model is indifferent to whether

changes in the number of migrants involve changes in the number of species that migrate or changes in the population sizes of migrant species. The essential point is that species are allowed to achieve an ideal free distribution.

DEFINITIONS

Resource levels in region X are X_1 during winter and X_2 during summer ($X_2 > X_1$). For region Y, these levels are Y_1 and Y_2 ($Y_2 > Y_1$). Resource levels are expressed in terms of number of individuals that can be supported.

Adult populations are designated by the letter A. Thus, A_x is the number of adults in region X. At the end of winter, $A_x = X_1$. Other populations are A_y (resident adults in region Y) and A_m (migrant adults in region Y). Density-dependent adult mortality occurs only during the nonbreeding season.

The number of independent offspring produced during the breeding season is designated by F. Thus, F_x represents the number of independent young having been produced by the adults A_x at the end of the breeding season.

The fraction of birds wintering in region Y that migrates to region X to breed is designated m; the number of these migrants is A_m. Thus, at the end of winter in region Y, $A_y + A_m = Y_1$, and $A_m = mY_1$.

These relationships are illustrated in Figure 1.

THE MODEL

(1) The simplest case is no migration; that is, each of the regions is treated independently. In this case, in region X, the adult population at the end of the winter, determined by winter resources, is $A_x = X_1$. At the end of the summer, assuming no adult mortality during the breeding season, $A_x + F_x = X_2$, and, therefore, $F_x = X_2 - X_1$.

I define B as per capita fecundity, S_0 as prereproductive survival (of independent offspring from the end of the breeding season), and S as adult survival.

To simplify the model, we further assume that adult and prereproductive survival are identical. Now,

$$S_0 = S = A_x/(A_x + F_x)$$
$$= X_1/X_2, \text{ and}$$

$$B = (X_2 - A_x)/A_x$$
$$= (X_2 - X_1)/X_1.$$

The geometric growth rate of the population $\lambda = S_0 B + S$. Thus,

$$\lambda = \frac{X_1}{X_2}\frac{(X_2 - X_1)}{X_1} + \frac{X_1}{X_2} = 1.$$

In this model, reproduction and adult survival are strictly determined by resource levels and the population remains constant from year to year. Fecundity is directly related to the seasonality of the environment (the excess of X_2 over X_1).

(2) The second case is with migration between region Y and region X, with X being the more seasonal region, that is, $X_2/X_1 > Y_2/Y_1$. In region X, the total number of young produced is

$$F_m + F_x = X_2 - A_x - A_m$$
$$= X_2 - X_1 - mY_1.$$

Assuming that migrants and residents are equally productive,

$$B_m = B_x = \frac{(X_2 - X_1 - mY_1)}{X_1 + mY_1}.$$

We assume now that there is no migration mortality and that survival rates (S) of adults and immatures, and of migrants and residents of region Y, are identical. Survival rates of all groups are thus equal to $(A_y + A_m)$, the number of adults surviving the winter, divided by $(A_y + F_y + A_m + F_m)$, the number of adults and immatures at the beginning of winter in region Y. This can be expressed as

$$S = \frac{Y_1}{\left[Y_2 + X_2 \left(\frac{mY_1}{mY_1 + X_1} \right) \right]}$$
$$= \frac{Y_1 (mY_1 + X_1)}{(mY_1 Y_2 + X_1 Y_2 + mY_1 X_2)}.$$

Given this life table, the geometric rate of increase of migrants is

$$\lambda_m = \frac{Y_1 X_2}{(mY_1 Y_2 + X_1 Y_2 + mY_1 X_2)}.$$

(3) In the preceding case, the migration fraction will be stably regulated at an equilibrium value ($\hat{m}$). Note that as m approaches zero, λ_m approaches $Y_1 X_2/X_1 Y_2$, which exceeds one (X is the more seasonal region); as m approaches one, λ_m approaches $Y_1 X_2/[Y_1 X_2 + Y_2(X_1 + Y_1)]$, which is always less than one. Thus, an equilibrium value of λ occurs at intermediate m. Further note that $d\lambda_m/dm < 0$, indicating that m will be stably regulated at $\lambda_m = 1$.

From the equation for λ in the migration model above, $\lambda_m = 1$ when $mY_1 Y_2 + X_1 Y_2 + mY_1 X_2 = Y_1 X_2$, or

$$\hat{m} = \frac{Y_1 X_2 - X_1 Y_2}{Y_1 (X_2 + Y_2)}.$$

Note that $\hat{m} > 0$ when $Y_1/Y_2 > X_1/X_2$, hence when region X is the more seasonal. Also, $\hat{m}$ is always less than $X_2/(X_2 + Y_2)$, hence $\hat{m} < 1$.

(4) The equilibrium ratio of migrants in the north during the breeding season can be expressed as

$$\hat{m}_x = \frac{Y_1 X_2 - X_1 Y_2}{X_2 (X_1 + Y_1)}.$$

Thus, if $X_1 = 0$, the ratio is 1. If $X_2 = Y_2$, then the ratio is $(Y_1 - X_1)/(Y_1 + X_1)$. That is, if breeding season productivity in the two regions is identical, the migration fraction depends on the difference in winter productivity between the two regions.

(5) When the migration fraction has achieved its equilibrium value, the following life table values can be calculated for each of the populations. For migrants, $B_m = X_2/(X_1 + mY_1) - 1$. Substituting the expression for $\hat{m}$ in place of m, we obtain

$$B_m = \frac{X_2 + Y_2}{X_1 + Y_1} - 1.$$

Similarly, $S_m = Y_1(mY_1 + X_1)/(mY_1 Y_2 + X_1 Y_2 + mY_1 X_2)$. Substituting the expression for $\hat{m}$, we obtain

$$S_m = \frac{X_1 + Y_1}{X_2 + Y_2}.$$

Solving for λ we obtain $S_0 B + S = 1$.

For the population of residents in area X, $B_x = B_m$. It can also be shown that $S_x = (X_1 + mY_1)/X_2$; substituting the expression for $\hat{m}$,

$$S_x = \frac{X_1 + Y_1}{X_2 + Y_2}.$$

that is, identical to the overwinter survival rate of migrants.

For the population of residents in area Y, $B_y = (Y_2 - A_y)/A_y$. Since $A_y = (1 - m)Y_1$, $B_y = Y_2/Y_1(1 - m) - 1$. Substituting the expression for m, we find again that

$$B_y = \frac{X_2 + Y_2}{X_1 + Y_1} - 1.$$

which is identical to the fecundity of migrants and residents of area X. S_y is equal to $(A_y + A_m)/(A_y + F_y + A_m + F_m)$, or

$$S_y = \frac{Y_1}{\left[Y_2 + X_2 \left(\frac{mY_1}{X_1 + mY_1} \right) \right]}$$

When the expression for $\hat{m}$ is substituted, this can be shown to be

$$S_y = \frac{X_1 + Y_1}{X_2 + Y_2}.$$

which is identical to the overwinter survival of migrants and residents of region X.

(6) What happens when the population of migrants is regulated independently of residents during the winter? The demographic parameters of the migrants and those of residents in the winter region become uncoupled. But the life tables of the migrants and residents on the breeding grounds remain coupled and identical. In general, fully coupled populations have identical life tables.

(7) What happens when density-independent mortality is associated with migration? If mortality occurs only during spring migration, the proportion of individuals surviving migration (k) enters into the model equations for B_m and S_m as the product km. Now, however, the geometric growth rate of the population is

$$\lambda_m = kS_m(B_m + 1)$$

and the equilibrium migration fraction is

$$\hat{m} = \frac{kX_2Y_1 - X_1Y_2}{kY_1(X_2 + Y_2)}.$$

The fecundity of migrants (and residents of region X) becomes

$$B_m = \frac{X_2 + Y_2}{X_1 + kY_1} - 1.$$

that is, slightly higher than in the absence of migration mortality. Overwintering survival is now

$$S_m = \frac{X_1 + kY_1}{k(X_2 + Y_2)}.$$

To obtain annual survival, one must multiply by k. Thus, annual survival is not changed by density-independent mortality on spring migration. Rather, migration mortality is balanced by increased production of offspring on the breeding grounds. The fecundity and survival rates of residents of regions X and Y are also adjusted, but not to the same levels. For example, in region Y, fecundity becomes

$$B_y = \frac{k(X_2 + Y_2)}{kY_1 + X_1} - 1$$

and adult survival,

$$S_y = \frac{X_1 + kY_1}{k(X_2 + Y_2)}.$$

One could extend these models to include mortality during fall migration. One could also estimate the magnitude of demographic adjustments, and, particularly,

the differences to be expected in the life tables of different types of populations.

Life table variables of residents and migrants

The models described above predict that when migrants demographically couple resident populations in different regions, the life table variables of residents and migrants should equilibrate at identical or near-identical values. This prediction can be tested by comparing annual adult survival rates and production of independent offspring by birds in each of these categories. If migrant and resident populations were only partially coupled, the life tables of these populations would be convergent but not identical. Thus, it is possible to reject the model of complete coupling by comparing the life tables of migrant and resident populations. But to evaluate the possibility of partial coupling, one must compare resident populations in the presence and absence of migrants under similar ecological conditions. This might be possible in some areas of the tropics that differ in their densities of wintering migrants.

ADULT SURVIVAL

The scattered literature on survival rates in tropical passerines (Fogden 1972, Willis 1974, Snow and Lill 1974, Fry 1980, Vernon 1984, McDonald 1989) and the more extensive information available for temperate-zone species (Lack 1954, Farner 1955, Henny 1972, Dobson 1990) indicate that many tropical species have higher annual survival than temperate-zone species. However, taxonomic, ecological, and methodological differences between the temperate and tropical samples make such comparisons difficult to interpret. Long-term mist-net studies in Panama and eastern North America led Karr et al. (1990) to conclude that survival rates of passerines do not differ between the two regions. Taxonomic differences detract from this comparison, however: the tropical species are mostly suboscines, the temperate species oscines. The analysis of Karr et al. also would be subject to biases if dispersal, net avoidance, or local movement patterns differed between tropical and temperate songbirds.

In an attempt to eliminate a taxonomic bias, and following Snow (1956), I have estimated adult survival rates of New World species of the genus *Turdus* from proportions of first-year birds in museum collections from 30 populations of 18 species (Ricklefs, unpubl. data). In *Turdus*, first-year birds can be distinguished until the postnuptial molt by subtle plumage characters not obvious at a distance in the field. Biases might nonetheless

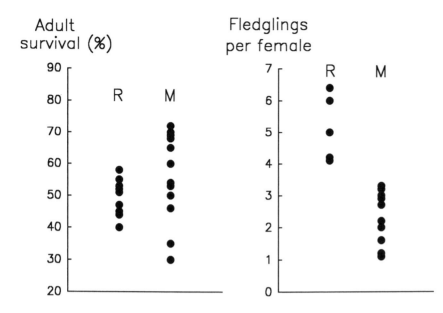

FIGURE 2. Survival and breeding productivity of North American resident (R) and migrant (M) passerine birds. Data from Greenberg (1980). Each symbol represents a single species; multiple values per species were averaged.

appear if adult and first-year birds, by behaving differently, are differentially vulnerable to collectors. The technique does, however, compare favorably with estimates of adult survival values obtained from banding programs. Proportions of samples that were first-year individuals indicated substantially higher survival of lowland tropical species (60–90%) and, especially, montane tropical species (78–91%) compared to temperate subspecies of *T. migratorius* (46–68%). Indeed, survival was inversely related to annual range of mean monthly temperature ($r = -0.79$).

Greenberg (1980) compared annual survival rates of resident and migrant species of passerines breeding in the north temperate zone. The distributions of values overlap considerably, but the highest values (> 60%) belonged to migratory species. The two samples did not differ significantly when comparisons were based on average values for each species represented by more than a single sample (residents, $S = 50 \pm 5$ SD, $n = 13$; migrants, $S = 56 \pm 13$ SD, $n = 13$; Kruskal-Wallis $\chi^2 = 2.6$, $P < 0.11$) (Fig. 2). In another comparison, Morse (1989) found, however, that survival rates of migratory paruline warblers (53–85%) significantly exceeded those of northern resident and short-distant migrants in other passerine families (37–60%). Therefore, apparently one can reject the hypothesis of complete coupling between migrant and resident populations, particularly on the breeding grounds. Survival rates of Neotropical residents and migrants might, however, be more similar.

BREEDING SUCCESS

The proper measure of breeding success in the model is the number of independent offspring produced per adult in the population. Presumably, density-dependent effects of resource availability on reproductive success are expressed primarily during the period of parental care, when foraging adults must satisfy the greatest resource demand. However, few studies have measured production of independent offspring. I assume here that the production of fledglings provides a reasonable index to breeding productivity; density-dependent factors relating breeding success to population size express themselves in good measure in brood size and the length of the nesting cycle. Although few studies have measured directly the annual production of fledged young, one can usually estimate this variable from brood size, nesting success, interval between nesting attempts, and the length of the breeding season (Ricklefs 1970). Variation in breeding productivity resulting from differences in clutch size and interclutch interval might reflect aspects of the food supply and thus behave in a density-dependent fashion, as required by the model. Although variation in nesting success caused by predation might not be density dependent (Ricklefs 1969a; but see Martin 1988a,b), it is largely compensated by renesting (Ricklefs and Bloom 1977, Ricklefs 1984).

Ricklefs and Bloom (1977) estimated breeding success in this manner for several samples of passerines

Fledglings per female

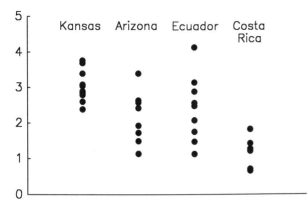

FIGURE 3. Breeding productivity of passerine birds from several areas of temperate and tropical America (from Ricklefs and Bloom 1977: Table 2). The Arizona and Ecuador localities are highly seasonal deserts.

from temperate and tropical areas. The estimated number of fledglings per female was greatest in Kansas (2.4–3.8), intermediate in arid habitats of Arizona and Ecuador, and least in Costa Rica (0.7–1.8), demonstrating substantial differences between temperate and tropical populations (Fig. 3; Kruskal-Wallis $\chi^2 = 14.6$, d.f. $= 3, P < 0.0022$).

Greenberg (1980) tabulated the number of fledglings per female from either field studies of color-banded birds or ratios of immature to adult birds at the end of the breeding season. In his sample of species, the five resident species had ratios between 4.1 and 6.4, whereas 13 species of migrants (wood-warblers and *Empidonax* flycatchers) had ratios between 1.1 and 3.4 (Kruskal-Wallis $\chi^2 = 9.7, P < 0.002$). Morse (1989), summarizing data from Palmer (1949), similarly concluded that the reproductive potential of Neotropical migrants (3.5–6.5 fledglings per pair per year) was statistically significantly lower than that of co-occurring resident oscine songbirds (4.5–11 per pair per year).

Ricklefs (1972) demonstrated that the ratio of immature to adult male Rough-winged Swallows (*Stelgidopteryx ruficollis*) at the end of the breeding season was higher in the temperate subspecies *serripennis* (1.75) than in the tropical subspecies *uropygialis* (0.76) and *aequalis* (0.42). Ricklefs (unpubl. data) estimated productivity in species of *Turdus* from the ratios of juveniles to adults in collections taken at the end of the breeding season. These ratios are not comparable to the data of

Ricklefs and Bloom (1977) and Greenberg (1980) but, as in the swallow data, they reveal the same pattern: north temperate populations (subspecies of *T. migratorius*) had higher juvenile/adult ratios (0.08–0.26) than did lowland tropical species (0.03–0.12). The data are rather consistent in pointing to higher breeding productivity in temperate than in tropical populations. Thus, in spite of longer breeding seasons in the tropics, the combination of smaller clutches, longer breeding cycles, and higher rates of nest predation results in lower production compared to temperate areas (Ricklefs 1969a,b, Skutch 1985).

Therefore, as in the case of adult survival, available data suggest a considerable difference in fecundity between migrants and temperate residents and between temperate and tropical residents. Whether migrants and tropical residents differ in fecundity is less clear. For migrants and temperate residents, however, the prediction arising from complete demographic coupling between populations can be rejected.

Ecological segration of migrant and resident populations

If migrant and resident populations are not fully coupled, different ecological factors must regulate their populations. The most plausible basis for divergence with respect to density-dependent factors is ecological segregation with respect to food resources. There are, however, several alternative explanations for the lack of demographic coupling. First, migrants and residents might be limited by different classes of density-dependent factors: for example, one group by food resources and the other by predators or disease organisms. Accordingly, residents and migrants might overlap substantially with respect to one class of factor (e.g., habitat or food resource) but not enter into density-dependent interactions with each other. Second, populations of migrants might be limited during one season only. For example, winter conditions might so depress populations both in the tropics and temperate regions that migrants and temperate residents share a superabundant food resource during the breeding season (Wiens 1977, Herrera 1978a, Schwartz 1980, O'Connor 1981).

Results from the literature on ecological segregation of migrants from both tropical residents during the winter and temperate residents during the summer are somewhat mixed. Although ecological and biogeographic studies have presented abundant evidence of partitioning by region, habitat, and food (e.g., Herrera 1978b, Hutto 1980, Keast 1980a, Willis 1980, Lack 1985, O'Connor 1985, Greenberg 1986), this partitioning certainly is not complete (e.g., Pienkowski and Evans 1985, Stanback 1987).

TABLE 1. Reclassification of migrant and resident species based on a discriminant analysis

From	Number of observations and percent classified into group			
	Temperate	Tropical	Migrant	Total
Temperate	41	12	15	68
	(60)	(18)	(22)	
Tropical	60	244	33	337
	(18)	(72)	(10)	
Migrant	9	9	50	68
	(13)	(13)	(74)	
TOTAL	110	265	98	473

NOTE: Percentages of group in parentheses.

AN ECOMORPHOLOGICAL ANALYSIS

The use of field observations of diet, substrate, and foraging behavior to estimate ecological segregation (e.g., Cody 1974) poses substantial difficulties of quantification and interpretation. An alternative approach to estimating segregation substitutes morphology for ecology (Ricklefs and Travis 1980). Morphology, foraging behavior, and substrate utilization are closely interrelated (Keast 1972, Karr and James 1975, Cody and Mooney 1978, Miles and Ricklefs 1984). It is reasonable, therefore, as a first approximation, to let morphology stand proxy for ecology (Ricklefs and Travis 1980) and to examine the segregation of species within morphological space.

Keast (1980a) noted that body dimensions of resident and migrant wood-warblers in the tropics did not differ significantly. However, Greenberg (1981) found that the bills of resident Neotropical foliage-gleaning insectivores were longer and narrower than those of migrant insectivores in the same forest habitats. He associated the distinction with dietary differences, the Neotropical residents including a larger proportion of large arthropods in their diets.

My analysis is based on measurements of 473 species of passerine birds from North, Central, and South America, and the Caribbean region. Eight dimensions were measured: total length, wing, tail, tarsus, midtoe, and the length, breadth, and depth of the beak. Measurements were log-transformed for analysis. Methods follow Ricklefs and Travis (1980) and Miles and Ricklefs (1984). Species were placed in three classes: tropical resident ($n = 337$), temperate resident ($n = 68$), and Neotropical migrant ($n = 68$). Fully migratory species that winter in the southern part of the temperate zone were classified as temperate residents because they do not interact with tropical species.

A discriminant function analysis (SAS Institute 1988, DISCRIM Procedure) revealed that the three groups of species differed significantly with respect to morphology. Overall, the posterior classification of species placed 335 out of 473 species (70.8%) in the proper group (Table 1). The canonical structure of the data calculated by SAS Procedure CANDISC (SAS Institute 1988) shows that the first canonical variable emphasizes beak size exclusively, species with smaller beaks having larger values on the first canonical axis (Table 2). The second canonical variable, which has about one-quarter the discriminating power of the first, emphasizes different components of size, particularly wing, tarsus, and midtoe length.

The distribution of species on the first and second canonical discriminant axes (Fig. 4) demonstrates substantial separation of tropical and temperate residents, and of migrants from both groups. In particular, migrants tend to have small beaks (high values of canonical axis 1) compared to residents in either area. Furthermore, the migrants tend to have short wings and legs, and shallow beaks (low values of canonical axis 2). These are characteristics of many small flycatchers, wood-warblers, and vireos.

Discussion

Complete ecological and demographic coupling between resident and migrant species would result in identical life tables for migrants, tropical residents, and temperate-zone residents. Comparisons of adult survival rates and per capita production of offspring allow one to reject the hypothesis of complete coupling. Migrants clearly are segregated to some degree from both tropical and temperate resident birds, if one can judge from differences between the life tables of migrants and those of both types of residents. This segregation is sup-

TABLE 2. Canonical structure of discriminant functions

	Discriminant function	
	1	2
Eigenvalue[a]	0.514	0.137
Likelihood ratio	0.581	0.897
Approximate F	18.1	9.1
Degrees of freedom		
Numerator	16	7
Denominator	926	464
Significance level	0.0001	0.0001
Between canonical structure (correlations)		
Total length	-0.46	0.81
Tail length	-0.35	0.38
Wing length	0.16	0.90
Tarsus length	-0.22	0.97
Midtoe length	0.05	0.99
Beak length	-0.98	0.17
Beak depth	-0.78	0.63
Beak width	-0.98	0.17
Group means		
Temperate	0.98	0.74
Tropical	-0.45	-0.02
Migrant	1.26	-0.62

a. Ratio of the between-group variance to the pooled within-group variance; a measure of discrimination.

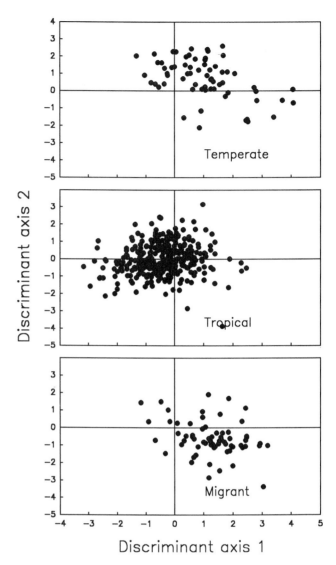

FIGURE 4. Positions of temperate residents, tropical residents, and migrants on canonical discriminant axes based on morphological measurements. On the first axis, species to the right have small beaks relative to those on the left. On the second axis, species with longer wings, legs, and toes have the higher values.

ported by observations of habitat and resource partitioning between wintering migrants and both tropical and temperate residents. Migrants appear to occupy at least partially distinctive ecological niches on both the breeding grounds and the wintering grounds.

Although ecological segregation is evident, migrants and residents clearly do interact. It is difficult to determine the degree to which this interaction has produced convergence in demographic traits, because one cannot easily judge the values of these traits in the absence of interactions. Yet the localized distribution of migrants in the Neotropics, and elsewhere throughout the tropics, affords opportunities to test the idea of convergence. As mentioned above, residents in the Greater Antilles, particularly Hispaniola, Cuba, and Jamaica, where migrants might comprise the majority of bird populations during the winter (Diamond 1974, Gochfeld 1985), exhibit higher brood sizes than similar resident species in the Lesser Antilles (Ricklefs 1980), where migrants are substantially less abundant (Terborgh and Faaborg 1980). More detailed comparisons of this type

might reveal evidence for convergence mediated by density-dependent interactions of migrant and resident populations. Furthermore, migrants and residents overlap partially in morphological space, and one might expect life tables of species in the region of overlap to exhibit convergence compared to species in regions of nonoverlapping morphology.

Have migrants achieved an ideal free distribution? What factors limit their populations? If one adopts the most interactive point of view and believes in density-dependent limitation of adult population size on the wintering grounds and density-dependent limitation of recruitment on the breeding grounds, one has to accept that migrants and residents are limited to a large degree by different factors, that is, they are uncoupled. On a broad scale, one might consider tropical residents, temperate residents, and migrants as occupying three mostly distinctive "niches" in a global-scale "habitat" that includes all of the Neotropical and Nearctic regions of the Western Hemisphere. That is, each group of species represents a distinctive megapopulation having only marginal demographic coupling with the others. But although interactions among species might occur primarily within each of these distinctive megapopulations, their segregation itself might reflect a long history of ecological and demographic interactions between migrant and resident populations. Although an ideal free distribution has undoubtedly been achieved overall (if only because each species has achieved an approximate equilibrium), migrants and residents partition the available resources as subsets of the total avifauna of each region, each subject, therefore, to mostly different population limitations.

Conclusions

(1) As a working hypothesis, tropical and temperate bird populations can be viewed as components of a vast megapopulation linked by movements of individuals between regions on a seasonal basis. However, ecological studies have shown that the migrants and the residents of each region comprise partially segregated components of the megapopulation because of the particular ecological requirements and opportunities of each way of life. Thus, the degree to which migrants couple with the population dynamics of resident populations is open to question.

(2) The model presented in this paper based on density-dependent regulation of population demography in summer and winter predicts identical life tables under conditions of complete coupling. Because this prediction is easily falsified by available data, the population dynamics of migrants and residents are at least partially uncoupled.

(3) Comparisons of tropical areas with and without abundant wintering migrants could provide evidence for partial coupling of resident and migrant populations. According to the model presented in this paper, demographic coupling should produce convergence in the life tables of resident tropical species toward those of migrants, relative to the life tables of counterparts in ecologically comparable tropical regions outside areas of abundant wintering migrants. Convergence would also be expected among groups of species that resemble each other ecologically or morphologically within areas, relative to comparisons between morphologically distinctive groups.

(4) Our limited ability to test the prediction of convergent life tables emphasizes a need for information on population densities, prebreeding and adult survival, and on breeding productivity, particularly of tropical species. Because of the small numbers of banders in tropical countries, these data can best be obtained at present by local, long-term studies of individually marked populations, where the breeding success and fates of individuals can be known with confidence.

(5) We need to explore the use of nontraditional sources of information on demography and ecological relations. In particular, I strongly advocate the use of morphological analyses to identify potential ecological relationships among species. I also believe that proportions of first-year birds in populations at the beginning of the breeding season can provide reasonable estimates of adult mortality rates, particularly when similar taxa can be compared over wide geographic areas. Museum collections house vast amounts of information, not only on systematics and biogeography, but on ecology and demography as well.

(6) In order to validate general patterns, we should compare migration systems in the western hemisphere with analogous systems in Europe, Africa, Asia, and Australia. An immense literature has been published on these systems. And, even though they generally resemble New World systems, important differences might provide clues to processes responsible for shaping the megapopulations of each region.

(7) Finally, although this study indicates general uncoupling of migrant and resident populations, the concept of the megapopulation, nonetheless, emphasizes the role of species interactions on a regional level in establishing geographic ranges and habitat selection, as well as local niche diversification among populations.

Literature cited

Alerstam, T., and G. Högstedt. 1980. Spring predictability and leapfrog migration. *Ornis Scand.* 11:196–200.

———. 1982. Bird migration and reproduction in relation to habitats for survival and breeding. *Ornis Scand.* 13:25–37.

Bell, H.L. 1982. Abundance and seasonality of the savanna avifauna at Port Moresby, New Guinea. *Ibis* 124:252–274.

Chipley, R.M. 1976. The impact of wintering migrant wood warblers on resident insectivorous passerines in a subtropical Colombian oak woods. *Living Bird* 15:119–141.

Cody, M.L. 1974. *Competition and the Structure of Bird Communities*. Princeton: Princeton University Press.

Cody, M.L., and H.A. Mooney. 1978. Convergence versus nonconvergence in Mediterranean-climate ecosystems. *Ann. Rev.*

Ecol. Syst. 9:265–321.

Cox, G.W. 1968. The role of competition in the evolution of migration. *Evolution* 22:180–192.

———. 1985. The evolution of avian migration systems between temperate and tropical regions of the New World. *Am. Nat.* 126:451–474.

Diamond, A.W. 1974. Annual cycles in Jamaican forest birds. *J. Zool.* 173:277–301.

Dickson, J.G. 1978. Seasonal bird populations in a south central Louisiana bottomland hardwood forest. *J. Wildl. Manage.* 42:875–883.

Dobson, A. 1990. Survival rates and their relationship to life-history traits in some common British birds. *Current Ornithol.* 7:115–146.

Farner, D.S. 1955. Birdbanding in the study of population dynamics. Pages 397–499 in *Recent Studies in Avian Biology,* A. Wolfson, ed. Urbana: University of Illinois Press.

Fogden, M.P.L. 1972. The seasonality and population dynamics of equatorial birds in Sarawak. *Ibis* 114:307–343.

Fretwell, S. 1972. *Populations in a Seasonal Environment.* Princeton: Princeton University Press.

———. 1980. Evolution of migration in relation to factors regulating bird numbers. Pages 517–527 in *Migrant Birds in the Neotropics: Ecology, Behavior, Distribution and Conservation,* A. Keast and E.S. Morton, eds. Washington: Smithsonian Institution Press.

Fry, C.H. 1980. Survival and longevity among tropical land birds. *Proc. IV Pan-Afr. Ornithol. Cong.:* 333–343.

Gauthreaux, S. 1982. The ecology and evolution of avian migration systems. Pages 93–167 in *Avian Biology,* Vol. 6. D.S. Farner and J.R. King, eds. New York: Academic Press.

Gochfeld, M. 1985. Numerical relationships between migrant and resident bird species in Jamaican woodlands. Pages 654–662 in *Neotropical Ornithology,* P.A. Buckley, E.S. Morton, R.S. Ridgely, and F.G. Buckley, eds. Ornithol. Monogr. 36.

Greenberg, R. 1980. Demographic aspects of long-distance migration. Pages 493–504 in *Migrant Birds in the Neotropics: Ecology, Behavior, Distribution and Conservation,* A. Keast and E.S. Morton, eds. Washington: Smithsonian Institution Press.

———. 1981. Dissimilar bill shapes in New World tropical versus temperate forest foliage-gleaning birds. *Oecologia* 49:143–147.

———. 1986. Competition in migrant birds in the nonbreeding season. *Current Ornithol.* 3:281–307.

Hall, G.A. 1984. Population decline of neotropical migrants in an Appalachian forest. *Am. Birds* 38:14–18.

Henny, C.J. 1972. An analysis of the population dynamics of selected avian species. *U.S. Fish and Wildlife Service, Wildl. Res. Rept.* 1:1–99.

Herrera, C.M. 1978a. On the breeding distribution pattern of European migrant birds: MacArthur's theme reexamined. *Auk* 95:496–509.

———. 1978b. Ecological correlates of residence and non-residence in a Mediterranean passerine bird community. *J. Anim. Ecol.* 47:871–890.

Holling, C.S. 1988. Temperate forest insect outbreaks, tropical deforestation and migratory birds. *Mem. Ent. Soc. Can.* 146:21–32.

Holmes, R.T., and T.W. Sherry. 1988. Assessing population trends of New Hampshire forest birds: Local vs. regional patterns. *Auk* 105:756–768.

Holmes, R.T., and F.W. Sturges. 1973. Annual energy expenditure by the avifauna of a northern hardwoods ecosystem. *Oikos* 24:24–29.

———. 1975. Bird community dynamics and energetics in a northern hardwoods system. *J. Anim. Ecol.* 44:175–200.

Hutto, R.L. 1980. Winter habitat distribution of migratory land birds in western Mexico, with special reference to small foliage-gleaning insectivores. Pages 181–203 in *Migrant Birds in the Neotropics: Ecology, Behavior, Distribution and Conservation,* A. Keast and E.S. Morton, eds. Washington: Smithsonian Institution Press.

Karr, J.R. 1976. On the relative abundances of north temperate migrants in tropical habitats. *Wilson Bull.* 88:433–458.

Karr, J.R., and F.C. James. 1975. Ecomorphological configurations and convergent evolution in species and communities. Pages 258–291 in *Ecology and Evolution of Communities,* M.L. Cody and J.M. Diamond, eds. Cambridge, Mass.: Belknap Press.

Karr, J.R., J.D. Nichols, M.K. Klimkiewicz, and J.D. Brawn. 1990. Survival rates of birds of tropical and temperate forests: Will the dogma survive? *Am. Nat.* 136:277–291.

Keast, A.E. 1972. Ecological opportunities and dominant families, as illustrated by the Neotropical Tyrannidae (Aves). *Evol. Biol.* 5:229–277.

———. 1980a. Spatial relationships between the migratory parulid warblers and their ecological counterparts in the Neotropics. Pages 109–130 in *Migrant Birds in the Neotropics: Ecology, Behavior, Distribution and Conservation,* A. Keast and E.S. Morton, eds. Washington: Smithsonian Institution Press.

———. 1980b. Synthesis: Ecological basis and evolution of the nearctic-neotropical bird migration system. Pages 559–576 in *Migrant Birds in the Neotropics: Ecology, Behavior, Distribution and Conservation,* A. Keast and E.S. Morton, eds. Washington: Smithsonian Institution Press.

Lack, D. 1954. *The Natural Regulation of Animal Numbers.* Oxford: Oxford University Press.

Lack, P.C. 1985. Ecological correlates of migrants and residents in a tropical African savanna. *Ardea* 74:111–119.

———. 1987. The structure and seasonal dynamics of the bird community in Tsavo East National Park, Kenya. *Ostrich* 58:9–23.

Lovejoy, T.E. 1983. Tropical deforestation and North American birds. *Biol. Conserv.* 1:126–128.

Lundberg, S., and T. Alerstam. 1986. Bird migration patterns: Conditions for stable geographical population segregation. *J. Theoret. Biol.* 123:403–414.

MacArthur, R.H. 1959. On the breeding distribution pattern of North American migrant birds. *Auk* 76:318–325.

Martin, T.E. 1988a. On the advantage of being different: Nest predation and the coexistence of bird species. Proc. Nat. Acad. Sci. USA 85:2196–2199.

———. 1988b. Processes organizing open-nesting bird assemblages: Competition or nest predation? *Evol. Ecol.* 2:37–50.

McDonald, D.B. 1989. Cooperation under sexual selection:

Age-graded changes in a lekking bird. *Am. Nat.* 134:709–730.

Miles, D.B., and R.E. Ricklefs. 1984. The correlation between ecology and morphology in deciduous forest passerine birds. *Ecology* 65:1629–1640.

Morel, G., and F. Bourlière. 1962. Relations écologiques des avifaunes sédentaire et migratrice dans une savane sahélienne du Bas-Sénégal. *Terre et Vie* 109:371–393.

Morse, D.H. 1980. Population limitation: Breeding or wintering grounds? Pages 505–516 in *Migrant Birds in the Neotropics: Ecology, Behavior, Distribution and Conservation*, A. Keast and E.S. Morton, eds. Washington: Smithsonian Institution Press.

———. 1989. *American Warblers*. Cambridge: Harvard University Press.

Murphy, M.T. 1989. Life history variability in North American breeding tyrant flycatchers: Phylogeny, size or ecology? *Oikos* 54:3–14.

Nix, H.A. 1974. Environmental control of breeding, post-breeding dispersal and migration of birds in the Australian region. *Proc. 16th Internat. Ornithol. Cong.* (Canberra): 273–305.

O'Connor, R.J. 1981. Comparisons between migrant and non-migrant birds in Britain. Pages 167–195 in *Animal Migration*, D.J. Aidley, ed. Soc. Exp. Biol. Seminar Series 13, Cambridge: Cambridge University Press.

———. 1985. Behavioural regulation of bird populations: A review of habitat use in relation to migration and residency. Pages 105–142 in *Behavioural Ecology: Ecological Consequences of Adaptive Behavior*, R.M. Sibly and R.H. Smith, eds. Oxford: Blackwell Scientific Publications.

Palmer, R.S. 1949. Maine birds. *Bull. Mus. Comp. Zool.* 102:1–656.

Pienkowski, M.W., and P.R. Evans. 1985. The role of migration in the population dynamics of birds. Pages 331–352 in *Behavioural Ecology*, R.M. Sibly and R.H. Smith, eds. Oxford, England: Blackwell.

Ricklefs, R.E. 1969a. *An Analysis of Nesting Mortality in Birds*. Smithsonian Contrib. Zool. 9.

———. 1969b. The nesting cycle of songbirds in tropical and temperate regions. *Living Bird* 8:165–175.

———. 1970. The estimation of a time function of ecological use. *Ecology* 51:508–513.

———. 1972. Latitudinal variation in breeding productivity of the rough-winged swallow. *Auk* 89:826–836.

———. 1980. Geographical variation in clutch size among passerine birds: Ashmole's hypothesis. *Auk* 97:38–49.

———. 1984. The optimization of growth rate in altricial birds. *Ecology* 65:1602–1616.

Ricklefs, R.E., and G. Bloom. 1977. Components of avian breeding productivity. *Auk* 94:86–97.

Ricklefs, R.E., and J. Travis. 1980. A morphological approach to the study of avian community organization. *Auk* 97:321–338.

Robbins, C.S., J.R. Sauer, R.S. Greenberg, and S. Droege. 1989. Population declines in North American birds that migrate to the neotropics. *Proc. Natl. Acad. Sci.* 86:7658–7662.

SAS Institute. 1988. *SAS/STAT Users' Guide, Release 6.03.* Cary, N.C.: SAS Institute Inc.

Schwartz, P. 1980. Some considerations on migratory birds. Pages 31–36 in *Migrant Birds in the Neotropics: Ecology, Behavior, Distribution and Conservation*, A. Keast and E.S. Morton, eds. Washington: Smithsonian Institution Press.

Skutch, A.F. 1985. Clutch size, nesting success, and predation on nests of neotropical birds, reviewed. Pages 575–594 in *Neotropical Ornithology*, P.A. Buckley, E.S. Morton, R.S. Ridgely, and F.G. Buckley, eds. Ornithol. Monogr. 36.

Snow, D.W. 1956. The annual mortality of the blue tit in different parts of its range. *Brit. Birds* 49:174–177.

Snow, D.W., and A. Lill. 1974. Longevity records for some neotropical land birds. *Condor* 76:262–267.

Stanback, M. 1987. Coexistence of migrant and resident birds in the neotropics. *The Biologist* 66:55–69.

Terborgh, J.W. 1980. The conservation status of Neotropical migrants: Present and future. Pages 21–30 in *Migrant Birds in the Neotropics: Ecology, Behavior, Distribution and Conservation*, A. Keast and E.S. Morton, eds. Washington: Smithsonian Institution Press.

Terborgh, J.W., and J.R. Faaborg. 1980. Factors affecting the distribution and abundance of North American migrants in the eastern Caribbean region. Pages 145–155 in *Migrant Birds in the Neotropics: Ecology, Behavior, Distribution and Conservation*, A. Keast and E.S. Morton, eds. Washington: Smithsonian Institution Press.

Vernon, C.J. 1984. Population dynamics of birds in Brachystegia woodland. *Proc. V Pan-Afr. Ornithol. Cong.*: 201–216.

Weiner, J., and Z. Glowacinski. 1975. Energy flow through a bird community in a deciduous forest in southern Poland. *Condor* 77:233–242.

Weins, J.A. 1977. On competition and variable environments. *Am. Scientist* 65:590–597.

Wilcove, D.S., and J.T. Terborgh. 1984. Patterns of population decline in birds. *Am. Birds* 38:10–13.

Willis, E.O. 1974. Populations and local extinctions of birds on Barro Colorado Island, Panamá. *Ecol. Monogr.* 44:153–169.

———. 1980. Ecological roles of migratory and resident birds on Barro Colorado Island, Panama. Pages 205–225 in *Migrant Birds in the Neotropics: Ecology, Behavior, Distribution and Conservation*, A. Keast and E.S. Morton, eds. Washington: Smithsonian Institution Press.

CHANDLER S. ROBBINS
Patuxent Wildlife Research Center
Laurel, Maryland 20708

JOHN W. FITZPATRICK
Archbold Biological Station
P.O. Box 2057
Lake Placid, Florida 33852

PAUL B. HAMEL
Tennessee Department of Conservation
Ecological Services Division
701 Broadway
Nashville, Tennessee 37219-5237

A warbler in trouble:
Dendroica cerulea

Abstract. The Cerulean Warbler, like other Neotropical migrants, has suffered extensive loss of breeding habitat during the past century. It differs from many other migrants in its preference for mature floodplain forest with tall trees, a habitat that has become scarce over much of the warbler's original nesting range. Sensitivity to fragmentation within remaining suitable tracts places this warbler at an additional disadvantage. Furthermore, Cerulean Warblers winter strictly in primary, humid evergreen forest along an extremely narrow elevational zone at the base of the Andes. This zone is among the most intensively logged and cultivated regions of the Neotropics. From 1966 to 1987 the Cerulean Warbler showed the most precipitous decline of any North American warbler (3.4% per year). Unless steps are taken to protect large tracts of habitat of this ecologically specialized species, both on the breeding grounds and in the Andean foothills, we believe the future of this warbler is in serious jeopardy.

Sinopsis. El Parúlido *Dendroica cerulea*, como otros migrantes neotropicales, ha sufrido grandes pérdidas de habitat reproductivo durante el último siglo. Se diferencia de otros migrantes en que prefiere selvas inundables maduras con árboles altos, un tipo de habitat que se ha vuelto muy escaso dentro de la distribución reproductiva inicial. La sensibilidad a la fragmentación pone a esta ave en mayor desventaja. Asimismo, esta ave pasa la estación no-reproductiva en selvas primarias perennes a lo largo de una gradiente elevacional extremadamente angosta. Esta zona es una de las cultivadas más extensamente en el Neotropico. Desde 1966 hasta 1987, esta ave ha mostrado la caída poblacional mas precipitosa de todos los parulidos de América del Norte (3.4% al año). Salvo que se tomen medidas para proteger grandes extensiones de habitat para esta ave especializada, tanto en las zonas reproductivas como en las no-reproductivas de los Andes, consideramos que el futuro de esta especie es muy oscuro.

We selected the Cerulean Warbler (*Dendroica cerulea*) for special study because it typifies many of the forest-dwelling Neotropical migrants whose traits make these birds subject to serious population declines. Specifically, we selected the Cerulean Warbler because (1) it has been undergoing a long-term decline as suggested by

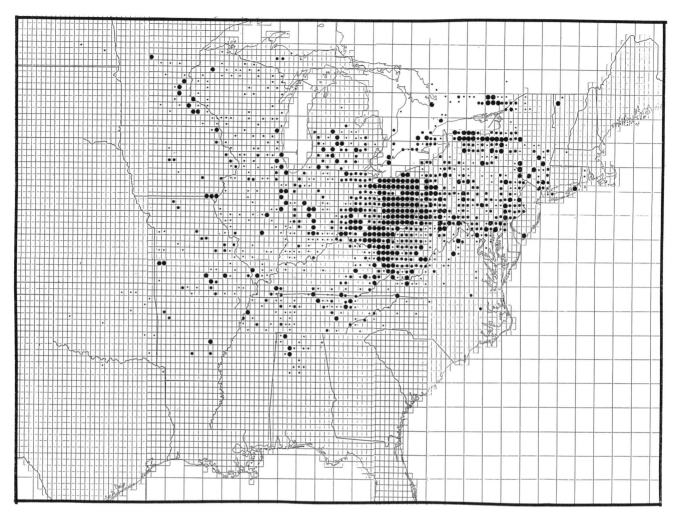

FIGURE 1. Present breeding distribution of Cerulean Warbler, based largely on Breeding Bird Atlas records. Each dot represents presence in from one to a maximum of 24 5 × 5-km atlas blocks during the breeding season. Large dots represent confirmed nesting records, medium dots represent probable nesting, small dots represent possible nesting based on single occurrences during the breeding season.

many historic references and as measured by the Breeding Bird Survey, and this decline is still continuing; (2) its principal nesting habitat, extensive floodplain forest of tall, mature, deciduous trees, has been disappearing at an alarming rate over the past 50 years; (3) its limited winter range on the east slope of the Andes has become threatened because of large-scale habitat destruction; and (4) its life history is poorly known. Furthermore, the Cerulean Warbler has just been added to the U.S. Fish and Wildlife Service's list of birds of management concern, making this an appropriate time to summarize the constraints that affect this species and to offer recommendations for assisting its survival.

Breeding range

The 6th edition of the A.O.U. Check-list (A.O.U. 1983) outlines the breeding range as extending "from southeastern Nebraska, northern Iowa, central and southeastern Minnesota, southern Wisconsin, southern Michigan, southern Ontario, southwestern Quebec, western and southeastern New York, northwestern Vermont and central Connecticut south to eastern Oklahoma, north-central Texas (to Dallas area), southern Arkansas, southeastern Louisiana (probably), central Mississippi, central Alabama and central Georgia, and east to northern New Jersey, northern Delaware, eastern Maryland, central Virginia and central North Carolina." This is essentially the same as was given in Chapman (1907), but includes the following range extensions since then: southwestern Quebec, northwestern Vermont, central Mississippi, and eastern Maryland (which, in the A.O.U. Check-list, should have read northeastern Maryland). Bagg and Eliot (1937), Bull (1974), and Ellison (*in* Laughlin and Kibbe 1985) have summarized the slow but steady expansion of the breeding range in the northeastern United States.

Breeding Bird Atlas projects are providing much new information about the breeding distribution of the Cerulean Warbler. Figure 1 is based largely on a condensation of atlas data, but for states for which atlas data are not available, other published sources (including Hands et al. 1989) were used. As might have been predicted, the intensive atlas field work resulted in the discovery of many new nesting populations of the species during the 1980s, including range extensions in several states. Without comparable coverage in the past, it is uncertain how many of the new locations reported are actually recent range extensions.

Michigan atlas observers, for example, recently documented the first occurrences of Cerulean Warblers in the Upper Peninsula. In Ontario, atlas observers discovered a new band of occurrence extending eastward from the Bruce Peninsula to north of Kingston, documented by records in more than 50 10-km atlas squares (Cadman et al. 1987). In New York, atlasers found many new populations that they believe represent range expansions (Andrle and Carroll 1988). In Vermont, the first state nesting record was obtained in 1977, during the atlas period, and the known state population by 1985 ranged from four to six pairs (Laughlin and Kibbe 1985). Kirkwood (1895) knew of only one summer record for Maryland, perhaps because 19th century Maryland observers did not recognize the song of this species. Maryland atlas workers found this species in 145 of the 1,250 5-km blocks in 1983–1987 (Maryland/DC Breeding Bird Atlas, in prep.), most of them within the range mapped by Stewart and Robbins (1958). The first nesting record for Cape May County, New Jersey, was obtained on 30 May 1989 (Bacinski 1989).

On the other hand, the literature abounds with references suggesting a drastic reduction in numbers during the 20th century (Wood and Tinker 1910, Blincoe 1925, Trautman 1940, Stine 1959, Mayfield 1977, Mossman and Lange 1982, Ambuel and Temple 1982, Graber et al. 1983).

Breeding densities

In their favored habitats, breeding populations of Cerulean Warblers can be as dense as those of most other species of *Dendroica*. The highest published breeding densities for the Cerulean Warbler in the first 35 years of Breeding Bird Censuses (1937–1971) are shown in Table 1, and the highest breeding densities reported for 14 *Dendroica* species in the same years are shown in Table 2. The greatest concentration of breeding Cerulean Warblers appeared to be on the Cumberland Plateau of southern West Virginia, eastern Kentucky, and eastern Tennessee, with an average of 2.6 birds per 50-stop Breeding Bird Survey route during 1966–1987. The highest statewide means were 1.8 for West Virginia, 0.7 for Kentucky and Tennessee, and 0.4 for Ohio (unpublished Breeding Bird Survey data).

TABLE 1. Highest breeding densities for Cerulean Warblers

Density (pairs/km^2)	Elevation (m)	State	County	Habitat	Reference[a]
290	165	OH	Hamilton	Climax deciduous	Hellman (1950)
206	275	WV	Wetzel	Mature oak-hickory	Harrison (1961)
189	400	WV	Kanawha	Upland oak-hickory	Hurley (1966)
132	290	WV	Gilmer	Deciduous hillside	Koch (1968)
132	810	WV	Greenbrier	Oak-hickory	Koch (1971)
124	285	MI	Livingston	Young oak-hickory	Snyder (1949)
115	815	WV	Greenbrier	Maturing oak-hickory	Rudy (1971)
99	360	WV	Wetzel	Mixed mature hardwoods	Hurley (1961)
99	250	WV	Mason	Mixed upland	Laitsch (1971)
94	230	IN	Marion	Mature mixed hardwood	Nading (1954)
82	220	WV	Wayne	Mature mesophytic	Koch (1969)

a. References are to the Breeding Bird Census issues of *Audubon Field Notes* in the years indicated.

TABLE 2. Highest breeding densities for *Dendroica* warblers

Species	Density (pairs/km^2)	State/Prov.	Habitat	Reference[a]
Yellow *(D. petechia)*	580	MAN	Green ash woodland	Jones (1971)
Blk-thr. Green *(D. virens)*	337	ME	Lowland forest & edge	Simmers (1961)
Cerulean *(D. cerulea)*	290	OH	Climax deciduous	Hellman (1950)
Chestnut-sided *(D. pensylvanica)*	280	WV	Cut-over oak-hickory	Olsen (1966)
Blackburnian *(D. fusca)*	271	MD	Virgin Hemlock	Robbins (1949)
Magnolia *(D. magnolia)*	247	WV	Young spruce forest	Aldrich (1948)
Bay-breasted *(D. castanea)*	234	ME	Young spruce-fir	Stewart (1951)
Prairie *(D. discolor)*	209	MD	Dry deciduous scrub	Robbins (1947)
Black-thr. Blue *(D. caerulescens)*	204	TN	Virgin hardwood	Aldrich (1946)
Pine *(D. pinus)*	188	MD	Loblolly-shortleaf pine	Springer (1948)
Audubon's *(D. coronata auduboni)*	124	CO	Red fir–lodgepole pine	Kingery (1951)
Blackpoll *(D. striata)*	106	VT	Mountain coniferous	Nichols (1968)
Myrtle *(D. coronata coronata)*	99	NWT	Virgin white spruce	Stewart (1955)
Yellow-throated *(D. dominica)*	71	MD	Loblolly-shortleaf pine	Springer (1948)

a. References are to the Breeding Bird Census issues of *Audubon Field Notes* in the years indicated.

Population trends

Cerulean Warblers were recorded on 255 Breeding Bird Survey routes during the period 1966–1987, and during this period they experienced an average decline of 3.4% per year ($P < 0.01$) (unpublished Breeding Bird Survey data). This was the greatest decline for any species of warbler. In fact, the only passerine species with a greater significant decline for those years were Olive-sided Flycatcher, *Contopus borealis* (3.5%), Gray Jay, *Perisoreus canadensis* (3.8%), Boreal Chickadee, *Parus hud-* *sonicus* (9.2%), Cassin's Sparrow, *Aimophila cassinii* (4.6%), Field Sparrow, *Spizella pusilla* (3.7%), and White-winged Crossbill, *Loxia leucoptera* (13.8%). The yearly means for Cerulean Warblers are depicted in Figure 2. The greatest rates of decline were recorded on the Ozark-Ouachita Plateau of Arkansas and Missouri, and on the Highland Rim in Tennessee and Kentucky. Major significant declines (1.9% per year or greater) were also found in Ohio and West Virginia. Thus declining population trends were most pronounced in the core of the breeding range rather than at the edges of the range.

Comments on the life history

Although the Cerulean Warbler was first described by Alexander Wilson in 1810 (AOU 1983), its nest was not found until about 50 years later (Bent 1953). The nests range in height above ground from 4.5 to 27 m, with the majority in the 9–12 m range (Forbush 1929, Bent 1953, Peck and James 1987); the actual mean height is probably greater than this, because the shallow nest on top of a branch or fork is very hard to detect at a great height.

Probably because of the difficulty of finding nests, no one has yet published a life history of this species. The nesting behavior, incubation period, number of broods per year, and normal reproductive success are still unknown. Even the food habits are poorly known. Also, because the birds typically remain in the treetops even during migration, fewer than 1,000 have been banded since 1950 (M.K. Klimkiewicz, pers. comm.).

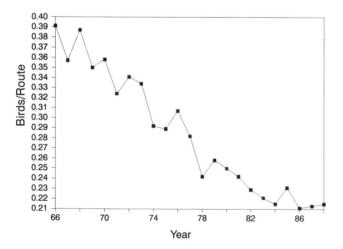

FIGURE 2. Mean number of Cerulean Warblers detected along 50-stop Breeding Bird Survey routes, 1966–1988.

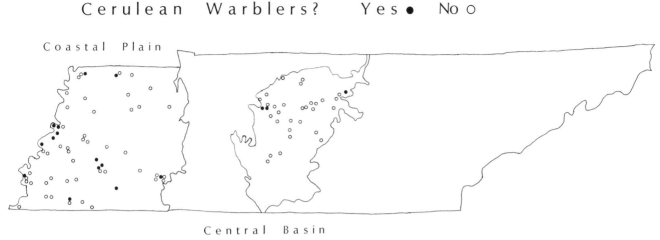

FIGURE 3. Cerulean Warbler study sites in the Coastal Plain and Central Basin of Tennessee.

Habitat requirements in Tennessee

To document critical habitat requirements on the nesting grounds, Hamel recently examined the following three hypotheses in Tennessee: (A) Cerulean Warblers consistently occur at or near the tops of tall trees, (B) Cerulean Warblers use the largest trees available, and (C) in the breeding season, Cerulean Warblers are associated with large forest tracts and not with smaller ones.

METHODS

Hamel chose Middle and West Tennessee, the Central Basin and Coastal Plain, respectively, as the study region (Fig. 3). Study sites had to be uniform in composition, roadless, and at least 40 ha in extent, with trees at least 20 years old. In the Central Basin, 32 sites that met these criteria were randomly selected from among 2500 latitude-longitude intersections (Ford and Hamel 1988). In the Coastal Plain, 60 qualifying sites were randomly selected by river miles in alluvial plains of major river drainages (Durham et al. 1988b).

Vegetation measurements at each site were taken according to standard protocols (Bridges et al. 1985, Durham et al. 1988a). Protocols involved identifying to species and measuring the diameter at breast height of each tree at least 3 cm dbh on three (in the Central Basin) or six (in the Coastal Plain) fixed plots of 0.1 ha. Canopy cover was estimated using the technique of James and Shugart (1970). Heights of the top, bottom, and densest layers of canopy and subcanopy were measured, as well as the diameter and height of snags and the length and diameter of downed vegetation at least 12.5 cm dbh. Additional measurements on 0.025-ha sub-

plots involved identification of species composition and estimates of height and coverage of vegetation in shrub and herbaceous layers and estimates of percentage cover of several types of ground cover. Slight variation in technique involved measurement of topographic position, slope, and aspect in the sites in the Central Basin but not in the Coastal Plain where each of these was essentially constant. In the Coastal Plain, measurements of flooding intensity and duration were made instead. Bird sampling was carried out according to a standard protocol of line transect and variable circular-plot counts (Järvinen and Väisänen 1975, Hamel 1984, Ford and Hamel 1988, Durham et al. 1988b, Ford 1990). Additional supporting data on the size of all forest tracts in the floodplains of West Tennessee rivers were measured on recent aerial photographs (Abernethy and Hamel 1987, Durham et al. 1988b).

Cerulean Warblers occurred on a subset of sites in each part of the study region. At these sites, additional vegetation measurements were taken beneath singing perches of territorial male Cerulean Warblers. Individual Cerulean Warbler territories were identified by the presence of a persistently singing male, present over several consecutive days or weeks on the study sites. Vegetation measurements on these territories were made using either the standard protocol on fixed plots or on variable radius plots sampled with a 20× basal area factor device (Renewable Resources Evaluation Project 1977). Among measurements made in each territory were the species, diameter, and height, and number of canopy and subcanopy trees.

Observations of behaviors of Cerulean Warblers consisted of detailed measurements of the location and activity of individual birds as they moved through the for-

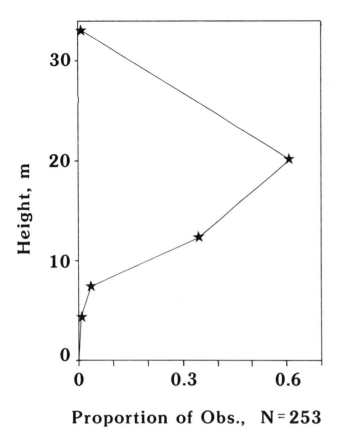

FIGURE 4. Feeding heights of Cerulean Warblers, expressed as a proportion of total observations (*n* = 253).

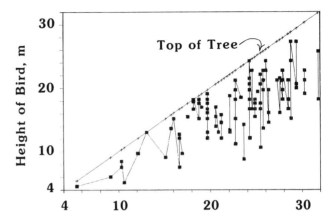

FIGURE 5. Feeding heights of Cerulean Warblers in relation to height of trees in which they were feeding.

est, using the protocol of Hamel (1981). The protocol involves noting the study area, date, time, sympatric warbler species, age and sex of observed individual, the tree species, and measuring the tree height, tree diameter at breast height, density of foliage in the tree on an ordinal scale, canopy level of tree, height of bird in the tree, distance of bird from center of the tree, size of the support on which the bird is perched, status of the support as alive or dead, orientation of the support as above or below 45° with respect to horizontal, position of the bird on the support as within or out of reach of vegetation, the relative position of the bird in the tree on a nine-step vertical and three-step horizontal scale, and the behavior in which the bird was engaged. Among other measurements, the protocol includes the species, height, and diameter of the tree as well as the height and location of the birds in the tree.

Tract-level data were summarized by available tract sizes, sampled tract sizes, and tract sizes in which Cerulean Warblers occurred, as well as effort-standardized numbers of registrations of Cerulean Warblers. An identical summary of occurrence of Brown-headed Cowbirds (*Molothrus ater*) was prepared for comparison of the two species in the Coastal Plain.

Vegetation data were summarized into diameter-class distributions of trees at four spatial scales: regional, the tract on which Cerulean Warblers occurred, the territories of Cerulean Warblers, and the trees used by Cerulean Warblers. Behavioral data were summarized by heights of the trees and the heights and locations of the birds in those trees, as well as by the heights at which Cerulean Warblers were observed.

Log-likelihood ratio and chi-square statistics were used to compare observed with predicted distributions, and *t*-tests to compare bird height and tree height.

RESULTS

Hamel examined the hypotheses in order of increasing scale from microhabitat use through regional to, by implication, rangewide occurrence, and determined the following:

(A) Height distributions of 253 measured locations of the warblers in the trees showed the birds unequivocally to be canopy-dwellers (Fig. 4). This pattern is similar to that for other canopy warblers such as Northern Parula (*Parula americana*), Yellow-throated Warbler (*Dendroica dominica*), Pine Warbler (*D. pinus*), and Black-throated Green Warbler (*D. virens*) (Hamel 1981). Cerulean Warblers typically occurred above the middle of the tree, but not at the top. The mean observation was at 77% of the height of the tree (Fig. 5), about 17 m up in a 22-m-tall tree. Thus, the hypothesis that Cerulean Warblers consistently occur at or near the tops of tall trees cannot be completely refuted based on this evidence; rather, it seems that the birds occur within a wide range of heights in the upper portion of the trees.

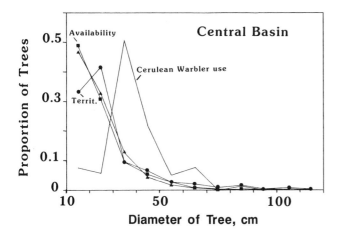

FIGURE 6. Tree diameters (cm, dbh) used by Cerulean Warblers in the Central Basin of Tennessee compared with availability in the forest and availability within their territories.

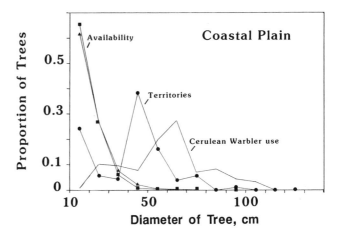

FIGURE 7. Tree diameters (cm, dbh) used by Cerulean Warblers in the Coastal Plain of Tennessee compared with availability in the forest and availability within their territories.

(B) Heights and diameters of nearly 30,000 trees were measured, and availability was compared with use by Cerulean Warblers (Figs. 6, 7). In each study region, four diameter class distributions were available for analysis, (a) the regional distribution indicated by all tree diameters measured in the respective region; (b) the distribution on those sites that contained Cerulean Warblers indicated by measurements from those sites; (c) the distribution of tree diameters within the actual territories of the birds in those sites; and (d) the distribution of diameters of trees actually selected by individual birds. Comparison of these four distributions involved calculation of log likelihood ratio statistics in which the observed distribution at the smaller scale in the sequence was compared with the expected distribution at that scale. Expected distributions were calculated from the observed distributions at the next larger scale. The null hypothesis of each of these tests was that use or habitat selection by Cerulean Warblers at one scale was not different from availability as indicated by the tree diameter distribution at the next larger scale. Twelve diameter classes were used in each instance to avoid small cell expectations. The critical value of the test statistic, G, at $P = 0.005$, with 11 d.f., is 26.7. In the Central Basin (Fig. 6), Cerulean Warbler territories tended to be in areas with larger-diameter trees than would have been expected from availability ($G = 341.7$, $P < 0.001$), and within those territories the birds spent more time in the larger trees ($G = 312.4$, $P < 0.001$). There was a similar preference for the larger trees in the Coastal Plain ($G = 448.2$, $P < 0.001$; and $G = 324.3$, $P < 0.001$ respectively; (Fig. 7). We reject the null hypothesis of no tree-size selection by Cerulean Warblers.

Manomet Symposium 1989

(C) The third hypothesis, that breeding Cerulean Warblers are associated with large forest tracts and not with smaller ones, was hard to examine in the Central Basin where Cerulean Warblers were found in only three sites; two of these were in Warner Parks (800 ha), among the largest forest tracts in the region. On the Coastal Plain, the 14 sites used were all in tracts of at least 1,600 ha, most of them on public land. Cerulean Warblers were most numerous in the larger tracts (Fig. 8, where compared with similar data for Brown-headed Cowbird). The distribution of Cerulean Warblers in the extensive forest tracts supports the conventional hypothesis that they are associated with large forest tracts.

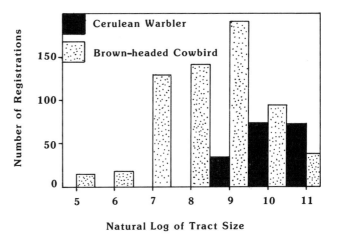

FIGURE 8. Distribution of Cerulean Warblers and Brown-headed Cowbirds as a function of forest tract size.

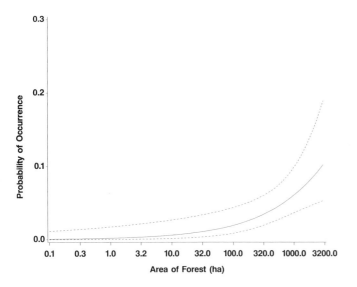

FIGURE 9. Probability of occurrence of Cerulean Warblers as a function of woodland size. Dashed lines are 95% confidence limits; $r = 0.308$. From Robbins et al. (1989).

Habitat requirements in the Middle Atlantic states

Robbins et al. (1989), in a study of 469 mature forest sites in Maryland and adjacent states, found that breeding Cerulean Warblers selected large tracts of mature, semi-open deciduous forest. Their analysis showed that the probability of occurrence of breeding Cerulean Warblers was positively correlated with the natural logarithm of the area of the forest ($P < 0.01$), the square root of the basal area of the trees ($P < 0.05$), and the percentage ground cover ($P < 0.05$), and negatively correlated with the arcsine of percent canopy cover by coniferous trees ($P < 0.05$).

The two smallest sites at which they found Cerulean Warblers contained 138 and 637 ha of contiguous forest habitat. The authors concluded that maximum density of Ceruleans occurred in woodlands of at least 3,000 ha. A computer-generated plot of probability of occurrence, as influenced by area of woodland, predicted that probability of occurrence would reach 50% of maximum for the species when woodland size reached 700 ha (Fig. 9).

Habitat summaries from other states

In Missouri, Kahl et al. (1985) found that habitat around song perches of Cerulean Warblers was most consistently characterized by a large number of live stems > 30 cm dbh (range 50–150), and a high (always > 18 m), closed canopy (> 85%, never < 65%). Other important features included an intermediate to closed subcanopy (always > 45%), an intermediate number of

woody stems < 2.5 cm dbh (1030–2800/ha, never < 1030), and few dead stems 2.5–9.9 cm dbh (always < 175/ha).

In a disjunct population in the Roanoke River basin of northeastern North Carolina, Lynch (1981) found that the highest densities occurred in old-growth, mature floodplain forest communities on well-drained, natural levees within 330 m of the Roanoke River. Dominant canopy species were sycamore (*Platanus occidentalis*), green ash (*Fraxinus pennsylvanica*), and sugarberry (*Celtis laevigata*). At the highest-density site, the canopy height was 24 to 30 m, the canopy was closed, the shrub layer was distinct, and ground cover (proportion of ground concealed by green vegetation < 1 m high) was 100%. The males characteristically used the tallest available canopy trees for singing perches. Lynch noted that segments of floodplain containing even-aged timber without old-growth trees contained few, if any, breeding pairs of Cerulean Warblers.

Constraints on the breeding ground

The chief constraints on the breeding ground are: (1) loss of mature deciduous forest, especially along stream valleys, (2) fragmentation and increasing isolation of remaining mature deciduous forest, (3) change to shorter rotation periods and even-aged management, so that less deciduous forest habitat reaches maturity, (4) environmental degradation from acid rain and stream pollution, (5) loss of key tree species, especially oaks from oak wilt and gypsy moths, sycamores from a fungus, elms from Dutch elm disease, and American chestnuts from chestnut blight, and (6) nest parasitism by the Brown-headed Cowbird.

(1) During the past 200 years most of the old-growth deciduous forest within the breeding range of the Cerulean Warbler was cut. The ensuing second-growth forests still persist in mountainous regions, but have largely given way to agricultural and urban uses away from the mountains. Stream valleys have been especially vulnerable to loss from reservoir construction, stream channelization, agricultural clearing, and other disturbances in and adjacent to the floodplain. Thousands of kilometers of floodplain habitat have been destroyed by construction of reservoirs and sewer lines, by stream channelization, and by construction of railroads, highways, transmission lines, and housing and commercial developments in the adjacent uplands. (See Hands et al. 1989 for other references to loss of floodplain habitat.)

(2) The Cerulean Warbler is sensitive to forest fragmentation, and now is rarely found nesting in forests less than 250 ha in extent (Robbins et al. 1989). The classic example of loss and fragmentation of woodland in Cadiz Township, Green County, Wisconsin, from 1831 to 1950 (Curtis 1956) might be typical of much of the

prairie cropland; forest cover was reduced by more than 90% and the 60 remaining fragments were all less than 80 ha, nearly all of them less than 40 hectares. Most of the virgin deciduous forest within the breeding range of this warbler has been cut, and old growth forest tracts continue to decline (Mengel 1965:17, Terborgh 1989:8).

(3) In forests managed for timber production, deciduous trees are not permitted to grow large enough to attract Cerulean Warblers (Lynch 1981).

(4) Pollution and disease problems certainly are not specific to Cerulean Warblers, but these problems seem to be especially severe in the major breeding areas of this warbler (Cowling 1983, Husar and Holloway 1983).

(5) The Cerulean Warbler tends to nest in tree species that either in the past or currently are experiencing problems with disease or pollution (chestnuts, elms, oaks, sycamores). Nearly one half of 32 Ontario nests were in oaks, elms were tied for third place with four nests, and one old nest record was in an American chestnut (Peck and James 1987). All 16 nests in Jackson County, Illinois, were in American elms (Graber et al. 1983). All but two of Smith's (1893) 40 Cerulean nests in Oklahoma were in sycamores.

(6) The scarcity of nest records for the Cerulean Warbler led Friedmann (1929) to conclude erroneously that this warbler was a very uncommon victim of the Brown-headed Cowbird. Peck and James (1987) stated that 7 of 39 Ontario nests (18%) were parasitized. This is comparable to the parasitism rate on the Common Yellowthroat, which Friedmann called a very common victim. The Brown-headed Cowbird has been increasing in the southeastern states in recent decades; and because it requires open country for feeding, birds nesting within a few hundred meters of a wood margin are especially vulnerable to cowbird parasitism (Brittingham and Temple 1983). As the eastern forests become more fragmented, cowbird parasitism can be expected to increase further. A new potential threat is the recent invasion of Florida, Georgia, Louisiana, South Carolina, North Carolina, Alabama, and Texas by the South American Shiny Cowbird (*Molothrus bonariensis*) (LeGrand 1989, 1990, Imhof 1989, Jackson 1990, Lasley and Sexton 1990). The rapidly expanding range of this immigrant brood parasite has already brought dozens of individuals within 350 km of the Cerulean Warbler's breeding range.

Migration casualties

Stoddard and Norris (1967) reported that 93 Cerulean Warblers (out of 29,451 birds) struck the Leon County, Florida, TV tower during 11 fall migration periods, 1956–1966. Extreme dates were 21 July and 15 October; they had no spring records. Stoddard (1962) commented that several times as many were picked up under the tower as were seen in "opera glass" birding over the re-

gion. Chapman (1907) stated that fall migrants reach the coast of Louisiana and Mississippi from 12 to 29 July. Burleigh's (1944) 17 fall specimens from coastal Mississippi ranged from 26 July to 26 September, with 7 August as the median date of occurrence (not the median arrival). Thus, this is one of the earliest fall migrant passerines to reach the Mississippi coast, surpassed only by the Louisiana Waterthrush. It is likely, therefore, that much of the fall migration is over before most observers begin to look for fall migrants or search for casualties at towers and ceilometers.

Winter distribution and ecology

The principal winter range of Cerulean Warblers is mature, humid evergreen forest of the Andean foothills, from Venezuela and Colombia to southern Peru (Fig.

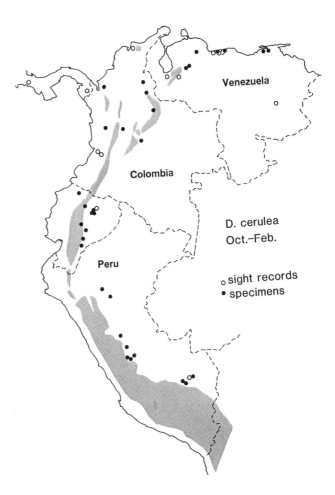

FIGURE 10. Documented winter distribution (October through February) of the Cerulean Warbler. Specimen localities and well-documented sight records (excluding several from Costa Rica) are plotted. Shaded areas show mountain elevations above 3000 meters. Extralimital records from October exist from Bermuda (*n* = 1) and Mexico (*n* = 1).

TABLE 3. Counts of Neotropical migrant passerines in 28 mixed-species canopy flocks censused by J. W. Fitzpatrick in the Cosnipata Valley, depts. Madre de Dios and Cuzco, Peru, 1981–1985

Flock Elev. (m)	Red-eyed Vireo	Canada Warbler	Cerulean Warbler	Blackburnian Warbler	Scarlet Tanager	Summer Tanager
500	1					
550						
620	5		1			
625	2	1				
640	1					
700	3					
750	1	1	1		1	1
750	2	1				
780						
800	3	1	1			
820	4	1		1	2	1
850	3		1		2	
850	1	2	2		1	
900	1				2	
920	2	1	2		4	2
950	4	1	1		2	
950	2	1	1		3	
950	4				2	1
950	2	1	1			
1000	2	2		1		
1030	2				2	
1150	3	1	1		2	1
1170	4	1				
1200	2	2	1		3	
1300	2				1	
1350	3	1		1	2	1
1350						
1400	2	1		2	5	

NOTE: Scientific names: *Vireo olivaceus, Wilsonia canadensis, Dendroica cerulea, D. fusca, Piranga olivacea, P. rubra.*

10). A survey of thirteen large systematic collections of Neotropical birds (see Acknowledgments) yielded 87 specimens with dates and complete locality information taken outside the United States and Canada. Only 37 of these were collected from November through February, all from South America: Venezuela (16), Peru (10), Ecuador (9), and Colombia (2). Of 23 additional specimens collected in October or March, 15 also were from these four Andean countries: the other 8 were from Costa Rica (2), Panama (2), Belize, Bermuda, Mexico, and United States.

Scattered sight records and a remarkable banding recovery indicate that a few individuals overwinter in the foothills of Costa Rica and Panama (the recovery was banded as immature at Powdermill Nature Reserve, Pennsylvania, on 22 July 1973, and found dead at Tor-

tuguero National Park, Costa Rica, on 12 December 1973). Recent sight records also reveal a small wintering population at middle elevations in the table-land region of eastern Venezuela (Fig. 10). In 1991, D. Stotz (pers. comm.) encountered several Cerulean Warblers on a forested mountain slope in southeastern Brazil. Most recent records, however, confirm the historical evidence that Cerulean Warblers winter almost exclusively in the Andes. August and September arrivals as far south as Ecuador show that Ceruleans are among the first passerine birds to arrive in South America from North America. All recent sight records and about half of the specimens were accompanied by habitat information. None of these records indicates a habitat other than mature evergreen forest.

In the Andean foothills of Peru and the coastal mountains of northern Venezuela, Cerulean Warblers arrive by mid-September and are found exclusively in large mixed-species flocks in the subcanopy or canopy of tall, virgin forest (Fitzpatrick, unpubl. data). At appropriate elevations (see below), about one half of the flocks censused contained at least one Cerulean Warbler, and none contained more than two individuals. In Peru, the species appears to occur only in the largest flocks, which can contain as many as 25 resident species and four other Nearctic migrant passerines (Table 3). Male Cerulean Warblers often reveal their presence by singing (the winter song is similar to the breeding song but less strident). Both sexes deliver a loud "chip" note irregularly while foraging.

Blackburnian Warblers (*Dendroica fusca*) also winter singly or in pairs within mixed-species flocks in the humid Andean forests. In Peru, no flock was found to contain both Cerulean and Blackburnian warblers (Table 3, and J.W. Fitzpatrick, unpubl. data), suggesting that these behaviorally similar species might avoid one another on the wintering grounds. As shown below, ecological segregation between these two warblers is further maintained by almost complete elevational separation, a feature characteristic of congeneric species pairs across Andean elevation gradients (Terborgh and Weske 1975).

Extensive sampling of forest bird communities in the Peruvian foothills during October, November, and December, 1981 through 1985, revealed Cerulean Warblers to be restricted to one of the narrowest elevational zones encountered among any Andean bird, migrant or resident (Fitzpatrick, unpubl. data). In our region of Peru the species occurred only between 620 and 1,300 m (Table 3). By contrast, Blackburnian Warblers in the same area were in mixed flocks from 800 to 3,000 m, and were common between 1,400 and 2,500 m. The same narrow elevational distribution appears to hold elsewhere in the Andes. Elevations of all specimens and documented sight records fall between 500 and 1,800 m, and most of these are between 600 and 1,400 meters (Fig. 11).

Constraints on the wintering grounds

Cerulean Warblers winter almost exclusively in large mixed-species flocks in tall, primary forest within an extremely narrow elevational zone in the Andes. The species' native distribution was exceedingly limited, confined to a thin, sinuous zone of forest along the Andean foothills from Venezuela to Peru. Today, this forest zone has been fragmented along its entire extent, leaving remnant lengths in only the most inaccessible regions of the foothills.

No reliable figures exist yet as to the extent of different vegetation types lost to habitat destruction across

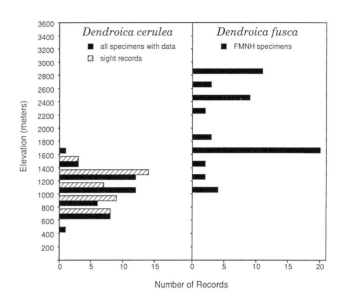

FIGURE 11. Elevations of wintering Cerulean and Blackburnian warblers in the Andes. All well-documented specimens with elevational data ($n = 43$), and reliable sight records with elevation ($n = 41$), are included for Cerulean Warbler. Elevations on labels of 56 specimens in the Field Museum of Natural History are shown for Blackburnian Warbler, for comparison.

the Neotropics. However, consensus among researchers familiar with both Central and South America is clear: proportional to its original extent, the humid forest zone of the montane foothills has been cut more extensively than any other forest type in the Neotropics except the nearly extirpated Atlantic coastal forests of Brazil. By the end of the 1980s, locating *any* accessible tract of Andean foothill forest not significantly altered by man had become extremely difficult outside of a few existing parks and preserves (Fitzpatrick, pers. obs.).

The Andean foothill forests are under escalating pressure from humans. In part this reflects the exploding human population. National figures for 1937 and 1985 (FAO 1956, 1986) show the population of Colombia increased from 8.53 million to 28.71 million (+237%), Venezuela from 3.52 million to 17.32 million (+392%), and Peru from 6.70 million to 19.70 million (+194%). Furthermore, the elevational zone of the foothills, which is inherently narrow, is also unusually attractive for human use. Foothill forests provide the highest rainfall in the Amazon Basin, very fertile soils, and agreeable climatic conditions, and are above the elevations where insect-borne tropical diseases remain rampant. Some of the most valuable commercial timber of South America grows in the foothills. This is the principal region for large, plantation-style cultivation of coffee, cacao, tea, hill rice, numerous staple vegetables, and coca.

Any bird species limited to the foothill forests of the eastern Andes should now be considered threatened because of habitat loss and fragmentation. The Cerulean Warbler is just such a specialist; its winter distribution is more restricted to this zone than any other migrant in South America. Outright loss of its specialized forest habitat, and degradation or fragmentation of remaining tracts to the point where they cannot support large mixed-species flocks, might already be increasing overwintering mortality among Cerulean Warblers. Because of its restriction to an extremely narrow ecological zone known to be severely threatened by rapid agricultural development, we would predict the Cerulean Warbler to be among the most likely of all Neotropical migrants to be severely affected by loss of its wintering habitat. The 24-year decline as reflected on BBS counts might in part be a result of this situation on the wintering grounds.

Conservation implications

The continuing loss, fragmentation, and degradation of breeding and wintering habitat for the Cerulean Warbler emphasize the importance of taking steps now to curb this decline. It is not likely that a massive conservation program specifically to benefit this warbler will be undertaken in the near future, but much can be done to promote habitat conservation beneficial to the Cerulean Warbler. By concentrating on protecting old-growth floodplain habitat required by the species, we shall be benefitting many other Neotropical migrants as well, especially the area-sensitive warblers of the southeastern United States.

Both Hamel's Tennessee study and studies of Robbins and colleagues in the Middle Atlantic states have shown the dependence of the Cerulean Warbler on large tracts of mature deciduous forest. These studies also revealed that the majority of summer records of this species in those states are on government-owned lands. We recommend, therefore, (1) that government agencies at all levels be informed of the need to protect extensive tracts of mature deciduous forest under their control. We also recommend (2) that each state and province identify extensive tracts of mature forest not under government control, and explore ways of preserving the most important of these by purchase, easement, or other means; (3) that where appropriate, younger or smaller tracts be identified and included in long-term management plans so they will ultimately develop into extensive mature tracts; (4) that more be done to educate the public (at all age levels) on the importance of habitat protection; (5) that habitat protection legislation, especially as it relates to floodplain habitats, be improved and better enforced; and (6) that more research on the life history and habitat requirements of the Cerulean Warbler be encouraged. This research should include finding ways to supplement even-age management with retention of enough old-age trees to make managed timber lands attractive to Cerulean Warblers.

Data of Fitzpatrick and others indicate unusually specialized winter habitat requirements of Cerulean Warblers. The key habitat is extremely limited, and remnant patches continue to be logged and converted to agricultural land. Furthermore, it is reasonable to suspect that this species is area sensitive on its wintering grounds as on the breeding grounds. Therefore, it appears that the best hope for long-term protection of wintering Cerulean Warblers (as well as large numbers of native Andean species) hinges on establishment of a series of preserves specifically designed to protect long tracts of primary forest encompassing elevations between 600 and 1,400 meters, along the montane foothills of Venezuela, Colombia, Ecuador, and Peru.

Acknowledgments

We thank our many colleagues and collaborators, most especially Bob Ford of the Tennessee Division of Ecological Services, Barbara Dowell and Deanna Dawson of the Patuxent Wildlife Research Center, and David Willard and Douglas Stotz of the Field Museum of Natural History, all of whom contributed substantially to the field research. Jay Buckelew, Daniel Brauning, Mark Hoffman, David Lee, Gail McPeek, Chuck Nicholson, Brainard Palmer-Ball, Sue Ridd, Sally Sutcliffe, and Rick West kindly provided unpublished atlas data. Robert Behrstock, Davis Finch, Steven Hilty, Ted Parker, Ken Parkes, and Robert Ridgely kindly provided unpublished sight records from Central or South America. We thank curators of the following systematic collections for information and access to specimens: British Museum, American Museum of Natural History, U.S. National Museum of Natural History, Field Museum of Natural History, Museum of Comparative Zoology, University of Michigan Museum of Zoology, Academy of Natural Sciences of Philadelphia, Carnegie Museum of Natural History, Museum of Vertebrate Zoology (Berkeley), Royal Ontario Museum, Los Angeles County Museum of Natural History, Louisiana State Museum of Natural Science, and the National Museum of Canada. We thank the government of Peru for permitting field work and the collecting of voucher specimens in that country. The assistance of the staff of the Warner Park Nature Center in Nashville was invaluable in studying Cerulean Warblers on that property. We thank the following colleagues who made helpful editorial suggestions for improving the manuscript: Sam Droege, Michael Erwin, John Hagan, Marshall Howe, David Johnston, and two anonymous reviewers.

Literature cited

Abernethy, R., and P. Hamel. 1987. Corridors of life. *Tennessee Recreation and Parks Association Magazine,* 2d Quarter 1987:6–7.

Ambuel, B., and S.A. Temple. 1982. Songbird populations in southern Wisconsin forests: 1954 and 1979. *J. Field Ornithol.* 53:149–158.

American Ornithologists' Union. 1983. *Check-list of North American Birds.* 6th ed. Washington: American Ornithologists' Union.

Andrle, R.F., and J.R. Carroll, eds. 1988. *The Atlas of Breeding Birds in New York State.* Ithaca, N.Y.: Cornell University Press.

Bacinski, P. 1989. Spring field notes, March–May 1989, Region No. 5. *Records of New Jersey Birds* 15(3):55–59.

Bagg, A.C., and S.A. Eliot, Jr. 1937. *Birds of the Connecticut Valley in Massachusetts.* Northampton, Mass.: Hampshire Bookshop.

Bent, A.C. 1953. *Life Histories of North American Wood Warblers.* U.S. Natl. Mus. Bull. 203.

Blincoe, B.J. 1925. Birds of Bardstown, Nelson County, Kentucky. *Auk* 42:404–420.

Bridges, E., D.C. Eagar, D.B. Durham, P.B. Hamel, L.R. Smith, and P. Somers. 1985. *Developing a Community-based Natural Area Survey Technique in the Central Basin Area of Tennessee.* Nashville: Tenn. Dept. Conserv.

Brittingham, M.C., and S.A. Temple. 1983. Have cowbirds caused forest songbirds to decline? *BioScience* 33:31–35.

Bull, J. 1974. *Birds of New York state.* New York: Doubleday.

Burleigh, T.D. 1944. The bird life of the Gulf Coast region of Mississippi. *Louisiana State Univ. Mus. Zool., Occ. Papers* 20:329–490.

Cadman, M.D., P.F.J. Eagles, and F.M. Helleiner. 1987. *Atlas of the Breeding Birds of Ontario.* Waterloo, Ontario: University of Waterloo Press.

Chapman, F.M. 1907. *The Warblers of North America.* New York: D. Appleton.

Cowling, E.B. 1983. The North American acid rain situation. Pages 53–73 in *Ecological Effects of Acid Deposition.* National Swedish Environment Protection Board Report PM 1636. Solna, Sweden.

Curtis, J.T. 1956. The modification of mid-latitude grasslands and forests by man. Pages 721–736 in *Man's Role in Changing the Face of the Earth,* W.L. Thomas, ed. Chicago: University of Chicago Press.

Durham, D.B., R.K. Abernethy, D.C. Eagar, R.P. Ford, and P.B. Hamel. 1988a. *The West Tennessee Bottomland Hardwood Evaluation System Model.* Nashville: Tenn. Dept. Conserv. and U.S. Army Corps of Engineers.

Durham, D.B., R.K. Abernethy, D.C. Eagar, R.P. Ford, P.B. Hamel, L.J. O'Neil, and T.M. Pullen, Jr. 1988b. Application of the Habitat Evaluation System to modeling bottomland hardwood forest communities in west Tennessee. *Trans. North Amer. Wildl. and Nat. Resour. Conf.* 53:481–490.

Food and Agricultural Organization. 1956. *1955 Yearbook of Food and Agricultural Statistics.* Vol. 9, part 1. Rome: FAO.

Food and Agricultural Organization. 1986. *1985 FAO Production Yearbook.* Vol. 39, FAO Statistics Series No. 70. Rome: FAO.

Forbush, E.H. 1929. *Birds of Massachusetts and Other New England States.* Vol. 3. Boston: Massachusetts Department of Agriculture.

Ford, R.P. 1990. Habitat relationships of breeding birds and winter birds in forested wetlands of west Tennessee. M.S. Thesis, University of Tennessee at Knoxville, Tennessee.

Ford, R.P., and P.B. Hamel. 1988. The breeding birds of forested habitats of the Central Basin of Tennessee. Pages 278–294 in *Proc. First Ann. Symposium on the Natural History of Lower Tennessee and Cumberland River Valleys,* D.H. Snyder, ed. Clarksville, Tenn.: Center for Field Biology of Land Between the Lakes, Austin Peay University.

Friedmann, H. 1929. *The Cowbirds: A Study in the Biology of Social Parasitism.* Springfield, Ill.: Charles C. Thomas.

Graber, J.W., R.R. Graber, and E.L. Kirk. 1983. *Illinois Birds: Wood Warblers.* Illinois Biol. Surv. Biol. Notes 118.

Hamel, P.B. 1981. A hierarchical approach to avian community structure. Ph.D. Dissertation, Clemson University, Clemson, South Carolina.

———. 1984. Comparison of variable circular-plot and spot-map censusing methods in temperate deciduous forest. *Ornis Scand.* 15:266–274.

Hands, H.M., R.D. Drobney, and M.R. Ryan. 1989. *Status of the Cerulean Warbler in the Northcentral United States.* Columbia: Missouri Coop. Fish and Wildl. Res. Unit.

Husar, R.B., and J.M. Holloway. 1983. Sulfur and nitrogen over North America. Pages 95–115 in *Ecological Effects of Acid Deposition.* National Swedish Environment Protection Board Report PM 1636. Solna, Sweden.

Imhof, T.A. 1989. The spring season, Central Southern Region. *Am. Birds* 43:491–95.

Jackson, G.D. 1990. The spring season, March 1–May 31, 1990, Central Southern Region. *Am. Birds* 44:439–444.

James, F.C., and H.H. Shugart. 1970. A quantitative method of habitat description. *Aud. Field Notes* 24:727–736.

Järvinen, O., and R.A. Väisänen. 1975. Estimating relative densities of breeding birds by the line transect method. *Oikos* 26:316–322.

Kahl, R.B., T.S. Baskett, J.A. Ellis, and J.N. Burroughs. 1985. *Characteristics of Summer Habitats of Selected Nongame Birds in Missouri.* Univ. Missouri-Columbia Agric. Exp. Sta. Res. Bull. 1056.

Kirkwood, F.C. 1895. A list of the birds of Maryland. *Trans. Maryland Acad. Sci.* 2:241–382.

Lasley, G.W., and C. Sexton. 1990. The spring season, March 1–May 31, 1990, Texas Region. *Am. Birds* 44:458–465.

Laughlin, S.B., and D.P. Kibbe, eds. 1985. *The Atlas of Breeding Birds of Vermont.* Hanover, N.H.: University Press of New England.

LeGrand, H.E. Jr. 1989. Spring 1989 report, Southern Atlantic Coast Region. *Am. Birds* 43:1302–1306.

———. 1990. The winter migration, Southern Atlantic Coast Region. *Am. Birds* 44:252–256.

Lynch, J.M. 1981. Status of the Cerulean Warbler in the Roanoke River basin of North Carolina. *Chat* 45(2):29–35.

Mayfield, H. 1977. Brown-headed Cowbird: Agent of extermination? *Am. Birds* 31:107–113.

Mengel, R.M. 1965. *The Birds of Kentucky.* Ornithol. Monogr. 3.

Mossman, M.J., and K.I. Lange. 1982. *Breeding Birds of the Baraboo Hills, Wisconsin: Their History, Distribution, and Ecology.* Madison: Wis. Dept. Nat. Resources and Wisc. Soc. Ornithol.

Peck, G.K., and R.D. James. 1983. *Breeding Birds of Ontario: Nidiology and Distribution, Vol. 2: Passerines.* Toronto: Royal Ontario Museum.

Renewable Resources Evaluation Project. 1977. *Forest Survey Field Instructions for South Carolina.* Asheville, N.C.: USDA Forest Service, Southeastern Forest Experiment Station.

Robbins, C.S., D.K. Dawson, and B.A. Dowell. 1989. *Habitat Area Requirements of Breeding Forest Birds of the Middle Atlantic States.* Wildl. Monogr. 103.

Smith, P.W., Jr. 1893. Nesting of the Cerulean Warbler. *Ornithol. and Ool.* 18:5.

Stewart, R.E., and C.S. Robbins. 1958. *Birds of Maryland and the District of Columbia.* North American Fauna 62.

Stine, P.M. 1959. Changes in the breeding birds of Bird Haven Sanctuary over a period of forty-five years. *Wilson Bull.* 71:372–380.

Stoddard, H.L., Sr. 1962. *Bird casualties at a Leon County, Florida TV tower, 1955–1961.* Tall Timbers Res. Sta. Bull. No. 1.

Stoddard, H.L., Sr., and R.A. Norris. 1967. *Bird Casualties at a Leon County, Florida TV Tower: An Eleven Year Study.* Tall Timbers Res. Sta. Bull. No. 8.

Terborgh, J. 1989. *Where Have All the Birds Gone?* Princeton: Princeton University Press.

Terborgh, J., and J.S. Weske. 1975. The role of competition in the distribution of Andean birds. *Ecology* 56:562–576.

Trautman, M.B. 1940. *The Birds of Buckeye Lake, Ohio.* Univ. Mich. Mus. Zool. Misc. Publ. 44.

Wood, N.A., and A.D. Tinker. 1910. Notes on some of the rarer birds of Washtenaw County, Michigan. *Auk* 27:129–141

RICHARD T. HOLMES
Department of Biological Sciences
Dartmouth College
Hanover, New Hampshire 03755

THOMAS W. SHERRY
Department of Ecology, Evolution,
and Organismal Biology
Tulane University
New Orleans, Louisiana 70118

Site fidelity of migratory warblers in temperate breeding and Neotropical wintering areas: Implications for population dynamics, habitat selection, and conservation

Abstract. We measured site fidelity from year to year in populations of two long-distance migratory paruline warblers in a temperate breeding area in New Hampshire USA and on a Neotropical wintering ground in Jamaica. Annual site return varied significantly among age and sex classes of American Redstarts (*Setophaga ruticilla*) in summer but not in winter. For Black-throated Blue Warblers (*Dendroica caerulescens*), site fidelity was similar for sex and age classes within each season, but varied among years in winter, probably because of the effects of a hurricane in one year. Both species, but especially American Redstarts, exhibited lower site fidelity and moved greater distances between years on breeding grounds than in wintering areas. We propose that lower site fidelity and site attachment in summer reflects habitat that varies strongly in suitability from place to place and probably from year to year. This variability in the breeding habitat results in intense competition among males for high quality sites and consequently for mates. We argue that habitat selection and competitive processes operating in summer have important influences on the population dynamics and potentially on the abundances of these temperate-nesting passerines. On the other hand, the higher site fidelity and site attachment of both species in winter suggests that winter habitats are crucial for survival and that major habitat destruction or alteration in winter quarters could have a severe negative impact on populations of such long-distance migrant species.

Sinopsis. Nosotros medimos la fidelidad al sitio de un año a otro en poblaciones de dos Parulinae migratorios de larga distancia en un área templada de anidación en New Hampshire, EUA y en un cuartel de invernada neotropical en Jamaica. El retorno anual al sitio varió significativamente entre sexos y clases de edad de *Setophaga ruticilla* en verano pero no en invierno. Para *Dendroica caerulescens,* la fidelidad al sitio fue similar para clases de edad y sexo dentro de cada estación, pero varió entre inviernos de diferentes años probablemente por los efectos de un huracán en un año. Ambas especies, especialmente *S. ruticilla,* exhibieron fidelidades a los sitios mas bajas y se desplazaron mayores distancias en los sitios de cría que en las áreas de invernada. Nosotros consideramos que la menor fidelidad y vínculo con el sitio en verano refleja un habitat que varía fuertemente en su calidad de un sitio a otro y probablemente de año a año. Esta variabilidad en el hábitat de cría produce una competencia intensa entre machos por sitios de alta calidad y consecuentemente por parejas. Argumentamos que la selección de habitat y los procesos competitivos que se presentan en verano tienen influencias importantes sobre la dinámica de las poblaciones y potencialmente sobre las abundancias de estas aves anidantes de zonas templadas. Por otra parte, la mas alta fidelidad y vínculo con el sitio de ambas especies en invierno sugieren que los habitats de invierno son cruciales para la supervivencia y que una destrucción o alteración mayor en los cuarteles de invierno podría tener un severo impacto negativo sobre las poblaciones de tales especies migratorias de larga distancia.

Many migratory passerine birds occupy specific sites in their habitats to which they return year after year. Most data on such site fidelity concern birds on their breeding grounds (Greenwood 1980, Greenwood and Harvey 1982). Likewise, explanations for the occurrence of site fidelity and for observed variation in year-to-year dispersal distances relate mostly to breeding season events, for example, the effects of previous breeding performance (Darley et al. 1977, Nolan 1978, Grieg-Smith 1982, Shields 1984, Beletsky and Orians 1987, Drilling and Thompson 1988) and the avoidance of inbreeding (Greenwood and Harvey 1982).

In recent years, it has become evident that migratory passerines also exhibit site fidelity to their wintering grounds. For example, Ketterson and Nolan (1982) and Rabenold and Rabenold (1985) documented winter site fidelity in Dark-eyed Juncos (*Junco hyemalis*), a short-distance migrant which winters mostly in the south temperate zone. Species that migrate longer distances and winter in the Neotropics also return to the same localities in successive winters (e.g., Nickel 1968, Loftin 1977, Diamond and Smith 1973, Faaborg and Arendt 1984, Kricher and Davis 1986). Unfortunately, most data on the site return of such Neotropical migrants are based on small sample sizes, usually of only a few marked individuals caught in mist nets operated in successive winters. The degree to which such long-distance migrants

return to specific winter quarters has rarely been quantitatively assessed, nor has there been discussion of its ecological or evolutionary significance.

In 1986, we initiated demographic studies of two migrant warbler species, the American Redstart (*Setophaga ruticilla*) and the Black-throated Blue Warbler (*Dendroica caerulescens*), in their Neotropical winter quarters in Jamaica. Using a playback technique to capture and color-mark individuals (Holmes et al. 1989), we were able to resight individuals returning from one year to the next, and thus determine site fidelity on a population basis. We have also gathered comparable information on breeding populations of these same two species in New Hampshire, USA. The objectives of this paper, then, are (1) to compare the site fidelity of these two migratory warblers in summer breeding areas and in winter quarters, (2) to relate these findings to published information, and (3) to consider the implications of site fidelity in both summer and winter for understanding population dynamics and habitat selection of migratory passerines and for developing strategies for their conservation.

Study sites and methods

We studied breeding populations of American Redstarts and Black-throated Blue Warblers in the Hubbard Brook Experimental Forest, part of the White Mountain National Forest, in central New Hampshire. American Redstarts were studied intensively on a 34-ha study area from 1983 through summer 1989 and Black-throated Blue Warblers on a 55-ha forest plot from 1986 to 1989. The habitat at Hubbard Brook is a relatively mature northern hardwoods forest, and has been described extensively by Holmes et al. (1986) and Holmes (1990).

We studied wintering populations of the two species on several small (5- to 11-ha) forested sites in Jamaica, West Indies, during the months of October, January, and March from 1986 to 1989. These were located along a north-south transect between Montego Bay and Black River in the western part of the island, and are described by Holmes et al. (1989).

Males in summer and individuals of both sexes and species in winter were caught mainly with the playback technique described by Holmes et al. (1989). Breeding females were caught mostly by placing a mist net near their nests. All birds captured received unique color-band combinations, which permitted subsequent identification of individuals in the field.

Males of both species were aged according to plumage characteristics (U.S. Fish and Wildlife Service 1977, Pyle et al. 1987). They were designated as yearlings (< 1 year of age, referred to as hatch year, HY, prior to December 31 or as second year, SY, as of 1 January and until their first prebasic molt in late summer of the

TABLE 1. Site fidelity of American Redstarts in summer at Hubbard Brook (1983–1989) and in winter in Jamaica (1986–1989)

	% Returning (n) in years following banding			
	1st	2nd	3rd	4th
A. SUMMER				
Males[a]				
Banded as SY	16% (51)	60% (5)	0% (2)	–
Banded as ASY	39% (83)	43% (30)	17% (12)	100% (1)
All (SY+ASY)	30% (134)	46% (35)	14% (14)	100% (1)
Females	19% (48)	50% (8)	0% (4)	–
Totals (males + females)	27% (182)	47% (43)	11% (18)	100% (1)
B. WINTER				
Males[a]				
Banded as HY	75% (12)	0% (1)	–	–
Banded as ASY	49% (57)	57% (21)	50% (8)	–
All (HY + ASY)	54% (69)	55% (22)	50% (8)	–
Females	46% (42)	47% (15)	40% (5)	–
Totals (males + females)	51% (111)	51% (37)	46% (13)	–

a. Males aged as HY (= hatch year, those caught and marked in their first autumn in Jamaica, i.e., in the October following their hatch), SY (= second year, those caught and marked at Hubbard Brook during their first breeding season), or ASY (= after second year, those in black-and-orange "adult" male plumage); see text and U.S. Fish and Wildlife Service Banding Manual (1977) for details.

year following their hatching, in accord with U.S. Fish and Wildlife Service (1977) terminology or as older males (individuals two-years-of-age or older or ASYs). Although criteria for aging females of these species have been developed recently (Pyle et al. 1987, T.W. Sherry and R.T. Holmes, unpubl.), we were unable to age them consistently during the early years of this study, and therefore do not distinguish between female age classes here.

Site fidelity to breeding and wintering areas was measured by recording the return of birds to the study areas in successive summers and winters, respectively. We visually searched each plot and surrounding habitat for returning color-marked individuals. The number of birds marked each season and their returns in subsequent years were then tabulated, that is, the number of birds marked in year x, and then returning in years x + 1, x + 2, . . ., and the columns summed for each year following capture (see Nolan 1978). We then calculated the percentage of birds returning in the first year following marking (x + 1), in the second year (x + 2), and so on. To obtain the largest possible sample size, we used data through the year 1989, which does not allow us, for example, to document the return rate after year 1 of those birds marked in 1988. This accounts for the marked decrease in sample sizes in subsequent years in the data set (see Tables 1 and 2).

The territories of color-marked individuals were

mapped on gridded census plots in both summer and winter (for procedures see Sherry and Holmes 1989 for summer, Holmes et al. 1989 for winter). The degree of site attachment of returning males in summer and both sexes in winter was determined from these maps, as the distance between territory centers from one June to the next (summer) and from one October to the next (winter). For breeding females, site attachment represents the distances between nest sites in successive breeding seasons.

Results

In this paper, we separate site fidelity into two components: (1) annual site return—percentage of marked individuals returning to a study area each year, and (2) site attachment—the distance between territory centers of individuals returning to the study areas in successive years. The latter in the breeding area has been referred to as "breeding dispersal" by Greenwood (1980) and others.

ANNUAL SITE RETURN IN SUMMER AND WINTER

AMERICAN REDSTARTS. Of 182 redstarts marked at Hubbard Brook between 1983 and 1988, 49 (27%) returned in the year following banding (Table 1A). Male redstarts returned at a higher rate than females (30% vs. 19%),

TABLE 2. Site fidelity of Black-throated Blue Warblers in summer at Hubbard Brook (1983–1989) and in winter in Jamaica (1986–1989)

	% Returning (n) in years following banding		
	1st	2nd	3rd
A. SUMMER			
Males[a]			
Banded as SY	42% (26)	38% (8)	100% (1)
Banded as ASY	35% (23)	50% (6)	67% (3)
All (SY+ASY)	39% (49)	43% (14)	75% (4)
Females	36% (50)	36% (11)	0% (1)
Totals (males + females)	37% (99)	40% (25)	60% (5)
B. WINTER			
Males[a]			
Banded as HY	40% (20)	0% (3)	–
Banded as ASY	62% (13)	0% (7)	–
All (HY + ASY)	48% (33)	0% (10)	–
Females	42% (24)	33% (6)	–
Totals (males + females)	46% (57)	13% (16)	

a. Males aged as HY (= hatch year, those caught and marked in their first autumn in Jamaica, i.e., in the October following their hatch), SY (= second year, those caught and marked at Hubbard Brook during their first breeding season), or ASY (= after second year, those in black-and-orange "adult" male plumage); see text and U.S. Fish and Wildlife Service Banding Manual (1977) for details.

although the difference was not statistically significant (G-test, G = 2.33, P > 0.10). Yearling (SY) males marked in their first breeding season returned at a significantly lower rate (16%) than did older ASY males (39%, Table 1A; (G = 8.39, P < 0.005). This difference, however, did not persist past the second year of return (Table 1A), that is, 60% of the SYs that returned in year 1 returned in year 2, a rate that was not significantly different from ASY returns in year 2 (43%, G = 0.47, P > 0.10). These data show that SY male redstarts exhibit low site return to their first potential breeding site, but that once a male has returned in his second breeding season, then the probability of his further return is relatively high.

In Jamaica, 55 of 111 (51%) color-banded redstarts returned in the first year following banding (Table 1B). Males and females returned at nearly equal rates (52% vs. 46%, respectively, G = 0.50, P > 0.10). Unlike yearlings in the breeding area, HY male redstarts marked in their first winter returned to those winter sites in the year following banding at an even greater frequency than did males marked initially in winter as ASYs (75% vs. 49%, respectively), although the difference was not significant (G = 3.17, P > 0.05). Because relatively few SY males were marked in the first two years of our study in Jamaica, we have few data on their return rates in years 2 and 3. ASY males, however, continued to return

to their winter sites in years 2 and 3 at rates ≥ 50% (Table 1B). In these seasons, these individuals would have been at least three and four years of age, respectively.

Comparisons of redstart site returns in summer and winter (Table 1A vs. 1B) show that American Redstarts exhibited significantly less site fidelity to breeding than to winter locations for the species as a whole (27% vs. 50%, G = 15.3, P < 0.005), for males considered separately (30% vs. 54%, G = 9.57, P < 0.005, and for females (19% vs. 46%, G = 4.0, P < 0.05). However, for those individuals (males and females considered both separately and combined) returning for a second or third year after first banding, there were no significant differences in site fidelity between summer and winter (G-tests, all P > 0.10).

BLACK-THROATED BLUE WARBLERS. Of the 99 Black-throated Blue Warblers marked at Hubbard Brook, 37 (37%) returned in the first year following banding (Table 2A). Males and females returned at very similar rates (39% vs. 36%, respectively, G = 0.08, P > 0.5). In contrast to SY redstarts, however, yearling (SY) male black-throated blues returned slightly more frequently (42%) than did older (ASY) males (35%, Table 2A), but not significantly so (G = 0.29, P > 0.50). Thus, once a yearling black-throated blue male has settled and bred in an area, even in its first breeding season, it is as likely to return to that place in subsequent years as are older males. Furthermore, males first marked either as SYs or as ASYs continued to return at approximately the same rates in subsequent years (e.g., 38% vs. 50% , respectively, in year 2, Table 2A; $G = 2.31, P > 0.10$). Thus, Black-throated Blue Warblers do not show the age-related differences in breeding-site return evident in redstarts.

In winter, 26 of 57 (46%) of the black-throated blues marked in Jamaica returned in the next year (Table 2B). Annual site return of males and females was nearly the same (48% vs. 42%, respectively, $G = 0.26, P > 0.50$). Male black-throated blues marked initially as ASYs tended to return at a higher rate than those marked as SYs (62% vs. 40%, respectively), although the difference was not significant ($G = 1.47, P > 0.10$). No marked males in Jamaica returned in year 2 after banding (Table 2B), probably because of the occurrence of a major hurricane in September of 1988 (see Discussion).

Comparisons of summer- and winter-site return of black-throated blues show that they return at a lower rate in summer than in winter (Table 2A vs. 2B). This was true for males (39% vs. 48%), for females (36% vs. 42%), and for both sexes combined (37% vs. 46%). However, in all cases, the differences were not statistically significant (G-tests, $P > 0.1$).

SITE ATTACHMENT IN SUMMER AND IN WINTER

The distances between territory centers of returning individuals in subsequent seasons, which we define here as site attachment, provide a measure of the degree of site fidelity. Because such distances were not distributed normally, we use the medians for comparisons.

AMERICAN REDSTARTS. Site attachment of male redstarts returning to the breeding grounds (68 m) was significantly higher (Mann-Whitney U-test, $P < 0.05$) than that of breeding females, 171 m (Fig. 1). The median distances between territory centers of returning SY and ASY males (85 m vs. 63 m, respectively) were not significantly different (Mann-Whitney $U, P > 0.10$).

Site attachment of male and female redstarts returning to their wintering grounds in Jamaica (29 and 27 m, respectively—Fig. 1) did not significantly differ (Mann-Whitney $U, P > 0.5$). However, both sexes exhibited significantly greater site attachment in winter quarters than on the breeding grounds (Mann-Whitney $U, P < 0.001$ for males, $P < 0.01$ for females).

It has frequently been shown that site attachment (dispersal) of breeding birds is often influenced by their previous nesting success (see Greenwood and Harvey 1982 and references in Introduction). To address this possibility, we tested the hypothesis that redstarts that returned to the breeding area were more likely to have

successfully fledged young in the preceeding season than those that failed to return. Combining data from all years yields a sample size of 67 males, 37 of which returned to the breeding area in a subsequent year and 30 which did not return. Twenty five (67%) of the 37 returning male redstarts had been successful (i.e., fledged ≥ 1 young) in the preceeding season, whereas 13 (57%) of 30 nonreturning males had also been successful in nesting the previous year. This difference is not statistically significant ($G = 0.84, P > 0.10$). Even considering only older ASY males, those not returning were just as likely to have been successful the previous season as those that did return (73%, $n = 22$ vs. 63%, $n = 27$, respectively; G-tests, $P > 0.10$). Likewise, although 80% of 10 returning females were successful in fledging one or more young the previous season, this was not statistically significant from the 55% of females ($n = 22$) that had also been successful but that did not return ($G = 2.06$, $P > 0.10$) Thus, the tendency was for successfully nesting individuals to return more frequently than those that failed in their nesting attempts, but the differences were not significant.

Another relevant measure would be to compare the breeding dispersal distances of returning birds that succeeded or failed in their previous year's nesting attempt(s). However, our sample sizes, particularly for those that failed in the previous season, were too low for testing this possibility.

BLACK-THROATED BLUE WARBLERS. Site attachment of Black-throated Blue Warblers returning to the breeding areas in successive seasons was 94 m for males and 153 m for females (Fig. 2). This difference in the distance moved by males and females was not statistically significant (Mann-Whitney $U, P > 0.1$). Males marked in summer as yearlings (SYs) returned the next year at a median distance of 156 m, which because of the high variability in the data did not differ significantly from that of ASY males (83 m; Mann-Whitney $U, 0.10 < P > 0.05$).

In winter, the comparable median values between territory centers of Black-throated Blue Warblers were 28 m for males and 41 m for females, which were not significantly different (Mann-Whitney $U, P > 0.1$). Both male and female black-throated blues moved significantly farther when they returned to breeding sites than to winter sites (Fig. 2, Mann-Whitney $U, P < 0.01$ for males, and $P < 0.001$ for females).

Also, as with redstarts, male black-throated blues that successfully fledged one or more young in a season were no more likely to return the next season than those that did not return (96%, $n = 27$, vs. 91%, $n = 35$; $G = 0.63, P > 0.10$). The comparable rates for returning females that had been successful the previous season (95%, $n = 21$) vs. for those not returning (82%, $n =$

AMERICAN REDSTART

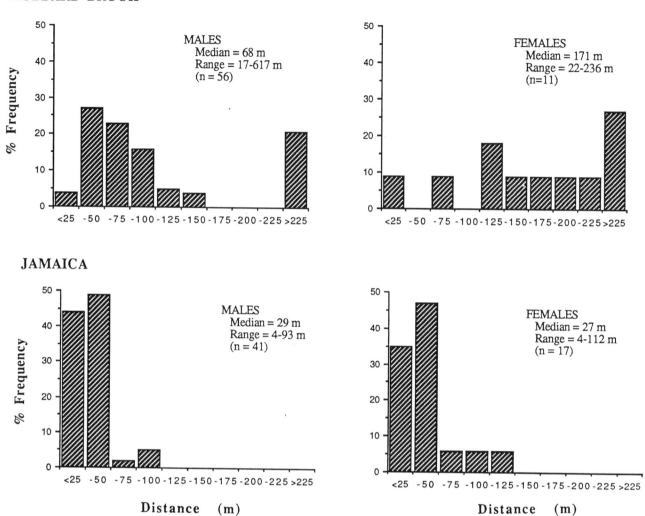

FIGURE 1. Distances between territory centers for male American Redstarts returning from one June to the next June (in summer at Hubbard Brook) and for male and female redstarts returning from one October to the next October (in winter in Jamaica, W.I.). For females in the breeding season, data represent distances between first nests in successive years.

39) were also not significantly different ($G = 2.37, P > 0.10$). Because black-throated blues often fledge more than one brood per season (R.T. Holmes, unpubl.), a better measure of nesting success might have been total number of young fledged. Unfortunately, data are insufficient at this time for adequate testing of this possibility.

Discussion and conclusions

The results presented above show that American Redstarts and Black-throated Blue Warblers exhibit site fidelity to both breeding and wintering grounds. The data also indicate that individuals of both species, but especially the redstart, exhibit higher site fidelity to winter habitats in the Neotropics than to breeding habitats in the north temperate zone. Furthermore, not only do individuals return at a higher rate to their wintering grounds, but they tend to return more precisely to the same places within that habitat. In the ensuing discussion, we consider (1) whether the site fidelity estimates are reasonable and how they compare to existing information, (2) why site fidelity might be lower in the breeding season and what factors influence it, and (3)

BLACK-THROATED BLUE WARBLER

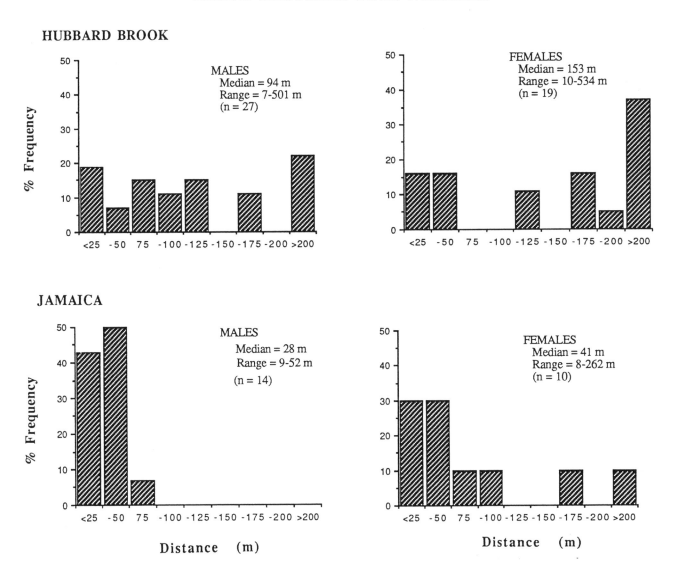

FIGURE 2. Distances between territory centers for male Black-throated Blue Warblers returning from one June to the next June (in summer at Hubbard Brook) and for male and female black-throated blues returning from one October to the next October (in winter in Jamaica, W.I.). For females in the breeding season, data represent distances between first nests in successive years.

SITE FIDELITY IN SUMMER AND WINTER: HOW REALISTIC ARE THE ESTIMATES?

Annual returns to breeding areas have been documented for a number of migratory passerines, although replicated estimates for the same species in the same or different habitats are rare. In most cases, the rates vary between 20 and 60%, with males returning more frequently than females. For example, Nolan (1978) found the implications of these findings for studies of migrant bird population dynamics and conservation.

that 60% of the male and 19% of the female Prairie Warblers (*Dendroica discolor*) returned to a breeding ground in Indiana in the first year following banding. Walkinshaw (1953) reported site return rates of male and female Prothonotary Warblers (*Protonotaria citrea*) in Michigan of 50% and 20%, respectively, whereas comparable values for Kirtland's Warblers (*Dendroica kirtlandii*) in the same state were 53% and 31% (Berger and Radabaugh 1968). For Yellow-breasted Chats (*Icteria virens*), Thompson and Nolan (1973) found that only 11% of 18 males returned in the year following banding, whereas none of 29 females did so. For Willow Warblers (*Phyllo-*

scopus trochilus) in northern Europe, Tiainen (1983) reported 24% of 122 males returning, and Jakobsson (1988) found a return rate of 29% for males of the same species (*n* = 151). For other migratory species, Drilling and Thompson (1988) found that 38% of male and 23% of female house wrens (*Troglodytes aedon*) returned, and Gavin and Bollinger (1988) report site fidelity of 44% for male bobolinks (*Dolichonyx oryzivorus*) and 25% for females.

Since breeding-site fidelity will undoubtedly vary among habitats occupied, influenced at least in part by reproductive success and mortality rates experienced by each species or population, it is difficult to generalize from such comparisons. Nevertheless, the site return rates reported here for breeding male and female American Redstarts of 30% and 19%, and for Black-throated Blue Warblers of 39% and 36%, are within the range of values reported previously, and appear to represent reasonable estimates for these small migratory passerines.

Site return of migrant birds to winter habitats has been less well studied. Diamond and Smith (1973) report return rates of American Redstarts to Jamaica of 11.9% (*n* = 126) and of Black-throated Blue Warblers, 16.1% (*n* = 85). Faaborg and Arendt (1984) found that 15% of 59 redstarts returned to their study site in Puerto Rico, whereas several other warbler species wintering in their study area returned at rates ranging from 3% (*n* = 29) for Northern Parula (*Parula americana*) to 50% (*n* = 4) for Prothonotary Warblers. McNeil (1982) found 44% of 9 American Redstarts returning to a site in Venezuela. Kricher and Davis (1986) reported return rates for warblers wintering in Belize ranging from 0% (*n* = 5) for Common Yellowthroats (*Geothlypis trichas*) to 35% (*n* = 35) for Kentucky Warblers (*Oporornis philadelphia*). Martin and Karr (1986) found that four migrant warblers in Panama returned at rates varying from 24 to 80%, although their sample sizes were small. Most of these values of winter-site return rates are low compared to those we report. However, they are all derived from birds captured in general mist-netting activities, which, unless intensively done, undoubtedly underestimate the number of marked birds returning. The procedure we have used of color-marking birds and then making intensive searches to resight them produces higher, and probably more realistic estimates of site fidelity. Note also that all of the estimates of breeding site fidelity given above are derived from observations of returning color-banded birds.

The importance of this methodology is supported by several other studies of migrants in winter which used the observation technique. Kelsey (1989) reports that 57% of 23 color-marked male Marsh Warblers (*Acrocephalus palustris*) returned to a study area in Zambia in

one year, whereas 27% of 18 did so in a second year. Similarly, 52% of 25 color-marked male Greenish Warblers (*Phylloscopus trochilis*) returned to a site in India (Price 1981). Nisbet and Medway (1972), using intensive mist-netting instead of color-marking, reported that 50% of 262 banded Great Reed Warblers (*Acrocephalus orientalis*) returned to their study site in Malaysia. At a second locality nearby, they found a return rate of 37% (*n* = 83).

These site return estimates for migratory warblers from other studies in the tropics are similar to those we report here for redstarts and black-throated blues in Jamaica. It, therefore, seems that a return rate of about 50% for migratory warblers in winter quarters might not be unusual. Also, these values of winter site fidelity are consistent with the 50–60% annual survivorship rates for many small migratory passerine birds, as estimated using more sophisticated methods such as Jolly-Seber models on mark-recapture data (e.g., Nichols et al. 1981).

SITE FIDELITY IN SUMMER VERSUS WINTER: WHY THE DIFFERENCES?

Both American Redstarts and Black-throated Blue Warblers exhibited lower levels of site fidelity in summer than in winter. For example, only 16% of the yearling male redstarts marked in their first potential breeding season (SYs) returned the following year, compared to about 40% of the ASY males. Note that we are not considering natal philopatry, which is almost always very low (Greenwood and Harvey 1982), but returns of individuals marked in the summer when they are about one year of age (SY) to the next breeding season when they are two years of age. These differences in site fidelity between summer and winter could be caused by a variety of factors. For example, we could be comparing different populations in summer and winter, the results could be an artifact of our sampling procedures, or there might be actual differences in the ways in which birds respond to, and are affected by, habitat in their breeding and wintering areas. Each of these is considered below, with particular reference to the redstart which exhibited the most pronounced differences.

DISTRIBUTIONAL PATTERNS: THE VALIDITY OF THE COMPARISONS. First, it is possible that we might be comparing different populations of birds in summer and winter, and these different populations might be affected by different mortality factors and thus differ in return rates. Unfortunately, little information is available to link particular breeding and winter areas of any individual or even population of American Redstart or Black-throated Blue Warbler, or for that matter for almost any other Neotropical migrant species. To examine the

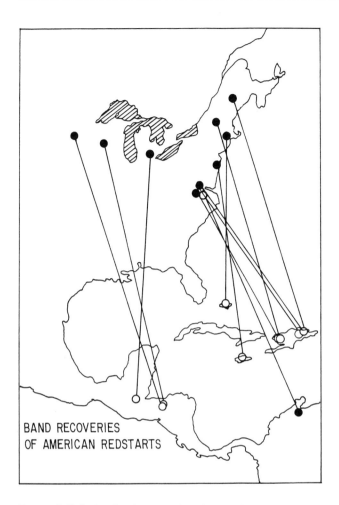

FIGURE 3. Relationship between breeding and wintering areas of American Redstarts, as indicated by recoveries of banded birds (data from U.S. Fish and Wildlife Service, Laurel, MD). Banding sites (solid circles) and recovery points (open circles) are connected with straight lines. The latter are not intended to represent actual migratory flight paths.

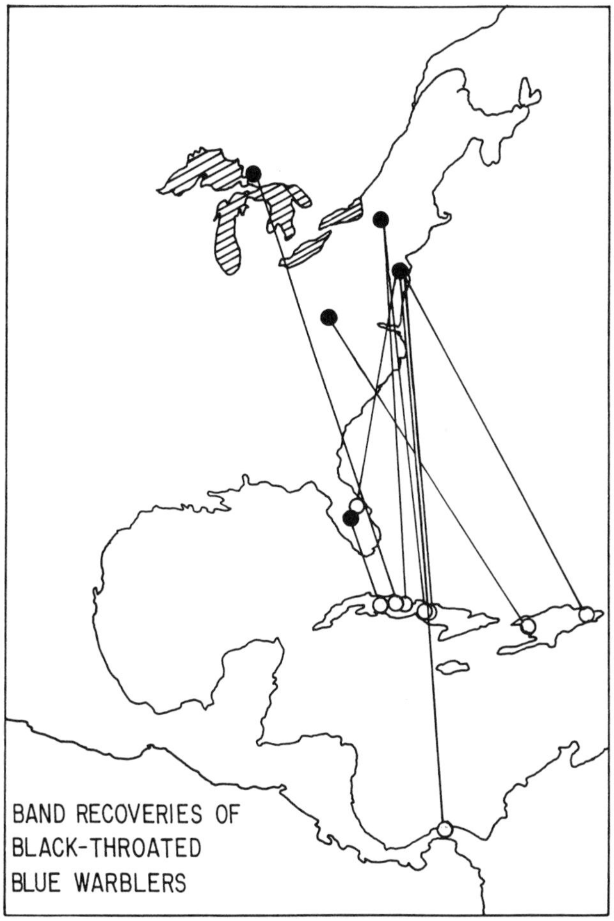

FIGURE 4. Relationship between breeding and wintering areas of Black-throated Blue Warblers, as indicated by recoveries of banded birds (data from U.S. Fish and Wildlife Service, Laurel, MD). See legend for Figure 3.

available distributional data for redstarts and black-throated blues, we reviewed the banding recoveries for these two species from the U.S. Fish and Wildlife Service records through 1988. Of 213 recoveries of banded redstarts and 26 of black-throated blues, most were of birds recaptured within the same area as banding. A few individuals of each species were recovered in potential winter areas (Figs. 3 and 4), but in all cases the banding occurred during migration, often in late summer or autumn, so no link could be established between a breeding and a wintering area. For example, a redstart recovered in Haiti (a probable winter site) in November had been banded in Virginia in mid-September (during fall migration).

Analyses of these band-recovery data do indicate the directions of migration, however, and provide strong evi-

dence linking breeding and wintering areas for migrant populations. From Figures 3 and 4, it can be seen that both American Redstarts and Black-throated Blue Warblers from the northeastern United States migrate to the Caribbean area, with their probable destination being the Greater Antilles. Moreover, redstarts from the more western portions of their breeding range have been recovered in more westerly wintering areas in Central America (Fig. 3). Such north-south migratory routes have been reported for other migratory species (Cooke 1904, Hutto 1985), and the evidence shown here, for redstarts at least, suggests that the pattern might hold for populations within species.

Although we would like to know more precisely the wintering locations of the warblers breeding in New Hampshire and the breeding areas for those wintering in Jamaica, the data here indicate that American Redstarts and Black-throated Blue Warblers from the northeast are migrating to or toward the Greater Antilles. It is thus likely that we are dealing with the same general populations.

METHODOLOGICAL PROBLEMS. Second, the differences in site fidelity between summer and winter might be an artifact of differences in methodology. Our study sites at Hubbard Brook are large (34–55 ha), whereas the winter sites in Jamaica are smaller (6–10 ha) and in some cases rather isolated from other, similar habitats (see Holmes et al. 1989). If this difference were important, however, we might expect lower site fidelity in winter, because if returning warblers settled far away from their previous winter's site, given the small size and partial isolation of the study areas, we would expect to have difficulty locating them. Yet, in fact, winter-site fidelity rates were higher than those in summer, suggesting that this is not a valid explanation for the differences between winter and summer site fidelity. Also, because the winter site fidelity rates of 50% approach the estimated annual survival rate for small paruline warblers (see above), it appears we resighted in winter most of the individuals expected to be alive, that is, they were all, or nearly all, back on their specific winter sites.

ECOLOGICAL DIFFERENCES IN SUMMER AND WINTER HABITAT. A third possible explanation for site fidelity differences, particularly the age-related patterns of breeding American Redstarts, relates to the habitat characteristics. The finding that male redstarts, even ASYs, often move considerable distances from one year to the next (Fig. 3) suggests that breeding habitat suitability varies considerably. This is evident each breeding season at Hubbard Brook by the appearance of new, unmarked ASY males that settle in our study area: we know that between 40 and 59% of all ASYs at Hubbard Brook each year are new to the area, because all of the males present in the previous seasons had been marked (T.W. Sherry and R.T. Holmes, unpubl.). If ASY male redstarts exhibited complete site fidelity, we would expect all or at least most new birds recruited to an area to be yearlings (SYs), which is not the case. These newly appearing ASY males must in part be the SYs from the previous season (now at least two years of age) moving onto the study area from elsewhere (the ones on our plot in the previous year having all been color-marked, with few returning), plus other ASYs shifting locations, perhaps to better or more preferred breeding sites.

Other observations and experiments indicate that both intraspecific (Sherry and Holmes 1989) and interspecific (Sherry 1979, Sherry and Holmes 1988) competition strongly affect the pattern of habitat selection by SY and ASY male redstarts in breeding areas. In addition, some SY male redstarts remain unmated each breeding season (Procter-Gray and Holmes 1981, Morris and Lemon 1988), while older males are almost always mated (T.W. Sherry and R.T. Holmes, unpubl.). These findings suggest a shortage of females and hence strong competition among males for mates or for good territories in which to attract mates (but see Morris and Lemon 1988). In all cases, it appears to be SY males that are constrained in their habitat choice, and perhaps also in mating success, by the older ASY male redstarts.

Given these habitat shifts and intraspecific competitive interactions of male redstarts in the breeding season, we suggest that suitability of these breeding habitats is highly variable, both from place to place and from year to year. The result is strong competition for the better habitat, which then causes at least some individuals to change locations between seasons. Habitat suitability might be related to food resource availability, good nesting sites, and/or the presence of competitors or predators (Holmes et al. 1986, Holmes 1988, 1990, Sherry and Holmes 1988, Reitsma et al. 1990). Although the relationship between redstart nesting success and site return was not statistically significant (see Results), other data from Hubbard Brook indicate that nesting success of these warblers there is affected severely by nest predation (Sherry and Holmes, this volume, and unpubl.). Such predation could be one of the factors causing such movements, especially for the older males and probably for females. For SY males which do not always obtain a mate and therefore do not always reproduce in their first potential breeding season, competition with older males for good territories (and indirectly for mates) is probably a more important factor. These site fidelity data indicate that events in the breeding areas have important effects on redstart habitat selection and reproductive activities, which could in turn influence population density, survivorship, and other population parameters. Further study of these processes is currently in progress.

The higher site fidelity rate and the close site attachment to particular places in the winter habitat for both species suggest that habitat suitability there might not vary as much as in breeding areas, and that surviving birds of both sexes and age classes can return to and occupy the same precise areas as the year before. However, both American Redstarts and Black-throated Blue Warblers, as well as many other warbler species (Rappole and Warner 1980, Greenberg 1986), are territorial in winter (Holmes et al. 1989). This suggests that there is a premium on those specific wintering sites that make them worth defending. Because there is no reproductive activity in winter, the main evolutionary "goal" of wintering migrants must be survival. For these small, mostly insectivorous warblers, the most successful way to do this appears to be to return to a local area with which they are familiar. Our studies in Jamaica show that 80% of the redstarts (87% of the males and 70% of the females) marked in October were still present on their territories in late March/early April (Holmes et al. 1989). Allowing for some movement of individuals out of the study area, this suggests that overwinter mortality is very low. Nisbet and Medway (1972) also reported that overwintering mortality of *A. orientalis* in Malaysia appeared to be minimal.

Finally, in contrast to American Redstarts, Black-throated Blue Warblers exhibit nearly equal summer and winter site fidelity, with no significant differences between age or sex classes. This species thus seems to respond in the same ways to summer and winter habitats, both of which might be equally important but for different reasons—reproduction in summer and survival in winter.

SITE FIDELITY IN WINTER AND SUMMER: IMPLICATIONS FOR POPULATION DYNAMICS, HABITAT SELECTION, AND CONSERVATION

Our findings are relevant to understanding the ecology and conservation of migratory passerine birds in several ways. First, the difference in site fidelity between breeding and winter populations suggests that measurements of annual survivorship based on breeding site fidelity, at least for a species like redstarts, will be biased. For this latter species, data on site return in winter will provide a more accurate estimate of the proportion of birds alive because they are more site specific at that time of year.

Second, if the estimate of winter site fidelity is closer to average annual mortality and if we are dealing with the same population in winter and summer (see above), then the lower return rate in the breeding area indicates that many marked birds in summer must survive but not return to their previous territories. The effect is seen most strongly among male redstarts, but the data on females indicate that they also return at lower rates and disperse farther in summer than in winter (Table 1). Thus, temperate forest habitats might vary in suitability for breeding migrants, and each spring newly arriving individuals must compete for the better places, leading to the possibility of density dependent habitat selection (Fretwell 1972, O'Connor 1985) in the breeding season. Because habitat variability and greater movement of redstarts appear to be more prevalent in the breeding areas than on wintering grounds, events in the breeding season might be particularly important in affecting the population dynamics of a species like the redstart. This is also supported by other analyses of redstart ecology as reported elsewhere in this symposium (Sherry and Holmes, this volume).

Third, the high site fidelity and site attachment of color-marked individual warblers to specific winter sites indicates that winter habitat is of critical importance to survival. Furthermore, it seems that birds obtaining a good site when reaching the wintering grounds survive well over the winter, because a high percentage of the redstarts and black-throated blues that we have marked in October are still present at the end of the winter (Holmes et al. 1989). These warblers occupy relatively exclusive winter territories as evidenced by contests with conspecifics for these sites (see above and Holmes et al. 1989). There is also some evidence from both observations and removal experiments of wintering migrants (Rappole and Warner 1980, Holmes et al. 1989, T.W. Sherry and R.T. Holmes, unpubl.) that vacant sites are quickly re-occupied by new individuals, indicating some degree of habitat saturation. High survival in winter might depend mostly on having a benign living place and an adequate food supply, both of which might be worth defending (Greenberg 1986). Finally, predation on warblers in winter does not seem to be a major threat, at least in Jamaica where resident bird-hunting predators are absent (Holmes et al. 1989).

Given the strong site fidelity and attachment of redstarts and black-throated blues to specific winter habitats, it seems likely that any disruption of those sites—deforestation, for example—will affect survival of wintering migrants. However, we have observed on one of our plots in Jamaica that color-marked birds of both species stayed in their territories even when local slash-and-burn agriculture greatly changed the nature of that habitat (R.T. Holmes and T.W. Sherry, pers. obs.). Although these birds shifted their locations slightly to nearby forest edges, they still fed in the recently burned areas and in the tops of trees isolated in the garden plots. The implication is that at least a modest amount of habitat alteration in winter does not seem to affect individual birds too drastically. For the purposes of developing conservation practices, it is important to know how much disturbance these species can tolerate or how easily they can be displaced into nearby areas. If, in fact, most winter habitat is saturated and density dependent processes are operating, such dispersal might be impossible or unsuccessful. Also, such habitat alterations resulting in even slightly depressed survival rates might have long-term population consequences.

Fourth, one source of variation in estimates of site fidelity is catastrophic events, such as hurricanes, that influence survivorship. This is illustrated here in the site return data for Black-throated Blue Warblers in Jamaica when no marked males returned to the Jamaican study sites in their second year following banding (Table 2B). A large cohort of marked birds (i.e., those marked in October 1986 whose survivors would have been expected to return for the second time in 1988) did not return after Hurricane Gilbert in the early autumn of 1988. This hurricane severely altered the vegetation in our main study site for black-throated blues (Copse Mountain), as well as that in other heavily forested areas of Jamaica (Holmes et al. 1989, J. Wunderle and R. Waide, pers. comm.). The hurricane could have directly caused mortality of these warblers or, alternatively, changed the habitat drastically enough to cause returning birds to settle elsewhere. Because the hurricane occurred in early autumn (September 12–13) before most black-throated blues arrive (R. Sutton, pers. comm.), the first hypothesis seems unlikely. However, we cannot discount the possibility that the older, returning warblers might have arrived early and been affected directly by the hurricane. The second hypothesis is feasible. Yet, by late October 1988, when we first visited these sites after the hurricane, the densities of black-throated blues were about the same as in previous years (Holmes et al. 1989), suggesting that the habitat had not been sufficiently altered to deter some black-throated blues from settling. Those that did settle, however, were mostly yearlings (HYs). Another possible explanation for the absence of returning birds is simply an artifact of small sample size: 10 males marked in the preceding winter perhaps, just by chance, did not return. It is worth noting that two of six color-banded females present in October 1987 did reoccupy the plot in 1988, despite the hurricane.

Our data do not indicate that American Redstarts were affected by this huricane, even though they often arrive by early to mid-September (R. Sutton, pers. comm.). This might have been due to differences in locations of our study sites within Jamaica. The areas on which we had the most marked redstarts (Luana and Paradise) were less severely hit by the storm than was the site (Copse) with most Black-throated Blue Warblers (see Holmes et al. 1989). Thus, redstarts might have been similarly affected but not in the areas for which we had data.

Fifth, and finally, it is important to emphasize again that the comparisons we have made are based on the assumptions that we have studied the same, or at least representative, "breeding" and "wintering" populations. There is essentially no information on how breeding populations for any migratory species settle in winter areas and vice versa. Do redstarts from New Hampshire spread throughout the Greater Antilles and Central America in winter, or do most individuals from a particular breeding area winter in a fairly restricted locality? Conversely, do the redstarts wintering on our study sites in Jamaica come from throughout the breeding range? For example, in some migratory populations whose morphological features distinguish subspecies, some mixing of breeding populations seems to occur in winter (Ramos and Warner 1980, Ramos 1988). If we are to un-

derstand the year-round ecology of these migratory species, as well as to develop conservation strategies, it is urgent that we obtain such basic data on winter distributions of breeding populations, and vice versa.

Acknowledgments

We thank L. Reitsma, F. Sturges, S. Baird, P. Marra, and many other colleagues, associates, and assistants for their efforts in support of this research. We greatly appreciate the advice, cooperation, and in many cases the permission to use their property, of the following individuals in Jamaica: Y. Strong (Natural Resource and Conservation Department), I. Goodbody, A. Haynes-Sutton, R. Sutton, L. Salmon, P. Reeson (Petroleum Corporation of Jamaica), T. Clark (Paradise Properties Ltd.), and the Williams at Kew Park. Field work at Hubbard Brook was conducted under the auspices of the Northeast Forest Experiment Station, U.S. Forest Service, Radnor, Pennsylvania, and we thank Drs. R. Pierce and W. Martin for their cooperation. The Banding Office of the U.S. Fish and Wildlife Service, Laurel, Maryland, kindly provided the band recovery data. J. Wunderle, V. Nolan, and P. Marra made many useful suggestions on the manuscript. The research was supported by grants from the National Science Foundation to Dartmouth College and Tulane University.

Literature cited

Beletsky, L.D., and G.H. Orians. 1987. Territoriality among Red-winged Blackbirds. I. Site fidelity and movement patterns. *Behav. Ecol. Sociobiol.* 20:21–34.

Berger, A.J., and B.E. Radabaugh. 1968. Returns of Kirtland's Warblers to the breeding grounds. *Bird-Banding* 39:161–186.

Cooke, W.W. 1904. Distribution and migration of North American warblers. *U.S. Dept. of Agric. Biol. Survey Bull.* 18:1–142.

Darley J.A., D.M. Scott, and N.K. Taylor. 1977. Effects of age, sex, and breeding success on site fidelity of Gray Catbirds. *Bird-Banding* 48:145–151.

Diamond, A.W., and R.W. Smith. 1973. Returns and survival of banded warblers wintering in Jamaica. *Bird-Banding* 44:221–224.

Drilling, N.E., and C.F. Thompson. 1988. Natal and breeding dispersal in House Wrens (*Troglodytes aedon*). *Auk* 105:480–491.

Faaborg, J., and W.J. Arendt. 1984. Population sizes and philopatry of winter resident warblers in Puerto Rico. *J. Field Ornithol.* 55:376–378.

Fretwell, S. 1972. *Populations in a Seasonal Environment.* Princeton: Princeton University Press.

Gavin, T.A., and E.K. Bolinger. 1988. Reproductive correlates of breeding site fidelity in Bobolinks (*Dolichonyx oryzivorus*). *Ecology* 69:96–105.

Greenberg, R. 1986. Competition in migrant birds in the nonbreeding season. *Current Ornithol.* 3:281–307.

Greenwood, P.J. 1980. Mating systems, philopatry and dispersal in birds and mammals. *Anim. Behav.* 28:1140–1162.

Greenwood, P.J., and P.H. Harvey. 1982. The natal and breeding dispersal of birds. *Annu. Rev. Ecol. Syst.* 13:1–21.

Grieg-Smith, P.W. 1982. Dispersal between nest-sites by Stonechats *Saxicola torquata* in relation to previous breeding success. *Ornis Scand.* 13:232–238.

Holmes, R.T. 1988. Community structure, population fluctuations, and resource dynamics of birds in temperate deciduous forests. *Acta 19th Internat. Ornithol. Cong.* (Ottawa): 1318–1327.

———. 1990. The structure of a temperate deciduous forest bird community: Variability in time and space. Pages 117–135 in *Biogeography and Ecology of Forest Bird Communities,* A. Keast, ed. The Hague: SPB Academic Publishing.

Holmes, R.T., T.W. Sherry, and L. Reitsma. 1989. Population structure, territoriality and overwinter survival of two migrant warbler species in Jamaica. *Condor* 91:545–561.

Holmes, R.T., T.W. Sherry, and F.W. Sturges. 1986. Bird community dynamics in a temperate deciduous forest: Long-term trends at Hubbard Brook. *Ecol. Monogr.* 50:201–220.

Hutto, R.L. 1985. Habitat selection by nonbreeding, migratory landbirds. Pages 455–476 in *Habitat Selection in Birds,* M.L. Cody, ed. New York: Academic Press, Inc.

Jakobsson, S. 1988. Territorial fidelity of Willow Warbler (*Phylloscopus trochilus*) males and success in competition over territories. *Behav. Ecol. Sociobiol.* 22:79–84.

Kelsey, M.G. 1989. A comparison of the song and territorial behaviour of a long-distance migrant, the Marsh Warbler *Acrocephalus palustris* in summer and winter. *Ibis* 131:403–414.

Ketterson, E.D., and V. Nolan, Jr. 1982. The role of migration and winter mortality in the life history of a temperate-zone migrant, the Dark-eyed Junco, as determined from demographic analyses of winter populations. *Auk* 99:243–259.

Kricher, J.C., and W.E. Davis Jr. 1986. Returns and winter-site fidelity of North American migrants banded in Belize, Central America. *J. Field. Ornithol.* 57:48–52.

Loftin, H. 1977. Returns and recoveries of banded North American birds in Panama and the tropics. *Bird-Banding* 48:253–258.

Martin, T.E., and J.R. Karr. 1986. Temporal dynamics of neotropical birds with special reference to frugivores in second-growth woods. *Wilson Bull.* 98:38–60.

McNeil, R. 1982. Winter residents repeats and returns of austral and boreal migrant birds banded in Venezuela. *J. Field Ornithol.* 53:125–132.

Morris, M.M.J., and R.E. Lemon. 1988. Mate choice in American Redstarts: By territory quality? *Can. J. Zool.* 66:2255–2261.

Nichols, J.D., B.R. Noon, S.L. Stokes, and J.E. Hines. 1981. Remarks on the use of mark-recapture methodology in estimating avian population size. Pages 121–136 in *Estimating Numbers of Terrestrial Birds,* C.J. Ralph and M.J. Scott, eds. Studies in Avian Biology No. 6.

Nickel, W.P. 1968. Return of northern migrants to tropical winter quarters. *Bird-Banding* 39:107–116.

Nisbet, I.C.T., and L. Medway. 1972. Dispersion, population ecology and migration of Eastern Great Reed Warblers *Acrocephalus orientalis* wintering in Malaysia. *Ibis* 114:451–494.

Nolan, V., Jr. 1978. *The Ecology and Behavior of the Prairie Warbler*

Dendroica discolor. Ornithol. Monogr. 26.

O'Connor, R.J. 1985. Behavioural regulation of bird populations: A review of habitat use in relation to migration and residency. Pages 105–142 in *Behavioural Ecology: Ecological Consequences of Adaptive Behavior,* R.M. Sibly and R.H. Smith, eds. Oxford: Blackwell Scientific Publications.

Price, T. 1981. The ecology of the Greenish Warbler *Phylloscopus trochiloides* in its winter quarters. *Ibis* 123:131–144.

Procter-Gray, E., and R.T. Holmes. 1981. Adaptive significance of delayed attainment of plumage in male American Redstarts: Tests of two hypotheses. *Evolution* 35:742–751.

Pyle, P., S.N.G. Howell, R.P. Yunick, and D.F. DeSante. 1987. *Identification Guide to North American Passerines.* Bolinas, Calif.: Slate Creek Press.

Rabenold, K.N. and P.P. Rabenold. 1985. Variation in altitudinal migration, winter segregation, and site tenacity in two subspecies of Dark-eyed Junco in the southern Appalachians. *Auk* 102:805–819.

Ramos, M.A. 1988. Eco-evolutionary aspects of bird movements in the northern neotropical region. *Acta 19th Internat. Ornithol. Cong.* (Ottawa): 251–293.

Ramos, M.A., and D.W. Warner. 1980. Analysis of North American subspecies of migrant birds wintering in Los Tuxtlas, southern Veracruz, Mexico. Pages 173–180 in *Migrant Birds in the Neotropics: Ecology, Behavior, Distribution and Conservation,* A. Keast and E.S. Morton, eds. Washington: Smithsonian Institution Press.

Rappole, J.H., and D.W. Warner. 1980. Ecological aspects of migrant bird behavior in Veracruz, Mexico. Pages 353–393 in *Migrant Birds in the Neotropics: Ecology, Behavior, Distribution and Conservation,* A. Keast and E.S. Morton, eds. Washington: Smithsonian Institution Press.

Reitsma, L.R., R.T. Holmes, and T.W. Sherry. 1990. Effects of removal of red squirrels (*Tamiasciurus hudsonicus*) and eastern chipmunks (*Tamias striatus*) on nest predation in a northern hardwoods forest: An artificial nest experiment. *Oikos* 57:375–380.

Sherry, T.W. 1979. Competitive interactions and adaptive strategies of American Redstarts and Least Flycatchers in a northern hardwoods forest. *Auk* 96:265–283.

Sherry, T.W., and R.T. Holmes. 1988. Habitat selection by breeding American Redstarts in response to a dominant competitor, the Least Flycatcher. *Auk* 105:350–364.

———. 1989. Age-specific social dominance affects habitat use by breeding American Redstarts (*Setophaga ruticilla*). *Behav. Ecol. Sociobiol.* 25:227–234.

Shields, W.M. 1984. Factors affecting nest and site fidelity in Adirondack barn swallows (*Hirundo rustica*). *Auk* 101:780–789.

Thompson, C.F., and V. Nolan, Jr. 1973. Population biology of the Yellow-breasted Chat (*Icteria virens* L.) in southern Indiana. *Ecol. Monogr.* 43:145–171.

Tiainen, J. 1983. Dynamics of a local population of the Willow Warbler *Phylloscopus trochilus* in southern Finland. *Ornis Scand.* 14:1–15.

U.S. Fish and Wildlife Service. 1977. *Bird Banding Manual.* Washington, D.C.

Walkinshaw, L.H. 1953. Life history of the Prothonotary Warbler. *Wilson Bull.* 65:152–168

Concluding remarks

EUGENE S. MORTON
Department of Zoological Research
National Zoological Park
Smithsonian Institution
Washington, D.C. 20008

What do we know about the future of migrant landbirds?

This symposium focused on the conservation of the world's largest vertebrate migration system, the Neotropical-Nearctic caterpillar-eating landbirds that comprise about 80% of the breeding individuals in large eastern North American forests. How will this system fare in the face of increasing human demands on the landscape? What information is needed and what can be done to conserve its present status? In introductory remarks to the symposium, Linda Leddy provided an organizational framework to these crucial questions. For as in any science, conservation biology must produce questions that are answerable as well as data that are unassailable. To this end, she mentioned central concerns such as what evidence do we have for population changes, what are the effects of forest fragmentation in the breeding areas versus forest elimination in the nonbreeding areas, and what are the effects on a species by species basis? Here, I will summarize our efforts to answer these and other questions, and outline critical growing concerns in research and conservation.

General trends and habitat predictions

There are two complementary means to assess the health of migrant populations and both are necessary. One is to take annual censuses using standardized methods to estimate trends in populations. Such data have been obtained only from surveys during the breeding season, when males make themselves obvious by singing and where large numbers of dedicated professional and amateur ornithologists tally them. Other censuses include radar estimates of trans-Gulf migration volume (Gauthreaux, this volume) and mist-netting efforts during migration (Hussell et al., this volume; Hagan et al., this volume). Species that decline significantly over a period of time should concern conservationists. Attempts to reverse declines must then use all available knowledge of the ecological bases for the declines. A second means is to use knowledge of habitats needed to sustain migrants. If these habitats are being degraded, declines of migrants can be predicted, and managers can put efforts into habitat restoration or suggest changes in land use.

In part, both means are devoted to avoiding crisis situations by detecting or predicting declines, but that was not the main thrust of this symposium. Here, the goal is to put together information that might preclude precipitous declines and crises—to keep common species common, to keep the New World migratory bird system intact, not to wait until, species by species, each becomes rarer and of increasing management concern. Some contributors suggested that we may be closer to crises than we think.

In 1980, John Terborgh listed 55 species that wintered primarily in tropical forests (Terborgh 1980). He noted that migrants in the tropics are spatially concentrated to about eight times their temperate densities due to the smaller area available for wintering. Forest-dwelling migrants must spill over into edge, extensive areas of young sapling growth without open understory, and brushy pastures, if forest areas are inadequate to support them. (Humid tropical forest is often termed "mature" or "second growth," terms of little use in describing them. Undisturbed old forests are characterized by frequent canopy openings through treefalls, resulting in a mosaic of forest tree ages and uneven canopy height (e.g., Browkaw 1982). Indeed, the age attained by tree species forming the canopy in such forests may be only about 100 years (Leigh et at. 1982). Species of ground-living migrants, such as the Kentucky Warbler, often use such treefall gaps for early morning foraging, perhaps because it becomes bright enough to permit foraging about 30 minutes earlier than in the forest interior, to which they return for most of the day. Therefore, a crucial question is not whether they "use" such natural "edges" but whether they can use unnaturally extensive areas of sapling growth that have no canopied, layered forest within a bird's daily range). Knowledge of the survival and numbers of migrants in spillover habitats becomes more important as forests are converted. Morphology-habitat relations (Bairlein, this volume) and psychological factors (Greenberg 1983, 1990) set limits on the adaptability of migrants to modified environments. Predicting the dynamic equilibrium between breeding and wintering population limitation (Morse 1980) will depend upon this knowledge.

Future predictions based on trends in tropical forest conversion are not bright (Morton and Greenberg 1989). John Terborgh (this volume) and Gary Hartshorn (this volume) emphasized that we have a 10-year time window before tropical conversion devastates the migratory bird system and 30–60 years before *all* tropical wintering grounds are rendered useless (see also Lovejoy 1989). This is a simple matter of human population growth: with greater than 100 people per km², there will be little room for other than a "manscape." This prediction of the future may or may not be compatible with past "trends." Furthermore, it suggests that it is not essential for past-to-present avian population trends to show declines before immediate action should be taken to save the migratory bird system. Hartshorn provides some examples of what can be done to change current directions. But are the declines already occurring?

The analysis by Robbins et al. (1989b) of Breeding Bird Survey (BBS) data coupled with an analysis of wintering vs. breeding habitat supports the conclusion that declines are occurring. They compared population trends from 1966 to 1978 with trends from 1978 to 1987. During the first period, 47 of 62 species (75.8%) showed increasing population trends (23 of which were statistically significant at $P < 0.05$). From 1978 to 1988, 44 of the 62 species (71%) showed negative population trends (20 with significant declines).

The turnaround was not found in species that migrate within the temperate zone, or are nonmigratory. There is nothing magical about 1978 as a turning point. Indeed, Sauer and Droege (this volume) show in the long-term data set, 1966–1989, that more species of Neotropical migrants were increasing than decreasing. Forest-dwelling migrants have declined significantly in the eastern areas of North America since 1977 (BBS). However, when the focus is on smaller subsets of this region, it is clear that regional trends in Neotropical migrants might not mirror overall population declines (Hagan et al. this volume). For eight of the most common species of warblers, James et al. (this volume) describe a complicated pattern of declines and increases for southeastern and southern United States using BBS data from 1966 through 1988. Common Yellowthroat, Prairie Warbler, Yellow-breasted Chat, and Kentucky Warbler declined in the uplands whereas five forest-dwelling species increased in lowland forests (Prothonotary, Hooded, Northern Parula, Yellow-throated, and Kentucky warblers). Prothonotary Warblers increased in the first half of the 22-year period but decreased in the second half in the Mississippi Alluvial Plain and the Lower Coastal Plain. Other species did not show downward trends, based on visual inspection of the LOWESS plots (Taub 1990; James et al. 1990). In contrast to these species in the southern United States, Witham and Hunter (this volume) analyzed BBS data in New Hampshire and Maine and territory-mapping data from a 40-ha mature pine/oak forest in Maine. Comparing the period 1966–1988 with 1983–1988, species showing declines increased from 10 of 16 to 13 of 16 in forest-breeding Neotropical migrants.

What is alarming is that the decade of declines is not likely to turn around, to be merely a random blip in the longer term, because it was predicted by knowledge of the natural history of Neotropical migrants in the tropics (e.g., Rappole et al. 1983) as well as by an example of migrant population dynamics in an intensively studied tropical site. John Rappole and I found a significant decline (33%/1000 net hr and 64% fewer individuals) in migrant numbers coincident with minimal forest alteration between 1974 and 1981 in Veracruz, Mexico (Rappole and Morton 1985).

There is no reason to suspect that Neotropical migrants are not suffering limitations during breeding, migration and wintering periods. However, Robbins et al. (1989b) provided evidence that tropical deforestation has had a significant recent effect. That evidence comes from a combination of BBS results with knowledge of natural history. Because most species use the same general habitat in both winter and summer it is not easy to factor out summer and winter effects on population survival. Rappole's Veracruz data, for example, could result from overall declines of migrants due to breeding season effects and not solely from the alteration of his tropical forest study site. But some species switch from forest to scrub habitats between seasons and it was this small subset of data (eight species) that was used to tease apart the effects of wintering and breeding conditions. Migratory species breeding in scrub but wintering in forests (White-eyed Vireo, Blue-winged Warbler, and Chestnut-sided Warbler) declined more from 1978 to 1988 than from 1966 to 1978. By contrast, three of five species breeding in temperate forests but wintering in tropical scrub (Eastern Wood-Pewee, Least Flycatcher, Blue-gray Gnatcatcher, but not Yellow-throated Warbler or Rose-breasted Grosbeak) showed trends that declined much less steeply in recent years compared to the 1966–1978 period. (The grosbeak and Yellow-throated Warbler may be more forest-oriented than "tropical scrub" suggests. The tropical perspective was from the Sian Ka'an Biosphere Reserve in Quintana Roo, where the warbler is uncommon compared to Pine Savannas in Belize and Honduras [Monroe 1968, Russell 1964]. The grosbeak feeds on fleshy fruit and, especially, on dried [wind-dispersed] seeds in scrub *and* forest canopy. Habitat used by the large grosbeak population wintering in South America has not been adequately described, but includes forest, where the birds occur in small flocks [Johnson 1980, Orejuela et al. 1980, Hilty 1980, Pearson 1980].) This analysis represented the strongest evidence to date that tropical deforestation can account for the declines in Neotropical migrants (Robbins et al. 1989b, Askins et al. 1990).

Breeding Bird Censuses (BBC) showed even more drastic declines that began earlier than BBS declines (Johnston and Hagan this volume; Askins et al. 1990). Neotropical migrants declined in the late 1960s and 1970s at most of 13 eastern deciduous forest sites. The

BBCs are much more intensive studies than the BBS, but lack the coverage of the hundreds of BBS 25-mile roadside surveys. Nonetheless, the parallel timing of declines at widely separated sites suggests a common underlying cause, a general decline in Neotropical migrants that is unlikely to be due to breeding season events. Indeed, many local BBCs show that the "Neotropicals," normally more abundant than residents, dropped below the numbers of breeding resident and short-distance migrants in the late 1960s and 1970s (Johnston and Winings 1987). Long-term BBCs in forest "islands" show extirpation of many Neotropicals to an alarming extent (Galli et al. 1976, Leck et al. 1988) and also in sites less insularized but perhaps more "peninsularized" by surrounding development (Briggs and Criswell 1979, Johnston and Winings 1987).

Corroborating the BBS and BBC data is Sidney Gauthreaux's radar study (this volume) of the volume of spring migration across the Gulf of Mexico. His preliminary findings show a decline of nearly 50% between 1965–1967 and 1987–1989 in the percentage of days birds migrated northward at Lake Charles, Louisiana when the weather conditions were favorable to trans-Gulf flights. These flights included birds that would become nonbreeding floaters as well as those that would be counted as breeders, for these in-transit individuals are not yet on breeding territories or singing. The radar results are valuable both as an independent source of trend data and because floaters are not counted in either the BBS or BBCs. It is the floater population that would decline before any marked decrease in breeders might be noticed (Wilcove and Terborgh 1984). Of course individual species cannot be identified by the weather radars, but the flow over the Gulf is comprised of the birds of concern, the Neotropical migrants.

Taken as a whole, the trend data from the BBS and BBCs, with preliminary corroboration by the radar data, show a marked decline in Neotropical migrants. Breeding declines are taking place most noticeably in smaller woodlots and in forest fragmented landscapes (e.g., Freemark and Collins, this volume; Robbins et al. 1989a and refs. therein; Robinson, this volume; Villard et al., this volume). Nonetheless, declines are occurring at a time when forest acreage on the breeding grounds is higher than a century ago, and which should continue to increase for the next 30 years (T.W. Birch, symposium presentation). Sauer and Droege (this volume) found no association between changes in forest acreages by state and population trends of Neotropical migrants breeding in forest (BBS data).

Migrant landbird populations respond differently to land use patterns in breeding and wintering areas. Breeding adults tend to return to the same areas for breeding, whereas these individuals are scattered far and wide in the tropics (Morton 1976, Ramos and Warner 1980). For example, Purple Martins marked in one winter roost in Sao Paulo State, Brazil, were later found breeding throughout their North American range (K. Klimkiewicz, unpubl. data). While return rates of individuals to prior breeding *and* wintering sites tend to be high (Rappole et al. 1983; Blake and Loiselle, this volume; Rappole et al., this volume; Sherry and Holmes, this volume), local tropical deforestation effects are likely to be diluted when breeding bird trends are evaluated. Declines because of tropical deforestation are spread out over the breeding areas. Can the effects of a 1–2% annual decline in tropical forest be detected easily through breeding counts—are we trying to pick up a weak signal in much statistical noise (Askins et al. 1990)? Because of this, it is disheartening that the signal *has* been detected.

The nonbreeding season

Predicting nonbreeding limitations for Neotropical migrants necessitates a short review of some of the myths that have died since the early 1970s. There is no heuristic value to the concept that migrants are avoiding competition with residents. Tropical bird numbers, in both of these artificial categories, reflect primary productivity. Neotropical migrants as a group converge on tropical residents in the nonbreeding season and join mixed-species flocks with insectivorous residents (Morton 1980a,b). There is little conservation value in the concept that migrants as a group are birds of successional habitats that chase after ephemeral, superabundant food, such that deforestation will not harm them (e.g., Beuchner and Buechner 1970). The single generality that separates migrants from residents is the explicit lack of sex recognition in migrant social behavior, but even here there may be rare exceptions (Morton 1980b, Greenberg and Gradwohl 1980). This has conservation implications: sexes (and age classes) are in competition and a reduction in wintering habitat often will not affect both sexes equally (Morton 1990; Lopez Ornat and Greenberg 1990; Wunderle, this volume). This competition is most noticeable, and probably most important, in species that defend nonbreeding territories for all or part of the nonbreeding season.

We need a classification of the modes of nonbreeding season habitat use that includes elements of site specificity vs. movement, social and foraging behavior and food habitats (Table 1), factors which augment data presented by Reed (this volume). The starting point is at the species level, for this is more conservative than a guild approach, from a conservation standpoint. The classification can be used to determine information needed, on a species-by-species basis, as well as conservation priorities. Using this classification, a higher score

TABLE 1. Vulnerability factors used to construct a conservation classification system for forest-dwelling migrants in the Neotropics

Factors	Points
A. Wintering site specificity	
Tracks tropical seasons, not site-specific	4
Homes to previous overwintering site:	
wide wintering range	1
medium range	3
small wintering range	5
B. Social tolerance (intra vs. interspecific)	
Low social intraspecific tolerance, territorial	4
Low intraspecific social tolerance, high interspecific tolerance (requires mixed species flock)	5
High intraspecific tolerance	0
Social tolerance flexible, often tracks local tropical season changes or food defensibility and quality	2
C. Diet and foraging specialization	
Strictly arthropod food (or carnivorous), plastic foraging mode	2
Arthropod food, specialized forager	5
Frugivorous	3
Omnivorous	2
D. Ability to use non-forest habitat	
Found in humid forest understory	5
Forest canopy foliage	4
Uses woody vegetation of any sort	0
More abundant in forest canopy or subcanopy but also in sapling, shrub, forest edge	2

NOTE: Forest-dwelling migrants refers to species more common in forest than earlier successional stages during all or part of the overwintering period.

indicates more vulnerability to tropical deforestation. What is *not* included are sex differences in habitat use, migration distance, and the impact of enroute habitat needs, all potentially important in predicting conservation priorities, but poorly known. Furthermore, regional differences, if any, in scoring are possible, because such differences in behavior/habitat/seasonality relationships are relevant but almost unknown (Hutto, this volume).

TABLE 2. **Examples of forest-dwelling migrants scored for vulnerability to tropical deforestation**

Species	Vulnerability factor[a]				Species score
	A	B	C	D	
Broad-winged Hawk	3	4	2	5	14
Whip-poor-will	3	4	5	5	17
Yellow-billed Cuckoo	3	3	5	2	13
Eastern Kingbird	4	0	3	2	9
Great Crested Flycatcher	1	4	2	4	11
Eastern Wood-Pewee	1	4	2	2	9
Acadian Flycatcher	3	4	2	2	11
Wood Thrush	3	4	2	5	14
Swainson's Thrush	4	2	2	5	13
Yellow-throated Vireo	3	5	5	3	16
Red-eyed Vireo	1	5	3	2	11
Philadelphia Vireo	3	5	2	4	14
Black-and-white Warbler	3	5	5	2	15
Swainson's Warbler	5	4	5	5	19
Worm-eating Warbler	3	5	5	5	18
Golden-winged Warbler	5	5	5	2	17
Blue-winged Warbler	3	5	5	2	15
Tennessee Warbler	4	2	2	2	10
Northern Parula	3	0	2	2	7
Magnolia Warbler	3	4	2	2	11
Cape May Warbler	5	5	2	2	14
Black-throated Green Warbler	3	0	2	2	7
Black-throated Blue Warbler	5	4	2	2	13
Cerulean Warbler	5	0	2	4	11
Yellow-throated Warbler	3	4	2	2	11
Blackburnian Warbler	3	0	2	2	7
Chestnut-sided Warbler	5	4	5	2	16
Bay-breasted Warbler	5	2	2	2	11
Blackpoll Warbler	1	2	2	2	7
Ovenbird	3	4	5	2	14
Kentucky Warbler	3	4	5	5	17
Hooded Warbler	5	4	2	2	13
Canada Warbler	5	5	2	2	14
American Redstart	1	4	2	2	9
Scarlet Tanager	5	0	3	2	10
Summer Tanager	1	4	2	4	11
Rose-breasted Grosbeak	1	0	2	2	5

a. See Table 1 for definition of vulnerability factors.

Ecologists have not produced quantitative surveys of habitat relations of individual migrant species in the Neotropics (Greenberg 1986; Petit et al., this volume).

Some examples of species in each category are provided in Table 2. Species with a score of 12 or higher are highly vulnerable to continued tropical deforestation.

Species overwintering chiefly in the Greater Antilles (Swainson's Warbler, Northern Parula, Cape May,

Black-throated Blue, Prairie, Kirtland's, Bachman's warblers, Bicknell's Grey-cheeked Thrush) are threatened by habitat destruction if only because of the limited area available. The first four species named above also occur along the Caribbean coast of the mainland. As Waide and Wunderle (symposium presentation) mentioned, widespread deforestation in the Antilles took place a long time ago relative to the mainland. We have no information on migrant populations prior to this deforestation. Most migrants probably use various modified habitats such as coffee plantations (with tree overstory), second growth, and mangroves because these habitats occupy most of the area. Nonetheless, González Alonso et al. (this volume) indicate that mature forest contains more migrants than modified habitats in Cuba. It is apparent that all remaining forest in the Greater Antilles needs to be preserved. Staicer (this volume) provides needed information on the wintering behavior of the Prairie Warbler and Cape May Warbler. The use of large trees for nocturnal roosting suggested that a few large trees may be an important component to the overwintering habitat of these species, even though the birds often forage in shrub vegetation (summarized in Nolan 1978, see also Fretwell 1980). The low interspecific dominance of Prairie Warblers suggests that they are a "fugitive species." Their decline in the Guánica dry forest of Puerto Rico may be related to this fact, for other species show high return rates between years (Faaborg and Arendt, this volume). The Cape May Warbler is highly aggressive and interspecifically dominant apparently throughout its wintering range, easily displacing from defended ripe cactus fruit even the large resident *Teretistris* warblers endemic to Cuba (González and Morton, pers. obs.). Even though Arendt (this volume) found mixed opinions on migrant population trends from longtime birders in the Greater Antilles, he suggested that the Lesser Antilles may become more important to migrants with continued habitat alteration in the Greater Antilles. Concurring with this, Askins et al. (this volume) found a richer migrant population on St. John, the more forested of the U.S. Virgin Islands, and suggested that this results from the widespread degradation and destruction of forest on St. Thomas.

With this volume, we now have fairly good descriptions of the occurrence, abundance, and habitat use of migrants from specific sites ranging from Mexico to Panama. What is still lacking are broad-scale surveys that would enable us to plot species by species abundances over most of, or entire, wintering ranges and to track geographic changes in abundance during the overwintering period for mobile species that track intratropical seasons (e.g., Swainson's Thrush, Eastern Kingbird). We lack information on South American habitats, in particular on the potentially crucial limited altitudinal distribution of migrants in Andean regions (Robbins et al., this volume; J.W. Fitzpatrick, pers. comm.). Some of North America's common breeding species may be affected by deforestation of mid-elevations (e.g., Cerulean Warbler, Scarlet Tanager). These and other species may not use extensive lowland Amazonian rainforest, as once thought. For Mexico, the papers by Richard Hutto (this volume) and James Lynch (this volume), covering

western Mexico and the Yucatan Peninsula, respectively, are the only broad-scale studies. Still broader geographic studies would be valuable.

There is still some confusion about the use of non-forest habitats by migrants. Studies relying on mist nets to assess the occurrence of migrants across habitats ranging from low to tall structure invariably show migrants to be apparently more common in low stature habitats amenable to mist netting (Petit et al., Kricher and Davis, Blake and Loiselle, all this volume). If mist nets were used to assess breeding season habitat use in North America, our picture of the effects of forest fragmentation on breeding populations of forest-related Neotropical migrants would be different. Many forest "interior" species would be moved into the "edge-interior" category. Observationally based surveys generally tally more forest-related migrants in forests (González Alonso et al., Greenberg, Hutto, Lynch, all this volume). It is possible that regional differences exist in the use of scrub habitats by forest-related migrant species. For example, in Quintana Roo, Mexico, the White-eyed Vireo is a forest canopy species, relying on the fruit of Gumbo Limbo trees (*Bursera simaruba*) to such an extent that this tree species is an essential component of its territories (Greenberg, this volume). It is found in both forest canopy, where it forages "above net height," and in "second growth" in Veracruz, Mexico (Rappole et al., this volume). However, in Belize, mist-net captures of this vireo would indicate that it avoids forest (Petit et al., this volume). This may be either a regional difference in habitat use, or because of the use of mist nets at one site, which is biased against tallying birds in forest canopy. At the same time, this method records species typical of forest canopy that follow the canopy to its lower edges, where they are netted in disproportionate numbers.

The best means to assess migrant use across habitats is through observation. It is important that researchers agree on a standard methodology to do this. A standardized point count method seems best because it is possible to cover more geographic area and to avoid some of the bias inherent in mist-net work (see Askins et al. 1990, for the latest discussion of mist-net bias in across-habitat comparisons). In tall forest it is difficult to census migrants in the canopy even with observational methods (Stiles 1983). The use of "spishing," squeaking (as produced with the Audubon device or with the hand), and owl whistles in conjunction with the point counts help to overcome this bias (Lynch 1989). Birds will become evident through callnote production even if seeing them remains difficult. It is not impossible to learn to identify species through callnotes, and this should be a necessary part of the point census process (the Cornell Laboratory of Ornithology may publish a recording of such callnotes, Greg Butcher, pers. comm.).

Lynch's methodology is the only type to employ such visual and aural techniques, and I recommend it as a standard procedure (Lynch 1989, this volume). Only point counts will produce broad-scale, between-habitat comparisons, that can provide a quantitative estimate of migrant use of various habitat structures. Mist nets are simply too biased for between-habitat comparisons although essential for intensive studies within like-structured habitats, marking birds for individual identification, behavior studies, and determining physiological and molt condition.

Future work will need to focus more on the biology of forest-related migrants in terms of carrying capacity in the tropics under various stages of habitat modification. It is apparent that some of these species will be found in "any woody vegetation" at a particular time of day or season. Only one paper addresses the use and survival of forest-related migrants in non-forest habitats throughout the overwintering period (Greenberg, this volume). The most common forest migrants in Greenberg's disturbed habitats were predators of foliage insects in the upper levels of the forest, reflecting the use of canopy of various heights characteristic of "undisturbed" forests (see above). It is possible that the use of Greenberg's early successional stages by these species reflects, not a recent accommodation to disturbance, but historic use of low canopy in treefall gaps, a characteristic of old forest. Numbers of several species declined in the early successional stages, and, of course, were less common to begin with, but the good news is that individuals survived there in good condition. Females of Northern Parula, American Redstart, Magnolia and Hooded warblers were significantly more common in the early successional stage than males. It is important that Greenberg's methodology be used in other geographic areas. He found that transect points near 8–10 or more small trees have nearly three times the number of forest migrant sightings than those without such a patch of small trees. This has important conservation value in the future "manscape." It means that a threshold effect of tree cover that could retain some migrants in cattle pasture, which they could otherwise not use, should be integrated in land use recommendations. And, while not preserving the normal abundance of Neotropicals as breeding birds, their endangerment might be mitigated.

More intensive work with individual species is also needed, to test hypotheses on habitat preferences by sex and age class, seasonal changes in habitat use on both local and broad geographic scales (e.g., Holmes and Sherry, Mabey and Morton, Staicer, Wiedenfeld, Wunderle, all this volume). Broad-scale surveys at intervals throughout the overwintering period are badly needed, coupled with Landsat imagery (Powell et al., this volume, Green et al. 1987).

Breeding season

Population trend determinations by the BBS have become the accepted measure of North American breeding bird populations. Because of the importance of BBS information to managers and conservation biologists more ecological data should be obtained so that correlations might be tied to potentially causative factors underlying population changes. Each roadside BBS route might be scored for a variety of habitat and climate factors on an annual basis if sufficient resources are available. Blake et al. (this volume) highlight the importance of drought on the breeding areas in Michigan and Wisconsin and suggest that long-term studies using transect census methodology are valuable adjuncts to the BBS. The important perspective provided by paleoecology is highlighted by Hunter (this volume) for boreal forest species. While documenting adaptability in the very long term, this perspective provides some optimism in the quest to maintain the migration system in the next decade.

Intensive studies provide the data needed to decipher underlying causes of population changes in North American breeding birds. Natal dispersal is an important factor that is best appreciated with information on return rates of breeding adults relative to breeding population size and breeding success. Robinson (this symposium) illustrates the importance of this information for Illinois woodlots. The low return rates for breeding adults (ca. 20%) coupled with high predation and cowbird parasitism show that *most* breeding adults came from somewhere else. (The Brown-headed Cowbird pressure he describes is extraordinary, especially for its nearly complete coverage of the temperate zone breeding season, to late July! In most areas, at least in the past, cowbirds stop egglaying by mid-to-late June. This cowbird pressure is surely due to abnormally high cowbird winter survival, likely due to agricultural practices in the south-central states. Indeed, John Rappole [pers. comm.] witnessed huge outdoor piles of sorghum in Texas, surplus grain that could be made unavailable to wintering cowbirds.) To appreciate the dynamics of localized breeding populations, mark and recapture techniques need to be utilized. Censuses, long-term or short-term, BBS or BBC, will not provide this information.

Robinson, Freemark and Collins, and Villard et al. (all this volume) emphasize the value of combining intensive study with a larger geographic scale (landscape ecology). Surveys of mated status of male Ovenbirds in relation to forest area showed that only 25% of male Ovenbirds on "islands" were mated (Faaborg et al. symposium presentation). Because unpaired males sing more, unpaired males might be more apt to be tallied on BBS routes than true reproductive units. Villard et al. (this vol.) provide an integration of landscape ecology with a metapopulation approach. They documented a large number of "winking patches," extinctions and re-colonizations by Wood Thrushs, Scarlet Tanagers, and Ovenbirds in sets of 71 forest patches representing five landscape types near Ottawa.

The metapopulation concept has important implications for conservation efforts directed at preserving remnant woodlands in highly suburbanized landscapes. It is important to preserve large tracts (e.g., Whitcomb et al. 1981), but often only small tracts, of 200–300 acres, are all that remain to provide future generations a taste of the natural environment, and within walking distance for the children that will learn from them. And, local citizens feel a direct involvement with preserving these remnants. Many Neotropical migrants use these, as in the "winking patches" described by Villard et al. (this volume). Unfortunately, biotechnicians hired by developers to assure local authorities that no environmental damage will occur from destroying small woodlands ("we will leave most of the trees and, after all, I will be living there too," is a common ruse used by developers) gain much support from forest fragmentation research that shows that forest area is the *cause* of declines of Neotropicals migrants in woodlands smaller than 300 acres, even though small numbers of "interior" species do breed in them (pers. obs.). That is, small woodlots are perceived to be of little ecological value. Developers push local authorities to continue to consider all land as a simple commodity, even though remnant woodlands are irreplaceable within suburban communities, and the marketplace rules. The destruction of remnant forest patches in man-dominated landscapes is a serious problem for the conservation of Neotropical migrants. Biologists should view the landscape with metapopulations in mind, rather than view individual woodlots as having self-contained breeding populations of migrants (Lynch and Whigham 1984).

Tying tropical deforestation to the breeding season, a case history: The Wood Thrush

The Wood Thrush provides a well-studied example of a species that should be relatively immune from forest fragmentation on its breeding grounds and vulnerable on its wintering grounds, scored at 14 in Table 2. More is known about the life history of this species than any other Neotropical migrant and, although its specific case may not be applicable to other species, the concepts under which we operate can be evaluated with data from this species. It is still a common, even backyard, bird—what is its future in the next decade?

All tropical studies of the Wood Thrush show that it is found in moist tropical forest understory. Unlike most territorial migrant species, a "floating" strategy is prob-

ably a normal social system in addition to territoriality, with floaters utilizing patchy fruit abundance in forest canopy as an alternative to territories when forests are saturated with territorial birds (Winker et al. 1990; Rappole et al., this volume). The floating population may consist largely of younger birds, at least historically, providing a potential buffer to tropical forest destruction (pers. obs.). The behavioral ability to "float" in other species needs more study. I doubt that it is a common strategy in most territorial species, but it is important in considering carrying capacity in disturbed landscapes. Wood Thrush floaters constitute about 5.8 birds/ha versus 2.4 birds/ha of territorial individuals in Veracruz (Rappole et al., this volume). Direct measure of survival was obtained by radio-tracking and showed lower survival for floaters (Rappole et al. 1989). Their floater sample incurred higher mortality from avian and mammalian predators. Maximum survival during the portion of the overwintering period their study covered would reduce the floating population to 4.2 birds/ha and the sedentary birds to 2.3 birds/ha. These estimates highlight the high selection pressure favoring sedentary behavior, resulting in territoriality, regardless of the benefits for food resource defense via territorial behavior. In the Tuxtla Mountains of southern Veracruz, the Wood Thrush is estimated to have declined 70% from 1960 to 1985 through deforestation. Throughout the Wood Thrush's wintering range, from Mexico southeast through Panama, its population is estimated to have declined 41%, from 68.9 to 28.1 million birds, since ;scA.D. 1500. More Wood Thrushes may be moving south, forced out of deforested areas farther north. In central Panama, at the southern end of their range, where they were uncommon in the early 1970s (Morton 1980a), they are now more common in Parque Nacional Soberania (pers. obs.).

In breeding areas, Wood Thrushes are a forest interior and edge species, tolerant of forest fragmentation, commonly found in woodlots of 1–5 ha (Whitcomb et al. 1981). Nevertheless, long-term studies of forest patches show declines. In the Hutcheson Memorial Forest on the Piedmont of central New Jersey, Leck et al. (1988) show declines in the Wood Thrush from 76 birds/yr from 1960–1968 to 52 birds/yr from 1971–1980 (excluding 1973). Returning breeders declined from 30% to 15% of the population per year in the same two time periods. Presumably, this wooded patch is a "sink," deriving most new breeders from other areas as the old breeders and their young move to larger forests. Or, is the decline and low return rate indicative of overall population limitation as predicted by wintering biology?

Unfortunately, the Wood Thrush decline, occurring at a rate of 4.0% per year from 1978 to 1987 (Robbins et al. 1989a) is not restricted to isolated woodlands (Witham and Hunter, this volume). Because North American management strategies are based on breeding season events, it is important to know what is happening in forest fragments. Are they "sinks" contributing to declines due to tropical deforestation? Can local losses be caused by breeding habitat fragmentation regardless of tropical events? The data needed to answer these questions for forest fragments can be obtained from long-term intensive banding of breeders together with study of reproductive success. Roth and Johnson (in press) provide these necessary ingredients in their 1974–1988 study of a 15-ha woodlot near Newark, Delaware. When the study began they found a saturated breeding population of the Wood Thrush in excellent thrush habitat, although isolated from the nearest forest patch by suburban development. Each year, they banded breeders and most fledged young, and studied nest success and cowbird parasitism. The number of breeding males and females declined similarly, at a rate of 3.4% per year. Return rates declined significantly with mean return rate for females (44%) significantly lower than for males (57%). Per capita reproduction remained the same over the study period and was adequate to maintain the population at the early levels. However, only 5% of all fledglings returned to breed and this low level remained the same over the study period. By checking other woodlots within 10 km of their site, they found no evidence of emigration of breeders to other areas (140 Wood Thrush were so checked and none were from their site). Nesting success remained sufficient to maintain the population, but high natal dispersal meant that immigration rates, which remained steady, were necessary to maintain the population. Roth and Johnson concluded that the population decline was not caused by dynamics intrinsic to the site, but more likely by low returns of breeders from tropical wintering grounds.

This example of Wood Thrush reproductive success and return rates in an isolated woodlot shows that patch size and isolation may not underlie declines. Roth and Johnson's study site is not unlike others in suburban eastern United States in its dynamics. In other areas, where parasitism and predation are higher (Robinson, this volume), local effects might indicate that the patch is, indeed, a population sink. But, this should not be inferred based on forest size without intensive work such as that of Roth and Johnson (in press).

The low return rates of breeding adults for the Wood Thrush are similar to the 30% return rate of breeding Kentucky Warblers during the 1980s found in an unfragmented forest at the Conservation and Research Center of the National Zoological Park near Front Royal, Virginia (E.S. Morton, M.V. McDonald, G. Saunders, unpubl. data). Intensive color banding and long-term study provide needed insight into the dynamics of local populations. As such, they are valuable additions to the BBS and BBCs, which cannot uncover more complicated

dynamics, such as low return rates compensated by immigration. A general summary of return rates in breeding Neotropical migrants is recommended, as are more intensive studies to provide new data. Low return rates of breeding populations indicate that a problem is occurring. Coupling return rate with immigration data should provide an index to the health of metapopulations.

We have learned much about the biology of Neotropical migrants as tropical birds since the 1970s. As one interested in the concept of island biogeography as applied to these animals, I observed that they used tropical forests of all sizes based on studies since the 1960s in Panama, Cuba, Mexico, Colombia, and Venezuela (see Robbins et al. 1989a). Management strategies are now firmly based on this concept, often ignoring tropical deforestation (Office of Migratory Bird Management 1990).

This example of the Wood Thrush illustrates one of several ways in which a declining overall population might be manifested on the breeding grounds: slow declines with low return rates of breeders but with normal reproductive output. This reflects the diluted effect that tropical deforestation has on the survival of breeders at any single site. But what about truly "area-sensitive" species that are found in normal abundance in large forest tracts but have disappeared from smaller tracts in a fragmented landscape? Surely, there is no other explanation for their declines except their response to local conditions, for overall decline in population should manifest itself without regard to forest size (Whitcomb et al. 1981). Unfortunately for our ability to "manage" breeding areas for such "interior" species, there is an alternative hypothesis to explain the unequal disappearance of these species from forests of differing size.

The reproductive ecology of migrant birds

The temperate climate and the migratory habit combine to produce a feature with great significance to natural selection. This feature is a concentration of fertile females in space and time unequalled in tropical latitudes with longer breeding seasons. It is becoming clear that natural selection has favored behavior patterns and habitat selection that increase a male's likelihood of increasing reproductive success through extrapair fertilizations (Gibbs et al. 1990, Morton et al. 1990, Petter et al. 1990, Westneat et al. 1990, Sherman and Morton 1988). The high cuckoldry potential relative to latitude (Morton et al. 1990) adds a new dimension to our conservation efforts and our concept of habitat requirements for Neotropical migrants. We must consider the mixed reproductive strategy along with the ecological structure of habitat requirements, as implied by "area sensitive," in our concept of what these birds "are."

Reproductive activity may be commonplace among Neotropical migrants even *during* migration, affecting the schedule and social behavior of migrating birds. Quay (1989) documented sperm transfer to female Tennessee Warblers during migration while the females were a thousand km from breeding territories. Morton and Derrickson (1990) suggest that the pressure of cuckoldry on young males might contribute to lower reproductive effort characteristic of first-time breeders.

All this strongly suggests that Neotropical migrants are looking for a population with which to interact reproductively, and not simply habitat. They are, in this sense, "colonial" breeders (Morton et al. 1990) and would most likely choose larger forest patches, where larger populations exist, to fulfill the requirements for extrapair reproductive potential.

This enlarged concept of what migratory birds "are" places overall population declines in a new light. We cannot accept the assumption that declines should be equally apportioned in forests of all sizes containing suitable species-specific habitat if the declines were caused by nonbreeding events such as tropical deforestation (e.g., Whitcomb et al. 1981). It is entirely possible, and for the Wood Thrush most likely, that small forest patches *could* be quite suitable for reproductive success. The cause of the correlation between fragment size and loss of many species of migrants, as opposed to resident species, may be a combined effect of lower overall population size (the loss of the floating population), in large part due to tropical deforestation, and the reproductive goals implied by extrapair fertilizations.

Acknowledgments

I thank all those involved with the planning of the Manomet Bird Observatory Conference on the conservation of migratory landbirds. It should have an important place in the history of conservation efforts and of conservation biology.

Literature cited

Askins, R.A., J.F. Lynch, and R. Greenberg. 1990. Population declines in migratory birds in eastern North America. *Current Ornithol.* 7:1–57.

Beuchner, H.K, and J.H. Beuchner, eds. 1970. *The Avifauna of Northern Latin America.* Smithsonian Contrib. Zool. 26.

Briggs, S., and J.H. Criswell. 1979. Gradual silencing of spring in Washington. *Atlantic Nat.* 32:19–26.

Browkaw, N.V.L. 1982. Treefalls: Frequency, timing, and consequences. Pages 101–108 in *The Ecology of a Tropical Forest, Seasonal Rhythms and Long-term Changes,* E.G. Leigh, A.S. Rand, and D.M. Windsor, eds. Washington: Smithsonian Institution Press.

Fretwell, S. 1980. Evolution of migration in relation to factors regulating bird numbers. Pages 517–528 in *Migrant Birds in the Neotropics: Ecology, Behavior, Distribution and Conservation,* A. Keast and E.S. Morton, eds. Washington: Smithsonian Institution Press.

Galli, A.E., C.F. Leck, and R.T.T. Forman. 1976. Avian distribution patterns in forest islands of different sizes in New Jersey. *Auk* 93:356–364.

Gibbs, H.L., P.J. Weatherhead, P.T. Boag, B.N. White, L.M. Tabak, and D.J. Hoysak. 1990. Realized reproductive success of polygynous Red-winged Blackbirds revealed by DNA markers. *Science* 250:1394-1397.

Greenberg, R. 1983. The role of neophobia in determining the degree of foraging specialization in some migrant warblers. *Am. Nat.* 122:444–453.

———. 1986. Competition in migrant birds in the nonbreeding season. *Current Ornithol.* 3:281–307.

———. 1990. Ecological plasticity, neophobia, and resource use in birds. Pages 431–437 in *Avian Foraging: Theory, Methodology, and Applications,* M.L. Morrison, D.J. Ralph, J. Berner, and J.R. Jehl, Jr., eds. Studies in Avian Biology No. 13.

Greenberg, R., and J.A. Gradwohl. 1980. Observations of paired Canada Warblers *Wilsonia canadensis* during migration in Panama. *Ibis* 122:509–512.

Green, K.M., J.F. Lynch, J. Sircar, and L.Z. Greenberg. 1987. Use of Landsat remote sensing to assess habitat for migratory birds in the Yucatan Penninsula. *Vida Silv. Neotrop.* 1(2):27–38.

Hilty, S.L. 1980. Relative abundance of North Temperate Zone breeding migrants in western Colombia and their impact at fruiting trees. Pages 265–272 in *Migrant Birds in the Neotropics: Ecology, Behavior, Distribution and Conservation,* A. Keast and E.S. Morton, eds. Washington: Smithsonian Institution Press.

James, F.C., C.E. McCulloch, and L.E. Wolfe. 1990. Methodological issues in the estimation of trends in bird populations with an example: The Pine Warbler. Pages 84–97 in *Survey Designs and Statistical Methods for the Estimation of Avian Population Trends,* J.R. Sauer and S. Droege, eds. U.S. Fish and Wildlife Service Biol. Rept. 90(1).

Johnson, T.B. 1980. Resident and North American migrant bird interactions in the Santa Marta Highlands, northern Colombia. Pages 239–248 in *Migrant Birds in the Neotropics: Ecology, Behavior, Distribution and Conservation,* A. Keast and E.S. Morton, eds. Washington: Smithsonian Institution Press.

Johnston, D.W., and D.I. Winings. 1987. Natural history of Plummers Island, Maryland. XXVII. The decline of forest breeding birds on Plummers Island, Maryland, and vicinity. *Proc. Biol. Soc. Wash.* 100:762–768.

Leck, C.F., B.G. Murray, and J. Swinebroad. 1988. Long-term changes in the breeding bird population of a New Jersey forest. *Biol. Conserv.* 46:145–157.

Leigh, E.G., A.S. Rand, and D.M. Windsor, eds. 1982. *The Ecology of a Tropical Forest, Seasonal Rhythms and Long-term Changes.* Washington: Smithsonian Institution Press.

Lopez Arnot, A., and R. Greenberg. 1990. Sexual segregation by habitat in migratory warblers in Quintana Roo, Mexico. *Auk* 107:539–543.

Lovejoy, T. 1989. Nothing, nothing at all? *Atlantic Nat.* 39:2–5.

Lynch, J.F. 1989. Distribution of overwintering Nearctic migrants in the Yucatan Peninsula, I: General patterns of occurrence. *Condor* 91:515–544.

Lynch, J.F., and D.F. Whigham. 1984. Effects of forest fragmentation on breeding bird communities in Maryland, U.S.A. *Biol. Conserv.* 28:287–324.

Monroe, B.L. 1968. *A Distributional Survey of the Birds of Honduras.* Ornithol. Monogr. 7.

Morse, D.H. 1980. Population limitation: Breeding or wintering grounds? Pages 505–516 in *Migrant Birds in the Neotropics: Ecology, Behavior, Distribution and Conservation,* A. Keast and E.S. Morton, eds. Washington: Smithsonian Institution Press.

Morton, E.S. 1976. The adaptive significance of dull coloration in Yellow Warblers. *Condor* 78:423

———. 1980a. Adaptations to seasonal changes by migrant land birds in the Panama Canal Zone. Pages 437–456 in *Migrant Birds in the Neotropics: Ecology, Behavior, Distribution and Conservation,* A. Keast and E.S. Morton, eds. Washington: Smithsonian Institution Press.

———. 1980b. The importance of migratory birds to the advancement of evolutionary theory. Pages 557–560 in *Migrant Birds in the Neotropics: Ecology, Behavior, Distribution and Conservation,* A. Keast and E.S. Morton, eds. Washington: Smithsonian Institution Press.

———. 1990. Habitat segregation by sex in the Hooded Warbler: Experiments on proximate causation and discussion of its evolution. *Am. Nat.* 135:319–333.

Morton, E.S., and K.C. Derrickson. 1990. The biological significance of age-specific return schedules in breeding Purple Martins. *Condor* 92:1040–1050.

Morton, E.S., and R. Greenberg. 1989. The outlook for migratory songbirds: "Future shock" for birders. *Am. Birds* 43:178–183.

Morton, E.S., L. Forman, and M. Braun. 1990. Extrapair fertilizations and the evolution of colonial breeding in Purple Martins. *Auk* 107:275–283.

Nolan, V., Jr. 1978. *The Ecology and Behavior of the Prairie Warbler* Dendroica discolor. Ornithol. Monogr. 26.

Office of Migratory Bird Management. 1990. *Conservation of Avian Diversity in North America.* Washington: U.S. Fish and Wildlife Service.

Orejuela, J.E., R.J. Raitt, and H. Alvarez. 1980. Differential use by North American migrants of three types of Colombian forests. Pages 253–264 in *Migrant Birds in the Neotropics: Ecology, Behavior, Distribution and Conservation,* A. Keast and E.S. Morton, eds. Washington: Smithsonian Institution Press.

Pearson, D.L. 1980. Bird migration in Amazonian Ecuador, Peru, and Bolivia. Pages 272–284 in *Migrant Birds in the Neotropics: Ecology, Behavior, Distribution and Conservation,* A. Keast and E.S. Morton, eds. Washington: Smithsonian Institution Press.

Petter, S.C., D.B. Miles, and M.M. White. 1990. Genetic evidence of mixed reproductive strategy in a monogamous bird. *Condor* 92:702–708.

Quay, W.B. 1989. Insemination of Tennessee Warblers during spring migration. *Condor* 91:660–670.

Ramos, M.A., and D.W. Warner. 1980. Analysis of North American subspecies of migrant birds wintering in Los Tuxtlas, southern Veracruz, Mexico. Pages 173–180 in *Migrant Birds in the Neotropics: Ecology, Behavior, Distribution and Conservation,* A. Keast and E.S. Morton, eds. Washington: Smithsonian Institution Press.

Rappole, J.H., and E.S. Morton. 1985. Effects of habitat alteration on a tropical avian forest community. Pages 1013–1021 in *Neotropical Ornithology,* P.A. Buckley, E.S. Morton, R.S. Ridgely, and F.G. Buckley, eds. Ornithol. Monogr. 36.

Rappole, J.H., E.S. Morton, T.E. Lovejoy, III, and J.L. Ruos. 1983. *Nearctic Avian Migrants in the Neotropics.* Washington: U.S. Fish and Wildlife Service.

Rappole, J.H., M.A. Ramos, and K. Winker. 1989. Wintering Wood Thrush movements and mortality in southern Veracruz. *Auk* 106:402–410.

Robbins, C.S., D.K. Dawson, and B.A. Dowell. 1989a. *Habitat Area Requirements of Breeding Forest Birds of the Middle Atlantic States.* Wildl. Monogr. 103.

Robbins, C.S., J.R. Sauer, R.S. Greenberg, and S. Droege. 1989b. Population declines in North American birds that migrate to the neotropics. *Proc. Natl. Acad. Sci.* 86:7658–7662.

Roth, R.R., and R.K. Johnson. In press. Decline of a Wood Thrush population: Loss of temperate or tropical habitat? *Auk.*

Russell, S.M. 1964. *A Distributional Study of the Birds of British Honduras.* Ornithol. Monogr. 1.

Sherman, P.W., and M.L. Morton. 1988. Extra-pair fertilizations in mountain White-crowned Sparrows. *Behav. Ecol. Sociobiol.* 22:413–420.

Stiles, F.G. 1983. Birds: Introduction. Pages 502–530 in *Costa Rican Natural History,* D.H. Janzen, ed. Chicago: University Chicago Press.

Taub, S.R. 1990. Smoothed scatterplot analysis of long-term breeding bird census data. Pages 80–83 in *Survey Designs and Statistical Methods for the Estimation of Avian Population Trends,* J.R. Sauer and S. Droege, eds. U.S. Fish and Wildlife Service Biol. Rept. 90(1).

Terborgh, J.W. 1980. The conservation status of Neotropical migrants: Present and future. Pages 21–30 in *Migrant Birds in the Neotropics: Ecology, Behavior, Distribution and Conservation,* A. Keast and E.S. Morton, eds. Washington: Smithsonian Institution Press.

Westneat, D.F., P.W. Sherman, and M.L. Morton. 1990. The ecology and evolution of extra-pair copulations in birds. *Current Ornithol.* 7:331–369.

Wilcove, D., and J. Terborgh. 1984. Patterns of population decline in birds. *Am. Birds* 38:10–13.

Whitcomb, R.F., C.S. Robbins, J.F. Lynch, B.L. Whitcomb, M.K. Klimkiewicz, and D. Bystrak. 1981. Effects of forest fragmentation on the avifauna of the eastern deciduous forest. Pages 125–205 in *Forest Island Dynamics in Man-dominated Landscapes,* R.L. Burgess and D.M. Sharpe, eds. New York: Springer-Verlag.

Winker, K., J.H. Rappole, and M.A. Ramos. 1990. Population dynamics of the Wood Thrush in southern Veracruz, Mexico. *Condor* 92:444–460.

Some suggestions for future cooperative work in Latin America: An outline

Algunas sugerencias para futuros trabajos cooperativos en Latinoamérica: Lineamentos

Luis G. Naranjo, Jorge Correa-Sandoval,
Jesús García-Barron, Hiram González-Alonso,
Daniel Hernández, Belkys Jiménez, Jorge E. Morales,
Adolfo Navarro, Rosa María Vidal-Rodriguez,
Laura Villaseñor, Fernando Villaseñor, and
José A. Colón

During this symposium, we have discussed how human disturbance of natural forests throughout the Americas might explain the significant decline of landbird migrants. At the same time, it is evident that unless we engage in an international effort to preserve this valuable part of our heritage, nothing can be done to stop such a decline of natural populations. We can think of many ways of accomplishing this goal, but we still lack the necessary framework that allows us to protect the migrant's nonbreeding grounds. Despite the acknowledged need of joint efforts between North American and Latin American ornithologists, it is apparent that we both poorly understand how those efforts can actually be channeled toward definite goals.

With these facts in mind, the few Latin American ornithologists present at the symposium have constructed an outline of suggestions for future cooperative work in our countries. The following are the main conclusions.

1. We can talk for eons about ways to help native Latin American communities to preserve the remnants of native forests. But we have to talk business before thinking of conservation. In a region where most people are striving for survival, you cannot expect to stop the expansion of the agricultural frontier. There are a few examples throughout Latin America of attempts to enhance the means of survival of small agricultural communities associated with natural parks and reserves.

Durante el simposio, hemos estado discutiendo acerca de como la perturbación humana de bosques naturales a través de toda América podría explicar la declinación significativa de aves migratorias terrestres. Al mismo tiempo, ha sido evidente que a menos que nos comprometamos en un esfuerzo internacional para preservar esta valiosa porción de nuestro legado, nada puede hacerse para detener tal declinación de poblaciones naturales. Podemos pensar en muchas formas de conseguir estas metas, pero como fue claro durante el foro de anoche, aún carecemos del marco contextual que nos permita defender los cuarteles de invierno de las aves migratorias terrestres. A pesar de la reconocida necesidad de esfuerzos conjuntos entre ornitólogos Norteamericanos y Latinoamericanos, al parecer tanto los unos como los otros tenemos un pobre entendimiento de como dichos esfuerzos pueden ser realmente canalizados hacia metas definitivas.

Con estos hechos en mente, los pocos ornitólogos Latinoamericanos presentes en este simposio hemos elaborado un bosquejo de sugerencias para futuro trabajo cooperativo en nuestros países. Las siguientes fueron las principales conclusiones de nuestra discusión.

1. Podríamos hablar durante siglos acerca de formas para ayudar a las comunidades nativas de Latinoamérica en la preservación de los remanentes de bosques nativos. Pero primero tenemos que hablar de negocios

590

While several of our scientists and technicians are already working to find these alternative solutions, we still urge you as a whole to help us find ways to improve land use and management through funding of our current projects or directly by means of research. The sustainable development of our natural resources is by far the most important goal toward achieving real conservation in the Neotropics.

2. For most Latin American naturalists, it is a surprise to learn how unaware of environmental issues the average citizen in the United States really is. Since conservation of tropical forests is not an isolated matter, we need to be sure that, while in Latin America we educate our people in environmental matters, North Americans help make the average "gringo" wake up and become aware of what is going on in other parts of the world. We have heard in this meeting the old story about pesticides and chemicals that are currently prohibited in the United States being exported to Latin America. While using these chemicals in the United States would cause considerable turmoil, thanks to the mass media, few are concerned that your labs still produce these substances and send them to ruin our nature.

3. In most Latin American countries there is a surplus of reasonably well-trained field biologists that cannot get a job and must abandon forever the dreams of working on research. We suggest that instead of hiring American graduate and undergraduate students to work as field assistants in the Neotropics, it is feasible to hire local naturalists. You can either have local research assistants, local coauthors, or both. Although we do not have a surplus of Ph.D. level scientists, most of our scientists that hold a B.S. are better trained than many unexperienced North American biologists. To get this kind of cooperation, you must establish an active correspondence with well-established biologists in our countries who can provide a list of qualified candidates for these positions. At the same time, North American researchers would benefit from enhanced mobility, direct contacts with local authorities, reduction in logistic costs, and access to some information up to now unavailable to North Americans.

4. For several years, North American ornithologists have complained about the poor local interest in ornithological research throughout Latin America. This is a misconception. In fact, a tremendous effort is currently being undertaken by our scientists. However, budget limitations and limited access to basic equipment and literature continue to hinder our research efforts. Through a well-established network of cooperation, North American researchers might consider donating some of their equipment to Latin American researchers after they finish their field work in the Neotropics. This has already been done by a few researchers (e.g., field studies in Mexico, Cuba, and Colombia), but we feel

antes de pensar en conservación. En una región en donde la mayoría de la población lucha por sobrevivir, no podemos pensar en simplemente detener la expansión de la frontera agropecuaria. Existen unos cuantos ejemplos, a través de Latinoamérica, de intentos para mejorar los medios de subsistencia de pequeñas comunidades agrícolas asociadas a parques nacionales y reservas. Aunque muchos de nuestros científicos y tecnólogos están trabajando para encontrar estas soluciones alternativas, queremos enfáticamente pedir a ustedes como grupo ayudarnos a buscar maneras de mejorar el uso y manejo de la tierra, bien sea mediante financiación de proyectos actuales o bien por medio de investigación. El desarrollo sostenible de nuestros recursos naturales es, sin lugar a dudas, la meta mas importante en la consecución de conservación real en el Neotrópico.

2. Para la mayoría de naturalistas Latinoamericanos, es una sorpresa saber que el ciudadano promedio de los Estados Unidos es tan poco consciente acerca de problemas medioambientales. Puesto que la conservación de bosques tropicales no es un asunto aislado, necesitamos estar seguros de que mientras en Latinoamérica nosotros educamos a nuestra gente en asuntos del medio ambiente, los Norteamericanos ayudan a despertar al "gringo" promedio para que se entere de lo que sucede en otras partes del mundo. Hemos escuchado en esta reunión la vieja historia de la exportación hacia Latinoamérica de pesticidas y químicos prohibidos. Mientras que el uso de estos químicos en los Estados Unidos causaría un escándalo considerable gracias a los medios de comunicación, muy pocas personas se preocupan porque vuestros laboratorios aún producen dichas sustancias y las envían a arruinar nuestra naturaleza.

3. En la mayoría de países latinoamericanos existe un exceso de biólogos de campo razonablemente bien entrenados, los cuales no pueden conseguir un empleo y deben abandonar para siempre sus sueños de trabajar en investigación. Sugerimos que en vez de contratar estudiantes Norteamericanos pregraduados y posgraduados para trabajar como ayudantes de campo en el Neotrópico, es factible contratar naturalistas locales. Así, ustedes pueden tener ayudantes de investigación locales, co-autores, o ambos. Aunque no tenemos un exceso de científicos con una preparación al nivel de Ph.D., la mayoría de aquellos con un título básico están mejor entrenados que muchos biólogos Norteamericanos sin experiencia. Para conseguir este tipo de cooperación, ustedes deben establecer una activa correspondencia con biólogos bien establecidos en nuestros países, quienes pueden proveer una lista de candidatos calificados para estos empleos. Al mismo tiempo, los investigadores norteamericanos se beneficiarían al obtener una mayor capacidad de movilización, contactos directos con autoridades locales, reducción en gastos logísti-

that few researchers have ever considered that possibility. With respect to scientific literature, current prices of most North American journals are too high to allow many young scientists in our countries to subscribe. We would greatly appreciate any effort that might provide reduced costs of subscriptions for Latin Americans.

5. Every issue of the Ornithological Newsletter carries announcements of available research assistantships in the United States. Although we do not know how accessible these positions may be to Latin American researchers, we consider it important that you urge, through Latin American universities, young people to apply for these short-term jobs. This would expand the professional horizons of our naturalists and allow you to have a permanent source of contacts, co-workers, and assistants throughout the Neotropics.

In addition, we have noticed a reduction in support for Latin American biologists to come to the United States for graduate studies. This situation seriously impairs the development of science, and ornithology in particular, in the Neotropics. Unless your universities improve the opportunities for scholarships and other grants for our students, we do not foresee an improvement in international cooperative ornithological research.

As a conclusion, we would like to summarize by saying that such cooperation is not possible unless we both give it our best effort. While we Latins can greatly benefit from your knowledge, expertise, and funding, you can also learn one or two things from us: (Spanish, for example), how to reduce the cumbersome dealings with Latin American bureaucracies, how to get to important research sites more easily, and how to actually change the rules of this destructive game of "progress." Migrant birds do not recognize political borders. To save these species we must begin to have a similar perspective of the hemisphere.

Acknowledgments

First of all, the authors of this document want to express our gratitude for the support provided by the Manomet Bird Observatory, the National Science Foundation, and the World Wildlife Fund to allow us to attend this enlightening symposium. We would like to have seen many other colleagues from our countries at this meeting, but, at the same time, we must recognize the effort made by the organizing committee to bring us all to Woods Hole.

cos y acceso a información hasta el momento generalmente inaccesible a Norteamericanos.

4. Durante varios años, los ornitólogos norteamericanos se han quejado por el escaso interés local en la investigación ornitológica a través de Latinoamérica. Esta es una falsa apreciación. De hecho, nuestros científicos están realizando actualmente un tremendo esfuerzo. No obstante, limitaciones de presupuesto y de acceso a equipo y literatura básicos continúan frenando nuestros esfuerzos investigativos. A través de una red de cooperación bien establecida, los investigadores Norteamericanos podrían considerar el donar algo de su equipo a investigadores Latinoamericanos al finalizar su trabajo de campo en el Neotrópico. Esto ya ha sido hecho por algunos investigadores (por ejemplo en estudios en México, Cuba y Colombia), pero nos damos cuenta que no muchos investigadores han siquiera pensado en esta posibilidad. Con respecto a la literatura científica, los precios actuales de la mayoría de las revistas Norteamericanas son demasiado altos como para permitir a muchos jóvenes científicos en nuestros países conseguir una suscripción. Agradeceríamos enormemente cualquier esfuerzo que pueda proveer costos reducidos de suscripciones para América Latina.

5. En cada número del "Ornithological Newsletter" se publican anuncios de ayudantías de investigación disponibles en los Estados Unidos. Aunque no sabemos que tan accesibles puedan ser estas posiciones para investigadores Latinoamericanos, consideramos importante el que ustedes impulsen, a través de universidades Latinoamericanas, a gente joven para concursar por estos empleos a corto plazo. Esto podría expandir los horizontes profesionales de nuestros naturalistas y les ayudaría a Ustedes a tener una fuente permanente de contactos, co-investigadores y ayudantes a través del Neotrópico.

Adicionalmente, hemos notado una reducción en el apoyo brindado a biólogos Latinoamericanos para venir a los Estados Unidos a proseguir estudios de postrado. Esta situación debilita seriamente el desarrollo de la ciencia y, en particular, de la ornitología en el Neotrópico. A menos que sus universidades mejoren las oportunidades de becas y otras ayudas para nuestros estudiantes, nosotros no prevemos para el futuro un mejoramiento de la investigación ornitológica internacional cooperativa.

Como una conclusión, quisiéramos resumir diciendo que la cooperación no es posible a menos que tanto Ustedes como nosotros hagamos nuestro mejor esfuerzo. Mientras que nosotros los Latinos nos podemos beneficiar enormemente con su conocimiento, experiencia y financiación, Ustedes también podrían aprender de nosotros una o dos cosas (Español, por ejemplo). Podrían reducir los complicados trámites con la burocracia Latinoamericana, llegar a sitios de importancia mas fácilmente y podrían igualmente cambiar de verdad las reglas de este destructivo juego del "progreso". Las aves migratorias no reconocen fronteras políticas. Para salvar a estas especies, debemos empezar a tener una perspectiva similar del hemisferio.

Agradecimientos

Primero que todo, los autores de este documento queremos expresar nuestra gratitud por el apoyo brindado por el Observatorio de Aves de Manomet, la Fundación Nacional de Ciencias y el Fondo Mundial de la Vida Silvestre para permitirnos asistir a este iluminador simposio. Hubiéramos querido ver a muchos otros colegas de nuestros países en esta reunión, pero al mismo tiempo debemos reconocer el esfuerzo hecho por el Comité Organizador para traernos a Woods Hole.

Resolutions
Program
Attendees
Author index

Symposium resolutions

These resolutions, read at the conclusion of the symposium, have been slightly modified based on subsequent comment from symposium participants

WHEREAS:

Neotropical migratory landbirds are a shared international resource and therefore require a major conservation initiative that transcends international boundaries, and

WHEREAS:

owing to their fragmentation or conversion to unsuitable habitat, North American forests continue to decrease in quality for many migrant landbird species, and

WHEREAS:

wintering habitats, including mature tropical forest, are also greatly reduced in quantity and quality in Latin America and the Caribbean, and habitat destruction continues today at a dangerously high rate, and

WHEREAS:

without improvements in land-use practices in North and Latin America, many Neotropical migrant landbird species face serious threats to their survival, and

WHEREAS:

there is particular urgency for forest-dwelling species, both on their breeding and wintering grounds, owing to the loss, conversion, and fragmentation of their habitats, and

WHEREAS:

species that use second-growth habitats are not immune from habitat alterations in North and Latin America, and their populations also require careful attention, and

WHEREAS:

there is a vital need to develop comprehensive, cooperative research and monitoring programs throughout the ranges of migratory landbirds to resolve uncertainties about the effects of environmental change, to identify population trends, and to suggest conservation measures, and

WHEREAS:

it is recognized that enacting migrant bird conservation measures must be concordant with the economic, social, and political well-being of people throughout the Americas, and

WHEREAS:

Neotropical migrant landbirds are only one valuable and deserving element of many broader, global conservation concerns that need immediate attention, such as overall loss of biodiversity and human population growth,

THEREFORE BE IT RESOLVED:

that the participants in this symposium on ecology and conservation of Neotropical migrant landbirds commit themselves, and call upon the scientific community and public and private institutions, to act upon the best information available, and to use all appropriate resources to conserve populations of migrant landbirds and the habitats on which they depend, and

BE IT FURTHER RESOLVED:

that in doing so, it is critical that the scientific community in North, Central, and South America form cooperative efforts in the conservation of this resource, and that nations of the Western Hemisphere recognize the value of migrant landbirds and the habitats on which they depend.

Symposium Program

Wednesday, 6 December 1989

12:00 Registration desk opens - Swope Hall

18:30 Swope dining hall open for dinner

20:00 Refreshments for weary travelers - Meigs Room, Swope Hall

Thursday, 7 December 1989

08:00 Welcome and Opening Remarks
      John M. Hagan III, Chairman, Symposium Organizing Committee
      Linda E. Leddy, Director, Manomet Bird Observatory

Plenary Session

08:10 *The current state of Neotropical migrant bird conservation.*
      John Terborgh

08:55 *The patch-corridor-matrix paradigm: from theory to landscape fragmentation and policy.*
      Richard T. T. Forman

09:40 *Past, present, and future of Neotropical forests.*
      Gary Hartshorn

10:25 Coffee Break - Swope Hall

General Paper Session

Topic: Population trends and distribution changes

10:50 Introduction to the Session - Raymond J. O'Connor

1 10:55 *Geographic patterns in population trends of Neotropical migrants in North America.* J. R. SAUER and S. DROEGE, Fish and Wildlife Service, Patuxent Wildlife Research Center Laurel, MD 20708 USA

2 11:15 *Trends in breeding populations of warblers: declines in the southern highlands and increases in the lowlands.* F. C. JAMES, D. A. WIEDENFELD, Department of Biological Sciences, Florida State University, Tallahassee, FL 32306, and C. McCULLOCH, Biometrics Unit, Department of Plant Breeding and Biometry, Cornell University, Ithaca, NY 14853 USA

3 11:35 *An analysis of long-term population trends from Breeding Bird Censuses in eastern deciduous forests.* D. W. JOHNSTON, 5219 Concordia Street, Fairfax, VA 22032 USA, and J. M. HAGAN, P. O. Box 936, Manomet Bird Observatory, Manomet, MA 02345 USA

4 11:55 *Population trends of Neotropical migrant landbirds in northern coastal New England.* J. W. WITHAM, JR., Holt Research Forest Old Stage Rd., Box 309, Arrowsic, Maine 04530, and M. L. HUNTER, Wildlife Department, 240 Nutting Hall, University of Maine, Orono, ME 04469 USA

12:15 Lunch

Population Trends and Distribution Changes (cont.) - Chairman, David W. Johnston

5   13:30 *Range expansions of Neotropical migrants in the southern Appalachians.* G. A. HALL, Department of Chemistry, West Virginia University, P. O. Box 6045, Morgantown, WV 26506-6045 USA

6   13:50 *Long-term patterns of winter resident warblers in a Puerto Rican dry forest: which species are in trouble?* J. FAABORG, 110 Tucker Hall, University of Missouri, Columbia, MO 65211, and W. J. ARENDT, U.S.D.A Forest Service, Calle 2, A-11 Brisas del Mar Luquillo, PUERTO RICO 00673 USA

7 14:10 *Migrant and resident warbler population trends on the Puerto Rico and St. Croix banks from Christmas Bird Counts, 1978-1988.* R. L. NORTON, Box 234, Cruz Bay, St. John, U. S. VIRGIN ISLANDS 00830

8   14:30 *Status of North American migrant landbirds in the Caribbean: A summary.* W. J. ARENDT, USDA Forest Service Calle 2, A-11 Brisas del Mar Luquillo, PUERTO RICO 00673 USA

14:50 Coffee Break - Swope Hall

9   15:20 *A cooperative bird-banding project in Peninsula de Zapata, Cuba 1988-1989.* H. GONZALEZ ALONSO, M. K. McNICHOL, P. B. HAMEL, M. ACOSTA, E. GODINEZ, J. HERNANDEZ, J. A. JACKSON, C. M. GREGO, R. D. McRAE, D. RODRIQUEZ, and J. SIROIS (corresponding author P. Hamel, Tennessee Dept. of Conservation, 701 Broadway Nashville, TN 37219-5237 USA

10 15:40 *Trends in numbers of tropical and temperate migrant landbirds in migration at Long Point, Ontario, 1961-88.* D. J. T. HUSSELL, M. MATHER, and P. SINCLAIR, Ministry of Natural Resources Wildlife Research Branch P. O. Box 50 Maple, Ontario CANADA L0J 1E0

11 16:00 *Are banding data consistent indicators of avian population trends?* C. M. FRANCIS, Biology Department, Queen's University, Kingston, Ontario CANADA K7L 3N6

12 16:20 *Detecting population changes using migration count data: A comparative approach.* J. M. HAGAN, T. L. LLOYD-EVANS, J. L. ATWOOD, P. O. Box 936, Manomet Bird Observatory, Manomet, MA 02345 USA, and D. S. WOOD, Carnegie Museum of Natural History, Pittsburgh, PA USA

16:40 Open Forum: General Discussion of population trend evidence

17:30 Cocktail Hour - Meigs Room, Swope Hall

18:30 Dinner

19:30 Poster Session Reception - Poster Display Area, Swope Hall

20:30 Live Entertainment, *Geese in the Bogs* , Meigs Room, Swope Hall

General Paper Session
Topic: Habitat Selection and Effects of Habitat Change

08:10 Introduction to the Session - Russell Greenberg

13 08:15 *Islands within islands: Problems facing forest warblers in a highly fragmented landscape.* J. FAABORG, Division of Biological Sciences, University of Missouri-Columbia, Columbia, MO 65211 USA, R. L. CLAWSON, Missouri Department of Conservation, 110 S. College Ave., Columbia, MO 65211 USA, J. GIBBS, D. WENNY, R. GENTRY, M. VAN HORN, R. O'CONNER, and K. KARLSON, Division of Biological Sciences, University of Missouri-Columbia, Columbia, MO 65211 USA

14 08:35 *Population dynamics of breeding birds in a fragmented Illinois landscape.* S. K. ROBINSON, Illinois Natural History Survey, 607 E. Peabody Dr., Champaign. IL 61820 USA

15 08:55 *Factors influencing the decline of Neotropical migrants in Sapsucker Woods Sanctuary, Ithaca, NY.* T. S. LITWIN and C. R. SMITH, Clark Science Center, Smith College, Northampton, MA 01063 USA

16 09:15 *Forest land conversion in the eastern United States.* T. W. BIRCH, Northeast Forest Experiment Station, USDA Forest Service, 370 Reed Road, Broomall, PA 19008 USA

17 09:35 *Landscape ecology of temperate forest birds.* K. FREEMARK, CWS, National Wildlife Research Ctr., Environment Canada, Ottawa, CANADA K1A 0H3

09:55 Coffee Break - Swope Hall

18 10:25 *Metapopulation dynamics as a conceptual model for Neotropical migrant birds: an empirical investigation.* M. A. VILLARD, Ottawa-Carleton Institute of Biology, Deptartment of Biology, Carleton University, Ottawa, Ontario, CANADA K1S 5B6, K. FREEMARK, CWS, National Wildlife Research Center, Environment Canada, Ottawa, CANADA K1A 0H3, and G. MERRIAM, Ottawa-Carleton Institute of Biology, Deptartment of Biology, Carleton University, Ottawa, Ontario, CANADA K1S 5B6

19 10:45 *Paleoecology, landscape ecology, and the conservation of boreal forest Neotropical migrant passerines.* M. L. HUNTER, JR, Wildlife Department, 240 Nutting Hall, University of Maine, Orono, ME 04469 USA

20 11:05 *The response of migrant birds to changing habitats in the Greater Antilles and the Bahamas.* R. B. WAIDE, Center for Energy and Environment Research, GPO Box 3682, San Juan, PUERTO RICO 00936 and J. M. WUNDERLE, JR., Departmento de Biologia, Universidad de Puerto Rico, Cayey, PUERTO RICO 00633 USA

21 11:25 *Effect of habitat fragmentation on wintering migrants in the U. S. Virgin Islands.* R. A. ASKINS, Department of Zoology, Connecticut College, New London, CT 06320, D. N. EWERT, The Nature Conservancy, 2840 East Grand River Ave., Suite 5, East Lansing, MI 48823 USA, and R. L. NORTON, British Virgin Islands National Park Trust, Ministry of Natural Resources and Labor, Road Town, Tortola, British Virgin Islands.

22 11:45 *Habitat management during the breeding season: what are the appropriate features?* T. E. MARTIN, Department of Zoology, University of Arkansas, Fayetteville, AK 72701 USA

12:05 Lunch

Habitat Selection and Effects of Habitat Changes (cont.) - Chairman, Tom Sherry

23 13:30 *On the habitat distribution of long-distance migratory landbirds in western Mexico.* R. L. HUTTO. Department of Zoology, University of Montana, Missoula, Montana 59812 USA

24 13:50 *Comparison of Neotropical migrants in tropical forest, isolated fragments, and agricultural habitats.* C. S. ROBBINS, B. A. DOWELL, D. K. DAWSON, J. A. COLON, A. & R. ESTRADA, A. & R. SUTTON, and D. WEYER (senior author, U. S. Fish and Wildlife Service, Patuxent Research Center, Laurel, MD 20708 USA)

25 14:10 *Use of native and man-modified vegetation by overwintering migrants in the Yucatan Peninsula.* J. F. LYNCH, Smithsonian Environmental Research Center, Box 28, Edgewater, MD 21073 USA

26 14:30 *Habitat use by migratory passerines wintering in Costa Rica.* G. V. N. POWELL, National Audubon Society, Research Department, 115 Indian Mound Trail, Tavernier, FL 33073 USA, J. A. RAPPOLE, P.O. Box 218 Texas A & I University, Kingsville, TX 78363 USA, and S. SADER, Department of Forestry Management, 201 Nutting Hall, Orono, ME 04469 USA.

14:50 Coffee Break - Swope Hall

27 15:20 *Eastern Bobolink populations: ecology and conservation in an agricultural landscape.* E. K. BOLLINGER, Department of Zoology, Miami University, Oxford, OH 45056 USA, and T. A. GAVIN, Department of Natural Resources, Cornell University, Ithaca, NY 14853 USA.

28 15:40 *Habitat distribution patterns of temperate migrants at La Selva Biological Station and Braulio Carrillo National Park, Costa Rica.* J. G. BLAKE and B. A. LOISELLE, Natural Resources Institute, University of Minnesota, 3151 Miller Trunk Highway, Duluth, MN 55811 USA

29 16:00 *Fate of forest migrants wintering in non-forest habitats in Quintana Roo, Mexico.* R. GREENBERG, Department of Zoological Research, National Zoological Park, Washington, DC 20008 USA

30 16:20 *Density, philopatry, and population estimates for songbird migrants wintering in Veracruz.* J. RAPPOLE, P.O. Box 218 Texas A & I University Kingsville, TX 78363, E. S. MORTON, Department of Zoological Research, National Zoological Park, Washington, DC 20008, and M. A. RAMOS, World Wildlife Fund U. S., 1250 24th St. N. W., Washington, DC 20009 USA

31 16:40 *Distribution of migratory birds overwintering in non-agricultural habitats in Belize, Central America.* D. R. PETIT, L. J. PETIT, and K. G. SMITH, Department of Zoology, University of Arkansas, Fayetteville, AK 72701 USA

17:00 Open forum - Responses to changing habitats and habitat selection

17:30 Cocktail Hour - Meigs Room, Swope Hall

18:30 Dinner

19:30 Open Discussion - Migrant bird policy and conservation strategies - Lillie Auditorium

21:00 Reception - Meigs Room, Swope Hall

General Paper Session
Topic: Behavior of Migrants and Migration Ecology

08:10 Introduction to the Session - Frank Moore

32 08:15 *Social behavior of the Northern Parula, Cape May Warbler and Prairie Warbler wintering in Puerto Rico.* C. A. STAICER, Department of Biology, Dalhousie University, Halifax, Nova Scotia CANADA B3H 4J1

33 08:35 *Foraging in temperate- and tropical-breeding and wintering Yellow Warblers.* D. A. WIEDENFELD, Department of Biology, Florida State University, Tallahassee, FL 32306 USA

34 08:55 *Ecological and behavioral factors contributing to the over-winter demography of Kentucky Warblers (Oporornis formosus) in Panama, Canal Zone.* S. MABEY and E. MORTON, National Zoological Park, Smithsonian Institution, Washington, DC 20008 USA

35 09:15 *Habitat segregation in wintering Black-throated Blue Warblers in Puerto Rico.* J. M. WUNDERLE, JR., Departmento de Biologia Universidad de Puerto Rico, Cayey, PUERTO RICO 00633 USA

36 09:35 *The Hooded Warbler (Wilsonia citrina): ecology, conservation, and non-breeding distribution.* W. C. BARROW, D. N. PASHLEY, School of Forestry, Wildlife, and Fisheries, Louisiana State University, Baton Rouge, LA 70803 USA, and R. B. HAMILTON, Louisiana Nature Conservancy, Baton Rouge, LA 70821.

09:55 Coffee Break - Swope Hall

37 10:25 *Pattern of trans-gulf southward migration to Central America by Neotropical migrant landbirds.* D. A. JAMES, Department of Zoology, University of Arkansas, Fayetteville, AK 72701 USA.

38 10:45 *Long-term patterns of trans-gulf migration in spring: A radar and direct visual study.* S. GAUTHREAUX, Department of Biological Sciences, Clemson University, Clemson, SC 29634-1903 USA

39 11:05 *Stopover site use by four Neotropic migrant species in the Saint Croix River Valley.* A. R. WEISBROD, National Park Service, Spring Creek Field Lab, Marine on St. Croix, Minnesota 55047-0168, D. W. WARNER, Bell Museum of Natural History, University of Minnesota, Mineapolis, MN 55455, and J. G. TURNER, Belwin Outdoor Education Lab, Afton, MN 55001 USA

40 11:25 *Morphology-habitat relationships in migrating songbirds.* F. BAIRLEIN, Physiological Ecology Section, Department of Zoology, University of Koeln 5000, Koeln 41, FED REP GER

41 11:45 *Habitat suitability and the stopover ecology of Neotropical passerine migrants.* F. R. MOORE, Department of Biological Sciences, Box 5018, University of Southern Mississippi, Hattiesburg, MS 39406-5018 USA, and T. R. SIMONS, National Park Service, Gulf Island National Seashore, 3500 Park Rd., Ocean Springs, MI 39564 USA

12:05 Lunch

General Paper Session (continued)
Topic: Population Dynamics and General Conservation

Session Chairman, Fran James

42 13:30 *A system for ranking conservation priorities for Neotropical migrant birds based on relative susceptibility to extinction.* J. M. REED, Department of Zoology, North Carolina State University, Box 7617, Raleigh, NC 27695-7617 USA

43 13:50 *Drought and annual variation in bird populations: effects of migratory strategy and breeding habitat.* J. G. BLAKE, G. E. NIEMI, and J. A. HANOWSKI, Natural Resources Research Institute, Center for Water and the Environment, University of Minnesota, Duluth, MN 55811 USA

44 14:10 *Potential effects of climatic change on Neotropical migrant landbirds.* N. RODENHOUSE, Department of Biological Sciences, Wellesley College, Wellesley, MA 02181

45 14:30 *Site fidelity and site attachment of migrant warblers in temperate and Neotropical wintering quarters: Implications for population dynamics, habitat selection, and conservation.* R. T. HOLMES, Department of Biological Sciences, Dartmouth College, Hanover, NH 03755 USA, and T. W. SHERRY, Department of Biology, Tulane University, New Orleans, LA 70118 USA

14:50 Coffee Break - Swope Hall

46 15:20 *Demography of a long-distance migrant: causes and consequences of variable yearling recruitment in the American Redstart.* T. W. SHERRY, Department of Biology, Tulane University, New Orleans, LA 70118 USA, and R. T. HOLMES, Department of Biological Sciences, Dartmouth College, Hanover, NH 03755 USA

47 15:40 *Population dynamics and migrancy status in North American birds.* R. J. O'CONNOR, Department of Wildlife, 240 Nutting Hall, University of Maine Orono, ME 04469 USA

48 16:00 *A model of demographic coupling between resident and migrant populations.* R. E. RICKLEFS, Department of Biology, Uinversity of Pennsylvania, Philadelphia, PA 19104-6018, USA

49 16:20 *A warbler in trouble: Dendroica cerulea.* C. S. ROBBINS, Patuxent Research Center, U. S. Fish and Wildlife Center Laurel, MD 20708, J. W. FITZPATRICK, Archbold Biological Station, and P. HAMEL, Tennessee Department of Conservation, 701 Broadway, Nashville, TN 37219-5237 USA

(Saturday agenda continued next page)

Saturday, 9 December 1989 (continued)

16:40 Symposium Summary - Eugene S. Morton

17:10 Closing Remarks

17:30 Cocktail Hour - Meigs Room, Swope Hall

18:30 Banquet - Swope dining hall

20:00 Banquet Lecture - Lillie Auditorium

<u>Conservation Beyond Our Borders</u>
Dr. Thomas Lovejoy,
Smithsonian Institution

Poster Presentations

50 *Common Yellowthroat (<u>Geothlypis trichas</u>) spring migration in coastal Massachusetts: a geographic analysis.* J. L. ATWOOD AND T. L. LLOYD-EVANS, P. O. Box 936, Manomet Bird Observatory, Manomet, MA 02345, USA

51 *Trends in Broad-winged Hawks and available nesting habitat, 1936 to 1988.* L. J. GOODRICH AND J. C. BEDNARZ, Hawk Mountain Sanctuary, Kempton, PA, 19529, USA

52 *Monitoring Neotropical warblers at a California island census station.* P. PYLE, R. P. HENDERSON, D. F. DeSANTE, N. NUR, AND G. R. GEUPEL Point Reyes Bird Observatory, 4990 Shoreline Highway, Stinson Beach, CA 94970.

53 *The influence of Aspen grove size on bird species richness in central Saskatchewan.* BRIAN W. JOHNS, Canadian Wildlife Service, 115 Perimeter Road, Saskatoon, Sask., Canada S7N OX4.

54 *Using aerial photography to assess guild species richness: The importance of habitat size and shape.* J. K. KELLER, Coastal Environmental Services, 1099 Winterson Road, Suite 130, Linthicum, MD 21090, USA

55 *Species richness patterns among bird communities in disturbed and undisturbed moist forest in southern Belize.* J. C. KRICHER, Wheaton College, Norton, MA 02766 AND W. E. DAVIS, JR., Boston University, Boston, MA 02215, USA

56 *Factors affecting reproductive success of a migrant landbird on an insular preserve.* R. A. LENT, Seatuck Research Program, Cornell Lab. of Ornithology, Box 31, Islip, NY 11751 USA, and Department of Ecology and Evolution, State University of New York at Stony Brook, Stony Brook, NY 11794 USA

57 *Frugivory and the evolution of Neotropical migration.* D. J. LEVEY. University of Florida, Gainesville, FL 32611, USA and F.G. STILES, University of Costa Rica, Ciudad Universitaria "Rodrigo Facio," Costa Rica.

58 *A baseline extinction curve for North American terrestrial birds*. B. A. MAURER, Department of Zoology, Brigham Young University, Provo, UT 84602.

59 *Abundance and return rates of Wood Thrush breeding in a forest fragment, 1974-1989*. R. R. ROTH and R. I. JOHNSON, University of Delaware, 248 Townsent Hall, Newark, Delaware 19717-1303

60 *Conserving migratory birds along the West palearctic-African flyways*. T. SALATHE, International Council for Bird Preservation, 32 Cambridge Road, Girton, Cambridge CB3 OPJ, U.K.

61 *Population trends of Oregon's Neotropical migrants*. B. SHARPE, U.S. Fish and Wildlife Service, 1002 N.E. Holiday Street, Portland, Oregon 97232-4181.

62 *Proposed migratory bird watch to encompass research, monitoring and interpretation*. T. SIMONS, National Park Service, Gulf Islands National Seashore, 3500 Park Road, Ocean Springs, Mississippi 39564.

63 *Integrating distribution and abundance information to assess management needs for migratory songbirds*. C. R. SMITH, 159 Sapsucker Woods Road, Cornell Lab of Ornithology, Ithaca, NY 14850.

64 *Bird migration patterns in the highlands of Chiapas, Mexico*. R. M. VIDAL RODRIGUEZ, Coodinadora Tecnica, Estacion Biologica PRONATURA, Adpo Post 219, S.C.L.C., Chiapas 29230, Mexico.

65 *The Northern Waterthrush and Swainson's Thrush as transients at a stopover site in the St. Croix River valley, Minnesota*. K. WINKER, D. W. WARNER, Bell Museum of Natural History, 10 Church Street, SE, Minneapolis, MN 55455 USA, and A. R. WEISBROD, U. S. National Park Service, St. Croix National Riverway, P. O. Box 168, Marine on St. Croix, MN 55047 USA.

Symposium attendees

Kenneth Able
Raymond Adams
Michael Amaral
Kathleen Anderson
Brad Andres
Edith Andrews
Ralph Andrews
Wayne Arendt
Felicity Arengo
Dorothy Arvidson
Robert Askins
Jonathan Atwood
Brent Bailey
Franz Bairlein
Richard Baker
Lynda Baldwin
Wylie Barrow
James Bednarz
Alan Bennett
Tom Birch
Denis Blais
John Blake
Jan Blew
Karen Blumer
Eric Bollinger
Marc Bosch
Craig Bower
Michael Bradstreet
Barbara Braeker
Margaret Brittingham
Nicholas Brokaw
Dirk Burhans
William Buskirk
Gregory Butcher
Michael Cadman
Meade Cadot
Peter Cannell
David Capen
Josette Carter
Nancy Claflin
David Clapp
José Colón
Beverly Collier
Molly Cornell
Jorge Correa-Sandoval
George Cox
Mary Jo Croonquist
Dick Cunningham
William Davis, Jr.
Deanna Dawson
Janette Dean

Michael DeJong
Diane DeLuca
Randy Dettmers
Hanni Dinkeloo
James Dinsmore
Morrill Donnald
Margaret Donnald
Terri Donovan
Mary Doscher
Barbara Dowell
Randall Downer
Pierre Drapeau
Susan Drennan
Sam Droege
Diane Dumanoski
Charles Duncan
Ricky Dunn
Phillip Elliott
David Emerson
Marilyn England
Rick Enser
Duncan Evered
David Ewert
John Faaborg
Craig Faanes
George Fairfield
Jean Fairfield
Celia Falzone
Brent Fewell
June Ficker
Davis Finch
Allen Fish
Jane Fitzgerald
John Fitzpatrick
David Flashpohler
Anna Forster
Richard Forster
Richard Forman
Charles Francis
Kathryn Freemark
Rick Fridell
Dan Froehlich
Cecilia Fung
Jesús García-Barron
Nicholas Gard
Alexander Gardner
William Gates
Jean Gauthier
Sidney Gauthreaux
Geoffrey Geupel
James Gibbs

Bill Giezentanner
Betty Gilbert
G. Tanner Girard
Hiram González-Alonso
Laurie Goodrich
Susannah Graedel
Russell Greenberg
Joseph Grzybowski
Michael Guilfoyle
Pamela Gunther
George Haas
John Hagan
George Halekas
George Hall
Margy Halpin
Robert Hamilton
Christopher Haney
Lisa Hartman
Gary Hartshorn
Alfred Hawkes
Scott Hecker
Ann Hecker
Steve Hess
John Hill
Laura Hill
Norman Hill
Regina Hirsch
Jeanne Holler
Richard Holmes
Lorraine Holowach
Rebecca Holverton
Libby Hopkins
Russ Hopping
Steve Hounsell
Marshall Howe
William Howe
Jane Huff
Katherine Hunt
Peter Hunt
Malcolm Hunter
William Hunter
David Hussell
Richard Hutto
Cindy Hyslop
Frances James
Douglas James
Belkys Jiménez
David Johnston
Kyle Jones
James Karr
Anne Kasprzyk

Mark Kasprzyk
John Keane
Jeff Keller
Paul Kerlinger
Lewis Kibler
Priscilla Kilbler
Douglas Kimball
Timothy Kimmel
Warren King
David Kirk
H. Kivela
William Kolodnicki
John Kricher
Don Kroodsma
Elissa Landre
Bruce Lauber
Sarah Laughlin
Charles Leck
Linda Leddy
Gaeten Lefebvre
Richard Lent
Douglas Levey
Thomas Litwin
Trevor Lloyd-Evans
Pat Loafman
Gordon Loery
Thomas Lovejoy
Jim Lyons
James Lynch
Sarah Mabey
Laurie MacIvor
Robert Maker
Elizabeth Mallory
Peter Marra
Robert Marshall
Thomas Martin
Larry Master
Monica Mather
Thomas Matthews
Brian Maurer
John McCracken
Mary McDonald
Anne-Margaret McKinnon
Dave Mckinnon
Janet McMillen
Doug McRae
Scott Melvin
David Merker
Lyla Messick
Eileen Miller
Brent Mitchell
Frank Moore
Jorge Morales-Sanchez
Eugene Morton
Michael Mossman
Pete Myers
Luis Naranjo
Adolfo Navarro

Thomas Nicholls
Blair Nikula
Greta Nilsson
Daniel Niven
Donald Norman
Raymond O'Connor
David Osborne
Janet Partlow
Danielle Perillat
Simon Perkins
Katharine Perkins
Betty Petersen
Wayne Petersen
Lee Pfannmuller
Jonathan Plissner
Peter Polshek
Bridgette Poulin
George Powell
Kerry Rabenold
John Rappole
J. Michael Reed
Robert Reitsma
Len Reitsma
Nancy Richards
Peter Richards
Robert Ricklefs
Sue Ridd
Chris Rimmer
David Rimmer
Alison Robb
Chandler Robbins
Scott Robinson
John Roche
Nick Rodenhouse
Tom Rogers
Camille Romano
Roland Roth
Frank Rowher
Tami Rudnicky
Robert Russell
Steve Sader
Tobias Salathe
Al Sandilands
Anne Sandilands
John Sauer
Susan Savage
Jean-Pierre Savard
Don Schwab
Glenn Seebaransingh
Stanley Senner
Michael Serio
Patricia Serrentino
Nancy Sferra
Tom Sherry
Myles Silman
Ted Simons
Pamela Sinclair
Jacques Sirois

Susan Skagen
Charles Smith
Kimberly Smith
Bruce Sorrie
Cynthia Staicer
Benjamin Steele
Tim Sullivan
Jack Swenson
Lisa Taboada
Randy Tate
John Terborgh
Scott Terrill
Diana Teta
Frank Thompson
Elliot Tramer
John Trapp
Cheryl Trine
Nellie Tsipoura
James Tucker
Jennifer Turner
Martha Van der Voort
Peter Vickery
Rosa María Vidal-Rodriguez
Marc-André Villard
Fernando Villaseñor
Laura Villaseñor
Robert Waide
Thomas Waite
Patricia Wainwright
Charles Walcott
James Waltman
Dwain Warner
Alan Weisbrod
Charles Weise
Daniel Welsh
Christopher Welsh
Lauren Wemmer
Dan Wenny
Christopher Whelan
Louise White
Donald Whitehead
Susan Whiting
Andrew Whitman
Paul Wieczoreck
David Wiedenfeld
John Wiley
Kevin Winker
Jack Witham
D. Scott Wood
Mark Woodrey
Joeseph Wunderle
Richard Yahner
Chuck Yohn
Kimberly Young
Mary Ann Young
Charles Ziegenfus
Elsie Ziegenfus

Author index

Martín Acosta, 131
Wayne J. Arendt, 57, 143
Robert A. Askins, 197
Jonathan L. Atwood, 115, 377
Franz Bairlein, 356
John G. Blake, 257, 419
Eric K. Bollinger, 497
Brian Collins, 443
José A. Colón, 207, 590
Jorge Correa-Sandoval, 590
William E. Davis, Jr., 240
Deanna K. Dawson, 207
Barbara A. Dowell, 207
Sam Droege, 26
Rosamond Estrada, 207
David N. Ewert, 197
John Faaborg, 57
John W. Fitzpatrick, 549
Kathryn E. Freemark, 443, 474
Jesús García-Barron, 590
Sidney A. Gauthreaux, Jr., 96
Thomas A. Gavin, 497
Esteban Godinez, 131
Hiram González-Alonso, 131, 590
Russell Greenberg, 175, 273
John M. Hagan III, 75, 115
Paul B. Hamel, 131, 549
JoAnne M. Hanowski, 419
Gary S. Hartshorn, 13
Daniel Hernández, 590
Jorge Hernández, 131
Richard T. Holmes, 431, 563

Malcolm L. Hunter, Jr., 85, 511
David J.T. Hussell, 101
Richard L. Hutto, 211
Jerome A. Jackson, 131
Frances C. James, 43
Belkys Jiménez, 590
David W. Johnston, 75
John C. Kricher, 240
Thomas S. Litwin, 483
Trevor L. Lloyd-Evans, 115
Bette A. Loiselle, 257
James F. Lynch, 178
Sarah E. Mabey, 329
Carmen Marcos Grego, 131
Thomas E. Martin, 455
Monica H. Mather, 101
Charles E. McCulloch, 43
Martin K. McNicholl, 131
R. Douglas McRae, 131
Gray Merriam, 474
Frank R. Moore, 345
Jorge E. Morales, 590
Eugene S. Morton, 329, 337, 579
Luis G. Naranjo, 590
Adolfo Navarro, 590
Gerald J. Niemi, 419
Robert L. Norton, 197
Raymond J. O'Connor, 23, 64
Daniel R. Petit, 247
Lisa J. Petit, 247
George V.N. Powell, 287
Mario A. Ramos, 337

John H. Rappole, 287, 337
J. Michael Reed, 524
Robert E. Ricklefs, 537
Chandler S. Robbins, 207, 509, 549
Scott K. Robinson, 405, 408
Daysi Rodríguez, 131
Steven A. Sader, 287
John R. Sauer, 26
Thomas W. Sherry, 431, 563
Ted R. Simons, 345
Pamela H. Sinclair, 101
Jaques Sirois, 131
Charles R. Smith, 483
Kimberly G. Smith, 247
Cynthia A. Staicer, 308
Ann Sutton, 207,
Robert Sutton, 207
John Terborgh, 9
Rosa María Vidal-Rodriguez, 370, 590
Marc-André Villard, 474
Fernando Villaseñor, 590
Laura Villaseñor, 590
Dwain W. Warner, 384
A.R. Weisbrod, 384
Dora Weyer, 207
David A. Wiedenfeld, 43, 321
Kevin Winker, 384
Jack W. Witham, 85
D. Scott Wood, 115
Joseph M. Wunderle, Jr., 299